St
M agement

Strategic Management

Seventh Edition

Richard Lynch

PEARSON

Harlow, England • London • New York • Boston • San Francisco • Toronto • Sydney • Auckland • Singapore • Hong Kong
Tokyo • Seoul • Taipei • New Delhi • Cape Town • São Paulo • Mexico City • Madrid • Amsterdam • Munich • Paris • Milan

PEARSON EDUCATION LIMITED
Edinburgh Gate
Harlow CM20 2JE
United Kingdom
Tel: +44 (0)1279 623623
Web: www.pearson.com/uk

First published 1997 (print) (as *Corporate Strategy*)
Second edition 2000 (print)
Third edition 2003 (print)
Fourth edition 2006 (print)
Fifth edition 2009 (print) (as *Strategic Management*)
Sixth edition 2012 (print)
Seventh edition published 2015 (print and electronic)

ISBN: 978-1-292-06466-6 (print)
978-1-292-06468-0 (PDF)
978-0-292-06470-3 (eText)

British Library Cataloguing-in-Publication Data
A catalogue record for the print edition is available from the British Library

Library of Congress Cataloging-in-Publication Data
Lynch, Richard L.
Strategic management / Richard Lynch. -- Seventh edition.
pages cm
ISBN 978-1-292-06466-6 (print) -- ISBN 978-1-292-06468-0 (PDF) -- ISBN 978-0-292-06470-3 (eText)
1. Strategic planning. 2. Business planning. I. Title.
HD30.28.L92 2015
658.4'012--dc23

2014039211

10 9 8 7 6 5 4 3 2 1
18 17 16 15 14

Cover image © Getty Images

Print edition typeset in 10/12pt Garamond MT Pro by 35
Print edition printed and bound in Slovakia by Neografia

NOTE THAT ANY PAGE CROSS REFERENCES REFER TO THE PRINT EDITION

BRIEF CONTENTS

CONTENTS

Supporting resources

Visit www.pearsoned.co.uk/lynch to find valuable online resources

Companion Website for students

- Video summaries of each chapter
- Videos to accompany the long case studies
- Additional material, including further cases studies, questions and checklists, to expand your knowledge and aid your understanding
- Case Study Guide offering help with reading, analysing and presenting cases
- A searchable online glossary to explain key terms

For instructors

- Complete, downloadable Instructor's Manual, including teaching notes on the book and the case studies
- A bank of additional case studies from the previous edition of the book
- PowerPoint slides that can be downloaded and used as OHTs

For more information please contact your local Pearson Education sales consultant or visit www.pearsoned.co.uk/lynch

ABOUT THE SEVENTH EDITION

Given that the topic of strategic management focuses essentially on developing and implementing the future direction of organisations, every edition of this text must reflect both the fundamentals of the subject and the new challenges that face organisations at any point in time. This new, seventh edition of *Strategic Management* therefore balances the basic concepts for identifying the future of organisations with the new challenges and opportunities that may lead to substantial change. It therefore explores new topics such as the significant changes in social internet media, the fundamentals of green strategy and the opportunities and problems of the global economy within the context of a structured and critical approach to the essential elements of strategic management.

The underlying theme remains the need to consider not only the *rational approach* to strategic decision making, but also the *creative aspects* of such decisions – an approach that remains unique to this strategy text. The book argues that both of these approaches are essential to enable students and practising managers to develop effective strategies. This two-pronged approach is entirely consistent with the survey amongst strategy academics conducted for the *Strategic Management Journal* published in 2007.[1]

In addition, the seventh edition presents three new areas of the topic:

1 Two new chapters, the first on sustainability and green strategy and the second on business models, to present new academic thinking in these areas.
2 Major updates to the case material that explore the shifting economic fortunes of companies around the world, the rise of the developing nations and the rapid changes in communications and other technologies.
3 Additional online and open-source teaching support material for both students and their professors.

These three areas are explained in more depth later in this section.

OBJECTIVES

The purpose of the book is to provide a comprehensive, well-structured and leading-edge treatment of strategic management, covering organisations in both the private and public sectors. The text has been specially designed in a modular format to provide both a summary of the main areas and a more detailed treatment for those wishing to explore issues in more depth.

More specifically, the objectives are:

- *To provide a comprehensive coverage of the main study areas in strategic management.* For example, it explores important subject areas such as innovation, knowledge and technology strategy.
- *To present the practical issues and problems of strategic management, so that the compromises and constraints of real organisations are considered.* Each chapter contains case studies which both illustrate the principles and raise subjects for group and class discussion. Objective-setting, green strategy and corporate governance are amongst the topics explored.

[1] Nag, R, Hambrick, D C and Chen, M-J (2007) 'What is strategic management really? Inductive derivation of a consensus definition of the field', *Strategic Management Journal*, Vol 28, pp 935–955.

- *To assist organisations to add value to their assets through the development of effective strategic management.* The search for best practice in the context of the organisation's resources and constraints is a constant theme.
- *To explore both the rational and the creative approaches to the development of strategic management.* This text takes the view that the classical approaches to rational corporate strategy development need to be complemented by ideas based on crafting strategy development. For example, entrepreneurship and learning processes are covered in depth.
- *To stimulate critical appraisal of the major theories*, particularly with regard to their practical application in organisations. Many of the leading conceptual approaches are first described and then subjected to critical comment. The aim is to encourage the reader to think carefully about such matters.
- *To outline the international implications of the strategic management process.* Most of the cases have an international dimension. A special chapter on international and global strategy explores the specific issues raised by this strategic area.
- *To explore the application of strategic theory to new areas.* In addition to the well-received chapters on leadership, entrepreneurial strategy and public sector strategy, wholly new chapters have been developed on green strategy and business models. In addition, many of the cases have been revised to reflect radical shifts in the world economy and in new technology.

WHO SHOULD USE THIS BOOK?

The book is intended to provide an introduction to strategic management for the many students in this area.

- *Undergraduate students* on Business Studies, modular and other courses will find the subject matter sufficiently structured to provide a route through the subject. No prior knowledge is assumed.
- *MBA students* will find the practical discussions and theoretical background useful. They will also be able to relate these to their own experience.
- *Postgraduate students* on other specialist taught masters' programmes will find that the extensive coverage of theories and, at times, critical comment, together with the background reading, provide a useful input to their thinking.

In addition, the book will appeal to practising middle and senior managers involved in the development of strategic management. The case studies and checklists, the structured approach and the comprehensive nature of the text will provide a useful compendium for practical application.

DISTINCTIVE FEATURES

Two-model structure

For some years, there was disagreement on the approach to be adopted in studying strategic management. The *rational* model – strategy options, selection and implementation – was criticised by those favouring an approach based on the more *creative* aspects of strategy development. Given the lack of agreement between the approaches, *both* models are presented throughout this book. Both models contribute to the development of effective strategy: two sides of the same strategic coin. According to a 2007 survey, this dual approach has now become accepted amongst leading academics in the field.

Clear chapter structure

Each chapter follows the same format: learning outcomes; short introduction; opening case study; later case studies linked to the theory points in the text; a specific project linked with one of the case studies; regular summaries of key strategic principles; chapter summary; review and discussion questions; critical reflection on a key issue in the chapter; recommended further reading; detailed notes and references. There is also a glossary of terms at the end of the book as an aid to comprehension. Finally, the book has a selection of strategy cases at the end of the text to stimulate broader strategic debate.

New open-access web videos, strategy cases and support material

After the change to open access for the sixth edition of this text, all the web material for seventh edition remains open-access. Earlier editions required an access code to read the support material for the text. This radical shift in publishing strategy recognises that technology has changed and influenced the way that students learn about strategic management. In addition, considerable extra video and written material has been added to provide additional support for the book. However, most of this extra material is best understood in the context of the chapters to which it relates.

Given the great success of the extended case video 'Battle for the European Breakfast Cereal Market', this has been retained for the seventh edition but is available free on the web. The film uses an in-depth case study to explore the main areas of strategy and show how they link together. Strategy is a complex topic with many different approaches – the aim of the web film is to show one way that the strategic decision-making process can be developed from the available data. The website icon (left) appears in the margin to highlight where the book and website content link.

Video Part 00

In addition, there are video summaries for each chapter of the book as well as video summaries of the longer cases at the end of the text. Again, these are all open-access from the book's website: **www.pearsoned.co.uk/lynch**.

The website also contains two more areas of support material. First, there are additional explanations and checklists of strategic management material that complement the basic text itself. Second, there are additional cases that contain not only the main case material but also indicative answers to some of the case questions. Importantly, 'indicative answers' means that these are only examples of answers to the case questions: many other responses are possible.

Two new chapters: green strategy and business models

Although the sixth edition covered green strategy for the first time in a strategy textbook, it was simply treated as a part of each relevant chapter. Part of the reason for this approach was that the topic had only received limited coverage in the leading strategy research journals up to that time. It has now been explored in sufficient depth to justify a separate chapter. In addition, many businesses now highlight this topic as a significant part of their strategies. To emphasise the importance and relevance of green strategy to strategic thinking, the green strategy icon (left) appears in the margin to highlight these issues.

In addition, both individual companies and the business press have made increased reference to the 'business model' of a company. This has been accompanied by some new academic thinking on the topic that deserves to be more widely studied. Hence, for the first time in a strategy textbook, there is a separate chapter on this topic.

Focused case material plus longer cases at the end of the text

There are 68 shorter case studies in this book with 14 longer, more integrative cases at the end of the text. The shorter cases have been written or adapted to explore strategy issues relevant to their location in the text. The shorter cases have been especially designed for the larger class sizes and shorter discussion sessions now prevalent in many institutions. Fifteen cases have been updated for the seventh edition and 12 are either completely new or radically updated. Most of the 14 cases at the end of the text are either new or substantially updated. Previous cases are still available via **www.pearsoned.co.uk/lynch**. The 14 longer cases are summarised in video case films available free on the book's website.

Key strategic principles and chapter summaries

To aid learning and comprehension, there are frequent summaries of the main learning points under the heading of *key strategic principles*. In addition, at the end of each chapter there is an integrated summary of the areas explored.

International coverage

There is extensive coverage of international strategic issues throughout the book with cases and examples threaded through the text covering many well-known European and American companies. The book now has cases covering China, Africa and India, North Africa and the Eastern Mediterranean (excluding Israel) and, for the first time, Russia. In addition, there is a separate chapter on the special issues involved in international and global strategy.

Public sector and not-for-profit strategy

After the widespread welcome for the new (and unique) chapter on public sector strategy in earlier editions, this has been retained in the seventh edition. *Strategic management* principles have been historically developed almost exclusively from a business perspective – for example, competitive advantage, customer-driven strategy and corporate governance. *Public sector* theory has historically had a completely different intellectual foundation – for example, the concepts of the public interest, the legal framework of the state and the role of public administrators. This chapter explores how they can come together. It will be particularly relevant to managers from the public sector studying for a business degree at both undergraduate and postgraduate level.

Entrepreneurial strategy

Ever since its first edition, this text has always placed strong emphasis on creativity in strategy development. The recent increased research emphasis on entrepreneurial strategy has now prompted this important chapter. It explores in particular the personal aspects of effective entrepreneurial strategy.

Critical reflection and recommended further reading

Every chapter ends with a short critical reflection on a key topic in the chapter. In addition, each chapter has a list of recommended further readings. The purpose is to allow the student to debate a topic from the chapter and to explore the subject matter further as the basis for further projects, assignments and dissertations.

Strategic project

Some, but not all, chapters include at least one suggestion for a strategic project. It is linked to a case study in the chapter and shows how the case topic might be extended. The projects are supported by further information available on the internet.

A useful feature of the text remains the selection of some case material from the *Financial Times*. These extracts are the copyright of the *Financial Times*, which has kindly given permission to reproduce them in this book.

Lecturer's guide

This is available to those professors adopting this textbook. It includes short commentaries on each chapter and comments on the cases, together with OHP masters.

NEW FOR THE SEVENTH EDITION

As a result of the helpful feedback on the six earlier editions, this new edition has some new material while maintaining the main topics of previous editions. The key changes are in three areas – two new chapters, new case material and new open-access material.

Two new chapters

As outlined earlier, the seventh edition has two new chapters: the first explores 'Green strategy and sustainability'; the second covers 'Strategy and business models.' In addition, *all* the company cases in the seventh edition have been scrutinised with regard to their green strategies with a brief comment or description at the end of each case on the relevant company strategies.

New case material

Except for a few classic, popular cases, many of the cases in the seventh edition have been updated. Twenty-seven cases are either totally new or substantially updated. In addition to the existing broad range of cases from European and North American companies, there is increased geographic coverage from the new and growing parts of the world: there are now two cases each from China, Africa and India. There are also three cases from North Africa and the Eastern Mediterranean and, for the first time, a case from the Russian Federation.

Video films, podcast material and ready-to-use PowerPoint material have also been developed further for this new edition. They are all downloadable from the book's open-access website.

All the cases have teaching notes in the *Lecturer's Guide* and any that have been dropped from the previous edition appear on the *Strategic Management* website.

The longer cases at the end of the book are summarised with short video films that can be downloaded from the book's open-access website. These short films can be used to introduce class discussion of the cases and to identify key strategic issues.

New and open-access material

- Video summaries of each chapter plus summaries of the long cases at the end of the text.
- Extensive, additional web-based strategic management material and checklists. These are linked to specific topics throughout the text.
- Web-based cases with indicative answers.

In addition, some parts of several chapters have been re-drafted and updated.

Front cover – why a chameleon?

As all good students and managers know, the chameleon is adaptable just like the best strategy. Many chameleons can change colour depending on the context of their environment: this is a characteristic shared with the best prescriptive and emergent approaches to strategic management. Moreover, such creatures represent a link with a natural world that needs to be protected by the new greener strategies adopted by the best organisations.

ABOUT THE AUTHOR

Richard Lynch is Emeritus Professor of Strategic Management at Middlesex University, London, England. He originally studied at UMIST, Leeds University and the London Business School. He then spent over 20 years in business with well-known companies such as J Walter Thompson, Kraft

Jacobs Suchard and Dalgety Spillers in positions in marketing and strategic management. During the early 1980s, he was a director of two public companies before setting up his own consultancy company specialising in European and international strategy. In the 1990s he became increasingly involved in Higher Education, eventually taking a full-time professorship in 1998. He retired from his full-time post in December 2004 but remains highly active in teaching, research and writing including work at Trinity College Dublin, Ireland, the School of Economics and Management at Wuhan University, China and Politecnico di Milano, Italy. He has written four previous books on international marketing and strategy as well as a number of original research papers with colleagues for various academic journals and research conferences. His current research interests include projects on global branding and global strategy particularly with regard to companies from emerging countries like China and India.

HOW TO USE THIS BOOK

Strategic management is complicated because there is no final agreement on what exactly should be included in the topic. There are two main strategic approaches worth mastering before venturing too far into the text. They are summarised in Chapter 1 – the *prescriptive* and the *emergent* strategic approaches. Since these approaches are discussed extensively later in the book, they should be studied in Chapter 1 before moving on to other chapters. If you have trouble understanding these two elements, then you might also like to consult the early part of Chapter 2, which investigates them in more detail.

Each chapter then follows the same basic format:

- *Learning outcomes and introduction.* This summarises the main areas to be covered in the chapter and is useful as a summary of what to expect from the chapter.
- *Opening case.* This is designed to highlight a key strategy issue in the chapter and to provide an example that will then be explored in the text. It is therefore worth reading and using the case questions to ensure that you have understood the basics of the case. You can return to it once you have read the chapter.
- *Key strategic principles.* Each chapter then explores aspects of the subject and summarises them. These can be used to test your understanding of the text and also for revision purposes later.
- *Comment.* After the outline of a major strategic theory, there may be a section with this heading to explain some of the theoretical or practical difficulties associated with that topic. The opinions contained in such a section are deliberately designed to be controversial. The section is meant to make you think about the topic. If you agree with everything I have written, then I have failed!
- *Later case studies.* These are designed to provide further examples and raise additional strategic issues. It is worth exploring the questions.
- *Strategic project.* For some of the cases, one of the case studies has been used to suggest a broader strategic project. There is data on the internet to assist the process and your lecturer or tutor will suggest how you can access this.
- *Critical reflection.* Each chapter ends with a short section highlighting a key theme of the chapter as the basis for further discussion and exploration. For example, it might form the basis of an essay on a strategy topic or the focus of a seminar after a class lecture.
- *End of chapter questions.* Some are designed to test your understanding of the material in the chapter. Others are present as possible essay topics and require you to undertake some research using the references and reading from the chapter. Some questions have been developed to encourage you to relate the chapter to your own experience: student societies and outside organisations to which you belong can all be considered using the chapter concepts. You may also be able to relate the chapter to your own work experience or to those of other members of your family or friends. All these will provide valuable insights and help you explore the concepts and reality of corporate strategy.
- *Further reading.* This is designed to help when it comes to essay topics and dissertations. This section tries to keep to references in the major journals and books in order to make the process as accessible as possible.

GUIDED TOUR

Two-model structure – two models of strategic management thought are used throughout this book – *prescriptive* and *emergent*. Both are treated as contributing to the development of optimal strategic management.

1 *The prescriptive approach.* Some commentators have judged strategic management to be essentially a linear and rational process, starting with where-we-are-now and then developing new strategies for the future (see Jauch and Glueck[25] and Argenti[26]). **A prescriptive strategy is one whose *objective* has been defined in advance and whose *main elements* have been developed before the strategy commences.**

Definition ▸

2 *The emergent approach.* Other commentators take the view that strategic management emerges, adapting to human needs and continuing to develop over time. It is evolving, incremental and continuous, and therefore cannot be easily or usefully summarised in a plan which then requires to be implemented (see Mintzberg[27] and Cyert and March[28]). **An emergent strategy is one whose *final objective* is unclear and whose *elements* are developed during the course of its life, as the strategy proceeds.** The theorists of this approach often argue that long-term prescriptive strategies are of limited value.

Definition ▸

In Chapter 2 we examine these important differences in more detail. There are, for example, differences in approach even amongst those who judge that the process is rational and linear. Mintzberg[29] captured the essence of the distinction:

Case studies – are woven into each chapter and referred to frequently in order to illustrate how strategic principles do and don't work in practice. There are more than 80 case studies throughout the book and many are new and updated. For ease of reference, see the Guide to the main focus of case studies on page xxii.

CASE STUDY 3.1

The rise and fall of Blockbuster video stores

The Blockbuster video store chain was the subject of an $8.4 billion takeover in 1994. Twenty years later, the business was just a memory. Why? What are the implications for analysing the strategic environment?

By 2014, Blockbuster stores were just empty shells, the victim of technology change and questionable strategy
Photo courtesy of Steve Corbett

Background

Back in 1994, the Blockbuster video store chain was a fast-growing group of retail stores that hired out video films. It had that were rented over night by customers to play on their home video recorders and then return the following day. The company had special contracts with the major film companies to ensure that it was able to stock the latest films soon after showing in cinemas. It kept 60 per cent of the rental income and passed the other 40 per cent back to the film studios: a viable business model at that time.

Blockbuster takeover

In 1994, the US media conglomerate Viacom acquired Blockbuster for $8.4 billion. Viacom was partially interested in Blockbuster's $1.5 billion cash which it needed for another acquisition, Paramount Pictures. It was also possible that it over-valued Blockbuster even at that time because the Blockbuster profits were much lower in the year after its sale. But Viacom continued to invest in the store chain over the next ten years. In addition, there were reported to be synergies from the purchase that would benefit both companies. They would come from cross-marketing Viacom's MTV television channels with Blockbuster and from selling

Key strategic principles – at regular intervals, frequent summaries are given of the main learning points.

Icons indicate where there is additional material to be found on the website.

KEY STRATEGIC PRINCIPLES

- Environmental analysis is important because it helps in developing sustainable competitive advantage, identifies opportunities and threats and may provide opportunities for productive co-operation with other organisations.
- There are three difficulties in studying the environment: the use to which the analysis will be put; uncertainty in the topic; coping with the wide range of environmental influences.
- Environmental analysis can be used to provide a *proactive* strategy outcome or highlight a *reactive* strategic situation that will need to be monitored.

3.2 STRATEGIC ENVIRONMENT – THE BASICS

In order to begin the environmental analysis, it is useful to start with some basic factors that are sometimes forgotten in the academic concepts but contribute to the strategic analysis of the environment.[4] We can divide the basics into three areas:

Video Part 4a

1 Market definition and size
2 Market growth
3 Market share

Strategic projects – some chapters include a suggestion for a strategic project, based on a theme developed within the cases in the chapter and offering you the chance to delve a bit deeper.

STRATEGIC PROJECT

McDonald's has gained some ground from its new ranges. Where does it go from here? Should it revert to the previous strategy of acquiring alternative restaurant chains? If so, which chains? If not, then just how much further growth is there in the concept of fast food? This is a real strategic problem for a company whose shareholders demand continued profitable growth. Perhaps the company should try a completely new approach? In addition to looking at greater depth at McDonald's, it would be interesting to examine some alternatives such as Subway described in Chapter 2. There are websites for both these companies. You might like to consider two further trends. These are green strategy issues and better nutritional content: McDonald's has faced some strong adverse criticism on both these matters in recent years. Yet the company would argue that it has made genuine progress to improve its performance. Perhaps it could be even more proactive with regard to green strategies and nutritional matters?

Critical reflections – every chapter ends with a short critical reflection on a key topic in that chapter.

CRITICAL REFLECTION

Is purpose over-complicated?

This chapter has argued that strategic purpose is complex and multifaceted. It needs to take into account such matters as leadership, corporate governance, ethics and corporate social responsibility. The problem is that all this makes purpose difficult to analyse, define and communicate to employees, managers, shareholders and other stakeholders. Moreover, there is no clear logical path to the development of purpose, with vague areas like 'managerial judgement' being used to justify particular goals.

Given these definitional and logical difficulties, perhaps it would be much better to simplify matters and focus on one area such as maximising profits? Or maximising shareholder wealth? Or even maximising the organisation's contribution to society after paying shareholders a minimum dividend?

Is there any merit in purpose being complex and multifaceted?

Chapter summaries – recap and reinforce the key points in each chapter succinctly.

SUMMARY

- Fundamental to the exploration of purpose is the definition of the organisation's activities. It needs to be narrow enough to be actionable and broad enough to allow scope for development. It will develop from a consideration of the organisation's customers and its competitive resources. Purpose will also be defined by any specific desire to grow the organisation and by an exploration of the demands of the environment in which the organisation exists.
- Organisations are multidimensional and unlikely to have a single purpose. However, for reasons of focusing on specific objectives and communicating with those in the organisation, a simplified definition of purpose is often developed. The polygon of purpose captures the many factors that will need to be taken into account in developing and defining the purpose of the organisation. Green strategy issues will be present in a number of elements, rather than be identified as one separate element.
- Stakeholders are the individuals and groups who have an interest in the organisation. Consequently, they may wish to influence its mission and objectives. The key issue with regard to stakeholders is that the organisation needs to take them into account in formulating its mission and objectives. The difficulty is that stakeholder interests may conflict. Consequently, the organisation will need to resolve which stakeholders have priority: *stakeholder power* needs to be analysed. Where conflict exists, negotiations are undertaken to reach a compromise.
- The *mission* of an organisation outlines the broad directions that it should and will follow and briefly summarises the reasoning and values that lie behind it. The *objectives* are then a more specific commitment consistent with the mission over a specified time period. They may be quantified, but this may be inappropriate in some circumstances.
- Corporate governance refers to the influence and power of the stakeholders to control the strategic direction of the organisation in general and, more specifically, the chief executive and other senior officers of the organisation. Corporate governance relates primarily to the selection, remuneration and conduct of the senior officers of the organisation. It is also concerned about their

End-of-chapter **Questions** – test your understanding of the key issues raised in each chapter.

QUESTIONS

1 Take an organisation with which you are familiar and attempt to define its purpose: how has this been influenced by the factors outlined in Section 6.1, including its environment, resources, culture and stakeholders? How has the purpose changed over time? Why have these changes occurred?

2 In 2013, Yahoo! claimed that its vision of the future was that of 'a global technology company focused on making the world's daily habits inspiring and entertaining.' Use the classification developed by Hamel and Prahalad to evaluate this vision critically (see Section 6.2).

3 Can *organisations* have vision or is it the *managers* inside the organisation who have the vision? What are the implications of your answer for the development of strategy, especially in terms of communication within the organisation?

5 Do companies always need to behave ethically, regardless of the costs?

6 Should 'green' environmental issues form part of the corporate social responsibility of a business? How, if at all, will your answer impact on the strategy of the business?

7 How is corporate governance related to strategic management? What systems, if any, does McDonald's need to put in place to ensure compliance with corporate governance issues? Use the example of Citibank to assist you.

8 Take an organisation with which you are familiar and assess the information that it supplies to its stakeholders in terms of corporate governance issues. Is it doing a good job by its own standards and by the likely standards of its stakeholders?

Recommended **Further reading** – allows students to explore the subject further, providing an ideal basis for essays and assignments.

FURTHER READING

On purpose: read Drucker, P (1961) *Practice of Management*, Mercury, London. For a more recent review of mission and goal literature, see the early part of Slater, S, Olsen, E and Hult, T (2006) 'The moderating influence of strategic orientation on the strategy formation capability–performance relationship', *Strategic Management Journal*, Vol 27, pp 1221–1231.

On vision: see Tregoe, B B *et al.* (1989) *Vision in Action*, Simon & Schuster, London. See also Hamel, G and Prahalad, C K (1994) *Competing for the Future*, Harvard Business School Press, Boston, MA. Both books are at the practical end of the subject.

On leadership: Bennis, W and Nanus, B (1997) *Leaders: Strategies for Taking Charge*, HarperCollins, New York is a readable text with some useful insights. See also the special issue of *Academy of Management Executive* (2004) Vol 18, No 3, pp 118–142, on leadership including: Conger, J A, 'Developing leadership capability: What's inside the black box?'

On ethical issues: a good basic text is Chryssides, G D and Kaler, J H (1993) *An Introduction to Business Ethics*, International Thomson Business Press, London. The special issue of *Academy of Management Executive* (2004) Ethical Behavior in Management, pp 37–91 with guest editor John F Veign constitutes a substantial review with thoughtful papers on various current topics. There was also a special issue on the same topic in *Academy of Management Learning and Education*, September 2006, Vol 5, Issue 3 co-editors Robert Giacalone and Kenneth R Thompson that will provide more discussion.

For a more general and critical commentary on ethics and management theory including a critique of shareholder theory, you should read the late Professor Sumanthra Ghoshal's paper written in 2005, 'Bad Management Theories are Destroying Good Management Practices', *Academy of Management Learning and Education*, Vol 4, No 1, pp 75–91. Not a 'difficult' paper to understand and containing some profound and well-argued positions.

On corporate social responsibility a more recent accessible paper is that by Basu, K and Palazzo, G (2008) 'Corporate Social Responsibility, A Process Model of Sensemaking', *Academy of Management Review*, Vol 33, pp 123–136. This paper has a useful summary of recent research literature and would make a good start for project work.

Longer case studies at the back of the book enable students to further explore the link between theory and practice by analysing the strategic issues of particular organisations in much greater depth.

CASE STUDY 2

Global beer and lager: exploring strategies in a mature market

Although the annual global market for beer was massive in 2013, it was only growing slowly at just around 3 per cent per year. Moreover, it was dominated by four companies with a combined market share of over 50 per cent. These are all characteristics of a mature market. What are the best strategies for companies in such markets?

Video and sound summary of this case

Consolidation in world beer markets – size, growth and share

The world market for beers and lagers was valued at a massive $140–210 billion in 2012. Customers worldwide consumed 2,000 million hectolitres of beer and lager. The leading countries by production are shown in Figure 1: apart from German exports, beer is mostly consumed in the home country. It will be self-evident why the world's largest brewers have all been targeting the Chinese market over the past few years. The problem with the Chinese market is that profit margins are very low because beer is relatively cheap.

Over the 13 years to 2013, global beer markets followed a consolidation strategy. The number of independent brewing companies reduced and their share of the total market grew. The world's five largest brewers accounted for 19 per cent of sales in year 2000. Twelve years later, the world's four largest brewers accounted for 50 per cent of world sales and 75 per cent of global profits. The fifth brewer, the UK-based Scottish and Newcastle, was finally acquired and broken up by two of the other four in 2009. The consolidation strategy is typical of mature markets where a few firms come to dominate an industry and consolidate their market shares by acquisition and merger.

World beer markets are becoming increasingly competitive with companies developing differing strategies for different parts of the world.

In the nine years 2005 to 2013, compound annual growth in beer sales worldwide was around 3 per cent. But this masked a decline in developed world markets of minus 3.5 per cent and a growth in developing markets of plus 7 per cent. The

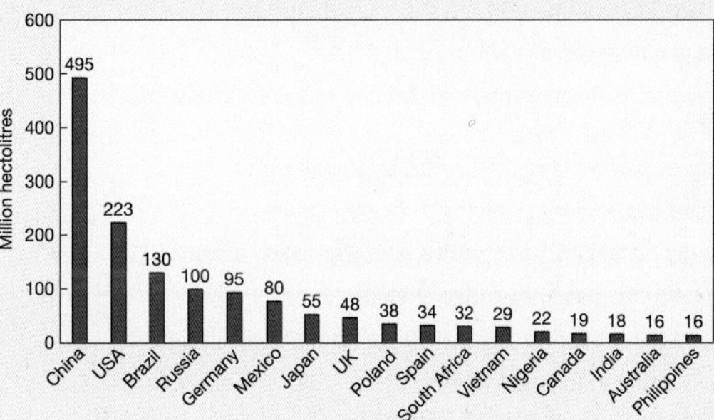

Figure 1 World beer production in 20 leading countries in 2012

Source: author from various industry estimates.

Guide to the main focus of case studies

Page	CASES WITHIN THE CHAPTERS		Main area/ country						Topic or theme														
			Global	UK	European	Asia/Pacific	USA	African	Emergent/prescriptive process	Competitive environment	Competitive resources	Culture and leadership	Developing purpose	Governance and social responsibility	Strategic options	International and global strategy	Corporate-level strategy	Acquisitions and alliances	Learning and knowledge	Managing change	Public and not-for-profit	SMEs and entrepreneurship	Green strategy
6	**1.1**	Why did Kodak collapse?	◆				◆		✓	✓	✓	✓	✓				✓			✓			
14	**1.2**	Corporate profit disaster at IBM	◆				◆			✓	✓	✓			✓								
23	**1.3**	Facebook's strategy: where is the sustainable competitive advantage?	◆							✓	✓								✓	✓		✓	
30	**2.1**	Attacking a dominant competitor: a joint venture strategy by Nestlé and General Mills	◆		◆				✓	✓	✓		✓		✓			✓	✓				
37	**2.2**	Prescriptive strategies to build world airlines at Singapore Airlines and Emirates Group	◆			◆		◆	✓							✓							
45	**2.3**	Building the Subway world franchise using emergent and prescriptive processes	◆				◆		✓							✓							
53	**2.4**	Africa calling: mobile phones open up new opportunities	◆					◆		✓	✓	✓	✓			✓		✓					
66	**3.1**	The rise and fall of Blockbuster video stores	◆						✓	✓		✓			✓		✓		✓				
77	**3.2**	Lifecycle impact on strategy in the European ice cream market			◆					✓					✓								
80	**3.3**	Bajaj Motorcycles: should the company move into cars?				◆			✓	✓	✓		✓		✓		✓						
86	**3.4**	Strategic bargaining to film *Lord of the Rings*	◆							✓													
103	**3.5**	Arçelik aims for Europe			◆					✓	✓				✓	✓							✓
110	**4.1**	How three European companies attempt to utilise their resources and capabilities			◆						✓												
125	**4.2**	Competitive advantage at Louis Vuitton and Gucci	◆						✓	✓	✓					✓							
148	**4.3**	Microsoft and Sony use their competitive resources to hit Nintendo hard	◆			◆	◆			✓	✓								✓				
156	**5.1**	Formula One 1 racing strategy: balancing brilliant driving with knife-edged bargaining	◆							✓	✓				✓	✓		✓					✓
163	**5.2**	L'Oréal beauty products: using financial data to explore the strategy dynamics of an industry	◆		◆					✓	✓												
171	**5.3**	Why are format wars important in strategy? The battle between Sony and Toshiba	◆							✓	✓					✓	✓						
196	**6.1**	The yawning gap at Yahoo!	◆				◆					✓	✓					✓					
202	**6.2**	McDonald's Restaurants: maintaining momentum by attacking Starbucks?	◆				◆						✓		✓								✓
208	**6.3**	Citigroup: rebuilding its corporate governance	◆				◆						✓	✓									
220	**6.4**	Coca-Cola: lowering the fizz in its objectives	◆				◆						✓				✓						✓
230	**7.1**	Maglev: Shanghai's innovative new transport system				◆			✓				✓						✓				
236	**7.2**	Developing new knowledge at Nike	◆				◆		✓			✓	✓						✓				
242	**7.3**	Egyptian innovation: the growing charm of Egypt's Sharm						◆		✓	✓				✓	✓			✓				
248	**7.4**	Revitalising innovation at 3M	◆				◆		✓										✓				
267	**8.1**	Walt Disney: building options for Mickey Mouse	◆				◆								✓								
275	**8.2**	Generic strategy options analysis: global ice cream	◆												✓								
277	**8.3**	Market-based strategies in global TV: exciting opportunities in a fast-changing market	◆												✓		✓						
288	**8.4**	News Corporation builds a global media empire but then decides on a new break-up strategy	◆			◆	◆		✓			✓			✓				✓				

Page		CASES WITHIN THE CHAPTERS	Main area/ country						Topic or theme														
			Global	UK	European	Asia/Pacific	USA	African	Emergent/prescriptive process	Competitive environment	Competitive resources	Culture and leadership	Developing purpose	Governance and social responsibility	Strategic options	International and global strategy	Corporate-level strategy	Acquisitions and alliances	Learning and knowledge	Managing change	Public and not-for-profit	SMEs and entrepreneurship	Green strategy
303	9.1	Corporate strategy at two multinationals – General Electric (USA) and Siemens (Germany)	◆		◆		◆				✓		✓		✓		✓						
313	9.2	The rise and fall of Nokia	◆		◆					✓		✓			✓		✓			✓			
322	9.3	Unilever: can product portfolio strategies help large corporations to grow?	◆		◆							✓	✓				✓						
333	10.1	Unilever ice cream defends its global market share	◆		◆					✓	✓				✓	✓							
341	10.2	Eurofreeze evaluates its strategy options: Part 1			◆								✓		✓								
353	10.3	Global ice cream: Nestlé goes on the attack	◆		◆				✓	✓	✓					✓		✓					
360	10.4	Eurofreeze evaluates its strategy options: Part 2			◆										✓								
369	11.1	How Honda came to dominate two major motorcycle markets				◆			✓				✓						✓				
373	11.2	Europe's leading telecom companies: how to dial up new demand?			◆				✓				✓		✓	✓	✓	✓	✓				
381	11.3	Buying travel online: choosing a strategy for the internet age	◆						✓				✓		✓				✓				
402	12.1	PepsiCo: organising to integrate its acquisitions	◆				◆										✓			✓			
416	12.2	Royal Dutch/Shell – what does it take to bring change?	◆		◆							✓		✓			✓			✓			
426	12.3	How ABB empowered its managers and then reversed the process	◆		◆								✓							✓			
440	13.1	European football: bad strategy? Or bad implementation?	◆		◆							✓								✓			
449	13.2	Strategic planning at Canon with a co-operative corporate style				◆											✓		✓	✓			
453	13.3	Informal strategic controls at Nestlé	◆									✓					✓			✓			
463	13.4	Prescriptive strategic planning at Spillers in the late 1970s		◆						✓					✓		✓						
472	14.1	Prescriptive and emergent strategies: profits from the sun, wind and sea? Even from nuclear energy?		◆	◆					✓	✓	✓									✓		✓
483	14.2	Green strategy; two problems with solar power				◆				✓	✓							✓			✓		✓
491	14.3	Green strategy in the world car industry: who makes the rules?				◆				✓	✓							✓			✓		✓
498	15.1	Strategic change at Nokia: the 'Doomsday Memo'	◆									✓					✓			✓			
506	15.2	Counting on Carly	◆				◆					✓								✓			
516	15.3	Risky strategic change at EMI?	◆	◆								✓					✓			✓			
532	16.1	How Anne Mulcahy rescued Xerox	◆				◆					✓								✓			
539	16.2	Ford Motors: strategy, leadership and strategic change	◆				◆			✓	✓	✓								✓			
546	16.3	Daimler: how three leaders influenced strategy	◆		◆					✓		✓	✓							✓			
557	17.1	Chocolate maker savours its sweet desserts			◆														✓			✓	
565	17.2	Strategy lessons from three entrepreneurs – Bill Gates, Luke Johnson and John Caudwell			◆	◆			✓			✓							✓				
571	17.3	Entrepreneurs pioneer a zero carbon house	◆	◆												✓			✓			✓	✓
581	18.1	Public sector strategy: how Galileo ended up in serious trouble	◆									✓			✓						✓		
594	18.2	Windfarm or wildlife? A public interest dilemma for green strategy		◆	◆																✓		✓
602	18.3	'Should we close the Kings Theatre?' A tough strategic decision for Portsmouth City Council		◆						✓		✓			✓						✓		
613	19.1	MTV: more local than global?	◆				◆			✓							✓						
620	19.2	TCL: global strategy at one of China's largest consumer electronics companies	◆			◆				✓	✓	✓				✓							
630	19.3	Cadbury: will it ever gain global market leadership in chewing gum?	◆	◆			◆			✓							✓						
652	20.1	The changing business model of Novartis	◆		◆		◆			✓		✓	✓						✓				
660	20.2	Success and failure of two business models at Tesco	◆	◆						✓	✓						✓			✓			
665	20.3	Why a bigger business model does not necessarily mean better, but a green strategy helps	◆													✓	✓						✓

Page		LONGER AND MORE INTEGRATIVE CASES (IN PART 6)	Main area/ country						Topic or theme														
			Global	UK	European	Asia/Pacific	USA	African	Emergent/prescriptive process	Competitive environment	Competitive resources	Culture and leadership	Developing purpose	Governance and social responsibility	Strategic options	International and global strategy	Corporate-level strategy	Acquisitions and alliances	Learning and knowledge	Managing change	Public and not-for-profit	SMEs and entrepreneurship	Green strategy
674	1	Europe's leading airlines: budget strategy or bust?	◆		◆				✓	✓	✓	✓	✓		✓	✓		✓		✓			
680	2	Global beer and lager: exploring strategies in a mature market	◆		◆	◆	◆			✓	✓	✓	✓		✓	✓	✓	✓					
685	3	SABMiller: South Africa goes quietly global	◆					◆		✓	✓	✓	✓		✓	✓	✓	✓					
689	4	Prescriptive and emergent strategy: global car markets and the battle between the world's top five car companies	◆							✓	✓		✓		✓	✓		✓					✓
699	5	PSA Peugeot Citroën: stuck in the strategy slow lane?	◆			◆	◆			✓	✓	✓	✓		✓	✓	✓			✓			✓
704	6	Risks and rewards in Russia: rescue strategy at AvtoVAz Cars			◆					✓	✓				✓	✓		✓					
706	7	Competitive strategies: good news and bad news at Tata Motors	◆			◆				✓	✓	✓			✓		✓			✓			✓
712	8	Strategic leadership and change: the rise and fall of CEO Carly Fiorina at Hewlett-Packard	◆			◆				✓	✓	✓						✓		✓			
716	9	Strategic leadership: what can companies learn from 'Chainsaw Al'?					◆					✓								✓			
718	10	Sony strategy: more restructuring or complete breakup?	◆			◆			✓	✓	✓	✓			✓				✓			✓	
722	11	Emergent strategy: what's the new smart strategy for PCs, media tablets and mobiles?	◆						✓				✓		✓							✓	
728	12	Prescriptive strategy: Dell's new strategy beyond commoditisation: too little and too late?	◆						✓	✓	✓					✓							
732	13	Emergent strategy: the competitive threat to Apple Music	◆						✓	✓	✓				✓			✓	✓				
738	14	Emergent strategy: how Google's search strategy opened up the web (and earned a fortune for its inventors)	◆							✓	✓	✓							✓	✓		✓	

CASES ON THE COMPANION WEBSITE

In addition to the above cases, the companion website student section also contains the following cases with indicative answers to the case questions:

Chapter 1: Apple's profitable but risky strategy

Chapter 2: Emergent strategy at Virgin Group

Chapter 5: How GEC Marconi used attack, co-operation and game theory strategies to make an extra US$3 billion

Chapter 7: Will traditional retail banks survive the threat of the new technologies – the internet and telephone banking?

Chapter 15: Shock tactics at BOC

Chapter 17: eBay – the auction market that spans the world

Chapter 18: Olympic Games 2012: five cities bid to host the games

Chapter 19: Tate & Lyle plc: globalisation to sweeten the profit line?

Chapter 20: Side effects leave Roche reeling

In addition, the companion student website also contains the following cases in the Integrative Cases section at the end of the text but without indicative answers:

Heineken: what's the best strategy? Build brands or acquire companies?

Toyota: does it rely too heavily on production for world leadership?

Disaster and recovery: thinking outside the box at IBM

Sorting out Sony: restoring the profits and the innovative fire

ACKNOWLEDGEMENTS

First edition

During the writing of the first edition of this book, the text has benefited enormously from a panel of reviewers set up by Pitman Publishing. They are: Drs Robert Bood, Vakgroep Bedrijfseconomie, Faculty of Economics, Groningen University; Stuart Bowie, Bristol Business School, University of the West of England; Ms Maria Brouwer, Department of Economics, Amsterdam University; Bruce Lloyd, Head of Strategy, Business School, South Bank University; Professor Bente R Lowendahl, Department of Strategy and Business History, Norwegian School of Management, Sandvika; Richard Morland, Senior Lecturer in Management, Department of Business Management, Brighton University; Dr Martyn Pitt, School of Management, Bath University; Professor Louis Printz, Department of Organisation and Management, Aarhus School of Business, Denmark; Professor Dr Jacob de Smit, Faculteit der Bedrijtskunde, Erasmus University, Rotterdam; and Bill Ramsay, Associate Fellow, Templeton College, Oxford.

In addition, others have also made a significant contribution: Dr Richard Gregson and Richard Cawley, European Business School, London; Professor Colin Haslam, Royal Holloway College, University of London; Dr Carol Vielba and Dr David Edelshain, City University Business School, London; Adrian Haberberg, University of Westminster, London; Professor Kazem Chaharbaghi, University of East London; Laurie Mullins, University of Portsmouth; and Val Lencioni and Dr Dennis Barker, Middlesex University Business School. I am also grateful to Middlesex University for a part-time sabbatical to write sections of the text.

Since becoming involved in higher education, I have lectured at universities in South East England, Singapore and elsewhere. The concepts and cases have benefited from the comments, challenges and contributions of many students over this time period and I am grateful to them all.

To provide real-life examples, I have been able to draw upon material provided by a number of organisations. In particular, I would like to thank Skandia, Ford Motor Company and Portsmouth City Council. I am also grateful to the *Financial Times* for permission to adapt a number of articles as case studies for use in the book. Numerous other authors and organisations have also given permission for extracts from their work to be used: these are acknowledged appropriately in the text.

Note that Chapter 10 presents a case study of two companies, Eurofreeze and Refrigor. These are wholly fictional names developed for the purposes of the case study. No link is intended with any real company that might be trading under these or similar names in frozen food or other products. As explained in the case, the data is derived from several real cases and has been disguised to protect confidentiality.

The first edition of this book would never have happened without the major support and encouragement of the editorial team at Pearson Education. Their professionalism, experience and knowledge have been invaluable. My thanks go to Catriona King in the very early days and, later, to the invaluable Stuart Hay, together with Simon Lake and Mark Allin. Elizabeth Tarrant worked magnificently on the editorial process, Colin Reed produced an excellent design and Helen Beltran notably improved the text. Finally, Penelope Woolf provided the bedrock of guidance and support on which all else has rested. My thanks to them all.

This book has a history stretching back over a number of years, including the author's experience in nearly 30 years as a line manager and consultant in industry. To all my many colleagues over the years, I offer my grateful thanks for all the lessons learnt.

Second edition

The second edition owes much to those who contributed to the first edition: they are acknowledged above. In addition, a new panel of reviewers set up by the publishers has commented on the second edition and the text has again benefited considerably from their guidance. They are: Greet Asselburgh, Management Department, RUCA Antwerpen; Peter Berends, Faculty of Economics and Business Administration, University of Maastricht; Andy Crane, Cardiff Business School; Steven Henderson, Southampton Institute; Tom Lawton, Royal Holloway, University of London; Judy Slinn, Oxford Brookes University.

In addition to all those named above across the two editions, others have also made a significant contribution to this edition: the many students who have commented on parts of the text; Professor Harold Rose and the Dean, Professor John Quelch, London Business School; Roger Lazenby, Middlesex University Business School; Gerry Scullion, Ulster University; the participants in the two *Financial Times* Corporate Strategy Workshops in early 1999; the anonymous respondents to the academic questionnaire from the publishers on the first edition; John Meehan and one of his student groups in Liverpool John Moores University. In addition to his comments, John has also taken over responsibility for the website that operates in conjunction with this text, for which my thanks.

Various companies and organisations have given permission for their material to be used in the text. They are thanked individually in the text.

Importantly, it is right to acknowledge the immense contribution of the publishers, Pearson Education, to the development of this second edition. Their policy of seeking the highest standards in educational publishing has been crucial to this work. Their significant resource commitment to promote and communicate strategic management writing and research has been a vital element in the development of the second edition. In addition to those named above at the time of the first edition, I am particularly grateful to Jane Powell and Beth Barber for their earlier guidance and advice. More recently, Sadie McClelland and Jacqueline Senior have taken over these roles and moved the process forward with considerable skill. I would also like to record my thanks to David Harrison for the desk editing job at Harlow.

Finally, I want to thank two of my nephews: Christian Lynch, who sorted out my computer software, and Stephen Lynch, who sorted out the hardware. Without them and all the others who have contributed to the text, this second edition would never have happened.

Third edition

Once again, Pearson Education set up a panel to comment on the second edition and provide invaluable comments for the third edition. The guidance of the following is much appreciated: John Ball, Swansea Business School; Jack Colford, Oxford Brookes University; Sandy Cripps, East London Business School; Bo Eriksen, University of Southern Denmark; Joyce Falkenberg, Norwegian School of Economics and Business Administration; Moira Fischbacher, University of Glasgow; Simon Harris, University of Stirling, UK; Paul Jackson, Coventry Business School; Tomi Laamanen, Helsinki University of Technology; Juha Laurila, Helsinki School of Economics; Tim Moran, University of Salford; Robert Morgan, University of Wales, Aberystwyth; Colin M Souster, University of Luton; Barry Witcher, University of East Anglia.

Fourth edition

As with previous editions, Pearson Education set up a panel to comment on the third edition and provide invaluable comments for this fourth edition. The comments of the following have been much appreciated: Dr Paul Baines, Middlesex University Business School; Dr David Lal, Aberdeen Business School, The Robert Gordon University; Dr Celine Abecassis-Moedas, Centre for Business Management, Queen Mary University of London; Bruce Cronin, University of Greenwich Business School; Marcin Wojtysiak-Kotlarski, Collegium of Business Administration, Warsaw School of Economics; Philippa Collins, School of Management and Languages, Heriot-Watt University; James

Rowe, Sunderland University Business School; Dr Denis Harrington, Business Postgraduate Centre, School of Business, Waterford Institute of Technology, Ireland; Dr James Cunningham, Department of Management, National University of Ireland, Galway; Dr Edward Shinnick, National University of Ireland, Cork; Colin Turner, University of Hull; Dr Paul Hughes, The Business School, Loughborough University; Dr Jonathan Moizer, Plymouth Business School, University of Plymouth; Professor Robert E. Morgan, Cardiff Business School, Cardiff University.

Fifth edition

As with previous editions, Pearson Education set up a panel to comment on the fourth edition and provide invaluable comments for the fifth edition. My grateful thanks are due to the following reviewers: Andrew Muir, University of Glasgow; David Lal, The Robert Gordon University; David Wornham, University of the West of England, Bristol; Donald Nordberg, London Metropolitan University; Kyle Bruce, Aston University; Laura Costanzo, University of Surrey; Ian Hipkin, University of Essex; Jonathan Lean, University of Plymouth; Dermot Breslin, University of Lincoln; William Sun, Leeds Metropolitan University.

Sixth edition

Again, it is right to acknowledge the major contribution of the publishers, Pearson Education, to the development of this and all the previous editions. Over the years, many Pearson people have contributed with professionalism, enthusiasm and real interest. For the first two editions, I listed all the major Pearson contributors individually. However, there have now been so many over the years that the list has become somewhat unmanageable. May I therefore simply record my thanks collectively to everyone involved.

As with previous editions, Pearson Education set up a panel to comment on the fifth edition and provide invaluable comments for this sixth edition. The comments of the following have been much appreciated: Poul Houman Andersen, The Aarhus University School of Business; Raluca Bunduchi, University of Aberdeen Business School; Kevin Burt, University of Lincoln; Annemarie Davis, University of South Africa; Johan Frishammar, Luleå University of Technology; Amie Heene, Ghent University; Anders McIlquham-Schmidt, The Aarhus University School of Business; Marius Ungerer, University of Stellenbosch Business School.

Seventh edition

As with previous editions, Pearson Education set up a panel to comment on the sixth edition and provide invaluable comments for this seventh edition. The comments of the following have been much appreciated: Dr Ian Heywood, The University of Aberdeen Business School; Dr Maria Emmanouilidou, Kent Business School; Omar Al-Tabbaa, University of Huddersfield; Christian Lebrenz, Hochschule Augsburg; Mark Holbourn, University of Bedfordshire; Dr M Oktemgil, University of Birmingham, Birmingham Business School; Richard Godfrey, University of Leicester; Professor Thomas Lawton, Open University Business School.

PUBLISHER'S ACKNOWLEDGEMENTS

We are grateful to the following for permission to reproduce copyright material:

Figures

Figure 1.6 adapted from *Managing Change for Competitive Success*, Blackwell Publishing Ltd. (Pettigrew, A. and Whipp, R. 1991) p. 26, Copyright © 1991 by Andrew Pettigrew and Richard Whipp, reproduced with permission of B. Blackwell in the format republish in a book via Copyright Clearance Center; Figure 3.2 adapted from K. Koopman and J.M. Montias, On the description and comparison of economic systems, in *Comparison of Economic Systems: Theoretical and Methodological Approaches*, Figure 3.3 (Eckstein, A. (ed.) 1971), University of California Press, Berkeley, CA, Copyright © The Regents of the University of California; Figure 3.5 from *Competitive Strategy: Techniques for Analyzing Industries and Competitors*, Free Press (Porter, M.E. 1998) p. 5, Figure 1.1, Copyright © 1980, 1998 Michael E. Porter, all rights reserved, reprinted with the permission of Simon & Schuster Publishing Group, a division of Simon & Schuster, Inc.; Figure 4.5 from *Competitive Advantage: Creating and Sustaining Superior Performance* (Porter, M.E. 1998) p. 37, Figure 2.2, Copyright © 1985, 1998 by Michael E. Porter, all rights reserved, reprinted with the permission of Simon & Schuster Publishing Group, a division of Simon & Schuster, Inc.; Figure 4.6 from *Competitive Advantage: Creating and Sustaining Superior Performance* (Porter, M.E. 1998) p. 35, Figure 2.1, Copyright © 1985, 1998 by Michael E. Porter, all rights reserved, reprinted with the permission of Simon & Schuster Publishing Group, a division of Simon & Schuster, Inc.; Figure 4.12 from Managing strategic change: strategy, culture and action, *Long Range Planning*, Vol. 25 (1), pp. 28–36 (Johnson, G. 1992), with permission from Elsevier; Figure 5.7 adapted from Sustainable competitive advantage: towards a dynamic resource-based strategy, *Management Decision*, Vol. 37 (1), pp. 45–50 (Chaharbaghi, K. and Lynch, R. 1999), with permission from MCB University Press; Figure 7.4 from *The Knowledge-Creating Company: How Japanese Companies Create Their Dynamics of Innovation*, Oxford University Press, Inc. (Nonaka, I. and Takeuchi, H. 1995) p. 72, Figure 3.2, Copyright © 1995 by Oxford University Press, Inc., reproduced with permission of Oxford University Press, Inc. in the format book via Copyright Clearance Center; Figure 7.5 from *Wellsprings of Knowledge*, Harvard Business School Press (Leonard, D. 1995) p. 9, Figure 1.2, Copyright © 1995 by the Harvard Business School Publishing Corporation, all rights reserved, reprinted by permission of Harvard Business Review Press; Figure 8.3 from *Competitive Advantage: Creating and Sustaining Superior Performance* (Porter, M.E. 1998) p. 12, Figure 1.3, Copyright © 1985, 1998 by Michael E. Porter, all rights reserved, reprinted with the permission of Simon & Schuster Publishing Group, a division of Simon & Schuster, Inc.; Figure 10.2 Copyright © Arthur D. Little, reproduced by permission of Arthur D. Little Ltd.; Figure 13.9 from *The Strategy-Focused Organization*, Harvard Business School Press (Kaplan, R.S. and Norton, D.P. 2001) p. 96, Copyright © 2001 by the Harvard Business School Publishing Corporation, all rights reserved, reprinted by permission of Harvard Business Review Press; Figure 14.2 from *Renewables 2010 Global Status Report*, REN21 Secretariat, Copyright © 2010 Deutsche Gesellschaft fur Technische Zusammenarbeit (GTZ) GmbH; Figure 14.3 from A. Hoffman and P. Bansal, Retrospective, Perspective, and Prospective: Introduction to The Oxford Handbook on Business and the Natural Environment, in *The Oxford Handbook on Business and the Natural Environment*, pp. 3–25 (Bansal, P. and Hoffman, A. (eds.) 2011), © Oxford University Press, Figure 1.1 from p. 5 by permission of Oxford University Press, www.oup.com; Figure 14.4 adapted from *Climate Change – A Business Revolution?* The Carbon Trust (2008) p. 3, Copyright © The Carbon Trust 2008; Figure 14.7 from *The Natural Advantage of Nations: Business Opportunities, Innovation and Governance in the 21st Century*, London: Earthscan (Hargroves, K. and Smith, M.H. 2005) p. 17, Figure 1.1; Figure 15.7 from *Managing Change for Competitive Success*, Blackwell Publishing Ltd. (Pettigrew, A. and Whipp, R. 1991) p. 104, Copyright © 1991 by Andrew Pettigrew and Richard Whipp, reproduced with permission of B. Blackwell in the format republish in a book via Copyright Clearance Center; Figure 17.3 from D.A. Kolb and R. Fry, Toward an applied theory of experiential learning, in *Theories of Group Process* (Cooper, C.

(ed.) 1975), Copyright © John Wiley & Sons Ltd.; Figure 18.3 from *Public Management Reform: A Comparative Analysis*, Oxford University Press (Pollitt, C. and Bouckaert, G. 2000), reproduced with permission of Oxford University Press in the format book via Copyright Clearance Center; Figure 19.3 from *The Competitive Advantage of Nations*, Free Press (Porter, M.E. 1998) p. 72, Figure 3.1, Copyright © 1990, 1998 by Michael E. Porter, all rights reserved, reprinted with the permission of Simon & Schuster Publishing Group, a division of Simon & Schuster, Inc.; Figure 19.7 from *Managing the Multinational Enterprise: Organization of the Firm and Ownership of the Subsidiaries* (Stopford, J.M. and Wells, L.T. 1972) Copyright © 1972 by Basic Books, Inc., reproduced with permission of Basic Books, Inc. in the format republish in a book via Copyright Clearance Center; also with permission of Pearson Education Ltd. and the authors; Figure 20.5 from From strategy to business models and on to tactics, *Long Range Planning*, Vol. 43 (2–3), pp. 195–215 (Casadesus-Masanell, R. and Ricart, J.E. 2010), with permission from Elsevier.

Screenshots

Screenshot on page 248 from 3M Canada homepage, http://www.3m.com./intl/ca, Copyright © 3M IPC. This material is reproduced by courtesy of 3M. No further reproduction is permitted without 3M's prior written consent.

Tables

Table 3.2 from *Implanting Strategic Management*, FT Prentice Hall (Ansoff, I. and McDonnell, E. 1990) reprinted by permission of the Ansoff Family Trust; Table 4.2 from How much does industry matter?, *Strategic Management Journal*, March, pp. 64–75 (Rumelt, R. 1991), Copyright © 1991 John Wiley & Sons, Inc., reprinted by permission of John Wiley & Sons, Inc.; Table 4.4 from *Gaining and Sustaining Competitive Advantage*, 2nd ed., Pearson Education, Inc. (Barney, J.B. 2002), printed and electronically reproduced by permission of Pearson Education, Inc., Upper Saddle River, New Jersey; Table 5.2 from Formula Money, *Financial Times*, p. 20, 17 March 2009, © The Financial Times Limited 2009, all rights reserved; Table 6.1 adapted from *Corporate Responsibility*, Pitman Publishing (Cannon, T. 1994), with permission from Pearson Education Ltd.; Table 15.1 from *Hewlett Packard Annual Report and Accounts 2001*; Table on page 725 Copyright © Portio Research.

Text

Case Study 3.4 adapted from Pete and Ken's excellent adventure, *FT Creative Business* (Hofmann, K.), 19 March 2002, Copyright © The Financial Times Limited 2002, all rights reserved; Exhibit 4.3 adapted from *The Economics of Strategy*, John Wiley & Sons, Inc. (Besanko, D., Dranove, D. and Shenley, M. 1996) p. 73, Copyright © John Wiley & Sons, Inc., reprinted by permission of John Wiley & Sons, Inc.; Exhibit 6.7 from Company Mission, Values and Guiding Principles, Ford Motor Company (1996), Copyright © Ford Motor Company 1996, reprinted with permission; Exhibit 7.2 from *Skandia Annual Report and Accounts 1997*, reproduced courtesy of Skandia Insurance Company Ltd. (publ); Exhibit 12.6 adapted from An integrative framework for strategy-making processes, *Academy of Management Review*, Vol. 17, pp. 327–351 (Hart, S. 1992), Copyright © 1992 Academy of Management; Case Study 17.1 adapted from Chocolate maker savours its sweet desserts, *Financial Times*, p. 13 (Rafferty, E.), 20 April 2004, Copyright © The Financial Times Limited 2004, all rights reserved; Case Study 20.3 adapted from Why bigger is not necessarily better, *Financial Times*, p. 10 (Owen, G.), 24 August 2010, © The Financial Times Limited 2010, all rights reserved; Case Study 9 adapted from Sunbeam chainsaw massacre victim: profile of Al Dunlap, Sunbeam Corporation, *Financial Times*, p. 15 (Lambert, R.), 17 June 1998, © The Financial Times Limited 1998, all rights reserved.

In some instances we have been unable to trace the owners of copyright material, and we would appreciate any information that would enable us to do so.

PART 1
Introduction

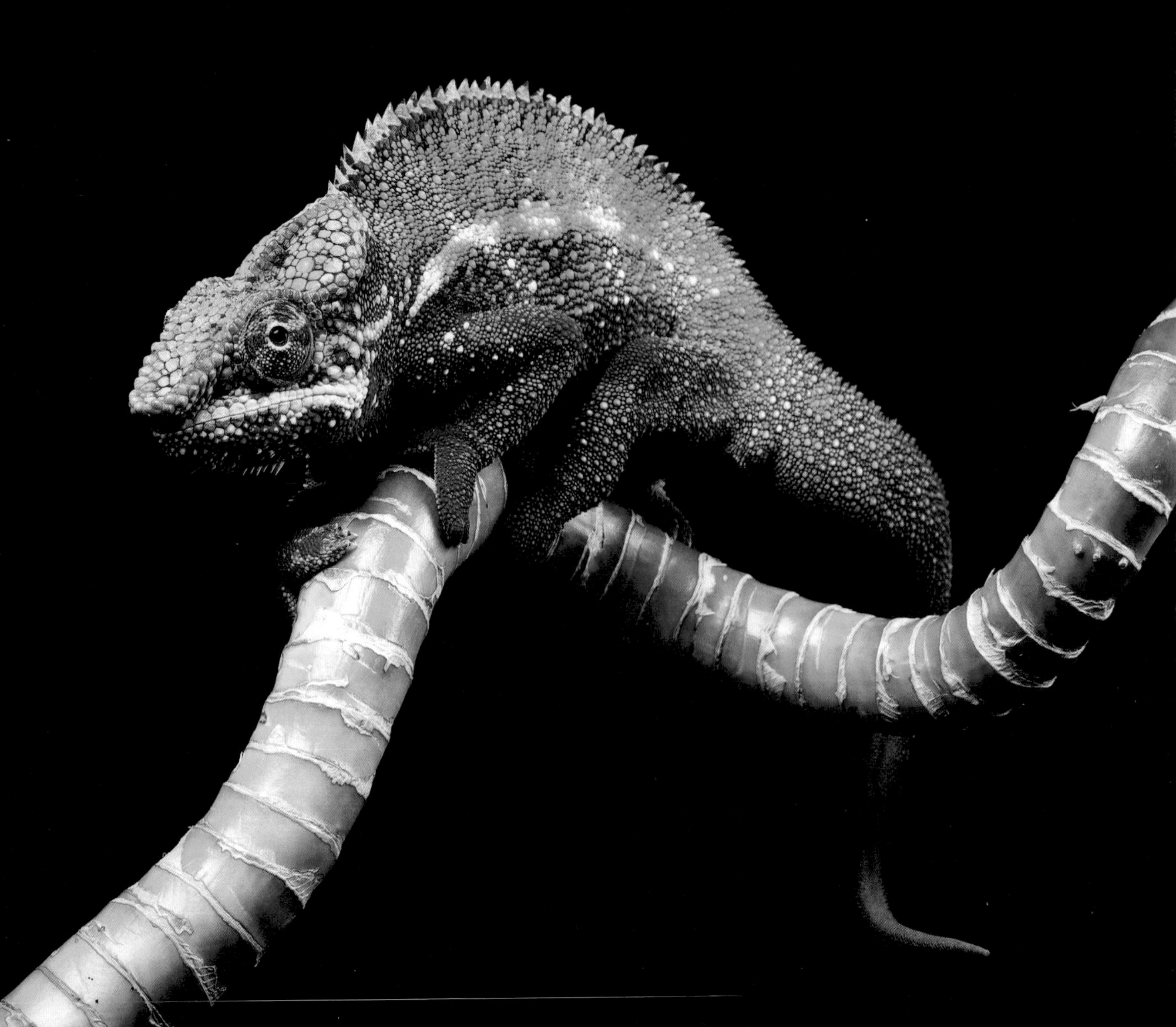

This part of the book introduces the concept of strategic management. Chapter 1 outlines the main elements of the subject and explains its importance and its role in delivering the purpose of the organisation. The two main approaches to the process of strategic management are outlined and explored. Chapter 2 gives a fuller review of how strategic management has evolved and discusses in greater depth the two main approaches in its development.

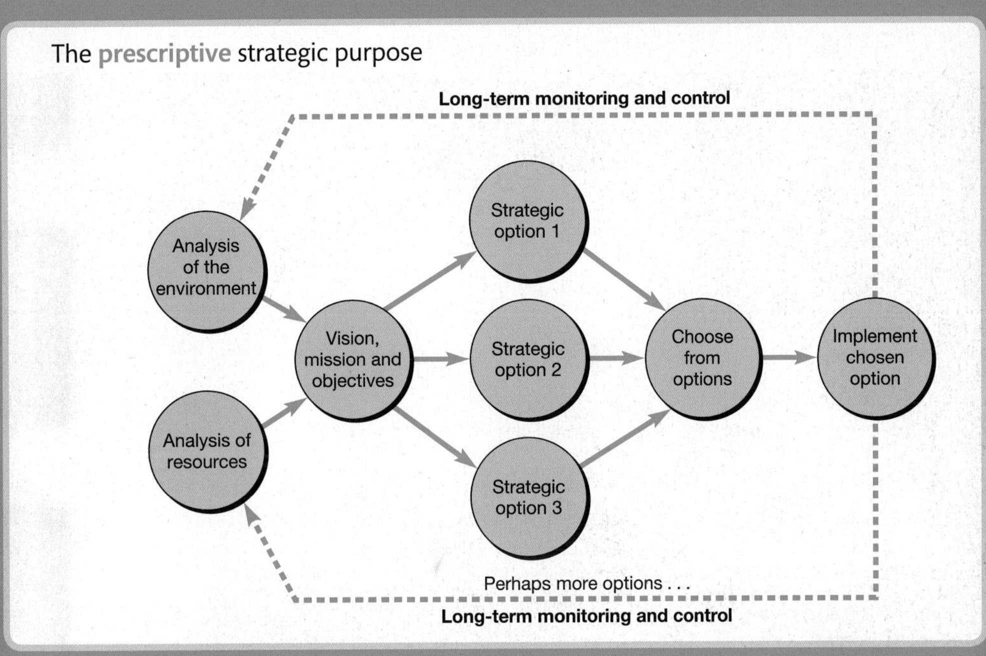

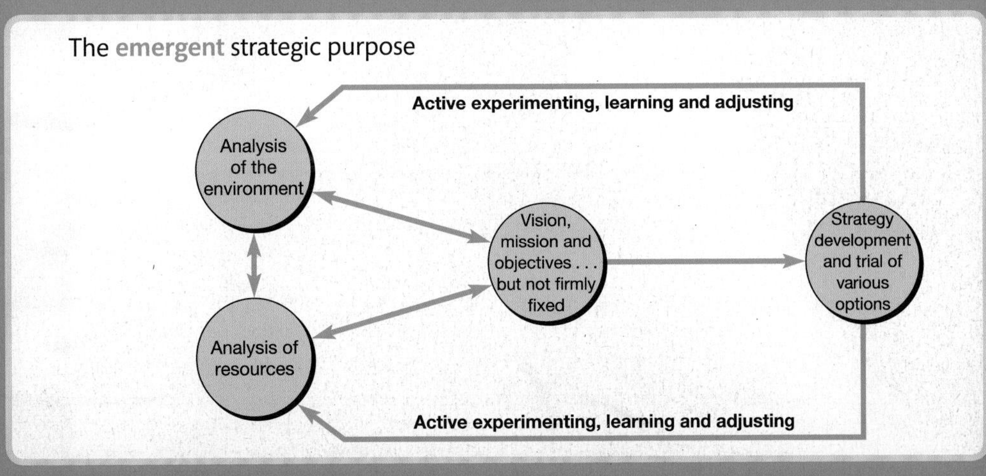

Key strategic management questions

CHAPTER 1
Strategic management

- What is strategic management and why is it important?
- What are the core areas of strategic management and how do they link together?
- Distinguish between process, content and context of a strategy.
- Outline the two main approaches to strategy development.
- Explain the differences between the prescriptive and emergent strategy models.

CHAPTER 2
A review of theory and practice

- How have current ideas on strategic management evolved?
- What are the main approaches to strategic management?
- What are the main prescriptive and emergent theories of strategy?
- How does the theory of strategic management relate to corporate practice?

CHAPTER 1
Strategic management

Video and sound summary of this chapter

LEARNING OUTCOMES

When you have worked through this chapter, you will be able to:

- define strategic management and explain its five special elements;
- explain the core areas of strategic management and how they link together;
- distinguish between process, content and context of a strategy;
- outline the two main approaches to strategy development;
- explain the differences between the prescriptive and emergent strategy models.

INTRODUCTION

Strategic management is exciting and challenging. It makes fundamental decisions about the future direction of an organisation: its purpose, its resources and how it interacts with the world in which it operates.

Every aspect of the organisation plays a role in this strategy – its people, its finances, its production methods and its environment (including its customers). In this introductory chapter we examine how these broad areas need to be structured and developed if the organisation is to continue to operate effectively.

Strategic management is complicated by the fact that there is considerable disagreement between researchers on the subject and how its elements are linked together. There are two main routes and these are examined in this chapter: the prescriptive process and the emergent process. As a result, two models have been developed to explain the subject. These are shown in the opening diagram to this part of the book (see p 3).

Video Part 1

In exploring strategic management, it is useful to begin by examining why it is important and what it contains. A useful distinction can also be drawn between its process, content and context. Finally, the two main strategy routes are then examined – see Figure 1.1.

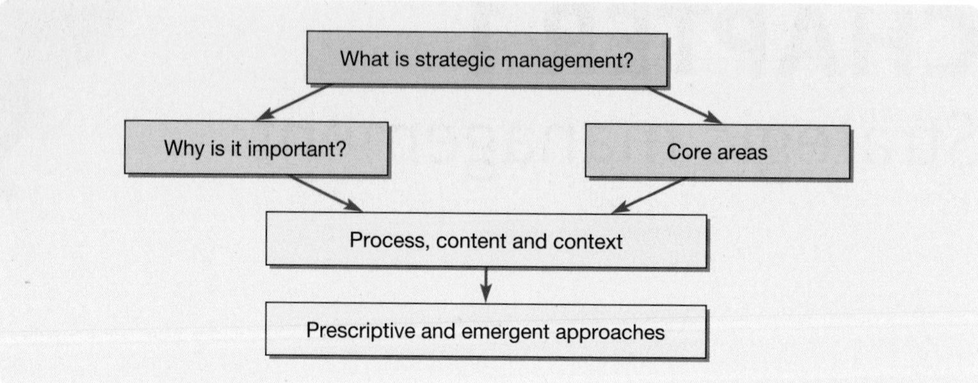

Figure 1.1 Analysing strategic management

CASE STUDY 1.1

Why did Kodak collapse?

Kodak, formerly one of the world's leading photographic companies, filed for Chapter 11 bankruptcy protection in 2012. Why? What went wrong with its business strategy?

Early years

Founded by the entrepreneur George Eastman in 1880, Kodak became the world leader in silver halide photographic film by the 1920s. It introduced the first cheap, mass market film camera, the Kodak Brownie, in 1900 - US$1 for the camera and 15 cents for each roll of film. Essentially, the strategy was to hook customers with a cheap camera so that they would repeat buy the film. Kodak had major economies of scale in film production: the profit margins, reportedly around 75 per cent, were described as 'luxurious'. This strategic resource – chemistry-based, continuous flow manufacturing – was part of its competitive advantage. The company's purpose was to grow profitably and thus generate more value added. By 1993, the company had annual sales of nearly US$13 billion. It had strong branding, wide distribution and quality products. But some Kodak executives could already see 'the oncoming freight train' of digital cameras: they did not need rolls of film. This would eventually undermine its major source of revenue. The real problem was that too many at Kodak were either unable or unwilling to jump out of the train's path.

The twenty years of change: 1993–2012

Although some senior managers at Kodak predicted the inevitable, others were more optimistic. Kodak itself invented one of the early digital cameras in 1975. The company had previously launched other film camera designs like the Kodak Instamatic camera in 1963. The problem for the company was that it was investing heavily in research and development expenditure, but it was not producing any major new winners. The contrast with one of its competitors, the Japanese printer, lens and camera company Canon, is quite striking. Kodak sales were essentially flat and then declining in the 20 years to 2013. Canon's sales increased steadily from new products and new markets: see Figure 1.2.

The declining revenue figures at Kodak in Figure 1.2 hide a more complex strategic story: the loss of film sales as customers moved to digital cameras was partially replaced by sales of Kodak digital cameras. But, unlike Canon, Kodak made no serious attempt to launch upmarket camera models where the profit margins were higher. Kodak's mindset was still cheap, mass market products. Moreover, competition was high in the mass market and Kodak had no clear competitive advantages beyond its well-known brand name and entrenched distribution position with some retailers.

At the same time as launching cheap digital cameras, Kodak was closing down most of its film-making factories: demand dropped as customers moved to digital cameras or mobile phones. The company closed 13 factories and 130 film processing labs with the loss of 47,000 jobs over the period to 2007. Kodak was loss-making and struggling to survive. The company spent US$3.4 billion restructuring itself alone in the period 2004–2007. In addition, Kodak offered generous pension and health insurance benefits to many of its former employees: these are often called 'legacy costs'. This built up a big company pension liability that resulted finally in the Chapter 11 bankruptcy protection filing in 2012.

What did Kodak do well in strategy?

Four areas stand out:

1 Strong marketing and branding with good reliable film products.

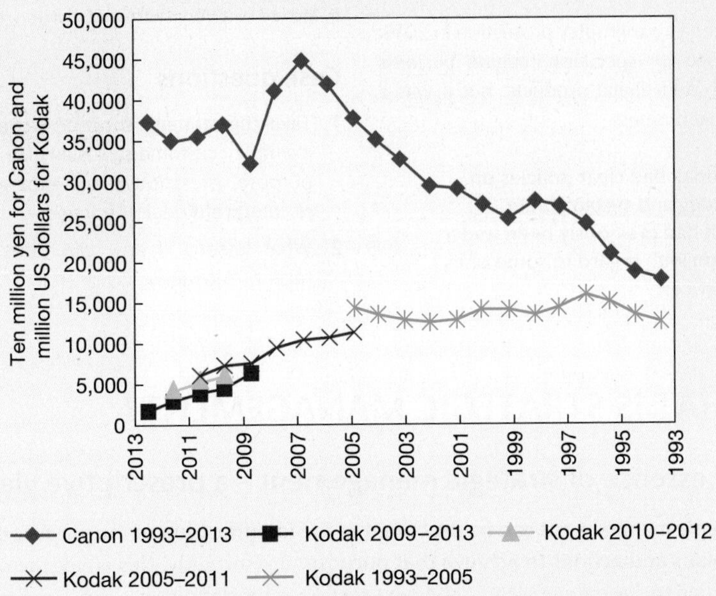

Figure 1.2 Comparing sales growth at Canon and decline at Kodak as it sold assets and ceased most film sales

Notes:

- The sales for the two companies are in different currencies, but the trend is clear and the two companies had similar starting sales levels in 1993: nearly $15 billion for Canon, nearly $13 billion for Kodak.
- The Canon sales declined during the world recession in 2008–2009.
- The Kodak accounting base was changed in 2005 and 2011 because parts of the company were sold. This meant that strict comparison with earlier years was no longer possible, but the trend is clear.

Source: author from company annual report and accounts for various years.

2 It identified digital cameras early as being a game-changer for the company. Former employee, Larry Matteson commented: 'I can't think of another major company in the US that has undergone as tough a transformational problem as Kodak.' The company completely relaunched its digital strategy in the years 2000 onwards.

3 It exploited its low-cost film manufacturing and processing base as a competitive advantage for as long as possible. It is still using this knowledge but for industrial and commercial customers where film has not yet replaced digital cameras – for example in the Hollywood film industry (though digital is now coming here as well).

4 It recognised the value of patenting its products to maintain its competitive advantage in digital camera technology. However, it has been involved in some recent expensive legal battles to preserve its rights (against Apple and RIM/ Blackberry).

So, what did Kodak do badly in its business strategy?

With the benefit of hindsight, it is possible to identify at least five major errors:

1 Although it moved into digital cameras, it focused mainly on low-end camera designs. Thus the company was moving from its dominance of the highly profitable roll-film business to the lower profit margin and highly competitive digital camera business.

2 More fundamentally, many (but not all) Kodak senior managers were never fully convinced about the death of film until it was too late. This meant that the move into digital was implemented slowly and with reluctance. The Kodak old guard were against digital.

3 Anticipating the change, Kodak attempted to diversify its product range into printers and scanners. But these were also competing against low-cost competition in fragmented markets: this was a poor product market choice with no clear competitive advantage. Kodak finally ceased to sell printers in 2012.

4 Kodak also diversified into other unrelated product areas, including chemicals, pharmaceuticals and health products. These divisions were later sold, some after running into profit problems. But, unlike its rival Fuji Film who had moved into components for LCD screens, Kodak had no other business to deliver profits while it sorted out digital.

5 Its pension benefits were too generous, leading to legacy cost issues that eventually led to the Chapter 11 filing.

Where is Kodak now?

Kodak came out of Chapter 11 bankruptcy protection in 2013: smaller, wiser and focused on specialist imaging business markets that still use film and digital products, but it was a shadow of its former global business.

In 2013, Kodak had clear policies on green strategy and sustainability. However, it had previously been under investigation with regard to some of its earlier practices.

Case questions

1 Take the strategy concepts covered in this chapter: for example, customers, sustainable competitive advantage, purpose, prescriptive and emergent strategies. Can you re-interpret Kodak's strategies using these concepts?

2 What lessons, if any, can other companies learn from recent strategies?

1.1 WHAT IS STRATEGIC MANAGEMENT?

1.1.1 The essence of strategic management – a prescriptive view

Definition ▶ **Strategic management can be described as the identification of the *purpose* of the organisation and the plans and actions to achieve that purpose.**[2] Importantly, this is not the only definition. We will consider an alternative view in the next section. This definition clearly carries the implication that it is possible to plan strategy in advance and then carry out that strategy over time: rather like a doctor writing out a prescription with the aim of curing an illness – hence the word *prescriptive* strategy.

Taking the well-known web search company Google as an example, the company's early sense of purpose was to provide work for the owners, friends and immediate employees. In later years, the purpose changed as the company grew larger and it was able to seek new customers and broaden its product range. The purpose became a broader concept that included dividends to independent shareholders beyond its original founders and offering its services to a far wider range of customers. All the time, the founders were developing new business opportunities through planned expansion of their operations – both internationally and in terms of the range of services offered by Google. The company's strategies are explored in more depth in Case 14 at the end of this book.

Video Part 1

Within this definition, strategic management consists of two main elements: corporate-level strategy and business-level strategy. Figure 1.3 captures these two important aspects of the topic of strategic management. Early commentators such as Ansoff[3] and Drucker[4] clearly refer to both these aspects of strategy: mapping out the future directions that need to be adopted against the resources possessed by the organisation.

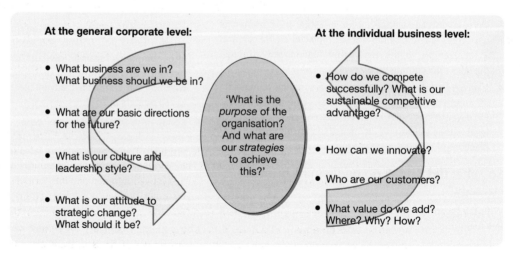

At the general corporate level:

- What business are we in? What business should we be in?
- What are our basic directions for the future?
- What is our culture and leadership style?
- What is our attitude to strategic change? What should it be?

'What is the *purpose* of the organisation? And what are our *strategies* to achieve this?'

At the individual business level:

- How do we compete successfully? What is our sustainable competitive advantage?
- How can we innovate?
- Who are our customers?
- What value do we add? Where? Why? How?

Figure 1.3 The essence of strategic management

- *At the general corporate or headquarters level,* basic decisions need to be taken over what business the company is in or should be in. The culture and leadership of the organisation are also important at this broad general level.[5] For example, Google developed a major new European headquarters to match its American operation: the basic strategic decision to move internationally was taken at the centre of the organisation. Importantly, Google decided that the original American spirit of the organisation needed to be replicated in Europe. Hence, the company designed its new headquarters in Zurich, Switzerland, with funky colours and bean bags and it began recruiting innovative team-players who would fit the special Google culture. Corporate-level strategy can also be seen in the following definition of strategic management:

  > Strategic management is the pattern of major objectives, purposes or goals and essential policies or plans for achieving those goals, stated in such a way as to define what business the company is in or is to be in and the kind of company it is or is to be.[6]

- *At the business level,* strategic management is concerned with competing for customers, generating value from the resources and the underlying principle of the sustainable competitive advantages of those resources over rival companies. For example, Google in the early twenty-first century was investing heavily in new internet services such as the Google earth mapping library archiving as described in Case 14 in Part 6. Business-level strategy can be seen in the following definition of strategic management:

  > The strategy of the firm is the match between its internal capabilities and its external relationships. It describes how it responds to its suppliers, its customers, its competitors and the social and economic environment within which it operates.[7]

However, as pointed out above, there is no universally agreed definition of strategy.[8] For example, some strategy writers, such as Campbell and others,[9] have concentrated on corporate-level activity. By contrast, most strategy writing and research, such as that by Porter,[10] has concentrated on the business level. This book explores *both* levels.

1.1.2 An alternative view of strategy – an emergent view

Some strategists dispute the approach to strategy described above.[11] Some writers, like Quinn, emphasise the uncertainty of the future and suggest that setting out to identify a purpose and a single strategy and then develop a complete strategic plan may be a fruitless task.[12]

They see strategic management as being essentially entrepreneurial and dynamic, with an element

Definition ▶ of risk. **Strategic management can be described as finding market opportunities, experimenting and developing competitive advantage over time.** The intended purpose of the strategy may not necessarily be realised in practice. This definition is clearly different from that mentioned earlier. For example, Google has changed the way that it sells advertising space on the internet on two separate occasions after its initial launch of the service: the company adapted its strategy as a result of market experience. This suggests that strategy evolves as the events both inside and outside the organisation change over time – hence the word *emergent* strategy.

1.1.3 What is strategic management? A modern consensus view

In view of the above two fundamental differences of view about the nature of strategic management, it is reasonable to enquire whether there is any modern consensus on the topic. Three strategists investigated this in the years 2002–2005: they surveyed the views of senior strategy writers and researchers on the topic over the period 1984–2003.[13] In summary, they concluded that there was an implicit agreement on the definition of the field of strategic management amongst leading

Definition ▶ strategy researchers and writers, as follows. **'The field of strategic management deals with the major intended and emergent initiatives taken by general managers on behalf of owners, involving utilization of resources, to enhance the performance of firms in their external environments.'**[14] Essentially, this definition combines the earlier two approaches above in that it contains reference to both intended (called prescriptive in this text) and emergent perspectives. This book explicitly employs this consensual definition.

Equally, this definition is also reflected in the recognition by business leaders that the traditional elements in strategy – such as competitive advantage, controlling costs, maintaining quality and seeking technological innovation – are necessary but insufficient for success. For example, A J Laffley, chief executive of the global multinational company Procter and Gamble, explained: 'The name of the game is innovation. We work really hard to try to turn innovation into a strategy and a process.'[15]

Within this framework, the main differences between the prescriptive and emergent approaches cannot be ignored. Therefore this text explores both prescriptive and emergent processes and their implications for strategy development. However, it focuses more on the former than the latter because the former has received more attention in the literature.

1.2 THE MAIN TOPICS COVERED IN STRATEGY

Examining the actions further at the *business level* of strategic management and focusing on this definition, every organisation has to manage its strategies in three main areas:

1 the organisation's internal *resources*;

2 the external *environment* within which the organisation operates;

3 the organisation's ability to *add value* to what it does.

Strategic management can be seen as the linking process between the management of the organisation's internal resources and its external relationships with its customers, suppliers, competitors and the economic and social environment in which it exists.[16] The organisation develops these relationships from its abilities and resources. Hence, the organisation uses its history, skills, resources, knowledge and various concepts to explore its future actions. Figure 1.4 shows some examples of this process.

For some large organisations, there are additional aspects of strategy that occur at their headquarters. This is called the *corporate level* of strategic management and covers such topics as raising finance and dealing with subsidiaries: these are explored in Chapter 9.

1.2.1 Resource strategy

The *resources and capabilities* of an organisation include its human resource skills, the investment and the capital in every part of the organisation. Organisations need to develop strategies to optimise the use of these resources. In particular, it is essential to investigate the *sustainable competitive advantage* that will allow the organisation to survive and prosper against competition. For example, Google (see Case 14 in Part 6) had advantages in its possession of unique and secret algorithms for handling large volumes of computer data and its established network of satisfied users. It had also invested heavily in branding its products and in the network of companies that use Google to advertise their services. All these were part of its resources and capabilities.

1.2.2 Environmental strategy

In this context, *environment* encompasses every aspect external to the organisation itself: not only the economic and political circumstances, which may vary widely around the world, but also competitors, customers and suppliers, who may vary in being aggressive to a greater or lesser degree. Customers and competitors are particularly important here. In strategy, the word 'environment' does *not* just mean the 'green, preserve the planet' issues, though these are important and are included in the definition.

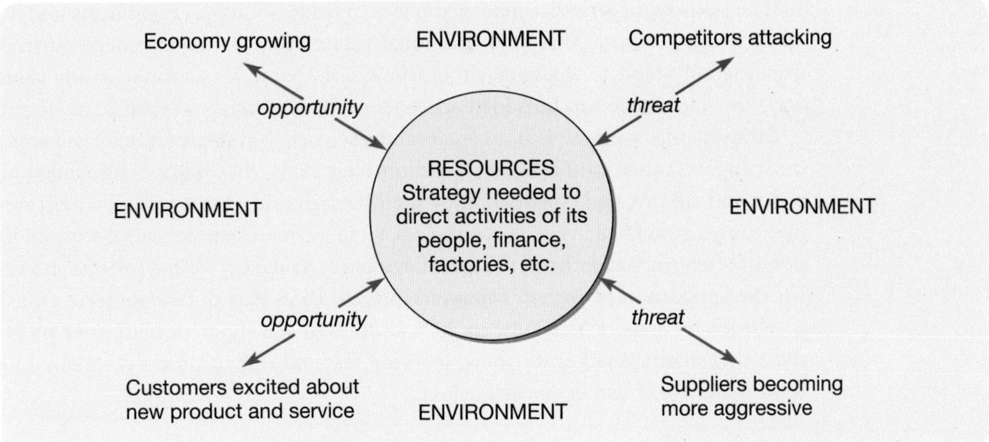

Figure 1.4 Examples of how strategic management links the organisation's resources with its environment

Organisations therefore need to develop strategies that are best suited to their strengths and weaknesses in relation to the environment in which they operate. For example, Google faced a highly competitive environment for the launch of its first information search engine from established American companies such as Yahoo! and Ask Jeeves. In addition, the company had to cope with changing levels of economic growth in many markets around the world, which influenced the decisions of its customers to search for new sources of products and services.

Some commentators, such as Ohmae,[17] suggest that a strategy is really only needed when an organisation faces competitors: no competitive threat means there is no need for strategy. This is a rather narrow view of strategy and its environment: even a monopoly without competitors could need a strategy to defend its position. With a general move to privatise the former nationalised monopolies around the world, strategic management may be required for this reason alone. Equally, charitable foundations compete for funds from donors and sometimes for the volunteers that make the wheels turn. Strategic management is no less relevant in this context.

Other commentators, such as Mintzberg,[18] have suggested that the environment is so uncertain, particularly at a global level, that it may be impossible to *plan* a long-term strategy. This may need to be *crafted*, i.e. built up gradually through a learning process involving experimentation. For example, the evidence from Case 1.3 suggests that Facebook learnt to adapt its social networking strategy over the first few years of its existence, adding and adapting new services as it developed. More generally, the organisation may be seeking to add value by operating effectively, but a fast-changing environment may offer little or no possibility for the management to plan in advance. Such commentators argue that unpredictable environments make the task of devising a realistic strategy more than mere prediction about the future. Strategies have to be devised to cope with such uncertainty.

1.2.3 Adding value

There is a need to explore further the purpose of strategic management beyond the requirements of environmental change and management of resources. In essence, the need is to *add value* to the supplies brought into the organisation. To ensure its long-term survival, an organisation must take the supplies it brings in, add value to these through its operations and then deliver its output to the customer.

For example, Facebook takes the supplies it buys in – such as software, energy, skills and computer equipment – and then uses its own resources and expertise to create a product from these supplies – essentially the contents of the Facebook page – that has a value which is higher than the combined value of all the supplies which have been used to make the product. Facebook adds value and then makes the service available to its customers.

The purpose of strategic management is to bring about the conditions under which the organisation is able to create this vital additional value. Strategic management must also ensure that the organisation adapts to changing circumstances so that it can continue to add value in the future. The ways in which value can be added and enhanced are crucial to strategic management.

Strategic management is both an art and a science. No single strategy will apply in all cases. While most organisations would like to build on their skills, they will be influenced by their past experiences and culture, and constrained by their background, resources and environment (just as we are in our own individual lives). Nevertheless, strategic management is not without logic, or the application of scientific method and the use of evidence. At the end of the process, however, there is a place for the application of *business judgement*. In Case 14 in Part 6, Google took a business judgement to go ahead and acquire YouTube in 2006 in spite of the apparent high price of $1.65 billion because the video sharing market was new, growing fast and difficult for a company to enter after the first sharing networks had been established.

1.2.4 Key elements of strategic decisions

There are five key elements of strategic decisions that are related primarily to the organisation's ability to add value and compete for customers in the market place. To illustrate these elements, examples are given from the highly competitive market for video computer games, which was worth around $35 billion globally in 2010:

1 *Existing and new customers.* Customers are crucial to strategic management because they make the buying decision, not competitors. This may seem obvious, but much of the literature on strategic management has focused more heavily on competitors than on customers. Even in the public sector and the non-profit sector, customers matter. For example, there would be little point in Microsoft launching its new *Xbox* games console if it was unable to attract substantial sales. Up to 2011, Microsoft had sold over 50 million units since its launch in 2001.

2 *Implementation processes to deliver the strategy.* Strategy is at least partly about *how* to develop organisations or allow them to evolve towards their chosen purpose. For example, Microsoft began by launching *Xbox* into the US market in Autumn 2001, followed by Japan in early Spring 2002 and Europe about one month later. It then launched its next generation product – the *Xbox 360* in 2006 and the *Kinect* controller in 2010. Importantly, the whole strategic decision of Microsoft to compete in this market was taken in the 1990s and then major investments were undertaken to achieve this purpose.

3 *Offer sustainable competitive advantage.* For the long-term survival of the organisation, it is important that the strategy is sustainable. There would be little point in Microsoft launching its new *Xbox* games console if the market disappeared after six months. Up to year 2007, the company had spent millions of dollars developing the product and this would take some years to recover.[19] In addition to being sustainable, a strategy is more likely to be effective if it delivers competitive advantages over actual or potential competitors. Microsoft was much later in entering the global computer games market than its main rivals, Sony and Nintendo. Microsoft therefore needed some special competitive advantages in its new machine to persuade customers of rival products to change. Initially, it was offering what it claimed to be the best video graphics and the ability to play its games online. Subsequently, it has claimed to offer superior games and more computing power than its competitors. Its main rival – Sony PlayStation – then announced a totally new computer chip in 2005 that would beat this advantage. One way of developing competitive advantage is through *innovation* – a constant theme of this book. As some readers will be aware, Sony had technical problems with its computer chip and related laser technology so that PlayStation 3 was launched late and had to play catch-up. This is often the risk associated with innovative technology.

4 *Exploit linkages between the organisation and its environment* – links that cannot easily be duplicated and will contribute to superior performance. The strategy has to exploit the many linkages that exist between the organisation and its environment: suppliers, customers, competitors and often the

government itself. Such linkages may be contractual and formal, or they may be vague and informal (just because they are not legally binding does not mean they have little importance). In the case of video games machines, Microsoft was able to offer compatibility and connections with its other dominant computer software products – Explorer and Windows XP/Vista/7/8 – not that this link appears to have proved particularly beneficial.

5 *Vision and purpose* – the ability to move the organisation forward in a significant way beyond the current environment. This is likely to involve innovative strategies. In the highly competitive video games market, it is vital to have a vision of the future and also a clear sense of purpose. This may involve the environment but is mainly for the organisation itself: a picture of how video games might look in five years' time will challenge and direct strategic decisions over the intervening period. For Microsoft, its vision of the *Xbox* would move it from its current involvement primarily with *office* activities like report writing and presentations to new, *home entertainment* applications like video games – thus providing a completely new source of revenue. It is highly likely to involve *innovative* solutions to the strategic issues facing the company such as the Microsoft *Kinect* controller launched in 2010. The vision then needs to be turned into a specific purpose for the company over time. Nintendo had a rival vision and purpose with the launch of its revolutionary Wii games machine in 2006: this is explained and explored in Case 4.3 later in this text.

The outcome of strategic management is concerned with delivering long-term *added value* to the organisation. Microsoft was reported in 2006 as still not making any significant profits on *Xbox*, but this had changed by 2014.

To summarise with regard to the topic of strategic management, it deals with the major intended and emergent initiatives taken by general managers on behalf of owners and other stakeholders, involving the utilisation of resources, to enhance the performance of organisations in their external environments and thereby add value to the organisation.

What makes effective strategy? Given the difficulty in developing effective strategy, it makes sense to explore and answer this important question.

KEY STRATEGIC PRINCIPLES

- The field of strategic management deals with the major intended and emergent initiatives taken by general managers on behalf of owners and other stakeholders, involving the utilisation of resources, to enhance the performance of organisations in their external environments and thereby add value to the organisation.
- Strategic management can be considered at two levels in the organisation: the corporate level and the business level.
- At the corporate level, strategic management is the pattern of major objectives, purposes or goals and the essential policies or plans for achieving those goals. It involves a consideration of what business the company is in or should be in.
- At the business level, strategic management is concerned with the match between the internal capabilities of the organisation and its external relationships with customers, competitors and others outside the organisation.
- A modern consensus view of strategy adds another dimension: prescriptive and emergent processes, to the existing processes.
- Strategy is developed by a consideration of the resources of the organisation in relation to its environment, the prime purpose being to add value. The added value is then distributed among the stakeholders.
- There are five key elements to strategy. They are principally related to the need to add value and to offer advantages over competitors: customers; implementation process; sustainable competitive advantage; the exploitation of linkages between the organisation and its environment; vision and purpose. Several of these elements may well involve innovative solutions to strategic issues.

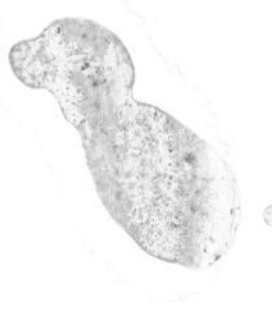

CASE STUDY 1.2

Corporate profit disaster at IBM

In the early 1990s, the world's largest computer company, International Business Machines (IBM), suffered one of the largest profit disasters in corporate history at that time. Essentially, its problems were rooted in poor strategic management. This case study examines how IBM got into such a mess. There is a free online webcase 'Thinking outside the box at IBM'. It is linked to the cases in Part 6 of this book and shows how IBM managed to retain its position as the world's largest computer company.

Over the period 1991–1993, IBM (US) suffered a net loss of almost $16 billion (half the total GDP of the Republic of Ireland at that time) – see Figure 1.5. During this period, the company had many of the characteristics of a supposedly good strategy: a dominant market share, excellent employee policies, reliable products (if not the most innovative), close relationships with national governments, responsible local and national community policies, sound finances and extensive modern plant investment around the world. Yet none of these was crucial to its profit problems, which essentially arose from a failure in strategic management. This case examines how this came about: see Figure 1.5. The reasons for the major losses are explored in the sections that follow – clearly the company was continuing to sell its products, but its costs were too high and it was unable to raise its prices because of increased competition.

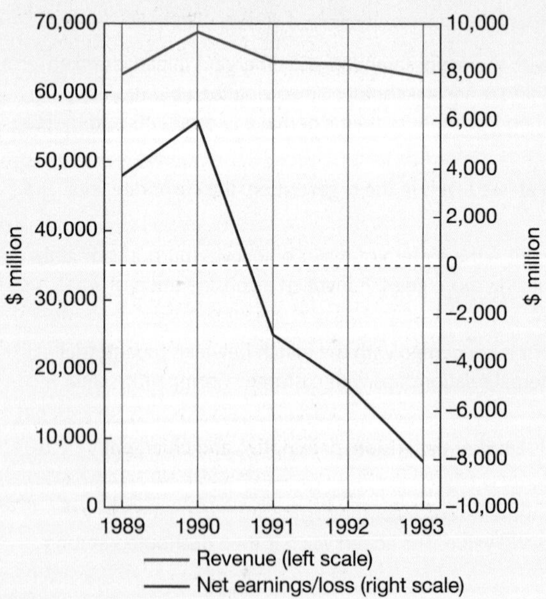

Figure 1.5 IBM Computers – sales and net income 1989–1993

IBM market domination 1970–1985

During the 1970s and early 1980s, IBM became the first-choice computer company for many of the world's leading companies: it had a remarkable global market share – approaching 60 per cent. It constructed its computers to its own proprietary standards so that they were incompatible with other computers but helped to maintain the company's domination of the market.

In essence, IBM offered large, fast and reliable machines that undertook tasks never before operated by machinery: accounting, invoicing and payroll. Above all, choosing IBM meant that risk was low for customers: 'No one ever got fired for buying IBM.' Hence, IBM was the market leader in large *mainframe* computers and earned around 60 per cent of its profits from such machines.

Reflecting its dominance of global computer markets, the IBM culture was relaxed and supremely confident of its abilities and resources. Because of its sheer size and global reach, the company was split into a series of national companies, each operating with a great degree of independence. This meant that central management control was limited, with many key strategic decisions being taken at national company level. Often, central management did not even know what was happening in key product groups until the end of the year, when all the figures for the group were added up. For major new market developments, the initiative was often taken by IBM's North American subsidiary. Throughout this period, IBM central HQ was content to rely on the success and profitability of its mainframe computer range and observe the rapid growth of another small but related market in which it had no involvement: the personal computer (PC) market.

Development of the PC market

During the late 1970s and early 1980s, small PCs with names like Osborne, Commodore and Sinclair were developed. Some of these were particularly user-friendly – for example, Apple computers. In these early years, IBM preferred to maintain a lofty technical distance. It took the view that the PC market was small and PCs would never handle the mainframe tasks. Some of these small machines were built around common computer chips and software. Although they did not have the capacity to handle any of the large computational problems of computer mainframes, the PC market was growing fast – over

In spite of its price (over $1,000) and performance, the new Atari ST was presented as good value for money in 1985. It was compatible with the new IBM-PC standard but did not use Microsoft Windows software – it used an alternative called GEM, which has now disappeared. The Atari Company itself ceased to trade around 1990.

100 per cent per annum in some years. In the late 1970s, IBM was exploring new growth areas and decided to launch its own small machine onto the market.

The launch of the IBM PC in 1981

Because IBM's existing company structure was large and nationally based and its culture was so slow and blinkered, it chose to set up a totally new subsidiary to manufacture and market its first PC. Moreover, it did not use its own proprietary semiconductor chips and operating software. It acquired them respectively from the medium-sized chip manufacturer Intel (US) and from what was then a small software company called Microsoft (US).

IBM took the view that it was doing Intel and Microsoft and all PC customers a favour by making the IBM designs into the world standard. Indeed, IBM was rather proud of establishing the global benchmark in what was a small specialist market sector, as well as holding the lead in the much larger mainframe market. IBM finally launched its first PC in 1981 without tying either Intel or Microsoft exclusively to itself. The new PC cost $3,000 and, by today's standards, was very small. Although the claim 'IBM-compatible' quickly became a common standard for most PCs, except Apple, these developments had two consequences for IBM:

1 its worldwide PC standard allowed competitors to produce to a standard design for the first time;

2 no restriction was placed by IBM on Intel and Microsoft supplying similar products to other companies.

IBM reasoned that these issues did not matter because it would dominate the small PC market just as it did mainframes. In addition, IBM judged that the small PC would never replace the large mainframe, so it posed no significant threat to its main business. As it turned out, the company was at least partially wrong on both counts.

Technological advance and branding in the later 1980s

Although computer markets were driven by new technology, the key development was IBM's establishment of the common technical design mentioned above. This meant that its rivals at last had a common technical platform to drive down costs. IBM was unable or unwilling to find some way of patenting its design. IBM's strategic mistake was to think that its reputation alone would persuade customers to stay with its PC products. However, its competitors were able to exploit the new common IBM-compatible PC design to produce faster, reliable and cheaper machines than IBM, using the rapid advances in technology that occurred during the 1980s.

IBM and other computer companies continued to spend funds branding their products. However, their suppliers, such as Intel and Microsoft, also began to spend significant sums on advertising. Microsoft's 'Windows' was launched in the late 1980s and Intel's 'Pentium' microchip was launched in 1993. Both were destined to dominate their respective markets.

IBM slips into disaster 1986–1993

In the late 1980s, IBM recognised the competitive threat from Microsoft and Intel. It launched its own proprietory software, OS/2 Warp, in 1994, to counteract this. It also negotiated with Apple to set up a new computer chip standard, the Power PC Chip, with the aim of attacking Intel. Although both initiatives had some innovations, they were too little and too late. IBM struggled on with the concepts, but the software made little headway against the established Microsoft and the chip was abandoned in the mid-1990s.

By 1993, IBM's advertising was forced into claiming that its PCs used the Microsoft 'Windows' operating system and its computer chips had 'Intel inside'. The IBM PC was just one of many computers in the small-computer market.

New organisation structure: 1991

Recognising the need for change, the company began to develop a new organisational structure in 1991. Up to this time, the organisation had been centred on two central aspects of the company:

1 *Products.* The company provided the most complete range of products from mainframes to telecommunications networks, from PCs to computer software. Each main product group sold its products independently of other groups.

2 *Country.* The company was the leading provider in most countries, with the ability to provide computer solutions tailored at national level for the particular requirements of each country. Each major country had its own dedicated management responsibilities.

While this provided strong local responsiveness, it meant that global and international company customers were not always well served through country companies and individual product offerings. In a new organisation announced in 1991, the major global industries such as banking, insurance, oil and gas, manufacturing, telecommunications companies and transport were tackled by dedicated teams with a *complete range of products* worldwide: the new structure involved the development of Industry Solution Units (ISUs). Each ISU had its own dedicated management team and was measured not only on sales but also on customer satisfaction. However, the country and the product managers were reluctant to give up control to the ISUs, which often operated internationally across many countries. This resulted in confusion among customers and some internal political battles inside IBM.

Future IBM strategy: 1993 strategic perspective

After the major profit problems of the early 1990s, IBM clearly needed a major shift in strategy. A new chief executive, Lou Gerstner, was recruited from outside the computer industry, but he was faced with a major task. The conventional strategic view in 1993 was that the company was too large. Its true strengths were the series of national IBM companies that had real autonomy and could respond to specific national market conditions, and the wide range of good IBM products. But the local autonomy coupled with the large IBM product range meant that it was difficult to provide industry solutions. Moreover, IBM's central HQ and research facility had difficulty in responding quickly to the rapid market and technological changes that applied across its global markets. The ISUs had been set up to tackle this but did not seem to be working. The most common strategy solution suggested for IBM was therefore to break up the company into a series of smaller and more responsive subsidiaries in different product areas – a PC company, a mainframe company, a printer company and so on. The solution adopted by IBM was to turn itself into a computer services company: this is described in the web-based case 'Thinking outside the box at IBM' (see weblink in Part 6).

Case questions

1 Use the five key elements of strategic decisions (see Section 1.2.4) to evaluate IBM's strategic management. What conclusions do you draw for these and added value?

2 What are the strengths and weaknesses of IBM? And what are the opportunities and threats that it faces from the competitive environment surrounding the company?

3 What strategies would you have adopted in 1993 to turn round the situation at IBM? When you have made your choice you might like to look at the book's free, online webcase to see what the company actually did next. The web link for this case 'Thinking outside the box at IBM' is located in Part 6 of this book.

Given the strategic disaster that hit IBM, this raises the strategic question, 'Why do companies fail?' There are some answers on the web.

1.3 CORE AREAS OF STRATEGIC MANAGEMENT

Definition ▶ The three core areas of strategic management are strategic analysis, strategy development and strategy implementation.

1 *Strategic analysis.* The organisation, its mission and objectives have to be examined and analysed. Strategic management provides value for the people involved in the organisation – its *stakeholders* – but it is often the senior managers who develop the view of the organisation's overall objectives in the broadest possible terms. They conduct an examination of the *objectives* and the organisation's *relationship with its environment.* They will also analyse the *resources* of the organisation. This is explored in Chapters 3 to 7.

2 *Strategy development.* The strategy options have to be developed and then selected. To be successful, the strategy is likely to be built on the particular skills of the organisation and the special relationships that it has or can develop with those outside – suppliers, customers, distributors and government. For many organisations, this will mean developing advantages over competitors that are

sustainable over time. There are usually many options available and one or more will have to be selected. This is covered in Chapters 8 to 12.

3 *Strategy implementation.* The selected options now have to be implemented. There may be major difficulties in terms of motivation, power relationships, government negotiations, company acquisitions and many other matters. A strategy that cannot be implemented is not worth the paper it is written on. This is explored in Chapters 13 to 15, including a special chapter on the important topic of green strategy.

If a viable strategic management is to be developed, each of these three areas should be explored carefully. For the purpose of clarity, it is useful to separate the strategic management process into three sequential core areas, as we have done above. It would be wrong, however, to think of the three core areas as being only sequential. While it is not possible to implement something that does not exist, many organisations will have some existing relationships with customers and suppliers that are well developed, and others that have not yet started. Even small, new companies will want to experiment and negotiate. This means that activities in all three areas might well be simultaneous – implementing some ideas while analysing and developing others.

Table 1.1 lists some of the working definitions used in the three core areas of strategic management, some of which will already be familiar to you. To clarify the distinction between the terms, the table also includes the example of an ambitious young manager, showing his or her strategy for career progression. However, the example in Table 1.1 highlights two important qualifications to the three core areas:

1 the influence of judgement and values;
2 the high level of speculation involved in major predictions.

The importance of *judgement and values* in arriving at the mission and objectives shows that strategic management is not a precise science. Equally, there are risks in many strategic decisions. For example, in the hypothetical career example in Table 1.1, the person has a clear view on what is important in life if their ambitions are to be achieved; some people would not share these ambitious values. Moreover, the career choice made will carry risks with regard to its achievement. We examine the role of value judgements further in Chapter 6 and risk in Chapter 10.

Moreover, strategic management may be *highly speculative* and *involve major assumptions* as it attempts to predict the future of the organisation. For example, many of the later stages of the career progression in Table 1.1 involve some very difficult projections – on marriage, family and health, for example – that may well not be achieved. Indeed, given such risks and uncertainties, it is difficult to see the example as anything more than an idealised series of wish-statements. In the same way, in the case of strategic management, there may be a largely false and perhaps unrealistic sense of direction.

Some books and research papers on strategic management do not recognise this problem and may be guilty of implying that strategic management has certainties about the future that it does not possess in reality.[21] Some companies also take this approach and work on the basis that strategy is set rigidly for a fixed time period.[22] This does not mean we should not explore the future directions of the subject, just that we should be cautious about their meaning and aware of the risks.

KEY STRATEGIC PRINCIPLES

- The three core areas of strategic management are: strategic analysis, strategic development and strategy implementation.
- There are two important qualifications to the three core areas. Judgement and values play an important role in determining the objectives and choice. Moreover, some elements are highly speculative and may involve major assumptions and risks.
- There is considerable overlap between the three core areas, which are separated out for the sake of clarity but, in practice, may operate concurrently.

Table 1.1 Definition of terms used in the three core areas of strategy[23]

	Definition	Personal career example
Mission statement	Defines the business that the organisation is in against the values and expectations of the stakeholders	To become a leading European industrialist
Objectives (or goals)	State more precisely what is to be achieved and when the results are to be accomplished. Often quantified. (Note that there is no statement of how the results are to be attained.)	To achieve a directorship on the main board of a significant company by the age of 42
Strategies	The pattern or plan that integrates an organisation's major goals or policies and action sequences into a cohesive whole. Usually deals with the general principles for achieving the objectives: why the organisation has chosen this particular route	1 To obtain an MBA from a leading European business school 2 To move into a leading consultancy company as a stepping stone to corporate HQ 3 To obtain a key functional directorship by the age of 35 in the chosen company
Plans (or programmes)	The specific actions that then follow from the strategies. They specify the step-by-step sequence of actions to achieve the major objectives	1 To obtain a first-class honours degree this year 2 To take the next two years working in a merchant bank for commercial experience 3 To identify three top business schools by December two years from now 4 To make application to these schools by January of the following year
Controls	The process of monitoring the proposed plans as they proceed and adjusting where necessary. There may well be some modification of the strategies as they proceed	Marriage and children mean some compromise on the first two years above. Adjust plans back by three years
Reward	The result of the successful strategy, adding value to the organisation and to the individual	High salary and career satisfaction

Case study exploring strategic decision making, including the judgements and risks involved in effective strategy: *Apple's profitable but risky strategy*. After you have read this case, you can see indicative answers to the questions at the end of this case on a separate page on the website.

1.4 CONTEXT, CONTENT AND PROCESS

Research[24] has shown that in most situations strategic management is not simply a matter of taking a strategic decision and then implementing it. It often takes a considerable time to make the decision itself and then another delay before it comes into effect. There are two reasons for this. First, *people* are involved – managers, employees, suppliers and customers, for example. Any of these people may choose to apply their own business judgement to the chosen strategy. They may influence both the initial decision and the subsequent actions that will implement it. Second, the *environment* may change radically as the strategy is being implemented. This will invalidate the chosen strategy and mean that the process of strategy development needs to start again.

For these reasons, an important distinction needs to be drawn in strategy development between *process, content* and *context*. Every strategic decision involves these three elements, which must be considered separately, as well as together.

Every strategic decision involves:

1 *Context* – the environment within which the strategy operates and is developed. In the IBM case during the 1980s, the context was the fast-changing technological development in personal computers. This is explored further in Chapter 11.

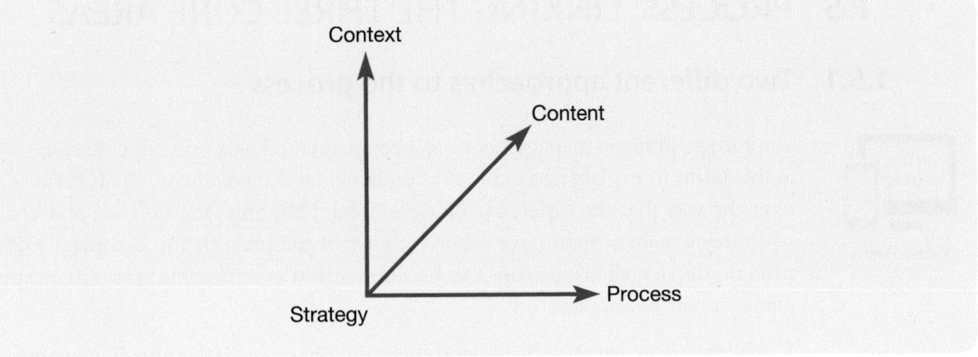

Figure 1.6 The three elements of the strategic decision

Source: adapted from Pettigrew, A and Whipp R (1991) *Managing Change for Competitive Success*, Blackwell Publishing Ltd, p 26. Reproduced with permission.

2 *Content* – the main actions of the proposed strategy. The content of the IBM strategy was the decision to launch the new PC and its subsequent performance in the market place. This is explored further in Chapter 10.

3 *Process* – how the actions link together or interact with each other as the strategy unfolds against what may be a changing environment. The process in the IBM case was the delay in tackling the PC market, the slow reaction to competitive actions and the interaction between the various parts of the company as it attempted to respond to competitor actions. Process is thus the means by which the strategy will be developed and achieved. This is explored further in Chapters 5, 10 and 11.

These three elements are the axes of the same three-dimensional cube of strategic management decision making (see Figure 1.6). The implications of this distinction are explored further in Chapters 5, 10 and 11.

In most strategic management situations, the *context* and *content* are reasonably clear. It is the way in which strategy is developed and enacted – the *process* – that usually causes the most problems. Processes need investigation and are vague and quixotic because they involve people and rapidly changing environments.

The difficulty is compounded by the problem that, during the implementation period, the process can influence the initial strategic decision. For example, as the process unfolded at IBM, competitive actions forced the organisation to make cutbacks that were not originally identified as part of the strategic content.

At various points throughout this book, the distinction between process, content and context will be useful in clarifying relationships. Much emphasis will be laid on process, which is one of the more difficult parts of strategy.

KEY STRATEGIC PRINCIPLES

- In strategic management development, it is necessary to distinguish between three elements: context, content and process.
- In most strategic management situations, the context and content are reasonably clear; it is the process that causes the problem because process may influence the way that people in the organisation develop and implement strategy.
- Process is the way actions link together or interact with each other as the strategy unfolds in the environment, which may itself be changing. It is often one of the more difficult parts of strategy development.

1.5 PROCESS: LINKING THE THREE CORE AREAS

1.5.1 Two different approaches to the process

Video Part 1

Until now, strategic management has been presented as a unified, cohesive subject. It is important at this point to explain and explore a fundamental disagreement which exists among commentators over the way that the topic may be developed. Differing views on the content, process and nature of strategic management have arisen because of the breadth and complexity of the subject. For the present, the overall distinctions can be summarised as representing two main approaches to strategic management development:

1 *The prescriptive approach.* Some commentators have judged strategic management to be essentially a linear and rational process, starting with where-we-are-now and then developing new strategies for the future (see Jauch and Glueck[25] and Argenti[26]). **A prescriptive strategy is one whose *objective* has been defined in advance and whose *main elements* have been developed before the strategy commences.**

Definition ▶

2 *The emergent approach.* Other commentators take the view that strategic management emerges, adapting to human needs and continuing to develop over time. It is evolving, incremental and continuous, and therefore cannot be easily or usefully summarised in a plan which then requires to be implemented (see Mintzberg[27] and Cyert and March[28]). **An emergent strategy is one whose *final objective* is unclear and whose *elements* are developed during the course of its life, as the strategy proceeds.** The theorists of this approach often argue that long-term prescriptive strategies are of limited value.

Definition ▶

In Chapter 2 we examine these important differences in more detail. There are, for example, differences in approach even amongst those who judge that the process is rational and linear. Mintzberg[29] captured the essence of the distinction:

> The popular view sees the strategist as a planner or as a visionary; someone sitting on a pedestal dictating brilliant strategies for everyone else to implement. While recognising the importance of thinking ahead and especially of the need for creative vision in this pedantic world, I wish to propose an additional view of the strategist - as a pattern recognizer, a learner if you will - who manages a process in which strategies (and visions) can emerge as well as be deliberately conceived.

It should be noted here that Mintzberg sees merit in *both* approaches. (Both approaches can make a contribution and are not mutually exclusive. In many respects, they can be said to be like the human brain, which has both a rational left side and an emotional right side. Both sides are needed for the brain to function properly.[30]) It can be argued that the same is true in strategic management. Reference is therefore made to both the prescriptive and emergent approaches throughout this book. However, it should be understood that these are main headings for a *whole series of concepts* of strategic management – explored in more detail in Chapter 2.

1.5.2 Impact on the three core areas

1 *The prescriptive approach* takes the view that the three core areas – strategic analysis, strategic development and strategy implementation – are linked together sequentially. Thus it is possible to use the analysis area to develop a strategy which is then implemented. The strategy is *prescribed* in advance (see Figure 1.7(a)).

2 The *emergent approach* takes the view that the three core areas are essentially interrelated. However, it is usual to regard the analysis area as being distinctive and in advance of the other two elements. Because strategy is then developed by an experimental process that involves trial and error, it is not appropriate to make a clear distinction between the strategy development and implementation phases: they are closely linked, one responding to the results obtained by the other. These relationships are shown in Figure 1.7(b).

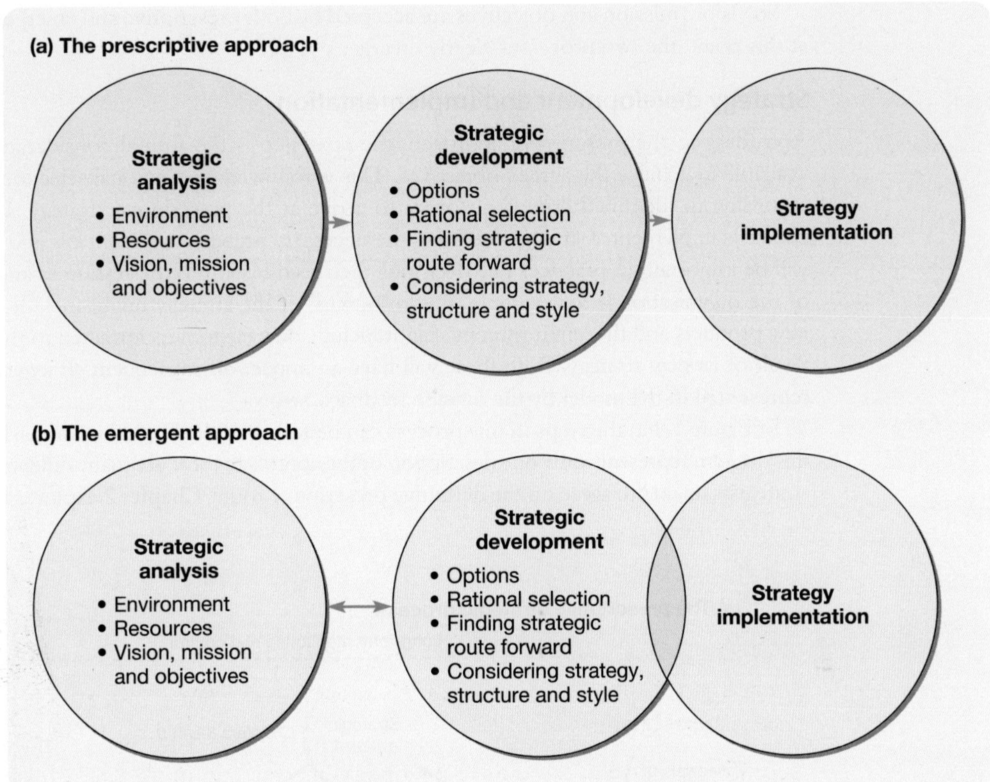

Figure 1.7 Prescriptive and emergent approaches to the three core elements

1.5.3 Developing models of strategic management

Based on the two approaches, it is possible to develop models to aid in understanding the way that strategic management operates. These models are explained here and will then be used throughout this book to structure our examination of the topic.

The two contrasting models are shown in Figure 1.8. Each element of the process is explored in more depth in the chapters of the book that follow.

Strategic analysis

The analytical phase of both the *prescriptive* and the *emergent* approach can be divided into two parts:

1 *Analysis of the environment* – examining what is happening or likely to happen outside the organisation (e.g. economic and political developments, competition).

2 *Analysis of resources* – exploring the skills and resources available inside the organisation (e.g. human resources, plant, finance).

These are followed by a third element:

3 *Identification of vision, mission and objectives* – developing and reviewing the strategic direction and the more specific objectives (e.g. the maximisation of profit or return on capital, or in some cases a social service).

Some strategists put this third element *before* the other two.[31] They argue that any organisation first sets out its objectives and then analyses how to achieve them. However, this book takes the view that it is necessary to set objectives in the *context* of the environment and competitive resources of the organisation. For example, a manufacturer of straw hats needs to take account of the very limited demand for that product and the limited likelihood of having superior competitive resources *before* setting its objectives.

So vision, mission and objectives are accepted by both prescriptive and emergent approaches but, at this point, the two processes clearly diverge.

Strategy development and implementation

According to the prescriptive approach, the next step is the formal consideration of the options available to achieve the agreed objectives. This is followed by a rational selection from the options according to identified criteria, in order to arrive at the prescriptive strategy. In most cases, this choice is implemented after considering the necessary organisation, controls and other matters that will be important in practice. The decisions then feed back into the resources and the environment of the organisation – for example, the 'resources' of the strategy might include new factories and new products and the 'environment' might include new customers attracted to the organisation as a result of its new strategy. Both these will have an impact on subsequent strategic decisions and are represented in the model by the outside feedback arrows.

In Figure 1.8(a) the steps in this process can be followed. It should be emphasised, however, that this diagram represents only one description of the approach; there are many different approaches, with strategists unable to agree on the definitive prescriptive route. Chapter 2 explores this in more depth.

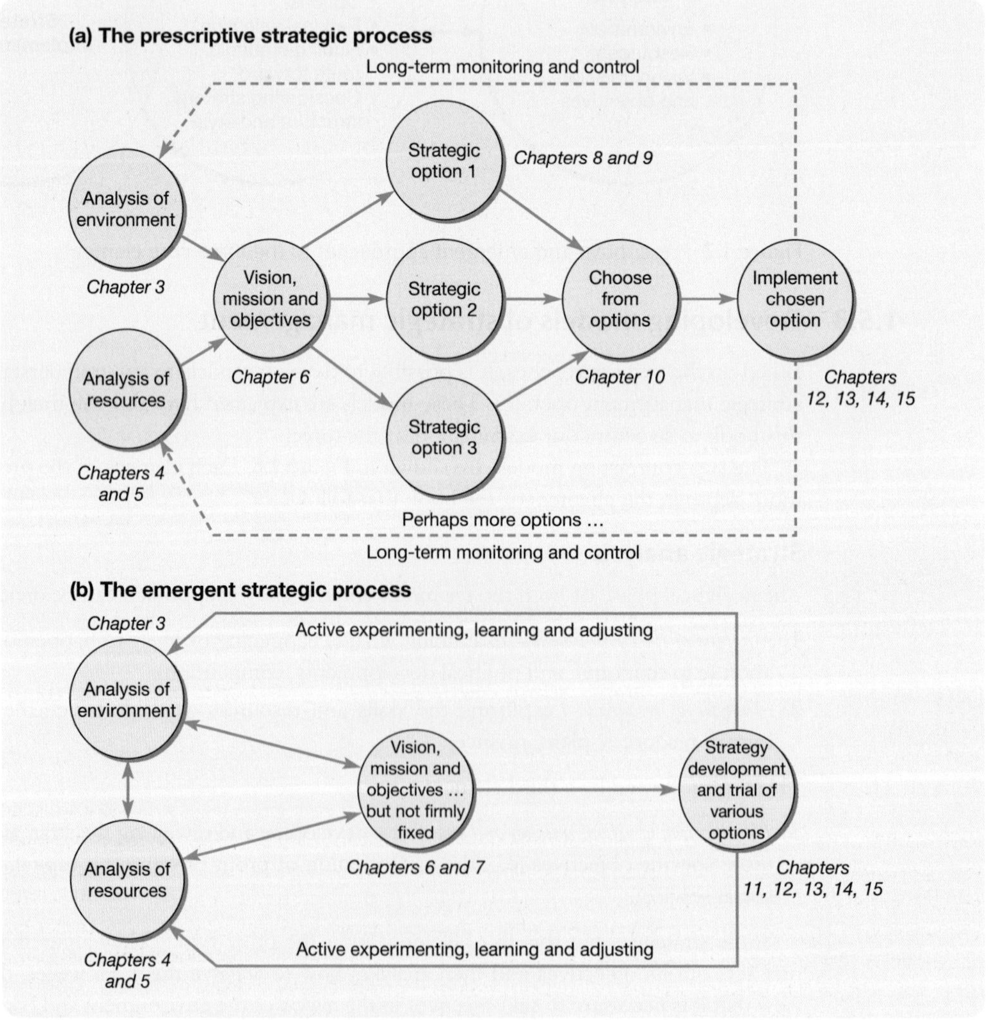

Figure 1.8 The prescriptive and emergent strategic approaches

Important: These two models illustrate two extremes of the strategic process. They over-simplify the reality, which is often more complex and interactive. But they are useful in emphasising and thinking about the different facets of the strategic process.

Strategy development and implementation – the emergent approach

Essentially, this takes a much more experimental view of the strategy choice and its implementation. It seeks to learn by trial, experimentation and discussion as strategies are developed. There is no final, agreed strategy but rather a series of experimental approaches that are considered by those involved and then developed further. Strategies emerge during a process of crafting and testing.

There is therefore no clear distinction in the emergent approach between the two stages of developing the strategy and its implementation. Moreover, there is no need to identify a separate stage of discussion involving the leadership, culture and organisation, since all these will occur inevitably during the strategy development and implementation phase. Importantly, there is then a strong link back to the earlier analytical phase, enabling changes in the environment and resources to be reflected quickly in the adaptive, learning strategy. This is shown in Figure 1.8(b).

By definition, there can be no single view of a process that emerges within an organisation – each one will be different. Figure 1.8(b) serves to indicate the circulatory nature of the decision-making process according to this approach. There is no definitive emergent route.

KEY STRATEGIC PRINCIPLES

- There are two main approaches to strategic management development: the *prescriptive* approach and the *emergent* approach. Each complements the other, and both are relevant to the strategy process.
- The *prescriptive* approach takes the view that the three core elements are linked together sequentially. The *emergent* approach regards the three core areas as being essentially interrelated.
- The two approaches can be used to develop models for the strategic management process. However, it should be recognised that every model is a compromise and may not reflect all the circumstances that exist in reality.

There are two areas of strategic management that deserve special strategies:

- public sector and not-for-profit strategies;
- international and global strategies.

The main areas are summarised on the free accompanying website. There is a more detailed discussion of each of the topics in Chapters 14, 18 and 19, respectively.

CASE STUDY 1.3

Facebook's strategy: where is the sustainable competitive advantage?

Over the nine years to 2013, Facebook's strategy has built the world's largest social networking site. But it is not so clear whether the company had sustainable competitive advantages over its rivals. Perhaps that was why it made three company acquisitions in 2013 and 2014?

Years of growth

Back in 2004, Mark Zuckerberg and some friends were Harvard University students writing computer programs to provide a social network connecting their fellow students. The result was the first version of Facebook – free, lively and popular. The service was so successful that it was first extended to other US universities, then across the USA and finally to other countries. By early 2013, it had become the world's largest social networking site with over 1.2 billion active users.

When it was decided to put Facebook on a commercial footing around 2006, the company invited outside investment beyond the founders. Various venture capital companies took shares to fund the company's growth. These included Microsoft which took a small share in return for exclusive priority for its advertising. Mark himself became Chief Executive Officer and some of his colleagues remained with the company in various positions. However, new people with more business experience were also recruited with the aim of ensuring that the business was profitable and soundly based.

Facebook was highly successful up to 2014, but will it continue?
© AKP Photos/Alamy

By 2013, leading entrepreneurs were attracted to the fast-growing, experimental nature of the business. They could see substantial potential in Facebook. The outcome was a business valued at a staggering $120 billion in 2013 on annual sales of around $3 billion. But did the company really possess assets that would justify this valuation?

Social networking customers and competitors

From its early beginnings, social networking began to capture the imagination of many people. It provided a way of exchanging news, photos, events and contacts for anyone with an internet connection. By 2010, it had taken over from search engines like Google and Bing and from entertainment sites like computer games as the main area of online activity. Essentially, social networking is a much broader range of activity that allows people to engage with each other in whatever way they choose. But it is essentially free, so Facebook only makes a profit from advertising and from links to commercial users who support the site and seek new customers.

Given the success of the format, there were a number of other social network providers. For example, in 2008 MySpace had a larger user base in the USA than Facebook: 62 million versus 31 million visitors, respectively. In the UK, Facebook was the leader by about 1 million customers over Bebo with MySpace third: 12, 11 and 9 million visitors, respectively. It was this type of evidence that persuaded the world's largest media company, News Corporation, to acquire MySpace for $580 million in 2008. Similarly, AOL acquired Bebo for $850 million in the same year.

Nevertheless, Facebook continued to innovate with new interactive sections on uploading photos, the Wall (where users can post messages), Pokes (which allows users to send a virtual 'poke' to each other), the Marketplace (free classified ads) and other related areas. Facebook became market leader by 2010 as its main competitors failed to offer the same innovative and easy-to-use range of social network services. But none of the Facebook services was totally unique and impossible to copy. Moreover, Twitter with a different network offering was coming up strongly with over 500 million registered users with revenues of $317 million, although Twitter was still loss-making in 2013.

Nevertheless, advertisers began to see potential in social networking in general and Facebook in particular. The reason was that it allowed them to reach their target groups through display advertising. By 2011, 'brands are still flocking to Facebook and its share of display advertising spending is rising fast,' according to the *Financial Times*.[32] But all was not well in the social networking business. MySpace was sold by News Corporation in 2011 for around $30 million and Bebo was sold by AOL for $10 million according again to the *Financial Times*. Was Facebook really different? Did it have a competitive advantage that would allow it to survive?

Facebook's competitive advantages?

In essence, Facebook was better at developing new services and re-aligning its offerings than its rivals. The main value of social networks comes not from the exchanges of geeky computer experts but from a wide range of people exchanging their interests, opinions and ideas. But such networks have a difficult history. 'As long as social networks are growing and pulling in millions of new members . . . they have great revenue potential. But when growth stalls, or even slows, they tend to implode as the network effect goes into reverse. This has been the pattern since Friendster became the pioneer of online social networking in 2002,' according to John Gapper in the *Financial Times* in 2011.[33] There are risks inherent in social networking businesses that require careful strategy.

From a strategy perspective, what does Facebook have that other networks do not? Why is it better than other companies? What are its competitive advantages? The most obvious one is the size of its social network. In addition, it clearly has some talented software engineers and managers that are able to read the markets and put together new services that customers find attractive. But it does not have the killer, patented software application that has distinguished Google's search engine from its rivals.

Moreover, Facebook still faces new competitors. For example, Twitter – the network that allows instant brief comment on anything – had 1.6 billion daily search hits by 2013. Google's Buzz was also launched in 2010 but had not been successful at the time of writing this case in 2014. Importantly, although Twitter had 500 million registered users in 2013, it was making a loss. Facebook was not the market leader in every country. QQ instant messaging service has at least 500 million active users in China and is highly effective (as the author of this case can confirm from his time at Wuhan University in 2012). These and other alternative networks suggest that it is relatively easy to set up a social network: the barriers to entry are low. Such social networks have little competitive advantage beyond the size of the networks themselves. This therefore raises the question of the business model of a social network. How does Facebook generate its revenue and make a profit?

Facebook's business model

At the time of its public share offering, Facebook had annual revenues of nearly $2 billion. These had risen to $7.9 billion by 2013. Its revenue was derived wholly from advertising by companies on its network. However, the Facebook business model is more complex than the model for a search engine like Google. When someone undertakes a search on Google and then clicks onto a company, there is a way of automatically registering whether the potential customer has migrated to a company website – the *clickthrough rate* in the jargon – on which revenues and profits are then generated.

Social networks are different. They do not exist to provide product or service search and follow-up sales. They exist for social purposes with advertising as a secondary reason for looking at the site. Hence, the most successful advertising on Facebook has been where customers have been asked to help choose something on a company's website: for example Starbucks in the UK invited Facebook users to choose seasonal drinks in late 2010. This resulted in boosting sales by 15 per cent. But this lack of a direct connection between the advertising and the click makes it more difficult to put a value on social network advertising and marketing. As a result, advertising is cheaper on social networks than search networks, but this reduces the value and makes it more difficult to see whether there is much added value in the business of social networks.

Importantly, there is little loyalty to social networks beyond the network of friends and family held by the network. Thus new users may decide to migrate to another network. Arguably, it was for this reason that Facebook made three company acquisitions between 2012 and 2014:

1 *Instagram* photo sharing website for $1 billion in 2012: the new company was reported to be growing faster than Facebook.

2 *WhatsApp* instant messaging service for $19 billion in 2013: the new company claimed over 200 million active monthly users.

3 *Oculus* virtual reality company for $2 billion in 2014: 'Every 10 or 15 years, there's a major new computing platform,' explained Facebook founder Mark Zuckerberg. 'To me, by far the most exciting platform is around vision . . . It's different from anything I've ever experienced in my life.'

Facebook still faces the task of monetising and developing these new ventures to preserve and enhance its business strategy.

In April 2011, Facebook announced a new initiative with regard to custom-engineered technology designed to increase energy efficiency and lower costs. It is sharing this specification and best practice with companies across the industry.

Case questions

1 What are the sustainable competitive advantages of Facebook? And where and how does it add value?

2 Do you think Facebook's strategy is sustainable over time? What would you do next if you were responsible for Facebook?

3 What lessons can other companies learn from recent strategies? Would you invest in developing a new social network?

CRITICAL REFLECTION

The nature of strategic management

One of the main disputes in strategic management over the past 20 years concerns the differences between prescriptive and emergent forms of strategy process. Companies argue that they need to have a 'strategic plan' in order to plan ahead in terms of both the competitive environment – sales, customers, new products and services – and of resources – finance and cash, people, factories. Some of these elements take years to develop and put into practice. A clear strategic plan is therefore essential and involves a *prescriptive* process to strategy development.

Other companies have a more entrepreneurial and experimental approach to strategy.

It is important to sense what is happening in fast-changing markets and to be able to respond to this. In addition, long-term strategic planning often turns out to be mistaken, with unintended outcomes. It is better therefore to be more creative in strategy development and to take an *emergent* approach to the process of strategy development.

What is your view? Which approach is better?

Or do both approaches have merit? If the latter is true, then how do you handle the differences of approach inside a company?

SUMMARY

- The field of strategic management deals with the major intended and emergent initiatives taken by general managers on behalf of owners and other stakeholders, involving the utilisation of resources, to enhance the performance of organisations in their external environments and thereby add value to the organisation.
- In this chapter, we have explored the nature of strategic management – linking process between the organisation and its environment – which focuses particularly on value added and the sustainable competitive advantages of the organisation and the need to be innovative. Adding value is of particular importance to most organisations, although for non-profit and government organisations this is not necessarily the case. Sustainable competitive advantage is also important.
- There are five key elements to strategy. They are principally related to the need to add value and to offer advantages over competitors: customers; implementation process; sustainable competitive advantage; the exploitation of linkages between the organisation and its environment; vision and purpose. Several of these elements may well involve innovative solutions to strategic issues.
- There are three core areas of strategic management: strategic analysis; strategic development; and strategy implementation. Although the three core areas are often presented as being strictly sequential, they will be simultaneous in some circumstances. There are two important qualifications to the three core areas: the use of judgement and values to derive the strategy and the need to make highly speculative assessments about the future and significant risks. Unless handled carefully, these may give a false sense of direction about the future.
- In developing strategic management, there is a need to distinguish between process, content and context. Process is the method by which the strategies are derived; content is the strategic decisions then made; context is the environment within which the organisation operates and develops its strategies. Process is usually the area that causes the most problems because it is difficult to measure precisely and because it is crucial to strategy development.
- There has been a fundamental disagreement between some strategists regarding how strategic management can be developed. There are two basic routes: the *prescriptive approach* and the *emergent approach*. The prescriptive approach takes the view that the three core areas are linked together sequentially; the emergent approach regards the three core areas as being interrelated. The two approaches have some common elements in the early stages: analysis and the development of a mission for the organisation. Beyond this, they go their separate ways and lead to two different models for the strategic management process. There has been some recent acceptance that both approaches may be valuable.

QUESTIONS

1 Summarise the main IBM strategies in Case 1.2. Take each element of your summary and compare it against the criteria for a successful strategy shown on the free web material for this chapter. How does each element measure up? Did IBM have an effective strategy?

2 As a work assignment, analyse the activities of Facebook. Investigate in particular how it has managed to stay ahead of its competitors. Compare your answer with the five key elements of strategic decisions in Section 1.2.4.

3 In commenting on strategy, Professor John Kay makes the comment that motivation of employees is not really part of strategic management. Do you agree with this? Give reasons for your views.

4 Take the three core areas of strategic management and apply them to a decision with which you have recently been involved. For example, it might be the organisation of a student activity or the purchase of a major item of equipment. Did you analyse the facts, consider the options and make a selection? Does this description over-simplify the process because, for example, it was necessary to persuade others to spend some money?

5 To what extent do you agree with Professor Mintzberg's description of strategies emerging rather than being prescribed in advance? If you agree with his description, what evidence do you have to support your view? If you disagree, then explain the basis of your rejection.

6 With the three core areas of strategic management in mind, identify how the strategy development process might vary for the following types of business: a global company such as IBM; a public service company such as a water provider (which might also be a monopoly); a non-profit organisation such as a student union or society.

7 If strategic management is so uncertain and has such a strong element of judgement, is there any point in its formal analysis? What arguments does the chapter use to justify such a process? Using your own value judgement, do you find them convincing?

FURTHER READING

Professor Kay's book *Foundations of Corporate Success* (Oxford University Press, 1993) remains an excellent introduction to the nature of strategic management; read the early chapters. In addition, the well-known book of readings and cases by Professors Mintzberg and Quinn, *The Strategy Process* (Prentice Hall, 1991), has a useful selection of material on the nature of strategic management; read Chapter 1 in particular. The article by Professor Mintzberg on 'Crafting strategy' in the *Harvard Business Review* (July–August 1987, p 65) is also strongly recommended.

For the counter-argument to Mintzberg, a useful paper is: Miller, C C and Ireland, R D (2005) 'Intuition in strategic decision making: friend or foe in the fast-paced 21st century', *Academy of Management Executive*, Vol 19, pp 19–30, which argues that intuition is troublesome in strategy.

See also Henry Mintzberg and Frances Westley (2001) 'Decision-making: It's not what you think', *Sloan Management Review*, MIT. Another interesting paper: Ireland, R D, Hitt, M A, Camp, S M and Sexton, D L (2001) 'Integrating entrepreneurship and strategic management actions to create firm wealth', *Academy of Management Executive*, Vol 15, No 1, pp 49–63.

For the most recent view on strategy definitions, see: Nag, R, Hambrick, D C and Chen, M-J (2007) 'What is strategic management really? Inductive derivation of a consensus definition of the field', *Strategic Management Journal*, Vol 28, pp 935–955.

For a more general but interesting view of theory development, see the special issue of *The Academy of Management Review*, Vol 36, No 2, April 2011: *Special topic forum on Theory Development: Where are the New Theories of Organization?* Some thoughtful papers that take a broader look at organisations but are relevant to future directions in strategic management are presented.

NOTES AND REFERENCES

1 References for the Kodak case: Annual Report and Accounts for Kodak 1997, 2000, 2005, 2010, 2011, 2013. Annual Report and Accounts for Canon Inc (in English) for the years 2002, 2004, 2009, 2013. *Financial Times*: 3 April 2012, p 12; 4 April 2012, p 14. Both are well-researched articles by Andrew Hill.

2 Adapted from Andrews, K (1987) *The Concept of Corporate Strategy*, Irwin, Homewood, IL, Ch 2.

3 Ansoff, I (1969) *Corporate Strategy*, Penguin, Harmondsworth, Ch 1.

4 Drucker, P (1961) *The Practice of Management*, Mercury, London, Ch 6.

5 Leadership is sometimes ignored as part of the topic of strategy, but is actually extremely important. For example, where would Microsoft be without Bill Gates? It might be argued that 'strategy' should stand separately from 'leadership', but this is like trying to separate an orange from its juice.

6 Andrews, K (1971) *The Concept of Corporate Strategy*, Irwin, Homewood, IL, p 28.

7 Kay, J (1993) *Foundations of Corporate Success*, Oxford University Press, Oxford, p 4.

8 Further definitions are discussed in Quinn, J B (1980) *Strategies for Change: Logical Incrementalism*, Irwin, Homewood, IL, Ch 1.

9 Campbell, A, Goold, M and Alexander, M (1995) 'Corporate strategy: the quest for parenting advantage', *Harvard Business Review*, March–April, pp 120–132.

10 Porter, M E (1985) *Competitive Advantage*, The Free Press, Harvard, MA.

11 See, for example, Quinn, J B (1980) Op. cit.

12 He argues that strategic decisions are those that determine the overall direction of an enterprise and its ultimate viability in the light of the predictable, the unpredictable and the unknowable changes that may occur in its most important environments. Quinn, J B (1980) Op. cit.

13 Nag, R, Hambrick, D C and Chen, M-J (2007) 'What is strategic management really? Inductive derivation of a consensus definition of the field', *Strategic Management Journal*, Vol 28, pp 935–955.

14 Ibid., p 944.

15 Quoted in Teece, D J (2007) 'Explicating dynamic capabilities: the nature and microfoundations of (sustainable) enterprise performance', *Strategic Management Journal*, Vol 28, p 1320.

16 Kay, J (1993) Op. cit., Ch 1.

17 Ohmae, K (1982) *The Mind of the Strategist*, Penguin, Harmondsworth, p 36.

18 Mintzberg, H (1987) 'Crafting strategy', *Harvard Business Review*, July–August, p 65.

19 Harney, A (2002) 'Microsoft fired up for console wars', *Financial Times*, 7 February 2002, p 28.

20 Case compiled by the author from the following published sources: Heller, R (1994) *The Fate of IBM*, Warner Books, London (easy to read and accurate); Carroll, P (1993) *The Unmaking of IBM*, Crown, London (rather one-sided); *Financial Times*: 7 August 1990, p 14; 5 June 1991, article by Alan Cane; 8 November 1991, article by Alan Cane and Louise Kehoe; 5 May 1993, p 17; 29 July 1993, p 17; 14 March 1994, p 17; 26 March 1994, p 8; 28 March 1994, p 15; *Economist*, 16 January 1993, p 23; *Business Age*, April 1994, p 76. Note that this case simplifies the IBM story by emphasising the PC aspects. There are further parts to the story that can be read in the references above.

21 For example, Gilmore, F F and Brandenburg, R G (1962) 'Anatomy of corporate planning', *Harvard Business Review*, Vol 40, November–December, p 61.

22 For example, the IBM Annual Report and Accounts for 1993 took a firm and inflexible view on what was required to recover from its major losses. It was only the arrival of a new chief executive that revised this picture in a more experimental way.

23 Partly adapted from Quinn, J B (1991) *Strategies for Change*, Ch 1, and Mintzberg, H and Quinn, J B (1991) *The Strategy Process*, Prentice Hall, Upper Saddle River, NJ.

24 See, for example, Pettigrew, A and Whipp, R (1991) *Managing Change for Competitive Success*, Blackwell, Oxford. See also Mintzberg, H (1987) Op. cit.

25 Jauch, L R and Glueck, W (1988) *Business Policy and Strategic Management*, McGraw-Hill, New York.

26 Argenti, J (1965) *Corporate Planning*, Allen and Unwin, London.

27 Mintzberg, H (1987) Op. cit.

28 Cyert, R M and March, J (1963) *A Behavioural Theory of the Firm*, Prentice Hall, Upper Saddle River, NJ.

29 Mintzberg, H (1987) Op. cit.

30 This analogy was inspired by Professor Mintzberg's brief comment in his article: Mintzberg, H (1994) 'The fall and rise of strategic planning', *Harvard Business Review*, January–February, p 114.

31 See, for example, Thompson, A A and Strickland, A J (1993) *Strategic Management: Concepts and Cases*, 7th edn, Irwin, Homewood, IL.

32 Bradshaw, T (2011) 'The fickle value of friendship', *Financial Times*, 31 March, p 16.

33 Gapper, J (2011) 'When the networks bubble over', *Financial Times*, 31 March, p 15.

34 Further references for the Facebook case beyond the two above: *Financial Times*: 14 March 2008, p 30; 6 April 2009, p 17; 8 July 2010, p 23; 4 January 2011, pp 16 and 22. *Economist*: 22 March 2008, p 81. BBC News: 16 September 2009, 'Facebook grows and makes money'; 14 October 2010, 'Emerging rivals threaten Facebook's dominance'; 21 February 2011, p 21; 21 February 2011, p 21; 22 February 2011, p 22; 7 July 2011, p 17; 31 January 2012, p 11; 6 February 2012, p 20; 3 May 2012, p 11; 18 December 2013, p 21; 20 December 2013, p 14; 20 February 2014, pp 1 and 16; 27 March 2014, p 19.

CHAPTER 2
A review of theory and practice

Video and sound summary of this chapter

LEARNING OUTCOMES

When you have worked through this chapter, you will be able to:

- describe and evaluate prescriptive strategic practice;
- describe and evaluate emergent strategic practice;
- identify the main theories associated with prescriptive strategic management;
- identify the main theories associated with emergent strategic management;
- explain the shift in stance on stakeholder and ethical thinking in many organisations.

INTRODUCTION

This chapter provides an overview of strategic management theories and practice. Each of the main theories is explored in further detail in later chapters, so it is possible to skip this chapter now and read it later, but you will miss the opportunity to gain an overview of the general theoretical structure of the topic.

To provide a more substantial foundation for strategic management development, the prescriptive and emergent approaches of Chapter 1 deserve further exploration. The first sections of this chapter therefore undertake this task. They will benefit from being set against the background of the historical developments that prompted and shaped them. Even within each route, prescriptive or emergent, there is substantial disagreement among strategists about how strategic management can and should be developed. Both routes contain many different interpretations and theories. If the dynamics are to be fully understood, it is important that some of these differences are explored.

Finally, it is argued that strategic management should be considered from an ethical perspective. Every organisation's strategy must be seen in the context of its responsibilities to its owners, its managers and employees and its role in society.

CASE STUDY 2.1

Attacking a dominant competitor: a joint venture strategy by Nestlé and General Mills

Kellogg (US) dominates the world's ready-to-eat breakfast cereal market. In 1989, Nestlé (Switzerland) and General Mills (US) agreed a joint venture to attack the market. The objectives of the new company were to achieve by the year 2000 global sales of $1 billion and, within this figure, to take a 20 per cent share of the European market. This case examines how this was achieved by the new joint company, Cereal Partners (CP).

More detailed film explaining and analysing the strategy of Nestle and General Mills. The video is divided into sections that explore various aspects of the complete strategic management process from a prescriptive and emergent perspective.

Background

In 1997, Kellogg was the breakfast cereal market leader in the USA with around 32 per cent share in a market worth $9 billion at retail selling prices. By 2002, the company was no longer market leader. Its great rival, General Mills (GM), had finally taken over with a share of 33 per cent while Kellogg's share dropped to 30 per cent. GM had achieved this important strategic breakthrough by a series of product launches over a 15-year period in a market that was growing around 2 per cent per annum. However, by 2004, Kellogg had regained market leadership again by one percentage share point. This reversal was the outcome of some clever marketing by Kellogg coupled with GM being distracted by the consequences of its acquisition of another American food company, Pillsbury, in 2003.

Outside the USA, the global market was worth around $8-10 billion and growing in some countries by up to 10 per cent per annum. However, this was from a base of much smaller consumption per head than in the USA. Nevertheless, Kellogg still had over 40 per cent market share of the non-US market. It had gained this through a vigorous strategy of international market launches for over 40 years in many markets. Up to 1990, no other company had a significant share internationally, but then along came the new partnership.

The video on the website accompanying this text explores the battle for the breakfast cereal market.

Development of Cereal Partners

After several abortive attempts to develop internationally by itself, General Mills (GM) approached Nestlé about a joint venture in 1989. (A joint venture is a separate company, with each parent holding an equal share and contributing according to its resources and skills; the joint venture then has its own management and can develop its own strategy within limits set by the parents.) Nestlé had also been attempting to launch its own breakfast cereal range without much success. Both companies were attracted by the high value added in this branded, heavily advertised consumer market.

GM's proposal to Nestlé was to develop a new 50/50 joint company. GM would contribute its products, technology and manufacturing expertise – for example, it made 'Golden Grahams' and 'Cheerios' in the USA. Nestlé would give its brand name, several under-utilised factories and its major strengths in global marketing and distribution – for example, it made 'Nestlé' cream products. Both parties found the deal so attractive that they agreed it in only three weeks. The joint venture was called Cereal Partners (CP) and operated outside North America, where GM remained independent.

Over the next 15 years, CP was launched in 70 countries around the world. Products such as 'Golden Grahams', 'Cheerios' and 'Fibre 1' appeared on grocery supermarket shelves. CP used a mixture of launch strategies, depending on the market circumstances: acquisitions were used in the UK and Poland, new product launches in the rest of Europe, South and Central America and South Africa, and existing Nestlé cereal products were taken over in South-East Asia. To keep Kellogg guessing about its next market moves and to satisfy local taste variations, CP also varied the product range launched in each country. By contrast with Kellogg, CP also agreed to make cereals for supermarket chains, which they would sell as their own brands.

By 2004, CP had reached its targets of $1 billion profitable sales and 20 per cent of European markets. Kellogg was responding aggressively, especially in the USA, where it had regained market leadership. CP was beginning to think that its innovative strategies would repeat US experience: it was beginning to attack a dominant competitor, Kellogg, worldwide.

Both General Mills and Nestlé have extensive programmes related to green strategy issues according to their annual reports.

Note: the video on the website accompanying this text has a detailed analysis of the competitive battle between Kellogg and Cereal Partners. You will find it helpful to look at the video to answer the question below and explore its implications.

Case question

Using the description of prescriptive and emergent strategies from Chapter 1 (and this chapter if you need it), decide the following: was CP pursuing a prescriptive strategy, an emergent strategy, or both?

Strategic management theories can be understood more easily against the background of the historical developments that prompted and shaped them. The historical context of strategic management is described on this book's free website.

2.1 PRESCRIPTIVE STRATEGIC MANAGEMENT IN THEORY AND PRACTICE

2.1.1 The basic concept

Definition ▸ **A prescriptive strategy is one where the *objective* has been defined in advance and the *main elements* have been developed before the strategy commences.** However, it should be noted that there are many variations on this basic approach.

On the website
Video Parts 4, 5 and 6

- As seen in Chapter 1, prescriptive strategy starts with an analysis of the competitive environment and resources of the organisation. For example, Cereal Partners (CP) – see Case 2.1 – began with data on the European breakfast cereals market.
- This is then followed by a search for an agreed purpose, such as the maximisation of the return on the capital involved in a business (Ansoff, Porter).[1] It should be noted that the objective is not necessarily profit maximisation: for example, in a publicly owned enterprise or social co-operative, the objective could have social service standards as its major aim. One test for prescriptive strategy is to see whether a clearly defined objective has been identified in advance of the commencement of the strategy. In the case of CP, the purpose was related primarily to the delivery of profits to shareholders.
- Against the background of the competitive environment and an agreed purpose, various options are identified to enable the business to achieve the purpose. One option is then selected which is best able to meet the objective. In Case 2.1, CP had a complete range of options with regard to choice of customer targets, possible countries for entry, choice of product range and choice of brand names.
- The chosen option is implemented by the organisation's managers. At CP, the strategic decisions to acquire a company in the UK and launch a special range in Spain and Portugal were then implemented by the actual purchase of a company, Shredded Wheat, and the launch of a range of products into south western Europe. You can see the more detailed story in the free film on the web.

This prescriptive process is shown in Figure 2.1. In summary, the advantages of the prescriptive process are that it assists in providing a complete overview of the organisation, thus allowing a comparison with the objectives of the organisation. In turn, this allows an assessment of the resources of the organisation, especially those that deliver competitive advantage, and the allocation of resources that are scarce. Finally, the prescriptive process lends itself to assessing the implementation and monitoring of an agreed plan.

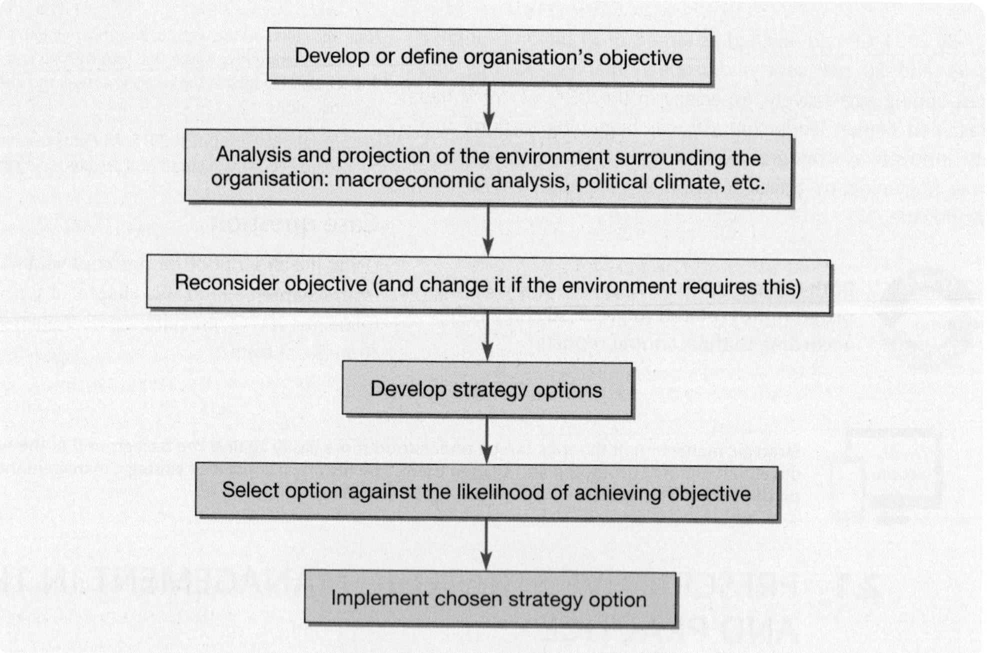

Figure 2.1 How the prescriptive strategic management process works

KEY STRATEGIC PRINCIPLES

- Prescriptive strategy begins with an analysis of the competitive environment and the competitive resources of the organisation. In this context, the purpose or objective of the strategy is then identified.
- The objective may be adjusted if the environment or other circumstances change.
- To test for prescriptive strategy, it is useful to examine whether a clearly defined, main objective has been identified.
- The advantages of the prescriptive process include the overview it provides; the comparison with objectives; the summary of the demands made on resources; the picture of the choices to be made; and the ability to monitor what has been agreed.

2.1.2 Foundations of prescriptive strategy

In studies of prescriptive strategy, close parallels have been drawn with what happens in *military strategy* – for example, as seen in the early Chinese military historical writings of Sun Tzu; the writings of the nineteenth-century German strategist, Clausewitz,[2] and those of Captain B H Liddell Hart[3] who wrote about the First World War. All these have been have quoted by corporate strategists.[4]

Prescriptive business strategy is sometimes seen as being similar to sending the troops (*employees*) into battle (*against competitors*) with a clear plan (*the prescriptive strategic plan*) that has been drawn up by the generals (*directors*) and then has been implemented (by launching innovatory products, etc.). The Kelloggs/CP breakfast cereals strategic battle is a good example – CP doing battle against Kelloggs worldwide.

Prescriptive strategic analysis has also borrowed from *economic theory*. Adam Smith, writing in the eighteenth century, took the view that human beings were basically capable of rational decisions that would be motivated most strongly by maximising their profits in any situation.[5] Moreover, individuals were capable of rational choice between options, especially where this involved taking a long-term view. Adam Smith has been quoted with approval by some modern strategists, economists and politicians. However, it should be noted that he lived in the eighteenth century and wrote about an era before modern organisations were conceived: for example, he had never seen a factory; only the craftsman's workshop.[6]

Subsequently, modern strategy theorists, such as Professor Michael Porter[7] of Harvard University Business School, have translated profit maximisation and competitive warfare concepts into strategy techniques and structure that have contributed to prescriptive strategic practice. Porter suggested that what really matters is *sustainable competitive advantage vis-à-vis* competitors in the market place: only by this means can a company have a successful strategy.

Others have taken this further: for example, the Boston Consulting Group used market data to develop a simple, strategic matrix that presented strategic options for analysis (we will explore this in Chapter 9). One of the early writers on strategic management was Professor Igor Ansoff, at that time at Vanderbilt University, Tennessee. He wrote a number of books and papers over the period from 1960 to 1990[8] that explored the practice of prescriptive strategy. Strategists such as Andrews[9] and Chakravarthy and Lorange[10] follow in the long line of those writing about strategic planning systems who employ many of these basic concepts. They are still widely used in many organisations around the world.

2.1.3 Critical comment on prescriptive strategy

Despite the advantages claimed for a prescriptive strategy system operating at the centre of organisations, there have been numerous critics of the whole approach. One of the most insightful is Professor Henry Mintzberg of McGill University, Canada. Along with other commentators,[11] Mintzberg has researched strategy decision making and suggested that a prescriptive strategy approach is based on a number of dangerous assumptions as to how organisations operate in practice (summarised in Exhibit 2.1).[12] There is significant research to show that these prescriptive assumptions are not always correct. For example, the market place can change, or employees may not like an agreed strategy – perhaps because it will mean that they lose their jobs – and will find ways to frustrate it. Given this evidence, theories of *emergent strategy* have developed, as an alternative view of the strategy process.

Although highly critical of the formal prescriptive planning process, Mintzberg has modified his views in recent years and accepted that some strategic planning may be beneficial to the organisation.[13]

EXHIBIT 2.1

Some major difficulties with the prescriptive strategic process

Mintzberg has identified six major assumptions of the prescriptive process that may be wholly or partially false:

1 *The future can be predicted accurately enough to make rational discussion and choice realistic.* As soon as a competitor or a government does something unexpected, however, the whole process may be invalidated.

2 *It is possible and better to forgo the short-term benefit in order to obtain long-term good.* This may be incorrect: it may not be possible to determine the long-term good and, even if it is, those involved may not be willing to make the sacrifice, such as jobs or investment.

3 *The strategies proposed are, in practice, logical and capable of being managed in the way proposed.* Given the political realities of many companies, there may be many difficulties in practice.

4 *The chief executive has the knowledge and power to choose between options.* He/she does not need to persuade anyone, nor compromise on his/her decisions. This may be extraordinarily naïve in many organisations where the culture and leadership seek discussion as a matter of normal practice.

5 *After careful analysis, strategy decisions can be clearly specified, summarised and presented*; they do not require further development, nor do they need to be altered because circumstances outside the company have changed. This point may have some validity but is not always valid.

6 *Implementation is a separate and distinctive phase that only comes after a strategy has been agreed: for example, a strategy to close a factory merely requires a management decision and then it just happens.* This is extraordinarily simplistic in many complex strategic decisions.

In conclusion, the period of the 1970s was the era when prescriptive strategic planning was particularly strong. Further strategic competitive concepts, such as generic strategies, would be proposed in the 1980s (see Chapter 8), but the basic process of analysis, strategic choice, selection and implementation formed the best practice of many companies. The major joint venture, Cereal Partners, was just one example of prescriptive strategy in action (see Case 2.1). Another example of prescriptive strategy is that associated with the development of two major airline companies, Singapore Airlines and Emirates, as leading world airlines later in this chapter (see Case 2.2). However, the outcomes have not always been those that were intended (see Case 14 on Google in Part 6).

KEY STRATEGIC PRINCIPLES

- A prescriptive strategy is a strategy whose objective has been defined in advance and whose main elements have been developed before the strategy commences.
- The objective may be adjusted if circumstances change significantly.
- After defining the objective, the process then includes analysis of the environment, the development of strategic options and the choice between them. The chosen strategy is then implemented.
- Mintzberg identified six assumptions made by the prescriptive process that may prove suspect in practice and invalidate the process.

2.2 EMERGENT STRATEGIC MANAGEMENT IN THEORY AND PRACTICE

2.2.1 The basic concept

Definition ▶

Video Parts 6 and 7

Emergent strategic management is a strategy whose *final objective* is unclear and whose *elements* are developed during the course of its life, as the strategy proceeds. However, it should be noted that there are many variations on this basic approach.

In the light of the observation that human beings are not always the rational and logical creatures assumed by prescriptive strategy,[14] various commentators have rejected the dispassionate, long-term prescriptive approach. They argue that strategy *emerges*, adapting to human needs, benefiting from new and unknown innovations and continuing to develop over time. Given this, they argue that there can be only limited meaningful prescriptive strategies and limited value from long-term planning.

Although this approach probably has its roots in the Hawthorn experiments of Elton Mayo in the 1930s,[15] it was not really until the research of Cyert and March in the 1960s[16] and Herbert Simon[17] around the same period that real progress was made. Research into how companies and managers develop strategic management in practice has shown that the assumption that strategies are always logical and rational does not take into account the reality of managerial decision making.

- Managers can handle only a limited number of options at any one time – called 'bounded rationality' in the literature.
- Managers are biased in their interpretation of data. All data is interpreted through our perceptions of reality.
- Managers are likely to seek a satisfactory solution rather than maximise the objectives of the organisation. In other words, the profit-maximising assumption of economic theory may over-simplify the real world.
- Organisations consist of coalitions of people who form power blocs. Decisions and debate rely on negotiations and compromise between these groups, termed 'political bargaining'. Researchers

found that the notion of strategy being decided by a separate, central main board does not accord with reality.

- To take decisions, managers rely on a company's culture, politics and routines, rather than on a rational process of analysis and choice. (Who you know and how you present your strategic decision is just as important as the content of the strategy.)

More recently, the research of Pettigrew,[18] Mintzberg,[19] Johnson[20] and others has further developed the *people* areas of strategy. Their empirical research has shown that the development of strategic management is more complex than the prescriptive strategists would imply: the people, politics and culture of organisations all need to be taken into account. Strategists such as Argyris[21] and Senge[22] have emphasised the *learning* approach to strategy: encouraging managers to undertake a process of trial and error to devise the optimal strategy.

As a result, according to these researchers, strategic management can best be considered as a process whereby the organisation's strategy is derived as a result of trial, repeated experimentation and small steps forward: in this sense, it is *emergent* rather than *planned*. Figure 2.2 presents a simplified and diagrammatic view of the emergent process. The process then proceeds as market conditions change, the economy develops, teams of people in the company change, innovations occur, etc. Clearly, such a process is hard to define in advance and therefore difficult to analyse and predict in

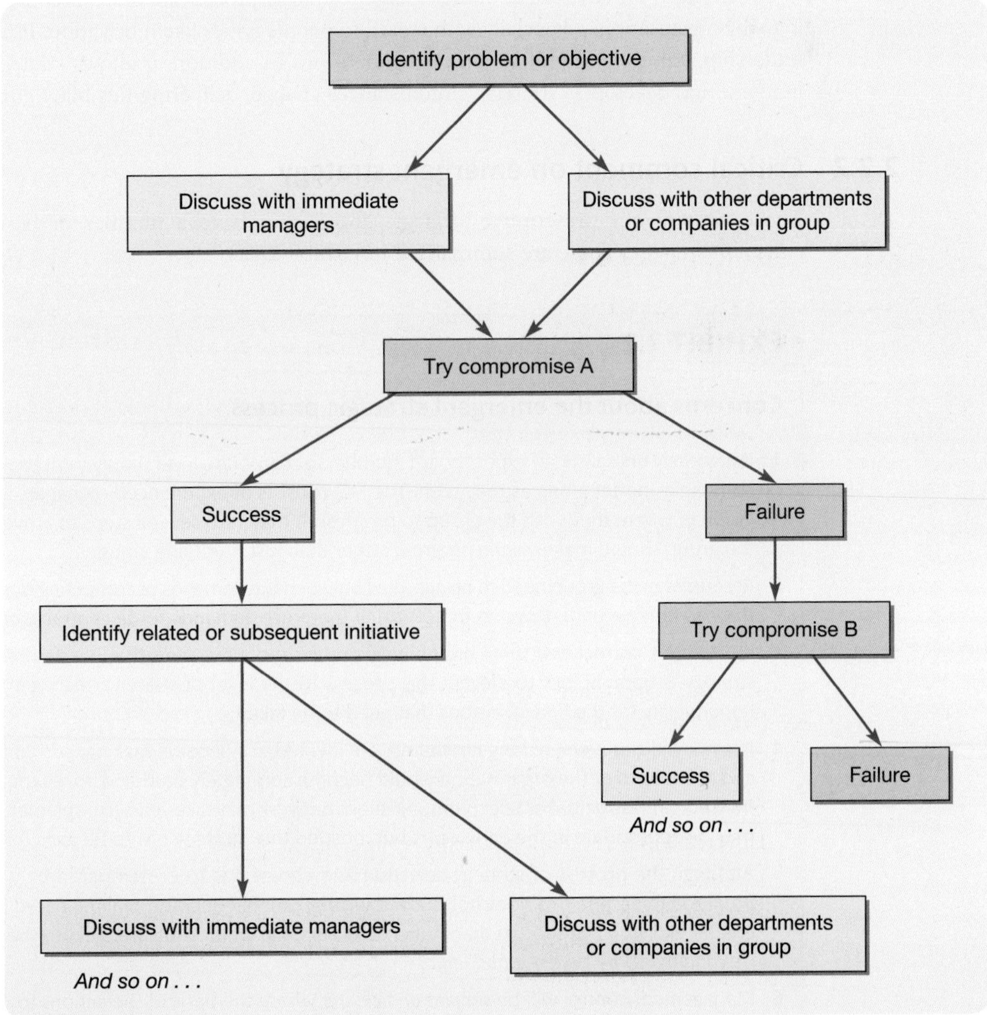

Figure 2.2 One view of how the emergent strategy process works

a clear and structured way. For example, when entering new breakfast cereal markets, CP in Case 2.1 adopted different strategies in accordance with the particular market circumstances. Equally, the Subway franchise operation described in Case 2.3 experimented with new forms of sub, new organisation for the serving team and new designs for its outlets before arriving at the current format: some were more successful than others.

If the emergent view of the strategy process is correct, then the implications for strategic management are profound:[23,24]

- Strategies emerge from a confused background and often in a muddled and disorganised way: the resulting strategies themselves may therefore be unclear and not fully resolved.
- The prescriptive strategic process is unlikely to reflect reality: options identified will not be comprehensive and the selection process will be flawed.
- Considering 'implementation' *after* the rest of the strategy process does not reflect what usually happens.
- Managers are unlikely to seek the optimal solution: it may not be capable of identification and, in addition, may not be in their personal interests.
- Working within an organisation's routines and culture will allow the optimal culture to emerge rather than be forced by an artificial planning process.

In summary, the advantages of the emergent strategy process are that it accords with actual practice in many organisations, especially with regard to people issues like motivation. It takes account of the leadership, culture and politics of an organisation. In addition, it allows strategies to experiment, innovate and develop as strategic circumstances change, delivering flexibility during the process.

2.2.2 Critical comment on emergent strategy

Those who favour prescriptive strategic approaches have a number of basic concerns about emergent strategy. These are summarised in Exhibit 2.2.[25]

EXHIBIT 2.2

Concerns about the emergent strategic process

1. It is entirely unrealistic to expect board members at corporate level simply to sit back and let operating companies potter along as they wish. The HQ consists of experienced managers who have a *unified* vision of where they wish the group to progress. It may take several steps to arrive at this vision, but the group should make visible progress rather than just muddling along.
2. Resources of the group need to be *allocated* between the demands of competing operating companies; this can only be undertaken at the centre. It therefore demands some central strategic overview.
3. It is entirely correct that there are political groups and individuals that need to be persuaded that a strategy is optimal, but to elevate this process to the level of strategic management is to *abdicate responsibility* for the final decisions that need to be taken.
4. In some industries where long timeframes are involved for decision making, decisions have to be taken and adhered to or the organisation would become completely muddled: for example, building a new transport infrastructure or telecommunications network may take years to implement. Experimentation may be appropriate in the early years but, beyond this, strategy has to be *fixed* for *lengthy projects.*
5. Although the process of strategy selection and choice has to be tempered by what managers are prepared to accept, this does not make it wrong; rational decision making based on evidence has a greater likelihood of success than hunch and personal whim. Thus the debate should take place but be *conditioned by evidence and logic.*
6. Management control will be *simpler and clearer* where the basis of the actions to be undertaken has been planned in advance.

In practice, many organisations treat the above comments as *limitations* on the prescriptive approach, rather than issues that cannot be overcome. To see how prescriptive strategy can emerge, you can read Case 2.3. Subway's strategy from a small sandwich shop to a global franchise shows the importance of experimenting. Moreover, an *extended time perspective* is useful in order to see how strategic decisions take shape according to the emergent approach.

KEY STRATEGIC PRINCIPLES

- Emergent strategic management is a strategy whose final *objective* is unclear and whose *elements* are developed during the course of its life, as the strategy proceeds.
- The process is one of experimentation to find the most productive route forward.
- Emergent strategy does not have a single, final objective; strategy develops over time.
- In fast-developing markets, the time period may be short; in slow-developing markets, it is likely to be longer.
- To test for emergent strategy, it is essential to examine how the strategy has developed in practice over a defined time period.
- The advantages of the process include its consistency with actual practice in organisations; it takes account of people issues such as motivation; it allows experimentation about the strategy to take place; it provides an opportunity to include the culture and politics of the organisation; it delivers flexibility to respond to market changes.
- Six problems have been identified with the emergent strategic process that make it difficult to operate in practice.

Checklist: Seven questions to help choose between prescriptive or emergent strategy . . . or choose both.

CASE STUDY 2.2

Prescriptive strategies to build world airlines at Singapore Airlines and Emirates Group

Widely regarded as world-leading airlines, Singapore Airlines and Emirates Group both started as small regional airlines. With the backing of their respective governments, the airlines chose to use prescriptive strategies to build their market positions. But both have had to contend with uncertainty and competitive pressures in air travel as they grew to their present size.

When the Prime Minister of Singapore, Mr Lee Kuan Yew (now the distinguished Senior Minister of that country), led his country to break away from the Malaysian Federation in 1965, he realised that a relatively small country of 6 million people needed a strong and distinctive strategy if it was to survive and grow.[26] His government allowed the existing airline - Malaysian-Singapore Airlines - to continue until 1972. At that time, both his government and the government of Malaysia judged that it would be better if the airlines of the two countries followed the distinctive paths set by their separate countries. Two airlines, Malaysian Airlines System (now called Malaysian Airlines) and Singapore Airlines were therefore founded. This case focuses in part on Singapore Airlines but acknowledges that Malaysian Airlines has also built a major international airline in the period up to 2012.

In a similar way, His Excellency Sheikh Mohammed bin Rashid Al Maktoum judged, from his base in Dubai, that the Gulf Kingdoms of the United Arab Emirates needed a strong airline in the early 1970s. Emirates launched its first flights in 1985 starting with routes to Pakistan and India. The company tells the story of a potential public relations disaster in 1985 on its first flight from Dubai to Karachi: 'A PR disaster is thwarted by recruiting 80 Emirates staff to travel incognito to disguise

Table 2.1 Traffic and business results 2009

	Passengers (000s)	Load factor (%)	Revenue ($m)	Operating profit ($m)
Emirates Airline Group	27,454	78.1	11,834	971
Singapore Airlines	16,480	78.4	9,083	45

Source: based on ATW World Airline Report 2010.

the dismal sales of tickets on the maiden flight.' Emirates Group has come a long way since that time.

From their foundation to the present, both governments held controlling shares in their respective airlines. The governments have therefore been at the centre of the development strategy of both airlines. Table 2.1 indicates how the two companies have grown since the early years. By 2012, the airlines were recognised world leaders with major fleets of aircraft serving many of the world's leading destinations. Importantly, both companies have developed strong home base operations. Singapore Airlines operates from Changhi Airport, Singapore, and Emirates Airlines operates from Dubai International Airport in Dubai, United Arab Emirates. Both are widely regarded as being amongst the most modern and smooth-running aircraft hub operations in the world. In addition, both companies have a strong service reputation with customers based on their use of modern aircraft, attractive in-flight food and extensive provision of in-flight entertainment. What were the strategies that led to this level of success?

The following prescriptive strategies were undertaken for the development of both Emirates Group and Singapore Airlines on the important assumption that significant growth in world travel would continue:

- From the beginning, the airlines decided that they would build a reputation based on *superior service* to their rivals. Thus, they introduced free drinks, hot towels and headsets from the outset – such amenities are relatively cheap and quick to introduce. In more recent years, they were among the first airlines to offer in-flight entertainment screens at each individual seat – even in economy class.
- Substantial investment in *staff training, employee welfare and related activities*. The airlines took the view that staff were crucial both to in-flight service delivery and also to aircraft safety through expertise in ground and related operations. Equally, as aircraft design changed and in-flight service operations became more complex, the airlines recognised the need to update continuously their knowledge and expertise in these areas.
- The investment in a *modern fleet of aircraft* with a policy of always seeking out the latest in terms of technology and aircraft design. For example, both airlines were amongst the first airlines to operate the new Jumbo Passenger Jet – the A380-800 – which was expected to add a new dimension to long-distance air transport.
- Development of *modern airports* at their main bases in Singapore and Dubai coupled with the related strategy of ensuring that the airports became an efficient handling facility for rival airlines. This would encourage other airlines to base their services at Changhi and Dubai International, respectively, when seeking stop-over locations on long-haul flights between the continents of the world.
- *Co-operation with other airlines* through code-sharing and ticket marketing arrangements to make it easier for customers to travel around the world and to lock them into certain airlines rather than rivals.

European and North American customers were increasingly travelling to the company's major Gulf and Asian markets. However, the prescriptive strategy assumption that growth in world travel would continue was cast into doubt by a number of major events that reduced airline travel:

- the disastrous attack in the USA on 11 September 2001;
- the highly infectious SARS virus in 2003;
- the world financial banking collapse in 2008;
- European flight disruption following the Icelandic volcanic eruptions in 2010 and 2011;
- fuel price rises in 2009–2010 – fuel accounts for 29 per cent of the total costs of Emirates Airlines;
- political unrest in several Middle Eastern countries following the change of government in Egypt in early 2011.

Hence, the market and financial predictions needed to support the prescriptive strategies outlined above were subject to increased uncertainty due to events outside the control of

Just like its competitors, Singapore Airlines will typically need years to negotiate, acquire and implement new aircraft and new routes. Prescriptive strategies are essential.
Munshi Ahmed/Corbis

the company. This does raise the question of whether it is appropriate to rely on prescriptive approaches when outside events can clearly undermine the outcome.

Both Singapore Airlines and Emirates Airline group have taken important initiatives on carbon emissions and energy saving according to their annual reports.

Case questions

1 What makes the Singapore and Emirates strategies prescriptive rather than emergent? Does it matter that the outcomes were not as predictable as assumed by prescriptive strategy?

2 Are there any weaknesses in using prescriptive strategy processes to develop strategy at the airline? You might like to use *Exhibit 2.1* to answer this question.

2.3 SOME PRESCRIPTIVE THEORIES OF STRATEGIC MANAGEMENT

The distinction between prescriptive and emergent strategies explored in the last two sections oversimplifies the reality of strategy development – there are many theories. The next two sections explore some of the theories that underlie this basic distinction. This section examines prescriptive strategy theories, while emergent strategy theories are explored in Section 2.4. It should be noted, however, that there is some overlap between the two areas. This will be explored further later in this chapter. In broad terms, it is useful to identify four main areas of prescriptive strategy theory:

1 industry- and environment-based theories of strategy;
2 resource-based theories of strategy;
3 game-based theories of strategy;
4 co-operation- and network-based theories of strategy.

2.3.1 Industry- and environment-based theories of strategy

For some companies, *profitability* is the clear goal, and the content therefore addresses this objective; over the long term, this is likely to override all other objectives.

Definition ▶ **Industry- and environment-based theories of strategy argue that profits are delivered by selecting the most attractive industry and then competing better than other companies in that industry.** Importantly, the word 'environment' here is not used in the sense of 'green, sustainability' but means *the external factors acting on the organisation*, markets, competitors, governments, etc. Figure 2.3 shows where the emphasis lies within the context of prescriptive strategy.

Such concepts derive from the assertion that organisations are rational, logical and driven by the need for profitability. They can be related back to three areas:

1 the eighteenth-century Scottish economist, Adam Smith, and his view that man was rational, logical and motivated by profit;
2 the concepts of military warfare quoted earlier in this chapter that show how the competitive war can be won;
3 the industrial organisational (I/O) model of above-average returns to a company deriving from the concept that the most important determinant of company profits is the external environment.

In terms of the development of strategy theory, much of this material only came together in the 1960s. Igor Ansoff,[28] Alfred Chandler[29] and Alfred Sloan[30] all had an early influence in this area. More recently, writers such as Wheelen and Hunger[31] have laid out the model for rational, analytical

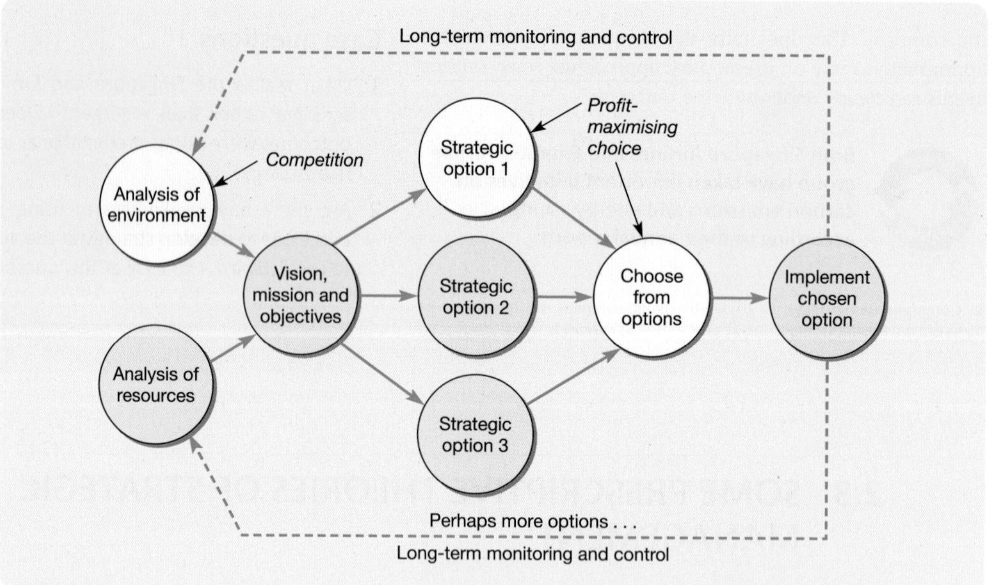

Figure 2.3 The prescriptive strategic process: the position of profit-maximising, competition-based theories

and structured development of strategy. During the 1980s, the work of Professor Michael Porter[32] added significantly to this material; he was a dominant influence during this period. Much of his work was based on the study of large companies and the application of industrial economic concepts to strategy, as has been pointed out by Rumelt, Schendel and Teece.[33] Porter's approach relied essentially on the view that the industry in which a firm chooses to compete and the way that it competes in that industry are the prime determinants of its long-run profitability.[34] This contribution will be examined in greater depth later in the book.

In fairness, it should be pointed out that earlier researchers such as Ansoff never saw their work in quite such stark prescriptive terms. For example, an Ansoff 1968 research paper on strategic management[35] refers with approval to the emergent strategy work of Cyert and March on human resources strategies, which we explore later in this chapter.

For all these writers, strategy involves formal, analytical processes. It will result in a specific set of documents that are discussed and agreed by the board of directors (or the public sector equivalent) of an organisation – a tangible strategic plan for some years ahead. Typically, the plan will include sections predicting the general economic and political situation; exploring industry characteristics including economies of scale and degree of concentration; analysing competitors, their strengths and weaknesses; identifying customer demand; considering the resources available to the organisation; and recommending a set of strategies to meet these requirements.

The strategy will primarily (but not exclusively) be driven by the objective of maximising the organisation's profitability in the long term (such profits may particularly accrue to the shareholders) by seeking and exploiting opportunities in particular industries. The Singapore Airlines and Emirate case is an example here – see Case 2.2. The major argument of the theorists is that the purpose of strategy is to develop sustainable competitive advantage[36] over competitors through choosing the most attractive industry[37] and then resolving how to compete within that industry.

Although these views were broadly endorsed by Kenichi Ohmae,[38] head of the Japanese part of the well-known consulting company, McKinsey, it has been pointed out by Wilks that they remain largely Western and Anglo-American in their orientation.[39] They are primarily concerned with profit and leave only limited room for social, cultural, governmental and other considerations. This view of strategy is therefore unlikely to appeal to countries which demand a higher social content from company plans – for example, within Europe: France, Poland, the Netherlands and Scandinavian countries.

Outside Europe, India has insisted on a strong social content to plans for many years and has only in the past few years come to accept that strong social policies need to be tempered by market forces.[40] Japanese companies also have other criteria, as we have already seen. Malaysian and Singaporean companies with their strong relationships with the governments of their respective countries might well also sacrifice profitability to other objectives, such as building market presence or providing extra training for workers – see Case 2.2 on Singapore Airlines and Emirates.[41] Content for companies in these countries will inevitably be broader.

These nation-state arguments are, however, a matter of degree and do not deny the need to make long-term profits in order to ensure the survival and growth of the enterprise. A more fundamental criticism of profit-maximising theories has been made by Hamel and Prahalad[42] and Kay.[43] They argue that, although competitors are important, the emphasis on competitive industry comparisons essential to such theories is misleading: it simply shows where organisations are weak. Such theories do not indicate how the company should develop its own resources and skills – the key strategic task in their view. Moreover, as soon as all companies have access to Porter's writings on industry analysis, Hamel and Prahalad[44] and Kay[45] have argued that the advantage ceases since all companies have the same knowledge and no company has an advantage.

Hannan and Freeman[46] took a differing view: they argued that markets are so powerful that seeking sustainable competitive advantage for the majority of companies is not realistic; only the largest companies with significant market share can achieve and sustain such advantage. For all the others, complex and detailed strategies are a distraction.

From a different perspective, Mintzberg[47] and others have criticised the industry-based approach by arguing that this is simply not the way that strategy is or should be developed in practice. In contrast, human-resource-based theories of strategy suggest that seeking to maximise performance through a single, static strategic plan is a fallacy. There are no clear long-term mission statements and goals, just a series of short-term horizons to be met and then renewed. Techniques that purport to provide long-term insights may be too simplistic. Using such arguments, Mintzberg in particular has been highly articulate in his criticisms of the formal strategic planning process. However, he has subsequently modified his criticisms and accepted that some strategic planning may be beneficial to the organisation.[48]

Chapter 3 explores the detailed concepts and useful insights offered by industry and environment-based theories.

2.3.2 Resource-based theories of strategy

Definition ▶ **Resource-based theories concentrate on the chief resources and capabilities of the organisation, especially those where the organisation has a competitive advantage, as the principal source of successful strategic management.** Essentially, competitive advantage comes from the organisation's resources rather than the environment within which the company operates (see Figure 2.4). This does not mean that *all* the resources of an organisation will deliver competitive advantage – perhaps not the canteen or legal facilities of Singapore Airlines, for example. But *some* of the resources must be able to provide a distinctive competitive advantage in the market place if the company is to deliver above-average profits in that industry – for instance, the Emirates brand name is a unique and powerful resource that allows the company to attract and keep customers.

Writing in the 1960s, Drucker[49] points out that it is important to '. . . build on strength . . . to look for opportunities rather than for problems'. Many basic economic texts have also stressed the importance of resources as the basis for profit development.

One particular aspect of resource-based strategy, emphasised by US and Japanese strategists beginning in the 1960s and 1970s, was operations (manufacturing) strategy and the emphasis on total quality management. Although Henry Ford had developed these areas early in the twentieth century, little emphasis was subsequently given to them. They were probably considered to be too ordinary and insufficiently concerned with overall strategic management. (Many strategic texts made no mention of them even in the late 1990s.) Deming, Ishikawa and Taguchi[50] worked on quality issues and Ohno[51] and many others worked on manufacturing strategy issues. Such issues are

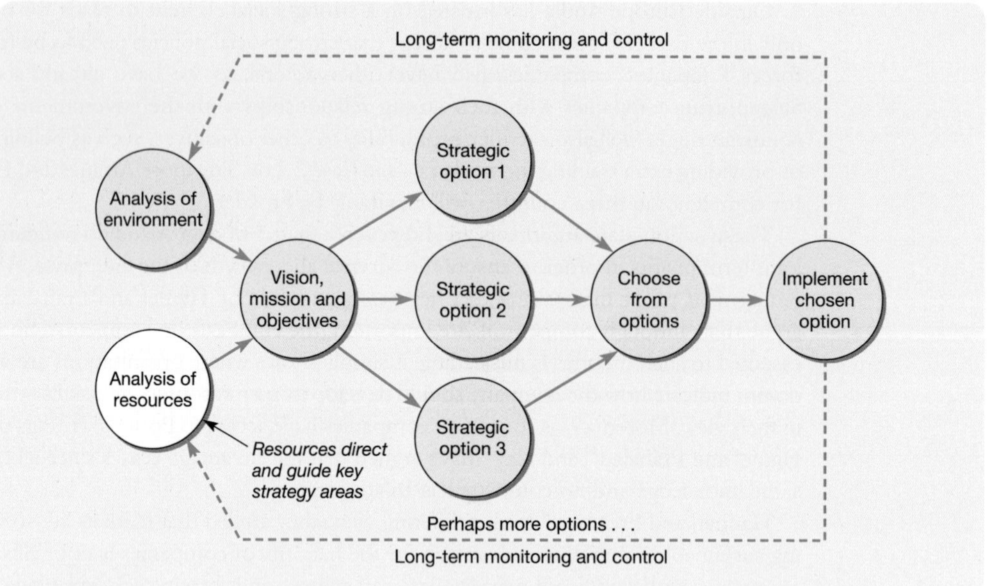

Figure 2.4 The prescriptive strategic process: the position of resource-based theories

beyond the scope of this edition of the book, but some recommendations are given in the references at the end of this chapter.[52]

From a different theoretical perspective, resource-based strategy development has emerged as one of the key prescriptive routes in recent years. Possibly as a reaction against the strong emphasis on markets and profit maximising of the 1980s (see Section 2.3.1 above), researchers began to argue that the organisation's resources were far more important in delivering competitive advantage:

> The traditional competitive strategy paradigm [e.g. Porter 1980] with its focus on product market positioning, focuses only on the last few hundred yards of what may be a skill-building marathon.[53]

Wernerfelt,[54] Peteraf,[55] Dierickx and Cool,[56] Kay[57] and others have all explored aspects of what has become known as the *resource-based view* of strategy development. Essentially, although competition is explored, the emphasis in this approach is on the organisation's own resources – its physical resources, such as plant and machinery; its people resources, such as its leadership and skills, and, above all, the ways that such resources interact in organisations. It is this combination of resources that delivers competitive advantage, because such a combination takes years to develop and may therefore be difficult for others to copy.

In this context, the resource-based view draws a distinction between the general resources that are available to any organisation, such as accounting skills and basic technology, and those that are special and, perhaps, even unique to the organisation. It argues that it is only those special resources that deliver sustainable competitive advantage. For example, the Nestlé brand name is a unique resource available to Cereal Partners' breakfast cereals and the Emirates name to that company – see Cases 2.1 and 2.2. The resource-based view is explored in Chapter 4.

An important recent development has been the treatment of the *knowledge* of the organisation as a key resource.[58] It has been argued that the knowledge possessed by an organisation – its procedures, its technical secrets, its contacts with others outside the organisation – will deliver significant competitive advantages to many organisations. Some strategists have gone so far as to suggest that such knowledge is the only resource that will deliver sustainable competitive advantage. While this may be over-stated, knowledge is important in strategy development and is explored in Chapter 7.

One of the main criticisms of resource-based theories is that, although they are good at analysing competitive advantage once it has been achieved, such theories have rather less insight into the pathways to developing competitive advantage and to responding to a constantly changing competitive environment.[59] New theories and concepts with regard to the *dynamics of resource-based theory* are now in the course of development: they rest principally on concepts associated with an organisation constantly seeking new entrepreneurial opportunities and responding to resource changes by competitors.[60] These theories are explored in Chapter 5.

2.3.3 Game-based theories of strategy

Definition ▶ **Game-based theories of strategy focus on an important part of the prescriptive process - the decision making that surrounds the selection of the best strategic option. Instead of treating this as a simple options-and-choice model, game theory attempts to explore the interaction between an organisation and others as the decision is made - the game** (see Figure 2.5). The theoretical background to such an approach is based on mathematical models of options and choice coupled with the theory of chance.[61]

Game theory begins by recognising that a simple choice of the 'best' strategy will have implications for other companies, such as suppliers and competitors. The consequences for others will be unknown at the time the initial choice is made by the organisation itself. The theory then attempts to model the consequences of such a choice and thereby allow for the choice itself to be modified as the game progresses. Game theory will include not only *competitors*, but also other organisations that might be willing to *co-operate* with the organisation. Such a theory considers that the options-and-choice prescriptive model over-simplifies the options and choices available. It will also involve negotiation with others, anticipation of competitive responses and the search for optimal solutions. Such a process may allow all competitors in the market place to win.

An example of game theory occurred when Virgin Media, part of the Virgin Group, attempted to acquire the British television channel ITV in 2005. A rival media company, British Sky Broadcasting (controlled by News Corporation – see Case 8.4), bought a shareholding in ITV to block the Virgin acquisition. Virgin was then forced to turn to the UK's competition office in an attempt to overturn this position.

Although game theory has been around since the 1940s, it is only relatively recently that it has been applied to strategy. The reason is that the complex world of strategy decisions is difficult to model adequately using the mathematical theory that lies at the foundation of game theory. In the last few years, strategists have begun to explore some key concepts without necessarily modelling every detail using strict mathematical analysis. The results have been some new insights into the

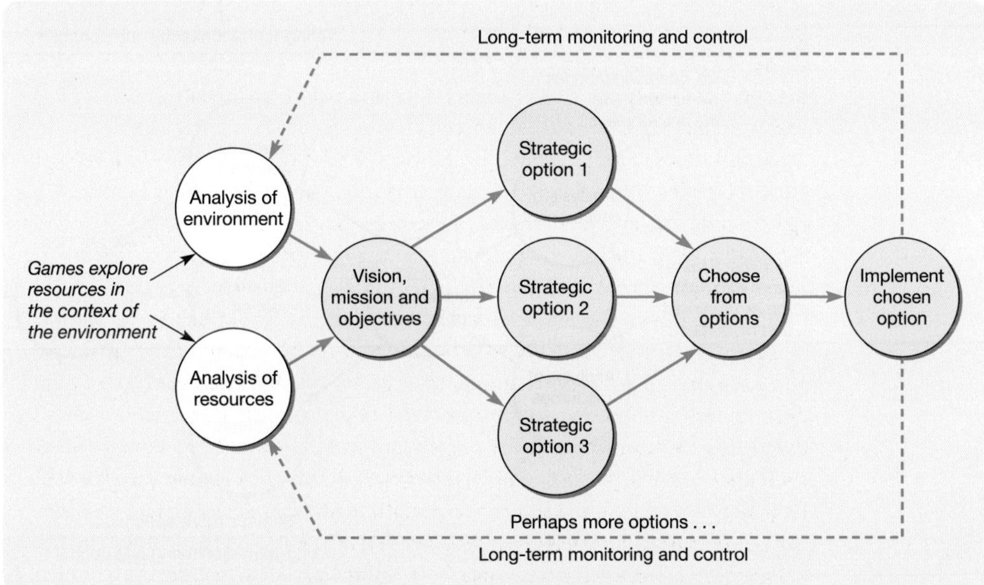

Figure 2.5 The prescriptive strategic process: the position of game-based theories

prescriptive strategic process which are explored in Chapter 5. However, game theory still remains only a partial view of a limited part of the strategic process.

2.3.4 Co-operation- and network-based theories of strategy

Definition ▶ **In co-operative strategy theory, at least two independent companies work together to achieve an agreed objective. In network theory, the focus rests on sharing networks of personal contacts, knowledge and influence both inside and outside the organisation.** Network theory is therefore a broader concept than co-operative theory. Both co-operation and network theories of strategy seek clearly defined, prescriptive strategies, but they stress the importance of the formal and informal relationship opportunities that are also available to organisations. Figure 2.6 shows where they fit into the overall model.

Such theories have arisen in recent times as a result of the realisation that organisations can deliver better value to customers and create competitive advantage over rivals by co-operating with other companies. Various forms of co-operation are possible. The main underpinning principle is that such activities deliver growth by developing links that are external to the organisation. Thus the external strategies may include strategic alliances, joint ventures and other forms of co-operation. For example, Singapore Airlines – see Case 2.2 – is a member of the Star Alliance with other airlines to share computer ticketing, passenger onward-booking and comprehensive airline services. This is a strategy external to the company that delivers both extra business and a competitive advantage that cannot be generated inside the company.

Eisenhardt,[62] Inkpen[63] and Child and Faulkner[64] all provide background on this increasingly important area of strategy development. They argue that such strategies are valuable for at least three reasons: first, because they may allow companies to move into restricted markets more quickly; second, because they may allow companies to adopt new technologies earlier than their rivals by gaining the technology from an outside company – perhaps from another country; third, they may allow the alliance to gain and increase its market power.

Some forms of co-operation occur at the corporate headquarters level rather than at the business level. These might take the form of diversification away from the existing business areas or the development of a network of alliances with its potential partners in order to spread the benefits into a number of business relationships. One form of co-operation that has been used increasingly around the world is the franchise operation.

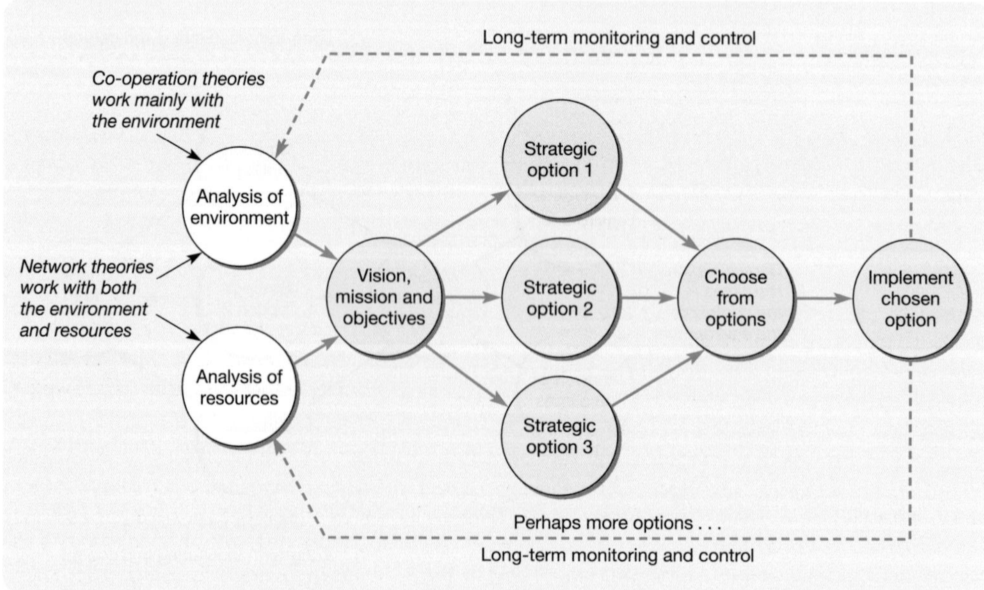

Figure 2.6 The prescriptive strategic process: the position of co-operation and network theories

Definition ▶ **A franchise is a form of co-operative strategy in which a firm (the franchisor) develops a business concept and then offers this to others (the franchisees) in the form of a contractual relationship to use the business concept.** Typically, the franchisee obtains a tried-and-tested business formula in return for paying a percentage of its sales and agreeing to tight controls from the franchisor over the product range, pricing, etc.[65] Case 2.3 describes the Subway franchise operation.

The main problems with co-operative and network strategies are that they are fragile and risk collapse if the contractual terms have not been carefully developed or one of the partners misrepresents the benefits that it brings to the agreement.[66] Co-operative agreements are explored further in Chapter 4. In addition, it is important to note that some forms of co-operation are *illegal* in most countries around the world. Such illegal activities involve collusion to reduce competition in the market place, thus increasing the prices of the goods on sale and thereby increasing profits. These activities are not only illegal but also unethical. They do *not* form part of the proper development of theories of strategic co-operation and networking.

KEY STRATEGIC PRINCIPLES

- Industry and environment-based theories emphasise the importance of the market place to deliver profits. Strategy should seek sustainable competitive advantage.
- Resource-based theories stress the competitive resources of the organisation in strategic development. Core competencies and other uniquely competitive resources need to be identified.
- Game-based theories of strategy focus on the options-and-choice stage of the prescriptive model. They explore the commercial realities of competitor reactions and possible counter-moves in the search for an optimal strategy.
- Co-operation and network-based theories focus on the formal and informal relationships that can be built to develop strategic management, such as strategic alliances and joint ventures. They have arisen as a result of the realisation that it is sometimes possible to develop competitive advantage by co-operating with rival companies. The main difficulty is to make such co-operation work over time: it often fails for a variety of reasons.

CASE STUDY 2.3

Building the Subway world franchise using emergent and prescriptive processes

Back in 1965, 17-year-old Fred DeLuca opened up a sandwich shop called Pete's Super Submarines in Delaware, USA. (Non-American readers might like to know that long bread rolls are known as 'submarines' in North America because of their shape.) By 2014, the business had grown into a chain – renamed Subway – with over 40,000 outlets in 104 countries. It was all done through a mix of emergent and prescriptive strategies.

Subway: the early years

When Fred DeLuca wanted to earn some money in 1965 to pay his college fees, he asked a family friend, Dr Peter Buck, for some advice on what he should do. Dr Buck suggested that he tried to open a sandwich store, having seen a successful operation in the local town. Buck loaned him $1,000 and the first store was opened in Bridgeport, Connecticut, USA in August 1965. It was called Pete's Super Submarines and sold a range of freshly-cut long sandwiches for which the customer could choose the fillings from a range on the counter. Fred himself ran the store and drove regularly to market to buy fresh vegetables and meat – obtaining the right quality at the right prices proved to be important to a successful shop. A second shop followed after one year and then a third in 1967. Importantly, the third shop – now really a 'restaurant' – was in a more visible location. This was found to be vital to success, even if the rents and related costs were higher.

Subway: developing the franchise concept

For the next few years, the store/restaurant experimented with different approaches to its product range, its marketing, its purchase of fresh produce and its in-store production. The company name was changed to 'Subway' and the familiar yellow logo was developed. Essentially, the founders developed

Subs can be bought everywhere from Valdez, Alaska, USA to Shanghai, China.

a business formula for their sandwich restaurant with the following characteristics:

- relatively low capital costs around $80–120,000 compared to around $1 million for a McDonald's, Jolly Bee or Burger King Restaurant (because the latter need to fit fryers and grills, etc.);
- around 6–8 employees per store compared to around 15–20 in a typical McDonald's;
- clean and simple design with strong logo – name changed to 'Subway';
- clear and simple in-store pricing and product presentation – hygiene factors and training are important to ensure that all food is fresh and clean.

This was the basis of the Subway franchise first offered in 1974. Over the next 35 years, Subway grew its operations mainly through franchising. Importantly, it began to experiment with different locations. Typically, a fast-food franchise like McDonald's needs to be located in a high customer traffic area like a shopping mall in order to be profitable because of the high start-up and wage costs. Subway found that its franchise could be operated in smaller and more specialist outlets – such as schools and factories – because of its smaller-scale business formula.

Subway in North America

By the mid-1990s, Subway had more outlets than McDonald's, although each individual outlet had a lower turnover than a McDonald's. The strategic problem for Subway in North America was that sales growth was beginning to slow around this time. Previous growth had come from opening more outlets but – as McDonald's also discovered: see Case 6.2 – eventually a franchise chain like Subway largely runs out of new locations. To tackle this, Fred DeLuca went back to his customers. He learned that an increasing number came to Subway because it offered a low-fat alternative to burgers and French fries. In 1998, Fred used this to develop a marketing campaign that focused on a line of seven low-fat sandwiches. The company claims that the sales were boosted significantly as a result – the precise figures are unclear because the company was private (and remains so to this day). In 2000, the company decided that it still wished to attract customers who wanted a full calorie meal. It therefore developed a range of big-eater sandwiches – for example, steak and cheese. Again, this had a positive impact on sales. By 2004, Subway had around 20,000 outlets in the USA and Canada.

Subway: worldwide expansion

In 1984, Subway opened its first franchise operation outside North America – in Bahrain in the Middle East. The company then continued to expand internationally and had opened 12,000 outlets by 2014 in 104 countries: locations included China, India, Australia, New Zealand, Africa, South America, Mexico, Germany and the UK. The opening of the 2000th outlet in 2004 was regarded as being particularly important. 'This milestone shows that we are right on track towards achieving our goals of our worldwide strategic plan and reaching the 7,500 restaurant count by the year 2010,' said Patricia Demarais, Subway's Director of International Business. In fact, Subway beat this target and by 2014 actually had more outlets than McDonald's worldwide.

Subway has an extensive commitment to green strategy initiatives. These are described on its website: www.subway.com.

Case questions

1 What precisely makes the development of Subway's strategy both prescriptive and emergent?

2 More generally, is it possible for a company to start with an emergent strategy and then develop a prescriptive strategy? Can a company continue with emergent strategies beyond its early years? Should a company continue with such emergent strategies as it continues to grow?

2.4 SOME EMERGENT THEORIES OF STRATEGIC MANAGEMENT

When strategies emerge from a situation rather than being prescribed in advance, it is less likely that they will involve a long-term strategic plan. This does not mean that there is no planning but rather that such plans are more flexible, feeling their way forward as issues clarify and the environment surrounding the company changes. Planning is short-term, more reactive to events, possibly even more entrepreneurial.

To understand the background to emergent strategy theory, it is useful to look back to the 1970s. At that time, prescriptive strategies with detailed corporate plans were widely used. Suddenly, oil prices rose sharply as a result of a new, strong Middle East oil price consortium. Many industrial companies around the world were hit badly in an entirely unpredictable way; the prescriptive plans were thrown into confusion. Emergent strategies that relied less on precise predictions about the future were sought. Around the year 2000, the economic bubble associated with new internet companies also highlighted the uncertainty of the environment. For this reason, some strategists argue that the whole basis of prescriptive strategy is false. They would claim that, even during periods of relative certainty, organisations may be better served by considering strategy as an emergent process.

For our purposes, we can usefully distinguish four sets of emergent strategy theories:

1 survival-based theories of strategy;
2 uncertainty-based theories of strategy;
3 human-resource-based theories of strategy;
4 innovation- and knowledge-based theories of strategy.

2.4.1 Survival-based theories of strategy

Definition ► **Survival-based strategies regard the survival of the fittest company in the market place as being the prime determinant of strategic management.** The theory begins by exploring how to survive in an environment which is highly competitive, shifting and changing. There is little point in sophisticated prescriptive solutions: much better to dodge and weave as the market changes, letting the strategy emerge in the process. Figure 2.7 shows where the emphasis is placed by survival-based strategies.

As Section 2.3 explained, industry- and environment-based approaches are concerned with selecting the optimal strategy to maximise the organisation's profitability and then implementing

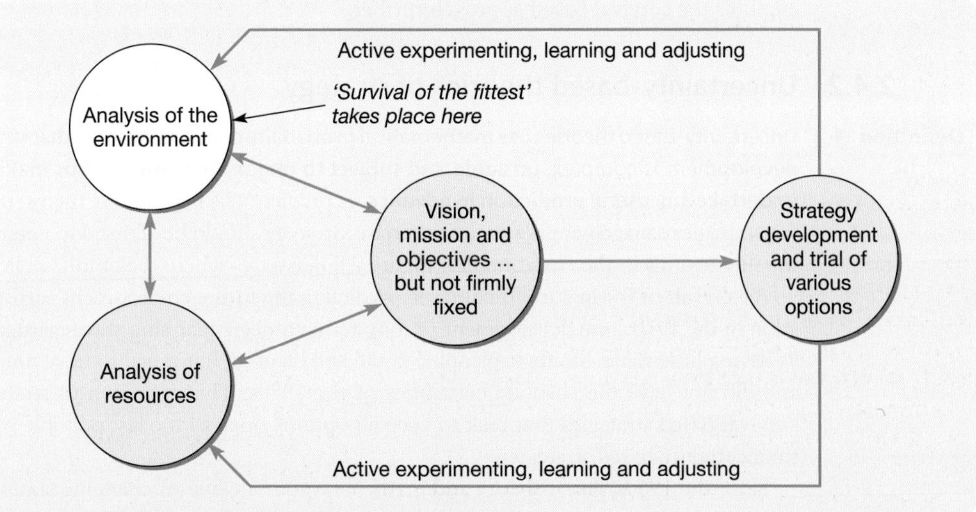

Figure 2.7 The emergent strategic process: the position of survival-based theories

that strategy. Critics have long known that this simple economic model is far from reality. For example, in the late 1930s, Hall and Hitch[68] surveyed companies and showed that they did not set output at the theoretical maximum level, i.e. where marginal cost equals marginal revenue. This was partly because decisions were not necessarily rational and partly because it was unclear what the revenue and cost relationships were anyway.

However, this does not mean that companies just muddle through. The competitive jungle of the market place will ruthlessly weed out the least efficient companies; survival-based strategies are needed in order to prosper in such circumstances. Essentially, according to the survival-based strategy theorists, it is the market place that matters more than a specific strategy; hence, the optimal strategy for survival is to be really efficient. Beyond this, companies can only rely on chance.

To overcome these difficulties, Henderson[69] suggested that what most companies needed in order to survive in these highly competitive circumstances was differentiation. Products or services that were able to offer some aspect not easily available to competitors would give some protection. However, other strategists doubt that true differentiation is possible because it takes too long to achieve and the environment changes too quickly. In these circumstances, theorists suggest that survival-based strategies should rely on running really efficient operations that can respond to changes in the environment. As Williamson commented:

> Economy is the best strategy.[70]

If the environment matters more than a specific strategy, then survival-based strategists argue that the optimal strategy will be to pursue a number of strategic initiatives at any one time and let the market place select the best.[71] Selection of strategy is therefore incorrect according to this theory. It is better to experiment with many different approaches and see which emerges as the best through natural selection. For example, Whittington[72] points to the example of Sony's Walkman strategy in the 1980s. The company launched 160 different versions in the North American market, never retaining more than about 20 versions at any one time. Ultimately, the market selected the best.

If survival-based theories are correct, then we need to study the organisation's environment carefully (we begin this process in Part 2). In addition to this, we would need to treat the prescriptive strategy selection process of Chapters 8, 9 and 10 with a great deal of caution.

Other strategy writers believe survival-based theories are too pessimistic; there are practical problems in a strategy that only takes small cautious steps and keeps all options open. Major acquisitions, innovative new products, plant investment to improve quality radically would all be the subject of much anxious debate and little action. The bold strategic step would be completely ruled out.[73] Perhaps Emirates would never have launched its highly successful airline, which has required extensive capital commitments over the years, if it had followed a survival-based strategy. Chapter 11 explores the survival-based approach further.

2.4.2 Uncertainty-based theories of strategy

Definition ▶ **Uncertainty-based theories use mathematical probability concepts to show that strategic management development is complex, unstable and subject to major fluctuations, thus making it impossible to undertake any useful prediction in advance.** If prediction is impossible, then setting clear objectives for strategic management is a useless exercise. Strategy should be allowed to emerge and change with the fluctuations in the environment. Figure 2.8 illustrates where the emphasis lies in such theories.

As a result of the major difficulties in predicting the future environment surrounding the organisation in the 1970s, the development of long-term strategic planning was regarded by some theorists as having little value. Strategic planning could still be used, but it had to have much greater flexibility and did not have the absolute certainties of the 1970s. This approach to strategy led not only to survival-based strategies that seek to keep all options open to the last possible opportunity but also to uncertainty-based strategies.

Since the 1960s, chaos theory and mathematical modelling of changing states have been used to map out the consequences of scientific experiments; such procedures were not developed for the business community but for other scientifically oriented topics, as in the mathematical modelling of

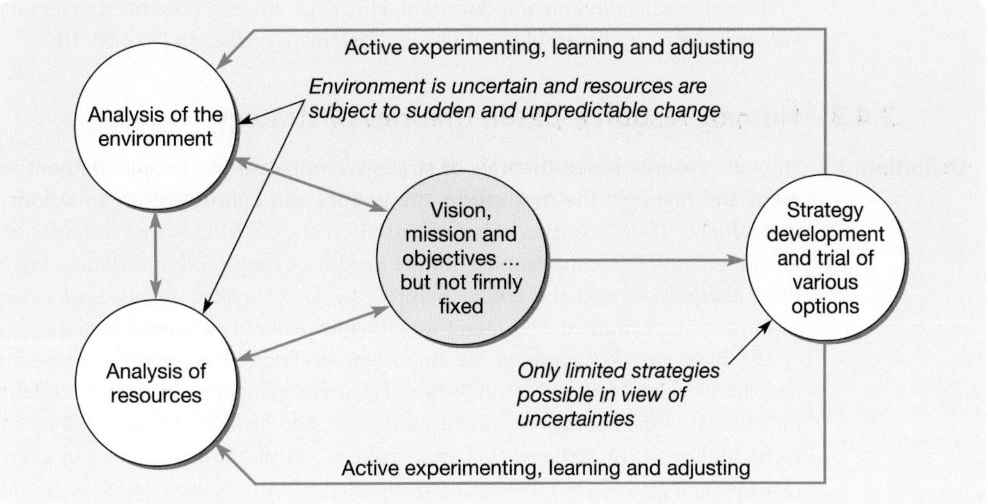

Figure 2.8 The emergent strategic process: the position of uncertainty-based theories

weather forecasting. Essentially, such techniques were able to demonstrate that, in particular types of uncertain environment, small perturbations in the early stages of a process can lead to major variances in the later stages – not unlike the multiplier effect in macroeconomics. A major implication of such environments – often called *chaotic systems* – is that it is simply not possible to predict sufficiently accurately many years ahead (see Gleick).[74]

One variant of this approach to strategy is provided by the empirical research study conducted by Miller and Friesen.[75] They found that significant strategic management occurs in revolutionary ways: there are sudden major shifts in the whole strategy and organisational structure of the company before they reach a new steady state. From a mathematical perspective, it is possible to model such systems and show that they oscillate between steady and turbulent states. Strebel[76] has used a similar argument, pointing particularly to changes in technology that are likely to lead to 'breakpoints' in the development of the organisation.

Business has been identified as such a chaotic system. Stacey[77] has suggested that the environment of many businesses, particularly those in rapidly growing industries such as computers, is inherently unstable. It will never be possible to forecast accurately profits five or ten years into a new project; hence, for example, the apparent accuracy of discounted cash flows and cash projections is largely spurious. It follows that business strategy has to emerge rather than try to aim for the false certainties of the prescriptive approach.

Several writers, such as Miller and Friesen,[78] have also applied the same arguments to the resources of the organisation. They argue that innovation is vital to successful strategy: this can only be achieved in a significant way if the organisation's resources are subjected to revolutionary change, rather than gradual change. Such an approach is likely to have a chaotic, free-wheeling element whose outcome cannot be planned or predicted by strategy in advance. Chapters 7 and 11 explore revolutionary innovation further.

Some companies would regard this whole approach as being partially true but probably too pessimistic. Although the weather is a chaotic system and cannot be predicted accurately, we do know that the Sahara Desert is hot and dry, Singapore is warmer and more humid than London, and so on. Similarly, it can be argued that there are some certainties about business, even though we are unable to predict accurately. Moreover, organisations (especially large ones) need a basic non-chaotic structure if they are to avoid dissolving into anarchy. Singapore Airlines could not afford to rely on uncertainty-based theory when placing an order for ten new SuperJumbo airliners – see Case 2.2 – back in 2003.

There are patterns of behaviour and trends that may be subject to change but can still be predicted with some accuracy. Business strategy may need to emerge and be adaptable, but it is not necessarily totally random and uncertain. However, strategy does need to identify and estimate risk. (We will return to the problem of risk and risk management in Chapter 10.)

2.4.3 Human-resource-based theories of strategy

Definition ▶ **Human-resource-based theories of strategy emphasise the people element in strategy development and highlight the motivation, the politics and cultures of organisations and the desires of individuals.** They have particularly focused on the difficulties that can arise as new strategies are introduced and confront people with the need for change and uncertainty. Figure 2.9 shows where these theories fit into the emergent process. They involve people and occur wherever human resources are prominent; it is therefore difficult to identify a precise position.

We have already examined the important findings of researchers such as Cyert and March[79] and the work of Herbert Simon[80] – strategic management needs to have a human-resource-based dimension. Organisations consist of individuals and groups of people, all of whom may influence or be influenced by strategy; they may make a contribution, acquiesce or even resist the strategic management process, but they are certainly affected by it. Nelson and Winter[81] developed this theme further, arguing that the options-and-choice model of the prescriptive process was completely misleading:

> It is quite inappropriate to conceive of firm behavior in terms of deliberate choice from a broad menu of alternatives that some external observer considers to be 'available' opportunities for the organization.

The human resource aspects of strategy development are further explored in Chapters 4, 11, 12 and 16. However, according to some writers, these matters are not just about peripheral issues of implementation; they are fundamental to the strategy process itself. Nelson and Winter[82] argued that organisations have in reality limited strategic choice. The strategy available is:

> not broad, but narrow and idiosyncratic; it is built on a firm's routines, and most of the 'choosing' is also accomplished automatically by those routines.

Strategic logic is restricted by the processes and people already existing in the organisation.

Mintzberg[83] has also developed this theme and argued that strategy emerges from an organisation as it adapts continuously to its environment. Implementation is not, therefore, some separate phase tacked on to the end of the strategy process, but intermingled with strategic management as it develops. Quinn[84] has described this gradualist, emergent approach that accepts that it is looking

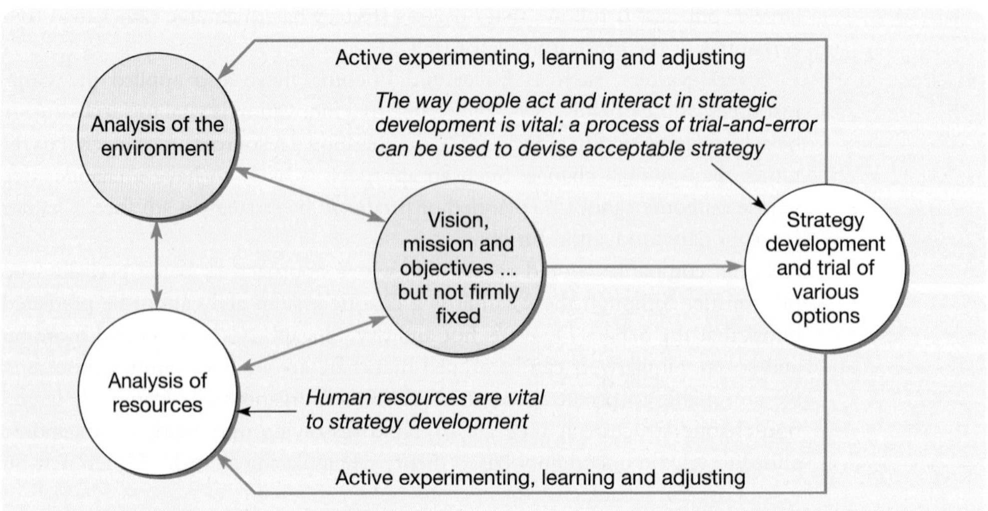

Figure 2.9 The emergent strategic process: the position of human-resource-based theories

at only a limited number of feasible options as *logical incrementalism*. In the words of Mintzberg's famous phrase:

> Smart strategies appreciate that they cannot always be smart enough to think through everything in advance.

We will explore these areas in greater depth in Chapter 11.

More recently, there has been considerable emphasis on the learning aspect of strategy development. Mintzberg emphasised the importance of learning. After him, Senge[85] and others have developed the learning concept, encouraging managers involved in strategy to undertake a process of trial and error to adopt the optimal strategy (see Chapter 11).

The main criticisms of the emergent approach to strategy development listed in Section 2.2 apply especially to human-resource-based strategy. Similar comments may have prompted Mintzberg to move more recently towards the modification of his argument outlined above.[86]

2.4.4 Innovation- and knowledge-based theories of strategy

Definition ▶ **Innovation- and knowledge-based theories of strategy privilege the generation of new ideas and the sharing of these ideas through knowledge as being the most important aspects of strategy development.** These theories came to prominence during the 1990s. Innovation here does not just mean inventing new products or production processes: it means the development and exploitation of any resource of the organisation in a new and radical way.[87] In particular, the way that the knowledge of the organisation is used to generate new and radical solutions has come to be recognised as an important contributor to strategy development.[88] 'Knowledge' here does not mean data so much as the collective wisdom and understanding of many people in the organisation developed over many years. Figure 2.10 shows where such an approach fits into the emergent strategic process.

According to those favouring innovation and knowledge theories, their advantage is that they begin to tackle a problem that has arisen with other, existing theories. The argument goes that the widespread study of existing theories – like resource-based competitive advantage, for example – means that every company knows about such thinking and therefore there is less chance for such theories to deliver new competitive advantage. By emphasising the new and evolving nature of knowledge and innovation, such theories help to overcome this difficulty. Innovation by its very nature moves forward the traditional thinking of the organisation and thereby delivers the possibility of new competitive advantage. Case 14.1 shows the way that companies involved in green

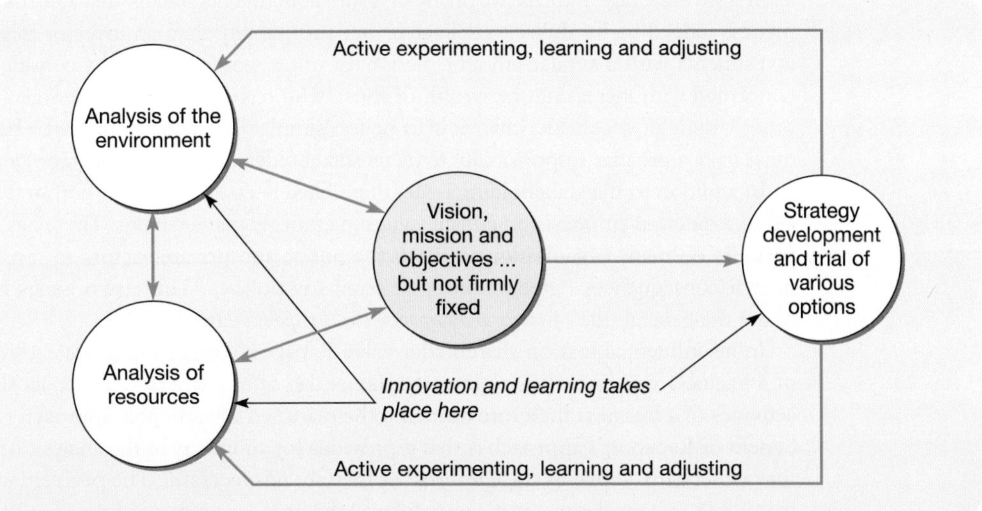

Figure 2.10 The emergent strategic process: the position of innovation- and knowledge-based theories

strategy are willing to explore new ideas, share knowledge and build new business activities through an innovative approach to business strategy.

In the process of innovating, one important aspect is that of sharing knowledge and ideas. This has been made much easier in the past ten years as a result of the internet and telecommunications technology. This area has now developed into an important topic in strategy with real potential to revolutionise strategic thinking. The rise and fall of some internet businesses around the year 2000 has made no difference to the potential of this important strategic route. Chapters 7 and 11 explore these concepts in more depth.

Case study: *Emergent strategy at the Virgin Group*. After you have read the case, you might like to look at the indicative answers to the Case questions. These are given on a separate page on the website.

KEY STRATEGIC PRINCIPLES

- Survival-based theories of strategy are based on the survival of the fittest in the market place. It is difficult to plan strategy actively and possible to survive by differentiation as events unfold.
- Uncertainty-based theories of strategy regard prediction as impossible because of the inherently unstable nature of business and its environment. Strategies must be allowed to react to the changing environment and emerge from the chaos of events. Some would regard this as being a pessimistic view of strategy.
- Human-resource-based theories emphasise the importance of the people element in strategy development. They highlight the motivation, the politics and culture of organisations and the desires of individuals. They also suggest that strategy would benefit from an element of learning and experimentation that empowers individuals.
- Innovation- and knowledge-based theories stress the value of radical new strategic thinking in order to move ahead of rivals. The sharing of knowledge through the internet may be an important part of such a process.

2.5 THE PURPOSE OF THE ORGANISATION: SHAREHOLDERS, STAKEHOLDERS AND 'ABOVE AVERAGE RETURNS'

In many treatments of strategic management,[89] the purpose of strategy is considered simply to be to 'earn above-average returns' of profit or value added. This means that effective strategic management is judged by its ability to deliver higher profitability than an investor might earn from other investments with a similar amount of risk. In other words, strategy is considered to be primarily concerned with increasing the wealth of those who have invested in the organisation. By contrast, other writers now consider this view to be too simplistic.[90] They argue that a business organisation must have a broader responsibility to *all* its stakeholders, not just its shareholders.

In addition to the stakeholding issue, there have been a number of corporate scandals that have led to a renewed emphasis on ethical values in strategic management. There has also been increased pressure on many organisations in both the public and private sectors to face up to the environmental consequences ('green issues') of company policies. These two issues have been captured under the general title of *ethics and corporate social responsibility*.

In his influential text on shareholder value Rapaport[91] argued in the late 1980s that the purpose of a business was essentially to increase the wealth of its owners – that is, its shareholders. All the activities of a business therefore needed to be managed towards this approach to adding value. The benefit of Rapaport's approach is that it provides for simplicity in the analysis of strategy proposals: they either earn 'above-average returns' or they are unsuccessful. The problem with this approach is that it fails to consider in any meaningful way the broader purpose of the organisation. To quote the strategist Charles Handy:[92]

> The idea of a corporation as the property of the current holders of its shares is confusing because it does not make clear where the power lies. As such, the notion is an affront to natural justice because it gives inadequate recognition to the people who work in the corporation and who are, increasingly, its principal assets. To talk of owning other people, as shareholders implicitly do, might be considered immoral.

Essentially, shareholders matter, but so do other *stakeholders* such as employees. We return to this issue in Chapter 6 when we examine the purpose of the organisation. We also explore the point that the strategy of an organisation is not an end in itself. It is the means to deliver the purpose of the organisation, which should in turn be shaped by ethical and social considerations.

To summarise, this text takes the view that the purpose of the organisation will be shaped by the *values* of the organisation, the *power* of the stakeholders in the organisation – amongst whom will be the shareholders – and the *contribution* that every organisation can make to the society within which it exists. Such a contribution will be formed, at least in part, by its ethical values and its view of its corporate social responsibilities. It will also concern itself with issues surrounding the sustainability of its policies in the context of green strategy. Effective strategic management will seek 'above-average returns' but these are not just the profits for the organisation's shareholders.

KEY STRATEGIC PRINCIPLES

- In the past, strategy was considered to be primarily concerned with increasing the wealth of its shareholders. This is now considered to be too simplistic a view because it does not clearly take into account the other stakeholders in the organisation.
- By ethics and corporate social responsibility is meant the standards and conduct that an organisation sets itself in its dealings within the organisation and outside with its environment. Such issues will include green strategy. These policy issues will influence the strategy of the organisation.

CASE STUDY 2.4

Africa calling: mobile phones open up new opportunities

Africa's leading nations have seen a dramatic growth in mobile telephone usage over the past ten years. This case explains the main reasons and explores the key strategic questions - Will it continue? If so, how?

Mobile telephone growth in Africa

Africa is the world's second largest continent with over 800 million people in over 50 countries. Unfortunately, it is also the only area of the world that has experienced a real decline in personal wealth over the past 30 years. Some of the reasons have been well documented by the United Nations - war and conflict, disease including AIDS/HIV and political upheaval. Yet, after years of watching the rest of the world benefit from new mobile telephone technology, African countries are now beginning to catch up. For example, the number of mobile telephones in Africa's largest country, Nigeria, increased tenfold between the years 2002 and 2007. Similarly, South African growth has also been dramatic - more than doubling, albeit from a higher base number, over the same period - see Table 2.2 for the data. By 2013, African mobile telephone growth was amongst the highest in the world - fuelled by increasing wealth and well-proven technology.

Some leading African mobile telephone companies

MSI Cellular becomes part of India's Airtel

One of the earliest companies into the African continent was MSI Cellular. It began back in 1998 with a Ugandan subsidiary called Celtel. By 2001, it had operations in 11 countries. By 2006, the company had 8.5 million customers in 14 countries and claimed to be market leader in ten of them. Apart from its Sudanese operation, Celtel has chosen to own a majority

Table 2.2 Telephone usage in selected African countries

	Population (millions)	Fixed telephone lines (thousands)		Mobile telephones (thousands)	
		2002	2007	2002	2007
Nigeria	135	700	1,200	1,200	22,000
South Africa	44	4,800	4,800	14,000	33,000
Tanzania	39	150	150	670	2,000
Kenya	37	300	300	1,300	6,500
Uganda	30	55	100	400	1,500
Ghana	23	270	320	450	2,800

Notes:
Fixed telephone lines: these are the fixed cables that connect homes, offices and businesses to a telephone exchange. They are often old and have the reputation in Africa of not being reliable.
Mobile telephones: all these networks have been set up since 1998 and use transmitters and GSM technology as in the rest of the world.

Source: author from various sources including the World Bank and the three leading African companies on the web. Note that the World Bank figures include some inconsistencies and are therefore not entirely reliable.

share in all its subsidiaries: 'in principle, we like to control the company,' explained its chief executive Marten Pieters. 'This supports our brand, our values, our strategy.'

In 2005, the Kuwait telecommunications company MTC acquired 85 per cent of Celtel for $3.4 billion. Given that Celtel itself only had annual sales of $58 million in 2000, this shows how sales, profits and valuations have grown over the succeeding years. The founder of MSI, Dr Mohamed Ibrahim, explained that the company has networks that achieve operational profits within six months and real profitability within two years. Return on capital was in excess of 30 per cent per year. 'By any yardstick, these projects are more rewarding than in Europe,' he commented.

In the early years, MSI Cellular made its profits by acquiring government licences as each African country market opened up from government control. There was relatively little competition and the main aim for each operator was to set up a basic country network in the main centres of population. However, after the initial acquisition of licences, the company's follow-up strategy was to deepen its coverage across each country and experiment with new services like higher quality 3G telephony.

In addition, Celtel had sufficient coverage across the African continent in 2006 to launch a new service called 'One Network'. This was claimed to be the first borderless network across Africa, enabling subscribers in some countries to roam free across neighbouring countries, scrapping roaming charges, making local calls and receiving incoming calls free of charge. Pieters explained: 'Africa's borders are colonial. They don't reflect economic or language relations, so there is a lot of inter-country traffic.' By 2007, Celtel coverage with its 'One Network' was working across 13 African countries - Kenya, Uganda, Tanzania, Gabon, Democratic Republic of Congo, Congo, Malawi, Sudan, Zambia, Burkina Faso, Chad, Niger and Nigeria.

In 2007, MTC announced that it was re-branding its company name to Zain, which means 'beautiful' in Arabic. Zain continued to manage and extend its African interests over the next two years. However, these were then sold to the major Indian telecommunications company Bharti Airtel for around $10.7 billion in 2010. The African networks of Zain were then re-branded with the company's Indian brand name 'Airtel' in 2010.

Importantly, Bharti Airtel attempted to merge with the South African-based MTN Group in 2009 - see below. This was refused by the South African telecom authorities, who wanted to retain some influence over the merged entity but were prevented by the terms of the proposed merger. It was after this failed merger with MTN that Bharti Airtel then turned to the acquisition of Zain described above.

MTN Group

Headquartered in South Africa, MTN claims to be the largest mobile telephone operator in the African continent. Its most profitable business lies in South Africa itself, but it also has substantial interests in 11 other African countries, including a profitable venture in Nigeria. In 2006, MTN extended its mobile interests into the Middle East by acquiring a company called Investcom for $5.5 billion. This extended its franchise into five West African countries plus Sudan, Cyprus, Syria, Iran, Afghanistan and Yemen. As a result of the acquisition, MTN increased its total number of subscribers from 23 to 28 million - substantially ahead of the 19 million subscribers of its main South African competitor, Vodacom (described below). By 2013, MTN Group had a subscriber base of 180 million customers of which nearly 57 million were in Nigeria.

A strong subscriber base is important for the profitability of any mobile telephone company: after its investment in networks and other infrastructure, increased profitability for a phone company comes from greater usage of the network - achieved both by larger numbers of subscribers and also by increased usage of the telephone.

One of the strategic problems for both of the leading South African mobile companies is that South Africa, as a country, has become a relatively mature mobile telephone market. According to World Bank data, mobile penetration had reached around 72 per cent of the South African market in 2005 - compared, for example, with only 13 per cent of the Nigerian market in the same year. MTN used its strong position in the South African market as the basis for expansion elsewhere: its position provided a useful cash flow and, more importantly, training and experience in the operation of a mobile telephone business. The company then used this knowledge as it expanded, sometimes by acquisition, and sometimes by setting up its own company in other African countries.

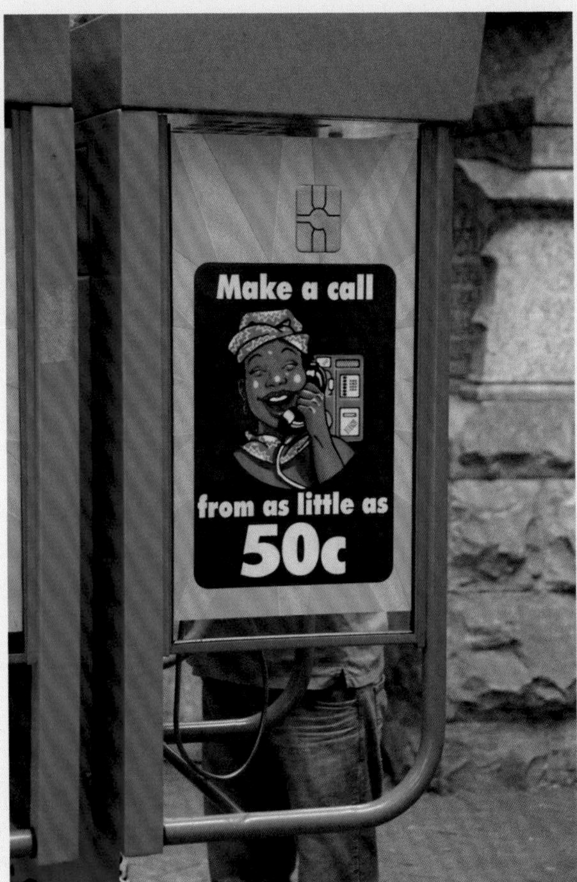

African telephone services are changing rapidly from public call boxes - in Cape Town, South Africa - to mobile telephones across the continent.

The maintenance of growth was the main reason behind MTN's expansion into other parts of Africa and the Middle East. Some of the new markets acquired by MTN had even lower levels of mobile penetration than its existing operations. According to MTN's Chief Executive Mr Phuthuma Nhleko, 'The combined companies' countries had, on average, just 9 per cent mobile penetration, giving [MTN] very meaningful potential for upside.'

Inevitably with its entry into some politically sensitive Middle Eastern countries, there was criticism of MTN with regard to political risk. Mr Nhleko commented: 'Our job is to be a mobile operator that delivers infrastructure, not to try to second-guess the politicians. Political risk is a politically loaded term. [But] there are countries where there are certainly challenges.'

Vodacom

Also based in South Africa, this company was a 50:50 joint venture between South Africa's largest individual telephone company called Telkom and the British-based, international mobile telephone company Vodafone until 2009. Telkom was for many years the leading South African provider of telephone services, particularly using fixed lines. It founded a mobile company in 1993, with Vodafone taking a minority share at that time. The British company then increased its stake to 50 per cent in 2005 because it was attracted by the growth potential of the African market. Vodafone then raised its share of Vodacom to 65 per cent in 2009 at a price of $2 billion. The British-based company was particularly interested because many of its existing European mobile phone markets - such as the UK - were highly mature and would no longer deliver its growth objectives.

Behind this change in control, Vodafone identified Vodacom as being its gateway into the fast-expanding African telephone market. In addition to its major share of the South African market, Vodacom also had mobile interests in Tanzania, Lesotho, Mozambique and the Democratic Republic of Congo. However, Vodacom had not expanded as rapidly as its rival MTN because there was a legal agreement when Vodacom was founded that it would not enter markets north of the Equator. However, Vodacom also had a reputation born out of its relationship with its South African parent, Telekom - reputedly a quasi-public, unionised and more bureaucratic organisation - that was also not conducive to growth. Whatever the background, Vodacom came under the control of the international mobile telephone company Vodafone in 2009. By 2013, Vodafone had eight African subsidiaries with ambitions to grow further.

Telkom

At the same time, the above move freed up the previous joint partner, South Africa's Telkom, to expand beyond its business into mobile phones not only in South Africa but elsewhere on the African continent. Importantly, the company is still effectively controlled by the South African state and has a monopoly of fixed line provision and international calls originating in South Africa. Its dominance of the domestic South African market is reflected in strong complaints from both customers about high prices and from competitors about network access. This dominance was confirmed in June 2013 when Telkom accepted a fine of 200 million Rand (US$18 million) for abusing its domestic market position.

In 2011, Telkom commented that it aimed to expand its fixed line and mobile business into other telecommunications areas and countries. Specifically, 'our strategy is to differentiate ourselves from competitors by moving from a provider of basic voice and data connectivity to become Africa's preferred ICT [Information and Telecommunications Technology] service provider, offering fully converged voice, data, video and Internet services.' This strategy - essentially based on new broadband and 3G technology - has been successful: by 2013, Telkom was involved in 38 African countries with regional hubs in Nigeria and Kenya.

Other African mobile telephone companies

In individual African countries, there were also other major telephone companies. For example, Safaricom was one of the dominant companies in the Kenyan mobile market. It was formed in 1997 as a wholly owned subsidiary of the government-owned Kenyan supplier of telephone services - Telkom Kenya. In 2000, the British company Vodafone acquired a 40 per cent stake in Safaricom and provided its international experience and coverage to its Kenyan associate.

For reasons of space, similar companies in other African countries are not described here. The main characteristic of all such companies is that they were all seeking to develop their networks and usage substantially over the next few years. They all believed that substantial growth was still possible.

Reasons behind the continued growth in African mobile telephones

Beyond the obvious point that existing penetration of mobile telephones remains low at 15–20 per cent of the population, it is possible to identify at least three reasons for the rapid growth in African mobile telephones:

1 *Political will.* African governments were willing to support and encourage new forms of telecommunication. They identified real benefits for their relatively poor populations through the wider spread of information technology. They accepted that the provision of fixed line telephone cables was so expensive as to be virtually unachievable in rural areas - better to have mobile than nothing at all.

2 *Risk-taking companies.* Companies like MSI Cellular and MTN took significant risks in investing in the mobile telephone infrastructure. For example, it was reported that MTN had to overcome significant infrastructure problems when it was building its Nigerian network in 2004 at a cost of $900 million. Commenting on its early investment in Africa, the Chairman of MSI Cellular, Dr Mohamed Ibrahim said: 'There is money willing to go to Africa as long as it is backed by credible people. African telecoms is no place for opportunists or amateurs. To survive requires a very experienced management team, a successful record and the ability to attract finance.'

3 *Increased demand for communication.* As the world has become more integrated and - in that sense - global, the demand for increased and instant communication has grown in Africa both for individuals and for multinational companies. Fixed line cables were incapable of providing enough links and capacity. Both companies and individuals needed more opportunities for contact. Two examples: individual farmers were able to check prices using their mobile phones and head for the best market; relatives were able to use a new mobile telephone service to transfer funds between families - it was no longer necessary to trek two hours by minibus to the local bank.

Importantly, these reasons suggested that there was still substantial growth in African mobile telephones over the next few years. But there would be some risks - political, economic and social.

There was also one remaining structural problem associated with the small number of fixed line telephone services in Africa. The growth of the internet and web relies, at present, for technical reasons on fixed lines rather than mobile phones. However, the new technologies associated with 3G and 4G mobile networks were overcoming this problem as such networks became widely available in Africa. Moreover, new and fast undersea cables had been laid that link Africa to regional and world markets. There were still plenty of opportunities for mobile telephone services in the African continent.

All four of the companies listed above have extensive policies with regard to green strategy according to their websites and annual reports.

Case questions

1 Where would you place the strategies of MTN and other African phone companies - prescriptive or emergent? And within this, which strategic theory represents the most appropriate explanation of the company's development?

2 What are the risks and benefits of African companies expanding beyond their home countries? What are the dangers of having a competitive advantage that relies largely on brand and geographical coverage?

3 Are there any more general lessons to be drawn for companies from the approach to expansion from Africa's leading mobile telephone companies?

STRATEGIC PROJECT

African mobile telephone companies still have plenty of opportunity for development. You might like to identify some of the leading companies, particularly in your own home markets. You might then consider how such companies can continue to grow. Should they stand alone or merge, for example? Is there any opportunity for co-operating with one of the large European companies that are currently not represented in Africa like Deutsche Telekom and France Telecom? What are the benefits and problems for both parties? How will they cope with maturing markets, as has already happened in South Africa? What should they do about growing demand for the internet and web services?

CRITICAL REFLECTION

Is the distinction between prescriptive and emergent strategy processes too simplistic to be useful?

This chapter has argued that there is a basic distinction to be made between prescriptive and emergent theories of strategy. However, it explained - see the beginning of Section 2.3 - that this basic distinction was simplistic. Many strategy theories rely on much more detailed insights than this simple difference - for example, 'game theory' or 'resource-based theory'. Examples of the specific theories are outlined in Sections 2.3 and 2.4. This might suggest that the basic split between prescriptive and emergent strategies is too simple and serves no useful purpose.

To explore this question, you might like to consider what precisely makes 'good' strategy. The topic - 'What makes effective strategy?' - on the book's open-access website linked to Chapter 1 - might give you some ideas. You could then apply them to the basic distinction between prescriptive and emergent strategy. You could also apply them to some of the more detailed prescriptive and emergent theories outlined in this chapter.

SUMMARY

- Prescriptive and emergent strategies can be contrasted by adapting Mintzberg's analogy:[94]
  - *Prescriptive strategy is Biblical in its approach*: it appears at a point in time and is governed by a set of rules, fully formulated and ready to implement.
  - *Emergent strategy is Darwinian in its approach*: an emerging and changing strategy that survives by adapting as the environment itself changes.

  Given the need for an organisation to have a strategic management, much of this chapter has really been about the *process* of achieving this strategy. As has been demonstrated, there is no common agreement on the way this can be done.
- On the one hand, there is the *prescriptive* process, which involves a structured strategic planning system. It is necessary to identify objectives, analyse the environment and the resources of the organisation, develop strategy options and select among them. The selected process is then implemented. However, there are writers who caution against having a system that is too rigid and incapable of taking into account the people element in strategy.
- On the other hand, there is the *emergent* process, which does not identify a final objective with specific strategies to achieve this. It relies on developing strategies whose final outcome may not be known. Managers will rely more on trial and error and experimentation to achieve the optimal process.
- In the early part of the twentieth century when industrialisation was proceeding fast, the prescriptive process was the main recommended route. As organisations came to recognise the people element and their importance to strategic development, emergent strategies were given greater prominence during the middle part of the century. In recent years, emphasis has switched between market-based routes and resource-based routes in the development of strategy. Social and cultural issues have also become more important as markets and production have become increasingly global in scale. New communications technologies like the internet have led to new opportunities and the need for new strategic concepts. In addition, the collapse of some companies through their lack of regard for the ethics of running a business has led to a new emphasis on ethical issues in the development of strategic management.
- Within the *prescriptive* route, four main groups of strategic theory have been identified:
  1. *the industry and environment-based route* – the market place is vital to profit delivery;
  2. *the resource-based route* – the resources of the organisation are important in developing strategic management;

3. *the game theory route* – concentrating on the way that strategic choice is decided and negotiated with others in the market place;
4. *the co-operation and network route* – this stresses the importance of the formal relationship opportunities that are available to organisations.

Each of these has different perspectives on the development of strategy.

- Within the *emergent* route, four main groups were also distinguished:
  1. *the survival-based route* – emphasising the 'survival of the fittest' in the jungle of the market place;
  2. *the uncertainty-based route* – regards prediction as impossible because of the inherently unstable nature of the environment and the need to have innovative processes;
  3. *the human-resource-based route* – places the emphasis on people in strategic development. Motivation, politics, culture and the desires of the individual are all important. Strategy may involve an element of experimentation and learning in order to take into account all these factors;
  4. *the innovation and knowledge-based route* – stresses the contribution of new ideas and radical ways of thinking and sharing knowledge if an organisation is to outsmart its competitors.
- In the past, strategy was considered to be primarily concerned with increasing the wealth of its shareholders. This is now considered to be too simplistic a view because it does not clearly take into account the other stakeholders in the organisation.
- By ethics and corporate social responsibility is meant the standards and conduct that an organisation sets itself in its dealings within the organisation and with its external environment. Such issues will include green strategy. These policy issues will influence the strategy of the organisation.

QUESTIONS

1. Is it possible for organisations to follow both prescriptive and emergent strategies or do they need to choose?
2. Examine the criticisms of prescriptive strategies in Section 2.1 and those of emergent strategies in Section 2.2. To what extent, if at all, do you agree with them? Why?
3. Consider the four emergent approaches to strategy outlined in Section 2.4. Which would you judge most closely described the route taken by Cereal Partners in Case 2.1? What conclusions do you draw from this about the viability of Cereal Partners' approach?
4. What predictions would you make for the environment over the next ten years? What influence will your predictions have on developments in strategic management over this period?
5. Take an organisation with which you are familiar. Analyse whether it has been following prescriptive or emergent strategies or both. Within these broad categories, how would you characterise its strategies according to the classifications laid out in Sections 2.3 and 2.4?
6. If you were asked to develop strategy for the following companies, which strategic management theory might you pick as a starting point for your assessment? A large, international car company; an advertising agency with global links; a government institution; a small travel agency with four branches, all in one region of a country.
7. *'When well-managed major organisations make significant changes in strategy, the approaches they use frequently bear little resemblance to the rational-analytical systems so often touted in the planning literature.'* (Professor J B Quinn) Discuss.
8. *'In turbulent environments, the speed at which changes develop is such that firms which use the emerging strategy formation advocated by Mintzberg endanger their own survival. When they arrive on a market with a new product or service, such firms find the market pre-empted by more foresightful competitors who plan their strategic moves in advance.'* (Professor I Ansoff) Explain and critically evaluate this comment.
9. Take an organisation with which you are familiar and explore the extent to which its current purpose is directed by its stakeholders and governed by ethical considerations. Use Section 2.5 to structure your answer.

FURTHER READING

For an alternative and interesting review of the way that the strategic management field developed, read the paper by Donald Hambrick and Ming-Jer Chen (2007) 'New academic fields as admittance-seeking social movements: the case of strategic management', *Academy of Management Review*, Vol 33, No 1, pp 32–54.

Richard Whittington's earlier text *What is Strategy and Does it Matter?* (Routledge, London, 1993) is lucid and well structured. Read Chapter 2 of Whittington for an alternative view and structuring of strategy theories and practice. For an approach to testing management theories, see K D Miller and E W K Tsang (2011) 'Testing Management Theories: Critical Realist Philosophy and Research Methods', *Strategic Management Journal*, Vol 32, No 2, pp 139–58.

Two major books of strategy research topics are strongly recommended: Michael Hitt, R Edward Freeman and Jeffrey S Harrison, *The Blackwell Handbook of Strategic Management* (Blackwell, Oxford, 2001); Andrew Pettigrew, Howard Thomas, Richard Whittington, *Handbook of Strategy and Management* (Sage, London, 2002).

J L Moore's *Writers on Strategy and Strategic Management* (Penguin, London, 1992) has a useful survey of some leading writers and theories which would be helpful for essay references and revision.

The book by Edith Penrose, *The Theory of the Growth of the Firm*, 3rd edn (Oxford University Press, Oxford, 1993), represents a classic early study of strategy development. Moreover, its precision of language and clarity of thought represent a model for us all to emulate.

NOTES AND REFERENCES

1 Ansoff, I (1969) *Corporate Strategy*, Penguin, Harmondsworth. Porter, M E (1980) *Competitive Strategy*, The Free Press, Harvard, MA, Introduction.

2 Clausewitz, C von, *On War*, Routledge and Kegan Paul, London, quoted in Kotler, P and Singh, R (1981) 'Marketing warfare', *Journal of Business Strategy*, Vol 1, Kotler, P and Singh, R (1981) pp 30–41.

3 Liddell Hart, B H (1967) *Strategy*, Praeger, New York, also quoted in Op. cit.

4 See, for example, James, B G (1985) *Business Warfare*, Penguin, Harmondsworth. See also Ries, J and Trout, A (1986) *Marketing Warfare*, McGraw-Hill, Maidenhead.

5 Whittington, R (1993) *What is Strategy – and Does it Matter?*, Routledge, London, p 16.

6 Wiles, P J D (1961) *Price, Cost and Output*, Blackwell, Oxford, p 78.

7 Porter, M E (1985) *Competitive Advantage*, The Free Press, Harvard, MA.

8 Ansoff, H I (1965) *Corporate Strategy: An Analytical Approach to Business Policy for Growth and Expansion*, McGraw-Hill, New York.

9 Andrews, K (1971) *The Concept of Corporate Strategy*, Irwin, Homewood, IL.

10 Chakravarthy, B and Lorange, P (1991) *Managing the Strategy Process*, Prentice Hall, Upper Saddle River, NJ. The first chapter is usefully summarised in: De Wit, R and Meyer, R (1994) *Strategy: Process, Context and Content*, West Publishing, St Paul, MN.

11 For example, see the following for an extended critique of prescriptive strategy: Stacey, R (1998) *Strategic Management and Organisational Dynamics*, 2nd edn, Pearson Education, London.

12 Mintzberg, H (1990) 'The Design School: reconsidering the basic premises of strategic management', *Strategic Management Journal*, Vol 11, pp 176–195.

13 Mintzberg, H (1994) 'The fall and rise of strategic planning', *Harvard Business Review*, Jan–Feb, pp 107–14.

14 Writing in the 1950s, Herbert Simon was amongst the first to argue that the unreliability and limitations of human decision making made Adam Smith's simple economic assumption that humans would usually take rational decisions somewhat dubious – see reference 29 below.

15 Mayo, E, *Human Problems in Industrial Civilisation*, along with other research on the *Bank Wiring Observation Room*, described in Homans, G (1951) *The Human Group*, Routledge and Kegan Paul, London, Ch III.

16 Cyert, R M and March, J (1963) *A Behavioral Theory of the Firm*, Prentice Hall, Upper Saddle River, NJ.

17 March, J G and Simon, H (1958) *Organisations*, Wiley, New York.

18 Pettigrew, A (1985) *The Awakening Giant: Continuity and Change at ICI*, Blackwell, Oxford.

19 Mintzberg, H (1990) Op. cit.

20 Johnson, G (1986) 'Managing strategic change – the role of strategic formulae', published in: McGee, J and Thomas, H (ed) (1986) *Strategic Management Research*, Wiley, Chichester, Section 1.4.

21 Argyris, C (1991) 'Teaching smart people how to learn', *Harvard Business Review*, May–June, p 99 summarises his many earlier papers.

22 Senge, P M (1990) 'The leader's new work: building learning organisations', *Sloan Management Review*, Fall, pp 7–22.

23 Lindblom, C E (1959) 'The science of muddling through', *Public Administrative Review*, Vol 19, pp 79–88.

24 Whittington, R (1993) Op. cit. He repeats Weick's true story of the Hungarian troops who were lost in the Alps during the First World War but found a map which they used to reach safety. They then discovered that they were using a map of a totally different mountain range, the Pyrenees. Whittington makes the point that taking *some* action, any action, will constitute strategy in these circumstances, even if the particular choice of strategy is wrong. The issue is not whether the *right* strategic choice has been made and then implemented, but rather whether any choice

has been made that will give direction to the people concerned.

25 These comments are taken from a variety of sources: the following is probably the best starting point: Ansoff, I (1991) Critique of Henry Mintzberg's 'The Design School', *Strategic Management Journal*, Vol 12, pp 449–461.

26 Lee Kuan Yew (1998) *The Singapore Story*, Simon and Schuster (Asia) Pte.

27 References for Singapore Airlines and Emirates Group case: airline website – www.singaporeair.com and www.theemiratesgroup.com/english/our-company/our-history.aspx; Singapore Airlines Annual Report and Accounts 2004, 2007 and 2010; Emirates Group Annual Report and Accounts 2010 (both are available on the web).

28 Ansoff, I (1965) *Corporate Strategy*, Penguin, Harmondsworth.

29 Chandler, A (1962) *Strategy and Structure*, MIT Press, Cambridge, MA.

30 Sloan, A P (1963) *My Years with General Motors*, Sidgwick & Jackson, London.

31 Wheelen, T and Hunger, D (1992) *Strategic Management and Business Policy*, Addison-Wesley, Reading, MA.

32 Porter, M E (1980) Op. cit. and (1985) Op. cit.

33 Rumelt, R, Schendel, D and Teece, D (1991) 'Strategic management and economics', *Strategic Management Journal*, Vol 12, pp 5–29. This contains an extensive and valuable review of this area.

34 Bowman, E H and Helfat, C E (2001) 'Does corporate strategy matter?' *Strategic Management Journal*, Vol 22, pp 1–23.

35 Ansoff, I (1968) 'Toward a strategy theory of the firm', in Ansoff, I (ed) (1969) *Business Strategy*, Penguin, Harmondsworth, p 39.

36 Porter, M E (1980) Op. cit.

37 Seth, A and Thomas, H (1994) 'Theories of the firm: implications for strategy research', *Journal of Management Studies*, Vol 31, pp 165–191.

38 Ohmae, K (1983) *The Mind of the Strategist*, Penguin, Harmondsworth.

39 Wilks, S (1990) *The Embodiment of Industrial Culture in Bureaucracy and Management*, quoted in Whittington, R (1993) Op. cit., p 160.

40 But problems remain: see Luce, E (2002) 'Investment in India "riddled with obstacles"', *Financial Times*, 19 March, p 14.

41 See, for example, the leading article in the *Financial Times Survey on Singapore*, 24 February 1995.

42 Hamel, G and Prahalad, C K (1990) 'The core competence of the corporation', *Harvard Business School Review*, May–June, pp 79–91. Their 1994 book *Competing for the Future* (Harvard Business School, Boston, MA) picks up many of the same themes.

43 Kay, J (1993) *Foundations of Corporate Success*, Oxford University Press, Oxford.

44 Hamel, G and Prahalad, C K (1990) Op. cit.

45 Kay, J (1993) Op. cit.

46 Hannan, M T and Freeman, J (1988) *Organisational Ecology*, Harvard University Press, Cambridge, MA.

47 Mintzberg, H (1987) 'Crafting strategy', *Harvard Business Review*, July–August, pp 65–75.

48 Mintzberg, H (1994) 'The fall and rise of strategic planning', *Harvard Business Review*, January–February, pp 107–114.

49 Drucker, P (1967) *The Effective Executive*, Harper and Row, New York, Ch 9.

50 Slack, N, Chambers, S, Harland, C, Harrison, A and Johnston, R (1995) *Operations Management*, Pitman Publishing, London, p 812.

51 Williams, K, Haslam, C, Johal, S and Williams, J (1994) *Cars: Analysis, History and Cases*, Berghahn Books, New York, Ch 7.

52 Slack, N, Chambers, S, Harland, C, Harrison, A and Johnston, R (1998) *Operations Management*, 2nd edn, Pitman Publishing, London, is a comprehensive text, clearly written and presented. This book explores manufacturing strategy issues in further detail. Another text is the book by Hill, T (1993) *Manufacturing Strategy*, 2nd edn, Macmillan, Basingstoke. This is a clear, basic text that is well referenced and directed at exploring strategic management issues.

53 Hamel, G and Prahalad, C K (1994) *Competing for the Future*, Harvard Business School Press, Boston, MA.

54 Wernerfelt, B (1984) 'A resource-based view of the firm,' *Strategic Management Journal*, Vol 5, No 5(2), pp 171–180.

55 Peteraf, M A (1993) 'The cornerstones of competitive advantage', *Strategic Management Journal*, Vol 14, pp 179–181.

56 Dierickx, I and Cool, K (1989) 'Asset stock accumulation and sustainability of competitive advantage', *Management Science*, Vol 35, pp 1540–1551.

57 Kay, J (1993) *Foundations of Corporate Success*, Oxford University Press, Oxford.

58 Nonaka, I (1991) 'The knowledge-creating company', *Harvard Business Review*, November–December, pp 96–104.

59 Priem, R L and Butler, J E (2001a) 'Is the resource-based view a useful "view" for strategic management research?', *Academy of Management Review*, January, Vol 26, No 1 and Priem, R L and Butler, J E (2001b), 'Tautology in the resource-based view and the implications of externally determined resource value: further comments', *Academy of Management Review*, January, Vol 26, No 1, pp 1–45.

60 Helfat, C, Finkelstein, S, Mitchell, W, Peteraf, M A, Singh, H and Teece, D J (2007) *Dynamic Capabilities: Understanding Strategic Change in Organisations*, Blackwell, Oxford, UK.

61 For a useful and accessible review, see Dixit, A K and Nalebuff, B J (1991) *Thinking Strategically*, W W Norton, New York. In addition to the references in Chapter 15, it is important to note that writers like Professor Michael Porter also employed game theory in their work without specifically discussing its theoretical background. See Chapter 3 for references to Porter.

62 Eisenhardt, K M (2002) 'Has the strategy changed?' *MIT Sloan Management Review*, Vol 43, No 2, pp 88–91.

63 Inkpen, A C (2001) 'Strategic alliances' in: Hitt, M A, Freeman, R E and Harrison, J S (eds) *Handbook of Strategic Management*, Oxford University Press, Oxford.

64 Child, J and Faulkner, D (1998) *Strategies of Co-operation: Managing Alliances, Networks and Joint Ventures*, Oxford University Press, Oxford.

65 Lafontaine, F (1999) 'Myths and strengths of franchising', *Financial Times Mastering Strategy*, Part Nine, 22 November, pp 8–10.

66 Dyer, J H, Kale, P and Singh, H (2001) 'How to make strategic alliances work', *MIT Sloan Management Review*, Vol 42, No 4, pp 37–43.

67 References for Subway case: Subway web pages 2005 – www.subway.com (incidentally, these give a clearer idea of the business formula than is possible in a short case); Biddle, R (2001) *Forbes Magazine*, 9 March; web franchise site – www.entrepreneur.com.

68 Hall, R C and Hitch, C J (1939) 'Price theory and business behaviour', *Oxford Economic Papers*, Vol 2, pp 12–45, quoted in Whittington, R (1993) Op. cit.

69 Henderson, B (1989) 'The origin of strategy', *Harvard Business Review*, November–December, pp 139–143.

70 Williamson, O (1991) 'Strategising, economising and economic organisation', *Strategic Management Journal*, Vol 12, pp 75–94.

71 Hannan, M T and Freeman, J (1988) Op. cit.

72 Whittington, R (1993) Op. cit., p 22.

73 Pascale, R (1990) *Managing on the Edge*, Viking Penguin, London, p 114.

74 Gleick, J (1988) *Chaos*, Penguin, London.

75 Miller, D and Friesen, P (1982) 'Structural change and performance: quantum versus piecemeal–incremental approaches', *Academy of Management Journal*, Vol 25, pp 867–892.

76 Strebel, P (1992) *Breakpoints*, Harvard Business School Press, Boston, MA. A summary of this argument appears in De Wit, R and Meyer, R (1994) *Strategy: Process, Content, Context – an international perspective*, 2nd edn, West Publishing, New York, pp 390–392.

77 Stacey, R (1993) *Strategic Management and Organisational Dynamics*, Pitman Publishing, London.

78 Miller, D and Friesen, P (1984) *Organisations: A Quantum View*, Prentice Hall, Englewood Cliffs, NJ.

79 Cyert, R and March, J (1963) Op. cit.

80 March, J and Simon, H (1958) Op. cit.

81 Nelson, R and Winter, S (1982) *An Evolutionary Theory of Economic Change*, Harvard University Press, Cambridge, MA, p 34.

82 Nelson, R and Winter, S (1982) Ibid.

83 Mintzberg, H (1987) Op. cit.

84 Quinn, J B (1980) *Strategies for Change: Logical Incrementalism*, Irwin, Burr Ridge, MN.

85 Senge, P M (1990) Op. cit.

86 Mintzberg, H (1994) Op. cit.

87 Major writers in this area include: Kay, J (1993) *Foundations of Corporate Success*, Oxford University Press, Oxford, Chapter 5. Professor Kay also reviews the earlier work of Professor David Teece – see references at the end of Chapter 5. For a more recent view, Markides C A (2000) *All the Right Moves*, Harvard Business School Press, Boston, MA.

88 Nonaka, I and Takeuchi, H (1995) *The Knowledge-Creating Company*, Oxford University Press, Oxford. See also Davenport, T H and Prusack, L (1998) *Working Knowledge*, Harvard Business School Press, Harvard, MA.

89 See, for example, the opening paragraph of the textbook by Hitt, M A, Ireland, R D and Hoskisson, R E (2003) *Strategic Management: Competitiveness and Globalization Concepts*, Thomson, South-Western, Fifth Edition, p 7.

90 See, for example, the writings of Professors John Kay and Charles Handy referenced elsewhere in this chapter.

91 Rapaport, A (1986) *Creating Shareholder Value: The new standard for business performance*, The Free Press, New York, Ch 1. An extract from the opening chapter of this book is also contained in De Wit, R and Meyer, R (1998) *Strategy: Process, Content and Context*, 2nd edn, International Thompson Business Press, London.

92 Handy, C (1997) 'The citizen corporation', *Harvard Business Review*, September–October, pp 26–28.

93 References for African Mobile Telecoms case: *Financial Times*: 21 August 2001, p 12; 30 October 2002, p 16; 27 November 2003, p 12; 4 November 2005, p 19; 13 February 2006, p 2 Digital Business Supplement; 3 May 2006, p 28; 8 May 2006, p 10; 13 June 2007, p 7; 4 September 2007, p 1; 9 October 2007, p 16; 24 October 2007, p 21; 29 November 2007, p 26; 25 April 2008, p 27; 12 May 2008, p 22; 3 June 2008, p 25; 10 June 2008, p 26; 10 October 2008, p 17; 7 November 2008, p 30; 18 November 2008, p 27; 15 February 2010, p 1; 16 February 2010, p 23; 19 March 2009, p 24; 13 August 2010, p 18; 1 October 2009, p 21; 5 October 2010, pp 20 and 25; *Economist*: 28 October 2006, p 93.

94 Mintzberg, H (1990) 'The Design School: Reconsidering the basic premises of strategic management', *Strategic Management Journal*, as adapted by De Wit, R and Meyer, B (1994) Op. cit., p 72.

PART 2
Strategic analysis and purpose

Both the prescriptive and the emergent approaches to strategic management consider an organisation's ability to understand its environment and its resources – its customers, its suppliers, its competitors and the organisation's own resources – to be an important element of the strategy process. This part of the book begins by examining the basic analytical tools and frameworks used in analysing an organisation's environment and its resources.

In addition, it is impossible to develop strategic management without first establishing the purpose of the organisation. Building on the analyses of the organisation's environment and resources, this part of the book then explores the general direction of the organisation. There are two chapters exploring purpose, first from a prescriptive perspective and then an emergent approach.

Some strategists argue that consideration of the organisation's purpose should come before analysing the organisation's environment and its resources. That is not the treatment adopted in this book. Any realistic view of purpose must be shaped by what is happening outside the organisation and what resources are available to deliver the organisation's purpose. This means that purpose comes *after* the analysis of these two areas.

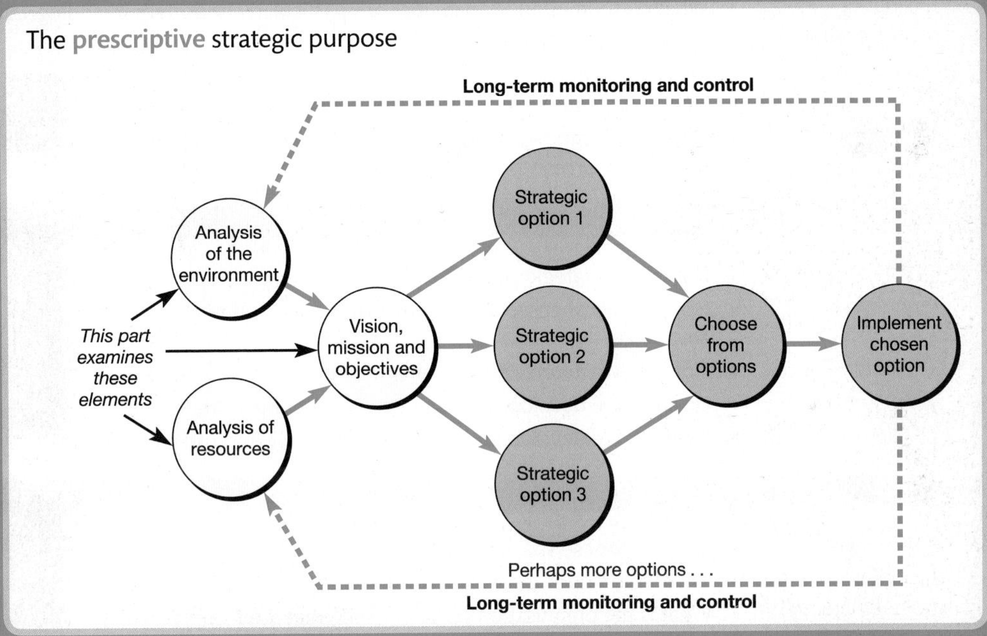

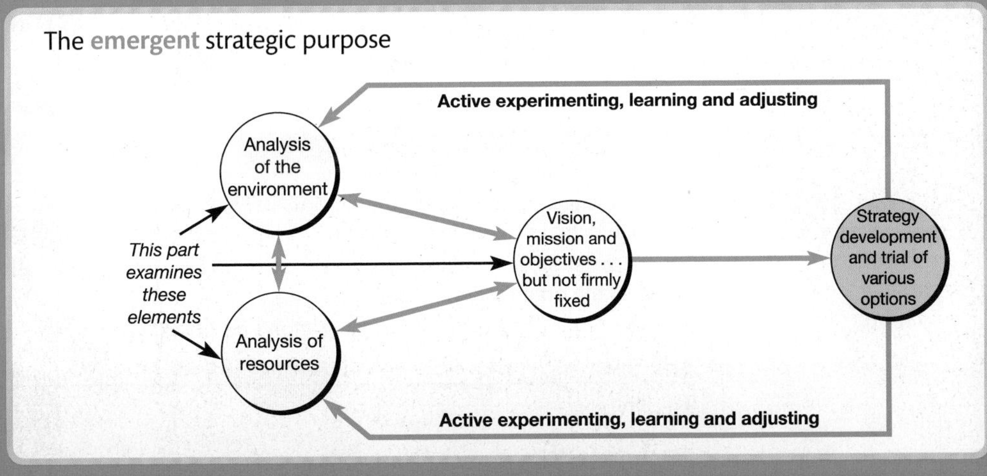

Key strategic management questions

CHAPTER 3
Analysing the strategic environment

- What is the strategic environment and why is it important?
- What key industry factors help to deliver the objectives of the organisation?
- What are the main background areas to be analysed?
- What is the strategic significance of market growth?
- How are the more immediate influences on the organisation analysed?
- How do we analyse competitors?
- What is the role of co-operation in environmental analysis?
- How important is the customer? And how do we position ourselves with customers?

CHAPTER 4
Analysing resources and capabilities

- How do resources and capabilities add value to the organisation?
- Which resources and capabilities are particularly important in adding value and competitive advantage?
- What are the main ways that resources and capabilities deliver competitive advantage?
- How can competitive advantage be enhanced?
- What other important resources does the organisation possess, especially in the area of human resources?

CHAPTER 5
Strategy dynamics

- How does strategic purpose change and why?
- How can we analyse the dynamics of the environment and its impact on competitive advantage?
- How can we analyse fast-moving markets and resource changes?
- How can we develop new aggressive competitive strategies?
- How can we develop co-operative strategies? And use game theory?

CHAPTER 6
Prescriptive purpose delivered through mission, objectives and ethics

- How is purpose shaped by the organisation and its environment?
- What vision does the organisation have for its future?
- What is the organisation's mission and what are its objectives?
- What is the relationship between purpose and the corporate governance of the organisation?
- What is the role and approach to green strategy?
- What are the organisation's views on ethics and corporate social responsibility? How will they affect purpose?

CHAPTER 7
Purpose emerging from knowledge, technology and innovation

- What knowledge does the organisation possess? How can it create and share new knowledge? What will be the impact on the organisation's purpose?
- What are the strategic implications of new technologies? How can technology shape the purpose of the organisation?
- Can innovation contribute to the organisation's purpose? If so, how?

CHAPTER 3
Analysing the strategic environment

Video and sound summary of this chapter

LEARNING OUTCOMES

When you have worked through this chapter, you will be able to:

- explain why it is important to study the environment of the organisation;
- outline the main environmental influences on the organisation and relate the degree of change to prescriptive and emergent strategic approaches;
- undertake a PESTEL analysis of the general influences on the organisation;
- understand the implications of market growth and market cyclicality for strategic management;
- identify the key factors for success in an industry;
- carry out a Five Forces Analysis of the specific influences on the organisation;
- develop a Four Links Analysis of the organisation's co-operators;
- undertake a competitor profile and identify the competitor's advantages;
- explore the relationship between the organisation and its customers.

INTRODUCTION

In recent years, the term 'environment' has taken on a rather specialised meaning: it involves 'green' issues and the poisoning of our planet by human activity. These concerns are certainly part of our considerations in this book, but we use the term 'environment' in a much broader sense to describe everything and everyone outside the organisation. This includes customers, competitors, suppliers, distributors, government and social institutions. The important topic of green strategy and sustainability has been moved for this edition to a separate chapter – Chapter 14.

As the starting point in the development of both prescriptive and emergent strategy, it is useful to begin by exploring the nine basic analytical tools of the environment that will influence the organisation's strategy (see Figure 3.1). Elements of the environment can change so the organisation needs to adjust its strategy accordingly. Prescriptive strategies will want to anticipate how the environment will change in the future in order to meet future needs ahead of competing organisations. Emergent strategies will be content with an understanding of the environment.

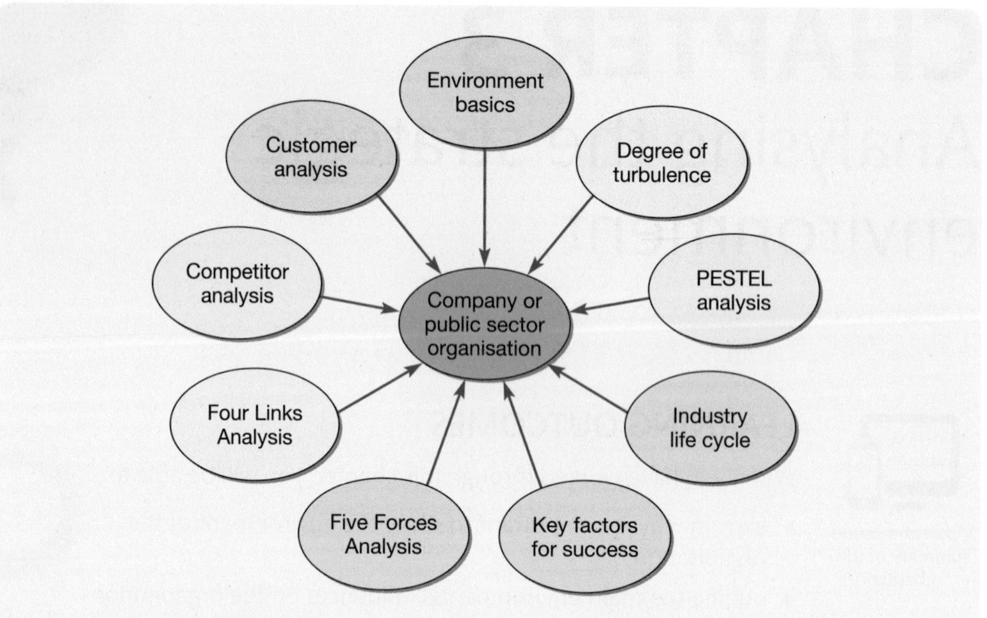

Figure 3.1 Analysing the strategic environment – the nine basic analytical tools

CASE STUDY 3.1

The rise and fall of Blockbuster video stores

The Blockbuster video store chain was the subject of an $8.4 billion takeover in 1994. Twenty years later, the business was just a memory. Why? What are the implications for analysing the strategic environment?

By 2014, Blockbuster stores were just empty shells, the victim of technology change and questionable strategy
Photo courtesy of Steve Corbett

Background

Back in 1994, the Blockbuster video store chain was a fast-growing group of retail stores that hired out video films. It had begun in the USA and was beginning to expand into Europe. Each store had a wide range of the latest Hollywood films that were rented over night by customers to play on their home video recorders and then return the following day. The company had special contracts with the major film companies to ensure that it was able to stock the latest films soon after showing in cinemas. It kept 60 per cent of the rental income and passed the other 40 per cent back to the film studios: a viable business model at that time.

Blockbuster takeover

In 1994, the US media conglomerate Viacom acquired Blockbuster for $8.4 billion. Viacom was partially interested in Blockbuster's $1.5 billion cash which it needed for another acquisition, Paramount Pictures. It was also possible that it over-valued Blockbuster even at that time because the Blockbuster profits were much lower in the year after its sale. But Viacom continued to invest in the store chain over the next ten years. In addition, there were reported to be synergies from the purchase that would benefit both companies. They would come from cross-marketing Viacom's MTV television channels with Blockbuster and from selling add-on merchandise like *Star Trek* watches – part of the Viacom franchise – through Blockbuster stores. None of this happened. According to one insider at Viacom, 'The MTV folks were very protective of their domain.'

Nevertheless by 2004, Blockbuster group was reported to employ 60,000 people and have 9,000 stores. It had moved to sell DVDs alongside its VHS tapes as the technology changed. It also expanded into DVD delivery by mail for those customers unable or unwilling to visit its stores. But it was facing major competition from other retail outlets. Blockbuster's suppliers, the film studios, had begun selling film videos directly to its competitors. These retail outlets included supermarkets who were able to sell rather than rent video tapes and discs. Moreover, they were able to compete at very low prices. Initially, Blockbuster had rejected the concept of selling low profit margin DVDs because it would cannibalise its more profitable rental income. But the competitive pressures were too great.

Perhaps to the surprise of some commentators, Viacom then sold the Blockbuster chain in 2004 for just under $900 million. Part of the reason for the sale was that Viacom had other media priorities such as further investment in its BET (Black Entertainment Television) and MTV (Music Television) networks. But Viacom could also see the future and Blockbuster was making losses by this time.

Technology change

Over the years to 2004, there was a substantial change in technology. Not only were DVDs replacing video tapes, but also broadband was beginning to deliver fast and large computer files to some customers. New companies were springing up to exploit this change. For example, a small company called Netflix was expanding: it was already selling DVDs by mail but it was also beginning to deliver the same content by broadband in the USA. It is reported that Blockbuster turned down the opportunity to acquire Netflix in year 2000 for $50 million.

The outcome

In 2004, Viacom sold its subsidiary at the right time. Blockbuster's brand name and range of film and television contracts were its chief assets. But the company's chain of retail stores was a liability when customers could obtain the same product without leaving their homes. The internet revolution was about to claim one of its early victims.

In 2010, Blockbuster still had 4,000 stores in the USA and 2,500 stores in other countries. The company could still see a future for its business up to that time. However, broadband speeds were increasing. More customers were learning how to download media. Companies like Netflix, LoveFilm in Europe and Hulu in the USA were expanding fast. Blockbuster filed for bankruptcy in late 2010. Some 1,700 stores were acquired by Dish TV for $300 million (including debts) with the rest being closed over the next three years.

By 2014, the Blockbuster company had completely disappeared. However, the name was still present in a chain of video rental kiosks called 'Blockbuster Express,' but this company had no connection with the original company and was still a viable business.

 This case was written by Richard Lynch from published information only.[1]

Case questions

1 What elements of strategic analysis are relevant here? Would scenario building have helped Blockbuster strategy around year 2000?

2 Are other industries threatened by the internet in the same way as Blockbuster? What strategy would you recommend for these industries?

3.1 EXPLORING THE COMPETITIVE ENVIRONMENT

3.1.1 Why studying the competitive environment is important

Definition ▶ **In strategy, the environment means everything and everyone outside the organisation: competitors, customers, suppliers plus other influential institutions such as local and national governments.** Strategists are agreed that an understanding of the competitive environment is an essential element of the development of strategic management. It is important to study the environment surrounding the organisation for three main reasons. First, most organisations compete against others – for example, films like *Lord of the Rings* compete against other films for finance from the film studios – see Case 3.4. Hence a study of the environment will provide information on the nature of competition as a step to developing *sustainable competitive advantage*.[2] Sustainable competitive advantage is an advantage over competitors that cannot easily be imitated. Second, most organisations will perceive *opportunities* that might be explored and *threats* that need to be contained.[3] For example, the *Lord of the Rings* trilogy was seen by some film backers to have more threats than opportunities. Such opportunities and threats may come not just from competitors but also from government decisions, changes in technology and social developments and many other factors. Third, there are opportunities for networks and other linkages, which lead to sustainable co-operation. For example, Peter Jackson met his old friend

Mark Ordesky when needing some help in the final negotiations to finance *Lord of the Rings*. Such linkages with others may strengthen an organisation in its environment by providing mutual support. By contrast, Blockbuster – see Case 3.1 – shows what can happen when companies fail to exploit such linkages.

However, there are three difficulties in determining the connection between the organisation's strategic management and its environment.

1 *The prescriptive versus emergent debate.* The first problem arises from the fundamental disagreement about the strategic management processes that were explored in Part 1 of this book. Some prescriptive strategists take the view that, in spite of the various uncertainties, the environment can usefully be predicted for many markets. Some (but not all) emergent strategists believe that the environment is so turbulent and chaotic that prediction is likely to be inaccurate and serve no useful purpose. Each of these interpretations implies a quite different status for the same basic topic. This difficulty is explored further in Section 3.2.

2 *The uncertainty.* Whatever view is taken about prediction, all strategists regard the environment as uncertain. New strategies have to be undertaken against a backdrop that cannot be guaranteed and this difficulty must be addressed as strategies are developed. For example, Case 3.4 shows that the risks were so high in financing the film *Lord of the Rings* that nearly every studio declined to finance it. Uncertainty was initially lower at Blockbuster, but new technology changed all that.

3 *The range of influences.* It is conceivable, at least in theory, that every element of an organisation's environment may influence strategic management. One solution to the problem posed by such a wide range of factors might be to produce a list of every element. This would be a strategic mistake, however, because organisations and individuals would find it difficult to develop and manage every item. In strategic management, the production of comprehensive lists that include every major eventuality and have no priorities has no value. A better solution is to identify the key factors for success in the industry and then to direct the environmental analysis towards these factors. This is considered later in this chapter in Section 3.6.

3.1.2 The main elements of environmental analysis

To analyse an organisation's environment, while at the same time addressing the three difficulties outlined in Section 3.1.1, certain basic analytical procedures can be undertaken (see Table 3.1).

3.1.3 The distinction between proactive and reactive outcomes

When analysing the environment, it is useful to draw a distinction between two types of results from the analysis:

1 *Proactive outcomes.* The environmental analysis will identify positive opportunities or negative threats. The organisation will then develop proactive strategies to exploit or cope with the situation. For example, film producers might develop cross-financing co-operation as a result of identifying new market opportunities.

2 *Reactive outcomes.* The environmental analysis will highlight important strategic changes over which the organisation has no control but to which, if they happen, it will need to be able to react. For example, new EU legislation on cultural content and investment might influence strategic activity in the European film industry.

On the website
Video Part 4a

On the website
Video Part 4b

On the website
Video Part 4b

On the website
Video Part 4a

On the website
Video Part 5b

On the website
Video Part 4b

On the website
Video Part 4b

On the website
Video Part 4c

On the website
Video Part 4c

Table 3.1 Nine basic stages in environmental analysis

Stage	Techniques	Outcome of stage
1 Environment basics – an opening evaluation to define and explore basic characteristics of the environment (*see* Section 3.2)	Estimates of some basic factors surrounding the environment: • Market definition and size • Market growth • Market share	Basic strategic analysis: • Scope the strategic opportunity • Establish future growth prospects • Begin to structure market competition
2 Consideration of the degree of turbulence in the environment (*see* Section 3.3)	General considerations: • Change: fast or slow? • Repetitive or surprising future? • Forecastable or unpredictable? • Complex or simple influences on the organisation?	Guidance on initial questions: • Is the environment too turbulent to undertake useful predictions? • What are the opportunities and threats for the organisation?
3 Background factors that influence the competitive environment (*see* Section 3.4)	PESTEL analysis and scenarios	• Identify key influences • Predict, if possible • Understand interconnections between events
4 Analysis of stages of market growth (*see* Section 3.5)	Industry life cycle	• Identify growth stage • Consider implications for strategy • Identify maturity, over-production and cyclicality issues
5 Factors specific to the industry: what delivers success? (*see* Section 3.6)	Key factors for success analysis	• Identify factors relevant to strategy • Focus strategic analysis and development
6 Factors specific to the competitive balance of power in the industry (*see* Section 3.7)	Five Forces Analysis	• Static and descriptive analysis of competitive forces
7 Factors specific to co-operation in the industry (*see* Section 3.8)	Four Links Analysis	• Analysis of current and future organisations with whom co-operation is possible • Network analysis
8 Factors specific to immediate competitors (*see* Section 3.9)	Competitor analysis and product portfolio analysis	• Competitor profile • Analysis of relative market strengths
9 Customer analysis (*see* Section 3.10)	Market and segmentation studies	• Strategy targeted at existing and potential customers • Market segmentation and positioning within segment

In both cases, the environment will need to be analysed but the strategic implications are very different.

> **KEY STRATEGIC PRINCIPLES**
>
> - Environmental analysis is important because it helps in developing sustainable competitive advantage, identifies opportunities and threats and may provide opportunities for productive co-operation with other organisations.
> - There are three difficulties in studying the environment: the use to which the analysis will be put; uncertainty in the topic; coping with the wide range of environmental influences.
> - Environmental analysis can be used to provide a *proactive* strategy outcome or highlight a *reactive* strategic situation that will need to be monitored.

3.2 STRATEGIC ENVIRONMENT – THE BASICS

In order to begin the environmental analysis, it is useful to start with some basic factors that are sometimes forgotten in the academic concepts but contribute to the strategic analysis of the environment.[4] We can divide the basics into three areas:

Video Part 4a

1 Market definition and size
2 Market growth
3 Market share

3.2.1 Market definition and size[5]

In analysing the strategic environment, most organisations will want an answer to the basic question – 'What is the size of the market?' This is important because it will assist in defining the strategic task. Markets are usually described in terms of annual sales. From a strategy perspective, a 'large' market may be more attractive than a 'small' market. The words 'large' and 'small' need to be defined carefully – for example, a 'large' opportunity to Peter Jackson who directed the major film trilogy *Lord of the Rings* might be $200 million – see Case 3.4 later in this chapter. However, a 'large' opportunity to Warner Brothers who ultimately funded the film and have much broader film interests might be $1 billion. Despite such problems, it is a useful starting point to attempt to assess the strategic opportunity (or the lack of it).

Measuring market size raises a related problem – how to define the 'market'. For example, is the annual market for the film trilogy *Lord of the Rings* (LOTR) defined as *fantasy films* only – worth, say, $500 million? Or is the annual LOTR market *all adventure films*, including *Lord of the Rings* but also covering others from James Bond films to those starring Clint Eastwood – worth, say, $10 billion? The answer will depend on the customers and the extent to which other products are a real substitute. Although some market definitions may seem obvious – for example, 'the ice cream market' would seem to be clearly defined – they need to be treated with care: perhaps another snack will substitute for ice cream and should be included within the definition?

3.2.2 Market growth

In establishing the size of the market, it is also common practice to estimate how much the market has grown over the previous period – usually the previous year. From a strategy perspective, the importance of growth relates to the organisation's objectives. An organisation wishing to grow rapidly might be more attracted to a market growing rapidly. Clearly any such estimate also needs to take into account the argument about market definition made above.

3.2.3 Market share

Although some strategists disagree, a large share of a market is usually regarded as being strategically beneficial.[6] The reason is that a large share may make it possible to influence prices and may also reduce costs through scope for economies of scale, thereby increasing profitability.[7] Clearly, there are definitional problems here – see Section 3.2.1 above – but some estimate of market share is desirable from a strategy perspective. In practice, it may be difficult to establish a precise market share – for example, the share of the film market taken by *Lord of the Rings* in 2002 will depend on the fact that it had a high share during the few weeks after its general release and greatest popularity – but this may not matter. From a strategy perspective, the important point is that *Lord of the Rings* took a significant share of the *fragmented* film market during that year. Equally, there will be other strategic circumstances where a *dominant* share may be identified – for example, the market share held by companies supplying domestic water to households – without necessarily being able to measure the precise share. This is explored further in Chapters 4 and 14.

KEY STRATEGIC PRINCIPLES

- Environmental analysis can usefully begin with a basic assessment of the market definition and size, the market growth and the market share.
- Market definition is important because it will determine the size and scope of the strategic opportunity. Market definition will be defined by a consideration of customers and the availability of substitute products.
- Market growth is commonly estimated early in any strategic analysis because of its importance with regard to the growth objectives of an organisation.
- A basic estimate of market share can be used to estimate whether an organisation has a significant share of a market as a starting point in exploring the strategic implications.

3.3 DEGREE OF TURBULENCE IN THE ENVIRONMENT[8]

Video Part 4b

At the general level of environmental analysis, it is important to consider the basic conditions surrounding the organisation. Special attention needs to be directed to the nature and strength of the forces driving strategic change – the *dynamics* of the environment. One reason for this consideration is that, if the forces are exceptionally turbulent, they may make it difficult to use some of the analytical techniques – like Porter's 'Five Forces', discussed later in this chapter. Another reason is that the nature of the environment may influence the way that the organisation is structured to cope with such changes.

The environmental forces surrounding the organisation can be assessed according to two main measures:

Definition ▶

1 **Changeability - the degree to which the environment is likely to change.** For example, there is low changeability in the liquid milk market and high changeability in the various internet markets.

Definition ▶

2 **Predictability - the degree to which such changes can be predicted.** For example, changes can be predicted with some certainty in the mobile telephone market but remain largely unknown in biogenetics.

These measures can each be subdivided further. Changeability comprises:

- *Complexity* – the degree to which the organisation's environment is affected by factors such as internationalisation and technological, social and political complications.
- *Novelty* – the degree to which the environment presents the organisation with new situations.

Table 3.2 Assessing the dynamics of the environment

	Environmental turbulence	Repetitive	Expanding	Changing	Discontinuous	Surprising
Changeability	*Complexity*	National	National	Regional Technological	Regional Socio-political	Global Economic
	Familiarity of events	Familiar	Extrapolable		Discontinuous Familiar	Discontinuous Novel
Predictability	*Rapidity of change*	Slower than response		Comparable to response		Faster than response
	Visibility of future	Recurring	Forecastable	Predictable	Partially predictable	Unpredictable surprises
	Turbulence level	*Low* 1	2	3	4	5 *High*

Source: Ansoff, I and McDonnell, E (1990) *Implanting Strategic Management*, FT Prentice-Hall. With permission.

Predictability can be further subdivided into:

- *rate of change* of the environment (from slow to fast);
- *visibility of the future* in terms of the availability and usefulness of the information used to predict the future.

Using these factors as a basis, it is then possible to build a spectrum that categorises the environment and provides a rating for its *degree of turbulence* (see Table 3.2).

When turbulence is low, it may be possible to predict the future with confidence. For example, film companies like Warner Brothers might be able to use data on their film customers around the world, along with international economic data, to predict future demand for different types of films.

When turbulence is higher, such predictions may have little meaning. The changeability elements influencing the organisation may contain *many* and *complex* items and the *novelty* being introduced into the market place may be high. For example, new services, new suppliers, new ideas, new software and new payment systems were all being launched for the internet at the same time. Turbulence was high. Predicting the specific outcome of such developments was virtually impossible.

If the level of turbulence is high – called *hypercompetition*[9] by some strategists – and as a result the environment is difficult to study, the analysis recommended in some of the sections that follow may need to be treated with some caution. However, for most fast-growing situations, including the internet, there is merit in at least attempting to understand the main areas of the environment influencing the organisation. It may not be possible to undertake formal predictions, but it will certainly be possible to identify the most important elements. Ways of coping with this situation are explored in Chapter 5 on Strategy Dynamics.

KEY STRATEGIC PRINCIPLES

- It is important to begin an analysis of the environment with a general consideration of the degree of turbulence in that environment. If it is high, then this will make prediction difficult and impact on prescriptive approaches to strategy development.
- There are two measures of turbulence: changeability, i.e. the degree to which the environment is likely to change; and predictability, i.e. the degree to which such change can be predicted.
- Each of the two measures can then be further subdivided: changeability can be split into complexity and novelty; predictability can be divided into rate of change and visibility of the future. All these elements can then be used to explore turbulence.

3.4 ANALYSING THE GENERAL ENVIRONMENT

Video Part 4b

Six political and economic trends that have affected strategic management.

Non-market strategies: what are they and why are they important?

In any consideration of the factors surrounding the organisation, two techniques can be used to explore the general environment: these are the PESTEL checklist and scenarios.

3.4.1 PESTEL checklist

It is already clear that there are no simple rules governing an analysis of the organisation. Each analysis needs to be guided by what is relevant for that particular organisation. However, it may be useful to begin the process with **the PESTEL checklist, which consists of the Political, Economic, Socio-cultural, Technological, Environmental and Legal aspects of the environment.**

Definition ▶

Exhibit 3.1 presents some of the main items that might be considered when undertaking a PESTEL analysis.

EXHIBIT 3.1

Checklist for a PESTEL analysis

Political future

- Political parties and alignments at local, national and European or regional trading-block level
- Legislation, e.g. on taxation and employment law
- Relations between government and the organisation (possibly influencing the preceding items in a major way and forming a part of future strategic management)
- Government ownership of industry and attitude to monopolies and competition

Socio-cultural future

- Shifts in values and culture
- Change in lifestyle
- Attitudes to work and leisure
- 'Green' environmental issues
- Education and health
- Demographic changes
- Distribution of income

Economic future

- Total GDP and GDP per head
- Inflation
- Consumer expenditure and disposable income
- Interest rates
- Currency fluctuations and exchange rates
- Investment – by the state, private enterprise and foreign companies
- Cyclicality
- Unemployment
- Energy costs, transport costs, communications costs, raw materials costs

Technological future

- Government and EU investment policy
- Identified new research initiatives
- New patents and products
- Speed of change and adoption of new technology
- Level of expenditure on R&D by organisation's rivals
- Developments in nominally unrelated industries that might be applicable

Environmental future

- 'Green' issues that affect the environment and impact on the company
- Level and type of energy consumed – renewable energy?
- Rubbish, waste and its disposal

Legal future

- Competition law and government policy
- Employment and safety law
- Product safety issues

Comment

Importantly, there is no underpinning logic to a PESTEL checklist, unlike many other strategy environmental concepts, such as the degree of turbulence or the market share and growth analysis explored above. PESTEL is purely a reminder checklist and should be used selectively.

Like all checklists, a PESTEL analysis is really only as good as the individual or group preparing it. Listing every conceivable item has little value and betrays a lack of serious consideration and logic in the strategic management process. Better to have three or four well-thought-out items that are explored and justified with evidence than a lengthy 'laundry list' of items. This is why this book does not recommend simple + and – signs and accompanying short bullet points, although these might provide a useful summary.

To the prescriptive strategists, although the items in a PESTEL analysis rely on *past* events and experience, the analysis can be used as a *forecast of the future*. The past is history and strategic management is concerned with future action, but the best evidence about the future *may* derive from what happened in the past. Prescriptive strategists would suggest that it is worth attempting the task because major new investments make this hidden assumption anyway. For example, when Warner Brothers invested several hundred million dollars in the first *Harry Potter* film, it was making an assumption that the fantasy film market would remain attractive; it might as well *formalise* this through a structured PESTEL analysis, even if the outcome is difficult to predict.

The emergent corporate strategists may well comment that the future is so uncertain that prediction is useless. If this view is held, a PESTEL analysis will fulfil a different role in *interpreting* past events and their interrelationships. In practice, some emergent strategists may give words of caution but still be tempted to predict the future. For example, one prominent strategist, Herbert Simon, wrote a rather rash article in 1960 predicting that, 'We will have the technical ability, by 1985, to run corporations by machine.'[10] The emergent strategists are correct in suggesting that prediction in some fast-moving markets may have little value. Overall, when used wisely, the PESTEL checklist has a role in strategic management.

More depth on 'analysing the role of government'.

3.4.2 Analysing the role of government

Although 'politics' appears as a checklist item in the PESTEL analysis above, this does not do justice to the importance of government in some areas of strategy development. At government policy level, politics and economics are inextricably linked. Strategic management is not concerned with forming such policies but does need to understand the implications of the decisions taken. Governments can stimulate national economies, encourage new research projects, impose new taxes and introduce many other initiatives that affect the organisation and its ability to develop corporate strategy. To analyse these influences, it is useful to identify three areas: the environment of the nation, its system of government and its policies. All these are summarised in the E–S–P paradigm – see Figure 3.2.

More generally, political decisions have been an important driver of industrial growth. Strategic management therefore needs to consider the opportunities and difficulties that derive from such policies. Other areas of government interest, such as public expenditure, competition policy and taxation issues, also need to be analysed. Influencing government policy in these areas may actually form an important part of an organisation's strategy: perhaps because the organisation is a government customer or perhaps because it is heavily dependent on some aspect of favourable government treatment such as tax. Finally, macroeconomic conditions – that is, economic activity at the general level of the national economy – can have a significant impact on strategic management. It therefore needs to be explored and assessed.

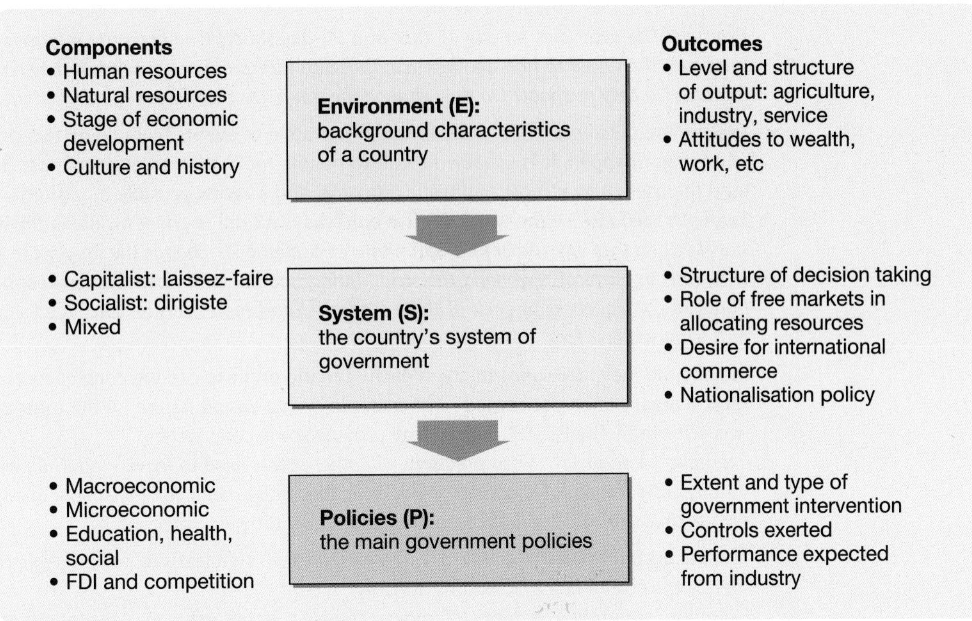

Figure 3.2 E–S–P paradigm: analysing the role of government

Source: adapted from Koopman, K and Montias, J M (1971) 'On the description and comparison of economic systems', in Eckstein, A (ed) *Comparison of Economic Systems: Theoretical and Methodological Approaches*, University of California Press, Berkeley, CA. Copyright © The Regents of the University of California. With permission.

3.4.3 Scenario-based analysis

In the context of a scenario-based analysis, a scenario is a model of a possible future environment for the organisation, whose strategic implications can then be investigated. For example, a scenario might be developed to explore the question: 'What would happen if broadband allowed every film to be delivered in-home by the year 2020 and demand for multi-screen cinema showings collapsed as a result? What impact would this have on film producers and cinema chains?'

Scenarios are concerned with peering into the future, not predicting the future. Prediction takes the *current* situation and extrapolates it forward. Scenarios take *different* situations with *alternative* starting points. The aim is not to predict but to explore a set of possibilities; a combination of events is usually gathered together into a scenario and then this combination is explored for its strategic significance. The organisation then explores its ability to handle this scenario – not because it necessarily expects it to happen but because it is a useful exercise in understanding the dynamics of the strategic environment. Exhibit 3.2 provides some guidance on the development of scenarios.

EXHIBIT 3.2

Some guidance on building scenarios . . . with an example from Case 3.4 on Hollywood blockbuster films

- Start from an *unusual viewpoint*. Examples might include the stance of a major competitor, a substantial change in technology, a radical change of government or the outbreak of war.
  Example: What are the consequences if one of the leading male actors dies half way through filming?
- Develop a *qualitative description* of a group of possible events or a *narrative* that shows how events will unfold. It is unlikely that this will involve a quantitative projection.

Example: The actor dies on day 45 (out of a 90-day shoot). The press are informed the same day. The producers then need to find another actor but also face problems over what they do about existing film footage: Do they re-shoot? Do they change the story? Do they invent another character?

- Explore the *outcomes* of this description or narrative of events by building two or three scenarios of what might happen. It is usually difficult to handle more than three scenarios. Two scenarios often lend themselves to a 'most optimistic outcome' and a 'worst possible outcome'.
  Example: Scenario 1 – the worst possible outcome is a total re-shoot including the withdrawal of other stars because they have other film commitments. Scenario 2 – change the storyline to fit the new situation with costs in terms of reworking the script, hiring another actor, perhaps re-shooting some scenes. The financial consequences of each of these scenarios (and more) can be calculated – what does it cost to hire script writers? Etc.
- Include the inevitable *uncertainty* in each scenario and explore the *consequences* of this uncertainty for the organisation concerned – for example, 'What would happen if the most optimistic outcome was achieved?' The PESTEL factors may provide some clues here.
  Example: Scenario 1 – When ***precisely*** *will other actors need to leave – after all, we still have another 45 days of contractual shooting? What does this really mean for the shoot? Surely we can do some rewrite that will help? Perhaps scenario 1 is actually too pessimistic?*
- Test the usefulness of the scenario by the extent to which it leads to *new strategic thinking* rather than merely the continuance of existing strategy.
  Example: Importantly in terms of radical thinking: if the actor was so important in the first place, why didn't we ***take out special insurance against his life*** *on the possibility of such an event before filming began?*
- Recall that the objective of scenario building is to develop strategies to cope with uncertainty, *not* to predict the future.
  Example: No-one wants a leading actor to die but imaginative scenarios help protect against uncertainties and unusual consequences.

KEY STRATEGIC PRINCIPLES

- The PESTEL checklist – the study of Political, Economic, Socio-cultural, Technological, Environmental and Legal factors – provides a useful starting point to any analysis of the general environment surrounding an organisation. It is vital to select among the items from such a generalised list and explore the chosen areas in depth; long lists of items are usually of no use.
- Prescriptive and emergent strategists take different views on the merits of projecting forward the main elements of the PESTEL checklist. The prescriptive approach favours the development of projections because they are often implied in major strategic decisions in any event. Emergent strategists believe the turbulence of the environment makes projections of limited value.
- In analysing the role and influence of government on strategy, the ESP Paradigm – Environment, System, Policies – can form a useful structure for this purpose. Influencing government policy may form an important element of strategy.
- A scenario is a picture of a possible future environment for the organisation, whose strategic implications can then be investigated. It is less concerned with prediction and more involved with developing different perspectives on the future. The aim is to stimulate new strategic thought about the possible consequences of events, rather than make an accurate prediction of the future.

CASE STUDY 3.2

Life cycle impact on strategy in the European ice cream market

During the period up to year 2004, the European ice cream market underwent significant change: some segments were relatively mature while some were experiencing strong growth. The North American market was more mature and fragmented with stronger regional brands. This case shows how the positions of the main European segments can be plotted in terms of the industry evolution (see Figure 3.3) and how strategies vary from one segment to another.

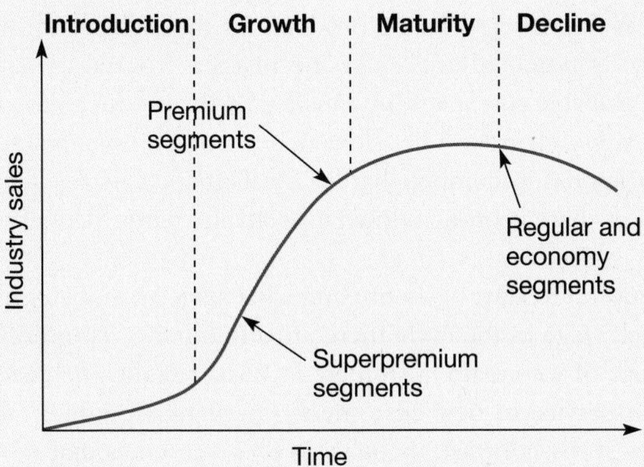

Figure 3.3 Industry evolution in the European ice cream market

The market can be divided into four distinct segments:

1 The *superpremium segment*, typified by Häagen-Dazs, was still in the early stages of its growth at this time. New companies were still entering the segment, for example Ben and Jerry's from the USA had been acquired by Unilever, but it had yet to be launched in some parts of continental Europe. New products were being tried using new methods of carton presentation and new high prices.

2 The *premium segment* had developed significantly in 1989 with the introduction of premium-priced Mars ice cream. By the year 2000, there were few new companies entering the market. The basic product ranges had become established among the leading players; the strategic battle was for distribution and branding.

3 The *regular* and 4 *economy segments* were typified by Unilever's bulk packs, sold under the name Carte d'Or across much of Europe. These had existed for many years but were still growing at around 5–6 per cent per annum (still regarded as a growth market according to some definitions). The segment also had a large number of other suppliers, not all of whom were national, let alone European. There was keen competition on price and with own-label products from grocery retailers. There was relatively little product innovation.

Some ice cream products – like traditional tubs – need little strategic investment. Others – like premium ice creams from Haagen-Dazs and Ben & Jerry's – need investment to support their high price/strong market position.

Case questions

1 What strategies are suggested for each segment of the market from the conventional view of the industry life cycle? (Refer to Table 3.3.)

2 Thinking of strategy as doing the unconventional, how might you modify the strategies identified in Question 1?

3.5 ANALYSING THE STAGES OF MARKET GROWTH

Video Part 4a

Definition ▶

The well-known strategy writer, Professor Michael Porter from Harvard University Business School, has described the *industry life cycle* as 'the grandfather of concepts for predicting industry evolution'. The basic hypothesis is that an industry – or a market segment within an industry – goes through four basic phases of development, each of which has implications for strategy – see Case 3.2 for an example. **The four main phases of the industry life cycle are usually identified as introduction, growth, maturity and decline** and are shown in Figure 3.4.

3.5.1 Industry life cycle

The nature of strategic management will change as industries move along the life cycle. In the *introductory* phase, organisations attempt to develop interest in the product. As the industry moves towards *growth*, competitors are attracted by its potential and enter the market: from a strategic perspective, competition increases. As all the available customers are satisfied by the product, growth slows down and the market becomes *mature*. Although growth has slowed, new competitors may still be attracted into the market: each company then has to compete harder for its market share, which becomes more fragmented – that is, the market share is broken down into smaller parts. Sales enter a period of *decline*.

To explore the strategic implications, it is useful to start by identifying what stage an industry has reached in terms of its development. For each stage in the cycle there are a number of commonly accepted strategies (see Table 3.3). In the case of ice cream customers in Case 3.2, the *introduction* phase will be used to present the product or service to new customers – perhaps a premium ice cream flavour to those who have never tasted it. By contrast, the *maturity* phase assumes that most customers are aware of the product and little new trial is required – perhaps a small tub of traditional chocolate ice cream.

As in other areas of strategic management, there are differing views regarding the choice of appropriate strategies for each phase of the industry life cycle. Table 3.3 represents the *conventional* view of the appropriate strategy for a particular stage in the industry's evolution. In strategic management, however, there are often good arguments for doing the *unconventional*, so this list would be seen as a starting point for analysing the dynamics of an industry. The most innovative strategy might well come by doing something different and breaking the mould.

As an example of the conventional view of such an analysis, the industry life cycle suggests that in the *early stages* of an industry's development there may be more opportunities for new and radical R&D. When an industry is more *mature*, rather less investment is needed in R&D.[11] However, the unconventional view argues that it is the mature industry that requires new growth and therefore

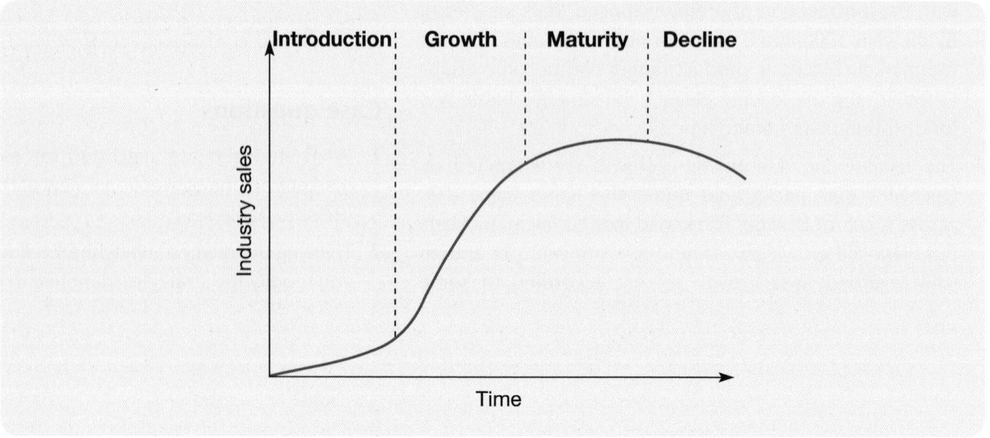

Figure 3.4 Stages of the industry life cycle

Table 3.3 The industry life cycle and its strategy implications – a conventional view

	Introduction phase	Growth phase	Maturity phase	Decline phase
Customer strategy	• Early customers may experiment with product and will accept some unreliability • Need to explain nature of innovation	• Growing group of customers • Quality and reliability important for growth	• Mass market • Little new trial of product or service • Brand switching	• Know the product well • Select on basis of price rather than innovation
R&D strategy	• High	• Seek extensions before competition	• Low	
Company strategy	• Seek to dominate market • R&D and production particularly important to ensure product quality	• React to competition with marketing expenditure and initiatives	• Expensive to increase market share if not already market leader • Seek cost reductions	• Cost control particularly important
Impact on profitability	• High price, but probably making a loss due to investment in new category	• Profits should emerge here, but prices may well decline as competitors enter market	• Profits under pressure from need for continuing investment coupled with continued distributor and competitive pressure	• Price competition and low growth may lead to losses or need to cut costs drastically to maintain profitability
Competitor strategy	• Keen interest in new category • Attempt to replicate new product	• Market entry (if not before) • Attempt to innovate and invest in category	• Competition largely on advertising and quality • Lower product differentiation • Lower product change	• Competition based primarily on price • Some companies may seek to exit the industry

R&D or some other strategic initiative. In the ice cream case, a market leader in traditional ice cream might benefit from investment in more modern facilities to reduce costs further. This suggests that, even in the mature phase of a market, heavy investment is often necessary to remain competitive in the market. It is for this reason that the life cycle concept can best be seen as a starting point for growth analysis.

It is important to note in the development of strategy the two consequences of the industry life cycle that can have a significant impact on industries:

1 *Advantages of early entry*. There is substantial empirical evidence that the first company into a new market has the most substantial strategic advantage. For example, Aaker[12] quotes a study of 500 mature industrial businesses showing that pioneer firms average a market share of 29 per cent, early followers 21 per cent and the late entrants 15 per cent. Although there are clearly risks in early market entry, there may also be long-term advantages that deserve careful consideration in strategic development.

2 *Industry market share fragmentation*. In the early years, markets that are growing fast attract new entrants. This is both natural and inevitable. The consequence as markets reach maturity is that each new company is fighting for market share and the market becomes more fragmented. Again, this has important implications for strategy because it suggests that mature markets need revised strategies – perhaps associated with a segment of the market (see Chapter 4).

For strategic purposes, it may be better to examine different *segments* of an industry, rather than the market *as a whole*, as different segments may be at different stages of the industry life cycle and may require different strategies (see the European ice cream industry example in Case 3.2). For example, it is possible to take a totally different industry such as the global travel industry and apply the same thinking: in recent years, some special-interest holidays, such as wildlife and photography, were still growing strongly whereas standard beach-and-sun holidays were in the mature stage of the life cycle.

3.5.2 Critical comment on the industry life cycle

The concept of the industry life cycle has both supporters and critics. Smallwood[13] and Baker[14] defend its usefulness and offer empirical support for the basic concept. Dhalla and Yuspeh[15] have led the criticisms, some of which certainly have a degree of validity (see Exhibit 3.3).

There are certainly some difficulties with the industry life cycle approach, but the reason for such an analysis is to identify the *dynamic factors that are shaping the industry's evolution*. The industry life cycle helps us to do this; it will then be possible to compare the organisation's own strategy with this analysis.

EXHIBIT 3.3

Criticisms of the industry life cycle

1 It is *difficult to determine the duration* of some life cycles and to identify the precise stage an industry has reached. For example, the Mars Bar was launched in the 1930s and is certainly not in decline - but is it in the growth or mature phase?

2 Some industries miss stages or *cannot be clearly identified* in their stages, particularly as a result of technological change. For example, has the bicycle reached the mature phase or has it reached a new lease of life as the petrol-driven car pollutes city atmospheres?

3 Companies themselves can instigate change in their products and can, as a result, *alter the shape of the curve*. For example, new life has been brought into the camera industry by the introduction of miniaturisation and, more recently, by the use of electronic storage in place of film.

KEY STRATEGIC PRINCIPLES

- The industry life cycle - charting the development of a market from introduction, through growth and maturity to decline - is useful to identify the dynamic factors shaping the industry's evolution, although there are criticisms of its use.
- It also helps to specify the conventional view of the strategies that are appropriate to each stage of the cycle, even if these are then changed for logical reasons.
- Aspects of life cycle analysis that are worthy of special consideration include: the advantages of early entry, the fragmentation of market share as markets mature, the incidence of cyclicality and its effect on demand in mature markets.

CASE STUDY 3.3

Bajaj Motorcycles: should the company move into cars?

One of India's largest motorcycle manufacturers, Bajaj Motorcycles, faces a major strategic decision over the next few years - whether to move into the Indian car market and, if so, with what model. This case explores the issues.

Background

Unlike Western countries, where motorcycles are a minority form of transport, the Indian transport market is dominated by motorcycles, scooters and three-wheelers. Over 7 million such vehicles were sold in 2010, rising to 16 million in 2013. Indian markets were growing at 5 per cent per year in 2010 but were virtually static by 2013 mainly because of national government economic policies. Their engine sizes are quite small by international standards - typically 120cc machines in India versus 400cc ones in the West - and relatively cheap in India with prices around $2,000 compared with $8,000 in more wealthy Western countries. In addition, motorcycles are family transport in India - two children on the handlebars and mother side-saddle on the back behind the father - whereas motorcycles are largely for individuals in Western countries. All this reflects the fact that family incomes are substantially lower on average in India than in the West - typically, $5,000 per year versus anything up to $25–30,000 in the West. But typical Indian customers are becoming more wealthy and there is a growing middle class with significantly higher incomes - hence the possible scope for a small family car.

Strategy at Bajaj for motorcycles and three-wheelers

In 1998, Bajaj sold 1.4 million vehicles. By 2013, the company's annual sales had grown to almost 3.8 million of which nearly 1 million were exported. Its major product area was motorcycles which accounted for around 90 per cent of the above sales.

In addition, the company had another important line of vehicles: Bajaj was the leading company in the Indian three-wheeler market and had a profitable revenue stream from this market segment. Three-wheelers are unusual in Western markets but form a major part of many Asian markets, including Indonesia and the Philippines. They are open at the sides and often have no doors. They can be used as passenger carriers and also as goods carriers. Bajaj was the market leader in this market with 480,000 unit sales in 2013 and a dominant 57 per cent market share of the Indian domestic market.

In order to develop its early motorcycle business, Bajaj signed an agreement with the Japanese motorcycle company Kawasaki back in the early 1990s to employ Kawasaki's technology. In the early years, Bajaj was motorcycle market leader in India. However, Bajaj Auto lost its market leadership in motorcycles to a rival company, Hero Honda, over the years. The Bajaj market share was a steady 31 per cent in 2014. It had declined slightly in 2009 and 2010 because the company had limited success in launching successful models into the fast-growing executive segment of the Indian motorcycle market, where its major rival, Hero Honda, had established market leadership. Table 3.4 gives examples of models and prices.

Bajaj Auto was well established in 2013 as a major motorcycle and three-wheeler manufacturer in India. It had created three major manufacturing facilities for motorcycles and three-wheelers. It had also developed a strong distribution and service network and an important R&D facility, which had led to the introduction of new Digital Twin Spark Ignition Technology. The company had also become a major exporter of motorcycles in the Asian region and had set up a manufacturing facility in Indonesia.

Table 3.4 Indian motorcycle market 2007

Company	Examples of models	Pricing
Hero Honda	CDDeLuxe (97cc), Splendor (125cc), Passion (125cc), Hunk, CBZ Xtreme	CD DeLuxe - $3,000 Hunk - $3,800
Bajaj	Platina (100cc), XCD, Pulsar (150 and 220cc), Discover	Pulsar 150 - $2,800 Pulsar 200 - $3,200
TVS	TVS Victor, Flame	
Yamaha	Gladiator (125cc)	Gladiator $2,000

Other manufacturers include Honda Japan and Suzuki Japan

Source: author direct visits to Indian and Nepali motorcycle stores November 2007 with some updating thereafter.

To refresh its market position in motorcycles, Bajaj developed three major strategies:

1 *New 'executive' top of the range machines.* This was the fastest-growing market segment in India. The company had set up a new R&D facility at its main manufacturing plant in Pune to deliver new technology. Importantly, it was the executive segment that had the highest profit margins as a result of a premium pricing strategy associated with the top of the range.

2 *Cost reduction.* Bajaj had in its early years some 900 suppliers of parts for its motorcycles. This large number meant that its suppliers were fragmented and unable to gain true economies of scale in production. Bajaj therefore spent considerable effort over the 10 years 1998 to 2007 reducing the numbers of suppliers back to around 80 and, at the same time, locating them closer to its assembly lines - similar to Toyota's 'just-in-time' delivery systems described in the free web-based case (Toyota: does it rely too heavily on production for world leadership?) linked to Part 6 of this book. Low costs were particularly important in the smaller motorcycle segment where price competition was particularly fierce and profit margins low.

3 *Exports and overseas production.* Bajaj promoted overseas sales from its three factories. By 2010, the company was selling over 800,000 motorcycles and three-wheelers annually to countries such as Sri Lanka, Nepal, Columbia, Bangladesh, Mexico, Peru and Egypt.

The one lakh car - a new threat or an opportunity for Bajaj?

Up to 2008, the annual market for cars in India was substantially smaller than motorcycles - nearly 2 million cars versus around 7 million motorcycles. The main reason was that typical car prices were $5,000 and upwards - affordable only to the more wealthy middle-class Indian family and substantially higher than motorcycle prices. (The detailed figures are given in Case 7 on Tata Motors in Part 6 of this book.)

Then along came one of India's most famous companies, the Tata Group, with a sensational new car launch in January 2008. Its brand name was the *Nano* and it was marketed as the 'One Lakh Car' being priced at 100,000 Indian rupees - 100,000 being called 'one lakh' in the Indian numbering system. Tata had produced the cheapest car in the world - one lakh was equivalent to around $2,500. The company had spent years working on a clever new car design that combined space, economy and simplicity. The on-road price would be somewhat higher - probably around 1.3 million lakh or $3,250 - but it would still be competitive with the top-of-the-range motorcycles. And this was the new threat and opportunity for Bajaj.

Initially, Tata Motors was planning to introduce the first prototypes from their new production line in June 2008 with 

Bajaj Motorcycles is one of India's leading companies. It faces a major strategic decision - whether or not to move into the fast-growing Indian car market.

full production in October 2008. The company planned to manufacture 250,000 Nano cars in the first year but expected this to rise towards 1 million cars after several years. The response to the new car was highly favourable. 'Nano is expected to change the automobile market in India. It would cater to a typical middle-income Indian family of four who want to avoid rain, wind and dust. It's freedom for four,' commented Dilip Chenoy of the Society of Indian Motor Manufacturers.

Even motorcycle manufacturers were impressed: 'It's a nice car and, as an Indian, I am proud of the product. I really liked it but I don't feel that it will impact two-wheelers very much. There is a huge market for two-wheelers and we are not worried about any market erosion.' That was the view of Pawan Munjal, the Managing Director of Hero Honda. But Tata was taking a different line: it argued that the Nano was far safer than a motorcycle and, if only 10 per cent of the motorcycle market switched to the Nano, then this would give Tata annual sales of 700,000 vehicles. It would bring down the cost of car ownership in India by at least 30 per cent and make cars affordable to many more people.

As Case 7 in Part 6 of this book explains in more detail, the Nano did not sell in the numbers originally predicted. By 2013, Tata was selling only around 50–60,000 Nanos per year - far short of the initial projections.

Implications for Bajaj strategy

Up to 2013, the sales of the Nano had no impact on the Indian motorcycle market. But companies like Bajaj were aware that the car's competitive price was much the same as its profitable executive model, the 'Pulsar'. They would have read the comment in the Indian press of one Bajaj Pulsar user: 'I would definitely consider buying the Nano as the cost of the car fits my pocket and above all it has good mileage.' However, the company was also aware of the widely publicised weaker sales of the Nano up to 2013.

Tata acknowledged that its own ideas for the Nano would help other manufacturers. 'It is not our god-given domain,' explained Rajan Tata, the Chairman of the Tata Group, when introducing the Nano. 'It will be an easier task for them than it was for us.' However, even allowing for this, it would be no easy task for Bajaj Group or any other company.

Back in 2008, Bajaj had discussions with the French car company Renault about the possibility of a joint venture in the Indian car market. This led to an outline joint agreement to produce an ultra low-cost car (code-named the ULC) for the Indian market similar to the Nano.

Subsequently, there were two changes in strategic thinking. First, Renault decided that it would like to enter the Indian domestic market with its own range and therefore began planning this for launch around 2013–2014. This meant that it was less interested in the ULC - possibly supported by the relatively poor sales of the Nano. Second, Bajaj itself became increasingly doubtful about the market demand for the ULC. As an alternative, it was actively examining the possibility of dropping the ULC and developing an extended version of its three-wheeler vehicles - one with four wheels - but with the open design body work of the three-wheeler with no doors, rather than the closed design of a car body.

At the time of writing this case, Bajaj clearly had some major strategic decisions to take: should it make a ULC car like the Nano? Should it make a four-wheeler to complement its existing three-wheel range? Or should it just stay with motorcycles?

According to its 2013 annual report, the company has clearly designed policies, including an extensive contribution in the related areas of education and health activities.

 This case was written by Richard Lynch from published data only.[16] The author is grateful to Binod Rai in Kathmandu, Nepal, for helping him initially understand the Indian and Nepali motorcycle markets. The original concept for this case came from a brief comment from a fellow professor when the author was lecturing in Delhi in November 2007. Unfortunately, he did not make a note of the professor's name at the time but would like to acknowledge this source.

Case questions

1 Why did Bajaj lose market share and how did it respond?

2 What are the most profitable segments of the Indian motorcycle market? Why were they threatened initially by the Nano?

3 Should Bajaj move into car manufacture? What are the arguments in favour and what against? What would you recommend?

Ten more questions to help identify key factors for success in an industry.

Case study: *Can the world's regional steel companies develop truly global strategies?*

3.6 KEY FACTORS FOR SUCCESS IN AN INDUSTRY

Video Part 5b

In a strategic analysis of the environment, there is an immense range of issues that can potentially be explored, creating a problem for most organisations, which have neither the time nor the resources to cope with such an open-ended task. The Japanese strategist Kenichi Ohmae,[17] the former head of the management consultants McKinsey, in Japan, has suggested a way of tackling this matter by identifying *the key factors for success (KFS)* that are *likely* to deliver the company's objectives. These can then be used to focus the analysis on particularly important industry matters.

Definition ▶ **Key factors for success in an industry are those resources, skills and attributes of the organisations in an industry that are essential to deliver success in the market place.** Ohmae argued that, when resources of capital, labour and time are scarce, it is important that they should be *concentrated* on the key activities of the business – that is, those most important to the delivery of whatever the organisation regards as success.

This concept of key factors for success is also consistent with Porter's view[18] that there are factors that determine the relative competitive positions of companies within an industry. Moreover, the foundation of Kay's approach[19] is that it is important to concentrate resources on the specific areas of the business that are most likely to prove successful. Amit and Schoemaker[20] provide a more extended theoretical framework for the same topic, but call their treatment 'Strategic Industry Factors'. All the above have said that identifying the key factors is not an easy task.

KFS are common to all the major organisations in the industry and do not differentiate one company from another. For example, in Case 3.3, the factors mentioned – low labour costs, servicing centres, parts suppliers of motorbikes, etc. – are common to other similar companies to Bajaj. Such factors will vary from one industry to another. For example, by contrast, in the perfume and cosmetics industry the factors will include branding, product distribution and product performance, but they are unlikely to include labour costs.

When undertaking a strategic analysis of the environment, the identification of the KFS for an industry may provide a useful starting point. For example, the motorbike KFS item of 'low labour costs' would suggest an environmental analysis of the following areas:

- general wage levels in the country;
- government regulations and attitudes to worker redundancy, because high wage costs could be reduced by sacking employees;
- trade union strength to fight labour force redundancies.

In the Indian motorbike industry, these elements of the environment would benefit from careful study, whereas, in the cosmetics and perfume industry, they might have some relevance but would be far less important than other areas.

3.6.1 Identifying the key factors for success in the industry

Key factors concern not only the resources of organisations in the industry but also the *competitive environment* in which organisations operate. There are three principal areas that need to be analysed – Ohmae's *three Cs*.[21]

1 *Customers*. What do customers really want? What are the segments in the market place? Can we direct our strategy towards a group?

2 *Competition*. How can the organisation beat or at least survive against competition? What resources and customers does it have that make it particularly successful? How does the organisation compare on price, quality, etc.? Does the organisation have a stronger distributive network than its competitors?

3 *Corporation.* What special resources does the company itself possess and how do they compare with those of competitors? How does the company compare on costs with its rivals? And on technologies? Skills? Organisational ability? Marketing?

Exhibit 3.4 sets out some key questions in more detail. No single area is more important than another. The *corporate* factors relate to the *resource* issues which are explored in detail in Chapter 4.

3.6.2 Critical comment on the concept

Criticism of the key factors for success has concentrated on four issues:[22]

1 *Identification.* It is difficult to pick out the important factors.

2 *Causality of relationships.* Even though they have been identified, it may not be clear *how* they operate or interact.

3 *Dangers of generalising.* The competitive advantage of a single organisation, by definition, cannot be obtained by seeking what is commonly accepted as bringing success to all organisations in an industry.

4 *Disregard of emergent perspectives.* Success may come from change in an industry, rather than the identification of the current key factors for success.

Beyond these specific criticisms, some strategists have a more general concern about industry analysis (this is explored in the next section). Some of the criticisms can be countered if key factors for success are regarded as *guidelines* for directing strategy development, rather than rigid rules. But the criticisms suggest that key factors for success should be explored with caution. They are only a starting point in strategy analysis – the 'best' strategy may be to reject the key factors and do something completely different!

EXHIBIT 3.4

Identifying key factors for success in an industry

Note that key factors for success are directed at *all companies in an industry*, not just the target company for strategy development.

1 Customers

Who are the customers? Who are the potential customers? Are there any special segments? Why do customers buy from us? And from our competitors?

- *Price.* Is the market segmented by high, medium and economy pricing? For example, the market for European ice cream.
- *Service.* Do some customers value service while others simply want to buy the product? For example, top-class fashion retailers versus standard clothing shops.
- *Product or service reliability.* Is product performance crucial to the customer or is reliability useful but not really important? For example, heart pacemakers and pharmaceuticals.
- *Quality.* Some customers will pay higher prices for actual or perceived quality differences. Does this provide a route to success? For example, organic vegetables.
- *Technical specifications.* In some industrial and financial services, technical details will provide major attractions for some customers. Is this relevant in this industry? For example, specialist financial bond dealers.
- *Branding.* How important is branding for the customer? For example, Coca-Cola and Pepsi Cola.

2 Competition

Who are the main competitors? What are the main factors in the market that influence competition? How intense is competition? What is necessary to achieve market superiority? What resources do competitors possess that we lack and vice versa?

- *Cost comparisons.* Which companies have the lowest costs? Why? For example, Toyota until the mid-1990s.
- *Price comparisons.* Which companies have high prices? For example, Daimler-Benz does not make cheap cars.
- *Quality issues.* Which companies have the highest quality? Why? How? For example, Xerox (USA) in the light of fierce competition from Japanese companies such as Canon.
- *Market dominance.* Which companies dominate the market? For example, Nestlé, with the strongest coffee product range in the world and the largest market share.
- *Service.* Are there companies in the industry that offer superior service levels? For example, industrial markets, such as those served by Asea Brown Boveri, which need high levels of service to operate and maintain sophisticated equipment.
- *Distributors.* Which companies have the best distributive network? Lowest costs? Fastest delivery? Competent distributors that really know the product or service? For example, major glass companies such as St Gobain (France) and Pilkington (UK).

3 Corporation

What are our key resources and those of our competitors? What do they deliver to customers? Where are the majority of the industry costs concentrated? A small percentage reduction to a large part of the total costs will deliver more than a large percentage reduction in an area of lower total costs.

- *Low-cost operations.* Are low-cost operations important for ourselves or our competitors? For example, Aldi (Germany) and Tesco (UK) are both low-cost supermarket operators.
- *Economies of scale.* Do these exist in the industry? How important are they? For example, large-scale petroleum chemical refinery operations such as those operated by Royal Dutch/Shell.
- *Labour costs.* Does our industry rely heavily on low labour costs for competitive operations? For example, Philips (Netherlands) has moved its production to Singapore and Malaysia to lower labour costs.
- *Production output levels.* Does our industry need full utilisation of plant capacity? For example, European paper and packaging companies.
- *Quality operations.* Do customers need consistent and reliable quality? How do we compare with others in the industry? For example, McDonald's has applied the same standards around the world in its restaurants.
- *Innovative ability.* Does our industry place a high reliance on our ability to produce a constant stream of new innovations? For example, computer hardware and software companies such as Apple, Epson and Microsoft.
- *Labour/management relations.* Is our industry heavily reliant on good relations? Are there real problems if disputes arise? For example, European large-scale steel production, at companies such as Usinor/Arbed.
- *Technologies and copyright.* Does the industry rely on specialist technologies, especially those that are patented and provide a real competitive advantage? For example, News International (Australia), which has exclusive global control over some forms of decoder cards for satellite television.
- *Skills.* Do organisations in the industry possess exceptional human skills and people? What are such skills? For example, advertising agencies and leading consultancy companies.

KEY STRATEGIC PRINCIPLES

- Identifying the key factors for success shapes the key areas of strategic analysis.
- Such factors can conveniently be considered under three headings: customers, competition and corporation. By 'corporation' is meant the resources of the organisation.
- Key factors can be found in any area of the organisation and relate to skills, competitive advantage, competitive resources of an organisation in the industry, special technologies or customer contacts.
- Four criticisms of key factors have been made: identification, causality of relationships, dangers of generalising, and disregard of emergent perspectives. Caution is therefore needed in their application.

Some background on Professor Porter's work: the nature and intensity of competition in an industry.

CASE STUDY 3.4

Strategic bargaining to film *Lord of the Rings*

FT

In the highly competitive and risky environment of Hollywood film-making, it is essential to analyse those who have the power to make things happen. This case explores the strategic environment surrounding one of the most profitable films ever made – and how the deal and the movie almost failed.

Background

It was one of the biggest gambles in movie history – handing $300 million to shoot an epic trilogy in one take to a virtually unknown director with no record of big-budget Hollywood pictures. And letting him do it 7,000 miles away, so that studio executives had little control over what actually happened on the set.

There were plenty of recent examples of how a huge investment in what seemed a sure-fire blockbuster had backfired, leaving massive dents in the studio's finances – *Waterworld*, *Heaven's Gate* and so on. Somehow, though, *Lord of the Rings* did get made and took over $500 million in its first year as well as winning four Oscars. It is easy to forget the scale of the risk involved and the convoluted strategic bargaining that was necessary before a single scene was shot.

For Peter Jackson, the film's New Zealand-born director, and his agent, Ken Kamins from ICM, the story behind *Lord of the Rings* is one of a project that very nearly failed to see the light of day.

Competitive environment

When Jackson and Kamins set out to make the film in 1995, they first had to secure the rights to JRR Tolkien's novels, *The Fellowship of the Ring*, *The Two Towers* and *The Return of the King*. Producer Saul Zaentz had bought the rights from Professor Tolkien for a rumoured $15,000 30 years earlier and he had no intention of selling them. Up to that point, Jackson was known only for low-budget horror movies such as *Braindead*. However, an Oscar nomination in 1995 for the screenplay of his $3.5 million arthouse drama *Heavenly Creatures* had earned him a first-look deal with Harvey Goldstein, head of Miramax, the independent studio allied to Disney. So Jackson and Kamins approached Weinstein that year with the idea for a *Lord of the Rings* adaptation.

'When we told Harvey that Saul held the rights, he was immediately enthusiastic,' says Kamins, 'as he had just helped Saul on *The English Patient* [Miramax had stepped in to pick up the film after Fox, part of News Corporation, dropped it on the eve of production]. That created the moral window by which Harvey could ask. But this wasn't charity either. Saul had Harvey pay a pretty penny – I've been told somewhere in the $3 million range.'

New bargaining problems

Having secured the film rights, the Miramax boss sent Jackson and his partner, Fran Walsh, off to write the scripts for a two-

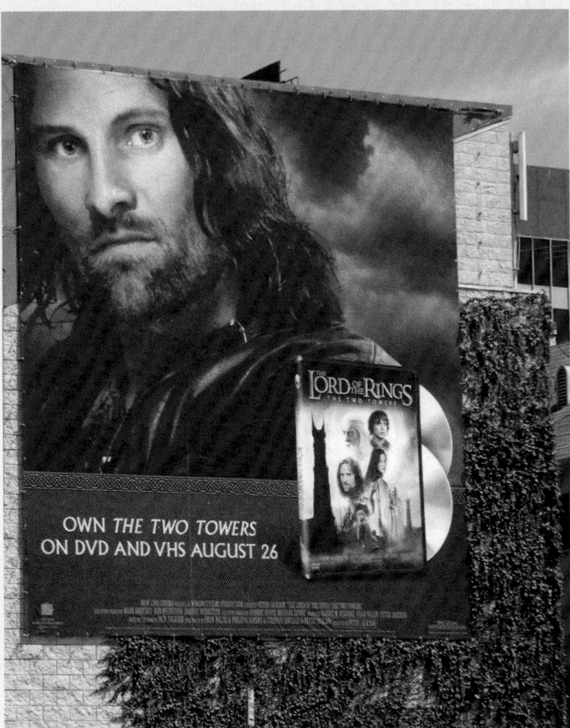

Outdoor advertising in Hollywood, USA. Even after the strategy was negotiated and implemented, it was important to promote the film.

part adaptation, with both parts being filmed one after the other. Production research was also to begin in New Zealand. Just when things seemed to be going smoothly, the next wave of problems emerged. 'It soon became clear to Miramax that it was going to be a very expensive proposition,' says Kamins, 'maybe more expensive than their brief as defined by Disney allowed them to get involved in. Harvey then went to Disney and asked whether they would want a partner in the project. When Disney said no, Miramax got concerned about the cost. And of course [started] asking obvious questions: what happens if the first movie doesn't work?'

Faced with such a risky and expensive project, Weinstein asked Jackson to make the trilogy as one film of no more than three hours. Jackson declined, and, instead, he and Kamins asked to take the project to another studio. Weinstein agreed, although he imposed very tough conditions. Says Kamins: 'We had three weeks to set it up somewhere else. Harvey also demanded that the $12 million that Miramax had already spent in development had to be repaid within 72 hours of the agreement being signed. Now this is highly unusual in the movie business. Normally, a studio would simply pay the former studio a 10 per cent option or they would work out a deal in the budget of the film once the movie got made. Most importantly, he and a partner insisted on 5 per cent of the gross, whether there was one movie, two movies or eight.'

The deal hangs on a knife-edge

With three weeks to find another studio, Jackson and Kamins decided to do two things. While Kamins started submitting the screenplays for the two-part adaptation to every studio in Hollywood, Jackson flew to New Zealand to produce a 35-minute documentary with $50,000 of his own money. The idea was that, if any of the studios was interested, the documentary would show them where Miramax's $12 million had gone, and, most importantly, why Jackson was the right director. But Kamins had little success – every studio said no, except two, Polygram and New Line, which was owned by Warner Brothers. Then Polygram pulled out at the last minute: 'So we went to New Line realising that they were the last Popsicle stand in the desert, and them not knowing that,' said Kamins.

But at New Line, they had some luck. Jackson's old friend, Mark Ordesky, turned out to be one of those making the decision. New Line then asked: 'Why are you making two movies? It's three books, so it's three movies.' Negotiations started the next day. Many in the business doubted the sanity of the decision, especially making three rather than two films. 'But Peter's presentation made it clear that he had an absolutely commanding vision for the film . . . You would be surprised how, in the movie business, some of these commitments are made on far less sturdy ground.'

By 2002, AOL Time Warner was estimated to have one of the biggest money-spinners in entertainment history on its hands. New Line and its distribution partners had turned *Lord of the Rings* into a worldwide franchise in the *Star Wars* mould, and were exploiting the brand name across a huge range of platforms – DVD, video games, the internet, merchandise of every sort. The gamble was starting to pay.

Heavily adapted by Richard Lynch from an article by Katja Hofmann in *FT Creative Business*, 19 March 2002, p 10. © The Financial Times Limited 2002. All rights reserved. Richard Lynch is solely responsible for providing this adapted version of the original article and the Financial Times Limited does not accept any liability for the accuracy or quality of the adapted version.

Case questions

1 Who has the bargaining power in this strategic environment? And who has the co-operating power? Identify and analyse the players – use the concepts from Sections 3.6 and 3.7 to help you.

2 What useful strategic concepts, if any, from this chapter can be used in analysing the strategic environment? And what cannot be used? Why?

3 If risk and judgement are important in business decisions, can prescriptive strategic analysis be usefully employed?

3.7 ANALYSING THE COMPETITIVE INDUSTRY ENVIRONMENT – THE CONTRIBUTION OF PORTER

Video Part 4b

An industry analysis usually begins with a general examination of the forces influencing the organisation. The objective of such a study is to use this to develop the *competitive advantage* of the organisation to enable it to defeat its rival companies. Much of this analysis was structured and presented by Professor Michael Porter of Harvard University Business School.[23] His contribution to our understanding of the competitive environment of the firm has wide implications for many organisations in both the private and public sectors.

This type of analysis is often undertaken using the structure proposed by Porter; his basic model is illustrated in Figure 3.5. This is often called *Porter's Five Forces Model* because he identifies five basic forces that can act on the organisation:

1 the bargaining power of suppliers;
2 the bargaining power of buyers;
3 the threat of potential new entrants;
4 the threat of substitutes;
5 the extent of competitive rivalry.

The objective of such an analysis is to investigate how the organisation needs to form its strategy in order to develop opportunities in its environment and protect itself against competition and other threats. Porter himself cautiously described[24] his analysis as being concerned with the 'forces driving industry competition'. However, the general principles can perhaps be applied to public service and not-for-profit organisations where they compete for resources, such as government funding or charitable donations – see Chapter 18 for a further discussion of this.

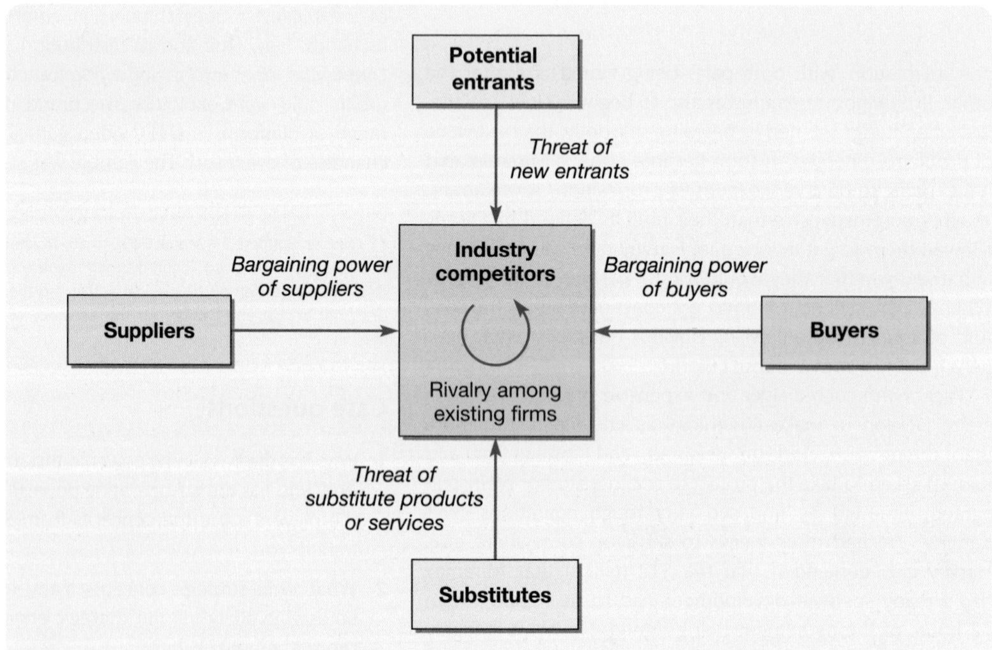

Figure 3.5 Porter's Five Forces Model

Source: reprinted with the permission of Free Press, a Division of Simon & Schuster, Inc., from *Competitive Strategy: Techniques for Analyzing Industries and Competitors* by Michael E Porter. Copyright © 1980, 1998 by The Free Press, All rights reserved.

3.7.1 The bargaining power of suppliers

Virtually every organisation has suppliers of raw materials or services which are used to produce the final goods or services. Porter suggested that suppliers are more powerful under the following conditions:

- *If there are only a few suppliers.* This means that it is difficult to switch from one to another if a supplier starts to exert its power.
- *If there are no substitutes for the supplies they offer.* This is especially the case if the supplies are important for technical reasons – perhaps they form a crucial ingredient in a production process or the service they offer is vital to smooth production.
- *If suppliers' prices form a large part of the total costs of the organisation.* Any increase in price would hit value added unless the organisation was able to raise its own prices in compensation.
- *If a supplier can potentially undertake the value-added process of the organisation.* Occasionally a supplier will have power if it is able to integrate forward and undertake the value-added process undertaken by the organisation; this could pose a real threat to the survival of the organisation.

In the case of motorcycle companies like Bajaj, suppliers' bargaining powers are in some respects low. There are many sources of supply for some motorcycle parts. However, in terms of more sophisticated electronic parts that make a substantial difference to the performance of the machines, suppliers may have higher bargaining power.

3.7.2 The bargaining power of buyers

In his model, Porter used the term *buyers* to describe what might also be called the *customers* of the organisation. Buyers have more bargaining power under the following conditions:

- *If buyers are concentrated and there are few of them.* When the organisation has little option but to negotiate with a buyer because there are few alternative buyers around, the organisation is clearly in a weak position: national government contracts in defence, health and education are obvious examples where the government can, in theory at least, drive a hard bargain with organisations.
- *If the product from the organisation is undifferentiated.* If an organisation's product is much the same as that from other organisations, the buyer can easily switch from one to another without problems. The buyer is even more likely to make such a shift if the quality of the buyer's product is unaffected by such a change.
- *If backward integration is possible.* As with suppliers above, the buyer's bargaining power is increased if the buyer is able to backward-integrate and take over the role of the organisation.
- *If the selling price from the organisation is unimportant to the total costs of the buyer.*

In the case of Indian motorcycle customers, private buyers are unlikely to have much bargaining power with companies of the size of Bajaj; a letter from an individual customer, threatening to switch from its motorcycle purchase to Hero Honda, is unlikely to have much impact – the threat is low. For the sake of clarity, this reasoning does not imply that Bajaj would ignore a letter from an individual customer – just that the bargaining power of that individual is not high according to Porter's theory. However, if a large purchaser of motorcycles like a police authority were to make such a threat, then it would clearly have to be taken more seriously because of the potential impact on sales. In this latter case, the threat is high.

3.7.3 The threat of potential new entrants

New entrants come into a market place when the profit margins are attractive and the barriers to entry are low. The allure of high profitability is clear and so the major strategic issue is that of barriers to entry into a market.

Porter argued that there were seven[25] major sources of barriers to entry:

1. *Economies of scale.* Unit costs of production may be reduced as the absolute volume per period is increased. Such cost reductions occur in many industries and present barriers because they mean that any new entrant has to come in on a large scale in order to achieve the low cost levels of those already present: such a scale is risky. We have already examined the computer and motorcycle industries where such cost reductions are vital.
2. *Product differentiation.* Branding, customer knowledge, special levels of service and many other aspects may create barriers by forcing new entrants to spend extra funds or simply take longer to become established in the market. Real barriers to entry can be created in strategic terms by long-established companies with such strengths in a market (see Chapter 4). Retailers such as IKEA with strong branding and specialist product lines and expertise are examples of companies with differentiated products.
3. *Capital requirements.* Entry into some markets may involve major investment in technology, plant, distribution, service outlets and other areas. The ability to raise such finance and the risks associated with such outlays of capital will deter some companies – for example, the high capital cost of investing in new motorcycle production capacity in Case 3.3 earlier in this chapter.
4. *Switching costs.* When a buyer is satisfied with the existing product or service, it is naturally difficult to switch that buyer to a new entrant. The cost of making the switch would naturally fall to the new entrant and will represent a barrier to entry. Persuading buyers to switch their purchases of computer software from Microsoft Windows to Apple has an obvious cost and inconvenience to many companies that would need to be overcome. In addition to the costs of persuading customers to switch, organisations should expect that existing companies will retaliate with further actions designed to drive out new entrants. For example, Microsoft has not hesitated to upgrade its products and reduce its prices to retain customers that might otherwise switch.
5. *Access to distribution channels.* It is not enough to produce a quality product; it must be distributed to the customer through channels that may be controlled by companies already in the market. For many years, the leading petrol companies have owned their own retail petrol sites to ensure that they have access to retail customers.
6. *Cost disadvantages independent of scale.* Where an established company knows the market well, has the confidence of major buyers, has invested heavily in infrastructure to service the market and has specialist expertise, it becomes a daunting task for new entrants to gain a foothold in the market. Korean and Malaysian car companies are attempting to enter the European and American car markets and face these barriers created by well-entrenched companies such as Ford, Volkswagen and Renault.
7. *Government policy.* For many years, governments have enacted legislation to protect companies and industries: monopolies in telecommunications, health authorities, utilities such as gas and electricity are examples where entry has been difficult if not impossible. The European Commission has been working alongside European governments to remove some but not all such barriers over the past few years. The Chinese government will not allow foreign steel companies to take a controlling interest in Chinese steel companies.

3.7.4 The threat of substitutes

Occasionally, substitutes render a product in an industry redundant. For example, SmithKline Beecham lost sales from its product Tagamet for the treatment of ulcers, due to the introduction of more effective products – first the introduction of Zantac from Glaxo in the 1980s and then, in the 1990s, Losec from the Swedish company Astra. Tagamet is still on sale as an over-the-counter remedy, but its major public health sales have largely ceased. More recently, Losec sales have also suffered as the drug patents protecting prices have come to an end and cheaper low-price substitutes have been launched by rival companies – the so-called 'generic' drugs, sourced from countries like India.

More often, substitutes do not entirely replace existing products but introduce new technology or reduce the costs of producing the same product. Effectively, substitutes may limit the profits in an industry by keeping prices down.

From a strategy viewpoint, the key issues to be analysed are:

- the possible threat of obsolescence;
- the ability of customers to switch to the substitute;
- the costs of providing some extra aspect of the service that will prevent switching;
- the likely reduction in profit margin if prices come down or are held.

In the motorcycle market, there is the possibility of substituting cars and three-wheelers depending on the price and usage. The threat of substitution may therefore be high, but this depends on the technology and end-use.

3.7.5 The extent of competitive rivalry

Some markets are more competitive than others. Higher competitive rivalry may occur in the following circumstances:

- *When competitors are roughly of equal size and one competitor decides to gain share over the others*, then rivalry increases significantly and profits fall. In a market with a dominant company, there may be less rivalry because the larger company is often able to stop quickly any move by its smaller competitors. In the UK market for electricity supply, there are only six major suppliers each with roughly equal market shares. If one was to bid for a major increase in share, then the others would have to follow.
- *If a market is growing slowly and a company wishes to gain dominance*, then by definition it must take its sales from its competitors – increasing rivalry.
- *Where fixed costs or the costs of storing finished products in an industry are high*, then companies may attempt to gain market share in order to achieve break-even or higher levels of profitability. Paper making, steel manufacture and car production are all examples of industries where there is a real case for cutting prices to achieve basic sales volumes – thus increasing rivalry.
- *If extra production capacity in an industry comes in large increments*, then companies may be tempted to fill that capacity by reducing prices, at least temporarily. For example, the bulk chemicals industry usually has to build major new plants and cannot simply add small increments of capacity. In the steel and oil industries, it is not possible to half-build a new processing plant: either it is built or not.
- *If it is difficult to differentiate products or services*, then competition is essentially price-based and it is difficult to ensure customer loyalty. Markets in basic pharmaceutical products such as aspirin have become increasingly subject to such pressures. In the steel market, flat-rolled steel from one manufacturer is much the same as that of another, so competition is price-based. However, where specialist steels are made with unique performance characteristics, the products are differentiated on performance and price rivalry is lower.
- *When it is difficult or expensive to exit from an industry* (perhaps due to legislation on redundancy costs or the cost of closing dirty plant), there is likely to be excess production capacity in the industry and increased rivalry. The steel industry has suffered from problems in this area during the past few years.
- *If entrants have expressed a determination to achieve a strategic stake in that market*, the costs of such an entry would be relatively unimportant when related to the total costs of the company concerned and the long-term advantages of a presence in the market. Japanese car manufacturing in the EU has advantages for Toyota and Nissan beyond the short-term costs of building plant, as EU car markets were opened to full Japanese competition around the year 2000.

3.7.6 Strategy implications from the general industry and competitive analysis

In strategic management, it is not enough just to produce an analysis; it is important to consider the implications for the organisation's future strategy. Some issues that might arise from the above include:

- *Is there a case for changing the strategic relationships with suppliers?* Could more be gained by moving into close partnership with selected suppliers rather than regarding them as rivals? The Japanese car industry has sought to obtain much closer co-operation with suppliers and mutual cost reduction as a result.[26] (See Case 4 on global cars in Part 6.)
- *Is there a case for forming a new relationship with large buyers?* Manufacture of own-label products for large customers in the retail industry may be undertaken at lower margins than branded business but has proved a highly successful strategy for some leading European companies.[27] Even Cereal Partners (from Chapter 2) is now engaged in this strategy in order to build volume through its plants.
- *What are the key factors for success that drive an industry and influence its strategic development?* What are the lessons for the future that need to be built into the organisation's strategic management? We looked at these questions in Section 3.6.
- *Are there any major technical developments that rivals are working on that could fundamentally alter the nature of the environment?* What is the timespan and level of investment for such activity? What action should we take, if any?

3.7.7 Critical comment on the Five Forces Model

Porter's Five Forces Model is a useful early step in analysing the environment, but it has been the subject of some critical comment:

- The analytical framework is essentially *static*, whereas the competitive environment in practice is constantly changing. Forces may move from high to low, or vice versa, rather more rapidly than the model can show.
- It assumes that the organisation's own interests come first; for some charitable institutions and government bodies, this assumption may be incorrect.
- It assumes that buyers (called customers elsewhere in this book) have no greater importance than any other aspect of the micro-environment. Other commentators such as Aaker,[28] Baker[29] and Harvey-Jones[30] would fundamentally disagree on this point: they argue that the customer is more important than other aspects of strategy development and is not to be treated as an equal aspect of such an analysis.
- In general, its starting point is that the environment poses a threat to the organisation – leading to the consideration of suppliers and buyers as threats that need to be tackled. As pointed out above, some companies have found it useful to engage in closer *co-operation* with suppliers; such a strategy may be excluded if they are regarded purely as threats. This is explained more fully in Section 3.8.
- Porter's strategic analysis largely ignores the human resource aspects of strategy: it makes little attempt to recognise, let alone resolve, aspects of the micro-environment that might connect people to their own and other organisations. For example, it considers neither the country cultures, nor the management skills aspects of strategic management.
- Porter's analysis proceeds on the basis that, once such an analysis has been undertaken, then the organisation can formulate a strategy to handle the results: *prescriptive* rather than *emergent*. As we saw in Chapter 2, some commentators would challenge this basic assessment.

In spite of these critical comments, the approach taken in this book is that Porter's model provides a very useful starting point in the analysis of the environment. It has real merit because of the issues it raises in a logical and structured framework. It is therefore recommended as a useful first step in strategy development.

Professor Porter presented his Five Forces Model as an early stage in strategic analysis and development. He followed it with two further analyses: an analysis of *industry evolution* – the extent to which the micro-environment is still growing or has reached maturity[31] – and the study of *strategic groups* within a market.

KEY STRATEGIC PRINCIPLES

- The purpose of industry and competitive strategic analysis is to enable the organisation to develop competitive advantage.
- Porter's Five Forces Model provides a useful starting point for such an analysis.
- Suppliers are particularly strong when they can command a price premium for their products and when their delivery schedules or quality can affect the final product.
- Buyers (or customers) are strong when they have substantial negotiating power or other leverage points associated with price, quality and service.
- New entrants pose a substantial threat when they are easily able to enter a market and when they are able to compete strongly through lower costs or other means.
- Substitutes usually pose a threat as a result of a technological or low-cost breakthrough.
- Competitive rivalry is the essence of such an analysis. It is necessary to build defences against competitive threat.
- The model has been the subject of some critical comment, but it remains a useful starting point for competitive strategic analysis.

3.8 ANALYSING THE CO-OPERATIVE ENVIRONMENT

3.8.1 The four links model

Video Part 4b

As well as competing with rivals, most organisations also co-operate with others, for example through informal supply relationships or through formal and legally binding joint ventures. Until recently, such links were rarely analysed in strategy development – the analysis stopped at Porter's Five Forces and some in-depth studies of one or two competitors (see Section 3.9). However, it is now becoming increasingly clear that *co-operation* between the organisation and others in its environment is also important as:

- it may help in the achievement of sustainable competitive advantage;
- it may open up new markets and increase business opportunities;
- it may produce lower costs;
- it may deliver more sustainable relationships with those outside the organisation.

It should be noted that an extreme form of co-operation – collusion between competitors to rig markets – is illegal in most countries and is not explored further here. But there are many other forms of co-operation that are highly beneficial and should form part of any analysis of the environment. For example, European steel companies have formed joint ventures with Brazilian steel companies for the benefit of both parties, and Krupp Thyssen Stahl is co-operating with its energy suppliers to reduce costs. Moreover, all the main European steel companies are co-operating with the government of the EU on policy matters affecting the industry. Equally, North American steel companies are co-operating with Federal and state governments for the benefit of the industry. Joint ventures, alliances and other formal methods of co-operation are explored in Chapter 5 – see Section 5.6.

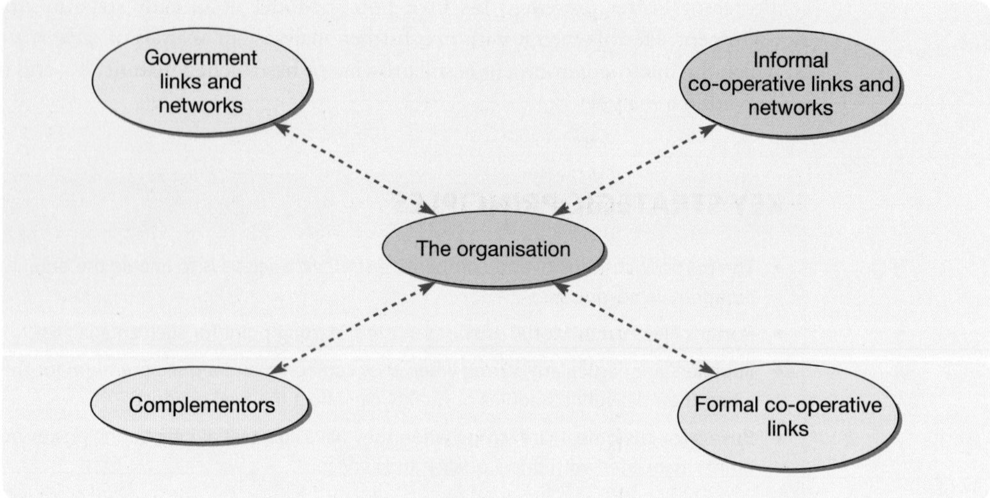

Figure 3.6 Analysing co-operation: the Four Links Model

The basic co-operative linkages between the organisation and its environment can usefully be explored under four headings:

1 informal co-operative links and networks
2 formal co-operative links
3 complementors
4 government links and networks.

The objective of such an analysis is to establish the strength and nature of the co-operation that exists between the organisation and its environment. It can be conducted through the *Four Links Model* – see Figure 3.6.

3.8.2 Opportunities and threats from informal co-operative links and networks

Informal co-operative links and networks are the occasions when organisations link together for a mutual or common purpose *without* a legally binding contractual relationship. They have long been recognised as providing an important means of understanding the strategy of the firm.[32] By their nature, they may well occur by accident as well as by design. They will include many forms of contact, ranging from formal industry bodies that represent industry matters with other interested parties – for example, the European Confederation of Iron and Steel Industries – to informal contacts that take place when like-minded individuals from a variety of industries meet at a social function – for example, a local Chamber of Commerce meeting.

The analysis will need to assess the opportunities that such links and networks present. Occasionally, there may also be threats from arrangements. In analysing them, it is the *strength or weakness* of the relationship that matters. For example, in some parts of the world such as Japan and Korea, the networks are called *keiretsu* and *chaebol*, respectively, and have provided strong mutual support to those companies that belong to them. In some services, such as international banking, it is the strength of the network that provides the competitive advantage for those involved in it and excludes those that are not.[33]

3.8.3 Opportunities and threats from formal co-operative linkages

Formal co-operative linkages can take many business forms but are usually bound together by some form of legal contract. They differ from the networks described above in the higher degree of formality and permanence of the link with the organisation. They are shown in alliances, joint ventures, joint shareholdings and many other deals that exist to provide competitive advantage and mutual support over many years. The benefits and problems of such linkages are explored in Section 5.6. Some companies like the UK retailer Marks & Spencer, the Japanese car manufacturer Toyota and the Italian clothing company Benetton have developed such linkages into vital contributors to the uniqueness of their strategies. Suppliers, distributors and other formal co-operators with such companies provide essential products and services at lower prices and higher service levels than those offered to others in the industry. Essentially, formal co-operative linkages develop out of many years of discussion and understanding. They are very difficult for other companies to copy.[34] The *strengths and weaknesses* of such linkages should therefore be measured in terms of their depth, longevity and degree of mutual trust. Although the main interest may come from opportunities offered by such formal linkages, threats may arise from those developed by competitors.

3.8.4 The opportunities and threats presented by complementors

Definition ▶ **Complementors are those companies whose products add more value to the products of the base organisation than they would derive from their own products by themselves.**[35] For example, computer hardware companies are worth little without the software that goes with them – one product *complements* the other. In strategic terms, there may be real benefits from developing new complementor opportunities that enhance both parties and contribute further to the links that exist between them. Typically, complementors come from different industries with different resources and skills that work together to present new and sustainable *joint offerings* to customers. Again, it is the *strengths and weaknesses* of the relationship that need to be analysed. Although the main interest may come from opportunities offered by complementors, threats may arise from the complementor linkages developed by competitors.

3.8.5 Opportunities and threats from government links and networks

Government links and networks concern the relationships that many organisations have with a country's national parliament, regional assemblies and the associated government administrations. In the case of the EU and other international treaties, these clearly extend beyond national boundaries. Such contact may be formal, through business negotiations on investment, legal issues and tax matters. It may also be informal, through representation on government/industry organisations in connection with investment and trade.

Government links and networks can be vital in tax and legal matters, such as the interpretation of competition law. Equally, governments can be important customers of organisations, for example in defence equipment and pharmaceuticals. Many organisations have come to devote significant time and effort to developing and cultivating such relationships through lobbying and other related activities. Because of the nature and role of government, it may need to remain relatively remote in its legislative and regulatory dealings with outside organisations. However, it is appropriate to evaluate the degree of co-operation or hostility between government and outside bodies. Thus outside organisations will wish to consider the *opportunities and threats* posed by government activities. These may form a significant part of their corporate strategic development, especially at very senior levels within an organisation.

3.8.6 Critical comment on Four Links Model

At least in part, such a model may not have the precision and clarity of the Five Forces Model and other competitor analyses: networks come and go, complementors may come to disagree, alliances may fall apart and democratic governments fail to be re-elected. All linkage relationships lack the simplicity of the bargaining power and competitive threat analyses of the Five Forces Model. However, the Four Links Model is essentially concerned with co-operation between organisations (see Figure 3.6). This will have many facets that go beyond simple bargaining relationships.

Developing such links is likely to involve, at least in part, an emergent approach to strategy development. Linkages may provide opportunities to experiment and develop new and original strategies. They may allow an unusual move in strategy development that will deliver sustainable competitive advantage. Hence, even though they may be imprecise and lacking in the simplicities of economic logic, such linkages deserve careful analysis.

Beyond the analysis of co-operation, companies have now come to recognise that co-operation provides new strategic opportunities. Strategic alliances, joint ventures and other forms of co-operation have been identified as possibilities for strategy development. These are explored in Chapter 5.

KEY STRATEGIC PRINCIPLES

- In addition to competing against rivals, most organisations also co-operate with other organisations. Such co-operation can deliver sustainable competitive advantage.
- The main elements that need to be analysed for co-operation are captured in the *Four Links Model*: informal co-operative links and networks, formal co-operative links, complementors and government links and networks.
- *Informal co-operative links and networks* are the range of contacts that arise from organisations joining together informally for a common purpose. *Formal co-operative linkages* are usually bound by some form of legal contract - examples include alliances and joint ventures. *Complementors* are those companies whose products add more value to the products of the base organisation than they would derive from their own products by themselves. *Government links and networks* concern the relationships that exist between national and international governments and organisations, including those concerning tax, legislation and formal government purchasing.
- Such relationships can be measured by the strength of the linkage in the case of the first three. In the case of government, they may be better measured by considering the opportunities and threats posed by the relationship. All such links are often less structured and formalised than those involving competitor analysis but may represent significant areas of long-term competitive advantage.

3.9 ANALYSING ONE OR MORE IMMEDIATE COMPETITORS IN DEPTH

Video Part 4c

In any analysis of competitors and their relationship to the organisation, it is useful to analyse some immediate and close competitors: this is often called competitor profiling. The purpose is to identify the competitive advantages (and disadvantages) of the organisation against its competitors.

3.9.1 What are the sustainable competitive advantages of our competitors?

Definition ▶ **Sustainable competitive advantage is an advantage over competitors that cannot easily be imitated.** Broad surveys of competitive forces are useful in strategy analysis. But it is normal to select one or two companies for more detailed examination to identify the competitive advantage of our company against one or two rivals. The reason is that sustainable competitive advantage becomes more precise and meaningful when we make a specific analysis of our competitors. Some rival companies will have competitive advantages that make them formidable opponents; for example, well-respected brand names like Coca-Cola and Volkswagen, specialist technologies such as laser printer production at the Japanese company Canon, and unique locations of hotels and restaurants, such as those owned by McDonald's. We return to the topics of competitive advantage and strategic resources in Chapter 4. We focus in this section on analysing the competitive advantages of our competitors in the strategic environment.

3.9.2 Competitor profiling

As a starting point, it is useful to undertake competitor profiling – that is, the basic analysis of a leading competitor, covering its objectives, resources, market strength and current strategies.

In many markets, there will be more than one competitor and it will not be possible to analyse them all. It will be necessary to make a choice – usually the one or two that represent the most direct threat. In public service organisations where the competition may be for *resources* rather than for *customers*, the same principle can be adopted, with the choice being made among the agencies competing for funds. In small businesses, the need to understand competitors is just as great, although here it may be more difficult to identify which company will pose the most direct threat; a *typical* competitor may be selected in these circumstances. Once the choice has been made, the following aspects of the competitor's organisation need to be explored:

- *Objectives.* If the competitor is seeking sales growth or market share growth, this may involve an aggressive stance in the market place. If the company is seeking profit growth, it may choose to achieve this by investing in new plant or by some other means that might take time to implement. If this is the case, there will be less of an immediate impact on others in the market place, but new plant may mean lower costs and a longer-term impact on prices. Company annual reports and press statements may be helpful here in defining what the competitor says it wants to do. These need to be treated with some caution, however, since the company may be bluffing or using some other competitive technique.
- *Resources.* The scale and size of the company's resources are an important indicator of its competitive threat – perhaps it has superior or inferior technology, perhaps over-manning at its plants, perhaps financial problems. Chapter 4 will provide a more detailed checklist in terms of competitive advantage.
- *Past record of performance.* Although this may be a poor guide to the future, it is direct evidence that is publicly available through financial statements and stockbrokers' reports.
- *Current products and services.* Many companies buy competing products or services for the sole purpose of tearing them apart. They analyse customers, quality, performance, after-sales service, promotional material and some will even interview former employees – unethical perhaps, but it does happen.
- *Links with other organisations.* Joint members, alliances and other forms of co-operation may deliver significant competitive advantage.
- *Present strategies.* Attitudes to subjects such as innovation, leading customers, finance and investment, human resource management, market share, cost reduction, product range, pricing and branding all deserve investigation.

Competitor profiling is time-consuming but vital to the development of strategic management. Some larger companies employ whole departments whose sole task is to monitor leading competitors. Small businesses also often have an acute awareness of their competitors, although this may be derived more informally at trade meetings, social occasions, exhibitions and so on. In strategic management, it is vital to gain a 'feel' for competitors.

3.9.3 Emergent perspectives on competition

One of the main dangers of competitive profiling is that it will be seen as essentially static. In practice, all organisations are changing all the time. Moreover, the competitive profiling process should be regarded as one of discovery and one that never finishes. Emergent perspectives on competitor analysis, which emphasise this changing nature, will deliver useful insights, especially where the environment is changing rapidly. For example, emergent perspectives are *essential* when analysing internet competitors in the recorded music industry – see, for example, Case 13 in Part 6.

3.9.4 Outcome of competitor profiling

However imprecisely, it is important to draw up a clear statement of the competitive advantages held by a rival organisation compared to ourselves. A useful means of summarising this is the SWOT analysis – see Section 8.1.

KEY STRATEGIC PRINCIPLES

- An environmental analysis needs to identify the competitive advantages of rival companies. This is undertaken using competitor profiling. It will seek to identify the competitive advantages by focusing on one or two rival companies in depth.
- More generally, it will explore the objectives, resources, past performance, current products and services, and present strategies of one or two competitors.
- Competitor profiling should be regarded as an ongoing task. Its emergent nature is particularly important in fast-moving markets.

3.10 ANALYSING THE CUSTOMER AND MARKET SEGMENTATION

Video Part 4c

Since customers generate the revenues that keep the organisation in existence and deliver its profits, customers are crucial in strategic management. In this context it is perhaps surprising that much greater emphasis has been given in some aspects of strategic development to *competition* rather than to the customer.[36] The reason is that the focus of the purchase decision for the customer is a competitive selection between the different products or services on offer. While this is undoubtedly true, it is easy to lose sight of the direct strategic importance of the customer.

There are three useful dimensions to an analysis of the customer:

1 identification of the customer and the market;
2 market segmentation and its strategic implications;
3 market positioning usually within a segment.

3.10.1 Identification of the customer and the market

Back in the 1960s, Levitt[37] wrote a famous article that argued that the main reason some organisations were in decline was because they had become too heavily product-oriented, and were not sufficiently customer-oriented. As a result, they defined their customer base too narrowly. To help this process, a useful distinction can be made between:[38]

- *immediate customer base* – for example, those travelling on railways; and
- *wider customer franchise* – for example, those travelling by public transport, including railways, aircraft and buses.

In order to define accurately this aspect of the environment it is important to develop strategies that identify customers and competitors. Ultimately, if the market environment is incorrectly defined, then competitors may creep up and steal customers without the company realising it until it is too late. Furthermore, it is vital to analyse *future* customers as well as the *current* customer profile.

Case study: *Two methods of segmenting products in the European ice cream market.*

3.10.2 Market segmentation

For many markets, customer analysis needs to move beyond the consideration of basic markets to an analysis of specific parts of a market – *market segmentation* – and to the competitive stance of organisations within the segment – their *market positioning*, which is explored in the next section.

Definition ▶ **Market segmentation is the identification of specific groups (or segments) of customers who respond to competitive strategies differently from other groups.**

The basic sequence for exploring the approach is shown in Figure 3.7. It employs a *prescriptive* approach as a first step in order to explore the elements. In practice, the sequence is likely to be more experimental and, in this sense, *emergent*, because it is often necessary to explore a number of positioning areas: this is also outlined in Figure 3.7.

The three prescriptive stages are:

1 *Identify market segment(s)*. Identification of specialist needs of segments will lead to customer profiles of those in the segments.

2 *Evaluate segment(s)*. Some segments are likely to be more attractive than others. They need to be identified and targeted.

3 *Position within market segment.* Within the segment, companies will then need to develop a differential advantage over competitors. See the example in Figure 3.8.

In the development of customer strategy, customer analysis will often move rapidly to an examination of market segmentation.[39] Market segmentation may be defined as the identification of specific groups (or segments) of customers who respond differently from other groups to competitive strategies. The advantages of identifying a market segment include:

- Strength in (and possibly dominance of) a group, even though the overall market is large. It may be more profitable to have a large share of a group than a small share of the main market. Thus competitive advantage may be stronger in a segment than in the broader market.
- Closer matching of customer needs and the organisation's resources through targeting the segment. This will enhance sustainable competitive advantage.
- Concentration of effort on a smaller area, so that the company's resources can be employed more effectively.

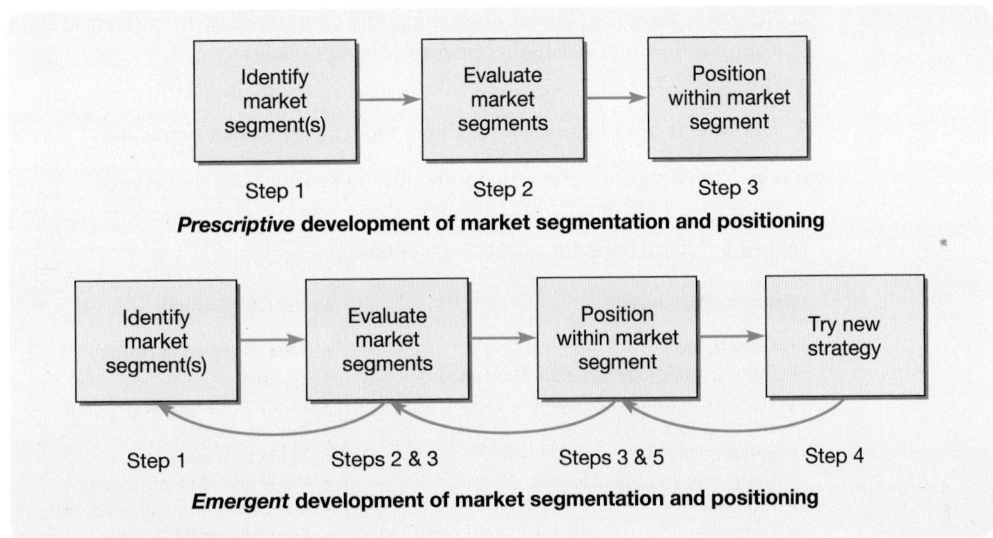

Figure 3.7 Market segmentation and position

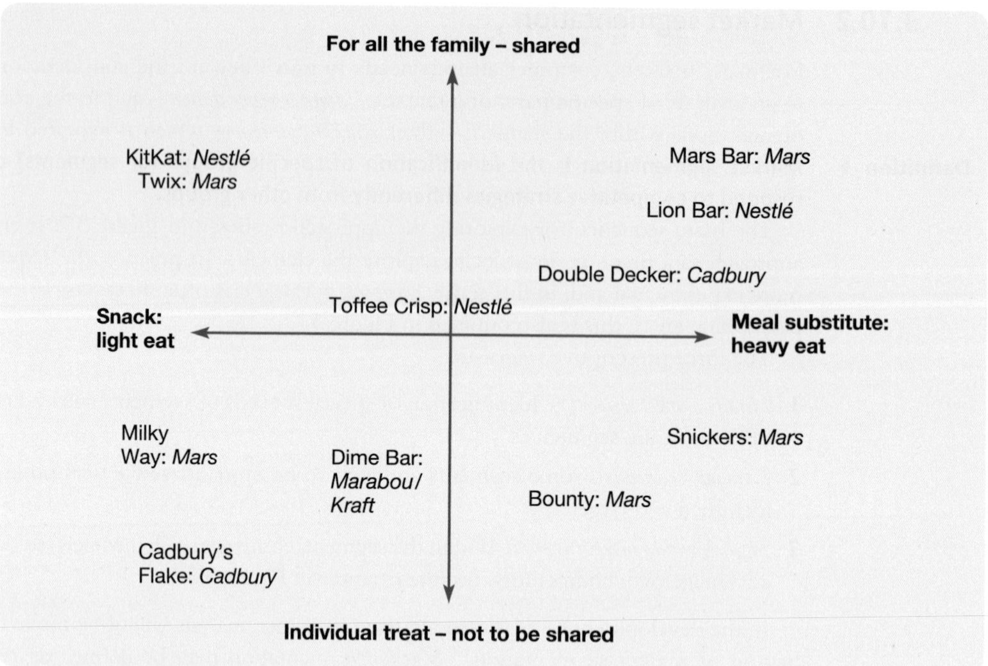

Figure 3.8 An example of market positioning – chocolate countlines

Hence, from a strategic viewpoint, the key advantage of market segmentation is probably the ability to dominate a sector of a market and then target benefits that will sustain this position, as in the case of Dyson's domination of the premium-priced vacuum cleaner segment.

Typical bases for segmentation in consumer and industrial markets are listed in Table 3.5. However, markets can be segmented by any criteria that prove helpful and do not necessarily need to conform to this list.

Having established the segments, strategic customer analysis then proceeds to evaluate the *usefulness* of each segment: Step 2 in Figure 3.7. It is not enough for a segment to be different. There are four important characteristics of any segment if it is to be useful in strategic customer analysis. It must be:

1 *Distinguishable.* Customers must be distinguishable so that they can be isolated in some way.
2 *Relevant to purchasing.* The distinguishing criteria must relate to differences in market demand. For example, they may pay higher prices for higher quality.
3 *Sufficiently large.* If the segment is too small, then it will not justify the resources needed to reach it.
4 *Reachable.* It must be possible to direct the strategy to that segment.

It is also important to assess the future growth prospects of the segment.

Table 3.5 Typical bases for market segmentation

Consumer products	Industrial products
• Geographic • Demographic (age, sex, education, etc.) • Socio-economic and income • Ethnic group • Benefits sought • Usage rate and brand loyalty • Attitudes • Lifestyle • Situation (where the consumption takes place)	• Area or region of country • End-use • Customer business • Buying situation • Market served • Value added by customer • Source of competitive advantage (price, service, etc.) • Emphasis on R&D and innovation • Professional membership

KEY STRATEGIC PRINCIPLES

- There are three prescriptive stages in developing market segmentation and positioning: identify potential segments, evaluate and select segment(s), and position within segment(s).
- Market segmentation is the identification of specific groups of customers who respond differently from other groups to competitive strategies. They can be important in strategy development because they provide the opportunity to dominate part of the market.
- Identification of gaps in segment provision may provide the basis of new strategic opportunities.

3.10.3 Competitive positioning[40]

Although a useful segment has been identified, this does not in itself resolve the organisation's strategy. The competitive position within the segment then needs to be explored, because only this will show how the organisation will compete within the segment. **Definition ▶** **Competitive positioning is the choice of differential advantage possessed by an organisation that allows it to compete and survive in a market place or in a segment of a market place.** A typical example of positioning is shown in Figure 3.8.

For example, both the Mars Company (USA) and Nestlé (Switzerland) compete in the market for chocolate products. However, the Mars' product Snickers is positioned as a 'meal substitute' – it can be eaten in place of a meal, whereas the Nestlé product KitKat is positioned as a 'snack' – it can be eaten as a break but is not substantial enough to be a substitute for a meal. Competitive positioning is thus the choice of differential advantage that the product or service will possess against its competitors. To develop positioning, it is useful to follow a two-stage process – first identify the segment gaps, second identify positioning within segments.

Identification of segmentation gaps and their competitive positioning implications

From a strategy viewpoint, the most useful strategic analysis often emerges by exploring where there are *gaps* in the segments of an industry: amongst others, Porter[41] and Ohmae[42] recommend this route. The starting point for such work is to map out the current segmentation position and then place companies and their products into the segments: it should then become clear where segments exist that are not served or are poorly served by current products. This is shown in Exhibit 3.5 using the European ice cream case as an example.

EXHIBIT 3.5

New or under-utilised segment gaps: Unilever's presence in the European ice cream market, early 2000s

Market basis for possible segmentation

	Buyer type 1	Buyer type 2	Buyer type 3, etc.
Product variety 1			
Product variety 2			
Product variety 3, etc.			

Step 1: Existing segments with Unilever's European presence shown

	Grocery supermarkets	Small grocery stores	Restaurants and takeaways	Newsagents and leisure facilities
Superpremium	✔ market test only			✔ few
Premium	✔	✔		✔ most
Regular	✔			
Economy	✔	✔ some		

Step 2: Some possible new segments in addition to the above

	Garages	Temporary facilities at sporting and cultural events	Factory canteens and restaurants: contract catering
Superpremium		✔	
Premium	✔		
Regular			✔
Economy			✔

Note: For the sake of clarity, only Unilever's presence is shown in the above. Moreover, the example is *illustrative only* and may not represent the actual practice of the Unilever subsidiaries in each country. Further segmentation analyses based on criteria such as the geographical country might also produce some useful additional information.

Comment: It will be evident that there are some gaps in the existing coverage of the market. The segmentation criteria outlined in the text above could be used to assess whether it would be worthwhile filling the gaps. One obvious area where Unilever could take action was in the superpremium sector.

Identifying the positioning within the segment[43]

From a strategy perspective, some gaps may be more attractive than others. For example, they may have limited competition or poorly supported products. In addition, some gaps may possess a clear advantage in terms of competitive positioning. Others may not. To explore the development of positioning, we can return to our earlier example of two chocolate countlines from Nestlé and Mars. The full positioning map for the range of such products was shown earlier in the chapter in Figure 3.8.

The process of developing positioning of chocolate countlines runs as follows:

1 *Perceptual mapping* – in-depth qualitative research on actual and prospective customers on the way that they make their decisions in the market place, for example, strong versus weak, cheap versus expensive, modern versus traditional. In the case of chocolate the dimensions of meal/snack and family/individual were established.

2 *Positioning.* Brands or products are then placed on the map using the research dimensions. Figure 3.8 presents the existing configuration.

3 *Options development.* Take existing and new products and use their existing strengths and weaknesses to devise possible new positions on the map. Figure 3.9 shows some gaps for some companies and some products that have an unclear position – Toffee Crisp at the time of the research.

4 *Testing* – first with simple statements with customers, then at a later stage in the market place.

It will be evident that this is essentially an emergent rather than a prescriptive process, involving experimentation with actual and potential customers.

KEY STRATEGIC PRINCIPLES

- Competitive positioning is the choice of differential advantage that the product or service will possess against its competitors.
- The sequence for developing competitive positioning has four main steps: perceptual mapping, positioning, options development and testing. The process is essentially emergent rather than prescriptive.

Conclusion: the danger of over-relying on strategic environmental analysis.

CASE STUDY 3.5

Arçelik aims for Europe

When Arçelik's home market demand declined in 2000, Turkey's leading domestic appliance company aimed its export strategy at Europe. This case explains its four main strategies and how they made the company the third largest in Europe.

Background: domestic strength in the 1990s

Arçelik has been making domestic appliances – washing machines, refrigerators, freezers and ovens – since the 1950s. It is controlled by one of Turkey's leading and most respected industrial groups, Koç Holdings. The holding company had sales of $43 billion in 2010 and, within this, Arçelik had sales of $3.5 billion – by any standards, an important company.

Back in the 1990s, Arçelik's domestic appliance business had been steadily expanded to dominate its Turkish home market. The country itself had a population of over 70 million with rapidly rising wealth. Arçelik's nearest competitor was another Turkish company called Vestel. But Arçelik's strategies were so successful that it had almost four times the sales of its rival. There were four key strategies:

1 branding under the Arçelik and Beko brand names;
2 quality-driven products;
3 efficient low-cost production;
4 extensive and dominant distribution outlets in all the main Turkish towns.

Arçelik's strategy in Turkey relies on distribution through its own retail stores. But this retail strategy would take too long and be too expensive to set up across Europe.

Change in the strategic environment: Turkey's economy takes a downturn

Around year 2000, Turkey's economy took a severe downturn. Arçelik was already exporting its domestic appliances outside Turkey in small quantities, but this only amounted to 15 per cent of its business. Suddenly, the company was faced with a serious profit problem. Economies of scale are a key factor for success in the domestic appliance business, but the local Turkish market was in decline. The company decided to export more of its products. But which countries and with what strategies?

Arçelik's export strategies in year 2000

Western European markets for domestic appliances - like Germany, the UK and France - were large but relatively mature. The lack of growth made it more difficult for new companies to enter, especially those from outside the European Union (EU). However, the EU had agreed to reduce its trade barriers with Turkey back in 1996, so EU markets were at least open to Arçelik in 2000. The problem was rather different in Eastern Europe. Markets were just beginning to open up after the fall of communism. Wealth and demand for consumer products was rising, but there were few good manufacturers.

As a result of these differences, Arçelik decided on a two-pronged strategy. In Western Europe, it would export domestic appliances from its Turkish factories and acquire some European brand names. In the east, it would also export but would also set up factories that would serve regional markets. The outcome was a significant increase in international sales - see Figure 3.9. Much of this increase was founded on the four home strategies outlined above. However, there was one difference. Arçelik judged that it would take too long and be too expensive to copy the home market competitive advantage of its own shops and distribution outlets. It would simply sell Arçelik products through existing stores.

Arçelik's strategies in Western Europe

In order to gain a rapid foothold, Arçelik bought a series of small companies in France, Germany and the UK. These acquisitions were not wholly successful because the company needed to manufacture its products from its efficient plants in Turkey so it was really only buying brand names and reputations such as its purchases of the Flavel brand in the UK and the Grundig name in Germany. There were also reported to be other brand and company acquisitions, for example Arctic in Romania, Blomberg in Germany and Elektra Bregenz in Austria with most of these becoming sales and service companies for the Arçelik/Beko range. In addition to its acquisitions, Arçelik had to make another strategic decision: whether to make OEM goods or sell branded products.

Original equipment manufacture (OEM) refers to products that are made by one manufacturer and then sold to a second company who will re-brand them with the name of the second company. For example, Arçelik had the opportunity to make washing machines which were then sold in the UK under the brand name of a well-known retailer such as Tesco. The problem with OEM is that such contracts depend largely on price. Customers can switch over time to rivals offering lower prices. Competitive advantage is therefore low. By contrast, branding is initially more expensive in terms with, for example, the costs of advertising and sponsorship. However, it has several advantages. It allows companies like Arçelik to develop innovative and patented products and to develop a widely respected brand name over time. Importantly, branding and quality products were closer to Arçelik's core competencies back in its home country and thus familiar strategies for this company to develop and manage.

Initially, Arçelik undertook some OEM contracts. But its main strategy in Western Europe was brand building with the *Beko* brand name: the Turkish name Arçelik had some problems in terms of spelling the specialist Turkish letter ç and pronunciation in Western markets. Its acquisitions were supported but the main strategic effort was put behind the brand name Beko. Arguably, the acquisitions were expensive and unnecessary in the long term. Moreover, Arçelik had registered over 130 patents across Europe in a range of domestic appliance applications, thus delivering potential competitive advantages for its Beko branded product range.

Over the years from 2001, Beko slowly built its branded sales in some Western European countries. By 2010, it had become the second largest brand in the UK using advertising and sponsorship, strong retail distribution, good design and relatively low prices. It was less successful in Europe's biggest market, Germany, where the international and local brand competition was particularly strong. International brands included Electrolux and domestic brands included the German companies Bosch and Miele.

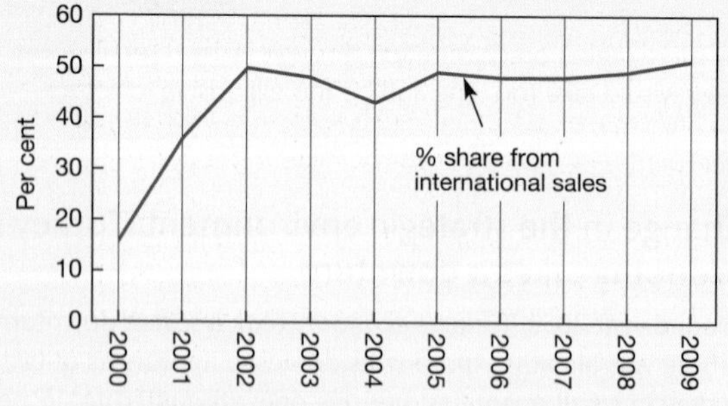

Figure 3.9 The outcome of Arçelik's export strategy

Source: author from Koç holding company report and accounts and research by Dr Tanses Gulsoy of Beykent University.

Arçelik in Eastern Europe and beyond

Given the low labour costs and potential for higher growth in Eastern Europe, Arçelik's strategy in this area was different. There were no acquisitions because there were no attractive companies. However, there were some opportunities, to set up new factories and build brands. As a result, by 2010, Arçelik had set up new plant in Romania and Russia and its brands held 35 per cent of the Romanian market and nearly 10 per cent of the Polish market.

Back in 2000, Arçelik opened up a sales office in China. Market demand was such that the company decided to expand its operations in 2007 by opening up its first factory in that country. It then followed this with a small number of Chinese domestic appliance stores - similar to those back in Turkey.

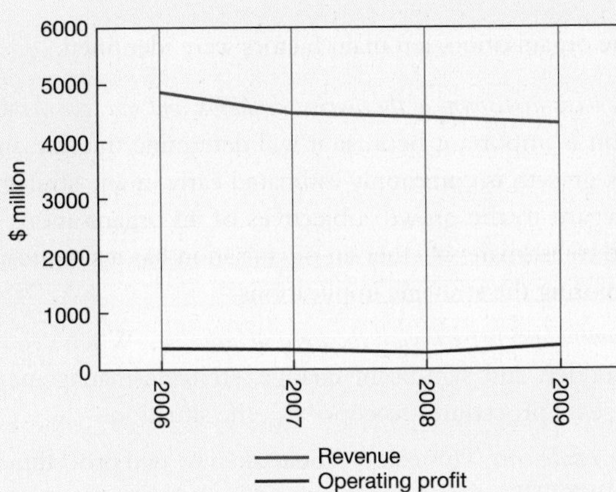

Figure 3.10 Arçelik's profit downturn with declining national economies

Source: author from Koç holding company report and accounts.

Arçelik's profit record

Although the company made major advances in Europe in the period to 2010, it also suffered a dip in profits over this time - see Figure 3.10. In 2008, its profits were still based largely on its Turkish production plants and had declined by 25 per cent compared with two years earlier. This was primarily due to a drop in sales as European market demand declined as a result of international economic pressures: economies of scale can be affected disproportionately by declines in sales. Arçelik reacted by new cost cutting and efficiency strategies inside the company: better inventory management and improved stock turnover resulting in lower working capital. By 2011, Arçelik had become the third largest domestic appliance brand in Western Europe behind Electrolux from Sweden and Indesit from Italy.

Arçelik has been using its R&D facilities to develop new, greener domestic appliances. The Koç group has a strong record of sustainability projects.

 This case was written by Richard Lynch from public information only. However, he acknowledges the considerable help in preparing this case from his co-research colleagues, Dr Tanses Gulsoy of Beykent University, Istanbul and Professor Dr Ozlem Ozkanli of Ankara University, Ankara.

Case questions

1 What strategic environmental factors have influenced Arçelik's strategic decisions? And with what outcomes?

2 What were Arçelik's competitive advantages? Why was OEM inconsistent with these? Given its profit problems in 2008, would you have advised Arçelik to change strategy and pursue some OEM contracts?

3 Thinking about the various possible growth markets around the world, would you advise Arçelik to open up more country markets as part of its growth strategy? Or should the company concentrate primarily on its existing countries? You can assume that Arçelik is typical of many companies with only a limited amount of resources - both financial and human - to undertake further expansion.

CRITICAL REFLECTION

What purpose is served by analysing the strategic environment?

There are two fundamental assumptions that underpin this chapter. First, strategic analysis assumes that it is possible to learn from past events. This assumption is important because strategy is essentially about future actions. Second, such a study implicitly assumes that the future is predictable in some way - otherwise, there would be little point in drawing any lessons from the analysis. Both these assumptions may rest on shaky foundations.

'Learning from the past' may examine a strategic environment with strategic perceptions and definitions that no longer apply: for example, the traditional market for air travel has been revolutionised by redefining it as being just like getting on a bus where aircraft seats are readily available without lengthy booking procedures. In the same way, 'Predicting the future' always runs the risk of making an incorrect prediction: for example, who would have predicted 15 years ago how the internet would develop?

Perhaps, in developing new strategies, we cannot learn much from the past. Perhaps we cannot usefully predict the future. In which case, what purpose is served by PESTEL Analysis, Porter's Five Forces, etc.?

SUMMARY

In analysing the environment surrounding the organisation, ten main factors were identified.

- *Environmental analysis can usefully begin with a basic assessment of the market definition and size, the market growth and the market share.* Market definition is important because it will determine the size and scope of the strategic opportunity. Market growth is commonly estimated early in any strategic analysis because of its importance with regard to the growth objectives of an organisation. A basic estimate of market share can be used to estimate whether an organisation has a significant share of a market as a starting point in exploring the strategic implications.
- *A general consideration of the nature of the environment and, in particular, the degree of turbulence.* When events are particularly uncertain and prone to sudden and significant change, strategic management needs to become more flexible and organise its procedures to cope with the situation.
- *A general analysis of the factors that will affect many industries.* This can be undertaken by two procedures: the PESTEL analysis and scenarios. The PESTEL analysis explores political, economic, socio-cultural, technological, environmental and legal influences on the organisation. It is important when undertaking such an analysis to develop a shortlist of only the most important items, not a long list under every heading. In analysing the role and influence of government on strategy, the E–S–P Paradigm – Environment, System, Policies – can form a useful structure for this purpose. Influencing government policy may form an important element of strategy. In developing scenarios, it should be recognised that they provide a different view of conceivable future events, rather than predict the future.
- *Growth characteristics* can be explored using the industry life cycle concept. Markets are divided into a series of development stages: introduction, growth, maturity and decline. In addition, the maturity stage may be subject to the cyclical variations associated with general economic or other factors over which the company has little control.
- Different stages of the life cycle demand different corporate strategies. The early stages probably require greater investment in R&D and marketing to develop and explain the product. The later stages should be more profitable on a conventional view of the life cycle. However, there is an argument that takes a more unconventional stance: it suggests that it is during the mature phase that investment should increase in order to restore growth.
- *Key factors for success in an industry*: identifying these can help focus strategy development on those areas that really matter. They can conveniently be considered under three headings: customers, competition and corporation. By 'corporation' is meant the resources of the organisation. Key factors can be found in any area of the organisation and relate to skills, competitive advantage, competitive resources of an organisation in the industry, special technologies or customer contacts. Four criticisms of key factors have been made: identification, causality of relationships, dangers of generalising, and disregard of emergent perspectives. Caution is therefore needed in their application.
- *A Five Forces Analysis.* This will involve an examination of buyers, suppliers, new entrants, substitutes and the competition in the industry. The aim is to analyse the balance of power between each force and the organisation in the industry.
- *A Four Links Analysis* of those outside bodies cooperating with the organisation. This will include a study of the complementors, networks and legal links that the organisation has with its environment. The purpose is to analyse the relative strengths of such links and their ability to enhance the competitive advantages of the organisation.
- *A study of selected direct competitors.* An environmental analysis needs to identify the competitive advantages of rival companies. This is undertaken using competitor profiling. It will seek to identify the competitive advantages by focusing on one or two rival companies in depth. More generally, it will explore the objectives, resources, past performance, current products and services, and present strategies of one or two competitors. Such a study needs to recognise the fluid and changing nature of competitors and their resources.

- *A study of customers, market segmentation and positioning.* The final area of analysis is concerned with actual and potential customers and their importance to the organisation. Segmentation of markets derives from customer analysis and plays an important role in strategic management development. Positioning then determines how products will compete to attract customers in a particular part of the market.

QUESTIONS

1 Using Case 3.4 and your judgement, determine the degree of turbulence in the Hollywood film industry. Give reasons for your views.

2 Undertake a general environmental analysis of an industry of your choice, using both the PESTEL format and scenarios to draw out the major strategic issues.

3 Develop and compare the key factors for success in the following three industries: the computer industry (see companies like Acer and Hewlett-Packard in Case 11 in Part 6), the ice cream industry (Chapter 10) and the Indian motorcycle industry (Chapter 3).

4 For the Indian motorcycle industry, analyse the competitive forces within the industry using the Five Forces Model. Identify also any forms of co-operation in the industry using a Four Links Analysis.

5 Based on your answers to the previous questions, what strategic advice would you offer Bajaj? Use Section 3.7.6 to assist you.

6 Undertake a life cycle analysis of an industry of your choice. What strategic conclusions would you draw for organisations in the industry, if any? Comment specifically on the difficulties of this approach.

7 Prepare a full environmental analysis for an industry of your choice and make recommendations on its future strategic management.

8 Undertake a customer analysis for your own organisation. What segments can you identify? What role is played by customer service and quality? What strategic conclusions can you draw?

9 Do you agree with the statement that stable environments favour prescriptive approaches to strategy whereas turbulent environments demand emergent strategies? Consider carefully the impact technology may have on a stable environment and the problem of long-term investment, even in turbulent industries - remember Blockbuster at the beginning of this chapter.

10 To what extent can competitive analytical techniques be applied to the public sector and charitable institutions?

FURTHER READING

M E Porter's *Competitive Strategy: Techniques for Analysing Industries and Competitors* (The Free Press, Harvard, MA, 1980) has careful and detailed studies for analysis of the immediate competitive environment. Mona Makhija's paper (2003) 'Comparing the resource-based and market-based views of the firm: empirical evidence from Czech privatisation', *Strategic Management Journal*, Vol 24, pp 433–451 presents some useful comments on the Porter approach as well as a more general comparison that is also relevant also to Chapter 4.

Professor Porter's article, 'How competitive forces shape strategy' (1979) *Harvard Business Review*, March–April, pp 136–145, is probably the classic short analysis here, but note that it says little or nothing about the importance of co-operation.

Finally, for a comprehensive review of the underpinning economic theory, read Séan Rickard's Chapter 5 entitled 'Industrial Organisation Economics Perspective' in the edited text: Mark Jenkins and Veronique Ambrosini with Nardine Collier (2007) *Advanced Strategic Management*, 2nd edn, Palgrave Macmillan, Basingstoke, pp 61–82.

NOTES AND REFERENCES

1 Sources for the Blockbuster case: *Financial Times*: 8 November 2011, p 23; 11 October 2011, p 17; 10 January 2012, p 18; 6 December 2012, p 28; Blockbuster website: http://web.archive.org/web/19961224035012/http://blockbuster.com/; *Blockbuster press releases*: 31 December 2003; 3 January 2007; 23 September 2010; *CNN Money*, 1 July 2003, 'He Began Blockbuster. So What? David Cook created a household name, but he refuses to become one', Joshua Hyatt; *New York Times*, 8 April 2011, 'Other Retailers Find Ex-Blockbuster Stores Just Right', Stephanie Clifford; *Los Angeles Times*, 7 April 2011, Dish network wins bidding for assets of bankrupt Blockbuster; *Digital Trends*: http://www.digitaltrends.com/home-theater/dish-network-shutting-down-a-third-of-all-remaining-blockbuster-stores/#!bh97ek.

2 Porter, M E (1980) *Competitive Strategy*, The Free Press, New York.

3 Andrews, K (1987) *The Concept of Corporate Strategy*, Irwin, Homewood, IL.

4 Many strategy texts (including previous editions of this one!) set out in great depth various environmental concepts and forget that it is useful to begin with some basic data.

5 Levitt, T (1960) 'Marketing myopia', *Harvard Business Review*, July–August, pp 45–56. Levitt's paper challenged the traditional definitions of the market.

6 There may be tautological problems here, but it is not appropriate to explore these at this early stage in strategy analysis. Suffice to say that it is possible to pursue this academic debate by starting with the well-known text by Buzzell, R D and Gale, B T (1987) *The PIMS Principles*, The Free Press, London. Follow this up with Baker, M (1993) *Marketing Strategy and Management*, 2nd edn, Macmillan, London.

7 Porter, M E (1980) Op. cit., Ch 2.

8 The early part of this section is based on Ansoff, I and MacDonnell, E (1990) *Implanting Strategic Management*, 2nd edn, Prentice Hall, Englewood Cliffs, NJ.

9 D'Aveni, R (1994) *Hypercompetitive Rivalries*, Free Press, New York.

10 Simon, H 'The corporation: will it be managed by machine?', in Leavitt, H and Pondy, L (eds) (1964) *Readings in Managerial Psychology*, University of Chicago Press, Chicago, IL, pp 592–617.

11 Baden-Fuller, C and Stopford, J (1992) *Rejuvenating the Mature Business*, Routledge, Ch 2.

12 Aaker, D R (1992) *Strategic Marketing Management*, 3rd edn, Wiley, New York, p 236.

13 Smallwood, J E (1973) 'The product life cycle: a key to strategic marketing planning', *MSU Business Topics*, Winter, pp 29–35.

14 Baker, M (1993) *Marketing Strategy and Management*, 2nd edn, Macmillan, London, p 100 *et seq*. presents a short defence and interesting discussion of the main areas.

15 Dallah, N Y and Yuspeh, S (1976) 'Forget the product life cycle concept', *Harvard Business Review*, January–February, p 101 *et seq*.

16 Sources for the Bajaj case: *Financial Times*: 12 May 1999, p 31; 4 September 2007, p 14; 9 January 2008, p 30. *DNA Money Mumbai*: 24 November 2007, p 27; 26 November 2007, p 25. *The Economist*, 10 January 2008. *Economic Times*, 11 January 2008 – extracted from the *Times of India* website. Websites: www.bajaj.com and www.herohonda.com. Bajaj Auto annual report and accounts 2010: all the market data is sourced from this well-presented and clearly written document.

17 Ohmae, K (1983) *The Mind of the Strategist*, Penguin, Harmondsworth, Ch 3.

18 Porter, M E (1985) *Competitive Advantage*, The Free Press, New York, Ch 7.

19 Kay, J (1993) *Foundations of Corporate Success*, Oxford University Press, Oxford, Chs 5 to 8.

20 Amit, R and Schoemaker, P (1993) 'Strategic assets and organizational rent', *Strategic Management Journal*, Vol 14, pp 33–46.

21 Ohmae, K (1983) Op. cit., p 96.

22 Ghemawat, P (1991) *Commitment*, The Free Press, New York.

23 Porter, M E (1980) Op. cit. Note that Porter's work owes much to the writings of Professor Joel Bain and others in the 1950s on industrial economies. However, it was Porter who gave this earlier material its strategic focus. See also Porter's article, 'How competitive forces shape strategy' (1979) *Harvard Business Review*, March–April, pp 136–145, which is a useful summary of the main points from the early part of his book.

24 Op. cit., p 4.

25 Porter (1980) actually refers in his book to 'six' areas and then goes on to list seven!

26 Cusumano, M and Takeishi, A (1991) 'Supplier relations and management: a survey of Japanese, Japanese transplant and US auto plants', *Strategic Management Journal*, Vol 12, pp 563–588.

27 Nielsen, A C (1988) *International Food and Drug Store Trends*, Nielsen, Oxford.

28 Aaker, D (1992) Op. cit.

29 Baker, M (1993) Op. cit

30 Harvey-Jones, J (1991) *Getting it Together*, Heinemann, London, Ch 14.

31 Porter (1980) Op. cit., Chs 7 and 8.

32 Reve, T (1990) 'The firm as a nexus of internal and external contracts', *The Firm as a Nexus of Treaties*, Aoki, M, Gustafson, M and Williamson, O E (eds), Sage, London. See also Kay, J (1993) *The Foundations of Corporate Success*, Oxford University Press, Oxford, Ch 5.

33 Kay, J (1993) Op. cit., p 80.

34 Kay, J (1993) Op. cit.: Ch 5 on architecture explores this topic in depth.

35 Nalebuff, B J and Brandenburger, A M (1997) *Coopetition*, HarperCollins Business, London.

36 For example, Porter, M E (1980) Op. cit.

37 Levitt, T (1960) 'Marketing myopia', *Harvard Business Review*, July–August, p 45.

38 Davidson, H (1987) *Offensive Marketing*, Penguin, Harmondsworth.

39 Aaker, D (1992) Op. cit., p 48.

40 It should be noted that, in theory at least, it is not necessary to segment a market before exploring its competitive positioning. However, it is usual and much easier to select part of a market before undertaking positioning. Many marketing strategy texts do not make this clear.

41 Porter, M E (1985) *Competitive Advantage*, The Free Press, New York, p 233.

42 Ohmae, K (1983) *The Mind of the Strategist*, Penguin, Harmondsworth, p 103.

43 Probably the best-known text exploring positioning issues in depth is: Hooley, G J and Saunders, J (1999) *Competitive Positioning*, Prentice Hall, Hemel Hempstead.

CHAPTER 4
Analysing resources and capabilities

Video and sound summary of this chapter

LEARNING OUTCOMES

When you have worked through this chapter, you will be able to:

- identify the main resources and capabilities of an organisation and the strategic decision on whether to make or buy;
- explain the concept of value added;
- analyse both the value chain and value system of an organisation and comment on their strategic significance;
- explain how resources deliver sustainable competitive advantage to the organisation;
- identify and explain the seven main concepts of sustainable competitive advantage;
- explain the roles of five special resources in the organisation and relate them to sustainable competitive advantage;
- outline three methods for improving the sustainable competitive advantage of the organisation's resources;
- identify other important resources in the organisation, especially its organisational culture.

INTRODUCTION

Analysing the resources and capabilities of an organisation involves not only exploring the role and contribution of the main resources, but also developing an understanding of two main issues: first, how resources can deliver superior profits in private companies and provide the best services in publicly owned organisations – called the delivery of *value added* in strategy; second, which resources and capabilities deliver competitive advantage to the organisation and how they can be improved over time. The resource and capabilities analysis therefore proceeds along two parallel and interconnected routes: value added and sustainable competitive advantage. Figure 4.1 identifies the elements involved. The *value-added* route explores how the organisation takes goods from its suppliers and turns them into finished goods and services that are then sold to its customers: essentially, adding value to the inputs from its suppliers is fundamental to the role of every organisation. The *competitive advantage* route attempts to find the special resources that enable the organisation to compete: how and why some resources deliver sustainable competitive advantage is crucial to strategy development.

Video Part 5

This chapter begins by exploring what precisely is meant by resources and capabilities. It then queries why organisations need to possess resources, rather than buying them in from outside. The chapter continues along two parallel routes, first exploring the concept of value-added and second examining competitive advantage and how this can be improved. The chapter also identifies the main issues related to green strategy in the section on value added.

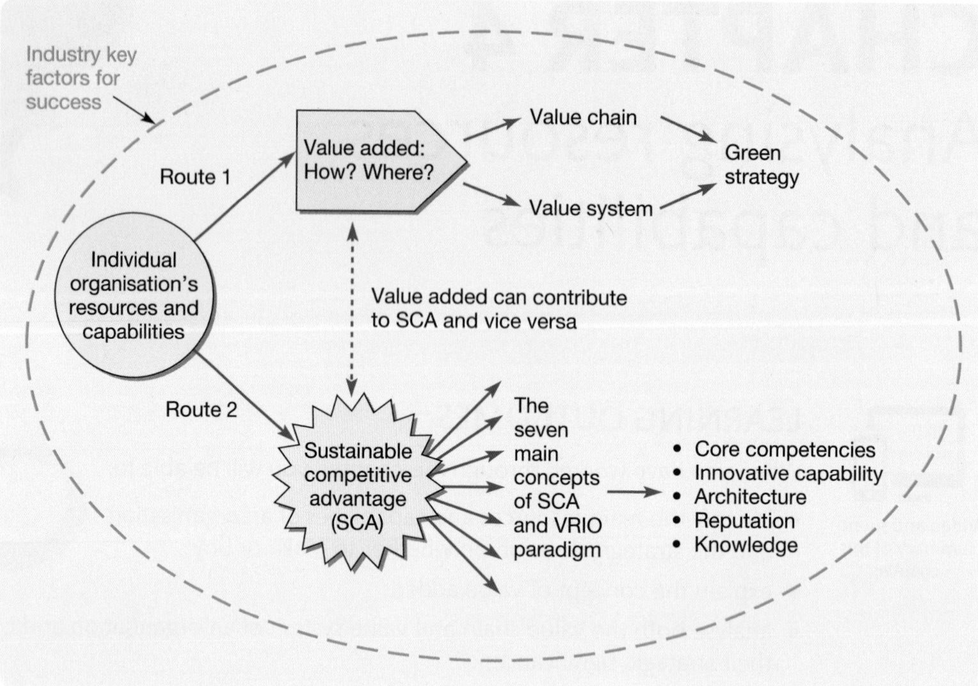

Figure 4.1 Analysing resources and capabilities

CASE STUDY 4.1

How three European companies attempt to utilise their resources and capabilities

In this case, three totally different companies are explored to see how each utilises its resources and achieves its corporate objectives. The first two companies operate in the pharmaceutical and national railway service industries, respectively; the third is a holding company with a range of activities mainly in construction, public services, mobile telephones and television broadcasting.

The three companies under consideration are the UK-based pharmaceutical company Glaxo, the Dutch national railway company Nederlandse Spoorwegen, and the French services holding company Bouygues. Each has totally different resources, skills and methods of working, and each is involved in very different environments, including pharmaceuticals, transport services and the construction of roads. The purpose of this case is to identify the *key* strategic resources – that is, those that will make a difference to the company's strategy.

Mission and objectives

As a starting point for any strategic analysis, it is important to consider *why* these three organisations are utilising the resources. What are they attempting to achieve? In principle, each is setting out to accomplish its *mission and objectives*. These need to be identified and explored.

Key resource and capability analysis

Each of these companies brings totally different types of resources, organisational skills and methods of operation to the achievement of its objectives. Figure 4.2 has used data taken from annual reports and other sources to construct the *cost profiles* for each of the three companies in this case. The costs of each major item of company expenditure are expressed as a percentage of sales, coupled with profits before tax and interest as a percentage of sales. They are calculated by taking each cost item and dividing it by the sales figure and expressing this as a percentage. The profile demonstrates how each element of *resource* in the company contributes to profit and sales.

Resources and capabilities for Glaxo

This company is one of the world's largest pharmaceutical companies. It makes a wide range of drugs, most of which are

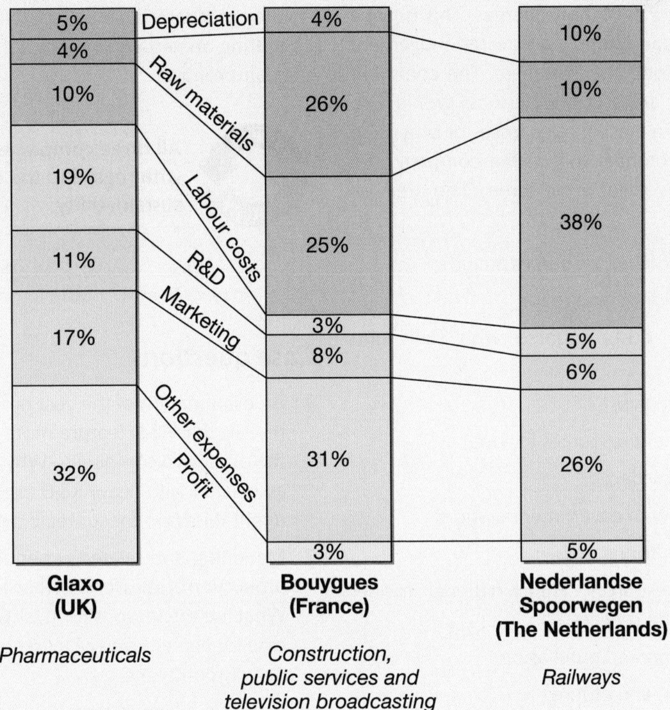

Figure 4.2 Cost profiles – costs as a percentage of sales

patented and therefore a source of competitive advantage. One of Glaxo's strategic problems is that patents do not last for ever. It therefore needs a continuing supply of new patent drugs. This means that it needs to possess a strong research and development capability. In addition, its global operations allow the company to market its products into many countries. Thus, its wide geographical coverage also offers competitive advantage.

Resources and capabilities for Nederlandse Spoorwegen

- *Increased utilisation of existing railway lines and rolling stock.* The investment in track and trains in most companies is largely complete. The key is to obtain greater usage of what is already present.
- *Marketing, sales and special prices.* These are to encourage customers to use the railways in preference to their competitors: road, air and bus traffic. This is particularly true in the Netherlands with its extensive and well-developed transport infrastructure.
- *High levels of service.* These involve the employees of the company and investment in new equipment on information and signalling to inform customers better of transport network problems.

Most national European railway companies are competing mainly within their national boundaries.[1] Resource analysis therefore needs to concentrate on national transport competitors in the first instance.

With the high fixed investment already made in track, signalling and rolling stock, strategic management has relied largely on encouraging *greater utilisation of the existing facilities* – that is, the marketing and sales activities mentioned above.

Another aspect of strategy that is important for most railway companies is *the relationship with government.* During the period from which the data shown in Figure 4.2 were taken, the Dutch railway company was receiving grants from the Netherlands government that amounted to 9 per cent of its total revenue. These were used to subsidise train fares and freight passage so that railways would be used in preference to roads.

Resources and capabilities for Bouygues

In this case, the resources and capabilities will be dictated by the precise nature of each of the activities in which the company is engaged. In theory, it will be necessary to analyse each of the hundreds of companies in the group. In practice, three areas of the company accounted for over 90 per cent of sales:

- Building and road construction 63%
- Public utilities management 15%
- Media and telecommunications 14%

For the purposes of *strategic analysis*, it is normally acceptable to ignore the remaining collection of areas. This is not a financial audit of the company, simply an overall judgement of the *main thrust* of the company's business. The comment on ignoring the remaining areas of the business would also be invalid if other areas were making huge losses or otherwise represented a significant potential shift in the company. We can identify the reasons involved in the three main areas of business:

1 Building and road construction resources include:
- raw materials for buildings and roads;
- labour construction costs coupled with skills and efficiency;
- design and engineering costs.

2 Public utilities management resources include:
- quality of services provided;
- management liaison with government owners;
- cost control and monitoring skills.

3 Media television station resources - French national channel TF1 and mobile telephone services:
- programme origination and purchasing;
- network management and costing;
- audience monitoring and assessment;
- mobile telephone service management and marketing.

It will be evident that analysing the resources in a diversified holding company is a major task. It has been simplified by concentrating on certain key areas of the business. However, this is a compromise.

All three companies have strong policies with regard to the environment and sustainability.

Case questions

1 An examination of the cost profiles of the three companies reveals that R&D feature more prominently in GSK than in the other two companies. Why is this? What risks, if any, are associated with heavy R&D expenditure? What implications might this have for strategic decisions?

2 Marketing and related expenditures are much higher as a proportion of sales for GSK than for Nederlandse Spoorwegen. What are the reasons for this? Can you make out a strategic case for higher levels of marketing expenditure at the Dutch railway company?

3 The case suggests that holding companies like Bouygues have a more complex task in managing their resources and capabilities. Do you agree?

A much more detailed case study about competitive advantage at the pharmaceutical company, now called Glaxo Smith Kline: *Resource strategy at GSK: organising capabilities for innovation and new business.*

4.1 ANALYSING RESOURCES AND CAPABILITIES

Definitions ▶ **The *resources* of an organisation are those assets that deliver value added in the organisation. The *capabilities* of an organisation are those management skills, routines and leadership that deploy, share and generate value from the resources of the organisation.** Analysing the resources and capabilities of an organisation has a dual purpose: to identify where value is added in the organisation and to explore and enhance the competitive advantages of the organisation's resources. Most strategists draw a distinction between the basic resources of an organisation and the additional abilities of an organisation to exploit these resources. For example, there is little point in the pharmaceutical company GSK possessing some important drug patents if it does not have the organisational capability to promote their sales to potential customers.

Although it might seem obvious that the analysis of the *environment* in Chapter 3 needs to be accompanied by an analysis of the *resources and capabilities* of the organisation, this was not so apparent until recently.[3] For many years in the 1970s, 1980s and 1990s, the main emphasis in strategy development was laid on analysis of the strategic competitive environment – for example, the work of Porter[4] and others outlined in Chapter 3.[5] However, this stress on industry analysis in turn represented a shift from the 1950s and 1960s, which took a more inclusive approach – for example, the work of Penrose[6] and others. It was the work in the 1980s and 1990s of strategists such as Wernerfelt[7] and Barney[8] that shifted the emphasis back towards the competitive resources of the organisation.

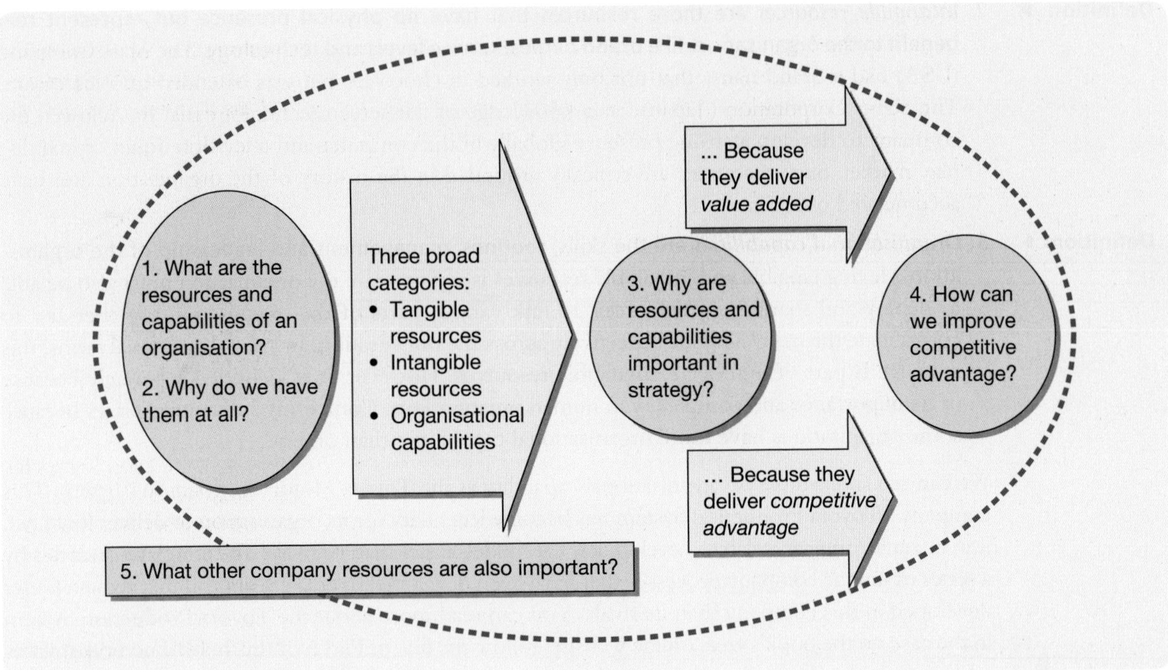

Figure 4.3 Five key questions related to strategic resources and capabilities

All the above areas take an economic perspective on resource analysis. But there are other aspects of the resources of a company: for example, its people, its finances and its production methods. These will also be also be important. Although the major emphasis of this chapter is on the *economic* aspects, the last section of this chapter will cover some of these other areas. Figure 4.3 summarises the questions and answers that we will explore in more depth during the course of this chapter.

4.1.1 Analysing the basic resources and capabilities of an organisation

Video Part 5a

In analysing an organisation's resources and capabilities, it is essential to begin by surveying the complete range of its resources. This is not easy because some resources are difficult to measure or even define in an unambiguous way. For example, the patents of the pharmaceutical company GSK represent resources whose future value cannot simply be determined by examining the company's accounts. The reason is that such assets will decline in value as the patents expire, and may not be fully valued in the accounts in any event.

Equally, an organisation's capabilities, for example its special skills in co-ordinating activities, may have no obvious money value but may be extraordinarily valuable to an organisation. Another example of organisational capability can be seen at GSK: the company's chief executive (Jean-Paul Garnier in 2002) provided an important resource called leadership, which is impossible to quantify but vital to strategy development. In strategy analysis, accounting and management systems data may represent a starting point, but little more.

We therefore need to take a broader and more inclusive approach to resource analysis. We begin with the definition that the resources and capabilities of the organisation are those assets that contribute to the generation of value added. As a starting point, it is useful to divide resources into three broad categories.[9]

Definition ▶

1 ***Tangible resources*** **are the physical resources of the organisation that contribute to its value added.** Plant and equipment at the German chemical giant Bayer can clearly be identified and valued. The location of McDonald's restaurants on busy highways, rather than obscure secondary roads, is clearly a valuable and tangible resource.

Definition ▶ 2 ***Intangible resources* are those resources that have no physical presence but represent real benefit to the organisation, like brand names, service levels and technology.** The Mars Company (USA) had a brand name that not only worked in chocolate but was extended into ice cream. The Sharp Corporation (Japan) has a knowledge of flat-screen technology that has allowed the company to develop a strong presence globally in the computer and television liquid crystal display market. Such resources are typically grounded in the history of the organisation and have accumulated over time.

Definition ▶ 3 ***Organisational capabilities* are the skills, routines, management and leadership of the organisation.** Having tangible and intangible resources is not enough: the organisation must also be able to deploy and share these resources, to link various parts of the organisation together and to co-ordinate the many activities effectively across the organisation. In strict definitional terms, this resource is part of number 2, intangible resources. However, it is identified separately because of its importance and complexity in human organisations. Competitive advantage arises because some organisations have more organisational capabilities than others.

We can see an example of organisational capability at the Toyota Motor Corporation (Japan). This company's Toyota Production System has become legendary for its organisation to deliver low-cost, lean manufacturing and also to develop new car models faster than its rivals. The company does this by a series of unique company processes that have been developed over the years and that remain better developed in this company than its rivals. You can read more about the Toyota Production System in the case on the book's free, online website: follow the link in Part 6 of this book. Such capabilities take years to develop and represent an important competitive advantage for the organisation.

Some strategists have other ways of defining the resources and capabilities of an organisation. These are a potential source of confusion and are therefore outlined in Exhibit 4.1. The important points are to understand the way that such definitions are used in this text and to be aware of the principles behind any chosen definition.

EXHIBIT 4.1

Differing definitions of strategic resources and capabilities: should we include 'core competencies'?

Some strategists and commentators include the words 'core competencies' as part of their basic definition of resources and capabilities. Such strategists begin by making a simple distinction between tangible and intangible resources.[10] They then define organisational capabilities in the way used in this text but include *all* capabilities, not just those that deliver competitive advantage. They then use the words 'core competencies' to identify those resources that deliver competitive advantage and value added.

Unfortunately, this is not the meaning originally attributed to 'core competencies' by their inventors - Hamel and Prahalad: see Section 4.6.3 later in this text - and is therefore a potential source of confusion to any reader of the original, well-known paper.[11]

In addition, other strategists make the point that certain key resources of a company, like a brand name or a patent, are not summarised accurately by the commonly understood meaning of the words 'core competencies'. Thus, for example, brand and patent resources may be the *outcome* of such competencies but have a value developed over time that goes beyond the skilled process of their development. Unilever paid $20 billion for the brand names *Hellmanns Mayonnaise* and *Knorr Soups*, not for the brand-building competencies that Unilever already possessed - see Case 9.3.

At the present time, there is no single agreed definition amongst strategists. The important point is to use all such definitions with precision as to their meaning and their implications for strategy.

In practice, such an analysis will concentrate on the main resource areas of the organisation, especially those that deliver added value and competitive advantage. It may also employ the *key factors for success* in an industry as a starting point to make sense of what might otherwise be a time-consuming and unproductive task – see Chapter 3. For example, in chocolate confectionery, a key factor for success for large companies is branding. Therefore, it is essential to examine the intangible branding resource of leading companies like Mars and Cadbury: it may not be possible to put a precise value on the brand but, in strategy resource analysis, this does not matter – the important point is to recognise that Mars and Cadbury have major competitive advantages in these areas.

For another example of the main resource advantages of an organisation, we can examine the pharmaceutical company Glaxo from Case 4.1 and from the more detailed case on the book's website:

- *Research and development* – the 'centres for excellence' in drug discovery that overcame the bureaucratic problems associated with its large size. In addition, the company's patents provide competitive advantage over other companies that exists while the patent lasts.
- *Marketing and sales* – the ability to develop effective advertising campaigns for the new drugs to large hospitals and other institutions, not only through direct selling but also via a well-organised and co-ordinated promotional campaign. The size and network contacts of the personnel employed at the Glaxo are a competitive advantage.
- *Human resources* – the skills and knowledge to motivate and retain employees, especially those who were especially skilled in drug development and sales contacts in pharmaceutical markets.
- *Manufacturing* – the skills required to operate large and complex drug manufacturing facilities, where quality and safety are paramount and are regularly monitored by outside government bodies like the US Food and Drug Administration.
- *Distribution and logistics* – the capability of co-ordinating, stocking and transporting drugs efficiently – often across international boundaries because drugs may be made in one region of the world and sold elsewhere.

Another example of the main points of a resources and capabilities analysis in a service industry is shown in Exhibit 4.2.

EXHIBIT 4.2

Resource and capabilities analysis at the worldwide hotel chain Holiday Inns

	Resource and capability
Tangible resources	• Physical locations at airports, city centres, holiday destinations, etc. • Size and facilities of individual hotels: rooms, restaurants, swimming pool, etc.
Intangible resources	• Brand name of Holiday Inns • Employees in management, reception, room cleaning, etc.
Capabilities	• Skills in co-ordinating suppliers of food, telephone services, etc. • Management training to maintain and improve levels of service • Management organisation and leadership to deliver detailed, consistent quality at each hotel • Organisational routines that allow each hotel to run smoothly and efficiently

4.1.2 Managerial and other difficulties in undertaking the analysis of resources and capabilities

Although it may seem simple enough to define the resources and capabilities of an organisation, the practical difficulties should not be under estimated. Managers need to undertake a resource and capabilities analysis at an early stage in order to identify where the profits are made in the organisation and to define and enhance their competitive advantages, if any. This is fraught with difficulty for three main reasons:

1. because there is often *uncertainty* about the industry conditions and the actions of competitors;
2. because the many factors making up the analysis are *complex* and the underlying causes difficult to understand;
3. because there is often *disagreement* within the organisation over what constitutes a competitive resource.

Particularly with the last point, the judgement and choice of competitive resources and capabilities may have implications for individual managers and departments: for example, if a resource was identified as providing no competitive advantage, it might imply that the organisation could dispose of the resource and its related managers. This is the topic of 'strategic change' which we explore in Chapter 15 of this text.

4.1.3 Prescriptive and emergent approaches to resource analysis

Both emergent and prescriptive approaches to strategy development regard resources as important. However, their perspectives are very different.

Prescriptive strategists take the view that it is important to use resources efficiently and build on resource strengths. Resources are to some extent regarded as objects to be manipulated. Hence it is possible for strategy to mould resources in order to provide a more efficient organisation. For example, the GSK pharmaceutical company came about from a merger of the two major companies, Glaxo (UK) with Smith Kline (USA). The merger benefits then came from significant job cuts resulting in annual savings of over $750 million. Prescriptive strategists argue that the company was stronger as a result.

Although there is not complete agreement among emergent strategists, they would certainly question the certainties of the prescriptive view of resources and capabilities. For some, doubts centre on the assumption made by prescriptive strategists that change is achievable. For example, the GSK job cuts were accompanied by considerable uncertainty and worry, which must have affected the ability of those carrying out the changes. For other emergent strategists, the environment is changing fast as a result of forces beyond the control of the organisation. Resources need to be flexible and aimed at survival. Analysing resources as static and unchanging therefore is not appropriate.

These differences of views are reflected in the two models used in this book. In the prescriptive model, resources deliver a definite result to the organisation and its future strategies. In the emergent model, the resources and subsequent strategies are much more fluid and interrelated.

This chapter concentrates on the prescriptive approach because it forms the basis of resource analysis for strategy development. This is because it is well developed, with useful insights, and, in addition, even those who doubt its usefulness still need to understand it first. Chapter 5 explores the emergent approach.

KEY STRATEGIC PRINCIPLES

- The *resources* of an organisation are those assets that deliver value added in the organisation.
- The *capabilities* of an organisation are those management skills, routines and leadership that deploy, share and generate value from the resources of the organisation.
- The purpose of a resources and capabilities analysis is to identify where value is added in an organisation and where the organisation possesses sustainable competitive advantage.
- In resource analysis, it is important to begin by analysing the complete range of resources and capabilities of the organisation: tangible resources, intangible resources and organisational capability. Such resources go beyond the usual definitions of accounting and finance concepts into areas like the value of patents and leadership.
- There are often practical managerial difficulties in analysing the resources of the organisation. These arise in three areas: uncertainty with regard to the environment and competition, complex and uncertain causality, disagreement within the organisation over what constitutes a competitive resource.
- Prescriptive approaches regard resources as objects to be moulded for maximum strategic benefit. Emergent approaches do not have a consistent theme with regard to resources. However, they tend to lay more emphasis on the uncertainty of the environment and thus the difficulty of a static analysis of competitive advantage.

4.2 WHY DOES AN ORGANISATION POSSESS ANY RESOURCES AT ALL? THE MAKE-OR-BUY DECISION

As a starting point in identifying the strategic role of individual resources, it is useful to explore the reasons for an organisation to possess and use *any* resources beyond the minimum amount needed to stay in existence. Arguably, in an efficient market, there will be outside more specialised suppliers that will be able to sell some activities more cheaply to the organisation than it can make them for itself. For example, GSK does not produce its own advertising campaigns but employs an outside agency. Nor does the company manufacture its own cartons, boxes and foil in which to pack its drugs, but buys them in – why? Because it is cheaper to buy from an outside supplier than make them for itself. The decision to use the outside 'market' to buy in products or services rather than use the organisation's own resources to make them is known in strategic terms as outsourcing. However, there are also problems with buying in from outside – see Exhibit 4.3 – otherwise all organisations would buy everything and make nothing. Essentially, to resolve the problem of what an organisation should make rather than buy, the costs of using the market must be higher than the benefits.

The make-or-buy decision is part of a broader strategic reappraisal of resources. Over the past 30 years, many organisations have come to redefine the boundaries of their resources – what they *make* is only part of the resources *owned* by the firm. For example, firms also have resources like brand names, which they do not manufacture on a production line but which are important contributors to value added. This profound re-think on the nature and role of resources by writers such as Coase, Penrose and Williamson has led to some important strategic resource decisions.[12]

Companies like Nike Sports (US) and Benetton Clothing (Italy) have achieved strategic success by buying in many of the activities that might previously have been undertaken in-house: both use networks of suppliers and, in the case of Benetton, distributors to make and sell their goods more cheaply. Nike designs and markets its new shoes but has them manufactured by outside suppliers in Asia – see Case 7.2. Benetton has a similar arrangement, using a group of local suppliers in northern Italy: this is called *outsourcing* supplies. Although it might appear that Benetton owns the resource of the shop chain that bears the company name, in fact most of the stores are not owned by the company. They are operated under the control of Benetton but owned by others outside the

EXHIBIT 4.3

Benefits and costs of using the market

Benefits

- Outside suppliers can achieve economies of scale that in-house departments producing only for their own needs cannot.
- Outside suppliers are subject to the pressures of the market and must be efficient and innovative to survive. Overall corporate success may hide the inefficiencies and lack of innovativeness of in-house departments.

Costs

- Production flows need to be co-ordinated through the value chain of the organisation. This may be compromised when an activity is purchased from an independent market firm rather than performed in-house.
- Private information may be leaked when an activity is performed by an independent market firm – such information may be crucial to the competitive advantage held by the organisation.
- There may be costs of transacting with independent firms that can be avoided by performing the activity in-house.

Source: adapted from Besanko, D, Dranove, D and Shenley, M (1996), *The Economics of Strategy*, p 73. Copyright © 1996 John Wiley & Sons, Inc. This material is used by permission of John Wiley & Sons, Inc.

company: this is called *franchising*. The concepts of branded clothing, franchised clothing stores and outsourced supplies formed the basis of Benetton's highly original new strategy in the 1970s. The starting point for such strategy development is an analysis of the resources of the organisation as they exist at present. We undertake this task during the rest of this chapter.

KEY STRATEGIC PRINCIPLES

- The *make-or-buy decision* concerns the choice that every organisation has of either making its own products or services or buying them from outside. Every organisation needs to reappraise its activities regularly in this area.
- Over the past 30 years, the make-or-buy decision has forced organisations to reappraise what they really own and why. Organisations have redefined the boundaries of what they possess.

4.3 RESOURCE ANALYSIS AND ADDING VALUE

Video Part 5a

Definition ▶

The fundamental role of resources in an organisation is to add value. All organisations need to ensure that they do not consistently lose value in the long term or they will not survive. For commercial organisations, adding value is essential for their future. For non-profit organisations, adding value may only be a minor part of the reason for their existence, other purposes being centred on social, charitable or other goals. Resources add value by working on the raw materials that enter the factory gate and turning them into a finished product. **Added value can be defined as the difference between the market value of the output of an organisation and the cost of its inputs.**

The concept is basically an economic one and is outlined, using GSK as an example, in Figure 4.4. For non-profit organisations, the concept of adding value can still be applied. The inputs to the organisation may be similar to those of commercial organisations – electricity, telephones, etc. – and may be very different, particularly voluntary labour, which has a zero cost. Equally, the outputs may be difficult to define and measure – service to the community, help for sick people, etc. But the *value added* is real enough, just difficult to quantify. To explore the basic concepts, commercial explanations *only* are examined in this section.

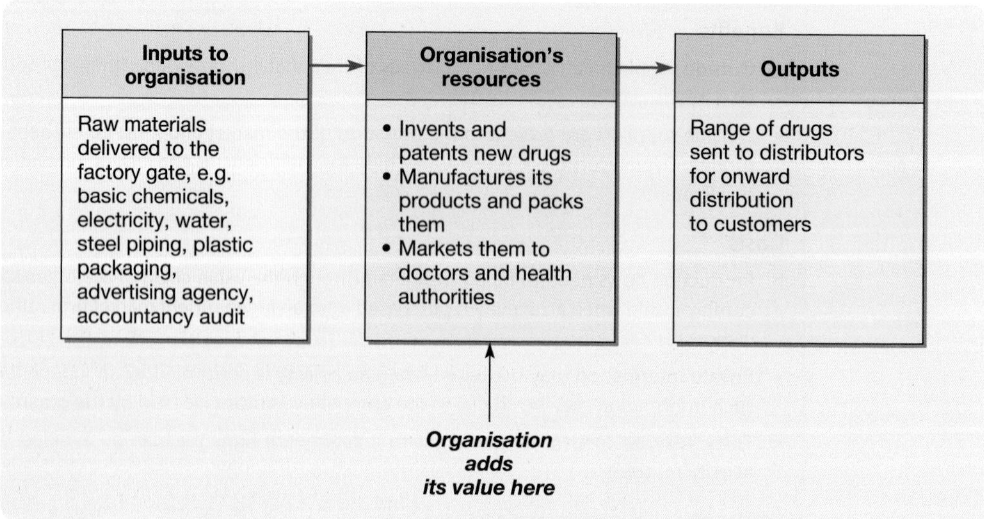

Figure 4.4 Value added by a pharmaceutical company such as GSK

From the above definition of value added (i.e. outputs minus inputs), it follows that value can be added in an organisation:

- *either* by raising the value of outputs (sales) delivered to the customer;
- *or* by lowering the costs of its inputs (wages and salaries, capital and materials costs) into the company.

Alternatively, both routes could be used simultaneously. Strategies therefore need to address these two areas.

Raising the value of outputs may mean raising the level of sales, either by raising the volume of sales or by raising the unit price. Both these methods are easy to state and more difficult to achieve. Each will involve costs – for example, the cost of advertising to stimulate sales – which need to be set against the gains made. *Lowering the costs of inputs* may require investment – for example, in new machinery to replace workers – at the same time as seeking the cost reduction. These two strategic routes need to be examined in detail. *Outputs* have already been covered in Chapter 3; *inputs* are considered later in this chapter.

A strategic analysis of value added needs to take place at the market or industry level of the organisation, not at a corporate or holding company level. If this analysis were to be undertaken at the general level, the performance of individual parts of the business would be masked. Value added is therefore calculated at the level of individual product groups.[13]

KEY STRATEGIC PRINCIPLES

- The added value of a commercial organisation is the difference between the market value of its output and the costs of its inputs.
- The value added of a not-for-profit organisation is the difference between the service provided and the costs of the inputs, some of which may be voluntary and have zero cost.
- All organisations need to ensure that they do not consistently lose value in the long term or they will not survive. For commercial organisations, adding value is essential for their future. For non-profit organisations, adding value may only be a minor part of the reason for their existence, other purposes being centred on social, charitable or other goals.
- In principle, there are only two strategies to raise value added in a commercial organisation: increase the value of its outputs (sales) or lower the value of its inputs (the costs of labour, capital and materials). In practice, this implies detailed analysis of every aspect of sales and costs.
- In companies with more than one product range, added value is best analysed by considering each group separately. Some groups may subsidise others in terms of added value. Not all groups are likely to perform equally.

4.4 ADDING VALUE: THE VALUE CHAIN AND THE VALUE SYSTEM – THE CONTRIBUTION OF PORTER

The concept of value added can be used to develop the organisation's sustainable competitive advantage. There are two main routes – the *value chain* and the *value system*. Much of this approach was developed in the 1980s by Professor Michael Porter of the Harvard Business School.

Every organisation consists of activities that link together to develop the value of the business: purchasing supplies, manufacturing, distribution and marketing of its goods and services. These activities taken together form its *value chain*. **The value chain identifies where the value is added in an organisation and links the process with the main functional parts of the organisation.** It is used for developing competitive advantage because such chains tend to be unique to an organisation.

Definition ►

When organisations supply, distribute, buy from or compete with each other, they form a broader group of value generation: the *value system*. **The value system shows the wider routes in an industry that add value to incoming supplies and outgoing distributors and customers. It links the industry value chain to that of other industries.** Again, it is used to identify and develop competitive advantage because such systems tend to be unique to companies.

Definition ▶

The contributions of the value chain and value system to the development of competitive advantage, and the links between the two areas, which may also deliver competitive advantage, are explored in this section.

4.4.1 The value chain

The value chain links the value of the activities of an organisation with its main functional parts. It then attempts to make an assessment of the contribution that each part makes to the overall added value of the business. The concept was used in accounting analysis for some years before Professor Michael Porter[14] suggested that it could be applied to strategic analysis. Essentially, he linked two areas together:

1 the added value that each part of the organisation contributes to the whole organisation; and
2 the contribution to the competitive advantage of the whole organisation that each of these parts might then make.

In a company with more than one product area, he said that the analysis should be conducted at the level of product groups, not at the level of company headquarters. The company is then split into the *primary activities* of production, such as the production process itself, and the *support activities*, such as human resources management, that give the necessary background to the running of the company but cannot be identified with any individual part. The analysis then examines how each part might be considered to contribute towards the generation of value in the company and how this differs from competitors.

Porter's outline process is shown in Figure 4.5. He used the word 'margin' in the diagram to indicate what we defined as *added value* in Section 4.4: 'margin is the difference between the total value and the collective cost of performing the value activities'.[15]

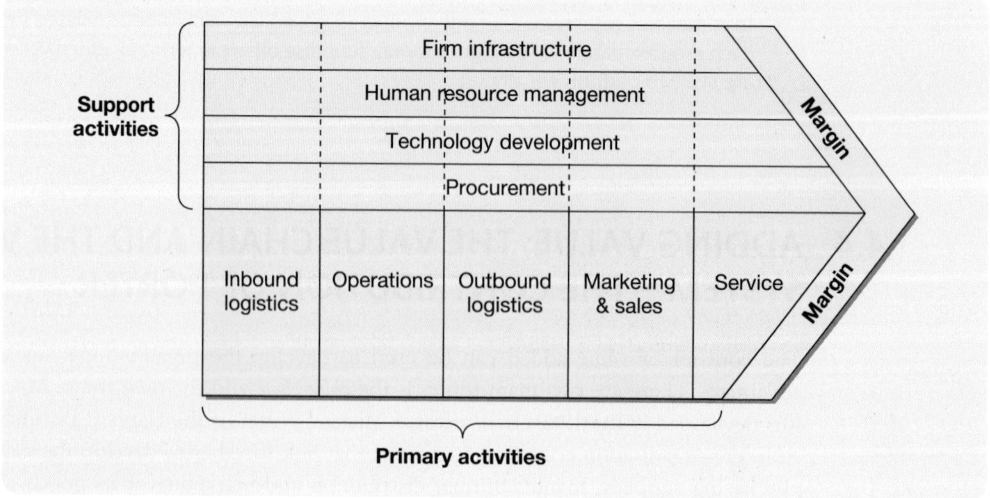

Figure 4.5 The value chain

Source: reprinted with the permission of Free Press, a Division of Simon & Schuster, Inc., from *Competitive Advantage: Creating and Sustaining Superior Performance* by Michael E Porter. Copyright © 1985, 1998 by Michael E Porter. All rights reserved.

According to Porter, the *primary activities* of the company are:

- *Inbound logistics.* These are the areas concerned with receiving the goods from suppliers, storing them until required by operations, handling and transporting them within the company.
- *Operations.* This is the production area of the company. In some companies, this might be split into further departments – for example, paint spraying, engine assembly, etc., in a car company; reception, room service, restaurant, etc., in a hotel.
- *Outbound logistics.* These distribute the final product to the customer. They would clearly include transport and warehousing but might also include selecting and wrapping combinations of products in a multiproduct company. For a hotel or other service company, this activity would be reconfigured to cover the means of bringing customers to the hotel or service.
- *Marketing and sales.* This function analyses customers' wants and needs and brings to the attention of customers the products or services the company has for sale. Advertising and promotions fall within this area.
- *Service.* Before or after a product or service has been sold, there is often a need for pre-installation or after-sales service. There may also be a requirement for training, answering customer queries, etc.

Each of the above categories will add value to the organisation in its own way. They may undertake this task better or worse than competitors: for example, with higher standards of service, lower production costs, faster and cheaper outbound delivery and so on. By this means, they provide the areas of *competitive advantage* of the organisation.

The support activities are:

- *Procurement.* In many companies, there will be a separate department (or group of managers) responsible for purchasing goods and materials that are then used in the operations of the company. The department's function is to obtain the lowest prices and highest quality of goods for the activities of the company, but it is only responsible for purchasing, not for the subsequent production of the goods.
- *Technology development.* This may be an important area for new products in the company. Even in a more mature industry, it will cover the existing technology, training and knowledge that will allow a company to remain efficient.
- *Human resource management.* Recruitment, training, management development and the reward structures are vital elements in all companies.
- *Firm infrastructure.* This includes the background planning and control systems – for example, accounting, etc. – that allow companies to administer and direct their development. It includes company headquarters.

These support activities add value, just as the primary activities do, but in a way that is more difficult to link with one particular part of the organisation. A worked example of the primary part of a value chain is shown in Case 4.2 on Louis Vuitton and Gucci later in this chapter.

Comment

The problem with the value chain in strategic development is that it is designed to explore the **existing** linkages and value-added areas of the business. By definition, it works within the existing structure. Real competitive strategy may require a revolution that moves **outside** the existing structure. Value chains may not be the means to achieve this.

4.4.2 The value system

In addition to the analysis of the company's own value chain, Porter argued that an additional analysis should also be undertaken. Organisations are part of a wider system of adding value involving the supply and distribution value chains and the value chains of customers. This is known as the *value system* and is illustrated in Figure 4.6.

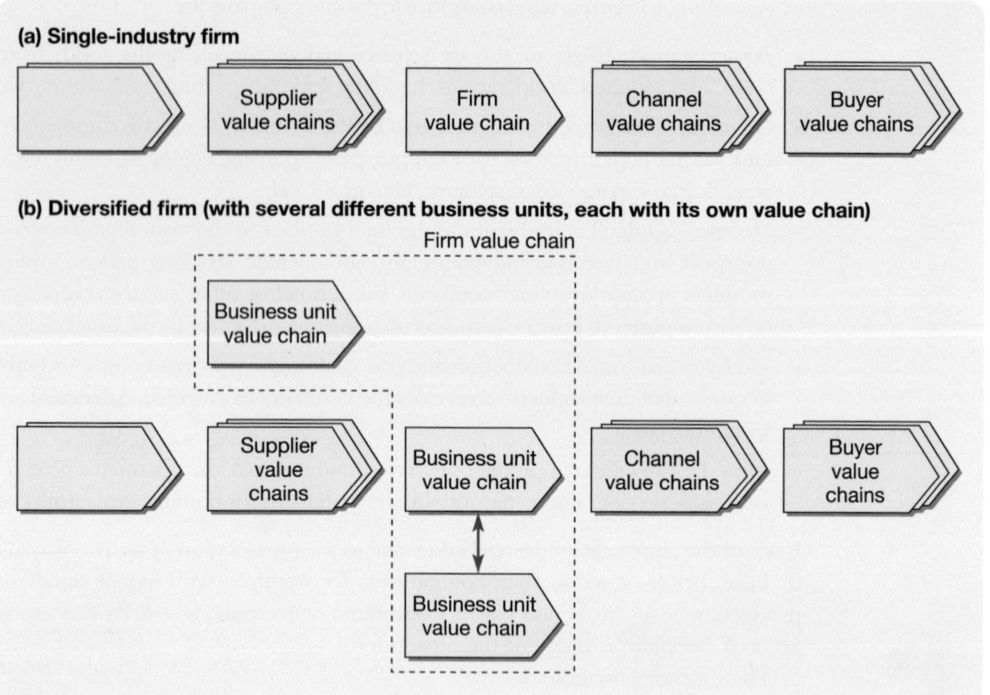

Figure 4.6 The value system

Source: reprinted with the permission of Free Press, a Division of Simon & Schuster, Inc., from *Competitive Advantage: Creating and Sustaining Superior Performance* by Michael E Porter. Copyright © 1985, 1998 by Michael E Porter. All rights reserved.

Except in very rare circumstances, every organisation buys in some of its activities: advertising, product packaging design, management consultancy, electricity are all examples of items that are often acquired even by the largest companies. In the same way, many organisations do not distribute their products or services directly to the final consumer: travel agents, wholesalers, retail shops might all be involved in this role.

Competitors may or may not use the same value system: some suppliers and distributors will be better than others in the sense that they offer lower prices, faster service, more reliable products, etc. *Real* competitive advantage may come from using the *best* suppliers or distributors. New competitive advantage may be gained by using a new distribution system or obtaining a new relationship with a supplier. An analysis of this value system may also therefore be required. This will involve a resource analysis that extends beyond the organisation itself.

Value chain and value system analysis can be complex and time-consuming for the organisation. This is where the *key factors for success* from the previous chapter can be used. If these have been correctly identified, then they will provide the focus for the analysis of added value that follows. Key factors may well be those factors that add value to the product or service.

In Section 4.3 we concluded that value added can only be raised by either increasing the outputs (sales) or by lowering the inputs (costs) of a company. Along with the key factors for success, these two value-added options now provide a method of analysing the value-added resources in the company. Such an enquiry will need to examine both the costs and the benefits of any proposed changes.

In the case of Glaxo Smith Kline (GSK), the company might be advised to concentrate its value analysis initially at least on its identified key factors for success: R&D, marketing and product performance. In fact, the company's strategy during recent years has been to invest very heavily in research and development – see Case 4.1 and the more detailed case on the book's website. As already explored, GSK spent considerable time and resources organising and then re-organising its valuable research and development facilities.[16] One of the main reasons for these activities was the strong range of new drugs that would complement the existing Glaxo product portfolio – another way of achieving R&D development. GSK might also usefully investigate ways of raising the value of key *outputs* and lowering key *costs*. The opening case showed that this is precisely the strategic activity undertaken by the company.

Comment

In common with the value chain, the value system is mainly concerned with the *existing* linkages and may miss totally new strategic opportunities.

4.4.3 Developing competitive advantage linkages between the value chain and value system

Analysis of the value chain and the value system will provide information on value added in the company. For an organisation with a group of products, there may be some common item or common service across the group, for example:

- a common raw material (such as sugar in various food products); or
- a common distributor (such as a car parts distributor for a group with subsidiary companies manufacturing various elements in a car).

Such common items may be *linked* to develop competitive advantage. Such possible linkages may be important to strategic development because they are often *unique* to that organisation. The linkages might therefore provide advantages over competitors who do not have such linkages, or who are unable to develop them easily.

It was Porter[17] who suggested that value chains and value systems may not be sufficient in themselves to provide the competitive advantage needed by companies in developing their strategies. He argued that competitors can often imitate the *individual* moves made by an organisation; what competitors have much more difficulty in doing is imitating the special and possibly unique *linkages* that exist between elements of the value chain and the value systems of the organisation.

In addition to analysing resources for value chains and value systems, therefore, competitive strategy suggests that there is a third element. It is necessary to search for special and possibly unique linkages that either exist or might be developed between elements of the value chain and between value systems associated with the company. Figure 4.7 illustrates this situation.

Examples of such linkages abound:

- Common raw materials used in a variety of end-products: for example, petrochemical feedstocks are used widely to produce various products.
- Common services, such as telecommunications or media buying, where a combined contract could be negotiated at a lower price than a series of individual local deals.
- Linkages between technology development and production to facilitate new production methods that might be used in various parts of a group – for example, direct telecommunications links between large retail store chains such as Marks & Spencer and their suppliers.
- Computer reservation systems that link airlines with travel ticket agents (proving to be so powerful that the European Commission has investigated their effects on airline competition).
- Joint ventures, alliances and partnerships that often rely on different members to the agreement bringing their special areas of expertise to the relationship (see Chapter 9).

All the above suggest that linkages that enhance value added may provide significant ways for companies to improve their resources.

Comment

One fundamental problem with the value chain, value system and its linkages is their broad perspective across the *range* of the company's resources. They are sometimes rather vague at identifying

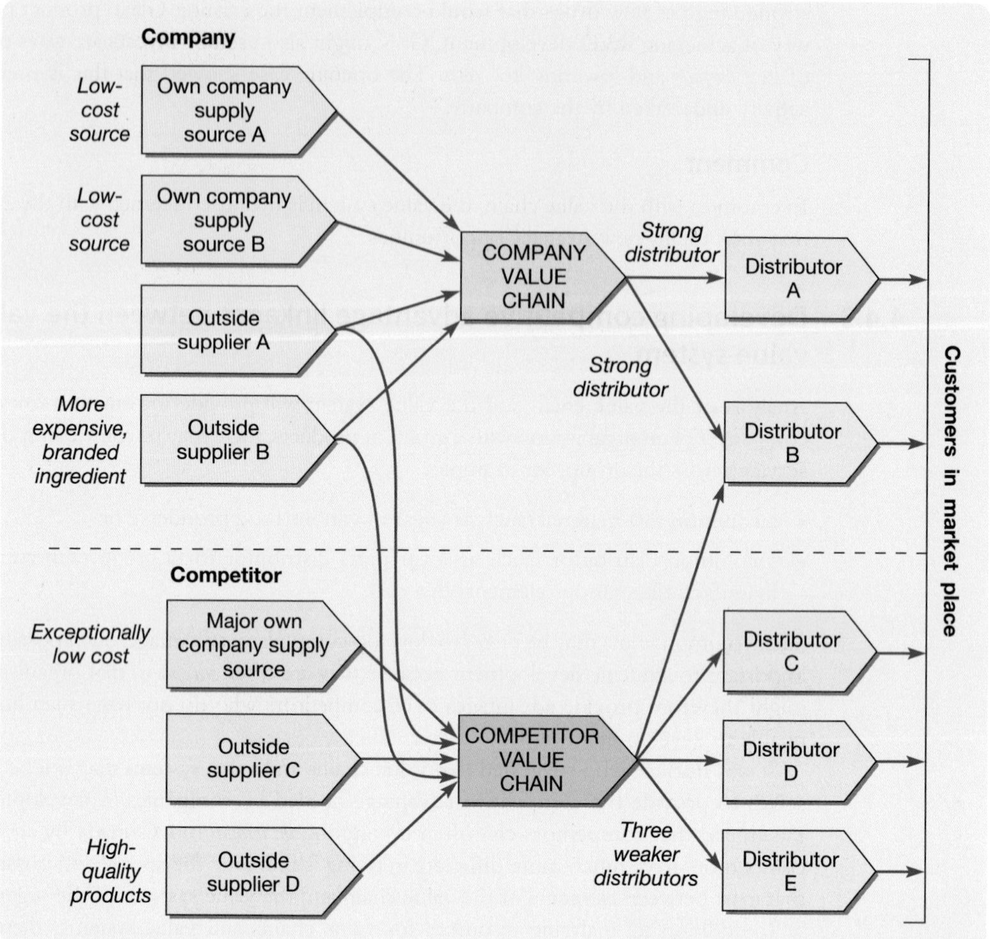

Figure 4.7 Competitive advantage through linkages between the value chain and value system

the *precise* nature and scope of the advantages such resources possess against competitors. Sustainable competitive advantage is not the primary target of the value-added analysis. The remaining sections of this chapter explore more direct ways of tackling this issue.

Another difficulty with value-added analysis is its focus on assets that can be clearly measured. This is a significant weakness because some of the organisation's most valuable assets may be difficult to quantify – such as branding or specialist knowledge. Moreover, some of the organisation's most important assets may be impossible to value, especially human resource assets like leadership and strong team building.

4.4.4 Improving value added

Despite its difficulties, value added is important in strategy development, especially when defined in broad terms rather than by the narrow (outputs minus inputs) definition used in the economic analysis explored in this chapter. The fundamental point remains that, unless organisations add some value to their inputs, their very existence may be in question. For most organisations, this suggests that an important issue is how to capture the value that is added by the organisation's resources. We will pick up this theme in Chapters 8 and 9 after exploring resources in more detail.

KEY STRATEGIC PRINCIPLES

- The value chain breaks down the activities of the organisation into its main parts.
- The contribution that each part makes can then be assessed for its contribution to sustainable competitive advantage.
- The value chain is usually analysed without any detailed quantification of the added value that each element contributes. It is undertaken at a broad general level and is compared with competitors.
- Most organisations are part of a wider system of adding value involving supplier and distributor channels: the value system.
- Analysing value chains and the value system can be complex. One way of reducing such difficulties is to employ the key factors for success as a means of selecting the items.
- Possible linkages of elements of the value chain and value systems need to be analysed because they may be unique to the organisation and thus provide it with competitive advantage.
- Significant weaknesses in the practical application of value added include a lack of precision in identifying areas of resource advantage and an inability to value clearly major assets like specialist knowledge and company leadership.

CASE STUDY 4.2

Competitive advantage at Louis Vuitton and Gucci

With annual sales of over $165 billion and gross profit margins of over 50 per cent, the major luxury goods companies rely on famous brands like Louis Vuitton and Gucci to deliver competitive advantage. But does the advantage come only from the brand name? Perhaps there are other advantages? This case explores competitive advantage in the world of high fashion luxury goods.

To explore competitive advantage in the industry, we begin by examining the *value chain* – where the profits are generated in the business. This is a useful starting point because it identifies those parts of the business that are particularly profitable and therefore likely to be linked with potential advantages. The second part of the case then uses the value chain to explore *competitive advantage* in luxury goods.

Value chain at a major fashion house

In practice in the luxury goods sector, the value chain is complex, with many interlocking parts. However, the key activity for most companies is the preparation and display of a new collection for its bi-annual fashion show. To explore this, we can take the example of a Paris fashion house, perhaps at the leading French company LVMH, which owns such brands as Louis Vuitton, Hennessy, Loewe, Kenzo, Givenchy and Thomas Pink. The lead designer at the fashion house has decided to make an embroidered silk *haute couture* dress as part of its next women's spring collection. This activity will generate profits through a value chain of business activities. The primary activities of the value chain are shown in Table 4.1. The support activities are not shown for reasons of simplicity, but the fashion designer, who oversees the whole process, is part of the firm infrastructure.

In order to make the dress, silk is supplied as thread mainly from China to a co-ordinating company, often in Northern Italy. The co-ordinating company has a network of associated companies in the geographical area to dye, spin and weave the silk. Importantly, the co-ordinating company will work very closely with the lead designer from LVMH on colours, patterns and textures relevant to the appropriate design collection.

For both the Chinese and Italian companies, the real driving force in terms of design, pricing and sales to the customer is the fashion house, rather than its suppliers. For this reason, the main value is generated at the fashion house, not the earlier parts of the value chain.

Turning to the fashion house itself, there are considerable variations in where and how value is added. Clearly, the fashion designer – for example, famous designers like John Galliano, Stella McCartney and Giorgio Armani – takes the lead in developing the new silk dress design. The designer's work is often better when supported by a business manager. The manager ensures that the business objectives of the fashion house are met and that the designer is not burdened with unnecessary administrative matters. The designer does not just focus on one silk dress but creates two complete fashion collections every year in each of the major fashion centres: Paris, Milan and New York. The designer may also develop

Competitive advantage in the fashion industry includes brand reputation. But for the leading fashion houses, the chief fashion designer is probably more important.
© Royalty-Free/Dex Image/Corbis

men's as well as women's collections, arrange a pre-collection briefing for department stores and other subsidiary buyers and also contribute to the design of the fashion house accessories range – scarves, bags, shoes, etc. The embroidered silk dress of our example will probably appear only once in one of these collections.

The designer begins each dress collection with fashion ideas that are simply draped as fabric on a static mannequin. Silk fabric might not even be used at this stage. The ideas are then refined over time, the silk fabric chosen and the brief given to the Italian suppliers to make this specific fabric – described above. When the material arrives from the Italian supplier, it is then cut to make up the finished garment. The final stages involve invisible stitching using highly skilled seamstresses who are an extremely important part of a top fashion house. The embroidery too demands great expertise. The silk dress then appears on the catwalk of the fashion show and subsequently in the showroom for sale after public presentation.

Each of these activities will add value to the finished garment – see Table 4.1. Even allowing for the expense of hand finishing, the resulting price of the silk dress may appear high – perhaps as much as $30,000 – and the value added may therefore seem high. However, there are only a relatively few *haute couture* customers – perhaps only 2,000 around the world – who are able to afford such prices. Thus the 'value' generated from the embroidered silk dress in absolute terms is relatively small. The real value added at the fashion house comes in at least three other related areas:

1 *Off-the-peg dresses from the same design label.* Many people may not be able to afford the $30,000 silk dress, but they will pay $2,000 for a *prêt-à-porter* (ready-to-wear) dress from the same designer.
2 *Shoes, scarves and other accessories.* Many customers will also pay $500 for shoes and other items from the same fashion house. Some of these may be made inside the fashion house, but many will be subcontracted to outside suppliers and then sold through the retail outlets owned by the fashion house.
3 *Other related and licensed items.* Customers will also pay $50–$100 for fragrances and other items related to the brand. Such items may not be manufactured by the fashion house but by licensees of the brand name.

The brand is therefore more than just a silk embroidered dress produced for a fashion show. Fashion houses license their brand names to outside companies but also understand the real danger of diluting the brand. An example of 'brand dilution' is the Pierre Cardin brand, which used to be a major high fashion brand in the 1970s. During the 1980s, the brand was licensed to over 800 products, including toilet seat covers. The Pierre Cardin brand is still important and well respected, but it is no longer a part of the high fashion luxury market in the sense explored in this case.

High fashion houses guard their brands carefully and will even revoke licences if they judge that the brand is being diluted: examples of activities leading to brand dilution include selling the ends of lines below normal pricing or attaching the brand name to an unsuitable product. From a more positive perspective, brand licensing across a number of related products means that a fashion house has a range of activities to exploit its major brands. For example, the world's leading fragrance company, L'Oréal, has bought licences from fashion houses for several of the L'Oréal luxury fragrance ranges – including Giorgio Armani, Ralph Lauren and Cacherel – see Case 5.2.

There are two additional aspects to value generation at fashion houses that are not captured in the simple design and manufacture of a single silk dress:

1 Most of the fashion houses have developed their *own retail outlets* to sell their products around the world. For example, the market leader in luxury goods is the French company LVMH: it has around 1,600 stores and derives around 80 per cent of its sales from these outlets.
2 Fashion houses also operate a *range of brands*, each with its own designer and fashion activity. For example, LVMH owns at least 50 brands, although not all are involved in fashion clothing. The purpose of such a strategy is to spread the risk: if one fashion house brand within the group suffers a temporary downturn, then another brand can take over. In total, LVMH employs 56,000 people, with two-thirds of them being located outside its home country, France.

Table 4.1 Value chain of a haute couture silk dress

Position in chain	Activity	Amount and location of value added
Suppliers	Silk thread from China Spinning, weaving and dyeing in Italy Design co-operation with fashion house on colours, patterns, styles and fabrics	Low – many suppliers Low/medium – several suppliers High – specialist work requiring good contacts and co-operation with fashion house
Inbound logistics – the goods arrive at the fashion house	Variety of importers, direct purchases	Low – many methods available, none exclusive
Operations – the design and manufacture of each *haute couture dress*	Famous designer, e.g. John Galliano or Stella McCartney Draping and sculpting new design, cutting and sewing up finished dress	High – crucial element – see text High but limited volume – see text
Outbound logistics – distributing the dresses to the shops and licensees	Mainly through the fashion house's own exclusive shops	Medium/high – need to keep control of brand
Marketing and sales	Fashion shows in Paris, Milan and New York Media coverage of show Special pre-collection briefing for department stores Brand-associated products like ready-to-wear and accessories like shoes, bags	High Valuable – cost of show $500,000 with value of media coverage into millions of dollars Medium – useful for brand promotion and aspiration Possibly highest value added here – see text
Service – exclusive and discreet levels of service to the wealthy clients Additional and important service for clients wishing to purchase *prêt-à-porter*	Through ownership of retail outlets	High, but small number of clients for *haute couture* Greater number of clients for *prêt-à-porter* (ready-to-wear)

Note: For reasons of simplicity, only the primary activities are identified in the value chain above. The fashion designer, who oversees the whole process, is arguably involved in every part of the primary activities and, in addition, is part of the firm infrastructure in the secondary activities.

Source: see references.

Competitive advantage in the luxury goods industry

Although the value chain locates the high profit margin activities, it does not necessarily follow that all will deliver competitive advantage for a company. The high profit margin activities may be the same at all the fashion houses and therefore not deliver a competitive advantage to a particular fashion house. Nevertheless, the value chain is a useful starting point because competitive advantage is more likely to be associated with high profits. In the case of the luxury goods market, it will be immediately evident that the competitive advantage rests only partly with a *brand name* like Gucci or Louis Vuitton. Table 4.2 examines the three leading luxury goods companies and describes the main attributes that will then generate competitive advantage.

Taking the elements of the value chain, we can explore them to test whether they deliver competitive advantage for a leading fashion house:

- *Brand*. This is a key ingredient that sets one company apart from another. The leading company has some well-known brands but so do its rivals. Importantly in fashion, the brand needs to be constantly renewed with advertising to support this. Part of the competitive advantage is therefore in brand support, including two items:
  - the amount of advertising spend – LVMH leads here;
  - the fashion house designer as part of the brand: examples include Jean Paul Gaultier and Yves St Laurent. Competitive advantage is strong here.
- *Designer*. The name, flair, skills and creative ability of the designer is a crucial factor in developing and maintaining a top fashion house. Designers can revive fashion houses – for example, Tom Ford (designer) and Domenico de Sole (business partner) who transformed Gucci in the early 1990s. They have now left the company after it was sold to the French store group, PPR, but their reputation lives on. In March 2005, it was reported that the new designer in charge of women's wear at Gucci Group after Mr Ford, Alessandra Facchinetti, resigned as a result of 'commercial concerns ruling the fashion world'. Clearly, the designer is a

Table 4.2 The three leading high fashion houses

Company	Sales 2002	Main brands – some in accessories and fragrances	Extra activities
LVMH • Louis Vuitton Moët Hennessy • Based in France	• $12 billion • 80 per cent of sales in own stores – around 1,600 stores • Advertising spend in 2004: $220 million	• Loewe, Celine, Kenzo, Givenchy, Marc Jacobs, Fendi, StefanoBi, Emilio Pucci, Donna Karan, Thomas Pink	• 15 wine and spirit brands, including Hennessy cognac • 10 perfume and beauty brands, including Christian Dior and Guerlain • 6 watch and jewellery companies including TAG Heuer and Zenith • 7 retail accessory companies
Richemont • Based in Switzerland	• $3.6 billion • 55 per cent of sales in own stores – around 3,500 stores • Advertising spend in 2004: $75 million	• Chloé, Cartier, Piaget, Van Cleef & Arpels, Dunhill, Hackett • More than half of sales come from Cartier, the jewellers. But the company plans to expand its Chloé high fashion brand	• pen companies – Mont Blanc brand • 6 watch companies
Gucci Group • Controlled by Pinault Printemps Redoute (PPR), the French department store chain	• $2.4 billion • 50 per cent of sales in own stores – around 1,500 stores • Advertising spend in 2004: $55 million	• Gucci, Yves St Laurent, Alexander McQueen, Stella McCartney, Balenciaga, Sergio Rossi	• Retail shops, department stores, mail order catalogue

Source: Rumelt, R. (1991) 'How much does industry matter?', *Strategic Management Journal*, March, pp 67–75, copyright © 1991 John Wiley & Sons, Inc. Reprinted by permission of John Wiley & Sons, Inc.

crucial competitive advantage in high fashion but also needs to deliver the results.

- *Range of brands*. Both LVMH and PPR argue that one of their real strengths is that they have many brands. If one declines over time, then there are others to take its place. In addition, the range means that it can make a more comprehensive offering to a wide range of customers – perhaps classic designs for some, with avant-garde for others. However, it is not entirely clear whether the brand range at LVMH is *superior* to the ranges at other leading companies. This is not necessarily a competitive advantage.
- *Licensing and franchising*. This is a major source of revenue for all the high fashion houses. There are dangers, as outlined above, but the benefits from controlled and monitored business activity are significant. Again, although these activities are important, there is no evidence that one of the leading fashion houses has a competitive advantage here – they are all good.
- *Retail outlets*. The leading high fashion houses control at least half of their sales directly. There are several reasons for this: first, because they retain the profit margin; second, because they retain control over how the brand is presented; third, because they are able to present the right ambience and level of discreet and exclusive service for their leading clients. But there is no clear competitive advantage between the three leading companies in this area – they all have strong and well-located store chains.
- *Location*. Paris, Milan and New York are vital for a real impact in high fashion. (Berlin, London, Madrid and Singapore are good but not as important.) Part of the reason for this is the major industrial infrastructure developed near Paris, Milan and New York to support the fashion industry. For example, France has some 2,000 firms, 200,000 jobs and 5 per cent of total industrial production directly associated with the fashion industry. These figures do not include the textile industry and media-related activities also connected to high fashion. But location does not deliver competitive advantage for one leading company over another.

Although the luxury goods industry faced some major profit problems in the immediate period after the world banking crisis of 2008–2009, it recovered relatively quickly. Cynics might argue that this was perhaps because the bonuses paid to the world's leading bankers were hardly affected. Their wealth made them major customers for luxury goods. This was in spite of the fact that they were at least partly responsible for the major economic downturn. Whatever the reason, the luxury goods market has proved remarkably resilient over the last few years.

Finally, let us remind ourselves that the fashion industry is about more than just making profits. To quote the fashion designer Valentino at the time of his retirement in 2007: 'Many women want to be extraordinary and feminine. That will never change. What I want is for a woman to walk into a room and everyone turns to look at her. I want a woman to be noticed and always arouse admiration.'

Neither LVMH nor Richemont discuss broader issues of green sustainability for the luxury goods industry in their annual reports. However, LVMH makes a contribution to supporting the arts and Richemont is an investor in a sustainability project in South Africa.

Case questions

1 Do you agree with the above comments and conclusions on the competitive advantages of luxury goods companies? What are the competitive advantages of such companies?

2 Can the competitive advantages listed above be reclassified using the resource-based concepts developed by strategists like Hamel and Prahalad and Kay? You should consult the sections that follow to review possible areas.

3 Can companies outside the fashion industry draw any useful lessons from the strategies used in this industry? In exploring this question, you might like to consider such topics as branding, licensing, control of retail outlets and the levels of service.

Resource analysis and economic rent - the contribution of David Ricardo: for those interested in the underpinning economic theory, this section explains why competitive advantages deliver high value added.

4.5 RESOURCE ANALYSIS AND COMPETITIVE ADVANTAGE – THE RESOURCE-BASED VIEW (RBV)

4.5.1 The reasons for the development of the RBV

If sustainable competitive advantage is fundamental to effective strategy,[19] then the question arises as to what makes a resource exceptional. Over the years 1984–2007, strategy writers developed a mainly prescriptive answer to this question. It did not happen all at once but emerged from various books and research papers over the period; some of the main contributors are summarised on this book's website.[20] Hence, it is not appropriate to attribute the development to one person. The overall title of the approach is the *resource-based view* (RBV) of strategy development. **Definition ▸** **The RBV stresses the importance of the individual resources of the organisation in delivering the competitive advantage and value added of the organisation.** It represents a substantial shift in emphasis away from the environment-based view that was emphasised in the 1980s and early 1990s through the work of Professor Michael Porter and others – see Chapter 3.

Summary of the reasons for the development of the RBV.

The change happened because strategists were puzzled by the different long-term profit performance of companies in the *same industry*. They argued that, if industry was the main determinant of profits, then all companies in an industry should have similar levels of profitability. But this clearly was not the case. For example, Kellogg (USA) had declining profits in its breakfast cereal business while General Mills (USA) continued to grow – see Chapter 2. Toyota (Japan) and Honda (Japan) made massive strides worldwide in the car industry, often at the expense of General Motors (USA) and Ford (USA), who were losing profits, even in their home markets – see the global cars case (Case 4) in Part 6. Why did this happen? Strategists argued that industry analysis was certainly not wrong: it was needed to identify sustainable competitive advantage and customer needs. But it was clearly not enough.

The essence of the RBV development is its focus on the *individual* resources of the organisation, rather than the strategies that are common to all companies in an industry. It is important to understand the industry, but organisations should seek their own solutions within that context. Sustainable competitive advantage then comes by striving to exploit the *relevant* resources of the individual organisation when compared with other organisations. Relevance means the identification of resources that are better than those of competitors, persuasive to the customer and available from the range of strengths contained inside the organisation. For example, GSK's strategy on pharmaceutical development should concentrate on drugs that will be more effective than those of the competition, offer genuine benefits to the customer and fit with its existing areas of drug strength in treating asthma, viral drugs, etc. It should not move into an area involving technology that is new to the company but where potential competitors like Johnson & Johnson (USA) are already well established, such as surgical equipment and dressings.

Within the context of industry analysis, the starting point for the RBV is a careful exploration of the resources of the organisation – see Section 4.3. But beyond this *general* analysis it is necessary to identify those attributes that give an individual organisation its *particular* strengths.

4.5.2 Sustainable competitive advantage and the RBV

Definition ▶ **Sustainable competitive advantage is an advantage over competitors that cannot easily be imitated.** Sustainable competitive advantage is often abbreviated to SCA. The main reason for analysing competitors is to enable the organisation to develop *competitive advantages* against them, especially advantages that can be *sustained* over time. SCA involves every aspect of the way that the organisation competes in the market place – prices, product range, manufacturing quality, service levels and so on. However, some of these factors can easily be imitated: for example, prices can be changed virtually overnight or other companies can make generic copies of drugs as soon as GlaxoSmithKline (see Case 4.1) loses its patent protection.

The real benefits come from advantages that competitors cannot easily imitate, not from those that give only temporary relief from the competitive battle. To be *sustainable*, competitive advantage needs to be more deeply embedded in the organisation – its resources, skills, culture and investment over time. For example, Louis Vuitton's advantages in the fashion industry come from its brand investment, its reputation for quality, its individual fashion designers and its network of relationships with both suppliers and customers.

4.5.3 Some sources of competitive advantage

In seeking the advantages that competitors cannot easily copy, it is necessary to examine not only the competitors, but also the organisation itself and its resources. There is no 'formula' for undertaking this task but here are some possible *starting points* for later study:

- *Differentiation.* This is the development of unique features or attributes in a product or service that position it to appeal especially to a part of the total market. Branding is an example of this source.
- *Low costs.* The development of low-cost production enables the firm to compete against other companies either on the basis of lower prices or possibly on the basis of the same prices as its competitors but with more services being added. For example, production in China and some South East Asian countries may involve lower labour costs that cannot be matched in the West.[21]
- *Niche marketing.* A company may select a small market segment and concentrate all its efforts on achieving advantages in this segment. Such a niche will need to be distinguished by special buyer needs. Fashion items such as those by Yves St Laurent or Dunhill are examples of products that are specifically targeted towards specialist niches.
- *High performance or technology.* Special levels of performance or service can be developed that simply cannot be matched by other companies – for example, through patented products or recruitment of especially talented individuals. The well-known global consulting companies and merchant banks operate in this way.
- *Quality.* Some companies offer a level of quality that others are unable to match. For example, some Japanese cars have, until recently, provided levels of reliability that Western companies have had difficulty in reaching.

- *Service*. Some companies have deliberately sought to provide superior levels of service that others have been unable or unwilling to match. For example, McDonald's set new levels of service in its fast food restaurants that were unmatched by others for many years.
- *Vertical integration*. The backward acquisition of raw material suppliers and/or the forward purchase of distributors may provide advantages that others cannot match. For example, in Chapter 3, the Arcelor steel company owned some steel distributors.
- *Synergy*. This is the combination of parts of a business such that the sum of them is worth more than the individual parts – that is, 2 + 2 = 5. This may occur because the parts share fixed overheads, transfer their technology or share the same sales force, for example. Claims are often made for this approach when an acquisition is made, but this synergy is not necessarily achieved in reality. Nevertheless, it remains a valid area of exploration.
- *Culture, leadership and style of an organisation*. The way that an organisation leads, trains and supports its members may be a source of advantage that others cannot match. It will lead to innovative products, exceptional levels of service, fast responses to new market developments and so on. This area is more difficult to quantify than some of the other areas above, but this only adds to its unique appeal. It is unusual to find such an area listed in strategy texts, but it is a theme of this book.

Some organisations and strategists have become almost obsessed with the first three of these sources of SCA – Porter's *generic strategies*, as they are often described – and these are discussed in Section 8.2. However, it is inappropriate to focus on three areas alone, because the others listed above (and many more not listed) are also important. In practice, Porter's books explore many possible areas in considerable detail. It could also be argued that several of the sources in the list above involve some form of differentiation. To group these all under 'differentiation', however, would be to ignore the *specific nature* of the form of advantage and to deny the important individual areas of strategy opened up by such concepts.

More generally, John Kay has argued that competitive advantage is based on the *stability* and *continuity* in relationships between different parts of an organisation.[22] He suggests that major advantages are not developed overnight or by some special acquisition or other miraculous strategy. Substantial advantages take many years to develop and involve the whole culture and style of an organisation. To this extent, it may even be misleading to see advantages as being summarised by the short list of items above. However, the list may provide a starting point for further analysis.

Importantly, there is no single route and no strategy 'formula' to finding SCA. Nevertheless, in particular types of business, it is possible to identify some possible areas of competitive advantage – see Table 4.3. In the next section, we examine the principles that underpin the concept.

Table 4.3 Typical sustainable competitive advantages in different types of business

High-technology business	Service business	Small business	Manufacturing business where the company is a market leader
Technical excellence	Reputation for quality of service	Quality	Low costs
Reputation for quality	High quality and training of staff	Prompt service	Strong branding
Customer service	Customer service	Personalised service	Good distribution
Financial resources	Well-known name	Keen prices	Quality product
Low-cost manufacturing	Customer-oriented	Local availability	Good value for money

Sources: see reference.[23]

4.5.4 The seven elements of resource-based sustainable competitive advantage

Over time, various strategists have explored the advantages that an individual organisation might possess to obtain competitive advantage. There is no agreement amongst them on the precise source of such advantages. For example, Prahalad and Hamel highlighted one key resource,[24] Kay[25] has identified three main areas, Peteraf[26] suggested four areas, and Collis and Montgomery[27] have described five. Certainly, these and other writers have made significant contributions and all are agreed on the importance of individual company resources within an industry. Taking all these views into account, it is useful to identify seven elements that comprise the RBV: see Figure 4.8. In addition, it should be noted that several of these elements have *additional* clarifying subordinate aspects – perhaps this is where the disagreement has arisen.

- *Prior or acquired resources.* Value creation is more likely to be successful if it builds on the strengths that are already available to the organisation, rather than starting from scratch in a totally new area. It does not guarantee that the strategy will be successful, but it is a major starting point. Moreover, building on existing strengths will exploit any real uniqueness that has been built as a result of the organisation's history and investment over many years – economists call this *path dependency*. It may be very difficult for competitors to develop the same complex resources. We explored this at the end of Chapter 2 in the section on strategy as history. Finally, one other prior strength that is of major importance in the development of future strategy is the existing reputation of the organisation. For example, the UK retailer Marks & Spencer has certain strengths in terms of *reputation* and quality that will form the basis of future strategy.
- *Innovative capability.* Some organisations are better able to innovate than others. Innovation is important because it is particularly likely to deliver a real breakthrough in competitive advantage that others will have difficulty in matching for a lengthy period. Innovation is explored at various points throughout this book, particularly in Chapter 11. For example, the Japanese consumer electronics company Sony has developed a consistent ability to produce new products over many years. We will return to innovation shortly.
- *Being truly competitive.* It is essential that any resource delivers a true advantage over the competition. This comes back partly to the test of *relevance* to customers, competitors and company strengths outlined in Section 4.5.1 above. But it emphasises that identifying the resource as being a real strength is not enough: the resource must be *comparatively* better than the competition. For example,

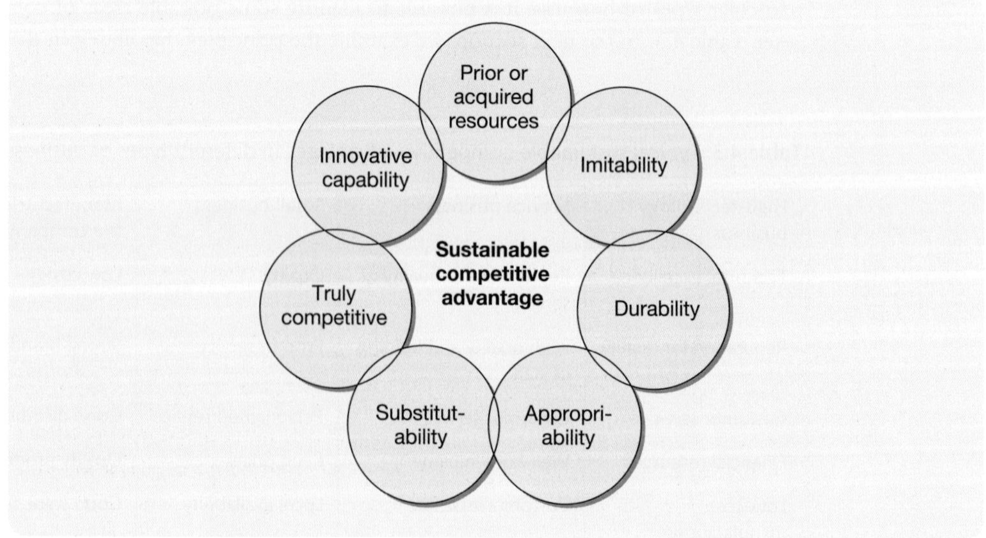

Figure 4.8 Resource-based view: the seven main elements

it is not enough to have a 'low-cost, high-quality' factory – it must have low*er* costs and high*er* quality than that of competitors. For example, the US company Microsoft has developed a computer software package and market position that is superior to any other in the world.

- *Substitutability*. Resources are more likely to be competitive if they cannot be substituted. Sometimes unique resources can be replaced by totally new alternatives. This element was explored in Chapter 3 in Porter's Five Forces Model and is equally valid here in the RBV. For example, there is no substitute for the US Walt Disney company's Mickey Mouse character.
- *Appropriability*. Resources must deliver the results of their advantage to the individual company and not be forced to distribute at least part of it to others. Just because a resource has competitive advantage does not necessarily mean that its benefits will come to the owners. They could be forced to give up some profits to others by the bargaining power of the various stakeholders of the organisation – customers, employees, suppliers and so on. We will explore bargaining in Chapter 5, in the section on game theory, and stakeholders in Chapter 6. Another method of maintaining appropriability is through the company patenting its products and processes. Whatever method is used, the company must be able to keep the profits that the resource generates. For example, the Italian company Benetton has organised its business such that it owns both manufacturing and distribution outlets, thus ensuring that it retains the value added that has been generated throughout its value chain.
- *Durability*. Useful resources must have some longevity. There is no point in identifying a competitive resource whose advantage is not sustainable. At some future time, it is likely that all competitive resources will succumb to the fate described in Chapter 5, Section 5.4.1, by Joseph Schumpeter and no longer deliver competitive advantage. But the longer a resource can keep its advantage, the better. Brand names like that owned by the US photographic company Kodak have that durability.
- *Imitability*. Resources must not be easy to imitate if they are to have competitive advantage. Although many resources can eventually be copied, such a process can be delayed by a number of devices:
  - *Tangible uniqueness*. Some form of specific differentiation, such as branding or a specific geographic location or patent protection, will delay imitability.
  - *Causal ambiguity*. It may not be obvious to competitors what gives a resource its competitive edge. There may be some complex organisational processes that have taken years to develop that are difficult for outside companies to learn or acquire.
  - *Investment deterrence*. When the market has limited or unknown growth prospects and it is difficult to make a small initial investment, a substantial investment by the organisation in the new strategy may well deter competitors from entering the market. This is particularly true where large capital plant or major advertising campaigns are essential to launch products and services.

  For example, the Japanese car company Toyota has developed a manufacturing process that has many human resource elements like team working that cannot easily be observed. This has made it difficult for other car companies to copy the superior Toyota practices.

You can learn more about the *other resources* of every organisation - for example the canteen, the car pool, the office location - and how they fit with the *key resources* that deliver competitive advantage as described in this section. The concept is called 'The Hierarchy of Resources'.

4.5.5 The VRIO Framework - a mechanism for testing competitive resources

Even if the resource hierarchy is useful in providing an initial assessment of the resources possessed by an organisation, there is still the question of identifying those resources that are most likely to provide the return potential associated with exploiting the firm's resources or capabilities. We need a mechanism for testing the competitive resources. Professor Jay Barney of Ohio State University has suggested the *VRIO Framework* to provide such a route – see Table 4.4. This is a sequential

Table 4.4 The VRIO Framework

Is a resource or capability . . .					
Valuable?	**Rare?**	**Costly to imitate?**	**Capable of being exploited by the organisation?**	**Competitive implications**	**Comparative economic performance to be expected from the resource**
No	–	–	No	Competitive disadvantage	Below normal
Yes	No	–	Yes/No	Competitive parity	Normal
Yes	Yes	No	Yes/No	Temporary competitive advantage	Above normal
Yes	Yes	Yes	Yes	Sustained competitive advantage	Above normal

Source: Barney, Jay B, *Gaining and Sustaining Competitive Advantage*, 2nd edn, © 2002. Printed and electronically reproduced by permission of Pearson Education, Inc., Upper Saddle River, New Jersey.

decision-making approach which starts by questioning each resource and asking if it is valuable. Having answered this question, the question then goes on to examine rarity, imitation and organisational capability as outlined below:

- *Valuable*. An organisation's resource needs to be valuable if it is to allow a firm to choose strategies that exploit environmental opportunities or neutralise a competitive threat.
- *Rare*. An organisation's resource needs to be rare. If the resource is available to competitors then exploiting the resource will not generate competitive advantage and economic performance will not be superior to rivals.
- *Cannot be imitated*. An organisation's resource needs to be costly to imitate. If it can be easily imitated then competitors will be able over time to take advantage of the profits generated in the market place to duplicate the rare resource.
- *Organising capability*. An organisation needs to be able to organise itself to exploit its valuable, rare and inimitable resource. In a sense, this is a balancing factor in relation to the three above.

These factors can then come together in the VRIO Framework as a series of cascading decisions. They start by asking whether a resource is valuable, then rare, then easy to imitate, then whether the organisation is well organised to exploit the opportunity. Table 4.4 shows the complete framework.

KEY STRATEGIC PRINCIPLES

- The resource-based view (RBV) argues that the individual resources of an organisation provide a stronger basis for strategy development than industry analysis. The reason is that the RBV will identify those resources that are exceptional and have sustainable competitive advantage (SCA).
- SCA is an advantage over competitors that cannot easily be imitated. There are numerous sources of SCA. These include: differentiation; low costs; niche marketing; high performance or technology; quality; service; vertical integration; synergy; and the culture, leadership and style of the organisation. Importantly, SCA develops slowly over time; such a list is only the starting point of a more detailed study.
- There are seven elements of resource-based competitive advantage: prior or acquired resources, innovative ability, being truly competitive, substitutability, appropriability, durability and imitability.
- It is not necessary for an organisation to possess all of them before it has some competitive advantages. Each organisation will have a unique combination of resources, some of which will involve SCA.
- The VRIO Framework – Valuable, Rare, Inimitable and Organisationally possible – can be used to test resources for their ability to contribute to competitive advantage.

Checklist: A company's competitive resources.

4.6 IDENTIFYING WHICH RESOURCES AND CAPABILITIES DELIVER SUSTAINABLE COMPETITIVE ADVANTAGE

We are now in a position to identify those resources of the organisation that are most likely to deliver SCA. However, it should be noted that this involves a degree of judgement. Moreover, strategic thinking is still developing in this area. The complete process related to SCA is summarised in Figure 4.9.

4.6.1 Basic resource analysis

Video Part 5a

In any resource analysis, we need to begin with a survey of all the basic resources of the organisation. We undertook this process at the beginning of the chapter when we defined resources, so we simply remind ourselves of those three areas:

- *Tangible resources*: the physical resources of the organisation.
- *Intangible resources*: the many other resources that are important but are not physically present.
- *Organisational capability*: the skills, structures and leadership of the organisation that bind all its assets together and allow them to interact efficiently.

Although there is no 'formula' for identifying the specific resources and capabilities that deliver competitive advantage, a number of strategists have suggested some possible areas for consideration – namely, distinctive capabilities, core competencies and knowledge. We examine these in the sections that follow.

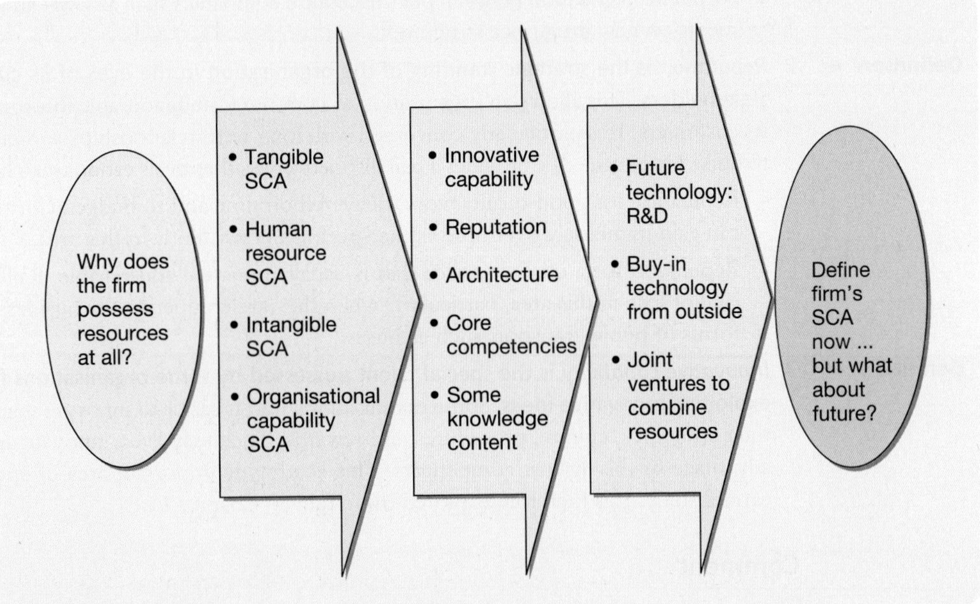

Figure 4.9 Identifying the resources that deliver SCA

4.6.2 The particular importance of three distinctive capabilities: architecture, reputation and innovation

Video Part 5a

As outlined above, different researchers have approached the issue of the resources that will deliver SCA in different ways. Two areas in particular deserve further exploration: distinctive capabilities and core competencies. Although they are contained within the framework outlined above, they represent particular areas of interest and insight. They also make the important point that different strategists lay the emphasis on different areas. For example, the distinctive capabilities approach treats 'innovative ability' as being no more important than any other core resources. This section explores distinctive capabilities in more depth and the next section examines core competencies.

In the analysis of resources, John Kay argued that the distinctive capabilities of an organisation's resources are particularly important in delivering competitive advantage. *Distinctive capabilities* relate to three possible unique resource areas in an organisation: architecture, reputation and innovative ability.[28] They are complex and not necessarily capable of quantified analysis but they will undoubtedly contribute to the distinctive development of a company's strategy. He introduced and explored them by explaining that an organisation has a series of contracts and more informal relationships:

- with its employees inside the organisation;
- with its suppliers, distributors and customers outside in the environment; and
- possibly between a group of collaborating firms inside and outside the immediate industry.

The relationships have been built over time. Some are formal and some informal. They are similar to, but more extended than, the linkages explored in the value system of Section 4.4.2 above. They provide the organisation with three major ways for their resources to be distinctive from competitors'.

Definition ▶ 1 ***Architecture* is the network of relationships and contracts both inside and outside the firm.** Its importance lies in its ability to create knowledge and routines, to respond to market changes and to exchange information both inside and outside the organisation. Long-term relationships with other organisations can lead to real strategy benefits that competitors cannot replicate. Examples include:
   - the contacts between major construction companies such as Bouygues and government departments which place substantial contracts;
   - negotiations between rail companies such as Nederlandse Spoorwegen and trade unions on new working practices to introduce new technologies and reduce costs;
   - corporate negotiation between pharmaceutical companies such as GSK and Merck and governments on new drug price structures.

Definition ▶ 2 ***Reputation* is the strategic standing of the organisation in the eyes of its customers and other stakeholders.** This allows an organisation to communicate favourable information about itself to its customers. It is particularly concerned with long-term relationships and takes lengthy periods to build. Once gained, it provides a real distinctiveness that rivals cannot match. Examples include:
   - Reputation for good-quality work, delivered on time and to budget. Construction companies can gain immensely over time as they perform consistently in this area.
   - Reputation for a quality service that is usually punctual and reliable. Railway companies can gain or lose in this area, particularly when they are competing for business against alternative forms of public transport such as buses.

Definition ▶ 3 ***Innovative capability* is the special talent possessed by some organisations for developing and exploiting innovative ideas.** Some organisations find it easier to innovate than others because of their structures, culture, procedures and rewards. They may even innovate and then fail to take advantage of this against competitors. This is a highly important area of strategy that deserves careful study. It is therefore explored more fully in Chapter 11.

Comment

The above areas of resource will apply to a greater or lesser extent to most organisations. In themselves, they are important but uncontroversial.

All three areas usually require years of development. The first two are easier to define than they are to develop in terms of options: the *method* by which architecture and reputation are to be improved begs numerous questions about their nature that are difficult to explore. There is a tendency towards worthy, but largely meaningless, wish-fulfilment statements about the desirability of improving them. Kay offers no clear exposition in this area. The third element, innovation, will be explored in Chapter 11. Some strategists judge that there are so many other potential areas of resource-based advantage that it is not worth highlighting these areas, as appears in this text. The point is correct but fails to take into account the broad nature of the RBV and thus the difficulty of making it actionable.

The real point is how they are understood and used to gain competitive advantage. Resource analysis in these areas needs to take into account the changes that can occur over time and the need to explore not only the area itself but how it can be developed further. This is where the alternative viewpoint of the seven elements of the RBV can make a contribution.

4.6.3 The particular importance of core competencies

Definition ▶

In a related area of study, Hamel and Prahalad have explored the area of core skills and competencies.[29] **Core competencies are a group of production skills and technologies that enable an organisation to provide a particular benefit to customers;** they underpin the leadership that companies have built or wish to acquire over their competitors.

Video Part 5a

Core skills are a fundamental resource of the organisation. The two authors describe the example of Sharp (Japan) and Toshiba (Japan), both of which identified *flat-screen electronic technology* as an opportunity area that they expected to see grow in the future. Both companies invested hundreds of millions of dollars in developing their technology and skills in the market for flat screens that would then be used in miniature televisions, portable computers, digital watches, electronic video recorders and other areas. Importantly, this investment was made *before* it was possible to build a product-specific business case that would justify this level of investment. Core competencies form the basis of core products which, in turn, form the basis of the business areas of the company.

Core competencies cover an integration of skills, knowledge and technology. This combination can then lead to competitive advantage. The analysis of such areas is derived from a study of its components in an individual organisation. A skills analysis needs to be conducted at a level that is detailed enough to reveal useful strategic insights but not so detailed that it is unmanageable. The two authors suggest that if only three or four skills are identified this may be too broad, but if 40 or 50 are identified this may be too detailed. They suggest there are three areas that distinguish the major core competencies:

1 *Customer value.* Competencies must make a real impact on how the customer perceives the organisation and its products or services.
2 *Competitor differentiation.* This must be competitively unique. If the whole industry has the skill, then it is not core unless the organisation's skills in the area are really special.
3 *Extendable.* Core skills need to be capable of providing the basis of products or services that go beyond those currently available. The skill needs to be removed from the particular product group in which it currently rests. The organisation needs to imagine how it might be exploited in the whole area of its operations.

Importantly, core competencies are a vital *prerequisite* for the competitive battle that then takes place for market share: the development of key resources has to come before and not during market place activity. It should be noted that Hamel and Prahalad couple core competencies with the organisation's *vision of the future* – this is explained and explored in Chapter 6.

Examples of core skills will include:

- *Glaxo* – not just its ownership of its drug patents, but also the whole range of skills and contacts that the company has in the pharmaceutical market place with customers, distributors and health authorities.

- *Nederlandse Spoorwegen* will have core skills related to its operation of a rail network. But, more importantly from a competitive viewpoint, it will have skills in customer handling, timetabling, service scheduling and so on, as against those related to buses and aircraft.
- *Bouygues* has core skills in road building that relate to road design and construction. But many companies will have such skills. Its real competencies will relate to its ability to gain large contracts and manage such assignments once agreed. It will need to deliver on time to an agreed standard and within the agreed budget.

Comment

David Sainsbury, the chairman of the leading UK retailer, has said that he believes that the ideas contained in the above have real merit.[30] But he also comments that:

- Core skills may be easier to apply to larger rather than smaller companies, which may not have the depth of management talent. Certainly, the examples on core skills quoted in the text are all from large companies.
- The ideas have been most thoroughly developed for electronics and related markets. The concepts may need to be adapted for others, e.g. medium-sized engineering companies.

Beyond these comments, one of the practical problems with core competencies is that the developers never really offer any clear checklist of points for their development – they are all rather vague. Ten guidelines that explore resource-based competencies and capabilities are offered in Chapter 8, Exhibit 8.3.

More fundamentally, core competencies ignore other areas highlighted by the RBV as contributing to resource analysis and development. Competitive advantage may be just as well served by a strong brand, an exclusive patent or a superior geographical location. These and other resources have little or no connection with core competencies.

4.6.4 Knowledge management as the main source of competitive advantage?

In recent years, some strategists have taken the view that the knowledge management of the organisation represents the main source of competitive advantage.[31] They argue that the retention, exploitation and sharing of knowledge are extremely important in the ability of companies to stay ahead of their rivals. In particular, the way in which knowledge is managed and disseminated throughout the organisation represents an important advantage, especially in international companies.[32] **By knowledge is meant the accumulation over time of the skills, routines and capabilities that shape the organisation's ability to survive and compete in markets.** In addition, as Leonard points out, 'Knowledge reservoirs in organisations are not static pools but wellsprings, constantly replenished with streams of new ideas and constituting an ever-flowing source of corporate renewal.'[33] We will explore the role of knowledge in the context of innovation in Chapter 7.

Definition ▶

Comment

Clearly, it is conceivable that, in some types of organisation, knowledge is extremely important – for example, consulting companies, some accountancy and legal practices. But to raise the role of knowledge to be the prime source of advantage for *all* organisations may be to exaggerate its importance. For example, Nederlandse Spoorwegen possesses a unique collection of rail track in the Netherlands and McDonald's has employed branding of the Big Mac to deliver competitive advantage that is sustainable. Neither of these has any substantive connection with knowledge.

4.6.5 Resource-based view and SMEs

Although it might at first appear that the RBV is particularly suited to large companies with vast resources, it is also relevant for small and medium-size enterprises (SMEs). Such organisations tend to have a smaller number of resources, but they can also be more flexible and entrepreneurial. Typically, organisations of this size often develop strategies that might include:

- higher levels of personal service;
- specialist expertise;
- design skills;
- regional knowledge;
- bespoke solutions.

All of these can be contained within the seven elements of the RBV. They suggest that core resources at SMEs need to be carefully developed to reflect these strategies – perhaps extra people, extra training, the use of local knowledge and so on. Some areas of the RBV may be difficult to develop in the early years, such as *tangible uniqueness* and *investment deterrence*. Microsoft was once an SME, but now it has the ability to develop some of these more capital-intensive resource areas. In principle, the elements therefore provide useful guidance for SMEs.

4.6.6 Comment on the RBV

Although the RBV represents greater clarity in strategy development, it still harbours a number of important weaknesses:

- It is still just a list of factors to consider – there is no guiding logic between the elements. Probably there never will be because, by definition, such logic might imply an industry solution.
- Beyond the concept of innovation (and this is not present in many explorations of the RBV), there is little guidance on how resources develop and change over time. The dynamics of resource development are an important element in strategy and the RBV adds little insight to this.[34] We will explore this in the next chapter.
- There is a complete lack of consideration of the human element in resource development.
- Some critical comment suggests that the whole concept is tautological, i.e. the logical process that identifies key resources is flawed because the solution is known from the opening definition of the process.[35]
- There is little or no emphasis on emergent approaches to resource development and almost no recognition of the process aspects of strategy development. The simple assumption that each element just needs to be defined and then it will happen automatically is a gross over-simplification of the reality of strategy development.

Finally, some proponents of various aspects of the RBV hold exaggerated views of its role as the solution to most strategic issues. It is clearly an advance, but it is no substitute for the comprehensive development of every aspect of strategy analysis.

KEY STRATEGIC PRINCIPLES

- There is no general agreement on what constitutes the best single approach to the development of SCA. Two approaches have proved useful - *distinctive capabilities* from Kay and *core competencies* from Hamel and Prahalad.
- Distinctive capabilities identify three possible unique resource areas in an organisation: architecture, reputation and innovative ability.
- Core competencies are a group of production skills and technologies that enable an organisation to provide a particular benefit to customers.
- The RBV has a number of weaknesses: it is simply a list of possible factors to consider; it ignores many aspects of human resource issues and it partially ignores the process aspects of strategy development.

4.7 RESOURCE AND CAPABILITY ANALYSIS – IMPROVING COMPETITIVE ADVANTAGE

After analysing resources, organisations often find that they have few assets that are *truly* competitive. This is quite normal since most organisations will consist of a range of resources, many being similar to those of competitors, with just a few being exceptional. In this context, the long lists of 'core competencies' seen in some analyses suggest that the compiler has not been sufficiently rigorous rather than that the company is multi-talented.[36] Regardless of the length of the list, the identification of the truly competitive resources based only on the analysis undertaken so far in this chapter may be misleading. The reason is that the approach so far has been largely static:

- the analysis of value added represents the picture at a point in time;
- the identification of the seven elements of RBV is usually based on current resources.

Although a static approach is useful, a resource analysis at a point in time is a distortion of reality. An organisation's capabilities will change over time, its competitors will invest in new assets and so on. For example, assets will be constantly consumed in an oil company and they will have a limited life in a fast-changing computer business. The real role of resource analysis is to act as the first step in improving resources. This is developed further in Chapter 5.

Any enhancement of value added and competitive advantage will come about through a course of action over time. This is a strategic *process* with all that this implies in terms of the human resources of the organisation, its change of culture and its leadership. The process may be *emergent* as well as *prescriptive*. For example, it may involve experimental, trial-and-error approaches to resource development (emergent) just as much as the strict application of RBV analysis (prescriptive). Our main exploration of the ways of improving our resources must await a more detailed look at resources and a clarification of the purpose of the organisation in Chapters 6 and 7. But it is convenient and relevant to consider three elements now:

1 benchmarking;
2 exploiting existing resources – leveraging;
3 upgrading resources.

4.7.1 Benchmarking

Definition ▶ One approach to the task of assessing the comparative performance of parts of an organisation is ***benchmarking* – the comparison of practice with that of other organisations in order to identify areas for improvement.** The other organisation does not necessarily have to be in the same industry. The comparison simply has to be with another whose practices are recognised as leading the field in that particular aspect of the task or function.

For example, the Ford Motor Company (USA) might wish to test the competitiveness of its supplier relationships. It might then identify a world leader in supplier relationships, such as the well-known UK retailer Marks & Spencer. Ford might then approach the retailer directly or indirectly through consultants or an industry association. Ford will ask to compare its performance against that of Marks & Spencer in this specific functional area. The differences in performance between Ford and the retailer in its chosen activity are then analysed to form the basis of improving the resource at Ford. The results are then used in the sequence shown in Figure 4.10.

Comment

Some commentators argue that benchmarking has an inherent weakness in improving competitive advantage because its aim is only to bring a resource up to the standards of other companies – on this interpretation, there is no *advantage* over other companies. However, this may not fully capture the essence of benchmarking, which is to bring up the resource standard compared with companies *in other industries* – for example, Ford in the car industry benchmarking with Marks & Spencer in UK

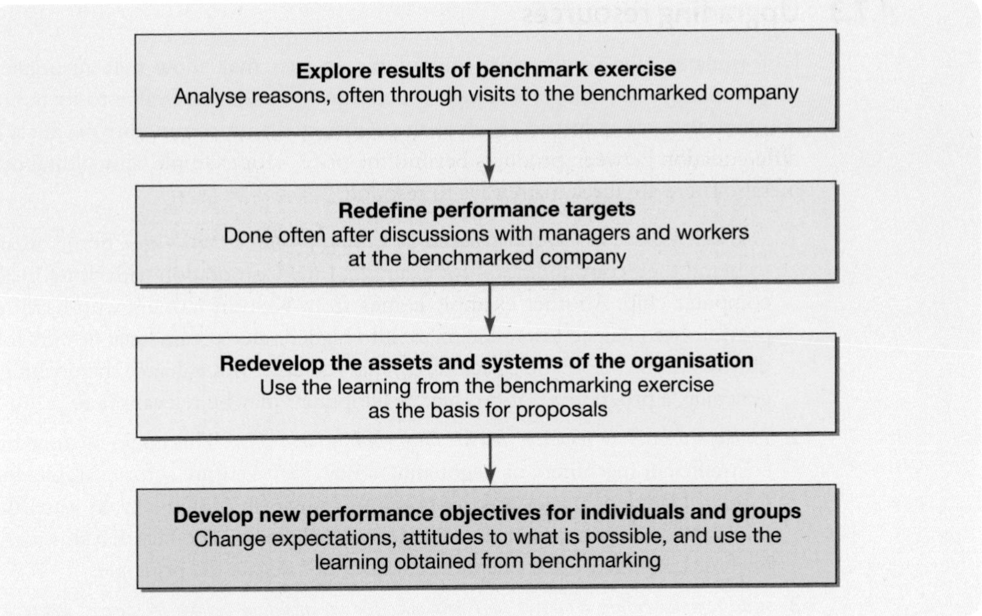

Figure 4.10 Typical benchmarking sequence

retailing. In other words, if Ford achieves the benchmark, then it may still be superior to other companies *in the car industry*.

4.7.2 Exploiting existing resources – leveraging

Definition ▶ **In any organisation, it is essential to exploit its existing resources to the full – this is sometimes called *leveraging resources*.**[37] For example, for many years after Walt Disney died, his film company continued to make good films but made no attempt to exploit the many characters in any other medium. It took the arrival of Michael Eisner at the head of Disney in the 1980s to exploit the Disney resources and move the company into hotels, brand merchandising and publishing. More generally, existing resources can be exploited in five areas:

1 *Concentration* – focusing resources on the key objectives of the organisation and targeting, in particular, those that will have the largest influence on value added.
2 *Conservation* – using every part of the resource, perhaps recycling where possible, with the aim of exploiting every aspect available to the organisation.
3 *Accumulation* – digging deep into the resources of the organisation to discover every scrap of accumulated knowledge and skill, coupled with the acquisition of outside skills and experience, where appropriate.
4 *Complementarity* – analysing resources from the perspective of blending new elements together, such as marketing and operations, and supporting stronger elements so that they do not suffer from weaknesses elsewhere in the organisation.
5 *Recovery* – ensuring that resources generate cash quickly where possible, thus achieving the full benefit of new and existing resources sooner rather than later.

These are all prescriptive routes towards exploiting existing resources and deserve careful study. A classic example in strategy development has been the way that News Corporation (Australia) used its existing strength in UK newspapers in the early 1990s to support and enhance its development of its new satellite television channels: they were heavily promoted in its leading UK newspapers the *Sun* and *The Times* – see Chapter 8.

4.7.3 Upgrading resources

Unfortunately, the results of a competitive analysis may show that an organisation has little or no competitive advantage, although it continues to add some value to its inputs. This situation is common in some industries, such as those involved with commodity products where there is little differentiation between products beyond the price – for example, agricultural products, mining and metals. There are three main ways to respond:

1 *Add new resources to support or enhance an existing product or service area.* Some organisations have tried to brand their commodities – for example, Intel Corporation with 'Intel Inside' and its Pentium computer chip. Another example comes from Kenyan farmers who have replanted fields that previously contained low-value maize into higher-value commercial flowers for export to Europe: they retain their land and agricultural skills resources but enhance them with new products. More generally, a programme of product development may be relevant here.
2 *Enhance directly the resources that are threatened by competition.* This could be done by buying new, more cost-efficient machinery or negotiating a new joint venture – for example, the 1998 merger that formed DaimlerChrysler was supposed to transform (potentially, at least) the resources of two medium-sized car companies to create a global player. The fact that this merger has now largely been unscrambled – see Chapter 16 – does not negate the principle.
3 *Add complementary resources that will take the organisation beyond its current competition.* Sometimes the industry will remain unattractive and it may be better to develop resources that will eventually allow the organisation to move beyond its current competitors – for example, some farmers have moved into the leisure industry, setting up golf courses, accommodation and similar activities and thus moving out of reliance on agricultural commodity pricing and into other areas with higher profit margins.

Upgrading resources raises the whole issue of how an organisation moves forward over time with regard to the resources at its disposal, the purpose of the organisation and the moves made by its competitors. Importantly, it relies on a strategic vision of where the organisation is headed – perhaps more of the same, perhaps moving into new areas. This issue is tackled in the next chapter.

KEY STRATEGIC PRINCIPLES

- There are at least three ways to improve sustainable competitive advantage (SCA): benchmarking, exploiting existing resources and upgrading resources.
- *Benchmarking* is a comparison of practice with that of another organisation considered to display best practice in its field of operation. The aim of benchmarking is to identify areas of improvement in the resources of the organisation.
- *Exploiting existing resources – leveraging.* There are five main methods for undertaking this task. They are: concentration, conservation, accumulation, complementarity and recovery.
- *Upgrading resources.* There are three main methods: developing new resources, enhancing those threatened by competitors and adding complementary resources.

4.8 ANALYSING OTHER IMPORTANT COMPANY RESOURCES: ESPECIALLY HUMAN RESOURCES

After analysing resources from the perspective of competitive advantage, it is important to explore other perspectives. Case 4.1 on the three different companies Glaxo, Nederlandse Spoorwegen and Bouygues illustrates the importance of taking a broader view of resources beyond competitive advantage. There are at least three approaches:

- *Financial perspective*, including cash flow, shareholding, tax and related issues.
- *Operations (production) perspective* involving such matters as lean production, inventory control and quality manufacturing and services.
- *Human resources perspective* examining topics such as organisational culture, leadership and change.

Many such areas are beyond the scope of this book, which focuses primarily on strategy as a separate subject. However, strategy inevitably involves *strategic change* which has an obvious human element. In addition, the *leadership* of the organisation will be crucial to developing and implementing the most effective strategy. Hence, one of the most important areas of company resource that is intertwined with strategy is the human resource. This deserves to be analysed at this stage of strategy development. In particular, the culture of the organisation needs to be studied. Chapter 16 examines strategic leadership.

Checklist: Analysing the human resources of an organisation from a strategy perspective.

4.8.1 Analysing the current organisational culture

Definition ▶ **Organisational culture is the set of beliefs, values and learned ways of managing of an organisation.** The culture of the firm will influence the structures, systems and approach to the development of strategic management. Company culture derives from its past, its present, its current people especially its leader(s), technology and physical resources. It will also derive from the aims, objectives and values of those who work in the organisation. For example, some people in GSK pharmaceuticals will recall the original merger of the UK Glaxo company with the American Smith Kline company: the merger strategy resulted in many changes that relied totally on a culture that was willing to accept change.

Because each organisation has a different combination of history, management and technology, each will have a culture that is unique. Analysis is important because culture influences every aspect of the organisation and leaders need to understand the starting point if they are to develop strategy that usually involves some changes.[38] Specifically, it is the filter and shaper through which the leaders, managers and workers develop and implement their strategies. For these reasons, it will be a major influence on the development of strategic management.

In spite of its importance, there is a significant problem in analysing culture. The difficulty is the lack of agreement amongst leading writers on its nature, structure and influence. This book explores the matter from a strategic perspective only and has therefore used this lens to select the most relevant theories.[39] The main elements of organisational culture are set out in Figure 4.11.

Outside the organisation itself, there will be a whole series of influences on the organisational culture of the organisation. These will include the changing values of people in society and political life, the corporate cultures of other similar companies and the employment policies of governments with which the organisation has to deal. There may also be some international issues associated with culture, if the organisation is involved in more than one country.

Within the organisation, there will also be a series of factors that will define the existing culture of an organisation. Leaders may find it useful to analyse them under the following headings.

History and ownership

A young company may have been founded by one individual or a small group who will continue to influence its development for some years. Centralised ownership will clearly concentrate power and therefore will concentrate influence and style. Family firms and owner-dominated firms will have clearly recognisable cultures.

Size

As firms expand, they may lose the tight ownership and control and therefore allow others to influence their style and culture. Even if ownership remains tight, larger companies are more difficult to control from the centre.

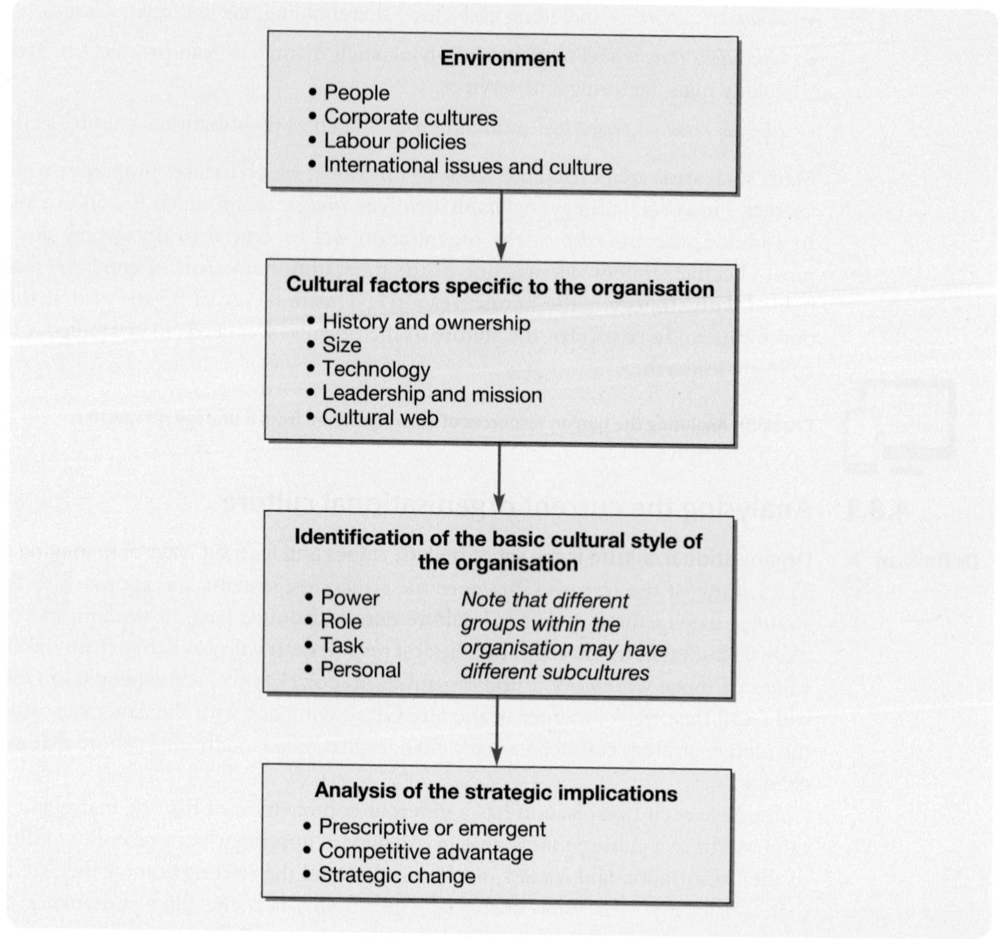

Figure 4.11 Analysing the main elements of organisational culture

Technology

This will influence the culture of the company, but its effects are not always predictable.[40] Those technologies that require economies of scale or involve high costs and expensive machinery usually require a formal and well-structured culture for success: examples might include large-scale chemical production or beer brewing. Conversely, in fast-changing technologies, such as those in telecommunications, a more flexible culture may be required.

Leadership and mission

Individuals and their values will reflect and change the culture of the organisation over time, especially the chief executive and immediate colleagues. These issues are vital to the organisation.

Cultural web

Definition ▶ **The cultural web consists of the factors that can be used to characterise some aspects of the culture of an organisation.** It is a useful method of bringing together the basic elements that are helpful in analysing the culture of an organisation (see Figure 4.12). It is important because culture can shape strategy. The main elements are:

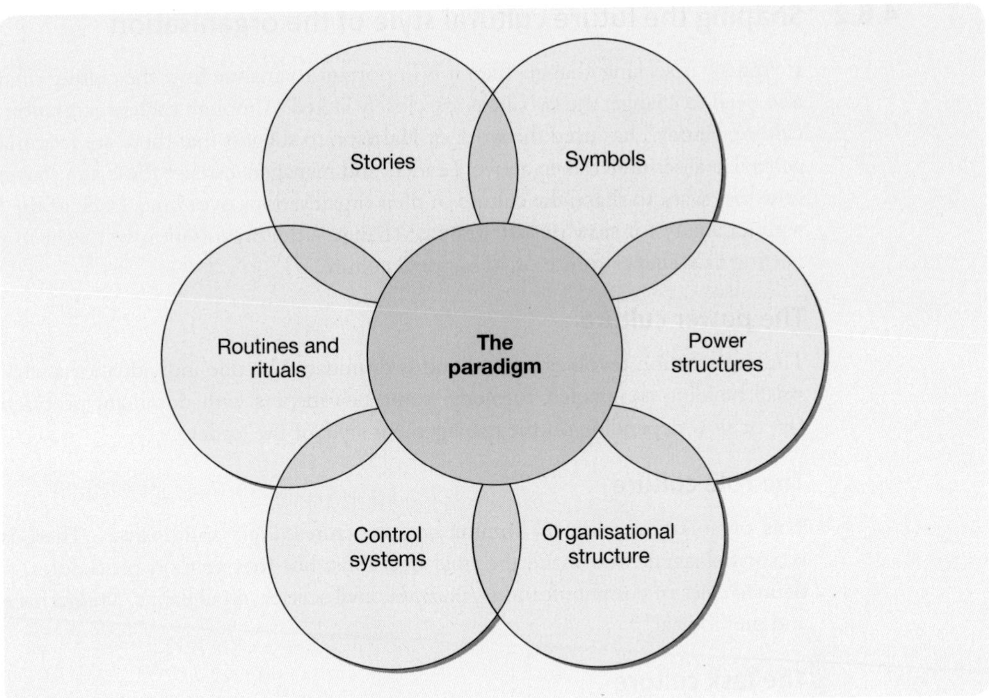

Figure 4.12 Developing the cultural web

Source: Johnson, G (1992) 'Managing strategic change – Strategy, culture and action', *Long Range Planning*, Vol 25 (1), pp 28–36. Copyright 1992, with permission from Elsevier.

- *Stories*. What do people talk about in the organisation? What matters in the organisation? What constitutes success or failure?
- *Routines*. What are the normal ways of doing things? What are the procedures (not always written down)?
- *Rituals*. Beyond the normal routine, what does the organisation highlight? For example, long service? Sales achievement? Innovation? Quality standards? How does it highlight and possibly reward such rituals?
- *Symbols*. What are the symbols of office? Office size? Company car size? Separate restaurants for different levels of managers and workers? Or the absence of these? How do employees travel: first, business or tourist class?
- *Control systems*. Bureaucratic? Well-documented? Oriented towards performance? Formal or informal? Haphazard?
- *Organisational structure*. Who reports to whom in the organisation on a formal basis and who has an informal relationship?
- *Power structures*. Who makes the decisions? Who influences the decisions? How? When?

The cultural web can usefully distinguish also between what is done *officially* in an organisation, such as press releases and post-project evaluation, and what is done *unofficially*, such as grapevine stories, office parties, e-mail messages and so on. The paradigm not only links the elements but may also tend to *preserve* them as 'the way we do things here'. It summarises the culture of the organisation. An example of the cultural web analysis for Ford Motor Company is given later in this book at Exhibit 16.2.

4.8.2 Shaping the future cultural style of the organisation

If strategy is seeking change, then it is important to analyse how the culture of an organisation may also need to change: the two areas are closely linked. Although each organisation has its own unique culture, Handy[41] has used the work of Harrison to suggest that there are four main types within the general analysis undertaken above. Leaders and managers can use these as a starting point in deciding how they want to shape the culture of their organisations over time. Each of the four styles is linked with an ability for slow or fast strategic change – the organisation will want to reflect on this connection as it shapes future organisational culture.

The power culture

The organisation revolves around and is dominated by one individual or a small group. *Examples*: small building companies; formerly, some newspapers with dominant proprietors. *Strategic change*: fast or slow depending on the management style of the leader.

The role culture

This organisation relies on committees, structures, logic and analysis. There is a small group of senior managers who make the final decisions, but they rely on procedures, systems and clearly defined rules of communication. *Examples*: civil service, retail banks. *Strategic change*: likely to be slow and methodical.

The task culture

The organisation is geared to tackling identified projects or tasks. Work is undertaken in teams that are flexible and tackle identified issues. The teams may be multidisciplinary and adaptable to each situation. *Examples*: advertising agencies, consultancies. *Strategic change*: will depend on the circumstances but may be fast where this is needed.

The personal culture

The individual works and exists purely for him/herself. The organisation is tolerated as the way to structure and order the environment for certain useful purposes, but the prime area of interest is the individual. *Examples*: co-operatives, communes and also individual professionals such as architects or engineers working as lone people in larger organisations such as health authorities. *Strategic change*: can be instant, where the individual decides that it is in his/her interests to make such a move.

Qualifying the four cultural types

In considering the four main types of organisational culture, there are four important qualifications:

1. *Organisations change over time.* The entrepreneur, represented by the *power culture*, may mature into a larger and more traditional business. The bureaucracy, personified by the *role culture*, may move towards the more flexible structure of the *task culture*. Hence, an analysis may need to be reassessed after some years.
2. *Several types of culture usually exist in the same organisation.* There may be small task-teams concentrating on developing new business or solving a specific problem and, in the same organisation, a more bureaucratic set-up handling large-volume production in a more formal structure and style. Strategic management may even need to consider whether different parts of the organisation should develop *different* cultures – for example, a team culture for a radical new venture, a personal culture for the specialist expertise required for a new computer network.
3. *Different cultures may predominate, depending on the headquarters and ownership of the company.* Hofstede's research[42] indicates that national culture will also have an influence and will interact with the above basic type.
4. *Organisational culture changes only slowly.*[43] It is important that leaders do not expect instant shifts in basic attitudes, beliefs and ways of acting in an organisation.

For the above four reasons, the analysis of strategic cultural change needs to be approached with caution. Nevertheless, there are many organisations, both large and small, where the mood, style and tone are clear enough as soon as you walk through the door: Google's bright colours, 'Lego' models and bean bags represent just one example. There is one prevailing culture that permeates the way in which business is done in that organisation.

4.8.3 Testing the analysis of culture for strategic relevance

Finally for the purposes of strategy development, the culture analysis needs to be tested for strategic relevance in at least the following five areas:

- *Risk*. Does the organisation wish to change its level of risk?
- *Rewards*. What reward and job satisfaction?
- *Change*. High or low degree of change needed?
- *Cost reduction*. Is the organisation seeking major cost reductions?
- *Competitive advantage*. Are significant new advantages likely or will they be needed?

Exploring international cultural perspectives on strategic management.

Leaders may need to direct and manage across country borders. In these circumstances, it is useful for leaders to have some understanding of *national* culture alongside the *organisational* culture that is already explored in this chapter.

Ten guidelines for analysing organisational culture and its strategy implications.

KEY STRATEGIC PRINCIPLES

- Organisational culture is the set of beliefs, values and learned ways of managing that govern organisational behaviour. Each organisation has a culture that is unique.
- Culture influences performance and strategic management. Leaders have the opportunity to shape culture over time.
- Factors within the organisation influencing culture include: history and ownership, size, technology, leadership and mission, along with the cultural web of the organisation.
- The cultural web provides a method of summarising some of the cultural influences within an organisation: stories, routines and rituals, symbols, power structures, organisation structure, control systems.
- Factors external to the organisation influencing culture include: people, national cultures, the corporate cultural environment, labour and employment policies.
- Within a general analysis of organisational culture, there are four main types: power, role, task and personal. Some types are better able to cope and manage strategic change than others. Leaders who wish to change strategy will want to identify and use these types with regard to specific strategic initiatives.
- Guidelines can be developed for analysing organisational culture. For the purposes of strategy development, such an analysis needs to be assessed against the strategy in areas such as attitudes to risk, change, reward, cost reduction and competitive advantage.

CASE STUDY 4.3

Microsoft and Sony use their competitive resources to hit Nintendo hard

In 2007, the Japanese computer games manufacturer Nintendo launched the innovative Wii to retake a major share of the computer games market. But Microsoft and Sony have struck back so hard that Nintendo became loss-making for the years 2012 and 2013.

Background – the early years

There is nothing new in the home video game machine battle. The Californian firm Atari was the early leader back in the 1980s. However, it had no proprietary software or hardware – competitors could copy its machines and software games developers had unrestricted access to its games. As in the case of the IBM personal computer – see Chapter 1 – this was not a recipe for success.

Then along came the Japanese company Nintendo. It had learnt some important strategic lessons about competitive resources. First, it used a branded character called Mario. Second, it sold the games consoles at low prices and made its profits from its exclusive software games. Third, it made sure that the games consoles were unique and could not work with other games. Finally, it restricted the number of software houses that it licensed to develop its games, thus ensuring that it had some control over the quality of the games.

Game wars hot up in the 1980s and 1990s

Such success attracted another Japanese company, Sega. This company picked up some of the best ideas from Nintendo; for example, it developed its own branded character, Sonic the Hedgehog. In addition, it launched a more advanced machine and stole market share from Nintendo in a rapidly expanding market. By the early 1990s, Sega had become market leader, with around 50 per cent market share. Then Sony entered the market in the mid-1990s.

Sony gains market leadership in the late 1990s

Sony used its competitive resources well. As a result of its involvement in films, it had the use of branded characters from its entertainment business. In addition, it used its financial resources to acquire a software development company and its expertise in consumer electronics to develop a new generation of games machines based on CD-ROMs. In 1998, Sega responded with its Dreamcast machine, which had superior graphics. Sony then hit back with PlayStation, which had even better graphics and was much faster than the Sega machine. Meanwhile, Nintendo was holding its own with Game Boy.

In 2001, Sega decided to throw in the towel on games machines – it had not made a profit for six years. Sony had invested $500 million in PlayStation and its successor, PlayStation 2. It was reaping the rewards, with market leadership of around 80 per cent in a global market worth around $20 billion per annum. Sony's games machine profits were the biggest contributor to its total business over this time. Then along came Microsoft in 2000.

After early success with the Wii, Nintendo's rivals have hit back with their own new games machines.
Getty Images/Justin Sullivan

Microsoft enters the home entertainment battle

Microsoft has been the market leader in personal computer software with its Windows system since the early 1980s. It has so dominated the global market that it has been the subject of anti-trust legal action in its home country, the USA, and also in Europe. Microsoft would not deny that it dominated this market worldwide. But the Windows system was largely employed for home *work* rather than home *entertainment*.

Market opportunity 2001–2005

If you are an aggressive company like Microsoft, you can see an obvious opportunity to expand into entertainment – especially when the video-games console market is worth around $30 billion and projected to grow at 10 per cent per annum up to 2015. Thus Bill Gates launched the new Microsoft games machine, the XBox, in the USA in late 2001 and in Japan and Europe in early 2002. Importantly, the new machine was in some respects more like a dedicated home computer, thus illustrating how the personal computer and the games machine may converge technically over the next few years. Arguably, this might threaten the Microsoft dominance of home PCs in the long term. Certainly, it also provided an opportunity for Microsoft to tackle a new and potentially lucrative market in the short term.

Around 2000 to 2005, Microsoft was not aiming to beat Sony's market share. Its machine was technically more sophisticated but was initially priced higher. Sony's PlayStation 2 largely matched the XBox performance. The Nintendo GameCube was simpler technically, but significantly cheaper. Both Sony and Nintendo had a wider range of software games in the early years than Microsoft. However, Microsoft claimed to have built into its new machine the technical ability for gamers to use the much faster broadband telecommunications system so that fast games could be played between homes. But, since broadband was only in 4 per cent of homes at the time of launch, this was not a major competitive advantage in the early years. More generally, after four years on the market, prices were settling down at levels substantially below those of the launch period.

Market opportunities 2006

In May 2005, Microsoft launched the XBox 360 with a new generation of graphics capability and new software games. Almost on the same day (what a coincidence!) Sony announced the launch of PlayStation 3 (PS3). Importantly, both these machines represented a real competitive threat to Nintendo's Game Boy because they had superior gaming facilities.

Throughout this whole competitive battle, commentators assumed that Nintendo would be completely eliminated from the games machine market. They argued that Nintendo did not have the financial resources and market dominance of Microsoft or the next-generation technical capacity of Sony. The whole discussion among market observers was whether Microsoft would be able to gain the upper hand from Sony in the games machine market: would game players wait for Sony? Or would they opt for the XBox?

Market response from Nintendo

In late 2006, along came Nintendo's response: a new games machine called the Wii that was truly innovative. Nintendo introduced a motion-sensitive wand that could be pointed and waved to control the game on the screen. It also helped that the Wii was priced at around $200, significantly cheaper than its rivals. Nintendo could not make enough of the machines and had stopped advertising. By the end of 2010, Nintendo had sold 85 million machines - nearly as much as the combined sales of both Microsoft and Sony.

Microsoft and Sony hit back

In late 2010, Microsoft launched its Kinect motion box. This was technically more advanced than the Wii because it was able to respond to visual and sound signals without the need for a hand-held controller. Nintendo's sales began to falter.

In 2013, this was then followed by completely new games machines from Microsoft and Sony: the Xbox One and the PlayStation 4 - see Table 4.5. Nintendo's only response had been the hand-held 3DS machine, followed later by a two-dimensional version of the same machine. In 2012 and 2103, Nintendo made operating losses on its worldwide business even before the launch of the two new games machines from Microsoft and Sony. Arguably, Nintendo needed another machine like the earlier Nintendo Wii to recover its position. Otherwise, it might go the same way as Sega.

All three companies have published extensive plans, which are available on their websites.

 This case was written by Richard Lynch from published sources only.[44]

Table 4.5 The rival products in 2014

Games machine	Maker	Launch prices	Total sales since launch	Facilities	Number of games available
Xbox One with updated Kinect controller - launched November 2013	Microsoft	$499 plus $60 per year for processor, Kinect	5 million units	Live TV, Blue Ray, 8 core processor, Kinect	Limited games at launch Good range after four years
Nintendo 3DS followed by cheaper 2DS	Nintendo	$170	'Disappointing' level of sales	Handheld, exclusive three-dimensional display but online services weak and closing down	Wide range of games, especially those aimed to broader target group than games players
PlayStation 4 - launched November 2013	Sony	$399 plus $50 per year for game playing online	7 million units	TV streaming services, Blue Ray, 8 core processor	Limited games at launch: primarily aimed at games players only

Source: author from various websites plus references listed at end of chapter.

Case questions

1 What conclusions do you draw about the competitive advantages of Microsoft? Are its advantages sustainable over time?

2 What core competencies does Nintendo possess? Is it capable of leveraging them further? If so, how?

3 How does Sony score on Kay's three areas of distinctive capabilities? What conclusions can be drawn on future resource development?

4 What is the strategic significance, if any, of the efforts of games machine makers to establish their own special technical standards? What are the risks of such strategies?

STRATEGIC PROJECT

Will Nintendo survive?

This case was written in early 2014. Nintendo was clearly struggling against the competitive resources of Sony and Microsoft. You can read the impact on Nintendo from its annual report and accounts for 2013 which is available at www.nintendo.co.jp/ir/en/library/annual/ What would *you* recommend?

CRITICAL REFLECTION

How useful is the resource-based view?

At the present time, the resource-based view (RBV) of strategy development is the focus of a significant body of research and development. Some strategists believe that its insights lie at the core of strategy development. But the RBV also faces significant criticism in at least three areas:

1 *Tautological*. The RBV is seeking truths that are part of the very definition of what is being sought. The RBV is supposed to identify the resources that lead to competitive advantage by identifying those resources that deliver value, rarity and inimitability. But competitive advantage itself is defined as something that is valuable, rare and inimitable. In this sense, the RBV only seeks to identify what it already knows or should know!

2 *Vague generalisations*. The resource areas identified by the RBV - core competencies, innovative capability, etc. - are vague. Some suggest that they are so generalised as to be of little value. They need to be seen in the context in which they arise if they are to have any meaning. Otherwise, they are merely slogans or aspirations that everyone can seek.

3 *Pathway to competitive resources*. The RBV is unclear on how organisations can develop and maintain their competitive resources. The destination of the superior, competitive resource is somewhat clearer than the path to develop it.

What is your view? Does the RBV have some useful insights? Or is it over-rated as a meaningful concept?

SUMMARY

- The *resources* of an organisation are those assets that deliver value added in the organisation. The *capabilities* of an organisation are those management skills, routines and leadership that deploy, share and generate value from the resources of the organisation.
- The purpose of a resources and capabilities analysis is to identify where value is added in an organisation and where the organisation possesses SCA.
- In resource analysis, it is important to begin by analysing the complete range of resources and capabilities of the organisation: tangible resources, intangible resources and organisational capability. Such resources go beyond the usual definitions of accounting and finance concepts into more ill-defined areas like the true value of patents and leadership.

- Prescriptive approaches regard resources as objects to be moulded for maximum strategic benefit. Emergent approaches do not have a consistent theme with regard to resources. However, they tend to lay more emphasis on the uncertainty of the environment and thus the difficulty of a static analysis of competitive advantage.
- One basic resource decision facing every organisation is whether to make or buy, i.e. whether to make its own products or buy them from outside in the market place. Every organisation needs to reappraise its activities regularly in this area. The decision will be based not only on simple cost considerations but also on broader aspects related to the maintenance of SCA.
- Resources add value to the organisation. They take the inputs from suppliers and transform them into finished goods or services. The value added is the difference between the market value of outputs of an organisation and the costs of its inputs. It is possible to calculate this accurately for an overall company but very difficult to do so for individual parts of the company. When used in developing competitive advantage for the individual parts of the company, the concept is therefore often left unquantified.
- In order to develop SCA, it is necessary to consider the various parts of the organisation and the value that each part adds, where this takes place and how the contribution is made. The value chain undertakes this task. It identifies where value is added in different parts of the organisation and where the organisation may have competitive advantage.
- It may also be necessary to consider the *value system*, i.e. the way that the organisation is linked with other parts of a wider system of adding value involving suppliers, customers and distributors. Unique linkages between elements of the value system may also provide competitive advantage.
- In searching for SCA, the resource-based view (RBV) argues that the individual resources of an organisation provide a stronger basis for strategy development than industry analysis. The reason is that RBV will identify those resources that are exceptional and deliver competitive advantage.
- SCA is an advantage over competitors that cannot easily be imitated. There are seven elements that may be associated with SCA: prior or acquired resources; innovative ability; being truly competitive; substitutability; appropriability; durability; and imitability. It is not necessary for an organisation to possess them all before it has some competitive advantages: each organisation will have some unique combination of resources, some of which will deliver SCA. The VRIO Framework – Valuable, Rare, Inimitable and Organisationally possible – can be used to test resources for their ability to contribute to competitive advantage.
- There is no general agreement on what constitutes the best single approach to the development of SCA. Two approaches have proved useful: distinctive capabilities – architecture, reputation and innovation – and core competencies. Another approach that has gained ground is that the knowledge of the organisation is the key resource.
- The RBV has a number of weaknesses: it is simply a list of factors to consider; the underpinning logic may be flawed; it largely ignores human resource factors; and it does not take into account the process aspects of strategy development.
- There are at least three ways to improve competitive advantage: benchmarking, improving existing resources and upgrading resources.
- Organisational culture is the set of beliefs, values and learned ways of managing that govern organisational behaviour. Each organisation has a culture that is unique.
- Culture influences performance and strategic management. Factors within the organisation influencing culture include: history and ownership, size, technology, leadership and mission, along with the cultural web of the organisation.
- The cultural web provides a method of summarising some of the cultural influences within an organisation: stories, routines and rituals, symbols, power structures, organisation structure, control systems.
- Factors external to the organisation influencing culture include: people, national cultures, the corporate cultural environment, labour and employment policies.

- Within a general analysis of organisational culture, there are four main types: power, role, task and personal. Some types are better able to cope and manage strategic change than others. Leaders who wish to change strategy will want to identify and use these types with regard to specific strategic initiatives.
- Guidelines can be developed for analysing organisational culture. For the purposes of strategy development, such an analysis needs to be assessed against the strategy in areas such as attitudes to risk, change, reward, cost reduction and competitive advantage.

QUESTIONS

1. Using your judgement, determine the key factors for success in the following industries: pharmaceuticals, fast food restaurants, charities helping homeless people, travel companies offering package tours.
2. Identify and develop the value chain for an organisation with which you are familiar. Outline the implications of your study for competitive advantage.
3. Take the value added and other data for Glaxo Smith Kline and outline the value chain for the company. Develop the value system within which the company operates. What strategy conclusions can you draw?
4. How do the seven elements of the resource-based view contribute to strategic management? What are their limitations?
5. Using the evidence from the case study on the fashion industry, identify the main elements of Gucci's competitive advantage. Use the seven elements of RBV to structure your answer and explain the relationship with the other resources possessed by the company.
6. Take an organisation with which you are familiar and identify its distinctive capabilities, using the key guidelines to assist the process. Compare the organisation with its competitors and comment on the strategy implications.
7. Identify the core competencies of fashion companies in general and Louis Vuitton in particular. What do your observations mean for strategic management development at Louis Vuitton?
8. Can core competencies be bought in as a short-term strategic solution or do they have to be developed over the long term? Use an example to support your answer.
9. Could Microsoft's XBox (see Case 4.3) use any of the three main ways to improve further its competitive advantage? Which methods might be used? Why?
10. Undertake an analysis of the organisational culture of an organisation of your choice - for example, a student society - using the concepts in this chapter. How does this analysis influence the competitive resources of the organisation outlined earlier in the chapter?

FURTHER READING

For the value chain and value system: Porter, M E (1985) *Competitive Advantage*, The Free Press, New York. An interesting review of the value chain appears in: Channon, D (2005) 'Value chain analysis', in McGee, J and Channon, D F (eds) *Encyclopedic Dictionary of Management*, 2nd edn, Blackwell Business, Oxford.

For core competencies: Hamel, G and Prahalad, C K (1994) *Competing for the Future*, Harvard Business School Press, Boston, MA.

For distinctive capabilities: Kay, J (1993) *Foundations of Corporate Success*, Oxford University Press, Oxford.

Two useful summaries of the resource-based view are contained in chapters in two major texts. The first is: Cool, K, Costa, L A and Dierickx, I (2002) 'Constructing competitive advantage', in Pettigrew, A, Thomas, H and Whittington, R (eds) *Handbook of Strategy and Management*, Sage, London, pp 55–71. The second is: Barney, J B and Arikan, A M (2001) 'The resource-based view: origins and implications', in Hitt, M A, Freeman, R E and Harrison, J S (eds) *The Blackwell Handbook of Strategic Management*, Blackwell, Oxford, pp 124–188.

For a more academic consideration of the problems with the RBV, see the critique by Priem and Butler in Priem, R L and Butler, J E (2001a), 'Is the resource-based view a useful "view" for strategic management research?', *Academy of Management Review*, January, Vol 26, No 1, pp 22–40 and Priem, R L and Butler, J E (2001b), 'Tautology in the resource-based view and the implications of externally determined resource value: further comments', *Academy of Management Review*, January, Vol 26, No 1, pp 1–45. Then read the response by Jay Barney in Barney, J B (2001) 'Is the resource-based "view" a useful perspective for strategic management research? Yes', *Academy of Management Review*, Vol 26, No 1, pp 41–56.

There are still substantial research projects on the RBV. Three suggested recent papers contain summaries of recent thinking and evidence: Lado, A A, Boyd, N G, Wright, P and Kroll, M (2006) 'Paradox and theorizing within the resource-based view', *Academy of Management Review*, Vol 31, No 1, pp 115–131. Acedo, F J, Barroso, C and Galan, J L (2006) 'The Resource-based Theory: Dissemination and main trends', *Strategic Management Journal*, Vol 27, pp 621–636. Newbert, S L (2007) 'Empirical research on the resource-based view of the firm: an assessment and suggestions for future research', *Strategic Management Journal*, Vol 28, pp 121–146.

For a well-developed exposition of culture: Brown, A (1995) *Organisational Culture*, Pitman Publishing, London. For some excellent and provocative reading on the relationship between human resources and strategy: Egan, C (1995) *Creating Organizational Advantage*, Butterworth–Heinemann, Oxford.

NOTES AND REFERENCES

1 Lynch, R (1994) *European Business Strategies*, 2nd edn, Kogan Page, London, p 43.

2 References for Case 4.1: Annual Reports and Accounts of GSK, Nederlandse Spoorwegen and Bouygues for various years.

3 Some early articles on this shift in position include: Wernerfelt, B (1984) 'A resource-based view of the firm', *Strategic Management Journal*, September–October, p 171; Barney J B (1986) 'Strategic factor markets: Expectations, luck and business strategy', *Management Science*, October, p 1231; Rumelt, R, 'Theory, strategy and entrepreneurship', in Teece, D J (ed) (1987), *The Competitive Challenge: Strategies for Industrial Innovation and Renewal*, Ballinger, Reading, MA.

4 Porter, M E (1980) *Competitive Strategy: Techniques for Analyzing Industries and Competitors*, The Free Press, New York. But note that this was based on earlier work, particularly that of Bain, J (1956) *Barriers to New Competition: Their Character and Consequences in Manufacturing Industries*, Harvard University Press, Cambridge, MA.

5 In particular, many marketing strategy texts make no mention of individual resource analysis. From this perspective, they should all be read with caution. However, many definitions of marketing have long recognised the importance of resources – one used at several universities in the UK makes explicit reference to the resources of the organisation.

6 For example: Penrose, E (1959) *The Theory of the Growth of the Firm*, Basil Blackwell, Oxford; Ansoff, I (1965) *Corporate Strategy*, McGraw-Hill, NY.

7 Wernerfelt, B (1984) 'A resource-based view of the firm', *Strategic Management Journal*, September–October, p 171.

8 Barney, J B (1986) 'Strategic factor markets: expectations, luck and business strategy', *Management Science*, Vol 32, pp 1231–1241; Barney, J B (1991) 'Firm resources and sustained competitive advantage', *Journal of Management*, Vol 17, pp 99–120.

9 Collis, D and Montgomery, C (1995) 'Competing on resources: strategy in the 1990s', *Harvard Business Review*, July–August, pp 118–128.

10 See, for example, Hitt, M, Ireland, D R and Hoskisson, R E (2003) *Strategic Management: Competitiveness and Globalization Concepts*, 5th edn, Thomson, OH, Chapter 3.

11 Prahalad, C and Hamel, G (1990) 'The core competence of the corporation', *Harvard Business Review*, May–June, pp 79–91.

12 See the pioneering work of Coase, R (1937) 'The nature of the firm', *Economica*, Vol 4, pp 386–405. Also Penrose, E (1959) Op. cit., and Williamson, O (1975) *Markets and Hierarchies*, The Free Press, New York.

13 For a more detailed example of value chain analysis, see Shepherd, A (1998) 'Understanding and using value chain analysis', in Ambrosini, V (ed) *Exploring Techniques of Analysis and Evaluation in Strategic Management*, Prentice Hall, Berkhamsted.

14 Porter, M E (1985) *Competitive Advantage*, The Free Press, Harvard, MA, Ch 2.

15 Porter, M E (1985) Ibid., p 38.

16 Cookson, C and Luesby, J (1995) 'Glaxo Wellcome giant changes the drug mixture', *Financial Times*, 9 March, p 33.

17 Porter, M E (1985) Op. cit., Chs 9, 10 and 11.

18 Sources for this case: Three trips by the author with Middlesex University MBA students to study the fashion industry in Como, Northern Italy. In particular, my thanks are due to Mantero SpA whose senior directors gave freely of their time. However, it should be noted that *no direct information* from Mantero is used in this case. All the data is from the publicly available sources listed below. The author also acknowledges the considerable guidance of his former colleague at Middlesex University, Mr Valeriano Lencioni, and two professors in the specialist fashion group at Bocchoni Business School in Milan, Professors Erica Corbellini and Stefania Saviolo, who also came to Como. The data used in this case comes from: LVMH Annual Report and Accounts 2003; PPR Annual Report and Accounts 2003; Gucci Annual Report and Accounts 2001 (the latest available); *Economist*, 'Rags and Riches – a survey of fashion', 6 March 2004; *Financial Times* Womenswear 'Business of Fashion' Supplement, Spring/Summer 2005, with newspaper in Feb 2005; *Financial Times* Menswear 'Business of Fashion' Supplement, Spring/Summer 2005, with newspaper in March 2005; *Financial Times* 9 March 2005, p 30 – 'Designer quits as Gucci seeks results'; *Fashion Business International*: April–May 2002, pp 52–53, Dec–Jan 2003, pp 16, 45–46; Times (UK) 5 September 2007, p 8.

19 For a more recent discussion on competitive advantage, see: Durand, R and Vaara, E (2009) 'Causation, counterfactuals and competitive advantage', *Strategic Management Journal*, Vol 30, No 12, pp 1245–1264.

20 Many of these research papers are referenced elsewhere in this text. The remainder are: Dierickx, I and Cool, K (1989) 'Asset stock accumulation and sustainability of competitive advantage', *Management Science*, Vol 35, pp 1504–1511;

Connor, K (1991) 'A historical comparison of resource-based theory and five schools of thought within industrial organisation economics: Do we have a new theory of the firm?', *Journal of Management*, Vol 17 No 1, pp 121–154; Amit, R and Schoemaker, P (1993) 'Strategic assets and organizational rent', *Strategic Management Journal*, Vol 14, pp 33–46; Grant, R (1991) 'The resource-based theory of competitive advantage: implications for strategy formulation', *California Management Review*, Vol 33, pp 114–122. Makadok, R (2001) 'Towards a synthesis of the resource-based and dynamic capability views of rent creation', *Strategic Management Journal*, Vol 22, pp 387–401. Hoopes, D G, Madsen, T L and Walker, G (2003) 'Why is there a resource-based view? Toward a theory of competitive heterogeneity', *Strategic Management Journal*, Vol 24, October, Special issue.

21 For those obsessed with the generic strategies outlined in Professor Porter's two books, it should be noted that no mention has been made of a company being the lowest-cost producer. This book will argue that sustainable advantage may be achieved by having both low costs and other qualities that take the company beyond being merely the lowest-cost producer.

22 Kay, J (1993) *Foundations of Corporate Success*, Oxford University Press, Oxford, p 367.

23 High technology and services columns developed from Aaker, D (1992) *Strategic Marketing Management*, 3rd edn, Wiley, New York, p 186; others from author.

24 Prahalad, C and Hamel, G (1990) 'The core competence of the corporation', *Harvard Business Review*, May–June, pp 79–91.

25 Kay, J (1993) Op. cit.

26 Peteraf, M (1993) 'The cornerstones of competitive advantage: a resource-based view', *Strategic Management Journal*, 14, pp 179–91.

27 Collis, D and Montgomery, C (1995) 'Competing on resources: strategy in the 1990s', *Harvard Business Review*, July–August, pp 119–128.

28 Kay, J (1993) Op. cit., Chs 5, 6 and 7.

29 Hamel, G and Prahalad, H K (1994) *Competing for the Future*, Harvard Business School Press, Boston, MA, Chs 9 and 10.

30 Sainsbury, D (1994) 'Be a better builder', *Financial Times*, 2 September, p 11.

31 Roos, J (1997) *Financial Times Mastering Management*, Pitman, London, Module 20.

32 Roos, J (1998) *Financial Times Mastering Global Business*, Pitman, London, Part 5, pp 14–15.

33 Leonard, D (1998) *Wellsprings of Knowledge*, Harvard Business School Press, Boston, MA, p 3.

34 See also Chaharbaghi, K and Lynch, R (1999) 'Sustainable competitive advantage: towards a dynamic resource-based strategy', *Management Decision*, Vol 37, No 1, pp 45–50.

35 Priem, R L and Butler, J E (2001) 'Is the resource-based view a useful perspective for strategic management research?', *Academy of Management Review*, Vol 26, No 1, pp 22–40 and Lynch, R (2000) 'Resource-based view: paradigm or checklist?' *International Journal of Technology*, Vol 3, No 4, pp 550–561. Professor Jay Barney is a strong supporter of the RBV. He responded to the Priem and Butler paper with the following: Barney, J (2001) 'Is the resource-based view a useful perspective for strategic management research? Yes', *Academy of Management Review*, Vol 26, No 1, pp 41–56.

36 Collis, D and Montgomery, C (1995) Op. cit., p 123, emphasise that lengthy lists of core competencies have sometimes become just a 'feelgood' factor.

37 Hamel, G and Prahalad, C K (1994) Op. cit., Ch 7.

38 Brown, A (1995) *Organisational Culture*, Pitman Publishing, London, p 198.

39 Brown, A (1998) *Organisational Culture*, 2nd edn, Financial Times/Pitman Publishing, London.

40 Handy, C (1993) *Understanding Organisations*, 4th edn, Penguin, Harmondsworth, pp 193–194.

41 Handy, C (1993) Ibid., p 183. Handy uses the work of Harrison, R (1972) 'Understanding your organisation's character', *Harvard Business Review*, (5)3, September-October, pp 119–128. Handy uses Greek gods to typify the four cultural types: they make an interesting read, but mean rather less to those of us who have not studied *The Aeneid*.

42 Hofstede, G (1980) *Culture's Consequences: International Differences in Work-related Values*, Sage, Beverly Hills, CA.

43 Brown, A (1995) Op cit, p 5.

44 References for computer games machine case: Brandenburger, A M and Nalebuff, B J (1997) *Co-opetition*, HarperCollins, London; *Economist*, 19 May 2001, p 83; *Guardian Newspaper*, 12 March 2002, p 21; *Financial Times*: 14 October 1999, p 31; 19 January 2000, p 28; 28 August 2000, p 9; 6 September 2000, p 3; 25 January 2001, pp 23, 29; 26 January 2001, p 24; 1 February 2001, p 32; 18 May 2001, p 11; 19 May 2001, p 12; 23 May 2001, p 36; 7 July 2001, p 14; 21 September 2001, p 34; October 2001, p 18; 8 January 2002, p 30; 7 February 2002, p 28; 8 March 2002, p 1; 12 March 2002, p 36; 10 April 2002, p 30; 23 April 2002, p 30; 10 September 2002, p 27; 4 October 2002, p 30; 13 May 2003, p 31; 14 May 2003, p 32; 24 July 2003, pp 11, 27; 25 July 2003, p 27; 5 November 2003, p 26; 14 November 2003, p 29; 30 March 2004, p 30; 5 May 2004, p 13; 12 May 2004, p 30; 17 September 2004, p 28; 22 September 2004, p 23; 18 February 2005, p 25; 25 February 2005, p 26; 8 March 2005, p 5; 11 March 2005, p 21; 6 November 2006, p 17; 10 November 2006, p 27; 17 November 2006, p 10; 23 March 2007, p 24; 15 June 2007, p 23; 22 June 2007, p 24; 4 July 2007, p 23; 10 July 2007, p 19; 13 July 2007, p 20; 17 September 2007, p 25; 6 December 2007, p 25; 8 May 2008, p 22; 7 April 2009, p 25; 5 June 2009, p 22; 20 August 2009, p 14; 28 August 2009, p 13; 7 September 2009, p 23; 3 September 2009, p 20; 23 February 2010, p 23; 25 September 2010, p 27; 30 September 2010, p 23; 12 November 2010, p 14; 8 December 2010, p 19. See also the websites for the three main companies with the 'investor' links showing company results for each company.

CHAPTER 5
Strategy dynamics

Video and sound summary of this chapter

LEARNING OUTCOMES

When you have worked through this chapter, you will be able to:

- develop a dynamic business framework;
- identify the three main ways of coping with an unpredictable environment;
- explore the dynamics of fast-moving environments, especially in the context of innovation;
- identify the dynamics of resource development;
- plan aggressive competitive strategies;
- plot the main ways to develop co-operation strategies;
- outline the main aspects of game theory and the implications for strategy dynamics.

INTRODUCTION

Video Part 7b

Both organisations themselves and the strategies that they pursue change continuously over time. They alter as the environment shifts and they change as the organisation's own resources and capabilities grow or decline. The mechanisms by which these processes occur are not fully understood because they are complex and our knowledge of the various elements requires further development. This chapter on the dynamics of strategy development explores the current state of knowledge.

To begin our study of strategy dynamics, we identify the main elements of the concept and how they fit together. The theory focuses particularly on the importance of flexibility in strategy. The process is therefore more emergent than prescriptive, emphasising particularly both innovation and strategic responses to external events. The chapter then follows the strategy distinction used in Chapters 3 and 4 between the strategic environment and the strategic resources of the organisation. However, it takes the concepts further by emphasising the changes rather than the constant elements of these concepts. Within the environment, the chapter looks particularly at the problems that can arise when an environment cannot be predicted and, specifically, when the environment is fast-moving and prescriptive strategies become difficult to use. The chapter then explores the changing resources of the organisation, including their origins, their development and their destruction.

In the last three sections of the chapter, we take a less analytical and more proactive approach.[1] We explore attack strategies against competitors. We then look at cooperative strategies with other organisations that might deliver a competitive advantage over our competitors. Finally, we tackle the benefits and problems of game theory strategy.

Within interpretive dynamics, the main focus rests on understanding the dynamics of purpose, the environment, competitive advantage and the way that competitive resources can change. In proactive dynamics, the emphasis is more on the activities that organisations can and will take to enhance their competitive advantage and value added. See Figure 5.1.

Figure 5.1 Exploring the dynamics of strategy development

CASE STUDY 5.1

Formula One racing strategy: balancing brilliant driving with knife-edged bargaining

In the glitzy world of Formula One Motor Racing, brilliant driving hits the headlines. But the serious business of knife-edged bargaining delivers the business strategy and even the possibility of a new green strategy, as this case explains.

Formula One Motor Racing: the three business players

Formula One (often shortened to F1) motor racing generates annual revenue in excess of $1 billion. It is, at least in part, in the entertainment business. It is also an important employer: there are several thousand directly employed by the teams and countless associated companies supplying everything from specialist testing equipment to catering at the race venues. It also claims to be a technology leader whose inventions have led to spin-offs in other areas. For example, the industry suggests that it originated non-slip footwear, improved fishing lines, lightweight medical leg braces and medical monitoring equipment based on racetrack telemetry technology.

But all the above is nothing without the entertainment that comes from brilliant driving by young and charismatic drivers. They are paid large sums to risk their lives at high speeds on specially designed racing circuits all over the world. The F1 Racing brand is glamorous, sexy and global. And it has three main business players: the F1 commercial rights owners, the F1 teams and the professional governing body – see Table 5.1. It

Table 5.1 Three main players in F1 Motor Racing: the members of the Concorde Agreement

Number	Description	Role
Formula One Group	Privately-owned company responsible for the promotion of the World Championship and exploitation of its commercial rights. The company's Chief Executive, Bernie Ecclestone, is one of the most famous and dominant figures in world motor sport.	Negotiates with racing circuits and leading sponsors as well as the other two partners. It also negotiates with television companies over media rights and with sponsors and track-side advertisers.
Formula One Teams Association (FOTA)	Each F1 team is a member of the Association with the lead often being taken by Luca di Montezemolo, the FOTA Chairman and president of Ferrari.	Drivers are contracted to an individual team. Each team also has directors, employees and suppliers of technology, parts, etc.
Fédération Internationale de l'Automobile (FIA)	Professional body governing all motor sport headed by its president, Max Mosley, until 2009, then Jean Todt.	Sets rules and judges disputes in all motor sport, including the F1. Also has a guiding role in car design to produce more environmentally friendly cars for competition.

is because these three did not always have the same interests that bargaining has taken place in recent years.

The issue was further complicated because the F1 commercial rights company was sold in a complex deal to a private venture capital company, CVC Capital Partners Ltd, in 2005 for a reported $2.8 billion. The purchase was funded by heavy loans with high interest repayment terms that meant the company was under pressure to take profits from its involvement in F1 Racing. In fact, it has been reported that the interest rates are so high that the company has been making a loss. This has put pressure on the company, but it has also put it in a weak negotiating position because it needs F1 Racing to be successful and generate revenue. One of its main strengths is that its chief executive is Bernie Ecclestone who is one of the most well-known and well-connected figures in the F1 Racing industry. He was paid a reported salary of £4.85 million ($6.35 mn) in 2010.

Up to and including the 2007 season, the three had a legal agreement governing the way F1 operated called the *Concorde Agreement*. The agreement essentially covered the terms by which teams compete in the races and share the television revenues and prize money. This finished at that time with the three parties then having an unofficial understanding that ran for the 2008 season. It was the re-negotiation of the Concorde Agreement that was on a knife edge during much of 2009.

Formula One Motor Racing: sources of income

With 2008 annual income of $1.25 billion, F1 Racing is a large global business. To understand the basis of the Concorde Agreement, it is important to understand the sources of income for F1 Racing. The main sources are shown in Table 5.2, but these do not capture the full revenue involved in this business. The reason is that some individual teams will also be subsidised by their owners (e.g. Ferrari) and by their team sponsors (e.g. the Virgin group). In addition, there are other sources of income such as support from tyre manufacturers: Bridgestone Tyres reported that it regularly supported F1 with around $70 million in tyres and technical support each year before withdrawing in 2010. The 2011 season used Pirelli tyres, no doubt also with substantial support.

Formula One Motor Racing: profit pressures

From the financial figures for 2009 and 2010, it would seem that F1 Racing was profitable – see Table 5.3. Revenue was slightly down on 2008, but the main company was reporting reasonable profits. However, these figures hide two difficulties:

- the heavy interest charges on the loan taken out by CVC to buy the company in 2005;
- the F1 team earnings were not enough in themselves for teams to survive: they needed to supplement their incomes by either sponsorship deals or private financial support in order to compete.

For example, Ferrari had private support from Italian family interests associated with Fiat, and Red Bull had finance from the owner of the parent drinks company. But Williams relied on commercial sponsorship that was under threat from the economic recession, and some other teams were in a similar position. This need for further funds did not help their negotiating positions when it came to demanding a higher contribution from F1 Racing. However, the races needed around 12 teams to make the sport entertaining: there would be little point in a race just between Ferrari and Red Bull. Hence, there was a strong incentive for the F1 Racing company and for the FIA to support the weaker teams financially.

Table 5.2 Formula 1 Motor Racing: sources of income 2008

	$million
Race hosting fees – paid by each race track	404
TV rights – paid by the media companies to broadcast F1	380
Trackside advertising	170
Corporate hospitality – paid by sponsors for race day coverage	150
F1 partner programme	60
Other – includes merchandising, internet and publishing	50
GP2 (F1 junior series)	40
Total	**1,254**

Source: Formula Money, published in the *Financial Times*, 17 March 2009, p 20.

Table 5.3 F1 Racing income in 2009 and 2010

	2009 $m	2010 $m	Comment
Revenue	1,063	1,082	Increase from the new Korean venue and the reinstatement of the Canadian venue. Also new sponsorship deals with UBS bank and LG electronics.
Operating profit	277	296	Some reports suggested that this level of profit was not enough to support the debt finance of CVC Capital Ltd.
F1 Team prize money	544	658	Three new teams were promised $30 million each for their participation in F1 Racing – hence the earnings rise.

Source: based on http://www.grandprix.com/ns/ns23091.html.

Although Formula 1 Racing is glamorous, it was under pressure from a number of sources in 2009:

- World economic recession was causing problems with sponsors, especially the banks like RBS and ING that were making substantial losses.
- In addition, fans in some countries were finding it difficult to afford the high ticket prices. This made it more difficult for host racing circuits to afford the race hosting fees that they had to pay F1 Racing.
- Direct costs for the racing teams were also rising in a number of areas.
- Motor manufacturers were under profit pressures - see Case 4 in Part 6 for details. The result was that three manufacturers withdrew completely from racing in late 2008: Honda, Toyota and BMW.

As a result, the FIA President, Max Mosley, could see that something needed to be done. He proposed a series of cost-cutting measures in 2008 to be applied to Formula 1 Racing, including a budget cap of $60 million on each team and other design restrictions. In response in March 2009, the FOTA teams came up with their own package of cost-saving measures that would reduce the cost of running an F1 team down from around $300 million to around half that figure in 2010. 'We are looking at this crisis with a positive attitude,' said Luca di Montezemolo, FOTA chairman and the Ferrari president. 'It is a huge opportunity to improve F1 in terms of cost and competition. We want to preserve the DNA of the sport. We want a stable F1, a positive F1, so international brands can be present and we want to increase the audience.' But there was a gap between the FIA proposal and the offer from FOTA.

Although all teams accepted the need to reduce costs, some teams, especially Ferrari, were not willing to accept the $60 million budget cap - at least initially. The company said that it would have led to race companies having to make numbers of their employees redundant. By late 2009, this led to a crisis between the FIA and FOTA with some very harsh words being exchanged. Ferrari 'issued a trenchant statement blaming the FIA for seeking to undermine the carmakers', according to the *Financial Times*. Referring to the possible withdrawal of Renault, Ferrari were reported as saying that, 'This gradual defection from the F1 fold has more to do with a war waged against the major car manufacturers by those who managed F1 over the past few years than the result of any economic crisis.'

At one stage in 2009, the FOTA teams threatened to leave the existing F1 Racing scene and set up their own rival series. Negotiations were on a knife edge. The teams judged that they had the ultimate bargaining advantage of owning the racing cars and teams. But they faced the problem that the existing circuits and the media rights were contracted to Formula One Racing Group rather than the teams. It was possible to negotiate new track and media contracts, but this would take time to organise. Importantly, it did not help the FOTA bargaining position in 2009.

A key person in bringing the three parties together was

Formula 1 Motor Racing is now big business. But what are the winning strategies that will deliver the largest share of the total business revenue? And what are the principles behind the bargaining that will be needed?
© Speedpix/Alamy

Bernie Ecclestone, the Chief Executive of F1 Racing. He knew all the participants well having been involved in the business for many years. Moreover, his company had no assets other than the F1 Racing company. Ecclestone was particularly concerned to ensure that F1 Racing continued to be entertaining. He recognised that the stronger financial resources of some teams like Ferrari meant that they had the potential to dominate the races. If this continued, then the races would not be so exciting and unpredictable as in the past. He was therefore in favour of restrictions on the team budgets. He also wanted some standardisation of design, which would reduce the costs for all the teams and therefore make the races more competitive and entertaining.

Eventually in late 2009, the three parties signed a new agreement that would run to the end of 2012. It included provisions for engine and design restrictions plus some changes in other aspects of the way that races were run. The aim of these changes was to reduce the costs of development for teams that did not have extensive funds and also to encourage the development of green technology in the sport. The agreement also raised the amount of money given to the F1 teams during each of the three years of the agreement. The outcome of the agreement at the time of writing this case was that the teams shared prize money in 2010 of $658 million, which was a 21 per cent increase over 2009. However, it was also reported that CVC Capital, the owners of F1 Racing, faced losses of $660 million on financing costs from its acquisition of the F1 series. It was not clear how long this state of affairs could continue. But at least, the new rules brought the teams closer and therefore made the sport more entertaining.

In April 2011, the FIA announced that it was working with the European Commission to create new electric car, go-kart and single-seater racing categories. There was the prospect of an F1-style car championship on the existing circuits. The FIA President, Jean

Todt, explained, 'We want as soon as possible to have new categories with new engines.' The first electric car racing season could come as early as 2013. The European Commission had a strong mandate to convert the car industry to more sustainable energy. It was hoping 'that the event would use F1's vast media muscle to stir consumers' interests in electric vehicles.'

In addition, new more sustainable and green energy designs became mandatory for all the existing F1 cars for the racing year 2014. This made an immediate difference to the race results with Mercedes overtaking Red Bull as the early leader. But it was still early days. . . .

Case questions

1 What are the strengths and weaknesses of using strategy dynamics to plot this strategic battle? Who appeared to be the winners in the negotiations? Why?

2 To what extent were aggressive competitive strategies used in the negotiations? What other aspects of strategy dynamics were involved?

3 What lessons can we draw from the case on the usefulness of strategy dynamics and aggressive competitive theory in strategy development?

5.1 DEVELOPING A DYNAMIC BUSINESS FRAMEWORK

Video Part 7b

In Chapter 4 on resource strategy, sustainable competitive advantage was identified as an important element of strategic management. Clearly, competitive advantage is unlikely to remain static forever: competitors, technology, managers, customers and many other factors are likely to change over time. Some strategists,[3] particularly those that have studied industries where advanced technology is involved, argue that the static identification of competitive advantage misses an important strategic opportunity. They suggest that competitive advantage should be seen as constantly evolving and that strategy can be more proactive in managing this process. The F1 Racing case illustrates how strategy is changing all the time because of external economic pressures, green strategy policy decisions and the desire of individual race teams to win the F1 Sports Car Championship.

Importantly from a strategy dynamics perspective, organisations should be seeking to *manage and shape* the dynamics of the environment. In other words, strategy is a dynamic concept that will provide a constant flow of new opportunities and threats to the organisation.

5.1.1 Dynamics starts with a strategy's history

To begin at the beginning, an organisation's previous history is a key determinant of its future dynamic development. Future purpose and strategy will be grounded in its past resources developed over time. **Definition ▶** **According to the historical strategy perspective, purpose and its outcomes must, at least in part, be seen as being influenced by the organisation's present resources, its past history and its evolution over time.** Back in 1959, before strategy was considered to be a distinct academic subject, the young academic economist Edith Penrose turned traditional economic thinking on its head. She argued that what happened *inside* the firm was just as important as the market place *outside* the firm.[4] Up to this time, it was this latter area that had been the main focus of economics with its consideration of market demand and supply issues. Moreover, in exploring how firms grow, Penrose argued that this was related to a firm's resources, its past history and its evolution over time. Thus the firm's previous history was a key influence on its future development including its purpose.

In 1962, the US strategist Alfred Chandler published a substantial study of the growth of four great US companies during the early twentieth century:[5] its arguments and language were similar to those of Penrose. Both writers showed that the development of a firm over time is an essential element of understanding strategy. To make sense of strategy, it is useful to consider the history of an organisation in the three areas originally identified in the well-known strategy research paper by Teece, Pisano and Shuen:[6]

1 *the processes* – how an organisation has developed its organisational structure, company relationships and leadership, especially in the areas of technology, institutional assets and market assets;
2 *the position* – how the organisation is placed with regard to its competitors, both at present and with regard to the future;
3 *the paths* – how its past history has developed and how its future is envisaged, covering its special resources, innovative ability and knowledge.

In common with us as individuals, organisations are creatures of their history, resources and experience. Strategic purpose needs to consider these if it is to understand how developments should proceed for the future. More specifically, the purpose of an organisation and its strategy are highly dependent on the leadership, culture and style of those who have come to form the company, especially at a senior level. Some of this will happen by design, some by chance. In the same way, purpose and strategy also need to be considered in the context of how resources were acquired and market positions obtained.[7] For example, expansion by acquisition brings the history of the acquired company into its new parent. This will include the good and bad aspects of the new resources, the knowledge, experience and organisational culture.

5.1.2 The structured yet dynamic strategy process

According to some strategists, the key issue is for a company to strike a balance between supporting its long-term sustainable advantages and at the same time engaging in the process of constant change and renewal. Such a company will begin by identifying some sustainable competitive advantages that are structured, supported and clear – for example, Intel Corporation supports its 'Pentium' brand name and individual new computer chips as they are launched into the market place – for example, the Pentium Dual Core in 2006. However, at the same time, such a company will also deliberately have some other aspects of its activities that fall essentially outside its existing areas of advantage – for example, Intel Corporation might experiment with some totally new technology or computer software in one of its laboratories that has no obvious relation to its current competitive advantage but would be an interesting point of departure for the company. Thus, the strategy process is both *structured* – advertising the brand name – and *dynamic* – exploring a totally new and unproven technology.

5.1.3 Dynamic business development - some guidelines, not rules

Clearly such a dynamic strategic process has the potential to be both immensely beneficial and also totally unmanageable. Strategists therefore suggest that there should be some guidelines laid down to exploit the real benefits of such an approach. In the words of Brown and Eisenhardt:

> Successful firms in fiercely competitive and unpredictably shifting industries pursue a competing on the edge strategy. The goal of this strategy is not efficiency or optimality in the usual sense. Rather, the goal is flexibility - that is, adaptation to current change and evolution over time, resilience to setbacks, and the ability to locate constantly changing sources of advantage. Ultimately, it means engaging in continual revolution.[8]

In practice, for such organisations, this means striking a balance between structure and dynamism – strong financial control systems are in place, but managers have significant free time to develop their own ideas in an entrepreneurial way. Thus the process may be flexible, inefficient and perhaps even have some failures. But it will be proactive in the sense of seeking positively after new entrepreneurial initiatives and accepting that there will inevitably be some failures. The process is often driven by a basic objective that the organisation will derive a significant percentage of its sales from totally new products over time – the 3M case in Chapter 7 and the Google case (Case 14 in Part 6) provide more details.

Fundamentally, the process is guided by the concept of the organisation having a *continuous flow* of resource changes and competitive advantages rather than a static list. For example, the F1 Racing case shows that there have been a series of technical developments and external pressures effectively demanding a flow of resource changes of each competing car company over the last few years. This has then led to the bargaining described in the case, which has been an ongoing process. Clearly this is an emergent rather than a prescriptive approach to strategy development. How is this possible?

5.1.4 Structuring a dynamic business – a possible framework

Given the present state of knowledge in the strategy field, we do not have a clear way of structuring the concept of a business that has a dynamic strategy. According to Professor David Teece, the aim is clear enough: To develop a business that is 'sustaining the evolutionary and entrepreneurial fitness of the organisation'.[9] It is certainly not possible to develop a model to show how this might work, but Figure 5.2 presents a framework that captures some of the major ideas at the current state of knowledge.[10]

Definition ▸ **The Three 'S' Framework is built around a three-stage approach to dynamics:**

1 **sensing the changes in the environment;**
2 **seizing the opportunities that such changes present;**
3 **surveying the outcomes of such changes, not just in a reflective way, but also in order to shape future change.**

Sensing

It is important to seek out opportunities far and wide. Clearly, these can come from technology and knowledge developments both inside and outside the organisation. But new possibilities can also come from suppliers and complementors along with customers and competitors. The important issue is for the organisation to be constantly seeking such changes.

Seizing

For all new opportunities, the organisation needs to be structured for these to be assessed and developed on a continual basis. There are various ways of undertaking this task: one way is to focus on research and development, particularly in cross-functional teams that will bring new and different

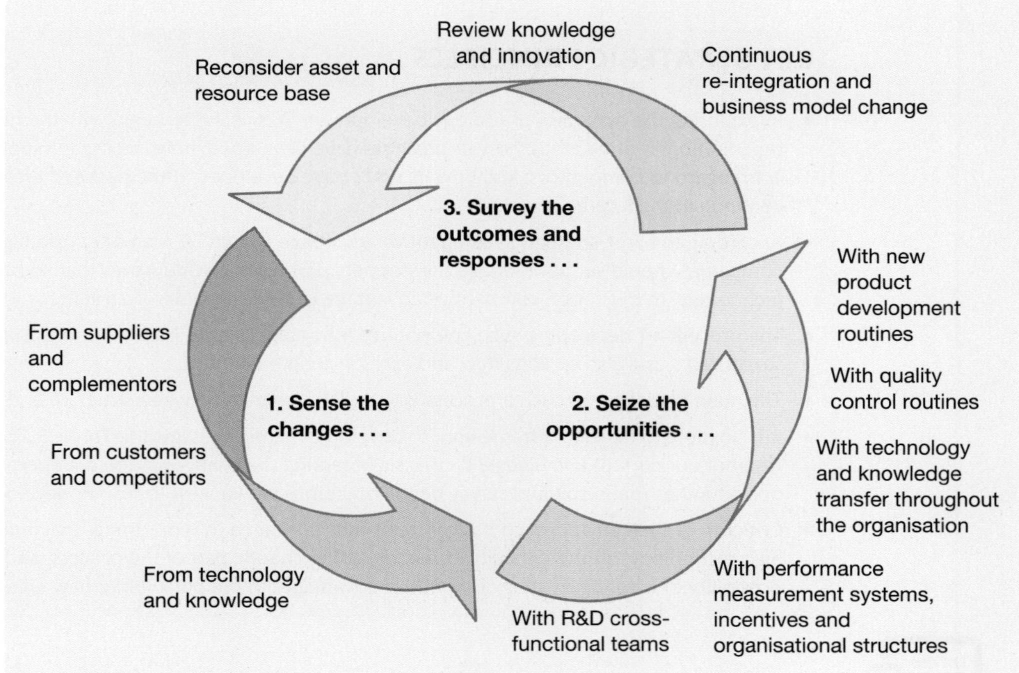

Figure 5.2 The Three 'S' Framework for dynamic strategy

perspectives to an issue. In practice, total quality procedures and performance management systems can also contribute by laying emphasis on the search for new areas. In addition, new product development through marketing and the wide circulation of new knowledge through web systems development also present further opportunities. Possibly the most important aspect of this part of development is a willingness to experiment and that means accepting the possibility of failure with its associated costs: a 'no-blame' culture is essential here to ensure that those who fail are not discouraged from trying again in the future.

Surveying

For senior managers in particular, a crucial aspect of this process is to survey what has happened and draw out the relevant lessons. These will include a review of the knowledge that has been gained and the related areas of innovation. It may reconsider the assets owned by the organisation – for example, back to the beginning of Chapter 4 about what the organisation makes and what it buys in from outside. Fundamentally, the survey will want to consider where the value is added in the business – back to the value added and the value chain of Chapter 4 – and the implications for the future direction of the business.

5.1.5 Critical comment on the concept

There are some obvious flaws in such an approach:

- It may be possible in high-technology industries, but difficult to achieve and even irrelevant elsewhere – see Case 10.1, where Unilever's competitive advantage in ice cream is real but does not depend on a technological advantage. The Unilever ice cream technology is available to competitors, who unfortunately may not necessarily have the economies of scale to justify the investment.
- There is a real difficulty in managing the difficult boundary between inspired development ideas and total chaos.
- Other important areas of competitive advantage, such as branding, may be largely discounted in the quest for technological benefits. This means that such advantages may be under-supported in a search for a totally new area of advantage.

KEY STRATEGIC PRINCIPLES

- In exploring the dynamics of strategy development, it is useful to begin with the history of an organisation in three areas: how its *processes* have developed; how the organisation is *positioned* with regard to competitors; and how its *paths* have developed in the past and are envisaged to continue in the future.
- According to some strategists, competitive advantage should be seen as constantly evolving and companies should set out to make this happen, particularly in industries that involve advanced technology. In this sense, competitive advantage is dynamic rather than static.
- The process for developing such competitive advantage is both built around existing strengths - structured - and also exploits new and exciting areas - chaotic.
- The main guideline for such a process is to strike a balance between structure and chaos.
- It is possible to develop a framework to develop dynamic strategy: the Three 'S' Framework is the result of our current knowledge. It consists of *sensing* the changes in the environment, *seizing* the opportunities that result and *surveying* the outcomes with a view to further developments.
- Criticism of such an approach has centred on its relevance to more traditional industries outside high technology, on the difficulty of managing the chaotic part of the process, and on the possibility of ignoring existing competitive advantages in the pursuit of a new area of advantage.

Checklist: Some factors to help develop dynamic strategies.

CASE STUDY 5.2

L'Oréal beauty products: using financial data to explore the strategy dynamics of an industry

How does the world market leader, L'Oréal, compare with its rivals? How has the company built its beauty products business? What strategies are likely to prove successful in the cosmetics and fragrances business?

This case provides some answers: importantly, all the data is available from publicly available resources – Company Annual Reports, the World Wide Web and library-based surveys. For reasons of space, the case focuses on one part of L'Oréal and then one section within this part. In a more complete strategic analysis, it would be essential to explore every part of the company.

Comparison of L'Oréal with two competitors

We begin by comparing the financial performance of L'Oréal with two major national competitors – Estée Lauder and Shiseido – see Table 5.4. What does the data tell us? Clearly, L'Oréal has been consistently profitable over the last ten years. Moreover from a strategy dynamics perspective, it has been more profitable than the two rival companies. We can see this more clearly by calculating the net profit margins for each company – see Table 5.4. Net profit margin is calculated by dividing the annual net profit, i.e. profit after tax and interest, by the turnover of that year and expressing the result as a percentage.

How has L'Oréal managed to increase its net profit margin over a number of years to levels not achieved by its competitors? We would need to examine all three companies in depth to answer this question fully. For this case, we will simply focus on L'Oréal.

L'Oréal's worldwide business strategy – including its Hungarian brands above – can be analysed in depth from company financial data available on the web. Data on rival companies like Estée Lauder (USA) and Shiseido (Japan) can also be sourced from the internet.

More detailed examination of the L'Oréal Annual Report and Accounts

We can look further at the company accounts of L'Oréal to see the *geographic spread* of sales – see Figure 5.3. The data shows

Table 5.4 Three companies in the world beauty business
All figures in $ billion

Year	L'Oréal, France		Estée Lauder, USA		Shiseido, Japan	
	Sales	Net profit	Sales	Net profit	Sales	Net profit
2003	16.8	2.0	5.8	0.3	5.2	0.2
2002	15.0	1.5	5.1	0.3	4.5	(0.2)
2001	12.1	1.1	4.7	0.2	4.7	0.4
2000	11.9	1.0	4.6	0.3	5.6	0.1
1999	10.8	0.7	4.3	0.3	5.1	0.1
1998	13.4	0.8	4.0	0.3	4.7	0.1
1997	11.5	0.7	3.6	0.2	4.8	0.2
1996	11.5	0.7	3.4	0.2	5.2	0.2
1995	10.9	0.6	3.1	0.2	6.2	0.1
1994	8.9	0.6	2.9	0.1	5.3	0.1

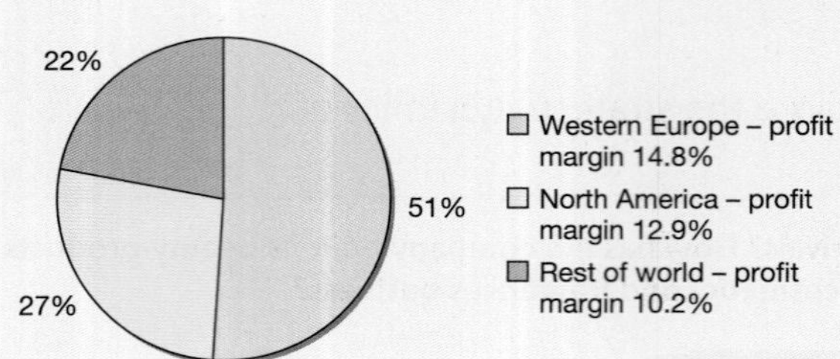

Figure 5.3 L'Oréal: Geographic location of sales and profit margins 2004

Source: company accounts for 2004 with graphic prepared by author.

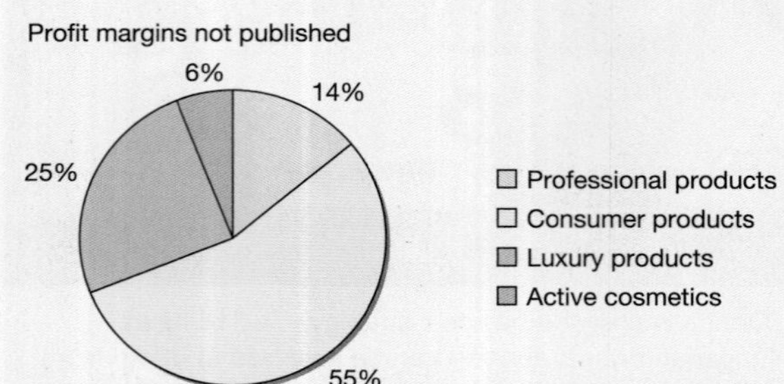

Figure 5.4 L'Oréal: share of sales by product group 2004

Source: company accounts with graphic prepared by author.

that the profit margin is higher in Western Europe than elsewhere. Moreover, Western Europe is the biggest contributor to sales and the most profitable part of the business. We can also examine data at the other two companies: not shown here for reasons of space. This shows that L'Oréal derives more of its sales from Western Europe than its two rivals, suggesting either that Western Europe is a more profitable market in itself or that L'Oréal's dominant position in Western Europe is particularly important in delivering profits. For reasons of space, this is not explored further here. But it is directly related to the dynamics of the cosmetics market and the three companies competing worldwide.

It would also be useful to examine in more depth which *products* have the highest product margins. The starting point is to examine the contribution that each product group makes to the overall sales of L'Oréal – see Figure 5.4 and Table 5.5.

Although the company accounts show the various products in L'Oréal's range, they do not show which products are the most profitable. Nevertheless, the annual report does give some further data on each product group. For our purposes, we will focus on the largest group – *consumer products*.

L'Oréal Consumer Products Division 2003

This product group uses mass-market retail channels to sell its products. Brand names included *L'Oréal Paris, Garnier Fructis, SoftSheen Carson* and *Maybelline*. The next two tables are taken from the web version of the annual report and accounts. They show sales by geographic zone and sales by business segment within the Consumer Products Division – see Tables 5.6 and 5.7.

Readers will see that some of the numbers appear to be inconsistent. For example, the sales appear to have *declined* between 2002 and 2003 whereas the web table claims that sales actually *grew* by 7.7 per cent on a like-for-like basis. We have to trust the accountants here – they will give the *actual* sales figures for 2002 and 2003. But in recording like-for-like comparisons, they will have adjusted for other events – for example, perhaps a product was discontinued or a subsidiary sold during the year and therefore removed from the accounting data.

L'Oréal Consumer Products Division was very satisfied with a +7.7 per cent sales growth, which it described as substantial.

Table 5.5 Net income margins at three cosmetics companies: net income divided by sales revenue

Year	L'Oréal Net profit margin	Estée Lauder Net profit margin	Shiseido Net profit margin
2003	11.9%	5.2%	3.8%
2002	10.0%	5.9%	–
2001	9.1%	4.2%	8.5%
2000	8.4%	6.5%	1.8%
1999	6.5%	6.8%	2.0%
1998	6.0%	7.5%	2.1%
1997	6.1%	5.5%	4.2%
1996	6.1%	5.9%	3.8%
1995	5.5%	6.4%	1.6%
1994	6.7%	3.5%	1.9%

Source: calculated by author from company accounts.

Table 5.6 L'Oréal: Consumer Products Division sales by geographic zone
Sales in € millions

	Sales 2002	Sales 2003	% of 2003 sales	Like-for-like sales growth 2003/02 (%)
Western Europe	3,837	3,991	53.2	5.3*
North America	2,319	2,080	27.7	6.7*
Rest of world	1,445	1,434	19.1	16.4*
Total	7,601	7,505	100.0	7.7*

* See text for comment.

Source: company accounts.

Table 5.7 L'Oréal: Consumer Products Division sales by business segment
Sales in € millions

	Sales 2002	Sales 2003	% of 2003 sales	Like-for-like growth 2003/02 (%)
Haircare	4,048	3,957	52.7	6.2
Make-up	2,100	1,983	26.4	5.9
Skincare	1,020	1,179	15.7	23.7
Perfumes	151	128	1.7	-11.9
Other	282	259	3.5	-6.4
Total	7,601	7,506	100.0	7.7

Source: company accounts.

This growth is much higher than the market growth in the more mature parts of the ice cream industry (see Case 3.2) so the conclusion is not unreasonable. The company then goes on to explain how it achieved this growth by the following strategies:

- Operational teams in each country adapted the product mix provided by the centre - *local* strategy within a *global* base. 'Garnier's success with shampoo in the United States and with skincare and colourants in Asia is a good example,' explains the company's report.
- Focusing on three flagship brands - L'Oréal Paris, Maybelline New York and Garnier - with each being targeted at a different customer segment. The report does not name the targets but looking at the products in-store would probably provide evidence for this.
- Launching new products patented by headquarters and then marketed globally.
- Targeting 'growth driver countries' like China with Maybelline make-up and the Russian Federation with Garnier skincare products in order to deliver growth objectives.
- Maintaining strong *co-operation* strategies with leading local country partners - the company comments that the 'point of sale' presentation is 'absolutely critical' to sales success and this can only be achieved with local partners and distributors.
- The skincare growth was exceptional at nearly 24 per cent. This was achieved using the L'Oréal Paris and Garnier brands along with new patented products in every part of the world.

The company claimed to outperform its competitors with such strategies. It also gives similar information on the other product areas. This information is available on the web at **www.l'oreal.com**.

L'Oréal describes many initiatives with regard to green strategy in its annual report and accounts.

 This case was written from published sources of information only.[11]

STRATEGIC PROJECT

1 Use the World Wide Web to call up the remaining L'Oréal data and explore the strategies that it has adopted.

2 Make a comparison with rival companies like Estée Lauder and Shiseido. You will find that Estée Lauder's sales are stronger in the USA and Shiseido in Japan. You might like to find the comment on the North American market by L'Oréal in its annual report 2003 that would then explain - at least in part - why Estée Lauder's sales were less profitable.

3 Use the web to identify other companies involved in beauty products. You may like to know that the second largest beauty products company in the world is the US company Procter & Gamble (P&G) (**www.pg.com/investors/annualreports.jhml**). The company has annual sales over $30 billion in beauty products. It has achieved this through the acquisition in the past few years of the three companies Gillette, Wella and Clairol, as well as products acquired some years ago, including Oil of Olay and Pantene. You could look up P&G on the web, but you may not find the full data - some large American companies choose to reveal only what is required by company law with regard to their trading performance and it may be that there is no such requirement to show such data. The other large cosmetics company is Unilever with brands such as Dove and Sunsilk - Unilever is explored in Case 9.3.

4 Use the web to find stockbrokers' reports that analyse the above companies. They will often provide market size, growth and share data that is lacking from the financial statements of the companies. This will be given to financial analysts so that they can understand the strengths and (maybe) the weaknesses of the companies that they are commenting upon.

Detailed definitions and guidance on using financial ratios in dynamic analytics.

5.2 THE DYNAMICS OF AN ORGANISATION'S CHANGING AND UNCERTAIN ENVIRONMENT

In strategy, the main environmental factors that influence strategy – including general policies and events like global warming, competitors, customers and suppliers – are continuously changing and often very difficult to predict. Outside events move both in relation to each other and to their influence on the organisation. Although strategists like Porter and Rumelt focus primarily on competitors, the influence of the dynamic environment on the organisation is actually much broader – as we explored in Chapter 3. For example, when L'Oréal acquired the retail cosmetics chain Body Shop in 2006, the purchase required the buyer to consider Body Shop's strong ethical stance against the testing of cosmetics on animals. L'Oréal was entirely supportive on an issue that went beyond competitive considerations.

Although there are many dimensions to the environment, it is useful to divide our consideration of the dynamics into four related areas:

1 *The nature and intensity of competition in an industry*. There are some basic factors that influence the dynamics – such as the number of firms and the barriers to entry. These need to be analysed first.
2 *The dynamics of competitor activities*. Although it is generally accepted that competitors matter in strategy development, their activities are often assumed to be static over time. In reality, both the strategies of our own organisation and those of our competitors will be changing continuously.
3 *The predictability of the environment*. When the environment is growing or declining steadily, the dynamics may be easy to predict – as outlined in Chapter 3. However, not all environments are predictable, so the issue needs to be explored.
4 *Resource inertia in response to environmental change*. Even though the dynamics of the environment may be *understood*, this does not necessarily mean that the organisation is able to *act* on that understanding. The relationship between the two areas needs to be investigated.

One final area – the degree of co-operation in an industry – is explored in Section 5.6.

5.2.1 The nature and intensity of competition in an industry

Governments will set the basic degree of competitiveness that they wish to see in industries. Having established this, it is useful to start any analysis of competition with Porter's *Five Forces Analysis* (see Chapter 3). This will provide a basic starting point in any development of the major factors driving the dynamics of the industry. From a dynamic perspective, there are some further factors that can also be analysed.

Industry structure and market characteristics have a significant impact on strategic management. However, the actions that companies take go well beyond the pricing activity often highlighted in microeconomic theory – for example, cost reduction, product differentiation, linkages with other companies through alliances and joint ventures. At L'Oreal, pricing was clearly important, but there were a whole range of factors associated with its cosmetic products that would also attract buyers. Three main areas of strategic significance can be analysed:

1 The *total number of firms in an industry* may influence their ability to exert buying power over suppliers. If there are few, then buying power may increase; if there are many, then their buying power will be lower. There are many firms in the cosmetics industry but the leading firms are clearly few in number.
2 The *mix of firms making up the industry* will also impact on profitability. If there are a few companies that are roughly equal in size, then there may be some tacit understanding between them to allow profits to grow. As the numbers increase and there is a likelihood of some giants and some

smaller companies, then there is a lower possibility of a tacit understanding, so profits will suffer. In cosmetics, there are clearly giants, like L'Oréal and P&G, and small specialist companies – perhaps selling fragrances under exclusive fashion labels like Chanel No 5.

3 The *barriers to entry* possessed by the existing firms in that industry. Economists identify three main types of barrier:[12] barriers based on production or distribution technology, barriers from brand name or reputation, and legal barriers. Strategists would argue that there are other barriers that are just as important such as knowledge barriers and networks of business contacts. We explore these latter areas in Chapters 7 and 11. In cosmetics, the main barriers to entry relate to the heavy expense of brand building, the high cost of product innovation and the difficulty of gaining retail distribution.

Overall, it is likely that strategy will vary with company size and the degree of market competition. Smaller companies, such as small shoe manufacturers, may have to adopt different strategies from larger organisations, such as the world's largest retail chain, Wal-Mart. Large companies have the resources to set up retail chains to sell their products – unlike small companies. Highly competitive markets with few competing companies may therefore require different strategies from those with lower degrees of competition. This has profound significance because it suggests that strategy will vary with industry.[13] There may be no single 'strategy' that will suit all industries.

5.2.2 The dynamics of competitor activities

Amongst strategists, there is a widely held view that the search for competitive advantage is fundamental to strategic success. To quote Michael Porter:

> Competitive strategy is the search for a favourable competitive position in an industry . . . Competitive strategy aims to establish a profitable and sustainable position against the forces that determine industry competition.[14]

There are two difficulties acknowledged by Porter in this statement. First, the forces determining industry competition are changing all the time. Second, the firm itself will not only respond to such forces but will also attempt to '*shape* that environment in a firm's favour' [my italics in this quote from Porter].[15]

In other words, Porter argues that the dynamics of competitive advantage have at least two dimensions:

1 the nature of the competitive advantage operating in an industry – called interpretive dynamics in this text;

2 the degree to which a firm is able or willing to shift the balance of competitive advantage towards itself by its new strategies in that industry – called proactive dynamics in this text.

However, according to Gary Hamel and C K Prahalad, this misses an important element in the dynamics because it concentrates on the *current* industry boundaries:

> Strategy is as much about competing for tomorrow's industry as it is about competing within today's industry structure. Competition within today's industry structure raises such issues as: What new features should be added to a product? How can we get better channel coverage? Should we price for maximum market share or maximum profits? Competition for tomorrow's industry structure raises deeper questions such as: Whose product concepts will ultimately win out? How will coalitions form and what will determine each member's share of power? And, most critically, how do we increase our ability to influence the emerging shape of a nascent industry?[16]

Although Hamel and Prahalad were addressing their remarks primarily to new industry opportunities like satellite television and internet record distribution, the same logic can be applied to existing and more mature markets like cosmetics. To quote Baden-Fuller and Stopford on mature market strategy: 'The real battles are fought among firms taking different approaches, especially those that counter yesterday's ideas.'[17] In other words, the dynamics of competitive advantage need to be viewed not just as a battle between the existing firms but also as an attempt to break out of the existing competitive framework. For example in the cosmetics industry, L'Oréal broke out of its existing boundaries when it acquired its first retail cosmetics shop chain – The Body Shop – in 2006 for $2.2 billion. Equally, Procter and Gamble broke out of its reliance on female cosmetics when it acquired the major men's personal products group – Gillette – in 2005 for $57 billion. This carries the significant difficulty of shaping such a dynamic so that it is still manageable within the resources of an organisation. Exhibit 5.1 shows a three-stage process that might elucidate the dynamics and identify the opportunity.[18]

EXHIBIT 5.1

Investigating the dynamics of the competitor activities

There are three possible steps:

1 *Develop a vision about the future direction of an industry and related areas.* For example, the Ford Motor Company has taken the view that strategy in the global car industry will involve control of distributors, second-hand cars and servicing in addition to car manufacturing. This is the organisation identifying the opportunity.

2 *Manage the paths that will service this vision.* This will involve building before rivals such areas as the key resources, the new products and services, the relevant networks and alliances. For example, the UK retailer Tesco was amongst the first to establish a home shopping service using the internet which required both a website and a well-organised home delivery service. This is the organisation shaping the strategy.

3 *Compete within the chosen market for market share.* This will involve such areas as the level of service, the marketing mix and the reduction in costs through operations strategies.

Keypoint: it is this last stage that is often portrayed as the conventional battleground of sustainable competitive advantage, whereas it may be the two earlier areas that contain the most useful dynamic opportunities.

5.2.3 The predictability of the environment

From a strategic management perspective, the dynamics of the environment can be managed better if the environment can be predicted. The changes are known in these circumstances and the strategic implications can therefore be actioned. For example in the cosmetics industry, it may be possible to predict changes in attitudes to recycling of cosmetics packaging. We examine this issue by first exploring some of the types of prediction that can be and have been undertaken. We then explore the argument of Mintzberg that much of this activity is a waste of time.

The purpose of prediction

The objective of undertaking prediction is to cope better with uncertainty in the environment. There will always be some residual risk, but prediction should help to reduce this and increase the chance of success. In other words, the dynamics of the environment may be at least partially controlled, if they can be predicted.

According to some strategists,[19] the key to tackling strategic prediction is to understand that some environments are more predictable than others. For example, the market for ice cream – see Cases 10.1 and 10.3 – can be predicted with some certainty. Some revolutionary new technology might invalidate this prediction, but this is unlikely. By contrast, the outcome of the DVD format battle – see Case 5.3 – could not be so easily predicted, because the future direction was highly uncertain. However, although the second is more open, there are some techniques that will reduce the uncertainty and make the environment partially predictable.

EXHIBIT 5.2

Coping with different levels of environmental uncertainty

Environment 1 Reasonably predictable, barring catastrophe	Environment 2 Alternatives clear, but precise outcome remains unknown	Environment 3 Many possible outcomes with no clear idea of way ahead
Techniques: market and competitor projections – see Chapters 3 and 10	*Techniques*: market projections, decision analysis plus options from game theory – see Chapters 3 and 10 plus game theory later in this chapter	*Techniques*: market outlook, technology forecasting and scenario planning – see Chapters 3, 10 and 11
Prediction: single outcome with upside and downside	*Prediction*: series of discrete outcomes that will encompass the main future possibilities	*Prediction*: some possible outcomes that provide a general sense of direction only; even this may be of only limited value
Example: Nestlé's food markets – see Case study 13.3	*Example*: Prediction of the likely outcomes to the consolidation of the European defence industry – see the GEC Marconi case on the book's open-access website	*Example*: The outcomes of the opportunities that will arise from the internet record industry – see Case 13 in Part 6

Note: Exhibit 3.2 contains a worked example on using scenarios.

For our purposes, it is useful to identify three types of environment and the techniques that might be employed in their prediction: these are shown in Exhibit 5.2. This book has explored the main techniques elsewhere so they are not repeated here. The main point is that, even where there is strong residual uncertainty, some prediction of the environment may be possible within broad limits.

The fallacy of prediction?

Within the context of this conclusion, we now turn to the comments of Professor Henry Mintzberg. He has argued that prediction is often a complete waste of time.[20] He describes how traditional prescriptive strategic planning will make a prediction about the environment and then expect the world to stay on this predicted course while the strategy is developed and implemented.

As an example of what he regards as the fallacy of prediction, Mintzberg quotes from one of the early pioneers of strategic management, Professor Igor Ansoff, who wrote in his book on *Corporate Strategy*: 'We shall refer to the period for which the firm is able to construct forecasts with an accuracy of, say, plus or minus 20 per cent as the planning horizon.'[21] Mintzberg comments:

> What an extraordinary statement! How in the world can any company know the period for which it can forecast with any accuracy? . . . While certain repetitive patterns, such as seasons, may be predictable, the forecasting of discontinuities, such as technological innovation or a price increase, is virtually impossible.

Thus Mintzberg argues that, where environmental prediction really matters, for example in predicting innovations, it is largely worthless. He dismisses the value of future visions of markets, explaining that they arise from essentially personal and intuitive approaches.

Comment

What does this mean for environmental dynamics? Mintzberg is right to dismiss the value of precise predictions in areas of great uncertainty. Thus if a strategist were to undertake financial discounted cash flow (DCF) calculations based on predictions about the size of the internet record industry in 10 years' time – see Case 13 in Part 6 – they would have little value, beyond the general implication that considerable growth is likely. However, Mintzberg takes his argument too far when he suggests that nothing can be done: scenarios, options and general forecasts may prove beneficial, as outlined in Exhibit 5.2. Moreover, where the environment is more stable, environmental dynamics can benefit from prediction.

5.2.4 Resource inertia response to environmental change

Even though organisations are able to see and understand changes in the environment, they are not always able to act upon them. There is an inertia in organisations that arises from the difficulties, costs and risks implied by such change. The result is that the dynamics of the environment will not necessarily be translated immediately into actions inside the organisation, especially in terms of resource-based change. The economist Professor Richard Rumelt has suggested that there are five reasons for this:[22]

1 *Distorted perception.* Although individuals in organisations may be able to see the environment clearly, the organisation taken as a whole may have more difficulty. The reasons may include a desire to stay with short-term certainties, a fear of what the future might bring or a selective desire to stay with current habits.
2 *Dulled motivation.* Even though organisations understand the environment, they may not perceive with sufficient clarity the threat that it poses. Thus they will not be sufficiently motivated to act on the information.
3 *Failed creative response.* The organisation may be unable to find a creative way out of the threat posed, even though it perceives it accurately.
4 *Political deadlocks.* Organisational politics may make it impossible to develop the best strategy to cope with the perceived opportunity or threat.
5 *Action disconnects.* Leadership, organisational routines and stakeholder interest groups may all make it impossible to react to environmental change.

We explore some of these areas in more depth in Chapter 11, but it is appropriate here that we acknowledge the difficulty of connecting the environment with the resources of the organisation.

KEY STRATEGIC PRINCIPLES

- To analyse the nature and intensity of competition in an industry, three areas have a signficant influence on strategy: the total number of firms in an industry; the mix of those firms in terms of numbers and size; the barriers to entry possessed by the existing firms in that industry.
- The dynamics of environmental development have many dimensions but can usefully be considered from three perspectives: the maintenance of competitive advantage; the predictability of the environment; the ability of the organisation's resources to respond to changes in the environment.
- The maintenance of competitive advantage will depend on the nature of the advantages operating in an industry. It will also involve the willingness of a firm to shape new advantages and the nature of the future advantages that might operate in an industry.

- If the environment is predictable then it allows the dynamics of the environment to be managed more easily. Although no environment is entirely predictable, some strategists argue that the process is largely a waste of time, with no meaningful results where it matters.
- Although an organisation may have understood the nature of environmental change, it may not be able to act upon it. Five major reasons have been identified for this: distorted perception; dulled motivation; failed creative response; political deadlocks; action disconnects.

CASE STUDY 5.3

Why are format wars important in strategy? The battle between Sony and Toshiba

Over the past few years, the two Japanese electronics giants - Sony and Toshiba - have been battling to win the format war for the next generation of high definition digital video discs (DVDs). Why does this matter? Not just for these companies but also for any company engaged in a technology standards battle?

The battle for the new DVD standard

'We won't lose this game, we will win. It's only a matter of time until slim-type HD-DVDs will be in notebook computers and costs will drop dramatically.' The chief executive of the Japanese electronics giant Toshiba, Atsutoshi Nishida, was comparing his company's new format digital video disc - called the HD-DVD - with the rival disc from another Japanese electronics giant, Sony - called the Blu-ray DVD. 'In Europe, there are many more HD-DVD [film] titles available than Sony.'

For the past few years, the two companies and their allies have been engaged in a war to develop a new format for DVDs. The customer benefits of the new standard over existing DVDs were three-fold: higher quality presentation especially for films, more capacity on each disc and greater protection against piracy (though some might say that this was more of a benefit for the companies than the customers). However, the new format of DVDs would require customers to invest in a new DVD player. The problem for customers - initially at least - was that there were at least two technologies for achieving such results: the HD-DVD from Toshiba and the Blu-ray DVD from Sony.

While two such formats existed, customers would initially refrain from buying the new DVD players. This would slow down the take-up of the new technology. In turn, the lower market volumes meant that it was more difficult to achieve the economies of scale that come with higher levels of production and lead to lower costs and lower prices. It would also mean that film companies would be forced to either present their film DVDs in the two formats and increase production costs or only offer one format and reduce sales.

Winning a format war has clear profit implications both for the companies immediately involved - like Sony and Toshiba - and for film companies relying on take-up within an industry - like Walt Disney and 20th Century Fox. But the high definition DVD battle was not the first technology format war in strategy.

Is this the only standards battle?

Ever since the QWERTY keyboard won the battle for the English language typewriter keyboard format in the early twentieth century, there have been standards wars at various times. Possibly the most famous was the battle between Sony and Philips against JVC over the standard for video tape recorders in the early 1980s: Sony and Philips claimed that its Betamax format was technically superior to that of the VHS rival. The latter format was owned by the Japanese company JVC and backed by at least three other Japanese companies - Matsushita (owners of the Panasonic brand), Pioneer and Toshiba. The formats were incompatible and launched into the market place for television video recorders. The outcome after some years was that the VHS format was the winner. Sony and Philips dropped the Betamax format and introduced VHS format machines. They then paid a licence fee to JVC for the VHS format technology.

What about other examples? In the early 1990s, Sony launched its MiniDisc to compete with the rival digital compact disc (DCC) - a miniaturised cassette tape developed jointly by Matsushita and Philips. Eventually, Sony won that war and Matsushita was forced to produce MiniDiscs on a large scale, after accepting the Sony product as the industry standard. Subsequently in 1999, Sony and Philips launched the Super Audio CD against a rival technology - the DVD Audio format - also from Matsushita. Neither was especially successful and both failed to replace the basic compact disc, which lasted at least until the arrival of Apple's iPod in year 2000.

At present, there are at least two further standards battles in progress. The first concerns *open-source software* for use on computers. For large commercial and government organisations, commercial software is important for operating many of their computer systems. Specialist companies can supply and maintain their own proprietary software. 'Proprietary' here means that it is owned by the supplying company who keep the underlying codes secret but guarantee to update the resulting company software: Microsoft and Sun are companies that operate in this way. By contrast, open-source software is developed by a loose community of developers from many companies and it is distributed under licence so its impact is much more widely and immediately available.

The second example concerned Microsoft and its battle to get its new Windows Office software - called Open XML - accepted as a standard by the International Standards Organisation (ISO). This involved a vote by various countries at a special meeting of the ISO in September 2007. It would be beneficial for Microsoft because the ISO standard is used by many large companies and governments when placing large software contracts. Microsoft's application was opposed by several other computer companies like IBM and Sun, who were supporting the rival standard - ODF (Open Document Format).

The Open XML/ODF battle was continuing at the time of writing. For example, Pieter Hintjens, chief executive of the non-profit-making Foundation for a Free Information Infrastructure, was campaigning against the Microsoft request. He commented: 'We've recorded fairly systematic manipulation of the voting process. We've seen what amounts to vote-buying in Italy, Portugal, Columbia. In Sweden and Denmark, much the same happened - Microsoft paying their business partners to join the vote.' Against this, Microsoft denied any improper influence: 'Our customers want to have an impact on this decision and we have encouraged that,' explained Tom Robertson, general manager for interoperability and standards at Microsoft.

Sony's Blu-ray format has won the DVD strategy battle. This case explains how the company beat Toshiba's rival technology.

How do companies win format wars?

Such activities raise the question of how format wars are influenced and won. There are five main methods:

1. *Develop superior technical performance*. HD-DVD has a capacity of 45 GB on three disc layers whereas Blu-ray has a higher capacity of 200 GB on two layers.
2. *Build industry support*. HD-DVD has its 'DVD Forum' with 230 members including Universal Pictures, Warner Brothers, Microsoft and Intel. Blu-ray has the 'BD Association' with 100 members including Walt Disney and 20th Century Fox.
3. *Make it cheap to produce*. HD-DVD can use existing DVD technology in current factories, which will also be able to continue producing existing DVD discs. Blu-ray uses new production technology that is not compatible with existing factories and is therefore more expensive.
4. *Gain early customer acceptance*. Blu-ray has the unique advantage that it is the technology introduced with the new P3 Sony PlayStation - finally launched in 2006 but still with limited take-up - see Case 4.3.
5. *Organise backward compatibility*. HD-DVD has close links with existing DVDs. Blu-ray introduces new designs and processes that require new production facilities.

The importance of format wars in strategy

What does all this mean for format wars? For several years and a cost estimated around $2 billion, the two main companies in the high definition DVD battle fought the video format war. 'The cost of the HD-DVD will be less than Blu-ray. In the US market, HD-DVD is now $499 which is half Blu-ray,' commented Toshiba's chief executive in March 2007. However, Sony was planning its own cut-price Blu-ray disc player in an attempt to maintain its lead over Toshiba with a price of $599. Just as important as pricing was the degree of acceptance by the major film companies of a particular format. Sony had some major backers like Disney and 20th Century Fox. But Toshiba had persuaded other film companies like Warner to back its format.

Then in early 2008, Warner changed sides and backed the Sony format. Within 48 hours of this announcement, Toshiba backed down and said that it would withdraw its DVD format. Sony had won.

Since both companies clearly suffered from lower profits in the medium term as a result of this battle, the question might be asked why they never agreed to co-operate and share the benefits. In fact, Sony and Toshiba had serious commercial discussions during the early part of 2005 but were unable to reach a contractual agreement. Each company judged that the benefits would be higher in the long run if it won the war. However, if it lost the war, then the costs of conversion for the loser to the rival format would be much greater. In practice, the profit consequences of failure were all too clear. Toshiba was estimated to have spent over $1 billion by 2008 on developing, promoting and subsidising its failed format.

Conclusion: do we really need a 'war'?

Finally, it is worth exploring whether a 'war' is really needed to decide a technology format. At the time of writing, the main mobile phone manufacturers - Nokia, Motorola, Samsung, etc. - and the leading mobile service providers - Vodafone, Verizon Wireless, China Mobile - were engaged in technical discussions about a new mobile telephone standard called 4G. This would enable phones to be used anywhere in the world - including Europe, North America, Africa and Asia. At present, there are rival second- and third-generation mobile technologies that make it difficult to obtain universal usage. There were still important technical and competitive issues to be resolved, but at least some companies were no longer engaged in costly format wars.

Both Sony and Toshiba have policies with regard to green strategy in their annual reports for 2013. But, arguably, the Sony report has more specific detail than the Toshiba report.

Case questions

1 What were the competitive advantages of the two rival DVD formats?

2 Using the innovation flow process in Section 5.3, how would you analyse the development position of the two companies? Could Toshiba still come up with a version when the technology became more mature? If so, what should be the strategy for such a development?

3 What lessons can we learn from format wars for strategy dynamics?

5.3 DYNAMIC STRATEGIES IN FAST-MOVING MARKETS

Fast-moving markets present real opportunities and challenges for strategists. The dynamics of the DVD industry and its format wars above show just what scope there is for strategic development, including real opportunities for small and medium-sized enterprises (SMEs). The dynamics of such fast-moving markets are mainly governed by the pace and change of innovation.

By its nature, innovation is difficult to define. Thus some innovations are relatively small, while others revolutionise whole industries. For example, the compact disc method of recording was innovative in producing increased sound quality in the record industry but was hardly revolutionary, whereas the possible distribution of music by the totally new technology of the internet may cause the market to open up significantly. This latter development will be both innovative and revolutionary. In exploring the dynamics of innovation, there are several interrelated areas that need to be explored: these are shown in Figure 5.5.

5.3.1 Fast-moving dynamics: market dominance issues

Where an industry is subject to rapid technological change, then there are two problems facing a company that dominates an industry and has *already* committed its resources to a specific technology:

1 *Sunk cost effect.* Firms that have already committed substantial resources to a specific technology may be reluctant to change. Resources and organisational abilities will have been developed for that technology and will be less valuable in any new technology. Such resources represent costs sunk into that technology: for example, the massive investment in record promotion networks to retail shops by the Big Three record producers (see Case 13 in Part 6) would be largely useless on the internet. In deciding whether to switch to new technology, the sunk costs should be ignored because they have been spent. But inevitably such costs may bias firms like the Big Five against making the innovative change.[24]

2 *Replacement effect.* Existing large firms have less incentive to innovate than new companies. The reason is that new companies might expect to gain market dominance by innovation, whereas existing large firms gain no further dominance by such a process. For existing large firms, their market dominance by one technology is simply replaced by that of a new technology – the replacement effect.[25]

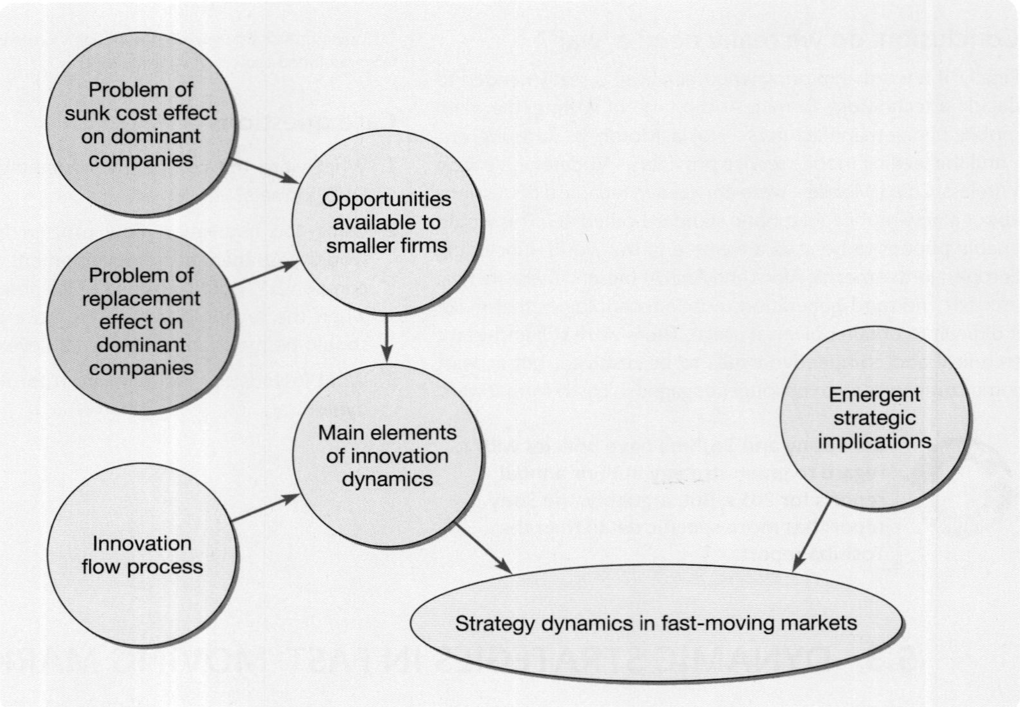

Figure 5.5 Exploring the dynamics of fast-moving markets

5.3.2 Fast-moving dynamics: the opportunities available to smaller companies

In fast-moving markets, SMEs that do not dominate the market should have significant opportunities. They should be faster and more flexible. Their cultures should be more entrepreneurial and seek out the opportunities presented by the market dynamics. For example, it is the smaller, independent record companies that have developed new artists over the years: as they have benefited from their growth, so they have been acquired in many cases by the Big Five.

Innovation is about process as well as product. For example, in the record industry it is not only about new artists and music (product) but also about new forms of internet distribution (process). Small companies that do not have vested interests in existing processes will also gain by new process methods, such as using the internet.

5.3.3 Fast-moving dynamics: the innovation flow process

Clearly, it is the substantive, major innovation that will provide important opportunities for SMEs to transform an industry and gain substantial new added value. Professor James Utterback of the Massachusetts Institute of Technology has explored innovation and its dynamics. In particular, he studied how substantial innovation has revolutionised a number of industries.[26] Other writers have also investigated the importance of innovation in revolutionising the structure of industries, especially the way that new firms come to dominate industries.[27]

From the various empirical studies, it is possible to identify the elements of the way that innovation changes whole industries over time: this is shown in Figure 5.6. Essentially, innovation starts with the existing resources of an organisation and an influx of new ideas from outside. In the early stages, there is often no dominant technology or design. This has the advantage of allowing many companies to participate but the disadvantage of making cost reduction of such a design difficult. Once a dominant design has emerged, then a small group of firms may come to dominate that

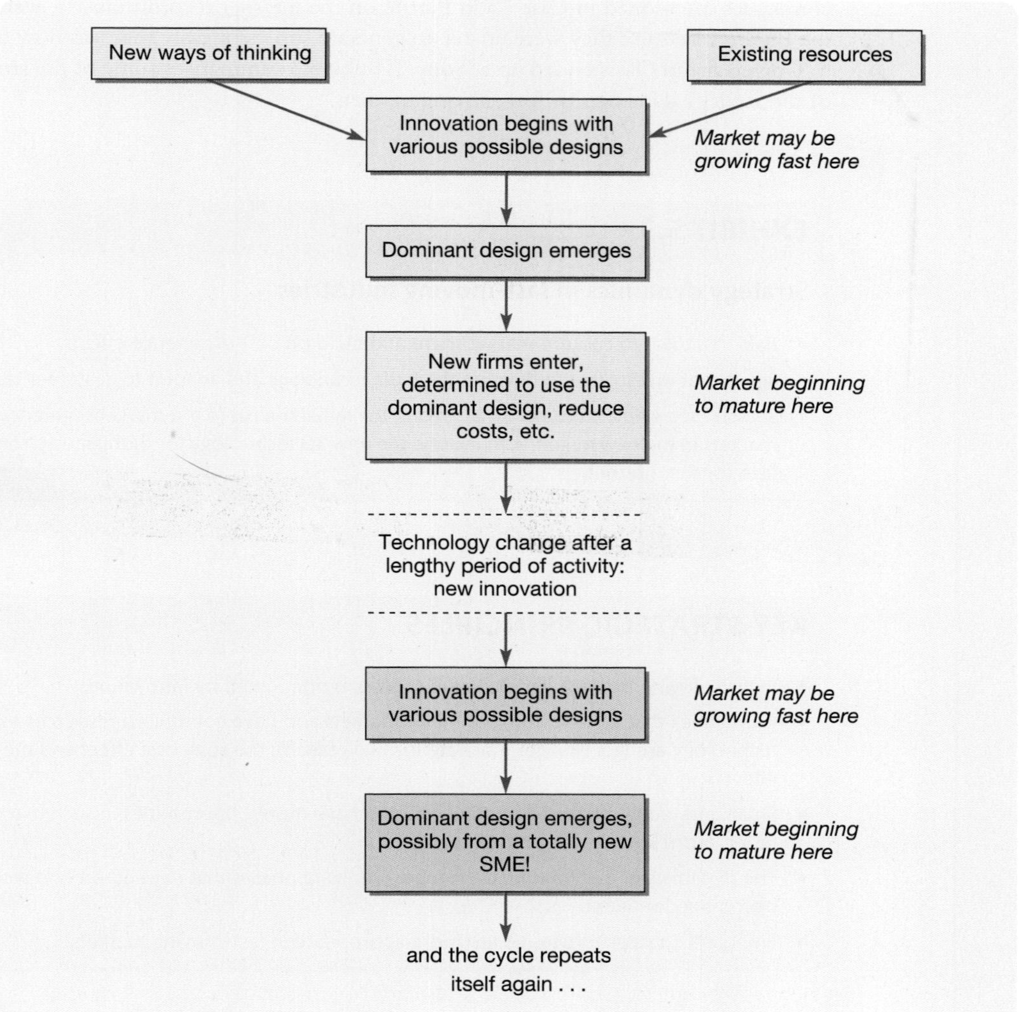

Figure 5.6 The innovation flow process

market and cost reduction begins. After a period of time, a totally new technology emerges and the process begins all over again. The significance of this is that it highlights the opportunities for small, new companies to come to dominate an industry as a result of innovative change: the classic example is the Microsoft dominance of personal computers with its Windows operating system – see Case 1.2.

5.3.4 The emergent strategic implications of fast-moving dynamics

When a market is new and growing fast, it is not clear how it will develop. Technology may still be in its early stages, with little agreement on industry standards. Companies will still be low on the experience curve (see Section 8.6.4) and will be operating emergent strategies to find the best route forward.

Dominant market shares will have less meaning because the market is changing fast. New customers will still be entering the market and will need to be introduced to the products. Competitors should all be experiencing significant sales growth, with the problem being to provide adequate finance for this and for further research at the same time. For example, some of the small record companies mentioned in Case 13 in Part 6, on the internet record industry, were swallowed up by the Big Five because they were unable to generate sufficient cash: that was how the group U2 came to Universal and Oasis ended up at Sony. Exhibit 5.3 summarises some of the strategic implications of the strategy dynamics of fast-moving markets.

EXHIBIT 5.3

Strategy dynamics in fast-moving industries

- *Bold initiatives* to capture market share and build on cost experience effects.
- Significant investment to develop the *basic technology* and adapt it to customer tastes.
- Search for a viable *customer base* beyond the initial trialists (e.g. a market segment). Examples of such markets in the new millennium include the new 3G technology for mobile telephones and some new uses for the internet.

KEY STRATEGIC PRINCIPLES

- In fast-moving markets, the dynamic process is dominated by innovation.
- Companies that already dominate their markets and have committed resources to a specific technology are less likely to innovate for two reasons: the sunk cost effect and the replacement effect.
- Small and medium-sized companies should have more opportunities in such markets if they are faster, more flexible and entrepreneurial.
- The dynamics of innovation go through a series of phases that depend on one technical design becoming dominant.
- Emergent strategic processes are more appropriate in fast-moving markets.

5.4 THE DYNAMICS OF RESOURCE DEVELOPMENT

In Chapter 3, the resources of the organisation were classified into four main areas and the concept of the *hierarchy of resources* was explored. However, the balance between the four areas does not stay static over time.[28] Figure 5.7 illustrates how resources might be expected to alter dynamically over time. This section explores how and why such changes might occur.

Resources will change as the organisation's purpose changes. In addition, they will also be influenced by what is happening outside in the environment. For example, following Sony's success with its DVD format, it will still face resource decisions with regard to licensing of the format technology to companies that have opted for the Toshiba format: Sony does not have the manufacturing capacity to supply the whole world with such discs. Thus competitive resources will also be influenced by the outside activities of competitors and by further changes in DVD technology.

Given that an organisation has made the normative and reasonable choice to increase its value added, the dynamics of resource development can be considered as having three main dimensions:[29]

1 *time* – resource configurations developed and destroyed over time;
2 *early-mover advantages* – resource developments when moving into a new market place;
3 *imitation pressures* – resource changes related to the existing resources.

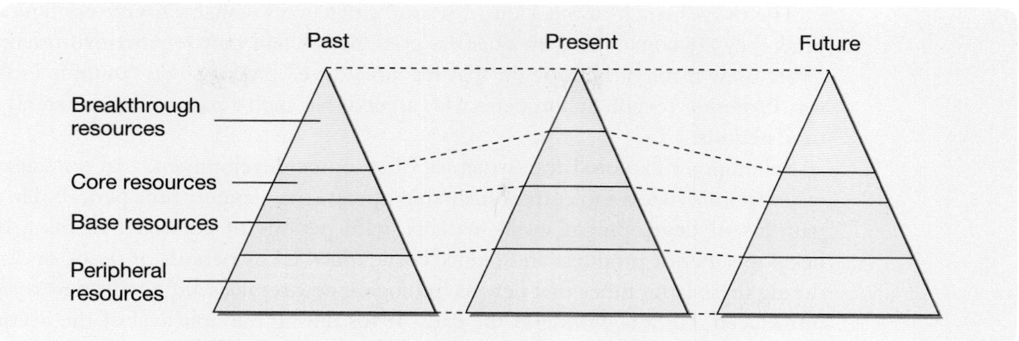

Figure 5.7 How resources alter dramatically

Source: Chaharbaghi, K and Lynch, R (1999) 'Sustainable competitive advantage: towards a dynamic resource-based strategy', *Management Decision*, Vol 37, No 1, pp 45–50. Adapted with permission.

5.4.1 Resource configurations developed and destroyed over time: the contributions of four leading economists

Four leading economists have explored aspects of resource dynamics, each making their own contribution:

- Penrose – the two sources of new resource growth;
- Nelson and Winter – the delaying effect of routines in companies;
- Schumpeter – the mechanism that destroys resources over time.

In exploring the future growth of the firm, Edith Penrose was very clear. It would partially come from the resources already present in the company: 'In planning expansion, a firm considers two groups of resources – its own previously acquired or "inherited" resources, and those it must obtain from the market in order to carry out its production and expansion programmes.'[30] The clear implication of this statement is that the starting point of resource dynamics will be these two aspects, which we can extend to any organisation rather than just the firm. It also follows that organisations may be constrained by their previous resources: this is an example of *strategy as history* as explored in the first section of this chapter.

Writing originally in the 1950s, Penrose considered the dynamics of the resources only in the context of the growth of the firm. Some 20 years later, Richard Nelson and Sidney Winter developed a view of evolutionary economics that examined how firms changed over time, possibly but not necessarily with growth as the objective. They identified the *routines* of the firm as being the basis of its resources and its strategic decision making.[31] They defined such routines as the well-practised patterns of activity inside the firm: for example, the Toyota production system described in the Toyota web case linked to Part 6 and the European branding policy introduced by Unilever on its ice cream products explored in Chapter 10. It is these routines that deliver some distinctive resources to the firm and therefore provide some of its competitive advantage. The concept of routines has three implications for resource dynamics:

1 Many routines have to be learned and take long periods to establish. This means that these resources will change relatively slowly. Such resources are *sticky*.

2 In so far as routines dominate the pattern of activity in an organisation, they may limit the innovative capacity of the firm to develop totally new resources. Such resources are relatively *blind* to new developments.

3 Routines often employ tacit knowledge and informal networks of people. This is beneficial in making it difficult for outsiders to imitate, but this imprecision will make it more difficult to replicate inside the company. Such resources will *require investment* so that they can be relearnt or they may atrophy and die.

The overall result of this view of resource dynamics is that resource configurations develop over time, they are constrained by what has gone before and they require investment if they are to continue. Now it might be thought that resource development could continue in this way for ever. It was Professor Joseph Schumpeter who argued that such a pattern was inherently unlikely over long time periods.

Schumpeter explored the dynamics of resource development.[32] In particular, he identified the way that innovation and entrepreneurship operate over lengthy time periods. He said that there were patterns of development in all markets, with periods of comparative calm, during which firms develop superior products and reduce costs, followed by periods of shock or discontinuities. It was during these latter times that new technologies, new services and totally new ways of operating were introduced. He was writing in the early 1940s during the upheaval of the Second World War and was also able to look back to the First World War and the relatively calmer period in between. He had no knowledge of the 'dot.com' boom-and-bust scenario of the period 1999–2000, but this is a more recent example of his concept. He argued that entrepreneurs who were able to exploit the market opportunities during such periods of shock would benefit during the subsequent periods of calm. Sony's winning format for the new higher quality DVD – see Case 5.3 – means that Toshiba's design and development will probably disappear. Schumpeter called this process *creative destruction*.

From the perspective of resource dynamics, the significance of creative destruction is that all resources should have a limited shelf-life. They cannot go on for ever and will be superseded by innovatory new products. Thus Schumpeter would argue that Bill Gates and his colleagues at Microsoft may have made a fortune with the Windows computer operating system, but it will ultimately be overtaken by some new development. Competitive resources will become uncompetitive over time as a result of innovation and new organisational knowledge.

If Schumpeter's argument is correct, then the strategic problem is that competitive resources never stand still. The strategic solution is to develop new resources before the competition. We examine this in the next section.

Comment

It is interesting to note that it took Microsoft several years to see the potential threat of Netscape's Internet Browser as an alternative means of delivering computer software services. No wonder Microsoft reacted so vigorously to the opportunities presented by the internet.[33] On this evidence, Schumpeter's view of *creative destruction* is useful in high-technology markets.

However, creative destruction may have less relevance as a resource dynamic in relation to more traditional markets. For example, the substantial worldwide market for chocolate products like Nestlé's KitKat or Mars' Milky Way does not seem, so far, to have been subject to creative destruction. In some product categories, evolutionary resources may continue for substantial periods without destruction.

5.4.2 The early-mover advantage: resource developments when moving into a new market place

In some markets, the firm that acquires a competitive advantage early in the life of a market may find that this sets in motion a resource dynamic that preserves the advantage during the life of the market: *the early-mover advantage*. For example, by being one of the early companies into the market for computer operating systems and by co-operating with the market leader at the time, IBM, Microsoft was able to establish a user base for its Windows system that other companies have been unable to match – see Case 1.2. Equally, by being one of the early companies to produce mobile telephones on a global scale, Nokia has established itself as one of the leaders in that market and delivered sustainable competitive advantages based on economies of scale and product design – see Case 9.2.

Importantly, being the early mover does not necessarily mean being *first* into a new market. The very first companies can make mistakes from which they never recover – perhaps from poor technical performance, perhaps in marketing. Learning from what others have already done may be useful, while still being one of the early-but-not-first movers may be all that is required.

There are at least five resource advantages delivered by an early move into a market:

1. *Establishment of the benchmark technical format.* Innovation may introduce a basic technology that will set the standard for the market. It may not even be the most efficient technology, but it may still deliver useful advantage. The example usually quoted is the QWERTY typewriter layout which was introduced in 1899 and is still used in keyboards today. Although this configuration of letters on the keyboard is technically not as fast as some others, it has become the dominant design.[34] Another example is in this chapter – DVD format wars, Case 5.3.
2. *Building networks of complementors.* For some products, such as computers, computer games and sound systems, it is not just the product itself that matters but the complementors who supply the software, the new games and the recording artists. These networks take time to establish and early movers have an advantage in terms of an installed base of suppliers and users that becomes difficult to shift. For example, in the early 1990s, both Sega and Nintendo video games companies placed considerable emphasis on gaining and keeping their installed base of games users. Nintendo made a major strategic mistake when it introduced its 16-bit machine in the 1990s and made no attempt to build on its previous users of its 8-bit machine.[35] Later it recovered in 2006 for the reasons explored in Case 4.3.
3. *Early move down the learning curve.* Early production experience should allow a company to learn before its competitors and move down the learning curve – see Chapter 8.
4. *Usefulness of reputation when buyers are uncertain.* When new products cannot be assessed fully by customers before they are purchased, the reputation of the company launching such a product becomes a useful customer guide to subsequent performance. For example, a new format DVD from Sony is more likely to carry conviction than the same product from an obscure brand name.
5. *Costs to the buyer from switching products.* When new products are launched, buyers may be reluctant to switch to them if the costs involved are high. For example, switching retail bank accounts used to be an immense administrative task with high costs. In the era of telephone banking, rivals have attempted to reduce such costs by using new technology, but there is still a resource advantage for those banks with an established customer base.

Thus the dynamics of resources are conditioned by the early-mover advantages. However, there are also obvious problems with being the early mover: most companies have to make a bet on the new technology and this may turn out to be incorrect. They may *choose the wrong technology*. For example as explored in Case 5.3, Sony took the view that its Betamax technology would become the dominant tape format for television videotape machines, but JVC ended up with the more widely accepted format and Sony was eventually forced to withdraw its system.[36]

Moreover, companies may be unable to understand or afford the organisational and administrative back-up that is necessary to support the introduction of a totally new technology: they may lack the *complementary assets*. For example, when it was first introduced, the EMI (UK) body scanner was technically the most advanced machine of its kind for scanning human bodies. But the company's resources were primarily engaged in recorded music and television rental and it simply lacked the resources to develop the market.[37] EMI was forced to withdraw and sell out to General Electric (USA) which had the relevant resources.

5.4.3 Imitation pressures: resource changes related to existing resources

For existing products and services, the luxury of being an early mover does not apply. Resource dynamics are driven by the need to deter rivals from imitation. The dynamics of gaining and improving resources that cannot be imitated lie in five main areas:

1. *Incremental improvements in the product or service.* Probably the most widely used way of preventing resources being imitated is a regular programme of product improvement. Consumer companies like Procter & Gamble (USA) in household detergents like Ariel, and PepsiCo (USA) in its Walkers and Frito-Lay snack products have ongoing activities designed to keep their products

one step ahead of the competition. None of the resource changes is radical in itself but all represent genuine improvements that allow these companies to maintain their competitive advantage. The dynamic is slow, steady resource change.

2 *Legal barriers to imitation.* Patents, copyrights and trademarks all represent means of reducing the ability of competitors to imitate products. For example, The Disney Corporation (USA) not only owns the exclusive rights to Disney characters like Mickey Mouse but has also acquired rights to other characters such as Winnie the Pooh. The resource dynamic is powerful and one-way, as long as the resources remain relevant to the customer.
3 *Developing superior relationships with suppliers and customers.* Networks that involve customers and suppliers have been explored extensively in this text – see Chapters 3, 4 and 11. Good supply networks can provide lower costs and higher quality from suppliers. Equally, strong and loyal customer networks can provide larger sales and greater profitability over time. The resource dynamic here is most likely to be broken if technology changes or the balance of power alters.
4 *Exploiting market size and scale economies.* Imitation will clearly be more difficult when profits are derived, at least in part, from a minimum size and economies of scale. Thus Asian car companies like Daewoo (Korea) and Proton (Malaysia) have had difficulty moving into European markets because of the need to provide adequate levels of service support. There are ways around this problem, so the resource dynamic tends to slow the rate of change rather than stop it completely.
5 *Developing intangible barriers to imitation.* There are a whole series of barriers here that are explored in Chapters 4 and 7. They include *tacit knowledge*, which is difficult for the company to codify, let alone for competitors to imitate; *innovative ability*, which is difficult to define but represents a real resource in companies like 3M; *causal ambiguity*, which makes it difficult for competitors to understand how a firm has developed a competitive advantage. The resource dynamics here can present real and practical barriers to imitation.

KEY STRATEGIC PRINCIPLES

- From a dynamic perspective, resources in organisations are developed and destroyed over time. There are three main dimensions: time; early-mover advantages; and imitation pressures.
- When exploring the time dimension, there are three main considerations: the two sources of new resource growth; the delaying effect of routines in companies; the mechanism that destroys resources over time.
- In terms of early-mover advantages, there are five main areas: the establishment of the benchmark technical format; the building of networks of contacts; the early movement down the learning curve; the usefulness of reputation; and the subsequent costs to the buyer when switching from the early mover.
- The pressures that arise from imitating an existing product or service can be countered by five resource activities: incremental improvements in the product or service; legal barriers to imitation, such as patenting; developing superior relationships with customers and suppliers; exploiting market size and scale economies; and developing intangible barriers to imitation.

5.5 AGGRESSIVE COMPETITIVE STRATEGIES[38]

Video Parts 6a and 6b

There is a whole range of aggressive strategies that competitors can undertake. These need to be analysed for two reasons:

1 to understand the strategies competitors may undertake;
2 to assist in planning appropriate counter-measures.

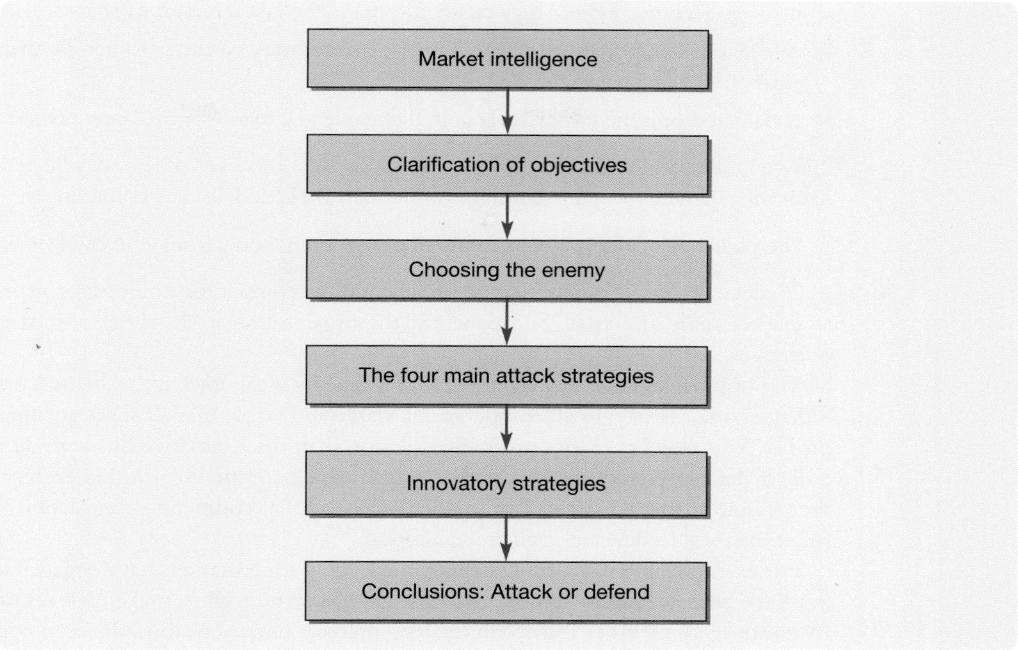

Figure 5.8 Analysing the aggressive strategies undertaken by competitors

In practitioner literature and even some more academic articles in this area, the language and style are often *militaristic* in tone.[39] For example: 'Find a weakness in the leader's strength and attack at that point'; 'Strong competitive moves should always be blocked'. Porter eschews some of the more colourful language but is in no doubt about the importance of this area. Professor Philip Kotler from North Western University, USA, has developed the material in his well-known marketing text, *Marketing Management*[40] and has collaborated with Singh to write an influential article on the topic.[41] The analytical process is summarised in Figure 5.8.

5.5.1 Market intelligence

In accordance with the well-known saying 'knowledge is the basis of power', many companies monitor the activities of their competitors constantly. Occasionally, a few may undertake snooping or eavesdropping activities which may be illegal and are probably unethical. Although such behaviour cannot be condoned, it is entirely correct for companies to seek an understanding of their competitors' strategies. There are many entirely legitimate means for investigating this area. For example:

- company annual reports;
- newspaper articles;
- stockbroker analyses;
- exhibitions and trade fairs.

5.5.2 Clarification of the objectives of competitors

In military situations, the objective is often the total defeat of the enemy. This is rarely appropriate in strategic management for the following reasons:

- It may contravene monopoly legislation, certainly in the EU, the USA and many other countries around the world.

- It often becomes increasingly costly to pursue the last remnant of share.
- A weakened opponent that is still in the market may be easier to handle than a new aggressive entrant.
- A defeated opponent may be acquired cheaply in a takeover by a new powerful entrant.

Even military strategists have recognised that the objectives of war may be better served by some form of stalemate or understanding. As Captain B H Liddell-Hart commented:

> The objective of war is a better state of peace, even if only from your own viewpoint.[42]

To develop this, it is necessary to understand the competitor's objectives, especially in such areas as market share and sales. Subsequently, the organisation itself will also need to develop its own objectives.

The optimal strategic management may define its ideal objective as being a *new market equilibrium* – that is, one that allows all competitors a viable and stable market share accompanied by adequate profits. This may be a more profitable solution than the alternative of continuing aggression, especially if the aggression involves a price war in which competitors outbid each other downwards in the pursuit of market share. Even under strict national competition legislation, it is often possible for companies to develop such an equilibrium.[43]

For example, in UK grocery retailing, the leading supermarkets have engaged in minor price wars but have been willing to settle for shares that allow them all to make high returns on their capital. By contrast, some other European retailing markets have been the subject of continuing aggressive price wars, especially where price discounters – such as Aldi and Netto – have become major players. The result has been that German and other retailers tend to operate with returns on capital that are below those of the UK. In this context, cut-throat competition may serve no one well: the profits of all companies are then reduced.[44]

From a strategic perspective, it is therefore important to clarify the true objectives of competitors in the industry.

5.5.3 Choosing the enemy

Not all competitors are the same: some may be immensely aggressive, with large financial resources, relatively passive shareholders, long-term objectives to take market share and considerable determination. Some well-known Japanese companies provide examples here. These are not the companies to choose to fight, although it may be inevitable that the organisation will compete with them.

Equally, attacking a market leader directly is a high-risk strategy because of the strength of such a competitor, even if the payoff appears to be attractive. Military strategists state that a superiority in people and machinery of 3:1 is needed before launching an attack, if the approach is to be successful. By definition, this is highly unlikely where the market leader is involved.

For these reasons, it may be better to analyse and target competitors of more equal size. Their weaknesses might then form the basis of an aggressive move. They might even be available for takeover.

5.5.4 The four main attack strategies

In any analysis of competitors, it is important to recognise the four main strategies that they may use against each other and any new entrant. It should also be noted that these represent a *checklist of strategy options* for use in Part 5 when it comes to further development of strategic management (see Chapter 8).

The four main attack strategies are shown in Exhibit 5.4. These are based on three main principles from military strategy:[45]

1 *the need to concentrate the attack on competition* so that it is overwhelming at that particular point and therefore more likely to be successful;

2 *the element of surprise* so that gains can be made while the competitor is still recovering (perhaps involving rewriting the rules of the game);
3 *the need to consolidate the attack* by continuing to invest for some period (except in the last option which is based on rapid withdrawal and limited losses).

EXHIBIT 5.4

The four main attack strategies

1 Head-on against the market leader

- Unless resources are sustained, the campaign is unlikely to be successful.
- Attack where the leader is weak.
- Pick a narrow front to open up the campaign.

2 Flanking or market segmentation

- Choose a flank that is relatively undefended.
- Aim to take a significant market share.
- Expect to invest in the flank for some years.
- Pricing and value for money are often distinguishing features of a successful flank.

3 Occupy totally new territory, i.e. where there is no existing product or service

- Innovate if possible.
- Seek market niches.

4 Guerrilla: that is, a rapid sortie to seize a short-term profitable opportunity

- Relies on good information to identify opportunities.
- Fast response needed and rapid withdrawal after success.
- Important not to stand and fight leaders on their own ground but pick new areas.

Again, as in military strategy, these principles:

- involve a reliance on brute force to achieve an objective only when it is useful and achievable;
- recommend concentrating such force so that it will achieve maximum effect;
- suggest following up the use of force by longer-term strategies that will secure the position permanently.

For these reasons, the head-on strategy is rarely successful.

It should be emphasised that other strategies are also possible and, for the underdog, may be crucial. They often involve some form of *innovation* in the competitive environment.

5.5.5 Innovatory strategies

There are many forms of innovation but it is useful to identify four for our purposes:

1 rewriting the rules of the game;
2 technological innovation;
3 higher levels of service;
4 co-operation.

Many of these are particularly suited to smaller companies that do not have substantial resources.

Rewriting the rules of the game

In competitive strategy, the existing players in the market will work according to a mutual understanding of how competitors are engaged – the rules of the game. For example, life and household insurance was sold by agents who personally advised their customers on the best product for their circumstances. All the major companies invested vast sums in recruiting and training their people to undertake this task. Ultimately, their heavy investment meant that it was in the interests of such insurance companies not to offer any alternatives. Then along came smaller companies with telephone insurance selling. They changed the rules of the game and sold the product without the heavy overhead of a large sales force, so that it was possible to offer much lower prices. The revolution has now largely happened across much of the European insurance industry. Rewriting the rules of the game is important in strategic management.

Technological innovation

Especially in the case of new, smaller players, it may be essential to introduce some form of innovation in order to take market share. This does not mean that this is the only way to enter a market and survive, but in certain types of industry it may represent a viable route. For example, the internet is set to revolutionise the distribution of recorded music – see Case 13 in Part 6. Smaller companies will be able to distribute their music more readily.

Higher levels of service

In some industries, technology may not be a dominant feature, but service levels may still be important. For example, in the shoe industry, there have been technical advances, but some companies have survived because they have offered high levels of personalised service and shoe design. Even in retailing, small shops have been able to survive by staying open for long hours in their local communities.

Co-operation

Formal partnerships or some other form of joint activity have proved useful innovatory strategies in recent years. Joint ventures, alliances and other forms of co-operation have been used with success to beat larger rivals (see Section 5.6).

5.5.6 Conclusions: attack or defend

In a static market, every company that identifies a market opportunity will present another company with a market problem. Attack strategies therefore invite defensive responses, but they are two sides of the same coin and need to be treated as such in strategic management.

The analysis of the range of aggressive strategies open to competitors is a useful starting point in the development of strategic management. However, Kay[46] has urged caution in the use of military analogies for two reasons:

1 *It may exaggerate the importance of size and scale.* The use of brute force is supported by the financial resources and market share that can be brought to bear. Kay points out that business success comes from *distinctive capabilities* rather than destroying the enemy. It is therefore important to recognise size and scale as useful but not conclusive devices in strategic terms.

2 *It invites excessive emphasis on leadership, vision and attack.* The generals plotting the strategy are the primary engines for successful military strategy. Kay observes that many successful companies rely on *teams*, rather than charismatic leaders – a theme that will be explored throughout this book.

In many respects, it is the *prescriptive* view of strategy that is best served by concepts of aggressive attack with plans that are carefully drawn up in advance. The more adaptive approach of *emergent* strategy does not lend itself so readily to such recipes, although the militarists would no doubt recognise the need for adaptation as the battle proceeds. Innovative strategies therefore have an important role.

KEY STRATEGIC PRINCIPLES

- In assessing the aggressive strategies of competitors, it is important to begin by monitoring competitive activity on a regular basis.
- Although total defeat may be appropriate as a military objective, it is rarely relevant in business. A new market equilibrium may be much more profitable, involving stable market shares, no price wars and viable levels of profitability.
- Some competitors may be naturally more aggressive than others and have more substantial resources. If it is possible to choose, then these may be the competitors to avoid.
- Choosing an enemy that can provide a successful outcome is important. Attacking the market leader is not usually wise.
- The four main attack strategies are: head-on, flanking, occupy totally new territory, and guerrilla.
- Innovatory strategies may prove particularly significant, especially for the underdog. These include rewriting the rules of the game, technological innovation, higher levels of service, and partnerships. (See further Chapter 11.)

5.6 THE DYNAMICS OF CO-OPERATION STRATEGIES

Definition ▶

Video Part 3a

Co-operation strategies involve organisations working with rivals or other related companies to the mutual benefit of both organisations. It is not essential to work with a competitor: the co-operation might be with another company offering a related product – for example, Dell Computers working with Microsoft to offer Windows software on Dell machines. **A co-operation strategy is therefore a strategy in which at least two organisations work together to achieve an agreed objective.**[47] Another example comes from the countries of the European Union who have agreed to co-operate with the agreed objective of launching the Galileo satellite system by 2006 – see Case 18.1. Recent business evidence suggests that co-operation strategy is becoming increasingly important when other forms of internal growth – such as those associated with portfolio matrices – become expensive.[48]

5.6.1 Types of co-operation

There are various forms of co-operation, amongst which are:

Definition ▶

- ***Strategic alliances*** **– co-operative strategies where organisations combine or share some of their resources.**[49] For example, car companies like General Motors have developed purchasing alliances with Fiat and Suzuki to purchase car parts from suppliers. The benefit of such alliances is that GM, Fiat and Suzuki obtain lower prices from their suppliers than they would be able to obtain from individual negotiations.

Definition ▶

- ***Joint ventures*** **– co-operative strategies where two or more organisations set up a separate jointly owned subsidiary to develop the cooperation.**[50] For example, Cereal Partners has been set up as a 50/50 joint venture by Nestlé and General Mills to develop products for the worldwide breakfast cereal market – see Case 2.1.

Definition ▶

- ***Franchises*** **– co-operation strategies in which a master company (the franchisor) develops a business concept which it then shares with others (the franchisees) to their mutual benefit.**[51] For example, Subway and McDonald's restaurants – see Cases 2.3 and 6.2.

Definition ▶

- ***Collusive alliances*** **– co-operative strategies in which firms seek to share information in order to reduce competition and/or raise prices.** For example, the EU has in the past investigated and heavily fined companies for colluding on price fixing in the organic peroxide market and in the PVC plastics market. Such forms of co-operation are illegal in many countries of the world because they are essentially anti-competitive. They are therefore not explored further in this chapter.

5.6.2 Benefits of co-operative strategies

In essence, co-operation strategy is used to create added value for the two or more co-operating organisations.[52] 'Value' means that the profits from the co-operation must exceed the costs involved in operating the form of co-operation. The benefits from co-operation can be generated in a number of ways, depending on the particular circumstances (sometimes called the 'strategic context') of the organisations involved and the markets in which they operate. In practice, this means that it is difficult to generalise about the specific benefits of an individual co-operative agreement. However, it is useful to identify two forms of strategic context that may influence the benefits of co-operation:[53]

- *Growth context* – where technological investment may still be heavy and risky, industry technical standards may still be under development and market opportunities still available. Benefits may include:
  - joint funding of technological investment;
  - development of industry standards;
  - access to new markets.

  These three are explained in more detail below.
- *Mature context* – where competitive advantage may be more stable and cost reduction opportunities more attractive as a method of increasing profitability. Benefits may include:
  - competitive advantage;
  - cost reduction;
  - sharing of knowledge and prior investment.

  These three benefits are also explained below.

Joint funding of technological investment: By combining individual resources, companies may be able to fund new research that would be beyond their available individual funds. In addition to sharing the costs, such co-operation also shares the risks and uncertainties of new technology development. For example, the Galileo satellite system described in Case 18.1 has some benefits to participants.

Development of industry standards: In some markets, particularly those associated with telecommunications and electronics, industry standards do not exist in the early years of development. This means that the manufacturing costs are higher because there are fewer economies of scale. For example, the early personal computers – before the IBM personal computer – were not standardised in design and therefore more expensive to produce: see Case 1.2. It is difficult for one company to develop an industry standard unless they dominate the industry, like IBM. An alternative strategy is therefore co-operation between companies to develop an industry standard. For example, in Case 5.3 on DVD formats, the two rival companies formed co-operative links with other interested companies in order to influence the outcome of the war. The benefits to the winning collaboration will come through royalty payments being paid by the losers.

Access to new markets: By combining the international resource of one competitor with the local knowledge resource of another competitor, it may be possible for the two companies to co-operate in the local market to mutual advantage.[54] In addition, such a co-operation may overcome trade barriers that would otherwise stop the international company entering the market. For example, a number of international car companies have entered the potentially large Chinese car market by setting up joint ventures with local, knowledgeable Chinese companies.

Competitive advantage: By combining resources, companies may be able to gain competitive advantages over rivals.[55] For example, in the world airline market, Singapore Airlines, Lufthansa and North West have formed the Star Alliance network to be able to offer superior ticketing and air transfer services that offer superior benefits to passengers when compared to rivals.

Cost reduction: By combining resources, companies may be able to develop cost reduction opportunities jointly that would be difficult to find as separate companies.[56] For example, various purchasing companies have been set up by EU farmers to buy agricultural supplies more cheaply than they would be able to obtain them individually.

Sharing of knowledge and prior investment: By co-operative agreements, companies may be able to achieve synergistic benefits from the cross-fertilisation of business activity.[57] For example, the franchise operation at Subway involves sharing Subway's knowledge of sandwich ingredients and preparation with its franchisees. Another example is Toyota's investment in developing its new Prius environmentally friendly car. The patents on its dual petrol-and-electric engine have been shared with rival companies like General Motors and Ford through licensing agreements, which are a form of co-operation.

5.6.3 Managing the risks of co-operative strategies

Co-operative strategies come with costs and risks that need to be managed. There are two broad approaches to this task:[58]

1 *Cost minimisation* – a formal contract specifying how the co-operation is to be developed and monitored. The aim is to minimise the costs of co-operation and ensure that each partner adheres to the deal in a structured way.

2 *Opportunity maximisation* – a more informal arrangement that allows the co-operators to exploit market opportunities as they are identified and also learn from each other as the co-operation progresses.

There are no clear guidelines for choosing between these two mutually exclusive approaches – they depend on the objectives of the parties involved, the nature of the opportunity and the risk-taking stance of each of the parties. Nevertheless, research has shown that there are two major factors that will determine the success or otherwise of many co-operative agreements:

1 The *clarity* with which the objectives and expectations of the co-operation between the parties have been explored, agreed and understood at the outset of such an agreement.

2 The *mutual trust* that has developed and persists between the co-operating parties.

Finally, it is sometimes said that, when the two parties have to resort to the detailed contract between them to resolve outstanding issues, then the co-operation agreement itself has run its course and should be terminated. In this context, it is worth noting that many co-operation agreements are fragile and need to evolve over time if they are to remain successful.[59]

KEY STRATEGIC PRINCIPLES

- Co-operation strategies involve companies working with rivals or other related companies to the mutual benefits of both organisations.
- There are at least four types of co-operation: strategic alliances, joint ventures, franchises and collusive alliances. The last of these is illegal in most countries of the world.
- The benefits of co-operation depend on the strategic context within which the co-operation occurs. It is useful to make a distinction between growth and mature market contexts. Within growth, co-operation may deliver joint funding of projects, the establishment of industry standards and access to new markets. Within the market context, co-operation may deliver competitive advantage, cost reduction and the sharing of knowledge.
- Managing the risks of co-operative strategies involves two mutually exclusive mechanisms: cost reduction and opportunity maximisation. Cost reduction depends primarily on written contracts, careful negotiation and monitoring of developments. Opportunity maximisation is more informal, with the aim of identifying and exploiting business opportunities as they emerge. Trust is often a key factor in the success of co-operative agreements.

Case study on game theory: ***How GEC Marconi used attack, co-operation and game theory strategies to make an extra US $3 billion.*** Indicative answers are provided to the questions raised at the end of the case.

5.7 STRATEGY DYNAMICS USING GAME THEORY

Definition ▶ **The game-theory route refers to structured methods of bargaining with and between customers, suppliers and competitors of the organisation, such structuring involving the quantification of possible outcomes at each stage of the strategy decision-making process.** For example, the free web case linked to this text describes how British Aerospace used game theory to complete the negotiation of the successful acquisition of GEC Marconi by British Aerospace. This was undertaken using an approach that quantified the various possible outcomes of different stages of the bidding and negotiating process, the purpose being to determine what and how British Aerospace should bid at each stage.

During the 1940s, mathematical models were first developed to handle in a structured way the commercial decisions that are involved: they are known under the general title of *game theory*.[60] Game-based theory is concerned with the immediate negotiation and its related strategy: it says little or nothing about the implementation stages that follow once the negotiation has been concluded. Game theory has two clear advantages for strategy development:

1 It clarifies the *nature of the negotiation*, identifying the players, setting out their options, identifying the outcomes of each option and the sequence of events that need to take place.
2 It can predict the *optimal outcomes of some games*, particularly by permitting the manipulation of the payoffs to the players. It does this by providing insights into the nature of the relationships that exist between players, including the identification of the competitors and co-operators.[61]

Game theory attempts to predict competitor reactions in the negotiating situation. The circumstances may be regarded as being similar to a game of chess, where anticipation of the opponent's moves is an important aspect of the challenge. Much of game theory has been modelled mathematically, with the rules specifying how the scarce resources of the company can be employed and what benefits will be obtained by particular moves or a combination of moves – the benefits are often called *payoffs*.[62]

- In a *zero-sum game*, there is ultimately no payoff because the gains of one member are negated by the losses of another.
- In a *co-operative game*, the benefits may add up to a positive payoff for all.
- In a *negative-sum game*, the actions of each party undermine both themselves and their opponents.

Although game theory has provided a useful basis for structuring negotiations and the consequences of each move, it has proved difficult to model strategic options and decisions which are often highly complex and interrelated. Probably the most interesting strategic insights provided by game theory are in the likely outcomes of various stages of the negotiation process. For example, when British Aerospace was negotiating the restructuring of the European defence industry, it used game theory to show that it was useful to acquire GEC Marconi for two reasons:

1 The increased size gave it much greater influence on the final shape of the pan-European consolidation game.
2 The acquisition reduced the number of options available in the industry, thus lowering the number of moves that it would take to achieve the consolidation required.

Given these advantages, the issue is how to make use of game theory to analyse and conduct competitive strategic games. There are six essential steps in what is essentially a prescriptive process.

Example: Game theory; six steps to playing strategic games in Formula 1 Racing strategy.

More generally, the mechanics and logical decision-making aspects of game theory are well represented in the various theoretical descriptions. But they say little about other vital aspects of most strategic negotiations. The leadership of the teams involved, the personalities and cultures of their members, the ambitions and the history of the players are not covered at all. The strategic context in which negotiations are taking place can lead to consequences that go well beyond the mathematics of game theory. For example, in the European defence industry case, the various personalities of the leading chief executives and their other responsibilities influenced the outcome of the game: George Simpson was determined to sort out the GEC Group that he had inherited, while Jürgen Schrempp at Daimler was preoccupied with the massive merger with Chrysler.

To capture some of these practical complexities of negotiation, the *Six Steps to Playing Strategic Games* checklist on the book's website has been constructed. Readers may care to note that it can be used not only for acquisitions but for many other negotiation situations, including personal strategies. There are four aspects of game theory in the checklist that are worth highlighting here:

1 *Viewpoint of the game.* It is important to assess the game not just from one player's perspective of the outcome. It is essential to gauge what rivals expect to take out of the game and possibly make some attempt to accommodate this.
2 *Rewrite the rules of the game.* The outcome of some games can be altered by totally rewriting the way that the game is played, even part-way through the game. In this sense, game theory is not like chess or football. This can provide a real opportunity.
3 *Reassessment of the game.* It is usually worth reconsidering whether a game is worth pursuing part of the way through the game. Some negotiations can simply be a waste of time and resources.
4 *Reassurance about the final outcome.* In any game, even where there are multiple winners, it is worth remembering that people are involved. Players need to be reassured after the outcome that it was the best that could be achieved.

Although game theory can be helpful in certain limited circumstances, it focuses mainly on one small area of the strategic process – the *options and choice* part of the prescriptive process. Game theory has nothing substantial to offer with regard to the earlier analysis phase or the later implementation phase of the prescriptive process.

Comment

There are three main problems with game theory in negotiation-based strategy:[63]

1 The mathematical complexity makes the analytical results useful but limited. Moreover, it assumes that a dynamic and interacting environment can be modelled by a series of static equilibria. This is a dangerously simple approximation of reality.
2 Many of its conclusions, especially about Nash equilibria, are ambiguous and based on a narrow view of context. For example, game theory largely excludes all psychological insight. Game theory has so far proved incapable of handling the many complexities of real business situations.
3 Importantly, game theory focuses on a small fraction of the strategic process. For example, it provides no insight whatsoever into the development of the competitive resources of the organisation, nor any useful guidance on the massive task of implementing whatever has been negotiated.

KEY STRATEGIC PRINCIPLES

- Game theory attempts to predict the outcomes of customer reactions or, in some cases, to show how the outcome of negotiations may well produce a suboptimal solution unless both sides of the negotiations realise the consequences of their actions.
- Game theory has some value in negotiations but suffers from three difficulties: mathematical complexity; ambiguous conclusions; being only one small part of the strategy process.

CRITICAL REFLECTION

Attack or co-operate?

Much of the strategic management literature emphasises the importance of gaining sustainable competitive advantage over other organisations. The assumption is that *competition* is vital to strategy development. However, some strategists have suggested in recent years that *co-operation* is far better as a strategy - less costly, more productive, more mutually beneficial - and the result has been a series of co-operative alliances of various kinds between organisations.

Perhaps it is better to co-operate with rivals rather than to attack them. There will be occasions when competition cannot be avoided and it is not suggested that an illegal collusion takes place. But are there strategic circumstances where co-operation is the superior strategy?

SUMMARY

- In exploring the dynamics of strategy development, it is useful to begin with the history of an organisation in three areas: how its *processes* have developed; how the organisation is *positioned* with regard to competitors; and how its *paths* have developed in the past and are envisaged to continue in the future.
- According to some strategists, competitive advantage should be seen as constantly evolving and companies should set out to make this happen, particularly in industries that involve advanced technology. In this sense, competitive advantage is dynamic rather than static.
- The process for developing such competitive advantage is both built around existing strengths – structured – and also exploits new and exciting areas – chaotic.
- The main guideline for such a process is to strike a balance between structure and chaos.
- It is possible to develop a framework to develop dynamic strategy: the Three 'S' Framework is the result of our current knowledge. It consists of *sensing* the changes in the environment, *seizing* the opportunities that result and *surveying* the outcomes with a view to further developments.
- Criticism of such an approach has centred on its relevance to more traditional industries outside high technology, on the difficulty of managing the chaotic part of the process, and on the possibility of ignoring existing competitive advantages in the pursuit of a new area of advantage.
- To analyse the nature and intensity of competition in an industry, three areas have a signficant influence on strategy: the total number of firms in an industry; the mix of those firms in terms of numbers and size; the barriers to entry possessed by the existing firms in that industry.
- The dynamics of environmental development have many dimensions but can usefully be considered from three perspectives: the maintenance of competitive advantage; the predictability of the environment; the ability of the organisation's resources to respond to changes in the environment.
- The maintenance of competitive advantage will depend on the nature of the advantages operating in an industry. It will also involve the willingness of a firm to shape new advantages and the nature of the future advantages that might operate in an industry.
- If the environment is predictable then it allows the dynamics of the environment to be managed more easily. Although no environment is entirely predictable, some strategists argue that the process is largely a waste of time, with no meaningful results where it matters.
- Although an organisation may have understood the nature of environmental change, it may not be able to act upon it. Five major reasons have been identified for this: distorted perception; dulled motivation; failed creative response; political deadlocks; action disconnects. In fast-moving markets, the dynamic process is dominated by innovation.

- Companies that already dominate their markets and have committed resources to a specific technology are less likely to innovate for two reasons: the sunk cost effect and the replacement effect. Small and medium-sized companies should have more opportunities in such markets if they are faster, more flexible and entrepreneurial.
- The dynamics of innovation go through a series of phases that depend on one technical design becoming dominant. Emergent strategic processes are more appropriate in fast-moving markets.
- From a dynamic perspective, resources in organisations are developed and destroyed over time. There are three main dimensions: time, early-mover advantages and imitation pressures.
- When exploring the time dimension, there are three main considerations: the two sources of new resource growth; the delaying effect of routines in companies; the mechanism that destroys resources over time.
- In terms of early-mover advantages, there are five main areas: the establishment of the benchmark technical format; the building of networks of contacts; the early movement down the learning curve; the usefulness of reputation; and the subsequent costs to the buyer when switching from the early mover.
- The pressures that arise from imitating an existing product or service can be countered by five resource activities: incremental improvements in the product or service; legal barriers to imitation, such as patenting; developing superior relationships with customers and suppliers; exploiting market size and scale economies; and developing intangible barriers to imitation.
- In assessing the aggressive strategies of competitors, it is important to begin by monitoring competitive activity on a regular basis. Although total defeat may be appropriate as a military objective, it is rarely relevant in business. A new market equilibrium may be much more profitable, involving stable market shares, no price wars and viable levels of profitability.
- Some competitors may be naturally more aggressive than others and have more substantial resources. If it is possible to choose, then these may be the competitors to avoid. Choosing an enemy that can provide a successful outcome is important. Attacking the market leader is not usually wise. The four main attack strategies are: head-on, flanking, occupy totally new territory, and guerrilla. Innovatory strategies may prove particularly significant, especially for the underdog. These include rewriting the rules of the game, technological innovation, higher levels of service, and partnerships.
- Co-operation strategies involve companies working with rivals or other related companies to the mutual benefits of both organisations. There are at least four types of co-operation: strategic alliances, joint ventures, franchises and collusive alliances. The last of these is illegal in most countries of the world.
- The benefits of co-operation depend on the strategic context within which the co-operation occurs. It is useful to make a distinction between growth and mature market contexts. Within growth, co-operation may deliver joint funding of projects, the establishment of industry standards and access to new markets. Within the market context, co-operation may deliver competitive advantage, cost reduction and the sharing of knowledge.
- Managing the risks of co-operative strategies involves two mutually exclusive mechanisms: cost reduction and opportunity maximisation. Cost reduction depends primarily on written contracts, careful negotiation and monitoring of developments. Opportunity maximisation is more informal, with the aim of identifying and exploiting business opportunities as they emerge. Trust is often a key factor in the success of co-operative agreements.
- Game theory attempts to predict the outcomes of customer reactions or, in some cases, to show how the outcome of negotiations may well produce a suboptimal solution unless both sides of the negotiations realise the consequences of their actions. Game theory has some value in negotiations but suffers from three difficulties: mathematical complexity; ambiguous conclusions; being only one small part of the strategy process.

QUESTIONS

1 Using the 'Three S' Framework, identify how the dynamics of an organisation of your choice. What have been the implications for the strategy of the organisation?

2 What are the main reasons for resource changes in an organisation? How do they affect sustainable competitive advantage and value added? Give examples to support your explanation.

3 Does the early-mover advantage have any relevance from the perspective of strategy development in more mature markets, like those for chocolate and beer?

4 If you were attempting to defend an existing pharmaceutical product against the announcement by a rival of a similar new drug, which of the five resource-based imitation strategies would you employ? Give reasons for your approach.

5 Why is it sometimes difficult for an organisation to act upon the changes that it sees taking place in the environment? What can it do to overcome such problems? Give examples to support your views.

6 *'A successful business strategy is affected by many amplifying feedback processes that are outside the control of its managers and produce effects that they did not intend.'* (Professor Ralph Stacey) Discuss this comment in the context of the dynamics of the environment.

7 Take a fast-moving market with which you are familiar - such as the provision of services on the web - and investigate the strategies that might be available for entering such a market. Identify those strategies, if any, that are more likely to deliver sustainable competitive advantage.

8 *'Military principles and strategies are not the whole answer to competitive strategy, but they do provide insight into what it takes for a company to succeed in attacking another company or in defending itself against an aggressor.'* (Philip Kotler and Ravi Singh) To what extent do you agree with this statement?

9 Bruce Henderson, founder of the Boston Consulting Group, commented: *'Induce your competitors not to invest in those products, markets and services where you expect to invest most . . . that is the fundamental rule of strategy.'* Briefly explain this statement and comment on its usefulness.

10 Take an industry with which you are familiar and estimate its degree of concentration. For example, you might pick the university and college of higher education market in a particular country. What conclusions would you draw from your analysis? (Clue: the market may look fragmented, but if you look more closely there are often groups of institutions that form segments that are more concentrated.)

FURTHER READING

Utterback, J M (1996) *Mastering the Dynamics of Innovation*, Harvard Business School Press, Boston, MA is an interesting read that has some excellent examples.

Peter Drucker's text might be old – Drucker, P (1961) *The Practice of Management*, Mercury Books, London – but it still has many valuable insights. It was the subject of a retrospective by the *Academy of Management Executive* in 2003. Equally, Tom Peters is always stimulating – Peters, T (1989) *Thriving on Chaos*, Pan Books, London – if somewhat over the top on occasions. Livengood, R S and Reger, R K (2010) 'That's our Turf! Identity Domains and Competitive Dynamics', *The Academy of Management Review*, Vol 35, No 1, pp 48–66 has a different and more recent perspective on dynamics.

Rita McGrath's chapter – McGrath, R G (2002) 'Entrepreneurship, small firms and wealth creation' in Pettigrew, A, Thomas H and Whittington, R, *Handbook of Strategy and Management*, Sage, London – provides a useful structure on entrepreneurship.

There is a special issue in *Long Range Planning* on Boundaries and Innovation – six papers covering topics from resource allocation to acquisition: guest editors – Gibbert, M and Valigangas, L (2004) Boundaries and Innovation: Special Issue, *Long Range Planning*, Vol 37, No 6, pp 493–601. See Day, G S and Schoemaker, P (2004) 'Peripheral vision: sensing and acting on weak signals', *Long Range Planning*, Vol 37, No 2, pp 117–123 plus many other well-known strategy writers for this special issue including Sidney G Winter and C K Prahalad.

An interesting perspective on game theory, negotiation and dynamics is Carmeli, A and Markman, G D (2011) 'Capture, Governance and Resilience: Strategy Implications From the History of Rome', *Strategic Management Journal*, Vol 32, No 3, pp 322–341. (Don't be put off by the title!)

Two chapters are useful from Mark Jenkins' and Véronique Ambrosini's edited text with Nardine Collier (2007) *Advanced Strategic Management*, Palgrave Macmillan: Chapter 3 'Military Strategy Perspective' by Sylvie Jackson and Chapter 6 'Game Theory Perspective' by Stephen Regan.

For an approachable comparison between the resource-based view, hypercompetition and complexity see Lengnick-Hall, C and Wolff, J (1999) 'Similarities and contradictions in the core logic of three strategy research streams', *Strategic Management Journal*, Vol 20, pp 1109–1132.

Finally the following text has the insights of another distinguished group of scholars: Helfat, C, Finkelstein, S, Mitchell, W, Peteraf, M A, Singh, H, Teece, D J and Winter, S G (2007) *Dynamic Capabilities: Understanding Strategic Change in Organizations*, Blackwell, Oxford.

NOTES AND REFERENCES

1 Note that the distinction between analytical and pro-active is not the same as that between theory and practice: Markides, C (2007) 'In search of ambidextrous professors', *Academy of Management Journal*, Vol 50, No 4, August, p 705.

2 References for F1 Racing case: *Financial Times*: 4 February 2008, p 16; 14 August 2008, p 12; 25 January 2009, p 16; 9 February 2009, p 16; 6 March 2009, p 17; 17 March 2009, p 20; 8 April 2009, p 5; 24 July 2009, p 12; 3 November 2009, p 23; 6 November 2009, p 12; 4 April 2011, p 1; 18 March 2014, p 4; Bloomberg, 6 April 2011, 'F1 Teams shared $658 million in prize money' by Alex Duff; BBC Sport, 11 May 2009 'F1 losing innovation race'; 13 May 2009 Andrew Benson's blog 'F1 battle lines drawn'; 10 September 2009 'Briatore bows out in unsavoury style'; 15 September 2009, 'Why Barrichello is beating Button'. Website accessed on 6 April 2011: http://www.grandprix.com/ns/ns23091.html.

3 See, for example, Brown, S L and Eisenhardt, K M (1998) *Competing on the Edge*, Harvard Business School Press, Boston, MA and Hamel, G and Prahalad, C K (1994) *Competing For the Future*, Harvard Business School Press, Boston, MA. For two more accessible papers, the following are worth reading: Eisenhardt, K M and Brown, S L (1998) 'Time pacing: competing in markets that won't stand still', *Harvard Business Review*, Vol 76 (March–April), pp 59–69; Eisenhardt, K M and Brown, S L (1999) 'Patching: restitching business portfolios in dynamic markets', *Harvard Business Review*, Vol 77 (May–June), pp 72–82; Eisenhardt, K and Martin, J (2000) 'Dynamic capabilities: what are they?' *Strategic Management Journal*, October–November Special Issue, Vol 21, pp 1105–1121; Helfat, C, Finkelstein, S, Mitchell, W, Peteraf, M A, Singh, H, Teece, D J and Winter, S G (2007) *Dynamic Capabilities: Understanding Strategic Change in Organizations*, Blackwell, Oxford; Teece, D J (2007) 'Explicating dynamic capabilities: the nature and microfoundations of (sustainable) enterprise performance', *Strategic Management Journal*, Vol 28, pp 1319–1350.

4 Penrose, E (1959) *The Theory of the Growth of the Firm*, Basil Blackwell, Oxford. Note that a third edition of the text was published in 1993 with a new preface by Professor Penrose: it has a historical perspective that is relevant to strategy development.

5 Chandler, A (1962) *Strategy and Structure*, MIT Press, Cambridge, MA. Chandler later developed this perspective further in his 1990 text: *Scale and Scope: Dynamics of Industrial Capitalism*, Harvard University Press, Cambridge, MA.

6 Developed by the author from the concepts outlined in: Teece, D J, Pisano, G and Shuen, A (1997) 'Dynamic capabilities and strategic management', *Strategic Management Journal*, Vol 18, No 7, pp 509–533.

7 The arguments here are not dissimilar to those used by the human-resource-based strategists outlined in Section 2.4.3. See in particular the views of Nelson and Winter.

8 Brown and Eisenhardt (1998) Op. cit.

9 Teece, D J (2007) Op. cit., p 1322.

10 This framework has been developed by the author and inspired specifically by the research papers of Teece, D J (2007) Op. cit. and Eisenhardt, K M and Martin, J (2000) Op. cit. However, the framework remains essentially an attempt to make sense of a whole group of recent research activity presented at the Strategic Management Society and Academy of Management Annual Conferences in 2005 and 2006 attended by the author. The work of Professors Sidney Winter, Sidney Finkelstein, Margaret Peteraf, Connie Helfat and Will Mitchell – who presented their work at AOM – is also acknowledged.

11 Sources for L'Oréal case: L'Oréal Annual Report and Accounts; Estée Lauder Annual Report and Accounts; Shiseido Annual Report and Accounts. Much of the detailed L'Oréal market commentary is available on www.loreal.com/enww/press-room; the L'Oréal financial data is available on www.loreal-finance.com.

12 Saloner, G, Shepard, A and Podolny, J (2005) *Strategic Management*, Wiley, NY, p 138.

13 See Porter, M E (1980) *Competitive Strategy*, The Free Press, Harvard, MA for an extended discussion of this topic.

14 Porter, M E (1985) *Competitive Advantage: Creating and Sustaining Superior Performance*, The Free Press, New York, p 1.

15 Porter, M E (1985) Ibid., p 2.

16 Hamel, G and Prahalad, C K (1994) *Competing for the Future*, Harvard Business School Press, Boston, MA, p 42.

17 Baden-Fuller, C and Stopford, J (1992) *Rejuvenating the Mature Business*, Routledge, London, Ch 2.

18 Based loosely on Hamel, G and Prahalad, C K (1994) Op. cit., p 47.

19 Courtney, H, Kirkland, J and Viguerie, M (1997) 'Strategy under uncertainty', *Harvard Business Review*, November–December, pp 67–79.

20 Mintzberg, H (1994) 'The fall and rise of strategic planning', *Harvard Business Review*, January–February, pp 107–114.

21 Ansoff, I (1969) *Corporate Strategy*, Penguin, Harmondsworth.

22 Rumelt, R (1995) 'Inertia and transformation', in Montgomery, C A (ed) *Resource-based and Evolutionary Theories of the Firm: Towards a Synthesis*, Kluwer Academic, Boston, MA, pp 101–132.

23 Sources for the DVD format wars case: *Financial Times*: 29 September 1998, p 8; 19 May 1999, p 6; 28 July 2004, p 11; 14 October 2004, p 19; 22 April 2005, p 30 (the announcement that the rivals were negotiating); 27 May 2005, p 24 (the announcement that the deal was breaking down); 26 August 2005, p 17 (still talking but no agreement); 28 September 2005, p 26; 30 November 2005, p 21; 15 March 2007, p 23; 7 January 2008, p 1 and p 25; 8 January 2008, p 16 (Lex) and p 22; 18 February 2008, p 25; 20 February 2008, p 29; 6 March 2008, p 26; 31 August 2007, p 19; 5 September 2007, p 24 (last two references on Microsoft format fight).

24 Besanko, D, Dranove, D and Shanley, M (1996) *The Economics of Strategy*, Wiley, New York, p 581.

25 Concept originally developed by Professor Kenneth Arrow: Arrow, K (1962) 'Economic welfare and the allocation of resources for inventions', in Nelson, R (ed) *The Rate and Direction of Inventive Activity*, Princeton University Press, Princeton, NJ. Concept outlined in Besanko, D, Dranove, D and Shanley, M (1996) Op. cit., p 584.
26 Utterback, J M (1996) Op. cit.
27 For example, see the references in the discussion on innovation in Chapter 11.
28 Chaharbaghi, K and Lynch, R (1999) 'Sustainable competitive advantage: towards a dynamic resource-based strategy', *Management Decision*, 37(1), pp 45–50.
29 Parts of this section have benefited from Chs 14 and 15 of Besanko, D, Dranove, D and Shanley, M (1996) Op. cit.
30 Penrose, E (1995) *The Theory of the Growth of the Firm*, Oxford University Press, Oxford, p 85.
31 Nelson, R R and Winter, S G (1982) *An Evolutionary Theory of Economic Change*, Belknap Press, Cambridge, MA.
32 Schumpeter, J (1942) *Capitalism, Socialism and Democracy*, Harper & Row, New York.
33 At one stage, Microsoft was the subject of a US Federal and State Government investigation into its competitive reaction against Netscape's browser success. Microsoft successfully defended its position and Netscape has now disappeared – just as Schumpeter would have predicted!
34 Utterback, J M (1996) *Mastering the Dynamics of Innovation*, Harvard Business School Press, Boston, MA, pp 10, 30.
35 Nalebuff, B J and Brandenburger, A M (1997) *Co-opetition*, HarperCollins Business, London, p 241.
36 Utterback, J M (1996) Op. cit., p 28.
37 There is a Harvard Business School case that explores this well.
38 This section is based on the work of Professors Porter and Kotler (see refs 13 and 40) and on a lecture given by Professor Ken Simmons at the London Business School in 1988.
39 For example, see Ries, A and Trout, J (1986) *Marketing Warfare*, McGraw-Hill, New York.
40 Kotler, P (1994) *Marketing Management: Analysis, Planning, Implementation and Control*, 8th edn, Prentice Hall, New York.
41 Kotler, P and Singh, R (1981) 'Marketing warfare in the 1980s', *Journal of Business Strategy*, Winter, pp 30–41.
42 Liddell-Hart, B H (1967) *Strategy*, Praeger, New York.
43 Kay, J (1993) *Foundations of Corporate Success*, Oxford University Press, Oxford, pp 236–238 provides an interesting discussion of the circumstances under which such an understanding can emerge without contravening monopoly legislation.
44 Lynch, R (1994) *European Business Strategies*, 2nd edn, Kogan Page, pp 119–121 supplies some evidence here.
45 Liddell-Hart, B H (1967) Op. cit.
46 Kay, J (1993) Op. cit., p 364.
47 Barney, J B (2002) *Gaining and Sustaining Competitive Advantage*, 2nd edn, Prentice Hall, Upper Saddle River, NJ, p 339.
48 Hitt, M A, Ireland, R D, Camp, S M and Sexton, D L (2002) 'Strategic entrepreneurship: integrating entrepreneurial and strategic management perspectives', in: Hitt, M A, Ireland, R D, Camp, S M and Sexton, D L (eds) *Strategic Entrepreneurship: Creating a New Mindset*, Blackwell, Oxford, Ch 8.
49 Doz, Y L and Hamel, G (1998) *Alliance Advantage: The Art of Creating Value Through Partnering*, Harvard Business School Press, Boston, p xiii.
50 Inkpen, A C (2001) 'Strategic alliances', in: Hitt, M A, Freeman, R E and Harrison, J S (eds) *Handbook of Strategic Management*, Oxford University Press, Oxford.
51 Shane, S A (1996) 'Hybrid organizational arrangements and their implications for firm growth and survival: a study of new franchisers', *Academy of Management Journal*, Vol 39, pp 216–234.
52 Inkpen, A C (2001) Op. cit.
53 Williams, J R (1998) *Renewable Advantage: Crafting Strategy Through Economic Time*, Free Press, New York.
54 Lord, M D and Ranft, A L (2000) 'Organizational learning about new international markets: exploring the internal transfer of local market knowledge', *Journal of International Business Studies*, Vol 31, pp 573–589.
55 Harrison, J S, Hitt, M A, Hoskisson, R E and Ireland, R D (2001) 'Resource complementarity in business combinations: extending the logic to organizational alliances', *Journal of Management*, Vol 27, pp 679–699.
56 Dyer, J H (1997) 'Effective interfirm collaboration: how firms minimize transaction costs and maximize transaction value', *Strategic Management Journal*, Vol 18, pp 535–556.
57 Doz, Y and Hamel, G (1998) Op. cit.
58 Dyer, J H (1997) Op. cit.
59 Inkpen, A C (2001) Op. cit.
60 Useful introductory texts include: Nalebuff, B and Brandenburger, A M (1997) *Co-opetition*, HarperCollins Business, London; Schelling, T C (1980) *The Strategy of Conflict*, 2nd edn, Harvard University Press, Cambridge, MA; also Dixit, A and Nalebuff, B (1991) *Thinking Strategically: the Competitive Edge in Business, Politics and Everyday Life*, W W Norton, New York.
61 Nalebuff, B and Brandenburger, A M (1997) Op. cit., Ch 2.
62 Dixit, A and Nalebuff, B (1991) Op. cit.
63 Amongst the critical comments on game theory, it is worth consulting: Camerer, C F (1991) 'Does strategy research need game theory?', *Strategic Management Journal*, 12, Winter, pp 137–152. Postrel, S (1991) 'Burning your britches behind you', *Strategic Management Journal*, Special Issue, 12, Winter, pp 153–155. See also Fisher, F M (1989) 'The games economists play: a noncooperative view', *RAND Journal of Economics*, 20, pp 113–124.

CHAPTER 6
Prescriptive purpose delivered through mission, objectives and ethics

Video and sound summary of this chapter

LEARNING OUTCOMES

When you have worked through this chapter, you will be able to:

- outline the main considerations in the development of purpose;
- explore the organisation's vision for the future and its strategic implications;
- analyse the balance of power amongst stakeholders in the organisation;
- develop a mission for the organisation;
- define the objectives of the organisation to be achieved by its strategies;
- outline the chief areas of corporate governance that will influence strategy and decision making at the centre of the organisation;
- show how ethics and corporate social responsibility shape the purpose of the organisation.

INTRODUCTION

Video Part 6

Strategic purpose is delivered by identifying and defining the mission and the objectives of the organisation. However, before considering these two subjects, we need to stand back and consider why the organisation exists, who it is meant to serve and how its value added should be generated and distributed amongst its stakeholders – the broader purpose at a more fundamental level of the organisation.

We also need to think about issues associated with *green strategy*. These will influence every aspect of the organisation's purpose, not just one specific element. Hence they can be seen as surrounding the whole development of the purpose of the organisation, rather than a distinctive box at a point in the process – see Figure 6.1. In this edition of this book, they are explored separately in Chapter 14.

In addition, it is important to take the process beyond the current horizons and explore future opportunities and challenges captured in the *vision* of the organisation. Some may conclude that the future is too turbulent to predict and therefore the result is worthless. However, in many strategic situations, this will not be the case, even in turbulent markets. The broader purpose of the organisation and its *vision of the future* will set the focus and stretch the organisation as it develops the more specific subjects of mission and objectives.

There are three additional areas that will help shape the purpose of the organisation and deserve early examination in its development. These are: the *stakeholders* in the organisation, the way that the directors *govern* the organisation and the *ethics and corporate social responsibility* policies that it will pursue.

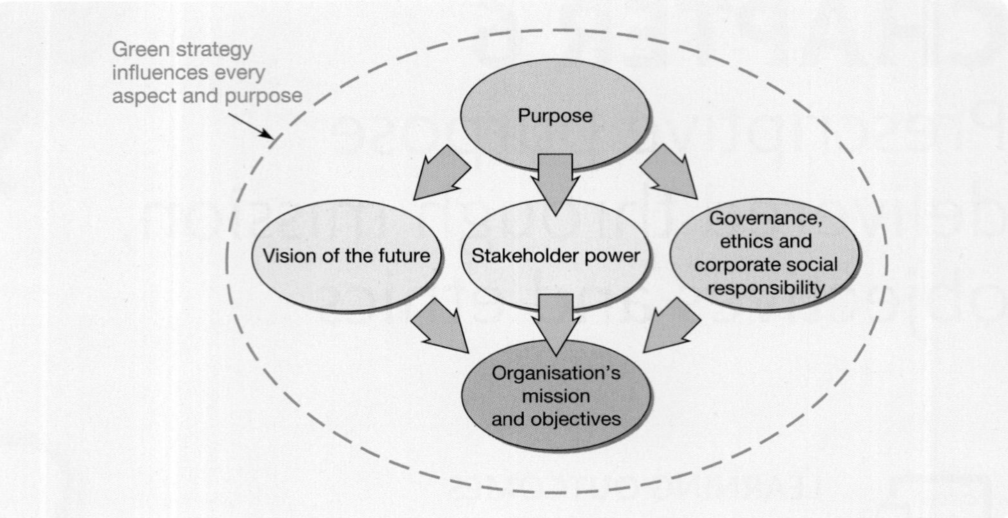

Figure 6.1 Purpose shaped by vision, stakeholders and ethical issues and delivered by mission and objectives

The power of the various stakeholders in the organisation – its shareholders, employees, customers, etc. – will be a key influence on the organisation's purpose. Corporate governance has become an important issue over the past few years because of new stricter rules and legislation after the failure of a few companies in this area. Ethics examines the way that the organisation sets its standards and conduct in society: such matters will clearly influence purpose. Corporate social responsibility defines the specific policies that organisations will adopt on matters such as poverty, AIDS and working conditions.

Having considered these issues, we are then in a position to develop the *mission* of the organisation and to define more precisely its *objectives*. The relationship between these areas is shown in Figure 6.1 and outlines the structure of this chapter. In parallel with the above areas, the strategic leadership of the organisation is also important: this is explored separately in Chapter 16.

Case study with indicative answer: *Starbucks – sacrificing dividends for global growth.*

CASE STUDY 6.1
The yawning gap at Yahoo!

Like many internet companies, the purpose of Yahoo! is continued growth. But the reality is that the five years to 2013 were different: it had stopped growing. Why? What happened to its strategy?

The yawning gap

When Jerry Yang and David Filo started Yahoo! back in 1994, they could hardly have foreseen the building of a $5 billion business by 2014. The company's problem was that growth seemed to have come to an end. There was a yawning gap between its purpose of continued growth and the reality of little or no growth. Both the company's revenue and its profits were, at best, static and, in some years, declining: see Figure 6.2.

Shareholders were able to compare Yahoo!'s performance with rival companies set up around the same time or later: Google, Facebook, Microsoft, Amazon, Pandora, Twitter and LinkedIn were all still showing substantial growth. But not Yahoo! What was the problem?

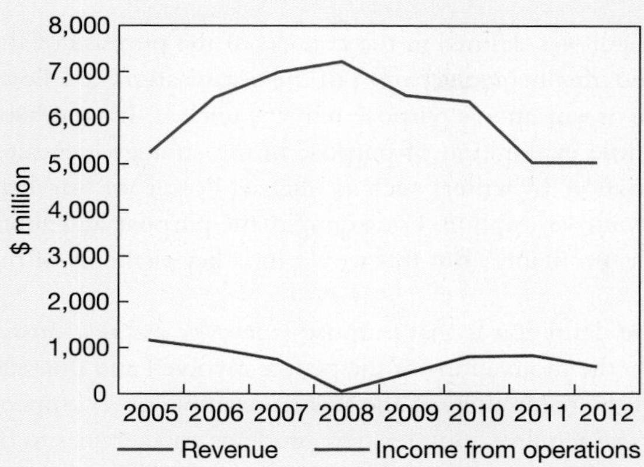

Figure 6.2 The problem at Yahoo!

Source: author from company reports for a number of years.

Sources of revenue at Yahoo!

The company was offering the following businesses through numerous content partners: Yahoo Finance, Yahoo Music, Yahoo Movies, Yahoo News, Yahoo Games and others. It was also offering shopping services through Yahoo Shopping, Yahoo Autos and others. Nearly three quarters of its turnover was in the Americas with 8 per cent in the region of Europe, Africa and the Middle East and 19 per cent in the Asia Pacific region. In addition to its own brand name, it had acquired the following businesses over the last few years:

- Flickr online photo and video sharing business was acquired in 2005 for over $30 million.
- Tumblr blogging site was acquired in 2013 for $1 billion.
- RockMelt social media web browser was purchased for an undisclosed sum in 2013. At the time of writing, it was reported that Yahoo! had closed down the site and was planning to use its technology in various other company products.
- Highly valuable 24 per cent minority stake in the Chinese e-commerce company Alibaba Group: Alibaba's turnover in China in 2013 was reportedly higher than eBay and Amazon combined. At the time of writing, Alibaba was about to offer its shares on the New York stock exchange. In many ways, this share is just an investment for Yahoo! It will not deliver business growth to Yahoo!

Yahoo! derives its revenue from two major sources: *searches* where it has text links with advertisers similar to Google and *display advertising* where it has graphical advertising on its various websites similar to MSN and other websites.

The reason for the lack of revenue growth at Yahoo! is partly that rival companies have been taking a greater share of both the above sources of advertising. Thus Yahoo!'s share of digital advertising revenues in the USA (its biggest market) declined from 6.8 per cent to 5.8 per cent between the years 2012 and 2013 with further declines projected. For the same period, Facebook's share rose from 5.9 per cent to 7.4 per cent and Twitter from 0.6 per cent to 1 per cent. However, the total US media market spend rose from $37 billion to $43 billion for these two years. This meant that the total revenue of Yahoo! was roughly static even though its share dropped. But there was no growth.

Some possible strategic problems at Yahoo!

The lack of growth at the company would seem to stem from at least three areas – maybe more:

1 *Yahoo's acquisitions.* They all replicate existing business areas: for example, Flickr versus Google's Picasa; Tumblr versus Twitter. The company purchases brought existing network users to Yahoo! In these cases at least, they have brought the company into competition with its rivals. Yahoo! is playing 'catch up' in these internet areas with no obvious competitive advantage. Moreover, good acquisitions are never cheap and can have an impact on the profit line for some years.

2 *Basic services like search and shopping.* These compete directly against two industry leaders, Google and Amazon. Again, the company has no obvious competitive advantage.

3 *Change of leadership at Yahoo!* The company has had six Chief Executive Officers in the five years to 2012. The leader at the time of writing this case, Marissa Mayer, has come from Google. She is beginning to give the company some shape and consistency. But such leadership changes over such a short period will inevitably mean that the company will have lost momentum.

The strategic way forward for Yahoo!

In the fast-changing market for web services and networking, the company should be able to grow again. It has a strong brand name, around 700 million users in 60 countries around the world and considerable technical expertise not necessarily possessed by some of the more recent start-ups. But it does need to re-think its strategy to deliver its purpose of continued growth.

The company describes its commitment in this area at the following web address: https://yodel.yahoo.com/blogs/general/sustainability.

Case questions

1 Do you agree with the three strategic problems identified in the case? Would you add any more from your experience and knowledge of the company?

2 What is your strategy recommendation for renewed profitable growth at Yahoo!?

6.1 SHAPING THE PURPOSE OF THE ORGANISATION

Video Parts 2 and 6

In Chapter 1, the topic of strategic management was defined in the context of the purpose of the organisation: strategy is only a means to an end, that being the *purpose* of the organisation. It follows that it is impossible to develop strategy if the organisation's purpose remains unclear. It is perhaps surprising therefore that there has been so little exploration of purpose in the strategy literature. Purpose is often simplified to 'profit maximisation' by writers such as Michael Porter[2] or 'survival' by Oliver Williamson[3] or some other simplifying assumption. For example, the purpose at Yahoo! might be summarised as to 'grow the business profitably'. But this would miss key elements of the Yahoo! business purpose.

The reason for such a simplification in the definition is that purpose is *complex and multi-faceted*, involving not only profit and survival but also the motivations of the people involved and the relationship of the organisation with society and the community. Yahoo! is an example of a company where its purpose of growth remains elusive and requires complex new products and services to be successful. Moreover, purpose will be *unique* to each organisation. Yet, however complex and singular, the general principles underlying the development of purpose need to be understood and clarified if the subsequent development of strategy is to be meaningful.

For many writers,[4] purpose is explored or defined solely in terms of business organisations. But many other not-for-profit organisations, such as government institutions, charities and public services, also generate value-adding activities that have a clear purpose and need strategies to attain that purpose. An exploration of purpose therefore needs to be broad enough to include such bodies. Whether private company or public body, every organisation needs to develop its purpose and develop a common understanding of the main elements.

There is a tendency for organisations to summarise their purpose in a few sentences. For example, an organisation will summarise its purpose as the maximisation of shareholder wealth, the achievement of growth targets, the delivery of market share or similar statements. Hamel and Prahalad[5] have even argued that purpose should be summarised in a few words under the heading of 'strategic intent'. But the purpose of the organisation deserves more thought than a single statement about profitability or some other phrase. The complexity of the topic is usually handled by identifying and concentrating on the essentials for that organisation. Such a process takes time and is best described as a process of *shaping* the purpose of the organisation. It is multifaceted with a number of important elements.

The six main questions that will shape the purpose of the organisation.

In summary, the exploration of purpose is fundamental to the strategy of the organisation. Purpose needs to be narrow enough to be actionable and broad enough to allow scope for development. It will develop from a consideration of the organisation's customers and its competitive resources. Purpose will also be defined by any specific desire to grow the organisation and by an exploration of the demands of the environment in which the organisation exists. Organisations are multidimensional and unlikely to have a single purpose. For reasons of focusing on specific objectives and communicating with those in the organisation, a simplified definition of purpose is often developed, but this ignores the complexity of the various elements of purpose.

To bring all the elements together, it is possible to construct the *polygon of purpose* shown in Figure 6.3. *Polygon* means a many-sided figure with no obvious dominant side. This is precisely the situation with the development of purpose, where there are a number of factors, none of which is usually crucial. Green strategy issues are not highlighted as a separate element because they are part of a number of elements: innovation, growth and ethical values, for example. The main elements of the polygon are explained below with examples from the Yahoo! case:

- *Time dimension* – long- and short-term perspectives will have a substantive impact on the purpose. Yahoo! has a new chief executive who was taking time to redirect the company at the time of writing this text.

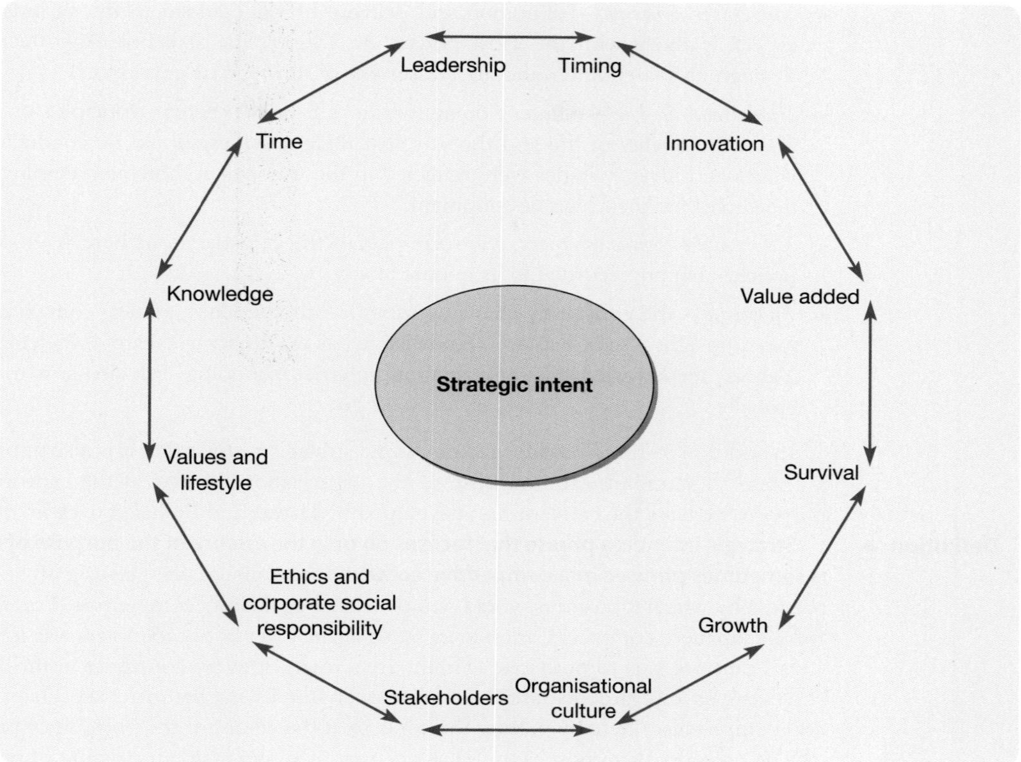

Figure 6.3 Polygon of purpose

- *Timing* – when to begin or end a new period of change. This will, in turn, depend on such issues as the cyclicality and the static or dynamic nature of the environmental forces. Yahoo! was forced into a shift in strategy in 2011 when its growth objectives in the USA were not being met.
- *Innovation* – the generation and exploitation of new ideas. These may have a profound impact on the purpose of the organisation – see Chapter 7. In its early years, Yahoo! was clearly innovative in many of its policies with regard to product range and employees – perhaps lost in more recent years.
- *Value-added dimension* – for every organisation, it is axiomatic that some value needs to be added for the organisation to continue to exist. Value here does not necessarily mean economic rent. It could mean service or some other concept associated with other aspects of purpose. For business organisations, it means profits and related issues. Yahoo!, both in North America and the rest of the world, was clearly in need of a reminder of this aspect of purpose in 2008.
- *Survival dimension* – the desire to survive. This is particularly important in some environments, perhaps all in the long term. Clearly Yahoo! was not immediately threatened in this regard in 2008, but the threat of competition from Amazon and eBay potentially has an impact on the survival of Yahoo!
- *Growth dimension* – the desire for sustained growth. This will not apply to all organisations, but certainly needs to be considered as an objective for some. As Case 6.1 demonstrates, this remains the principal purpose of Yahoo!
- *Leadership* – the style and substance of the way the organisation is led. The impact of this on purpose may be substantial – see Chapter 16. The judgement of Marissa Mayer will be crucial to the development of company purpose at Yahoo! over the next few years.

- *Stakeholder dimension* – definition and delivery of value added to the various interested parties, especially those with the most power. At Yahoo!, the stakeholders influenced the company through its shareholders and, to a lesser extent, through its employees.
- *Values and lifestyle* – different organisations will hold different principles on what is important about the quality of life and the way that their activities should be conducted. At Yahoo!, the values and lifestyle issues were reflected in the way that it motivated employees and gave them incentives for their own development.
- *Ethics and corporate governance* will form part of the considerations here. Yahoo! has quite specific policies that are recorded in its annual report.
- *Knowledge* – the constantly changing mixture of experience, values, contextual information and expert insight – see Chapter 7. Knowledge has the ability to create new elements of purpose. At Yahoo!, the knowledge is not just about internet technology but also how to market its services globally.

In addition to these broader factors, some strategists argue that it is also appropriate to develop a phrase to summarise the purpose of the organisation. Hence, at the centre of the polygon of purpose, we have the concept first developed by Hamel and Prahalad back in 1989:[6] *strategic intent*.

Definition ▶ **Strategic intent is a phrase that focuses on only the *essence* of the purpose of the organisation. It is sometimes phrased in a competitive context.** It was first developed as a way of encapsulating the process by which a business would win over time against its competitors. For example, the phrase for the Japanese company Canon in its battle against Xerox photocopiers was to 'Beat Xerox'; Coca Cola's purpose was to put Coke 'within arm's reach of every consumer in the world'. While some strategists have regarded strategic intent as over-simplifying the many aspects of purpose, the polygon compromises here by putting the concept at the centre of the polygon of purpose.

The polygon of purpose is useful as one way of summarising the nature of purpose. But it is not conclusive and other factors not covered in the list may be more important for some organisations – for example, aspects of service delivery in the public services and power and wealth creation for some entrepreneurs. It is for this reason that it has been called a many-sided polygon rather than the 12-sided polygon that is actually drawn in Figure 6.3.

KEY STRATEGIC PRINCIPLES

- Fundamental to the exploration of purpose is the definition of the organisation's activities. It needs to be narrow enough to be actionable and broad enough to allow scope for development. It will develop from a consideration of the organisation's customers and its competitive resources.
- Purpose will also be defined by any specific desire to grow the organisation and by an exploration of the demands of the environment in which the organisation exists.
- Organisations are multidimensional and unlikely to have a single purpose. However, for reasons of focusing on specific objectives and communicating with those in the organisation, a simplified definition of purpose is often developed.
- The polygon of purpose captures the many factors that will need to be taken into account in developing and defining the purpose of the organisation. Green strategy issues will be present in a number of elements, rather than being identified as one separate element.

6.2 DEVELOPING A STRATEGIC VISION FOR THE FUTURE

Video Part 2

Vision can be defined as 'a mental image of a possible and desirable future state of the organisation'.[7] In developing the purpose of the organisation, there are two views on the value of developing a strategic vision for its future: first, that it is irrelevant; second, that it has value. We deal with these in turn.

6.2.1 The irrelevance of strategic vision

Where the short-term needs to take priority, it may not be appropriate to develop a strategic vision for an organisation. A famous example comes from the major computer company IBM in 1993 – see IBM 'Thinking outside the box' on the book's free, online website. The link can be found in Part 6 at the end of this book. The company had just appointed a new chief executive, Lou Gerstner, to tackle its major profit problems. He commented: 'The last thing IBM needs right now is a vision.' What he meant was that the strategic context of the circumstances surrounding IBM made any strategy beyond an *immediate focus on turnaround* irrelevant. In this sense, strategic vision may be inappropriate in a strategic context where the short-term needs to take priority.

Given that a vision of the future is not always appropriate, the difficulty then comes in the correct definition of the strategic problem facing the organisation. There are no simple methods of undertaking this difficult task, which remains one of the most difficult facing any strategist. For example, McDonald's Restaurants – see Case 6.2 – shows the company's difficulty over the period 2004–2008 in identifying what should be the focus of the strategy at the company – is it to revitalise the lack of growth in North America? Is it to increase profitability in its overseas operations? Is it to branch out into the fast-growing segment of coffee shops? Is it to move into more healthy foods and away from burgers?

6.2.2 The value of strategic vision

Definition ▸ Vision can be defined in more complete terms than the opening statement of this section. **Vision is a challenging and imaginative picture of the future role and objectives of an organisation, significantly going beyond its current environment and competitive position.** In spite of such difficulties, some strategists are convinced that there are at least five reasons to develop a strategic vision:[8]

1 Vision refers to an organisation's ambitions that go well beyond the immediate future and *any full investigation of purpose needs to explore this vision.* Even not-for-profit organisations or those in the public sector usually need to compete for charitable or government funds and often desire to increase the range of services that they offer; such organisations will also benefit from a picture of where they expect to be in the future.

2 The organisation's *mission and objectives may be stimulated* in a positive way by the strategic options that are available from a new vision.

3 There may be major strategic opportunities from exploring new development areas that go *beyond the existing market boundaries and organisational resources.*[9] These require a vision that deserves careful exploration and development.

4 Simple market and resource projections for the next few years will miss the opportunities opened up by a whole new range of possibilities, such as new information technologies, biogenetics, environmental issues, new materials and lifestyle changes. Virtually every organisation will feel the impact of these significant developments. *Extrapolating the current picture is unlikely to be sufficient.*[10]

5 Vision provides a desirable *challenge* for both senior and junior managers.

Vision is therefore a backdrop for the development of the purpose and strategy of the organisation.

To be clear, vision is not the same as purpose: vision is the *future* picture, with purpose being the more immediate and broader role and tasks that the organisation chooses to define based on the current situation. However, it may be that the vision will lead to the purpose: for example, the Yahoo! vision of a wide-ranging internet service company led to the specific purpose of acquiring two companies, Flickr and Tumblr, in the last few years.

How to judge the vision of the organisation.

KEY STRATEGIC PRINCIPLES

- Strategic vision may be inappropriate in a strategic context where the short-term needs to take priority. The difficulty then becomes defining correctly the strategic problem facing the organisation. There are no simple methods of undertaking this difficult task.
- When developing purpose, there is a need to develop a vision of the future within which the organisation will operate. The main reason is to ensure that every opportunity is examined.
- Vision is not the same as the organisation's purpose, though the two may be related.

CASE STUDY 6.2

McDonald's Restaurants: maintaining momentum by attacking Starbucks?

After growth problems in the late 1990s, McDonald's was firmly set on a growth path in 2005 in terms of sales revenue and profits. But this success has brought a new strategic problem: how to maintain the momentum. Move into the coffee bar market and attack Starbucks?

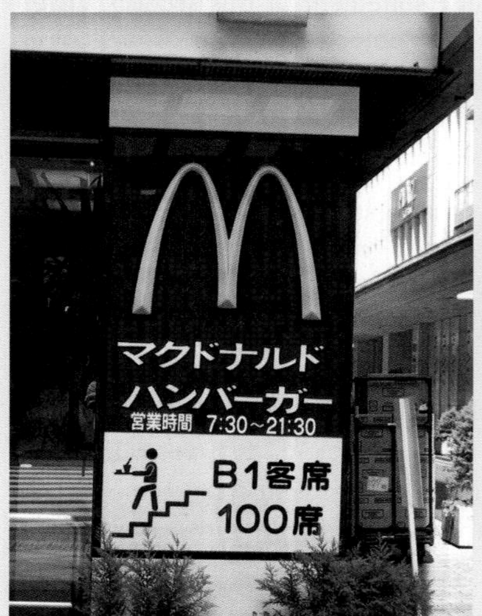

McDonald's has developed into the world's largest restaurant chain – Tokyo in Japan, Shanghai in China and Lima in Peru. To maintain its growth objectives, it has been developing a new strategy to attack the Starbucks business.

1990s: International expansion followed by acquisitions

In spite of its dominant market position in the $60 billion global fast food market, McDonald's faced a serious problem with regard to sales and profit targets in the late 1990s. It was struggling to achieve the double-digit growth target of 10–15 per cent increase in annual profits that it had previously announced to its shareholders. This was not surprising since a 10 per cent increase in annual profits might need a rise of up to $1.4 billion in annual sales – a challenging increase in the mature market for fast food.

In the early 1990s, McDonald's had achieved its strong growth targets by moving from the mature North American market into Europe and Asia Pacific. Essentially, there had been a rapid expansion of new outlets around the world. By 1998, this growth strategy had taken its course. There had even been some cutbacks in the number of openings because some new stores were not profitable.

For the period 1999–2001, McDonald's judged that further growth in its existing restaurant chain was so difficult that it would need to look elsewhere. The traditional burger and fries market was slowing in North America in terms of growth and there was strong competition from companies like Burger King and Wendy's. McDonald's therefore began a new strategy of acquiring what it called 'partner brands'. Essentially, it bought companies engaged in other parts of the restaurant business - for example, it acquired the Chipotle Mexican grill restaurants, the Donato's pizza chain and a share in the Pret à Manger sandwich shop chain based in the UK.

2002: 'We took our eyes off the fries'

Unfortunately, the new acquisition strategy did not produce the required growth over the period 1999–2002. The chief executive officer (CEO) who had introduced this shift in policy, Jack Greenburg, was ousted from his job in late 2002 and a new, experienced 59-year old CEO was appointed - James Cantalupo. He was assisted by a new younger chief operating officer, Charlie Bell, who had previously been the head of European operations for McDonald's. Before that, he was the CEO in his native Australia. The new executive team undertook a thorough review of the strategy. They concluded that the 'partner brands' strategy was flawed, not only because of the lack of profitable growth from the new outlets, but from its impact on the traditional McDonald's Restaurants business. There was even some evidence that the basic McDonald's service, quality and cleanliness had declined during this period because the company was focused too strongly on the new expansion strategy. In Cantalupo's memorable phrase: 'We took our eyes off the fries.' Thus around the year 2002, McDonald's decided that it needed to return to its core restaurant strengths.

2003: Back to basics with a healthy twist

Because of difficulties in meeting its targets from the 1990s, McDonald's began by reconsidering its earlier sales growth targets of 10–15 per cent per annum. The company considered that they were not realistic, so produced much lower targets of 1–2 per cent sales increase in mature fast food markets - like the USA and Western Europe - coupled with 2–3 per cent sales increase in the faster growing markets - like Asia and Eastern Europe. These very low sales growth figures would nevertheless translate into profit increase targets of 6–8 per cent. The more challenging profit targets would be achieved through new strategies of cutting costs, working more efficiently and more productively. However, although the company recognised that it needed to focus on its basic restaurants, simply doing more of the same was not enough. It also needed to revise its strategy.

McDonald's' largest business and biggest profits were generated in the USA: 35 per cent of sales and 60 per cent of profits came from this one country in 2006. The difficulty was that the fast food market in the USA was without any significant growth. In addition, it remained a highly competitive market, with aggressive competitors such as Burger King and Wendy's. Moreover, there were *some* customers - but by no means all - who criticised McDonald's for its high-calorie, high-saturated-fat menu with items like the *Big Mac* and the milk shake. In the years 2002–2004, McDonald's responded by launching new salad main meals and fruit ranges in all its stores. The company also promoted these products heavily to a new, health-conscious target group outside its traditional customer base. Such a switch in menu strategy was not quite as simple as it might seem. In order to launch the new range, McDonald's needed to restructure its supplies, its packaging and, importantly, to cut its existing in-store menu range. Fast food is only possible if the menu range is limited. Introducing new items meant that some part of the existing range had to be cut, thus losing the sales and profits from the deleted items.

In spite of the difficulties, the new strategy was successful. Unfortunately, Cantalupo was taken ill with a heart attack later in 2004. He was replaced by his assistant, Charlie Bell. Sadly, Mr Bell was diagnosed with cancer five weeks into taking up the post and died in early 2005. In a sense, the financial results are their legacy to the company. Together, the two men had refocused McDonald's on its growth purpose. They had produced major growth in its traditional North American markets by introducing the new main course salad range. They had tightened up the basic standards of food service and cleanliness by a new system of inspectors who visited individual franchise restaurants. They also prompted the launch for the first time of a global McDonald's marketing programme with a common worldwide payoff line: 'I'm Lovin' It'.

As both executives would acknowledge, the company had to continue in spite of the pressures on its senior managers. But there were still problems. The new chief executive, Jim Skinner, explained that there was pressure to increase profitability around the world. Ultimately, this meant that the company decided that it needed to focus on the basics and sell its outside operations like its interest in the Mexican restaurant chain. In addition, it needed to sort out the lack of profitability in its Latin American operations which were losing money.

Recovery and growth

In 2006, McDonald's began to refocus its operations. There were three main strategies. First, it decided to sell its peripheral operations such as its chain of Mexican restaurants and interest in the *Pret à Manger* sandwich chain. Second, it needed to sort out its losses in its Latin American operations. Third, it needed to find new growth in Europe and America: Figure 6.4 shows how important these two areas were to the company. Over the next two years, the company disposed of its non-McDonald's operations. In addition, it resolved its problems in Latin America essentially by selling the chain to a franchise holder. This led to the drop in turnover over the period around 2008 but it meant that profits recovered since the company was no longer carrying its unprofitable Latin American business. It was therefore able to focus on the third strategy - renewed and profitable growth at McDonald's itself.

As Figure 6.5 shows, McDonald's was able to grow its profitabiltity over the years from 2006. The fundamental problem was the company's business model was beginning to seem a little tired. The model was (and remains) to sell essentially the same products around the world - for example, the 'Big Mac' and the Filet-o-Fish - and in similar design settings - for example, illuminated menu boards behind the servers, unmovable plastic

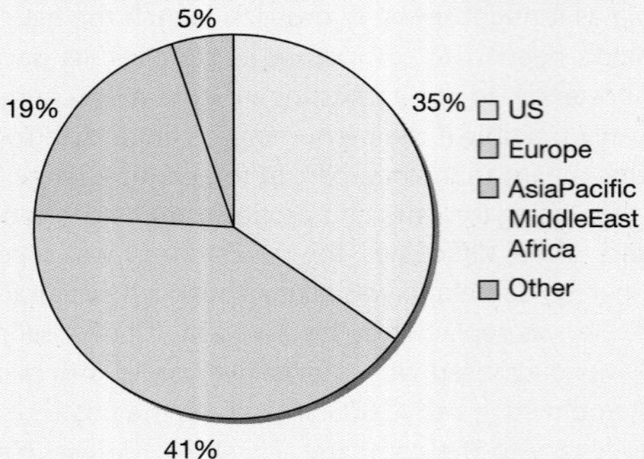

(b) McDonald's operating income 2009 by geographic area

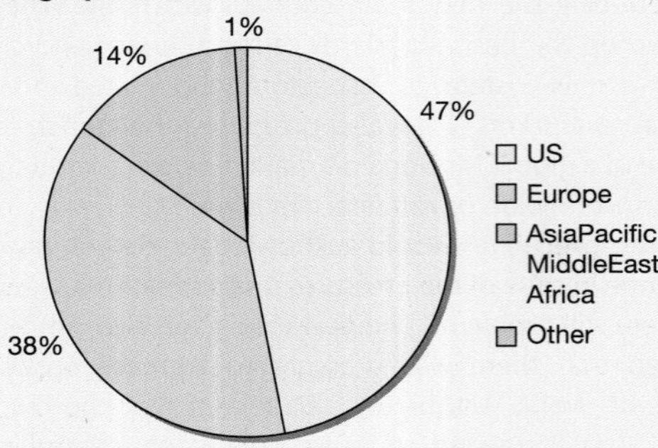

Figure 6.4 McDonald's revenue and operating income (profit) by geographic region

Source: author from company report and accounts.

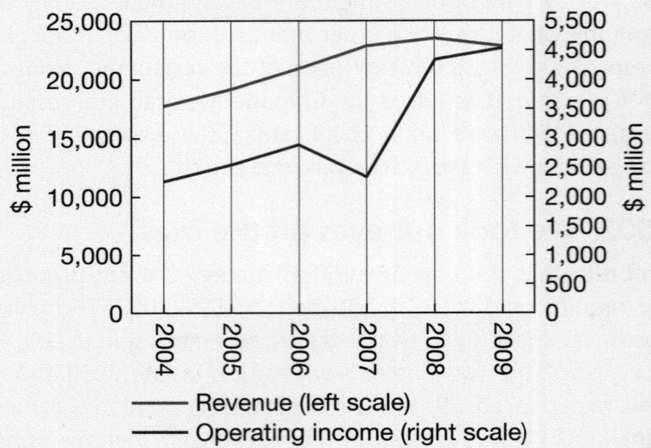

Figure 6.5 McDonald's recovers its impressive profit record in 2008

Note: 'Operating income' effectively means the trading profit of the company.

Source: author from company annual report and accounts.

chairs and tables. But there were new trends in worldwide eating that were moving towards more local items and also more local forms of restaurant design. Pressure was put on the company by shareholders to generate new growth in these more mature markets.

After careful analysis, McDonald's came up with two strategies: first, to be more local as well as global; second, to develop the McCafé concept. The company began developing more local menu items – for example rice burgers in Taiwan and a McOz burger in Australia with a slice of beetroot. McDonald's encouraged its regional directors to experiment with new tastes and menus for their parts of the world. At the same time, country directors were relocated out of the US headquarters and into their regions in order to be closer to local tastes and styles. But this ran the real risk of moving away from the basic global McDonald's Restaurants concept.

Around the same time, an even more radical shift was undertaken: the McCafé. It was originally developed in Australia by the late CEO, Charlie Bell. Essentially, it is a coffee bar inside a McDonald's Restaurant complete with a barista serving items such as cappuchinos and blueberry muffins, surrounded by bags of Guatemalan coffee beans and relaxed seating. Why do this? Essentially, McDonald's regular coffee typically sells for 50 cents per cup, whereas coffee in the McCafé sells for around $2.50 per cup. Both the profit margins and the ambience are much higher in a coffee bar – as Starbucks had already proved.

In 2005, the McCafé concept was extended into Europe where it was found to help profit margins and be consistent with the more general brand image. In the same year, the same concept was trialled in five US stores. Early in 2008, McDonald's launched coffee bars in nearly 14,000 locations across the USA. Clearly, there were risks in attempting to attract new customers to a fast-food outlet like McDonald's from the more relaxed style of a Starbucks. But the company was willing to invest millions of dollars in redesigning parts of its restaurants to attract new coffee bar customers. The outcome of these strategies was the return to substantial profit growth, as shown in Figure 6.5.

McDonalds has an extensive report on its sustainable practices on its website.

Case questions

1 Clearly the growth from new restaurants and healthy menu items was beginning to slow down by 2005: would you have persisted for longer? Or would you have lowered the growth objectives?

2 Was McDonald's risking too much on the McCafé concept to deliver its 2009 growth targets? Would the company have been better advised to go down the route of more local menu items?

3 McDonald's solved its strategic problem in the early 2000s by going 'back to basics' and introducing new healthy products. Can other companies use the same approach? What are the limits to such a strategy, if any?

STRATEGIC PROJECT

McDonald's has gained some ground from its new ranges. Where does it go from here? Should it revert to the previous strategy of acquiring alternative restaurant chains? If so, which chains? If not, then just how much further growth is there in the concept of fast food? This is a real strategic problem for a company whose shareholders demand continued profitable growth. Perhaps the company should try a completely new approach? In addition to looking at greater depth at McDonald's, it would be interesting to examine some alternatives such as Subway described in Chapter 2. There are websites for both these companies. You might like to consider two further trends. These are green strategy issues and better nutritional content: McDonald's has faced some strong adverse criticism on both these matters in recent years. Yet the company would argue that it has made genuine progress to improve its performance. Perhaps it could be even more proactive with regard to green strategies and nutritional matters?

6.3 STAKEHOLDER POWER ANALYSIS

6.3.1 Identifying the stakeholders

Definition ▶ **Stakeholders are the individuals and groups who have an interest in the organisation and, therefore, may wish to influence aspects of its mission, objectives and strategies.** For example at McDonald's, the stakeholders include the shareholders, the managers and the employees. In addition they also include the McDonald's *franchisees*: these are independent companies and individuals who operate many of the McDonald's Restaurants around the world under the parent's brand name. Franchisees have a significant influence on McDonald's headquarters and its strategy because the franchisees have to *deliver* aspects of this McDonald's strategy. In fact, stakeholders can be an area of competitive advantage, if managed well.[12]

An organisation's mission and objectives need to be developed bearing in mind two sets of interests:

1 the interests of those who have to carry them out – for example, the managers and employees; and

2 the interests of those who have a stake in the outcome – for example, the shareholders, the franchisees, the government, customers, suppliers and other interested parties.

Together these groups form the *stakeholders*.

Stakeholders are likely to have conflicting interests: for example, McDonald's shareholders will want to ensure that profits are high in order to pay reasonable share dividends. By contrast, McDonald's employees may want higher wages which will reduce profits. It is perhaps not surprising that the organisation's purpose is not formulated overnight. It can take months of debate and consultation within the organisation to balance out the various interests. Even after discussion with the directors, managers and employees may not necessarily accept the purpose without question: there may be objections when it is realised that individuals will have to work harder, undertake new tasks, or face the prospect of leaving the company. The individuals and groups affected may want to debate the matter further. Such individuals and groups have a *stakeholding* in the organisation and therefore wish to influence its purpose. For example, McDonald's Restaurants announced in early 2008 that it was going to introduce coffee bars into many of its US restaurants. This involved new dispensing equipment, new staff training and new menu presentations – all impacting on its stakeholders, including its employees, managers, directors.

This concept of stakeholding also extends *beyond* those working in the organisation. Shareholders in a public company, banks which have loaned the organisation money, governments concerned about employment, investment and trade may also have legitimate stakeholdings in the company. Customers and suppliers will also have an interest in the organisation. The interests may be informal, such as government involvement in a private company, or formal, such as through a shareholding in the company. All can be expected to be interested in and possibly wish to influence the future direction of the organisation. To summarise, it is not necessary to have a *shareholding* in order to have a *stakeholding*.

6.3.2 Conflict of interest amongst stakeholders

As indicated above, the difficulty is that stakeholder interests may be in conflict. Examples of these are summarised in Table 6.1. Consequently, the organisation will need to resolve which stakeholders have priority: this means that *stakeholder power* needs to be analysed.

Importantly in many organisations, it is no longer the case that the shareholders who own the organisation automatically have absolute power. For example, ever since the 1930s, there has been evidence of an increasing gap between shareholders and senior managers as companies grow larger. Berle and Means[13] surveyed top management in the USA and produced evidence that there was an increasing gap between what senior managers wanted – such as larger offices and more perks – and what attracted shareholders – such as increased profitability and dividends.

Managers may be more interested in size than profits: as companies grow, they are more protected from takeover and can afford to offer larger and more prestigious rewards to their leading managers.[14] By contrast, owners are more likely to be concerned with maximising profits and seeking only moderate growth. Unless managers in large organisations are threatened by takeover or incentivised financially, they may take a broader view of the purpose of the organisation than shareholders:[15] for example, shareholder dividends may be less important to senior managers than power and prestige. Because shareholding is fragmented in large companies, such managers have considerable power.

6.3.3 Analysing and applying stakeholder power

Checklist: The analysis of stakeholder power.

From a strategic management viewpoint, the major issue is to identify the influence of *stakeholder power* on the direction of the organisation, typically its mission and objectives. Importantly, this can be positive as well as negative – many organisations will welcome the contributions of and discussions with those who have power. For example, the Ford car company shareholders ultimately used their power in 2001 to force a change in leadership at the company – see Case 16.2.

Some of the major possible stakeholders are shown in Figure 6.6. The analysis of their relative power is likely to vary country by country. In addition, there is likely to be variation by industry: the

Table 6.1 Stakeholders and their expectations

Stakeholder	Expectations	
	Primary	Secondary
Owners	Financial return	Added value
Employees	Pay	Work satisfaction, training
Customers	Supply of goods and services	Quality
Creditors	Creditworthiness	Payment on time
Suppliers	Payment	Long-term relationships
Community	Safety and security	Contribution to community
Government	Compliance	Improved competitiveness

Source: adapted from Cannon, T (1994) *Corporate Responsibility*, Pitman Publishing. With permission.

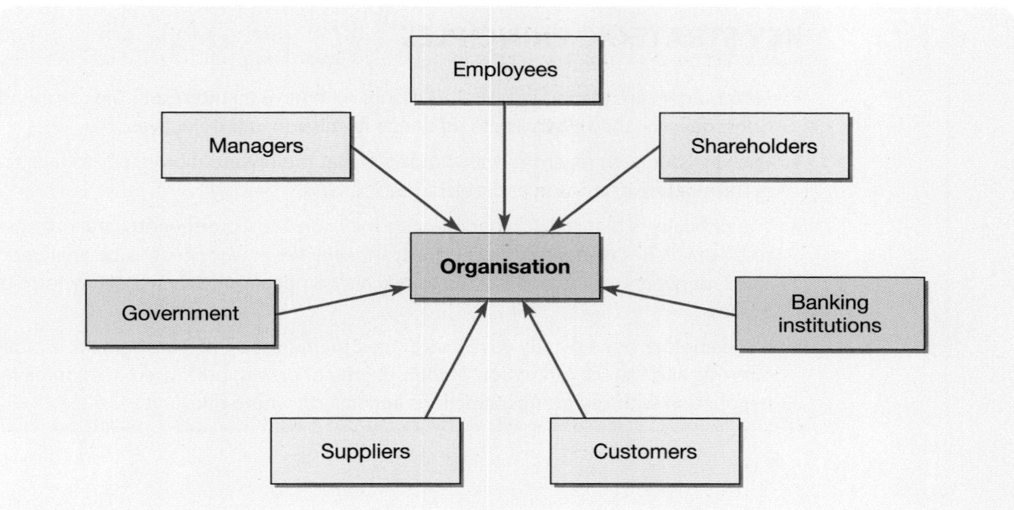

Figure 6.6 Stakeholder power analysis: the balance of power

volume car industry may well have a different profile from a more fragmented industry such as the textile garment industry with its smaller companies and family shareholdings. It is difficult to generalise, but a free checklist on the book's website may provide a useful guide to analyse a particular organisation.

However welcome contributions may be to the development process, the fact remains that there are likely to be conflicts of interest. Those with the most power therefore need to be considered most carefully. A *stakeholder power study* needs to be undertaken. This is shown in Exhibit 6.1.

EXHIBIT 6.1

Stakeholder power study

There are six major steps:

1 Identify the major stakeholders.
2 Establish their interests and claims on the organisation, especially as new strategy initiatives are developed.
3 Determine the degree of power that each group holds through its ability to force or influence change as new strategies are developed.
4 Development of mission, objectives and strategy, possibly prioritised to minimise power clashes.
5 Consider how to divert trouble before it starts, possibly by negotiating with key groups.
6 Identify the sanctions available and, if necessary, apply them to ensure that the purpose is formulated and any compromise reached.

As part of the analysis of stakeholder power, some explicit investigation needs to be undertaken of the *sanctions* available against specific stakeholder groups. These might be used to ensure that, where conflict exists between stakeholder groups, some resolution is achieved. Such an analysis may be the beginning of a *bargaining process* between the various groups. This is likely to involve compromise, depending on the power of groups of stakeholders and their willingness to agree. However, it may also involve the use of sanctions to bring pressure to bear on particularly difficult groups. Such a negotiation process can involve the game theory outlined in Chapter 5.

KEY STRATEGIC PRINCIPLES

- Stakeholders are the individuals and groups who have an interest in the organisation. Consequently, they may wish to influence its mission and objectives.
- The key issue with regard to stakeholders is that the organisation needs to take them into account in formulating its mission and objectives.
- The difficulty is that stakeholder interests may conflict. Consequently, the organisation will need to resolve which stakeholders have priority: *stakeholder power* needs to be analysed. Where conflict exists, negotiations are undertaken to reach a compromise. Sanctions may form part of this process.
- A stakeholder power study covers six stages: identification of stakeholders; establishment of their interests and claims; estimation of their degree of power; prioritised mission development; negotiation with key groups; sanctions application where relevant.

CASE STUDY 6.3

Citigroup – rebuilding its corporate governance

Citigroup is the world's largest financial institution, dealing every day in billions of dollars of banking instruments such as currencies, shares and bonds. It is a lead-bank in the financing of major world capital projects as well as handling over 200 million customers worldwide. Yet it was involved in a series of financial scandals in the last few years that led the company to rebuild its corporate governance. This case explains how this came about and what is now being done.

Citigroup's growth

Starting as a bank around 200 years ago in New York City, Citigroup has grown over the last 20 years by a series of aggressive acquisitions and mergers in many parts of the world. The major change took place in 1998 when Citigroup itself merged with Travelers to 'create a new model of financial services to serve its clients' financial needs'. In addition, there were large numbers of smaller firms acquired over the period 1995–2003. By 2004, the company was the world's largest financial institution, with dealings in over 100 countries around the world and major activities in all the leading financial centres.

In the period 1998–2004, Citigroup's net revenue almost doubled and its net income went up even faster – see Table 6.2 – and this all happened in a company that was already large by international standards. Importantly, its employee numbers never increased as fast, implying that each employee delivered increasing amounts of business and profits over that time. In practice, what happened was that each of the acquisitions added to turnover, but the 'back office' of most of the takeover candidates – the administration, systems, financial compliance, the IT support – was substantially reduced by Citigroup and replaced by Citigroup's own systems. This produced substantial cost savings and justified the company purchases but it had two other effects:

1 It reduced the people available for undertaking governance activities in the new subsidiaries.

2 It made central monitoring of a large group even more complex – there were not enough people.

Table 6.2 Citigroup: major growth in revenue and net income, but not in employees

	1998	1999	2000	2001	2002	2003	2004
Total net revenues $ billions	45.00	54.80	63.60	67.40	71.30	77.40	86.20
Net income $ millions	6,950	11,243	13,519	14,126	15,276	17,853	17,046
Employees	202,400	212,500	233,000	268,000	250,000	253,000	287,000

Source: company annual report and accounts 2004.

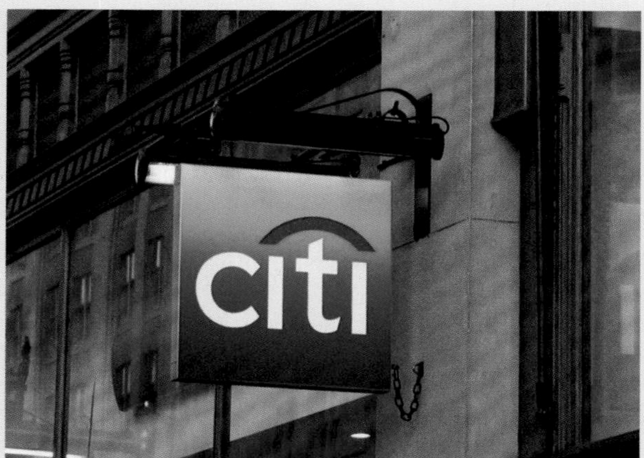

Citibank became the world's largest bank by a series of acquisitions and mergers that eventually led the company itself to redefine its ethics and corporate governance.

The new, much-enlarged Citigroup of 2003 was a mixture of many different types of financial operations. It included investment banking, credit card operations, retail banking and lending to poorer people. Importantly, this vast range of banking activity resulted in two further issues:

3 It meant that there were possible conflicts of interest between these different operations which would impact on governance. For example, the investment banking business might be advising on a new takeover at the same time as the private banking part of Citigroup was considering investing in the takeover candidate.

4 The knowledge and skills needed in the various parts of the bank are quite varied - for example, investment banking is quite different from credit card handling. This made it difficult for Citigroup to transfer people between parts of the company - useful if Citigroup wanted to develop a new company organisational culture.

Citigroup's rule breaking

Over the period 1998–2003, Citigroup was governed by the style of its chief executive, Sanford Weill. It was Weill who prompted many of the deals and mergers that doubled the size of Citigroup. Specifically, Weill put pressure on his colleagues to make such deals work financially - he set tough profit targets for the operating subsidiaries and they were then given considerable autonomy to achieve them. According to the *Financial Times* commenting on Citigroup, 'Executives who cut corners to hit quarterly profit targets could earn large performance bonuses.'[16] Amey Stone, a journalist with the financial magazine *Business Week*, co-authored a book on Weill: '[He] was a very hands on and controlling manager who oversaw a lot of operations. He did have an aggressive style, he emphasised profits, he was very strict about divisions delivering profits. I think questions of ethics really took a back seat.'[17]

Whatever the pressures on its employees, Citigroup became involved in a series of financial rule-breaking deals:

- Citigroup paid nearly $5 billion to cover legal actions arising from its relationship with the bankrupt telecoms company Worldcom - see Exhibit 6.2.[18] It also faced similar difficulties with regard to Enron - see Exhibit 6.2.[19]
- Citigroup paid around $20 million in fines to resolve US federal regulators' allegations that it kept from customers the fact that brokers were paid to recommend certain mutual funds, creating a conflict of interest. In a related action, the US National Association of Securities Dealers disclosed that Citigroup, American Express Co and JPMorgan Chase and Co had agreed to pay a total of $21.25 million for alleged violations in sales of mutual funds - within this, Citigroup itself agreed to pay $6.25 million.[20]
- Citigroup paid the American Securities and Exchange Commission almost $200 million after an investigation into commission payments.[21]
- Citigroup paid $75 million to settle a class action suit over its role in the collapse of the telecom network provider Global Crossing.[22]
- Citigroup was forced to close its Japanese private bank after 'repeatedly breaking local rules'.[23]

In addition, Citigroup was facing legal action by the administrators of the Italian food group Parmalat. However, it is important to note that Citigroup denied any wrongdoing with regard to this activity. Citigroup had also been cleared by the German financial market regulator of criminal wrongdoing with regard to bond trading in European government bonds in August 2004: 'Like in cases of fraud, there must be evidence of deception in order to press charges,' the German federal prosecutors explained. The bank allegedly made a profit of $17.5 million on the trade.[24] Importantly, when Citigroup was given permission by the US central reserve bank - the US Federal Reserve - to take over a privately held Texas bank in 2005, the Fed was prompted to advise Citigroup to delay big takeover plans 'until it tightens internal controls and addresses many regulatory problems inside and outside the United States'.[25]

In practice, Citigroup had already decided that it needed to make a major change in its practices: '2004 was not a good year for us. There are places where we have done some things we should not have done. We need to make things right and express our regret. We need to move on and make sure we're learning from it,' explained Sallie Krawcheck, Citigroup's chief financial officer.

Citigroup's new corporate governance approach

In 2003, Citigroup appointed a new chief executive, Charles (Chuck) Prince. He undertook a major survey of the company during 2004 and formed the view that radical change was required. In a message to employees in February 2005, he said:

'Let me be very clear: to be the most respected company does not require a sea change in our culture. Citigroup already has one of the world's most respected names in financial services with a legacy and record of accomplishment few companies could even dream to match. Yet at times our actions have put at risk our most precious commodity – the trust of our clients, the patience of our employees, and the faith of our shareholders.'

The company developed a five-point plan to enhance corporate governance at Citibank: this included expanded training, new performance appraisal and compensation arrangements and better controls. In addition to its five-point plan, Citigroup also developed a 13-page set of guidelines on corporate governance, especially for its board of directors. These covered such issues as the directorial independence of two-thirds of the board; qualifications to ensure board directors were adequately skilled and experienced; insistence that board directors should offer to resign if they were given major new responsibilities in other organisations; annual reviews of directors' performance; regular attendance at board meetings; direct access to senior managers to review important issues; rules on insider transactions and other business relationships.[26]

Commenting on the changes, the *Financial Times* concluded: 'Focused financial services companies find themselves involved in scandals from time to time. It will be much harder for a diversified group to avoid such lapses, given the nature of the industry. Mr Prince's plans are welcome, but it will require laser-like execution to make them effective.'[27]

And then came the subprime loan problems . . .

In Autumn 2007, Citigroup's investment bank announced that there were $1.4 billion writedowns on leverages loans, another $1 billion on mortgage-backed securities, $250 million on collateralised loan obligations and $600 million on other credit trading losses. 'If it went wrong, we were in it, we were bigger in it and we were slower to react,' explained one senior Citigroup executive. Later in the year, the company revealed potential mortgage-related losses of up to $11 billion, with the full extent of the problem still not fully clear some years later.

What was certainly known was that Citigroup Chairman and Chief Executive, Chuck Prince, resigned in December 2007 as a result of these losses. Vikram Pandit was appointed to succeed him as Chief Executive with a pledge to simplify the bank's organisation and reshape its business. He had clearly taken on a tough assignment.

By late 2008, Pandit was still having trouble resolving the many issues. He instituted a reduction in assets of $308 billion and announced job cuts of around 75,000 people by end 2008. There were problems not only with subprime mortgages issues but also with the way that the group had been assembled under his predecessors. To quote one financial analyst, 'This is no easy fix, even for the best of managers.'[28]

Citibank publishes wide-ranging material on its sustainability policies on its website.

Case questions

1. How do you assess the changes in corporate governance at Citigroup? Will they be successful?
2. Can other companies learn anything from Citigroup or is the company so different from others that no useful conclusions can be drawn?

6.4 CORPORATE GOVERNANCE AND THE PURPOSE OF THE ORGANISATION

As the Citigroup case shows, corporate governance has become increasingly important in strategic management. The chief executive can influence every aspect of an organisation, including the way that it treats its employees, its customers, its shareholders and other stakeholders. But it is the chief executive and other executive directors who take strategic decisions on behalf of the stakeholders.

Definition ▶ **Corporate governance refers to the influence and power of the stakeholders to control the strategic direction of the organisation in general, especially the authority of the chief executive and other senior officers of the organisation.** The corporate governance relationship with strategy arises from the opportunities given to senior managers to influence the future purpose of the organisation. The senior officers are usually the directors of the organisation. However, they may also include senior representatives of workers and senior outside advisers with no daily responsibility for strategy development. In some European countries such as Germany, Sweden and the Netherlands, this latter group would constitute a supervisory board that oversaw the work of the directors.

Many public bodies will also have corporate governance structures. These are likely to cover the major issues of the not-for-profit sector, including the monitoring of the quality of public services and the value-for-money obtained by taxpayers and charity givers.

For most organisations, corporate governance goes beyond selecting, remunerating and reviewing the conduct of the senior officers. It will also include a review and approval process for the main corporate strategies that have been developed by the officers. Typically, such a procedure might take place on an annual basis. In addition, to quote the corporate governance statement of the major international oil company British Petroleum,[29] there may be additional monitoring during the year to test 'the confidence in or risks to the achievement of the performance objectives and the observance of the strategy and policies'. Such policies have been tightened up in the wake of a number of corporate scandals in recent years – see Exhibit 6.2.

STRATEGIC PROJECT

You might like to follow up the examples of malpractice given in Exhibit 6.2, along with some others: there are references on the *Strategic Management* website to assist you. Are such offences rare? What actions have companies taken to stop them happening again? What has been the impact on the purpose, costs and strategies of other companies?

It should be emphasised that the majority of companies do not behave corruptly. However, the serious consequences of major scandals in this area have led to considerable tightening of corporate governance in recent years. These are described in the sections that follow.

6.4.1 Separation of ownership and control

Because the senior officers are responsible for taking strategic decisions and then acting upon them, they act as *agents* for the stakeholders. In this sense, there is a separation of the *interests* of the organisation represented by the stakeholders and the *control* of the organisation vested in the directors. Corporate governance has become important because the interests of the stakeholders in recent years have not always coincided with the interests of the directors. For example at Citibank, the directors appear on occasions in the past to have been willing to cut corners in order to grow the company, but have incurred significant penalties that then have to be deducted from shareholder dividends.

Larger companies now separate ownership and control. For example at BP plc, the company has a clear separation between the *executive* directors who manage the business affairs of the company and the *non-executive* directors whose task is to monitor this management activity. However, this did not stop BP's prime responsibility for the Deepwater Horizon oil spill in 2010 – one of the worst in global history.

6.4.2 The power of corporate governance

The importance of corporate governance lies in the *power* that is given to the senior officers to run the affairs of the organisation. In recent times, this power has not always been used in the best interests of the shareholders, employees or society in general. Examples of the abuse of this power abound, but are illustrated by a consideration of the UK company magnate Robert Maxwell. This man was chairman of a major international publishing and media group in the late twentieth century. By all accounts, he was corrupt, yet continued to operate with impunity for some years; the situation was only discovered after he died in a boating accident in 1993. Some other examples are shown in Exhibit 6.2.

EXHIBIT 6.2

Some examples of extreme problems in corporate governance

Company	Situation
Enron – an American company trading in energy futures	Enron was valued at $60 billion in 2000 but filed for bankruptcy in 2001. In late 2001, the company admitted inflating its profits. Various senior executives were prosecuted for corrupt practice and many found guilty. The company's accounting auditors – Andersen – were at that time one of the world's Big Five: their financial audits did not identify the Enron problems and they collapsed in the wake of the scandal.
WorldCom – an American company involved in telecommunications services	WorldCom's chief executive officer, Bernie Ebbers, was found guilty in 2005 of engineering an $11 billion accounting fraud in order to keep WorldCom's share price high and prevent margin calls on his personal outstanding loans totalling $400 million. Ebbers was imprisoned.
Vivendi – a French company that acquired one of the world's largest entertainment companies – Universal	In December 2003, the chief executive of Vivendi Universal, M. Jean-Marie Messier, was fined $1 million by the US Securities and Exchange Commission. He was denied a $25 million golden payout and barred from being an officer in a publicly listed US company for 10 years. He was accused of fraudulently disguising cash flow and liquidity problems by improperly accounting to meet earnings targets and by failing to disclose huge off-balance-sheet financial commitments.
Skandia – a Swedish company engaged in offering insurance services in Scandinavia and the USA	In 2002, the company was forced to sell its flagship US operation with a loss of $600 million because of a collapse in profitability through inflated share prices. It was also suggested that a small group of senior executives extracted around $100 million as bonuses from the company in the period 1997–2000 and gained the benefit of luxurious residences in the centre of Stockholm. There was particularly strong criticism of the way that Skandia used the funds of its insurance policy holders to prop up such plans: 'Skandia's troubles provide an example of what can happen when strong management is left unchecked by a weak board.'[30]
News Corporation – the media company controlled by the Murdoch family – see Case 8.4	By 2013, News Corporation had made payments of $340 million to settle the legal claims of people whose mobile telephones had been hacked.[31] There was one particularly notorious example: the hacking of the mobile of the dead UK schoolgirl, Milly Dowler.

EXHIBIT 6.3

Typical information available to different stakeholders in a company

Stakeholder	Information regularly obtained	Comment
Shareholders	Annual report and accounts	Limited to what the organisation wants its shareholders to know
Investment analysts, e.g. in stockbroking companies; also journalists	Regular updates of progress, sometimes face-to-face meetings	Better informed but still possible for the organisation to mislead
Main company board	Relatively full information but possible to mislead; legal obligation to be properly informed and to inform	Full disclosure of all issues is assisted by the character and independence of any non-executive directors
Senior managers	Detailed information in some areas but rely on managers to bring issues to their notice – remember Nick Leeson of Barings Bank	Likely to be without the full picture available to the main board; can be the 'whistleblower' on unethical, illegal or improper conduct but may also engage in such conduct
Managers	Some information but often incomplete	Can sometimes be the 'whistleblower' but under considerable pressure to conform to company rules
Employees	Usually only limited information unless the workers have representatives on a supervising board	New EU directives make senior representation more likely and offer some protection here

More recent governance incidents may not be so extreme. They have often related to the pay and other privileges that board members have awarded themselves to the detriment of others inside and outside the organisation – for example, the 'fat cat' company directors of the UK gas and electricity companies who gave themselves large share options at the time of privatisation in the late 1980s and early 1990s and ended up with vast fortunes at the expense of the nation.

As a result of these and other matters, professional bodies (especially those in the accounting profession) have set up standards to govern the ethical and professional conduct of the senior officers of organisations. Several commissions on such standards have also produced reports: for example, the Cadbury, Greenbury and Hampel committees in the UK, the Vienot report in France and the Dutch Governance Commission. In the USA, the corrupt behaviour at some companies led to the passing in 2002 of the Sarbanes-Oxley Act. This act made it essential for all companies operating in the USA (including foreign companies) to keep an *audit trail* of all decisions taken by the company. For many companies, this has involved totally new procedures that have been lengthy, costly and time-consuming. It has also involved clear communication with the many stakeholders of the company: Exhibit 6.3 shows some examples.

More on corporate governance, information flows and corporate conduct.

KEY STRATEGIC PRINCIPLES

- Corporate governance refers to the influence and power of the stakeholders to control the strategic direction of the organisation in general and, more specifically, the chief executive and other senior officers of the organisation.
- Corporate governance relates primarily to the selection, remuneration and conduct of the senior officers of the organisation. It is also concerned about their relationships with the owners, employees and other stakeholders of the organisation. The senior officers act as agents on behalf of the stakeholders in the organisation.
- The importance of corporate governance lies in the power that it gives the senior officers to run the affairs of the organisation. The problem with power is that it needs to be used responsibly.
- One check on the responsible conduct of the organisation is the information relayed to all the stakeholders - good-quality information will encourage responsible conduct. The problem is that such information may be commercially sensitive. Confidential independent advisers, such as accountants in an audit, may be the means of keeping check on corporate conduct.
- Another way of checking on the conduct of the company is by the appointment of non-executive directors who have no other commercial connection with the company.
- Beyond the matter of information availability, corporate governance is more a matter of the principles of conduct than simple rules. The main aim is to ensure that the value generated by the assets of the organisation is distributed equitably amongst the stakeholders.

Nine key ethics and corporate governance questions for company directors based on guidance from the former governor of the Bank of England.

6.5 PURPOSE SHAPED BY ETHICS AND CORPORATE SOCIAL RESPONSIBILITY

Decisions on ethics and corporate social responsibility are at the heart of strategic management. They particularly influence the purpose of the organisation. **By ethics and corporate social responsibility is meant the standards and conduct that an organisation sets itself in its dealings within the organisation and outside with its environment.**

Definition ▶

Ethics is particularly concerned with the *basic* standards for the conduct of business affairs – for example, policy with regard to honesty, health and safety and corrupt practice. Corporate social responsibility has a wider remit to include the organisation's responsibility beyond the minimum to its employees and those outside the organisation. Topics will vary with each organisation but may include environmental 'green' issues, treatment of employees and suppliers, charitable work and other matters related to the local or national community.

Corporate social responsibility is often abbreviated to CSR. To clarify the simple definition offered above, CSR has been further defined as **the process by which managers within an organisation think about and discuss their relationships with stakeholders as well as their roles in relation to the common good, along with the behavioural disposition with respect to the fulfilment and and achievement of these roles and relationships.**[32] Such a definition immediately raises many questions. What does 'common good' mean? Who decides about the 'common good' of society? The government? The individual? The managers? The directors? Why should any business be concerned about the common good of society? Why should any organisation devote resources to achieve the common good? We explore the value judgements involved in answering these questions in this section. In summary, these questions are captured from a business perspective in the question: 'What is business expected to be or to do to be considered a good corporate citizen?'[33]

Definition ▶

In practice, both ethics and corporate social responsibility are interrelated and are therefore treated as one topic in this section. Such issues concern not only business organisations like BP plc and Citigroup but also public and not-for-profit organisations. In the new millennium, both businesses and not-for-profit organisations can wield significant power both inside and outside their organisations. Most therefore now accept that some form of ethical standards and governance should govern and guide their activities. There are plenty of examples of the significance of such issues: for example, the *Exxon Valdez*, disposal of a Royal Dutch/Shell North Sea oil platform; the international ivory trade that threatens to wipe out an endangered species; the case of the American company Enron.[34] There is no one appropriate time to introduce a consideration of such standards, but it is appropriate to examine them in the development of the organisation's purpose.

6.5.1 Ethics and corporate social responsibility: basic issues[35]

To study such issues is to try to identify what is morally correct behaviour for the organisation. There are four main reasons for considering the ethical conduct of organisations:

1. In every society, such considerations are sometimes *inescapable*, e.g. legal limits on conduct.[36]
2. They may be *important* to conduct in that society, e.g. respect for 'green issues' in the environment that go beyond legal limits.[37]
3. A consideration of ethics is part of the *professionalisation* of business, e.g. the treatment of workers and ethnic groups.[38]
4. The *self-interest* of organisations is often best served by developing attitudes to ethical issues before they become acute, e.g. bad publicity as a result of accusations of incorrect behaviour.

EXHIBIT 6.4

Ethical and corporate social responsibility issues

Some basic examples of ethical issues that might impact on purpose

- *Espionage.* How does a company find out about competition? Where does reasonable enquiry finish and aggressive search for additional data commence? Perhaps anything goes?
- *Tyrannical regimes.* Does a company sell weapons or even life-saving equipment to a country that is run by regimes retaining power by unjustified use of force and human rights abuses? After all, the argument might be that lives might be saved in that country and jobs could be preserved in the selling company.

- *Bribery and corruption.* Should all organisations refuse to engage in such activity in every circumstance? Jobs may be saved and contracts won for only limited sums to a small number of people. On the other hand, the organisation itself would not wish to be on the receiving end of such conduct so why should it encourage it in others? Moreover, might it be profoundly unacceptable in society?
- *Telling half-truths and operating misleading negotiating tactics.* If such practices are unacceptable in general society, are they also unacceptable in business negotiations? Or does business operate by a different set of rules?

Some basic examples of corporate social responsibility issues that might impact on purpose

- *Treatment of suppliers.* Some global clothing companies have been criticised for allowing the workers in Asian and African companies who make up their clothes to employ very young workers and also pay them very low wages in relation to the price paid by the final customer.
- *'Green issues'.* Some companies have been criticised for failing to stop the destruction of the world's forests in order to feed customer demand for quality wood like mahogany. Other companies have been criticised for over-fishing some of the world's oceans in order to satisfy customer demand for fish products, regardless of the long-term impact on the environment.
- *Education.* On a more positive note, some companies judge that they have a role to help educate and inform the community in which they live, thereby contributing to the social development of society.

Exhibit 6.4 shows some examples of the type of issues that can readily arise. Any one of these would justify the exploration of ethics and corporate social responsibility issues. They raise three basic areas that need to be explored in the context of purpose and strategy development:

1 the extent and scope of ethical and social responsibility considerations;
2 the cost of such considerations;
3 the recipient of the responsibility.

In more detail:

- *Extent and scope.* Beyond the legal minimum, to what extent does the organisation wish to consider the ethical and social responsibility issues that could arise in its conduct of its business? Does it wish to be involved in every area or lay down some basic principles and then leave parts of the organisation or individuals to conduct themselves appropriately?
- *Cost.* Some actions will have a cost to the organisation. Many of the real conflicts arise here because if the actions were without cost then they would be easily undertaken. There are no abstract rules but each organisation will need to consider this area.
- *Recipient.* Is it considered that the organisation has a responsibility to the state? To the local community? To individuals? To special interest groups? These matters will need careful consideration in the light of the particular circumstances of the organisation.

In responding to these issues, it is important to bear in mind that developing and sustaining an ethical code is not easy.[39] It takes time, resource and vigilance. In many respects, the easy part is to set up an ethical code; the more difficult part is to ensure that everyone in the organisation *adheres* to that ethical code. Essentially, this means that the formal and informal business practices and culture of the organisation are aligned to such a code: 'Cultural messages about the importance of trust and long-term relationships with multiple stakeholders must get at least as much attention as messages about the bottom line, and employees must be held accountable for ethical conduct through performance management and reward systems.'[40] Business is more than making a profit at any cost.

Beyond these matters, ethical and social responsibility considerations may influence strategic management at a number of levels – these are shown in Exhibit 6.5. The values of the organisation will then need to be reflected in its purpose and possibly its mission statement; even the *absence* of values in the mission is itself a statement about the organisation and its view about its role in society. Such matters may well reflect the role that the organisation sees itself playing in society, if any, and the responsibilities that flow from this.

EXHIBIT 6.5

Ethical and social responsibility considerations: some connections with strategic management

- *The national and international level* – the role of the organisation in society and the country. Political, economic and social issues such as those explored in Chapter 3 will impact here: *laissez-faire* versus *dirigiste*, the role and power of trade blocks and state social policies. The organisation is entitled to have a view on these matters and seek to influence society, if it so desires.
- *The corporate level* – ethical and corporate issues over which the organisation has some direct control. Such matters as the preservation of the environment, contributions to political parties, representations to the country's legislative parliament are all examples of direct corporate activities that need to be resolved.
- *The individual manager and employee level* – standards of behaviour which organisations will wish to set for individual managers and workers. Some of these matters may not be strategic in nature in the sense that they are unlikely to affect the future direction of the organisation overall but rather the future of individuals. However, there may well be some general policies on, for example, *religious, ethnic and equality issues* that involve both the individual and fundamental matters relating to the direction of the organisation. These general matters of policy deserve to be treated at the highest possible level and therefore come within the ambit of strategic management.

6.5.2 Approaches to corporate social responsibility issues

After the corporate scandals of the last few years, there has been significant research on corporate social responsibility (CSR) and ethical issues. The approaches can be summarised under three main headings:[41]

1 *Stakeholder driven.* According to this approach, CSR is largely seen as a response to pressures from stakeholders that are external to the organisation – for example, consumer lobby groups or government organisations putting pressure to adopt policies with regard to global warming or reduce the cost of AIDS drugs.

2 *Performance driven.* Research in this area has focused on measuring the effectiveness of CSR actions in terms of their purpose by the organisation and their impact on the outside world. For example, research has explored the impact on profitability.

3 *Motivation driven.* This approach explores the reasons why organisations undertake CSR. For example, business may see this as enhancing the corporate reputation, lowering risk and generating customer loyalty. There may also be reasons that are more fundamental relating to the duties that businesses may have in relation to society at a theoretical and ethical level.

In summary, these three approaches illustrate the complexity of a subject that is both complex and important. From our perspective, the most relevant aspect is that it must form part of the purpose of the organisation. It is not just an afterthought that can be added later.

6.5.3 Corporate social responsibility: shareholder and stakeholder perspectives[42]

It should be noted that not all commercial organisations believe that they have a role beyond their own business. They take the view that society is perfectly capable of looking after itself and the prime responsibility of the enterprise is to care for its shareholders: this view was particularly prevalent during the stock market boom of the late 1990s. It was captured in the film *Wall Street* in which Michael Douglas played the crooked financier Gordon Gecko, who infamously believed that 'greed is good'. Such a view would probably mean that the company's purpose is unlikely to include any explicit comment on business ethics. It should be emphasised that this does *not* mean that such a company would behave unethically: simply that there is no need to reflect this in its purpose; its responsibilities are limited to the interests of the company. This is related to the *shareholder perspective* explored earlier in the chapter.

There are other companies that take the view that it is in the long-term benefit of both the company and the shareholders for the company to play a role in society beyond the minimum described by law. Sponsorship of outside initiatives, welfare provisions for workers, strong ethical beliefs and standards may all follow from such a view and be reflected in comments *associated with* the purpose and possibly the mission statement. This is the *stakeholder perspective* explored earlier in the chapter.

Beyond this again, there are organisations that exist primarily or wholly for their social functions in society, for example, those engaged in providing social services. Clearly, for these latter groups, it will be vital to specify the relationship with society. This group may well wish to include some statement of its beliefs and values in its overall purpose and also in its mission statement.

As an example of how business can both work within the community and at the same time focus on its more obvious commercial concerns, the UK charity *Business in the Community* provides a useful model. Essentially, it allows those businesses that believe that they should have a role in the community to *channel their efforts* while at the same time focusing on what they do commercially. No doubt similar organisations exist in other countries, ranging from Chambers of Commerce to some specific industry initiatives.

Comment

While this book needs to reflect a broad range of views on ethics and corporate social responsibility, this does not mean that it has no opinion on such matters. Companies do have a clear responsibility that goes beyond their immediate shareholders because they live in society, serve customers in one or more countries and interact with every aspect of the nation or nations in which they exist. The idea that the organisation's purpose is to serve *only* the selfish interests of the owners and the senior directors is morally and ethically wrong. Moreover, the 'Chicago School' argument that morals are largely matters for individuals is ethically and socially bankrupt.[43] This does make purpose more complex to develop in strategic management, but that is the price we pay for co-existing with others in society and contributing to its welfare. Readers are naturally entitled to disagree with this view.

KEY STRATEGIC PRINCIPLES

- By ethics and corporate social responsibility (CSR) is meant the standards and conduct that an organisation sets itself in its dealings within the organisation and outside with its environment. These need to be reflected in the mission statement.
- There have been three main approaches to the study of CSR: stakeholder driven which focuses on the pressures of outside organisations; performance driven which concentrates on the outcomes of CSR; and motivation driven which explores the reasons behind CSR policies.
- There are three prime considerations in developing ethics and social responsibility: the extent and scope of such considerations, their cost and the recipient of the responsibility.
- There are numerous differences between organisations over what should be covered under ethics and social responsibility, reflecting fundamentally different approaches to doing business.

6.6 DEVELOPING THE MISSION

Definition ▶ **The *mission* of an organisation outlines the broad directions that it should and will follow and briefly summarises the reasoning and values that lie behind it.** Such a mission needs to be defined in the context of the purpose explored earlier. The *objectives* are then a more specific commitment consistent with the mission over a specified time period. They may be quantified, but this may be inappropriate in some circumstances. For example, McDonald's Restaurant mission statement is: 'To be its customers' favourite place and way to eat. The company aims to provide its customers with food of a high standard, quick service and value for money.'[44]

As explored in Chapter 1, the strategies that will achieve the objectives then follow from the mission. These two areas define the whole strategic process and are therefore important in the development of strategic management.

6.6.1 What is the role of a mission statement?

If the mission statement outlines the broad directions that the organisation will follow, then the role of the mission statement is to *communicate* to all the stakeholders inside and outside the organisation what the company stands for and where it is headed. It therefore needs to be expressed in a language and with a commitment that all of those involved can understand and feel relevant to their own circumstances.[45]

Amongst strategists, there is some dispute over the definition of a mission statement.[46] There is really no agreed definition. There has been a high degree of interest by companies and other practitioners but relatively limited definition and research of a more academic nature. In addition, some researchers have questioned the lengthy nature and content of such statements: some[47] have even suggested that companies should concentrate on short and concise statements of their 'strategic intent' as outlined earlier in Section 6.1.

There are considerable differences of view on the form, purpose and content of such statements. At the same time, many leading companies in Europe and North America have developed and quoted their mission statements in their annual reports and accounts. Even if there is no agreed definition, companies still find the process of developing their mission statement useful because it encourages debate and commitment within the organisation. Some criteria for judging the results of attempting to draft a mission statement are shown in Exhibit 6.6.[50]

EXHIBIT 6.6

Some criteria for judging mission statements

Mission statements should:

- be specific enough to have an impact upon the behaviour of individuals throughout the business;
- reflect the distinctive advantages of the organisation and be based upon an objective recognition of its strengths and weaknesses;
- be realistic and attainable;
- be flexible enough to take account of shifts in the environment.

6.6.2 How to formulate a mission statement

Because no two organisations are exactly the same in terms of ownership, resources or environmental circumstances, the mission statement is specific to each organisation. Essentially, there are five elements:

1 Consideration of the *nature* of the organisation's business. Typical questions include: 'What business are we in? What business *should* we be in?'

2 The responses need to be considered from the *customer* perspective, rather than the organisation itself: 'We are in the business of developing books that will inform and educate our readers about strategy', *rather than* 'We are in the business of developing textbooks on strategic issues.'

- **Employee Involvement is Our Way of Life** – We are a team. We must treat each other with trust and respect.
- **Dealers and Suppliers are our Partners** – The Company must maintain mutually beneficial relationships with dealers, suppliers and our other business associates.
- **Integrity is Never Compromised** – The conduct of our Company worldwide must be pursued in a manner that is socially responsible and commands respect for its integrity and for its positive contributions to society. Our doors are open to men and women alike without discrimination and without regard to ethnic origin or personal beliefs.

Source: copyright © Ford Motor Company 1996. Reprinted with permission.

KEY STRATEGIC PRINCIPLES

- The *mission* of an organisation outlines the broad directions that it should and will follow and briefly summarises the reasoning and values that lie behind it.
- The *objectives* are then a more specific commitment consistent with the mission over a specified time period. They may be quantified, but this may be inappropriate in some circumstances.
- Prescriptive approaches emphasise the need to set out a mission and objectives for the organisation for the next few years.
- Some emergent approaches doubt the usefulness of a mission and objectives because the future is so uncertain. Other emergent approaches accept the need for a mission and objectives but place great emphasis on the need to include the managers and employees in their development.
- The purpose of the mission statement is to *communicate* to all the stakeholders inside and outside the organisation what the company stands for and where it is headed.
- There are five elements in formulating a mission statement: nature of the organisation; customer perspective; values and beliefs; competitive advantage or distinctiveness; main reasons for the approach.
- Mission statements rely on business judgement but criteria can be developed to assess the results.

CASE STUDY 6.4

Coca-Cola: lowering the fizz in its objectives

Coca-Cola, the world's largest soft drinks company, reduced its key earnings objective in 2002 and again in 2005. This case examines the reasons for the downgrade and shows how the company achieved its lower target in 2007.

Objective setting at Coca-Cola

For most companies in relatively mature markets like soft drinks, the starting point in setting the future objective of the company is what has happened in the past. Coca-Cola achieved annual growth in its earnings for shareholders of between 15 and 20 per cent in the years 1991 to 1997. There then followed three years of sharply declining earnings before a rebound in 2001. The company's operating income hardly moved ahead in the years to 2004 – see Figure 6.7. There were some one-off gains in net income (not shown in Figure 6.7), but these were exceptional and would not be repeated.

It was against this background that the company needed to define its purpose and then set its sales and operating profit objectives. In 2001, the company's chief executive – Douglas Daft – set what he regarded as a more realistic objective for the next few years of 11–12 per cent per annum operating income growth. This target was reduced to 10 per cent in 2003 as the company clearly was unable to meet the target. A new chief executive, Neville Isdell, then reduced it even further to 6–8 per cent in late 2004. 'It was part of the problem that I inherited,' he explained. 'Trying to meet numbers that could not be met over the near term.'

Coca-Cola is one of the world's leading global brands – an Indian delivery vehicle and a Mexican shoeshine stall.

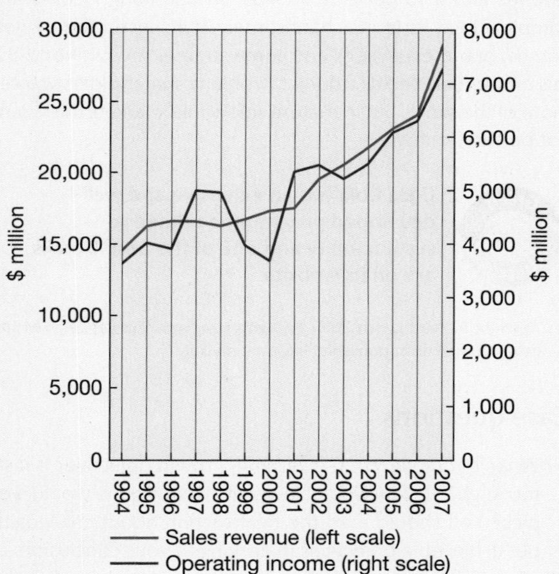

Figure 6.7 How Coca-Cola delivered its objectives in 2007

Source: company accounts 2007 and various previous years with some adjustments by the author for perfectly proper changes in accounting reporting for earlier years.

Yet at that time, there were at least four reasons to question whether this new, lower objective would be achieved.

Soft drink market growth

The first problem is the low growth in the market. Carbonated soft drink markets grew by only 2 per cent by volume worldwide during 2001. By 2005, the growth was only 1 per cent in Coca-Cola's leading market, North America, with a decline of 1 per cent in the following year. Coca-Cola dominates the carbonated soft drink market, from which it derives 87 per cent of its total sales. If the market is growing so slowly and the company is heavily reliant on the market, it is difficult to see how the company can outpace market growth without other measures.

Drinks markets that were growing faster include bottled water, fruit juices and sports drinks. Coca-Cola's chief rival, Pepsi, was much stronger in these markets, having spotted the trends to higher growth in these markets earlier than Coke. Coca-Cola's own attempt to enter the bottled water market in 2002 included the launch of the *Dasani* brand, which had success in some countries but was bungled and eventually withdrawn in the UK. In 2005 and 2006, the company had some success with new variations and brands in areas beyond the cola segment of the soft drinks market. However, the fact remains that Coca-Cola was under-represented in some growing soft drink market sectors.

Coca-Cola and its bottling companies

The second problem was the way that Coca-Cola earns its profits. The company does not just sell products in the market place. It works around the world through local bottling companies, some of which it owns and some of which it does not. Essentially, the company makes part of its profits by charging its local bottlers for the concentrates and syrups supplied from its headquarters – the bottlers add carbonated water, bottle and distribute the finished product. During the 1990s, Coca-Cola was reported to be buying up small bottling companies around the world and then selling them at a higher price to larger regional bottling companies, putting the profits from the sale into the Coca-Cola profit line.[51] The company was also charging ever-higher prices for its concentrates, again taking the profits.

Such strategies did not necessarily result in losses at its bottling companies or higher prices for bottles of Coke. The reason is that the consolidation from smaller to larger regional bottlers produced economies of scale that cut costs. But

Coca-Cola has now recognised that this process could not continue indefinitely and that it must share more of its profits with the bottlers, some of which were owned by the company anyway. For this reason, it reduced its earnings growth objective for the latest period.

New product development

The third reason for doubt about the earnings growth objective related to the successful introduction of new products. Coca-Cola's record here was disappointing. Its great rival, Pepsi, had a significantly smaller market share in most countries than Coke. But it had a good, possibly even superior, record on new product introductions - Pepsi was first to launch a diet cola and first to introduce cola with a lemon twist in 2001. Coke beat Pepsi to the launch of cherry Coke but this was back in 1985 and the variety still only accounted for 3 per cent of the volume generated by classic Coke. In addition, customers, employees and bottlers still remembered the major protests generated when Coca-Cola attempted to replace classic Coke with a more modern version in the early 1990s and eventually had to bring back the original variety.

In the years up to 2005, Coca-Cola undertook some new product launches and they were moderately successful. But there had been no dramatic breakthrough and none was likely. The company's strategy was to focus on marketing its main brand, Coke: 'Unless we have a healthy Coca-Cola [brand], we will not have a healthy Coca-Cola company,' explained the new chief executive, Neville Isdell.

Earnings growth through acquisition

The fourth problem was the reluctance of the company to make acquisitions that might enhance earnings growth. Coca-Cola bought the Schweppes mixer drink brand from Cadbury Schweppes (UK) in some parts of the world in 1999 and it made a series of bottling plant acquisitions in subsequent years. Yet the Coca-Cola board failed to support the recommendation of its then chief executive, Douglas Daft, to acquire the Quaker Oats company in 2001. The attraction of the purchase was the Quaker sports drink brand called Gatorade. This would have moved Coca-Cola firmly into a new market segment in which it is currently unrepresented and which is growing fast. However, the board felt that the price of $16 billion was too high. Pepsi bought Quaker in 2001.

Situation in 2007 - success but how long will it last?

After another three years of management upheaval - including a chief executive officer, Neville Isdell, brought back out of retirement - the company was still struggling to grow. The revised earnings growth objective of 11–12 per cent per annum was reduced to 5–6 per cent volume *sales* growth sometime in 2003. It was then reduced further in 2004 to 3–4 per cent late in 2004 after the arrival of a new chief executive. The sales growth objective was accompanied by the *operating income* growth of 6–8 per cent mentioned earlier in this case. According to Isdell, the operating income target would be achieved by a focus on the 'thousands of little things' that go into managing and promoting the world's biggest brand. For example, the company was beginning to explore global advertising rather than rely on national advertising, to develop more sophisticated pricing structures and to identify more product development in its core carbonated soft drink products.

In 2007, Coca-Cola achieved a 20 per cent increase in revenue and a 15 per cent increase in operating income: the company beat its targets handsomely. It achieved this by new brands, brand extensions and some strategic acquisitions. But this only underlined its strategic problem: shareholders wanted more of the same, but in mature soft drinks markets this would not be easy to achieve.

Coca Cola has an extensive and well-developed programme related to sustainability and one of the best. Details are on its website.

Case questions

1 What is your view of the earnings growth objective? Is it set too high? If you would lower it, what figure would you pick? You should read the next section about challenging but achievable objectives in arriving at your conclusion.

2 How should organisations set objectives? Past experience? Current market performance? Challenging objectives? Or what?

6.7 DEVELOPING THE OBJECTIVES

Definition ▶ **Objectives take the generalities of the mission statement and turn them into more *specific* commitments.** Usually, this process will cover what is to be done and when the objectives are to be completed. Objectives may include a *quantified* objective – for example, a specific increase in market share or an improvement in some measure of product quality. For example, Coca-Cola reduced its quantified objectives for income growth over the years 2001 to 2005, as described in Case 6.4. But business objectives will not necessarily be quantified – for example, Coca-Cola might have objectives related to job satisfaction for its senior employees that will essentially remain individual and unquantified.

The purposes of objectives therefore are:

- to focus the management task on a specific outcome;
- to provide a means of measuring whether that outcome has been achieved after the event.

6.7.1 Different kinds of objectives

In the 1960s and 1970s, several writers were keen to make the objectives quantified and thus measurable.[53] It is now generally recognised that some objectives cannot easily be quantified (e.g. those associated with business ethics and employee job satisfaction) yet they may represent extremely important parts of the activities of companies.

Nevertheless, a company that has a mission but no quantified objectives at all would be in danger of engaging in meaningless jargon. It is usual for companies to set objectives in two types of areas, the first of which is likely to be quantified and the second only partially:

1. *financial objectives*, e.g. earnings per share, return on shareholders' funds, cash flow;
2. *strategic objectives*, e.g. market share increase (quantified); higher product quality (quantified); greater customer satisfaction (partially quantified); employee job satisfaction (supported by research survey but not necessarily quantified).

None of the areas above is necessarily more important than any other. Individual organisations will devise their own lists depending on their stakeholders, culture, leadership, mission and future direction.

6.7.2 Conflict between objectives

There are some objectives that ensure the *survival* of the organisation, for example adequate cash flow, basic financial performance. These need to come early in the process. But for many organisations, survival is not really the main issue for the future: for example, companies like McDonald's and Coca-Cola are not about to disappear tomorrow. A major issue for these organisations concerns *development and growth* – for example, the Ford statement in Exhibit 6.7 contains the phrase 'survive and grow'. Equally, the McDonald's case earlier in this chapter revolves around the issue of delivering growth objectives.

Development and growth take time and require investment funds. Money invested in growth is not available for distribution now to shareholders. Growth objectives are therefore potentially in conflict with the short-term requirement to provide returns to shareholders, the owners of the company. Taking money out of the business today will not provide the investment for the future. Objectives therefore need to reach a *compromise* between the short and long term. It is for this reason that the Ford mission statement refers to providing a '*reasonable* return for our stockholders, the owners of our business'. This comment will then be translated into a numerical objective in terms of a dividend payout at McDonald's or Coca-Cola that reflects the need to invest as well as satisfy the shareholders.

Where a *competitive environment* exists, as in the global car industry, it is particularly important to recognise that any funds distributed now make it much more difficult to maintain performance against competitors in the future. For any organisation that needs to distribute the value that it adds, there will always be a potential conflict between the short and long term.

6.7.3 Implications of shareholder structure

The conflict between the long and short term becomes even more acute in some national markets where *shareholder power* is particularly demanding. The North American and UK stock markets have a reputation for *short-termism*:[54] that is, companies need to maintain their dividend record or face the threat of being acquired. Other European, Japanese and South-East Asian companies have had less pressure here because their shares are often held by governments and banking institutions, which have been able to take a longer-term view. For example, German car companies such as Volkswagen and DaimlerChrysler have had large share interests held by leading German banks. By contrast, Ford and General Motors have had their shares largely held on the open stock exchanges of Europe and North America. Thus the US companies have faced more acute shareholder pressures than the German companies. These priorities are bound to be reflected in how the objectives for the company are devised initially and monitored later.

6.7.4 Challenging but achievable objectives

When developing objectives, one of the real issues that arises is just how *challenging* the objectives should be. Do we merely set objectives that are easy to achieve so that we can then show real success beyond this? Or do we set objectives that are more challenging but still achievable? If we set the latter, to what extent are these open to negotiation with those who will be responsible for delivering them? Do we need a contract? And a reward?

These are difficult questions to resolve and will depend on the culture and style of the organisation and its senior managers, along with the nature of the organisation's mission and its competition, if any. Some will set demanding objectives and assess performance accordingly; others will discuss and agree (rather than set) a balance between demanding and easy objectives. In spite of Peter Drucker's optimism that this might be done more scientifically by the late 1990s,[55] this aspect of objective setting still requires great business judgement.

Developing objectives in larger organisations.

KEY STRATEGIC PRINCIPLES

- Objectives take the generalities of the mission statement and turn them into more *specific* commitments: usually, this will cover *what* is to be done and *when* the objective is to be completed.
- Different kinds of objectives are possible. Some will be quantified and some not.
- There may be conflict between objectives, particularly between the long- and short-term interests of the organisation.
- Shareholding structures will impact on objectives. UK and US companies are under greater pressure for short-term performance.
- Objectives need to be challenging but achievable.

CRITICAL REFLECTION

Is purpose over-complicated?

This chapter has argued that strategic purpose is complex and multifaceted. It needs to take into account such matters as leadership, corporate governance, ethics and corporate social responsibility. The problem is that all this makes purpose difficult to analyse, define and communicate to employees, managers, shareholders and other stakeholders. Moreover, there is no clear logical path to the development of purpose, with vague areas like 'managerial judgement' being used to justify particular goals.

Given these definitional and logical difficulties, perhaps it would be much better to simplify matters and focus on one area such as maximising profits? Or maximising shareholder wealth? Or even maximising the organisation's contribution to society after paying shareholders a minimum dividend?

Is there any merit in purpose being complex and multifaceted?

SUMMARY

- Fundamental to the exploration of purpose is the definition of the organisation's activities. It needs to be narrow enough to be actionable and broad enough to allow scope for development. It will develop from a consideration of the organisation's customers and its competitive resources. Purpose will also be defined by any specific desire to grow the organisation and by an exploration of the demands of the environment in which the organisation exists.
- Organisations are multidimensional and unlikely to have a single purpose. However, for reasons of focusing on specific objectives and communicating with those in the organisation, a simplified definition of purpose is often developed. The polygon of purpose captures the many factors that will need to be taken into account in developing and defining the purpose of the organisation. Green strategy issues will be present in a number of elements, rather than be identified as one separate element.
- Stakeholders are the individuals and groups who have an interest in the organisation. Consequently, they may wish to influence its mission and objectives. The key issue with regard to stakeholders is that the organisation needs to take them into account in formulating its mission and objectives. The difficulty is that stakeholder interests may conflict. Consequently, the organisation will need to resolve which stakeholders have priority: *stakeholder power* needs to be analysed. Where conflict exists, negotiations are undertaken to reach a compromise.
- The *mission* of an organisation outlines the broad directions that it should and will follow and briefly summarises the reasoning and values that lie behind it. The *objectives* are then a more specific commitment consistent with the mission over a specified time period. They may be quantified, but this may be inappropriate in some circumstances.
- Corporate governance refers to the influence and power of the stakeholders to control the strategic direction of the organisation in general and, more specifically, the chief executive and other senior officers of the organisation. Corporate governance relates primarily to the selection, remuneration and conduct of the senior officers of the organisation. It is also concerned about their relationships with the owners, employees and other stakeholders of the organisation. The senior officers act as agents on behalf of the stakeholders in the organisation. The importance of corporate governance lies in the power that it gives the senior officers to run the affairs of the organisation. Checks on this power include information given to stakeholders, the use of confidential independent advisors and non-executive directors. Ultimately, corporate governance is more a matter of principle than the application of rigid rules.
- By ethics and corporate social responsibility (CSR) is meant the standards and conduct that an organisation sets itself in its dealings within the organisation and outside with its environment. These need to be reflected in the mission statement. There have been three main approaches to the study of CSR: stakeholder driven that focuses on the pressures of outside organisations; performance driven that concentrates on the outcomes of CSR; and motivation driven that explores the reasons behind CSR policies.
- There are three prime considerations in developing ethics and social responsibility: the extent and scope of such considerations, their cost and the recipient of the responsibility. There are numerous differences between organisations over what should be covered under ethics and social responsibility, reflecting fundamentally different approaches to doing business.
- The purpose of the mission statement is to *communicate* to all the stakeholders inside and outside the organisation what the company stands for and where it is headed. There are five elements in formulating a mission statement: nature of the organisation; customer perspective; values and beliefs; competitive advantage or distinctiveness; main reasons for the approach. Mission statements rely on business judgement but criteria can be developed to assess the results.
- Objectives take the generalities of the mission statement and turn them into more *specific* commitments: usually, this will cover *what* is to be done and *when* the objective is to be completed. Different kinds of objectives are possible. Some will be quantified and some not. There may be

conflict between objectives, particularly between the long- and short-term interests of the organisation. Objectives need to be challenging but achievable. In larger organisations and those with scarce resources, the objectives may need to be adjusted to take into account the circumstances and trading situation of different parts of the organisation.

QUESTIONS

1 Take an organisation with which you are familiar and attempt to define its purpose: how has this been influenced by the factors outlined in Section 6.1, including its environment, resources, culture and stakeholders? How has the purpose changed over time? Why have these changes occurred?

2 In 2013, Yahoo! claimed that its vision of the future was that of 'a global technology company focused on making the world's daily habits inspiring and entertaining.' Use the classification developed by Hamel and Prahalad to evaluate this vision critically (see Section 6.2).

3 Can *organisations* have vision or is it the *managers* inside the organisation who have the vision? What are the implications of your answer for the development of strategy, especially in terms of communication within the organisation?

4 In what strategic circumstances should a leader be dominant? And in what circumstances should a leader work with a shared vision? Give examples to support your views and show how other factors can also influence leadership style.

5 Do companies always need to behave ethically, regardless of the costs?

6 Should 'green' environmental issues form part of the corporate social responsibility of a business? How, if at all, will your answer impact on the strategy of the business?

7 How is corporate governance related to strategic management? What systems, if any, does McDonald's need to put in place to ensure compliance with corporate governance issues? Use the example of Citibank to assist you.

8 Take an organisation with which you are familiar and assess the information that it supplies to its stakeholders in terms of corporate governance issues. Is it doing a good job by its own standards and by the likely standards of its stakeholders?

9 Can the concept of purpose and competitive advantage be applied to the whole of Coca-Cola? Compare your answers with the statements in the text from the company and comment on any differences.

FURTHER READING

On purpose: read Drucker, P (1961) *Practice of Management*, Mercury, London. For a more recent review of mission and goal literature, see the early part of Slater, S, Olsen, E and Hult, T (2006) 'The moderating influence of strategic orientation on the strategy formation capability–performance relationship', *Strategic Management Journal*, Vol 27, pp 1221–1231.

On vision: see Tregoe, B B *et al.* (1989) *Vision in Action*, Simon & Schuster, London. See also Hamel, G and Prahalad, C K (1994) *Competing for the Future*, Harvard Business School Press, Boston, MA. Both books are at the practical end of the subject.

On leadership: Bennis, W and Nanus, B (1997) *Leaders: Strategies for Taking Charge*, HarperCollins, New York is a readable text with some useful insights. See also the special issue of *Academy of Management Executive* (2004) Vol 18, No 3, pp 118–142, on leadership including: Conger, J A, 'Developing leadership capability: What's inside the black box?'

On ethical issues: a good basic text is Chryssides, G D and Kaler, J H (1993) *An Introduction to Business Ethics*, International Thomson Business Press, London. The special issue of *Academy of Management Executive* (2004) Ethical Behavior in Management, pp 37–91 with guest editor John F Veign constitutes a substantial review with thoughtful papers on various current topics. There was also a special issue on the same topic in *Academy of Management Learning and Education*, September 2006, Vol 5, Issue 3 co-editors Robert Giacalone and Kenneth R Thompson that will provide more discussion.

For a more general and critical commentary on ethics and management theory including a critique of shareholder theory, you should read the late Professor Sumanthra Ghoshal's paper written in 2005, 'Bad Management Theories are Destroying Good Management Practices', *Academy of Management Learning and Education*, Vol 4, No 1, pp 75–91. Not a 'difficult' paper to understand and containing some profound and well-argued positions.

On corporate social responsibility a more recent accessible paper is that by Basu, K and Palazzo, G (2008) 'Corporate Social Responsibility, A Process Model of Sensemaking', *Academy of Management Review*, Vol 33, pp 123–136. This paper has a useful summary of recent research literature and would make a good start for project work.

NOTES AND REFERENCES

1 Sources for the Yahoo! case: Company annual reports for the years 2008, 2009, 2020, 2011, 2012. *New York Times*, 16th January 2014, 'Bumps on a road to revival for Yahoo', Goel, V and Millerjan, C sourced from the web. *Advertising Age*, 19 December 2013, 'Yahoo slips behind Google, Facebook and even Microsoft', Peterson, T sourced from the web. *Financial Times*, 26 March 2014, p 17.

2 Porter, M E (1980) *Competitive Strategy*, The Free Press, New York.

3 Williamson, O (1991) 'Strategizing, economizing and economic organization', *Strategic Management Journal*, Vol 12, pp 75–94.

4 For example, see Drucker, P (1961) *Practice of Management*, Mercury, London, p 5.

5 Hamel, G and Prahalad, C K (1989) 'Strategic intent', *Harvard Business Review*, Vol 67, No 3, pp 63–76.

6 Hamel, G and Prahalad, C K (1989) Ibid.

7 Bennis, W and Nanus, B (1997) *Leaders: Strategies for Taking Charge*, HarperCollins, New York, p 82.

8 Bennis, W and Nanus, B (1997) Ibid.

9 Hamel, G and Prahalad, C K (1994) *Competing for the Future*, Harvard Business School Press, Boston, MA, p 31.

10 Hamel, G and Prahalad, C K (1994) Ibid, p 29.

11 Sources for McDonald's case: McDonald's Annual Report and Accounts 2004 and 2007. *Financial Times*: 3 September 1998, p 20; 13 December 2000, p 14; 15 April 2002, p 13; 26 April 2002, p 21 (Burger King); 23 October 2002, p 21; 1 March 2003, p 3; 29 August 2003, p 15; 26 November 2003, p 7; 5 February 2004, p 11; 9 March 2004, p 31; 9 January 2005, p M6; 18 January 2005, p 29; 13 October 2005, p 29; 1 February 2006, p 27; 7 February 2006, p 26; 9 February 2006, p 9; 22 February 2007, p 12; 21 August 2007, p 22; 8 January 2008, p 16; 11 August 2008, p 16; 14 December 2010, p 25; 25 February 2011, p 16; 17 March 2011, p 24. McDonald's' websites have extensive and useful information – www.mcdonalds.com

12 Hillman, A J and Keim, J D (2001) 'Shareholder value, stakeholder management and social issues: what's the bottom line?', *Strategic Management Journal*, Vol 22, pp 125–139.

13 Berle, A A and Means, G C (1967) *The Modern Corporation and Private Property*, Harvest, New York (originally published in 1932).

14 Marris, R (1964) *The Economic Theory of Managerial Capitalism*, Macmillan, London.

15 Holl, P (1977) 'Control type and the market for corporate control in large US corporations', *Journal of Industrial Economics*, Vol 25, pp 259–273; Lawriwsky, M L (1984) *Corporate Structure and Performance*, Croom Helm, London; Whittington, R (1993) *What is Strategy and Does it Matter?* Routledge, London.

16 Editorial (2005) *Financial Times*, 18 February, p 16.

17 Cooper, L (2005) 'Scandal-hit Citigroup rebuilds its image', *BBC World Service Report* on the World Wide Web, 14 March.

18 Cooper, L (2005) Ibid.

19 Reuters (2005) 'Citigroup completes Texas deal that alerted Fed', 31 March.

20 Associated Press (2005) 'Citigroup, Putnam pay SEC fines over funds', 23 March.

21 Cooper, L (2005) Op. cit.

22 Cooper, L (2005) Op. cit.

23 Cooper, L (2005) Op. cit.

24 Associated Press (2005) 'German prosecutors won't probe Citigroup', 21 March.

25 Reuters (2005) Op. cit.

26 Available on the web at www.citi.com/citigroup/.

27 Editorial (2005) Op. cit.

28 *Financial Times*: 9 October 2006, p 13; 13 December 2006, p 26; 2 October 2007, p 26; 12 December 2007, pp 1 and 29 (interview with new chief executive); 19 July 2008, p 18; 18 November 2008, p 26. *The Economist*: 28 October 2006, p 89; 19 January 2011, p 22.

29 British Petroleum (2004) *Annual Report and Accounts*.

30 *Financial Times*, 2 December 2003, p 31.

31 Source: Press Gazette, 7th February 2013, 'Phone hacking scandal: News Corp costs rise to $340 million' sourced from the web at http://www.pressgazette.co.uk/phone-hacking-scandal-news-corp-costs-rise-360m (sic).

32 Basu, K and Palazzo, G (2008) 'Corporate social responsibility: a process model of sensemaking', *Academy of Management Review*, Vol 33, No 1, pp 122–136. This paper is a useful starting point in researching this area.

33 Carroll, A B (1998) 'The four faces of corporate citizenship', *Business and Society Review*, Vol 4, pp 497–505.

34 Useful survey of Enron ethics: Chaffin, J and Fidler, S (2002) *Financial Times*, 9 April, p 30.

35 This section has benefited from Chryssides, G D and Kaler, J H (1993) *An Introduction to Business Ethics*, International Thomson Business Press, London.

36 Dickson, T (1995) 'The twelve corporate commandments', *Financial Times*, 11 October, p 18.

37 *Financial Times* (1998) *Visions of Ethical Business*, Vol 1, October. Various authors.

38 Dickson, T (1994) 'The search for universal ethics', *Financial Times*, 22 July, p 11.

39 Trevino, L K and Brown, M E (2004) 'Managing to be ethical: Debunking five business ethics myths', *Academy of Management Executive*, Vol 18, No 2, pp 69–81.

40 Trevino, L K and Brown, M E (2004) Ibid, p 80.

41 Basu, K and Palazzo, G (2008) Op. cit.

42 For a fuller discussion, see Chryssides, G D and Kaler, J H (1993) Op. cit., Ch 5. See also Badaracco, J L and Webb, A (1995) 'Business ethics: a view from the trenches', *California Management Review*, Vol 37, Winter, pp 8–29, and reply in *California Management Review*, 39 Spring 1997, Letter to the Editor, p 135. See also Reich, R B (1998) 'The new meaning of corporate social responsibility', *California Management Review*, Vol 40, Winter, pp 8–17.

43 You can read more about the 'Chicago School' and its views in Ghoshal, S (2005) 'Bad management theories are

destroying good management practices', *Academy of Management Learning and Education*, Vol 4, No 1, pp 75–91. Essentially, Professor Ghoshal's arguments are correct, in my judgement.

44 From McDonald's Restaurants UK website: www.mcdonalds.co.uk.

45 Christopher, M, Majaro, S and McDonald, M (1989) *Strategy: a Guide for Senior Executives*, Wildwood House, Aldershot, Ch 1.

46 Bart, C K and Baetz, M C (1998) 'The relationship between mission statements and firm performance: an explanatory study', *Journal of Management Studies*, Vol 35, No 6, pp 823–854; Hooley, G, Cox, A and Adams, A (1991) 'Our five year mission to boldly go where no man has been before', *Proceedings, Marketing Education Group Annual Conference*, Cardiff, pp 559–577.

47 Prahalad, C and Doz, Y (1987) *The Multinational Mission*, The Free Press, New York; Hamel, G and Prahalad, C (1989) 'Strategic intent', *Harvard Business Review*, May–June, pp 79–91.

48 Campbell, A and Nash, L (1992) *A Sense of Mission: Defining Direction for the Large Corporation*, Addison-Wesley, Wokingham.

49 Christopher, M *et al.* (1989) Op. cit.

50 Based on Christopher, M *et al.* (1989) Op. cit., p 8.

51 Tomkins, R (2002) 'Added spice', *Financial Times*, 5 April, p 16 and Hope, K (2002) 'A world wide bottling empire looks to Athens', *Financial Times*, 19 April, p 13.

52 Sources for Coca-Cola case: *Financial Times*: 19 June 1999, p 11; 22 July 1999, p 2; 29 January 2000, p 15; 27 March 2000, p 20; 1 August 2000, p 15; 15 March 2001, p 20; 15 March 2001, p 20; 5 April 2002, p 16; 17 April 2002, p 29; 19 April 2002, p 13; 15 May 2002, p 25; 17 April 2003, p 24; 18 June 2003, p 31; 11 December 2003, p 18; 24 February 2004, p 32; 10 March 2004, p 17; 25 March 2004, p 1; 20 April 2004, p 27; 5 May 2004, p 21; 11 May 2004, p 31; 23 June 2004, p 31; 16 September 2004, p 33; 28 September 2004, p 28; 12 November 2004, p 1; 6 January 2005, p 20; 12 February 2005, p 19; 17 February 2005, p 19; 18 February 2005, p 27; 25 April 2005, p 22; 29 April 2005, p 28; 22 September 2005, p 17; 6 December 2005, p 38; 10 July 2006, p 26; 21 November 2006, p 10; 26 February 2007, p 11; 9 December 2007, p 20; 4 September 2008, p 20; 26 February 2010, p 27; 7 January 2011, p 21; 20 January 2011, p 16. Coca-Cola Annual Reports and Accounts for 2001, 2004, 2007 and 2009, available on the web at www.coca-cola.com.

53 Ansoff, I (1968) *Corporate Strategy*, Penguin, Harmondsworth, p 44.

54 There are many papers on this controversial topic: see, for example, Williams, K, Williams, J and Haslam, C (1990) 'The hollowing out of British manufacturing and its implications for policy', *Economy and Society*, Vol 19, No 4, pp 456–490.

55 Drucker, P (1961) Op. cit., p 54.

CHAPTER 7 Purpose emerging from knowledge, technology and innovation

Video and sound summary of this chapter

LEARNING OUTCOMES

When you have worked through this chapter, you will be able to:

- define and explore the implications of tacit and explicit knowledge;
- explain how purpose emerges from knowledge creation;
- examine the implications of developments in technology for the organisation's purpose and strategy;
- identify the main innovation processes relevant to purpose;
- show how purpose changes with innovation;
- explain why an organisation's purpose may sometimes be emergent rather than prescriptive;
- relate knowledge, technology and innovation to green strategy issues.

INTRODUCTION

Video Part 7

Chapter 6 concentrated on shaping purpose in a defined and explicit way. Essentially, it adopted a *prescriptive* approach. Typically, many organisations seek to define purpose in such terms – for example, they might develop a defined code of ethical conduct, a target for earnings per share, a specific increase in the return on capital employed, a gain in market share and so on. One of the consequences of shaping purpose explicitly in this way is that it will exclude, by definition, alternative purposes and strategies whose outcomes are unknown and non-specific or whose outcomes are predicted to fail to meet the defined prescriptive criteria. The danger of such approaches is that they may exclude purposes and strategies that may be more rewarding in the long term and deserve some early exploration as part of strategy development. The objective of this chapter is to redress the balance.

In open-ended investigations, purpose might be allowed to be more experimental and developed from the process itself – an *emergent* approach to purpose. The issue is how to set about this task. There are many routes, three of which are explored in this chapter: knowledge creation, technology development and innovation. Ultimately, all three processes need to be related back to the organisation, especially with regard to their ability to contribute to increased revenue, enhanced value added and stronger competitive advantage. These three areas are useful criteria for judging this more open-ended approach to the development of purpose – see Figure 7.1. Issues surrounding green strategy are explored in Chapter 14.

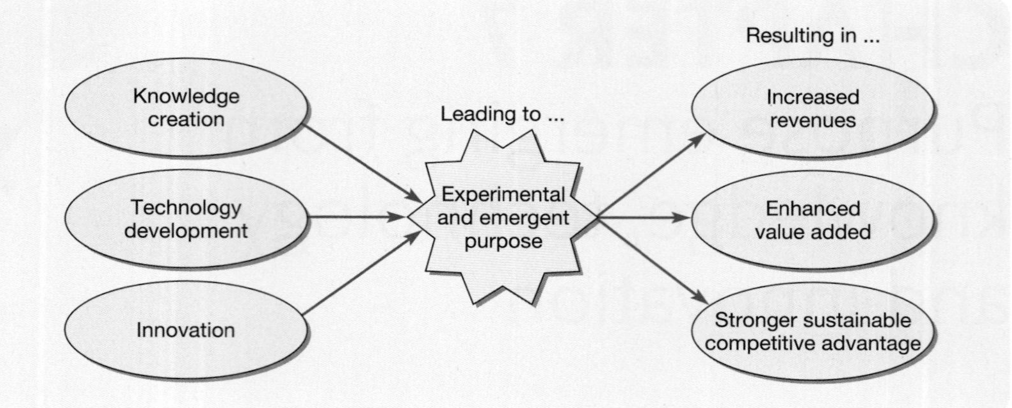

Figure 7.1 An emergent approach to purpose

CASE STUDY 7.1

Maglev: Shanghai's innovative new transport system

Opened in December 2002 in the presence of the Chinese premier and the German chancellor, the Maglev railway is the fastest public transport system in the world. It runs between Pudong Airport and the city of Shanghai but, unfortunately, has not carried as many passengers as expected. Just what are the implications for innovation?

Maglev background

'Maglev' means *electromagnetic levitation* and refers to a system whereby a public transport carriage runs on railway-like tracks. Magnetism holds the carriage in the air just above the track itself so that there is very little friction between the track and the carriage - unlike a normal carriage that sits on the track itself. The power for the system is in the track rather than carried on board, so that the carriages are also lighter than normal. The resulting low friction means that much greater acceleration, higher speeds and very smooth rides are possible. Maglev is faster than the Japanese 'Bullet Train' - the *Shinkansen* - and faster than the French and German high-speed trains, *TGV* and *ICE*, respectively. But the system does require a special track and carriages and, until the Shanghai development, had not been used on a large commercial scale anywhere else in the world. It was originally a British patent, but was developed commercially by a German company who persuaded the Chinese authorities to experiment with the new system in 2000.

Shanghai, People's Republic of China

With a population of around 18 million, Shanghai is one of China's great cities, both as a commercial port and as the major centre of commercial and financial activity in Eastern China. In order to provide room for substantial further growth, the city decided in the early 1990s to develop an area of muddy agricultural land east of the existing city. The *Pudong* area - with its massive skyscrapers, television tower, apartments and hotels - was then built over a 10-year period. Unquestionably, this development took considerable imagination on the part of the city's leading officials and its developers and it paid off in terms of the city's increased wealth, status and urban renewal.

Shanghai's existing airport was located south west of the city and could not cope with the resulting increased demand for both internal and international air travel. It was therefore decided to build a completely new airport on the other side of the city, beyond Pudong, and 30 km (19 miles) from the city centre. The new airport would be connected to the city with a new rapid transit system. Maglev was chosen and built at a cost of $1.2 billion in the relatively short time of two and a half years for a complex project. In addition to the Maglev, the authorities also built motorways to allow taxis and buses to carry passengers and visitors to the airport. A single journey to the airport by taxi costs around $10–15 and takes at least 1 hour, depending on the time of day - Shanghai's tunnels and flyovers under and over the river system can be very crowded at peak periods.

Maglev trains run on specially built overhead double tracks. They run every 20 minutes between 08.30 and 17.30 and can carry 440 people in modern comfortable carriages. The journey takes around 8 minutes to cover a distance of 30 kilometres at speeds up to 430 km/hour (270 miles/hour). Unfortunately, for planning reasons, the track does not end in the centre of Shanghai but finishes several kilometres outside.

Shanghai's Maglev train was not chosen in 2010 for China's new high-speed rail services, which are now the largest in the world.

It stops next to one of Shanghai's busy subway stations, Longyang Road. Passengers therefore have to leave the Maglev and carry their bags and cases down into the subway before buying a ticket for the rest of the short journey into the centre of town.

Maglev prices and financial situation

For the first experimental year 2003, the Maglev tickets were priced at 75 yuan (about $9) for a single journey. The final subway ride was a small, additional cost for those wishing to continue into the city centre. Unfortunately, the trains were running with an average of only 73 passengers per trip for the first year, so it was decided to reduce the fare to 50 yuan in Spring 2004. Even with this reduction, the Maglev was still only carrying around 8,000 passengers per day during 2004. This brought revenues of around 130 million yuan annually – 'less than half the yearly bank loan interest at over 300 million yuan'. Essentially, this meant that the Maglev was not covering its cost of capital and needed to be subsidised by the city's transport authority.

What of the future?

With the Summer Olympic Games coming to Beijing in 2008, the authorities were exploring upgrading the existing rail track between Beijing and Shanghai. Initially, it was thought that the Maglev system might be used because it would shorten the 14-hour journey time dramatically. But other systems – including the Shinkansen, the TGV and ICE – were also under consideration. After much debate, it was decided that the Maglev would be too expensive: the technology was still only proven over relatively short distances and the capital costs were high at $30 billion. However, In spite of this decision, it was then proposed to extend the Maglev to the new Shanghai World Exhibition site and onwards to Shanghai's second airport south west of the city. After protests from residents worried about harmful magnetic rays and after considering the costs and feasibility, all further extensions were cancelled.

The Maglev train still has some experimental interest but China's high-speed rail development has now moved along a totally different path. High-speed rail has become a major investment area in China using designs based on the Japanese Shinkansen and the European ICE trains and acquired as result of technology transfer agreements with foreign suppliers. By 2012, China had the largest high-speed rail network in the world and was even bidding for overseas export contracts. At the same time, the Maglev had become essentially a technical footnote in the history of Chinese high-speed rail.

 This case was written from published information only.[1] The author is grateful to Edward Zhang of Pearson Education Shanghai for introducing him to the Maglev, but all conclusions and comments remain solely those of the author.

Case questions

1 Maglev was an innovative new transport system: what are the risks and rewards of undertaking such an innovation?

2 Can other companies learn anything from the city of Shanghai's decision to experiment with the Maglev transport system or is the situation unique?

7.1 UNDERSTANDING AND MEASURING KNOWLEDGE

Video Part 7a

Over time, city authorities like those in Shanghai can develop considerable knowledge about new technologies, customers and their preferences: that is why they invest in experimental systems like the Maglev. In the same way, commercial companies can develop knowledge about existing and new technologies, customers, suppliers and other aspects of the various manufacturing processes that are important to the company's purpose. In this sense, knowledge is a *resource* of the organisation and deserves to be analysed along with other resources in Part 2 – see Chapter 4. However, knowledge can also be explored from another perspective – that of *creating future knowledge* – and it is this approach that opens up new opportunities. It is this second perspective that we will concentrate on in this chapter. Plainly, such a viewpoint could have a considerable impact on the future purpose of the organisation.[2]

In order to clarify knowledge creation, it is helpful to begin by exploring the nature of the knowledge of an organisation and by assessing its existing knowledge resources. Having explored these two areas, we can then move on to consider the issue of knowledge development, which is essentially an *emergent* process. Finally, we can relate knowledge development to the purpose of the organisation and explore the implications of this approach.

7.1.1 Knowledge: its strategic origins and definition

For many years in strategy development, the topic of knowledge never received any substantive or explicit attention.[3] Some early writers on strategy recognised its importance, but only Drucker made any significant attempt to explore its significance. He wrote in 1964:

> Knowledge is the business fully as much as the customer is the business. Physical goods or services are only the vehicle for the exchange of customer purchasing - power against business knowledge.[4]

However, beyond pointing out that each business is likely to have areas of distinctive knowledge, Drucker offered no clear definition of the topic. Even in the new millennium, there is no widely agreed definition of the main aspects of knowledge from a strategic perspective. But if we are to use knowledge in strategy development then we need to be able to recognise it, so some form of definition is important. For our purposes, we will adopt the definition of knowledge proposed by Davenport and Prusack:[5]

Definition ▸

> Knowledge is a fluid mix of framed experience, values, contextual information and expert insight that provides a framework for evaluating and incorporating new experiences and information. It originates and is applied in the minds of knowers. In organisations, it often becomes embedded not only in documents or repositories but also in organisational routines, processes, practices and norms.[6]

The keys to this lengthy but helpful definition lie in such words as 'fluid mix . . . embedded . . . practices'. The most useful knowledge in many organisations is often the most difficult to understand, codify and replicate. Just as it is difficult to pin down a simple definition of knowledge, it is also problematic to identify the knowledge of an organisation. To explore this point, we will use the example of the Nike Sports company, which is described in Case 7.2 later in this chapter. Importantly, the above definition also tells us what knowledge is not:

- Knowledge is not just *data* – a set of discrete, observable facts about events, e.g. the market share data on Nike quoted in the case. The weakness of such data is that it only describes a small part of what happened at Nike and gives little idea of what made the company so successful.
- Knowledge is not just *information* – the information message, often in a document or some other form of communication, certainly has meaning, but it has little depth. And knowledge requires depth from a strategy perspective. For example, it is useful to know that Nike's positioning was summarised in the phrase 'just do it'. But the meaningful part is to understand *why* such wording was chosen and *how* it was developed – essentially a knowledge-based process.

More generally, Nike's experience of dealing with its customers and suppliers cannot be usefully summarised in statistical data and information, although this might form part of a broader whole. Nike's knowledge will have two main parts:

1. a range of manufacturing contracts, procedures and practices built up over time – the 'routines and processes' part of its knowledge;
2. a whole series of working experiences, personal friendships and other activities also developed over time that are much more difficult to summarise – the 'framed experiences, values' part of the definition above.

Because it is difficult to define knowledge, most organisations have taken a broad view on what should be included. This has the disadvantage of possible information overload but avoids pre-judging what will be important for individuals in developing new areas of purpose.

Whatever view is taken of knowledge, the information age will certainly mean that it will be central to strategic management. Knowledge will go well beyond basic market share, financial data and management accounting information and involve people and unquantifiable assets. To paraphrase Gary Hamel,[7] Madonna may have been the material girl but what sets her apart are her immaterial assets – her knowledge-based copyrights, recording deals, television and film contracts and so on. In addition, her reputation, her life and her relationship with her audience will also represent important assets. Many of these items are less easy to measure, but represent the real wealth and knowledge at the centre of the global information environment. These knowledge-based assets are Madonna's sustainable competitive advantage.

7.1.2 Knowledge: the distinction between tacit and explicit knowledge

With hindsight, some knowledge assets are clear enough. But the company itself may be unclear on what knowledge is needed for future product developments. Moreover, some knowledge – called *explicit knowledge* – may be clearer than other, rather more vague but equally valuable, knowledge – called *tacit knowledge*.

Definition ▶ **Explicit knowledge concerns knowledge that is codified and transmittable in formal, systematic language - often, but not necessarily, written down. Tacit knowledge is personal, context specific and much harder to formalise and communicate - often, but not necessarily, hidden and not formally recorded.**

This useful distinction between two types of knowledge was first employed by Nonaka and Takeuchi to explore knowledge strategy.[8] They researched the experiences of the Japanese domestic appliance company Matsushita Electric in 1985. The company was attempting to develop a new home bread-baking machine. For months, dough was analysed and X-rayed and prototype machines were built. But none produced a decent loaf. They were all under-cooked, burnt, unevenly cooked or simply dried out. Finally, a software developer, Ikuko Tanaka, proposed a practical solution: find the best bread maker in the local town and watch how bread was made. She discovered that it was made in a distinctive way, involving stretching and kneading the dough. After a year of study and experimentation, Matsushita was able to launch its bread-making machine, which made good bread and achieved high sales. Nonaka and Takeuchi drew two specific conclusions on the nature of knowledge from this and other studies:[9]

1 Some knowledge is difficult to specify. It is fuzzy, often complex and unrecorded; they called this *tacit* knowledge.

2 After such knowledge has been carefully analysed, it is often possible to define it more precisely; they called this *explicit* knowledge.

All organisations have tacit and explicit knowledge. It is the tacit knowledge that often delivers the sustainable competitive advantage because it is this part that competitors have trouble in replicating. For example, the managing director of one of Toyota's car manufacturing plants in the USA never had any doubts about inviting competitors to tour his plant. He knew that they would never discover the real secrets of the Toyota Production System (TPS) – which gave the company one of its major competitive advantages – because much of the TPS knowledge was tacit and impossible to observe on one factory visit.

However, explicit knowledge may also provide sustainable competitive advantage – for example, a company's patents will be recorded for other companies to examine, but remain exclusively owned by the originating company. Although both types may contribute to the sustainable competitive advantage of the organisation, tacit knowledge may be particularly important because it is less easy for competitors to comprehend and therefore copy. Exhibit 7.1 shows examples of tacit and explicit knowledge in a company.

EXHIBIT 7.1

Examples of tacit and explicit knowledge in a company

Tacit knowledge	Explicit knowledge
• Practical and unwritten procedures for unblocking production stoppages • Informal networks and procedures for sales order processing • Multifunctional team working on new projects that rely on informal contacts • Experience of what has worked in practice in branding development over a number of years • Specific company treatments of some detailed aspects of management accounting	• Costing procedures codified in company accounting manuals • New product development through formal company review procedures • Company patents and legal contracts • A company's written history of its past events and experiences, successes and failures - often very limited • Training schemes and apprenticeship programmes that develop and teach best practice

Importantly, the description of the interrelationship between tacit and explicit knowledge shows that one can lead to the other. Taking the bread-making example above for example, Matsushita was able to write down the tacit knowledge of the bread maker and thus turn it into explicit knowledge in order to build a bread-making machine. Thus a mechanism is provided for emergent strategy development.

7.1.3 Knowledge audit and management

If knowledge creation is important for purpose, the question arises as to whether it is possible to draw up an inventory of existing knowledge and renewal capacity as a starting point for future development. In the phrase of the Swedish insurance company Skandia, can we assess the *intellectual capital* of an organisation? It is this company that has provided a lead in this area. In the early 1990s, it argued that many of the accounting laws and rules developed after the Second World War were outmoded because they did not measure a company's intellectual assets, only its physical assets such as land, plant and raw materials. Skandia defined the intellectual capital of its operations as its:

> future earnings capacity from a deeper, broader and more human perspective than that described in [its financial reports]. It comprises employees as well as customers, business relations, organisational structures and the power of renewal in organisations. Visualising and interpreting these contexts can provide better insight into future development at an earlier stage.[10]

The company then divided the basic concept of intellectual capital into a number of components, each of which contributes to the creation of market value. It pointed out that in traditional economics only one of these aspects is measured – the financial capital – but, in reality, there are many other contributors to a company's future profits summarised in its intellectual capital. These elements are shown in Exhibit 7.2.

Intellectual capital has two main components: *human capital*, which is similar to the tacit knowledge outlined in the previous section, and *structural capital*, which is similar to the explicit knowledge also covered. Structural capital can then be divided into two further elements related to the *customer capital* and the *organisational capital* of a company. The organisational capital includes information systems, databases, information technology solutions and other related knowledge areas. The company has then developed a method of exploring the implications of this knowledge valuation exercise that lays particular emphasis on the future value of knowledge.

Over the past few years, similar approaches to knowledge assessment and its transferral around the organisation have been adopted in varying ways by many other organisations.[11] Rather than concentrating on the calculation of the total sum of knowledge in an organisation – the intellectual capital approach – such efforts have focused on the gathering and sharing of knowledge around an organisation – the *knowledge management* approach. But they cover similar areas.

EXHIBIT 7.2

Skandia value scheme

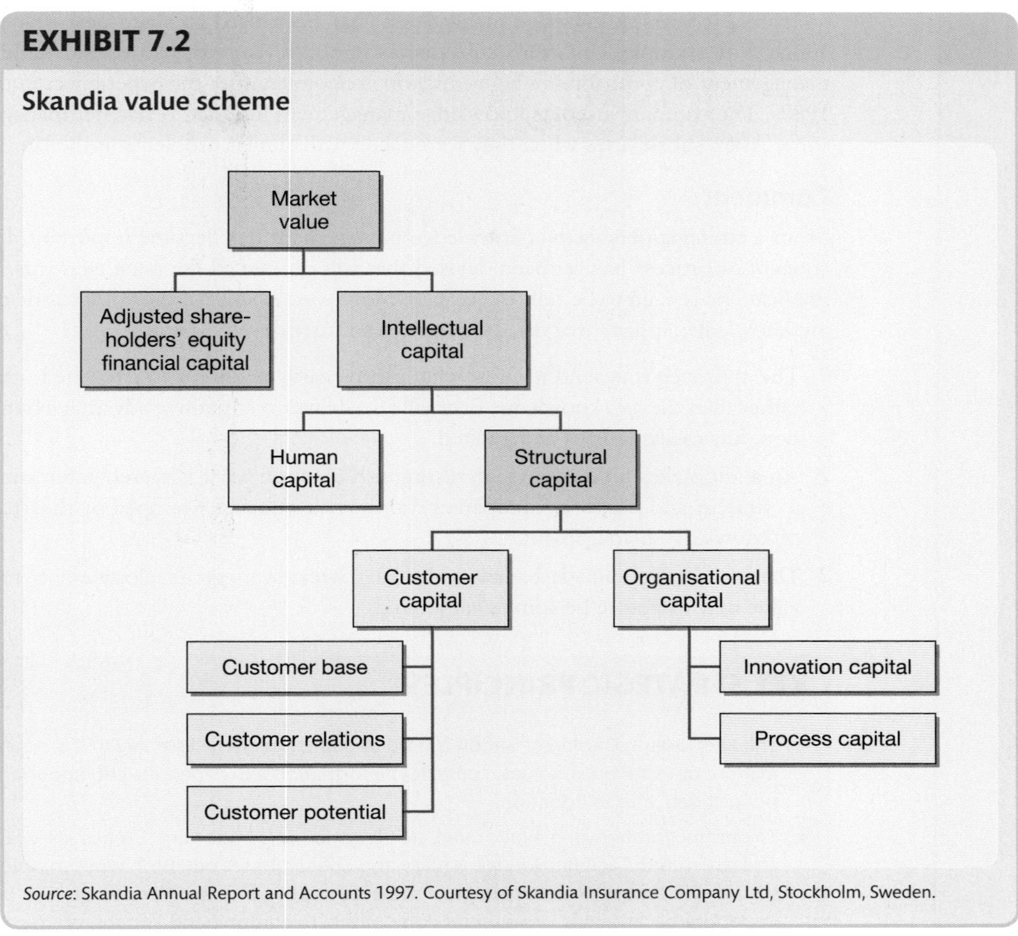

Source: Skandia Annual Report and Accounts 1997. Courtesy of Skandia Insurance Company Ltd, Stockholm, Sweden.

Particularly in service and consultancy organisations, knowledge management has come to be regarded as the prime source of competitive advantage. Hence, the collection and dissemination of knowledge around the organisation has become a top strategic priority. Assessments have been made of the factors that are most likely to contribute to the success of knowledge management.[12] These are shown in Exhibit 7.3. The first point is particularly important because, for some groups in an organisation, 'knowledge is power'.[13] These groups may not be willing to share such knowledge and may regard knowledge networks as a threat. Care therefore needs to be taken when introducing such new initiatives.

EXHIBIT 7.3

Factors contributing to success in knowledge management

- Building a knowledge-sharing community inside the organisation, both in technical terms and in terms of a willingness to share knowledge
- Contribution of knowledge to economic performance and value, e.g. profits and cost savings
- Technical and organisational infrastructures, which need to be wide-ranging to succeed
- The need to gather both the tacit knowledge, which is difficult to record, and the explicit knowledge, which is easier to record and circulate
- Clarity on the background history of how the knowledge was derived, its context in relation to other areas and the learning that has resulted
- Recognition that many channels are needed for knowledge gathering and transfer
- Senior management support and encouragement

In recent years, knowledge management has been used to share best practice across organisations. For example, Unilever's subsidiaries in South America had considerable knowledge of the management of companies in high-inflation economies, after the experiences in the continent in the 1980s. The company used its knowledge management intranet to transfer management practices to some Asian subsidiaries when they were faced with similar problems in the late 1990s.

Comment

From a strategic perspective, knowledge management has become important. However, no single concept or process has yet been devised that will capture all the main elements.[14] The audit and its implications remain to be fully developed. Moreover, in spite of the enthusiastic reception for auditing knowledge, it has three disadvantages in strategy development:

1 The approach may lend itself to what can be easily audited and circulated – *explicit* knowledge – rather than the *tacit* knowledge that will also deliver competitive advantage but remains, by definition, less easily defined and audited.
2 An audit makes little attempt to distinguish between what is merely interesting and what is vital to strategy and purpose. Companies run the risk of being swamped by the irrelevant in the name of knowledge management.
3 The knowledge audit is backward-looking while strategy development is forward-looking. Its value may therefore be somewhat limited.

KEY STRATEGIC PRINCIPLES

- The knowledge of an organisation is hard to define precisely. Essentially, it is a constantly changing mixture of experience, values, contextual information and expert insight. Importantly, knowledge is not just data and information.
- The distinction between explicit and tacit knowledge is important. Explicit knowledge is recorded and structured. Tacit knowledge is fuzzy and difficult to set out. Both types may contribute to the sustainable competitive advantage of the organisation, but tacit knowledge may be particularly important because it is less easy for competitors to comprehend and therefore copy.
- An organisation's knowledge can be audited, but the process is easier with explicit than tacit knowledge. The audit might form the basis of strategy development but suffers from several disadvantages.

CASE STUDY 7.2

Developing new knowledge at Nike

When Phil Knight founded Nike with $500 in 1964, he could hardly have seen his purpose as building the biggest sports company in the world. Yet this is what Nike had become by 2014. This case examines the foundations of the company's growth, especially the knowledge developed and retained within the company over the years.

The early knowledge years: the 1960s

Back in 1958, Phil Knight was a middle-distance runner in the University of Oregon's track team, where his coach was Bill Bowerman, who later trained the US Olympic team. It was Bowerman who considered the existing running shoes were too heavy and designed and made his own lighter version. After graduating from Oregon, Knight studied for an MBA at Stanford University, where he was inspired by Bowerman to write a thesis on trainer manufacture. Knight then went on a world tour that included a visit to Japan, where he found the leading shoe brand called Tiger. He decided that this was a superior product and set up an importing company to bring Tiger running shoes to the USA while still continuing to work as an accountant. Then in 1964, he and Bowerman each put up $500 to found the Nike shoe company, named after the Greek goddess of victory. Its first 'office' was the laundry room at Knight's family home.

To start the company, Knight used his athletics contacts to sell Tiger running shoes from a station wagon at track and field events. He bought the shoes from Japan, but both he and Bowerman always felt that there was potential for a US-designed shoe. This led Bowerman to invent the 'waffle' trainer. In the early 1970s, demand for Nike shoes was sufficient for the company to consider developing its own shoe manufacture. However, he was concerned to use Japanese experience of shoe production. In 1972, he placed his first contract in Japan to begin shoe manufacture to a Nike all-American design.

Developing new knowledge: the 1970s

Over the next few years, the yen moved up against the dollar and Japanese labour costs continued to rise. This made Japanese shoe production more expensive. In addition, Nike itself was gaining more experience of international manufacture and making more contacts with overseas shoe manufacturers. In order to cut production costs, Nike switched its operations in 1975 from Japan to two newly industrialised nations, Korea and Taiwan, whose wage costs were exceptionally low at that time. In this context, the company had to learn how to handle overseas production, how to brief manufacturers on new designs and models, and how to set and maintain quality standards.

The decade of difficulty and renewal: the 1980s

By the early 1980s, Nike was profitable and continuing to develop its role as a specialist US sports shoe manufacturer with no production facilities in its home country. It became the leading brand of sports trainers in the USA. Then along came competition in the form of a new sports shoe manufacturer, *Reebok*. From a start-up company in 1981, Reebok went into battle against Nike under its founder and chief executive, Paul Fireman. Reebok launched a strong and well-designed range of sports shoes with great success.

To hit back against Reebok, Nike then began to invest considerable sums on developing new and innovative sports shoe designs. The most successful of these was begun in the late 1980s, the Nike Air shoe. 'It was an intuitively simple technology to understand,' said John Horan, publisher of *Sports Goods Intelligence*, a US industry newsletter. 'It's obvious to consumers that if you put an airbag under the foot, it will cushion it.' But it was not until 1990 that the Nike Air shoe was launched and began to deliver success for Nike. Thus the 1980s were both the decade of difficulty and the time for renewal. Nike had learned about the heat of competition and the need for innovation and continual R&D in its shoe designs.

The new heights of the 1990s – sponsorship and brand building

Coupling the new Nike Air shoe with advertising featuring Michael Jordan was a touch of marketing inspiration. The US basketball star, top of his chosen sport, was signed up to promote the new product in a multimillion-dollar deal that added a new dimension to sports sponsorship. Over the next few years, this was enhanced by the heavy funds Nike was prepared to invest. For example, in 1995 Nike invested almost $1 billion in sports marketing, compared with Reebok's spending at around $400 million.

In addition, Nike began sports sponsorship deals. These included the golf star Tiger Woods and, for a previously unheard-of sum, the whole Brazilian football team. By signing a 10-year deal in 1996 worth between $200 million and $400 million, Nike broke new ground in football sponsorship. Importantly, this moved the company into totally new areas of sports goods. The sponsorship gave Nike credibility in a new market area along with knowledge of that area. For example, the technology of a football boot is not the same as that of an athletic running shoe.

But it was not just the Nike sports sponsorship that was important. The brand and the message were also important. During the 1980s and 1990s, the company had come to understand its target market well – young, cool and competitive teenagers. The 'swoosh' logo was highlighted on all its goods to help brand the product and the main message, 'just do it', was developed to express the individuality of the target group. The accompanying slogan of 'winning your own way'

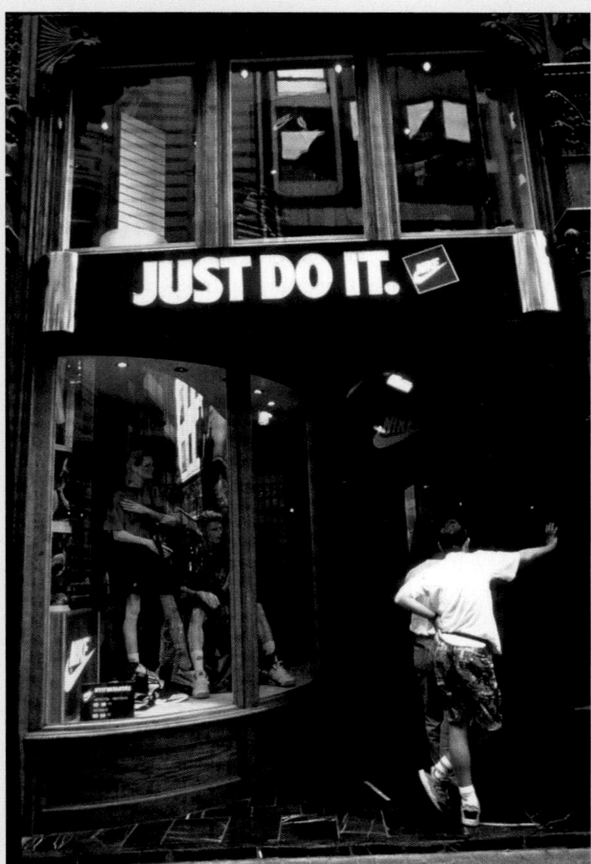

Nike's leadership of the world's sports goods markets developed from modest beginnings – selling sports shoes from the back of a pickup truck in North America.

captured the aggression, competition and individual success epitomised by the sports stars who were signed up. However, Nike was criticised for its use of cheap labour in some countries and was forced to take steps to deal with this. The company's approach to this matter still rankles with some members of the target group to this day.

Sports clothing, equipment and total fitness: the 2000s

Over the next 10 years, Nike continued to develop rapidly in two further, related activities. It used its involvement in new sports areas to develop into sports clothing using the Nike brand and into sports equipment, in some cases by company acquisition. At the same time, it began rapid international expansion, for example using its sponsorship in Brazil to expand in Latin America and its sponsorship of Arsenal Football Club to expand its position in Europe. It was using its resource-based competitive advantages to build into related markets. By the year 2010, Nike was the biggest sports and fitness company in the world, with a truly global spread of sales - see Figure 7.2.

In the late 1990s, the Asian economic downturn hit the company hard. There was also heavy over-stocking of its products in the US retail trade that hit the company in 2000. Trading profits soon recovered to record levels in 2004. In the same year, Phil Knight became the chairman and Tom Clarke took over as chief executive. Clarke was quite clear:

> You grow a lot, then you need a period when things aren't booming to ask what works and what doesn't. . . . Remember, we're a fairly self-critical bunch. We're running the company for the long term, not to keep people happy for the next couple of quarters.

The company continued to grow after Knight's retirement. Like many companies, its profits did not always hold up over the years. For example, there was a company rationalisation in 2009 that impacted on profits although the company was still the largest sports company in the world with continuing profitable growth - see Figure 7.3.

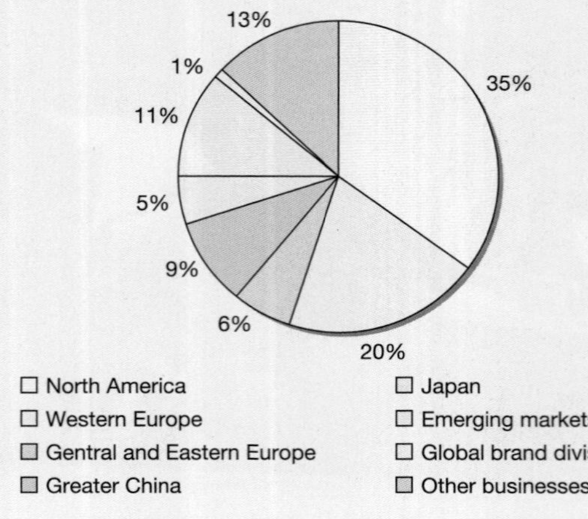

Figure 7.2 Nike's global sales 2010 ($ millions)

Source: Nike Annual Report 2010 from the web.

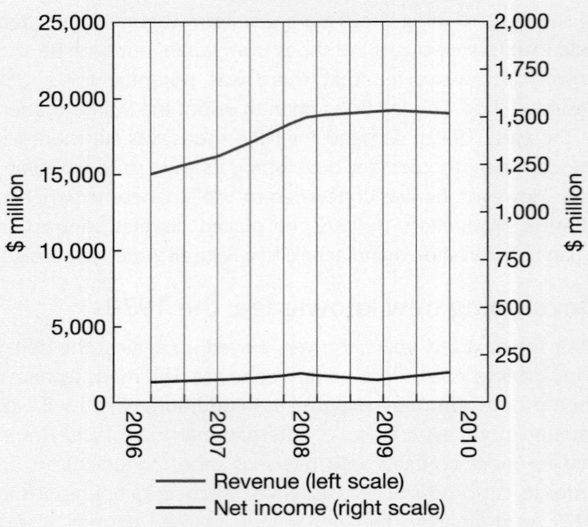

Figure 7.3 Nike growth slows but it's still the world leader

Source: Nike Annual Report and Accounts 2010.

It was in early 2005 that Phil Knight announced that his retirement from Nike. It was just over 40 years since he and his friend Bill Bowerman had started selling trainers from the back of a station wagon in 1964. He had built a global company. The purpose of Nike had therefore changed over time, sometimes through prescriptive strategies and sometimes through experimental, emergent strategies. But fundamentally Nike grew as a result of building competitive resources like sports branding, taking risks and employing and sharing knowledge across the company.

Nike has substantive policies on green strategy. These can be viewed at: http://www.nikebiz.com/responsibility.

Case questions

1 What knowledge has Nike acquired over the years? Use the definitions of knowledge contained in this chapter to help you move beyond the obvious.

2 What other resources beyond knowledge does the company possess that offer clear sustainable competitive advantage?

3 From a consideration of this case, what conclusions can you draw on the emergent purpose of Nike in relation to its knowledge?

7.2 KNOWLEDGE CREATION AND PURPOSE

Having considered existing knowledge in the last section, we can now move on to consider the development of new knowledge. Knowledge creation can be considered as the development and circulation of new knowledge within the organisation. Although the knowledge audit helps to define the starting point, its role is essentially static. Knowledge creation arguably requires a more dynamic approach and offers a new strategic opportunity. The full mechanisms for knowledge creation remain to be resolved, but some key elements can be distinguished:

- conversion and communication of existing knowledge;
- knowledge creation and acquisition processes;
- knowledge transfer processes.

7.2.1 Conversion and communication of existing knowledge

The creation of new knowledge in an organisation can usefully start from an exploration of the existing knowledge base of the organisation, especially how this is converted and communicated within the organisation. One useful method is to structure this using Takeuchi and Nonaka's Model of Knowledge Conversion – see Figure 7.4. This concept starts from the assumption that there are two main types of knowledge in any organisation – tacit and explicit – as explored in the previous section. If this is the case, then it follows that there are only four ways that these two types can be communicated and shared within the existing knowledge base:

1 *From tacit knowledge to tacit knowledge: socialisation.* One way that companies can share unwritten knowledge across the firm is to socialise, sharing unwritten experiences and information, perhaps in informal meetings or working together. For example, the Nike company will have informal contacts between their sponsored sports stars and the Nike marketing and advertising agencies that can be used to develop specific sponsorship timing opportunities, work on topical campaigns, etc. None of this is necessarily written down but may be helpful in increasing Nike brand awareness and loyalty.

2 *From tacit knowledge to explicit knowledge: externalisation.* Companies can also exchange unrecorded knowledge and other vague concepts by making them more formal. This may mean conceptualising

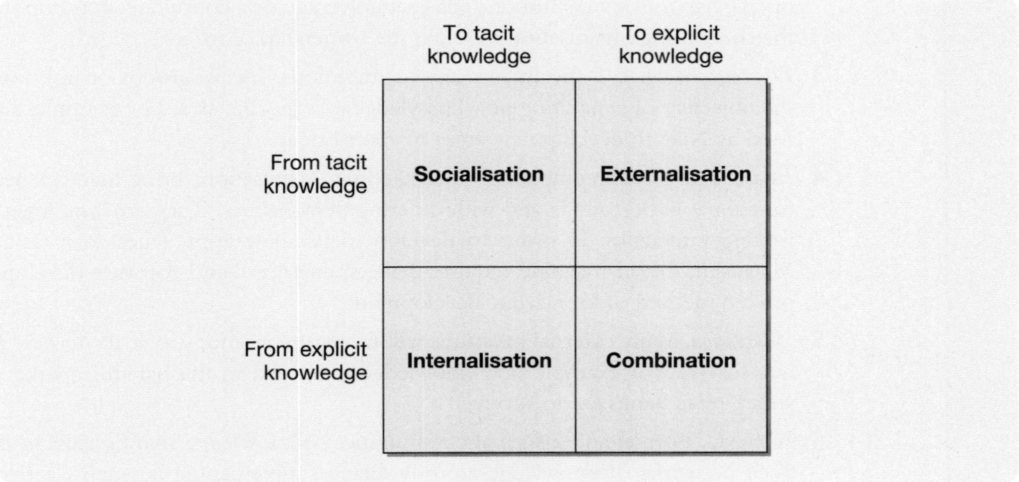

Figure 7.4 Four modes of knowledge conversion

Source: 'Fig. 3.2: Four modes of knowledge conversion', from *the Knowledge-Creating Company: How Japanese Companies Create Their Dynamics of Innovation* by I Nonaka and H Takeuchi, copyright © 1995 by Oxford University Press, Inc. Used by permission of Oxford University Press, Inc.

and modelling vague ideas – perhaps again in meetings, but this time attempting to record and structure what was previously hidden. For example at Nike, this approach might involve a new unwritten idea for a training shoe, which is then turned into an experimental model or drawing for market research.

3 *From explicit knowledge to explicit knowledge: combination.* Companies can also take previously recorded explicit knowledge and share this more widely within a company – perhaps using an intranet system or some other company-wide means of communication. For example at Nike, the company could use its web-based communications to distribute Nike customer data between different parts of the world.

4 *From explicit knowledge to tacit knowledge: internalisation.* Companies can also take written and recorded information and use this as a starting point for further shared experiences which are not necessarily written down. For example at Nike, this could involve taking a general training manual on in-store merchandising at a Nike shop and using this to examine what informal lessons need to be applied in an individual Nike retail store.

Comment

While the above four areas are helpful, they do rely on a rather simplistic assumption about the tacit/explicit nature of existing knowledge in an organisation. There will be many variations in the range and type of information and knowledge. Yet they need to be forced into only one of the four boxes of the matrix. Such knowledge may benefit from a broader view of their usage. However, the underpinning concepts of sharing, conceptualising and communicating both unwritten and recorded knowledge more widely are useful when it comes to knowledge creation.

7.2.2 Knowledge creation and acquisition processes

Beyond exploring and sharing the knowledge already in the organisation, there are also processes for creating new knowledge. Davenport and Prusak recommend six mechanisms that will assist in knowledge creation.[16] They are:

1 *Acquisition.* New knowledge does not necessarily come from inside the organisation. British Petroleum is reported by Davenport and Prusak to award a 'Thief of the Year' award to the employee who has 'stolen' the best ideas in applications development from other companies.

2 *Rental.* Knowledge can also be rented or leased in the sense that it can be sponsored and developed by an outside institution such as a university or a consultant. It is important in this case for the sponsoring organisation to retain the ownership of its use.

3 *Dedicated resources.* Typically in many organisations, special groups or task forces are set up with the objective of generating new knowledge in a specific area. For example, a task force might be used by Nike to develop new areas of sponsorship.

4 *Fusion.* For certain complex problems, some organisations bring together people from different functional backgrounds and with differing personalities. They are *fused* together in the sense of forcing interaction in order to develop totally new approaches to a task. For example, the Matsushita bread machine required bakers, engineers and software developers. This is a well-proven method of knowledge development.[17]

5 *Adaptation.* Many external pressures will force organisations to adapt to new realities or they will not survive: for example new knowledge is needed in the banking market if traditional, high street, retail banks are to survive.

6 *Networks.* Formal and informal communities of knowledge sharing exist in many organisations. Such networks of knowledge are now being supplemented by such electronic mechanisms as the intranet, a formal computer network inside an organisation for the exchange of knowledge. For example, Heineken set up a new company-wide intranet site in 1998 under the heading 'Knowledge is Power'.[18]

7.2.3 Knowledge transfer processes

New knowledge is unlikely to deliver its full potential if it remains with the originators in an organisation – it needs to be transferred to others. Knowledge transfer is related to the areas explored in the first section above on knowledge conversion and communication, but the process is taken further by the *proactive decision* to share knowledge.

Knowledge transfer is not a simple task because such a process involves people and groups. People may not understand each other, may feel threatened by new developments and may be unwilling to tolerate the mistakes or ambiguity that will surely occur during the process of transferral. In addition, groups of people may judge themselves to be the main owners of certain types of knowledge and also judge that their status will be lowered if such knowledge is shared.[19] These matters need to be addressed if the knowledge transfer process is to be successful. They may involve changes in the culture of the organisation, which cannot be achieved quickly.

Beyond these difficulties, there are some mechanisms that will assist in the transfer of knowledge. The 3M company is a well-known and successful exponent of them. The reader is therefore referred to the description of these mechanisms in Case 7.4.

7.2.4 Conclusion – knowledge creation and purpose

If new knowledge is significant in its impact, then it may well change the purpose of the organisation, perhaps providing the opportunity for global market leadership, as happened at Nike, perhaps threatening the survival of a business, as occurred when mechanical typewriter companies were replaced by the personal computers in many parts of the world.

The important point here is that the purpose of the business will only be changed *after* the new knowledge has been developed and made explicit. In this sense, a new definition of purpose *emerges* from the new acquisition of knowledge and cannot be easily defined in advance. This has not stopped companies attempting to define purpose in advance of a specific breakthrough in their knowledge: Hewlett-Packard (USA), 3M (USA) and GlaxoSmithKline (UK) are examples. But the attempt is usually made to focus minds and energy inside the company, rather than anything more explicit. It follows that the success rate is mixed – just look at the poor growth in the 3M case study later in this chapter for the years 2000–2002 from a company that had consistently set innovative growth targets and then struggled to meet them.

Within this caution about the emergent nature of purpose, it is possible to be more explicit about the way that knowledge management will contribute to the purpose of the organisation. This book has argued that, fundamentally, the purpose of an organisation is to *add value* and that this is assisted by the development of *sustainable competitive advantage*. It is therefore appropriate to explore how knowledge contributes to these two areas. Knowledge is essentially a resource of the organisation, so these two issues can be explored by considering the *resource-based view* of the organisation, outlined in Chapter 4. Teece has argued that knowledge can contribute to competitive advantage through two related mechanisms:[20]

1 *Replicabililty*. As outlined above, knowledge is often only useful when it is transferred and replicated in other parts of an organisation. This is particularly difficult where tacit knowledge is the main asset. Even where knowledge is explicit, organisations may have difficulty in replicating it where such knowledge is complex, relies on local cultures and faces other impediments.

2 *Imitability*. This simply means the ability of competitors to replicate the knowledge of the first organisation. If replication is difficult for the original owner, then it will surely be more difficult for competitors. However, when knowledge becomes explicit and published, then it is more likely to be imitated. This is particularly possible where an organisation has failed to defend its knowledge through the acquisition of intellectual property rights, such as patenting.

Finally, knowledge adds value through a circular mechanism that will impact on purpose at various stages of development. This is best seen in Dorothy Leonard-Barton's model of the creation and diffusion of knowledge – see Figure 7.5. This makes a clear distinction between the current and future tasks of an organisation: *in the present*, the organisation can problem-solve, whereas *in the future*

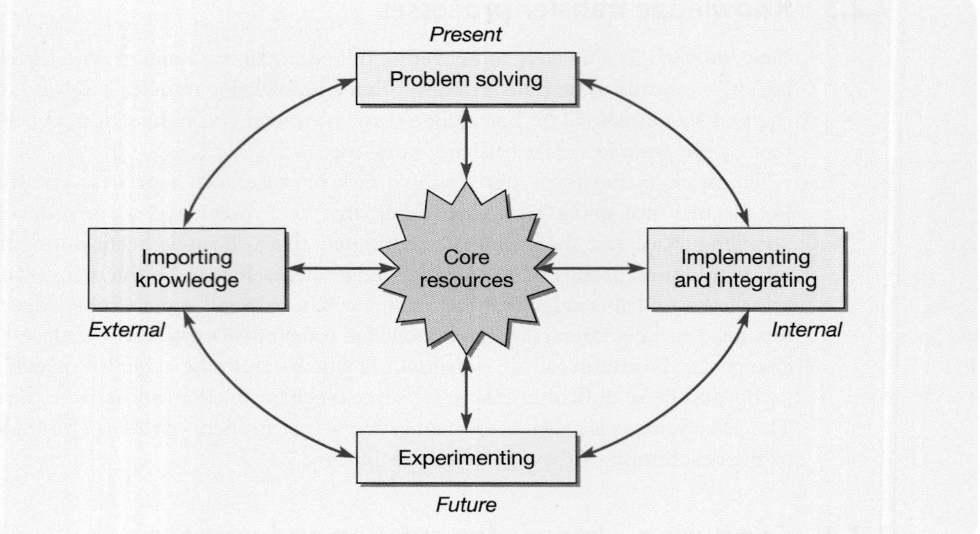

Figure 7.5 Creation and diffusion of knowledge

Note: 'Core resources' refers to those resources that are particularly likely to possess sustainable competitive advantage.

Source: reprinted by permission of Harvard Business School Press. From *Wellsprings of Knowledge*, by D Leonard, Boston, MA 1995, Fig. 1.2, p 9. Copyright © 1995 by the Harvard Business School Publishing Corporation; all rights reserved.

it can experiment without being clear about the outcome. The model also separates two mechanisms for the acquisition of knowledge: *internally* through discussion, implementation and integrating mechanisms, and *externally* through the knowledge acquisition.

KEY STRATEGIC PRINCIPLES

- Conversion and communication of existing knowledge can take place through four mechanisms: socialisation, externalisation, combination and internalisation. All four processes relate to the basic distinction between tacit and explicit knowledge existing in any organisation.
- Knowledge creation – the development and circulation of new knowledge – offers a dynamic strategic opportunity. There are three mechanisms: organisational learning, knowledge creation and acquisition, and knowledge transfer.
- If new knowledge is significant in its impact on the organisation, then it may well change the purpose of the organisation. Importantly, the purpose will only change after new knowledge has been developed. In this sense, the purpose of the organisation emerges from knowledge creation.

CASE STUDY 7.3

Egyptian innovation: the growing charm of Egypt's Sharm

Forty years ago, Egypt's Sharm el-Sheikh was just a small fishing port next to a very large desert. Today, 5 million visitors every year enjoy the sun, the sea and provide work and income for many local people. How did it happen? What was the strategy?

Background: building the business

Sharm el-Sheikh lies at the southern tip of Egypt's Sinai Desert. It has become a major tourist destination in the Middle East with a large, modern airport, a wide range of hotels and tourist attractions, especially those associated with water sports and scuba diving. But it did not happen overnight.

When the Israelis took over the Sinai Desert after the 1967 war, they had the imagination to see that Sharm could be more than just a fishing village: it had tourist potential. They built the first small hotels, a seafront promenade and a marina. But it was only after the whole Sinai peninsula was handed back to the Egyptian nation in 1982 that Sharm el-Sheikh began to expand. It was not easy for developing nations like Egypt to undertake such a task. There was little infrastructure for large-scale tourism and few people trained in all the services required to operate modern hotels and resorts such as cooks, cleaners, waiters and managers. Nevertheless, international companies were encouraged to invest in the area because of support from the Egyptian government and because they could see the potential demand in the area.

Changing demand for Egyptian tourism

For hundreds of years, tourists have come from around the world to see Egypt's historic sites: the pyramids, the temples and the Nile itself. Egypt actually has around one-third of all the world's ancient monuments still preserved. Tourism became one of the major contributors to the Egyptian economy. The strategic problem for the country was two-fold. First, many tourists visit foreign countries for the sun and sea rather than history: Egyptian antiquities simply did not meet this demand. Second, there was some evidence of flattening demand for ancient Egyptian history possibly because many other historic sites were becoming accessible around the world. The expansion of Sharm el-Sheikh as a leisure tourist destination was one answer to this changing and unmet demand.

Developing Sharm

From a strategy viewpoint, Sharm had the benefit from the start of its development of year-round sun, calm seas, good swimming and sandy beaches. But there were other resorts with similar attributes so that this was not a competitive advantage. However, Sharm was different because it also had coral reefs suitable for snorkelling and scuba diving. It was also largely undeveloped so it had clear space for new marinas and large hotels and an international airport. Hotel and resort companies like Marriott, Accor, Four Seasons and Le Meridien then invested in the area. The Egyptian government developed a major conference centre, road infrastructure and a new airport. A new marina and golf courses were also built. The scuba diving demand was supported by the construction of a full medical centre for diving related illnesses. At the same time, an area of 600 square kilometres was designated as a protected area of coral reefs, sand dunes and wildlife.

Over the next few years, there were setbacks. Sharm was hit by a series of terror attacks in 2005 aimed at the tourist industry with over 80 people being killed. However, the attack was never repeated as a result of greatly increased security in the area. In 2010, five people were attacked by a shark off the coast of Sharm with one fatality. In 2011, there was substantial political change in Egypt, though at the time of writing this case it appeared to have a limited impact on Sharm. More generally, the area was able to bounce back from its difficulties.

The government was so encouraged by its strategy that it was supporting developments further north in Sinai, in towns like Dahab and even in selected parts of the Sinai Desert itself. This was all part of the government's national tourist strategy to increase Egyptian visitor numbers from 12 million in 2008 to 30 million in 2020: an ambitious target by any standards. But travel innovation in Sharm el-Sheikh had shown the way: it had started with 20,000 annual visitors in the mid-1980s building up to 5 million in 2010.

Diving and water sports are major visitor attractions at Sharm el-Sheikh, Egypt. But this has required the resort to develop totally new tourist resources and infrastructure.

 This case was written by Richard Lynch from published information and from a personal visit to the area in 2010. He is grateful to Dr Samaa Attia of the British University of Egypt for comments on an earlier version of this case. For case references, see the endnote.[21]

Case questions

1 To what extent did the Egyptian government need to acquire new knowledge and new technology? How did it undertake this task?

2 Given the dramatic increase in visitors to Sharm el-Sheikh over 20 years, does this mean that it was an innovative development? What makes it innovative? And, if it was not innovative, why?

3 To what extent is government support needed in new developments like Sharm el-Sheikh? Are they essential or merely desirable? Should governments take the lead or merely respond to initiatives taken by private developers?

Case study: ***will traditional retail banks survive the threat of the new technologies the internet and telephone banking?*** After you have read the case, you might like to look at the answers to the case questions which are contained on a separate page on the website.

7.3 USING TECHNOLOGY TO DEVELOP PURPOSE AND COMPETITIVE ADVANTAGE

7.3.1 Technology and competitive advantage[22]

Given the pace of change over the past 20 years, technology has come to play an important role in the development of sustainable competitive advantage. Even in mature industries, not-for-profit organisations and small businesses, it is technology that has on occasions added the extra element to differentiate the organisation. For these reasons, technology strategy deserves careful investigation.

New technology developments are just as likely to alter the vision and purpose of the organisation as any other area. They can extend and enhance the existing position of the company. However, it should be noted that this will take time and resources – there may be no short-term impact on strategy. There are two main phases to this task:

- Phase 1 Survey of existing technologies
- Phase 2 Development of technology strategy.

Phase 1 Survey of existing technologies

This phase has four elements:

1 *An organisation-wide survey of existing technologies.* This should examine areas in detail rather than making broad generalisations, in order to ensure that no opportunities are missed. The result will be an audit of which technologies are used and where in the organisation they are used. The *audit* data are then classified into three areas:
   - *base technologies* that are common to many companies;
   - *core technologies* that are exclusive to the organisation itself, possibly delivering real competitive advantage;
   - *peripheral technologies* that are useful but not central to the organisation.

2 *An examination of related areas inside the organisation.* For example, patents and intellectual property may form the basis of important areas of competitive advantage. Some companies have special skills that have never been patented but come from years of experience and training; these may also present real advantages over competitors.

3 *A technology scan external to the organisation.* This will identify opportunities that are available for later consideration.

4 *A technology/product portfolio.* A matrix can be constructed relating products and technologies (see Figure 7.6).

Phase 2 Development of technology strategy

To develop technology strategy, it is important to take one technology at a time or risk muddle and confusion. It may also be important to develop both the technology and the *operations* (manufacturing) processes at the same time because the two areas are interrelated and because lead times need to be shortened.

The technology development initiative then needs to be analysed in two ways:

1 the technological developments of the organisation compared with those of competitors; and

2 the costs of further development compared with the time that this will take. (There is always a trade-off here.)

In addition to these two tasks, it is important to consider the possibilities of *acquiring* new technology – possibly through company acquisition, joint ventures or the purchase of a licence to use technology, probably from a company outside the home market.

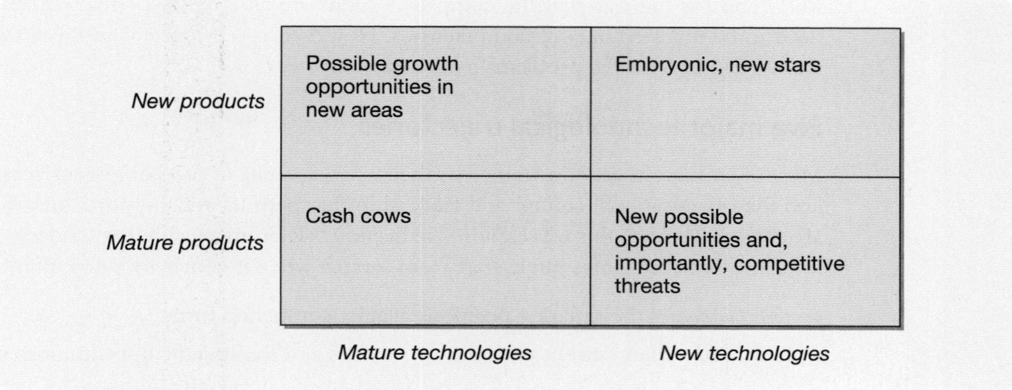

Figure 7.6 Technology/product portfolio mix

Two final issues then need to be considered:

1 *the speed of imitation.* It is important to estimate how quickly any technology development could be imitated by competitors;

2 *issues of globalisation.* It may be possible to exploit the new area on a worldwide scale and thus alter the attractiveness of the business proposition.

The above procedure may be too elaborate for some small companies and for not-for-profit organisations. However, small companies often gain their initial advantage from a technology edge. Larger companies may fail to consider the benefits of a clear drive on technology development, especially when they are operating in mature industries. The area has considerable potential strategic importance.

Technology developments are probably prescriptive in their overall approach in the sense that there needs to be a definite objective. However, they may be emergent in their detailed processes and by the nature of the experimental process.

7.3.2 Technology and innovation strategy

Given that companies and industrial sectors differ so much, it is extraordinarily difficult to develop a single framework that embraces all technology and all innovation strategy. For example, ethical drugs require *product innovation* through new patented drugs, whereas retailing services in recent years have relied largely on *process innovation* through new IT systems to improve such areas as stock delivery and stock control. In spite of such difficulties, there are two underpinning principles for technology and innovation strategy:

1 core competencies;

2 five major technological trajectories.

Core competencies

As identified by Prahalad and Hamel, core competencies focus on an individual company's competitive technological resources that deliver competitive advantage: 'The real sources of advantage are to be found in management's ability to consolidate corporate-wide technologies and production skills into competencies that empower individual businesses to adapt quickly to changing opportunities.'[23] Core competencies need to be identified and harnessed in the development of technology strategy. They go deeper than the immediate technologies employed by organisations – examples of core competence include Sony in miniaturisation, Philips in optical media and 3M in coatings and adhesives. Having identified core competencies, it is then possible to consider the implications for

R&D and for the way that the company's funds are allocated – perhaps more money and people need to be invested in core competencies. However, it is important to recall the words of caution from Chapter 6 on the problems with core competencies.

Five major technological trajectories

Most organisations are constrained by their existing range or products or services, their past histories and the organisational culture and leadership that permits and supports innovation. In short, they are *path-constrained*:[24] this was explored in Section 5.1. From a technology and innovation perspective, it means that companies rarely start from scratch when it comes to innovation because of:

- *their positions* – their market positions against competing firms;
- *their paths* – their current products or services and the specific opportunities now open;
- *their processes* – their current methods by which they achieve innovation.

These three will guide and limit the innovation process. Within these constraints, recent research[25] suggests that there are *five major technological trajectories* that will guide specific types of industry. They are:

1 *Supplier-dominated firms* – examples are agricultural companies, traditional manufacturers like textiles and some services. Technical change comes mainly from the suppliers to these companies. Hence such companies need to develop close links with their suppliers when seeking technology innovation.

2 *Scale-intensive firms* – examples are consumer durables, automobiles and bulk chemicals. Technical innovation will come from the building of complex plant and products. Given the high cost of such plant and consequent risks of failure, innovation tends to come in stages. Hence, technological innovation is concerned with small, frequent improvements in plant efficiencies – the Toyota cars case on the book's website is a good example.

3 *Science-based firms* – examples include pharmaceutical and electronics companies. Technological innovation will often come from a central R&D facility or from a university special incubator. Innovation is often associated with new discoveries and new patents. Hence the task of innovation is to find and exploit such new technologies – perhaps by looking outside the company.

4 *Information-intensive firms* – examples include publishing, banking, telecommunications and travel booking. Technological innovation will come both from in-house systems in the large companies and bought-in systems in both large and small companies. In both cases, the aim is to develop large and often complex systems for handling large quantities of data processing and also making such systems user- and customer-friendly. Totally new services may also result.

5 *Specialised supplier firms* – examples are small specialist companies that supply specialised, high-performance machinery, instruments and specialist software. Technology innovation comes from such firms understanding their customers' needs, their competitors' activities and new developments in their specialised areas of operation. Such companies will innovate by constantly searching for new technologies – perhaps internationally – and from keeping close to their customers.

7.3.3 Three specific technologies and their implications for strategic management

Three fundamental developments in technology may have implications for innovative developments over the next 10 years.[26] They are:

1 *Biotechnology and healthcare developments* – mapping of the human genome and developments in medical technology promise a revolution in healthcare over the next 20 years. Such changes

have already led companies like 3M and Philips – see Case 7.4 and the Philips case on the book's website – to redefine their company purpose in terms of such new opportunities in healthcare. Not every company will be interested or able to benefit from such technological advances but they have the potential to deliver some revolutionary strategies.

2 *Developments in microchip technology* – the increased miniaturisation and extra controls that come from embedded microchips in some products. Many companies produce products that require delivery to customers – an embedded microchip could keep such companies and their customers informed of the status of delivery. Increased chip miniaturisation will also change fundamentally some manufacturing processes and some domestic products. Mobile telephones are one example of technological innovation that has changed the lives of millions. The potential changes here remain to be fully exploited.

3 *Improvements in information technology* – the increased information that comes from the adoption of new IT systems, especially in a global context. We are in the middle of what has been called the third industrial revolution – *the information age*. Moreover, the information is global, not just local or national. For example, a major UK company now has a permanent *three-way* telecommunications link between its engineering design teams in the USA, UK and India. The communications use the specialist engineering knowledge of the US team, the skills but low labour costs of their Indian colleagues, and the overall co-ordination and marketing skills of the UK headquarters. Such activity was simply not possible some years ago. New information technology has also opened up the possibility of greater strategic control in companies. Again, the possibilities from such technological innovations will provide continued strategic opportunities for companies.

Comment

With regard to all the above, it is important to note that all such competitive advantages last only for a limited period of time – for example, traditional banks and insurance companies have begun telephone selling, where required. It is conceivable that technology advantages are not sustainable unless they involve some form of patent and, even then, the patent expires after a set time.

Case study: ***How the Dutch electronics company Philips exploits its technology edge.***

KEY STRATEGIC PRINCIPLES

- An internal and external scan of technologies is vital to strategic management development. It may alter the purpose of the organisation over time. Technologies should be classified into base, core and peripheral. Base areas are common to many companies. Peripheral areas are not mainstream to the organisation. The core areas are most likely to deliver competitive advantage, along with patenting and special skills.
- Each technology should be assessed separately against competition along with the costs of further development against the time taken. The speed of imitation and possible global exploitation also deserve examination. Core competencies - corporate-wide technologies and production skills - can form the basis of new areas of technology innovation.
- Organisations are constrained by their current products, competitors and organisational culture. Five main technology *path constraints* have been identified - supplier-dominated, scale-intensive, science-based, information-intensive, specialised suppliers.
- Three new areas of technology may provide major opportunities for companies in innovation technology over the next ten years: biotechnology and healthcare improvements, developments in microchip technology, improvements in information technology.

CASE STUDY 7.4
Revitalising innovation at 3M

Ever since the US multinational 3M invented Scotch tape and Post-it notes in the mid-twentieth century, the company has been held up as an example of innovative growth. Yet 3M had a problem when growth stalled in recent years. This case examines its famed innovation processes and how 3M began to grow again.

Early years

To give the company its full title is to reveal its early origins. The Minnesota Mining and Manufacturing Company – commonly known as *3M* – started when a group of investors bought a mine in 1902 that was understood to contain the valuable and highly abrasive mineral corundum. When they discovered that only low-grade minerals were present, they decided to branch out into other products that would be more profitable. This approach typifies some of the spirit of the present company, which has made its purpose to seek out high profitability from a wide range of products.

Ever widening product range

By 2010, the 3M turnover was nearly $27 billion and its wide product range included Scotch tape (clear adhesive tape), scrub sponges, tooth-filling materials, microflex electrical circuits and replacement CFC chemicals. Figure 7.7 shows the broad product areas in which the company was involved.

The reasons for this breadth of product range relate to the development style and investment criteria of the company:

- Does a proposed new product deliver high profit margins?
- Does a proposed new product provide innovative growth opportunities?

Importantly, there is no requirement for the product range to stay within the existing core markets of the company – the strategic concept of the resource-based view is interpreted broadly if it is recognised at all. New products can come from any part of the company. Some outsiders regarded the company as a conglomerate, which is rather unfashionable in the context of 'core competencies' – see Chapter 6. However, 3M's former chief executive, Livio DeSimone stoutly defends its range of 50,000 products: 'A very large part of what this company does has sticky stuff on it. Whether you talk about Post-it notes, or office tape, or bonding tape for industry, they're clearly sticky,' explained Mr DeSimone. 'The knowledge we have [allows us] to make those [basic products] valuable.' In practice, the core competencies of 3M probably lie in its deep knowledge of coatings and adhesives, which it then applies across a broad range of products.

3M's innovative process: two examples

The company is famed for its innovative processes. Its Annual Report for 2000 commented: 'In 2000, the company experienced one of the highest levels of innovation in our history, generating $5.6bn – nearly 35 per cent of total sales – from products introduced in the past four years, with over $1.2bn of sales coming from products introduced in 2000.' Innovation is at the essence of its business strategy and this is stimulated and supported throughout the organisation. But it did not prevent the company from having a period of much slower growth later in the decade, as we will see shortly.

To illustrate the 3M approach to innovation, it is useful to consider two famous 3M examples – Scotch tape and Post-it notes. These two major products came about as a result of the company's support for the personal initiatives of two of its managers, Dick Drew and Art Fry. Drew developed the former product and Fry invented the latter. The way that these developments happened is important in exploring innovation at 3M.

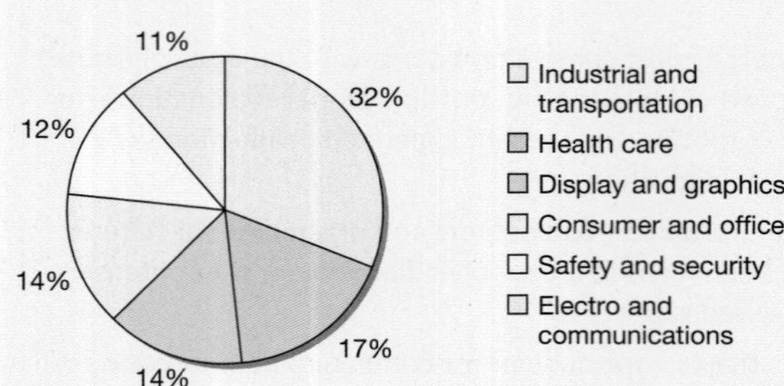

Figure 7.7 The wide range of 3M products in 2010 (sales in $ million)

3M prides itself with justification on its innovative record which it has written into its company description in Canada.

Dick Drew was a 3M sandpaper salesman who had customers in the automobile industry. He noticed one day that they were having difficulty painting two-tone cars: it was difficult to stop the paint spreading from one area to the other. He had an idea for a sticky tape that would protect and separate the areas. He approached his company, which at that time did not make sticky tape, and was allowed to work on the project over the ensuing months. At one stage, he had so little success that he was told by the president of his division at 3M to stop work on the project. But after some persuasion, he was allowed to continue. The product was eventually perfected and was used five years later as the basis of Scotch tape, which became market leader in North America.

Art Fry sang in his local church choir and needed some markers for his hymn book that would not fall out. He had the idea of taking a peelable adhesive that had been developed some years earlier at the 3M research laboratories and spreading it on the markers. It worked well and he asked if he could develop the product commercially. He was given permission and, after some persistence, developed a manufacturing process. But the marketing team was discouraging. They pointed out that customer research suggested that a weak adhesive would not sell. Fry then decided to make some markers anyway and distributed them to colleagues to try in the company. The result was a highly successful product, which became known as Post-it notes.

3M's innovative company culture

The stories above are important because they illustrate the style of 3M: 'Pursue your dream with freedom'. Employees can spend up to 15 per cent of their total time developing their own ideas. They are given extensive support, especially from their superiors, who act as coaches and mentors, rather than judges and leaders. Failure is accepted without criticism as part of the process. The company claims that there is an obsession right across the company with new ideas that have no boundaries. Regular meetings and knowledge fairs are held to allow researchers to exchange ideas. The company online knowledge base is extensive and widely used. The whole company culture is supportive of new ideas. This style of innovation management has led to 3M being held up as a classic example of the best practice in the area. The company has often been in the top 10 of *Fortune* magazine's most admired US companies. In spite of these skills and company culture, 3M failed to grow.

Slower growth, then recovery – how?

For all the innovation practices at 3M, the company failed to maintain its growth rate: sales growth in 1994–1995 was around 11 per cent per annum. By 2000, this had dropped to 6 per cent per annum. Profits followed a similar pattern. Again in the late 2000s, sales and profits failed to grow. Sales in 2010 were barely above the level of those in 2007, though profits were finally on an upward trend.

Part of the reason for the slower growth in the late 1990s was the Asian economic crisis: around 25 per cent of the

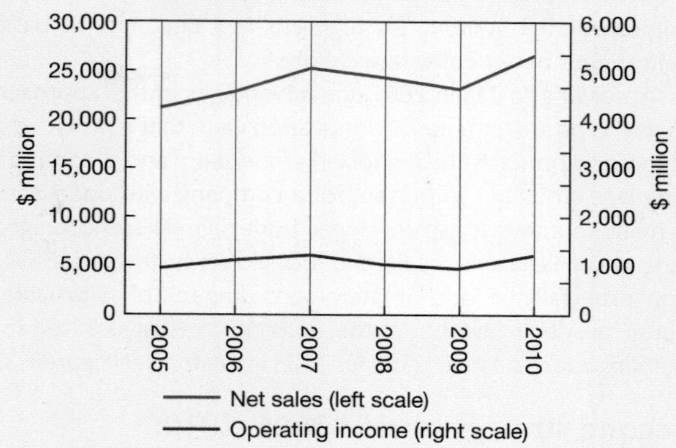

Figure 7.8 Six-year revenue and profit growth at 3M ($ million)

company's sales were in that region and its profit margins were also under pressure there. This was then followed by a slowdown in its home country economy – the USA – which accounted for 45 per cent of turnover. Again, sales and profits dipped in the years 2008 and 2009 partly because of significant economic problems in the USA – see Figure 7.8.

How did 3M turn around the situation over the years to 2010? The company made two attempts, the first of which was not successful and the second remains to be proven at the time of writing this case.

First strategy period 2001–2006: structured innovation

In 2001, 3M answered its critics by progressively introducing a new approach to growth. It was called the Six Sigma initiative. The Six Sigma name comes from total quality management (TQM) statistical concepts about the number of acceptable defects in any production process. (These are beyond the scope of this book to detail, but it is not necessary to understand such concepts in depth in order to see their contribution to 3M's innovation.) Moreover, the company appears to use Six Sigma as a name for two broad concepts, the second of which has little connection with TQM:

1 DMAIC – Define, Measure, Analyse, Improve, Control – a structured method for directing project teams at 3M to improve the quality of their products in the production process. (In other words, a form of TQM.)
2 DFSS – Design for Six Sigma – a standardised methodology for creating and accelerating new products into the market place. (Not necessarily related to TQM.)

3M began with the two Six Sigma concepts in early 2001 by introducing them to the senior leaders of the company. By 2004, all employees had been trained in the two methodologies and processes. The structure introduced by 3M contained a detailed Six Sigma hierarchy of 'directors, champions, master black belts, black belts, green belts and six sigma coaches' to implement the system. 'Six Sigma is fast becoming a basic component of our corporate culture.'

According to 3M in 2001, the advantages of this approach to analysing and structuring innovation were that it provided a common approach throughout the company and a common language globally - important for a company with operations in many countries. It also developed leadership skills, encouraged tangible, measurable results and focused on customer satisfaction, especially DFSS. Ultimately, according to 3M, it 'provides better products faster'. But the outcome was, at best, disappointing as the financial data for 2008 indicates (see Figure 7.8).

Second strategy period 2006–2010: technology-based innovation

In 2005, the company then began to move to a new approach. 'Five years ago, we set out to move 3M, gradually but permanently, to a higher growth regimen,' explained George Buckley, CEO in 2010. 'After the high growth rates of the 1960s and 1970s we had been stuck in a low growth mode since 1979 . . . [New growth] would require a step change in our approach to growth and especially in our approach to investments in growth. It would require a rekindling of our creativity, the taking of more calculated risks and pressing into new growth spaces and geographies . . . While everyone in the company has played a vital role in driving [innovation], 3M's scientists, process engineers and innovators still remain the single most important competitive advantage we have. They are the engine room of progress, and the collective imagination of our creative people is ultimately the birthplace of our success.' The early results from this shift towards technology-based innovation appeared to be more successful, especially when delivered against a backdrop of low national economic growth around the world. But it was still not clear at the time of writing this case whether 3M would be able to recover its fabled growth record.

3M has developed a series of global sustainability initiatives based on the criteria set down in the Global Reporting Initiative's G3 Guidelines: see http://www.globalreporting.org/Home. These guidelines provide a framework for companies to measure and report their activities. 3M has prepared a comprehensive survey of its activities in these areas. See: http://solutions.3m.com/wps/portal/3M/en_US/3M-Sustainability/Global/Resources/

 This case was written by Richard Lynch from published information only.[27]

Case questions

1 What are the main elements of the innovative process at 3M? Is it possible and desirable for other companies to emulate them?

2 It would appear that Six Sigma was unsuccessful: can you think of reasons why this might be?

3 To what extent, if at all, does innovation matter in setting the purpose of an organisation?

7.4 INNOVATION AND PURPOSE

Video Part 7a

The analytical process described in Chapters 3 and 4 of this book brings three potential dangers:

1 *Backward looking*. Inevitably, historical data forms the starting point for future action. However, whether the strategy intends to build on past success or to fight its way out of problems, it cannot rely just on the past. There needs to be a determined attempt to move forward.

2 *Sterility*. Too much analysis may stifle creativity. New ideas, new approaches to old problems, may be weakened by overemphasis on analysis and data collection.[28]

3 *False sense of security*. Because they have already happened, events in the past can be viewed with some certainty. However, it would be wrong to see the future in the same way. Whatever is predicted stands a high probability of being at least partially incorrect.[29]

Innovation is an important antidote to these real problems. In strategic management, we need to move beyond the obvious and comfortable into the new and interesting. The 3M example in Case 7.4 shows how a company has attempted to use a highly structured innovation process – the Six Sigma methodology – to achieve its stated organisational purpose: innovative and profitable growth.

7.4.1 The strategic role of innovation

Definition ▶ By definition, innovation moves products, markets and production processes beyond their current boundaries and capabilities. **An innovation is the implementation of a new or significantly improved product (good or service), or process, a new marketing method, or a new organisational method in**

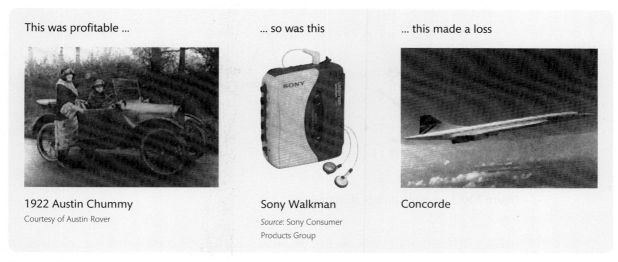

This was profitable ... | ... so was this | ... this made a loss

1922 Austin Chummy
Courtesy of Austin Rover

Sony Walkman
Source: Sony Consumer Products Group

Concorde

Figure 7.9

business practices, workplace organisation or external relations.[30] It also provides organisations with the ammunition to move ahead of the competition. Hence, innovation can deliver three priceless assets to strategic management:

1 substantial future growth;
2 competitive advantage;
3 ability to leapfrog major competition, even dominant competitors.

However, none of the three above areas will automatically deliver future profitability to innovating companies – see Figure 7.9. Consider the cases of Canon (Japan) and EMI (UK). Both companies developed major new innovations during the 1970s:

- *Canon* set out to compete with and beat Xerox (USA) in world photocopying markets. It developed a series of new processes that did not infringe the Xerox patents yet produced products that turned Canon into one of the world's leading photocopying and printing companies. By the mid-1990s, it had a larger market share than Xerox.[31]
- *EMI* was so badly wounded by its foray into medical electronics that its scanner business had to be sold off at a knock-down price. This happened despite the fact that its product was truly innovative and was the first in the market place by a significant period.[32]

Innovation is not without risk. Yet, if it is successful, the payoff is significant. There are two principal sources of innovation to be examined, neither of which is sufficient in itself:

1 customer needs analysis – *market pull*;
2 technology development analysis – *technology push*.

7.4.2 Customer needs analysis: market pull

Baker[33] suggests that innovation occurs when companies identify new market opportunities or a segment of an existing market that has been neglected. Essentially, it is important to develop such opportunities in terms of the *customer need served* in broad general terms – for example, transport, convenience – rather than by examining current products and how they meet demand. For example, Canon photocopiers were innovatory in meeting the general demand for photocopying rather than the needs of the existing customer base, which was biased towards large companies. The company developed new machines requiring little maintenance or repair, which were sold to a much broader range of customers – the medium-sized and small businesses. This process is known as *market pull* – see Figure 7.10.

As Whittington points out,[34] the importance of market pull in successful innovation has been well validated by research. It relies on identifying a market need that needs to be satisfied by a technological advance – essentially a *prescriptive* approach to strategic management. It is used in

Figure 7.10 Two major drivers of innovation

research and development of some new pharmaceuticals, consumer electronics and other areas of technology that are market driven.

However, prescriptive approaches to the study of market demand carry the danger that customers are often constrained in their vision by their current experience and knowledge. More experienced approaches to market need may also be worthwhile.

7.4.3 Technology development analysis: technology push

Market pull procedures do not fully describe the way that many real innovations happen, however.[35] Innovation may be born out of developments at small companies, often in a two-way process with their customers, who may be larger companies. Alternatively, innovations may start as narrow solutions to particular problems. For example, Thomas Watson, President of IBM, said that a new calculator built by his company in 1947 (the Selective Sequence Electronic Calculator) would be able to solve many of the world's major scientific problems but had no commercial applications. It proved to be one of the first IBM computers.

Successful technology often takes time to diffuse through to other industries. It follows that, in addition to monitoring customer needs, an innovatory company should also survey other industries for their technology developments and assess their relevance to its own – essentially an emergent approach to strategic management. This process is sometimes known as *technology push* – see Figure 7.10.

The Philips case on the book's website describes how technology push works at the Dutch electronics company Philips. Importantly, it shows that how the company is organised and how it handles the human side of technology are just as important as the new product derived from technology push.

7.4.4 Disruptive innovation – a variation of customer pull and technology push

Definition ▶ In the mid-1990s, Professor Clayton Christensen of Harvard University Business School suggested that there was another form of innovation, which he called 'disruptive innovation'.[36] **Disruptive innovation takes an existing market and identifies existing technologies that will offer simpler, less expensive products or services than have been offered previously.** This may result in some existing customers switching to the cheaper product or the lower costs and prices of the new product may attract new customers to that market. Disruptive innovation may not involve breakthrough technology but rather the repackaging of existing technology in a way that brings a new and possibly cheaper offering to the market place. The customers for such an offering might be those who would not previously have bought the product or those who would be happy with a low-performing version of the product. For example, customers who had not previously acquired an expensive hi-fi sound system might be attracted to purchase a lower-priced system that worked adequately, but was produced using mature technology, cheaper standardised components and was assembled using labour from low wage-cost countries like China. The importance of this approach is that the existing companies may not regard such a new segment as having much attraction. This therefore allows the disruptive company to enter the new market segment.

Disruptive innovation differs from the main thrust of technology push in so far as the latter involves the development of leading-edge new technology. It also differs from customer pull in the sense that disruptive innovation does not seek to identify a totally new area of consumer demand, but to attract those who currently are not part of an existing market demand. One way to identify where disruptive technology might operate is to analyse the *value chain* of a product or service – see Chapter 4. The location of highest value within the chain might suggest the area to attack.

KEY STRATEGIC PRINCIPLES

- Innovation contributes growth, competitive advantage and the possibility of leapfrogging major competition. However, innovation can be risky and can result in major company losses.
- There are two major drivers for innovation: customer needs analysis (often called *market pull*) and technology development analysis (often called *technology push*).
- Disruptive innovation takes an existing market demand and identifies existing technologies that will offer simpler, less expensive products or services than have been offered previously.

STRATEGIC PROJECT

The Dutch-based consumer electronics company, Philips, is a very interesting company from a strategy perspective because it is beginning to change. For many years, it produced exceptionally innovative solutions from a technical perspective but was less successful at marketing them. It is now changing and there is a good presentation on the web at www.philips.com which explains the company's progress. An interesting project would be to re-evaluate Philips one year on from the original presentation - just how much progress has it made? What principles has it used to develop its technology strategy? Do you think that it will be successful? There is a case study on Philips on the book's website that explores some possible answers to these questions.

Checklist: Six structural aids for the innovative organisation.

7.5 HOW TO INNOVATE: THE 'IDEAS' PROCESS

7.5.1 The phases of innovation

Innovation often occurs through a diffusion process.[37] It may well be adopted slowly at first, then the pace quickens until finally there are just a few late-adopters left to take up the process. Diffusion thus follows the S-shaped curve shown in Figure 7.11.

Sometimes the early pioneering companies fail to make profits because there are still few purchasers and large sums have been invested in developing the process. It is at this stage that business failures like that of the EMI scanner occur. The real profits are made during the rising part of the curve when there is major demand, pricing is still high to reflect the genuine innovation or costs have been dramatically reduced as a result of a technological breakthrough.

In some respects, strategic management may therefore be better served by those who are 'fast seconds' into the market place: the curve is still rising and the original innovator has still not come to dominate the market. For example, the antiulcer drug Zantac (Glaxo Wellcome, UK) was second

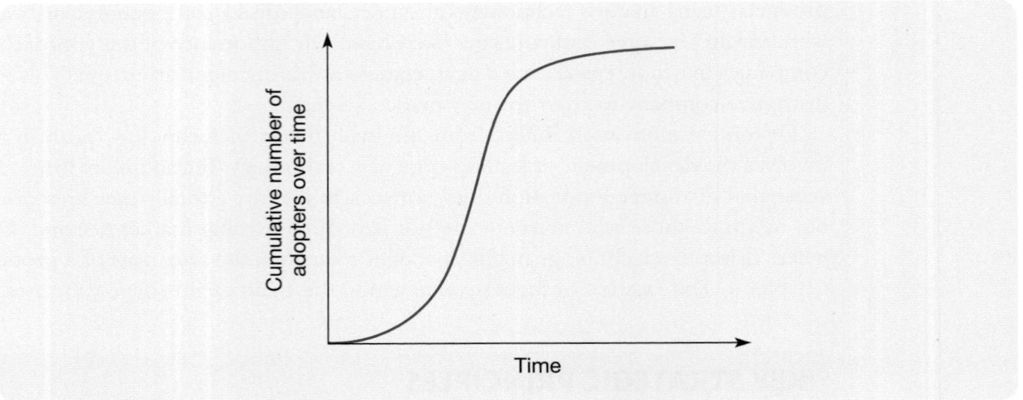

Figure 7.11 The S-shaped curve of the innovation adoption process

into the market after Tagamet (SmithKline Beecham, UK/USA) yet came to dominate the market eventually and make a substantial contribution to Glaxo profitability.

This finding is supported by the research of Mansfield,[38] who tracked innovations over a 30-year period. He estimated that on average those who were second into a market could make a new product for two-thirds of the cost and time of the original innovating company. The strategic problem is how to identify correctly and react quickly to the truly new innovation – not an easy task. Utterback[39] has identified three phases in individual innovation that may help in this identification process:

1 *Fluid phase.* In the early days of an innovation, the market is in a state of flux. The products are not standardised. There are often very few small-scale producers and the manufacturing equipment is general-purpose and small-scale. Competition is limited, with heavy reliance on further product development initiatives. Innovation comes from new product development.
2 *Transitional phase.* After a period, demand has risen sufficiently to justify dedicated production machinery. At least one product design has established itself to deliver volume sales. More competitors have entered the market, but the rate of entry is beginning to decline as a dominant design emerges and some companies adopt this and get ahead of competition. The competitive threat is likely to come, for the first time, from producers with lower costs and higher quality. Innovation is more likely to come from developments in the manufacturing process.
3 *Specific phase.* Over time, innovation slows down and becomes small and incremented. A few large-scale manufacturers dominate the market. They produce their goods on a relatively large scale, using specialist and dedicated machinery. Competition is more likely to be based on price and branding, until a new and genuine innovation is again developed.

With respect to the above areas, we observe that they are founded on two basic assumptions and empirical observations:

1 that economies of scale and scope are possible in an industry and remain the chief means of reducing costs;
2 that custom demand can be satisfied by standardised products.

These may not be true in all industries – see the other means of reducing costs described in Section 8.6. Moreover, the flexible manufacturing of Toyota Car Company described in the free online Toyota case linked to Part 6 of this book.

7.5.2 The routes to delivering innovation

Given its value to the organisation, the real issue is how to deliver innovation.

For the original innovators, the payoff can be substantial with the right product. Professor James Quinn[40] of Dartmouth College, USA, investigated the innovation process of a variety of companies and concluded that large companies need to behave like small entrepreneurial ventures to be truly successful. He suggested that innovatory companies should ideally follow the process he called 'controlled chaos' (see Exhibit 7.4) – not an easy task.

EXHIBIT 7.4

The controlled chaos approach to generating innovation

- *Atmosphere and vision* - with chief executives providing support, leadership and projecting clear, long-term ambitions for their company
- *Small, flat organisation* - not bureaucratic, but flexible
- *Small teams of innovators* - multidisciplinary groups of idea makers
- *Competitive selection process* - with innovatory ideas selected from a range in the company, and encouragement and support, not penalties, for the losing team
- *Interactive learning* - random, even chaotic, consideration of ideas from many sources and from a range of industries

Quinn believed strongly in the *emergent process* for innovation strategy. Writing around the same time, Fred Gluck[41] of the consulting company McKinsey took largely the opposite view. He argued that the really innovatory achievements needed a '*big bang*' approach. They need masses of information, a decision-making process that can discern patterns in these undigested data and the functional skills to implement the decisions once they were made. He urged the larger corporations, to which he was addressing his remarks, to become more sensitive to major environmental changes and to create a better climate to explore *big bang* ideas.

This conflict of views as to the best way forward for innovation would appear to be equally true for Japanese researchers. One study[42] describing Japanese practice was based on a survey of products in eight major companies including Honda, NEC, Epson and Canon. It found that the process was informal, multifunctional and involved excess information over that initially identified to solve the problem. The conclusion was that the most successful innovation processes often involved redundant information that interacted through chance, even chaotic, processes to produce the innovatory result. By contrast, another study[43] of Japanese innovation processes concluded that a more analytical approach can also be employed in some circumstances.

The overall conclusion is probably that there is no one route to innovation: both prescriptive and emergent approaches have been successfully used. There are, however, seven general guidelines that might be used to encourage the innovation process.[44] These are summarised in Exhibit 7.5.

EXHIBIT 7.5

Guidelines to encourage the innovation process

- Question the present business strategies and market definitions
- Consider carefully the current products or services
- Explore external timing and market opportunities
- Seek out competitors' weaknesses
- Deliver new and better value for money
- Search wide and far
- Seek to challenge conventional wisdom

An extended version of these guidelines with examples.

7.5.3 Blue Ocean strategy: the contribution of Kim and Mauborgne

Consistent with the above approaches to innovation and as an extension of how companies can become more innovative, Kim and Mauborgne have proposed a concept which they call *Blue Ocean strategy*.[45] The approach is built upon three underpinning principles:

1 The importance of analysing markets to find new opportunities – see Chapter 3.

2 The key role of value added which can be enhanced both by lowering costs and by raising prices – see Chapter 4.

3 The identification of new innovation through focusing on the key elements that will provoke new ways of thinking and acting: one of the themes of this chapter.

Kim and Mauborgne begin by arguing that much of strategy is focused on existing markets and the competitive advantages possessed by companies in these markets. They call existing markets *red oceans*. They then point out that there are many markets that did not exist 20 years ago. Although the authors do not use these examples, we can name, for example, internet, television and car satellite navigation systems. The authors name the industries that do not exist today *blue oceans*. **Blue ocean strategy is a strategy that focuses on untapped market space, demand creation and the opportunity for highly profitable growth.** Essentially, it looks beyond existing markets in an entirely new way. It seeks out those opportunities that will have high value by being able to develop new market offerings that go beyond existing boundaries. Importantly, the blue ocean concept does not dismiss red oceans. There will always be a need to develop strategies in existing markets against existing competitors: the red oceans. However, to gain higher returns as existing markets mature and competition becomes stronger, it is necessary to re-think boundaries and create new blue oceans.

Definition ▶

The essence of the blue ocean strategy is value innovation. The authors suggest that blue oceans permit the creation of new value added, both because costs can be re-configured and because new customers and products will allow new pricing models to flourish that move beyond existing competitive price comparisons. The identification of blue ocean opportunities then develops along four dimensions:

1 *Elimination*. Which current aspects of an industry are really important to customers and which can be eliminated as being peripheral?

2 *Reduction*. Which current features of products in an industry have been over-designed and can be reduced without affecting the fundamental product or service offering?

3 *Raising*. Which current features of products in an industry could be improved in ways that would be attractive to customers and avoid the compromises of current product offerings?

4 *Creation*. Which aspects of products and services in an industry can be employed to generate new value added for customers by creating new demand and new pricing models?

Blue ocean strategy then explores each of these elements in more depth and identifies a process to implement the outcome that involves specifying both the pricing and the cost implications of the new innovative offerings in the blue ocean.

Comment

The value of blue ocean strategy comes from its consistent focus on developing new innovative solutions in a structured way. It poses some important questions and provides a structure for answering them. However, some strategists will find difficulty in recognising the rather blunt distinction between red and blue oceans. Others will have difficulty in understanding how blue ocean strategy differs from market segmentation and positioning – see Chapter 3 – and from existing concepts related to raising value added – see Chapter 4.

7.5.4 How purpose can emerge from innovation

If the purpose of the organisation is defined in terms mainly of survival, then it can be argued that such a purpose is present in most organisations in advance of any process of innovation. In this sense, purpose cannot be said to emerge from innovation but, rather, to precede it. However, if the purpose of the organisation is defined in some broader way to include, for example, the delivery of additional value, quality or service, then innovation can take on a very different role.

Given the right circumstances and people, innovation can occur anywhere in an organisation. It is not confined to corporate technologists or marketing managers. Innovation can thus provide new opportunities to move beyond the current position in an industry. But until the full extent and implications of an innovation have been explored, its true potential cannot meaningfully be assessed. In this sense, the new purpose that will be presented by a radical innovation – such as some aspect of bioengineering or the internet – cannot be defined in advance but must be left to *emerge* as the innovation proceeds. Strategic management may be better served if at least some part of it is free from the straitjacket of a tightly defined purpose.

International perspectives on innovation.

KEY STRATEGIC PRINCIPLES

- The innovation process is complex and risky - early innovation pioneers did not always gain the full financial benefit from their work.
- Innovation development often follows an S-shaped curve, with the real profit being made during the growth phase, after the initial development.
- There are three phases in industrial innovation: fluid, transitional and specific. Change from the first to the second phase occurs when a product design becomes dominant. Change from the second to the third phase occurs through large-scale production.
- The innovation process can be emergent, with ideas freely generated from many sources. It can also be prescriptive, with a more analytical and directed approach to the task.
- The seven guidelines offered on innovation to start this process do not claim to be comprehensive. They have as their central theme the need to challenge conventional understanding and wisdom.
- Blue ocean strategy is a strategy that focuses on untapped market space, demand creation and the opportunity for highly profitable growth. Essentially, it looks beyond existing markets in an entirely new way.
- If the purpose of the organisation includes an element of growth, then it may be better to allow such a purpose to emerge from an innovative opportunity, whose full potential cannot be known in advance.

CRITICAL REFLECTION

Innovation: emergent or prescriptive?

- This chapter has argued for an experimental, emergent approach to purpose, based on knowledge, new technologies and seeking out innovation in every area of an organisation. Crucially, the purpose of an organisation to develop this approach needs to be left open and undefined.
- The difficulty is that this open-ended approach to purpose is completely contrary to the way that many organisations like to work. They make commitments to their shareholders about growth targets; they allocate funds for research on the basis of the likely benefits from such activities; they manage their employees on the basis of sales and profit development targets. In other words, they adopt highly prescriptive approaches to innovation and research.
- Should these two approaches be reconciled? Can they be reconciled? If so, how?

SUMMARY

- The knowledge of the organisation can be used to deliver and maintain sustainable competitive advantage. Knowledge is hard to define precisely but can be considered as a constantly changing mixture of experience, values, contextual information and expert insight. It will be evident that such areas might well be exclusive to the organisation and provide distinctiveness from competition.
- Knowledge needs to be divided between its tacit and explicit forms. Explicit knowledge is recorded and structured. Tacit knowledge is fuzzy and difficult to set out. Both can lead to competitive advantage, but tacit knowledge may be particularly important because it is less easy for competitors to comprehend and copy. An organisation's knowledge can be audited as the basis for strategy development, but the audit has several disadvantages.
- Conversion and communication of existing knowledge can take place through four mechanisms: socialisation, externalisation, combination and internalisation. All four processes relate to the basic distinction between tacit and explicit knowledge existing in any organisation.
- Knowledge creation – the development and circulation of new knowledge – offers a dynamic strategic opportunity. There are three mechanisms: organisational learning, knowledge creation and acquisition, and knowledge transfer.
- If new knowledge is significant in its impact on the organisation, then it may well change the purpose of the organisation. Importantly, the purpose will only change after new knowledge has been developed. In this sense, the purpose of the organisation *emerges* from knowledge creation.
- An internal and external scan of technologies is vital to the development of strategic management. It may alter the purpose of the organisation over time. Technologies need to be classified into base, core and peripheral. It is the core area that is most likely to deliver sustainable competitive advantage. Each technology then needs to be assessed against its competitors and for the time and costs involved in its development. Core competencies – corporate-wide technologies and production skills – can form the basis of new areas of technology innovation.
- Organisations are constrained by their current products, competitors and organisational culture. Five main path constraints have been identified – supplier-dominated, scale-intensive, science-based, information-intensive and specialised suppliers. Green strategy has benefited from technology breakthroughs and from process technology to reduce the cost of manufacturing greener products.
- Innovation contributes growth, competitive advantage and the possibility of leapfrogging competition. However, it can also be risky and result in major losses to the organisation. There are two major drivers for innovation: customer needs analysis (market pull) and technology development analysis (technology push). The innovation process can be both prescriptive and emergent.
- There are three phases in industrial innovation: fluid, transitional and specific. Change from the first to the second phase occurs when a product design becomes dominant. Change from the second to the third phase occurs through large-scale production. The first of these is primarily concerned with product innovation. The second and third phases are more likely to be associated with manufacturing process innovation.
- If the purpose of the organisation includes an element of growth, then it may be better to allow such a purpose to *emerge* from an innovative opportunity, whose full potential cannot be known in advance.

QUESTIONS

1 Take an organisation with which you are familiar and identify its areas of explicit and tacit knowledge. To what extent, if at all, does the process assist in identifying the sustainable competitive advantage of the company?

2 In what ways might a company like Nike use a 'knowledge audit' as part of its strategy development process? What are the problems with this approach? Would you recommend it?

3 *'In an economy where the only certainty is uncertainty, one sure source of lasting competitive advantage is knowledge.'* (Ikijuro Nonaka) Do you agree with Nonaka about the unique importance of knowledge?

4 Take an organisation with which you are familiar and classify its technologies into basic, core and peripheral. What conclusions can you draw on sustainable competitive advantage for the organisation's strategy?

5 With the introduction of the web, it has been argued that this: *'will give consumers increased access to a vast selection of goods but will cause a restructuring and redistribution of profits amongst stakeholders along the [value] chain'* (Robert Benjamin and Rolf Wigand). Discuss the strategic implications of this comment from the viewpoint of (a) a major retailer and (b) a small to medium-sized supplier of local building services.

6 Do you think that the increased use of information technology will affect all organisations equally? Will some remain relatively unaffected apart from the introduction of a few computers and a link to the internet? What are the strategic implications of your answer?

7 Identify some recent innovations and classify them into market pull and technology push. Explain how each innovation has been delivered into the market, using the S-shaped curve to show the process.

8 Quinn argues that large companies need to behave like small entrepreneurial ventures to be truly innovative. Gluck suggests that major innovations only come from a 'big-bang' push that needs major resources. Can these two views of the innovative process be reconciled? (See references 40 and 41.)

9 *'Innovate or fall behind: the competitive imperative for virtually all businesses today is that simple.'* (Dorothy Leonard and Susan Straus)

Is this true? Is innovation fundamental to all business strategy?

FURTHER READING

On knowledge: Davenport, Thomas and Prusack, Lawrence (1998) *Working Knowledge*, Harvard Business School Press, Boston, MA, is comprehensive and insightful. Nonaka, I and Takeuchi, H (1995) *The Knowledge-Creating Company*, Oxford University Press, Oxford, is one of the leading texts. Leonard, Dorothy (1995) *Wellsprings of Knowledge*, Harvard Business School Press, Boston, MA, is also about innovation. A good compendium of interesting papers is Morey, D, Maybury, M and Thuraisingham, B (eds) (2002) *Knowledge Management: Classic and Contemporary Works*, The MIT Press, Cambridge, MA. See also Krogh, G, Nonaka, I and Aben, M (2001) 'Making the most of your company's knowledge', *Long Range Planning*, Vol 34, No 4, pp 421–440. Read the chapter in Mark Jenkins' and Véronique Ambrosini's edited text with Nardine Collier (2007) *Advanced Strategic Management*, Palgrave Macmillan: Chapter 11 'Knowledge Perspective' by Spender, J C. See also the following special issue: Agarwal, R, Audretsch, D and Sarkar, MB (2010) 'Special Issue: Knowledge Spillovers and Strategic Entrepreneurship', *Strategic Entrepreneurship Journal*, Vol 4, No 4, with an interesting series of papers on this relationship.

On technology and strategic management: Contractor, F-J and Narayanan, V K (1990) 'Technology development in the multinational firm', *R&D Management*, Basil Blackwell, Oxford, republished in Root, F R and Visudtibhan (eds) (1992) *International Strategic Management*, Taylor and Francis, London, pp 163–183, is well developed, thoughtful and comprehensive. Although the paper's title does not suggest technology, the following paper has precisely this focus alongside the more general topic of intelligence: March J (2006) 'Rationality, foolishness, and adaptive intelligence', *Strategic Management Journal*, Vol 27, pp 201–214. A thoughtful and interesting paper.

On IT and strategic management: Porter, M E and Millar, V E (1985) 'How information gives you a competitive advantage', *Harvard Business Review*, July–August is useful. See also Benjamin, R and Wigand, R (1995) 'Electronic markets and virtual value chains on the information superhighway', *Sloan Management Review*, Winter, p 62.

On innovation: Tidd, J, Bessant, J and Pavitt, K (2001) *Managing Innovation*, 2nd edn, John Wiley, Chichester, is comprehensive, with a useful academic foundation. For a more recent academic review, see Stieglitz, N and Heine, K (2007) 'Innovations and the role of complementarities in a strategic theory of the firm', *Strategic Management Journal*, Vol 28, pp 1–15. Finally, Utterback, J (1996) *Mastering the Dynamics of Innovation*, Harvard Business School Press, Boston, MA, is an excellent earlier text with strong empirical research base. A more recent text is Lester, R K and Piore, M J (2004) *Innovation – the Missing Dimension*, Harvard University Press, Harvard, MA. For an alternative view on generating innovation: Kim, WC and Mauborgne, R (2005) *Blue Ocean Strategy*, Harvard Business Review Press, Harvard, MA.

For a more general review: Lichtenthaler, U (2011) 'Open Innovation: Past Research, Current Debates and Future

Directions', *Academy of Management Perspectives*, Vol 25, No 1, pp 75–93.

A useful general text that summarises *technical* innovation but says nothing about *non-technical* innovation is the Oslo Manual available on the web: Oslo (2005) *Oslo Manual: Guidelines for Collecting and Interpreting Innovation Data*, OECD and Eurostat. The text is strong on technology-led innovation but weaker on market-led innovation. It has some good definitions and references.

NOTES AND REFERENCES

1 Sources for Maglev case: Visits by author to Shanghai, June 2004 and April 2007. *Financial Times*, 28 June 2003, p 8; 5 July 2003, p M5; 7 August 2003, p 7; 5 November 2008, p 25; 24 September 2010, p 11; 6 January 2011, p 23; 9 February 2011, p 22; 11 April 2011, p 3 of Rail and Transport section; www.shairport.com/en; *China People's Daily*, 31 December 2002 'World's first commercial Maglev line debuts in Shanghai'; *Shenzen Daily*, 15 April 2004 'Shanghai Maglev ticket prices cut by 1/3'. See also http://englishpeople.com.cn 'Rail track beats Maglev in Beijing-Shanghai high speed railway'; www.cnn.com/2004/TRAVEL/Shanghai Maglev – 30 November 2004 'Shanghai to extend Maglev rail'; http://en.ce.cn/Industries/Transport/200412/15/ 'German Maglev technology abandoned?'

2 Nonaka, I (1991) 'The knowledge-creating company', *Harvard Business Review*, November–December, pp 96–104.

3 Nonaka, I and Takeuchi, H (1995) *The Knowledge-Creating Company*, Oxford University Press, Oxford, Ch 1. This chapter traces the development of knowledge as a topic area and clearly demonstrates that it was tangential to strategy development for many strategy writers. It should also be noted that many strategy texts make no significant reference to the subject even to the present time.

4 Drucker, P (1964) *Managing for Results*, William Heinemann, London, Ch 6.

5 Davenport, T H and Prusack, L (1998) *Working Knowledge: How Organizations Manage What They Know*, Harvard Business School Press, Boston, MA, pp 2, 3.

6 Davenport, T H and Prusack, L (1998) Ibid., p 5.

7 Hamel, G (1995) Foreword, *FT Handbook of Management*, Financial Times, London. See also his article in *Financial Times*, 5 June 1995, p 9, for an abridged version of the article (highly entertaining phraseology but somewhat confused argument).

8 Nonaka, I and Takeuchi, H (1995) Op. cit., pp 109–111. As they point out themselves, they did not invent the important distinction between tacit and explicit knowledge. That distinction comes from the Hungarian philospher Michael Polanyi.

9 Nonaka, I and Takeuchi, H (1995) Op. cit., p 27.

10 Skandia, Annual Report and Accounts 1997, p 62. See also Edvinsson, L (1997) 'Developing intellectual capital at Skandia', *Long Range Planning*, Vol 30, No 3, pp 366–373. Mr Edvinsson has made a significant contribution in this area at Skandia. For a more recent paper: Miller, K D (2002) 'Knowledge inventories and managerial myopia', *Strategic Management Journal*, Vol 23, pp 689–706.

11 For example, see Davenport, T H and Prusack, L (1998) Op. cit., p xv.

12 Davenport, T H, De Long, D W and Beers, M C (1998) 'Successful knowledge management projects', *California Management Review*, Vol 39, No 2, pp 43–57. See also Norman, R and Ramirez, R (1993) 'From value chain to value constellation', *Harvard Business Review*, July–August, p 65 (which explores knowledge and elements of key resources). Chan, Kim W and Mauborgne, R (1997) 'Fair process: managing in the knowledge economy', *Harvard Business Review*, July–August, p 65 (which explores the impact on employees). Evans, P B and Wurster, T S (1997) 'Strategy and the new economics of information', *Harvard Business Review*, September–October, p 70 (which discusses the internet). Woiceshyn, J. and Falkenberg, L (2008) 'Value creation in knowledge-based firms: aligning problems and resources', *Academy of Management Perspectives*, Vol 22, No 2, pp 85–99.

13 This is actually the headline in the 1998 Annual Report and Accounts of Heineken NV (see Case 2 in Part 6 and Heineken on web) introducing its new knowledge management world network. It is not clear whether the company was aware of the political significance of this phrase and its impact on some groups within the company.

14 Boshyk, Y (1999) 'Beyond knowledge management', *Financial Times Mastering Information Management*, 8 February, pp 12–13. For an alternative view of related issues: Arikan, A T (2009) 'Interfirm knowledge exchanges and knowledge creation capability of clusters', *Academy of Management Review*, Vol 34, No 4, pp 658–677.

15 References for the Nike case: Nike Annual Report and Accounts 2007 and 2010 available on the web at www.nikebiz.com; *Financial Times*: 15 July 1996, p 9; 15 December 1996, p 9; 22 December 1996, p 18; 2 April 1997, p 22; 11 October 1997, p 17; 17 January 1998, p 6; 16 July 1998; 20 March 1999, p 19; 20 March 2001, p 6 of Creative Business Supplement; 4 November 2003, p 19; 19 August 2004, pp 10, 25; 4 August 2005, p 21; 21 March 2006, p 25; 2 June 2006, p 24; 23 May 2007, p 32; 31 May 2007, p 9; 4 March 2010, p 23; 19 March 2010, p 18; 20 March 2010, p 14; 27 August 2010, p 19; Seth, A (1998) *Marketing Business*, February; *Guardian*, 17 June 2003, p 15 – interesting interview with Phil Knight.

16 Davenport, T H and Prusack, L (1998) Op. cit., Ch 3.

17 For example, see case studies quoted in Davenport and Prusak, and Nonaka and Takeuchi above. But also see researchers like Kanter, R (*Changemasters*) and Quinn explored in Chapter 12.

18 Heineken Annual Report and Accounts 1998.

19 For an extended discussion of this important area, see Davenport, T H and Prusack, L (1998) Op. cit., Ch 5. The author (RL) will never forget the months of negotiation

with his fellow finance director on one such knowledge issue.

20 Teece, D (1998) 'Capturing value from knowledge assets', *California Management Review*, Vol 40, No 3, pp 55–79.

21 Sources for Sharm el-Sheikh case: tourist material collected during visit in 2010. UN World Tourism Organization (2009) *Tourism Highlights Facts and Figures* available at www.unwto.org. *Financial Times*, 16 December 2010, p 10.

22 This section has benefited from Contractor, F J and Narayanan, V K (1990) 'Technology development in the multinational firm', *R&D Management*, Basil Blackwell, Oxford, republished in Root, F R and Visudtibhan (eds) (1992) *International Strategic Management*, Taylor and Francis, London, pp 163–183. Well developed, thoughtful and comprehensive. See also Zhou, K Z and Wu, F (2010) 'Technology capability, strategic flexibility and product innovation', *Strategic Management Journal*, Vol 31, No 5, pp 547–561 for a more recent review and perspective.

23 Prahalad, C K and Hamel, G (1990) 'The core competencies of the corporation', *Harvard Business Review*, May–June, pp 79–91. Prahalad, C K and Hamel, G (1994) *Competing for the Future*, Harvard Business School Press, Cambridge, MA.

24 Teece, D, Pisano, G and Shuen, A (1997) 'Dynamic capabilities and strategic management', *Strategic Management Journal*, Vol 18, No 7, pp 509–533.

25 This section has benefited from Tidd, J, Bessant, J and Pavitt, K (2001) *Managing Innovation*, 2nd edn, Wiley, Chichester, Ch 5.

26 Tidd J, *et al.* (2001) Ibid.

27 Sources for the 3M case study: Annual Report and Accounts 1997, 2000, 2007 and 2010. The quotes from Mr Buckley are taken from the 2010 report, pp 1 and 2. Takeuchi, I and Nonaka, H (1995) Op. cit., pp 135–140; Davenport, T H and Prusak, L (1998) Op. cit., pp 104–106; *Financial Times*: 7 September 1998, p 14; 28 February 2011, p 16.

28 Hamel, G and Prahalad, C K (1994) *Competing for the Future*, Harvard Business School Press, Boston, MA, p 274.

29 Stacey, R (1993) *Strategic Management and Organisation Dynamics*, Pitman Publishing, London, p 115.

30 Oslo Manual (2005) *Guidelines for Collecting and Interpreting Innovation Data*, OECD and EuroStat.

31 Harvard Business School (1983) *Canon (B)*, Case 9–384–151 plus note on world photocopying industry.

32 Harvard Business School (1984) *EMI and the CT Scanner (A) and (B)*, Case 383–194 and the *Economist Survey on Innovation*, 11 January 1992, p 21.

33 Baker, M (1992) *Marketing Strategy and Management*, 2nd edn, Macmillan, London, p 28.

34 Whittington, R (1993) *What is Strategy and Does it Matter?*, Routledge, London, p 82.

35 *The Economist* (1992) Loc. cit.

36 Christensen, C (1997) *The Innovator's Dilemma*, Harvard Business School Press, Boston, MA.

37 Baker, M (1992) Op. cit., p 110, and *The Economist* (1992) Op. cit., p 22.

38 *The Economist* (1992) Op. cit., p 22.

39 Utterback, J M (1996) *Mastering the Dynamics of Innovation*, Harvard Business School Press, Boston, MA, pp 94–95.

40 Quinn, J B (1985) 'Managing innovation: controlled chaos', *Harvard Business Review*, May–June, p 73.

41 Gluck, F (1985) 'Eight big makers of innovation', *McKinsey Quarterly*, Winter, p 49.

42 Nonaka, I (1990) 'Redundant, overlapping organisations: a Japanese approach to managing the innovation process', *California Management Review*, Spring, p 27.

43 Kawaii, T (1992) 'Generating innovation through strategic action programmes', *Long Range Planning*, Vol 25, June, p 42.

44 Developed principally from two sources: Hamel, G and Prahalad, C K (1994) Op. cit., Ch 4, and Day, G S (1987) *Strategic Marketing Planning*, West Publishing, St Paul, MN, Ch 6.

45 Kim, WC and Mauborgne, R (2005) *Blue Ocean Strategy*, Harvard Business Review Press, Harvard, MA.

PART 3
Developing the strategy

Having analysed the environment and resources of the organisation and defined its purpose, it is now possible to develop the strategy. With no single process agreed by all strategists, this part of the book first examines the *prescriptive* approach to strategy development: this involves generating a number of *strategy options*, followed by a *rational selection* between them, using agreed strategic criteria. It also involves a consideration of green strategy issues.

We then consider *emergent* approaches that may adjust the basic prescriptive recommendations. We also consider more radical emergent alternatives because some strategists reject the prescriptive process and rely solely on the emergent route.

Finally, the organisation structure and the style of the company are explored as these elements may have an important influence on the strategy, possibly even entailing a further reworking of the strategy itself. However, some strategy writers regard the structure as something to be resolved *after* the strategy has been agreed and would therefore not include a consideration of the organisation structure at this stage in the development process. For the reasons explained in Chapter 12, this book disagrees and takes the view that it is better to consider strategy, organisation structure and style together.

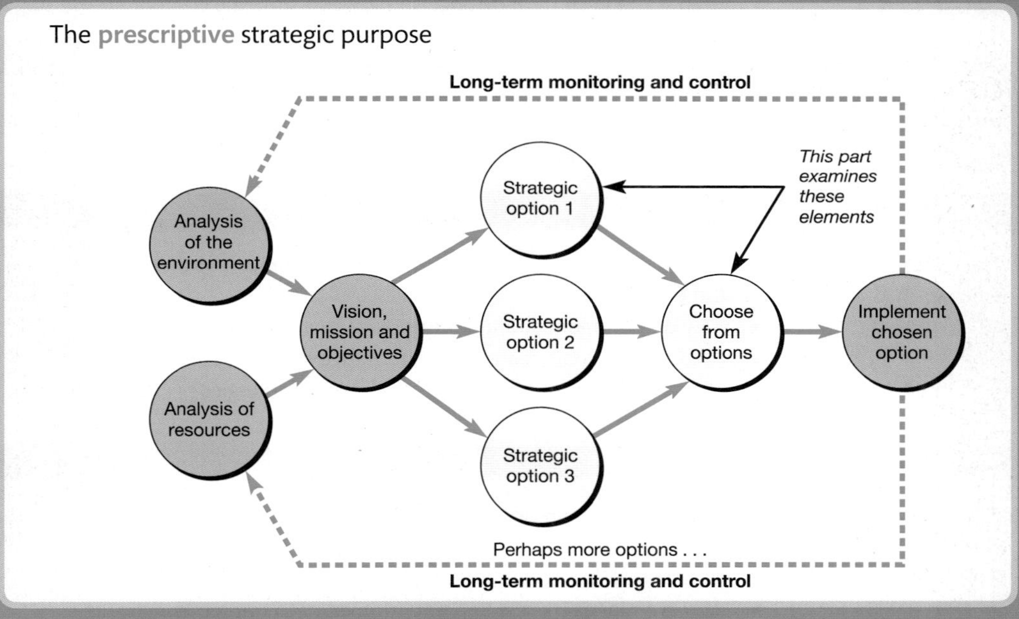

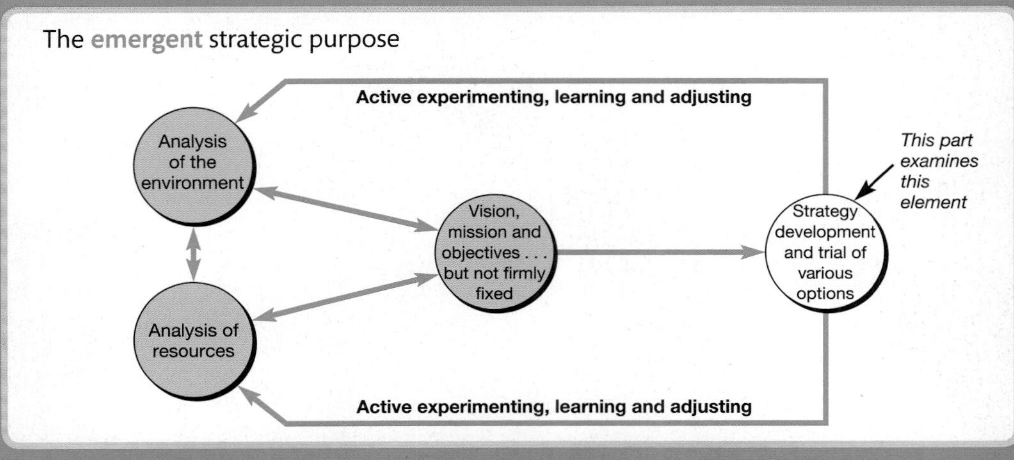

Key strategic management questions

CHAPTER 8 Developing business-level strategy options	• What are the main environment-based opportunities available to the organisation? • What are the main resource-based opportunities available to the organisation? • What strategy options arise from these opportunities?
CHAPTER 9 Developing corporate-level strategy options	• What are the benefits of being part of a group? And the problems? • What options arise from being part of a corporation? • How do we develop and decide strategic management?
CHAPTER 10 Strategy evaluation and development: the prescriptive process	• What is the important distinction between strategic content and strategic process? • Which options are consistent with the purpose of the organisation? • Which options are particularly suitable for the environmental and resource conditions facing the organisation? • Which options make valid assumptions about the future? Are feasible? Contain acceptable business risks? And are attractive to stakeholders?
CHAPTER 11 Finding the strategic route forward: mainly emergent approaches	• What is the distinction between strategic context and the other two elements – content and process? • How do emergent strategic considerations alter the decisions? • What are the main features of alternative strategic approaches? • What are the consequences for the chosen strategies?
CHAPTER 12 Organisational structure, style and people issues	• What are the main principles involved in designing an organisation's structure to implement its strategy? • What special considerations apply when seeking innovatory strategies? • How are managers selected and motivated to implement strategies?

CHAPTER 8
Developing business-level strategy options

Video and sound summary of this chapter

LEARNING OUTCOMES

After working through this chapter, you will be able to:

- undertake a SWOT analysis;
- generate options on the environment-based view of the organisation;
- explore generic strategy options and evaluate their potential;
- outline the market options matrix and its contribution to developing industry-based options;
- investigate the options prompted by the expansion method matrix and their implications for industry-based options;
- generate options from the resource-based view of the organisation;
- use the value chain in the development of resource-based options;
- develop options based on the distinctive capabilities and the core competencies of the organisation;
- identify resource options based on cost reduction in the organisation;
- critically evaluate the contributions of all these routes to the strategic development process.

INTRODUCTION

In many prescriptive approaches to strategy development, it is usual to define the purpose of the organisation and then develop a range of *strategy options* that might achieve that purpose. (Many of the popular texts take this approach.) After developing the options, a selection is made between them. This chapter is concerned with the options development part of this sequence at the level of individual businesses and markets. The following chapter then considers options at the corporate level of those companies that are involved in a number of diverse markets.

In Part 2 of this text we analysed the organisation's environment and its resources. Before embarking on an exploration of the strategic options that emerge from this study, it is useful to summarise the situation. One approach is to produce an analysis of the organisation's strengths and weaknesses and explore the opportunities and threats that connect it with the environment – this is often called a SWOT analysis. In addition, such an analysis might be supported by a consideration of such issues as vision, innovation and technology. In addition to these considerations, most organisations would also draw up a summary of the main elements of the organisation's purpose as a starting point for options development.

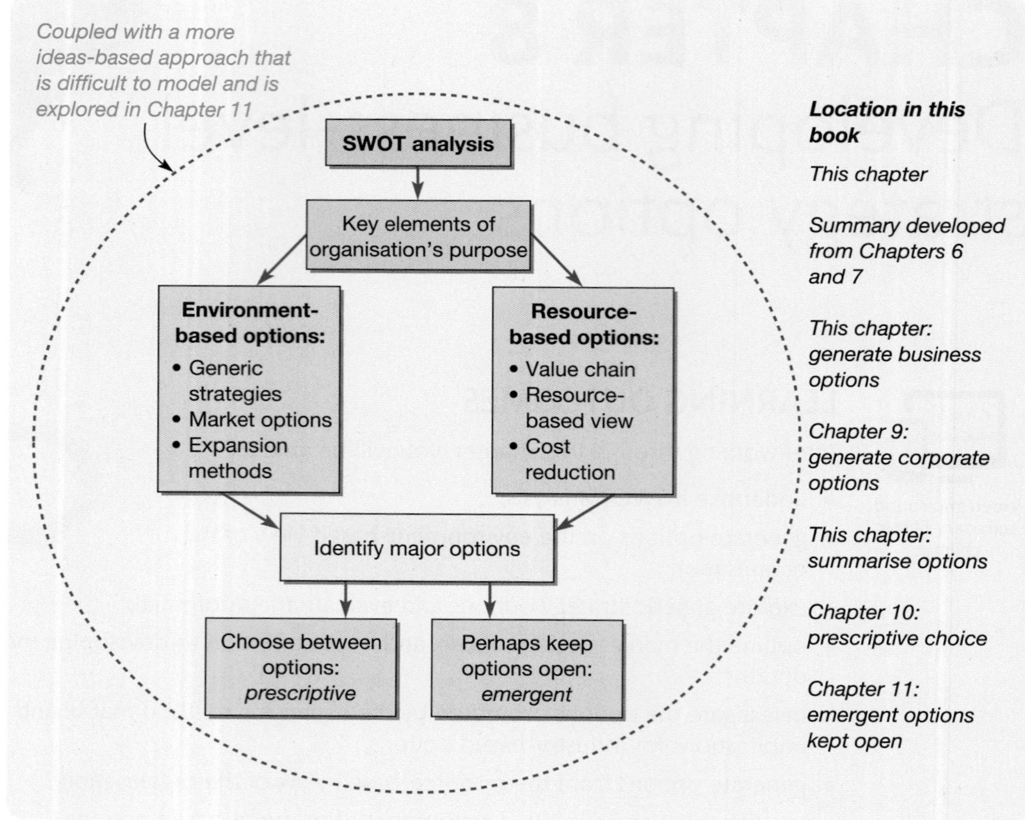

Figure 8.1 Developing business strategy options

To develop the strategic options, both rational and more imaginative processes can be used. Inevitably, because of the difficulty of modelling imagination, strategic research papers and books tend to concentrate on the more rational aspects, which are easier to outline, structure and study. Thus this chapter concentrates on the more rational approaches, but it acknowledges the importance of the creative process in options generation – see Figure 8.1.

In this chapter, we begin the options development process by exploring the *competitive environment* through three rational strategic routes: generic strategies, market options and expansion methods. We then turn to the organisation's *own resources* and explore another three rational areas: the value chain, the resource-based view and cost-cutting options. Importantly, there are considerable *cross-linkages* between the competitive environment and resource-based routes: for example, the market environment considers the resources of competitors and the company's own resources need to be considered in the context of its competitors.

Video Part 6a

In theory, there are a very large number of options available to any organisation, probably more than it can cope with. Some final comments are therefore offered on how to reduce these to a more manageable size. The structure of the chapter is summarised in Figure 8.1.

CASE STUDY 8.1

Walt Disney: building options for Mickey Mouse

In spite of its considerable competitive strengths, the Walt Disney Company was under pressure in the early 2000s to deliver further growth. Its best-known character and strategic resource, Mickey Mouse, represented one way forward. This case explores some strategic options for the company.

The Walt Disney Company

Founded by Walt and his brother Roy, the Walt Disney Company first made its name with brilliant and innovatory animated cartoons in the early 1920s and 1930s. In addition to characters such as Mickey and Minnie Mouse there were famous cartoons such as *Snow White and the Seven Dwarfs*, *Fantasia* and *Bambi*. The first theme park using such characters was opened in California in 1952. Subsequently, the company branched out into other types of filmed entertainment and into the ownership of one of America's major television broadcasters – the ABC television network. By the year 2005, the company was the second-largest media conglomerate in the world. Its interests included 70 radio stations, several cable TV channels such as ESPN (80 per cent owned), A&E television (38 per cent owned), Walt Disney Pictures, Touchstone, Miramax and Pixar. It also operated Walt Disney Parks and Resorts in the USA, in Japan (under licence), in Europe (majority share) and also in a new resort in Hong Kong. A new Disney resort will open in Shanghai, PRC, around the end of 2015. The company also owned an important and valuable range of brands, particularly those like Mickey Mouse and Winnie the Pooh, which were linked with children. The company used these to develop merchandise sold in its theme parks, Disney Shops and other direct marketing business activities. The main elements of its sales and profits are shown in Figure 8.2. The figure also shows how these have changed over the three years 2011 to 2013: for example, the interactive business was growing in terms of sales but still making losses.

Need for profitable growth

For many years, the Walt Disney Company had been able to deliver consistent and profitable growth to its shareholders. However, in recent years, various problems arose and profits began to stagnate. Its media networks suffered from competition from all the other major television stations in the USA and its income from advertising declined, although there was a major recovery here in 2004. Its parks and resorts were hit by various problems – the Florida parks were hit by several hurricanes in 2004, resulting not so much in damage but people staying away; its European theme park had rarely made any profits since its launch in 1992: it was too far north for year-round sun and also competed with the company's own parks in Florida; the Japanese theme park was profitable, but Disney was only a minority shareholder; the new Hong Kong park was still in its early stages.

However, Disney had successfully begun a new venture – family cruise ships to a Caribbean holiday location – as part of a holiday resort complex. Probably the biggest turnaround in 2004 was in filmed entertainment: the company had major successes in 2003 with *Finding Nemo* (co-production with Pixar) and *Pirates of the Caribbean*. But 2004 included the film *The Alamo*, which cost $100 million and was unsuccessful at the box office. The branded consumer products increased steadily but would never be the major part of the business.

The following years produced major profitable growth. The principal area was in its media networks, not just ABC television but also its dedicated sports channels, including ESPN. In addition, it produced a succession of quality films – called 'studio entertainment' in the company – including more *Pirates of the Caribbean* and the highly profitable *High School Musical*. Figure 8.2 also shows how sales and profits developed over 2011–2013.

New growth at Disney: what resources and what options?

Having survived a takeover attempt by a rival American media company – Comcast – in 2004, the Walt Disney Company had delivered new growth over the following years. It had been hampered by a considerable disagreement over strategy between some of the shareholders led by Roy E. Disney, son of one of the company's founders. He was in dispute with the company's dominant chief executive, Michael Eisner. Eisner had been with the company for 20 years and had been behind many of its recent major strategic moves. But Eisner had fallen out with some major shareholders who felt that he had become an obstacle to growth and did not recognise some of the major strengths of the Disney Company. For example, it was Eisner who decided that the remaining highly skilled studio animators should be asked to leave. He was criticised by Roy Disney, who commented: 'It is not cost-effective to fire a lot of talented artists and make mediocre movies. The safe decision is always the most dangerous one.' Disney even set up a website to fight the company's management – www.SaveDisney.com. The outcome of this was that Eisner was stripped of his Disney chairmanship in 2004 and he finally left the company in September 2005.

The competitive resources of the Disney company were formidable: its library of filmed material, its branded characters, its ownership of the method of delivering media, its theme parks and its experience in studio entertainment. It was particularly strong in family entertainment, with the Disney brand

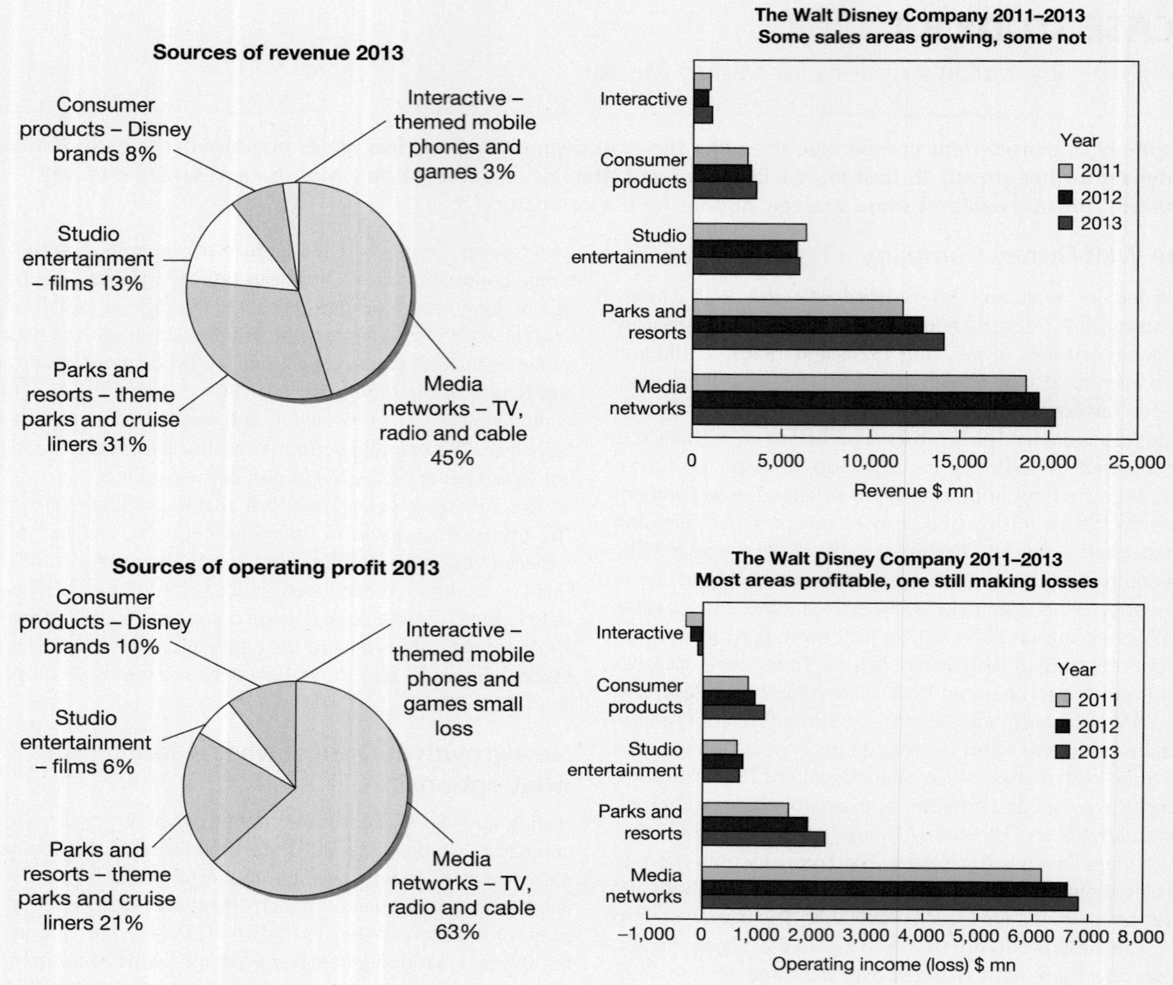

Figure 8.2 Walt Disney Company: sources of revenue and operating profit 2011–2013

itself being particularly powerful in this area. For several years, it had also combined with the animation company Pixar to distribute its films – *Finding Nemo*, etc. – and eventually acquired Pixar in 2007. In spite of producing substantial growth over the years, Disney was under pressure to continue the good performance. It needed new strategies.

Disney's future strategic options included the following:

- *Further development of its theme parks.* It was negotiating a possible site in Shanghai, China. The problem with theme parks is that they are capital-intensive and take a lengthy period to develop: for example, the Hong Kong park on Lantau Island was first agreed in 1999.
- *Media network development.* This would be difficult in the saturated US market, but the company was looking to the increasingly fragmented European market, especially the UK.
- *Studio filmed entertainment.* This was essentially a risky business. There are good payoffs if the judgement is right but a strong downside if the film is unsuccessful.

Options in 2013

Arguably, Disney could also look more broadly at its strategic options. The company is already using its considerable resource-based advantages wisely. It has used recent acquisitions to enhance its media content portfolio paying $15 billion to acquire Pixar (above) and subsequently Marvel Comics (Spider-Man, X Men) and Lucas Films (Star Wars). Content strategy remains crucial to competitive advantage in global media. Disney has spent wisely but needs to continue exploiting its new brands.

Disney has announced a series of long-term goals to reduce its environmental impact. Progress to achieving these is described in the Disney material available on the web at: http://corporate.disney.go.com/citizenship2010/environment/overview/ourapproach/

Case questions

1 What are the competitive advantages of the Disney group? Which, if any, are sustainable over time?

2 Using concepts from this chapter, what are the options available to Disney over the next five years?

3 Can companies in the media and travel industries, like television stations and theme parks, gain and retain competitive advantage simply by offering new products? Or do they need to rethink other aspects of their strategy? If so, which aspects?

Checklist for identifying company strengths.

8.1 PURPOSE AND THE SWOT ANALYSIS – THE CONTRIBUTION OF ANDREWS

As a starting point for the development of strategic options, Kenneth Andrews first identified the importance of connecting the organisation's purpose – its mission and objectives – with its strategic options and subsequent activities. 'The interdependence of purposes, policies, and organised action is crucial to the particularity of an individual strategy and its opportunity to identify competitive advantage.'[2] We explored the purpose of the organisation in Part 2 of this book, so we will assume here that we have some agreed definition against which to develop some options.

Andrews went on to argue persuasively that the rational analysis of the possibilities open to organisations was an essential part of strategy development. As a starting point in developing options, it is useful to summarise the current position using a SWOT analysis of the organisation. **Definition ▸** **SWOT is an analysis of the Strengths and Weaknesses present internally in the organisation, coupled with the Opportunities and Threats that the organisation faces externally.** This approach follows from the distinction drawn by Andrews between two aspects of the organisation:

1 strengths and weaknesses – explored in the *resource-based* analysis in Chapter 4;

2 opportunities and threats – explored in the *environment-based* analysis in Chapter 3.

Each analysis will be unique to the organisation for which it is being devised, but some general pointers and issues can be drawn up. These are indicated in Table 8.1, which provides a checklist of some possible factors.

In devising a SWOT analysis, there are several factors that will enhance the quality of the material:

- Keep it brief – pages of analysis are usually not required.
- Relate strengths and weaknesses, wherever possible, to industry key factors for success.
- Strengths and weaknesses should also be stated in competitive terms, if possible. It is reassuring to be 'good' at something, but it is more relevant to be 'better than the competition'.
- Statements should be specific and avoid blandness – there is little point in stating ideas that everyone believes in.

Table 8.1 Some possible factors in a SWOT analysis

INTERNAL Strengths	Weaknesses
• Market dominance • Core strengths • Economies of scale • Low-cost position • Leadership and management skills • Financial and cash resource • Manufacturing ability and age of equipment • Innovation processes and results • Architecture network • Differentiated products • Product or service quality	• Share weakness • Few core strengths and low on key skills • Old plant with higher costs than competition • Weak finances and poor cash flow • Management skills and leadership lacking • Poor record on innovation and new ideas • Weak organisation with poor architecture • Low quality and reputation • Products not differentiated and dependent on few products
EXTERNAL Opportunities	**Threats**
• New markets and segments • New products • Diversification opportunities • Market growth • Competitor weakness • Strategic space • Demographic and social change • Change in political or economic environment • New takeover or partnership opportunities • Economic upturn • International growth	• New market entrants • Increased competition • Increased pressure from customers and suppliers • Substitutes • Low market growth • Economic cycle downturn • Technological threat • Change in political or economic environment • Demographic change • New international barriers to trade

Note: See text for dangers of lists and bullet points!

- Analysis should distinguish between where the company *wishes to be* and where it is *now*. The gap should be realistic.
- It is important to be realistic about the strengths and weaknesses of one's own and competitive organisations.

Probably the biggest mistake that is commonly made in SWOT analysis is to assume that it is certain to be 'correct' because it contains every conceivable issue and is truly comprehensive. Nothing could be further from the truth. This merely demonstrates a paucity of real thought and a lack of strategic judgement about what is really important for that organisation.

Another common error is to provide a long list of points but little logic, argument and evidence. A short list with each point well argued is more likely to be convincing. Arguably, Table 8.1 with its bullet points and lack of any explanation is thoroughly misleading on this point. Whittington has a useful summary of some more general criticisms of SWOT analysis.[3]

8.2 ENVIRONMENT-BASED OPTIONS: GENERIC STRATEGIES – THE CONTRIBUTION OF PORTER

Definition ▶ We begin our exploration of environment-based options by considering the *generic strategies* first outlined by Professor Michael Porter of Harvard Business School. **Generic strategies are the three basic strategies of cost leadership, differentiation and focus (sometimes called niche) open to any business.** Porter's contribution was based on earlier work in industrial economics, exploring how firms compete.[4] Porter made the bold claim that there were only three fundamental strategies that any business could undertake – that is why he called them *generic*. During the 1980s, they were regarded as being at the forefront of strategic thinking. Arguably, they still have a contribution to make in the new century in the development of strategic options. However, strategists concentrating on the resource-based view now regard generic strategies as being largely historic. We return to a consideration of their merits at the end of this section.

Generic strategies were first outlined in two books from Porter, *Competitive Strategy*[5] in 1980 and *Competitive Advantage*[6] in 1985. The second book contained a small modification of the concept. The original version is explored here. After exploring the basic elements, a case example is considered and some comments on their theoretical validity and practical usefulness are offered. Porter confined his books to business situations and did not explore not-for-profit organisations.

8.2.1 The three generic competitive strategies: the three options

Porter argued that there were three basic, i.e. *generic*, strategies open to any business:

1 cost leadership
2 differentiation
3 focus.

According to the theory, every business needs to choose one of these in order to compete in the market place and gain sustainable competitive advantage. Each of these three strategic options represents an area that every business and many not-for-profit organisations can usefully explore. The three options can be explained by considering two aspects of the competitive environment:

1 *The source of competitive advantage*. There are fundamentally only two sources of competitive advantage. These are *differentiation* of products from competitors and *low costs*. We explore these two areas below.
2 *The competitive scope of the target customers*. It is possible to target the organisation's products as a *broad target* covering most of the market place or to pick a *narrow target* and focus on a niche within the market.

Porter then brought these two elements together in the well-known diagram shown as Figure 8.3.

In his second book, Porter modified the concept to split the niche sector into:

- niche differentiation and
- niche low-cost leadership.

The figure is sometimes shown in this modified form.

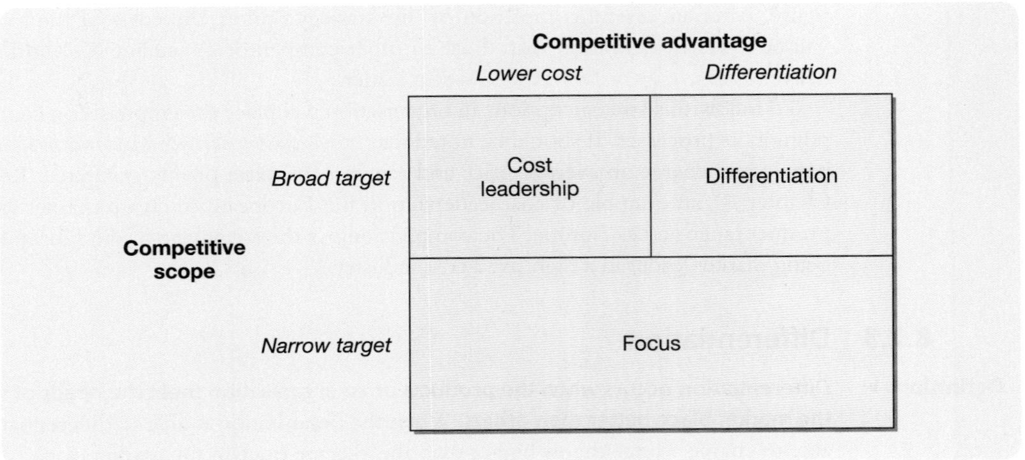

Figure 8.3 Generic strategic options

Source: reprinted with the permission of Free Press, a Division of Simon & Schuster, Inc., from *Competitive Advantage: Creating and Sustaining Superior Performance* by Michael E Porter. Copyright © 1985, 1998 by Michael E Porter. All rights reserved.

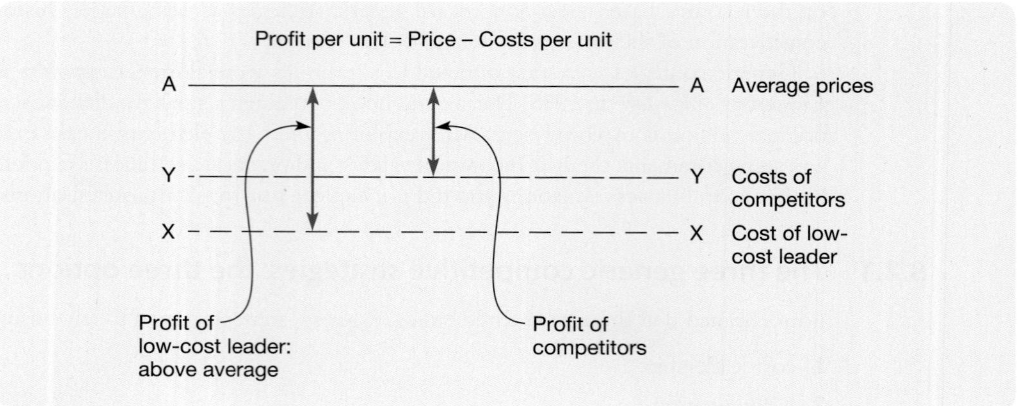

Figure 8.4 How low-cost leadership delivers above-average profits

8.2.2 Low-cost leadership

Definition ▶ **The low-cost leader in an industry has built and maintains plant, equipment, labour costs and working practices that deliver the lowest costs in that industry.** Later in this chapter, we will explore a number of options that organisations can follow for reducing costs – see Section 8.6. The essential point is that the firm with the lowest costs has a clear and possibly sustainable competitive advantage. However, in order to cut costs, a low-cost producer must find and exploit *all* the sources of cost advantage. Low-cost producers typically sell a standard, or no-frills, product and place considerable strategic emphasis on reaping scale or absolute cost advantages from all sources. In practice, low-cost leaders achieve their position by shaving costs off every element of the value chain – the strategy comes from attention to detail. McDonald's Restaurants achieves its low costs through standardised products, centralised buying of supplies for a whole country and so on.

The profit advantage gained from low-cost leadership derives from the assertion that low-cost leaders should be able to sell their products in the market place at around the average price of the market – see line A–A in Figure 8.4. If such products are not perceived as comparable or their performance is not acceptable to buyers, a cost leader will be forced to discount prices below competition in order to gain sales.

Compared with the low-cost leader, competitors will have higher costs – see line Y–Y in the figure. After successful completion of this strategy option, the costs of the lowest-cost producer will be lower by definition than those of other competitors – see line X–X in Figure 8.4. This will deliver *above-average profits* to the low-cost leader.

To follow this strategy option, an organisation will place the emphasis on cost reduction at every point in its processes. It should be noted that *cost leadership does not necessarily imply a low price*: the company could charge an average price and reinvest the extra profits generated. Referring forward to Chapter 10, an example of cost leadership in the European ice cream market would be Unilever's product range across Europe. The company enjoys the advantage of the substantial cost benefits of being market leader in a high fixed cost industry.

8.2.3 Differentiation

Definition ▶ **Differentiation occurs when the products of an organisation meet the needs of some customers in the market place better than others.** When the organisation is able to differentiate its products, it is able to charge a price that is higher than the average price in the market place.

Definition ▶ Underlying differentiation is the concept of *market segmentation*, which was explored in Chapter 3: **Market segmentation is the identification of specific groups who respond differently from other groups to competitive strategies.** Essentially, some customers will pay more for a differentiated

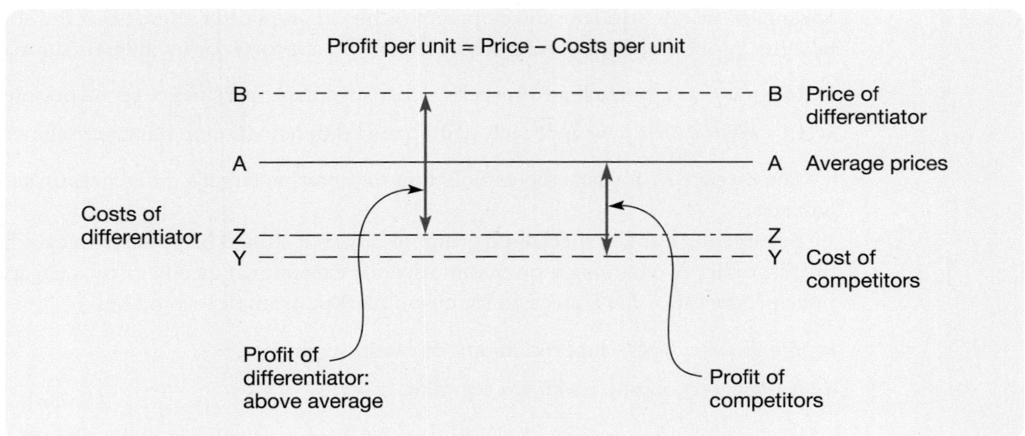

Figure 8.5 How differentiation delivers above-average profits

product that is targeted towards them. Examples of differentiation include better levels of service, more luxurious materials and better performance. McDonald's is differentiated by its brand name and its 'Big Mac' and 'Ronald McDonald' products and imagery. Another example can be taken from the European ice cream industry. The Mars Ice Cream range is clearly differentiated by its branding and its consequent ability to charge a premium price.

In order to differentiate a product, Porter argued that it is necessary for the producer to incur *extra costs*, for example, to advertise a brand and thus differentiate it. The differentiated product costs will therefore be higher than those of competitors – see line Z–Z in Figure 8.5. The producer of the differentiated product then derives an advantage from its pricing: with its uniquely differentiated product it is able to charge a premium price, i.e. one that is higher than its competitors – see line B–B in Figure 8.5.

There are two problems associated with differentiation strategies:

1 It is difficult to estimate whether the extra costs incurred in differentiation can be recovered from the customer by charging a higher price.

2 The successful differentiation may attract competitors to copy the differentiated product and enter the market segment. There are often costs associated with being first into a market, so there may be additional cost advantages from moving in second – for example, other companies have followed McDonald's and Mars Ice Cream.

Neither of the above problems is insurmountable, but they do weaken the attractiveness of this option.

8.2.4 Focus strategy (sometimes called niche strategy)

Sometimes, according to Porter, neither a low-cost leadership strategy nor a differentiation strategy is possible for an organisation across the broad range of the market. For example, the costs of achieving low-cost leadership may require substantial funds which are not available. Equally, the costs of differentiation, while serving the mass market of customers, may be too high: if the differentiation involves quality, it may not be credible to offer high-quality and cheap products under the same brand name, so a new brand name has to be developed and supported. For these and related reasons, it may be better to adopt a *focus* strategy.

Definition ▶ **A focus strategy occurs when the organisation focuses on a specific niche in the market place and develops its competitive advantage by offering products especially developed for that niche.** Hence the focused strategy selects a segment or group of segments in the industry and tailors its strategy to serve them to the *exclusion* of others. By optimising its strategy for the targets, the focuser seeks to achieve a competitive advantage in its target segments, albeit it does not possess a competitive advantage overall. In a later development of his theory, Porter argued that the company may undertake this process either by using a cost leadership approach or by differentiation:

- In a *cost focus* approach a firm seeks a cost advantage in its target segment only.
- In a *differentiation focus* approach a firm seeks differentiation in its target segment only.

The essence of focus is the exploitation of a narrow target's differences from the balance of the industry.

By targeting a small, specialised group of buyers it should be possible to earn higher than average profits, either by charging a premium price for exceptional quality or by a cheap and cheerful low-price product. For the European ice cream market, examples would be:

- *differentiation focus* – superpremium ice cream segment;
- *cost focus* – economy ice cream segment.

In the global car market, Rolls-Royce and Ferrari are clearly niche players – they have only a minute percentage of the market worldwide. Their niche is premium product and premium price.

There are some problems with the focus strategy, as follows:

- By definition, the niche is small and may not be large enough to justify attention.
- Cost focus may be difficult if economies of scale are important in an industry such as the car industry.
- The niche is clearly specialist in nature and may disappear over time.

None of these problems is insurmountable. Many small and medium-sized companies have found that this is the most useful strategic area to explore.

8.2.5 The danger of being stuck in the middle

Porter concluded his analysis of what he termed the main generic strategies by suggesting that there are real dangers for the firm that engages in each generic strategy but fails to achieve any of them – it is stuck in the middle. A firm in this position

> will compete at a disadvantage because the cost leader, differentiators, or focuser will be better positioned to compete in any segment . . . Such a firm will be much less profitable than rivals achieving one of the generic strategies.

Several commentators, such as Kay[7], Stopford and Baden-Fuller[8] and Miller,[9] now reject this aspect of the analysis. They point to several empirical examples of successful firms that have adopted more than one generic strategy: for example, Toyota cars and Benetton clothing manufacturing and shops, both of which are differentiated yet have low costs.

8.2.6 Comment on Porter's generic strategies

Hendry[10] and others have set out the problems of the logic and the empirical evidence associated with generic strategies that limit its absolute value. We can summarise them as follows:

Low-cost leadership

- If the option is to seek low-cost leadership, then how can more than one company be *the* low-cost leader? It may be a contradiction in terms to have an *option* of low-cost leadership.
- Competitors also have the option to reduce their costs in the long term, so how can one company hope to maintain its competitive advantage without risk?
- Low-cost leadership should be associated with cutting costs per unit of production. However, there are limitations to the usefulness of this concept, which are described in Section 8.6. They will also apply here.

- Low-cost leadership assumes that technology is relatively predictable, if changing. Radical change can so alter the cost positions of actual and potential competitors that the concept may have only limited relevance in fast-changing, high-technology markets.
- Cost reductions only lead to competitive advantage when *customers* are able to make comparisons. This means that the low-cost leader must also lead *price* reductions or competitors will be able to catch up, even if this takes some years and is at lower profit margins. But permanent price reductions by the cost leader may have a damaging impact on the market positioning of its product or service that will limit its usefulness.

CASE STUDY 8.2

Generic strategy options analysis: global ice cream

It is useful to explore some of the benefits and problems of options that have been developed from generic strategies. To undertake this, we can use the market data from Chapters 3 and 4 to analyse the possible strategy options in this industry in the late 2000s. The generic strategies are shown Figure 8.6.

Competitive scope		Competitive advantage: *Lower cost*	Competitive advantage: *Differentiation*
	Broad target	**Cost leadership** Unilever	**Differentiation** • Nestlé • Mars Ice Cream?
	Narrow target	**Cost focus** Economy ice cream made by small, local ice cream companies with low overheads	**Differentiation focus** Superpremium, e.g. Häagen-Dazs, Ben & Jerry's

Figure 8.6 Generic strategies in European ice cream

Although the market is still growing, it is relatively easy to position the basic companies in the global ice cream market. The positions of Nestlé and Mars are important. Whereas Nestlé has developed global scale it is still considerably smaller than the low-cost leader, Unilever. However, Nestlé does have a strong range of existing ice cream brands that will allow a premium price to be charged. Mars has differentiated products by the nature of its strong brands, but still remains a relatively small player: arguably it should be repositioned in the 'differentiated niche' category.

To develop new options, ice cream companies can move into niche strategic areas like ready-to-serve ice cream at Ben & Jerry's.

Case questions

1 If you were Nestlé in the global ice cream market, what strategy options would you pursue?

2 If you were Häagen-Dazs and someone recommended a low-cost option, what would your reaction be?

3 Are there any weaknesses in using Porter's generic strategies to generate market-based options in the European ice cream market? Make sure that you have read and understood the text before answering this question.

Differentiation

- Differentiated products are assumed to be higher priced. This is probably too simplistic. The form of differentiation may not lend itself to higher prices.
- The company may have the objective of increasing its market share, in which case it may use differentiation for this purpose and match the lower prices of competitors.
- Porter discusses differentiation as if the *form* this will take in any market will be immediately obvious. The real problem for strategy options is not to identify the *need* for differentiation but to work out what *form* this should take that will be attractive to the customer. Generic strategy options throw no light on this issue whatsoever. They simply make the dubious assumption that once differentiation has been decided on it is obvious how the product should be differentiated.

Competitive scope

- The distinction between broad and narrow targets is sometimes unclear. Are they distinguished by size of market? Or by customer type? If the distinction between them is unclear then what benefit is served by the distinction?
- For many companies, it is certainly useful to recognise that it would be more productive to pursue a niche strategy, away from the broad markets of the market leaders. That is the easy part of the logic. The difficult part is to identify *which* niche is likely to prove worthwhile. Generic strategies provide no useful guidance on this at all.
- As markets fragment and product life cycles become shorter, the concept of broad targets may become increasingly redundant.

Stuck in the middle

As was pointed out above, there is now useful empirical evidence that some companies do pursue differentiation *and* low-cost strategies at the same time. They use their low costs to provide greater differentiation and then reinvest the profits to lower their costs even further. Companies such as Benetton (Italy), Toyota (Japan) and BMW (Germany) have been cited as examples.

Resource-based view

In Chapter 4, we explored the arguments supporting this view of strategic analysis. They also apply to strategy options and suggest that options based on the uniqueness of the *company* rather than the characteristics of the *industry* are likely to prove more useful in developing competitive strategy. We return to these issues later in this chapter, but comment now that the resource-based view does undermine much of Porter's approach.

Fast-moving markets

In dynamic markets such as those driven by new internet technology, the application of generic strategies will almost certainly miss major new market opportunities. They cannot be identified by the generic strategies approach.

Conclusions

Faced with this veritable onslaught on generic strategies, it might be thought that Porter would gracefully concede that there might be some weaknesses in the concept. However, he hit back in 1996 by drawing a distinction between basic strategy and what he called 'operational effectiveness' – the former concerned the key strategic decisions facing any organisation while the latter is more concerned with such issues as total quality management (TQM), outsourcing, re-engineering and the like[12]. He did not concede any ground but rather extended his approach to explore how companies might use *market positioning* within the concept of generic strategies – this topic was explored in Chapter 3.

Given these criticisms, it might be concluded that the concept of generic strategies has no merit. However, as long as it is treated only as part of a broader analysis, it can be a useful tool for generating basic *options* in strategic analysis. It forces exploration of two important aspects of strategic management: the role of *cost reduction* and the use of *differentiated products* in relation to customers and competitors. But it is only a starting point in the development of such options. When the market is growing fast, it may provide no useful routes at all. More generally, the whole approach takes a highly *prescriptive* view of strategic action.

KEY STRATEGIC PRINCIPLES

- Generic strategies are a means of generating basic strategy options in an organisation. They are based on seeking competitive advantage in the market place.
- There are three main generic options: cost leadership, differentiation and focus.
- Cost leadership aims to place the organisation amongst the lowest-cost producers in the market. It does not necessarily mean having low prices. Higher than average profits come from charging average prices.
- Differentiation is aimed at developing and targeting a product against a major market segment. Because the product is especially developed, it should be possible to add a small premium to the average price. Differentiation has a cost, but this should be more than compensated for in the higher price charged.
- Focus involves targeting a small segment of the market. It may operate by using a low-cost focus or differentiated focus approach.
- According to the theory, it is important to select between the options and not to be 'stuck in the middle'. Some influential strategists have produced evidence that has cast doubt on this point.
- There have been numerous criticisms of the approach based on logic and empirical evidence of actual industry practice. Undoubtedly these comments have validity, but generic strategies represent a useful starting point in developing strategy options.

CASE STUDY 8.3

Market-based strategies in global TV: exciting opportunities in a fast-changing market

Over the past 15 years, global television has become a major business opportunity. This case explores how such opportunities have arisen and been exploited by some of the leading companies. It also outlines some further market possibilities for both national and global companies over the next few years.

Industry-based change: technology and politics bring new opportunities

Until recently, newspapers have been highly competitive in many countries of the world, but TV has not. Because of technical limitations on the numbers of TV channels that could be broadcast and the deep influence of TV on its audience, TV companies were often controlled by the state or by a small number of commercial interests. However, by the late 1990s, the global media market was growing rapidly. Major new profit opportunities came from two new sources: technology and politics.

- *Technology* – via new satellite channels, cable TV and, more recently, the internet. At the beginning of the twenty-first century, technology has been augmented by the advent of digital broadcasting, the essential effect here being to allow many more TV channels to appear on air and through the internet.
- *Politics* – through national governments either privatising government-owned channels or simply allowing new, private, commercial TV channels to broadcast.

The two main profit streams of global media: production and broadcasting

Media companies can generate revenue and profits in TV in two main ways: TV production and network broadcasting.

1. *TV production* – the manufacture of programmes for broadcast. Creative ideas, popular stars and strong entertainment values can deliver competitive advantage. TV production facilities, such as studios, can be hired and are relatively inexpensive. Production costs can range from cheap game shows to expensive TV drama. Revenue then comes from the sale of such programmes to the TV broadcasters and the worldwide syndication of programme formats like *Big Brother* and *Who Wants To Be A Millionaire?*

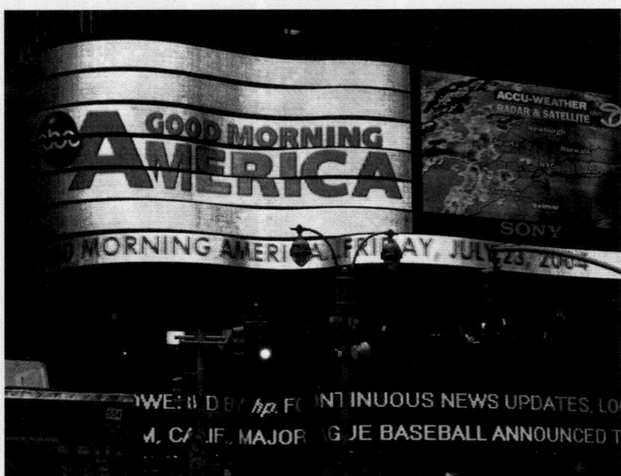

ABC television's *Good Morning America* Is broadcast live from New York but is facing increased competition from many new satellite and cable channels.

2 *Network broadcasting*. Traditionally, this has involved competition between a limited number of companies broadcasting across the airwaves. In recent years, new forms of transmission using cable, satellite and the internet are extending dramatically the number of channels available. Although the capital cost of cabling to homes is high, the new technology of streaming across telephone cabling using the internet will potentially revolutionise broadcasting in countries where fixed line telephone cables are present. Revenues are then derived from advertising or from subscription revenues to the cable (or satellite) channel or both.

Many companies are engaged in both production and broadcasting. However, there are also a large number of independent production companies because the barriers to entry have been much lower than for broadcasting. The costs of setting up a production company to make TV programmes might typically be $1 million, but these are much smaller than the costs of developing a broadcasting station – typically $10–100 million. However, this is beginning to change as internet broadcasting and cheap television cameras become more widespread. YouTube has demonstrated the power and success of simply-made new television films.

Strategically, the broadcasters have had the greater bargaining power because they controlled access to large numbers of viewers, whose only bargaining power is to turn off the TV. In practice, the broadcasters with their large budgets still have the main power but the situation is changing.

International TV markets: becoming more global?

Although some programmes are regularly broadcast around the world – ranging from *Star Trek* to World Cup football – both customer tastes and the various competitors vary from one continent to another. Some specialist niche categories such as coverage of the *Olympics* and *Formula 1 Motor Racing* may be considered global. It is these areas where large international media companies – like News Corporation and Disney – have the opportunity to use their international media coverage to negotiate stronger media deals in areas such as sport.

However, in many respects, there is no single global market. Language and cultural preferences still produce differences in approach and content. In terms of size, there are at least five main areas:

1 North America: USA and Canada.
2 Europe: the European Union.
3 Asia-Pacific: China and India are the largest, but Australia/New Zealand is also important.
4 Spanish-speaking North and South America with Portuguese-speaking Brazil as a special case.
5 African markets with a wide but rapidly growing franchise.

The new media challenge from the internet

Perhaps the most interesting and exciting new threat to all broadcast and cable television comes from the internet. The new technology of broadband telecommunications over telephone wires and cable has the power to alter television in at least three fundamental ways:

1 It will allow many more channels to reach homes and therefore potentially *fragment* the power of the traditional broadcasters. To offset this, such broadcasters are already developing their own offerings to saturate such channels. In addition, they are using their libraries of previously broadcast popular programmes – films, dramas, etc. – to entice viewers. However, fragmentation is already happening through existing cable channels and will continue.
2 It will allow viewers to select when they view programmes: digital technology can be used to store programmes. This means that advertising may lose some of its impact.
3 New channels, like YouTube and Facebook, have the power to create new outlets for material that go beyond any media previously seen. We have already observed how Google is taking substantial advertising revenue from existing media providers – see Case 1.3. The full potential for this route remains to be explored.

Overall, global media has the potential to change in ways that remain unpredictable at the present time. Arguably, emergent strategy will never be more relevant than in this market place.

TV business strategies: the choice between software and hardware and the need for innovation and negotiation skills

There is some disagreement between the leading companies about the most effective business strategies for the 2000s. Sony believes the best approach is through 'software', i.e. the purchase of exclusive rights to films, TV programmes and books. Other companies such as Viacom, News Corporation and Disney have spent at least part of their efforts on 'hardware' – i.e. the devices that deliver the TV signal to the final customer – through ownership of TV stations in some countries, satellite or cable channels. Both these routes can produce high barriers to entry in terms of the substantial investment required.

However, the internet is beginning to alter the high barriers because it is cheap and relatively easy to set up a website. The rapid introduction of broadband has allowed much more sophisticated picture signals to be delivered to individual homes. This has the potential to make the possession of the *content* of television programmes much more significant than the method of delivery: *software may begin to win over hardware.* Other strategies in the TV market include:

- delivery of *attractive programmes* such as live and exclusive TV sport or recent films;
- *restrictive access,* meaning that the viewer has no choice but to buy into the network – supply is via cable or an encrypted TV signal that takes a special box to decode;
- *outright acquisition of old films,* delivering unique competitive advantage here;
- *heavy investment in new cable and satellite channels* – for example, cable companies are investing around $10 billion in the USA and a similar amount in the UK;
- *company acquisitions and joint ventures* – for example, Disney acquired the ABC TV network and other assets for $19 billion; News Corporation is attempting to acquire the UK broadcaster BSkyB $12 billion;
- *cross-promotion deals* across the different media (e.g. from book to film or video to satellite).

Because the necessary investment often amounts to billions of dollars, companies may not have the resources to pursue *both* strategies and need to make a choice. More generally, it will be evident that the fast-moving environment has required two strategies above all others:

1 *Innovation* – seizing opportunities in film and sports deals, new channels, new technologies, etc.
2 *Negotiation skills* – many of the new strategies needed deals to be struck with governments, competitors, sports bodies, technology companies, etc.

Key factors for success in TV: how to build sustainable competitive advantage and value added

Because there is some disagreement on strategic management across the industry, the key factors cannot be identified with certainty. However, it is likely that on a global basis they would include the following:

- highly creative and innovative people to create programme content;
- strong financial base in order to fund the high market growth;
- real strengths in selected markets in terms of market share, at least in some market segments – this might be built using sports contracts, media contracts, a strong film library and even total control over subscribers to their channels;
- means of overcoming barriers to entry – either access to programmes or channels of distribution – perhaps via the internet;
- commercial acumen and deal-making skills.

Apart from some programmes that explore this issue, green strategy does not seem to feature in the activities of broadcasters or television production companies. One exception is Facebook which invested in new lower-energy servers for its networks. Perhaps the reason is that television broadcasters may not see themselves as high energy users.

Case questions

1 Do Porter's generic strategies provide any useful insights in structuring the strategic opportunities in global TV? Think carefully about the criticisms before you answer this question.
2 If you were developing strategy options for a small company, what strategy options would you consider? What problems might you encounter?
3 What strategy options would you consider if you were given the task of developing a truly global TV network? Would it be profitable?
4 What lessons, if any, can be drawn from the global TV market on the broad task of developing strategic options?

STRATEGIC PROJECT

This case only touches on the many media changes that have occurred in every part of the world over the past ten years. A more detailed study of the potential in one country would be both challenging and interesting. It needs to start with the national broadcaster(s) and then expand to cover the competition, how the national market is becoming increasingly fragmented and which channels are particularly popular. It should also cover the new methods of delivery using the internet and broadband. Much of this can be gained from websites and broadcast magazines. It would be particularly interesting to explore emergent strategies over the next five years because further change is certain.

8.3 ENVIRONMENT-BASED STRATEGIC OPTIONS: THE MARKET OPTIONS MATRIX

Definition ▸

Video Part 6a

The market options matrix identifies the product and market options available to the organisation, including the possibility of withdrawal and movement into unrelated markets. The distinction is drawn between *markets*, which are defined as customers, and *products*, which are defined as the items sold to customers. Thus, for example, one customer could buy several different products, depending on need.

The market options matrix examines the options available to the organisation from a broader strategic perspective than the simple market/product matrix (called in some texts the *Ansoff matrix*). Thus the market options matrix not only considers the possibility of launching new products and moving into new markets, but also explores the possibility of *withdrawing* from markets and moving into *unrelated* markets. Nevertheless, the format is based on product/market options: it is shown in Figure 8.7. The foundation in 'product/market options' suggests that such options are primarily at the *business* level of the organisation. In practice, some options may need to be considered at the *corporate* level in an organisation: the reason is that some decisions like withdrawal or diversification may impact on other areas of the business and also make it more difficult for the group in total to employ core competencies, block competitive moves, etc. Such decisions will need to be decided on a case-by-case basis.

Each of the strategic options is now considered in turn.

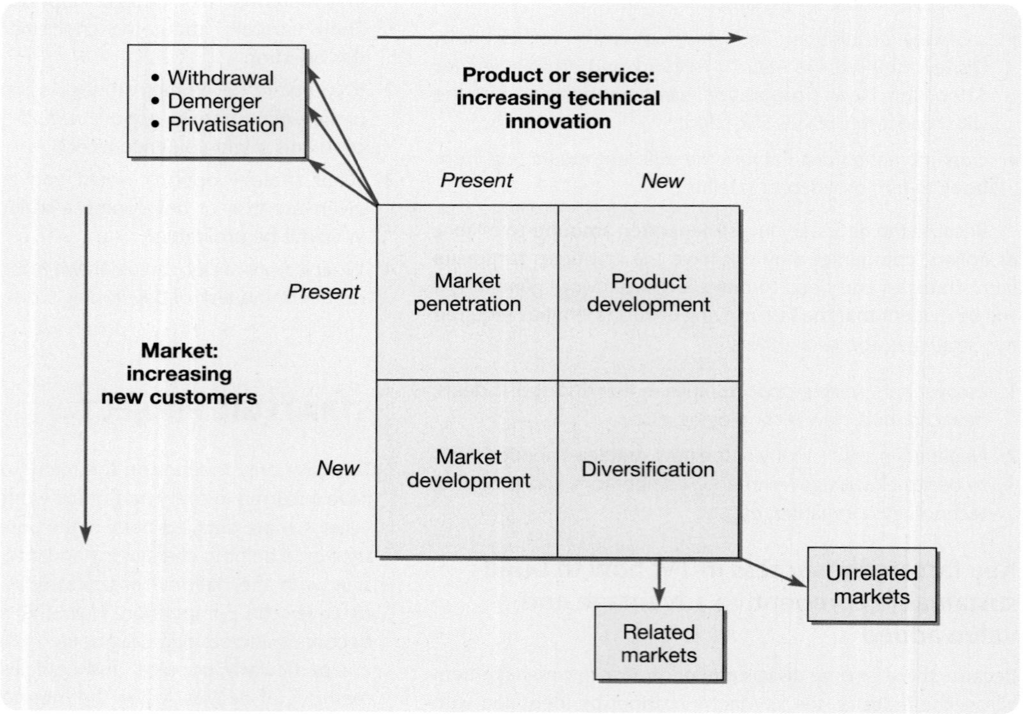

Figure 8.7 Market options matrix

Note: Although the developments are shown as *options* in separate boxes, there may in reality be a gradual movement from one area to another. They are not absolutes. To avoid confusion, it should be noted that market *penetration* differs from market *development* because penetration concentrates on existing or potential customers, whereas development seeks totally new segments of customers or totally new customer groups.

Source: author based on Ansoff, I (1989) *Corporate Strategy*, rev edn, Penguin, Harmondsworth. The matrix also uses concepts outlined in Day, G S (1987) *Strategic Management Planning*, West Publishing, St Paul, MN.

8.3.1 Withdrawal

It may seem perverse to begin the consideration of market options with the possible strategy of withdrawing from them. But strategy must always consider the unpredictable if it is to develop competitive advantage. There are a number of circumstances where this option may have merit, for example:

- *Product life cycle in decline phase with little possibility of retrenchment.* In the context of global TV, the time will come in the next 20 years (or sooner) when digital TV channels will take over from analogue broadcasts and all the old products will simply be scrapped.
- *Over-extension of product range which can only be resolved by withdrawing some products.* In television, some of the many channels now being offered may have such small audiences that they do not justify even the minimal expense of keeping them operating.
- *Holding company sales of subsidiaries.* Such companies often see their subsidiary companies, perhaps in diverse industries, as being little more than assets to be bought and sold if the price is attractive. US TV companies regularly sell local TV stations and withdraw from that market for reasons associated with finance, ability to link with other stations, change of corporate objectives, etc.
- *Raise funds for investment elsewhere.* Organisations may be able to *sell* the asset they are planning to withdraw from the market. Even without a sale, the working capital and management time devoted to the asset might be redeployed to other more productive uses. Government-owned companies faced with restrictions on outside funds might regard withdrawal and sale as a useful strategy here.

8.3.2 Demerger

In a sense, this is a form of withdrawal from the market, but it has a rather specialist meaning with some attractive implications. For some companies whose shares are openly traded on the stock exchange, the value of the *underlying assets* may be rather larger than the value implied by the *share price*. For example, the UK-based chemical company ICI was split into two companies in 1993 by issuing two sets of shares to its existing shareholders. The shares of the two companies were then separately traded on the London Stock Exchange at a greater value than when they had been combined. The reason was that part of the company's product range was in basic and specialist chemicals. A separate part was in agrochemicals and pharmaceuticals, the latter being highly attractive to stockholders. ICI was *demerged*, with the first part keeping the name ICI and the second part taking the name Zeneca. Subsequently, other chemical companies – such as the major German chemical company Hoechst – have followed a similar strategy.

This strategy has been used increasingly to realise the underlying asset values in publicly quoted companies. It also has the benefit that companies with totally unrelated market activities allow each part to focus on its own activities without competing for scarce resources. It has the disadvantage that it may destroy the benefits of size, cross-trading and uniqueness of a larger company.

8.3.3 Privatisation

In many countries around the world, there has been a trend to privatise government-owned companies – that is, to sell the company's shares into private ownership. This has become a major option for some institutions. For example, many national telecommunications companies have now been privatised, except in the USA, where they have always been in the private sector. The results in terms of management style, public accountability, ownership and strategy changes have been substantial. The changes in the product range, levels of service and public perceptions have also been significant.

8.3.4 Market penetration in the existing market

Without moving outside the organisation's current range of products or services, it may be possible to attract customers from directly competing products by penetrating the market. Market penetration strategy should begin[14] with *existing* customers. A direct attack on *competing* customers invites retaliation that can nullify the initial gains and erode the company's profit margins. Retaining an existing customer is usually cheaper, especially in consumer goods markets. Car companies such as Toyota and BMW make great efforts to retain customers when they change cars.

If a direct attack is to be mounted on a competitor in order to penetrate the market, it is likely to be more effective[15] if a *combination* of activities is mounted – for example, an improvement in product quality and levels of service along with promotional activity. Clearly, this is likely to be more expensive in the short term but should have benefits in the long run in terms of increased market share. News Corporation satellite operations regularly combine new TV channels with advertising and special deals on decoders as part of its strategy to penetrate the market.

Market penetration may be easier if the market is *growing*. The reason is that existing customer loyalties may be less secure and new customers entering the market may still be searching for the most acceptable product. The most attractive strategy in these circumstances will vary with the company's market share position:

- Existing companies with *low relative market share* in a growing market have little to lose from aggressively attacking the market or a segment of it. For example, the smaller Burger King (Grand Metropolitan, UK) has attacked McDonald's hard over the last few years with some success.
- Existing companies with a *high relative market share* in a growing market have potentially an attractive position which might be lost. Predatory price cutting is a strategy sometimes employed to keep out the smaller new entrants. It will work well and move the company down the experience curve, as long as it has the production capacity. This strategy has been employed by Intel to launch new-generation computer chips and hold off the smaller new entrants such as Cyrix and AMD (all US companies).

8.3.5 Market development using existing products

For this strategic route, the organisation moves beyond its immediate customer focus into attracting new customers for its existing product range. It may seek new *segments* of the market, new *geographical areas* or new *uses* for its products or services that will bring in new customers.

Expansion to bring totally new customers to the company for its existing products could easily involve some slight repackaging and then promotion to a new market segment. It will often involve selling the same product in new international markets – there are many examples of such a strategy throughout this book. Using core competencies and a little ingenuity, it may be possible to find new uses for existing products. For example, the pharmaceutical company Glaxo (UK) has sought to develop the markets for its anti-ulcer drug Zantac as markets have matured in Western Europe and North America. Thus it has marketed the product to an increasing range of countries and it has also developed a lower-strength version to be sold without prescription as a stomach remedy in place of antacid remedies.

We explore the methods by which organisations can undertake such expansion in the next section.

8.3.6 Product development for the existing market

We refer here to significant new product developments, not a minor variation on an existing product. There are a number of reasons that might justify such a strategy:[16]

- to utilise excess production capacity;
- to counter competitive entry;
- to exploit new technology;
- to maintain the company's stance as a product innovator;
- to protect overall market share.

Understanding the reason is key to selecting the route that product development will then follow. Probably the area with the most potential is that associated with innovation: it may represent a threat to an existing product line or an opportunity to take market share from competition. Sometimes product development strategies do not always fall neatly into an existing market. They often move the company into markets and towards customers that are not currently being served. This is part of the natural growth of many organisations.

8.3.7 Diversification: related markets

When an organisation diversifies, it moves out of its current products and markets into new areas. Clearly, this will involve a step into the unknown and will carry a higher degree of business risk. However, the organisation may minimise this risk if it moves into related markets. (*Related* here means a market that has some existing connection with its existing value chain.) It is usual to distinguish three types of relationship based on the value chain of Chapter 4 and explored in the section on corporate strategy in Chapter 9:

1 *Forward integration.* A manufacturer becomes involved in the activities of the organisation's *outputs* such as distribution, transport, logistics – for example, the purchase of glass distributors by Europe's two leading glass manufacturers, St Gobain (France) and Pilkington (UK).[17]

2 *Backward integration.* The organisation extends its activities to those of its *inputs* such as its suppliers of raw materials, plant and machinery – for example, the purchase by the oil company Elf (France) of oil drilling interests in the North Sea.[18]

3 *Horizontal integration.* The organisation moves into areas immediately related to its existing activities because either they compete or they are complementary – for example, the acquisition by BMW (Germany) of the UK car company Rover in 1994.

News Corporation has engaged in forward integration by purchasing cable and satellite channels to deliver TV programmes directly to customers. It has integrated backwards into film production companies. It has undertaken horizontal integration by extending the range of its activities from newspapers to books, TV and electronic media.

Synergy is the main reason given for such activities.[19] It means essentially that the whole is worth more than the sum of the parts: the value to be generated from owning and controlling more of the value chain is greater because the various elements support each other. This concept is relatively easy to understand but rather more difficult to analyse precisely. This means that it is difficult to assess its specific contribution to strategic management. It is related to the concept of *linkages* in the value chain that were explored in Chapter 4 and is probably best assessed using these concepts.

8.3.8 Diversification: unrelated markets

When an organisation moves into unrelated markets, it runs the risk of operating in areas where its detailed knowledge of the key factors for success is limited. Essentially, it acts as if it were a *holding company*. Some companies have operated such a strategy with success, probably the best known being Hanson plc (UK, but with strong interests in the USA) and General Electric (USA). The logic of such an expansion is unlikely to be market-related, by definition, since the target market has no connection with the organisation's current areas of interest. There are two reasons why the strategy may have some merit:

1 There could be other connections in finance with the existing business that would justify such expansion.

2 There may be no connection, but the diversification could still be operated successfully if the holding company managed such a venture using tight but clear financial controls.

Clearly, such strategies are directly related to the discussion on strategic parenting in Chapter 9. However, it should be pointed out that unrelated diversification is not popular at present: it flies against the evidence and logic of the resource-based view.

Comment

The market options matrix is a useful way of structuring the options available. However, it does not in itself provide many useful indicators of which option to choose in what circumstances. Thus its value lies in *structuring* the problem rather than *solving it*. The main strategic insights come from the possibilities that it raises to challenge current thinking by opening up the debate.

Such routes may involve the expenditure of some funds on new product development, research, advertising and related matters. Hence, the options are more likely to be favoured by those organisations with significant financial resources. Many of the options are more likely to be considered by profitable companies, rather than those attempting to recover from substantial losses. However, by disposing of some assets, market-based options may actually raise funds and provide greater freedom of action for those remaining in the organisation. Typically, these might include the sale of parts of companies.

The market options matrix may be more appropriate in the commercial, non-government-owned sector because state companies are usually set up to fill a specific role with little room for development beyond this definition.

KEY STRATEGIC PRINCIPLES

- By examining the market place and the products available, it is possible to structure options that organisations may be able to adopt: the overall structure is called the *market options matrix*.
- Options include moving to new customers and new products. As these are developed further, they may involve the organisation in diversifying away from its original markets.
- Synergy is the main reason behind diversification into related markets: the whole being more than the sum of the parts. This concept is associated with linkages in the value chain.
- The market options matrix is a method of generating options but provides no guidance on choosing between them. The main strategic insights come from the possibilities that it raises to challenge the current thinking by opening up the debate.

8.4 ENVIRONMENT-BASED STRATEGIC OPTIONS: THE EXPANSION METHOD MATRIX

Definition ▶ **The expansion method matrix explores in a structured way the methods by which the market opportunities associated with strategy options might be achieved.** By examining the organisation's internal and external expansion opportunities and its geographical spread of activity, it is possible to structure the various methods that are available.

Video Part 6a

In addition to exploring the routes to develop strategy options, it is also important to explore the methods by which these can be achieved. For example, launching a new product could be done using an existing company or an acquisition, merger or joint venture with another firm. As companies have moved outside their home countries, the methods used for such development have also increased. We have already seen how News Corporation has used a variety of contractual arrangements in different countries in the world to develop its global presence. The full list of options is set out in Figure 8.8.

8.4.1 Acquisitions

Probably the most important reason for this method of market expansion is that associated with the particular assets of the company: brands, market share, core competencies and special technologies may all represent reasons for purchase.[20] News Corporation acquired its encryption technology by buying a company in 1990. The obvious disadvantage is that, if a company really has an asset, there

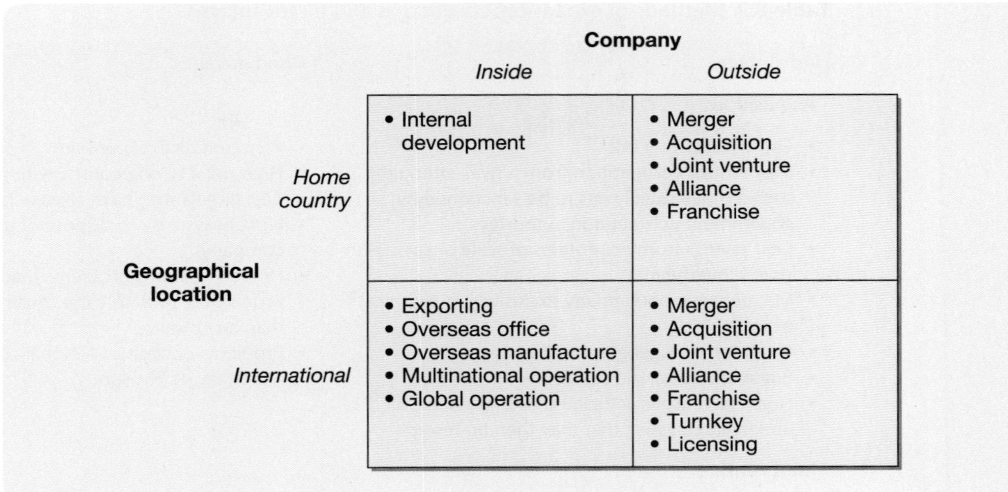

Figure 8.8 Expansion method matrix

Note: All the above methods must add value to the organisation if they are to justify the costs.

may be a substantial premium to pay over the asset value of the company. For example, Nestlé paid double the value at which the shares of Rowntree had previously been quoted on the stock exchange when it bought the chocolate company in 1989.

Acquisitions may also be made for competitive reasons. In a static market, it may be expensive and slow to enter by building from the beginning. For example, in the slow-growing coffee market, Philip Morris/Kraft General Foods has made a series of company purchases to add to its Maxwell House brand: Café Hag and Jacobs Coffee. In fast-growing markets, acquisitions may be the means to acquire presence more rapidly. For example, the purchase of the Biogen Company by Roche (Switzerland) moved the Swiss company at a stroke from its traditional drugs market into the totally new area of biomedical sciences.

8.4.2 Mergers

Mergers are similar to acquisitions in the sense of two companies combining. However, mergers usually arise because neither company has the scale to acquire the other on its own. This has the potential benefit of being more friendly but requires special handling if the benefits are to be realised. In other respects, it is similar to an acquisition in terms of the main strategic issues.

8.4.3 Joint ventures and alliances

A *joint venture* is the formation of a company whose shares are owned jointly by two parent companies. It usually shares some of the assets and skills of both parents. Cereal Partners Inc. is a 50/50 joint venture between Nestlé and General Mills (USA) whose purpose is to attack Kellogg's breakfast cereals around the world except in North America – see Case 2.1.

An *alliance* is some form of weaker contractual agreement or even minority shareholding between two parent companies. It usually falls short of the formation of a separate subsidiary. Several of the European telecommunications companies have built alliances as the basis for international expansion.

8.4.4 Franchise

A franchise is a form of licensing agreement in which the contractor provides the licensee with a preformed package of activity. It may include a brand name, technical service expertise and some

Table 8.2 Methods of expansion: advantages and disadvantages

Advantages	Disadvantages
Acquisition	
• Can be relatively fast • May reduce competition from a rival, although such a move usually has to be sanctioned by government competition authorities • Cost savings from economies of scale or savings in shared overheads • Maintenance of company exclusivity in technical expertise • Extend to new geographical area • Buy market size and share • Financial reasons associated with purchase of undervalued assets that may then be resold	• Premium paid: expensive • High risk if wrong company targeted • Best targets may have already been acquired • Not always easy to dispose of unwanted parts of company • Human relations problems that can arise after the acquisition: probably the cause of more failures than any other • Problems of clash of national cultures, particularly where target 'foreign'
Joint venture	
• Builds scale quickly • Obtains special expertise quickly • Cheaper than acquisition • Can be used where outright acquisition not feasible • Can be used where similar product available	• Control lost to some extent • Works best where both parties contribute something different to the mix • Can be difficult to manage because of need to share and because parent companies may interfere • Share profits with partner
Alliance	
• Can build close contacts with partner • Uses joint expertise and commitment • Allows potential partners to learn about each other • Locks out other competitors	• Slow and plodding approach • Needs constant work to keep relationship sound • Unlikely to build economies of scale
Franchise	
• Lower investment than outright purchase • Some of basic testing of business proposition undertaken by franchise holder: lower risk • Exclusive territory usually granted	• Depends on quality of franchise • Part of profits paid over to franchise holder • Risk that business built and franchise withdrawn

Source: adapted from Lynch, R (1994) *European Business Strategies*, 2nd edn, Kogan Page, London.

advertising assistance. Payment is usually a percentage of turnover. McDonald's Restaurants are among the best-known franchises.

The main advantages and disadvantages of the various methods of market expansion are summarised in Table 8.2.

8.4.5 International options

In spite of the publicity on some occasions across Europe, acquisitions are relatively infrequent outside the UK and North America.[21] They are also used sparingly in many countries of South-East Asia and in Japan. There are two main reasons: shares are more openly traded in Anglo-Saxon countries than in parts of Europe and Asia, where bank and government holdings are more important; and there is a stronger tradition in some countries of interlocking shareholdings that makes outright acquisition difficult, if not impossible.

Beyond this basic issue, the greater degree of global trading has made options that might have applied in a few Western countries now available around the world. There are two that have some importance for overseas operations:

1 *Turnkey*. A contractor who has total responsibility for building and possibly commissioning large-scale plant. Payment can take many forms.

2 *Licensing*. Technology or other assets are provided under licence from the home country. Payment is usually by royalty or some other percentage of turnover arrangement.

More generally, overseas expansion for many companies may take the form of the following sequence:[22]

- *Exporting* as a possible first expansion step.
- An *overseas office* may then be set up to provide a permanent presence.
- *Overseas manufacture* can take place, but this clearly increases the risk and exposure to international risks such as currency.
- *Multinational operations* may be set up to provide major international activity.
- *Global operations* may be introduced. The distinction from multinational operations lies in the degree of international commitment and, importantly, in the ability to source production and raw materials from the most favourable location anywhere in the world.

There are various risks and opportunities associated with all the above operations. Probably the most important of these is currency variation – that is, the difficulty of trading in currencies that are volatile and may cause significant and unexpected losses.

Comment

The expansion method matrix suffers from the same disadvantage as the previous matrix – i.e. it is useful at structuring the options but offers only limited guidance on choosing between them.

Finally, there is further coverage of the main expansion methods in the next chapter on strategic management options: the reason is that in practice many of such options are driven from the centre of large companies rather than at the individual business level.

KEY STRATEGIC PRINCIPLES

- The *expansion method matrix* explores in a structured way the methods by which market options might be achieved. By examining the organisation's internal and external expansion opportunities and its geographical spread of activity, it is possible to structure the various methods that are available.
- Within the home country, the four main methods of expansion are: acquisition, joint venture, alliance and franchise. Each has its advantages and problems.
- Beyond the home country, there are additional means of international expansion, including exporting, setting up overseas offices and undertaking full manufacturing. The most important risk associated with international expansion is probably currency fluctuation.

CASE STUDY 8.4

News Corporation builds a global media empire but then decides on a new break-up strategy

From a small Australian/UK newspaper operation, News Corporation has built a global media empire over the past 25 years. But it split the company into two in 2013. This case challenges the conventional 'strategic options' approach and identifies the new strategic challenges facing the company.

Company early years: newspapers developed by risk taking and innovation

Over the past 20 years, News Corporation has been shaped by its chairman and chief executive, Rupert Murdoch. He had the reputation as a young man of being something of a rebel. However, he was born into a wealthy family and inherited his father's chain of newspapers in Australia at the age of 21. He then used these as the starting point for his ambitions.

Murdoch radically repositioned his Australian newspapers by taking some downmarket and others upmarket. Building on this success, he moved from Australia to the UK and acquired control of a similar range there during the 1960s and 1970s. The newspapers included the brash and breezy *Sun* and the prestigious *Times*. Murdoch had the reputation of being aggressive, plain speaking and a good judge of managers. He knew what he wanted and controlled the main elements of his company with clarity and vision. He did not hesitate to plan and pick a fight with the UK print trade unions in the 1970s in order to break their power over the industry – he won and added to his reputation for ruthless efficiency. His companies were prepared to take risks and innovate in order to advance strategically, but they were still small by international standards and had no significant TV interests. From 1980 onwards, News Corporation shifted its focus to the television industry.

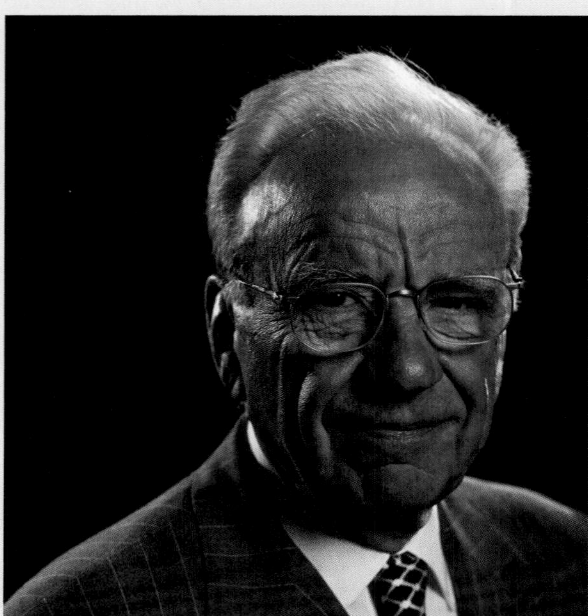

Rupert Murdoch has built News Corporation into a global media organisation over the past 30 years. But the company faces many new media challenges from both digital technology and the internet.
© Louie Psihoyos/Corbis

News Corporation: television and newspaper deals focused on its core resources

The company changed radically during the 1980s when Murdoch developed his first foray into television. He set up Sky television as the satellite broadcaster in the UK competing against the official UK rival. He contracted, for the first time, an exclusive deal with the UK football authorities to show the English football league games. This was the innovative, break-through deal that eventually established the British satellite broadcaster BskyB in which the Murdoch family still own a 39 per cent controlling share.

This deal was followed by moving into the USA with the acquisition of the film company 20th Century Fox and the founding of the Fox television channel. Further acquisitions and launches then followed in China, India, Italy and, more recently, Germany. Many of the early purchases were accompanied by considerable risk of bankruptcy and by major battles with well-established national companies and, in some cases, government bodies. For example, major US and European companies like Google (USA), Disney (USA), Bertelsmann (Germany) and Mediaset (Italy) put considerable competitive obstacles in the expansion path of News Corporation. Some governments also made it difficult for the company to expand, mainly through insisting on some form of national media ownership. Exhibit 8.1 lists some selected deals.

EXHIBIT 8.1

Some selected News Corporation deals

Year	Strategic deal	Comment
1980	Launched Sky Television UJ	Almost bankrupted the group
1985	Acquired 20th Century Fox and launched Fox television in the USA	Major success: established first major broadcaster to challenge existing US national channels - ABC, NBC and CBS
1990s	Acquired Israeli company's world rights to encryption of satellite broadcast signal	Secured subscription income for satellite channels: much larger income than advertising, mainly from sports exclusive content
2002	Acquired Telepiu satellite broadcaster in Italy	Developed into Sky Italia
2006	Bought the peer-to-peer website MySpace for US$560m.	Sold 2011 for US$35m
2007	Acquired the distinguished US business newspaper *Wall Street Journal* for US$5.6 billion	Wrote off US$2.6 billion of investment in 2009
2013	Finally acquired control of the leading German satellite broadcaster named Sky Deutschland	After 12 years, a determined strategic move into the German, Austrian and Swiss German markets

The key to understanding the News Corporation TV strategy is its vision of the future: 'Our evolution from primarily a newspaper publisher to an electronic media powerhouse' sums up the company's intentions. It also envisaged only four or five leading global TV companies by the end of the decade and News Corporation would be one of them.

In 2010, News Corporation made a bid to acquire complete control of British Sky Broadcasting: it already held 39 per cent of the company. This would give News Corporation complete dominance of both UK print and television media and provide a major cash cow for the group's further worldwide growth. The move was challenged by many other media groups in the UK as being anti-competitive. But News Corporation was so powerful in the UK that, up to 2011, the UK government was minded to approve the acquisition. The reason was the powerful influence of Mr Murdoch's UK press empire. And then came the hacking scandal . . .

In mid-2011, it was revealed that a UK newspaper within News Corporation, the *News of the World*, had been listening to the private mobile phone calls of leading personalities and distressed private individuals. Both Rupert Murdoch and his son, James, were called before a British Parliamentary Committee where they apologised and closed the paper. At the time of writing this case, News Corporation senior executives were under criminal police investigation in the UK. This serious matter meant that News Corporation withdrew its bid to buy BSkyB.

News Corporation: opportunistic, risk-taking and innovative strategies

From a standing start in the mid-1980s, News Corporation has built one of the world's largest media networks. Many of its strategies have been *negotiation-based* and derived from the rapid growth in world electronic media. In some respects, News Corporation's main strategy has also been opportunistic and risk-taking: for example, buying and selling companies as new deals have become available. The company has enhanced its core resources in the development and management of global TV and newspaper operations.

News Corporation has identified five basic strategies underlying these emerging business opportunities:

1 *Vertical integration* from film-making through to delivery of the electronic signal to the final customer. Thus it acquired the film company, 20th Century Fox, as well as having an interest in the satellite broadcaster BSkyB.

2 *Content creation*, not only through creative skills but also by negotiating exclusive new sports deals that buy up the media rights to world sporting events. For example, the company's deals for Southern Hemisphere Rugby, exclusive live coverage of Premier League football in the UK, and the US TV rights to American football were all dramatic ways to build a new, loyal audience. They delivered real sustainable competitive advantage to the company while the contract lasted.

3 *Globalisation* to give world coverage of electronic media. This is particularly important for news and sports events. It is less important for entertainment, which is more culture-specific. There are competitive risks from such a strategy – see below.
4 *Convergence* of newspapers, books and TV so that they all support each other and promote each other's interests. For example, the cross-promotion of News Corporation's TV channels in the company's newspapers, which had a much wider audience in the early days, was an important contributor to their success.
5 *Shift from print to electronic media*: the company took the view that newspapers were mature and would be replaced over time by web-based news. Importantly, advertising would shift from print to the web. But this has risks also.

News Corporation: the break-up in 2013

In 2013, Rupert Murdoch decided to break News Corporation into two separate publicly-traded companies: one focused on television called *21st Century Fox* and the other focused on newspapers and other print media renamed as *News Corp*.

In essence, the television empire was highly profitable, but the newspapers were beginning to be highly unprofitable. The reasons were linked to the widespread availability of the internet which meant that news was free and advertising was shifting to companies like Google that had strong internet activities.

There were three major changes in the strategic environment:

1 *Free news on the internet*. By tradition, information is free on the internet. In the past, News Corporation has supplied free news on its newspaper websites. But the company is only able to make profits if it charges for its news. In late 2010, it decided to make some of its internet newspaper sites subscription only. At the time of writing this case, it was not clear whether sufficient people would take out and maintain their subscriptions. In an era where other news is still available free on the internet, this strategy represents a risk for the company.
2 *Shift of advertising from press to internet*. The success of search engines like Google in terms of the numbers of hits has meant a radical shift in advertising revenue away from newspapers to the internet. Traditionally, advertising was a major source of revenue for newspapers, but some have now lost so much revenue that they have had to close. News Corporation's papers have seen a decline in advertising but, so far, have avoided closure. Both the *New York Daily Post* in the USA and the *Times* and *Sunday Times* in the UK were reported to be losing money.
3 *Move from satellite broadcasting to internet broadcasting*. News Corporation relies heavily on subscription to its satellite channels in some countries. But internet television is either here already – see Case 8.3 – or on its way. The News Corporation business model will need to cope with this fundamental shift over time.

All these issues were a major strategic problem for Mr Murdoch. In addition, he was 83 years old in 2014 and needed to find a successor, ideally within his family. Strategy was becoming a problem at the company.

News Corporation has been an early pioneer in the achievement of net-zero carbon emissions. In addition, it also announced plans for further environmental sustainability initiatives to year 2015. These can be accessed at: http://gei.newscorp.com/.

Case questions

1 Among the media companies, there is disagreement on the best route forward for strategic management: the software route versus the hardware route. Where does News Corporation stand in this debate? Do you judge that News Corporation has chosen the most successful long-term strategies?
2 How and where does News Corporation add value to its services? And where does it obtain its competitive advantage? What strategies has it adopted on barriers to entry?
3 In such a fast-changing market, is it possible to follow the prescriptive approach of options development and selection? Would News Corporation perhaps be better advised to have a general vision and then grab business opportunities as they arise?
4 Why has News Corporation been so successful? Where does it go from here?

Resource-based strategic options derived from the value chain.

8.5 RESOURCE-BASED STRATEGIC OPTIONS: THE RESOURCE-BASED VIEW

As explored in Chapter 4, resource-based strategies need to consider the opportunities presented by the resource-based view. The identification of those resources that are particularly important in delivering sustainable competitive advantage will represent an important starting point in the development of strategic options – for example, the brands of the organisation, its special and unique locations, its patents and its technologies. New resources might also be licensed from other companies or obtained through acquisition.[24]

8.5.1 Finding resource-based options: architecture, reputation and innovation

Essentially the resource-based view argues that organisations need some form of *distinctiveness* over competitors. In seeking out options, one method would be to test our resources against the criteria of architecture, reputation and innovation.[25] This would focus the process in terms of both current resources and those needed for the future. For example, using these three concepts, we can specify the ways in which News Corporation has been developing in this area:

- The network of relationships and contracts both within and around the organisation: the *architecture*. News Corporation has built a range of companies that are all focused in the areas of news, sport and entertainment. They make the company quite distinctive from Disney or Time Warner. This is clearly an asset that the company has developed.
- The favourable impression that News Corporation has generated with its customers: *reputation*. Again, News Corporation has developed a clear image in this area, based on its newspapers in particular. Its aggressive, open and iconoclastic style has set it apart from its rivals. This is clearly an asset of the organisation.
- The organisation's capacity to develop new products or services: *innovation*. Several examples of the innovative ability of News Corporation are recorded in Case 8.4. This may well cover core competencies as well as resource assets at the company.

8.5.2 Finding resource-based options – core competencies

Core competencies are defined as a group of skills and technologies that enable an organisation to provide a particular benefit to customers.[26] We explored them in Chapter 6 and can use them again here to guide the development of strategy options. Options that do not address core competencies are less likely to contribute to strategy than those that do. This suggests that a careful exploration of this topic in the context of strategy development is desirable. (Readers are referred to the earlier chapter for an exploration of this area.)

One way of generating options based on core competencies is to consider them as a *hierarchy of competencies*, starting with low-level individual skills and rising through the organisation to higher-level combined knowledge and skills. The basic assumption behind such an approach is that some competencies are formed from the integration of more specialised competencies.[27] Exhibit 8.2 shows the basic hierarchy of competencies, which might be used to identify and structure new areas.

8.5.3 Strategic options based on the resource-based view

Beyond the two areas outlined above, there are no detailed structures to conduct such an examination because every organisation is different. It will be necessary to survey each of the functional areas of the organisation for their resources. The aim of such an exercise is to explore those areas for their contribution to value added and competitive advantage.

EXHIBIT 8.2

The hierarchy of competencies

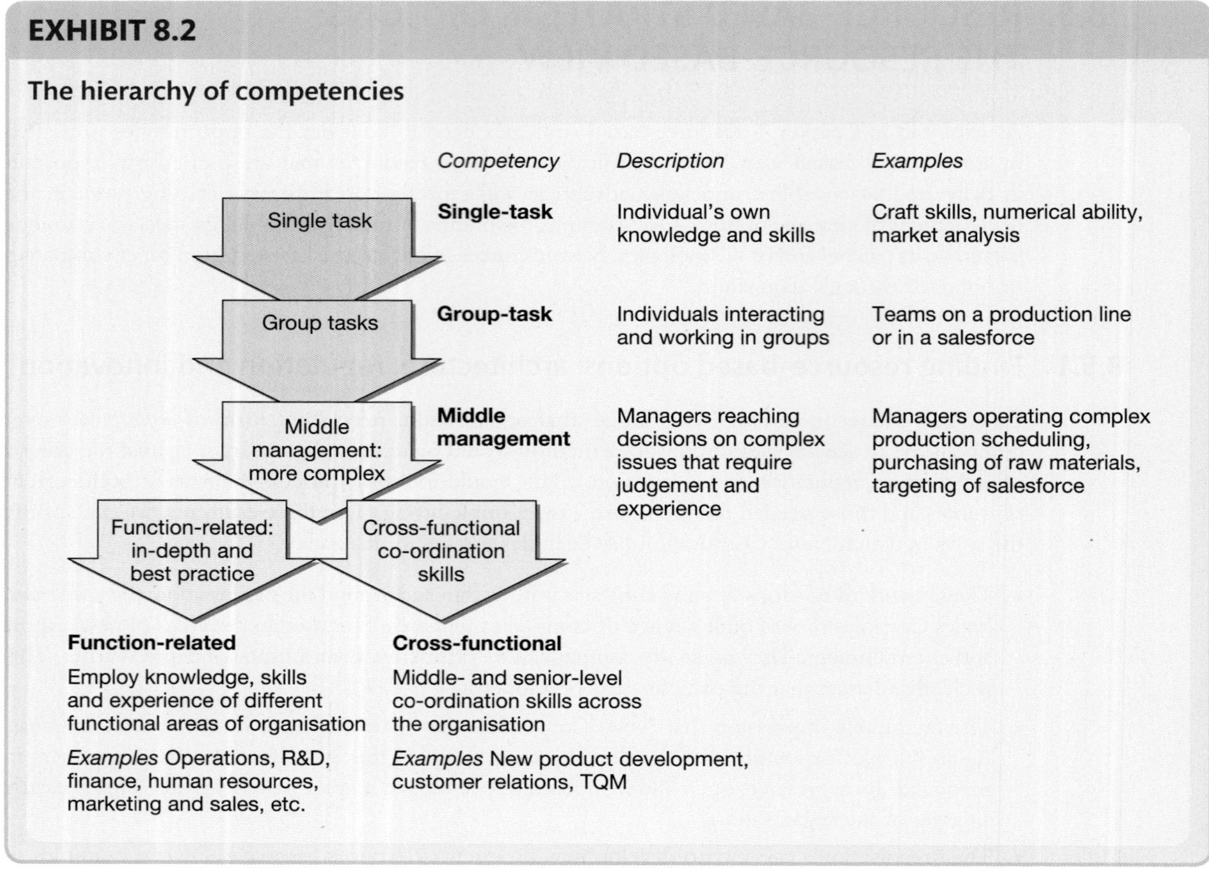

The checklist presented in Exhibit 8.3 has been prepared to assist the search for key resource options. However, such a list is not without its strategic dangers – readers are referred to the comments on SWOT analysis at the beginning of the chapter for a discussion. Moreover, a mechanistic combination of resources would miss the important issue that unique resources may derive from the *tacit knowledge* of the organisation. Such knowledge is unlikely to be discovered by a checklist.[28]

EXHIBIT 8.3

Ten guidelines for the options based on the resource-based view

1 What *technology* do we have? Is it exclusive? Is it at least as good as the competition? Is it better?
2 What *links* are there between the products that we manufacture or services that we operate? What common ground is there?
3 How do we generate *value added*? Is there anything different from our competitors? Looking at the main areas, what skills are involved in adding value?
4 What *people skills* do we have? How important is their contribution to our competencies? How vital are they to our resources? Are there any key workers? How difficult would they be to replace? Do we have any special values? What is our geographical spread?
5 What *financial resources* do we have? Are they sufficient to fulfil our vision? What is our profit record (or financial record in not-for-profit organisations)? Is the record sufficiently good to raise new funds? Do we have new funding arrangements, tax issues or currency matters?

6 How do our *customers* benefit from our competencies and resources? What real benefits do they obtain? Are we known for our quality? Our technical performance against competition? Our good value for money (*not* low cost)?

7 What *other skills* do we have in relation to our customers? What are the core skills? Are they unique to our organisation or do many other companies have them? How might they change?

8 What *new resources, skills and competencies* do we need to acquire over the next few years? How do they relate to our vision?

9 How is the *environment* changing? What impact will this have on current and future core skills and resources?

10 What are our *competitors* undertaking in the area of resources, skills and competencies?

Note: Caution is required in using this checklist - see text.

KEY STRATEGIC PRINCIPLES

- The resource-based view argues that it is important to identify and develop the key resources of the organisation, i.e. those that deliver value added and sustainable competitive advantage.
- Some resource areas are more likely to be important in developing options than others; those relating to architecture, reputation and innovation may represent one useful starting point.
- Core competencies explore options deriving from such areas as the basic skills, knowledge and technology of the organisation. They may also represent a way of structuring new strategic options in an organisation. A hierarchy of competencies can be built to explore the potential for new options.
- Because such resources are unique to each organisation, it is not possible to develop a general formula that will generate new options. However, a general checklist of some key areas can be developed, though caution is required in using it.

Resource-based options in some special types of organisation such as small businesses and not-for-profit organisations.

8.6 RESOURCE-BASED STRATEGIC OPTIONS: COST REDUCTION

Strategic options are not only concerned with expansion into new resource capabilities and core competencies. The organisation may also need to consider cutting back its current operations in order to reduce costs. Given the increasingly global nature of competition in some markets, it is quite possible that low-wage-settlement countries such as Thailand, Malaysia and the Philippines will provide real competition. This will mean that companies are unable to survive in Western countries unless they can cut costs drastically. Cost reduction strategy options therefore need to be considered. The main routes to cost reduction are:

- *Designing in cost reduction*. In some industries, large cost reductions come not from activity in the production plant, but *before* the product ever reaches the factory. By carefully designing the product – for instance, so that it has fewer parts or is simpler to manufacture – real reductions in costs can be achieved.
- *Supplier relationships*. If a supplier is willing and able to maintain quality and reduce costs, then the organisation will achieve a cost reduction.
- *Economies of scale and scope*. For a large plant, unit costs may fall as the size of the plant increases. It may also be possible for different products to share some functional costs.

- *The experience curve.* As a company becomes more experienced at production, it may be able to reduce its costs.
- *Capacity utilisation.* Where plant has a high fixed cost, there may be cost reductions to be obtained by running production as close to capacity as possible.

8.6.1 Designing in cost reduction

In some cases, up to 70 per cent of the cost of manufacturing a product is determined at the design stage – that is, before the product ever reaches the factory.[29] The reason is that it is at the design stage that major savings can be made on components, plant and procedures. It is more difficult to make them once products have reached the factory floor because of the inflexibility of installed machinery and the high cost of changing over time.

In addition, efficiency in the design procedures themselves has become an important element in the process. It can take years to design some products, with all the consequent costs involved. If time can be saved, this reduces the cost of the process. For example, Renault Cars (France) announced a new design and development facility in 1995 costing $1.22 billion.[30] The aim was to reduce design time from 58 months to 38 months for a new car launch in the year 2000. The facility's current cost per car was between $1 billion and $5 billion, depending on the model: this would be reduced by $200 million per model simply by producing each design more quickly.

8.6.2 Supplier relationships

Both in manufacturing and service industries, one of the ways of reducing costs is by negotiating cost reductions with suppliers to the organisation. This can be undertaken in one of two ways:[31]

1. *Closer relationships with suppliers.* As used by Toyota, this will involve sharing technical and development information in order to lower the cost of the finished product. It implies closer co-operation over many years, often with a small number of key suppliers. Inevitably, some of the value added is passed from the manufacturer to the supplier. However, it can help to drive down costs overall and raise quality.
2. *More distant relationships with suppliers.* This will involve aggressive negotiating to obtain the lowest possible price for an agreed specification. For example, Saab Cars (part-owned by General Motors) actually telephoned its suppliers of car mirrors twice a day for two weeks requesting lower quotes before deciding.[32] In this case, supplier relationships are at arm's length and obtain the lowest prices.

There is some evidence that the first of the two options above is becoming the preferred strategy.[33]

8.6.3 Economies of scale and scope

Definition ▶ **Economies of scale are the extra cost savings that occur when higher volume production allows unit costs to be reduced.** When it is possible to perform an operation more efficiently or differently at large volumes, then the increased efficiency may result in lower costs. Economies of scale can lead to lower costs – for example, in major petrochemical plants and in pulp and paper production.

Economies of scale need to be distinguished from capacity utilisation of plant. In the latter case, costs fall as the plant reaches capacity but would not fall any further if an even larger plant were to be built. With economies of scale, the larger plant would lead to a further cost reduction.

Definition ▶ **Economies of scope are the extra cost savings that are available as a result of separate products sharing some facilities.** An example might be those products that share the same retail outlets and can be delivered by the same transport.

Economies of scale are also available in areas outside production. They may occur in areas such as:

- *Research and development.* On some occasions, only a large-scale operation can justify special services or items of testing equipment.

- *Marketing.* Really large companies are able to aggregate separate advertising budgets into one massive fund and negotiate extra media discounts that are simply not available to smaller companies.
- *Distribution.* Loads can be grouped and selected to maximise the use of carrying capacity on transport vehicles travelling between fixed destinations.

In the analysis of resources, economies of scale are a relevant area for analysis. It is important to make an assessment for at least one leading competitor if possible. Factors to search for will include not only size of plant, but also age and efficiency of equipment.

Although writers such as Porter[34] are clear about the basic benefits of economies of scale and scope, real doubts have been expressed about the true reductions in costs to be derived from them – see for example, Kay.[35] The doubts centre on the argument that larger plant will have lower costs. When Henry Ford built his massive new Baton Rouge car plant in the 1930s, he was driven by this view. In practice, he encountered a number of problems.[36] They included:

- *machine-related issues* – the increased complexity and inflexibility of very large plant;
- *human-related issues* – the increasingly depersonalised and mechanistic nature of work in such plant, which made it less attractive or interesting for workers to perform to their best ability.

Although there were other management problems associated with the relative failure of this plant, some of the major reasons lay in the above areas. In the 1990s, large-scale steel plant was held up as providing lower costs, but new technologies have now allowed much smaller-scale operations to make the same profits.

The competitive advantage of large plant is lost if the market breaks into segments that are better served by higher-cost plants that produce variations on the basic item which more directly meet customers' needs. Car markets and consumer electronics markets are examples where, respectively, four-wheel-drive vehicles and specialist hi-fi systems are not the cheapest in terms of production but meet real customer demand.

The conclusion has to be that economies of scale have their place but are only part of a broader drive for competitive advantage.

8.6.4 Using the experience curve effect

Definition ▶ **The experience curve is the relationship between the unit costs of a product and the total units *ever produced* of that product, plotted in graphical form, with the units being cumulative from the first day of production.**

In the 1960s, a large number of unrelated industries were surveyed in terms of their costs and the cumulative production *ever achieved*: it is important to understand that this is cumulative production ever achieved, not just the production in one year. It was shown that an empirical relationship could be drawn between a cost reduction and cumulative output. Moreover, this relationship appeared to hold over a number of industries, from insurance to steel production. It appeared to show dramatic reductions in costs: typically, costs fall by 15 per cent every time overall output doubles. It is shown in Figure 8.9. The relationship was explained by suggesting that, in addition to economies of scale, there were other cost savings to be gained – for example through:

- technical progress;
- greater learning about the processes;
- greater skills from having undertaken the process over time.

The cost experience concept can be seen at both the *company* level and the *industry* level.

- At the company level, the market leader will, by definition, have produced cumulatively more product than any other company. The leader should have the lowest costs and other companies should be at a disadvantage.
- At the industry level, costs should fall as the industry overall produces more. Every company should benefit from knowledge that is circulated within its industries.

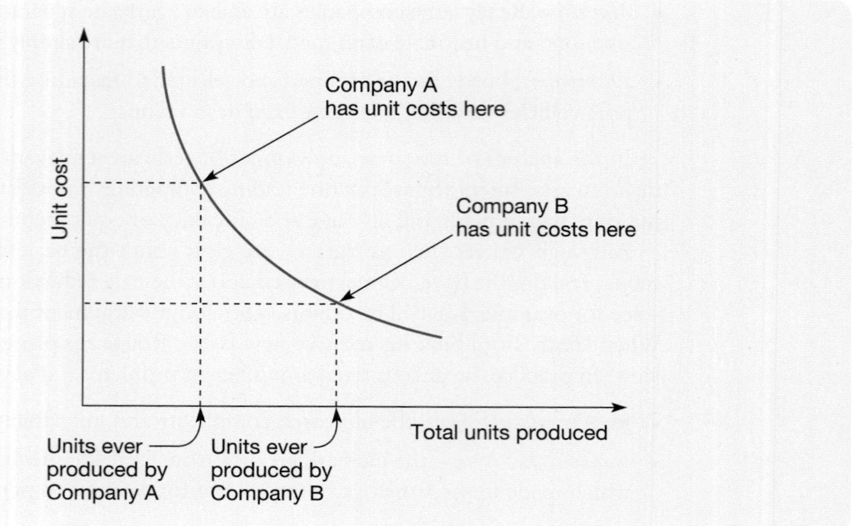

Figure 8.9 How the experience curve can deliver lower costs

When comparisons are drawn across different and unrelated industries, the similarities in the cost-curve relationship are remarkable for industries as far apart as aircraft manufacture and chicken broiler production. But there are few, if any, broad lessons for strategic management. As Kay points out,[37] the only similarity between aircraft and chickens is that they both have wings. There may be an *apparent relationship* in that the cost-curves look similar, but the *causes* are entirely different. Hence, the strategy implications are entirely different. Aircraft production is essentially global. Chicken production relies largely on national markets and requires somewhat less sophisticated technology and totally different forms of investment from aircraft manufacture and assembly. It is essential to consider the concept of experience curves *within an industry* only.

Even within an industry, there are ways of overcoming experience curve effects, the most obvious being by new technology. Another way would be to entice an employee of a more experienced company to join the organisation. As Abernathy and Wayne[38] point out, there are real limits to the benefits of the experience curve:

- Market demand in market segments for a special product change or variation cannot easily be met: to achieve scale, production flexibility may have to be sacrificed.
- Technical innovation can overtake learning in a more fundamental way: a new invention may radically alter the cost profile of an existing operation.
- Demand needs to double for every significant proportionate cost reduction. In markets where growth is still present but slowing down, this is only possible if an ever-larger market share is obtained. As market share becomes larger, this becomes progressively more difficult and expensive to achieve. In a static market where a company already has 51 per cent market share, this becomes logically impossible.

Within a defined market, the experience curve may suggest a significant route to cost reduction, but it is not always a key source of cost advantage.

8.6.5 Capacity utilisation

Definition ▶ **Capacity utilisation is the level of plant in operation at any time, usually expressed as a percentage of total production capacity of that plant.** In the global iron and steel industry discussed in

Chapter 3, we saw an example of the cost benefits to be gained by full utilisation of plant capacity. But we also saw how companies cut their prices as they scrambled to fill their plant, thus reducing their profit margins. High-capacity utilisation is useful but relies on competitors allowing such activity to take place, which may weaken its effect.

8.6.6 Structured process to achieve cost reduction options

We explored the basic issue of cost reduction above. However, Ohmae has suggested a model which structures this process in a logical and cross-functional way. It deserves to be examined for its implications in this area, and is shown in Figure 8.10. Overall, the model does not pretend to be comprehensive but rather to show the options that are possible, their logical flow and the interconnections between the various elements. For example, News Corporation over the last five years has emphasised the need to cut costs in order to remain competitive. It has introduced various programmes to achieve this.

Checklist: Comparing your costs against competitors.

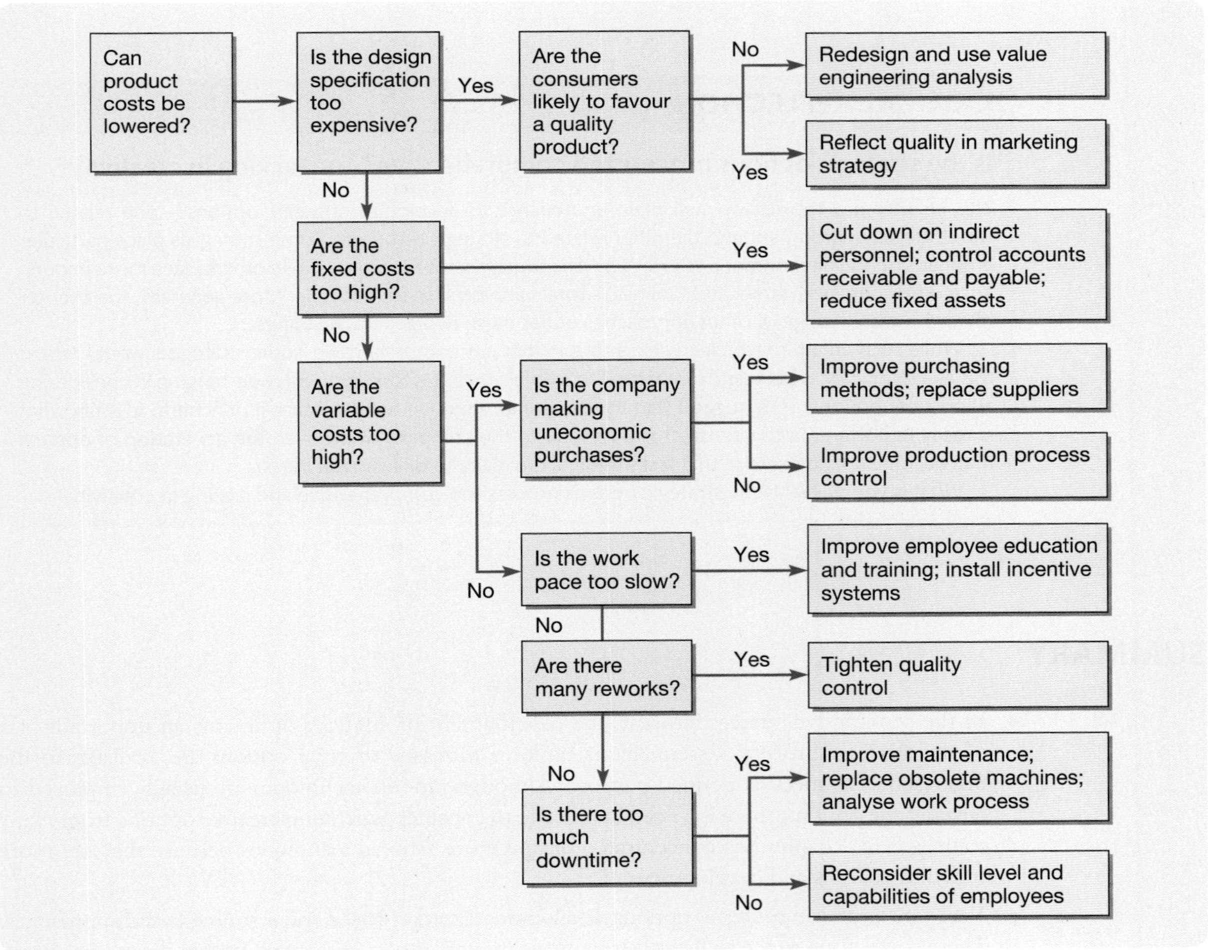

Can product costs be lowered?

Is the design specification too expensive?
Yes → Are the consumers likely to favour a quality product?
No → Redesign and use value engineering analysis
Yes → Reflect quality in marketing strategy

No → Are the fixed costs too high?
Yes → Cut down on indirect personnel; control accounts receivable and payable; reduce fixed assets

No → Are the variable costs too high?
Yes → Is the company making uneconomic purchases?
Yes → Improve purchasing methods; replace suppliers
No → Improve production process control

No → Is the work pace too slow?
Yes → Improve employee education and training; install incentive systems

No → Are there many reworks?
Yes → Tighten quality control

No → Is there too much downtime?
Yes → Improve maintenance; replace obsolete machines; analyse work process
No → Reconsider skill level and capabilities of employees

Figure 8.10 Structured approach to cost reduction options

Source: Ohmae, K (1983) *The Mind of the Strategist*, McGraw-Hill, pp 24–25.

KEY STRATEGIC PRINCIPLES

- There are *at least* six routes to cost reduction: design, supplier relationships, economies of scale and scope, the experience curve, capacity utilisation and synergistic effects.
- Economies of scale and scope are generally seen to reduce costs and raise value added, but the lack of production flexibility and the depersonalised nature of the work may be significant drawbacks.
- The experience curve suggests that significant reductions in costs are achieved as companies and the whole industry produce more product. The cost reductions relate to the cumulative production ever achieved, not just in one year.
- Experience curve cost reductions arise from a whole series of sources. They need to be sought and do not just happen automatically.
- Comparisons of experience curves across industries have little meaning, if any, in terms of the strategy lessons to be drawn.
- Utilising existing plant capacity is an important consideration in cost reduction.
- In exploring cost-cutting options, it is possible to develop a model which examines this in a structured and cross-functional way.

CRITICAL REFLECTION

Is the strategic options process too comprehensive? Too lacking in creativity?

This chapter has focused on two main approaches to developing strategic options – one related to the strategic environment and the other related to strategic resources. Some strategists place particular emphasis on the environment – Porter's *generic strategies*, for example – while others place more importance on resources – Hamel and Prahalad's *core competencies*, for example. More generally, the chapter reviews a whole range of other approaches under these two general headings.

While such an approach clearly has merit in that it is comprehensive, some strategists would regard this as a significant weakness. They argue the whole concept is too rigid, too wide-ranging in considering all possible options. They suggest that its very comprehensive nature makes it difficult to identify what is really important. In this sense, it is unhelpful to the company. Moreover, the generation of options may become a rigid exercise that lacks the real creativity to deliver new ideas.

What is your view? Is the strategic options process too comprehensive and lacking in creativity?

SUMMARY

- In the prescriptive strategy process, the development of strategic options is an important part of the strategic process. Essentially, it explores the issue of what options are available to the organisation to meet its defined purpose. Although rational techniques are usually employed to develop the options, there is a need in practice to consider generating creative options from many sources. This chapter has concentrated on the more rational techniques because they are more suited to analysis and development.
- There are two main routes to options development: market-based and resource-based approaches. These correspond to the analytical structure of the earlier part of the text. Within the market-based approach, there are three main routes: generic strategies, market options and expansion methods. Each of these can usefully be considered in turn.

- According to Porter, there are only three fundamental strategic options available to any organisation – he called them *generic strategies*. The three options are:
  1. *cost leadership*, which aims to place the organisation amongst the lowest-cost producers in the market;
  2. *differentiation*, which is aimed at developing and targeting a product that is different in some significant way from its competitors in the market place;
  3. *focus*, which involves targeting a small segment of the market. It may operate by using a low-cost focus or differentiated focus approach.

  According to generic strategy theory, it is important to select between the options and not to be 'stuck in the middle'. Some influential strategists have produced evidence that has cast doubt on this point. There have been numerous criticisms of the approach based on logic and on empirical evidence of actual industry practice. Undoubtedly, these criticisms have validity, but generic strategies may represent a useful starting point in developing strategy options.
- By examining the market place and the products available, it is possible to structure further options for organisations to adopt: the overall structure is called the *market options matrix*. The matrix represents a method of generating options but provides no guidance on choosing between them. The main strategic insights come from the way that such options challenge current thinking and open up the debate.
- The *expansion method matrix* explores in a structured way the methods by which market options might be achieved. By examining the organisation's internal and external expansion opportunities and its geographical spread of activity, it is possible to structure the various methods that are available.
- In addition to the market-based options, there is a range of options based on the resources of the organisation. There are three main approaches to the development of such options: the value chain, the resource-based view and cost reduction. Each of these approaches may be useful in options development.
- First, value can be added early in the value chain, *upstream*, or later in the value chain, *downstream*. Upstream activities add value by processing raw materials into standardised products. Downstream strategies concentrate on differentiated products, targeted towards specific market segments.
- Second, the resource-based view argues that each organisation is unique in terms of its resources. This means that there can be no formula that will identify the strategic options. However, the criteria developed by Kay – architecture, reputation and innovation – may provide some guidance. In addition, Hamel and Prahalad's core competencies may also provide some strategic options. A hierarchy of competencies may be developed to identify and develop new competencies in the organisation.
- Third, cost reduction options also deserve to be explored. Opportunities exist in many organisations to reduce the costs incurred by the resources of the organisation. There are five main opportunity areas for cost reduction: designing in cost reductions, supplier relationships, economies of scale and scope, the experience curve and capacity utilisation.

QUESTIONS

1 Do small firms have anything useful to learn from a consideration of the options available from generic strategies?

2 Plot the position of News Corporation on the generic strategies matrix. What conclusions, if any, can you draw from this about future strategies for the company? (Note the hint in the 'if any' phrase.)

3 *'Generic strategies are a fallacy. The best firms are striving all the time to reconcile opposites.'* (Charles Baden-Fuller and John Stopford) Discuss this statement.

4 Take an organisation with which you are familiar, such as a small voluntary group, and consider the possibilities of expansion: apply the market options matrix and expansion method matrix to your choice. What conclusions can you draw about future expansion strategy?

5 *'A recurring theme to criticisms of strategic planning practice is the pedestrian quality of the strategic options that are considered.'* (George Day) By what methods might this legitimate concern be overcome, if at all?

6 Choose an organisation with which you are familiar and identify the upstream and downstream parts of the value chain for that organisation. Which is the most important for that organisation or do they contribute equally?

7 Identify the probable key competitive resources of the following: a charity like UNICEF; a major consumer electronics company; a holiday travel tour operator; a multinational fast-moving consumer goods company.

8 *'During the 1990s, top executives will be judged on their ability to identify, cultivate and exploit the core competencies that make growth possible.'* (Gary Hamel and C K Prahalad) Discuss whether this is still relevant in the twenty-first century. Was it appropriate in the last century?

9 If key competitive resources are important, can they be acquired in the space of a few months or do they take years to develop? What are the implications of your response for the development of competitive advantage?

10 Take a small student society or charitable institution with which you are familiar. What strategic options based on its resources does it have for development?

11 It has been argued in this chapter that small businesses can develop competitive advantage over larger companies by offering higher degrees of service. What are the possible problems with this approach?

FURTHER READING

The two books that need to be read on environment-based options are Porter, M E (1980) *Competitive Strategy*, The Free Press, New York, and Porter, M E (1985) *Competitive Advantage*, The Free Press, New York. It should be noted that they also provide a much broader view of strategy than this single topic.

The market options matrix and expansion method matrix are covered in many marketing texts in a more limited form. George Day's book is probably the best at providing a breadth of viewpoint beyond the marketing function: Day, G S (1984) *Strategic Marketing Planning*, West Publishing, St Paul, MN.

On distinctive capabilities, the book by John Kay represents an important, well-referenced text on the topic: Kay, J (1993) *Foundations of Corporate Success*, Oxford University Press, Oxford.

On core competencies, you should read Hamel, G and Prahalad, C K (1994) *Competing for the Future*, Harvard Business School Press, Boston, MA. See also by the same authors, 'The core competence of the corporation', *Harvard Business Review*, May–June, 1990.

NOTES AND REFERENCES

1 References for the Walt Disney Company case: Annual Report and Accounts 2013. Available at http://corporate.disney.co.com. *Financial Times*: 28 October 1998, p 26; 3 November 1999, pp 14, 35; 16 March 2002, p 18; 2 August 2003, p M4; 9 October 2003, p 16; 30 October 2003, p 14; 29 April 2004, pp 21, 27; 21 January 2005, p 18; 27 January 2005, p 30; 19 February 2005, p M6. BBC News Website – 15 March 2005 – 'How Mickey Mouse made Disney a giant'; 27 July 2011, p 21; 1 November 2012, p 19; 26 March 2014, p 14.

2 Andrews, K (1987) *The Concept of Corporate Strategy*, Irwin, Homewood, IL.

3 Whittington, R (1993) *What is Strategy and Does it Matter?*, Routledge, London, pp 73–4.

4 Bain, J (1956) *Barriers to New Competition: Their Character and Consequences in Manufacturing Industries*, Harvard University Press, Cambridge, MA.

5 Porter, M E (1980) *Competitive Strategy*, The Free Press, New York.

6 Porter, M E (1985) *Competitive Advantage*, The Free Press, New York.
7 Kay, J (1993) *Foundations of Corporate Success*, Oxford University Press, Oxford, Ch 1.
8 Stopford, J and Baden-Fuller, C (1992) *Rejuvenating the Mature Business*, Routledge, London.
9 Miller, D (1992) 'The generic strategy trap', *Journal of Business Strategy*, Vol 13, No 1, pp 37–42.
10 Hendry, J (1990) 'The problem with Porter's generic strategies', *European Management Journal*, December, pp 443–450.
11 References for global ice cream case: see data sources for Cases 10.1 and 10.3.
12 Porter, M E (1996) 'What is strategy?', *Harvard Business Review*, November–December, pp 61–78.
13 References for the global TV case: earlier references before 2011 are listed in *Strategic Management*, 6th edn. New references are: *Financial Times*: 25 March 2011, p 11; 24 June 2011, p 17; 24 January 2012, p 23; 30 January 2012, p 21; 11 April 2013, p 13; 1 February 2013, p 18; 14 February 2013, p 18; 21 February 2013, p 20; 13 March 2013, p 16; 5 September 2013, p 18; 12 November 2013, p 1; 17 December 2013, p 19. *Economist*: 17 March 2012, p 67.
14 Day, G S (1987) *Strategic Market Planning*, West Publishing, St Paul, MN, p 104.
15 Buzzell, R and Wiersema, F (1981) 'Successful share-building strategies', *Harvard Business Review*, January–February, pp 135–144.
16 Kuczmarski, T and Silver, S (1982) 'Strategy: the key to successful product development', *Management Review*, July, pp 26–40.
17 Lynch, R (1994) *European Business Strategies*, 2nd edn, Kogan Page, London, p 208.
18 Lynch, R (1993) *Cases in European Marketing*, Kogan Page, London, p 31.
19 Synergy is explored in Ansoff, I (1989) *Corporate Strategy*, rev. edn, Penguin, Harmondsworth, Ch 1, p 22.
20 An interesting view on this relationship: Lee, G K and Liebermann, M B (2010) 'Acquisition vs internal development as modes of market entry', *Strategic Management Journal*, Vol 31, No 2, pp 140–158.
21 Kay, J (1993) Op. cit., p 146.
22 More information on international expansion is available in Lynch, R (1992) *European Marketing*, Kogan Page, London, Ch 8.
23 References for the News Corp. case: News Corporation Annual Report and Accounts 2004, 2007 and 2012–2013. References before 2011 are listed in *Strategic Management*, 6th edn. New references: *Financial Times*: 19 June 2011, p 14; 1 February 2012, p 22; 28 June 2012, p 13; 25 September 2013, p 4. *Guardian*: 5 January 2014, 'The Rupert Murdoch era is all but over' sourced from the web.
24 Stalk, G, Evans, P and Shulman, L (1992) 'Competing on capabilities', *Harvard Business Review*, April–May, pp 57–69. Hamel and Prahalad make no reference to this paper and its criticism of core competencies in their book published in 1994. However, their letter to the *Harvard Business Review* in 1996 stated that they could see no essential difference between core competencies and core capabilities.
25 Kay, J (1993) Op. cit., p 64.
26 Hamel, G and Prahalad, C K (1994) *Competing for the Future*, Harvard Business School Press, Boston, MA, p 221 and Ch 10 that follows.
27 Grant, R M (1998) *Contemporary Strategy Analysis*, 3rd edn, Blackwell, Oxford, pp 122–123. I am grateful to one of the reviewers of the second edition for suggesting this approach to options generation.
28 I am grateful to one of the reviewers of the second edition for making these important points.
29 Whitney, D (1988) 'Manufacturing by design', *Harvard Business Review*, July–August, p 83.
30 Ridding, J (1995) 'Renault unveils plant to speed launches', *Financial Times*, 17 February, p 24.
31 See, for example, Cusumano, M and Takeishi, A (1991) 'Supplier relations and management; a survey of Japanese, Japanese-transplant and US auto plants', *Strategic Management Journal*, Vol 12, pp 563–588. Also Macduff, J P and Helper, S (1997) 'Creating lean suppliers: diffusing lean production throughout the supply chain', *California Management Review*, Vol 39, No 4, pp 118–151.
32 Marsh, P (1995) 'Car mirror rivalry turns cut-throat', *Financial Times*, 14 June, p 10.
33 *Economist* (2002) 'Incredible shrinking plants', *Special Report on Car Manufacturing*, 23 February, pp 99–101.
34 Porter, M (1985) Op. cit., Ch 3.
35 Kay, J (1993) Op. cit., pp 170–175. It is difficult to convey fully the interesting data that Kay brings to this discussion in summary format in the text.
36 Abernathy, W and Wayne, K (1974) 'Limits of the learning curve', *Harvard Business Review*, September–October, p 108.
37 Kay, J (1993) Op. cit., p 116, where he reproduces the two charts.
38 Abernathy, W and Wayne, K (1974) Op. cit., p 128.

CHAPTER 9
Developing corporate-level strategy options

Video and sound summary of this chapter

LEARNING OUTCOMES

When you have worked through this chapter, you will be able to:

- define and explain the two main elements of corporate-level strategy;
- outline the benefits and costs of corporate-level strategy options;
- identify the levels of diversification in corporate strategy and their implications for strategy options;
- describe the role of corporate headquarters and identify the implications for strategy development;
- use the product portfolio matrix to choose between corporate-level strategy options;
- outline the main corporate-level strategy tools available to a corporate headquarters.

INTRODUCTION

Video Parts 2 and 6

Having examined strategy options at the *business* level in the last chapter, we now consider options at the *corporate* level. The business level focuses on individual markets and firms that operate in a single industry. Some firms will choose to diversify beyond a single area and operate in several markets, each with its own strategy, business team and profit centre. In this case, there will be a requirement for a corporate strategy to co-ordinate, manage and communicate with each business area and with outside organisations such as banks and shareholders. It is the corporate level that is the focus of this chapter.

For example, News Corporation in Case 8.4 operates at the separate *business* levels of newspapers, television broadcasting and film production amongst others. Each subsidiary has its competitors and strategic decisions at the business level. News Corporation headquarters acts at the *corporate* level when it makes decisions across *all* the various companies – for example, new investment in the internet along with a reduction in its interests in satellite transmission. Such corporate decisions may be about *diversification* issues into new media and beyond. They may also be about *existing* business areas that do not involve diversification – for example, using the high cash flow from News Corporation's British newspapers to invest further into German pay-television stations.

Definition ▶ Corporate-level strategy has two meanings in the literature that are related but are not necessarily the same. **First, corporate-level strategy means the strategic decisions that lead companies to *diversify* from one business into other business areas, either related or unrelated. Second, corporate-level strategy means the role of the *corporate headquarters* in directing and influencing strategy across a multi-product group of companies.**

Some of the strategic literature and research confuses these two areas and discusses them as if they were the same topic. They are not. We tackle these two separate issues in this chapter. The first

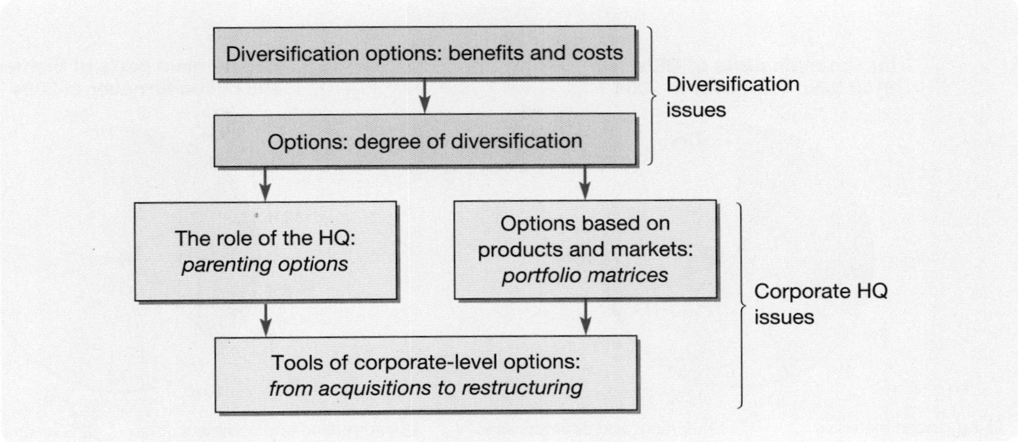

Figure 9.1 Developing strategic options at the corporate level

section of this chapter explores the benefits and costs of a corporate strategy from a diversification perspective. In practice, the benefits and costs are likely to change with the degree of diversification involved in a corporate strategy. The next section of the chapter then examines the degree of diversification and the options that are available.

The third section of this chapter explores the strategic options related to the role and function of the headquarters of the organisation: this is called *parenting* in the literature. The fourth section of this chapter examines the way that the headquarters makes decisions in terms of its different products and their markets in each of its subsidiary companies: this is called *portfolio matrix management* in the literature. Finally, the chapter surveys the broad range of strategy tools that exist mainly at the corporate level – from acquisitions to restructuring the organisation – because these will provide the strategic options needed for strategy development in larger companies. The structure of the chapter is shown in Figure 9.1.

CASE STUDY 9.1

Corporate strategy at two multinationals - General Electric (USA) and Siemens (Germany)

Multinationals are supposed to make superior profits from their internal resources and from their external market positions. But a comparison of two leading companies suggests that pursuing profitability is more complex in practice.

General Electric (GE)

As one of the world's largest multinational companies, GE has a wide range of commercial activities, ranging from financial services to media companies and heavy engineering - see Figure 9.2. Essentially, this wide range of essentially unrelated business activities is co-ordinated and managed through a highly focused corporate headquarters. The group's corporate purpose for many years has been to achieve high cash flow and drive down costs. Jack Welch, who retired as chief executive officer from GE group headquarters in 2001, was regarded as one of America's leading managers. He guided the multinational towards its current high profitability through mergers, acquisitions and divestments. Importantly, he also had a robust view of the performance of his senior managers in each of the company's divisions and sanctioned employment cuts where necessary to achieve the company's purpose.

Siemens

Siemens is one of Germany's largest multinational companies, with a long and distinguished history of invention, especially in engineering. In fact, the company has a reputation of being dominated for many years by engineers in senior management positions, with a consequent focus on the engineering excellence of its products. According to the *Financial Times*,

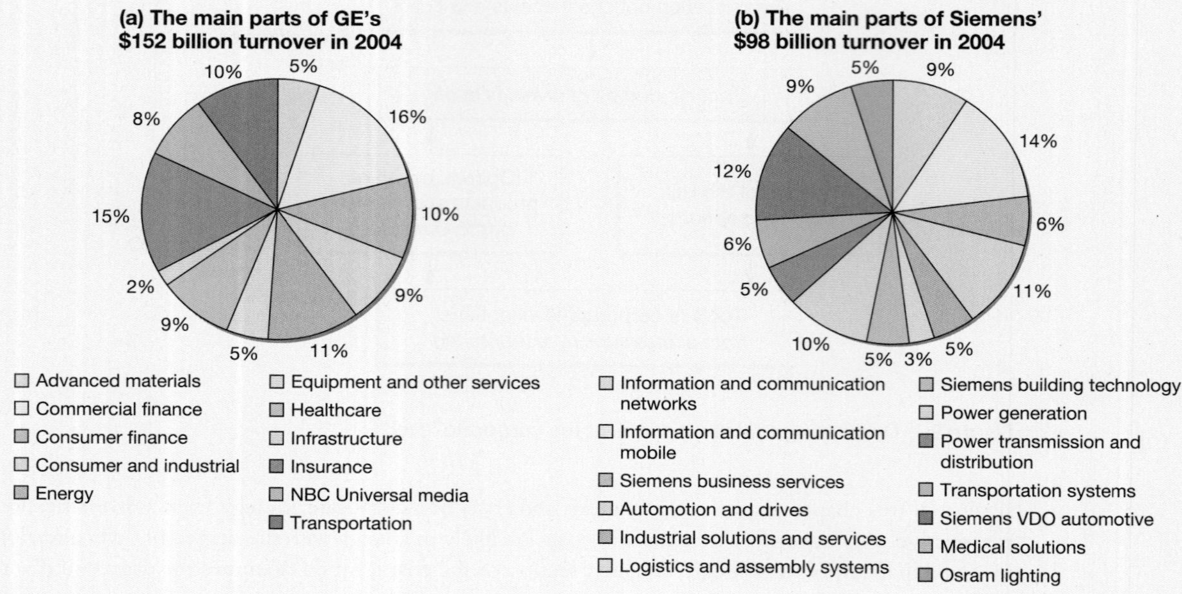

Figure 9.2 GE and Siemens – both massive conglomerates

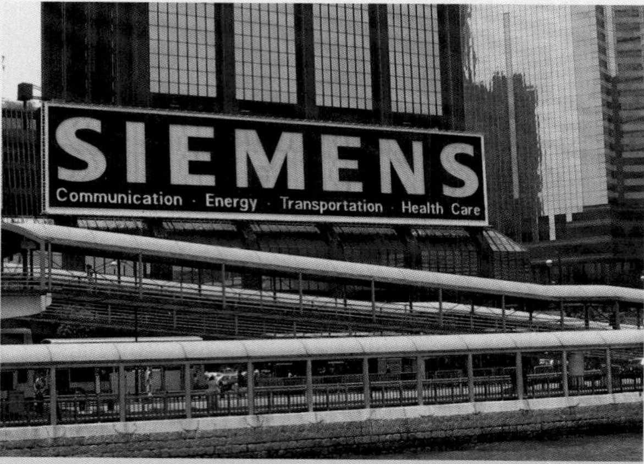

An intriguing strategic question is why the German conglomerate Siemens has lower profitability than its comparable American rival, General Electric.

Getty Images/Robert Nickelsberg/Getty Images News

'[It] had management methods rooted in the 19th century and financial returns to match. Much of its manufacturing was based on rigid production processes that could not be easily adapted to new products.' But Siemens' chief executive officer for the period 1992–2004, Heinrich von Pierer, guided the company towards a more market-oriented approach.

Siemens' headquarters then continued with this realignment under his successor, Klaus Kleinfeld, until Kleinfeld's sudden resignation in 2007. Unfortunately, Siemens found that there were suspicious payments amounting to $1.9 billion in 2006 which may have been related to bribery at the company. At the time of writing, this matter was still under investigation. Nevertheless, Kleinfeld judged that he should resign and a new chief executive, Peter Löscher, was appointed. 'We are using the crisis and the positive elements to create something better,' explained Löscher. 'One thing is clear: this company failed based on leadership responsibility and culture.' Essentially, the corporate headquarters team was then engaged in tackling the

Table 9.1 Comparison of sales margins for 2004

General Electric		Siemens	
• Total 2004 turnover across all divisions: $152 billion • Total number of employees in 2004 across all divisions: 227,000		• Total 2004 turnover across all divisions: $98 billion • Total number of employees in 2004 across all divisions: 430,000	
Division	**Sales margin %**	**Division**	**Sales margin %**
Advanced materials	8.6	Information and communication networks	3.2
Commercial finance	19.0	Information and communication mobile	3.1
Consumer finance	4.6	Siemens business services	0.8
Consumer and industrial	20.7	Automation and drives	12.2
Energy	16.4	Industrial solutions and services	2.2
Equipment and other services	7.1	Logistics and assembly systems	0.1
Healthcare	16.9	Siemens building technology	2.5
Infrastructure	16.3	Power generation	12.8
Insurance	2.5	Power transmission and distribution	6.6
NBC Universal media	1.8	Transportation systems	(10.1) loss
Transportation	20.6	Siemens VDO automotive	6.2
		Medical solutions	14.8
		Osram lighting	10.5

Note: Sales margin is defined as divisional operating profit divided by divisional revenue and expressed as a percentage. Some of the business activities of the two companies are different. However, directly comparable business activities between GE and Siemens are highlighted in the above table. They show that GE has higher sales margins than Siemens in similar business areas.

Source: annual report and accounts with sales margins calculated by author.

corruption accusations surrounding the company while at the same time allowing the various parts of the multinational to develop profitably.

Beyond this matter, Siemens appears to have been in a constant state of re-organisation and flux since the mid-1990s, when it had a major downturn in its profits. Siemens' corporate headquarters sold a range of poorly performing businesses in the late 1990s. Around 1999, the company HQ introduced a new three-part concept to improve its performance across the group called *Top*. It had three main pillars – cost-reduction, growth and innovation – directed at increasing the long-term profitability of the company. Cost-reduction was particularly important because Siemens' costs in many product areas were 20–30 per cent higher than those of its competitors. Growth was set as an additional target – 'Managers did not set themselves a static target, but one that was dynamic and took into account changes that competitors were likely to make,' explained the main board member responsible for *Top*, Edward Krubasik. Although the senior managers of Siemens' various divisions grumbled, this meant that they had to benchmark themselves against competitors. The third part was innovation through the introduction of new products that would compete better on world markets.

Even after seven years of *Top* and similar initiatives, Siemens still remained a distant second to GE in fields where a comparison could be made – see Table 9.1. While the overall product mix is different for the two companies, they do have some similar products, particularly in heavy engineering: compare the profit margins at GE's energy and transportation divisions with the similar product ranges of Siemens' power generation, power transmission and transportation systems businesses.

GE and Siemens

In some senses, the product ranges of the two multinationals are so different that it is not appropriate to make comparisons of performance. However, it might be argued that they are both diversified groups (sometimes called *conglomerates*) and therefore able to work with the special strategies associated with such groups – for example, the ability to seek economies of scope and the possibility of employing core competencies across the divisions of the conglomerate. In practice, Siemens has a range of companies that include those built on its earlier engineering tradition rather than modern areas of market growth. In addition, the company has other modern divisions where it struggles to compete because it is smaller than its rivals and competition is fierce – for example, its business in mobile telephones and telecommunications equipment. For some years, Siemens had been divesting itself of poorly performing parts of the group but it still compared poorly against GE in 2007.

GE's annual reports show that the company has had a long-term focus on clean energy through its 'ecomagination initiative'. For example, the company has ordered 25,000 electric vehicles to encourage the development of local electricity powerpoints.

Siemens annual report says that it has sustainability targets for all relevant areas of the company. It gives examples of its investment and practices at www.siemens.com/sustainability.

Case questions

1. Can Siemens ever achieve the profit margins of GE? What should it do now – continue to divest under-performing parts and invest in the profitable parts? Or is something more radical required – perhaps to break itself up and cease to be a conglomerate?
2. What conclusions do you draw on the strategic benefits of operating a corporate strategy? Does the theory outlined in this chapter help?

9.1 CORPORATE-LEVEL STRATEGY: THE BENEFITS AND COSTS OF DIVERSIFYING

Corporate-level strategy is important because multi-business corporations are major contributors to all the economies of the leading nations of the world. In the USA and Western Europe, such corporations account for around 60 per cent of industrial output. Even in the developing countries, 'groups' are becoming widespread as the means of generating output.[2] Such businesses may be multinational in their scope in the sense that they have significant operations outside their home countries: this certainly applies to both GE and Siemens in Case 9.1. But the important point here is that such companies are usually also multi-product companies with a diversified portfolio of business interests. Hence, whether in one main country or in many, the largest contributors to economic growth are the multi-business corporations, all of whom will need a corporate-level strategy.

In multi-product companies, each of the subsidiaries will have a large or a limited trading connection with another part of the group. For example at GE, the consumer finance division will have only limited connections with the media division because these divisions have few common customers and resources. By contrast at GE, the consumer and industrial division may have some common interest with the energy division because they both have common industrial customers.

In multi-product companies, each subsidiary will have its own resources, its own markets and therefore its own business strategy: for example, the resources in the media division at GE include the NBC Television studios; the resources at the GE consumer finance division include the network contacts with banks and other financial institutions. Above these subsidiaries, the enterprise will have a corporate headquarters, where corporate-level strategy options are generated.[3] For example, the headquarters of GE is located in Bridgewater, Connecticut, USA, from where it directs worldwide operations. The corporate activity of such a headquarters will include:

- the selection of businesses to be part of the group;
- the management and leadership of each business within the group;
- the selection, incentivisation and motivation of senior managers in each business;
- the resources to be allocated by the centre to individual businesses.

Corporate strategy options are concerned with the maximisation of value added and the additional competitive advantage contributed by the central headquarters of the group of companies. Importantly, the corporate headquarters must add value to the group if it is to justify its existence.

9.1.1 The benefits of corporate-level strategy diversification

By definition, multi-business companies are those trading in more than one market, each with its relatively autonomous and discrete operating companies: such operations are *diversified*. Opinions on the benefits of diversification have changed quite markedly over the past 30 years. It used to be said that being involved in a series of unrelated industries meant that the risks of overall failure were lower because the upswing in one market – such as healthcare at GE – would counterbalance any downswing in another market – such as transportation in the same company.[4] In addition, it was also argued that basic technological linkages between some diversified companies meant that they could provide mutual technical support: see the 3M Case in Chapter 7 for an example of this approach. At one stage in the 1960s and 70s, there were corporations with hundreds of semi-independent subsidiaries.[5] As we will see later in this section, this scatter-gun approach changed later in the century in Western countries. However, even today, there are many companies – including South Korean firms like Samsung and Indian firms like Tata – that still have a broad range of different semi-independent businesses.

In recent years, the benefits of a corporate strategy have come from the suggestion that the competitive resources and strong market position of one division of an organisation might be used to support another division.[6] For example, it might be possible to transfer the competitive advantages of one part of the business to another. One obvious example is the Virgin Group where the strong Virgin brand has been used to support quite different businesses from cosmetics to airlines.

Corporate strategy benefits can also occur through sharing resources and activities across a range of related businesses within a corporate group. For example, the US consumer products group Procter and Gamble (P&G) is market leader in both paper towels and in Pampers babies' nappies (diapers). Both of these products are manufactured from paper that is produced in a P&G joint factory to gain *economies of scale* and jointly reduce their costs. In addition, the marketing and sale of both product groups will be conducted through some of the same distribution outlets: this means that each business can employ some of the same transport companies and sales networks to gain further cost reductions. Essentially, these separate companies are able to gain the *economies of scope* that arise from a P&G corporate strategy.

In addition, there are benefits from corporate strategy associated with financial economies. Financial economies are cost savings that arise from two sources:

1 Because of the greater size that arises from the combination of all its subsidiaries, the corporate headquarters may obtain funds at a lower cost of capital than might be available to an individual subsidiary of the corporation.

2 Because of its position at the centre of the organisation, the corporate headquarters may be in a better position to allocate funds between the competing individual businesses and thereby make more efficient use of limited financial resources.

It is the role of the group headquarters to find and then manage the financial and other capital resources of the firm.[7] For example, GE's size and special contacts through its banking operations – see Case 9.1 – give the GE headquarters access to funds at very low rates of interest. This is a real competitive advantage for that group. In addition, the corporate headquarters of GE is very active in examining each of its major businesses and allocating funds to those that appear to have the best growth prospects.

It is also argued that it is beneficial for a group of companies to have a range of knowledge, technical skills and technologies around which to learn and build the company's resources.[8] For example at GE, each of the divisions is engaged in R&D in its own areas. But there is also a group headquarters view on research and knowledge that focuses on three areas that are relevant to a number of divisions: environmental impact issues, nanotechnology and security safety matters. Such knowledge development is shared across the GE group.

In the diversified group, the corporate strategy should earn above-average profits as a result of the special contribution of the group's headquarters over and above the contribution of the individual companies. This means that the diversified firms that make up the corporate group are worth more as part of that group than they would be worth individually. For example at GE, the theory suggests that the commercial finance division is worth more because it is located in the same group as the divisions making steam turbines and broadcasting NBC national television programmes across the USA. Some may find it difficult to understand what conceivable benefit could possibly be gained by combining such diversified elements. But according to corporate strategy theory, benefits are possible – for example, as we have seen at GE, the corporate headquarters is able to provide access to cheaper finance and lower capital costs than would be available to individual companies such as GE's subsidiaries in commercial finance, steam turbines and television stations.

Listing of the benefits delivered by a corporate-level strategy.

9.1.2 The costs of a corporate-level strategy diversification

Set against these possible benefits, some strategists have argued that the costs of a corporate strategy outweigh the benefits. In particular, they argue that diversifying into totally unrelated areas carries higher risks and makes managing such businesses difficult.[9] There are three principal cost areas associated with the higher risks of diversification:

1 the size and cost of the headquarters staff;
2 the complexity and management of the diversified firm;
3 the lack of a competitive resource-based focus.

The size and cost of headquarters staff

The most obvious disadvantage of operating a diversified firm is the need to employ a corporate headquarters. There have been few formal surveys regarding size, but one survey found that there was a 'wide variation in the absolute size of corporate headquarters'.[10] This study of 536 corporations found that the numbers of staff in headquarters varied from two for a company in Chile to 17,100 for a company in Germany. Typically, headquarters staff might include general management, legal, financial, reporting and control, and taxation.

The complexity and management of the diversified firm

As mentioned earlier, there was a strong belief in diversification in the late 1960s in order to reduce the risks of being exposed to any problems that arose from relying on just one business. However, during the 1980s, corporations began to realise that such diversification carried costs associated with the internal management of the diversification strategy. Some of the large corporations were broken up into their constituent parts, at least in part because they became too complex to manage.[11] In addition, some divisions were worth more as individual businesses than as part of a corporation – perhaps because the share price of the group was dragged down by a poorly performing division while, in the same group, there were highly profitable divisions that could be sold individually.

Complexity can also lead to increased costs across the corporation. Some of these are easily measured such as the bureaucracy associated with reporting periodically to HQ. However, other costs are less easily measured but equally important: for example, the need to gain economies of scope requires a degree of sharing amongst managers that may not be easily achieved; equally, the unequal distribution of resources by the HQ to subsidiaries can lead to conflict if the managers of subsidiaries believe that they are not being treated fairly.[12]

The lack of a competitive resource-based focus

During the 1990s, the resource-based view (RBV) of the firm – see Chapter 4 – became increasingly prominent in strategy development. From a corporate perspective, such an approach suggested that the heavily diversified firm is lacking in competitive focus and therefore has few competitive advantages.[13] From this viewpoint, it would be better to break up the corporation. On a more positive note, RBV theory also suggests the areas into which a firm might wish to diversify based on its existing strengths.

To summarise the costs and the benefits, we can recall the work of Alfred Chandler on the centre of the corporation.[14] He argued that the headquarters of multidivisional firms were primarily engaged in two activities: 'entrepreneurial' to create value for the corporation and 'administrative' to prevent losses and ensure efficient resource usage. If diversification is to be justified, then the costs associated with these two areas must be less than the benefits of operating a diversified group.

KEY STRATEGIC PRINCIPLES

- The benefits of corporate-level diversification lie in three areas: internal to the group, external to the group and financial benefits. Internal benefits include economies of scope, core competencies and share activities. External benefits include vertical integration, market power and competitive blocking. Financial benefits cover lower cost of capital, business restructuring and efficient capital allocation.
- The costs of corporate-level diversification arise from three areas: the size and cost of headquarters staff; the complexity and management of the diversified firm; and the lack of a competitive resource-based focus.

9.2 CORPORATE OPTIONS: DEGREES OF DIVERSIFICATION

After exploring the benefits and costs of the corporate diversification, we examine the degree of diversification in groups of companies.[15] Both in theory and in practice, companies have the choice over the degree to which they diversify from their original business over time.

Definition ▶ **Diversification strategy occurs when an organisation moves away from a single product or dominant business area into other business areas, which may or may not be related to the original business.** Some diversified groups seem to have very little connection across parts of the group – for example, at GE, its healthcare division does not appear to have much connection with its commercial finance division. Equally, other diversified groups have a clear connection between the various parts – for example, at the multinational company Nestlé, its global ice cream business with the same brand symbol around the world – see Case 10.3 – has at least one connection with its worldwide Nescafé coffee business: both companies call on the same supermarket customers. For the purposes of strategy options development, it is useful to identify three main levels of diversification:

1 close-related diversification,

2 distant-related diversification,

3 unrelated diversification.

9.2.1 Close-related diversification

Definition ▶ **With close-related diversification, the different companies within the group may have different products or services but have some form of close affinity such as common customers, common suppliers or common overheads.** For example, the Unilever group includes separate companies in such businesses as Magnum ice cream, Flora margarine, Hellman's mayonnaise and Knorr soups – see Case 9.3. Each of these businesses has its own competitors, markets and brands. But each company shares similar supermarket customers, some common suppliers and some common competitors. It makes commercial sense for such companies to seek the benefits of co-operation where appropriate. However, if the group's headquarters judges managers on their *individual* divisional performances, there is less incentive for such managers to co-operate and share competitor and supplier knowledge and contacts. There can be real tensions in close-related diversification.

9.2.2 Distant-related diversification

Definition ▶ **In distant-related diversification, although the different companies in the group will have quite different products or services, possibly using wholly different technologies, they will share the same underpinning core competencies or some other area of technology or service that would benefit from co-ordination by a central headquarters.** For example, 3M has many diversified businesses, but its underpinning core competencies in adhesives and coatings are used widely throughout the group – see Case 7.4. Another example is the Japanese company Canon, whose underpinning core competencies in optics are used in a range of applications from cameras to photocopiers – see Case 13.2.

9.2.3 Unrelated diversification

Definition ▶ **In unrelated diversification, the different companies in the group have little in common with regard to products, customers or technologies. However, they benefit from the resources of the headquarters with regard to the availability of lower-cost finance, quality of management direction and other related matters** – for example, GE and Siemens in Case 9.1.

9.2.4 Which diversification option?

Which option should corporations choose with regard to diversification? What degree of diversification should they follow? There are no simple theoretical answers to these questions at this time. The answers probably depend on the strategic context of the company's headquarters, the leadership and management style of the organisation, and the opportunities and resources available at any point in time.[16]

KEY STRATEGIC PRINCIPLES

- Diversification occurs when a company moves away from a single product into other business areas that may or may not be related to the original business. There are three levels of diversification in such companies: close-related, distant-related and unrelated. Each is important in assessing the benefits from operating a corporate-level strategy.
- Close-related diversification involves some form of affinity with the original business such as common customers or suppliers. Distant-related diversification occurs when there is some underpinning sharing of core competencies or other basic attributes. Unrelated diversification arises when the benefits relate solely to those associated with headquarters management such as lower financial costs.
- The choice of diversification option probably depends on the strategic context of the company's headquarters, its leadership and management style, and the opportunities and resources available at that time.

9.3 CORPORATE STRATEGY AND THE ROLE OF THE CENTRE – THE PRINCIPLE OF PARENTING

Within corporate strategy, it is important that the headquarters itself considers and sets out its role and relationships with its subsidiaries: for obvious reasons, this is called *parenting* in some texts.

The corporate headquarters' role might include the following possible areas:

- corporate functions and services such as international treasury management and central human resource management;
- corporate development initiatives, such as centralised R&D and new acquisitions;

- additional finance for growth or problem areas, on the principle of the product portfolio outlined in the next section of this chapter;
- development of formal linkages between businesses such as the transfer of technology or core competencies between subsidiaries;
- detailed comments on and evaluation of the strategies developed by the subsidiary companies.

For example at News Corporation, the company's leading shareholder and founder – Rupert Murdoch – is involved in all the leading strategic decisions about subsidiaries from his position at the group headquarters – see Case 8.4. Beyond this and as an example only, the film library of the News Corporation subsidiary 20th Century Fox is available to its other subsidiaries, including its TV stations in both the USA and the UK. This service operates even though they are operating totally independent schedules and are completely independent companies. In addition, the News Corporation centre is the major provider of funds for the main growth areas such as its new internet and media ventures – Sky Italia broadband service, *Wall Street Journal*, etc. – and the new, exclusive sports channels and contracts – Fox TV, etc.

Clearly, such parenting resources are formidable if carefully developed. Each group will have its own combination of resources, depending on its mix of businesses and the relevant strategic issues. However, corporate headquarters have a cost. The purpose of parenting is to add value to the subsidiaries that are served, otherwise the parental cost cannot be justified.[17] Subsidiaries need to perform better with the parent than they would independently.

9.3.1 Corporate headquarters characteristics

For the full benefits of corporate strategy, it is not enough for the headquarters to provide a few add-on services. It means developing the core skills of the parent itself; these are called the corporate or *parenting characteristics* of the headquarters.[18]

The parent needs three attributes:

1. an understanding of or familiarity with the *key factors for success* relevant for all of the diverse industries in which each of its subsidiaries is engaged;
2. an ability to *contribute something extra* beyond the subsidiaries that it manages – these might be from any of the areas identified earlier (e.g. R&D, finance);
3. following from the above two points, an ability to define its HQ role accordingly. Essentially, if the diversified group is *highly related*, then HQ has a strong strategy linking role; if the group is *highly diversified*, then HQ has a role closer to a banker who leaves the strategy to the subsidiaries, raises the finance for the group and assesses the performance of subsidiaries. The next section explains this is in more depth.

9.3.2 Determinants of the size and role of corporate headquarters

There are three principal determinants of the size and role of corporate headquarters in multi-product corporations:[19]

1. *The overall size of the group.* Because larger companies have scale economies in information processing, the largest corporate groups do not necessarily have the largest numbers of people in headquarters.
2. *The governance system of the group.* The shareholding structure will influence the activities of the HQ, and the geographical location of the HQ may also be important. If there are few shareholders, then there will be no need for an extensive staff to deal with this. If the group is government owned, then the evidence suggests that the HQ tends to be larger. Some countries such as Japan also seem to have larger headquarters than others.
3. *The corporate strategy of the group.* This is the most important determinant of the size and role of the HQ. If the group has related diversification – for example, Unilever in Case 9.3 – then the headquarters typically discusses and actively influences the strategies of the subsidiaries. The HQ

numbers to undertake this task are high. By contrast, if the group consists of a series of unrelated companies – such has GE in Case 9.1 – then the HQ typically acts more as a banker and does not engage in detailed strategy discussions. Such activity requires fewer numbers at HQ and its role is more limited.

To summarise, there is no simple formula to determine the size and role of the corporate headquarters. Senior directors need to consider precisely what contribution the headquarters makes to the group as a whole. This will then lead to proposals with regard to policy, staff numbers and reporting relationships with the subsidiaries. 'The end result should be a headquarters that delivers on the added-value components of the chosen corporate strategy, but which may well bear little resemblance to other superficially similar companies that follow similar strategies.'[20]

9.3.3 What are the main activities undertaken by the corporate headquarters?

To explore and define parenting further, we can identify the main tasks typically undertaken by a corporate headquarters. They fall into five areas and are shown in Figure 9.3. Some of these areas have already been explored in Chapter 6 earlier, so are not pursued further here.

The five main areas of corporate headquarters activity are:

1. *Ethics and corporate social responsibility issues.* These are explored in Chapter 6.
2. *Stakeholder management and communication, including shareholders.* These are explored in Chapter 6.
3. *Control and guidance of subsidiaries.* The degree of control will depend on the degree of diversification. If a group is highly diversified, then the control will be largely financial and profit oriented. If the diversification is closely related, then it is highly likely that the headquarters will engage in discussion with subsidiaries on topics such as markets, customers and competitive advantage. Both Nokia and Unilever have closely related subsidiaries with strong engagement from the centre, as illustrated in Cases 9.2 and 9.3.
4. *Remuneration, incentives and people evaluation.* For many multi-product groups and corporations, including GE in Case 9.1, this is a vital role of the headquarters. Each company will have its own approach, but any company that values its employees will regard this as a key topic – certainly true of all the four main companies in this chapter. This subject is explored in Chapters 12 and 16.
5. *Legal and treasury.* All companies have legal requirements with regard to tax and company reporting that must be coordinated from the centre. In addition, many companies will have a treasury function at HQ: the role here is to manage the cash across the group and to raise new funds for the group, as required. There is an important strategic financial element involved here, but it is beyond the scope of this book.

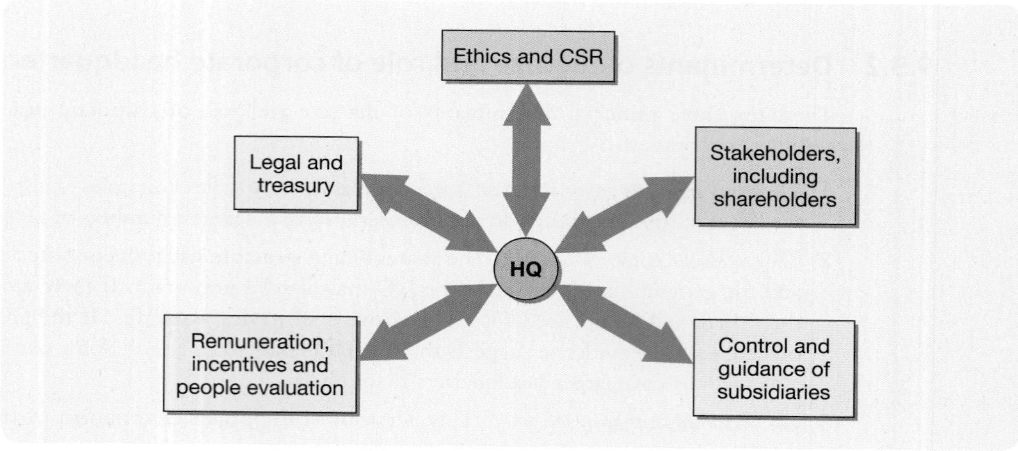

Figure 9.3 The five main activities of corporate HQ

KEY STRATEGIC PRINCIPLES

- Parenting concerns the corporate headquarters of a group of subsidiaries, whose areas of business may be unrelated to each other. Such a business still needs to define its purpose and develop its mission and objectives. This may be difficult where the activities are widely spread.
- The role of the corporate headquarters is to add value to the subsidiaries that are associated with the organisation, otherwise the cost of running a corporate headquarters cannot be justified.
- The corporate headquarters can make offerings in four areas: corporate functions; corporate development initiatives; additional finance for growth or problem areas; and the development of formal linkages between parts of the group.
- Corporate headquarters need two special attributes to operate effectively: an understanding of the key factors for success in the diverse industries of their subsidiaries and an ability to make a special contribution.
- There are five main areas of activity typically undertaken by a corporate headquarters: ethics and corporate social responsibility; stakeholder management and communication; control and guidance of subsidiaries; remuneration incentives and people evaluation; and legal and treasury.

CASE STUDY 9.2

The rise and fall of Nokia

Over the 20 years to 2014, the Finnish company Nokia built global leadership in mobile telephones before losing out to rivals. This case explores the strategic options chosen by the company and how they went both right and wrong.

Early strategic options: the late 1980s

In the late 1980s, the small Finnish company Nokia was involved in a wide range of businesses. For example, it made televisions and other consumer electronics in which it claimed to be 'third in Europe'. It also had a thriving business in industrial cables and machinery and manufactured a wide range of other goods from forestry logging equipment to tyres. It had been expanding fast since the 1960s and was beginning to struggle under the vast range of goods that it sold.

In 1991 and 1992, Nokia lost FM482 million ($120 million) on its major business activities. The company had to find new strategies to remedy this situation. It had already cut out some of its activities but was still left with a telephone manufacturing operation, an unprofitable TV and video manufacturing business and a strong industrial cables business. Nokia began the process by seeking a new group chief executive. Its choice was Jorma Ollila, who had previously run the small Nokia mobile phone division, which was loss-making at the time. 'My brief was to decide whether to sell it or keep it. After four months, I proposed we keep it. We had good people, we had know-how and there was market growth opportunity,' explained Ollila.

There were four criteria to justify the strategic choice to focus on mobile telephones:

1 It was judged that the mobile telephone market had great worldwide growth potential and was growing fast.

2 Nokia already had profitable businesses in this area.

3 Deregulation and privatisation of telecommunications markets around the world were providing specific opportunities.

4 Rapid technological change – especially the new pan-European GSM mobile system – provided the opportunity to alter fundamentally the balance between competitors.

Clearly, all the above judgements carried significant risk. In addition, the company's strategic choice was limited by constraints on its resources. The heavy losses of the group overall were a severe financial constraint. In addition, it was not able to afford the same level of expenditure on research and development as its two major rivals, Motorola (USA) and Ericsson (Sweden). Moreover, although it had the in-house skills and experience of working with national deregulated telecommunications operators through competing in Nordic markets in the 1970s and 1980s, it would need many more employees if it was to develop the market opportunities. However, by selling off its other interests and concentrating on mobile telephones it was able to overcome some of the difficulties.

Nokia became market leader in mobile telephones after shedding other product areas. But its new heavy reliance on mobiles proved its downfall when it was overtaken by better mobile technology.

Looking back on that time, Ollila commented: 'We were earlier than most in understanding . . . that in order to be really successful you have to globalise your organisation and focus your business portfolio . . . We have been able to grow and be global and maintain our agility and be fast at the same time.' What Ollila did not say was that Finland is a small country, so to build any sizeable business, it is essential to think beyond the country's national boundaries.

Building global leadership: the late 1990s

To build global leadership in mobile telephones, Nokia identified three important factors. First, it was important to find a new technology that would change the rules of the game and turn all existing competitors into beginners. Second, it was essential to move fast internationally and respond flexibly as international markets developed. Third, the company had to assess and deliver what customers really wanted from mobile telephones.

Around the late 1990s, Nokia had some luck. This was the agreement within the European Union to adopt the GSM technical standard for mobile telephones. This allowed a company like Nokia to have access to a large market where the technology was standardised and major economies of scale were therefore possible. Such a development was important because the GSM standard was subsequently used worldwide, with around 500 million of the world's 700 million mobiles using this standard by 2000.

In fact, the Nokia headquarters team was highly successful in its expansion. It moved rapidly to design phones that would appeal to global customers by designing mobile phones that offered flair, reliability and ease of use. This meant that it had to invest heavily in software development and it formed an alliance with the British company, Symbian. Subsequently, Nokia acquired a majority share in order to ensure that developments remained on track. Nokia was also single-minded in its investment in factories in order to deliver economies of scale, reduce costs and raise profit margins. The result was that by 2000 Nokia was world leader in mobile telephone manufacture, with 35 per cent global share.

The challenge of a new technology: the early 2000s

Around the year 2000, mobile phone technology changed. The new '3G' pure digital technology introduced a whole new market for telephone services that needed a totally new series of product designs. In turn, this would require new manufacturing processes inside companies like Nokia. The result was that all the mobile telephone manufacturers, including Nokia, were hit by falling profits in 2001–02. In addition, some of the Asian electronics manufacturers like Samsung and Sony realised that the new technology gave them another chance to enter the global mobile markets, particularly if they had missed out on the benefits of the GSM standard. Sony combined with Ericsson to launch a new joint venture and Samsung invested heavily in new 3G technology. The result was that Samsung had built a global market share of 14 per cent by 2005 and Sony Ericsson had a share of 6 per cent. However, Motorola still kept its second position with 17 per cent of the market. Competition was therefore increasing for Nokia, but it managed to hold its global market share around 35 per cent.

All change at Nokia: 2006–2010

In 2006, a new Chief Executive Officer was appointed at Nokia: Olli-Pekka Kallasvuo. But he did not last long. He was asked to leave in Autumn 2010 after the company's performance took a serious downturn – see Figure 9.4. The new chief executive

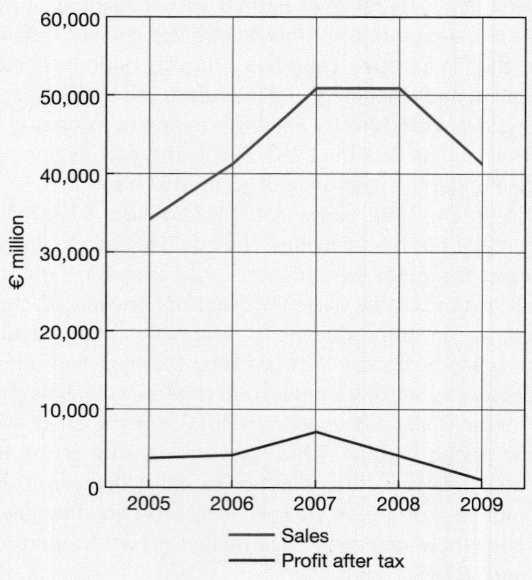

Figure 9.4 Nokia takes a downturn (2005–2009)

was Stephen Elop, formerly a senior director of Microsoft. The reasons for the change of leadership were a mixture of strategic mistakes by Nokia internally and success by its competitors externally. Nokia remained the world's leading mobile phone manufacturer, but both its global market share and its profitability were under serious threat.

Internally, Nokia was excellent at manufacturing mobile phones profitably, exploiting its 40 per cent global market share to deliver economies of scale and building on its strong relationships with the main mobile phone service companies. But Nokia had at least three strategic weaknesses:

1 Its mobile phones aimed at the lower end of the market were under attack from cheap Asian phone manufacturers. Basic mobile phone design and manufacture had become mature. This had allowed manufacturers with very low labour costs from Asian countries to undercut even the low-cost manufacturing processes of Nokia in its home country, Finland.

2 Nokia was using its own proprietary Symbian software to deliver its phone services. This was designed in the 1990s and worked well in the early years. But it was not easily adapted to the latest types of smart phones, like Apple's iPhone and various Blackberry models from RIM, with touch-screen interfaces and instant email and web access. Nokia launched a series of upgrades, for example Symbian 3 in 2010. But commentators said that the new Nokia phones like the N8 were still 'clunky' compared with the iPhone.

3 Nokia's design problems were made worse because the technical development of its mobile phone software was not well organised. Its smart phone software engineers were not focused as a single group directly linked to smart phone development until early 2010. Moreover, unlike its competitors, Nokia did not use exactly the same software across all its models. Any developer – both internally within Nokia and externally developing applications – had to write extra software for each Nokia model.

The result was a lack of design focus and effort that cost the company dearly. Basic mobile phones had become a mature market worldwide. The major growth was in smart phones, beginning with Apple's iPhone in 2007 and RIM's Blackberry to be followed by the launch of Google's open-source phone software in 2008 – called *Android*. Nokia was still the market leader in mobile phones – see Figure 9.5 – but its market share was falling and its profit margins slipping. It was good at basic phones but these were under attack at the bottom end of the market from cheap Asian phones and from the top end from smart phones. And it was the smart phone segment of the market that was growing fastest and had the highest profit margins.

Nokia's smart phone strategy: 2010 onwards

In addition to its internal failures, Nokia also failed to recognise fully the strength of two competitive threats: the launch of the App store in mid-2008 and the arrival of Android software in late 2008. Nokia's Chief Executive, Olli-Pekka Kallasuovo, acknowledged Nokia's weakness in internet services for mobiles after his appointment back in 2007. But he claimed that, 'We are second-to-none when it comes to having the ingredients of taking mobility to the internet. It is a natural extension of the business.' The problem was that this missed some of the real benefits of smart phones.

Although Apple launched its first iPhone in 2007, the full potential had to wait for a development that only came 18 months later: the iPhone App Store. The iPhone was technically advanced but premium priced with a relatively small market share – still only 12 per cent even in early 2010. The strategy that really boosted the iPhone was the company's policy of encouraging outside software companies to produce applications that would work on mobile phones – 'apps' in the jargon. These were then approved by Apple and ranged from simple services to games that could be downloaded onto the iPhone by Apple's customers. Naturally, Nokia responded by launching its own range of apps, but it was not nearly as successful as Apple. By late 2010, there were over 225,000 apps for the iPhone and 13,000 for Nokia phones.

In addition to the iPhone, Nokia also faced a major competitive threat from Google. In 2008, Google launched its own phone with a totally new software system called *Android*. Google's phone itself has not had great success in the market place up to the time of writing this case. However, Google made the Android software open source, meaning that other manufacturers had access to the complete software infrastructure and design for a fee. This meant that Android could be used under licence from Google by other mobile companies wanting to develop the smart phone market, especially in the area of apps. Thus companies like Samsung from South Korea, Motorola from the USA and HTC from Taiwan were able to

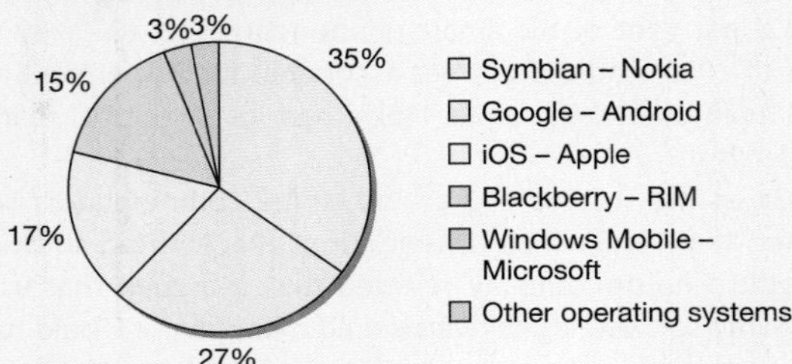

Figure 9.5 Nokia was still smartphone market leader in 2010 but its lead was slipping fast

Note: (1) Chart shows smartphones only. Nokia is still the market leader in basic phones, but smartphones are the main global growth area. (2) Nokia's market share was reported to have declined to 25% by mid-2011. Companies using Google's Android had made most of the gains.

Source: author from various market estimates.

design and launch attractive new smart phones that outperformed Nokia, which was based on its Symbian software. As evidence of the power of this strategy, Android systems had 3 per cent of the smart phone market in 2009. By the end of 2010, Android phones accounted for 27 per cent and had even overtaken Apple. Nokia had lost its global market leadership.

Given the success of Android, some commentators suggested that Nokia should itself adopt the Android software, but the Finnish company rejected this. It argued that using the same software as its rivals would mean that it would have no competitive advantage in the market place. Nokia was determined to keep its own proprietary software at that time, late 2010. The head of Nokia's smart phone unit, Ansi Vanjoki, explained that handset makers using Android would have low operating margins and claimed that they were likely to enjoy only temporary relief with Google's operating system. He compared such companies to Finnish boys who 'pee in their pants' for warmth during the cold winter.

Decline of Nokia: 2011–2013

In early 2011, Nokia was still working on the new software to upgrade or replace Symbian. It had re-organised its software technology teams to focus exclusively on this task. And its new Chief Executive Officer from outside Nokia, Stephen Elop from Microsoft, was thinking hard about what to do. Initially, Elop was keen to build Nokia's own apps. He told an audience of apps companies: 'Fundamentally at Nokia, we are capable of building great devices and getting them out there. But without you guys we can't create vibrancy within the ecosystem. It isn't that I love developers but you bring the system to life.'

A few weeks later, Mr Elop announced his bombshell. Nokia was going to discontinue Symbian software completely and switch to Microsoft's new *Windows* 7 mobile software system. His announcement to all Nokia staff in his famous 'doomsday memo' is described in Case 15.1. This decision was taken in spite of Nokia spending over $24 billion on R&D – much of it on Symbian – over the three years 2008–2010. The problem was that the Symbian software was simply not good enough and it was taking too long to get it right. The only alternative for Nokia to Windows 7 had been Google's Android software but this was rejected for the reasons outlined above.

Crucially, the strategic decision to use Windows 7 software carried real risks for Nokia. In the beginning, Nokia did not have a working Windows 7 mobile phone. Moreover, Windows 7 was only a small player in the mobile phone market place with few apps and Microsoft still had the right to sell its software to any other manufacturer: Nokia did not have competitive exclusivity. In addition, Nokia had openly admitted to its customers that its Symbian software did not perform well. It was perhaps not surprising that analysts were expecting Nokia's share of the smartphone market to decline even further before it could launch new Nokia smartphones in 2012. As the *Financial Times* commented in early 2011, 'Nokia needs this deal to work. And so does Microsoft or they could both end up like two drunks trying to support each other'. By 2013, Nokia's market share continued to decline. It had become a relatively small player in the global mobile phone market.

In 2013, Nokia accepted a bid from Microsoft to buy the mobile phone business for US$5 billion. The Nokia brand name would continue but the company was largely disbanded.

As a prominent Finnish company, Nokia has been committed to green strategies for a number of years: 'Nokia aims to be a leading company in environmental performance.' You can read more at www.nokia.com/environment/strategy-and-reports/environmental-strategy.

Case questions

1 Why did Nokia select only one area for development? What is the strategic risk involved in selecting one area out of four?

2 What was the significance of the introduction of the new Android software for Nokia's chosen strategy? Do companies always need such a technological development to ensure strategic success? Do they need other factors as well as technology – if so, what?

3 How important were the management teams to strategic choice? Did it really have to changes in 2004, 2007 and 2010?

STRATEGIC PROJECT

At the time of writing this case, Nokia was being hit hard by the strategies of Google, Apple and RIM. This case was written as the competitive market was still unfolding. To what extent has Nokia been able to overcome its problems as a result of becoming part of Microsoft? It would be interesting to track this market over the next few years from a strategy perspective. Examining app availability, prices, smartphone models and market initiatives will produce some interesting insights into strategy development. Much of this information is available on the web.

How to use market growth and market share data to identify the position in the BCG matrix . . .

. . . and how market growth and market share impact on company cash flow and profits.

9.4 CORPORATE STRATEGY: DECISIONS ABOUT THE COMPANY'S DIVERSIFIED PORTFOLIO OF PRODUCTS

Definition ▶ **Diversified companies have a range of products serving many customers in different markets: such companies have a *diversified portfolio of products*.** There are good strategic reasons for this: to be reliant on one product or customer clearly carries immense risks if, for any reason, that product or service should fail or the customer should go elsewhere.

Decisions on strategy usually involve a range of products in a range of markets – often referred to as 'balancing the product portfolio'. However, readers will immediately recognise that this view about diversifying the product portfolio runs totally counter to the resource-based view of strategy development. This was explored in Chapter 4 and is currently one of the more highly regarded theories of strategy development. Readers will also know that there are various conflicting views on strategy development: one of the themes of this book. For the purposes of this chapter, we will accept the premise of diversification and explore the concept of 'balancing the product portfolio'.

When an organisation has a number of products in its portfolio, it is quite likely that they will be in different stages of market development: some will be relatively new and some much older. For example at Nokia in Case 9.2, there will be some mobiles that have been around for some years based on simple and well-proven technology. At the same time, there will be others based on the latest 3G technology that will have much greater growth potential but be at an early stage of market development.

Many organisations will not wish to risk having all their products in the same markets and at the same stages of development: they will follow a strategy of diversification. It is useful to have some products with limited growth but producing profits steadily, as well as having others that have real potential but may still be in the early stages of their growth. Indeed, the products that are earning steadily may be used to fund the development of those that will provide the growth and profits in the future.

According to this argument, the key strategy is to produce a *balanced portfolio of products* – some low-risk but dull growth, some higher-risk with future potential and rewards. The results can be measured in both *profit* and *cash* terms. (Cash is used as a measure here because, both in theory and in practice, it is possible for a company to be trading profitably and yet go bankrupt. This is because the company is earning insufficient *cash* as the profits are being reinvested in growth in the business. It is important to understand this distinction.) The key strategic issue for corporate headquarters is how to arrive at this balance based upon the twin needs for new growth while maintaining current stability: the starting point is *product portfolio analysis*.

Portfolio analysis was originally suggested by the Boston Consulting Group (BCG) in the 1970s and, as a result, one version of the approach is known as the BCG portfolio matrix. **Definition ▶** **The portfolio matrix analyses the range of products possessed by an organisation (its portfolio) against two criteria: relative market share and market growth.** It is sometimes called the growth–share matrix and was subject to a number of criticisms that are important to understand. Other versions of portfolio matrices were later developed to overcome weaknesses in the BCG approach – for example, the *directional policy matrix* explained in Section 9.4.3. Portfolio analysis is one method of arriving at the best balance of products within a multi-product company.

9.4.1 The BCG growth–share matrix

This matrix is one means of analysing the balance of an organisation's product portfolio, the purpose being to produce the best balance of growth versus stable products within a diversified company. According to this matrix, two basic factors define a product's strategic stance in the market place:

1 *relative market share* – for each product, the ratio of the share of the organisation's product divided by the share of the market leader;[22]

2 *market growth rate* – for each product, the market growth rate of the product category.

Relative market share is important because, in the competitive battle of the market place, it is advantageous to have a larger share than rivals: this gives room for manoeuvre, the scale to undertake investment and the ability to command distribution. Some researchers, such as Buzzell and Gale,[23] claim to have found empirical evidence to support these statements. For example, in a survey of major companies, the two researchers found that businesses with over 50 per cent share of their markets enjoy rates of return three times greater than businesses with small market shares. There are other empirical studies that also support this broad conclusion.[24] However, Jacobsen and Aaker[25] have questioned this relationship. They point out that such a close correlation will also derive from other differences in businesses. High market share companies do not just differ on market share but on other dimensions as well: for example, they may have better management and may have more luck. However, Aaker himself in a more recent work[26] has conceded that portfolios do have their uses, along with their limitations.

Market growth rate is important because markets that are growing rapidly offer more opportunities for sales than lower growth markets. Rapid growth is less likely to involve stealing share from competition and more likely to come from new buyers entering the market. This gives many new opportunities for the right product. There are also difficulties, however – perhaps the chief being that growing markets are often not as profitable as those with low growth. Investment is usually needed to *promote* the rapid growth and this has to be funded out of profits.

Relative market share and market growth rate are combined in the growth–share matrix, as shown in Figure 9.6. It should be noted that the term 'matrix' is misleading. In reality, the diagram does not have four distinct boxes, but rather four areas which merge into one another. The four areas are given distinctive names to signify their strategic significance.

Definition ▶

- *Stars*. The upper-left quadrant contains the **stars: products with high relative market shares operating in high-growth markets.** The growth rate will mean that they will need heavy investment and will therefore be cash users. However, because they have high market shares, it is assumed that they will have economies of scale and be able to generate large amounts of cash. Overall, it is therefore asserted that they will be cash neutral – an assumption not necessarily supported in practice and not yet fully tested.

Definition ▶

- *Cash cows*. The lower-left quadrant shows the **cash cows: product areas that have high relative market shares but exist in low-growth markets.** The business is mature and it is assumed that lower levels of investment will be required. On this basis, it is therefore likely that they will be able to generate both cash and profits. Such profits could then be transferred to support the stars.

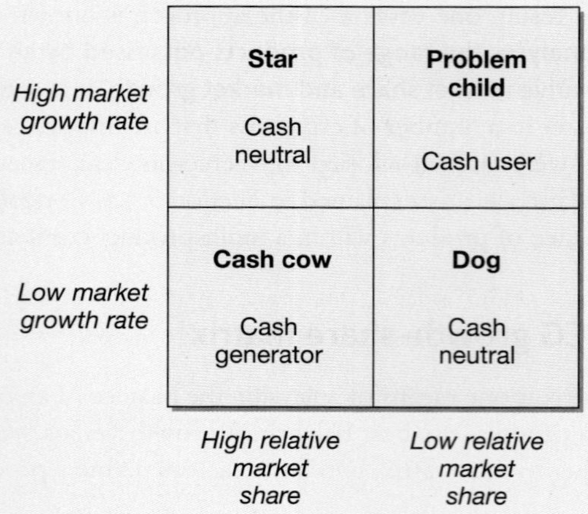

	High relative market share	*Low relative market share*
High market growth rate	**Star** Cash neutral	**Problem child** Cash user
Low market growth rate	**Cash cow** Cash generator	**Dog** Cash neutral

Figure 9.6 The growth-share matrix – individual products or product groups categorised by market growth and share

However, there is a real strategic danger here that cash cows become under-supported and begin to lose their market share.[27]

Definition ▶

- *Problem children*. The upper-right quadrant contains the **problem children: products with low relative market shares in high-growth markets.** Such products have not yet obtained dominant positions in rapidly growing markets or, possibly, their market shares have become less dominant as competition has become more aggressive. The market growth means that it is likely that considerable investment will still be required and the low market share will mean that such products will have difficulty generating substantial cash. Hence, on this basis, these products are likely to be cash users.

Definition ▶

- *Dogs*. The lower-right quadrant contains the **dogs: products that have low relative market shares in low-growth businesses.** It is assumed that the products will need low investment but that they are unlikely to be major profit earners. Hence, these two elements should balance each other and they should be cash neutral overall. In practice, they *may* actually absorb cash because of the investment required to hold their position. They are often regarded as unattractive for the long term and recommended for disposal.

Overall, the general strategy is to take cash from the *cash cows* to fund *stars* and invest in future new products that do not yet even appear on the matrix. Cash may also be invested selectively in some *problem children* to turn them into *stars*, with the others being milked or even sold to provide funds for elsewhere. Typically in many organisations, the *dogs* form the largest category and often represent the most difficult strategic decisions. Should they be sold? Could they be repositioned in a smaller market category that would allow them to dominate that category? Are they really cash neutral or possibly absorbing cash? If they are cash-absorbers, what strategies might be adopted?

Clearly the strategic questions raised by the approach have a useful function in the analysis and development of strategy. In Chapter 10, we will examine these further in the context of strategic choice. Some care needs to be taken in calculating the positions of products on the matrix and Chapter 10 has a worked example to show how it can be done (see Case 10.4 and Chapter 10 Appendix).

9.4.2 Difficulties with the BCG growth–share matrix

There are a number of problems associated with the matrix. The most obvious difficulty is that strategy is defined purely in terms of two simple factors and other issues are ignored. Further problems include:

- *The definition of market growth*. What is high market growth and what is low? Conventionally, this is often set above or below 5 per cent per annum, but there are no rules.
- *The definition of the market*. It is not always clear how the market should be defined. It is always possible to make a product dominate a market by defining the market narrowly enough. For example, do we consider the *entire* European steel market, where Usinor would have a small share, or do we take the *French segment* only, when the Usinor share would be much higher? This could radically alter the conclusions.
- *The definition of relative market share*. What constitutes a high relative share and a low share? Conventionally, the ratio is set at 1.5 (the market share of the organisation's product divided by the market share of market leader's product) but why should this be so?

Hence, although the BCG matrix has the merit of simplicity, it has some significant weaknesses. As a result, other product portfolio approaches have been developed.

9.4.3 Other product portfolio approaches – the directional policy matrix

In order to overcome the obvious limitations of the BCG matrix, other product portfolio approaches have been developed. Essentially, rather than relying on the simplistic (but easily measurable) axes of market growth and market share, the further developments used rather more comprehensive measures of strategic success. Three examples will suffice:

1. In the case of the matrix developed by the well-known management consultants McKinsey, the two matrix axes were market attractiveness and business competitive strength.[28]
2. In the case of strategy planners at the major oil company Royal Dutch/Shell, the matrix axes were called industry attractiveness and business competitive position:[29] Shell called its matrix development the *directional policy matrix* (DPM).
3. Another very similar matrix was developed around the same time by the large US conglomerate GE, and is called the *strategic business-planning grid.*

Most of these matrices have much in common, so our exploration is confined to the DPM. Taking the example of the DPM matrix, the axes for this approach are:

- *Industry attractiveness.* In addition to market growth, this axis includes market size, industry profitability, amount of competition, market concentration, seasonality, cycles of demand, and industry profitability. Each of these factors is rated and then combined into a numerical index. The industry attractiveness of each part of a multi-product business can be conveniently classified into high, medium or low.
- *Business competitive position.* In addition to market share, this axis includes the company's relative price competitiveness, its reputation, quality, geographic strengths, customer and market knowledge. Again, the factors are rated and classified into an index shown as strong, average or weak.

The complete matrix can then be plotted: see Figure 9.7. It will be evident that, where an organisation has a strong competitive position in an attractive industry, it should invest further. For example, Unilever has continued to invest worldwide in ice cream, with major acquisitions in the USA, China and Brazil in recent years. Conversely, where a company has a weak competitive position in an industry with low attractiveness, it should strongly consider divesting itself of such a product area. For example, Unilever divested its Speciality Chemicals Division in 1997, where it was relatively weak compared with other companies and the market was subject to periodic downturns in profitability.

Other positions in such matrices suggest other solutions. For example, a strong competitive position in an industry with low attractiveness might imply a strategy of cash generation, since there would be little point in investing further in such an unattractive industry, but there would be important cash to be generated from such a strong competitive position. In Unilever's case, such a product group might be its oils and fats business, where it has a strong share in many countries, but the market prospects are not as attractive as in its consumer toiletries business.

All this may seem clear and highly valuable in strategy development. The first problem comes in developing the two axes: for example, exactly how do you develop an index that represents market

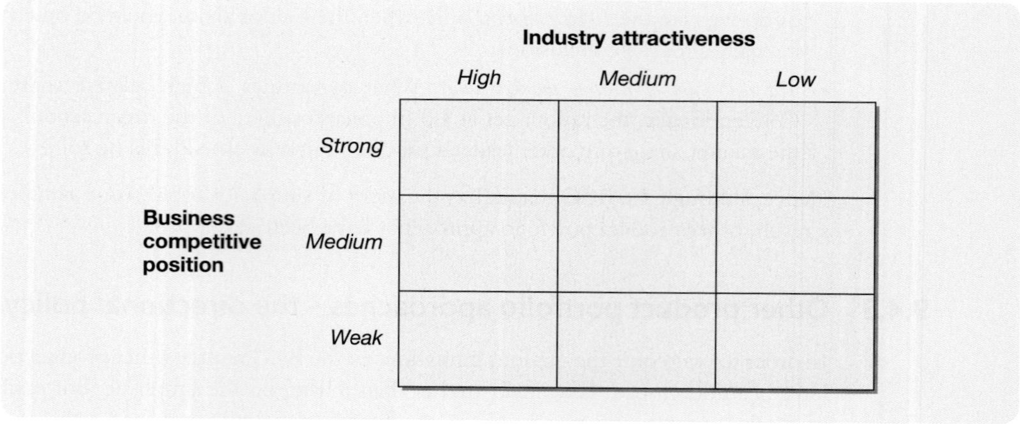

Business competitive position	Industry attractiveness: High	Medium	Low
Strong			
Medium			
Weak			

Figure 9.7 Directional policy matrix

growth, market size, industry profitability and so on? It can be done, but it is time-consuming and, partly at least, dependent on judgement. This means that it is open to management politics, influence and negotiation rather than the simple rational process of the BCG matrix. Beyond this, there are other problems associated with all product portfolio matrices which are discussed in the next section.

9.4.4 Difficulties with all forms of product portfolio matrices

In spite of their advantages, all such matrices present a number of analytical problems:

- *Dubious recommendations*. Can we really afford to eliminate dogs when they may share common factory overheads with others? Are we in danger of under-investing in valuable cash cows and diverting the funds into inherently weak problem children? Similar questions can be asked about the DPM.
- *Innovation*. Where do innovative new products fit onto the matrix? Do they have a small share of a tiny market and so deserve to be eliminated before they have even started? What meaning can be given to 'competitive position' in these circumstances?
- *Divesting unwanted product areas*. In many Western countries, there may be substantial redundancy costs that make divestment unattractive. Even if there are not, divestment assumes that other companies might be interested in buying such a product range at a fair market price, which may be equally doubtful.
- *The perceived desirability of growth and industry attractiveness*. This assumption is not necessarily appropriate for all businesses. Some may make higher longer-term profits by seeking lower levels of growth.
- *The assumption that competitors will allow the organisation freedom to make its changes*. Competitors can also undertake a product portfolio analysis for both their own and competing products. Competitor reactions may negate the proposed changes in the organisation's portfolio.

Although the development of the product portfolio is useful in raising and exploring strategic issues, it is not a panacea for the development of corporate strategy options. To overcome some of the issues raised above, various other formats for the product portfolio have been developed. Aaker[30] has provided a useful recent review of these. In 1977, Day[31] concluded that product portfolios were useful as a *starting point* in choosing between corporate level strategy options; such a comment still holds today.

KEY STRATEGIC PRINCIPLES

- Portfolio analysis provides a means of analysing a company that has a range of products.
- The BCG portfolio analysis is undertaken using only two variables: relative market share and market growth. It is clearly a weakness that other variables are not included.
- The portfolio is then divided into four areas: stars, cash cows, problem children and dogs. These outline categories are then used as the basis for developing a balanced product portfolio. The technique is useful as a starting point only in developing corporate strategy options.
- Because of weaknesses in the BCG matrix, other matrices have been developed – for example, the *directional policy matrix* based on industry attractiveness and competitive position. But such dimensions remain vague and unsubstantiated.

CASE STUDY 9.3

Unilever: can product portfolio strategies help large corporations to grow?

Unilever is one of the world's largest food and consumer goods companies. In 1999, it introduced its new 'Path to Growth' strategy with the objective of focusing on its leading brands in order to deliver new profitable growth. This was classic product portfolio strategy - cutting weak brands in low-growth markets - but Unilever's profits were hardly higher in 2012 than a decade earlier. Why? And where now?

Unilever's profit problem

Unilever has some areas of significant market strength: for example, it is the world's largest maker of ice cream products, tea beverages, margarine and cooking oils and some hair care and skin care products - see Exhibit 9.1. Its competitors worldwide include the multinational companies Procter & Gamble (USA) and Nestlé (Switzerland). Although Unilever has been trading successfully over many years, it has been operating in some relatively mature markets and with limited worldwide co-ordination. As a result, the executive committee decided in the late 1990s to weed out under-performing product areas and focus on strengths. Unfortunately, Unilever's product portfolio growth strategy was taking a long time to deliver: Figure 9.8 shows that its sales in 2012 were virtually the same as those in 2001. However, profits were beginning to increase.

To understand the circumstances leading to such prescriptive strategic solutions, it is useful to begin by exploring Unilever's history.

EXHIBIT 9.1

Unilever's key statistics

- Worldwide turnover €51.3 billion in 2012 with operating profit €6.9 billion
- Over 165,000 employees in over 100 countries worldwide
- Leading food brands include Flora/Becel, Knorr, Hellmann's, Heartbrand ice creams, Blue Band, Ben & Jerry's, Lipton
- Leading personal care and cleaning brands include Radox, TRESemmé, Rexona, Dove, Lux, Pond's, Axe/Lynx, Sunsilk, Omo, Cif
- Since the 'Path to Growth' strategy launched in 1999, Unilever has reduced the main brands from 1,600 to 12 leading brands each with sales of over €1 billion with another eight brands achieving sales of €0.5 billion: the top 20 brands represent around 70 per cent of sales.

Background - strategy as history

Unilever began as a merger between the British soap and detergent manufacturer Lever Brothers and the group of Dutch margarine and food oil companies Van Den Bergh and Jurgens after the First World War. Both parents already had extensive international activities which they sought to consolidate and extend through the new joint company. But the national sensitivities were such that the new company had some special characteristics that still affect the way that Unilever operates in the twenty-first century: it still has two worldwide headquarters, in the Netherlands and the UK, and has only recently moved to having one chief executive. Especially in the 1970s and 1980s, it also had a strong tradition of international co-operation and human resource development between the semi-autonomous national companies that made up the group: it was not a globally integrated company.

In the early years, the various national companies were allowed to manage their

Unilever's acquisition of Hellmann's Mayonnaise and Knorr Soups, including its Russian range, gave the company added presence in major world brands. But competition is fierce and retail pressures high. Some strategists have argued that Unilever should now focus on acquisitions in personal products like cosmetics where the profit margins are higher.

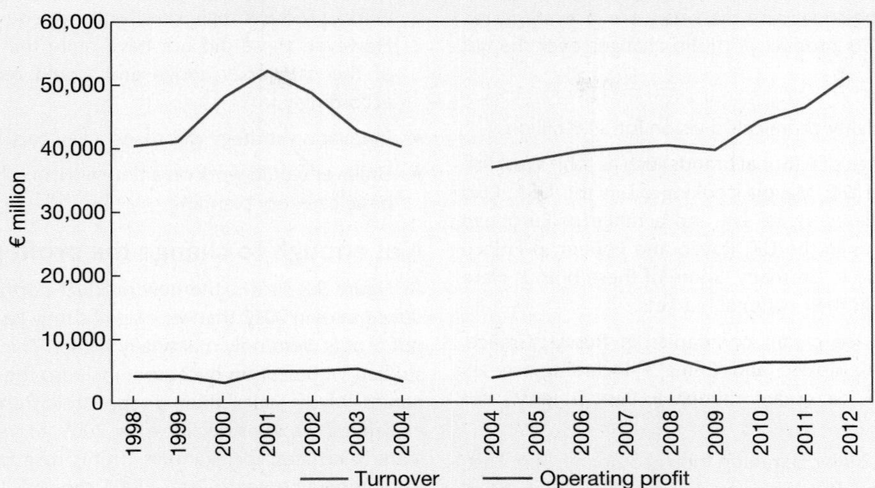

Figure 9.8 Unilever's turnover and profit growth from 1998–2012*

* In common with many companies, Unilever changed the basis of its accounting rules in 2004. This means that we need to be cautious in comparing the years before and after this change. But the broad, overall picture remains one of slow growth. Indeed, if world price inflation was taken into account, then arguably Unilever would show a *decline* in 2010 sales and profits in real terms compared with 10 years earlier.

Source: author from Unilever annual report and accounts for various years.

own affairs. In the 1960s, global co-ordination was introduced at the joint headquarters in product areas like detergents.[32] But national companies were still allowed to keep their own national brands, strategies and manufacturing facilities. Thus, for example, Unilever's detergent activities across Europe in the period 1965–1990 were a patchwork of national brands – Persil in the UK, Skip in France and Portugal, Omo in the Netherlands, Austria and parts of Africa – each with its own production operation. By contrast, its rival Procter & Gamble (P&G) was developing a more focused global branding and manufacturing operation under the brand names Ariel and Tide. Profit margins at P&G were consequently significantly higher than at Unilever. However, there was more co-ordination in some newer Unilever product areas – for example, Dove skin care, Liptons Tea and ice cream products like Cornetto and Magnum were encouraged to develop worldwide under the heart-shaped logo.

Unilever's prescriptive approach

In the late 1990s, the relative independence of Unilever's national companies began to give way to much a greater international co-ordination and global strategy, at least in some product areas. In 1997, Unilever's headquarters executive committee announced a new organisational structure that had several specific objectives:

- to clarify worldwide management responsibilities and stimulate growth;
- to inject some new life into a company whose culture had become worthy but dull;
- to increase product co-ordination with a view to stimulating greater responsibility and innovation across the group.

In 1999, the same Unilever executive then coupled this reorganisation with a new, bold strategy: the 'Path to Growth'. This would concentrate the company's resources on its 400 leading brands. It would either sell or slowly run down its other 1,200 brands. Marketing, research and personnel were focused on its leading power brands. The objective was to achieve annual sales growth of 6 per cent by 2004 and to boost profit margins from 11 to 15 per cent. Major costs savings would result from simplifying operations and reducing suppliers – over $1 billion per annum. The sales growth would come from investing more in marketing and advertising.

Subsequently, and in spite of approving a mission statement that was both bland and boring at that time ('Our purpose at Unilever is to meet the everyday needs of people everywhere'), the small executive committee at the centre took some bold strategic decisions to divest some products and invest in others – classic portfolio management strategy. Specifically, it decided to get out of low-branded areas like Speciality Chemicals and invest in global brands, for example its acquisition of Hellmann's Mayonnaise. In later years, this was followed up by another initiative to invest in personal care products, such as Lynx deodorant and Dove skin care, because these had higher profit margins than margarine and tea, and the personal care markets were growing faster. Here are some of its product portfolio changes over the last 10 years:

- It sold the speciality chemicals division for $4.6 billion.
- It divested a range of national brands such as John West fish products in the UK, Mazola cooking oil in the USA, Oxo cooking ingredients in the UK and a range of European soups: Batchelors in the UK, Royco and Lesieur in France and Heisse Tasse in Germany. Some of these brands were market leaders in their national markets.
- It bought new ice cream companies in Russia, Greece, Brazil, the USA, Mexico and China – including the US super-premium ice cream company Ben & Jerry's for $125 million.
- It acquired the major slimming foods company, Slim Fast, for $2.3 billion. This was just before the 'Atkins Diet' became popular, which was quite different from Slim Fast. Unilever's acquisition proved unsuccessful in the sense that it never covered the cost of its investment.
- It acquired the global food company, Bestfoods, which owned Hellmann's Mayonnaise and Knorr Soups and Sauces, for $20 billion. Unilever's acquisition was successful in that it delivered two major global brands. However, with hindsight, some commentators felt that the company might have been better investing in the faster-growing personal products category rather than slow-growing foods.
- In 2010, it acquired the shower gel and European detergents business of Sara Lee Corporation for €1.2 billion.
- Unilever sold its Birds Eye and Findus frozen food businesses in the UK and Italy in 2006 and 2010, respectively.
- In 2011, the company bought the personal products interests of the US company Alberto Culver, including TRESemmé and VO5 shampoo brands, for $3.7 billion.

In addition to these changes, Unilever decided to re-organise its entire operation to give more emphasis to key product groups and brands. Globalisation, even with local variations, meant that each national company could no longer go entirely its own way. The group's new structure included the following:

- Business product groups would now have more power. National companies would continue, but the business groups would be pre-eminent.
- Some seven product groups were identified with significant international growth potential for the first time: laundry, ice cream, yellow fats, personal wash, tea-based beverages, prestige products, and skin care. These were considered to have real growth potential and would receive priority investment accordingly.
- Another three categories were also identified as established world products: hair care, oral hygiene and deodorants. However, these did not have quite the growth potential of the categories above and would receive investment accordingly.
- Innovation strategy was made a key part of each company.
- Unilever would work on a time horizon of 8–10 years for its basic category planning.

Not enough to change the profit portfolio

As Figure 9.8 shows, the new product portfolio strategy produced sales in 2012 that were significantly higher than in 1996, but profits were only marginally higher. The data needs to be studied with caution because it includes the disposal of companies whose sales then disappeared from the total, thus explaining the sales decline after 2001. Moreover, there were some successes: for example, profits rose in 2010–2012. But the intervening years, 2001–2004 showed that the company needed to go beyond product portfolio strategies.

In 2005, Unilever decided that further re-organisation of management responsibilities was needed. A new, smaller executive team replaced the previous executive committee, the two divisions and 11 business groups. The new team would have three regional presidents for Europe, the Americas and Asia/Africa. It would also have two product category presidents, one for the food division and one for the home and personal care division. The new executive team would be completed by a chief finance officer, a chief human resources officer and one group chief executive (not two as previously). The new chief executive, Patrick Cescau, commented: 'I am excited to have been entrusted with this new challenge. These changes are designed to make us more competitive in the market place. The fusion of our businesses under three regional presidents gives us the ability to truly leverage our scale and to service our customers more effectively. The two category (product) presidents will concentrate on brand management and activation driven by consumer needs and aspirations.'

In 2008, Mr Cescau retired and a new CEO was appointed, Paul Polman. He then re-organised the board further by combining the two product directors into one area and appointing additional main board directors for supply chain management and marketing. Importantly, the strategic emphasis shifted from cost cutting to building volume through the existing portfolio of branded products, through innovation and marketing within this product range and through better service to its key retail supermarket customers like Tesco and Wal-Mart (ASDA in the UK). He was also beginning to move Unilever further along the focused product portfolio path on two dimensions: first, he focused more on increasing sales in developing countries where growth prospects were higher; second, he increased investment in personal care products where profit margins were higher. Figure 9.9 shows the outcome of these two trends.

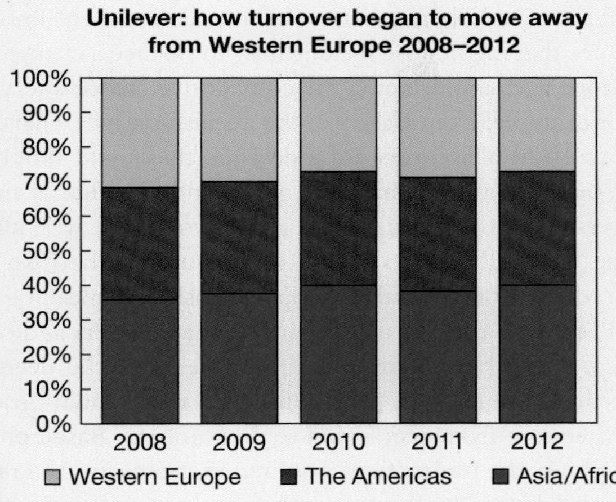

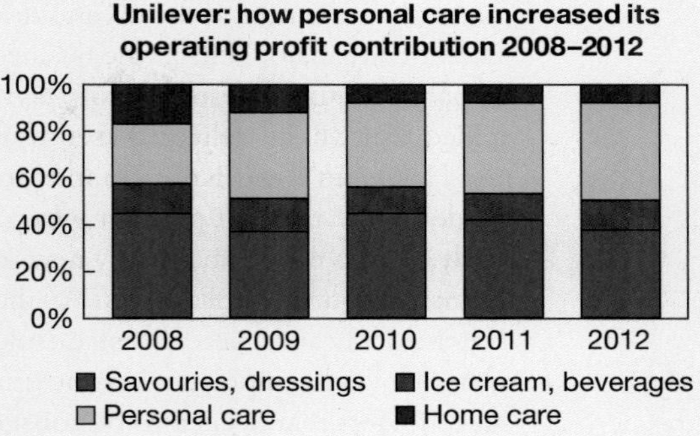

Figure 9.9 Unilever's increased emphasis on developing countries and personal care products

Note: (1) some developing countries like Brazil, Mexico, Chile and Argentina are included in The Americas data. Over 50 per cent of Unilever's turnover came from developing countries in 2010; (2) part of the personal care increase derived from new acquisitions, not just the from margin improvement.

Source: author from Unilever annual report and accounts.

As indicated above, Unilever is developing further its green strategies: *'Our Compass strategy sets out our ambition. It is to double the size of Unilever while reducing our environmental footprint.'* More details at www.unilever.com/sustainability.

Case questions

1 In what way is the Unilever strategic planning process prescriptive? How, if at all, does it help innovation?

2 To what extent is Unilever's strategic decision-making process a result of its history?

3 Given the size of the operation, would you make any changes to Unilever's strategic decision-making process? Are you convinced that the new structure and product focus will be any better at delivering results?

9.5 THE TOOLS OF CORPORATE-LEVEL OPTIONS: FROM ACQUISITIONS TO RESTRUCTURING

Eight key guidelines for takeovers and joint ventures.

Having explored the role of the corporate headquarters and the product portfolio decisions that are made at the centre of the organisation, we can now explore the tools of corporate strategy. What strategic options are actually available to corporate strategists? Typically, these are called *HQ transaction decisions*. Essentially, the headquarters of a multi-product group will take the final decisions on major company issues like acquisitions and diversification. We can see these areas at Unilever in Case 9.3, where transaction decisions included the sale of some of the subsidiary companies and the prioritisation of others.

The Unilever business units were involved in developing the strategy options but it was the Unilever headquarters that took the final decisions.

Definition ▶ **In any multidivisional company, HQ transaction decisions involve the headquarters in making the final decision with regard to acquisitions and other major restructuring.** The principal reason is that only the centre of the organisation will have the full picture in order to understand the implications of any major shift in the business. Issues that might arise include how to finance a change, the impact on human resources of such a change and, importantly, the competitive stance and value added that will be delivered as a result. For example, from Case 9.3, the acquisition by Unilever of the Hellmann's and Knorr brands for around $20 billion was not a decision that could simply be made by the relevant product group. The purchase transformed the group and stretched it financially. It also meant that many new managers and workers joined the group worldwide with all the human resource implications. At the same time, other parts of the group such as the Oxo and Batchelors brands were divested (sold) in order to comply with monopoly legislation, meaning that other Unilever employees left the group. There was also a major impact on shareholders and other stakeholders that needed to be considered. Unilever headquarters was fundamental to this decision.

HQ transaction strategic decisions are therefore capable of transforming many multi-product groups. Such decisions run across a clear spectrum from acquisition to divestment.[34] Definition ▶ **Based on the principle of the level of ownership by the group, the transactions continuum represents the range of options that are available for ownership and control by the group: they begin at one end with an acquisition with 100 per cent ownership and end with divestment at the opposite end with zero per cent ownership.** In between, there are various forms of alliance, including joint ventures and other forms of collaboration which may involve some form of partial ownership by the group. Figure 9.10 sets out the main options that are available to any group.

Strategists have researched corporate transactions extensively, especially in terms of their impact on company profitability.[35] For our purposes, we can note that many such strategies have a poor record of success, particularly those involving acquisitions. Divestments are less prone to failure because they are more fully under the control of the corporate headquarters, who can see the implications more clearly because they own the business to be sold. The reasons for failure amongst acquisitions are many and varied. Unfortunately, there is no simple underpinning logic for failure – just a long list produced by researchers of possible company purchases that have gone wrong over time.

Given the amount of energy and publicity expended, this conclusion may be regarded as somewhat disappointing. Various researchers have reviewed the main evidence, which is summarised in Exhibit 9.2. Essentially, they concluded that: 'The typical effect of merger and acquisition (M&A) activity on firm performance has been well documented and, on average, M&A activity does not lead to superior financial performance . . . Despite decades of research, what impacts the financial performance of firms engaging in M&A activity remains largely unexplained.'[36]

More positively with regard to acquisitions, it is possible to produce some guidance on what makes for successful acquisitions – such a checklist is shown on the website. However, the evidence suggests that this list provides no guarantee of success.

Checklist: Pointers towards successful acquisitions.

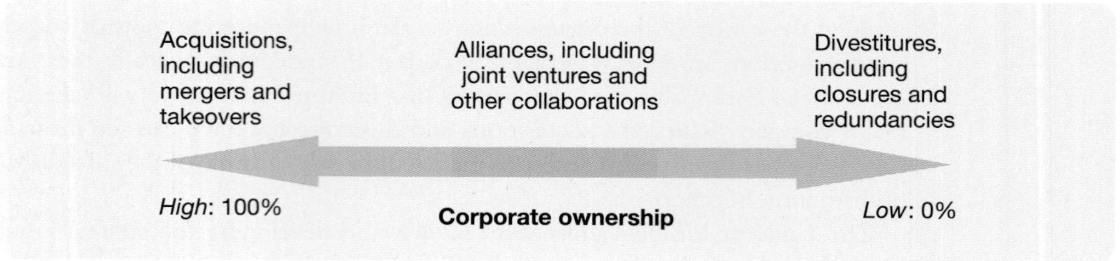

Figure 9.10 The HQ transactions continuum

EXHIBIT 9.2

The performance of mergers and acquisitions

Method of evaluation	Examples of studies	Conclusions
1 Cumulative studies of research findings	King *et al.* (2004)	On average, mergers do not lead to superior financial performance
2 Whether acquired business is held in the long term	Datta (1992)	More divested than retained
3 Impact of acquisitions remains 'inconclusive'	Ravenscraft and Scherer (1987)	No clear evidence of benefits
4 Benefits of M&A to acquirors often resource-based or market-based	Roll (1988); Haspeslaugh and Jemison (1991); Sirower (1997); Anand and Singh (1997); Ahuja and Katila (2001); Hayward (2001)	Benefits possible but not fully proven: note the relationship with resource-based (Chapter 6) and environment-based strategy (Chapter 3)

Source: compiled by the author from various research papers. The full references can be found by examining two papers: (1) King, D R, Dalton, D R, Daly, C M and Covin, J G (2004) 'Meta-Analysis of Post-Acquisition Performance: Indications of Unidentified Moderators', *Strategic Management Journal*, Vol 25, pp 187–200. (2) Hayward, M L A (2002) 'When do Firms Learn from their Acquisition Experience?' *Strategic Management Journal*, Vol 23, No 1, pp 21–40. There is a useful summary of the broader issues in M&A activity by Michael Hitt, R Duane Ireland and Jeffrey S Harrison in Chapter 12 of Hitt, M A, Freeman, R E and Harrison, J S (2001) *Handbook of Strategic Management*, Blackwell Business, Oxford.

KEY STRATEGIC PRINCIPLES

- In any multi-divisional company, HQ transaction decisions involve the headquarters in making the final decision with regard to acquisitions and other major restructuring. Such decisions can take place along a transactions continuum from acquisition to divestment of subsidiary companies.
- There is significant evidence that acquisitions do not have a high level of success, but the reasons remain obscure. Divestments are more likely to be successful because the subsidiary to be divested is better known to the corporate headquarters.
- It is possible to devise a checklist of pointers that will increase the probability of success from acquisitions. However, there is no guarantee of success.

CRITICAL REFLECTION

Can corporate strategy co-exist with the resource-based view?

One of the main arguments in favour of a corporate strategy is that the multi-product company has interests in a variety of markets: the profit downturn in one market may be offset by a rise in another rmarket. However, this approach runs contrary to the resource-based view of strategy development: strategies that build on competitive resources are more likely to be successful than those that do not.

Potentially, this risk-spreading aspect of corporate strategy conflicts with the resource-based view. What do you think? Which theory is more useful?

SUMMARY

- The benefits of corporate-level diversification lie in three areas: internal to the group, external to the group and financial benefits. Internal benefits include economies of scope, core competencies and share activities. External benefits include vertical integration, market power and competitive blocking. Financial benefits cover lower cost of capital, business restructuring and efficient capital allocation.
- The costs of corporate-level diversification arise from three areas: the size and cost of headquarters staff; the complexity and management of the diversified firm; and the lack of a competitive resource-based focus.
- Diversification occurs when a company moves away from a single product into other business areas that may or may not be related to the original business. There are three levels of diversification in such companies: close-related, distant-related and unrelated. Each is important in assessing the benefits from operating a corporate-level strategy.
- Close-related diversification involves some form of affinity with the original business such as common customers or suppliers. Distant-related diversification occurs when there is some underpinning sharing of core competencies or other basic attributes. Unrelated diversification arises when the benefits relate solely to those associated with headquarters management such as lower financial costs. The choice of diversification option probably depends on the strategic context of the company's headquarters, its leadership and management style and the opportunities and resources available at that time.
- Parenting concerns the corporate headquarters of a group of subsidiaries whose areas of business may be unrelated to each other. Such a business still needs to define its purpose and develop its mission and objectives. This may be difficult where the activities are widely spread.
- The role of the corporate headquarters is to add value to the subsidiaries that are associated with the organisation, otherwise the cost of running a corporate headquarters cannot be justified.
- The corporate headquarters can make offerings in four areas: corporate functions; corporate development initiatives; additional finance for growth or problem areas; and the development of formal linkages between parts of the group.
- Corporate headquarters need two special attributes to operate effectively: an understanding of the key factors for success in the diverse industries of their subsidiaries and an ability to make a special contribution.
- There are five main areas of activity typically undertaken by a corporate headquarters: ethics and corporate social responsibility; stakeholder management and communication; control and guidance of subsidiaries; remuneration incentives and people evaluation; and legal and treasury.
- Portfolio analysis provides a means of analysing a company that has a range of products.
- The BCG portfolio analysis is undertaken using only two variables: relative market share and market growth. It is clearly a weakness that other variables are not included. The portfolio is then divided into four areas: stars, cash cows, problem children and dogs. These outline categories are then used as the basis for developing a balanced product portfolio. The technique is useful as a starting point only in developing corporate strategy options.
- Because of weaknesses in the BCG matrix, other matrices have been developed – for example, the directional policy matrix based on industry attractiveness and competitive position. But such dimensions remain vague and unsubstantiated.
- In any multi-divisional company, HQ transaction decisions involve the headquarters in making the final decision with regard to acquisitions and other major restructuring. Such decisions can take place along a transactions continuum from acquisition to divestment of subsidiary companies.

- There is significant evidence that acquisitions do not have a high level of success, but the reasons remain obscure. Divestments are more likely to be successful because the subsidiary to be divested is better known to the corporate headquarters.
- It is possible to devise a checklist of pointers that will increase the probability of success from acquisitions. However, there is no guarantee of success.

QUESTIONS

1 Considering the Unilever case earlier in the chapter, does the 'path-to-growth' strategy represent an option available only to Unilever or can other companies benefit from such an approach?

2 Using Siemens as an example (see Case 9.1), why would this company choose to acquire other companies rather than grow from within? What are the benefits and problems with such a corporate strategy?

3 This chapter suggests that corporate headquarters should make the final decision with regard to acquisitions and other major activities. Do you agree with this? What are the difficulties of this approach?

4 Choose two organisations with which you are familiar, one from the commercial sector (perhaps from work or from your place of study) and one voluntary body (perhaps from a hobby, sport or society to which you belong). Do they ever make corporate decisions - related either to diversification and/or to the general direction of the organisation? Should they engage in such activities?

5 Can small companies benefit from any of the corporate-level strategy concepts explored in this chapter? If so, which ones and why? If not, then does that mean that small companies cannot diversify?

6 What are the benefits and problems of unrelated diversification? Do multi-product companies need to find degrees of relatedness in all their subsidiaries?

7 Using the Nokia case (Case 9.2) as an example, what are the benefits and costs of focusing on one product area such as mobile telephones? Would you recommend Nokia to diversify in such a way again?

8 *'Good corporate parents constantly search for ways in which they can improve the performance of their businesses.'* (Michael Goold) Is it wise for corporate parents to interfere in the strategies of diversified groups of companies?

9 Given that emergent approaches to strategic management are important, are there any circumstances in which you might use such an approach with regard to corporate-level strategy options?

FURTHER READING

On corporate strategy see Markides, C (2002) 'Corporate strategy: the role of the centre', Chapter 5 in Pettigrew, A, Thomas, H and Whittington, R (eds) *Handbook of Strategy and Management*, Sage, London. This is a very useful summary of the background theory with useful references. See also Collis, D, Young, D and Gould, M (2007) 'The size, structure and performance of corporate headquarters', *Strategic Management Journal*, Vol 28, pp 383–405.

On parenting strategy read Campbell, A, Goold, M and Alexander, M (1995) 'Corporate strategy: the quest for parenting advantage', *Harvard Business Review*, March–April pp 120–132. See also their book: *Corporate-level Strategy: Creating Value in the Multibusiness Company*, Wiley, New York, 1994. Michael Goold has also written a useful article: Goold, M (1996) 'Parenting strategies for the mature business', *Long Range Planning*, June, p 359.

On corporate strategy, see also Bergh, D D (2001) 'Diversification strategy research at a crossroads', Chapter 12, pp 362–383, in Hitt, M, Freeman, R E and Harrison, J S, *Handbook of Strategic Management*, Blackwell, Oxford.

On corporate transactions, see the readable Chapter 5, Markides, C (2002) mentioned above, which also addresses this topic. See Hoffmann, W H (2007) 'Strategies for managing a portfolio of alliances', *Strategic Management Journal*, Vol 28, pp 827–856. See also Lavie, D (2007) 'Alliance portfolios and firm performance: a study of value creation and appropriation in the US software industry', *Strategic Management Journal*, Vol 28, pp 1187–1212. Finally, a useful cross-comparison research paper is Villalonga, B and McGahan, A M (2005) 'The choice among acquisitions, alliances and divestitures', *Strategic Management Journal*, Vol 26, pp 1183–1208.

NOTES AND REFERENCES

1 Sources for GE/Siemens case: GE Annual Report and Accounts 2004 – available on the web at www.ge.com. Siemens Annual Report and Accounts 2004 – available on the web at www.siemens.com. *Financial Times*: 21 September 1998, p 28; 13 October 1998, p 27; 18 June 1999, p 33; 5 November 1999, p 32; 8 August 2000, p 10; 27 November 2000, p 18; 12 July 2001, p 9; 18 October 2001, p 28; 21 January 2002, p 10; 30 June 2003, p 26; 9 August 2004, p 24; 19 August 2003, p 10; 2 March 2004, p 9; 8 July 2004, p 29; 3 August 2004, p 10; 8 November 2004, p 26; 26 January 2005, p 28; 25 March 2005, p 26; 26 April 2007, p 30; 10 December 2007, p 30.

2 Collis, D, Young, D and Gould, M (2007) 'The size, structure and performance of corporate headquarters', *Strategic Management Journal*, Vol 28, pp 383–405.

3 Markides, C (2002) 'Corporate strategy: the role of the centre', Ch 5 in Pettigrew, A, Thomas, H and Whittington, R (eds) *Handbook of Strategy and Management*, Sage, London. Many reasons are given for corporate-level strategy: Markides provides a useful and structured argument of the main areas in this summary chapter. See also: Chatterjee, S and Wernerfelt, B (1991) 'The link between resources and type of diversification', *Strategic Management Journal*, Vol 12, pp 33–48; Farjoun, M (1998) 'The independent and joint effects of relatedness in diversification', *Strategic Management Journal*, Vol 19, pp 611–630.

4 See, for example, Heller, R (1967) 'The legend of Litton', *Management Today*, October, pp 60–67. But note that the claim is made in the article that subsidiaries were interconnected. It was only later that this proved to be overstated and Litton was broken up.

5 Bergh, D D (2001) 'Diversification strategy research at a crossroads', Ch 12, pp 362–383, in Hitt, M, Freeman, R E and Harrison, J S, *Handbook of Strategic Management*, Blackwell, Oxford. This chapter is a thoughtful review of research on diversification within corporate strategy – useful for essays and research.

6 Hamel, G and Prahalad, H K (1994) *Competing for the Future*, Harvard Business School Press, Boston, MA.

7 Williamson, O E (1975) *Markets and Hierarchies: Analysis and Antitrust Implications*, Free Press, New York.

8 Markides, C C and Williamson, P J (1994) 'Related diversification, core competencies and corporate performance', *Strategic Management Journal*, Vol 15, Special issue: pp 149–165. A similar issue is explored from a different perspective in Zhou, Y M (2011) 'Synergy, coordination and diversification choices', *Strategic Management Journal*, Vol 32, No 8, pp 624–39.

9 Bergh, D D (2001) Op. cit., Ch 12.

10 Collis, D, Young, D and Goold, M (2007) Op. cit., p 385.

11 Bergh, D D (2001) Op, cit., Ch 12. This topic is reviewed and applied using transaction cost economics.

12 Author's personal experience working at the corporate centre. Also described in various strategy texts.

13 Bergh, D D (2001) Op. cit. Ch 12. The chapter has an extensive review of this topic.

14 Chandler, A D (1991) 'The functions of the HQ unit in the multibusiness firm', *Strategic Management Journal*, Vol 12, Winter Special Issue, p 31.

15 Rumelt, R P (1974) *Strategy, Structure and Economic Performance*, Harvard Business School Press, Boston, MA.

16 While there is no formula, Chandler's study of multinationals that are often engaged in multi-product companies arguably provides the best evidence and guidance at the present time: Chandler, A D (1962) *Strategy and Structure*, MIT Press, Cambridge, MA.

17 Goold, M (1996) 'Parenting strategies for the mature business', *Long Range Planning*, June, p 359.

18 Campbell, A, Goold, M and Alexander, M (1995) 'Corporate strategy: the quest for parenting advantage', *Harvard Business Review*, March–April.

19 Collis, D, Young, D and Goold, M (2007) Op. cit., pp 400–403. The author acknowledges the value of this paper in developing this section.

20 Collis, D, Young, D and Goold, M (2007) Ibid., p 403.

21 Sources for Nokia Case: For earlier data and comment on Nokia see Lynch, R (1994) *European Business Strategies*, 2nd edn, Kogan Page, London, p 151. See also Lynch R, *Strategic Management*, 6th edn, for references prior to 2011. *Financial Times*: 28 April 2011, p 23; 17 August 2011, p 12; 19 August 2011, p 16; 19 January 2012, p 20; 9 February 2012, p 20; 12 April 2012, p 16; 15 June 2012, p 20; 18 April 2013, p 13; 4 September 2013, pp 1, 11, 14 & 17; 22 October 2013, p 12.

22 Readers may care to note the wording used here. It is not the *absolute* market share that matters according to the BCG matrix. It is the market share relative to the market leader, i.e. relative market share is a *ratio* not an absolute percentage number. The appendix to Ch 10 shows how to calculate relative market shares.

23 Buzzell, R D and Gale, B T (1987) *The PIMS Principles*, The Free Press, New York.

24 Aaker, D R (1992) *Strategic Marketing Management*, 3rd edn, Wiley, New York, pp 160–161.

25 Jacobsen, R and Aaker, D (1985) 'Is market share all that it's cracked up to be?', *Journal of Marketing*, Fall, pp 11–22. A vigorous debate still continues in the academic press on the benefits of portfolio analysis. For example, a research paper from Armstong and Brodie in the *International Journal in Research in Marketing* (Vol 11, No 1, Jan 1994, pp 73 ff.) criticising such matrices produced a strong defence from Professor Robin Wensley in the same journal and a further reply from the two authors.

26 Aaker, D (1992) Op. cit., p 176.

27 See McKiernan, P (1992) *Strategies for Growth*, Routledge, London. Ch 1 has an excellent discussion of some of the problems that can arise.

28 Covered in many marketing strategy texts. For example, Kotler, P, Armstrong, G, Saunders, J and Wong, V (1999) *Principles of Marketing*, 2nd European edn, Prentice Hall Europe, pp 98–99.

29 Hussey, D E (1978) 'Portfolio analysis: Practical experience with the directional policy matrix', *Long Range Planning*, August, pp 78–89.

30 Aaker, D (1992) Op. cit., pp 167 ff.

31 Day, G S (1977) 'Diagnosing the product portfolio', *Journal of Marketing*, April, pp 29–38.

32 From the personal knowledge of the author who worked on his MBA project at Unilever headquarters in London over the summer of 1967. Subsequently, he worked on soap and detergent Lever brands at J Walter Thompson Co advertising agency 1968–1972.

33 References for the Unilever case: Unilever press release 10 February 2005 available on the web at www.unilever.com. Unilever 1997, 2001, 2004, 2010 and 2012 Annual Report and Accounts. *Financial Times*: 10 June 1997, p 26; 1 July 1997, p 27; 27 September 1997, p 19; 3 October 1997, p 24; 23 December 1997, p 9; 6 January 1998, p 18; 11 February 1998, p 28; 12 March 1998, p 1; 15 March 1998, p 22; 17 March 1998, p 25; 22 April 1998, p 10; 28 April 1998, p 14; 15 May 1998, p 15; 4 June 1998, p 15; 10 July 1998, p 33; 19 January 1999, p 32; 24 February 1999, p 31; 22 September 1999, p 25; 24 September 1999, p 27; 25 November 1999, p 25; 11 December 1999, p 15; 23 February 2000, p 27; 30 May 2000, p 29; 30 October 2000, p 28; 22 January 2001, p 1; 30 January 2001, p 27; 9 February 2001, p 24; 27 April 2002, p 13; 8 May 2003, p 25; 30 October 2003, p 25; 29 April 2004, p 21; 29 July 2004, p 21; 23 August 2004, p 15; 11 February 2005, p 21; 8 February 2008, p 22; 5 September 2008, pp 16 and 22; 3 October 2008, p 15; 6 February 2009, p 19; 19 March 2010, p 20; 28 September 2010, p 19; 16 November 2010, p 19. Polman, P. (2010) Unilever Annual Report and Accounts, Chief Executive Officer's Review, p 6; 15 June 2012, p 22; 6 December 2013, p 28.

34 Villalonga, B and McGahan, A M (2005) 'The choice among acquisitions, alliances and divestitures', *Strategic Management Journal*, Vol 26, pp 1183–1208.

35 There are a number of reviews of the literature. For example: Hitt, M, Ireland, D and Harrison, J (2001) 'Mergers and acquisitions: a value creating or value destroying strategy?' in Hitt, M, Freeman, R E and Harrison, J, *Handbook of Strategic Management*, Blackwell, Oxford.

36 King, D R, Dalton, D R, Daly, C M and Covin, J G (2004) 'Meta-analysis of post-acquisition performance: indications of unidentified moderators', *Strategic Management Journal*, Vol 25, pp 187–200. See also: Schreiner, M, Kale, P and Corsten, D (2009) 'What really is alliance management capability and how does it impact alliance outcomes and success?' *Strategic Management Journal*, Vol 30, No 13, pp 1396–1419.

CHAPTER 10
Strategy evaluation and development: the prescriptive process

Video and sound summary of this chapter

LEARNING OUTCOMES

After working through this chapter, you will be able to:

- distinguish between the content and the process of the prescriptive approach;
- identify the six main criteria that might typically be used to evaluate the content of strategic options;
- outline the main prescriptive procedures and techniques used in selecting between strategy options;
- undertake an evaluation of strategic options in order to select the most appropriate option;
- apply empirical evidence and guidelines to the various options in order to assist the selection procedure;
- describe the main elements of the classic prescriptive process for developing strategic management;
- comment on the weaknesses in the classic process and suggest how these might be overcome.

INTRODUCTION

After identifying the options available, classical prescriptive strategic management has always argued that the next strategy task is to select between them.[1] The selection procedure is the subject of this chapter. It follows on from the options development process explored in Chapters 8 and 9.

Strategy selection involves two aspects that should be clearly distinguished: content and process.

Definition ▶ 1 **By *strategy content* is meant the actual strategy that is finally selected to meet the objectives of the organisation.** Content is about *what* is in the plan.

Definition ▶ 2 **By *strategy process* is meant the process of communication and discussion amongst those contributing to and implementing the strategy.** Process explores such questions as *who* develops the plan, *how* they undertake the task and *where* they are located in the organisation.

The first part of the chapter is about content and the second about process.

To select strategy content, the chapter begins by exploring, in Section 10.1, the main criteria that might be used. It then identifies, in Section 10.2, the main procedures and techniques that might be

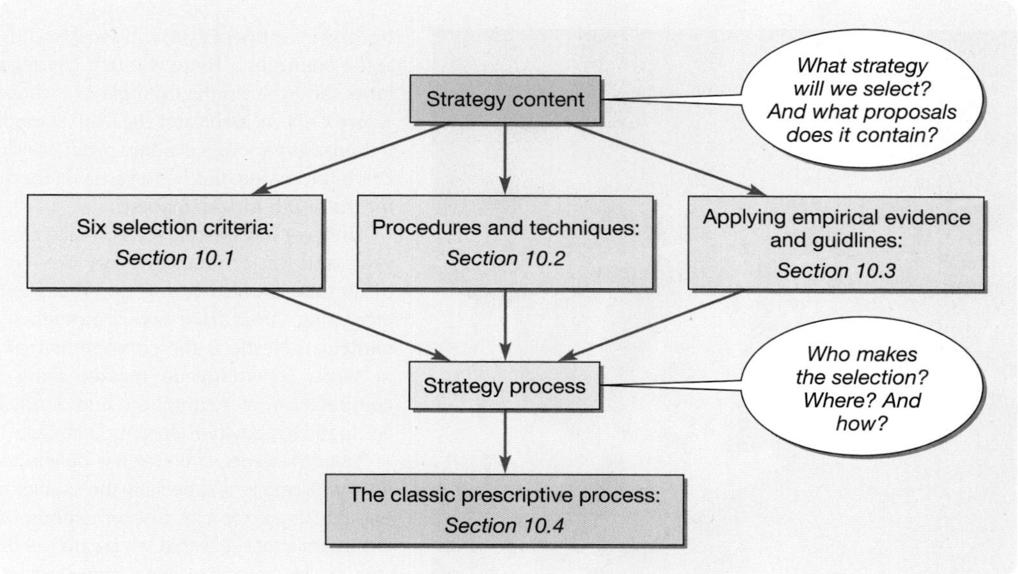

Figure 10.1 Selection between strategy options

employed in selection. Finally, to assist the process, it also outlines, in Section 10.3, some general guidelines and empirical evidence that might suggest which options would work best.

Finally, to identify the strategy process, the classic prescriptive route is described in Section 10.4 and the main contributors and their responsibilities are identified. This chapter focuses almost entirely on prescriptive processes. The next chapter explores alternative emergent processes.

Video Parts 6b and 6c

In addition to the cases throughout the chapter, there is a longer case at the end of this chapter (Case 10.4) which sets out the various options available to a company and invites the reader to select one of them (or perhaps even reject all of them) using the techniques explored in the chapter. The structure of the chapter is shown in Figure 10.1.

CASE STUDY 10.1

Unilever ice cream defends its global market share

With sales of $9.5 billion and around 18 per cent of the world ice cream market, Unilever is the dominant global company. It has built its leading market position with innovation and acquisition strategies.

The major Dutch/British multinational, Unilever, operates across many countries of the world with well-known brand names like Dove soap, Hellmann's mayonnaise, Flora margarine, Knorr soup and Fabergé personal products. Total sales amount to over $60 billion - see Case 9.3 for more information.

In its ice cream operations, Unilever works through a series of local brand names but with a heart-shaped symbol that is the same everywhere around the world. It employs strategies in the ice cream market that combine both global and local activities. As well as the heart-shaped logo, global activities cover certain common products: Magnum ice cream, Cornetto wafer cone, Carte d'Or take-home packs of ice cream, etc. This product range has been developed in a highly innovative way over the past 15 years. In order to obtain economies of scale, such products are not necessarily manufactured in the country in which they are sold - transport costs are a sufficiently small part of total costs to justify regional manufacture. Products are chosen for a country, depending on local demand and the availability of freezer cabinet space. Table 10.1 identifies some of the leading global Unilever products in selected countries.

For Unilever, local ice cream products are also important. There are two reasons: first, to meet local ice cream tastes and price expectations - not every country likes a particular flavour and can afford expensive ingredients; second, to exploit the

Unilever has attempted to bring uniform branding, using a heart-shaped symbol, to its many different global ice cream companies.

historic investment made in local brands over many years in some countries – there is much to be gained by building on local names. A simple example of local activity is South Africa where Unilever associates the heart symbol with the 'Ola' brand. It then sells various ice cream products like Magnum under the Ola brand name, but has also developed some local products for the South African market.

Unilever has been involved in ice cream markets for many years and this product category delivers around 10 per cent of its total profits. During the 1980s and 1990s, it faced an increasing threat from two competitors, Nestlé and Mars. In particular, Nestlé is the competitor that is catching Unilever in terms of worldwide market share through a different combination of acquisition and innovative strategies. This competitive activity is described in Case 10.3.

Over the years, Unilever has developed strong distribution links with retailers, especially the smaller outlets that only have enough space for one freezer cabinet. A crucial factor in all ice cream strategy is that ice cream needs freezers for in-store storage. Unilever has been highly active in ensuring that its products gain the maximum amount of freezer space through frequent deliveries and, in the case of smaller stores, through renting its freezers to the store. It used this distribution strength to keep out Mars Ice Cream from smaller stores in Europe for many years. However, in 2003 the European Courts ruled that

Table 10.1 Unilever's global ice cream products in selected countries

Country	Brand	Magnum	Cornetto	Carte d'Or	Solero	Viennetta	Ben & Jerry's	Local brands
Argentina	Kibon	✓	✓					✓
Australia	Heart	✓		✓			✓	✓
Brazil	Kibon	✓	✓	✓	✓			✓
China	Wall's	✓	✓	✓				✓
Germany	Langnese	✓	✓		✓	✓	✓	✓
Holland	Ola	✓	✓		✓		✓	✓
India	Kwality Wall's	✓	✓		✓		✓	
Ireland	HB	✓	✓	✓	✓	✓	✓	✓
Malaysia	Wall's	✓	✓	✓	✓			✓
Poland	Algida	✓		✓				✓
Russia	Algida and Inmarko	✓	✓	✓		✓		✓
Sweden	GB Glace	✓		✓	✓			✓
Turkey	Algida	✓	✓	✓		✓		✓
UK	Wall's	✓	✓	✓	✓	✓	✓	✓
USA (3 brands for historic reasons)	Breyers, Klondike, Good Humor						✓	✓

Source: from Unilever world websites and *China Daily*. Note that Unilever purchased ice cream companies in Denmark and Greece in 2010. However, much of the company's growth is now centred on its existing product areas.

Unilever's strategy was uncompetitive and Unilever was forced to allow Mars products into its freezer cabinets.

Unilever's large market share has delivered economies of scale that newer entrants cannot match, preventing them from achieving the same low-cost structure. For this reason, Unilever has been the most consistently profitable of the major ice cream companies. Mars ice creams were launched in 1989 but were unprofitable for much of the next ten years. Nestlé ice creams were also being developed over the past 15 years, but they again were not major profit earners for the company until recent years - see Case 10.3.

Probably Unilever's greatest weakness is that the group has no involvement in the confectionery market, unlike Nestlé and Mars. Unilever thus had difficulty in responding to the 1990s trend amongst rival companies to use confectionery brands in ice cream - like Mars ice cream. Eventually, Unilever developed its own global brands like Magnum and Cornetto. But investing in these new brands has been an expensive strategy with lengthy time horizons.

To counteract this weakness, Unilever began a new strategy in 2005. It licensed two global brands from other manufacturers. In the Carte D'Or range, the company launched Toblerone ice cream - the brand name being used under licence from Kraft Jacobs Suchard - and Lavazza coffee ice cream - with the brand name under licence from the Italian coffee company. The problem with a licence is that part of the profits is passed on to the owner of the brand rather than being retained by Unilever.

Case questions

1 What is the source of Unilever's advantages over its competitors?

2 What are Unilever's main strengths? Where do its weaknesses lie? What, if anything, should Unilever do about its weaknesses?

3 Given Unilever's market dominance, what strategies would you adopt if you were entering the ice cream market? How do you attack a dominant competitor?

10.1 PRESCRIPTIVE STRATEGY CONTENT: EVALUATION AGAINST SIX CRITERIA

Video Parts 6b and 6c

Prescriptive strategy has taken the approach that a rational and fact-based analysis of the options will deliver the strategy that is most likely to be successful: logic and evidence are paramount in choosing between the options. The content of strategy options therefore needs to be evaluated for their contribution to the organisation. We need to be able to understand in a structured way such comments as, 'Plausible . . . but not very likely.'[3] We need *evaluation criteria*.

In practice, each organisation will have its own criteria – for example, those for Nokia that led to the company selecting mobile telephones over other areas were described in the early part of Case 9.2. However, and as a starting point, we can identify six main criteria[4] that can be used in evaluating strategy options: consistency, suitability, validity, feasibility, business risk, stakeholder attractiveness. This section examines each of these.

10.1.1 Criterion 1: consistency, especially with the mission and objectives

If the main purpose of the organisation is to add value, then the way that this is defined for the purposes of strategic management is through the organisation's mission and objective – Chapter 6 explored this in detail. In a non-profit-making organisation, the prime purpose may be better defined in terms of some form of service. Whatever the purpose of the organisation, a prime test of

Definition ▶ any option has to be its consistency. **Consistency means whether it is in agreement with the objectives of the organisation.** In a business context, this is likely to be the mission and its ability to deliver the agreed objectives of the organisation. If an option does not meet these criteria, there is a strong case for:

- either changing the mission and objectives, if they are too difficult or inappropriate;
- or rejecting the option.

If the mission and objectives have been carefully considered, then the rejection option is the most likely course. For example, the European consumer products company Reckitt Benckiser has a net revenue growth rate of 5–6 per cent for all areas of its business at constant exchange rates.[5] This means that strategy options that do not deliver this *in the long term* are rejected by the company. The qualification 'in the long term' relates to the fact that there may well be a period in the very early years of a new option when the project will fall short, but it must deliver over a longer period.

10.1.2 Criterion 2: suitability

In addition, some options may be more suitable for the organisation than others: how well does each option match the environment and resources and how well does it deliver competitive advantage? **Suitability means to be appropriate for the context of the strategy of the organisation both internally and externally.** The environment can be explored from the mixture of opportunities to be taken and threats to be avoided. Competitive advantage can be built on the organisation's strengths, especially its core competencies, and may try to rectify weaknesses that exist.

Definition ▶

The SWOT analysis at the beginning of Chapter 8 summarises the main elements that have been identified here. Strategy options can also be examined for their consistency with the elements of the SWOT analysis. For example, Unilever ice cream has strengths in terms of its dominant brand share in many markets. A new option that ignored this strength and pursued a policy of new branding with totally new products would need careful study and possibly (but not necessarily) rejection. In fact, this option has been used to expand into other market segments – the obvious example being the acquisition of the Ben & Jerry's brand by Unilever to expand into the superpremium ice cream segment.

10.1.3 Criterion 3: validity

Most options will involve some form of *assumptions* about the future. These need to be tested to ensure that they are valid and reasonable, i.e. that they are logically sound and conform with the available research evidence. **Validity means that the calculations and other assumptions on which the plan is based are well-grounded and meaningful.** In addition, many options will use *business information* that may be well grounded in background material or, alternatively, doubtful in its nature. For example, some of the information that Unilever has about its competitors is soundly based (e.g. the market share data), but some is likely to be rather more open to question (e.g. information on the future plans and intentions of Nestlé).

Definition ▶

For both the above, it will be necessary to test the validity of the assumptions and information in each option. In practice, there is some overlap between suitability and validity. Because of the element of judgement in such issues, this is done under the general heading of applying business judgements and guidelines.

10.1.4 Criterion 4: feasibility of options

Definition ▶

Feasibility means that the proposed strategies are capable of being carried out. Although options may be consistent with the mission and objectives, there may be other difficulties that limit the likelihood of success. An option may, in practice, lack feasibility in three areas:

1 culture, skills and resources *internal* to the organisation;
2 competitive reaction and other matters *external* to the organisation;
3 *lack of commitment* from managers and employees.

Constraints internal to the organisation

In practice, an organisation might not have the culture, skills or resources to carry out the options. For example, there might be a culture in the organisation that is able to cope with gradual change but not the radical and sudden changes required by a proposed strategy option. For example, the difficulties experienced by the highly centralised company Metal Box (UK) when it merged with the decentralised company Carnaud (France) were largely in this area and caused the group major problems.[6]

Equally, an organisation may lack the necessary technical skills for a strategic option. It may not be possible for a variety of reasons to acquire them by recruiting staff.

In addition, some organisations have insufficient finance for an option to succeed. For example, the French computer company Groupe Bull had real problems financing its strategic development during the mid-1990s as it struggled to survive after a series of over-ambitious strategy initiatives earlier in the decade.[7]

EXHIBIT 10.1

Ten-point checklist on internal feasibility

1. Capital investment required: do we have the funds?
2. Projection of cumulative profits: is it sufficiently profitable?
3. Working capital requirements: do we have enough working capital?
4. Tax liabilities and dividend payments: what are the implications, especially on timing?
5. Number of employees and, in the case of redundancy, any costs associated with this: what are the national laws on sacking people and what are the costs?
6. New technical skills, new plant and costs of closure of old plant: do we have the skills? Do we need to recruit or hire temporarily some specialists?
7. New products and how they are to be developed: are we confident that we have the portfolio of fully tested new products on which so much depends? Are they real breakthrough products or merely a catch-up on our competition?
8. Amount and timing of marketing investment and expertise required: do we have the funds? When will they be required? Do we have the specialist expertise such as advertising and promotions agency teams to deliver our strategies?
9. The possibility of acquisition, merger or joint venture with other companies and the implications: have we fully explored other options that would bring their own benefits and problems?
10. Communication of ideas to all those involved: how will this be done? Will we gain the *commitment* of the managers and employees affected?

Exhibit 10.1 summarises some of the main internal feasibility issues.

Constraints external to the organisation

Outside the organisation, there are four main constraints that may make a strategic option lack feasibility: customer acceptance, competitive reaction, supplier acceptance and any approvals from government or another regulatory body.

Because it is customers who buy a new product or service, we observed that customers need to find a new strategy attractive. In addition, competitors who are affected by a strategy option may react and make it difficult to achieve. For example, the US software company Microsoft has around 90 per cent of the world market for personal computer software with its Windows operating system. In the past, it has been accused by competitors of deliberately pre-announcing some of its products to stall sales of new, competing software products.[8] The likelihood of competitive response is an area that must be assessed.

There may also be other constraints outside the organisation that make strategy options difficult if not impossible. For example, the Unilever ice cream product group has had to consider carefully the implications of the scrutiny of the European Union with regard to Unilever's policies on green issues. The company had both opportunities to develop strategies with regard to new packaging while at the same being constrained by the many pressures to reduce its use of packaging material.

The questions that might probe this area are summarised in Exhibit 10.2.

EXHIBIT 10.2

Four-point checklist on external feasibility

1 How will our *customers* respond to the strategies we are proposing?
2 How will our *competitors* react? Do we have the necessary resources to respond?
3 Do we have the necessary support from our *suppliers*?
4 Do we need government or regulatory approval? How likely is this?

Lack of commitment from managers and employees

If important members of the organisation are not committed to the strategy, it is unlikely to be successfully implemented. For example, the major US toy retailer Toys 'Я' Us had major problems implementing its business strategy in Sweden some years ago because the local managers and employees considered it to be inconsistent with the Swedish approach to labour relations.[9]

This constraint may arise because some organisations make a clear distinction between strategy development by senior managers and day-to-day management by more junior managers.[10] Hence in such organisations, junior managers and employees are unlikely to have been involved in the strategy development process: in essence, they have the results communicated to them and they may not feel *committed* to its implications.

Some strategic decisions may need to be made by a senior management centralised group – for example, the Nokia decision at the beginning of the 1990s to divest some companies – see Case 9.2. In spite of Nokia's commitment to an open Finnish culture, the key decisions on the new strategy were taken by a group of *senior* managers. The more junior managers and employees were not really consulted. Since the proposals included divesting part of Nokia, this is not really surprising.

Six key ways to reduce risk.

10.1.5 Criterion 5: business risk

Definition ▶ Most worthwhile strategies are likely to carry some degree of risk. In this context, **risk means that the strategy does not expose the organisation to unnecessary hazards or to an unreasonable degree of danger.** Such areas need to be carefully assessed. Ultimately, the risks involved may be unacceptable to the organisation. There are countless examples in strategic management of organisations taking risks and then struggling to sort out the difficulties. For example, Germany's largest industrial company, Daimler-Benz, took considerable risks with its expansion strategy over the past 20 years (see Chapter 16). In 1998, the company chose to merge with the US car company Chrysler, involving significant risk if the benefits were to be achieved.[11] By 2006, hindsight showed us that Daimler was unsuccessful and had to unscramble the merger. However, the risks were at least containable and both companies were still looking forward to their separate futures – see Case 4 in Part 6 for what happened next at Chrysler.

It is easy to see business risk only as a major strategic constraint. The Japanese strategist Kenichi Ohmae comments that this may stop a company from breaking out of the existing situation.[12] Some degree of business risk is likely in most worthwhile strategy development: should we really be so critical of Daimler-Benz for attempting some years ago to merge with Chrysler? The important aspects of risk are:

- to make an explicit *assessment* of the risks;
- to explore the *contingencies* that will lessen the difficulties if things go wrong;
- to decide whether the *risks are acceptable* to the organisation.

There is no single method of assessing risk in the organisation, but there are a number of techniques that may assist the process. Two are explored below – financial risk analysis and scenario building – and other techniques are examined in Sections 10.2.4 and 10.2.5.

Financial risk analysis[13]

For most strategy proposals in both the private and public sectors, it is important to undertake some form of analysis of the financial risks involved in strategy options. There are a number of types of analysis that can be undertaken:

- *Cash flow analysis.* This analysis is essential. An organisation can report decent levels of profitability at the same time as going bankrupt through a lack of cash. Each option needs to be assessed for its impact on cash flow in the organisation – explored in Section 10.2.4 later in the chapter.
- *Break-even analysis.* This is often a useful approach: it calculates the volume sales of the business required to recover the initial investment in the business. The important point about such a result is to explore whether this volume is reasonable or not – see Exhibit 10.4 later in this chapter. Break-even analysis on the main options at Eurofreeze, discussed in Case 10.2, would be useful.
- *Company borrowing requirements.* The impact of some strategies may severely affect the funds needed from financial institutions and shareholders. This area represents a real area of risk for strategy analysis and needs to be explored with financial experts both inside and outside the organisation.
- *Financial ratio analysis.* Liquidity, asset management, stockholding and similar checks on companies can be usefully undertaken. It might be argued that they are not needed since the company should know in detail about these areas. But what about key suppliers? And key customers? The knock-on effects of bankruptcy in one of these, when the company itself is stretched financially, deserve consideration: the starting point is the cash flow analysis explored in Section 10.2.4.

For international activities, there is one other area that is also important: *currency analysis.* A major shift in currencies can wipe out the profitability of an overseas strategy option overnight (or, more optimistically, increase it). A number of major companies have discovered the impact of this over the past few years. Specialist help may be required.

Scenario building

This is a most useful form of analysis and would be regarded as part of the basic strategy proposals in many organisations. Essentially, it explores the 'What if?' questions for their impact on the strategy under investigation. The basic assumptions behind each option, for example, economic growth, pricing, currency fluctuation, raw material prices, etc., are varied and the impact is measured on return on capital employed, cash and other company objectives. The key factors for success may be used to identify the major points that need to be considered.

The sensitivity of each these factors, as they are moved up or down by arbitrary variations, is then assessed in order to determine which are crucial. Those variations that turn out to be particularly sensitive can then be re-examined carefully before the strategy is accepted. They can also be monitored after it has been put into operation.

For example with regard to Case 9.2 on Nokia's mobile smartphone problems, the key assumptions might be tested by examining what would happen if they varied:

- What impact would there be if Nokia was unable to work with the new Microsoft software? This is quite specific and the result could be used to assess the strategy.
- What impact would there be if Nokia lost one third of its 2010 global market share? Perhaps it might lose half its market share as a result of waiting to introduce the new smartphones? Again specific calculations could be undertaken to test the sensitivity of this change.

- What impact would there be if Nokia lost its market leadership in developing countries where cheap mobiles were more important than smartphones? Perhaps the simplest calculation would be to assume that one of its low-cost rivals like ZTE became the market leader and the result was recalculated. The sensitivity to share variation could then be assessed.

Clearly, the results of all sensitivity analyses can provide those selecting the strategies with a useful estimate of the risks involved.

10.1.6 Criterion 6: attractiveness to stakeholders

Definition ▶ **Attractiveness to stakeholders means that the strategy is sufficiently appealing to those people that the company needs to satisfy.** As we explored in Chapter 6, every organisation has its stakeholders, such as the shareholders, employees and management. They will all be interested in the strategic options that the organisation has under consideration because they may be affected by them. But stakeholder interests and perspectives may not always be the same. For example, an option might increase the *shareholders'* wealth but also mean a reduction in *employees* in the organisation. Hence, stakeholders may not find all the strategic options equally attractive.

One way of resolving this issue is to *prioritise* the stakeholders' interests – for example, by putting the shareholders' interests first and raising dividends, cutting costs and possibly even sacking some workers. Some writers and companies would have no hesitation in pursuing this route. However, it may be over-simplistic for strategic management.

KEY STRATEGIC PRINCIPLES

- Evaluating strategy options relies on criteria for the selection process. There are six main criteria: consistency, especially with the organisation's mission and objectives, suitability, validity, feasibility, business risk and attractiveness to stakeholders.
- Consistency with the purpose of the organisation is a prime test for evaluating and selecting strategies.
- Suitability of the strategy for the environment within which the organisation operates is clearly important.
- Validity of the projections and data used in developing the option must be tested.
- In examining whether an option is feasible, there are three main areas to explore: first, those that are internal to the organisation, which are mainly those that arise from a lack of resources; second, those external to the organisation, such as customer acceptance and customer reaction; finally, special consideration needs to be given to employee and manager acceptance and commitment.
- The risks that a strategy option may bring to an organisation also need to be assessed because they may be unacceptably high. Such risks can be assessed under two broad headings: financial risk and sensitivity analysis.
- Stakeholders also need to be assessed for their reactions to major strategy initiatives. It may be necessary to prioritise the interests of stakeholders: shareholders may or may not come first. Stakeholder reactions need to be assessed under five headings, each of which is related to the prime interests of the stakeholder group in question.

CASE STUDY 10.2

Eurofreeze evaluates its strategy options: Part 1

With sales in 2003 of $1.05 billion, Eurofreeze was one of Europe's larger frozen food companies. However, it was being squeezed between two major competitive forces: its larger rival Refrigor, and the grocery supermarket own brands, which were becoming increasingly powerful across Europe. The time had come for a complete strategic re-think at Eurofreeze: the company was part of a large multinational and the group headquarters had turned up the heat.

This case begins the process by exploring the objectives, the environment and the resources of the company. At the end of the chapter, there is a follow-up case that examines the options identified by Eurofreeze.

Mission and objectives

As a starting point for the exploration of its options, Eurofreeze decided to re-examine its mission and objectives. It decided that it still wished to remain strong in European frozen food and therefore defined its mission as: 'To be a leading producer of frozen food products in the European Union'. This mission was based on its core strengths, its competitive position as the second largest in the EU, and the way it envisaged freezing technology would retain its position in preserving food over the next five years. Within this context, it then reviewed its current profitability, shareholder performance and market share position and defined its objectives over the next five years as being:

- to raise its return on capital from the current level of 12 per cent by 0.5 per cent per annum with the aim of reaching 15 per cent after six years;
- to raise its contribution to its earnings per share at a similar rate over time, but allow for some lag as it reinvested in the immediate future;
- to hold its overall market share but to move from low-value-added items (like frozen vegetables) to higher-value-added (like prepared pizza dishes).

To understand fully the implications of these demanding objectives, it was necessary for Eurofreeze to explore the background to the frozen food market and the competitive trends that were operating.

Some areas of frozen food are becoming increasingly like a commodity, with little competitive advantage and the main competition being based on price.

Frozen food products and added value

The first products to be frozen commercially were vegetables and fish in the 1940s. For many years, the higher food quality resulting from the freezing process allowed such products to be sold at premium prices compared to the competition from cans, glass jars and other forms of preserved food. But by 2000, freezing was old technology – there was no sustainable competitive advantage in this as such. Specifically, this meant that products like frozen vegetables and frozen meat, whether carrying a nationally recognised brand or not, had little value added to them before arriving in the shops.

Thus, the major supermarkets negotiated their own branded versions of many basic products and obtained keen prices from suppliers such as Eurofreeze. By the mid-1990s, the profit margins on basic vegetables and other commodities were very low: added value was minimal.

Over the same period, household incomes had risen across Europe, home freezers were more widespread, and tastes had become more international. For example, people across Europe had come to know and like a wider range of fresh recipe dishes and international products, everything from 'quattro stagioni' pizza to double layer chocolate gateaux. Such products had much higher added value. They were sold as branded items, usually under a name that had been well established over the years: Birds Eye, Dr Oetker, Heinz Weight Watchers and Findus were examples of the brand names that had become familiar in this context. The brand name was used across all products from the company so that it supported the strong, well-advertised products along with the weaker ones – a group branding policy.

Key factors for success

The following factors were considered to be critical to success in the industry:

- experienced and talented buyers to negotiate price and quality on low-value-added items;
- fast and efficient freezing processes coupled with good freezer storage and distribution;
- excellent relationships with the main supermarket chains;
- strong and consistent group branding;
- vigorous and innovative new product development programmes.

Eurofreeze core resources

As a result of its history and present market position, the company had core competencies in the following areas:

- purchase of raw materials such as vegetables, including the buying function;
- freezer technology;
- recipe development for new frozen dishes;
- frozen food distribution;
- supermarket negotiating and service;
- developing branded food products (it had a well-known brand name across Europe).

Within these areas, its key resource advantages over its leading rival were its brand names, its European market leadership in branded meat and fish products, and its corporate parent, which was one of the world's leading fast-moving consumer goods companies, with extensive financial resources.

The competition

During the 1990s, companies such as Eurofreeze sought new strategies to avoid the low-priced competition – the own-branded supermarket sales of vegetables and other low-value-added items had become a real problem. Profit pressures were such that Eurofreeze was even considering phasing out its range of branded vegetables. The giant supermarket companies like Tesco, Carrefour and Aldi had much of the bargaining power in basic frozen food.

In addition, many large grocery chains wanted *only one* market-leading frozen brand to put alongside their own brands. In this context, Eurofreeze faced a specific problem: in some European product categories, it was not the market leader. Eurofreeze was second in its markets to its major rival, Refrigor.

Refrigor had invested heavily in frozen food brands, manufacturing and grocery distribution over the last few years at a rate in excess of Eurofreeze. However, the company had been rather less profitable. It had much the same grocery customers as Eurofreeze. Both competitors offered a full range of frozen branded food products and, at the same time, supplied own-label versions to the leading grocery chains.

In total, Eurofreeze faced four competitive threats, the first two below being particularly strong:

1 The market leader, Refrigor, the low-cost leader.

2 In many supermarkets such as Sainsbury (UK) and Albert Heijn (part of Ahold, the Netherlands), increasing freezer space was given to supermarket chains' own-branded products at the expense of the manufacturer's branded product.

3 In other supermarkets with strong cut-price positioning, such as Aldi and Netto, the same freezer space was used for local or regional branded products that had no national advertising or promotional support but were low-priced.

4 In some specific product lines, such as French fries or gateaux, specialised companies such as McCain (USA) and Sara Lee (USA), respectively, sold branded products that had a significant share of that particular market segment.

Overall, the market was becoming volume-driven and highly competitive in many sectors. It was also becoming increasingly difficult to afford the investment in advertising and promotions to support branded lines. And group headquarters was beginning to think that it might be more profitable to sell the company from a corporate strategy perspective – see Chapter 9.

Case questions

1 What is your assessment of the mission and objectives of Eurofreeze? How do they stack up against the pressures of the highly competitive market? Are they too demanding?

2 Should the objectives be expanded? What about branded and non-branded items, for example? Clearer on the competitive threat? Further reference to financial objectives such as the precise relationship with headquarters? Specific reference to other matters such as ecological issues and employee job satisfaction? If your answer is yes to any of these questions, then what considerations should Eurofreeze take into account in making its decision? If your answer is no, then what are the implications for strategy selection?

3 What are the possible implications of the customer and competitive trends on the development of strategy options for Eurofreeze? You may wish to undertake some of the analyses contained in Chapter 13 in preparing your answer.

Evaluating international strategy options.

10.2 STRATEGY EVALUATION: PROCEDURES AND TECHNIQUES

Video Parts 6b and 6c

In examining the many criteria that can be employed, it is sometimes useful to consider whether some criteria are more important than others. It is possible that no useful prioritisation can be undertaken in this case.

10.2.1 Criteria in commercial organisations

For most organisations, the criteria will be prioritised by the mission and objectives. Within these, the following three questions represent the areas that may need exploration:

1 Is each strategy option consistent with the mission of the organisation? How well does it deliver the objectives? For example, at Eurofreeze how does each option meet the stated desire for a return on capital of 15 per cent and rising? How does each option contribute to the shift to higher-value-added products?

2 Does each option build on the *strengths* of the organisation? Does it exploit the *opportunities* that have been identified? And the *core resources* of the organisation? Thus at Eurofreeze, it should be possible to test the option for its usefulness in contributing to freezer technology or to supermarket opportunities. If it is not consistent with these issues, then there *may* be a case for rejecting it. However, it should be noted that rejection is not automatic.

3 Does each option avoid, or even overcome, the weaknesses of the organisation? And does it do the same for the threats that have been identified? At Eurofreeze, an option that involved development of its basic vegetable business would move the company further into this weak area and would invite rejection.

Question 3 has *lower priority* than questions 1 and 2.[14] It is much more important to deliver the organisation's mission and objectives and to build on its strengths than to worry about its weaknesses. However, there will be occasions when the weaknesses cannot be ignored and strategy options need to consider these.

It would be a great mistake to consider only those criteria that can be put into numbers. For example, many organisations will have guidelines related to *customer quality and satisfaction*; others will include *service to the broader community*. These may not be easy to quantify but are no less important in spite of this. All of them need to be reflected in the criteria for selection of strategy options. Such matters simply underline the importance of carefully defining the purpose of the organisation.

10.2.2 Criteria in not-for-profit organisations

Great care needs to be taken in such organisations that any quantified criteria do not come to dominate the selection between strategies when such selection measures are inappropriate. All not-for-profit organisations will need to create added value. However, beyond this, the criteria may need to reflect strongly the important aspects of the service or the value to the community appropriate to the mission.

Criteria in not-for-profit organisations also need to take into account the different decision-making processes and beliefs that motivate many such organisations. The reliance on voluntary support, the strong sense of mission and belief in the work of the organisation, and the style of the organisation may not lend themselves to a simple choice between a series of options.

Not-for-profit organisations may involve high loyalty to a mission, which is often clear, but the organisation may be decentralised, with local decision making. If this is the case, then a centralised evaluation of options is difficult. A comparison of the objectives with commercial organisations is shown in Exhibit 10.3. The evaluation of strategy options in not-for-profit organisations may be more diffuse and open-ended.

EXHIBIT 10.3

Comparison of possible criteria in commercial and not-for-profit organisations

Commercial organisation	Not-for-profit organisation
• Quantified • Unchanging • Consistent • Unified • Operational • Clear • Measurable	• Qualitative • Variable • Conflicting • Complex • Non-operational • Ambiguous • Non-measurable

10.2.3 Taking the first steps in selection

Before exploring the problems associated with strategic options, it is usual to make some initial selection of one or more options. To some extent, the initial evaluation will depend on the type of organisation. In commercial circumstances, the selection might start with the *profitability* of the venture. In a not-for-profit situation, other factors, such as the ability to *deliver the service*, might be more important. These are the reasons that make careful exploration of the mission and objectives so important. Sometimes, it is useful to eliminate the obvious strategic options that have no hope of long-term success. The steps that might be involved in the initial evaluation are summarised in Exhibit 10.4.

EXHIBIT 10.4

Ten steps towards an initial strategy evaluation

1 Screen out any *early no-hopers* that are highly unlikely to meet the objectives.
2 Estimate the *sales* of each of the remaining options based on market share, pricing, promotional support and competitive reactions.
3 Estimate the *costs* of each of the remaining options.
4 Estimate the *capital and other funds* necessary to undertake each option.
5 Calculate the *return on capital employed* for each option.
6 Calculate the *break-even* of each option.
7 Calculate the *net cash flow* effects of each option.
8 Evaluate whether the *projected sales levels* imply exceptional levels of market share or unusually low costs. Are these reasonable? Real strategic weaknesses can emerge here.
9 Assess the likely *competitive response* and its possible impact on each strategy option.
10 Assess the *risks* associated with each option.

10.2.4 Evaluation techniques: financial[15]

Having removed any options that have no hope of meeting the basic evaluation criteria, the next step is to undertake a financial evaluation of the remaining options. As a first step, most evaluations of strategic options in commercial organisations attempt to analyse the profit against the capital employed. In this case, it is important to note that extra capital will be needed in most organisations[16] *as soon as sales rise*, not just when new buildings or plant are bought. This arises because of the need to fund new debtors and pay for the extra stocks required for the new business activity. There are at least five main financial techniques:

1 return on capital employed (ROCE);
2 net cash flow;
3 payback period;
4 discounted cash flow (DCF);
5 break-even.

There are some important words of caution to note in the use of any financial evaluation of strategic options. These are summarised in Exhibit 10.5.

EXHIBIT 10.5

Caution on the use of financial criteria

Following on from the discussion in Chapter 8, there are some clear difficulties with these methods of appraisal of strategic options:

- The cost of capital is a vital element in two of the calculations above. The difficulties associated with its calculation were explored in Chapter 8. It is especially difficult to estimate where investment takes place over a lengthy period.
- There are real problems in estimating the future sales accurately up to ten years away, which is a typical period in many DCF calculations, even in consumer goods companies. However, direct costs can usually be estimated satisfactorily. The projections are therefore doubtful. Payback may be better here.
- With shorter product life cycles and greater product obsolescence in some product categories such as computers, the DCF process may rely on an over-extended timespan. Payback may again be better here and this is the justification used by some Japanese companies for using this approach.
- Comment was made above on the difficulty of isolating incremental from ongoing capital. This applies not only to ROCE calculations but to all such appraisals.
- Because of the emphasis on cash generated in the project itself, the appraisal tends to concentrate on the quantified financial benefits and may ignore some of the broader strategic benefits that are more difficult to quantify – for example, synergies and value chain linkages.
- ROCE is by definition an accounting calculation that looks back at a project's past rather than forward to its future potential. It may therefore not be suitable for strategic use.

Return on capital employed (ROCE)

Definition ▶ This is a measure of the profitability of a strategic option. **ROCE is defined as the ratio of profits to be earned divided by the capital invested in the new strategy.** Profits are usually calculated *before* any tax that might be charged, because tax matters go beyond the assessment of individual strategy options.

This ratio is commonly used to assess strategies. The expected operating profit is assessed after the strategy has been in operation for an agreed number of years, usually defined before tax and interest. It is divided by the capital employed in the option, which is commonly averaged across a year, given the tendency of capital to vary during the course of a year.

One of the major difficulties is defining the *incremental* capital used purely for that strategy. It is easy where a new piece of plant has been installed, but more difficult where the strategy involves using existing plant or a service where the capital involved cannot be easily distinguished from more general trading.

For ongoing business investments, companies often have *hurdle rates* for ROCE: if they do not earn at these rates then there is serious discussion about abandoning that strategy. Such rates are usually set in relation to the company's *cost of capital*: if capital is cheap, then a lower rate can be set.

Net cash flow[17]

Definition ▶ **The net cash flow is the profit *before* depreciation less the periodic investment in working capital that is required to undertake the project.** The importance of this calculation of cash flow lies in the ability of a negative cash flow to bankrupt a company. It is perfectly possible to deliver significant profits in the distant future, so that the return on capital looks good. However, there may be major negative outflows of cash in the short term, with the implication that the firm will go bust – the company may be unable to pay its current bills while waiting for its distant profits. An approximation of the net cash flow calculation is obtained by regarding it as the sum of pretax profits from the new strategy option, plus depreciation, less the capital to be invested in the new strategy.

In strategic investment appraisal, the difficulties with cash flow usually arise in two areas:

1 in the initial period, where the project is likely to be a cash user rather than a cash generator; and

2 with projects that have a long payback, where there may be a major cash requirement some years into the venture before it starts to earn major revenues.

Cash flow analysis is particularly important in periods of uncertainty such as national economic decline or rapid currency fluctuation. The additional pressures from such events can worsen an already tight cash situation and cause real problems. Hence, in addition to conducting a normal cash flow analysis, it is usual to undertake a *sensitivity* or *worst-case analysis* for such events – that is, a cash flow analysis of the worst possible combination of events for that particular strategy.

Payback period

Payback period is used where there is a significant and specific capital investment required in the option. In the early years of the option, capital is invested in it. As the company earns profits from the venture, it recovers the capital that has been invested. **Payback is the time it takes to recover the initial capital investment and is usually measured in years.** The cash flows in payback are not discounted but are simply added and subtracted equally, whatever year they occur.

Definition ▶

Typically, payback on a capital project in the car industry will be around three to five years. This is because of the large amounts of capital involved (often into $ billions) and the competitive nature of the industry, which makes profit margins low. In consumer goods, the period may be shorter, not because markets are any less competitive but because the profit margins on some items are higher, e.g. in fashion clothing and cosmetics. By contrast, the payback period may be 20–60 years for some highly capital-intensive items such as telecommunications infrastructure and roads.

Discounted cash flow (DCF)

Definition ▶ **Discounted cash flow is the sum of projected cash flows from a future strategy, after revaluing each individual element of the cash flow in terms of its present worth using the cost of capital of the organisation.** DCF is now used extensively for the assessment of strategic options. Essentially, DCF takes account of the fact that cash in five years' time is worth less than cash today, unlike payback above. It begins by assessing the net cash flow for each year of the life of the option, as in payback above. The cash is usually assessed after subtracting the taxation to be paid to the government. Each annual cash amount is then discounted back to the present using the organisation's *cost of capital*. It is probably negative in the early years as capital is expended and then positive as the option increases its sales. There are discounting tables or computer spreadsheet programs that make this process relatively easy. The net present value (NPV) is the sum in today's values of all the future DCFs. Case 10.4 shows the procedure for some Eurofreeze options – the analysis is typical of that undertaken by many organisations when exploring the consequences of strategic options.

There can be little doubt that, if markets are fast moving, then there are real difficulties in predicting future cash flows accurately. Even markets with steady growth will have real uncertainties as technology changes, government policies alter, social values and awareness evolve, wars occur and so on. This is the most difficult problem to overcome with discounted cash flow techniques.

Break-even analysis[18]

Definition ▶ **Break-even is defined as the point at which the total costs of undertaking the new strategy are equal to the total revenue.** It is often restated as the number of units of a product that need to be sold before the product has covered all its fixed costs.

Break-even analysis is directed at finding the break-even point, i.e. that point where fixed and variable costs equal total revenue. It is based on a number of assumptions that make its use in practice rather crude in strategy options analysis:

- Costs can easily be split into fixed and variable elements.
- Fixed costs are constant.
- Variable costs and revenue are linear in their relationship with volume over the range used in the analysis.
- Variable costs vary proportionately with sales, within given limits.
- It is possible to predict the volume of sales at various prices.

In spite of these problems, break-even has the great merit of being easily understandable and therefore communicable across an organisation. Used with caution, it can therefore be a useful tool in strategy options analysis.

10.2.5 Evaluation techniques: shareholder value added (SVA)[19]

Although many Western companies continue to use DCF techniques in their evaluation of strategies,[20] they became conscious in the 1980s of the difficulties of ignoring the broader strategic benefits. There were also two other developments:

1. Michael Porter's work emphasising the value chain and its relevance in strategy development – see Chapter 6.
2. Other writers[21] began to doubt the wisdom of seeking a steady increase in earnings per share as a measure of shareholder wealth. Such wealth can be measured in terms of a company's share price. It was shown empirically that share price was more closely correlated with long-term cash generation in a business than it was with earnings per share.

Taking the goal of a public company as being to maximise shareholder value, the concept of shareholder value added (SVA) was developed from DCF techniques and the above difficulties. Its purpose is to develop strategy, 'maximising the long-term cashflow of each SBU [strategic business unit]'.[22] Thus SVA evaluation differs in the following areas from the profitability approaches above:

- SVA takes the concept of cash flow but applies it to the complete business rather than to individual strategy options.
- It takes into account the cost of capital of the company and measures shareholder return against this benchmark.
- It lays particular emphasis on the critical factors for success in that business, defining them as being those that are particularly important in generating cash or value added. It calls these critical factors *value or cost drivers*. Such critical factors may bear some relationship to the key factors for success in an industry explored in Chapter 6. However, the value or cost drivers are different in that they relate to the *individual* business, not the *industry*.
- It supports the interrelationship of value or cost drivers in the development of cash generation. In this sense, it differs from the simpler DCF view that an option can be analysed by itself.

Comment

Although SVA represents an advance on some simpler DCF techniques, it still relies on a prescriptive view of strategy projections – a projection of future profit over an extended period of time is required. Moreover, it makes the crucial assumption that maximising shareholder value is the prime objective of strategy development. This may be true in UK and US companies but does not necessarily apply in some other leading industrialised countries.

10.2.6 Evaluation techniques: cost/benefit analysis[23]

Definition ▶ **Cost/benefit analysis evaluates projects especially in the public sector, where an element of unquantified public service beyond commercial profit may be involved, by attempting to quantify the broader social benefits of such a project.** Ever since cost/benefit analysis was used to assess the justification for building London Underground's Victoria Line in the 1960s, this has been an appraisal method favoured when the benefits go beyond simple financial benefits: for example, they might include lower levels of pollution or greater use of recycled materials. It is regularly used in public service investment decisions. It attempts to quantify a much broader range of benefits than sales, profits and costs.

When the benefits of some forms of public service go beyond simple financial appraisal, cost/benefit analysis may be used. It may be especially valuable where the project delivers value to users who are not directly investing their own funds. Thus, for example, in the analysis of the new Victoria Line on the London Underground, it attempted to assess:

- the faster and more convenient travel to be enjoyed by passengers on the London Underground;
- the ability of road transport to move more freely because roads were less congested.

As well as the benefits, there may also be social costs that need to be assessed. In the case of underground transport, these might include building subsidence or inconvenience while the line is being built.

The key point in cost/benefit analysis is that all such broader benefits and costs are still assessed in monetary terms. Much of the research in this area is concerned with the quantification of such benefits and the costs that may be associated with them. The direct investment costs are usually rather easier to determine and form another element in the equation.

The difficult part of such a cost/benefit analysis is usually where to place the limit on the possible benefits and costs. For example, it might be argued that easier travel would mean that there would be less atmospheric pollution, more healthy people and therefore a need to quantify the health benefits. There might also be benefits in terms of a more stress-free lifestyle that need to be quantified, and so on. In spite of this difficulty and the more general problem of quantifying the intangible, cost/benefit analysis does serve a useful function in the appraisal of public projects and strategy initiatives.

Evaluating options when the business is in trouble: Corporate Rescue.

KEY STRATEGIC PRINCIPLES

- In making an initial selection of the best option, it is important to clarify the basis on which this is to be done. Evaluation against the mission and objectives is important but needs to be rigorous and precise if it is to provide real benefit. Non-quantified objectives may be just as important for some organisations.
- Additional criteria for evaluation include the ability to build on the strengths and core competencies of the organisation and avoid its weaknesses. Generally in evaluation, strengths are more important than weaknesses, but occasionally a weakness cannot be ignored.

- Different parts of an organisation, such as the headquarters, the strategic business unit (SBU) and those involved in individual projects, will have different perspectives on the evaluation process. There is a need to recognise this in selection.
- In not-for-profit organisations, the criteria need to reflect the broader aspects of their service or contribution to the community. They also need to take into account the different decision-making processes and beliefs that motivate many such organisations. This may make the evaluation of strategy options more diffuse and open-ended.
- To undertake the initial evaluation in commercial organisations, it may be worth eliminating any options that have little chance of success. It is then usual to calculate initially for each option the profitability, break-even and net cash flow.
- Beyond this, ten steps can be undertaken to make an initial evaluation. From a *strategic* perspective, it is particularly useful to examine whether the projected sales levels of each option imply *exceptional* levels of market share or low costs in order to achieve their targets. If these occur, then it may imply that the option has real weaknesses.
- Evaluation usually employs common and agreed criteria across the organisation, such as contribution to value added and profitability. The strengths and weaknesses of these criteria need to be understood.
- The shareholder value approach (SVA) takes a broader perspective on evaluation than that provided by the specific project. It seeks to determine the benefit of such developments in the context of the whole SBU in which the project rests. However, it still relies on the assumption that shareholders are always the prime beneficiaries.
- Cost/benefit analysis has been successfully employed in public sector evaluation, where it is important to assess broader and less quantifiable benefits. The main difficulty is where to place the limit on such benefits and costs.

10.3 APPLYING EMPIRICAL EVIDENCE AND GUIDELINES

Video Part 6c

In addition to the logic of strategy development covered in the previous section, there is also empirical evidence of strategies adopted by other organisations in the past that have succeeded or failed. Such evidence also provides guidance that can be used to select the optimal strategy from the options available. We will consider this under three headings:

1. Generic industry environments
2. Evidence on the link between profitability and three key strategic issues
3. Mergers and acquisitions

10.3.1 Generic industry environments[24]

Some strategies have been shown through logical thought to provide a higher chance of success than others. Such insights may aid the selection of strategy options. Exploration and understanding of the main concepts is called the study of generic strategy environments.[25] **Generic industry environments proposes that strategies can be selected on the basis of their ability to cope with a particular market or competitive environment.** One of the best-known examples of this general approach is the *ADL matrix*. The well-known management consultants Arthur D Little (ADL) developed the matrix during the 1970s. It relies on matching an organisation's own strength or weakness in a market with the life cycle phase of that market. Specifically, it focuses on:

Definition ▸

- *stage of industry maturity* – from a young and fast-growing market through to a mature and declining market;
- *competitive position* – from a company that is dominant and able to control the industry through to one that is weak and barely able to survive.

Maturity / *Competitive position*	*Embryonic*	*Growing*	*Mature*	*Ageing*
Clear leader	**Hold position** Attempt to improve market penetration *Invest slightly faster than market dictates*	**Hold position** Defend market share *Invest to sustain growth rate (and pre-empt potential competitors)*	**Hold position** Grow with industry *Reinvest as necessary*	**Hold position** *Reinvest as necessary*
Strong	**Attempt to improve market penetration** *Invest as fast as market dictates*	**Attempt to improve market penetration** *Invest to increase growth rate (and improve position)*	**Hold position** Grow with industry *Reinvest as necessary*	**Hold position** *Reinvest as necessary or reinvest minimum*
Favourable	**Attempt to improve position selectively** Penetrate market generally or selectively *Invest selectively*	**Attempt to improve position** Penetrate market selectively *Invest selectively to improve position*	**Maintain position** Find niche and attempt to protect it *Make minimum and/or selective reinvestment*	**Harvest, withdraw in phases, or abandon** *Reinvest minimum necessary or disinvest*
Defensible	**Attempt to improve position selectively** *Invest (very) selectively*	**Find niche and protect it** *Invest selectively*	**Find niche or withdraw in phases** *Reinvest minimum necessary or disinvest*	**Withdraw in phases or abandon** *Disinvest or divest*
Weak	**Improve position or withdraw** *Invest or divest*	**Turn around or abandon** *Invest or disinvest*	**Turn around or withdraw in phases** *Invest selectively or disinvest*	**Abandon position** *Divest*

Figure 10.2 Evaluation using life cycle portfolio matrix

Note: The boxes indicate suggested strategies depending on life cycle and share position held by the company. They can be used both to stimulate options and to *evaluate proposed options* to ensure they are consistent with the company's strategic position.

Source: reproduced with permission from Arthur D Little Limited. © Copyright Arthur D Little.

It would be wrong to over-simplify the strategies that can be adopted depending on a company's competitive position in the above. As a starting point, the matrix shown in Figure 10.2 was developed in order to illustrate some of the choices that might be made. For example, if a company was in a *strong* position in a *mature* market, then the strategic logic of the matrix would suggest that it:

- sought cost leadership *or*
- renewed its focus strategy *or*

- differentiated itself from competition
- while at the same time growing with the industry.

Hence, if other strategy options for this market and competitive combination were presented and they did not conform with one of the above proposals, there would be a case for rejecting them. However, it will be evident from any of the technology-change cases in this text – see for example Case 9.2 on Nokia – that such analyses can be flawed where major technological change and marketing initiatives are introduced.

10.3.2 Profitability and three key strategic issues[26]

According to some research evidence, profitability in commercial organisations is linked to three key strategic issues:

1 the role of quality as part of strategic decision making;

2 the importance of market share and marketing expenditure as a contributor to strategy development;

3 the capital investment required for new strategic initiatives.

The evidence in this area comes from the Strategic Planning Institute (SPI), located in the USA. For the past 20 years, the SPI has been gathering data on about 3,000 companies (some 600 of which are located in Europe). The information collected covers three major areas:

1 the *results* of strategies undertaken (profits, market share, etc.);

2 the *inputs* by the company to this activity (plant investment, finance, productivity, etc.);

3 the *industry conditions* within which the company operates (market growth, customer power, innovation, etc.).

The data are often described as the *PIMS Databank* (PIMS is short for Profit Impact of Market Strategy), which is unique in the extent of its empirical database on strategic management coupled with its inputs and outputs. It collects data and calculates statistical correlations between various elements; whether such relationships have any real meaning has been the subject of fierce academic debate.[27] This book takes the view that it has made a useful contribution to empirical strategy research. The overall results have been published and a few of the key findings are explored below. In addition to its general work, the results are also fed back to contributing companies on a detailed and more confidential basis for them to assess their performance and draw relevant conclusions. From the results of these extensive studies, three key factors emerge – namely: quality, market share and marketing spend, and capital investment.

Quality

In the long run and according to the PIMS Databank, the most important single factor affecting a business unit's performance is the quality of its products and services, relative to those of its competitors. Strategy options that seek to raise quality are more likely to be successful than those that do not, and strategy options that consider quality in relation to the price charged are more likely to have a greater chance of success.

Market share and marketing expenditure[28]

In Chapter 3, we explored the strategic importance of a company having significant power in the market place. This is usually measured using market share and will be related, at least in part, to the marketing expenditure by the company on the product or service. PIMS monitors market share and has shown a strong correlation with return on investment. It also monitors marketing expenditure, where the results depend on whether the company already has a high or low market share.

The PIMS evidence suggests that there is a correlation between high levels of marketing activity and market share.[29] For those companies that already have a high share, there is merit in maintaining their levels of expenditure. For those companies with low market share, the correlation implies that it may not be the best strategy to spend funds on marketing activity to increase market share. Strategy options that attempt to buy market share with additional marketing activity may result in low return on investment.

However, it should be noted that the evidence is circular in the sense that, if high-share firms have higher profits, then they have more funds to invest in cost-saving devices, higher quality and more marketing activity. This will, in turn, raise their market share and profitability even further. Moreover, such evidence may be of little strategic help to the majority of companies that do not have a high share: what can they possibly do to catch up? It may be prohibitively expensive to invest in marketing and plant economies. However, Japanese car and electronics companies were in much that position in the 1960s, but have developed to become a major force in the world car industry. Innovation and the mistakes of the market leaders provide clues on the strategies needed.

Capital investment[30]

In the context of the cost reduction strategies explored in Chapter 8, it might be argued that it will usually be worthwhile to invest in extra capital equipment to reduce costs and thus increase return on investment. The PIMS Databank suggests that this does not necessarily follow. Companies that have *high* levels of capital investment as a percentage of their sales tend also to have *lower* profitability. The higher productivity and lower costs gained from such capital investment may not completely offset the initial costs.

There are several reasons for this: capital-intensive plant usually needs to be run at high production capacity to make profits, as the global steel industry web-based case linked to Chapter 3, Section 3.5, illustrates. Such production requirements need steady or increasing sales to deliver the profits and, as we have seen, this may be a dubious assumption. There may even be a temptation to keep production running at capacity by offering special deals to customers, stealing sales from competitors and so on, all of which will reduce profitability. By contrast, direct labour is more flexible and can be switched around when demand fluctuates. Moreover, if the company decides to leave the industry, the investment in fixed capital may make it more difficult, as we also saw in the web-based steel industry case linked to Chapter 3. Such companies may be tempted to reduce prices in order to survive, which will in turn reduce the profitability of all companies in the industry, even those that have invested in the latest capital-intensive equipment.

Strategy options that rely on heavy capital expenditure to generate profits need to be examined carefully. In some industries, there may be no choice. But there is no automatic likelihood that such expenditure will always deliver higher profitability.

10.3.3 Mergers and acquisitions[31]

Mergers and acquisitions often form part of the strategy options that are expected to transform company performance. Chapter 9 summarised the main reasons for seeking this approach, particularly as part of strategic management and as a means of entry into new markets. However, it should be stated that these activities are mainly confined to the UK, France and the USA. They are less common in the rest of Europe and the Far East. Although there are clear reasons for seeking mergers and acquisitions, the empirical evidence on their performance suggests that they add little value to the companies undertaking the activity.

In Chapter 9, we reviewed some of the evidence that suggested that mergers and acquisitions were unlikely to be successful. None of these data suggests that it is impossible for mergers or acquisitions to succeed in adding value. What the evidence does suggest is that many do not and the main reason would appear to be over-optimistic and vague objectives rather than some deeper inherent flaw.[32] Generally, they are more likely to be successful where the partners are of similar size. In addition, cost cutting and asset downsizing may not be the most effective ways of improving performance. It may be more useful to consider ways of transferring competencies and exploiting revenue synergies.[33] Beyond this, such options have no proven record of success in terms of delivering value.

KEY STRATEGIC PRINCIPLES

- Business judgement needs to be applied to selection because no one can be certain about the outcomes of strategy proposals.
- Generic industry environments have been analysed to provide some guidance on strategy evaluation. They are based on two broad categories: the *stage of industry maturity* and the *competitive position* of the organisation involved. After identifying where the organisation fits on these two parameters, simple choices then suggest themselves.
- Beyond this general work, further guidance on appropriate strategies has been developed for specific types of industry situation: fragmented industries, emerging industries, mature markets, declining markets have all been identified.
- Empirical evidence based on the PIMS Databank also exists on the connection between strategic actions and the results in terms of profitability and other criteria.
- According to PIMS, high quality and strong market share can make a positive contribution to profitability. High capital intensity is less likely to have a positive impact. Some researchers doubt the cause and effect relationships here.
- Acquisitions and mergers have also been studied for their impact on profitability. The evidence is, at best, mixed and, at worst, suggests that many are unsuccessful.

CASE STUDY 10.3

Global ice cream: Nestlé goes on the attack

Unilever is the market leader in the global ice cream market. But it is under competitive attack from Nestlé along with a competitive threat from the multinational grocery chains. Will Unilever stay on top?

Global ice cream market: growing in some parts of the world

In 2012, the global market for ice cream and other frozen products was worth around $100 billion at manufacturers' selling prices. But markets were very different around the world. For example, there were major differences in consumption patterns in different countries. For example, one estimate suggests that people in the USA consume on average 19.8 quarts per year, Dutch people eat 7.2 quarts, Chinese only 0.9 quarts and Indians only 0.1 quarts. There were also differences in the flavours, prices and presence of international brands. This is reflected in the geographical location of ice cream sales around the world – see Figure 10.3. Some world regions were mature markets – particularly North America and Europe – and others were still growing. It was for this reason that companies like Unilever and Nestlé were focusing their major growth strategies on the developing Asian and other markets.

The global market for ice cream was growing around 3 per cent annually – an average of low growth in countries with high living standards coupled with higher growth in countries where wealth was still growing. Even up to the year 2014, the global market was still projected to grow at this level. Such growth is attractive both because the market is already large by comparison with other food markets and because such levels of market growth are unusual in food. Food markets are mainly mature, with levels of growth largely in line with changes in the population. There are at least two reasons for the relatively high growth rate in ice cream:

1 *increased wealth* – people consume more ice cream as their income rises;

2 *increased convenience* – busier working lives and an increased desire for leisure time mean that customers like consuming products that are ready-to-eat like ice cream.

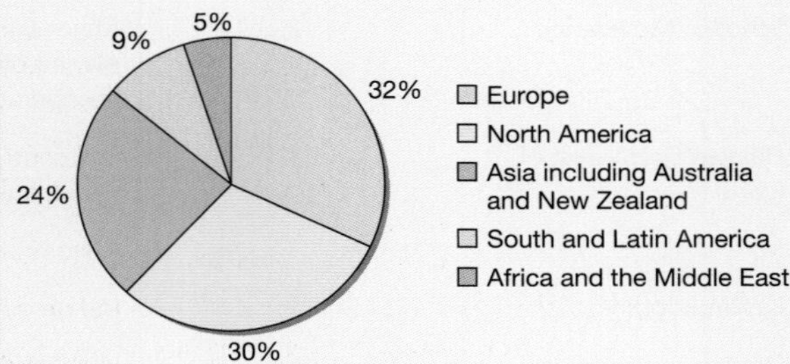

Figure 10.3 Location of global ice cream sales 2009

Source: author from trade estimates.

Nestlé regarded its move into ice cream as a significant strategic opportunity.

In northern countries, the cooler climates mean that ice cream consumption varies from year to year, depending on the temperature. More ice cream is consumed in hot weather. Such variations can have a significant impact on company profitability but do not deliver competitive advantage to one company, so they are not explored further in this case. However, it should be noted that some leading companies have been developing ice cream products that can be eaten throughout the year (e.g. take-home packs of dessert ice creams), so that there are opportunities regardless of the weather.

Global ice cream market: Unilever dominates but for how long?

In 2012, Unilever had around 18 per cent market share and was the largest player in this market - see Case 10.1. But mainly by a series of acquisitions, its main rival Nestlé was catching up and had amassed a market share of around 16 per cent - see Table 10.2.

The world market is highly fragmented beyond the market leaders. For example, there are over 4,000 ice cream companies in China and similar numbers in India. The many companies manufacture a wide range of products, including frozen water ice (sorbet) and frozen yogurt. There are companies with simple ingredients, production and overheads, leading to low costs and prices. There are also specialist companies with high-quality ingredients and premium prices.

Barriers to entry: branding, plant technology and retail distribution

It is not difficult to produce ice cream on a small scale: the ingredients need to be mixed and then frozen. However,

Table 10.2 World market shares by value for leading companies

Company	World share (%) 2001	Strategies 2001–2007	World share (%) 2012
Unilever	17	Focus on developing world brands - see Case 10.1 - plus some acquisitions where there were previous gaps in coverage in a particular country	18
Nestlé	9	Acquisition and technical innovation - see text	
Dreyer - USA	2	Dreyer is the market leader in USA - the main source of its business: acquired by Nestlé 2002	
Häagen Dazs - USA only	1	Acquired by Nestlé 2002	16
Scholler/Mövenpick	2	Major European ice cream company, previously owned by SüdZucker, a German sugar farming co-operative: acquired by Nestlé 2003	
Häagen Dazs - rest of world	1	Still controlled by General Mills (USA) - came with GM acquisition of Pillsbury in 2001	1
Mars	1	Major independent family US company - see text	1
Baskin Robbins	1	Independent - US headquarters	1
Other	66	Highly fragmented - many national, regional and local brands along with supermarket own brands	59

Note: The market shares in Table 10.2 are defined by *value*: this raises the overall share of the leading global companies like Unilever and Nestlé. If the shares were defined by *volume*, they would show the 'other' category to be even higher because of the large volume of ice cream sold at low prices.

Source: author's best estimate from a variety of trade sources, not all of which are entirely consistent with each other.

there are significant barriers to entry if manufacturers are more ambitious. Some products, such as Unilever's Magnum and Nestlé's Extrême, require heavy investment in branding to become established in the market place. They also need sophisticated machinery for their manufacture. Unilever, Nestlé and Mars have all invested heavily in modern technology to produce significantly different products.

More generally, the barriers to entry are not high: smaller companies can easily develop simple mixing and freezing of ingredients. They can buy commercially available packaging and then sell their products from small kiosks. Even for the large supermarket chains such as Carrefour, Tesco and Aldi, there are plenty of national ice cream manufacturers able to manufacture and pack ice cream. For all these reasons, the 'other' category in Table 10.2 is quite high – there is plenty of fragmented competition in the ice cream market.

The differentiating feature that distinguishes ice cream from some other food markets, such as confectionery, is that it requires a special distribution infrastructure: ice cream needs low temperatures to survive. Thus a specialised distribution network involving cold stores, special vehicles and retailers with freezer cabinets is essential.

In the global ice cream market, distribution has proved the most difficult entry barrier for leading manufacturers to resolve. It is easy and cost-effective to hire vans to deliver ice cream in bulk to individual shops, but maintaining retail shop distribution is more difficult. There is no problem in larger grocery supermarkets with substantial freezer cabinet space. But smaller shops with only one small freezer can be a barrier to entry when your competitor (usually Unilever) owns the cabinet and insists that only the competitor's products are stocked. Building and maintaining distribution in such retail shops proved a strategic problem for Mars Ice Cream in the early years.

Table 10.3 Customer segmentation in ice cream by purchase intention

Occasion	USA (%)	South Africa (%)	China (%)	UK (%)	Germany (%)
Impulse	40	80	90	30	50
Take-home	60	20	10	70	50

Source: author's estimates based on various trade articles.

Customers and market segmentation: significant growth in the branded and luxury segments

Ice cream purchases can usefully be segmented into two areas – *impulse* and *take-home*: the former are bought for immediate consumption while the latter are usually taken home in bulk for consumption later. Impulse purchases typically take place in small shops such as beach kiosks and newsagents' stores whereas take-home products are normally bought in larger grocers and supermarkets. It would be wrong to draw a rigid distinction between the two segments: bulk packs are purchased by retailers to sell as scoops for impulse demand; impulse items such as chocolate bars are sold in multipacks and may then be consumed on impulse later at home.

In practice, detailed segment data is available for some national markets, but no true global study has been published. Best estimates from a variety of sources for some are shown in Table 10.3.

During recent years, there has been growth in ice creams using expensive ingredients, high prices and exotic flavours: some customers (but not necessarily all) have become more adventurous in taste, more wealthy and more demanding in terms of quality. There has been a new attempt to redefine customers by *price and quality*. Table 10.4 shows the main areas.

Table 10.4 Customer segmentation by price and quality

Segment	Product and branding	Pricing	Market growth in around year 2012
Superpremium	High quality, exotic flavours, e.g. Häagen-Dazs Mint Chocolate Chip, Ben & Jerry's Fudge	Very high unit prices: very high value added	Up to 5% p.a. from a small market base – some countries only because of very high prices
Premium branded	Good quality ingredients with individual, well-known branded names such as Mars, Magnum and Extrême	Prices set above regular and economy categories but not as high as above: high value added	Up to 3% p.a. from a larger base than superpremium – leading brands available in many countries
Regular	Standard-quality ingredients with branding relying on manufacturer's name rather than individual product, e.g. Wall's, Scholler	Standard prices: adequate value added but large-volume market	Static in developed countries from a large base – available in many countries – leading brands available in many countries
Economy	Manufactured by smaller manufacturers with standard-quality ingredients, possibly for supermarkets' own brands	Lower price, highly price-competitive: low value added but large market – perhaps high-quality ingredients	Static from a large base, particularly in some countries such as the UK – many local brands

Source: author's estimates from trade articles. The segments in this table need to be treated with some caution since no precise information on the four market segments has been published.

Nestlé ice cream objective: build a global business

Nestlé is one of Unilever's global rivals, but it came late to the European ice cream market: it had virtually no presence until the late 1980s. It has adopted four main growth strategies:

1. the acquisition of existing national ice cream companies;
2. the introduction of a heavily branded product range;
3. the development of patented and proprietary products that are visibly different from rivals;
4. the flexibility to develop and offer local flavour ice creams and target local ice cream price points.

Nestlé acquisitions

In 1996, Nestlé had annual European ice cream sales around $1 billion compared to its total turnover of over $50 billion. By 2005, the company had ice cream sales of $7.6 billion compared to a total turnover of $60 billion. Much of this sales increase had been built from acquisitions of national companies. Between the early 1990s and the year 2000, Nestlé had acquired ice cream companies in over 30 countries. Major acquisitions then came in 2002. They were Dreyers, the US market leader, and Scholler, an important European ice cream company with involvement in a number of European markets.

Such a programme of acquisition will rest on the quality of companies that it is able to acquire. In the case of North America, it bought the market leader – Dreyers – and rolled its existing ice cream activities into Dreyers. Nestlé's acquisition strategy has not always been successful. In order to enter the mature UK ice cream market, Nestlé purchased the Clarkes Foods ice cream company in 1993. In 2001, Nestlé sold its UK subsidiary, Clarkes, for $10 million to a local UK ice cream manufacturer – Richmond Ice Cream. Nestlé commented that it had never made a profit since it bought the company: for example, it made a loss of $18 million on sales of $70 million in 2001. The new owner, Richmond, was a major manufacturer for the leading UK supermarket chains such as ASDA/Wal-Mart and Tesco. Richmond agreed to continue to make the Nestlé ice cream range under licence – but in this case, all Nestlé would receive from its continued UK market presence was a fee for the use of the licence.

Heavily branded product range

Like its major rival Unilever, Nestlé was determined to develop an international heavily branded range of products. It used a similar device to Unilever in that it made use of a local company name alongside the Nestlé logo. It then developed some global products – mainly the range of Extrême ice cream cones – to establish its position in individual markets. In addition to its own specialist branded range, Nestlé has also developed products under licence – such as Disney characters like Mickey Mouse – in order to appeal to specific market segments. Such a strategy reduces the profit margin because a royalty has to be paid to another company. But it does allow Nestlé to become associated with well-known characters and therefore become more established.

Patented and proprietary products

As an important part of its global strategy, Nestlé has set up two research laboratories – one in North America and the other in Europe – to develop new technologies in ice cream. They are mainly in the area of production technology – for example, introducing twists into frozen ice or biscuit layers between ice cream. The purpose is to develop a sustainable competitive advantage over rival companies with products that are both popular and unique to Nestlé.

Flexibility for local flavours, costs and price points

In addition to offering the global products, Nestlé has followed the global/local strategy of allowing its individual national companies to develop local flavours for local tastes and levels of wealth. For example, Nestlé China has a product range that sells low-price ice creams starting at just 1 yuan (about 12 US cents) and flavours including red and green bean flavour ice creams especially for Shanghai. The problem faced by companies like Nestlé is that they compete – at least in part – against local companies with very low overhead costs.

Nestlé strengths and weaknesses

After its acquisitions, Nestlé had become a strong player in the ice cream market. In addition, it was much stronger than the market leader, Unilever, in confectionery brands, having developed its chocolate products particularly over the last 20 years – Nestlé owns such brands as Kit Kat and Lion Bar. During the early 1990s, it then borrowed a strategy from Mars: it reformulated its confectionery brands as ice cream products and launched some as product extensions – for example, KitKat Dairy Ice Cream and Smarties. In addition, it has launched a series of patented ice cream products that rely on sophisticated manufacture beyond the scope of smaller, national manufacturers. To achieve economies of scale, Nestlé has chosen to limit the number of manufacturing sites around the world.

Despite these strengths, Nestlé has some major problems. The first is that it has developed its business by acquisition, with all the risks that this entails. In addition, it faces competition from local companies with much lower overheads in markets where the unit price is sometimes very low – this makes it difficult to build a profitable business. It also faces competition in its more mature markets from the supermarket chains – see below.

Finally, where Nestlé has been able to acquire the market-leading company, it has developed a profitable business. But where it has only acquired a relatively small share of the market, it has struggled to achieve profitability. The reason is that the fixed costs of developing and distributing ice cream are high, meaning that high volumes are needed to achieve high profits: these are much more likely with a high market share.

Supermarkets – the new competitors

Supermarket chains – like Aldi and Tesco in much of Europe, Wal-Mart in North America and Carrefour in Europe and Asia – offer increased competition in the ice cream market through two mechanisms. First, they bargain with Nestlé and Unilever to gain good prices and promotions for their branded ice cream products. Second, they approach companies like Richmond Ice Cream in the UK to manufacture products that are very similar in quality and technology to those from Unilever and Nestlé but at much lower prices – the so-called supermarket own brands. The effect of such competitive activity is to reduce the profit margins of the major multinational ice cream manufacturers.

In the more mature markets of Europe and America, Unilever and Nestlé have therefore been forced to find alternative outlets for their products – like shopping malls, kiosks and cinemas – with all the distribution and other costs involved in such activities. In such markets, there is therefore a high fixed cost to ice cream strategy. There are also low barriers to entry for smaller companies. It is therefore advantageous to have built a high market share, like Unilever, and costly to develop market share in the early years.

Case questions

1 What are the main features of the Nestlé strategy in ice cream? How do they differ, if at all, from those of Unilever?
2 Why has Nestlé adopted the strategy of attempting to take a large market share? Do you think that this is viable? What alternative strategies could Nestlé have adopted?
3 What strategy lessons can we learn from a market where the barriers to entry are low and the fixed costs are high for the market leaders?

10.4 THE CLASSIC PRESCRIPTIVE MODEL OF STRATEGIC MANAGEMENT: EXPLORING THE PROCESS

Having made our choice of the *content* of a strategic plan, we now turn our attention to the related issue of who will make the choice and how it will be made – the strategic *process*. Clearly, in practice the two topics of process and content will be interlinked, but it is useful to separate them in our exploration here. The aim of this section is not merely to describe the process but also to evaluate its usefulness because it is important to be aware of such issues. We consider the matter under three headings:

1 The prescriptive process of strategic management
2 Some problems with the prescriptive process
3 Solutions within the prescriptive process to its problems.

10.4.1 The prescriptive process of strategic management

In describing their version of the classic prescriptive model, Wheelen and Hunger[34] state that the process of strategic management involves five major elements:

1 *environmental scanning* – the external opportunities and threats of the SWOT analysis;
2 *internal scanning* – the strengths and weaknesses of the SWOT analysis;
3 *strategy formulation* – mission, objectives, strategies and policies;
4 *strategy implementation* – including programmes, budgets and other procedures;
5 *evaluation and control* – to ensure that the strategic process remains on its predicted path.

For example, at Unilever the company is constantly scanning its major competitors such as Procter & Gamble (USA) and Nestlé (Switzerland) – environmental scanning. It is also examining its own resources – internal scanning. It then considers its business objectives and develops new strategies such as its investment in global ice cream markets – strategy formulation. It implements such strategies by building or acquiring ice cream companies as described in Case 10.1 – strategy implementation. After it has begun its strategies, it will monitor their profits to ensure that they meet group strategic objectives and it will then take corrective action if necessary – evaluation and control.

Some commentators on the classical model, such as Jauch and Glueck,[35] put the mission and objectives before environmental scanning. This book puts the objectives after the environmental and internal scanning for the reasons given in Chapter 1. However, in practice, the process is circular, with no firm rule at this point. Figure 10.4 sets out a typical sequence for the classical model with, in this case, the objectives first.[36]

Just as important as the precise sequence of events in the process is *who* undertakes them. This becomes particularly acute when the organisation consists of a group of industries that are possibly unrelated. In these circumstances, it is likely that there will be a corporate centre that might undertake some tasks and SBUs that will undertake others. But who does what tasks? There is no single answer to this question. For example, Unilever's approach described in Case 9.3 is unique to the opportunities, history and products of that company.

Although there are dangers in generalising, several commentators have identified which groups are particularly likely to be involved at each stage.[37] In a large multinational like Unilever, the group's SWOT analysis is usually undertaken at the corporate level and it is also the corporation that defines the overall mission and objectives. The reason is that only the corporation can have the overview needed to direct the main strategic thrusts and the resources to fund them. The results are then passed down for the strategy *option* process to be developed by the SBUs. In the case of Unilever, some SBUs would be given specially favoured treatment – such as ice cream and tea-based beverages – while others would have a tougher evaluative regime. The strategy *selection* might then be undertaken

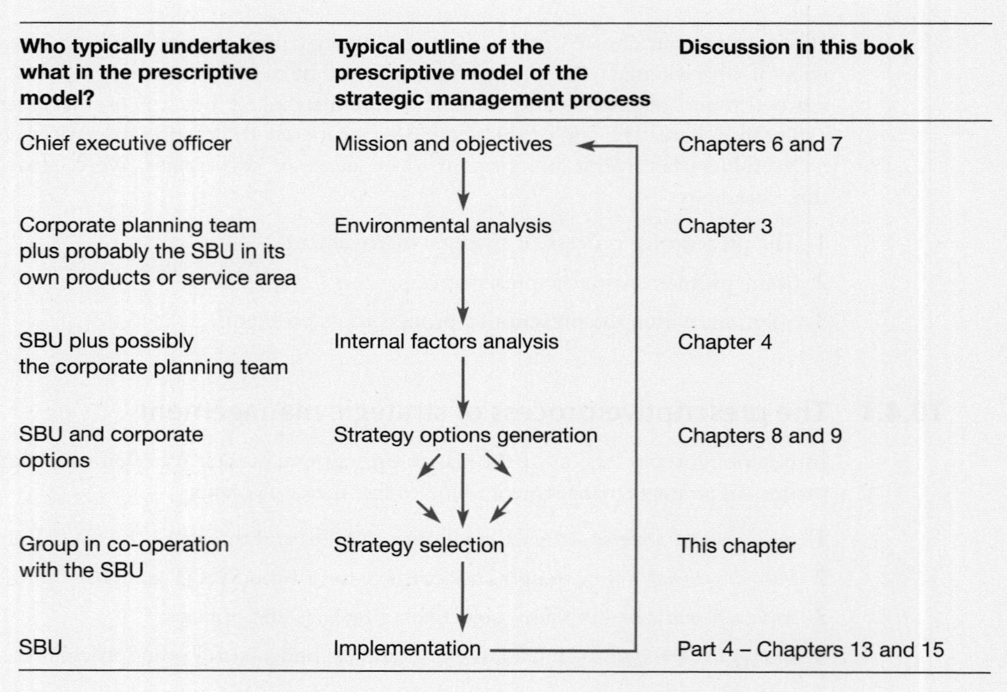

Who typically undertakes what in the prescriptive model?	Typical outline of the prescriptive model of the strategic management process	Discussion in this book
Chief executive officer	Mission and objectives	Chapters 6 and 7
Corporate planning team plus probably the SBU in its own products or service area	Environmental analysis	Chapter 3
SBU plus possibly the corporate planning team	Internal factors analysis	Chapter 4
SBU and corporate options	Strategy options generation	Chapters 8 and 9
Group in co-operation with the SBU	Strategy selection	This chapter
SBU	Implementation	Part 4 – Chapters 13 and 15

Figure 10.4 The prescriptive model of the strategic management process

Note: The process is largely linear but with feedback mechanisms at various points to ensure that the objectives, analysis and strategies are all consistent with each other. This is shown by the directions of the arrows, whose significance will become clearer when we examine alternative processes in Chapter 11.

at corporate headquarters, in consultation with the SBU and in the context of the available funds that the group has at its disposal. The SBU then implements the agreed strategies.

The process is therefore usually driven by corporate headquarters, on the basis that it is the only part of the organisation to have a complete picture of all aspects. However, individual businesses are often given considerable freedom within the guidelines to develop their strategy, as is the case at Unilever. Although many companies around the world have adopted the classical prescriptive process, there are a number of well-documented problems with this approach. We now explore them.

10.4.2 Some problems with the prescriptive process

There are a number of assumptions or simplifications in the prescriptive process that may not be valid in reality. We summarise four here but should note that other difficulties have been identified.

1 *Environment.* It is assumed that this is predictable, so that a clear direction can be used to develop the opportunities and threats to the organisation. There have been numerous instances of major variations in the environment that make this difficult to sustain.
2 *Clear planning procedure.* The major strategic decisions are initiated by this procedure that, once set in motion, can arrive at a clear and simple decision point: the strategy selection. In many companies, planning procedures are complicated by the need to persuade managers to undertake specific strategies. They may be reluctant for a variety of reasons, from a loss of power to a personality clash.
3 *Top-down procedures.* These procedures from corporate headquarters to the SBUs represent the most efficient method of developing new and innovative strategies. It is assumed that they can cope with the environment and gain commitment from the managers who will implement them. Many research studies have shown that managers find such a process demotivating. By contrast, the Japanese Honda company – see Case 11.1 – has reportedly more consultation and dialogue, which may be far more effective.
4 *Culture.* The culture of organisations will allow the classical model to operate. Culture here has two meanings: the style, beliefs and practices of the *organisation itself* and, more broadly, the culture of the *country* in which the organisation operates. Both of these are assumed to be consistent with the top-down classical model. In practice, some cultures are clearly more suited to a dominant top-down approach than others. The ABB case at the end of Chapter 12 provides an example of how the company's culture was actually changed.

Hence, all the above assumptions have been shown to have significant flaws.

Marx[38] quotes the former chairman of the giant US corporation General Electric – see Case 9.1 – Jack Welch, on the problems encountered in strategic planning in the 1960s using the classical process:

> Our planning system was dynamite when we first put it in. The thinking was fresh, the form mattered little - the format got no points. It was idea-oriented. We then hired a head of planning and he hired two vice-presidents and then he hired a planner, and the books got thicker and the printing got more sophisticated, and the covers got harder and the drawings got better. The meetings kept getting larger. Nobody can say anything with 16 or 18 people there.

Welch became increasingly concerned about the whole planning process in General Electric and moved to change it, being concerned about three areas:

1 the *bureaucracy* that may breed under classical strategy processes;
2 the *judgement* required to make choices, which may not be as rational as the simple options and choice selection process suggests;
3 the need to encourage a *culture of ideas* rather than a top-down approach as in the classical strategy process.

10.4.3 Solutions to problems within the prescriptive process

To explore the solutions available within the prescriptive process, it is useful to carry out a careful survey of the difficulties encountered. One such survey in the early 1980s observed that the prescriptive model had become excessively rational, bureaucratic and formalised.[39] There are a number of ways to overcome these problems. They involve a more open strategic planning culture with less emphasis on quantification of data. Stress can also be laid on two aspects of the actual process:

1 exploring with the proposers of the strategy the *assumptions* on which the strategy is based. When such assumptions are incorrect, the whole strategy is open to doubt;

2 during the strategy review sessions, requesting a simple *verbal summary* of the main proposals. If this cannot be done, then the proposals themselves may be suspect.

The whole process and system by which a strategy is developed should also be re-examined periodically in companies: this is a *planning process audit.* The aim would be to remove the impediments that creep in over time. It was just such an audit that led Unilever to rethink its strategy decision-making processes during 1996–1997. The company felt the need to redefine its direction, highlight key business areas and clarify the procedures that linked them together. It is notable that it also coincided with the appointment of a new co-chairman, Niall FitzGerald. Two specific aims were to gain greater individual ownership of strategic decisions and more emphasis on innovation. It is then notable that, when the 'Path to Growth' appeared to falter in the mid-2000s, the company made changes to its *management team* and *organisation structure* as well as to its products – see Case 9.3.

KEY STRATEGIC PRINCIPLES

- The prescriptive model of the strategic *process* is largely linear. It has feedback mechanisms at various points to ensure that objectives, options and strategy choice are consistent with each other.
- Problems with the prescriptive approach cover four main areas: environment unpredictability; planning procedures; top-down approaches driven by the centre; and the culture of the organisation that will allow the model to operate.
- Specific criticisms include the need for more dialogue, a greater flow of ideas and more adaptation to the environment.
- It may be possible to solve these problems within the prescriptive process, but some strategists take a more critical view.

CASE STUDY 10.4

Eurofreeze evaluates its strategy options: Part 2

After developing its mission and objectives, Eurofreeze began to examine the strategy options that were available and the important strategic decisions that would follow. Importantly, the case presents the strategic options in the form used by many companies to reach strategic decisions.

Future strategy options for Eurofreeze

The company was now considering a number of strategy options. It had undertaken the basic analysis using a cost of capital of 9 per cent. To help analyse the options, it gathered basic market data for its own products and those of its main competitor, Refrigor. The information covered all its main European markets and is shown in Table 10.5. Within the product groups, there was little useful additional information: product sales data were available on individual items, but varied so much by country and by store chain that there was little to be gained from analysing the data.

Refrigor was market leader in vegetables and fruit. Eurofreeze was market leader in branded meat and fish dishes, with Refrigor

Table 10.5 Market data on the European frozen products market 1999

	Eurofreeze		Refrigor		Market share of product category	
	Sales ($m)	Market share of product	Sales ($m)	Market share of product category (%)	2003	2012
Branded vegetables and fruit	400	10	800	20	+2%	-
Private label vegetables and fruit	200	5	300	7.5	+2%	-
Branded meat and fish	300	30	200	20	+4%	+6%
Private label meat and fish	150	15	100	10	+4%	+6%
Branded savoury dishes including pizza	30	6	80	16	+7%	+5%
Private label savoury dishes including pizza	none	-	40	8	+7%	+5%
Branded cakes and gateaux	25	12	25	12	+8%	+6%
Private label cakes and gateaux	none	-	20	9.6	+8%	+6%

second. Neither company was market leader in savoury dishes (including pizza) or gateaux. (McCain was leader in savoury dishes, with a 30 per cent share, and Sara Lee in gateaux, with a 25 per cent share.)

The company undertook a portfolio analysis in 2003. This is shown as Figure 10.5. The calculation of the relative market shares for this analysis is shown in the Appendix at the end of the chapter.

Eurofreeze then proceeded to consider each of the options that were available to it. The results are outlined below. (There could be some further combination of options but it was felt that the following reflected the main routes available to the company.)

Eurofreeze options

The strategic options available to Eurofreeze are summarised in Table 10.6; their financial implications are then explored in the following text.

Full 10-year financial projections for all five options below.

Option 1

Stop supplying all basic frozen products, including its branded and own brand (i.e. with the retailer's private brand name)

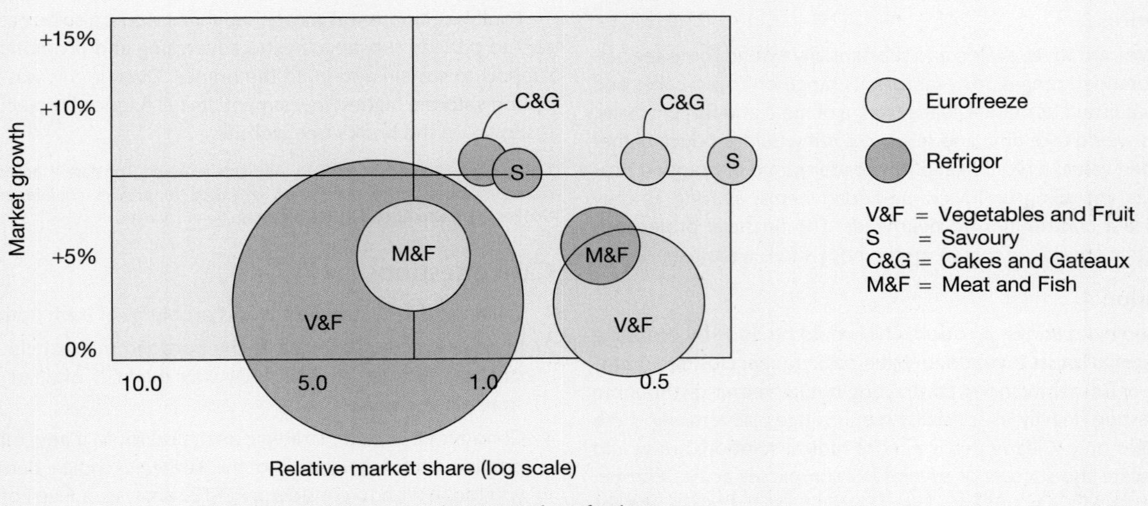

Figure 10.5 The European frozen foods market: portfolio matrices for Eurofreeze and Refrigor

Evaluating options in frozen food might begin by favouring products with more added value and higher profit margins - like the pizza and gateaux - and dropping products with lower margins - like simple frozen vegetables.

vegetables. Dropping this range would mean that the overhead contribution made by carrying these products would no longer be available to the group. The financial projections for this option are shown on the book's free website.

Option 2

Cancel its current branded range of basic frozen food products such as vegetables, but continue to manufacture own brand versions. This would keep some overhead contribution but would have very low added value. At the same time, the company would keep and slowly extend its range of higher-added-value branded items. The financial projections are shown on the book's free website.

Option 3

Drive hard to redevelop and substantially extend some specialist branded ranges; for example, its range of frozen cakes and gateaux and its market-leader range of meat and fish products. This would take time and resources but would produce higher added value. It would keep its broader range of branded products, including its low-value-added items, as long as they made a contribution to overheads. The financial projections for this option are shown on the book's free website.

Option 4

Become a specialist producer. This would be done by dropping almost all of its low-added-value basic range, closing a number of freezer factories, contracting out its freezer distribution, investing heavily in specialist menu ranges, advertising these ranges only. Clearly this is a more radical solution, but would emulate the success of several US companies across Europe, such as McCain and Sara Lee. The full financial projection for this option is shown on the book's free website.

Option 5

Becoming the lowest-cost producer. This would be done by building on existing sales to all major customers: major investment in new factories, new warehouses and new transport networks would be needed. This would be coupled with major (and largely unknown) manufacturing innovation, all with the aim of reducing costs, so that they would move below those of its competitor, Refrigor. Although this option was available in theory, it was based on three assumptions that carried some risk:

1 Refrigor would slow down its current rate of investment and allow itself to be overtaken.
2 Major cost savings of the order of 20 per cent below existing costs were still available in the industry.
3 Market leadership could be gained through a low-cost route.

For this option, it was recognised that it would also be necessary to provide substantial extra advertising and promotional support to sustain and build the brands. Overall, this was the option with the highest investment. Its full financial projection is shown on the book's free website.

Table 10.6 Summary of the Eurofreeze strategy options

Option	Implication for sales
1 Stop selling branded and own label vegetables and fruit	Sales decline $400 million in Year 1, $200 million in Year 2
2 Stop selling branded vegetables and fruit but continue own label	Sales decline $400 million in Year 1
3 Extend specialist branded food ranges, e.g. pizza and gateaux	Sales gain $50 million each year
4 Major cutback of range in first two years, then rebuild specialist areas from Year 4 onwards	Sales decline $205 million in Year 1, $300 million in Years 2 and 3. Sales gain $50 million in Year 4, $100 million in each year from Year 5 onwards
5 Become lowest-cost producer through major investment	Build sales by at least $100 million per annum

Case questions

1 What are the relative merits and problems of each option?
2 In what way does the use of the portfolio matrix help the strategic debate? And in what way might it mislead the strategic decisions?
3 Consider what other strategic analytical tools, if any, might provide useful insights into the strategic choice debate: you might wish to consider a PESTEL analysis, a Five Forces Analysis, generic strategies, a market options matrix, value chain and an innovations checklist (in Chapter 11).
4 Which option, if any, would you recommend to Eurofreeze? Give reasons for your choice and explain the strengths and weaknesses of your choice.

CRITICAL REFLECTION

Should companies engage in strategic plans?

This chapter has focused on prescriptive strategic decision making, which is widely used in many companies. It has explored both the strengths and weaknesses of such an approach, pointing out the many difficulties. Some strategists believe that prescriptive strategic planning has so many problems that it is not worth undertaking: in other words, it is counterproductive to produce a 'strategic plan'. What is your view? Should companies engage in strategic plans?

SUMMARY

- In evaluating strategic options, it is useful to distinguish between the content of the option (What strategy will we select?) and the process by which the selection will be undertaken (How will we undertake the selection task?).
- In considering strategy content, the chapter provides an overview of the classic prescriptive evaluation approach. Such an approach relies on developing criteria as a starting point for selection. These need to be developed bearing in mind the nature of the organisation: for example, commercial and non-profit-making organisations will clearly require different criteria.
- There are six main criteria usually employed in commercial organisations: consistency (especially with the organisation's mission and objectives), suitability, validity, feasibility, business risk, attractiveness to stakeholders.
  1. Consistency with the purpose of the organisation is a prime test for evaluating and selecting strategies.
  2. Suitability of the strategy for the environment within which the organisation operates is clearly important.
  3. Validity of the projections and data used in developing the option must be tested.
  4. Feasibility will depend on two factors: constraints internal to the organisation, such as technical skills and finance; and constraints external to the organisation, such as the response of competitors.
  5. Business risk also needs to be assessed because it may be unacceptable to the organisation.
  6. Attractiveness to stakeholders such as shareholders and employees is important: some options may be more attractive to some stakeholders than others.
- There may be international variations in evaluation criteria, depending on national differences in the roles and values of stakeholders and governments.
- In making an initial selection of the best option, it is important to clarify the basis on which this is to be done. Evaluation against the mission and objectives is important but needs to be rigorous and precise if it is to provide real benefit.
- Financial criteria can also be used as the basis of selection. The shareholder value approach takes a broader perspective on evaluation than that provided by the specific project. It seeks to determine the benefit of such developments in the context of the whole company against the cost of the company's capital. Major weaknesses are that it still relies on the assumption that shareholders are always the prime beneficiaries. In addition, it makes the dubious prescriptive assumption that revenue and profit streams can be forecast with accuracy some years into the future.
- Cost/benefit analysis has been successfully employed in public sector evaluation, where it is important to assess broader and less quantifiable benefits. The main difficulty is where to place the limit on such benefits and costs.

- Beyond the issues of criteria to aid strategy selection, business judgement is important. General empirical evidence is available through a number of routes. The ADL matrix summarises some broad decision-making parameters. It is based on two broad categories: the stage of industry maturity and the competitive position of the organisation involved. After the position of the organisation on these two parameters has been identified, simple choices then suggest themselves.
- Empirical evidence based on the PIMS Databank also exists on the connection between strategic actions and the results in terms of profitability and other criteria. According to PIMS, high quality and strong market share can make a positive contribution to profitability. High capital intensity is less likely to have a positive impact. Some researchers doubt the cause and effect relationships here. Acquisitions and mergers have also been studied for their impact on profitability. The evidence is, at best, mixed and, at worst, suggests that many are unsuccessful.
- After exploring the likely *content* of the selected strategy above, it is important to consider the *process* by which the selection is undertaken. The prescriptive model of the strategic process is largely linear. It has feedback mechanisms at various points to ensure that objectives, options and strategy choice are consistent with each other.
- Problems with the prescriptive approach cover four main areas: environment unpredictability; planning procedures; top-down approaches driven by the centre; and the culture of the organisation that will allow the model to operate. In addition, there are some specific criticisms which include the need for more dialogue, a greater flow of ideas and more adaptation to the environment. It may be possible to solve these problems within the prescriptive process model but some strategists take a more critical view.

QUESTIONS

1 Using Section 10.1, what criteria would you consider were particularly important if you were evaluating strategy options in the following organisations: a small chain of petrol stations; a large multinational developing a global strategy; a government telecommunications company that was about to be privatised; a student career planning service?

2 If you were developing strategy for a small company with 50 employees and a turnover of around $5 million, would you use all the selection criteria outlined in Section 10.1 or would you select only some for this purpose? Give reasons for your answer and, if only choosing some, explain which you would pick.

3 Japanese companies have tended to favour payback criteria while US/UK companies have been more inclined to use DCF criteria in evaluating strategic options. What are the merits of the two approaches? Can you suggest any reasons why one might be preferred to another?

4 *'Discounting techniques rest on rather arbitrary assumptions about profitability, asset deterioration and external investment opportunities.'* (Robert Hay) Explain the implications of this comment for strategy evaluation and comment on its application in strategy selection.

5 What are the dangers, if any, of using quantified and precise evaluation criteria in strategy selection?

6 *'Strategy evaluation is an attempt to look beyond the obvious facts regarding the short-term health of a business and appraise instead those more fundamental factors and trends that govern success in the chosen field of endeavour.'* (Richard Rumelt) Discuss this statement.

7 A well-known German company is primarily engaged in supplying motor components such as car radios and gearboxes to car companies in the EU, such as Ford and Toyota. It is considering acquiring a medium-sized US company as the basis for its first expansion outside Europe. What would you advise in this relatively mature and fiercely competitive industry?

8 With regard to new, fast-growing markets such as that for mobile telephones, the ADL matrix would suggest that weak and dominant companies face quite different strategic opportunities and problems. Is this really true when the market is changing so rapidly?

9 *'Merger and acquisition is the most common means of entry into new markets.'* (John Kay) What is the evidence of success from such ventures? What are the strategic implications of your answer for organisations considering this option?

10 *'Most firms rarely engage in explicit formal strategy evaluation . . . rather, it is a continuing process that is difficult to separate from normal planning, reporting and control.'* (Richard Rumelt) Discuss the implications for the evaluation criteria explored in this chapter.

APPENDIX

Calculation of relative market shares for portfolio analysis in association with Case 10.4

For Eurofreeze

Vegetables and fruit: (10% + 5%) + (20% + 7.5%) = 0.54

(Note that these could be redefined as separate branded and private product categories. Given the low added value from both routes, this has not been undertaken here. There are no clear rules.)

Meat and fish: (30% + 15%) + (20% + 10%) = 1.5

Savoury dishes: 6% + 30% = 0.2

(Note that McCain is market leader in this category and it is this share that has been used.)

Cakes and gateaux: 12% + 25% = 0.48

(Note that Sara Lee is market leader in this category and it is this share that has been used.)

For Refrigor

Vegetables and fruit: (20% + 7.5%) + (10% + 15%) = 1.1

Meat and fish: (20% + 10%) + (30% + 15%) = 0.67

Savoury dishes: (18% + 16%) + 30% = 0.8

Cakes and gateaux: (12% + 9.6%) + 25% = 0.86

FURTHER READING

On criteria for selection, see Day, G S (1987) *Strategic Market Planning*, West Publishing, St Paul, MN; Tiles, S (1963) 'How to evaluate business strategy', *Harvard Business Review*, July–August, pp 111–122; Rumelt, R (1980) 'The evaluation of business strategy', originally published in Glueck, W F, *Business Policy and Strategic Management*, McGraw-Hill, New York, but republished in two more recent texts: De Wit, Bob and Meyer, R (1994) *Strategy: Process, Content and Context*, West Publishing, St Paul, MN; Mintzberg, H and Quinn, J B (1991) *The Strategy Process*, Prentice Hall, New York.

On financial evaluation, Glautier, M W E and Underdown, B (1994) *Accounting Theory and Practice*, 5th edn, Pitman Publishing, London, is a useful summary of the main areas. See also Arnold, G (1998) *Corporate Financial Management*, Financial Times Pitman Publishing, London, which provides an excellent review of the topic.

For a rational view on the use and abuse of investment criteria: Hay, R (1982) 'Managing as if tomorrow mattered', *Harvard Business Review*, May–June, pp 72–79.

Feasibility is explored along with other criteria in Professor Richard Rumelt's article on 'The evaluation of business strategy' mentioned above.

For a view of the problems of planning versus autonomy see Anderson, T J (2000) 'Strategic planning, autonomous actions and corporate performance', *Long Range Planning*, Vol 33, pp 184–200, which contains some interesting empirical data.

NOTES AND REFERENCES

1 See, for example, Gilmore, F and Brandenburg, R (1962) 'Anatomy of corporate planning', *Harvard Business Review*, November–December, pp 61–69.

2 The two case studies of the global ice cream market in this chapter are based on data from published sources. These include: Unilever Annual Report and Accounts 2004 and 2010, Nestlé Annual Report and Accounts 2004 and 2010, General Mills Annual Report and Accounts 2004. Websites of these three companies plus individual country websites accessed from www.unilever.com. UK Monopolies and

Mergers Commission (1994) *Report on the supply in the UK of ice cream for immediate consumption*, Mar, HMSO, London Cmd 2524; *European Court of First Instance Ruling* – Case T-65-98 R, Van den Bergh Foods Ltd v Commission, Order of the President of the Court of First Instance, 7 July 1998; Final ruling report in *Financial Times* on 24 October 2003, p 8; *Financial Times*, 19 May 1993, p 24; 17 March 1994 and 13 June 1995, p 18; 23 November 1997, p 10; 30 July 1998, p 26; 31 July 1998, p 23; 18 August 1998, p 5; 15 February 1999, p 6; May 1999, p 9; 10 June 1999, p 19; 20 July 1999, p 12; 21 July 1999, p 7; 24 February 2000, p 3; 17 March 2000, p 8; 17 August 2001, p 17; 12 September 2001, p 25; 18 June 2002, p 30; 5 March 2003, p 31; 7 March 2003, p 23. *Dairy Industry International*, May 1994, p 33; August 1994, p 17 and September 1994, p 19; *Food Manufacture*, June 1994, p 24 and July 1994, p 28; *Sunday Times*, 7 June 1992, pp 1–8. Nestlé press release on acquisition of Dreyers – 'Strategic move to gain leadership in the US ice cream market' on the Nestlé website. http://app1chinadaily.com.cn/star3 March 2005; www.checkout.ie/Market Profile on ice cream; Hindu Business Line – Hot battles on ice cream, 17 April 2003; *Beijing Youth Daily*, 19 March 2004; Competition Tribunal of the Republic of South Africa, Case no 61/LM/Nov01; 'Nestlé cutting back ice cream capacity,' *Quick Frozen Foods International*, 1 October 2002.

3 Used with some effect to dismiss options by the late Professor 'Mac' MacIntosh in 1967 in London Business School MBA lectures and case discussions.

4 Different commentators have employed other criteria. Those used here have been developed from Day, G S (1987) *Strategic Market Planning*, West Publishing, St Paul, MN; Tiles, S (1963) 'How to evaluate business strategy', *Harvard Business Review*, July–August, pp 111–122; Rumelt, R (1980) 'The evaluation of business strategy', originally published in Glueck, W F, *Business Policy and Strategic Management*, McGraw-Hill, New York, and republished in two more recent texts: De Wit, Bob and Meyes, R (1994) *Strategy: Process, Content and Context*, West Publishing, St Paul, MN; Mintzberg, H and Quinn, J B (1991) *The Strategy Process*, Prentice Hall, New York.

5 Reckitt Benckiser Presentation to Financial Analysts 9 February 2005, available on the web at www.reckitt.com.

6 See Lynch, R (1993) *Cases in European Marketing*, Kogan Page, London, Ch 16.

7 See *Financial Times*, 15 April 1995, p 9; 13 October 1994, p 2; 1 March 1994, p 29; and Lynch, R (1993) Op. cit., p 84. Groupe Bull is a company with some real strategic problems that would make an interesting strategy project.

8 Kehoe, L (1995) 'Restrictive practice claims put Microsoft back in firing line', *Financial Times*, 6 February, p 6.

9 Carnegy, H (1995) 'Bitter Swedish dispute to end', *Financial Times*, 3 August, p 2.

10 See Chapter 2 for details.

11 Munchau, W and Norman, P (1995) 'Planes, trains and automobiles', *Financial Times*, 7 November, p 19.

12 Ohmae, K (1982) *The Mind of the Strategist*, Penguin, Harmondsworth, p 86.

13 For a more detailed treatment of this topic, see Arnold, G (1998) *Corporate Financial Management*, Financial Times Management, London, Chs 2–6.

14 This is consistent with the emphasis on core competencies in Chapter 13.

15 Further detailed exploration of the financial techniques outlined in this chapter is contained in Glautier, M W E and Underdown, B (1994) *Accounting Theory and Practice*, 5th edn, Pitman Publishing, London and Arnold, G (1998) *Corporate Financial Management*, Financial Times Pitman Publishing, London.

16 The main exceptions are the large grocery multiple retailers which sell for cash to the general public and buy on credit from the manufacturers. Retailers have relied on their suppliers to fund increased sales for many years, but they do need careful stock control procedures to handle the situation.

17 See Arnold, G (1998) Op. cit., Ch 3.

18 This section is based on the example in Chapter 31 of Glautier, M W E and Underdown, B (1994) Op. cit., p 540.

19 This was essentially proposed by Rappaport, A (1983) *Creating Shareholder Value*, The Free Press, New York. See also Rappaport, A (1992) 'CEO and strategists: forging a common framework', *Harvard Business Review*, May–June, p 84. A clear and careful discussion of this area is also contained in Ellis, J and Williams, D (1993) *Corporate Strategy and Financial Analysis*, Pitman Publishing, London, Ch 10.

20 It is not true of some Japanese companies according to the work of Williams, K, Haslam, C and Williams, J (1991) 'Management accounting: the Western problematic against the Japanese application', *9th Annual Conference of Labour Progress, University of Manchester Institute of Science and Technology*. The authors examined car and electronics companies only and made no claim to have extended their research to the *whole* of Japanese industry. Professor Toyohiro Kono also comments that 'DCF is not used very often' in his interesting survey of Japanese practice, which is more broadly based: Kono, T (1992) *Long Range Planning of Japanese Corporations*, de Gruyter, Berlin, pp 277, 281.

21 Rappaport, A, quoted above, and Woolridge, G (1988) 'Competitive decline and corporate restructuring: Is a myopic stock market to blame?', *Continental Bank Journal of Applied Corporate Finance*, Spring, pp 26–36, quoted in Ellis, J and Williams, D (1993) Op. cit.

22 Quoted from the UK chemist retailer Boots plc definition of strategy: Buckley, N (1994) 'Divide and thrive at Boots', *Financial Times*, 4 July, p 12.

23 See, for example, Rowe, A, Mason, A and Dickel, K (1985) *Strategic Management and Business Policy*, 2nd edn, Addison-Wesley, New York.

24 This section is based on Porter, M E (1990) *Competitive Strategy*, The Free Press, New York, Chs 9 to 13. The comments on leaders and followers also draw on Kotler, P (1994) *Marketing Management*, 8th edn, Prentice Hall International, Englewood Cliffs, NJ, Ch 15.

25 Porter, M E (1990) Op. cit., p 191.

26 This section relies heavily on Buzzell, R and Gale, B T (1987) *The PIMS Principles*, The Free Press, New York,

and other researchers who are individually acknowledged below.

27 Described in Buzzell, R and Gale, B T (1987) Ibid.

28 Described in Buzzell, R and Gale, B T (1987) Ibid.

29 PIMS (1991) 'Marketing: in pursuit of the perfect mix', *Marketing Magazine, London*, 31 October.

30 Described in Buzzell, R and Gale, B T (1987) Op. cit.

31 This section relies essentially on the work and data in Kay, J (1993) *The Foundations of Corporate Success*, Oxford University Press, Oxford, Ch 10.

32 Ghemawat, P and Ghadar, F (2000) 'The dubious logic of global mega-mergers', *Harvard Business Review*, July–August, pp 55–72.

33 Capron, L (1999) 'The long-term performance of horizontal acquisitions', *Strategic Management Journal*, November, 20, pp 987–1018.

34 Wheelen, T and Hunger, D (1992) *Strategic Management and Business Policy*, 4th edn, Addison-Wesley, Reading, MA.

35 Jauch, L R and Glueck, W F (1988) *Business Policy and Strategic Management*, 5th edn, McGraw-Hill, New York.

36 The prescriptive model presented in this chapter is shown in a number of texts in one format or another. In addition to reference 2 above, similar versions of the model are also to be found in the well-known text by Thompson, A and Strickland, A (1993) *Strategic Management*, 7th edn, Irwin, Homewood, IL. The leading and well-respected European text is that by Johnson, G and Scholes, K (2002) *Exploring Corporate Strategy: text and cases*, Prentice Hall International, Harlow, and is also essentially built around the options-and-choice model of prescriptive strategy with implementation of the agreed strategic choice.

37 See, for example, Andrews, K (1987) *The Concept of Corporate Strategy*, Irwin, Homewood, IL; also Chakravarthy, B and Lorange, P (1991) *Managing the Strategy Process*, Prentice Hall, Englewood Cliffs, NJ.

38 Marx, T (1991) 'Removing obstacles to effective strategic planning', *Long Range Planning*, 24 August, pp 21–28. This research paper is reprinted in De Wit, Bob and Meyer, R (1994) *Strategy: Process, Content and Context*, West Publishing, St Paul, MN.

39 Lenz, R T and Lyles, M (1985) 'Paralysis by analysis: Is your planning system becoming too rational?', *Long Range Planning*, 18 August, pp 64–72. This is also reprinted in De Wit and Meyer (1994) Op. cit.

CHAPTER 11
Finding the strategic route forward: mainly emergent approaches

Video and sound summary of this chapter

LEARNING OUTCOMES

When you have worked through this chapter, you will be able to:

- understand the importance of context in the development of strategy;
- explain five approaches to strategy development that go beyond the classic prescriptive approach;
- identify the relevance of a survival-based route forward in the context of the circumstances of the organisation;
- outline the importance of the uncertainty-based route forward and comment on its relevance, depending on the organisation's context;
- explain the two main elements of the network-based route forward and comment critically on its usefulness;
- decide the extent to which a learning-based strategy is needed as part of an organisation's strategy process.

INTRODUCTION

Video Parts 7a and 7b

Although the classic prescriptive model is probably the most widely used approach in strategy development, its simplifying assumptions have long been recognised. In this chapter, we explore alternative approaches to strategy development that are mainly emergent in approach.

In Chapter 10, we distinguished between the *content* (What?) of strategy development and the *process* (Why? Who? How?). In this chapter, we add a third element that helps to move beyond the simplifying assumptions of the classic prescriptive approach: the *context* within which strategy is developed.

Definition ▶ **Context means the circumstances surrounding and explaining the way that strategy operates and develops.** For classic prescriptive strategy, context is assumed to involve slow, steady circumstances which are easy to predict.[1] However, this may be an over-simplification of real strategic situations: for example, context may contain periods of upheaval and rapid growth. Context is therefore developed further in the opening section of this chapter to explore some of the realities and uncertainties of real situations. Four routes forward for strategy development are identified; each of them relies on different contexts and implies alternative strategic approaches. All of them include this more complex view of context but also consider other aspects of the strategic process and content. The four routes forward are shown in Figure 11.1.

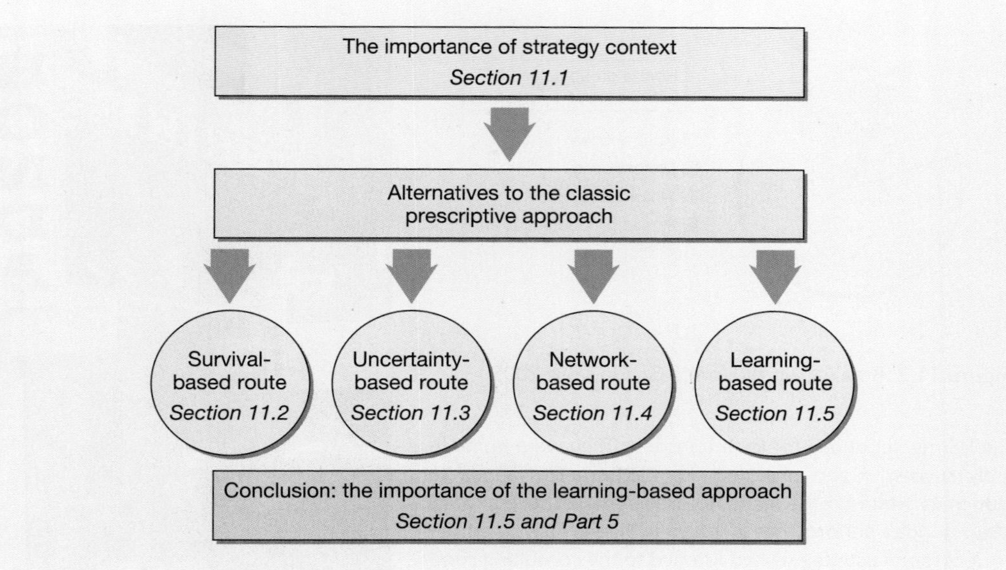

Figure 11.1 Finding the strategic route forward

Amongst the four routes, the chapter argues that the learning-based approach can usefully be added to the classic prescriptive approach developed in Chapter 10 in order to find the strategic route forward for all organisations. The other routes may also be useful depending on the context within which the strategy is being developed.

CASE STUDY 11.1

How Honda came to dominate two major motorcycle markets

This case study describes how Honda Motorcycles achieved its dominant market share of the US and UK markets. Although the strategic approach was originally seen as prescriptive, it was shown that, in reality, the strategies were much more emergent in their development.

During the period 1960–1980, Honda Motorcycles (Japan) came to dominate motorcycle markets in the USA and UK. Professor Richard Pascale has researched and described two perspectives on the process that Honda used to develop its strategies over this period.[2] They resulted in Honda moving from zero market share to domination of the US and UK markets, leaving the home-based industries with only small, niche-based market shares.

Pascale first examined a study undertaken by Boston Consulting Group for the UK motorcycle industry in 1975 on the strategic reasons for the success of Honda. Two key factors for the success of Honda were identified:

1 an advantage in terms of Honda's economies of scale in technology, distribution and manufacturing;

2 the loss to other companies of market share and profitability as a result of the Honda attack.

The diagnosis appeared to be an example of the classical model and its prescriptive solutions in action.

Pascale then interviewed the Honda executives who had actually launched the motorcycles in the USA and subsequently in the UK. He discovered that Honda's strategy had at first been a failure and that it was as a result of sheer desperation that they had stumbled on the strategy that proved so successful. The executives at Honda had a full range of motorcycles that could be imported into the USA. They ranged from small scooters to very large machines. All were more reliable and had higher performance than equivalent US competitors.

Honda US initially tried to compete head-on against the US main competition by using their large machines. However, Japanese motorbikes lacked credibility in the US market against the well-known US brands, even though the Honda bikes were better. The launch programme was unsuccessful. By chance, Honda then tried to sell some small scooters into

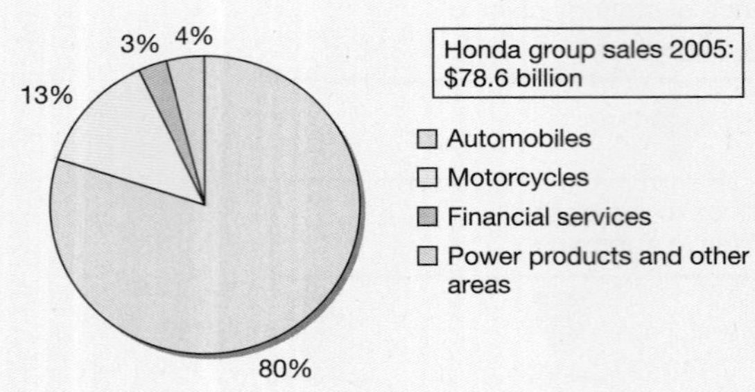

Figure 11.2 Breakdown of Honda Group sales 2005

For many years, Honda has dominated the motorcycle market, both in its home country - Japan pictured here - and around the world by a combination of segmented products, quality and competitive prices.

the US market purely for local transport. They were immediately successful and provided the platform for Honda to launch its attack on the main motorbike market several years later. Honda's performance is shown in Figure 11.2.

If corporate strategists had listened to the consulting company, they might have concluded that a major strategic initiative had been undertaken by Honda, based on careful strategic analysis and evaluation of options. But the reality was more haphazard and opportunistic, especially in the early days of the programme.

In conclusion, Pascale commented that Japanese managers at Honda and elsewhere did not use the term *strategy* to outline a *prescriptive* strategic plan. They were more inclined to see the process as providing an emerging process of trial and error, with the strategy evolving from experimentation as the process unfolded. According to his findings, Japanese companies were unlikely to develop a single strategy that was set to guide the company unerringly forward into the future.

In the Honda case, the strategy was developed from the managers in the market experimenting to find the most effective strategy. As each success was obtained, the Honda managers reported this back to Japan, with their ideas and suggestions for the next phase. There was frequent dialogue between Japan and the individual markets, with consensus being far more important to the emergence of the final strategy. Pascale concluded that strategy needed to be redefined as:

All the things necessary for the successful functioning of an organisation as an adaptive mechanism.

It should be noted, however, that during the 1980s Professor Toyohiro Kono repeatedly surveyed strategic planning in Japanese companies.[3] His conclusions suggested that, in large Japanese companies at least, there is rather more strategic planning than was observed by Pascale. Other recent examples, such as the Canon planning process described in Case 13.2, also exist that suggest that Japanese companies have now adopted some aspects of the prescriptive process, although there is still a strong element of experimentation and consensus in deriving the final plans.

Honda describes its detailed policies and initiatives on its main world website: http://world.honda.com/CSR/environment/.

Case question

Does prescriptive strategy need to be modified or would it be better, as Pascale suggests, to redefine the strategic process completely?

11.1 THE IMPORTANCE OF STRATEGY CONTEXT

Definition ▶ **Strategy context means the circumstances surrounding and influencing the way that a strategy develops and operates.** As the Honda case demonstrates, the company's success in the US motorcycle market was the result of three interrelated strategic factors:

1 *strategy content* – Honda's use of small machines as an entry point, followed by its launch of the larger machines;
2 *strategy process* – the way this strategy was developed by a combination of luck, product performance and management persistence in the face of initial difficulties;
3 *strategy context* – the historical dominance of the US manufacturers initially led to the failure of Honda's prescriptive entry strategy, but the industry's relative weakness in the small market provided an opening for Honda.

Although all three elements are important in strategy development, this section of the book concentrates on context (Chapter 10 explored the other two).[4] Strategy context is concerned with the circumstances surrounding and influencing the way that a strategy develops and operates. The definition of context covers three main elements:

1 *factors outside the organisation* – customers, competitors and other areas that may also be important;
2 *factors inside the organisation* – its resources, particularly the way that they interact through leadership, organisational culture and management decision making;
3 *strategy as history* – the situation that the organisation finds itself in at the time of the strategic decision: its procedures, pathways, culture and history.

To make sense of these aspects of context, it is useful to begin by considering some problems of context associated with the classic prescriptive strategy route. We then explore the relationship of context with the other two aspects of strategy development – process and content – before finally using context to identify five alternative strategic routes forward.

11.1.1 Some context problems with the classic model of prescriptive strategy

In some circumstances, the classic approach works adequately. However, it assumes that growth or decline is largely linear, continuous and predictable. Such simplifying assumptions enable new strategy to be developed and implemented. The difficulty is that there are a number of circumstances, particularly involving a more turbulent or uncertain context, where such assumptions are incorrect. In these circumstances, prescriptive strategic solutions are, at best, suboptimal and, at worst, irrelevant. Exhibit 11.1 outlines some typical contextual problems that can arise from the use of the classic prescriptive approach. They do not mean that the model is 'wrong', but (like all models) it may over-simplify the strategic context in some important circumstances.

11.1.2 The importance of context and its relationship with strategy process and content

Strategy context is important because it suggests that those alternatives to classic prescriptive strategy that include a fuller treatment of context may work better. There are two main reasons:[5]

1 *The external context.* This may be particularly uncertain – for example, internet banking may revolutionise the retail banking industry in ways that remain essentially unknown at the time of writing. This makes the prescriptive route, which relies on predicting the environment, largely meaningless.
2 *The internal context.* The organisation's resources and decision making are undoubtedly more complex than the simple options and choice of the classic prescriptive strategy model – for example, organisational politics, formal and informal networks, styles of leadership and many other issues all undermine the assumptions of the classic approach.

The *context* in which the strategy is developed may thus influence the *process* of strategy development. For example, an uncertain context may make a simple decision-making process irrelevant. As a result, the *content* of the strategy may therefore differ from that suggested by classic prescriptive strategy. For example, it will be difficult to decide the content of a strategy if the context within

EXHIBIT 11.1

How context can weaken classic prescriptive strategy

Typical outline	Some assumptions and characteristics of classic prescriptive strategy	Some resulting problems of context
Mission and objectives	• Objectives can and should be identified in advance	• Objectives may need to be more flexible in fast-moving markets
Environmental analysis	• Environment sufficiently predictable	• Technology, war and economic disaster may make this assumption meaningless
Resource analysis	• Resources can be clearly identified and developed	• Tacit knowledge needs to be seen in the company context in which it was developed (see Chapter 11) • The context of a leadership change may fundamentally alter resources (see Chapter 16)
Strategy options generation	• It is only necessary to identify options once • It is possible to identify options clearly	• May want to keep options open where the context is unclear • Competitor reactions may be unknown, context will alter
Strategy options selection	• Only one option can be chosen • It is possible to make a clear choice between options	• Why choose only one option? Surely this depends on the context of the time, resources, etc.
Implementation	• Implementation only needs to be considered at this late stage in strategic development	• Context may make this highly dubious (see opening sections of Part 5 and Chapter 17)

which it is being developed remains uncertain. It is this *combination* of context, process and content that will guide us in the search for alternative approaches to strategy development.

11.1.3 Alternative approaches to strategy development

Strategic management is not rocket science – combining context, process and content involves judgement that may go beyond the simple logic of classic prescriptive strategy. There is no well-tried and generally agreed scientific formula for finding the strategic route forward. As a consequence, there are many alternative approaches to strategy development.

Some approaches still have a strong prescriptive element, while others are more emergent in their exploration of strategic issues. The difficulty is how to explore the many alternative ways forward that have been suggested by strategy writers. This book has chosen four main routes for reasons of contrast and because each provides an insight into strategy development:[6]

1 *Survival-based.* This route puts heavy emphasis on organisations being able to survive in a hostile and highly competitive context. It does this through an emergent process, seeking out opportunities in strategy content as they occur.

2 *Chaos-based.* This route also emphasises the importance of context, treating the environment as uncertain and the processes as opportunistic and transformational. The process is therefore *emergent.*

3 *Network-based.* This route has two related elements: network externalities and network co-operation. The first element examines the way that networks for a product can be self-reinforcing and benefit members. The second element explores the ability of markets, industries and companies

to form co-operative networks. Both these aspects of the route have *emergent* elements because they have evolving outcomes and unknown elements during the process.

4 *Learning-based.* This route lays heavy emphasis on the context and the process derived from the existing knowledge and experience of the organisation. This essentially involves learning from the past and from the contributions of those involved at present. Thus both the historical context and the current process will influence strategy content – the process is, essentially, *emergent.*

This book places special emphasis on the learning-based route above. The reason is that most organisations will benefit from its insights on the strategy process. However, all four (and more not covered in this text) have their place in finding the most appropriate strategic route forward for the organisation.

KEY STRATEGIC PRINCIPLES

- In developing strategy, it is important to distinguish three distinct elements: the content of the strategy; the process by which it has been derived; and the context in which it has been developed.
- In the classic prescriptive model, context is assumed to be largely linear and predictable. This is not always the case, particularly when the context is turbulent and uncertain. Alternative approaches to strategy development may therefore be required.
- The context, process and content of a strategy are interconnected and it is this combination that is important in strategy development.
- There are a number of alternatives to the classic prescriptive approach to strategy development. Four are explored in the remainder of this chapter, but others may also be relevant.

CASE STUDY 11.2

Europe's leading telecom companies: how to dial up new demand?

After years of steady expansion to 2012, Europe's leading telephone companies needed to find new growth strategies. But that was not proving so easy, as this case explains. We begin by looking at general trends and strategies around the world to provide the necessary strategic context. We then explore European markets in more depth.

World telecom markets

Over half the world's population now has a mobile phone: there were 4.7 billion customers in 2010. Two billion of these were added in the previous three years. World markets grew fast at around 20 per cent per year for the three years to 2010. However, much of this growth was in the developing world with European and North American markets growing more slowly. As a result, the world's largest markets were no longer in Europe - see Figure 11.3. In theory, European telecom companies could find further growth by expanding into developing country markets. In practice, this has proved difficult because of barriers to market entry.

Barriers to developing world telecommunication services

Although many mobiles can be used freely around the world, there have been no world markets from a company perspective until relatively recently. Individual national markets remain highly regulated by national governments. Typically, there are only a limited number of companies in each country with governments often favouring local national companies. However, new companies that offer the same service worldwide have begun in recent years, *Skype* being a well-known example. But such companies still represent a small part of the total business in most countries at the time of writing this case.

The barriers to entry have made it difficult for European telecom service companies to enter new markets. The main entry method has been to acquire an existing local company, but that is expensive: for example, Vodafone's acquisition of the Indian company Hutchison Essar cost at least $11.1 billion. Some of the European companies have therefore expanded mainly within their own European geographic area: there are some exceptions which are described later in this case. Because national markets are highly regulated, competition mainly focuses on price tariffs, geographic coverage and new models to attract

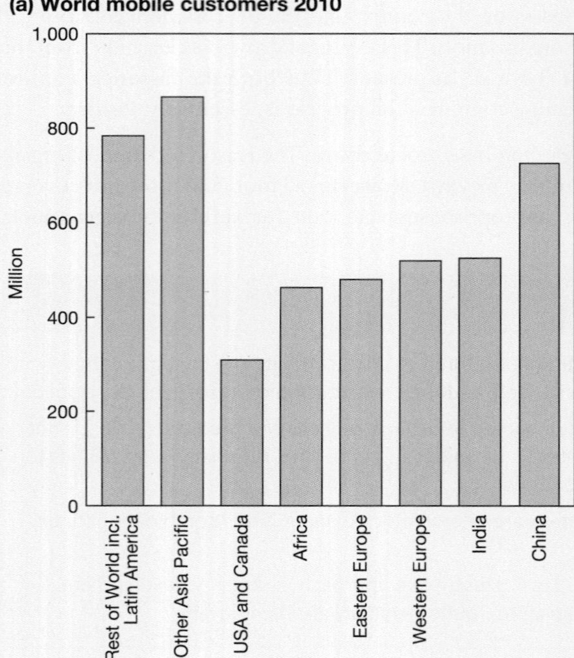

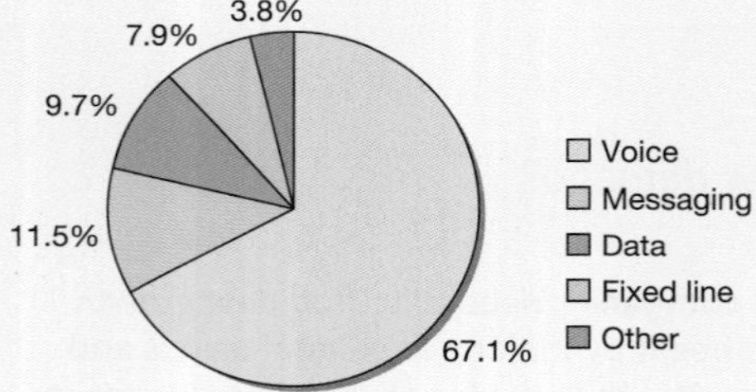

Figure 11.3 World's largest mobile telephone markets and service companies

Source: author from Vodafone annual report and accounts 2010.

European companies like the German market leader Deutsche Telekom - seen here in San Francisco, USA - have been expanding outside their home countries. The growth strategy has sometimes been at the expense of profit, as the case explains.

customers. Competitive advantage is limited to the brand names and the extent of coverage of an individual company.

World telecom growth areas

Despite the launch of smartphones which can access the internet, the majority of calls are still voice calls - see Figure 11.3. The mobile phone has now become the prime means of telephoning even in markets where the alternative - the fixed line - is also available. Nevertheless, data services are growing, especially in European and North American markets. But this growth is being offset by two problems for the telephone companies:

1 increased price competition from new entrants;
2 government regulation to drive down prices, especially by the European Union.

As a result of all these considerations, the European telecommunication companies faced some difficult strategic problems in 2010. How could they grow? The issue was particularly difficult because their growth record had been good for many years.

European telcos: the early years of plenty

Back in the 1980s and early 1990s, mobile telephones were heavy, chunky machines. They had no text messaging facility and no internet, not even a screen. But those were good years for Europe's leading telephone companies (the 'telcos' for short.) Most countries had a monopoly supplier of telephone services. The company owned and operated the fixed lines and a limited mobile service. The majority shareholder was often the national government itself. Profits were regulated externally but were attractive. But all this was about to change.

European telcos: privatisation and new technologies in the 1990s

Change came first from privatisation with the national companies being sold to the private sector and additional companies being encouraged to enter to provide competition and drive down prices. In addition, mobile phones became smaller, more reliable and with many more features, thus attracting more customers. Finally, new technologies in the form of new transmission frequencies and more advanced phones - the 3G phones - were introduced. This latter change had a serious impact on telco company profitability. Unfortunately for the companies, the new 3G licences were sold by national governments at highly inflated prices, thus putting extra profit pressures on the companies. However, the companies were still making good profits in the 2000s, especially as data demand was continuing to grow.

More regulation, more competition and maturing markets

By the late 2000s, pressures were increasing on the European telcos. The European Union introduced new regulations that forced down the price of calls when phones were used in Europe outside the home country: this had previously been a highly profitable source for the companies. New competitors emerged as companies like Skype and low-cost broadband providers began to establish themselves. In addition, European markets were beginning to slow down generally and a new round of '4G' licences was about to be announced.

In spite of all these pressures, it is perhaps surprising that the traditional European monopoly telecommunications companies were still amongst the largest in Europe when ranked by revenue - see Table 11.1. Some had managed to expand outside Europe. For example, Vodafone had purchased companies in Africa - see Case 2.4 - and India. Telefonica had acquired companies in Latin America and Deutsche Telekom had interests in North America. But some companies had also made mistakes in terms of overseas expansion. For example, British Telecom made several attempts to expand abroad by acquisition and alliances without success. Equally, Deutsche Telekom never made substantial profits on its North American operations, but at least the company obtained a good price when its North American subsidiary was sold in 2011.

Importantly, all these various pressures left many of the European telcos wondering about their future growth prospects. What strategies were now needed to grow? The answer from the leading companies was two-fold: first, consolidation into larger cross-border companies. Second, and more fundamentally, the leading companies were attempting to copy companies like BskyB in the UK: the companies were beginning to seeking to offer the new *triple play strategy* of the telephone, a television service and an internet broadband connection. For the traditional telephone companies, this has meant moving

Table 11.1 Selected European telephone companies

Company	Home country	Revenue 2010 ($ million)	Comment
Deutsche Telekom	Germany	92,000	Owns T-mobile but sold its US subsidiary 2011
Telefonica	Spain	88,800	Owns O2 mobile
Vodafone	UK	73,400	–
France Telecom	France	66,500	Owns Orange mobile
Telecom Italia	Italy	36,600	–
British Telecom	UK	34,500	Developed O2 mobile and then sold it to Telefonica

Source: author from company annual reports.

from a telephone service into television delivery via cable networks that also offer the other two services. At the time of writing, this strategy is still in its early stages.

All the leading telecommunications companies have policies in this area.

 This case was written by Richard Lynch from published data and his past experience as a consultant in the telecommunications industry.[7]

Case questions

1 Given the changes in technology and the declining market share of the existing telcos, what are the advantages and problems with adopting the classic prescriptive strategy process to develop strategies in this market?

2 Some strategists argue that it is useless to predict what will happen when technology is uncertain. What would be the consequences, if any, of following this advice in the European telecommunications market and not making any predictions? What implications does your answer have for a prescriptive strategy process that is built on the need to make predictions?

3 Can smaller companies attempting to find opportunities in this market also employ the prescriptive process? Or would they be better to use a process that is more radical and innovative to structure their approach? If so, do you have any suggestions on the process that might be employed?

11.2 THE SURVIVAL-BASED STRATEGIC ROUTE FORWARD

Definition ▶ **Survival-based theories of strategy regard the survival of the fittest in the competitive market place as being the prime determinant of strategy.** As the European mobile telephone market has grown, competition has increased. Companies have entered each other's markets on a limited basis and made the necessary investments. Markets have shown reasonable growth rates but are now beginning to mature. Hence, the sales increases from such growth are unlikely to satisfy the objectives of the major companies. Moreover, in spite of high levels of debt finance, some European telecom companies still wish to expand. One important conclusion that some strategists have therefore drawn about the European telephone industry is that by the year 2010 only five major global companies will remain: the rest will have been swallowed up in a shakeout of the industry. The contrast with the relative stability of the state monopoly companies of the 1980s and 1990s is striking. Survival-based strategy processes provide one explanation of the likely outcome after liberalisation.

11.2.1 The nature of survival-based strategies

Essentially, the survival-based process begins with the concept of *natural selection* first introduced in the nineteenth century by Charles Darwin to explain the development and survival of living creatures. He argued that survival was a constant battle against the environment. The species most likely to survive were those best suited and adapted to their surroundings. On this basis, adaptation to the environment is the main strategy that needs to be developed in a business context. Those that fail to change quickly enough will be the ones that select themselves for extinction.[8] The fittest companies survive because they are selected on the basis of the demand for their goods or services and the profits that they make.[9]

In the survival-based process there are two mechanisms in operation: adaptation to the environment and selection among those present for survival.

Using these two processes, together with principles and concepts from sociology, researchers have analysed the way that some industrial companies have developed.[10] They noted that, of the top 500 companies listed in *Fortune* magazine in 1955, only 268 were still listed in 1975: 46 per cent had disappeared, merged or otherwise declined over the 20-year period. They suggested that *adaptation to the environment* was the preferred mechanism for change in many companies because it was less painful than selection. This was influenced by a built-in inertia with regard to change in many industrial situations (see Exhibit 11.2).

Most strategy literature takes an *adaptive* perspective as its starting point in developing strategy options. Importantly, some survival-based strategists argue that this may not be sufficient. It may be necessary to add a *selection* perspective. There may come a time, precisely because of the inertia in the industry, when some organisations do not or cannot adapt quickly enough to the changes in the environment, and will not survive against the powerful forces ranged against them. Nevertheless, there may be an element of chance in selecting precisely who will disappear. For example, some European telephone companies may adapt to the changed environment of the new millennium, while others will change too slowly, and the pressures on them will be so great that they will not survive in their present form and will have to amalgamate with more efficient or luckier enterprises.

From a strategy *selection* perspective, the industry environment is the main determining factor of strategy development and survival. There is only a limited amount that individual companies can do in the time available before changes arrive. The only companies for which this may not apply are those that already have substantial market power and can influence the way their markets develop. However, even these may be overtaken by events – for example, in the case of European telecommunications, the advent of new communications technologies such as 3G mobile or the World Wide Web.

EXHIBIT 11.2

Examples of inertia towards change in company environments

Internal inertia

- Existing investment in plant and machinery
- Previous experience and history of the company

Example: in European telephone companies, the existing bureaucracy, which had been built up during many years in government ownership, was very difficult to shift.

External inertia

- Barriers to entry and exit from an industry
- Difficulty and cost of acquiring information on how the environment itself might be changing

Example: European telephone companies' existing investment in exchanges and telephone equipment, coupled with external government restrictions that would prevent new companies entering until 1998, had created an inertia towards change within the industry.

11.2.2 Consequences for the strategic management process

On this basis, strategic management has a limited ability, if any, to influence the environment. Moreover, an organisation may not be able to adapt quickly enough to change. In addition, the techniques recommended by the prescriptive process will be so well publicised that they will provide no competitive advantage to individual companies. As a result, and for those companies without real market power, Williamson[11] has recommended that the best strategy is to develop the most cost-effective operation possible, which he calls *economising*. He distinguishes this from new strategic moves beyond basic cost-effectiveness, which he calls *strategising*.

> I aver that, as between economizing and strategizing, economizing is much the more fundamental . . . A strategizing effort will only prevail if a program is burdened by significant cost excesses in production, distribution or organization. All the clever ploys and positioning, aye, all the king's horses and all the king's men, will rarely save a project that is seriously flawed in first-order economizing respects.[12]

What, therefore, can be done? Figure 11.4 summarises the main strategies that can be undertaken if this view of the strategy process is correct. It is clearly important to be cautious. It will also be necessary to seek clues from the environment on possible change and what is needed to survive. Finally, it will be useful to generate plenty of options so that whatever happens in the environment can be accommodated by the organisation.

Overall, if this view of the strategy process is correct, then the organisation is severely restricted in its strategies. Arguably, the way in which the European telephone companies have been building alliances and cross-shareholdings suggests that they cannot see the way ahead clearly and have chosen these mutually supportive strategies as the best protection.

Comment

This is a pessimistic view of the role of strategic management and the ability of organisations to shape their destiny. It rejects the insights offered by the prescriptive process but offers little alternative. It is useful in rapidly changing and turbulent environments, but offers only limited solutions in other circumstances.

Another strategic route forward: transaction cost economics (TCE). TCE is another strategic route forward related to survival-based strategy. Both routes emphasise the importance of low costs as a fundamental aspect of effective strategy development.

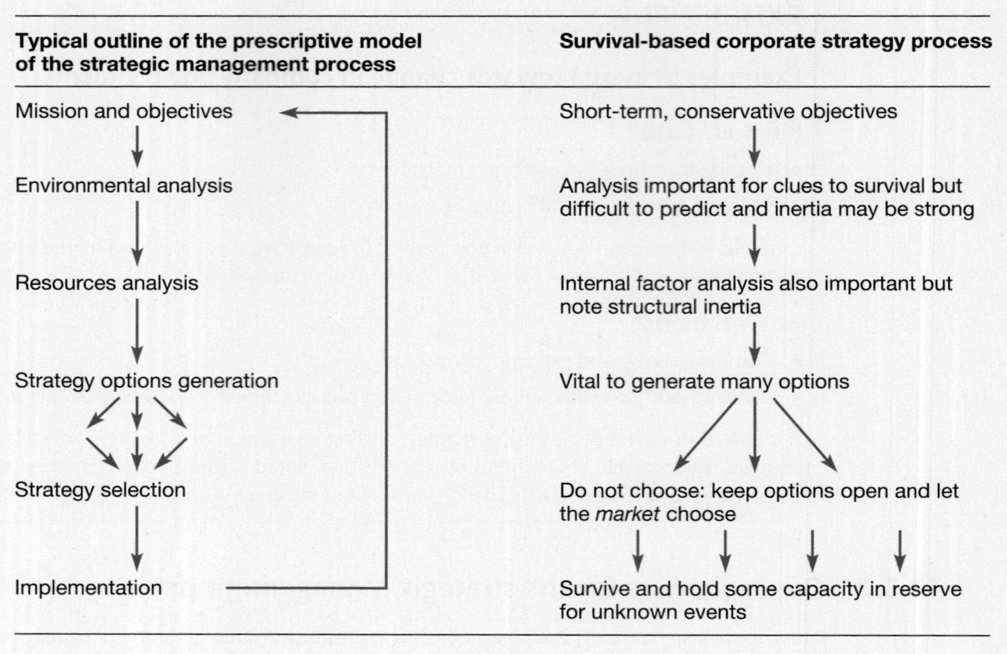

Figure 11.4 The survival-based strategy process compared with the prescriptive process

KEY STRATEGIC PRINCIPLES

- Survival-based strategies emphasise the importance of adapting strategies to meet changes in the environment. The ultimate objective is survival itself.
- The approach adopted is to develop options for use as the environment changes. Options that seek low costs are particularly useful.
- Beyond taking the precaution of developing strategic options, there is little that the individual organisation can do. There is an element of chance in whether it will survive or not.

11.3 THE UNCERTAINTY-BASED STRATEGIC ROUTE FORWARD

Definition ▶ **Uncertainty-based theories of strategy regard a prescriptive, defined strategy as being impossible to develop because the strategic process is unpredictable, unstable and liable to chaotic outcomes.** According to uncertainty-based strategists, Europe's telephone companies are wasting their time developing corporate strategies to cope with the events of the new millennium. They would argue that the environment is too uncertain and the outcomes largely unknown. Even striving for survival-based efficiency is useless. To understand the reasoning behind this, we need to examine the origins and thinking behind this approach.

11.3.1 Rationale

The key to understanding this route forward is its assumption about the purposes of most organisations: success will come from the ability of an organisation to survive by *innovating* and *transforming* itself.[13] Uncertainty-based strategists argue that it is not enough for most organisations simply to co-exist with others. In today's rapidly changing world, renewal and transformation towards new directions are key tasks for strategic management. To paraphrase the title of the strategy director at the mobile telephone company Orange, strategy is at least partially about 'imagineering and futurology' in an unknown world.[14]

Given this definition of success, the strategic process by which this is achieved will inevitably involve uncertainty. However, uncertainty can be modelled mathematically and its consequences set out in the science of *chaos theory*[15] – a system of modelling originally applied to scientific processes such as flow of liquid through a tube and subsequently to weather forecasting. The theory demonstrates that, in certain types of uncertain environment, *small* changes in the early stages of a process can lead to *major* variances in the later stages. This is not unlike the multiplier effect in macroeconomics.

In the classic strategy process, there is a mechanism of cause and effect that controls the dynamics of change. *Feedback* arises from an initial strategic decision, but goes *beyond* such a decision by multiplying its effects. *Uncertainty* is the unknown result of a strategic decision which may be affected by chance events along with those that are more predictable.

An example will help to clarify the concept. When the price of an item such as a telephone call is raised relative to competing products, the sales of the item are predicted to fall. According to uncertainty-based theory, this simple process may not represent the *full* outcome of events. The *feedback mechanism* suggests that the rise in telephone prices may not only affect sales but may also feed back into a lower level of loading at the telephone exchange. This may in turn influence the ability of the company to recover overheads from the exchange. Thus, the exchange loading, overheads and overall profitability may all be influenced by the one pricing decision. As soon as these items are affected adversely, there may be some attempt to recover profitability by a *further* price increase, i.e. the initial problem has fed back on itself. This will have a deleterious effect on the organisation, and so is usually referred to as *negative feedback*.

Conversely, in the above example, a reduction in price might have the opposite effect. It might cause profitability to rise more than the initial move in pricing, as a result of other consequences in the organisation. This is called *positive feedback*.

Uncertainty theory then adds another possibility. It can be proved mathematically that, where positive and negative feedback mechanisms operate, the system can *flip* between the positive and negative states. Importantly, it is not possible to predict in advance which of these three outcomes – that is, positive, negative or flip – will occur. The long-term consequences are therefore unknown and cannot be foreseen.

11.3.2 Consequences for the strategic management process

Uncertainty-based strategists argue that there is little to be gained by predicting the future, because virtually all strategy is composed of feedback mechanisms and involves uncertainty; therefore the outcome cannot be predicted. If the future is unknown, the effects of long-term strategic actions will also be unknown and the classical prescriptive process has little meaning.

This does not mean that uncertainty-based strategists believe that nothing can be done. They take the view, however, that actions should be much shorter-term in nature. Organisations must be able to learn and adapt to changed circumstances. Thus workers and managers in organisations are capable of assessing the results of their actions – in the example above, the effects of raising or lowering the price of telephone calls. They are also capable of learning to adapt to the consequences. More generally, for strategy purposes, they are capable of experimenting and innovating in the organisation and assessing the results of their work.

The implications of such theories are profound for strategic management. The majority of organisations need to innovate in order to survive and they exist in the increasingly turbulent world of the early twenty-first century, and yet uncertainty-based strategists would suggest that it is not possible to predict how innovation will succeed in the long term. According to these strategists, however, new ideas and new directions are necessary to survival and growth and should be pursued using the learning mechanisms mentioned above in order to refine and adapt strategies to a rapidly changing environment.

As an example of uncertainty-based strategy in action, you might like to consider the consequences of the launch of Sky television by News Corporation in 1990 and its later dominance of digital television broadcasting in the UK – see Case 8.4. Such an outcome was clearly impossible to predict at the time of the launch. According to the uncertainty-based theorists, strategic management based on, for example, a prescriptive approach would have been largely irrelevant in these circumstances.

For the uncertainty-based strategist, long-term strategy is a contradiction in terms. The only possible objectives are short-term, possibly with a strong innovative content.[16] There is no point in undertaking environmental analysis because it is essentially unpredictable, but it is useful to understand the organisation's resources in order to assess their contribution to the innovative process. As for strategy options and selection, this has no relevance to the strategy process that actually occurs. What is important is the way the company is organised to learn and respond to its changing environment: loose, informal networks of managers are required, rather than rigid functional divisions. Exhibit 11.3 presents some of the implications suggested by Stacey.[17]

Overall, there is no clear flow process, unlike in prescriptive strategy – only constant monitoring of the environment in order to take advantage of opportunities that occur. Figure 11.5 makes a comparison between the prescriptive and uncertainty-based processes.

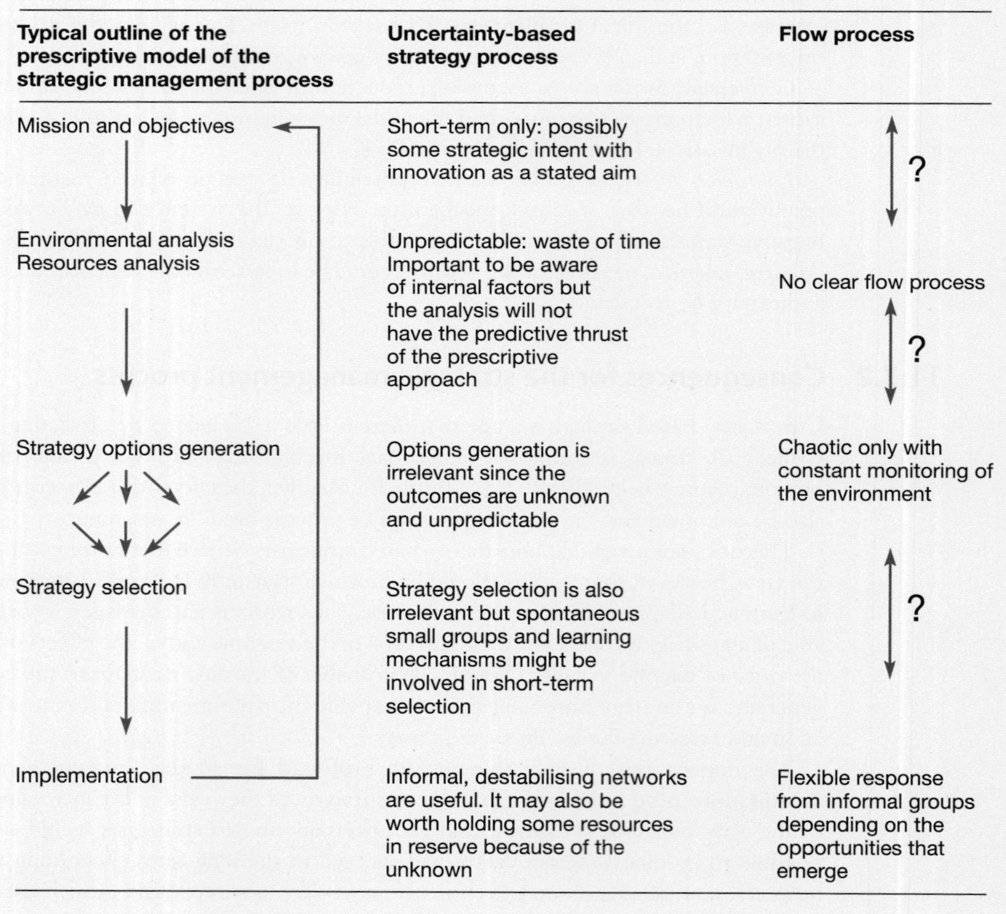

Figure 11.5 Comparison of the uncertainty-based strategic route with the prescriptive process

EXHIBIT 11.3

Some practical implications of uncertainty for the strategic management process

Basic objectives: develop new strategic directions and innovate.

Eight actions consistent with the uncertainty-based approach are:

1 Loosen control – let things happen.
2 Reconfigure power in groups to make them less competitive and more co-operative.
3 Allow groups to develop and set their own challenges, objectives and processes.
4 Encourage new organisational cultures in order to develop new perspectives.
5 Set open challenges ('Develop a new initiative in . . .') rather than defined objectives ('Your job is to double our profits in . . .').
6 Expose the business to demanding and challenging situations.
7 Spend time and resources developing the learning skills of groups in the organisation.
8 Develop time and space for managers to experiment.

Comment

The approach may be useful when market conditions are turbulent, but it has few insights into some of the areas of strategic decision making, such as the short-term pressure to deliver profits or service. However, the approach is still in its early stages of development.

KEY STRATEGIC PRINCIPLES

- Renewal and transformation are vital aspects of strategy. Inevitably, they will involve uncertainty. Such uncertainty can be modelled mathematically. However, the long-term consequences are unknown and cannot be foreseen or usefully predicted.
- Uncertainty-based approaches therefore involve taking small steps forward. Management needs to learn from such actions and adapt accordingly.
- Because of the uncertainty about the future, strategy options and selection between them using the prescriptive approach are therefore irrelevant.

CASE STUDY 11.3

Buying travel online: choosing a strategy for the internet age

Internet technology is revolutionising the $100 billion global market for travel booking. This case explores the changes and the uncertainty. It raises the question of which strategic route to choose when developing a strategy, especially for smaller travel companies.

Travel agencies and package tours

For much of the past 50 years, many travellers have used independent travel agencies to book their tickets and accommodation for national and international travel. Such agencies have the relevant networks and contacts with the hotels, airlines, rail operators, car hire agencies and other companies engaged in providing travel services. They are knowledgeable in the complicated arrangements required and can take the pain out of booking a two-week holiday or a week-long business trip. Travel agents are located in town shopping centres or at the end of a telephone. More recently, they are available online through the internet.

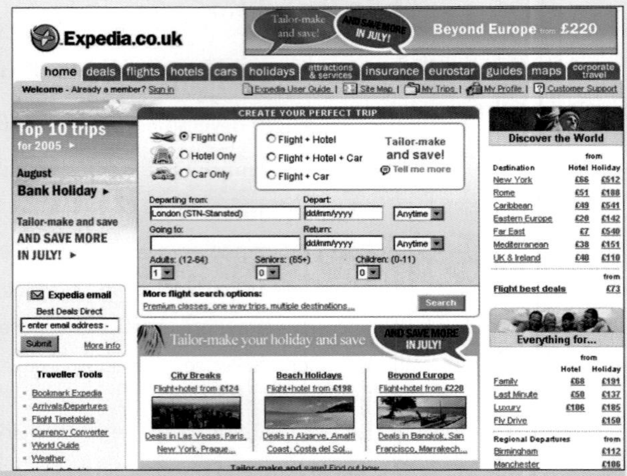

Whether you are travelling to the Taj Mahal in India, Hurrah's Casino in Las Vegas, USA or the Pudong area of Shanghai, China (pictured), internet online booking opens up the possibilities.
www.expedia.co.uk

In North America, travel agencies are largely independent of the companies offering particular aspects of the travel itinerary – air tickets, hotels, etc. In Asia, Africa and the Middle East, travel agencies are also largely independent. However, travel agencies in Europe are often connected with a particular travel organisation offering the complete holiday package covering flights, transfers, hotels and other activities – this approach is often called the 'package tour'. The package tour is particularly popular in some European countries like the UK and Germany. It is also important in China and Japan. Major European travel companies – like Thomas Cook, My Travel and Kuoni – were built on such business.

Even today, package tour companies are big business because they offer good value for money, especially where clients just want a single-location holiday destination. For example, package trips accounted for around 43 per cent of all booked holidays in 2012 in the UK. However, this figure was down from 54 per cent in 1998. This suggests that independent travel is growing, but it has not reached the levels of North America, where it accounts for 80 per cent of the business. Part of the reason for this higher percentage is that more North Americans holiday in their home countries: domestic travellers are more confident about booking independently than those who take holidays in new countries with different languages, laws and travel facilities.

Package tour operators across Europe expect package holidays to survive over the next few years but they will need to adapt their products – offering holidays that are complicated for individuals to organise, all-inclusive of children's activities, accompanied by comprehensive travel insurance and guaranteed hotel quality, perhaps through the operator owning the hotel. Such measures will provide protection against the advance of those booking independent holidays and it is this group that remains the major focus of internet travel booking.

Independent travellers and the internet

For independent travellers – perhaps on short-break destinations, perhaps on long-distance business travel, perhaps backpacking around the world – individual journey plans are often required. However, it does not follow that individual travellers will immediately turn to the internet – the STA student travel agency and Trailfinders are examples of travel agents offering individually tailored travel itineraries. Travel agencies, telephone bookings and postal bookings still account for the majority of such activity. For example in the UK in 2009, it has been estimated that bookings via the internet accounted for 40 per cent of the total spent by the independent traveller. But the figure was growing and was expected to be over 50 per cent of the total within two years. The figures were slightly lower in Germany, but in Scandinavia internet usage was much the same as in the UK. In France, a simplified form of online booking has been operated for many years – the French Minitel service – but this is now being replaced by internet web-based services.

In North America, internet booking already accounts for around 50 per cent of all bookings, but this depends on good internet access. For countries without widely available private, individual internet access – such as parts of Africa, China and India – travel agencies were still the main method of making travel arrangements. In spite of such barriers, however, the internet has become a significant source of booking for such travel services around the world. Although internet booking only began about 15 years ago, it was estimated in 2009 to account for \$20–30 billion worth of travel bookings every year around the world.

In a sense, there is nothing new in travel booking using telecommunications. Travel agencies have been using direct telephone links to central computers to book airline tickets

EXHIBIT 11.4

Some internet travel companies

All the main hotels, airlines and train companies operate internet booking sites: these are not listed here.

(GDS is short for Global Distribution System – see text.)

Parent company	Internet travel company	Internet subsidiary of travel company	Comment
Sabre Inc	Travelocity.com IgoUgo.com LastMinute.com Sabre GDS	Travelchannel.de and other related sites Travelocity also powers the search on Yahoo! Travel	Blocks metasearch Sabre is a private company
Travelport GDS	Galileo Worldspan	Sprice: French metasearch company acquired in 2010	Private company – failed IPO in 2010
Orbitz Worldwide	Orbitz ebookers.com CheapTickets HotelClub RatesToGo AwayNetwork		Spun off from Travelport in 2007
Amadeus GDS	Amadeus reservation system		Publicly quoted company, floated 2010
Opodo GDS	Airline reservation system		Acquired by Axa Private Equity and Permira in 2011 for €450 million
Expedia Inc	Expedia.com Hotels.com Hotwire.com Venere.com TripAdvisor.com	TripAdvisor subsidiaries include: CruiseCritic.com BookingBuddy.com SmarterTravel.com SeatGuru.com AirFareWatchdog.com IndependentTraveler.com	
Metasearch companies	Skyscanner Kayak.com mobissimo		

Source: see references for case.

online for at least 20 years. What has changed in the last ten years is that the internet has allowed such linkages to take place at the level of *individual* customers: the travel agencies have been cut out of the value chain. In addition, computer software has been developed to allow such access to be handled easily by individual travellers. Internet booking began with airline ticketing but has now extended into car hire, hotel booking and other aspects of travel service. In 2012, internet booking accounted for 60 per cent of all travel bookings and was still growing. For example, internet booking now accounts for over 95 per cent of the travel business of the budget airlines like Ryanair and easyJet. Travel companies therefore need a strategy to cope with this opportunity.

Internet travel market – online booking

With a large and growing internet travel booking market, it is difficult to gain a complete picture of the various services and booking agencies that are available. Moreover, they are in continual change and development as this case is being written. Exhibit 11.4 attempts to set out some of the leading internet players in 2011, but the picture will almost certainly have changed subsequently. In order to provide some focus to internet activity, it is useful to divide the internet travel service providers into three broad categories: primary providers, online travel agencies and metasearch travel websites. Each of these has different methods of operating – see Exhibit 11.5.

EXHIBIT 11.5

The main providers of internet online travel services

- *Primary providers.* These include the main airlines, the budget airlines, the main hotel chains, the main car rental companies and the main rail companies. It is time-consuming for individuals to search each of these internet sites for prices, availability and special deals. However, some of the leaders buy headline space on the main internet search engines like Yahoo and Google.
- *Online travel agencies.* These include those that offer a wide range of travel services – like Expedia, Travelocity and Orbitz – and those that have been primarily driven by a specialist sector like Opodo, which was set up by the airlines to sell travel tickets (but now also offers hotels and car hire through internet links). Some of the leading companies are shown in Exhibit 11.4.
- *Metasearch travel websites.* These are relatively new and use sophisticated search engine technology to trawl across all available prices and make price comparisons. Some of these are listed in Exhibit 11.4. Some main brand name hotel and travel sites block metasearch activity. The metasearch activity is called 'scraping' for obvious reasons.

Profits from internet travel

Hotel chains like Accor, Peninsula Hotels and InterContinental Hotels sell spare rooms at discount prices to the online internet travel agencies – like Expedia and Travelocity. These room prices are then raised by 30 per cent by the online agency and the rooms offered to the individual traveller. In one sense, the hotel operator is losing profits but, if the hotel room would otherwise be empty, then any revenue is useful extra business. This is called *yield management* in the hotel business. However, the hotel companies are now beginning to realise that they may be able to claw back the profit passed on to the travel agencies by offering rooms through their own websites and bypassing the agencies.

For example, the InterContinental Hotel chain has developed several internet strategies to counter the effect of the online travel agencies. In 2002, it began offering the lowest guaranteed prices on the internet for its rooms. It also started asking for significant sums from operators who wanted to use the InterContinental brand names – which also cover Crowne Plaza and Holiday Inn in the USA – on their websites. InterContinental has also registered apparently independent travel-sounding internet agency names that in practice direct the searcher to the hotel group. Finally, the company began registering foreign language websites – German, French, Spanish, Japanese, Chinese, amongst others – with the aim of making it easy for travellers in those countries to book with InterContinental. Other hotel groups like the world's largest hotel group – Accor, with brand names like Sofitel and Novotel – now also guarantee that prices offered directly on their websites are the lowest available. Such activities protect profit margins but provide no competitive advantage between rival hotel chains.

The large international airlines like American, British Airways and Air France/KLM sell tickets directly, if possible. Again the purpose is to cut out any profit margin that would be taken by the online travel agencies. However, in addition to developing their own websites, some airlines jointly work with websites like Opodo and Amadeus. Such websites are called Global Distribution Systems (GDS) and earn their profit by charging a percentage booking fee in addition to the ticket price. Airlines are also operating the sophisticated computer pricing software used by the budget airlines – see below.

For the budget airlines like Ryanair and easyJet, there is a strong desire to keep costs to a minimum and therefore such companies only offer seats on their own websites. However, they have a sophisticated computer pricing mechanism that alters the seat prices on a daily, even hourly, basis as and when the aircraft fills up. It pays independent travellers to book early with such airlines, but not all travellers have the flexibility to make early choices.

Metasearch internet sites operate in a different way. They generate revenue by collecting a small commission when they direct traffic to a hotel or travel website. In addition, they make – or at least hope to make – much higher profits from sales of sponsored links from hotel chains and internet travel agencies on their websites.

All this suggests that the profits from internet operations depend on the nature of the business involved:

- *For the primary providers* like hotels and airlines, the opportunity to fill empty hotel rooms or airline seats provides one source of profitability. There is a particular benefit if travellers book directly with the provider since the profit is then retained by the provider rather than passed on to a travel agent.
- *For the online travel agencies*, the profit comes from charging a margin beyond the basic cost of the travel service. Such margins can be quite small – not always the 20–30 per cent quoted earlier.
- *For the metasearch travel companies*, the profit margins are very small from each actual transaction but can be significant from sponsored advertising on the site. In addition, the high volume of searches – even at a low profit per search – will generate significant profits in total.

Internet travel opportunities for smaller companies

What about new companies thinking of setting up travel websites? The cost of registering and maintaining a new internet website is actually quite small. But this is not the key to internet travel strategy. The real success is attracting enough customers to be able to generate sufficient business. The chief executive officer of Lastminute.com, Brent Hoberman explains: 'This is a scale game and you're always facing global competition. I've always said that you need £1 billion ($1.9 billion) of bookings to be able to carry the right amount of technology, marketing and branding spend.' However, Hoberman would be the first to acknowledge that his own company is young and began only a few years ago with nothing like $1 billion of business.

Moreover, the internet offers three great advantages in the travel business. The first is that the fixed costs of operation in the early days of a small internet travel business are quite small - despite the comments of Brent Hoberman above. There are no expensive office premises, no major colour printing and brochure costs, direct contact with potential customers, etc. Such arrangements are ideally suited to small business start-ups. For this reason, many small travel companies are beginning to develop, especially those specialising in particular types of holiday - exclusive chalet skiing holidays, specialist adventure travel holidays and so on.

The second great benefit of the internet is the wide, *even global*, reach of the internet. This makes it much easier for a small business in a specialist area to find sufficient clients for a profitable operation by offering its services across national boundaries.

The third benefit is that business activities can be monitored constantly and changes in pricing, packaging and other services automated to reflect traffic flows. For example, seat prices on Ryanair and easyJet budget airlines are adjusted using computer modelling from constant monitoring of internet booking.

The internet has opened up the new opportunities, but what strategy process should small businesses adopt?

 This case was written from published information only.[18] The author is grateful to Pat Wood of London Metropolitan University for her comments on an earlier draft of this case. He is also grateful to Alison Bell of Trinity College Dublin for new information and guidance for the 2012 version of this case.

Case questions

1 If you were moving into the market for internet travel as a small company, which, if any, of the five routes described in this chapter would you employ? You can also consider the use of classic prescriptive strategy if you wish.

2 Are there any strategic routes that you would definitely not employ as a small company? Why?

3 If you were an established internet provider, which strategic routes would you select to develop your presence further? Why? Give examples of current practice where possible.

4 How will the internet impact on travel in the future? Would it be more beneficial to use emergent strategies - if so, which strategies and how should they be used?

STRATEGIC PROJECT

There are so many opportunities for both large and small companies that internet online strategy presents a most interesting challenge. Research opportunities exist because of the worldwide accessibility of the web in terms of pricing, product, presentation and market positioning. One approach would be to start with the companies identified in the case and explore how they have developed. Another approach would be to take an area of travel - for example, adventure travel or cruise liners - and explore their use of the internet and possible future strategies. Another approach would be to consider likely future changes in the internet - text messaging, mobile telephone booking, more sophisticated presentation technology, etc. - and explore their impact on travel company strategy.

11.4 THE NETWORK-BASED STRATEGIC ROUTE FORWARD

Definition ▶ **The network-based strategic route forward explores the links and degree of co-operation present in related organisations and industries and places a value upon that degree of co-operation.** There are two major aspects of networks from a strategy perspective covered in this section: network externalities and network co-operation. In order to understand these, it is useful to explore the online travel case from these two perspectives.

Network externalities[19]

Definition ▶ **Network externalities arise when an organisation is part of an external network that is seeking to standardise some aspect of operations across an industry.** Benefits arise for all those in the network when the standardisation has been achieved and they will increase as more organisations adopt the standard. The benefit is *external* to an individual organisation in the network. For example in Case 11.3, the network of travel agents will benefit from a standardised network of ticketing by the airline companies: this makes it easier for travel agents to book tickets and for airline companies to fill their aircraft. The outcome of such a network might be an agreement on a standard for the information required to book a ticket. This represents a real benefit to those taking part in the agreement because it allows those that are part of the network to develop new ticketing services based on the standard. Such an agreed standard may result in shared development costs and perhaps even economies of scale in network development. If others join the network and adopt the standard, then all the existing members of the network will benefit even further. We explore this relatively new aspect of strategy development in Section 11.4.1.

Network co-operation

Definition ► **Network co-operation arises when companies engage in formal and informal agreements with each other for their mutual benefit.** For example, even after some travel companies began to develop co-operative networks, it was important from a strategy perspective to see this as only the beginning of a new phase in world industry alliances and consolidation. Further developments will involve negotiation between companies like Expedia and others involved in the travel industry. The purpose will be to extract the full added value from the various moves towards consolidation and develop other forms of co-operation, while at the same time developing the sustainable competitive advantage of a company like Expedia. We have previously explored some aspects of this in Chapter 5 in our analysis of co-operation. However, we are now seeking new strategies, so it is important to return to this network co-operation at this point. This is examined further in Section 11.4.2.

11.4.1 Network externalities[20]

Definition ► **Network externalities refer to the development of an overall standard for a network that allows those belonging to the network to benefit increasingly as others join the same network.** It is called an *externality* because the concept is driven not by an activity internal to the company but by the external membership of all that belong to the network. Probably the best-known example of an industry *network externality* is that owned by Microsoft: its Windows operating system is used in 90 per cent of all personal computers around the world. Those using this computer system gain increased benefits because many other users also use the same system. In other words, *the value of the system is enhanced because it can be shared with others who are part of the same external network.*

Importantly, the network has a benefit as the total number of users increases and reaches a critical mass of users – this is sometimes called the '*tipping point*'. Essentially, the tipping point is reached when the installed base of network users moves towards one company supplying the network and away from rival suppliers. This is quite different from the normal microeconomic concepts of supply and demand, which assume that the sale and price of each product or service is independent of other purchases. Under network externalities, the more of one product that is purchased, the more valuable it becomes.

Comment

Although this is a useful concept, it applies mainly to organisations that have a high and formal co-operative content, for example the need for consumer electronics companies to agree a common standard for DVD players – see Case 5.3. Once the standard has been agreed, there will usually be some winners and losers, but strategy then needs to move on to its many other dimensions. In other words, network externalities have a role, but they will often apply only once in the technological lifetime of a product and will have more limited relevance where a single technology standard is less important in strategy development.

11.4.2 Network co-operation

Definition ► **Network co-operation refers to the value-adding relationships that organisations develop *inside* their own organisation and *outside* it with other organisations.** For example, European telecommunications companies have their own telephone exchange resources and employees that generate profits. In addition, they compete with each other in some national European telephone markets while, at the same time, developing co-operative linkages with other telephone companies in global markets. It is this complex web of internal and external activities that constitutes the network and delivers added value to the organisation.

From a strategic perspective, the issue is how to optimise the value added from such internal and external activities. As a starting point, we can refer to the two principles explored in Chapter 4:

1 *The benefits of owning and managing resources, rather than buying them in from outside.*[21] This can be used to identify the important relationships that organisations have both inside and outside their own organisation.

2 *The value chain and value linkages.*[22] The chain provides a picture of networks inside the organisation and the linkages do the same for the outside relationships.

In order to develop network-based strategy, these general principles need to be used to map out the networks that exist in and with every organisation. A largely prescriptive approach to this task is shown in Exhibit 11.6.

As a result of optimising value added, network co-operation also influences sustainable competitive advantage. For example, at the European telephone companies, those with superior value-added activities, based on an attractive combination of keen prices and high-quality service, are also likely to be able to compete strongly with competitors: high profits are likely to be associated with sustainable competitive advantage. However, such a combination of price and service will probably also derive, at least in part, from the valuable co-operative linkages that such superior companies have with others.

In more general economic terms, the 'invisible hand' of market competition should drive companies to greater efficiency in the use of their internal resources. At the same time, the 'visible hand' of co-operative linkages will generate real, and perhaps unique, external networks and value for organisations. In a sense, networks rely both on invisible and visible guidance in the generation and maintenance of relationships – a relationship more like a 'continuous handshake' than an intermittent hand clasp.[23]

Thus in network co-operation strategy, value is added and competitive advantage is developed by the precise *combination* of competition and co-operation that organisations have with others. As a result, organisations will construct a unique network of relationships both inside and outside their own organisation. For example, over time salespeople may strike up relationships with customers, purchasing managers with suppliers and so on. Long-term relationships with outsiders may be a crucial element of the company's strategy, as those in the aerospace, defence, telecommunications equipment and other industries negotiating with government will quickly confirm.

EXHIBIT 11.6

How networks can add value to the organisation

From *internal networks*, value added can be increased by:

- economies of scale and scope;
- development of superior, even unique, knowledge and technologies;
- investment in customer service, marketing and reputation;
- skills, knowledge and expertise in cash handling, financial transactions and other financial instruments.

From *external networks*, value added can be increased by:

- cost-effective logistics, stock handling and other outside transport facilities;
- superior purchasing from suppliers;
- skilled external sourcing of new technical developments, licensing of new technologies and other technical advances;
- strong and stable relationships with government and other influential organisations.

Note: These are only examples of the many networks that exist in and between organisations.

Negotiation is a vital strategic aspect of such relationships and the process becomes effectively one of the key determinants of success. Thus, for example, in the case of mobile telephones, governments may well be involved in the purchase or specification of such items. More generally, direct government control may be achieved by access to preferential credit, joint ownership, a threat to call in new suppliers, the allocation of R&D contracts and assistance in export sales.[24] Developing strategic management without negotiating with a government may be an expensive luxury. The bargaining power that each side has in such negotiations will depend on the maturity of the market and the technology involved.

In many respects, therefore, the organisation can be seen as a *network of treaties* both outside and inside the company.[25] Moreover, if such agreements are important for the development of strategy, then it follows that it is important to understand the dynamics of these networks in order to develop optimal strategy.[26] Because of the sheer complexity of this task, it may be better to use critical success factors to focus attention on the important areas of the process (see Chapter 3).

Comment

Some strategists argue that what matters is not the *combination* of competitive and co-operative networks but the *primacy* of one or the other:

- either competitive relationships are paramount: 'The essence of strategy formulation is coping with competition', according to Michael Porter;[27]
- or co-operative networks represent the main scope for strategic development: 'The realisation is growing that cooperative behaviour is at the root of many success stories in today's management', to quote J Carlos Jarillo.[28]

Such a choice is profoundly misleading.[29] All organisations both compete and co-operate and there is no 'strategic paradox' between these two that needs to be resolved. The only issue is the *balance* between the two. This will depend on the context within which the strategy is being developed. For example, in the European telephone companies in the late 1990s, *competition* was the main driving force. It was increasing inside countries like the UK and Germany, though co-operation was also important in providing international telephone networks. By contrast, in the European defence industry in the late 1990s, increased *co-operation* was being developed on a pan-European basis in order to allow European companies to compete more successfully in the global market place against the big US defence companies.

11.4.3 Consequences of all these aspects for strategic management

Essentially, networks are fluid and may change. Members of such networks can often leave without cost. In this sense, nothing is fixed and everything is open to negotiation. Therefore, objectives may need to be revised and selection may be compromised by the need to persuade groups to join or remain in the network. In a sense, the implementation process itself is now part of the selection process and part of the strategy.

Figure 11.6 illustrates the major implications of such a network-based route forward. It should be noted that the timetable for any strategic change may need to be lengthened to accommodate this process. It is not possible to show this adequately in the table.

Comment

There can be little doubt that networks are a part of many organisations, both large and small. However, there is still a need to drive the strategy process forward. This is where *leadership* is probably vital. Network-based strategies are unlikely to represent a complete route in themselves, but need to take place alongside prescriptive and learning-based strategy processes.

Another strategic route forward: agency theory. Agency theory is founded on similar principles to network-based theory. However, agency theory focuses on the relationships between different people involved in strategy rather than the broader communication networks of the network-based strategic route forward.

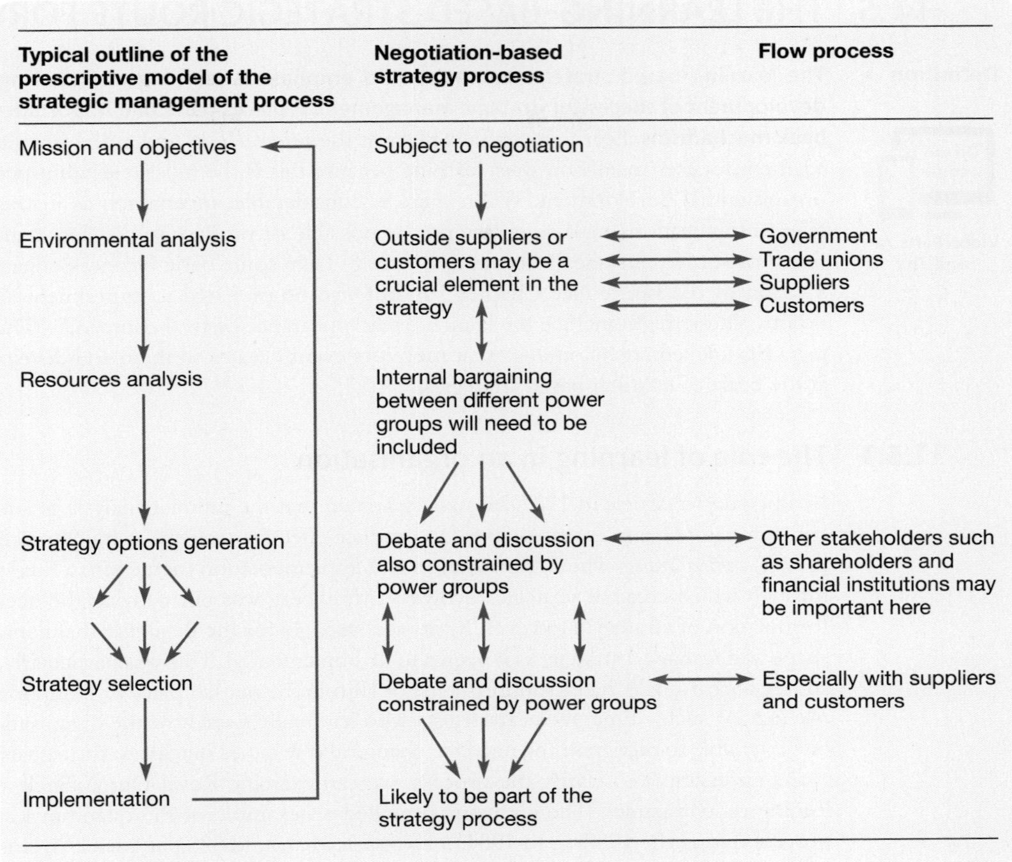

Figure 11.6 Comparison of the network-based process with the prescriptive process

KEY STRATEGIC PRINCIPLES

- *The network-based strategic route forward* explores the links and degree of co-operation present in related organisations and industries and places a value upon that degree of co-operation. The route has two aspects – network externalities and network co-operation.
- Network externalities refer to the development of an overall standard for a network that allows those belonging to the network to benefit increasingly as others join the same network.
- In such externalities, the key moment is the 'tipping point', which is reached when the installed base of network users moves towards one company supplying the network and away from rival suppliers.
- Network co-operation explores the links and degree of co-operation present in related organisations and industries and places a value upon that degree of co-operation.
- In network co-operation strategy, value is added and competitive advantage is developed by the precise *combination* of competition and co-operation that organisations have with others. Such a strategic approach also needs to be seen in the context of negotiations with powerful customers and suppliers where bargaining and trade-offs will take place.

11.5 THE LEARNING-BASED STRATEGIC ROUTE FORWARD

Definition ▶

Video Parts 7a and 7b

The learning-based strategic route forward emphasises learning and crafting as aspects of the development of successful strategic management. It places particular importance on trial and feedback mechanisms. Learning can take place at the *personal* level and at the *group* level: strategic management focuses mainly on *group* learning because this is the most relevant aspect in the context of organisational development. When there is considerable uncertainty, as in the European mobile telecommunications market, it may not be possible or prudent to develop a strategy that is firmly fixed for some years ahead. It may be better to have some basic business objectives, possibly even a vision of the future (see Chapter 10), but also be prepared to experiment and react to market events. These might include the launch or disappearance of rival companies. The process of adopting a flexible, emergent strategy that monitors events, reacts to them and develops opportunities is at the heart of learning-based strategies.

11.5.1 The role of learning in an organisation

In a persuasive article in 1987, Mintzberg argued that the rational analysis of such areas as markets and company resources was unlikely to produce effective strategy. A much more likely process was that of *crafting strategy* where 'formulation and implementation merge into a fluid process of learning through which creative strategies evolve'.[30] Mintzberg was not denying the need for planning and formulation of strategy. However, he argued strongly for the flexibility that comes from learning to shape and reshape a strategy as it begins to be implemented. This was particularly important because strategy occasionally had to address a major shift in the market place or in internal practice – a *quantum leap*. At such a time, those strategists who had really *learnt* how the organisation operated would be better able to recognise the need for change and respond quickly to the signals of the major shift.

As an example to clarify the process, we can examine Royal Dutch/Shell, one of the world's leading oil companies. The company provided an example of the quantum leap and the learning process during the 1980s.[31] In 1984, oil was priced around $28 per barrel. Against this background, the company's central planning department developed a speculative scenario based on the price dropping to $16 per barrel. Purely as an exercise, they urged senior management to speculate on the consequences of such a radical price drop. Some senior managers felt it was unlikely but were willing to enter into the spirit of the exercise. The consequences were explored well enough so that, when the price actually dropped to $10 per barrel in 1987, the company was well prepared.

One of Royal Dutch/Shell's leading planners later concluded:

> Institutional learning is the process whereby management teams change their shared mental models of their company, their markets and their competitors. For this reason, we think of planning as learning and of corporate planning as institutional learning.

The key words here are *change their shared mental models* and the process of *learning*. Most companies explore strategic issues not just as individuals but also as a management team or group that meets together. It is this *group* that develops assumptions about the company and its environment: these need to be made explicit and shared. These may then need to be changed, depending on the circumstances – for example, a quantum leap as mentioned above.

11.5.2 The relationship of learning with knowledge – the contributions of Argyris and Garvin

Learning may be seen as the process of expanding the knowledge of the organisation. It involves a *loop* of activity consisting of acquiring new knowledge, checking this against reality and then feeding back the result – for example, reading the room temperature on a thermostat, checking the room temperature to ensure comfort and adjusting the thermostat if required. The learning process may involve study, tuition and practical experience. In the complex world of business and not-for-profit organisations, learning will involve all three mechanisms and thus become complex.

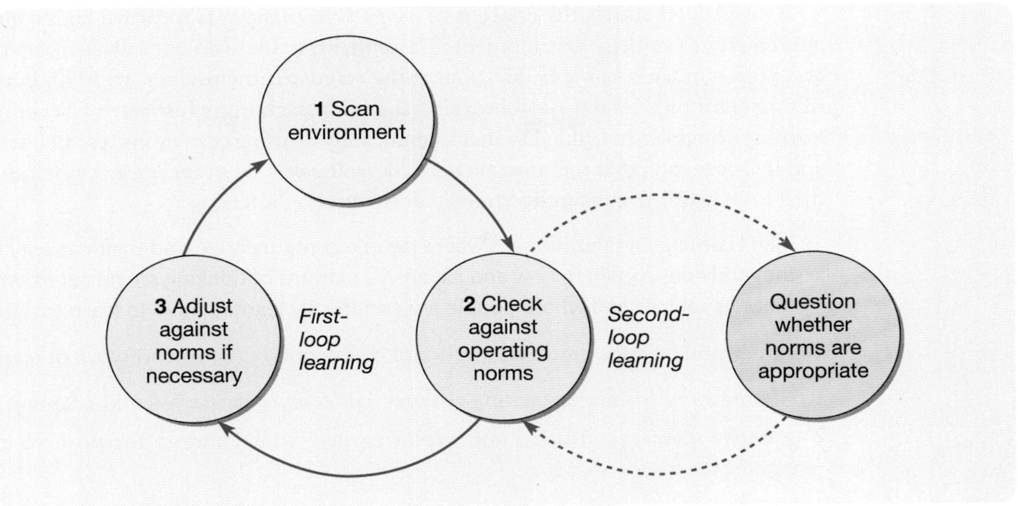

Figure 11.7 Double-loop learning

For organisations, learning has a further degree of difficulty because periodically it needs to embrace a fundamental review of the organisation's purpose and objectives. This will involve the managers of the organisation asking difficult questions and will place demands on them that go beyond mere data gathering and checking against reality. It was Professor Chris Argyris of Harvard Business School who first coined the term *double-loop learning* to explain this extra complexity. In addition to the first learning loop described in the paragraph above, there is a second learning loop which questions the whole mechanism served by the first loop. To take the example from the previous paragraph, he likened it to checking whether a thermostat was really needed and whether a completely different temperature control mechanism would produce better and cheaper results.[32] It is this fundamental reappraisal that is important to strategic management and to the process by which companies learn in organisations – see Figure 11.7.

Definition ► Hence, **double-loop learning consists of a *first* loop of learning that checks performance against expected norms and adjusts where necessary, coupled with a *second* loop that reappraises whether the expected norms were appropriate in the first place.** Given some imprecision over the criteria for the first and second loops, it is not surprising that there is no agreed definition of the learning organisation. Most people accept that organisations learn over time and that increased knowledge will deliver increased performance, but the processes beyond this are open to dispute. Some argue that organisations must change the way that they behave for true learning to occur, whereas others argue that simply acquiring new ways of thinking is sufficient. Recognising these difficulties, Professor Daniel Garvin, also from Harvard University Business School, has provided the following definition:[33]

> A learning organisation is an organisation skilled at creating, acquiring and transferring knowledge, and at modifying its behaviour to reflect new knowledge and insights.

Video Part 7a

It is the second part of this definition, 'and modifying its behaviour', that constitutes the second learning loop. The mechanisms identified by this definition – knowledge creation, acquisition, transferral and modification – were explored in Chapter 7 with regard to knowledge creation. Importantly, the latter point that organisations will only show that they have learnt when they have modified and changed their past behaviour is one that was developed by Peter Senge.

11.5.3 How groups can learn better – the contribution of Senge

The contribution of Senge was to extend the learning concept from the *individual* as a learning unit to the *group*. To understand this contribution, we begin by reviewing the main elements of the emergent strategy process and the theory of learning.

As explained above, the concept of *double-loop learning* was to prove highly influential in learning approaches to strategy development.[34] Essentially, it involved not only learning by comparison with accepted standards but also questioning the standards themselves. In 1990, Peter Senge, Professor of Organisational Systems and Learning at the Massachusetts Institute of Technology, employed the learning principles but added to them significantly by using operations research feedback mechanisms and by suggesting that the most powerful learning was by *groups or teams*, not individuals. He applied the group learning concept to strategy development, referring to:

> [t]he Learning Organization . . . where people continually expand their capacity to create the results they truly desire, where new and expansive patterns of thinking are nurtured, where collective aspiration is set free and where people are continually learning how to learn together.[35]

Importantly, Senge draws an important distinction between two types of learning. These are:

1 *adaptive learning* – understanding changes *outside in the environment* and adapting to these;

2 *generative learning* – creating and exploring new strategy areas for positive expansion *within the organisation itself*.

Both types of learning will come from experimentation, discussion and feedback within the organisation. Rigid, formal, hierarchical organisations are unlikely to provide this. New, more fluid structures are needed, according to Senge. It is interesting to note that, in the high-growth economies of Japan in the 1970s and 1980s and in South-East Asia in the 1990s, one of the major distinguishing features has been participation in the planning process, coupled with flexibility and adaptability, rather than rigid, formal plans.[36]

Senge went on to argue that learning is intimately involved with knowledge, which was best acquired by setting interesting and challenging targets and by encouraging group interaction. These ideas move strategy generation forwards from simply searching for simple, prescriptive solutions. A key point of Senge's text was that strategy development involved the *knowledge creation* process, which was best undertaken by groups. The aim was to develop a new 'mental model' of an issue through the group dynamic.

There are a number of well-recognised mechanisms for developing and sharing mental models as part of the learning process.[37] Probably the best known of these are the five learning disciplines of Peter Senge.[38] They are crafted to help organisations and individuals learn. However, *learning* here does not mean memory work or even merely coping with a changing environment. Learning has a more positive and proactive meaning: *active creativity* to develop new strategies and opportunities. The five learning disciplines developed to achieve this are summarised in Exhibit 11.7.

EXHIBIT 11.7

The five learning disciplines

1 *Personal mastery* – not only developing personal goals but also creating the organisational environment that encourages groups to develop goals and purposes

2 *Mental models* – reflecting and speculating upon the pictures that managers and workers have of the world and seeing how these influence actions and decisions

3 *Shared vision* – building commitment in the group to achieve its aims by exploring and agreeing what these aims are

4 *Team learning* – using the group's normal skills to develop intelligence and ability beyond individuals' normal abilities

5 *Systems thinking* – a method of thinking about, describing and understanding the major forces that influence the group

Source: based on the writings of Peter Senge.

To survive in today's turbulent business climate, it has been argued that strategy must include mechanisms that transfer learning from the individual to the group.[39] There are then three advantages from the learning process for the group and for the whole organisation:

1 It will provide fresh ideas and insights into the organisation's performance through a commitment to knowledge.
2 Adaptation through renewal will be promoted so organisations do not stultify and wither.
3 It will promote an openness to the outside world so that it can respond to events – for example, the quantum change of an oil price shock or the rapid developments in the European mobile telephone market.

It is often the well-educated, highly committed senior professional in an organisation who has the most difficulty with this process.[40] Such an individual may misunderstand the meaning of the word 'learning' and interpret it too narrowly as being purely about problem solving. It may also not be understood that the *process* of learning is about more than just instructions from the teacher or the senior management. The implications for strategic management are that learning is a two-way process and is more open-ended than prescriptive strategy would suggest.

11.5.4 Developing learning into heuristics

Definition ▶ **Heuristics are informal rules-of-thumb that provide simple decision rules to capture and summarise what has been learnt by one part of the organisation and then communicate this to other parts of the organisation.**[41] They are particularly valuable when facing new strategic decisions, especially those concerned with new business opportunities. For example, internet travel companies might develop simple decision rules on which countries to offer their services based on their learning experience – for example, 'Take one country at a time', 'Focus on the golf-playing customer', 'Synchronise new hotel web pages with newly opened air routes'. Many of these heuristics will derive from learning experiences, i.e. trial-and-error to see what works best. However, the key to heuristics is not the *initial* learning within part of an organisation, but the ability to *spread* this learning by summarising it as a decision rule that can be applied across the organisation.

Video Part 7b

There are three reasons why heuristics may help:[42]

1 They focus attention and save time. Many organisations cannot afford the time to go back to basics and undertake a learning study every time that they wish to make a new strategic decision.
2 They allow for improvisation – or, at least, they *should* be flexible if they are guidelines and not rigid laws. It is important that heuristics are able to respond to the specific opportunity.
3 They help to limit errors. 'They provide guidelines and rough preliminary plans for how individuals should respond to future events, thereby reducing the amount of learning that needs to take place through pure trial-and-error.'[43]

The difficulty with heuristics is that this can lead to the rigidities of dominant logic explored in the next section.[44]

11.5.5 Learning and the problem of dominant logic

The essence of the learning model is to explore widely and without pre-conceived ideas about a particular strategic issue, experimenting and trying various options. After a time, one or more solutions will prove to be more successful than others. Resources will then be allocated according to the results of such experimentation. This will become the basis of more general decision making in the organisation and a model will emerge of how the business should operate. That model is the dominant logic.

Definition ▶ **Dominant logic is 'the way in which managers conceptualise the business and make critical resource allocation decisions'.**[45] Although learning organisations can be interesting and demanding, there is evidence to suggest that learning can sometimes become stale and rely on past knowledge.[46]

Managers evolve their mental models of how profits are made in a business or how procedures deliver good levels of service in a public organisation. The difficulty is that such mental models can fail to sense the new circumstances that may subsequently influence the organisation. Such models are rooted in the past and provide a set of answers for past strategic decisions.

When a logic becomes dominant, then it can become a barrier to the organisation continuing to learn. The difficulty is not only that such logic may no longer be appropriate but that it can become embedded in the routine tasks and procedures of the organisation. It may even be that managers are rewarded on their ability to deliver the dominant logic. The organisation may even revert to single-loop learning and will only be jolted out of its actions when performance declines to the point that its survival is threatened. A new learning experience is then essential.[47]

11.5.6 The myopia of learning – the contribution of Levinthal and March

Reviewing Senge's contribution and other papers on learning, Levinthal and March[48] explored the myopia (short-sightedness) of learning. They acknowledged that learning has many virtues but argue that the learning process also has a number of limitations. They argued that learning has to maintain a difficult balance between developing *new knowledge* – exploring – and at the same time exploiting *current competencies* with the balance often tilting in favour of one or the other. They identified three constraints on organisational learning:

1. *Temporal myopia.* Learning tends to sacrifice the long run to the short run. As we learn about new competencies and market niches, we simultaneously focus on these and exclude other areas outside these competencies and niches. Clearly an organisation cannot survive in the long run if it is unable to survive its immediate future. But learning does present a problem here.
2. *Spatial myopia.* Learning tends to favour effects that occur near to the learner. Organisations tend to focus on the issues surrounding survival in the near future rather than the broader issues that will help the organisation to grow over time.
3. *Failure myopia.* Organisational learning over-samples successes and under-samples failures. By its nature, learning tends to eliminate failure and focus on success. Learning does not easily correct such biases in experience and may even make organisations over-confident of future success.

For these reasons, learning may not be as useful as sometimes suggested. Learning organisations can have difficulty in sustaining adequate exploration. Organisations should be conservative in their expectations from learning: 'Magic would be nice, but it is not easy to find.'

11.5.7 Improving an organisation's ability to learn

Clearly, the leaders of the organisation can ensure that such a trap is avoided by being aware of the danger of dominant logic. Senge himself was concerned to emphasise the role of the leader in building the shared vision, challenging mental models and helping those involved in the organisation to develop their group learning in many different ways.

Three other mechanisms can help to overcome the difficulty of dominant logic:

1. *Awaydays* – organising an occasion – perhaps a whole day – to take managers away from their daily routines in order to undertake a fundamental review of the business.
2. *Storytelling* – converting strategy development into a series of stories can also assist by emphasising the creative aspect of the learning, by highlighting the more dramatic aspects of the strategy development, and by presenting the rich detail that brings alive the relationships and breaks down the barriers that preclude sharing knowledge.[49]
3. *'No blame' culture* – developing an organisation that encourages and supports critical informed comment.

Underpinning all such initiatives and others is the realisation that organisations will improve their strategic decision making if they challenge existing ways of thinking and provide a supportive, 'no-blame' environment in which to undertake such a task. We return to this theme in Chapter 16.

11.5.8 Consequences for the strategic management process

In the learning process, the concept of 'top-down' management handing semi-finished objectives to the more junior managers and employees clearly carries no meaning. Generative learning needs to have a greater element of co-operation and discussion. Nevertheless, the analytical element of the process can proceed, though perhaps more openly and with more people involved. This will inevitably slow it down, but it may be a small price to pay for the greater commitment achieved and the alternative insights on strategy from group members. Strategy options and selection are still conceivable, but the process may be more complex and multilayered than the prescriptive route. However, it is clearly possible that the implementation phase may actually be faster because people will be better informed and more committed to strategies that they themselves have helped to form.[50]

Figure 11.8 outlines the main elements of the learning-based process. The key point is that the learning process itself is part of the strategy, not something added after the strategy has been developed. This means that the fully developed strategy only emerges over time.

Comment

The learning-based route has real value in the development of strategic management. However, it has to be said that it is sometimes vague and non-operational in its proposals, beyond the need to consult everyone. Moreover, there is still a need in some circumstances for senior managers to take decisions *without* consultation (see Case 9.2 on Nokia and Case 12.3 on Asea Brown Boveri). More generally, *how* and *when* organisations should adopt the learning-based approach has been the basis for fully justified criticism of this route forward.[51] In spite of these weaknesses, the route does not preclude the use of the prescriptive process. It will be explored further in later chapters of this book.

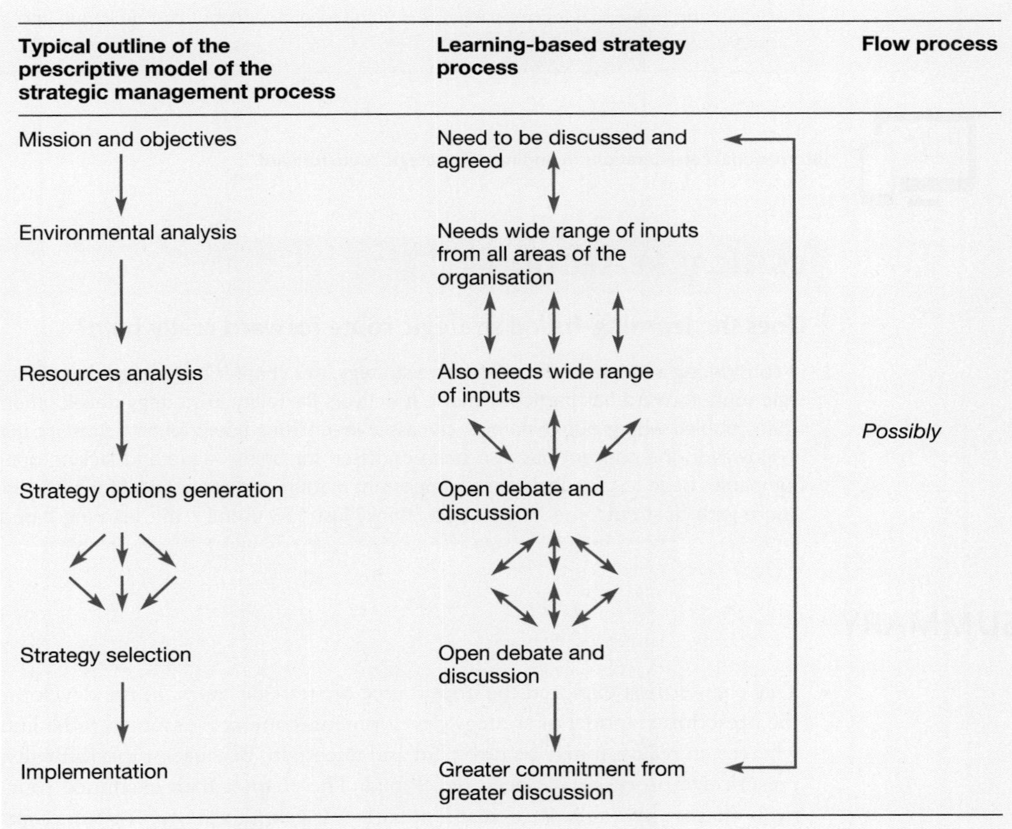

Figure 11.8 Comparison of the learning-based process with the prescriptive process

KEY STRATEGIC PRINCIPLES

- The learning-based strategic route forward emphasises learning and crafting as aspects of the development of successful strategic management. It places particular importance on trial and feedback mechanisms in developing unique strategies. Learning is not concerned with memory work, but with active creativity in developing new strategic opportunities.
- Double-loop learning consists of a *first* loop of learning that checks performance against expected norms and adjusts where necessary, coupled with a *second* loop that reappraises whether the expected norms were appropriate in the first place.
- In strategy development, group dynamics are more important than individuals in developing new, experimental strategies. There are five principles to group learning: personal mastery, group mental models, shared vision, team learning and systems thinking.
- Learning can be passed on to other parts of the organisation using *heuristics* - decision rules that capture and summarise what has been learnt by one part of the organisation and then passed on to others.
- One of the dangers associated with learning is that the 'successful solution' at the end of the process becomes the 'dominant logic' and this stops the organisation continuing to learn. There are ways of overcoming this, including good leadership, storytelling and organising opportunities for a thorough reappraisal of an organisation's strategy.
- Within the learning concept, there is a difficult balance to be struck between the learning that comes from developing new knowledge and the learning that comes from exploiting existing competencies. There are three fundamental problems with the learning concept: *temporal myopia* - learning tends to sacrifice the long run to the short run; *spatial myopia* - learning tends to favour effects that occur near the learner; and *failure myopia*; organisational learning over-samples success and under-samples failure.
- Group and individual learning have real value as concepts but can be vague and lack operational guidance in practice.

International considerations in finding the strategic route forward.

CRITICAL REFLECTION

Does the learning-based strategic route forward really help?

In considering alternatives to prescriptive strategy, this chapter has argued that the learning-based strategic route forward has particular merit. It delivers flexibility in strategy development and, particularly when coupled with group dynamics, can assist in initiating powerful new strategic insights.

However, the concept has also been criticised for being vague and lacking operational guidance. Companies need to take decisions on important matters and cannot wait for a learning process to commence with clear outcome. What do you think? Just how useful is the 'learning-based' approach?

SUMMARY

- This chapter first explored the importance of strategic *context* in the development of strategy. In the prescriptive model of strategy development, context is assumed to be linear and predictable, whereas, in reality, it may be turbulent and uncertain. Because of this difficulty, alternatives to the prescriptive process have been developed. The chapter then examined four models out of the many that are available. Particular emphasis was given to the *learning-based strategy* approach as one that has a contribution to make in conjunction with prescriptive approaches.

- *Survival-based* strategies emphasise the importance of adapting strategies to meet changes in the environment. The ultimate objective is survival itself. The approach adopted is to develop options for use as the environment changes. Options that seek low costs are particularly useful. Beyond taking the precaution of developing options, there is little that the individual company can do. There is an element of chance in whether the company will survive.
- *The uncertainty-based approach* concentrates on the difficult and turbulent environment that now surrounds the development of strategic management. Renewal and transformation are vital aspects of such strategy. Inevitably, they will involve uncertainty. Such uncertainty can be modelled mathematically. However, the long-term consequences are unknown and cannot be foreseen or usefully predicted. Uncertainty approaches therefore involve taking small steps forward. Management needs to learn from such actions and adapt accordingly. Because of the uncertainty about the future, it is argued that the prescriptive approach of looking at strategy options and selecting between them is irrelevant.
- *The network-based strategic route forward* explores the links and degree of co-operation present in related organisations and industries and places a value upon that degree of co-operation. The route has two aspects – network externalities and network co-operation.
- Network externalities refer to the development of an overall standard for a network that allows those belonging to the network to benefit increasingly as others join the same network. In such externalities, the key moment is the 'tipping point', which is reached when the installed base of network users moves towards one company supplying the network and away from rival suppliers.
- In network co-operation, value is added and competitive advantage is developed by the precise *combination* of competition and co-operation that organisations have with others. Such a strategic approach also needs to be seen in the context of negotiations with powerful customers and suppliers where bargaining and trade-offs will take place.
- *The learning-based strategic route forward* emphasises learning and crafting as aspects of the development of successful strategic management. It places particular importance on trial and feedback mechanisms in developing unique strategies. Learning is not concerned with memory work, but with active creativity in developing new strategic opportunities. Double-loop learning consists of a *first* loop of learning that checks performance against expected norms and adjusts where necessary, coupled with a *second* loop that reappraises whether the expected norms were appropriate in the first place.
- In strategy development, group dynamics are more important than individuals in developing new, experimental strategies. There are five principles to group learning: personal mastery, group mental models, shared vision, team learning and systems thinking.
- Learning can be passed on to other parts of the organisation using *heuristics* – decision rules that capture and summarise what has been learnt by one part of the organisation and then passed on to others. However, one of the dangers associated with heuristics is that the 'successful solution' at the end of the process becomes the 'dominant logic' and this stops the organisation continuing to learn. There are ways of overcoming this, including good leadership, storytelling and organising opportunities for a thorough reappraisal of an organisation's strategy.
- Within the learning concept, there is a difficult balance to be struck between the learning that comes from developing new knowledge and the learning that comes from exploiting existing competencies. There are three fundamental problems with the learning concept: *temporal myopia* – learning tends to sacrifice the long run to the short run; *spatial myopia* – learning tends to favour effects that occur near the learner; and *failure myopia* – organisational learning over-samples success and under-samples failure.
- Group and individual learning have real value as concepts but can be vague and lack operational guidance in practice.

QUESTIONS

1 Charles Handy has described recent technological breakthroughs in global development as discontinuous. He commented that *'Discontinuous change required discontinuous upside-down thinking to deal with it, even if thinkers and thought appear absurd at first sight.'* Can discontinuities be handled by the prescriptive process or is an emergent process required? If so, which one?

2 Why does context matter in strategy development? What are the main elements of context in the case of European telecommunications? How do they influence strategy development?

3 Take an organisation with which you are familiar and consider to what extent it plans ahead. How does it undertake this task? Is it reasonably effective or is the whole process largely a waste of time? To what extent does any planning process rely on 'people' issues and negotiation? What model from this chapter does the process most closely follow, if any?

4 Is it possible for the prescriptive strategy process to be creative?

5 Some have argued that the survival-based strategic route is over-pessimistic in its approach. Do you agree?

6 For organisations, such as the telecommunications companies, involved in lengthy investment decisions that take many years to implement, the uncertainty-based route forward, with its very short time-horizons, appears to have little to offer. Can this strategic route provide any useful guidance to such companies?

7 Why is negotiation important in strategic management? Why is it not better to have a strong leader who will simply impose his/her will on the organisation?

8 The learning-based strategic route emphasises creativity in strategy development. Why is this important and how might it be achieved?

9 *'Management theories are judged, among managers at least, by the demonstrable results that they deliver,'* comments Colin Egan. Apply this comment to the strategic routes described in this chapter and outline your conclusions.

10 If you were advising Honda Motorcycles about its strategies in the 1990s, what strategic approach or combination of approaches would you adopt? Give reasons for your views.

FURTHER READING

For an early comparative review of strategic approaches, the book by Dr Richard Whittington remains one of the best: Whittington, R (1993) *What is Strategy – and Does it Matter?*, Routledge, London. For a more recent paper, see Farjoun, M (2002) 'Towards and organic perspective on strategy', *Strategic Management Journal*, Vol 23, pp 561–594.

For a discussion of survival-based approaches, see Rumelt, R, Schendel, D and Teece, D (1991) 'Strategic management and economics', *Strategic Management Journal*, Vol 12, pp 5–29. This is a very useful general review and would provide a good link for those who have already studied economics. An interesting paper: Wiltbank, R, Dew, N, Read, S and Sarasvathy, S D (2006) 'What to do next? The case for non-predictive strategy', *Strategic Management Journal*, Vol 27, pp 981–998.

For a description of the uncertainty-based approach, see Stacey, R (1996) *Strategic Management and Organisational Dynamics*, 2nd edn, Pitman Publishing, London. See also Professor Robert Grant's paper (2003) 'Strategic planning in a turbulent environment: evidence from the oil majors', *Strategic Management Journal*, Vol 24, pp 419–517.

On network-based approaches, one of the most useful sources is the *Academy of Management Executive* special issue on building effective networks: Vol 17, No 4, November 2003.

For a useful discussion of learning approaches, see Senge, P (1990) *The Fifth Discipline: the Art and Practice of the Learning Organisation*, Century Business, London. For a critical examination of learning, Professor Colin Egan's book is strongly recommended: Egan, C (1995) *Creating Organizational Advantage*, Butterworth–Heinemann, Oxford. On linking learning to entrepreneurial activity, Anderson, B S, Covin, J G and Slevin, D P (2009) 'Understanding the Relationship Between Entrepreneurial Orientation and Strategic Learning Capability', *Strategic Entrepreneurship Journal*, Vol 3, No 3, pp 218–240.

One of the best papers on learning is Levinthal, D A and March, J G (1993) 'The myopia of learning', *Strategic Management Journal*, Vol 14, Special Issue, Winter. Don't be put off by this academic journal. Unlike some of its research papers, this one is easier to read and it has some major insights. It won the *SMJ* best paper prize 2002.

An interesting paper is one comparing strategic planning (prescriptive) and learning (emergent) processes: Brews, P J and Hunt, M R (1999) 'Learning to plan and planning to learn: resolving the planning school/learning school debate', *Strategic Management Journal*, Vol 20, pp 889–913. Another interesting paper on learning versus performance goals: Seijts, G H and Latham, G P (2005) 'Learning versus performance goals: when should each be used?', *Academy of Management Executive*, Vol 19, No 1, pp 124–31.

NOTES AND REFERENCES

1 Thus, for example, classic prescriptive strategy might explore 'Gap analysis': see Jauch, L R and Glueck, W F (1988) *Business Policy and Strategic Management*, 5th edn, McGraw-Hill, New York, pp 24–26.

2 Pascale, R (1984) 'Perspectives on strategy: the real story behind Honda's success', *California Management Review*, Vol XXVI, No 3, pp 47–72. This article was extracted in Mintzberg, H and Quinn, J B (1991) *The Strategy Process*, 2nd edn, Prentice Hall, Englewood Cliffs, NJ, pp 114–123. This is well worth reading to illustrate the problems of the classical model.

3 Kono, T (1992) *Long Range Planning of Japanese Corporations*, de Gruyter, Berlin.

4 See Chapter 1 for a basic discussion on context, process and content. Also Pettigrew, A and Whipp, R (1993) *Managing Change for Competitive Success*, Blackwell, Oxford, Ch 1.

5 For a fuller exploration, see Chaharbaghi, K and Lynch, R (1999), 'Sustainable competitive advantage: towards a dynamic resource-based strategy', *Management Decision*, Vol 37, No 1, pp 45–50.

6 These four routes were identified and set in the context of other strategic approaches in Chapter 2.

7 References for European telcos case: Isern, J and Rios, M I (2002) 'Facing disconnection – hard choices for Europe's telcos', *McKinsey Quarterly*, No 1; Annexes to Seventh Report on the implementation of the telecommunications regulatory package, Commission Staff Working Paper, SEC (2001) 1922 Brussels – 26 November; *Financial Times*: 1 August 1998, p 5 Weekend Money; 24 April 1999, p 21; 27 January 2000, p 1; 3 February 2000, p 24; 1 May 2000, p 11; 3 June 2000, p 15; 28 March 2001, p 23; 3 April 2001, p 26; 2 May 2001, p 15; 11 May 2001, p 22; 13 June 2001, p 27; 7 September 2001, p 13; 13 October 2001, p 16; 17 October 2001, p 23; 18 December 2001, p 23; 11 January 2002, p 20; 12 January 2002, p 11; 6 February 2002, p 19; 8 February 2002, pp 20, 24; 13 February 2002, p 16; 23 February 2002, p 19.

8 Alchian, A A (1950) 'Uncertainty, evolution and economic theory', *Journal of Political Economy*, Vol 58, pp 211–221, first proposed this. 2010 company annual report and accounts of the following companies: Deutsche Telekom, France Telecom, British Telecom, Telecom Italia, Vodafone, Telefonica. The market data used in the case comes from the Vodafone annual report.

9 Hofer, C W and Schendel, D (1986) *Strategy Formulation: Analytical Concepts*, 11th edn, West Publishing, St Paul, MN. This book used the same approach in the 1970s and 1980s.

10 Hannan, M and Freeman, J (1977) 'The population ecology of organisations', *American Journal of Sociology*, Vol 82, March, pp 929–964.

11 Williamson, O E (1991) 'Strategizing, economizing and economic organisation', *Strategic Management Journal*, Vol 12, pp 75–94.

12 This represents one particular view of the relationship between economics and strategy. For a more general discussion, see Rumelt, R, Schendel, D and Teece, D (1991) 'Strategic management and economics', *Strategic Management Journal*, Vol 12, pp 5–29.

13 Stacey, R (1993) *Strategic Management and Organisational Dynamics*, Pitman Publishing, London, p 211.

14 Roberts, D (2000) 'Orange renegade', *Financial Times*, 3 June, p 15.

15 Gleick, J (1988) *Chaos: the Making of a New Science*, Heinemann, London.

16 Lloyd, T (1995) 'Drawing a line under corporate strategy', *Financial Times*, 8 September, p 10. This provides a short, readable account of some of the consequences of this strategic approach.

17 Stacey, R (1993) 'Strategy as order emerging from chaos', *Long Range Planning*, Vol 26, No 1, pp 10–17.

18 References for the online travel case: *Financial Times*: 16 November 2001, p 24; 21 May 2003, p 15; 6 August 2003, p 21; 19 April 2004, p 10; 21 May 2004, p 28; 25 June 2004, p 28; 3 September 2004, p 26; 30 September 2004, p 30; 9 November 2004, p 13; 9 February 2005, p 11; 8 March 2011, p 25. In 2011, websites of Orbitz, Sabre Holdings, Amadeus, Travelport and Expedia.

19 Katz, M and Shapiro, C (1985) 'Network externalities, competition and compatibility', *American Economic Review*, Vol 75, pp 424–440.

20 This section has benefited from McGee, J, Thomas, H and Wilson, D (2005) *Strategy – Analysis and Practice*, McGraw-Hill, Maidenhead, Ch 12.

21 This refers to the work of Coase and Williamson.

22 This refers to the work of Porter.

23 Gerlach, M (1992) *Alliance Capitalism*, University of California Press, Berkeley, CA. Quoted in De Wit, R and Meyer, R (1998) *Strategy: Process, Content and Context*, 2nd edn, International Thomson Business Press, London, p 512. But note my rephrasing of this relationship.

24 Doz, Y (1986) *Strategic Management in Multinational Companies*, Pergamon, Oxford, pp 95, 96.

25 Reve, T (1990) 'The firm as a nexus of internal and external contracts', in Aoki, M, Gustafsson, M and Williamson, O E (eds), *The Firm as a Nexus of Treaties*, Sage, London.

26 Johanson, J and Mattson, L-G (1992) 'Network positions and strategic action', in Axelsson, B and Easton, G (eds), *Industrial Networks: a New View of Reality*, Routledge, London.

27 Porter, M E (1985) *Competitive Advantage*, The Free Press, New York.

28 Jarillo, J C (1988) 'On strategic networks', *Strategic Management Journal*, June–July, pp 31–41.

29 This choice is presented as the prime focus of the 'debate' in De Wit, R and Meyer, R (1998) Op. cit., Ch 7.

30 Mintzberg, H (1987) 'Crafting strategy', *Harvard Business Review*, July–August, pp 66–75.

31 De Geus, A (1988) 'Planning as learning', *Harvard Business Review*, March–April, p 70.

32 Argyris, C (1977) 'Double loop learning in organisations', *Harvard Business Review*, September–October, pp 115–125.

33 Garvin, D (1993) 'Building a learning organization', *Harvard Business Review*, July–August, pp 78–91. The precision and care of its wording make this article particularly valuable.

34 Argyris, C (1977) 'Double loop learning in organizations', *Harvard Business Review*, May–June, pp 99–109.

35 Senge, P (1990) *The Fifth Discipline: The Art and Practice of the Learning Organisation*, Century Business, London, Ch 1.

36 Pucik, V and Hatvany, N (1983) 'Management practices in Japan and their impact on business strategy', *Advances in Strategic Management*, 1, JAI Press Inc, pp 103–131. Reprinted in Mintzberg, H and Quinn, J B (1991) Op. cit.; World Bank (1994) *World Development Report 1994*, Oxford University Press, New York, pp 76–79.

37 See *The Economist* (1995) 'The knowledge', 11 November, p 107.

38 Senge, P (1990) 'The leader's new work: building learning organisations', *Sloan Management Review*, Fall, and Senge, P (1990) *The Fifth Discipline*, Op. cit.

39 Quinn, S, Mills, D and Friesen, B (1992) 'The learning organisation', *European Management Journal*, 10 June, p 146.

40 Argyris, C (1991) 'Teaching smart people how to learn', *Harvard Business Review*, May–June, p 99.

41 Bingham, C B, Eisenhardt, K M and Furr, N R (2007) 'What makes a process a capability?' *Strategic Entrepreneurship Journal*, Vol 1, pp 27–47. Note that the authors draw a distinction between learning and cognition in their interesting paper towards the end (p 40) but then confuse this by combining the two concepts earlier in the paper (p 31). For the purposes of this book, this distinction is ignored and the topic treated as the one subject of learning.

42 Bingham *et al.*, (2007) Op. cit., p 31.

43 Bingham *et al.*, Ibid., p 31.

44 Bingham *et al.*, Ibid., p 31. Note that the research evidence mainly covered firms at the beginning of their lives and therefore did not explore such rigidities – as acknowledged by footnote number 2 on p 31.

45 Prahalad, C K and Bettis, R A (1986) 'The dominant logic: a new linkage between diversity and performance', *Strategic Management Journal*, Vol 7, pp 485–501.

46 Bettis, R A and Prahalad, C K (1995) 'The dominant logic: retrospective and extension', *Strategic Management Journal*, Vol 16, pp 5–14.

47 Bettis, R A and Prahalad, C K (1995) 'The dominant logic: retrospective and extension', *Strategic Management Journal*, Vol 16, pp 5–14. See also: Cote, L, Langley, A and Pasquero, J (1999) 'Acquisition strategy and dominant logic in an engineering firm', *Journal of Management Studies*, Vol 36, pp 919–52.

48 Levinthal, D A and March, J G (1993) 'The myopia of learning', *Strategic Management Journal*, Vol 14, Special Issue, Winter.

49 Shaw, G, Brown, R and Bromiley, P (1998) 'Strategic stories: how 3M is rewriting business planning', *Harvard Business Review*, May–June, pp 41–50.

50 Burgoyne, J, Pedler, M and Boydell, T (1994) *Towards the Learning Company*, McGraw-Hill, Maidenhead.

51 Jones, A and Hendry, C (1994) 'The learning organisation: adult learning and organisational transformation', *British Journal of Management*, Vol 5, pp 153–162. See also a thoughtful critique of the learning approach in Egan, C (1995) *Creating Organizational Advantage*, Butterworth–Heinemann, Ch 5. Finally see the major review of learning: Levinthal, D A and March, J G (1993) Op. cit.

CHAPTER 12
Organisational structure, style and people issues

Video and sound summary of this chapter

LEARNING OUTCOMES

When you have worked through this chapter, you will be able to:

- evaluate critically the arguments that strategy and structure have a more complex relationship than that suggested by the early strategists;
- understand the basic principles involved in designing the structure of an organisation to meet its chosen strategy;
- evaluate the importance of changing an organisation's management style at the same time as changing its strategy;
- outline the six main types of organisation structure and assess their advantages and disadvantages in relation to a particular strategy;
- develop the special organisation structures that are more likely to lead to innovative strategies;
- explain the formal organisation needed to motivate staff and implement the chosen strategies.

INTRODUCTION

Alongside a well-considered strategy, there exists the need for an organisation, management team and people to deliver the strategy. One important academic debate in the past has been whether the strategy is planned first and then the organisation developed to implement that strategy. This book takes the view that it is preferable to consider both elements at the same time: that is why we examined aspects of human resource strategy back in the analysis phase in Chapter 7. Nevertheless, the argument for putting strategy first and organisation structure second needs to be understood. We begin this chapter with this topic.

We then explore the more general principles associated with developing the organisation structure. One particular aspect that deserves highlighting is the choice of management style. Having considered these matters, we then explore how to design organisation structures in different types of business. Given the importance of innovation in successful strategy – especially from an emergent strategy perspective – we examine this topic separately. We explore the role of effective reward structures and selection procedures in providing capable and well-motivated senior managers to implement strategy successfully. Finally, in the light of these considerations, an appropriate organisation structure can then be developed, as summarised in Figure 12.1.

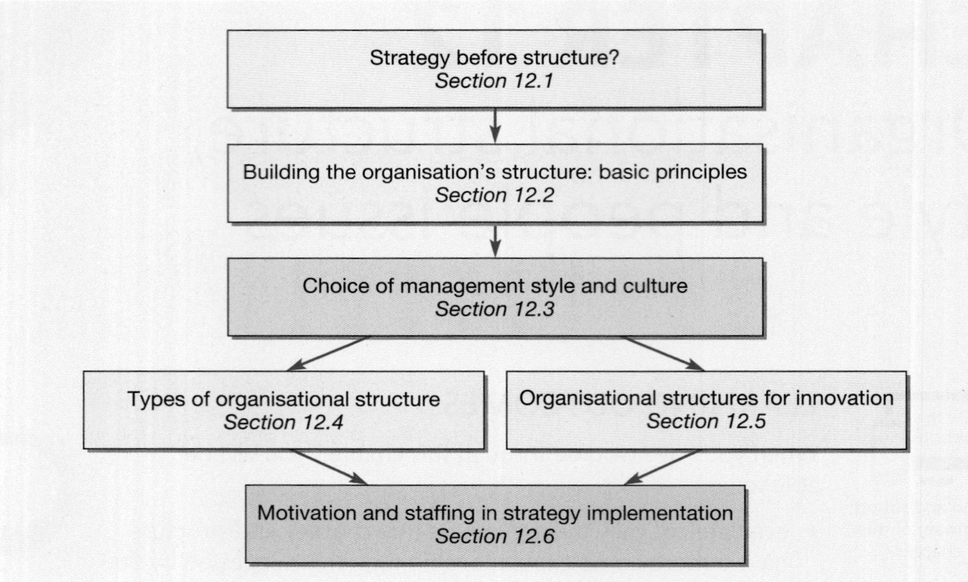

Figure 12.1 Organisation structure and people issues

CASE STUDY 12.1

PepsiCo: organising to integrate its acquisitions

Over a three-year period from 1998 to 2001, the US food and drink company PepsiCo made two major acquisitions. Each purchase was bought for a price premium that could only be repaid by finding new synergies and economies of scale. This required PepsiCo to develop new organisation structures designed to deliver these benefits in the years that followed.

Background – the company itself

PepsiCo is probably best known for its carbonated cola drink, Pepsi-Cola, which it sells in most countries around the world, often in second place to its great rival Coca-Cola. However, in terms of total sales, PepsiCo is actually much larger than Coca-Cola – sales of $29 billion in 2004 compared with Coke's $22 billion. The main reason for the greater size is that PepsiCo is also the world's largest snack and crisp manufacturer, with a series of brands in regions of the world – including Frito-Lay in North America and Walkers in the UK. However, the company also has some other famous brand names like Gatorade, Tropicana fruit juices and Quaker breakfast cereals. Table 12.1 sets out some of its leading products, including those that arrived through its acquisition strategy in the six years to 2004.

Company major acquisitions – Tropicana and Quaker

Both the Tropicana range of fresh fruit drinks and the Quaker range of products came from PepsiCo acquisitions in the period 1998–2001. Tropicana was bought from Seagram for $3.3 billion in 1998 and Quaker for $15 billion in 2001. In both

Table 12.1 PepsiCo's top ten products at retail prices

Brand	Worldwide sales ($ bn)
Regular Pepsi	17.0
Diet Pepsi	6.0
Mountain Dew	5.5
Gatorade Sports Drink	5.2 Acquired 2001
Lays Potato Chips	5.0
Doritos Tortilla Chips	3.0
Tropicana Juice Drink	2.9 Acquired 1998
7Up Drink (outside the USA)	2.4
Aquafina bottled water	2.3
Cheetos Cheese Flavored Snacks	2.0
Quaker Cereals	1.5 Acquired 2001

Source: company report and accounts 2004.

cases, PepsiCo paid a significant premium over the asset book value of the companies. It took the view that there were significant synergies and economies of scale to be gained from these two acquisitions. With regard to Quaker, PepsiCo was particularly interested in the sports drink Gatorade, which delivered the market leader in a new and fast-growing segment of the beverage market. The same purchase came with the Quaker cereal range, which was under heavy competitive pressure from Kellogg and General Mills - see Case 2.1. However, the Quaker brand also brought the possibility of new snack products. PepsiCo then began to organise the company to exploit this advantage, not only in North America but also in Europe.

PepsiCo company re-organisation to exploit the full acquisition potential

Building on its strong competitive resources was the prime starting point in developing the revised organisation structure for PepsiCo. Such resources included its major network of contacts with supermarkets across North America and, to a lesser extent, other countries. They also included its existing brand franchises in names like Pepsi and Frito-Lay, Quaker, Gatorade and Tropicana. The company had a specialist distribution structure designed to deliver fresh and fragile snacks every week directly to 15,000 outlets across the USA and indirectly to around 500,000 outlets. It also had a strong network of bottlers who were responsible for delivering Pepsi. The company had a record of product and packaging innovation which came from its Pepsi and Frito-Lay technical development units, the Gatorade Sports Science Institute and the Tropicana Nutrition Center. All were skilled at developing new products and packaging. Such units were kept centrally at headquarters on behalf of all operating companies.

Because PepsiCo was particularly strong in North America in virtually every product category, it was decided to set up North American divisions and separate these from its other, international operations. In addition, although the sports drink Gatorade and the Quaker cereal products were important in North America, they had a more limited franchise internationally - especially Gatorade, which was largely unknown outside the American continent. It was decided to combine these product areas internationally with some of its other product groups.

PepsiCo main organisation structure - 2001

In 2001, PepsiCo therefore had the following organisational divisions, each reporting to headquarters:

- *Pepsi-Cola North America* was responsible not only for the largest brand but also for building a new product range of non-carbonated drinks such as bottled water. The company was not expecting this area to yield major savings from its two acquisitions. In 2004, this was combined with Tropicana/Gatorade - see below.
- *PepsiCo Beverages International* contained the combined international operations of Pepsi-Cola, Tropicana and Gatorade. It was planned to combine general and administrative functions and gain 'very substantial cost savings'. One of the problems here was that, although the Pepsi brand was strong in the USA, its international brand share was weaker - especially in parts of Europe. It was therefore more cost-effective to combine it with Tropicana (Gatorade was too small to be important) and gain cost savings from shared overheads. In 2004, this was combined with Frito-Lay International - see below.

Faced with increased competition and slow growth, PepsiCo has responded by a strategy of moving into more rapidly growing markets - soft drinks, mineral water and snack products. But this has meant reorganising the company.

- *Frito-Lay North America* had part of the Quaker range of sweet cereal bars, energy bars and similar products, combined with its existing savoury crisps and snacks. The aim was to gain substantial cost savings and at the same time to offer the broader range of products to its existing outlets, thus increasing sales.
- *Frito-Lay International*. The snack and crisp products were sold across some 40 countries. The company already had some strong market positions, for example, 80 per cent of the Mexican snack market and 40 per cent of the UK snack market with Walkers Crisps. The aim here was to add the Quaker food distribution and gain major cost savings on distribution. The Quaker international cereal product range was also included in this area - probably because it was convenient and PepsiCo had to buy this product range in order to obtain Gatorade, as mentioned above. In 2004, this was combined with PepsiCo Beverages International.
- *Gatorade/Tropicana North America*. These two major product areas - sports drinks and fruit juices - were combined as a separate area from cola drinks because they were used and sold in different ways and through different outlets. More specifically, there was a common 'hot-fill' manufacturing process that could be used to deliver substantial cost savings. In 2004, this was combined with PepsiCo North America - see below.
- *Quaker Foods North America*. PepsiCo decided to keep the Quaker cereals and related products, like Aunt Jemima

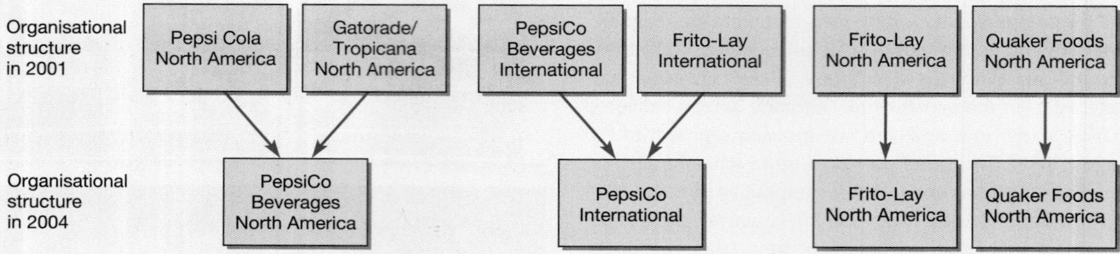

Figure 12.2 How PepsiCo re-organised in 2004

syrup and mixes, together in North America. Some commentators suspected that this separate division would also allow the product range to be sold more easily at some later stage – it simply did not fit in with the main strengths of PepsiCo and faced strong competition in both North America and internationally. The well-established warehouse distribution capabilities of Quaker and Gatorade brought important new scale to a new delivery/distribution system for PepsiCo.

PepsiCo further re-organisation – 2004

By 2004, PepsiCo had decided to combine several of the above divisions – see Figure 12.2. The reasons for this change in organisation structure were:

- *PepsiCo Beverages International was combined with Frito-Lay International.* The new division was called PepsiCo International. The logic here was to build on the company's different international strengths in different international markets. For example, its snack brands were particularly strong in Mexico with the Sabritas brand, in the UK with the Walkers brand and in Australia with the Smiths brand. In other countries, Pepsi-Cola was stronger and the snacks brands were relatively weak. Whatever was the strongest product category would be the lead brand and would then support the other weaker brands. This could best be done if there was one organisation rather than separate organisations.
- *Gatorade/Tropicana North America was combined with Pepsi Cola North America for financial reporting.* The new division was called PepsiCo Beverages North America. The reasoning here was to allow the company to exploit its strengths in non-carbonated and healthy fruit drinks across a wider range of outlets. Coca-Cola was leader in the carbonated drinks market, but Pepsi with Tropicana and Gatorade was easily the market leader in the total soft drinks market. To exploit this leadership, it was essential to drive the various brands as part of one team. This was particularly important given the increased bargaining power of the large retail supermarket chains like the world's largest retailer, Wal-Mart – PepsiCo Beverages became 'the No 1 liquid refreshment beverage company in measured channels'.

PepsiCo organisation in 2010

Like many other organisations, the company re-organised further over the years from 2004. The latest organisation structure is fully described in the report for 2010 but includes separate structures for Latin America, Europe and Asia, the Middle East and Africa as these parts have become more significant to the overall business of the company.

PepsiCo has an extensive range of activities associated with green strategy:
'Environmental initiatives help us identify business synergies and cut our operating costs. Equally important is improving efficiencies in packaging materials, water and energy use, so we may continue to minimize waste and move toward significant environmental goals . . .'
(PepsiCo, Inc. Annual Report 2010).

Case questions

1 Why was PepsiCo essentially organised into North American and international divisions? Why were there some variations in this structure? Examining the organisation structures outlined in this chapter, in which category would you put PepsiCo?

2 What benefits was the company seeking from its acquisitions? How did the change in organisation structure contribute to such benefits? In order to achieve such benefits, what actions would have to be taken? Would they have any human consequences? If so, what?

3 What lessons, if any, on strategy and organisation structure can be drawn from the approach of PepsiCo in developing its new organisation structure?

Exploration of prescriptive and emergent perspectives in human resource analysis.

12.1 STRATEGY BEFORE STRUCTURE?

A major debate has been taking place over the past 30 years regarding the relationship between the strategy and the structure of the organisation. In the past, it was considered that the strategy was decided first and the organisation structure then followed. For example, PepsiCo's strategy of building on its strengths in different markets then led to its decision to combine its international and beverage operations. Recent research has questioned this approach and taken the view that strategy and structure are interrelated. From this perspective, PepsiCo combined its North American operations in 2004 without necessarily knowing fully in advance the outcome of such a move: its new structure and strategy were part of a new combination approach. In this section we examine the reasons why views have changed: strategy no longer comes before structure.

12.1.1 Strategy before structure: Chandler's contribution

To understand the logic behind this prescriptive approach to the development of organisational structures, it is helpful to look at the historical background. Prior to the early 1960s, the US strategist Alfred Chandler Jr studied how some leading US corporations had developed their strategies in the first half of the twentieth century.[2] He then drew some major conclusions from this empirical evidence, the foremost one being that the organisation first needed to develop its strategy and, after this, to devise the organisation structure that delivered that strategy.

Chandler drew a clear distinction between *devising* a strategy and *implementing* it. He defined strategy as:

> [t]he determination of the basic long-term goals and objectives of an enterprise, and the adoption of courses of action and the allocation of resources necessary for carrying out these goals.[3]

The task of developing the strategy took place at the centre of the organisation. The job of implementing it then fell to the various functional areas. Chandler's research suggested that, once a strategy had been developed, it was necessary to consider the structure needed to carry it out. A new strategy might require extra resources, or new personnel or equipment which would alter the work of the enterprise, making a new organisational structure necessary: 'the design of the organisation through which the enterprise is administered', to quote Chandler.

The principle that strategy came before organisational structure was formed, therefore, by considering the industrial developments of the early twentieth century.[4] Whether such considerations are still relevant as we move into the new millennium will be considered next.

12.1.2 Changes in the business environment and social values

To understand why it is no longer appropriate to develop an organisation structure after deciding a strategy, the earlier theory needs to be placed in its historical strategic context. Since Chandler's research on early twentieth-century companies, the environment has changed substantially.[5] The workplace itself, the relationships between workers and managers, and the skills of employees have all altered substantially. Old organisational structures embedded in past understandings may therefore be suspect. Exhibit 12.1 summarises how the environment has changed.

12.1.3 Managing the complexity of strategic change – the contribution of Quinn

Much of the prescriptive approach is built around the notion that it is possible to choose precisely what strategies need to be introduced. The issue then becomes one of building the organisation and plans to achieve the chosen strategy. From empirical research, J B Quinn[6] has suggested that this grossly over-simplifies the process in many cases:

- Simple strategic solutions may be unavailable, especially where the proposed changes are complex or controversial.

EXHIBIT 12.1

A comparison of the early twentieth- and early twenty-first-century business environments

Early twentieth century	Early twenty-first century
• Uneducated workers, typically just moved from agricultural work into the cities • Knowledge of simple engineering and technology • The new science of management recognised simple cause-and-effect relationships • Growing, newly industrialising markets and suppliers • Sharp distinctions between management and workers	• Better educated, computer-literate, skilled • Complex, computer-driven, large-scale • Multifaceted and complex nature of management now partially understood • Mix of some mature, cyclical markets and some high-growth, new-technology markets and suppliers • Greater overlap between management and workers in some industrialised countries

- The organisation structure may be unable to cope with the 'obvious' solution for reasons of its culture, the people involved or the political pressures.
- Organisational awareness and commitment may need to be built up over time, making it impossible to introduce an immediate radical change.
- Managers may need to participate in the change process, to learn about the proposed changes and to contribute specialist expertise in order to develop the strategic change required.

Quinn suggests that strategic change may need to proceed *incrementally*, i.e. in small stages. He called the process *logical incrementalism*. The clear implication is that it may not be possible to define the final organisation structure, which may also need to evolve as the strategy moves forward incrementally. He suggests a multistage process for senior executives involved in strategy development: this is shown in Exhibit 12.2. Importantly, he recognises the importance of informal organisation structures in achieving agreement to strategy shifts. If the argument is correct, it will be evident that any idea of a single, final organisation structure – after deciding on a defined strategy – is dubious.

Comment

The description of the process certainly accords with the evidence of other researchers. Formal organisation structures are important for day-to-day responsibilities and work, but are only part of the strategy process when it comes to implementing complex and controversial strategic change. The validity of the above description relies on the extent to which radical change is required. Quinn's assumption that change needs to be radical enables him to conclude that the final organisational structure may have to emerge at the end of this period.

12.1.4 Specific criticism of strategy before structure

According to modern strategists, strategy and structure are interlinked. It may not be optimal for an organisation to develop its structure *after* it has developed its strategy. The relationship is more complex in two respects:

1 Strategy and the structure associated with it may need to develop *at the same time* in an experimental way: as the strategy develops, so does the structure. The organisation *learns to adapt* to its changing environment and to its changing resources, especially if such change is radical.

2 If the strategy process is emergent, then the learning and experimentation involved may need a *more open and less formal* organisation structure.

EXHIBIT 12.2

Quinn's logical incremental strategy process and its organisational implications[8]

Strategic stage	Organisational implications
1 Sensing the need for change	Use informal networks in organisation
2 Clarify strategy areas and narrow options	Consult more widely, possibly using more formal structures
3 Use change symbols to signal possible change	Communicate with many who cannot be directly consulted: use formal structure
4 Create waiting period to allow options discussion and newer options to become familiar	Encourage discussion of concerns among interested groups: use formal and informal organisational structures
5 Clarify general direction of new strategy but experiment and seek partial solutions rather than a firm commitment to one direction	General discussion without alienation, if possible, among senior managers. Use formal senior management structure
6 Broaden the basis of support for the new direction	Set up committees, project groups and study teams outside the formal existing structures. Careful selection of team members and agenda is essential
7 Consolidate progress	Initiate special projects to explore and consolidate the general direction: use more junior managers and relevant team members from the existing organisation
8 Build consensus before focusing on new objectives and associated strategies	Use informal networks through the organisation. Identify and manage those people who are key influencers on the future strategic direction
Over time, possibly years	
9 Balance consensus with the need to avoid the rigidity that might arise from over-commitment to the now successful strategy	Introduce new members to provide further stimulus, new ideas and new questions
10 New organisation	Re-organise the organisation's formal structure to consolidate the changes: at last!

In recent years, it has been suggested[7] that the impact of process and organisation on strategy has been constantly under-played. The contribution of employees in energising the organisation and promoting innovation may often be under-estimated. Moreover, the quality of management and the organisational structure itself will all have an impact on strategy and may even be a source of competitive advantage. In this sense, it cannot be said that people and process issues arise after the strategy has been agreed.

It has also been pointed out that there are some companies that have broadly similar resources but differ markedly in their performance. The reasons for this disparity may be associated with the way that companies are organised and conduct their activities, rather than with differences in strategy. The five main weaknesses of the strategy before structure approach are summarised in Exhibit 12.3.

12.1.5 Implications of strategy and structure being interlinked – the concept of 'strategic fit'

Although it may not be possible to define which comes first, there is a need to ensure that strategy and structure are consistent with each other. For example, PepsiCo re-organised its North American

EXHIBIT 12.3

Summary of the five main criticisms of the strategy-first, structure-afterwards process

1. Structures may be too *rigid, hierarchical and bureaucratic* to cope with the newer social values and rapidly changing environments of the 1990s.
2. *The type of structure* is just as important as the business area in developing the organisation's strategy. It is the structure that will restrict, guide and form the strategy options that the organisation can generate. A learning organisation may be required and power given to more junior managers. In this sense, strategy and organisational structure are interrelated and need to be developed at the same time.
3. *Value chain configurations* that favour cost cutting or, alternatively, new market opportunities may also alter the organisation required.
4. *The complexity of strategic change* needs to be managed, implying that more complex organisational considerations will be involved. Simple configurations such as a move from a functional to a divisional structure are only a starting point in the process.
5. *The role of top and middle management* in the formation of strategy may also need to be reassessed: Chandler's view that strategy is decided by the top leadership alone has been challenged. Particularly for new, innovative strategies, middle management and the organisation's culture and structure may be important. The work of the leader in empowering middle management may require a new approach - the organic style of leadership.

business to ensure that its strengths in the growing non-carbonated drinks market could be exploited across its full range of drinks – see Case 12.1. For an organisation to be economically effective, there needs to be a matching process between the organisation's strategy and its structure: this is the concept of *strategic fit*.[9] **Strategic fit is the matching process between strategy and structure.**

Definition ▶

In essence, organisations need to adopt an internally consistent set of practices in order to undertake the proposed strategy effectively. It should be said that such practices will involve more than the organisation's structure. They will also cover such areas as:

- the strategic planning process (see Chapter 13);
- recruitment and training (see later in this chapter);
- reward systems for employees and managers (see later in this chapter);
- the work to be undertaken (see Chapter 13);
- the information systems and processes (see Chapter 13).

This means that issues of strategic fit may not be fully resolved by considering only strategy and structure. It may be necessary to revisit strategy, even when the implementation process is formally under consideration (see Chapter 13).

There is strong empirical evidence, from both Chandler and Senge, that there does need to be a degree of strategic fit between the strategy and the organisation structure.

Although the environment is changing all the time, organisations may only change slowly and not keep pace with external change, which can often be much faster – for example, the introduction of digital technology. It follows that it is unlikely that there will be a perfect fit between the organisation's strategy and its structure. There is some evidence that a minimal degree of fit is needed for an organisation to survive.[10] It has also been suggested that, if the fit is close early on in the strategic development process, then higher economic performance may result. However, as the environment changes, the strategic fit will also need to change.

KEY STRATEGIC PRINCIPLES

- According to some modern strategists, Chandler's concept of strategy first and then structure to deliver it may over-simplify the situation. There have been five major criticisms.
- Changes in the business environment and social values of the late twentieth century suggest that others beyond top management may need to contribute to strategy. This is called empowerment of the middle and junior ranks of managers. This can best take place before the organisation structure is finalised.
- New processes for developing strategy are adaptive and involve learning mechanisms. They also need open, fluid structures that may not be best served by simple functional structures.
- When strategic change is radical, it may not be possible to define clearly the final organisation structure. It may be necessary to let the structure emerge as strategy changes and develops.
- If strategy and structure are interlinked, then it is essential that they are consistent with each other - the concept of 'strategic fit'.

12.2 BUILDING THE ORGANISATION'S STRUCTURE: BASIC PRINCIPLES

12.2.1 Consistency with mission and objectives

The organisation's structure is essentially developed to deliver its mission and objectives. Building the organisation structure must therefore begin at this point. Before considering the possible structures in detail, it is useful to explore some basic questions in the context of the analysis and development undertaken in Chapter 6.

- *What kind of organisation are we?* Commercial? Non-profit making? Service-oriented? Government administration? (These questions are not an exhaustive list.)
- *Who are the major stakeholders?* Shareholders? Managers? Employees?
- *What is our purpose?* What does our purpose tell us in broad terms about how we might be structured?

There is no simple or 'right' answer to the last question; it deserves careful thought. Every organisation is unique in size, products or services, people, leadership and culture. Exhibit 12.4 shows some of the possible implications for designing organisation structures. It can be useful to think in this general unformed way before plunging into the detail of organisation design, which is explored in the next section.

12.2.2 The main elements of organisation design

Before embarking on the design process, it is important to note that many organisations have existing structures and that the primary task of organisation design is usually not to invent a totally new organisation but to adapt the existing one. These matters are reflected in the nine primary determinants of organisation design:

1. *Age.* Older organisations tend to be more formal.
2. *Size.* Essentially, as organisations grow, there is usually an increasing need for formal methods of communication and greater co-ordination, suggesting that more formal structures are required.
3. *Environment.* Rapid changes in any of the *Five Forces* acting on the organisation will need a structure that is capable of responding quickly (see Chapter 3). If the work undertaken by the organisation is complex, then this will make its ability to respond to the environment more difficult to organise and co-ordinate.[11]

EXHIBIT 12.4

Examples of the connection between purpose and organisation design

Purpose	Implications for organisation design
'Ideas factory' such as an advertising or promotions agency	Loose, fluid structure with limited formalised relationships. As it grows in size, however, more formal structures are usually inevitable
Multinational company in branded goods	Major linkage and resource issues that need carefully co-ordinated structures, e.g. on common suppliers or common supermarket customers for separate product ranges
Government civil service	Strict controls on procedures and authorisations. Strong formal structures to handle major policy directions and legal issues
Non-profit-making charity with a strong sense of mission	Reliance on voluntary members and their voluntary contributions may require a flexible organisation with responsibility devolved to individuals
Major service company such as a retail bank or electricity-generating company	Formal structures but supported by some flexibility so that variations in demand can be met quickly
Small business attempting to survive and grow	Informal willingness to undertake several business functions such as selling or production, depending on the short-term circumstances
Health service with strong professional service ethics, standards and quality	Formalised structure that reflects the seniority and professional status of those involved while delivering the crucial complex service provisions
Holding company with subsidiaries involved in diverse markets	Small centralised headquarters acting largely as a banker, with the main strategic management being undertaken in individual companies

4 *Centralisation/decentralisation decisions.* To some extent, most organisations have a choice over how much they wish to control from the centre. In summary, there are four main areas that need to be explored:
   - the nature of the business, e.g. economies of scale will probably need to be centralised;
   - the style of the chief executive: a dominant leader will probably centralise;
   - the need for local responsiveness;
   - the need for local service.
5 *Overall work to be undertaken.* Value chain linkages (see Chapter 6) across the organisation will clearly need to be co-ordinated and controlled. They may be especially important where an organisation has grown and become more diverse. Divisional or matrix structures may be needed, with the precise details depending on the specific requirements and strategies of the organisation.
6 *Technical content of the work.* In standardised mass production, the work to be undertaken controls the workers and their actions.[12] However, Japanese production methods have recently shown that flexibility may be highly desirable in mass production.
7 *Different tasks in different parts of the organisation.* It is clear that the tasks of operations (production) are not the same as those of the sales and marketing areas. Different organisations have different balances of such functions – for example, the strong role of *research* in a major pharmaceutical

company versus the dominance of *creative* people in some media companies: the different tasks need to be reflected in the way the organisation structure is designed.

8 *Culture*. The degree to which the organisation accepts change, the ambitions of the organisation and its desire for experimentation are all elements to be considered.[13]

9 *Leadership*. The style, background and beliefs of the leader may have an important effect on organisation design. This will be particularly true in *innovative* and *missionary* organisations. The innovative organisation is explored later in this chapter. The missionary organisation is described on the book's website material about the Mintzberg configurations.

In bringing all the above elements together, there is a danger of over-complicating the considerations and arguments. *Simplicity in design* should guide the proposals because the structure needs to be understood and operated after it has been agreed. We return to this area later in this chapter.

It is usual in undertaking such an analysis to consider the *responsibilities* and *powers* of the main individuals and groups involved, even if they are deliberately left vague in some structures. Responsibility and power need to be *controlled* and *monitored* and this needs to be built into the organisational structure. However, the control systems of the organisation can usually be considered after the proposed structure has been resolved (see Chapter 13).

12.2.3 Design configurations based on the external environment and internal organisation – Mintzberg's contribution

According to Mintzberg,[14] there are four main characteristics of the environment that influence structure (see Exhibit 12.5).

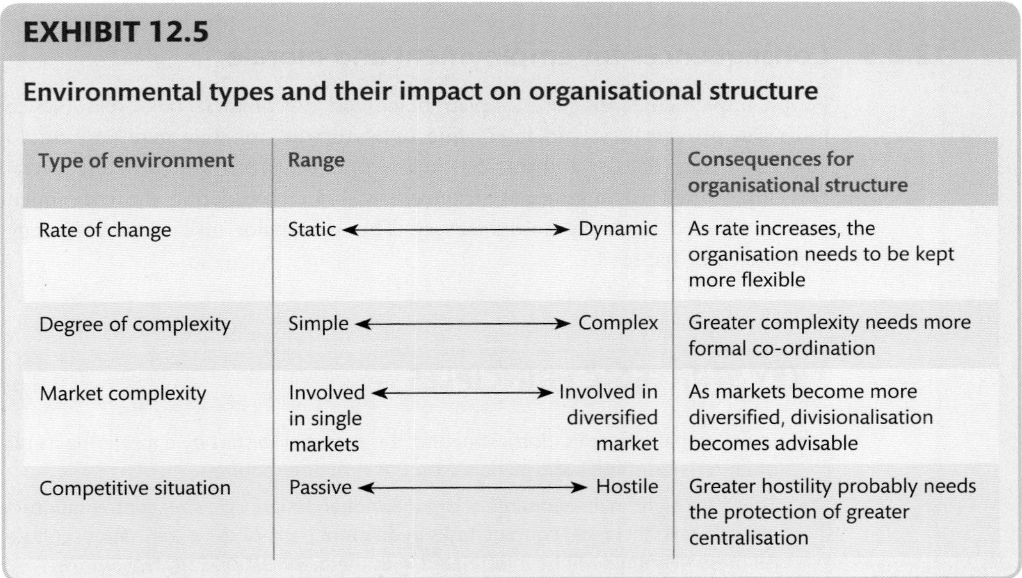

EXHIBIT 12.5

Environmental types and their impact on organisational structure

Type of environment	Range	Consequences for organisational structure
Rate of change	Static ⟷ Dynamic	As rate increases, the organisation needs to be kept more flexible
Degree of complexity	Simple ⟷ Complex	Greater complexity needs more formal co-ordination
Market complexity	Involved in single markets ⟷ Involved in diversified market	As markets become more diversified, divisionalisation becomes advisable
Competitive situation	Passive ⟷ Hostile	Greater hostility probably needs the protection of greater centralisation

Using these principles, Mintzberg then developed six major types of organisational structures that combine:

- the environment;
- the internal characteristics of the organisation (age, size, etc.) discussed earlier;
- the key part of the organisation in delivering its objectives; and
- the key co-ordinating mechanism that binds it together.

He then gave each of these combinations a name that would characterise its main features. There are six main types of structure – entrepreneurial, machine, professional, divisionalised, innovative and missionary – but they need to be used with caution.

More on Mintzberg's six design configurations for designing the structure of organisations.

12.2.4 The strategy to be implemented

Every organisation is to some extent unique – the result of its past, its resources and its situation. In addition, the key factors for success (see Chapter 3) and the major strategies chosen by whatever process will depend on the situation at that time. It is difficult to specify clear and unambiguous rules to translate strategy into organisational structures and people processes. Thompson and Strickland[15] recommend five useful steps that will assist this process but they caution against certainty:

1 Identify the tasks and people that are crucial to the strategy implementation.
2 Consider how such tasks and people relate to the existing activities and routines of the organisation.
3 Use key factors for success to identify the chief areas around which the organisation needs to be built.
4 Assess the levels of authority needed to action the identified strategies.
5 Agree the levels of co-ordination between the units in the organisation necessary to achieve the strategy.

The above are all rather generalised but this is inevitable in view of the unique nature of each organisation.

12.2.5 Consequences for employment and morale

People implement strategies, not plant machinery nor financial resources. New organisational structures can provide new and interesting opportunities for managers and employees. Alternatively, structures may deliver a threat to their scope for work and possibly even their employment. Developing new organisational structures without considering the consequences for those who will be affected is clearly unsatisfactory. This is a major task for any strategy and is considered separately in Chapter 15.

KEY STRATEGIC PRINCIPLES

- In building the organisation's structure, it is essential to start by considering its purpose. This will often provide some basic guidance on the structure required.
- There are eight main elements of organisational design: age; size; centralisation/decentralisation; overall work; technical content; tasks in different parts of the organisation; culture; and leadership. All these elements will be interrelated with the organisation's strategy.
- Environmental factors such as market change and complexity will impact on the proposed structure. In general, increased change and complexity suggest more flexible, less centralised structures. There are six main types of structure - entrepreneurial, machine, professional, divisionalised, innovative and missionary - but they need to be used with caution.
- Each organisation is unique and so it is difficult to develop unambiguous rules to implement strategy in terms of organisation structure and people issues.
- The impact of strategic change on employees and managers is a major consideration that deserves separate and detailed work.

12.3 THE CHOICE OF MANAGEMENT STYLE AND CULTURE

Alongside the issues of organisational purpose and design, there is also a choice to be made with regard to the style of management organisational culture. The organisation's culture was first analysed in Chapter 4. We now use this analysis because of its potential impact on strategy development. There is a related topic of the leadership of an organisation: this is explored in more depth in Chapter 16 but some issues related to the culture of an organisation are examined below.

12.3.1 Background

In addition to the discussions that have taken place over the past few years on the relationship between strategy and structure, there has been another equally vigorous debate about management style and culture. This has spanned both practitioner books and academic journals. Early writers included Peter Drucker, who started writing in the 1950s but was still producing books of interest in the 1990s.[16] In the 1980s, Peters and Waterman wrote their influential book *In Search of Excellence*, though Tom Peters has subsequently repudiated some of the guidance.[17] The writings of Charles Handy also represent a significant contribution.[18] Most are a good read but they also present research on how to operate companies, especially from the viewpoint of culture and style.

12.3.2 Culture, style, leadership and the relationship with strategy

Although every organisation is the result of its history, products and people, it periodically has the chance to renew itself. In other words, it is able to change its management culture and style. Inevitably, this will have an impact on strategy – both in obvious ways, such as the attitude to risk taking, and in more subtle ways, such as the ability of the company to innovate.

To some extent, an organisation will evolve in response to its continually changing environment. Furthermore, the leadership and top management at any point in time will clearly influence the organisation's culture and style. Nevertheless, organisations can also make the deliberate choice to change their culture and style as part of a major shift in strategy. The issues are therefore:

- Should the organisation change its culture and style?
- If so, in what way should the company change these?

It should be noted that this is not just an issue of implementation *after* the strategy has been chosen, but a fundamental choice available as part of the process. That is why the analysis of the organisation's culture was included at an early stage in Chapter 4.

Most of the writers and researchers quoted earlier in this section would argue that a shift in culture and style is essential if a fundamental change in strategy is proposed. They would support this view for three reasons:

1. Fundamental strategic change needs to impact on people in the organisation as well as on decision making. People issues are essentially summarised in culture and style.
2. Leadership is usually important for major changes in strategy. This is likely to encompass some shift in style and, occasionally, a change of leader.
3. Such a shift in culture and style is a *powerful symbol* of the related change in strategy.

12.3.3 The choice of a new culture and style

As a starting point, it is important to note that any change in this area will only happen slowly. In addition, the final decision will clearly be related to the proposed strategic changes. There will also need to be a degree of *strategic fit* between the strategy and the style, just as there was between strategy and structure earlier in the chapter. More generally, Hart has suggested a range of styles from which the choice can be made: they vary from the *imperial* to the *organic* and are shown in Exhibit 12.6. The content of each style can be matched to how the organisation sees itself developing over the period of the strategy.

Comment

Culture and style can rarely be changed overnight: it is often possible to introduce a new strategy more quickly than bring about a related change in style. Culture and style take time to develop so the strategic fit may need some adjustment. Hence, the process of introducing a new style needs careful thought.

EXHIBIT 12.6

Strategy and style options

Descriptors	Command	Symbolic	Rational	Transactive	Generative
Style	**Imperial** Strategy driven by leader or small top team	**Cultural** Strategy driven by mission and a vision of the future	**Analytical** Strategy driven by formal structure and planning systems	**Procedural** Strategy driven by internal process and mutual adjustment	**Organic** Strategy driven by the initiatives of those empowered in the organisation
Role of top management	**Commander** Provide direction	**Coach** Motivate and inspire	**Boss** Evaluate and control	**Facilitator** Empower and enable	**Sponsor** Endorse and sponsor
Role of organisational members	**Soldier** Obey orders	**Player** Respond to challenge	**Subordinate** Follow the system	**Participant** Learn and improve	**Entrepreneur** Experiment and take risks

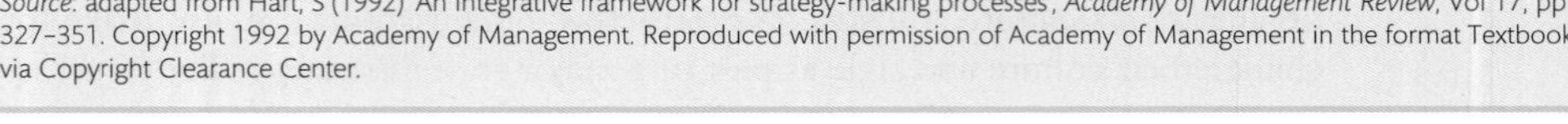

Source: adapted from Hart, S (1992) 'An integrative framework for strategy-making processes', *Academy of Management Review*, Vol 17, pp 327–351. Copyright 1992 by Academy of Management. Reproduced with permission of Academy of Management in the format Textbook via Copyright Clearance Center.

Description and critique of Professor Peter Senge's argument for a new organisational style based on modern ideas about co-operative management: 'Coping with the pressure for change: the new organic leadership style.'

12.3.4 Bridging the gap between strategy, structure and style: the contribution of Miles and Snow

Given the complexity of the relationships between strategy, structure and styles of management, there is a clear case for attempting to capture the main elements into some simpler format. Originally researched in the 1970s, the four strategic organisational types identified by R E Miles and Charles Snow have stood the test of time and are still relevant today.

Miles and Snow[19] identified four main strategic types of organisation:

1 *Defender organisations* produce products or services with the objective of obtaining market leadership. They may achieve their objectives by concentrating on a market niche through specialisation and cost reductions. The market may be mature and stable. The organisation is able to cope with sudden strategic change but would be more comfortable with steady strategic change. The organisation's style is more likely to be *command* or *rational* – see Exhibit 12.6.

2 *Prospector organisations* are involved in growing markets where they actively seek new opportunities through innovation. They are typically flexible and decentralised in their approach to the market and able to respond quickly to change. Their objectives are to seek new opportunities. Strategic change is no problem for such companies. The style is more likely to be *symbolic* or *generative* – see Exhibit 12.6.

Table 12.2 Four strategic types and their approaches to strategy

	Strategic environment	Strategic approach	Resource strategy	Simplified process approach
Defender	Stable	Protect market share Hold current position	Efficient production Tight control Centralised Manage via rules	Prescriptive
Analyser	Slow change	Hold market share but with some innovation Seek market opportunities but protect existing areas	Efficient production but some flexibility in new areas Tight control in existing areas but lower control in new products	Prescriptive
Prospector	Growing, even, dynamic	Find new opportunities Exploit and take risks	Flexible production Innovate with decentralised control	Emergent
Reactor	Growing or slow	Responding only to others Often late and inadequate	Muddled, centralised Slow	Prescriptive

Source: based on Miles, R E *et al.* (1978) 'A strategy typology of organisations', *Academy of Management Review*, July. Copyright 1978 by Academy of Management.

3 *Analyser organisations* seek to expand but also to protect what they already have. They may wait for others to innovate and delay while others prove new market opportunities before they enter. Large and small organisations can take this route, using mass production to reduce costs but also relying on some areas such as marketing to be more responsive and provide flexibility where required. Strategic change would need careful analysis and evaluation before it could be adopted. The style is more likely to be *command*, *transactive* or *rational* – see Exhibit 12.6.

4 *Reactor organisations* are those that respond inappropriately to competitors and to the more general environment. They rarely, if ever, take the initiative and, in a sense, may have no strategy: they always react to other strategies. Even if they have a strategy, it is entirely inappropriate to the environment and hence the resulting reactor organisation is bound to be inadequate. Strategic change will therefore be a problem. The style is likely to be *rational* – see Exhibit 12.6.

Table 12.2 summarises the main elements with a comment on the strategic process likely in each type of organisation. Reflecting on the four types, some readers (including this author) will wonder how *reactor* organisations ever manage to survive in the modern world. It is possible that the Miles and Snow classification over-simplifies the real situation and needs to be treated with some caution. Nevertheless, it does provide some guidance on these complex issues.

KEY STRATEGIC PRINCIPLES

- Every organisation has the choice of changing its culture and style when it changes its strategy.
- In many cases, a change of style is essential when a fundamental change of strategy is proposed.
- The content of the culture and style depends on the strategies proposed. There needs to be a degree of strategic fit between the two areas. Importantly, culture and style take time to change and may move more slowly than the proposed strategy.
- Given the complexity of the relationships between strategy, structure and style, Miles and Snow identified four different types of organisation that capture these. The four organisational types are: defender, prospector, analyser and reactor, each having associated styles of management and leadership.

CASE STUDY 12.2

Royal Dutch/Shell – what does it take to bring change?

In a bid to improve growth and profitability, the world's largest oil company Royal Dutch/Shell announced a radical re-organisation in 1995 that would sweep 'barons out of fiefdoms'. In 1999, the company's problems were unchanged and the barons – the managing directors of its national companies – were still there. In 2004, the company had major corporate problems, which at last forced the company into action. But would it be enough to bring real change?

Background

Royal Dutch/Shell is one of the world's great oil companies. It is based on a joint holding company set up in 1907 between the UK company Shell Transport and the Dutch oil company Royal Dutch. Over the years, the combined enterprise grew, becoming the largest oil company in the world in 1998, measured by turnover. However, global leadership was lost in 1999 – as we shall see later.

Unlike other oil companies, which had become more centralised, the delicate balance between the UK and Dutch interests was still preserved up to 1998. There was no overall holding company but two owners of all the subsidiaries: Royal Dutch owned 60 per cent of each subsidiary and Shell owned the other 40 per cent. This arrangement had originally been negotiated when the group was founded. There was no strong central core, nor any combined board of directors. The nearest that the company came to full co-ordination was a central management forum called 'the Conference'. This was a meeting of the management boards of the two operating companies, but it had no legal existence. The obvious strategic weakness was that this massive oil company could never use its shares – since they did not exist – to acquire another company.

Although managers and employees referred to themselves as members of Royal Dutch/Shell, they were in fact members of one of its various subsidiaries. This meant that all decision making was slow, laborious and careful – not necessarily a bad thing in an industry where time horizons for oil investment are typically 30 years. By 1998 the structure 'has become part of the problem – reducing accountability, blurring responsibility and increasing costs,' commented stockbrokers BT Alex Brown.

Proposed strategy and organisational changes in 1995

One result of the company's consultative style was that it had no chief executive to take final decisions. There was a committee of managing directors, but its decisions were achieved by consensus and its chairman was simply the 'first amongst equals'. Decisions on capital expenditure were often decidedly odd. The national companies were legal entities and demanded a share of the capital budget, regardless of whether they could make the best strategic case. Until 1995, the collegiate style of the committee of managing directors had limited powers to resist such demands.

In practical terms, this meant that key strategic decisions either took lengthy periods to emerge or were taken lower down in the organisation by the powerful national companies that made up the Royal Dutch/Shell empire, namely the barons referred to above. It also meant that there were large numbers of staff in London and Rotterdam whose job it was to co-ordinate the national policies associated with the regional barons. For many years, this had served the company well. However, by the mid-1990s, the company's return on capital was stuck below 10 per cent and was set to decline further.

Royal Dutch Shell had traditionally allowed its subsidiaries – like this one in Nagasaki, Japan – considerable freedom to take strategic decisions.

The 1995 re-organisation was supposed to sweep away such a decision-making structure and its consequences in terms of poor investment decisions based on national company interests rather than the global good of Royal Dutch/Shell. The national companies would report to a series of global operating companies and some 1,170 co-ordinating jobs would go at the centre. The aim was to save costs and focus decisions on the regional and global decision making. Figure 12.3 shows the change that was to be undertaken from 1995 onwards.

But the re-organisation quickly ran out of steam. Although some 900 staff jobs were cut, there was considerable resistance to the proposed changes. The consultation culture of the company led to 'laborious' negotiations with staff, especially in the Netherlands. Moreover, the barons were still in power through their membership of the new business committees and the company's profitability was declining – see Figure 12.4. According to many outside observers, much more drastic strategic change was required.

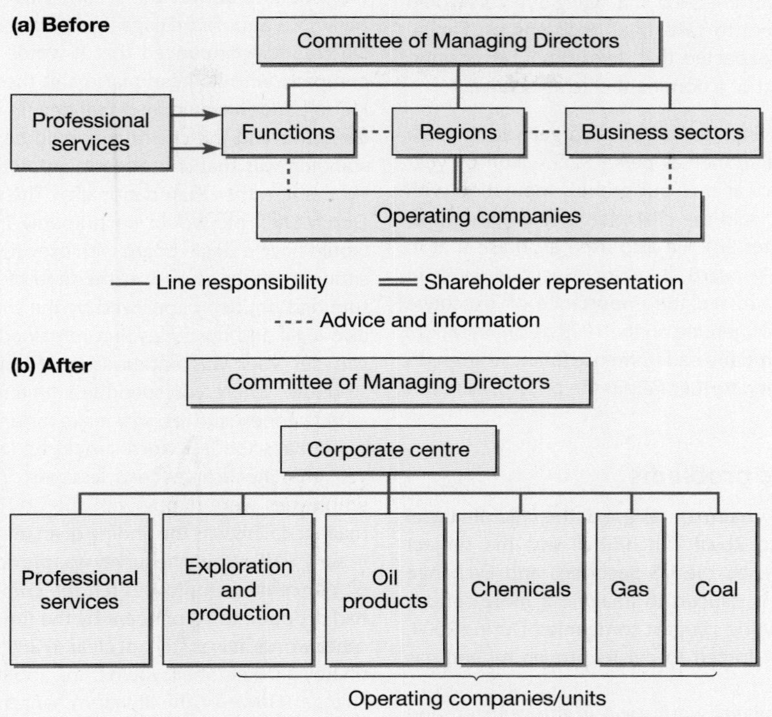

Figure 12.3 The 1995 re-organisation of Royal Dutch/Shell

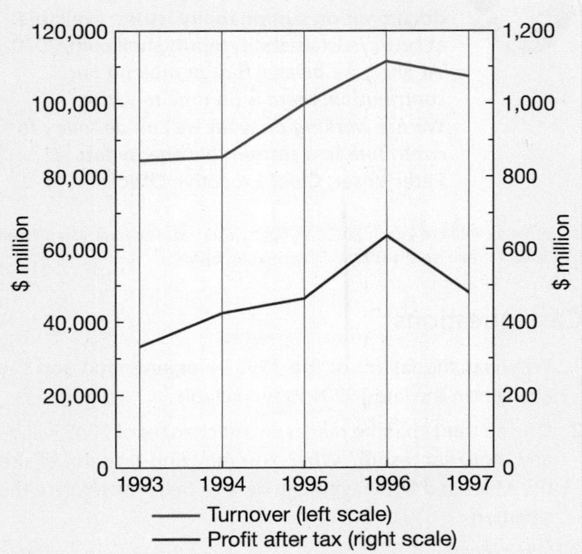

Figure 12.4 Operating performance at Royal Dutch/Shell

The 1998–1999 strategic re-organisation

By the late 1990s, it was much more difficult for all the world's oil companies to make profits than earlier in the decade. There were four main reasons for this.

1. Higher environmental standards meant that capital investment in oil refineries was much higher than in earlier decades.
2. Oil prices had declined from $15 per barrel in the early 1990s to around $10 in the late 1990s because supply worldwide outstripped demand.
3. Political uncertainty was higher in some leading oil-producing countries such as Russia and Indonesia.
4. Rival companies like Esso (USA), BP (UK) and Total (France) were acquiring or merging with rivals in order to gain further economies of scale: Exxon had acquired Mobil; BP had acquired Amoco, Atlantic Richfield and Castrol-Burmah; Total had merged with Fina and then with Elf. The subsequent success of these moves made Royal Dutch/Shell look weak strategically.

Royal Dutch/Shell realised that new and more drastic strategies were required, so it announced the following:

- closure of its national company headquarters in the UK, Germany, France and the Netherlands;
- write-off of $4.5 billion assets;
- sale of underperforming subsidiaries, especially 40 per cent of its chemicals business;
- cutbacks in annual capital investment from $15 billion to $11 billion per annum;
- several substantial acquisitions around the world that had been made earlier in the 1990s would be put up for sale;

- the chairman of the committee of managing directors would be given new powers to take final decisions on capital expenditure. It was expected that, over time, his position would emerge as that of a dominant chief executive.

The annual cost savings from this re-organisation were projected by Royal Dutch/Shell as being $2.5 billion by year 2001. 'I am absolutely clear that our group's reputation with investors is on the line,' said the chairman of the committee, Mark Moody-Stuart (later Sir). He also used a phrase that in the past has been rarely heard at senior executive levels in Royal Dutch/Shell: he stressed the importance of 'executive accountability' when commenting on the 1998 re-organisation. He also said that the company had immense financial strength and flexibility to withstand further falls in the price of oil, even below $10 per barrel.

The 2004 strategic problems

In 2004, the company's chairman resigned, the chief financial officer lost her job and Royal Dutch/Shell was the subject of a major investigation by the US Securities and Exchange Commission (SEC) – it is difficult to imagine a more serious situation in one of the world's largest companies. During 2004, the company had been forced to cut its proven oil and gas reserves by 23 per cent.

The seeds of the difficulty were sown in the years around the time of the 1998 re-organisation and its related cost savings. In the period 1996–1999, the group invested $6 billion per year exploring for new oil and gas deposits when it should have been spending around $8 billion. It was not until 2000 that Royal Dutch/Shell raised its level of investment to $9 billion per year, much closer to that of its rivals.

In 2001, a new chairman, Sir Philip Watts, took over at Royal Dutch/Shell. It is reported that he was warned in 2002 that the company was over-stating its oil and gas reserves in its annual accounts. This was a most serious situation since it affected the overall valuation of the company. However, it was not until early in 2004 that investors were told about this matter. Sir Philip and his head of exploration and production, Walter Van de Vijver, left the company in March 2004. The chief financial officer, Judy Boynton, also lost her job because she was 'not effective' in her compliance function. It was Judy Boynton's role to satisfy herself about the facts relating to the posting of reserves and compliance with the relevant financial statutes.

Outcome in 2004–2005

In March 2004, Jeroen van der Veer was appointed to succeed Sir Philip as chairman of the committee of managing directors of Royal Dutch/Shell. He had two major tasks. The first was to repair the damage to the company's reputation as a result of the problems above. The second was to re-organise the company into a more manageable whole. In October 2004, Royal Dutch/Shell announced that it would be reformed into one company with its headquarters in the Netherlands. The dual HQ in London would be disbanded. In addition, both the chief executive and the chairman would be Dutch, but the understanding was that subsequent appointments would be made on merit, rather than nationality. The newly combined Royal Dutch Shell plc would be primarily listed in London and it would have a single board with executives and non-executives sitting together as one. At the time of writing, this new structure had not been approved by the shareholders. There were also legal and tax issues that remained unresolved. However, van der Veer was enthusiastic: 'If you have a more simple structure, where you spend less time in lots of meetings, and with fewer executives, you make faster decisions.'

Perhaps the last word should be left to the employees. A year after the reserves crisis, less than one half of the company's employees were happy with the way that the company was managed. This was the finding of an internal survey undertaken in early 2005. When the survey was previously conducted in 2002, 67 per cent of employees felt the company was well led. This had dropped to 47 per cent by the time of the 2005 survey. In other words, it was still not clear in 2005 whether the pressures on Royal Dutch/Shell would bring about the necessary strategic changes. However, the situation changed over the next two years with the company beginning to put its problems behind it.

As part of its 2010 annual report, Royal Dutch Shell has prepared a 40-page document on sustainability issues: available at http://sustainabilityreport.shell.com/2010. *'At Shell, we believe that in making our contribution, there is no time to waste. We are working on what we can do today to contribute to a sustainable energy future.'* Peter Voser, Chief Executive Officer.

Case questions

1 Why was the failure of the 1995 re-organisation and the changes in the late 1990s so predictable?

2 Do you think that the management changes of 2005 will be any more successful? Why? You may find it useful to use the Miles and Snow typology here to help you analyse the situation.

3 What lessons, if any, can we draw about the human resource aspects of strategy analysis from this case?

Strategy and structure in international organisations – the role of headquarters.

12.4 TYPES OF ORGANISATIONAL STRUCTURE

Royal Dutch/Shell shows that changing the structure of an organisation can be slow and complex, possibly with unintended results. Nevertheless, there are some basic principles associated with the different types of organisational structure and these are explored in this section. Essentially, it is possible to identify six basic types of organisational structure that can serve to implement the chosen strategy:

- small organisation structure;
- functional organisation structure;
- multidivisional structure (sometimes shortened to *M-form* structure);
- holding company structure (sometimes shortened to *H-form* structure and discussed in Chapter 9 as the *corporate* headquarters company);
- matrix organisation structure;
- innovative organisation structure.

Each of these is explored in this section.

12.4.1 Small organisation structure

Definition ▸ **The small organisation structure consists of the owner/proprietor and the immediate small team surrounding that person.** In small organisations, there will often only be limited resources. Individuals will need to be flexible and undertake a variety of tasks. The informality of the structure will allow fast responses to market opportunities and customer service requirements. However, problems may be caused by the duplication of roles, confusion of responsibilities and muddled decision making, and it may not be realistic to draw up a clear organisational structure. Depending on the management style of the owner/leader, there may be many people or only the leader contributing to the organisation's strategy. Examples of such a company are a small family business or a specialist local computer service supplier.

12.4.2 Functional organisation structure[21]

Definition ▸ **The functional organisation is based on locating the structure around the main activities that have to be undertaken by the organisation, such as production, marketing, human resources, research and development, finance and accounting.** As the organisation grows from being a small company, the functional organisation structure is often the first structure that is adopted (see Figure 12.5). It allows experts in a functional area to be grouped together and economies of scale to operate. For example, a single product range production or service company, such as a regional bus company, is likely to have a functional structure. Exhibit 12.7 lists some of the advantages and disadvantages of this type of organisation structure.

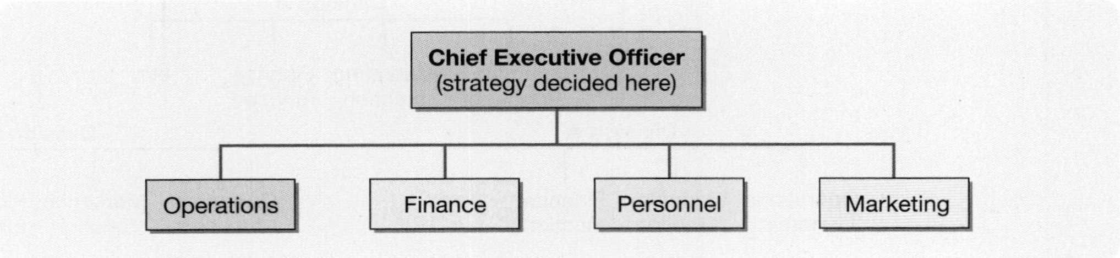

Figure 12.5 The functional organisational structure

EXHIBIT 12.7

Advantages and disadvantages of the functional organisation structure

Advantages	Disadvantages
• Simple and clear responsibilities • Central strategic control • Functional status recognised	• Co-ordination difficult • Emphasis on parochial functional areas in strategy development rather than company-wide view • Encourages interfunctional rivalry • Strategic change may be slow

12.4.3 Multidivisional structure

Definition ▶ **The multidivisional organisation is structured around separate divisions formed on the basis of products, markets or geographical areas.** This form of organisational structure was developed in the early 1920s by the future head of General Motors, Alfred Sloan, and was recorded by Alfred Chandler,[22] as explored in Section 12.1.1.

As organisations grow, they may need to subdivide their activities in order to deal with the great diversity that can arise in products, geographical or other aspects of the business (see Figure 12.6). For example in Case 12.1, there would be little to be gained by PepsiCo combining its Quaker Foods North America division with its PepsiCo International division because they have different product ranges, different customers and different strategic priorities. Chandler argued that strategy was decided at the centre, but in modern companies it is often partially determined by the divisions. However, the centre does influence strategy and allocate resources. See also Exhibit 12.8.

12.4.4 Holding or corporate company structure

Definition ▶ **A holding company is a company that owns various individual businesses and acts as an investment company with shareholdings in each of the individual enterprises.** The holding company strategy is

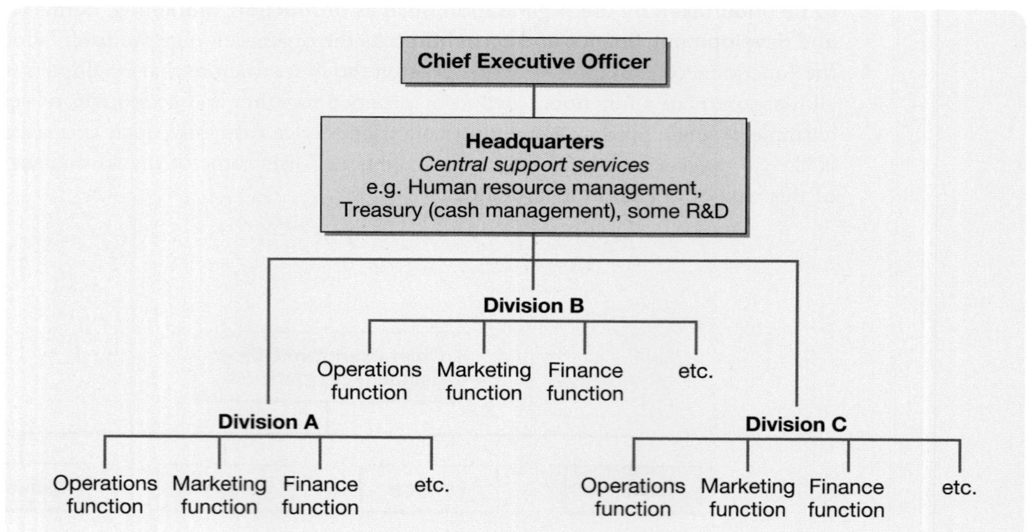

Figure 12.6 The multidivisional organisational structure

EXHIBIT 12.8

Advantages and disadvantages of the multidivisional organisation structure

Advantages	Disadvantages
• Focuses on business area • Eases functional co-ordination problems • Allows measurement of divisional performance • Can train future senior managers	• Expensive duplication of functions • Divisions may compete against each other • Decreased interchange between functional specialists • Problems over relationships with central services

often referred to as a *corporate strategy* across the range of individual businesses – see Chapter 9 for more detail.

Further growth in organisations may lead to more complex arrangements between different parts of the organisation and outside companies. For example, joint ventures with totally new companies outside the group, alliances, partnerships and other forms of co-operation may be agreed. As a result, the original company may take on the role of a central shareholder for the various arrangements that may be set up: it becomes a holding company (see Figure 12.7). Its role becomes one of allocating its funds to the most attractive profit opportunities. The holding company structure became more prominent in the period from 1970 onwards and was explored by Williamson. See also Exhibit 12.9.

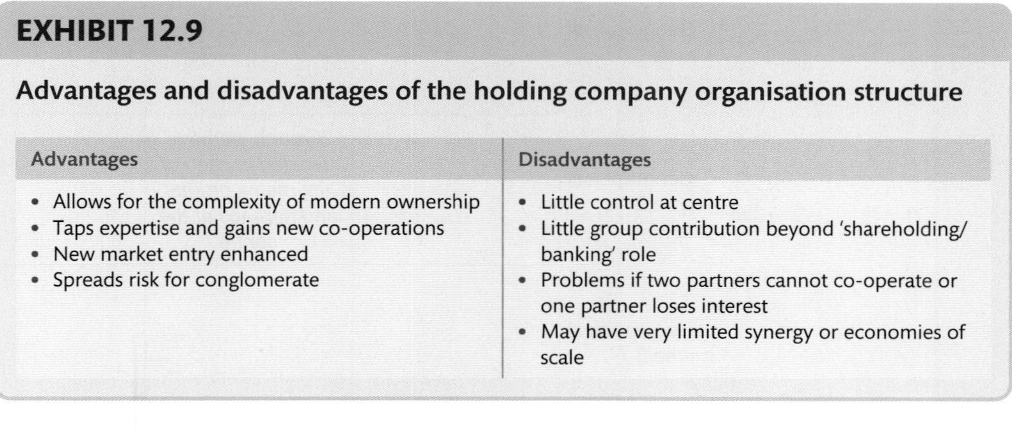

EXHIBIT 12.9

Advantages and disadvantages of the holding company organisation structure

Advantages	Disadvantages
• Allows for the complexity of modern ownership • Taps expertise and gains new co-operations • New market entry enhanced • Spreads risk for conglomerate	• Little control at centre • Little group contribution beyond 'shareholding/banking' role • Problems if two partners cannot co-operate or one partner loses interest • May have very limited synergy or economies of scale

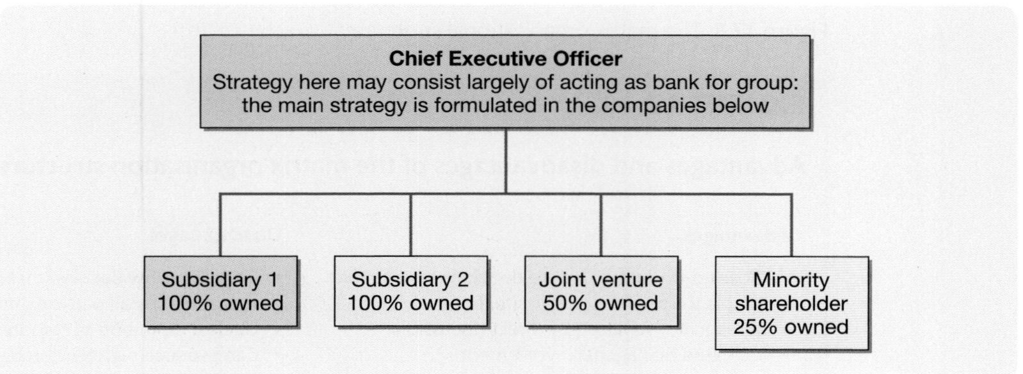

Figure 12.7 The holding company organisational structure

Siemens and General Electric (described in Case 9.1) is an example of a larger company that is well known for such arrangements:[23] it has extended its involvement into new markets and products. Some small companies have also become increasingly involved in such strategies in order to develop rapidly and exploit new opportunities. This is also seen in some of the large Japanese, Hong Kong and South-East Asian conglomerates.

12.4.5 Matrix organisation structure

Definition ▶ **A matrix organisation is a combination of two forms of organisation – such as product and geographical structures – that operate jointly on all major decisions.** In some cases, it may be advantageous for a large company to organise for its separate divisions or product groups to co-operate on business strategy with another method of organising the company, often a geographical one. For example, an oil company such as Royal Dutch/Shell may need to take strategic decisions not only for its oil, gas and chemical *products* but also for *countries* such as the UK, Germany, the USA and Singapore. It may be necessary to set up an organisation which has responsibilities along both product and geographical dimensions. Such dual-responsibility decision-making organisation structures are known as *matrix organisations*. The two dimensions do not necessarily have to be geography and product: any two relevant areas could be chosen (see Figure 12.8). Readers are referred to Case 12.3 on Asea Brown Boveri for the problems in a matrix structure. See also Exhibit 12.10.

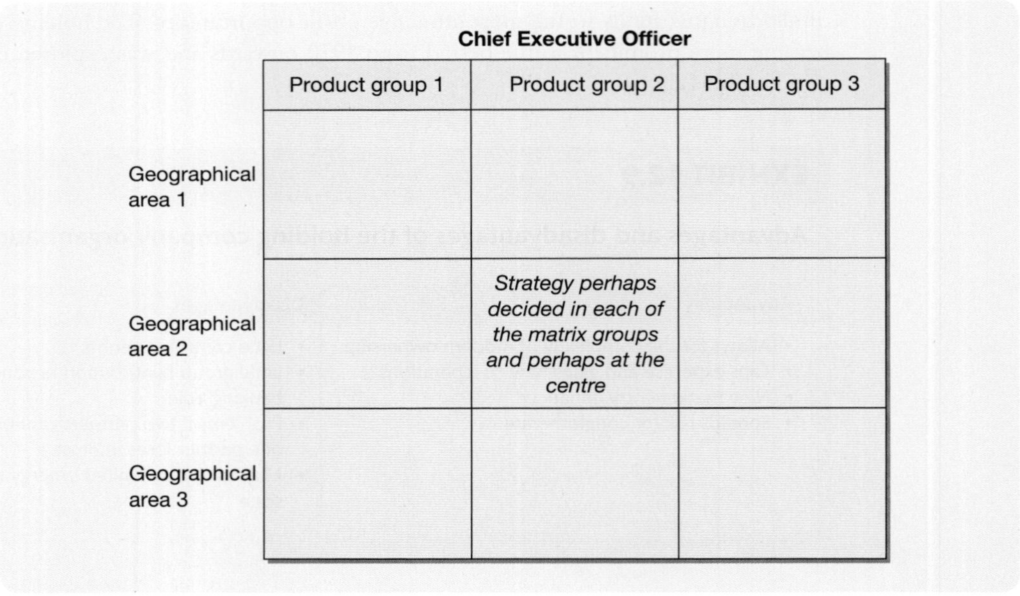

Chief Executive Officer

	Product group 1	Product group 2	Product group 3
Geographical area 1			
Geographical area 2		*Strategy perhaps decided in each of the matrix groups and perhaps at the centre*	
Geographical area 3			

Figure 12.8 The matrix organisational structure

EXHIBIT 12.10

Advantages and disadvantages of the matrix organisation structure

Advantages	Disadvantages
• Close co-ordination where decisions may conflict • Adapts to specific strategic situations • Bureaucracy replaced by direct discussion • Increased managerial involvement	• Complex, slow decision making: needs agreement by all participants • Unclear definition of responsibilities • Can produce high tension between those involved if teamwork of some parts is poor

12.4.6 Innovative organisation structures

Definition ▶ **Innovative organisation structures are characterised by their creativity, lack of formal reporting relationships and informality.** In some cases, large organisations need to lay special emphasis on their creativity and inventiveness – for example, advertising agencies, some service companies and innovative design companies. In these circumstances, there is a case for having strong teams that combine experts with different skills and knowledge, work without much hierarchy and have an open style of operation. The free-flowing nature of the group and its ideas may be important in the development of some aspects of strategy. In essence, strategy will be developed anywhere and everywhere. No simple organisation diagram can usefully be drawn.

12.4.7 Summarising the link between strategy and structure

For most organisations, it is essential to have some structure – even if it is fluid and ill-defined in small organisations; the choice lies between what the organisation has now and what it might have as its strategy changes. In summary, there is a connection between an organisation's business strategy and the most appropriate organisational structure[24] (see Exhibit 12.11).

EXHIBIT 12.11

Nature of business strategy and organisational structure

Nature of business strategy	Likely organisational structure
Single business - one major set of strategies for the business	Functional
Range of products extending across a single business - several strategies for each product area but business still run as one entity, perhaps with some common functions	Functional but monitor each range of products using separate profit and loss accounts
Separate businesses within group with limited links - assuming that each business is not related and operates in a separate market	Divisional
Separate businesses within group with strong links needed across parts of the group	Matrix (or divisional with co-ordination if matrix is difficult to manage)
Ideas factory - strategy needs to be strongly experimental and emerge	Innovative structure
Unrelated businesses - series of businesses each with its own strategic issues	Holding company
Related businesses owned jointly or by minority shareholdings - series of businesses where each needs to have its own strategies and be managed separately	Holding company

KEY STRATEGIC PRINCIPLES

- There are six main types of organisational structure, each having advantages and disadvantages.
- The small organisation has limited resources but an informal structure, allowing flexibility in response, but giving unclear lines of responsibility.
- The functional organisation has been used mainly in small to medium-sized organisations with one main product range.

- As organisations develop further ranges of products, it is often necessary to divisionalise them. Each division then has its own functional structure, with marketing, finance, production, etc.
- As organisations become even more diverse in their product ranges, the headquarters may just become a holding company.
- An alternative form of structure for companies with several ranges of products is the matrix organisation, where joint responsibility is held by two different structures, e.g. between product divisions and another organisational structure such as geographical or functional divisions. This type of organisation has some advantages but is difficult to manage successfully.
- Innovative organisations may have cross-functional teams.
- The place where strategy is developed depends on the organisational structure.

12.5 ORGANISATIONAL STRUCTURES FOR INNOVATION

Innovative structures and processes were introduced in the previous section, but innovation is too important to the whole corporate strategic process for it to be described as only suitable for some specialist organisation types. *Every* organisation needs an element of innovation: hence, *every* organisation needs structures capable of producing this, even if these structures are only temporary, for example, a team is formed for a particular project and disbanded once the work is completed.

12.5.1 Innovation needs to be commercially attractive

Before exploring how an organisation can best structure itself to be innovative, it is useful to examine what is required. In a competitive market place, it is not enough to be innovative: the new product or service has to be commercially attractive to potential customers, i.e. it must offer value for money compared with existing products and services. Gilbert and Strebel[25] call this the *complete competitive formula*.

It may be desirable to include a broader range of benefits in addition to the innovation itself. Often, the real breakthrough comes not with the technical development but with the extended package of promotion, distribution, support and customer service. All of these elements are geared towards making the innovation user-friendly and more commercially attractive. This requires an *integrated* organisation structure across all functions of the business. For example, one of the reasons that the web has taken off on the internet over the past few years has been the introduction of innovative user-friendly software such as that used by Adobe for picture and video editing. However, the real breakthrough for the company came when it arranged for free distribution through computer magazines of certain types of its software for evaluation by personal use. The result has been that, at the time of writing, Adobe has become the dominant software on this new, growing medium. From the organisational viewpoint, such developments need integration and co-ordination across all the functions if innovative solutions are to be obtained.

12.5.2 The nature of the innovative process

In Chapter 7, we examined Quinn's use of the concept of 'controlled chaos' to describe the innovative process. Innovation is flexible, open-ended and possibly without a clearly defined or fixed objective. The process needs to be free-wheeling and experimental. Within this, it is useful to distinguish between:[26]

- *simple innovation*, which might be possible in any organisation and relies on one person or a small group, and
- *complex innovation*, which may require experts drawn from a variety of business functions to form project teams. This is likely to involve larger resources and greater organisational complexity.

Mintzberg's comments on the innovative process had complex innovation particularly in mind when outlining three guidelines for organising project teams, which are summarised in Exhibit 12.12.

EXHIBIT 12.12

Guidelines for organising innovative project teams

1 *Flexible structures* are needed that allow experts not just to exercise their skills but to break through conventional boundaries into *new* areas.
2 *Co-ordination* within the team needs to be undertaken by experts with a technical background in the area, rather than a superior with authority from outside.
3 *Power* in the team needs to be distributed among the experts, where appropriate. Much of the activity will consist of liaison and discussion among the experts as they progress their innovative ideas.

Ultimately, the strategy that emerges from the innovative process may remain vague and ill-defined. This has the advantages of being flexible, responsive and experimental. However, the disadvantages associated with a lack of definition may not satisfy the culture of organisations wanting quick and precise results.

12.5.3 Organisational structures and procedures for innovative companies

Kanter[27] surveyed a number of US companies in the 1970s and 1980s in an attempt to identify the organisation structures and processes that were most conducive to innovation. Among her conclusions were:

- *The importance of matrix structures.* These were more likely in innovative companies. They tended to break down barriers and lead to the more open reporting lines that were important to the innovative process. Decision making may have been slow and complex in matrix structures, but it provided the network for individuals to move outside their own positions and make the interconnections useful to innovation.
- *The need for a parallel organisation.* A separate group to run in tandem with the existing formal hierarchy was often highly valuable. It was specifically tasked with finding innovative solutions to problems, especially where a matrix structure was not in operation. It was able to act independently, without the day-to-day pressures and politics of the existing structure. It was then left to the existing organisation to define routine jobs, titles and reporting relationships. Instead of contacts and power flowing up and down the existing structure, the parallel organisation allowed new relationships and ideas to develop.
- *The work of a parallel organisation.* This had to be problem solving, possibly focused on a single business problem and structured around the team. The work was integrative, flexible and with little hierarchical division. The function of such a group was often to re-examine existing routines and systems, concentrating especially on areas that were partially unknown and needed challenging. It often provided a means of empowering people lower down in the organisation.[28]
- *Participative/collaborative management style.* This was often employed to encourage innovation. It involved persuading rather than ordering, seeking advice and comments and sharing the favourable results of successful initiatives.[29]

From her research, Kanter recommended five pointers to action that could be taken to encourage innovation in weaker organisations[30] (see Exhibit 12.13). The most successful global companies, such as Toyota and McDonald's, have been particularly successful at pursuing such policies.

EXHIBIT 12.13

Five pointers to encourage innovation

1. Publicise and take pride in existing achievements.
2. Provide support for innovative initiatives, perhaps through access to senior managers, perhaps through project teams.
3. Improve communication across the enterprise by creating cross-functional activities and by bringing people together.
4. Reduce layers in the hierarchy of the organisation and give more authority to those further down the chain.
5. Publicise more widely and frequently company plans on future activity, giving those lower down in the organisation a chance to contribute their ideas and become involved in the process.

Comment

All of Kanter's ideas were researched and proposed in the context of the North American corporation. Some may not work at all or may need to be substantially modified in other national cultures. Moreover, the problems that were observed in terms of innovation may not be the same in other countries. What they do illustrate is that, for strategic innovation at least, the flexible, *open structure* of the organisation may need to come before the *innovatory strategies* that subsequently emerge.

KEY STRATEGIC PRINCIPLES

- All companies need to be able to innovate as part of the strategic process.
- Such innovation needs to be commercially attractive if it is to be viable. An organisation structure that integrates and co-ordinates all the functional areas of a business is desirable.
- Innovation is open-ended and flexible, so the process needs to be experimental, with flexible structures, close co-ordination and power distributed throughout the innovating group.
- In terms of structure, a matrix organisation may be more effective because it is more integrative. In some circumstances, a separate, parallel organisation tasked with developing innovative solutions can be usefully employed.

CASE STUDY 12.3

How ABB empowered its managers and then reversed the process

When the world's largest electrical engineering company, ASEA Brown Boveri (ABB), was formed in 1987, one of its earliest strategic decisions was to re-organise and move power from the centre to its operating companies: empowerment. In the beginning, this was hailed as being a classic example of modern management under its famous chairman, Percy Barnevik. By 2004, the empowerment strategy was regarded as being a complete failure. This case explains what happened at ABB.

Rise and fall of ABB

With 2004 revenue of over $20.7 billion and 100,000 employees around the world, ABB was one of the world's largest traditional electrical engineering companies. Its products included electrical power transmission and distribution, building technologies and automation. It operated in global markets and competed against such major companies as General Electric (USA), Westinghouse (USA), Siemens (Germany) and Alsthom

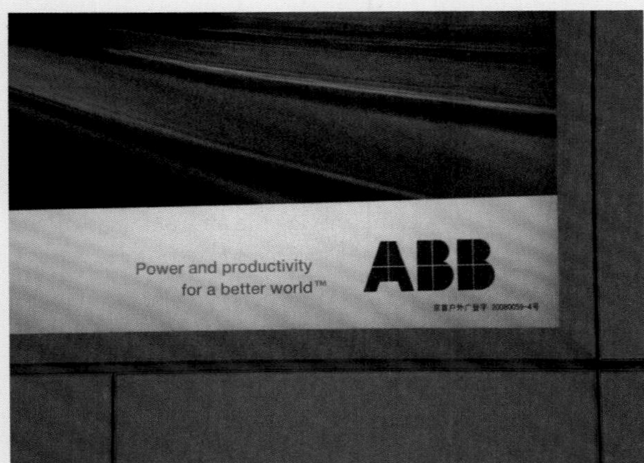

ABB's global strategy became famous in the 1990s for empowering its managers. This case examined what happened at that time

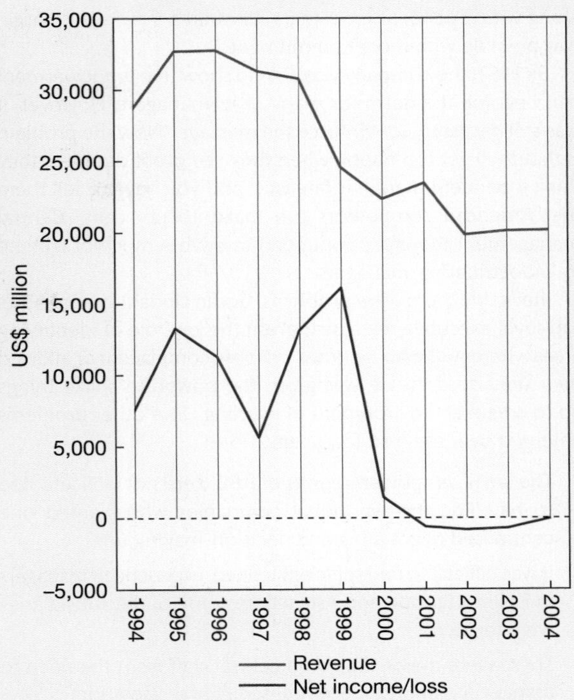

Figure 12.9 ABB's sales and profit record

Source: ABB annual report and accounts from various years.

(France) as well as with the major Japanese groups Mitsui and Mitsubishi. But ABB was not profitable during the latter part of this period.

After success in building its turnover during the 1990s, ABB's sales and profits hit their peak in 1999. The company then made a loss in the four years 2001–2004, although the loss was very small by the end of this period. Its staff dropped by 57,000 employees between the years 2000 and 2004 as a result of the closure and sale of subsidiaries. The reasons for this decline included fierce competition and a weak world economy. The company was also hit by one of its subsidiaries having to bear the considerable costs associated with the medical liabilities of asbestos products. However, ABB's manufacturing costs were also higher than those of its competitors: many commentators judged that its whole organisation structure needed simplifying and further costs taking out. Figure 12.9 shows the whole difficult record.

Company history

ABB was formed in 1987 from the engineering interests of the Swedish company ASEA and the Swiss engineering company Brown Boveri. Over the period 1988–1990, the company was completely re-organised by its new chairman, Percy Barnevik. The central HQ in Switzerland was reduced to a total of 150 people, with a matrix management structure introduced worldwide. The company was split into 1,300 smaller companies and around 5,000 profit centres, functioning as far as possible as independent operations. Several layers of middle management were stripped out and directors from the central HQ moved into regional co-ordinating companies. Costs were not necessarily lower because many of the central headquarters operations had to be duplicated in each company.

At the same time, the company engaged in a major programme of acquisitions that grew the order intake of ABB from $16 billion to $25 billion over two years. Major companies were purchased in the USA, Spain, Italy, the UK, France, Spain and Germany. All the negotiations for these major decisions were handled centrally by ABB. A period of consolidation then followed from 1991 to 1993.

Company strategy to empower management

Under the direction of its chief executive (later chairman), Percy Barnevik, ABB pursued its bold initiative of breaking up the company into 1,300 smaller units, each with profit responsibility. The company became a well-known strategy case for business school study during this period. The moves were essentially aimed at empowering managers to move closer to their customers and at giving them the incentives to act as smaller and more entrepreneurial units. Even research and development was decentralised, with the new operating companies controlling 90 per cent of the group's $2.3 billion budget. This made the centralised sharing of knowledge more difficult, but the company judged that this was more than compensated by the empowerment of individual companies. Importantly, central finance and cash management were excluded from the decentralisation process and then used to monitor the performance of the empowered companies across the world.

Barnevik considered that the greatest strategic challenge in running a group of this size was motivating middle and lower managers and shifting entrenched corporate values. As he explained, previously managers had been happy to coast along with 2 per cent gross margins when a 5 per cent margin was possible with more commitment.

By 1991, the company was able to show that empowerment had become the norm for many of its managers. However, it was still necessary to reinforce the message: 'Now the problem is that they get too happy when they see profit doubled; they think 4 per cent margin is fantastic, and you have to tell them that American competitors can make 10 per cent.' Central management therefore continued to devote much of its time to 'indoctrinating' managers.

Inevitably there were problems. Goran Lindahl, one of ABB's top-level executive team, was given the key role of identifying areas where ABB managers had become complacent or allowed their units to drift. He was given the power 'to shake things up to create an environment of learning'. Five other problems emerged over the next few years:

1 The small, empowered units of ABB were not well adapted to handling the big global companies who wanted one centralised negotiating and decision-making unit.
2 It was difficult to find sufficient trained, experienced managers in Eastern Europe and Asia where some of the subsidiaries were located.
3 There were major strains on central staff from the need to manage a complex, decentralised global operation.
4 Extra costs were incurred in duplicating management positions in a large number of small companies.
5 Small companies were not always able to gain the economies of scale that would be available to larger, more centralised organisations.

New leadership and new organisation structure – 1997

In 1997, Percy Barnevik gave up his position of chief executive. His successor was Goran Lindahl. Their leadership styles were quite different: Barnevik was eloquent, conceptual and led from the front, whereas Lindahl was more down-to-earth, consensual and interested in detail. Nevertheless, Barnevik stayed on as non-executive chairman.

In 1998, Lindahl announced two major strategic moves. First, he accelerated the shift to using Asian labour. Another 10,000 jobs would be lost in Europe and the USA and be replaced by the same number of jobs in Asia. The cost for shareholders was estimated at $1 billion. Second, he scrapped the group's matrix organisational structure and brought in some new, younger executives to the group's managing board. This was later followed by the sale of two unprofitable divisions – power generation and transport – over the next 18 months. Then, in 2000, Lindahl suddenly gave up his job. His explanation was that he believed ABB should be led by someone who 'understands how to exploit the IT revolution' and he was not that person. It is fair to say that his sudden departure halfway through his expected term caused some shock among outside observers.

New leadership and new organisation structure – 2000 onwards

The new chief executive, Jorgen Centermann, lost no time in completely restructuring ABB. He developed an organisation with four worldwide customer segments, coupled with two back-up product segments. He cut the number of subsidiaries from over 1,000 to 400, thus having the effect of undoing the 'empowerment' strategy of the early 1990s. He gave three reasons:

1 the need to focus more on ABB's main large, global customers;
2 the need to cut costs, especially those associated with the duplication of management essential to decentralisation;
3 the need to exploit the power of the internet.

In addition, he appointed two new main board directors, one with responsibility for 'corporate processes' and the other for 'corporate transmission'. These were both associated with his desire to turn ABB into an 'agile, knowledge-based company' and to develop 'brain power' as a corporate motto. Jorgen Centermann decided that ABB could not compete successfully in its power-related businesses so he scaled them back. He also sold the ABB nuclear power business to British Nuclear Fuels. In 2002, Centermann negotiated the sale of ABB's financial services division to one of its main competitors, General Electric of the USA. The funds raised by this latter sale helped ABB, which was in significant financial difficulties at that time. The company had been hit by the downturn in the world economy, the asbestos claims against two of its subsidiaries and strong competition. Having undertaken this restructuring, Centermann felt that he should resign. He was replaced as chief executive of ABB by Jurgen Dormann. It was Dormann who had previously taken over the chairmanship of ABB from Percy Barnevik in 2001 when it was obviously in trouble. Around this time and after adverse public criticism, Barnevik and Lindahl returned $82 million in controversial pension benefits that they had received from ABB.

Jurgen Dormann remained chief executive until 2004 during a difficult business period. He oversaw major cutbacks at the company from the centre and then handed over this position to Fred Kindle, who remained chief executive at the time of writing this case. With such a series of senior management changes, the company had clearly gone through a period of considerable turmoil. However, ABB claimed at the end of 2004 that, 'The company is now in good health.' The previous decentralised structure had been largely dismantled, with key decisions reverting to the centre of the company.

ABB is still one of the world leaders in power and automation companies. The company's range of products used in green strategy includes such items as wind power electricity generators. ABB has introduced a separate report on sustainability issues available at: http://www400.abbext.com/2010/sr/servicepages/welcome.html.

Case questions

1 How important to the strategy of empowerment is a sophisticated financial control system? And how vital is the central monitoring (e.g. Lindahl)? What does this mean for empowerment?

2 If the world is becoming increasingly global, do you think that ABB's unit empowerment ever stood any chance of success?

3 To what extent, if at all, can large, global companies empower local managers? What are the implications for strategy development – centralised or decentralised?

STRATEGIC PROJECT

This is a particularly interesting company because it was presented as a revolutionary new form of organisation in the 1990s and a model for other companies. You might like to use the references for this case to look back and see how the company has changed. You might also like to consider how the company should now move forward. It still faces significant difficulties that will need considerable effort and skill from all its employees.

12.6 MOTIVATION AND STAFFING IN STRATEGY IMPLEMENTATION

If ever there was a company that worked at motivating its managers (e.g. through its empowerment strategy) it was ABB. But the evidence suggests that the company was unsuccessful: its empowerment strategy was ultimately dismantled and power returned to the centre. Nevertheless, capable and well-motivated people are essential to strategy implementation, especially at senior management level. This section explores the *formal organisation* needed to achieve this:

- reward systems that can increase motivation;
- staff appraisal, training and selection procedures for a successful strategy.

The *informal* aspects of this subject, associated with strategy implementation, such as leadership and culture, are left to Chapter 15.

12.6.1 Reward systems

Definition ▶ **Reward systems are the structured benefits paid to individuals and groups who have delivered strategies that add value to the organisation consistent with its agreed purpose.** The measurement of achievement and the reward for good performance against the organisation's objectives can be powerful motivators for the delivery of strategic management. The linkage between reward and motivation has been extensively researched over the past few years and the connection well established.[32] Rewards need to be seen more broadly than simple payment: they may involve other forms of direct remuneration but also promotion and career development opportunities.

In designing reward systems to achieve strategic objectives, several factors need to be considered:

- *Strategic objectives*. These tend to have a longer-term element, whereas managers may well need to have short-term rewards. Hence, there may be a conflict between rewarding achievement of strategic objectives and a personal desire for short-term recompense. Moreover, not all strategic objectives are easily measurable, thus making accurate assessment difficult. To some extent, these problems have been resolved by rewarding individuals with shares in the enterprise, but this incentive may not be available to all organisations and is still subject to manipulation.
- *Rewards focusing on individual performance*. These may not be appropriate when group objectives have been identified as crucial to strategy. Careful consideration of the impact of reward systems may therefore be required.

- *Rewards encouraging innovation and risk taking.* These may need to move beyond quantitative measures of performance, such as an increase in return on capital or earnings per share, to qualitative assessments based on the number and quality of the initiatives undertaken. There may well be a greater element of judgement involved, which may in turn lead to accusations by others of unfairness unless handled carefully.

In recent years, reward systems have been given new emphasis by the introduction of *performance contracts*. Some companies have developed a system whereby strategy implementation is split into a series of measurable milestones. Individual directors and senior managers then sign contracts to deliver these targets and their performance is reviewed accordingly. There is a free web-based case that describes this procedure. It is linked to Chapter 15 and describes performance-based contracts at the UK company BOC Group.

12.6.2 Formal staff appraisal, training and selection procedures

New strategies may well call for new business approaches, new skills and new knowledge. Existing members of staff will not necessarily have these. It may be necessary therefore to introduce formal structures and procedures to appraise and train existing staff or to recruit new people in order to implement the strategy successfully.[33]

For motivational reasons, it is often appropriate to begin with existing staff members and assess their suitability for new positions – called appraisal. However, they may not possess the required knowledge and skill levels required, in which case training or outside recruitment becomes essential.

In strategic management, staffing issues primarily concern the most senior managers in the organisation. In cases of major strategic crisis, the chief executive officer may need to be replaced: there are countless cases during recent years of this one act being crucial to strategic change. However, it should be said that this may only be the *beginning* of a new strategy, rather than its implementation. When Lou Gerstner was recruited to head IBM after its spectacular profit problems in 1994 (see Case 1.2 on IBM), he was hired on the basis that he had complete freedom to identify the main strategic problems, solutions and strategies. In this case, the first stage of the new IBM strategy was to hire an outsider to rescue the company. However, it should be pointed out that the previous chief executive was also aware of the difficulties and the need for change. It will be evident that, in general, recruiting senior talent to implement identified strategies can be a crucial element in an organisation's continued success or failure.

For the many companies that do not experience major crises, the provision of a sound *performance appraisal system* will be a major contribution to successful strategy implementation. Staff training and broader staff development programmes to build up the people elements in strategic management may accompany this. These are part of the area of human resource management strategy for the company. Coupled with recruitment and reward, they underline the crucial importance of this functional area at the highest levels of strategic management development.

KEY STRATEGIC PRINCIPLES

- Measurement of achievement and the subsequent reward for good performance can be powerful methods for directing strategic management.
- However, reward systems may be difficult to develop that fully coincide with the organisation's strategic objectives for a variety of reasons.
- Staffing issues, such as recruitment, appraisal and training, are essential to the implementation of strategy. Formal procedures need to be built into the consideration of new or revised human resource management procedures.

CRITICAL REFLECTION

Should organisations put stronger emphasis on human resources issues much earlier in strategy development?

This chapter has explored the issues surrounding an organisation's culture, leadership style and structure after the previous chapters have considered the development of the organisation's strategy. The chapter has argued that strategy and structure are interrelated and, in that sense, suggested that the human aspects of the organisation need to be considered earlier in strategy development.

However, many of the leading strategy theorists seem to suggest that strategy is mainly concerned with competitive and customer issues, not human resource issues. But might human resource aspects - like leadership, organisation structure, culture and style - be more important? Should they perhaps come much earlier in strategy development? What are the consequences of your views for the way you would develop an organisation's strategy?

SUMMARY

- According to modern strategic thinking, Chandler's concept of strategy first and then structure to deliver it may over-simplify the situation. There have been some major criticisms of Chandler. First, changes in the business environment and social values of the late twentieth century suggest that others beyond top management may need to contribute to strategy. This is called empowerment of the middle and junior ranks of managers. This can best take place before the organisation structure is finalised. Second, new processes for developing strategy are adaptive and involve learning mechanisms. Third, such processes also need open, fluid structures that may not be best served by simple functional structures. When strategic change is radical, it may not be possible to define clearly the final organisation structure. It may be necessary to let the structure emerge as strategy changes and develops.
- If strategy and structure are interlinked, then it is essential that they are consistent with each other – the concept of 'strategic fit'.
- In building the organisation's structure, it is essential to start by reconsidering its purpose. This will often provide some basic guidance on the structure required. In addition, there are eight main elements of organisational design: age; size; centralisation/decentralisation; overall work; technical content; tasks in different parts of the organisation; culture; and leadership. All these elements will be interrelated with the organisation's strategy. There are six main types of structure – entrepreneurial, machine, professional, divisionalised, innovative and missionary – but they need to be used with caution. Each organisation is unique and so it is difficult to develop unambiguous rules to implement strategy in terms of organisation structure and people issues. The impact of strategic change on employees and managers is a major consideration that deserves separate and detailed work.
- Every organisation has the choice of changing its culture and style when it changes its strategy. In many cases, a change of style is essential when a fundamental change of strategy is proposed. The content of the culture and style depends on the strategies proposed. There needs to be a degree of strategic fit between the two areas. Importantly, culture and style take time to change and may move more slowly than the proposed strategy. Given the complexity of the relationships between strategy, structure and style, Miles and Snow identified four different types of organisation that capture these. The four organisational types are: defender, prospector, analyser and reactor, each having associated styles of management and leadership.
- There are six main types of organisational structure, each having advantages and disadvantages. The *small organisation* structure is self-explanatory. The *functional organisation* structure has been mainly used in small to medium-sized organisations with one main product range. As organisations develop further ranges of products, it is often necessary to *divisionalise*. Each division then

has its own functional structure – marketing, finance, production, etc. As organisations become even more diverse in their product ranges, the headquarters may just become a *holding company*. An alternative form of structure for companies with several ranges of products is the *matrix organisation*, where joint responsibility is held between the products structure and another organisational format such as the functional structure. This type of organisation has some advantages but is difficult to manage successfully. The *innovative organisation* is quite different from the others, involving less formal structures and more informal reporting procedures.

- In building the most appropriate organisation structure, it is important to keep in sight the need for simple, cost-effective structures. Environmental factors, such as market change and complexity, will also impact on the proposed structure. In general, increased change and complexity suggest more flexible, less centralised structures.
- All organisations must be able to innovate as part of the strategic process, but such innovation needs to be commercially attractive if it is to be viable. An organisation structure that integrates and co-ordinates all the functional areas of a business is desirable. Because innovation is open-ended and flexible, the process needs to be experimental, with flexible structures, close co-ordination and power distributed throughout the innovating group.
- In terms of innovative structures, a matrix organisation may be more effective because it is more integrative. In some circumstances, a separate, parallel organisation tasked with developing innovative solutions can be employed.
- Measurement of achievement and the subsequent reward for good performance can be powerful methods for directing strategic management. However, it may be difficult to develop reward systems that coincide fully with the organisation's strategic objectives. Staffing issues, such as recruitment, appraisal and training, are essential to the implementation of strategy. Formal procedures need to be built into the consideration of new or revised human resource management procedures.

QUESTIONS

1 Explain the structure of an organisation with which you are familiar, using the elements outlined in Sections 12.2 and 12.3 as your guide.

2 What structure would you expect the following organisations to have?

   (a) A small management consultancy company based in one country only.

   (b) A voluntary group providing volunteers to visit the elderly and house-bound.

   (c) A medium-sized company with 1,500 employees, two factories and a separate headquarters.

   (d) A leisure park business owned and operated by a family company.

   (e) A medium-sized computer company with 80 employees which writes software for games machines.

3 *'If structure does follow strategy, why should there be a delay in developing the new organisation needed to meet the administrative demands of the new strategy?'* (Alfred Chandler) How would you answer this question?

4 If you were asked to make PepsiCo – see Case 12.1 – more innovative, what would you do? In answering this question, you should take into account the existing culture of the company.

5 'Every organisation needs an element of innovation' (see Section 12.5). Is this correct?

6 *'All any company has to do to explore its own potential to become a more innovatory organisation is to see what happens when employees and managers are brought together and given a significant problem to tackle.'* (R M Kanter) Discuss.

7 Why is it difficult to develop reward systems to deliver the organisation's objectives? How might such difficulties be overcome in a small entrepreneurial business venture?

8 The managing director of a large company making bicycles has become worried by the lack of growth in sales, believing the company has lost its earlier innovative spark, and has turned to you for advice. What would you recommend?

9 *'The hallmark of many successful business organisations is the attention given to the human element.'* (Laurie Mullins, author of the well-known text *Management and Organisational Behaviour*) Is the human element more important than competitive strategy?

FURTHER READING

Professor Henry Mintzberg has a useful discussion on organisation structure and strategy in 'The structuring of organisations', in Mintzberg, H and Quinn, J B (1991) *The Strategy Process*, 2nd edn, Prentice Hall, New York, p 341.

Laurie Mullins (2006) *Management and Organisational Behaviour*, 7th edn, Pearson Education, Harlow, can be consulted for an extended discussion on organisational issues.

Professor Gerry Johnson's paper (1989) 'Rethinking incrementalism', *Strategic Management Journal*, January–February, pp 75–91, is worth reading. It is reprinted in De Wit, B and Meyer, R (1994) *Strategy: Process, Content and Context*, West Publishing, St Paul, MN.

Professor Rosabeth Moss Kanter (1985) *The Changemasters*, Unwin, London, has a useful empirical study of innovative practice. Note: there was a major and timely retrospective on Kanter's work in *Academy of Management Executive* (2004), Vol 18, No 2, pp 92–110.

There was a special issue of *Long Range Planning* in 2000 on executive pay and recruitment: five papers including the editorial, Vol 33, No 4, pp 478–559.

NOTES AND REFERENCES

1 Sources for PepsiCo case: Tropicana website 2002 and 2004; PepsiCo Annual Report and Accounts 2001, 2004 and 2010; *Financial Times* 22 July 1999, p 2; 28 February 2000, p 25; 15 March 2001, p 20; 5 April 2002, p 16.

2 Chandler, A (1987) *Strategy and Structure: Chapters in the History of the American Industrial Enterprise*, MIT Press, Cambridge, MA, pp 8–14.

3 Chandler, A (1987) Op. cit., pp 13–14.

4 Pugh, D (1984) *Organisation Theory*, Penguin, London. This book brings together various papers, including those of other influential theorists of the early twentieth century such as Taylor and Fayol.

5 This section has been adapted from the ideas of Kanter, R M (1983) *The Changemasters*, Unwin, London, pp 42–43 and pp 398–399. This is a well-researched, thoughtful and provocative book.

6 Quinn, J B (1980) 'Managing strategic change', *Sloan Management Review*, Summer, pp 59–76. Reprinted in Mintzberg, H and Quinn, J B (1991) *The Strategy Process*, Prentice Hall, New York and De Wit, B and Meyer, R (1994) *Strategy: Process, Content and Context*, West Publishing, St Paul, MN.

7 Prahalad, C K and Hamel, G (1994) 'Strategy: the search for new paradigms', *Strategic Management Journal*, Summer Special Issue, p 11.

8 Lynch, R, based on reference 6.

9 Galbraith, J R and Kazanjian, R K (1986) *Strategy Implementation*, 2nd edn, West Publishing, St Paul, MN, Ch 7.

10 Galbraith, J R and Kazanjian, R K (1986) Op. cit., p 113.

11 Laurence, P R and Lorsch, J W (1967) *Organisation and the Environment*, Richard D Irwin, Burr Ridge, IL, contains a full discussion of this important area.

12 Mintzberg, H (1991) 'The structuring of organisations', p 341 in Mintzberg, H and Quinn, J B (1991) Op. cit.

13 Johnson, G (1989) 'Rethinking incrementalism', *Strategic Management Journal*, January–February, pp 75–91. Reprinted in De Wit, B and Meyer, R (1994) *Strategy: Process, Content and Context*, West Publishing, St Paul, MN.

14 Mintzberg, H (1979) *The Structuring of Organisations*, Prentice Hall, New York.

15 Thompson, A and Strickland, A (1993) *Strategic Management*, 7th edn, Irwin, Homewood, IL, p 220.

16 Examples: Drucker, P (1961) *The Practice of Management*, Heinemann/Mercury, London, and (1967) *Managing for Results*, Pan Books, London.

17 Peters, T (1992) *Liberation Management*, Macmillan, London.

18 Handy, C (1989) *The Age of Unreason*, Business Books, London, and (1991) *The Gods of Management*, Business Books, London.

19 Miles, R E and Snow, C C (1978) *Organisational Strategy, Structure and Process*, McGraw-Hill, New York. See also Miles, R, Snow, C, Meyer, A and Coleman (1978) 'Organizational Strategy, Structure and Process', *Academy of Management Review*, July, pp 546–562, and reprinted in De Wit, R and Meyer, R (1994) Op. cit. There is clearly some overlap here with the classification developed by Handy on types of culture described in Chapter 16. It is hardly surprising that the two areas are consistent; it would be alarming if they were not.

20 Sources for the Royal Dutch/Shell case: Annual Report and Accounts 2004. *Financial Times*: 1 September 2003, p 20; 14 January 2004, p 12; 4 March 2004, p 23; 20 April 2004, p 25 (contains quotes from the explosive emails between Mr van de Vijver and Sir Philip); 30 July 2004, p 23; 23 September 2004, p 23; 29 October 2004, p 21; 16 December 2004, p 25; 2 February 2005, p 19 (the employee survey).

21 Mintzberg, H (1979) Op. cit.

22 Chandler, A (1962) *Strategy and Structure*, MIT Press, Cambridge, MA. See also Channon, D (1973) *The Strategy and Structure of British Enterprise*, Macmillan, London, for evidence in the UK.

23 Bouygues moved from construction into media and mobile telephones in the 1990s.

24 Developed from Galbraith, J R (1987) 'Strategy and organisation planning', *Human Resource Management*, Spring–Summer. Republished in Mintzberg, H and Quinn, J B (1991) Op. cit., pp 315–324.

25 Gilbert, X and Strebel, P (1989) 'From innovation to outpacing', *Business Quarterly*, Summer, Vol 54, pp 19–22. Reprinted in De Wit, B and Meyer, R (1994) Op. cit.

26 Mintzberg, H (1991) 'The innovative organisation', Ch 13 in Mintzberg, H and Quinn, J B (1991) Op. cit., pp 731–746.

27 Kanter, R M (1985) *The Changemasters*, Unwin, London, p 146.

28 Kanter, R M (1985) Ibid, p 205.

29 Kanter, R M (1985) Ibid, p 237.

30 Kanter, R M (1985) Ibid, pp 361–362.

31 ABB case study references: Ghoshal, S and Bartlett, C (1995) 'Changing the role of top management: beyond structure to process', *Harvard Business Review*, January–February, pp 86–96; *Financial Times*, 15 November 1989; 21 March 1990, p 27; 5 April 1991, p 11; 15 November 1991; 20 August 1993, p 15; 25 August 1993, p 19; 15 March 1994, p 32; 12 August 1994, p 17; 18 August 1994, p 18; 13 August 1998, p 27; 24 August 1998, p 8; 24 March 1999, p 26; 1 March 2000, p 28; 26 October 2000, p 28; 30 October 2000, p 16; 12 January 2001, p 24 (Lex) and p 29; 18 January 2001, p 13; 25 April 2001, p 24 (Lex); 25 July 2001, p 28; 19 September 2001, p 30; 25 October 2001, p 28; 22 November 2001, p 22 (Lex) and p 28; 23 November 2001, p 28; 31 January 2002, p 30; 14 February 2002, p 30; 21 February 2002, p 29; *ABB Annual Report and Accounts*, 1993, 1994 and 2001; video interview with Percy Barnevik on Tom Peters' 1993 video film: *Crazy Times Call for Crazy Organisations*. See also reference 17 above and the interview with Mr Barnevik.

32 Galbraith, J and Kazanjian, R (1986) Op. cit. Chapter 6 contains a thoughtful review of the evidence.

33 Hunger, J and Wheelen, T (1993) *Strategic Management*, 4th edn, Addison Wesley, Reading, MA, Ch 9.

PART 4
The implementation process

This part of the book addresses implementation – the process by which the organisation's chosen strategies are put into operation. It may involve planning new activities, developing methods to control the implementation and considering what benchmarks will be needed to assess the strategy.

However, empirical research has shown that the implementation process itself may influence the organisation's strategy. In other words, the distinction between the implementation process and the strategy choice may be overstated. Nevertheless, many organisations often consider planning and control separately from the generation of strategy, while also recognising the interaction between the two. These issues are fully explored in the following chapters.

As part of the implementation process, this part also tackles two more topics: first, the development and implementation of a green strategy and policies of sustainability; second, the important topic of strategic change and its implications for strategy outcomes.

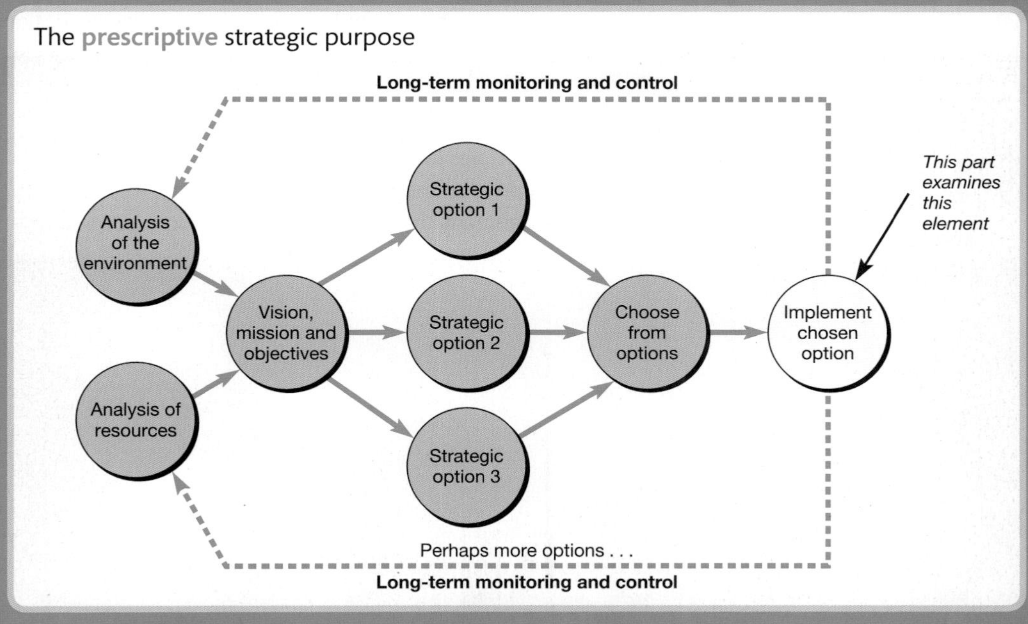

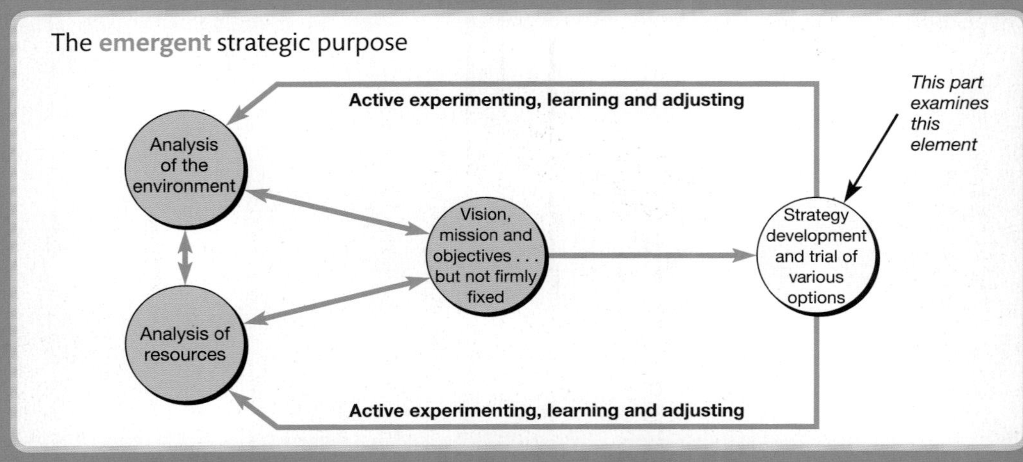

Key strategic management questions

CHAPTER 13
Implementing and controlling the strategic plan

- What is the process of implementation?
- How are tasks and objectives set?
- How are resources allocated?
- How is strategic planning conducted and what is its influence on strategy?
- How is strategy controlled?
- What is the role of information processing and systems?

CHAPTER 14
Green strategy and sustainability

- What are the main elements of green strategy and sustainability?
- What additional elements are involved in analysing the green strategy environment and in identifying sustainable resources and capabilities?
- How does purpose change as green strategy and sustainability principles are adopted?
- What are the implications of green strategy for knowledge, technology and innovation?
- What is the impact of green strategy and sustainability on strategic options and choice?

CHAPTER 15
Managing strategic change

- Why do people resist strategic change?
- What are the main principles involved in strategic change?
- How can we devise a programme to manage such change?
- How is strategic management changing?

CHAPTER 13
Implementing and controlling the strategic plan

Video and sound summary of this chapter

LEARNING OUTCOMES

When you have worked through this chapter, you will be able to:

- outline the nature and limitations of the implementation process;
- understand the way that the objectives, tasks and timing are implemented;
- describe how resources are allocated between parts of the organisation;
- outline the main elements of control and monitoring, and investigate their importance for strategic management implementation;
- show how the Balanced Scorecard brings together the various elements of the implementation process;
- explore how strategic planning can be conducted and critically evaluate its merits.

INTRODUCTION

By whatever method strategies are selected, there will come a time when every organisation will need to put its strategies into practice, i.e. to implement them. This chapter explores the basic steps involved in this process and the links between strategy development and implementation. It begins by exploring the meaning and limitations of the implementation process itself, including its relationship with green strategies.

Because the prime aim in implementing strategy is to deliver the mission and objectives of the organisation, the chapter then discusses these. After this, it considers the implications for the tasks to be undertaken by individuals and the allocation of the necessary resources for that work. As the strategies are then implemented, they clearly need to be monitored and controlled. To bring all these areas together, the chapter then explains the use of the *Balanced Scorecard*. Finally, the chapter considers the whole principle of prescriptive strategic planning, which has been criticised by some commentators in recent years. The way in which these activities are linked together is shown in Figure 13.1.

Effective strategies for investing in sport.

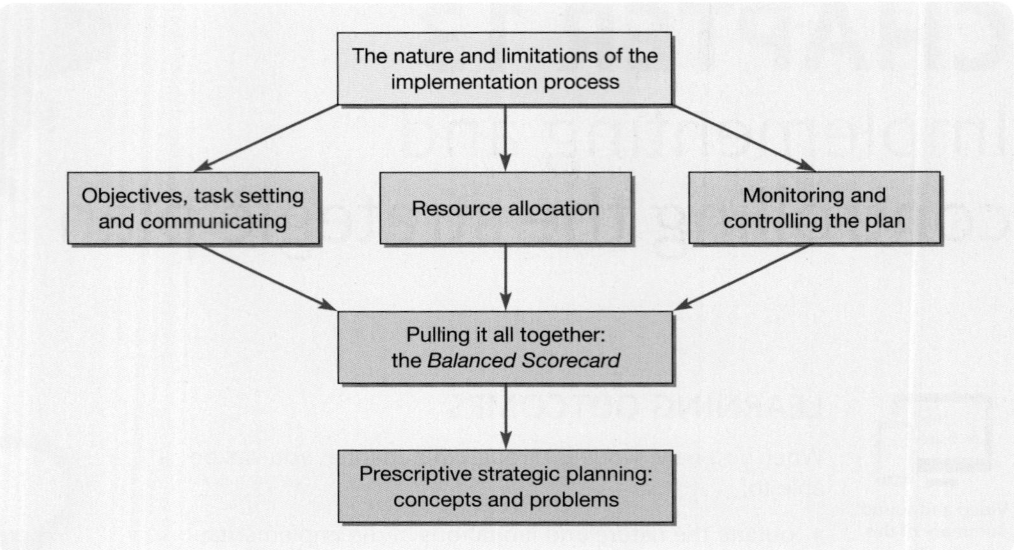

Figure 13.1 Main elements of the implementation process

CASE STUDY 13.1

European football:* bad strategy? Or bad implementation?

Half of Europe's leading football clubs were running at a loss in 2010 with 20 per cent incurring 'huge' deficits. Yet the money pouring into the leading football clubs has soared in recent years. This case explores the strategic issues.

There are real difficulties across European football: for example, the famous Italian club Lazio, the 2010 English Premier League winners Chelsea and the leading Spanish club Real Madrid have all reported significant losses in recent years. The European Union Football Association (UEFA) study in 2009 showed that the reported income of the 733 top European clubs was €11.7 billion and the expenditure was €12.9 billion. Beyond the leading clubs, the situation was worse: some 30–40 English League football clubs have either gone into administration or been threatened with financial pressures in recent years.

What is the basic strategic problem?

Even wealthy football clubs, like Barcelona and Bayern München, have to watch their profits carefully. But from a strategy perspective, they cannot survive by themselves – they need other clubs to make up a league to play against. Moreover, such a league must inevitably have winners and losers if the game is to be interesting. This means that clubs will go through periods when they achieve success and then periods when success may be more elusive. Manchester United were English League Champions in 2009 but were beaten by Chelsea in 2010. During the losing periods, strategic game theory can be used to show that this is likely to have financial consequences.

If this is correct then it follows that football clubs will always face strategic uncertainty. But does it mean that the losing clubs will always make losses and can never recover the situation? For example, the English League club Bradford City was relegated from the Premiership in 2001. In the following football year 2001–2002, Bradford lost revenue from television and other sources amounting to around $45 million and simply could not cut its costs fast enough. Its alternative strategy was to fund the loss from its bank for one year, hope that it would gain promotion in the season ending in 2002 and then pull in the funds again. In practice, it ended up filing for administration in May 2002 with the prospect that this proud club could totally disappear. The club then went on to survive – at least in the short term – but it was still in financial difficulties. More recently, Portsmouth was the first English Premier League club to file for bankruptcy during the 2010 season. At the time of writing, it still had another four years of debt-clearing before

* Readers in North America and some parts of Asia need to know that football is what you might call 'soccer'. It has many of the same strategic issues as American baseball and American football teams – stars paid vast sums, strong competition between clubs and private sector finance that never seems to be sufficient.

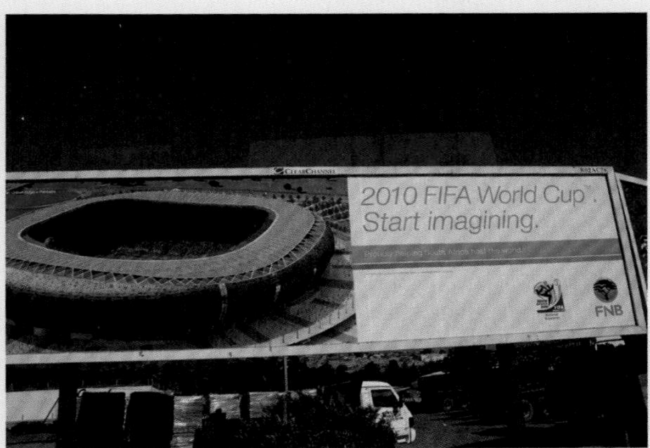

Football strategy has been revolutionised by the considerable sums earned from television rights and the promotion of football worldwide – including the 2010 World Cup in South Africa.

it would be free. More generally, other clubs faced similar financial difficulties, not only in the UK but across Europe: 123 football clubs across Europe were refused licences by UEFA in 2009 with 41 per cent being for financial reasons.

Is this endemic to football strategy across Europe at the present time? Or just a feature of a few foolish clubs who have not realised that any strategy needs to be implemented carefully? To explore this question, it is useful to explore the way that football clubs generate and use their funds.

Where does football money come from and where does it go?

Across Europe's main football leagues, the sources of funds will vary, depending on whether the club has a rich patron like Chelsea; whether it is famous like InterMilan and has a loyal fan base; the extent of television deals and the size of the league: for example, the Belgian league is inevitably smaller than the German Bundesliga or UK Premiership and therefore generates less funds. Even after its takeover by the American Glazer family, Manchester United has strong obligations to the banks that have financed the deal; Real Madrid is a mutual company owned by its 50,000 fans and therefore not able to raise funds in the same way. However, there are broadly five main sources of funds:

1 *Gate money*: typically, this makes up 15–30 per cent of a club's total income.

2 *Transfer fees*: these could be anything between 10 and 40 per cent of total income. Some of the smaller clubs have survived by selling players. Even large clubs can benefit: Italy's Juventus sold Zinedine Zidane for $70 million in 2001 to Real Madrid and Filippo Inzaghi to AC Milan for $25 million. (And then the club promptly spent the money on Pavel Nedved from Lazio, Lilian Thuram from Parma and Gianluigi Buffon from Parma.)

3 *Television rights*: typically, these could account for up to 60 per cent of total income for the three leading Italian clubs but down to 25 per cent for the smaller leading clubs. For example, BSkyB spent $1.8 billion buying the rights to three years of live games in the English Premiership – shared equally between the clubs that survive each year. The Italian Serie A television rights for three years cost around $500 million in 2005. Some commentators have suggested that such television payments across Europe will be lower in the future, but there is no evidence to support this. On the contrary, a new worldwide television deal was negotiated by the English Premier League in 2007 that would bring nearly $2 billion to the members of the league over three years. This funding route is growing.

4 *Merchandising and sponsorship*: typically, this could be worth around 15–50 per cent of total income for many clubs, the highest percentages being for the leading German clubs. Clearly, the most famous clubs are able to negotiate major deals.

5 *Wealthy owners*: these could be responsible for anything from zero to 80 per cent of total income. For example, the Agnelli family (who control Fiat cars) have ploughed well in excess of $100 million into Juventus over the years and Mohamed Al Fayed (who owned the London department store Harrods) has invested some $90 million into the English league club Fulham in recent years. There are plenty of other examples.

Where is the money spent? Apart from administration and management, there are obvious costs like football training and medical fees, hotel accommodation costs and travel costs. Some funds are also taken by the national and European leagues to invest and develop the game. But the majority of the funds go in players' wages – for instance, David Beckham's 2002 contract paid him nearly $7 million per year for three years. With a typical squad of some 40 players, the leading clubs spend most of their income in this area. It might be argued that Beckham and his colleagues are over-paid, but his wages can be justified by the concept of economic rent – see the free web text note linked with Chapter 4.

How will the strategy change?

Nothing stands still in strategy, including football. For example leading teams in the Italian and Spanish leagues like Juventus and Real Madrid have negotiated individual broadcasting deals for their games, rather than negotiate as part of their respective national football leagues. This means that individually these clubs earn more than the others in the same league and are beginning to pull away from the others in their respective leagues. But in 2010, Manchester United was still earning more than Juventus in spite of remaining part of the English Premier League collective television contract. The English Premier League itself had negotiated a new television rights deal and saw its member clubs like Manchester City, Chelsea and Liverpool as world-class brands. The League had even considered playing some of its games outside the UK in order to support its foreign fans, though the world football governing body FIFA was quick to condemn this proposal.

But the issue still hinged on what would happen to the funds generated by such deals and whether such funds could continue to rise faster than the costs. 'I don't think that you go into sport to make a profit,' explained the new Liverpool Football Club owner, John W Henry. 'We hope some day that Liverpool will be much more valuable than it is today.' Even allowing for low profitability, European football was moving into a new era of funding without having resolved some basic issues like the wage structure and the purchase of new players.

Green strategy **The world football governing body is FIFA and the main European organisation is UEFA. These two bodies have announced policies on sustainability linked to the World Football Cup in Brazil in 2014.**

Case question

Is this a problem of the correct strategy – finances and costs essentially sound but the implementation – players' wages and so on – needing some adjustment? Or does the strategy itself need to be changed in the face of fundamental problems across European football?

13.1 THE NATURE AND LIMITATIONS OF THE IMPLEMENTATION PROCESS

13.1.1 Basic elements of the implementation process

Whether the organisation faces the strategic problems of European football or the opportunities of new technologies such as the internet, it will have to draw up plans to carry out its strategies. Essentially, these implementation issues need to address the following questions:

- What activities need to be undertaken in order to achieve the agreed objectives?
- What is the timescale for the implementation of these plans?
- How will progress be monitored and controlled?

To turn general strategies into specific implementation plans involves four basic elements:[2]

1 *Identification of general strategic objectives* – specifying the general results expected from the strategy initiatives.
2 *Formulation of specific plans* – taking the general objectives and turning them into specific tasks and deadlines (these are often cross-functional).
3 *Resource allocation and budgeting* – indicating how the plans are to be paid for (this quantifies the plans and permits integration across functions).
4 *Monitoring and control procedures* – ensuring that the objectives are being met, that only the agreed resources are spent and that budgets are adhered to. Importantly, monitoring also takes place against the projections on which the strategies are based – for example, national economic change and competitive activity.

The relationship between these activities is shown in Figure 13.2.

13.1.2 Types of basic implementation programme

Implementation programmes will vary according to the nature of the strategic problems which the organisation faces. These problems will range from the extreme and urgent need for change, such as at a bankrupt European football club, to the more ongoing strategic development processes

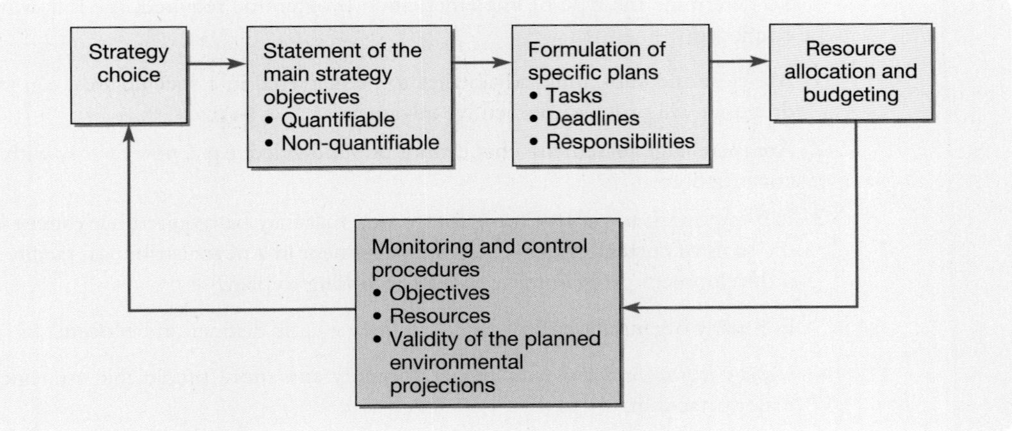

Figure 13.2 The basic implementation process

of Canon or Nestlé (described in the case studies later in this chapter). The two essential causes of variation in implementation programmes are:[3]

1 the degree of uncertainty in predicting changes in the environment;

2 the size of the strategic change required.

In response to these issues, several types of basic implementation programme can be carried out. At one extreme, there is the *comprehensive implementation programme* for fundamental changes in strategic direction. At the other extreme, there is the *incremental implementation programme*, where implementation is characterised by small changes and short time spans within the general direction implied by the strategy. Both these approaches have their difficulties, so a compromise may be chosen in practice: the *selective implementation programme.*

- *Comprehensive implementation programmes* are employed when the organisation has made a clear-cut, major change in strategic direction, as in the crisis faced by bankrupt European football clubs at the beginning of this chapter. Other reasons might include a new competitive or new technological opportunity. Implementation then becomes a matter of driving through the new strategies, regardless of changes in the environment and the reactions of those affected. Close co-ordination across the organisation is usually essential for success.
- *Incremental implementation programmes* may be used where there are conditions of great uncertainty – for example, rapidly changing markets or the unknown results of R&D. As a result, timetables, tasks and even objectives are all likely to change, depending on the outcome of current activities. Important strategic areas may be left deliberately unclear until the outcome of current events has been established. Essentially,[4] the uncertainty is handled by a flexible strategic approach.
- *Selective implementation programmes* may be used where neither of the above represents the optimal way forward. Comprehensive programmes involving radical change may require such fundamental changes that they encounter substantial resistance, such as negative reactions from fans to the collapse of their favourite European football club. Incremental programmes may be inappropriate when it is necessary to make a significant change that needs the impetus generated by a single, large step. Selective programmes represent the compromise required: a major programme developed in selective areas only.

Readers will recognise that the above two extremes are related to the prescriptive and emergent strategic approaches explored throughout this book.

To determine the type of implementation programme required, the following three criteria can be employed:

1. Are clear and substantial advantages to be delivered in a specific area, e.g. investment in a new drug that will provide competitive advantage?
2. Are there large increments that cannot be subdivided, e.g. a new factory with long lead times for construction?
3. Is it important to protect some future step that may be required but cannot be fully justified on the basis of current evidence, e.g. an investment in a new distribution facility that will be needed if development programmes proceed according to plan?

For many organisations, it is useful to draw a basic distinction between:[5]

- *ongoing, existing activities* with higher certainty and more predictable strategic change, barring a major cataclysm;
- *new activities* with higher uncertainty and possibly major strategic change.

Implentation in small and medium-sized companies.

13.1.3 Limitations of implementation: the empirical research of Pettigrew and Whipp

In a series of research studies between 1985 and 1990, the UK-based researchers Pettigrew and Whipp analysed how strategic change occurred in four sectors of UK industry.[6] Their evidence did not extend beyond the UK, but their conclusions are likely to be applicable to other geographic areas. They suggested that strategic change can most usefully be seen as a *continuous* process, rather than one with distinct stages, such as the formulation of strategy and then its implementation. In this sense, they argued that strategy was not a linear movement with discrete stages but an experimental, iterative process where the outcomes of each stage were uncertain. A first small step might be actioned and then the strategy itself adjusted, depending on the outcome of the actions.

Pettigrew and Whipp[7] concluded that there were three interlinking aspects to strategic change with clear implications for implementation:

1. *Analytical aspects.* Implementation must involve many aspects of the organisation. These are the areas that have been emphasised in various strategic models and frameworks and were explored in Chapters 3 and 4 of the book.
2. *Educational aspects.* 'The new knowledge and insights into a given strategy that arise from its implementation have to be captured, retained and diffused within the organisation' (Pettigrew and Whipp). Thus implementation cannot be regarded as immutable and unchanging. The organisation will learn about its strategies as it implements them.
3. *Political aspects.* 'The very prospect of change confronts established positions. Both formulation and implementation inevitably raise questions of power within the organisation. Left unattended, such forces can provide obstacles to change . . . Indeed, in the case of Jaguar [Cars] in the 1970s, ultimately such forces can wreak havoc' (Pettigrew and Whipp). These important issues are explored in the chapter on strategic change – Chapter 15.

Comment

The empirical evidence to support this view is significant. The description of the continuous process is similar to, but not necessarily the same as, the incremental implementation programme described in Section 13.1.2. According to this interpretation, strategy implementation at bankrupt European football clubs outlined in Case 13.1 might have been better served by a series of separate smaller actions, conducted on an experimental basis, rather than one major restructuring announcement. Chapter 15 will explore further the research of Pettigrew and Whipp.

13.1.4 Limitations of implementation: bounded rationality and minimum intervention

In exploring how managers develop their implementation plans, the strategists Hrebiniak and Joyce[8] have suggested that the implementation process is governed by two principles: bounded rationality and minimum intervention.

1 *Bounded rationality* derives from the work of researchers. They showed that managers in practice have difficulty in considering every conceivable option. They therefore reduce their logical choices to a more limited, 'bounded' choice. Arguing in a similar way, Hrebiniak and Joyce suggest that implementation is also likely to be limited: managers will act in a rational way but will reduce the overall task to a series of small steps in order to make it more manageable. Thus the strategic goals and implementation are likely to be split into a series of smaller tasks that can be more easily handled but may not be optimal.

   In addition, the authors suggest that *individuals* will make rational decisions but will include in this process their *personal* goals which are not necessarily the same as those of the organisation itself. Implementation needs to ensure that there is consistency between personal and organisational goals.

2 *Minimum intervention* has been summarised by the authors as follows:

   > In implementing strategy, managers should change only what is necessary and sufficient to produce an enduring solution to the strategic problem being addressed.

   Practising managers might recognise this principle as the rather more basic sentence: 'If it ain't broke, don't fix it.' The implication here is that implementation may be constrained by the need to consider the impact on the strategy itself.

KEY STRATEGIC PRINCIPLES

- Implementation covers the activities required for an organisation to put its strategies into practice. There are several basic elements to this process: general objectives, specific plans and the necessary finances, coupled with a monitoring and control system to ensure compliance.
- Within the implementation process, it is useful to draw a distinction between different types of implementation. There are three major approaches: comprehensive, incremental and selective.
- Implementation in small and medium-sized businesses may be less elaborate but needs to follow the same general principles.
- According to Pettigrew and Whipp, implementation is best seen as a continuous process, rather than one that simply occurs after the formulation of the strategy.
- Hrebiniak and Joyce placed boundaries on implementation in terms of the ability of managers to consider every choice rationally and to evaluate the impact of implementation on strategy itself.
- Emergent approaches to strategy imply that implementation needs to be considered not just as a single event but rather as a series of activities, the outcome of which may to some extent shape the strategy.

Ten practical guidelines on implementation.

13.2 OBJECTIVES, TASK SETTING AND COMMUNICATING THE STRATEGY

Over the next few years, all the main European football clubs will have clear sporting and business objectives that will need to be met – see Case 13.1. In particular, the well-paid managers will have to be told what is expected of their teams and what resources they will be given in terms of new players, training facilities and so on. Essentially, it is important to set out such resources clearly and agree the tasks with those individuals who will need to deliver them: typically, this process of task setting and communications will cover what is to be done, by what time and with what resources. This is a significant implementation issue and involves five basic questions, which are summarised in Exhibit 13.1.

EXHIBIT 13.1

Task setting and communications: the basic questions

1 Who developed the strategies that are now being implemented?
2 Who will implement the strategies?
3 What objectives and tasks will they need to accomplish?
4 How can objectives and tasks be handled in fast-changing environments?
5 How will the implementation process be communicated and co-ordinated?

In reality, the answers to these questions will depend primarily on the way that the strategies have been developed. In this sense, the strategy development phase and the strategy implementation phase are interconnected.

13.2.1 Who developed the strategies that are now being implemented?

In the past, some strategy writers have taken the view that the strategies in large corporations will be largely developed at the centre:

> Most of the people in the corporate centre who are crucial to successful strategy implementation probably had little, if anything, to do with the development of the corporate strategy.[9]

If this is the case, then the implementation process is very different from one where there has been a lengthy debate and agreement on the strategies. In this latter case, managers will know that they are likely to be responsible for implementing something that was discussed with them some weeks or months earlier. For example, if strategies have been produced using the procedures described at Canon (see Case 13.2), then most managers will be clear on who will be doing what because they will have been closely involved in developing them. Ignorance will be higher and commitment to the new strategy will be lower among those managers who have had no involvement in developing the strategy.

It is important therefore to address the question of who developed the strategy, rather than simply the question of who will implement it. For example, was it just a central team or was there full consultation? The response to this question will shape the implementation process.

13.2.2 Who will implement the strategies?

This question is important because it will define who is responsible for implementing a specific strategy. It is difficult to review progress at a later stage if no one is accountable for the way the strategy is being carried out. In many small companies, it is possible that a number of managers will be involved in the strategy development process because of the small size. The question needs more elaboration as organisations grow in size.

One important issue here is who makes the decision: is it the centre telling the managers or is the matter open for discussion and negotiation? Generally, this book takes the view that discussion is preferable because it is more motivating and rewarding all round. However, it may occasionally be necessary to instruct those involved.

13.2.3 What objectives and tasks will they need to undertake?

In Chapter 6, we examined the concept of the hierarchy of objectives – corporate, divisional and functional – cascading down from the top of the organisation. The main objectives and activities for implementation can also be considered as following a similar process. The overall corporate objectives need to be translated into objectives for each of the main areas of the business and then these objectives need to be reinterpreted into the tasks and action programmes that need to be undertaken in order to achieve them.

Figure 13.3 gives an example in a functional company of how the overall objective is reinterpreted in this way. The corporate objectives are translated into functional objectives that are each designed to make a contribution to the whole. This is not necessarily a simple task and may require several iterations before a satisfactory result is achieved. The marketing, operations and other tasks are defined from the functional objectives. These are then broken down into plans: timetables, resources to achieve the objectives and other matters. Deadlines are usually set to indicate the date for completion of a particular task, as are *milestones* – interim indicators of progress so that those monitoring events can review implementation while there is still time to take remedial action.

In practice, the definition of objectives, tasks and plans may be simpler in smaller companies and more complicated in larger companies. For example, at Canon three sets of objectives and plans are

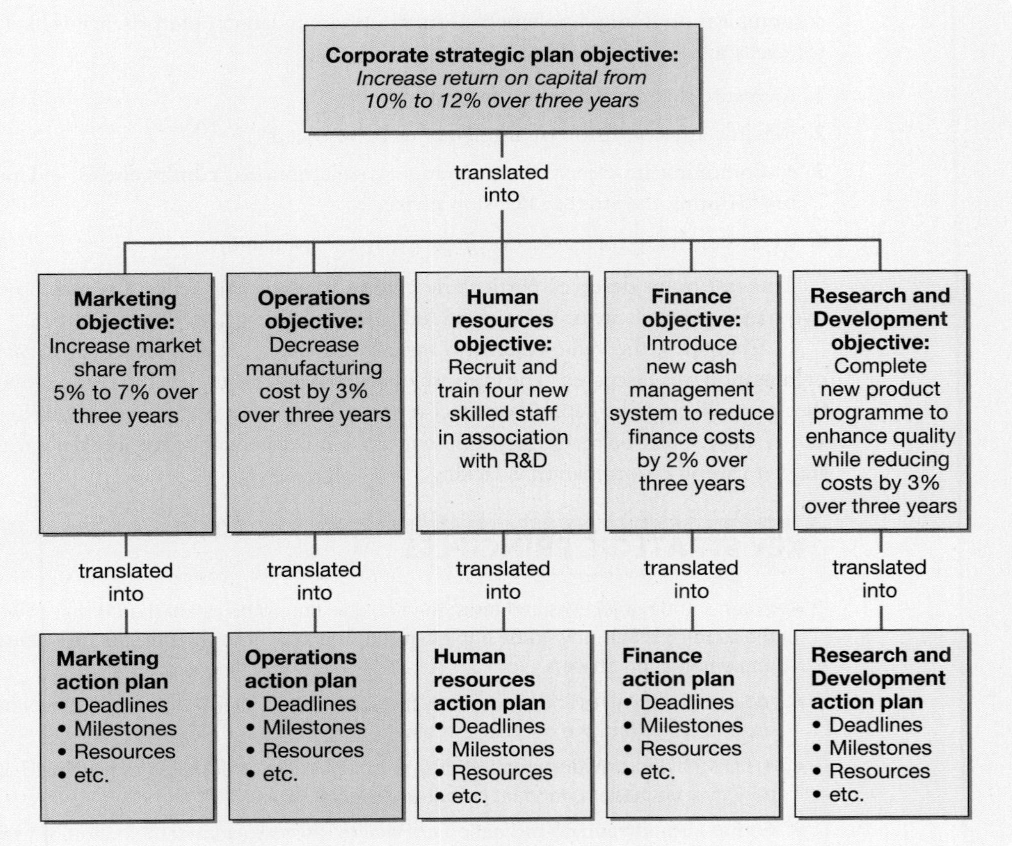

Figure 13.3 An example of translating corporate objectives into tasks in a functional organisation

prepared: on six-year, three-year and one-year time-horizons. They do not all have the same degree of detail but they are all fully co-ordinated across the company.

13.2.4 How can objectives and tasks be handled in fast-changing environments?

When environments are changing fast, it may be exceptionally difficult to specify satisfactory objectives and tasks: by the time they have been agreed and communicated, the environment may have changed. As changes occur, the objectives may rapidly become impossible or straightforward, depending on the nature of the changes. In this situation, it makes little sense to adhere to objectives developed for earlier situations. Three guidelines can be applied:

1 flexibility in objectives and tasks within an agreed general vision;
2 empowerment of those closest to the environment changes, so that they can respond quickly;
3 careful and close monitoring by the centre of those reacting to events.

The purpose of such surveillance is to ensure that actions taken do not expose the centre itself to unnecessary strategic or financial risk. This is vital if the organisation wishes to avoid the fate of companies such as Barings Bank in 1995, which crashed with debts of over $1.5 billion, partly as a result of inadequate controls in such a rapidly changing environment.

13.2.5 How will the implementation process be communicated and co-ordinated?

In small organisations, it may be unnecessary, over-complex or inappropriate to engage in the elaborate communication of agreed strategies. People who have explored the strategic tasks together during the formulation of the strategy and meet each other on a regular basis may not need lengthy communication during implementation. However, in larger enterprises, it is likely to be essential for four reasons:

1 to ensure that everyone has understood;
2 to allow any confusion or ambiguity to be resolved;
3 to communicate clearly the judgements, assumptions, contingencies and possibly the choices made during the strategy decision phase;[10]
4 to ensure that the organisation is properly co-ordinated.

This last point deserves particularly careful thought and action because co-ordination involves two major strategic areas: value chain linkages and synergy.

In Chapter 4, the value chain was introduced and its ability to deliver *unique linkages* across the organisation was discussed. The purpose of such linkages is to develop competitive advantage because they are unlikely to be capable of exact replication by other companies whose history, competencies and resources will be marginally different. Such linkages will be meaningless at the implementation stage if careful co-ordination is lacking.

KEY STRATEGIC PRINCIPLES

- When setting objectives and tasks, the first question to be established is that of who developed the strategy that is now to be implemented. The answer to this question will influence the implementation process.
- Individual objectives and tasks follow from the agreed overall objectives. It may be necessary to experiment to find the optimal combination of events.
- In fast-changing environments, it may not be possible or desirable to have rigid objectives because they may be made redundant by outside events.
- Communication and co-ordination are vital to satisfactory implementation. These are especially important to ensure understanding of the plan and its underlying assumptions.

CASE STUDY 13.2

Strategic planning at Canon with a co-operative corporate style

Since 1957, the Japanese company Canon has operated strategic planning. However, it has not been a rigid, inflexible process imposed by top management. Instead, it has been a free-flowing, open approach, driven by the strategic vision of Canon's senior and other managers. This vision covered the values of the company, the market position it expected to hold over many years and the resources needed to develop and sustain it. The strategies and their implementation have proved highly successful. This case examines the planning process in more detail.

Canon's sales have grown from ¥4.2 billion in 1950 to ¥3,468 billion in 2004 ($26 billion). The company has developed a strong market share in its leading products: for example, 70 per cent of the world laser beam printer engine market, 40 per cent of the world bubble jet printer market, second only to Hewlett-Packard. Overall, it has a strong global base in its major product areas: photocopiers, computer peripherals, computer and fax equipment, cameras, video recorders and optical products. The main business areas are shown in Figure 13.4. In terms of profitability, Canon has an excellent 10-year record, which is shown in Figure 13.5.

As an example of its strategic vision, Canon identified the world photocopying market back in the 1960s as an area for growth. Xerox Corporation (USA) had been the world leader since the 1950s, with its exclusive, patented technology. However, this did not stop Canon declaring its intention in 1967 of taking 30 per cent of the world market by the 1980s and its vision 'to catch Xerox through technological differentiation'. Through the 1960s and 1970s, it went about this by developing technology that was totally different from the Xerox patents and pursuing the small photocopier market niche, which remained poorly served by Xerox. Today, Canon is world market leader and has developed its core competencies out of photocopiers into laser printers, digital scanners, colour bubble jet printing, digitised optical images and other areas. It will be noted that printing was only one of Canon's areas of competence by the 1990s (see Table 13.1).

Strategic planning at Canon, however, is not just a matter of vision and the identification of core competencies. Exhibit 13.2 outlines the strategic planning process at Canon. It is driven initially by the centre and its strong belief in customer satisfaction. Typical of large Japanese companies, the centre has also defined its main growth plan under the headline 'Excellent Global Corporation Plan'. Some Western

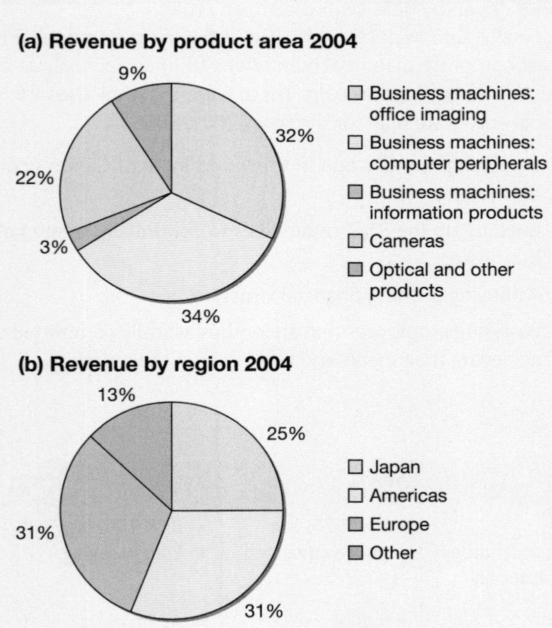

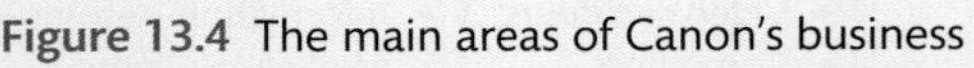

Figure 13.4 The main areas of Canon's business

Source: Canon annual report and accounts 2004.

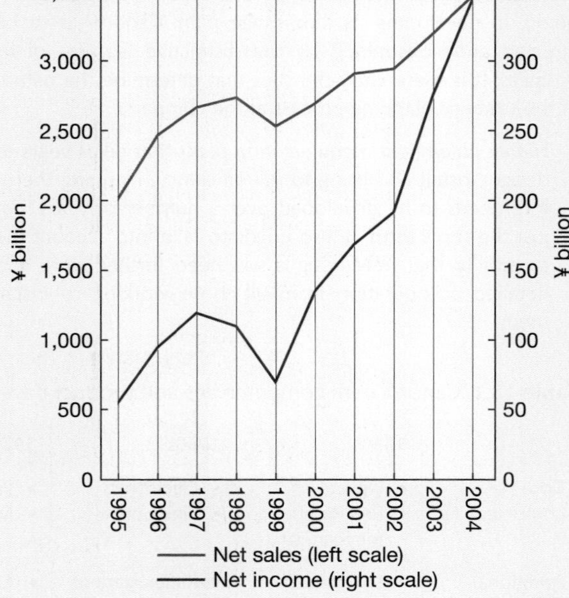

Figure 13.5 Ten-year record of Canon Inc

Source: Canon annual report and accounts 2004.

The patented optical and miniaturisation core competencies employed in Canon cameras have underpinned the company's strategic planning for many years.
With permission from Canon (UK) Limited.

companies might find this title vague and lacking in commercial directness, However, the detail from Canon is clear with its focus on 'gaining and maintaining top market shares. At Canon, top share and profitable operations must go hand in hand'. In other words, there is no question of driving for market share at the expense of profits.

Such elements appear regularly in strategic planning in Japanese companies and are employed in order to shape the approach to strategy development in its early stages. They appear in the basic analysis along with the assumptions and projections about the future (as explored in Part 2 of this book). In developing its long-range plan, Canon has to be directed and constrained by the distinctive features of its business. It is these characteristics that determine the nature of the strategic planning process at the company:

- *Highly automated manufacturing plant* that takes years to design, install and bring to full efficiency. Planning therefore needs to be developed over a number of years, not just the short term. It also needs to take into account the possibility that new designs will need further work and detailed co-operation from all those working to install them.
- *High-technology products* that take years to develop and perfect, including the possibility of some failures. Planning will again need to be experimental but will also need to be open and not involve criticism of failure to implement a new, experimental product.
- *Synergy and core competencies* that provide linkages across a number of product areas. These take time and resources and rely on strong co-operation across different divisions. Planning will act as co-ordinator and will also direct the divisions towards the areas that have been identified: it is likely to be centralised.

Although the centre sets the long-term strategy, the product divisions begin the *medium-range planning* within the constraints set by the centre. Considerable emphasis is placed on scenarios and contingency planning so that Canon is not caught out by an unexpected event, such as a sudden rise in the value of the yen. These plans are then consolidated by the centre.

For the short-term plan, financial objectives take greater precedence. They are usually prepared as budgets which are derived from the medium-term plan. Each division prepares its budget and these are then consolidated by the centre. From this amalgamation, the corporate HQ then prepares short-term plans on personnel, capital investments and cash flow. The data are also used to build the balance sheet and profit and loss account.

Although this might appear bureaucratic and unwieldy, Canon actually operates the process in an open, friendly and challenging fashion. Employees are encouraged to debate the issues, to take risks and to present new ideas. Strategy planning is regarded as an opportunity and a challenge, rather than a chore driven by hide-bound company rules.

Finally, Canon published some of the main elements of its latest corporate plan in presentations to financial analysts on the web – **www.canon.com**. These were the objectives for its global corporate plan for the years 2001–2005:

1. Becoming number one in the world in all of Canon's core businesses.
2. Building up the R&D capabilities to continually create new businesses.
3. Achieving a strong financial structure.
4. Fostering employees that are enthusiastically committed to achieving their ideals and take pride in their work.

Table 13.1 Canon's core competencies and product development

	1950s	1960s	1970s	1980s	1990s
Core competencies	• Optical • Precision mechanical	• Electronics • Fine optical	• Printing • Materials technology • Communications	• As 1970s but more advanced	• Biotechnology • Energy saving
Additional new products	• Still camera • Movie camera • Lenses	• Reflex camera • Calculators	• Copier • Laser printer • Word processing • Fax	• Office • Automation • Video recorders • Computers	• Audio visual • Energy saving • Information systems • Medical equipment

EXHIBIT 13.2

The process of strategic planning at Canon

Activity	Content		Example in 2004
Basic assumptions, analysis and projections (prepared by the centre, but after open discussion)	• Canon's strengths and weaknesses • Opportunities and threats • Business philosophy and beliefs		• Customer satisfaction • Cost reduction • Competitive products
Long-range strategy: six years (decided by centre but with input and discussion from division)		• Vision • Long-term objectives • Key strategic projects	• Maintain No 1 position • World class • Develop global markets • Reduce cost base • Digital cameras • New screen displays and rear projectors
Medium-range strategy: three years (started by divisions and then consolidated at HQ)	• Canon itself: resources, cultures, etc. • Environment: general outlook; competition; scenarios if major shift in assumptions • Basic assumptions and projections • Resource allocation • Goals and policies • Contingency • Timetables		• Specific quantified goals developed • Resources include capital projects, human resources and the key strategic projects • Invest in R&D
Short-term plan: one year (developed by the divisions)		• Budgeting: financial goals are stressed • Build on the medium-range plan	

Canon has clear policies with regard to sustainability. They can be read at www.canon.com/environment/report/pdf/report2010e.pdf

 This case was written by Richard Lynch from published data only.[11]

Case questions

1 What are the main problems of large companies such as Canon in managing the strategic planning process?

2 How has Canon succeeded in remaining innovative? Could it do even better? If so, how?

STRATEGIC PROJECT

In strategic terms, Canon was made famous by Hamel and Prahalad for its use of core competencies to develop into new product areas – their book *Competing for the Future* used Canon as an important example. An interesting strategic project would be to follow up Canon's progress and test to see just what the company is now doing. The Canon website is quite helpful, with several presentations made to financial analysts that go further than is possible in this case. There is much material for future exploration of this interesting and important company.

13.3 RESOURCE ALLOCATION

Most strategies need resources to be allocated to them if they are to be implemented successfully. The Canon case shows clearly the need to find resources for the new strategic directions that the company was seeking over the next few years in areas such as Canon's research and development and in recruiting new managers. This section explores the basic processes and examines some special circumstances that may affect the allocation of resources.[12]

13.3.1 The resource allocation process

In large, diversified companies, the centre plays a major role in allocating the resources among the various strategies proposed by its operating companies or divisions.[13] In smaller companies, the same mechanism will also operate, although on a more informal basis: product groups, areas of the business or functional areas may still bid for funds to support their strategic proposals.

There are four criteria which can be used when allocating resources.

1 *The contribution of the proposed resources towards the fulfilment of the organisation's mission and objectives.* At the centre of the organisation, the resource allocation task is to steer resources away from areas that are poor at delivering the organisation's objectives and towards those that are good. Readers will recognise this description as being similar to that employed when considering the movement of funds in the BCG *product portfolio matrix* in Chapter 4: in that case, cash was diverted from cash cows towards stars and so on. The principle is similar here but relies on centrally available funds rather than the diversion of funds.

2 *Its support of key strategies.* In many cases, the problem with resource allocation is that the requests for funds usually exceed the funds that are normally available. Thus there needs to be some further selection mechanism beyond the delivery of the organisation's mission and objectives. This second criterion relates to two aspects of resource analysis covered in Chapter 6:

   - *the support of core competencies*, where possible, in order to develop and enhance competitive advantage;
   - *the enhancement of the value chain*, where possible, in order to assist particularly those activities that also support competitive advantage.

   Although both of these should underpin the organisation's objectives in the long term, they can usefully be treated as additional criteria when resources are allocated.

3 *The level of risk associated with a specific proposal.* Clearly, if the risk is higher, there is a lower likelihood that the strategy will be successful. Some organisations will be more comfortable with accepting higher levels of risk than others so the criterion in this case needs to be considered in relation to the risk-acceptance level of the organisation.

4 *The support of green strategy initiatives.* If the organisation is serious about implementing green strategy, then it needs to allocate resources to achieve this. Such resources will include physical and financial resources and also the necessary managerial resources to implement such policies. It may even be necessary to prioritise the allocation of resources to those that support green strategy over those that do not.

13.3.2 Special circumstances surrounding the allocation of resources

Special circumstances may cause an organisation to amend the criteria for the allocation of resources. Still on the basis of the common principle of *bargaining* for the centre's funds, some organisations will consider the following:

- *When major strategic changes are unlikely.* In this situation, resources may be allocated on the basis of a *formula*, for example, marketing funds might be allocated as a percentage of sales based on past history and experience. The major difficulty with such an approach is its arbitrary nature. It may, however, be a useful shortcut.

- *When major strategic changes are predicted.* In this situation, additional resources may be required either to drive the strategic process or to respond to an expected competitive initiative. In both cases, *special negotiation* with the centre is required rather than the adherence to dogmatic criteria.
- *When resources are shared between divisions.* In this situation, the centre may seek to enhance its role beyond that of resource allocation. It may need to establish the degree of collaboration and, where the areas disagree, *impose* a solution. The logical and motivational problems associated with such an approach are evident.

13.3.3 Caution regarding the resource allocation process

Hamel and Prahalad have reservations about the whole resource allocation process.[14] They view it as offering the wrong mental approach to the strategy task, arguing that it is more concerned with dividing up the existing resources than with using the resources more effectively and strategically.

> If top management devotes more effort to assessing the strategic feasibility of projects in its resource allocation role than it does to the task of multiplying resource effectiveness, its value added will be modest indeed.

They make an important cautionary point.

KEY STRATEGIC PRINCIPLES

- The resource allocation process is used to provide the necessary funds for proposed strategies. In circumstances of limited resources, the centre is usually responsible for allocating funds using various decision criteria.
- Criteria for allocation include the delivery of the organisation's mission and objectives, its support of key strategies such as core competencies, its risk-taking profile and its contribution to green strategy development. Some special circumstances such as unusual changes in the environment may support other resource allocation criteria.
- There is a risk that the resource allocation process will ignore the need to use resources more effectively and strategically.

CASE STUDY 13.3
Informal strategic controls at Nestlé

Because of the diversity of its product portfolio, Nestlé has chosen in the past to devolve strategy to its main operating areas and control them informally from the centre. This case study describes the strategic planning procedures, but also shows how they are becoming more centralised as the company attempts to improve its performance and operational efficiency.

With sales of over $72 billion, Nestlé (Switzerland) is the world's largest food and consumer goods company. Its main product areas include coffee (Nescafé), milk and baby foods, confectionery, pet foods and frozen foods. It operates globally through a series of geographical zones and a set of product *strategic business units* (SBUs). For example, zone 1 is Europe and there is an SBU for the confectionery and ice cream product area operating on a worldwide basis. Figure 13.6 shows the true global nature of the company and its main product areas. Figure 13.7 shows the Nestlé revenue and profit record for four years to 2004 – somewhat patchy with no significant growth in revenue and earnings.

Because of the wide variation in the SBUs in its portfolio, Nestlé has chosen to give *strategic* control of its operations to the individual SBUs. Each SBU has a full range of functional expertise in its business area: marketing, production, research and so on. However, *operational* decisions rest with the zones and below them the national companies. In the past, the role

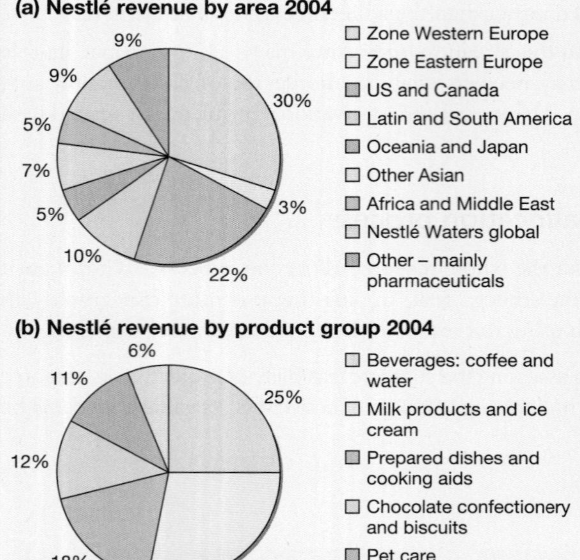

Figure 13.6 Nestlé activities around the world and by product group

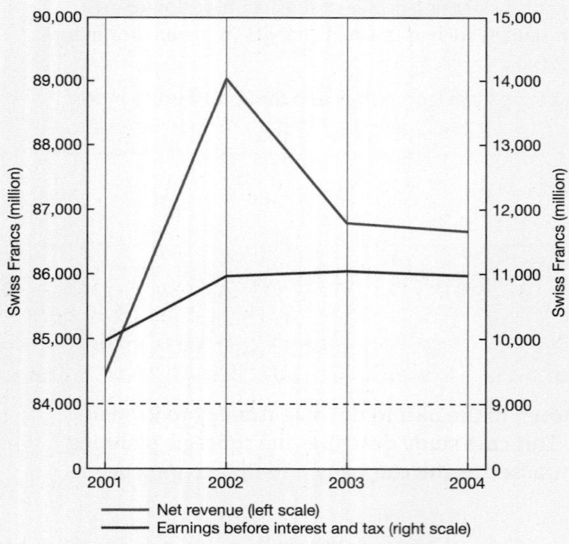

Figure 13.7 Nestlé four-year revenue and profit record

Source: Nestlé annual report and accounts 2004.

of the centre has been to co-ordinate and to allocate resources and this continues to the present with some modifications, described later in the case. The Nestlé structure for strategic planning, budgets and reporting is shown in Figure 13.8. The

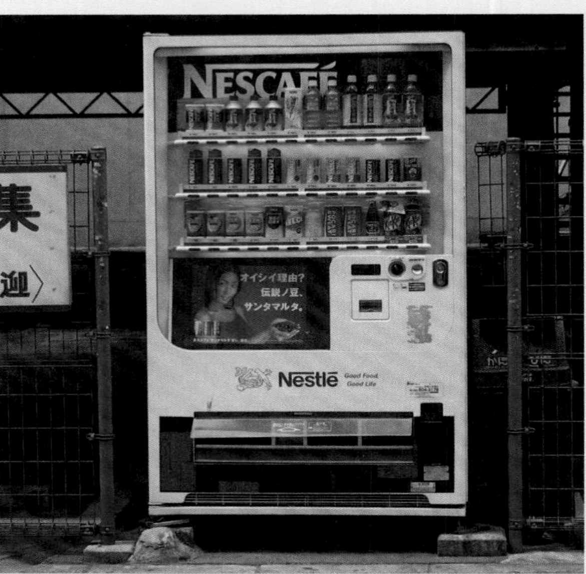

Nestlé's food range is founded on two major areas – milk products and instant coffee – Nescafé. The company's strategy has been to expand from this base into other food areas with a carefully planned series of acquisitions and in-house technology developments.

centre begins the process by issuing instructions to the SBUs for the next planning cycle. The SBUs then work on their three-year long-term plans (called LTPs). Every SBU prepares an LTP each year but some are merely updates from previous years. In order to promote strategic discussion with the centre, the LTPs are then circulated. They will include such areas as brand positioning, market share and competitive activity, pricing, capital proposals and new product development. However, as from 2000, the centre has initiated an additional layer of co-ordination and control on an experimental basis that will take some five years to be fully implemented.

Because the company operates in relatively mature markets, it is able to operate a system of checks and balances with more lengthy debate between the centre and the SBUs than might be appropriate where markets are changing fast and quick decisions are required. Hence, following the LTP preparation early in the year, discussions are held on content in the period from April to June between the SBUs, zones and the centre. The Nestlé executive committee has to give its approval. Later in the year, there is an investment and revenue budget review. The strategies and activities can be changed at this point if the market situation or competitive positions have altered significantly.

However, the controls and balances do not simply take the form of the official committees described above but are more subtle. A Nestlé manager commented on the control procedures: 'You could achieve your monthly budget targets by disturbing the strategy; for example, by repositioning brands or chang[ing] media expenditure. But if you did so, it would

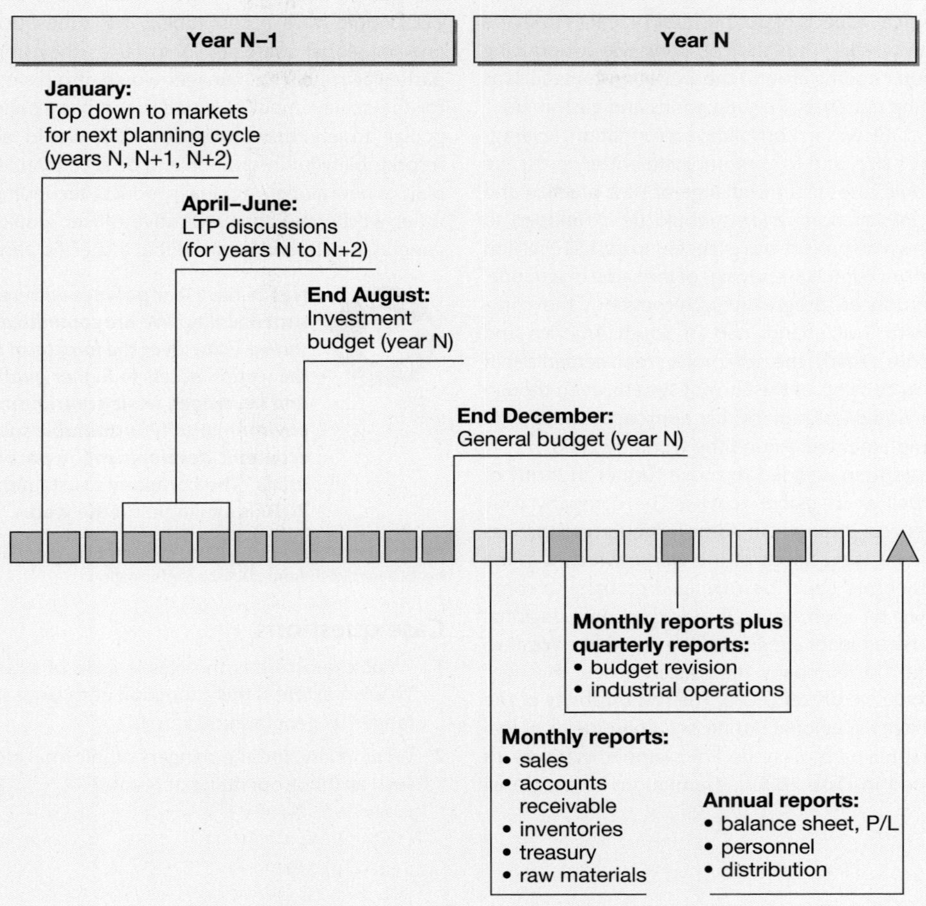

Figure 13.8 The Nestlé structure for strategic planning, budgeting and functional organisation

Source: after Goold, M and Quinn, J J (1991) *Strategic Control*.

quickly be noticed by the product group director at the centre. This would not be through a formal report, but through informal contacts with the country in question.'

In a similar way, although the SBUs and zones are separated in decision-making terms from the centre, most are located in the same geographical location – at Nestlé's HQ in Vevey, Switzerland. Here is a senior manager talking about the chocolate strategy group, which was at one time located in York, England. 'I got increasingly sucked into Vevey because of the need to talk to the various zone managers, and to all the corporate functions and services . . . I don't believe in electronic communication: face-to-face discussions are vital, especially in a group the size of Nestlé.' This principle of direct informal contact is encouraged, even if it means that some managers have extensive travel commitments. The aims are to produce an integrated team and to maintain the informal communications that provide the real checks and balances to the Nestlé style of strategic planning.

Nestlé believes that such informal approaches to planning and monitoring by the centre are useful in guiding and developing strategic management. They are probably just as effective as the formal reporting against strategic objectives. Financial rewards for achieving strategic targets are not an important aspect of the strategic process. Peer pressures, promotion and personal competitiveness are greater incentives in ensuring that strategies are delivered. A longer-term view is taken of management performance and competence by the centre rather than specific achievement against targets. This is reflected in the tendency for managers to serve the company for many years in long and stable relationships.

However, in 2000, the company realised that its devolved approach to planning meant that it was not able to take full advantage of the benefits of globalisation – economies of scale, shared R&D expenditure and so on. Hence, the company introduced a new information technology programme called GLOBE. The aim was 'to improve the performance and operational efficiency of our businesses worldwide. In the process, we will revisit all aspects of our business practices to shape new ways to run Nestlé'. Thus the company was introducing common computer coding around the world for items such as raw and packaging materials, finished goods and customers.

The aim of GLOBE was to consolidate information, leveraging the company's size, and to communicate better across the world. There would also be an exchange of best practice and data: common information systems would be developed to achieve this. The whole project was expected to cost $1.9 billion and, by 2006, deliver cumulative savings of the same magnitude. It would be introduced progressively throughout the company, starting with Switzerland, part of South America and Malaysia/Singapore. Clearly, the new project represented a shift from the informal controls of the current system, even though the new system would not replace that approach. The GLOBE IT system was implemented around the world by 2005.

In 2004, Nestlé then decided to move further in terms of its *regional* as well as its *global* activity. The company took the view that its real strength in some product groups was not global but in certain regions of the world, which it called zones. Such businesses could be managed globally to some extent, but would be even better if managed on a regional basis. 'Regional' here meant a region of the world like Western Europe or Africa. The company introduced a new manager called a zone executive officer (ZEO). The responsibility of the ZEO was to manage its regional businesses alongside its global management of some parts of Nestlé. For example, its ice cream business described in Case 10.3 had ambitions to be global but was particularly strong in certain parts of the world. The ZEO would have accountability for zone business strategies and for global strategies in so far as they impacted on that particular zone. The manager would also have responsibilities for the achievement of broader company policies in the particular zone. Importantly, the ZEO would also have clear responsibility for innovation and be accountable for the 'launch plan of new global/regional products/technologies/brands'. In other words, the zone executive officer would have a broad general management role within a specific part of the world.

Nestlé has clear policies with regard to sustainability. *'We are committed to create shared value over the long term by increasing the world's access to higher quality food and beverages, while contributing to environmentally sustainable social and economic development, in particular in rural areas.'* The company's sustainability report 2010 is available on the web.

Case questions

1 What characterises the Nestlé style of strategic planning? To what extent is this a function of its large size? Its product range? Its geographical spread?

2 What, if any, are the dangers of informal strategic controls such as those operating at Nestlé?

13.4 INFORMATION, MONITORING AND CONTROL[16]

13.4.1 Why are monitoring and controls important?

Once the strategy has begun, then monitoring and controls become operational. Monitoring and control procedures are an important aspect of implementation because information can be used:

- to assess resource allocation choices;
- to monitor progress in implementation;
- to evaluate the performance of individual managers as they go about the achievement of their implementation tasks;
- to monitor the environment for significant changes from the planning assumptions and projections;
- to provide a feedback mechanism and the fine-tuning essential for emergent strategy implementation, especially in fast-changing markets.

More generally, monitoring becomes increasingly important as the *concept* of strategy moves from being an isolated event towards being an ongoing activity.

> Strategy creation is seen as emerging from the way a company at various levels acquires, interprets and processes information about its environment.[17]

For all these reasons, companies like Nestlé and Canon spend significant resources on monitoring their activities. Because of the vast range of potential information, they may concentrate on the *key factors for success* as a first step (see Chapter 3). Some major companies have complete departments whose sole task is to monitor competitors. It is also a characteristic of some small businesses that they are acutely aware of their immediate competitors and customers, the market prices and other forms of strategic activity.

13.4.2 What are the main elements of a strategic control system?

Strategic control systems monitor the main elements of the strategy and its objectives. The crucial point of this is to obtain information in time to be able to take action. Information for its own sake has limited value: the real test is whether it is useful and timely in revising the implementation process, where required. Strategic control systems will include some financial measures but will also involve:

- customer satisfaction;
- quality measures;
- market share.

In many organisations, they now also include monitoring the achievement of green strategy objectives on sustainability, energy use, recycling and other relevant activities.

It may also be necessary to apply such indicators externally to monitor competition in order to assess the *relative* performance of the organisation against others in the market place.

It is important to distinguish between *financial monitoring* (cash flow, earnings per share, etc.) and *strategic controls* which may include these financial elements but will also have a broader perspective.

13.4.3 How can strategic controls be improved?[18]

To some extent, this question cannot be fully answered unless the precise strategy style has been established. Nevertheless, there are some useful guidelines designed to obtain the best from such systems:

- *Concentrate on the key performance indicators and factors for success.* There is a real danger that too many elements will be monitored, with resulting information overload.
- *Distinguish between corporate, business and operating levels of information and only monitor where relevant.* For example, not everyone at the centre needs to know that a minor product has just achieved its sales target. Equally, a division may have limited interest in market share data from another division, even if this is important at the centre.
- *Avoid over-reliance on quantitative data.* Numbers are usually easier to measure but may be misleading and simplistic. Qualitative data and information that is difficult to quantify in such areas as service may be far more relevant to strategy monitoring.
- *As controls become established, consider relaxing them.* Eventually, they may interfere with the most important task of clear and insightful strategic exploration. For example, it was for this reason that Jack Welch at GE reduced controls, but he did not do so until the principles had been learnt. Every organisation may need to go through this stage of learning before controls are relaxed.
- *Create realistic expectations of what the control system can do as it is being introduced or upgraded.* Some managers may regard strategic controls as a waste of time. Their reasoning is that it is difficult to see early results because of the long time scales involved. Such an objection cannot be avoided but can be anticipated. It is better to acknowledge that the benefits in terms of improved strategy, resources and results will not be immediately obvious.

13.4.4 Linking strategy monitoring with financial budgets

Bungay and Goold[19] state that it is 'vital' to link strategy monitoring into the budget process. They argue that, if the two processes are controlled by two different departments, there is a danger that short-term budget considerations will take precedence over longer-term important strategic decisions. This is a realistic but short-term Anglo-American view of the way that business operates. It is particularly associated with the financial control style described on the book's website under the heading 'Planning Strategies and Styles.' It holds the real danger that *strategy controls* and *budgeting variances* will be confused. Budgeting is concerned with the achievement of targets planned monthly or quarterly on the basis of revenue and costs. Strategy rarely concerns itself with such short-term matters.

KEY STRATEGIC PRINCIPLES

- Monitoring and control systems are important for their contribution to assessing how strategies are being implemented and how the environment itself is changing.
- The important point about information and control is the necessity of obtaining information in sufficient time to take action, where required.
- There are a number of ways in which strategic controls can be improved. All of them rely on the establishment of simple, cost-effective and useful information about the organisation and its environment.
- It has been argued that strategy control and budgeting should be linked. This is not recommended because strategy monitoring is more concerned with exploration, while budgeting is more focused on achieving specific short-term targets.

13.5 THE BALANCED SCORECARD: THE CONTRIBUTION OF KAPLAN AND NORTON

Definition ► **The Balanced Scorecard uses strategic and financial measures to assess the outcome of a chosen strategy. It acknowledges the different expectations of the various stakeholders and it attempts to use a 'scorecard' based on four prime areas of business activity to measure the results of the selected strategy.**

During the course of researching and implementing strategy at a number of US corporations in the early 1990s, Professor Robert Kaplan of the Harvard Business School and David Norton of the international strategy consultants Renaissance Solutions developed the *Balanced Scorecard*. 'The scorecard is not a way of formulating strategy. It is a way of understanding and checking what you have to do throughout the organisation to make your strategy work.'[20]

The Balanced Scorecard arose from their perceptions about two significant deficiencies in the implementation of many corporate strategic plans:

1 *Measurement gap*. Although most companies measure performance ratios, quality and productivity, these are mainly focused on historical figures – for example, 'How are we doing, compared with last year?' The two authors discovered that such measures may have little to do with future success. In addition, although such ratios were important, they did not measure other important aspects of future strategy, especially those that were more difficult to quantify. For example, future strategy might stress the importance of customer satisfaction and loyalty, employee commitment and organisational learning, but none of these might be measured.

2 *Strategy gap between general plans and managerial actions*. The authors claimed that many companies began major new strategic initiatives but that these often had little impact on the organisation. The reason was that the strategic plans were often not translated into measures that managers and employees could understand and use in their daily work.

Kaplan and Norton were particularly keen to move beyond the normal financial ratio data such as return on capital employed and earnings per share. They claimed that these are essentially functional measures and that what really matters in strategy implementation is the process: 'Processes have replaced (or are replacing) departments and functions.'[21] They identified three main types of process that are important:

1 *management* – how the leader runs the organisation, how decisions are made and how they are implemented;
2 *business* – how products are designed, orders fulfilled, customer satisfaction achieved and so on;
3 *work* – how work is operationalised, purchased, stored, manufactured and so on.

They argued that these are the activities that implement the agreed strategies but they are not the same as return on capital, market share and growth data and the other measures that often summarise the outcome of a strategic management.

13.5.1 The four key principles of the Balanced Scorecard

Kaplan and Norton developed the Balanced Scorecard to overcome these problems.[22] The Balanced Scorecard combines quantitative and qualitative measures of the selected strategy. It acknowledges the different expectations of the various stakeholders and it attempts to link scorecard performance measures to the chosen strategy. There are four key principles behind the scorecard:

1 *translating the vision* through clarifying and gaining consensus;
2 *communicating and linking* by setting goals and establishing rewards for success;
3 *business planning* to align objectives, allocate resources and establish milestones;
4 *feedback and learning* to review the subsequent performance against the plan.

While recognising that every strategy is unique, they then identified four strategy perspectives that need to appear on every scorecard. These are summarised in Exhibit 13.3. The four areas are:

1 *Financial perspective*. This translates the purpose of the organisation into action through clarifying precisely what is wanted and gaining commitment to it. For example, if the survival of the business is important, then cash flow features prominently on the scorecard.
2 *Customer perspective*. Purpose needs to be seen in the context of customer-oriented strategy. This should include not only market share data but also areas explored in Chapter 5, such as customer retention, customer profitability measures and customer satisfaction. For example, if the strategy highlights the introduction of a new product, then the scorecard might go beyond sales and share data to explore the extent of customer satisfaction and repeat business.
3 *Internal perspective*. This concerns internal performance measures related to productivity, capital investment against cost savings achieved, labour productivity improvements and other factors that will indicate the way that the organisation was undertaking the strategy inside the company. This might also involve setting internal strategy targets and establishing milestones for the implementation of the strategy. For example, the development of a new website will involve not only the customer satisfaction mentioned above but also registration of the web page, design of the site, maintenance of the site – all of these elements might be specified and targeted with dates and costs.
4 *Innovation and learning perspective*. This provides feedback and learning through strategy reviews and sharing comments on the outcome of events. It has the effect of highlighting the importance of communicating and linking people with the purpose through education, goal setting and rewards for achieving the required performance. For example, the achievement of a market share objective might be accompanied by a review of what was done well and what could be improved next time.

EXHIBIT 13.3

Balanced Scorecard: summary of strategy perspectives

Strategy perspective	Example	Example of scorecard measure – called a Key Performance Indicator (KPI)
Financial perspective	Shareholders' views of performance	• Return on capital • Economic value added • Sales growth • Cost reduction
Customer perspective	Customer satisfaction	• Customer satisfaction • Customer retention • Acquisition of new customers
Internal perspective	Assess quality of people and processes	• Manufacturing cost • Job turnover • Product quality • Stock turnover and inventory management
Future perspective	Examine how an organisation learns and grows	• New product development record • R&D core competencies • Employee retention • Employee profitability

13.5.2 Key performance indicators

These four strategy perspectives are then translated into Key Performance Indicators – called KPIs for short – for each of the areas as shown in the right-hand column of Exhibit 13.3. The KPIs are numerical measures of the target that will deliver the organisation's objectives from that particular perspective. There are therefore four steps, of which the KPI is the second, which we can examine with reference to a football club like the famous English soccer club Manchester United (ManU) from Case 13.1. Readers in other countries and followers of other sports can easily substitute their own favourite sports teams and individual sports stars for the example that follows.

1 *Step 1.* Take a *strategy objective* from the ManU strategic plan – for example, let us assume that a strategic objective is to raise the profitability of the club. ManU had low profitability in 2005 – it spent a large sum on the young, talented footballer Wayne Rooney and was not sufficiently successful in the European Football Championship. Its takeover by the Glazer family in 2005 has only increased the pressure to raise its profitability.

2 *Step 2.* Decide how the company is going to *measure* this particular objective – for example, the ManU profitability might be measured by the club's ability to deliver a return on capital that exceeds its cost of capital. A specific measure needs to be agreed – this measure is called the KPI in the Balanced Scorecard. Note that KPI measures are often relatively easy for the *financial* part of the Balanced Scorecard but much more difficult to define in other areas – for example, how do you agree a KPI for 'customer satisfaction' or 'innovation processes' at ManU?

3 *Step 3.* Translate this specific measure into a specific *numerical target* for the next period of the strategic plan – for example, ManU does not publish figures for its cost of capital, but let us assume that it is currently 7 per cent. The numerical target might be to achieve a return on capital of 8 per cent (versus the 7 per cent cost of capital).

4 *Step 4.* Generate some specific *initiatives* to achieve this numerical target.

Setting out the steps in this way raises many implementation issues that need in practice to be resolved. Taking each step in turn, *Step 1* is valuable in that it links the strategic plan with the implementation actions of the company. But there will be other objectives as well as a profitability objective and it will require some judgement to strike a balance between them.

The KPI identified in *Step 2* then becomes important because it will indicate whether Step 1 has been achieved. The scorecard will return to the KPI at various times throughout the life of the strategic plan to judge whether it has been achieved. There are a whole range of issues here: for example, there may be more than one way of measuring the objective and the KPI itself may represent a distortion of the underpinning strategy from Step 1. Careful thought therefore is needed, but the KPI has the great merit that it takes the strategic plan into the realm of what can be measured and controlled.

Step 3 takes the KPI and translates this into targets for the coming period of the strategic plan. Such targets require considerable judgement in practice and the Balanced Scorecard offers no substantive guidance on such matters – readers are referred back to the discussion on objective setting in Chapter 12 for some insights into this difficult area.

Step 4 is easy to summarise but more difficult to achieve in reality for two reasons. The first is that not all strategic initiatives will be successful, so judgement will be involved. The second reason is that each initiative is likely to have a cost that needs to be set against the likelihood and benefits of achievement. To take an extreme example, ManU might choose to achieve the financial KPI by copying the Chelsea Football Club strategy 2002–2004. This consisted of Chelsea buying every expensive, highly skilled football player that became available in the world. This would certainly be an initiative, but the cost might be beyond the financial reach of ManU, which has become a heavily indebted private company without the private financial resources of Chelsea's owner, Roman Abramovich. In addition, such an initiative might carry unacceptable levels of risk, especially in the uncertain world of sport and football.

Importantly, the Balanced Scorecard does not have just one KPI. Typically, there may be 20 KPIs for each organisation, possibly more. Each KPI in each of the main areas – financial, customer, internal and learning – needs to be identified from the strategy, measured, targeted and the initiatives identified. This is a substantial task for any organisation, but some have found it beneficial.

13.5.3 The benefits of the Balanced Scorecard

The real benefit of the Balanced Scorecard is that it provides a link between strategy and implementation. Kaplan and Norton argue that the final purpose of any strategy is to increase value to the shareholders of the organisation – a form of shareholder value added explored in Chapter 8. This is reflected in the way that the two writers have presented their approach, linking all the elements back to 'improve shareholder value' – see Figure 13.9. The four strategy perspectives shown in Figure 13.9 are linked with possible examples of the areas that might be chosen as KPIs for a particular company.

Comment

With reference to Figure 13.9, some strategists will disagree that the definition of purpose is mainly to 'improve shareholder value'. Moreover, we have seen that the Balanced Scorecard is complex to manage and some KPIs are difficult to define in practice.

In addition, some of these areas represent nothing new: educating, obtaining feedback, setting targets and milestones have been known for many years. Furthermore, as Norton himself has acknowledged, the danger of the scorecard is that it lays strong emphasis on what is measurable, which is not necessarily what is important strategically, rather than on gaining commitment and action. The scorecard may also lead to excessive measurement in larger companies, turning the whole process into a bureaucratic nightmare. However, the scorecard does represent a useful attempt in two major areas:

1 translating the abstract vision of strategic purpose into practical and useful action areas;
2 moving the strategy beyond a few overly simple measures such as earnings per share and return on capital employed.

For these reasons, it is worthy of serious exploration in many organisations.

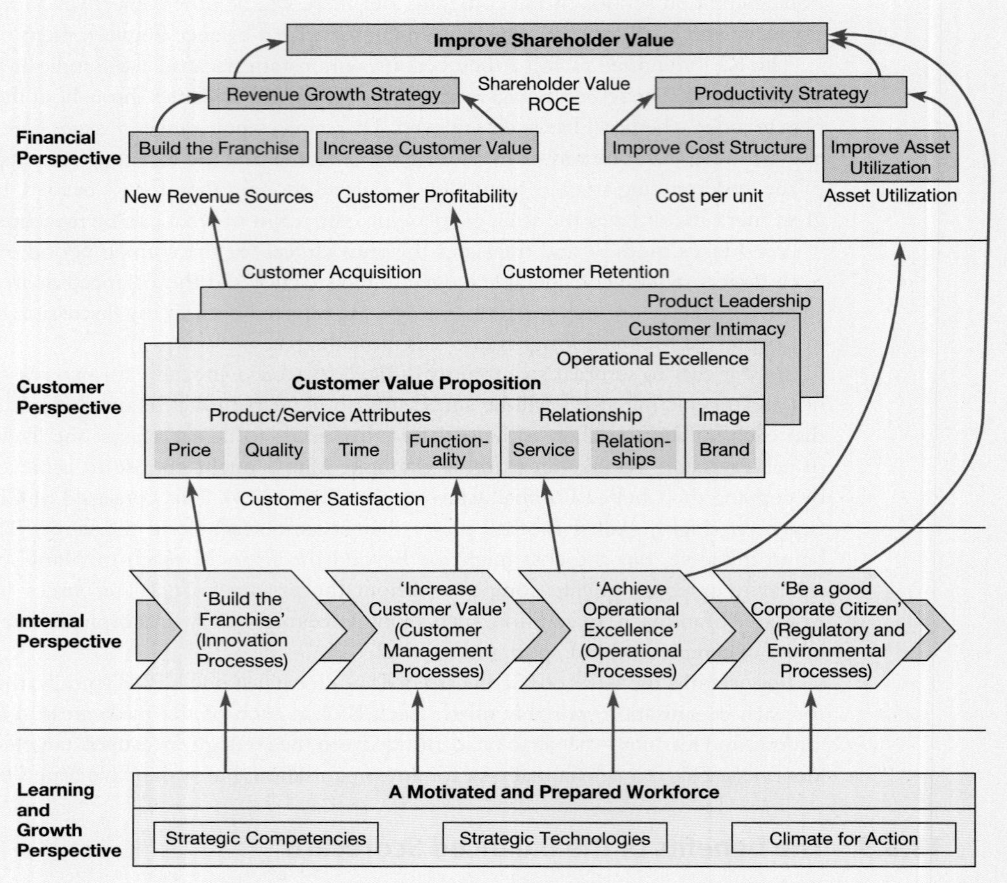

Figure 13.9 How the Balanced Scorecard strategy links back to strategy development

Source: reprinted by permission of Harvard Business School Press. From *The Strategy-focused Organization* by R S Kaplan and D P Norton, Boston, MA 2001, p 96. Copyright © 2001 by the Harvard Business School Publishing Corporation; all rights reserved.

KEY STRATEGIC PRINCIPLES

- The Balanced Scorecard was developed as a method of translating abstract strategy into specific areas of company action to help strategy to work. The Balanced Scorecard combines quantitative and qualitative measures of the selected strategy. It acknowledges the different expectations of the various stakeholders and it attempts to link scorecard performance measures to the chosen strategy.
- There are four key principles behind the scorecard: translating the vision through clarifying and gaining consensus; communicating and linking by setting goals and establishing rewards for success; business planning to align objectives, allocate resources and establish milestones; and feedback and learning to review the subsequent performance against the plan.
- The four strategy perspectives that appear on every scorecard are: financial, customer, internal, future. These are translated using four steps – strategy objectives, setting targets, identifying measurement criteria and developing strategy initiatives – that are summarised as Key Performance Indicators (KPIs).
- The main benefits lie in the focus of the scorecard on turning strategy into implementation and the development of objectives that go beyond simple financial measures.

CASE STUDY 13.4

Prescriptive strategic planning at Spillers in the late 1970s

Under the guidance of a leading North American consulting company, a strategic management system was introduced into Spillers plc in 1978–1979.[23] The company had a turnover of around £700 million ($1,200 million) and had been largely without any form of central direction up to that time.[24]

Spillers plc consisted of a number of operating companies:

- flour milling and bread baking (Spillers Homepride Flour);
- food coatings (Lucas Food Ingredients);
- meat slaughtering and processing (Meade Lonsdale Group);
- branded petfoods (Winalot);
- restaurant chain (Mario and Franco Italian Restaurants);
- branded canned meats and sauces (Tyne Brand).

Spillers was one of the UK's major food and food services companies in the 1970s. However, as the case explains, the company had completely disappeared by the end of the 1980s in spite of prescriptive strategic planning.

Spillers had increased its turnover, but its profits were static as it faced severe price competition in the milling and baking area of its business - see Figure 13.10.

The new strategic planning system consisted of an annual plan prepared to a common format by each of the above operating groups. Each plan had to address how it conformed with the Spillers' mission statement and objectives, e.g. with regard to return on capital, market share, capital investment, etc. The plans were gathered together and presented by the operating groups to the Spillers Group Board.

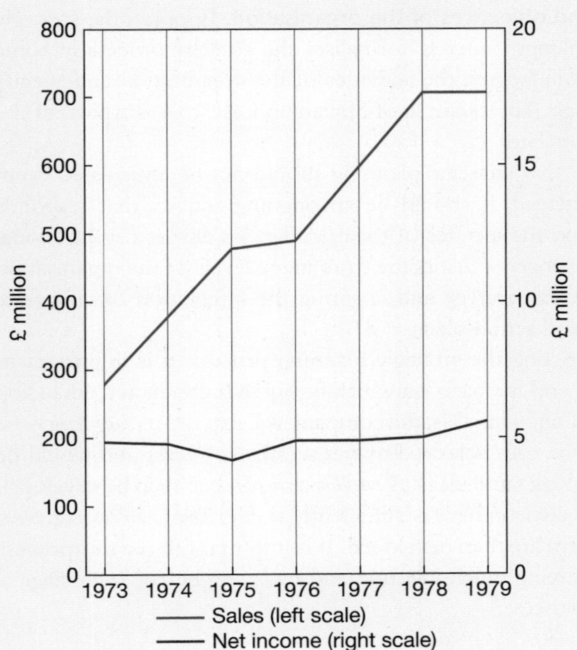

Figure 13.10 Spillers plc: sales and net income levels 1973–1979

This prescriptive strategy process certainly gave the centre of Spillers a degree of central knowledge and direction that it had never possessed before. It allowed the centre to debate with the senior managers and directors representing the various parts of the group what they judged to be the major strategic issues facing the company. Moreover, for the first time, it gave the company an ability to allocate scarce resources among the competing requests of the operating companies within the group:

- £2 million investment in a new ingredient production line at Lucas Ingredients near Bristol, UK;
- £1.5 million investment in a major expansion of the Mario and Franco restaurant chain;
- expansion of Spillers petfood branded products and production facility in Cambridgeshire, UK - estimated cost £3 million capital and a net loss for two years of £2 million in this product group;
- £20 million capital requirement spread over three years for a new abattoir at Reading, UK. (The existing facility cannot meet the new higher EU standards in the long term, yet it provides over half the profits of the Spillers Meat Group.)

The company did not have the financial resources to meet all the requests. It had to make a selection; techniques such as portfolio matrices (see Chapter 8) were used to analyse and present the results. Even under the new system, however, the operating companies rarely presented a full range of strategic options to group headquarters: for example, the Meat Group's strategic plan was for either a new abattoir or nothing.

Nevertheless, rational choice was considered by the main board. Moreover, beyond the centre, shareholders could now be told about the future plans and direction of the company. Employees were equally interested in the success of their own areas of the group.

Group strategic planning at Spillers had not previously existed. The success of Spillers' operating subsidiaries in obtaining funds up to that point had depended upon which operating company had asked first and who happened to make the most attractive financial case at the time when funds were available. Once prescriptive strategic analysis and rational debate were introduced into this process during 1979, the main board at last had a clear picture of the strategies of each major operating company and their requests for funds to implement these proposals. There had been a few complaints by the operating companies that the estimated system had been too rigid. Overall, however, the new Spillers system was fairer and less open to individual favouritism.

In practice, for Spillers in 1979 the prescriptive solutions offered by its strategic planning process were too little and too late; the strategic problems that would ultimately lead to its downfall were already evident.

All of this came to an end when Spillers was at the receiving end of a takeover bid by the UK company Dalgety in 1979. Spillers was swallowed up by an audacious acquisition and its strategic plans were used to provide a useful, if static, picture of what had been acquired. Prescriptive strategic planning had its uses for Dalgety, even if this was not quite the purpose originally intended by Spillers.

Case questions

1 Using the list of major failures in strategic planning in Exhibit 13.4 (see p. 466), what were the main weaknesses of Spillers' proposals?

2 Bearing these in mind, was it a worthwhile exercise for Spillers to develop a strategic plan in your judgement?

13.6 PRESCRIPTIVE STRATEGIC PLANNING

13.6.1 What is prescriptive strategic planning?

Definition ▶ **Prescriptive strategic planning is a formal planning system for the development and implementation of the strategies related to the mission and objectives of the organisation.** Importantly, strategic planning is no substitute for strategic thinking; it merely formalises the strategy process in some organisations. More specifically, the plan will *integrate* the activities of the organisation and specify the *timetable* for the completion of each stage. The example of Spillers in Case 13.4 is typical of the activity required – even today, some 30 years later.

George Day is right when he suggests[25] that strategic planning should not be an isolated event that culminates in a clear-cut decision. Instead, it should be an ongoing activity that responds simultaneously to the pressure of events and the dictates of the calendar. To ensure organisational commitment, involvement in the planning process must come from many levels of the organisation – each with a distinct role in formulating the strategy and ensuring the integration of corporate resource allocations, strategies, objectives and action plans.

Many companies believe that, in undertaking the strategic planning process, it is important to establish first the background assumptions and the basis on which business is conducted, including the key factors for success (see Chapter 3). Following this, the company will explore its *long-term vision* and broad strategic direction: these might be only achieved over a number of years and would be expected to include the input of new technologies and ideas. A *medium-term plan* can then be developed for the next two or three years, where the environment is sufficiently stable. *Short-term annual plans* and budgets consistent with the medium term are then developed. It is important to see this process as not just happening in sequence but involving much iteration and revisiting before each stage is finalised. Figure 13.11 illustrates the basic process.

Strategic planning in small companies and in the public and not-for-profit sectors.

Sometimes such a cycle is repeated by the company every year – Case 13.3 describes such a process at Nestlé. However, because of the potential complexity and length of such investigations,

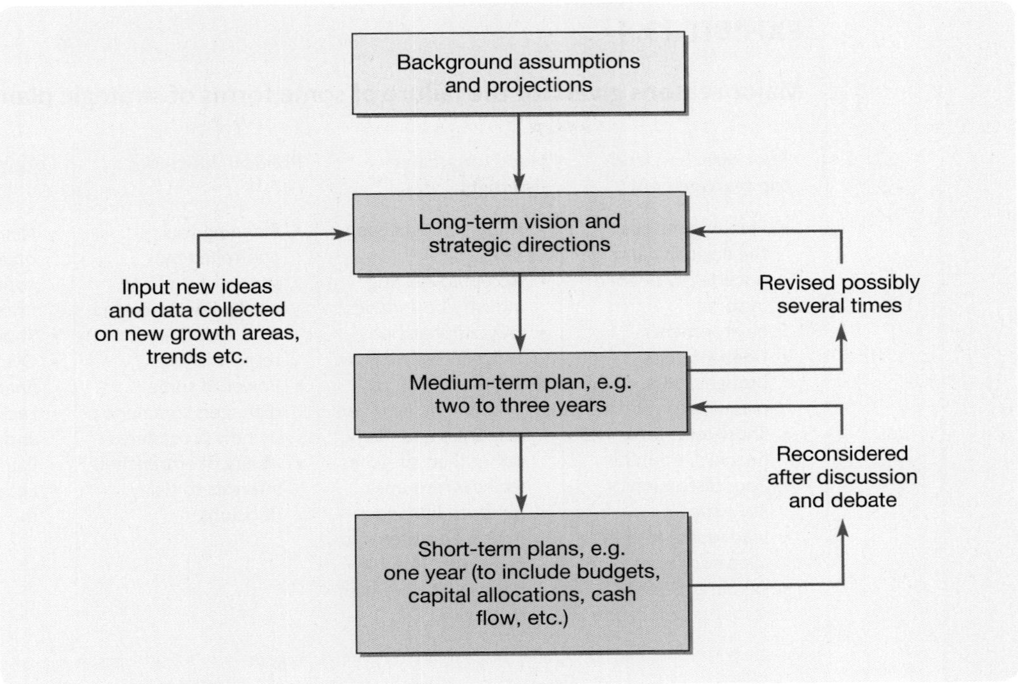

Figure 13.11 The basic strategic planning process

it would be most unusual if *every* aspect of the business were reviewed every year from a long-term perspective. Product groups, special topics, core competencies, different group objectives are often chosen as starting points for exploring strategic issues and fed into the long-term review. As Arie de Geus, the former head of planning at Royal Dutch/Shell, wrote:[26]

> The real purpose of effective planning is not to make plans but to change the . . . mental models that . . . decision makers carry in their heads.

13.6.2 The changing status of strategic planning

During the 1960s and 1970s, strategic planning promised to deliver superior financial returns. When these did not materialise and unpredictable events, such as the oil price crises of the 1970s, made a nonsense of planning (though not at Shell, as we saw in Chapter 12), strategic planning fell into some disarray.[27] Essentially, according to its critics, strategic planning had become too bureaucratic and rigid in its application.[28] These and similar comments were still being made in the 1990s.[29] Exhibit 13.4 summarises the major critical onslaught on strategic planning. It should be noted that some of the writers do not use the narrow definition of strategic planning, confined to formalising the broader process, used in this chapter. Their criticisms rely on a broader view of the role of strategic planning and may therefore be inappropriate for the narrow definition used here.

Given all these considerations, it might be argued that strategic planning is no longer appropriate as a means of formalising the strategy process. However, many companies still need to look beyond the short term and to co-ordinate their main activities, especially where significant commitments have to be made over lengthy timespans. Attitudes to strategic planning are beginning to change again and Nestlé and Canon which form the focus of the two main case studies in this chapter have been chosen from successful companies which still use some form of strategic planning. Even Mintzberg, who has been highly critical of strategic planning in the past, has now conceded that it does fulfil a useful function within certain limits.[31]

EXHIBIT 13.4

Major reasons given for the failure of some forms of strategic planning[30]

Poor direction from top management	Need for greater flexibility	Political difficulties	Corporate culture
• Planning replaced the flexibility and uncertainty needed in some environments • Deep strategic thought replaced by planning formulae • Short-term focus and financial emphasis • Poor discussion of key issues • Inadequate resources allocated for plans • Whole process of resources allocation	• Annual budget took priority • Accepted existing industry boundaries • Overemphasis on procedures and form filling • Tests for 'fit' between resources and plans rather than stretches for new resources • Better to introduce improved systems to cope with flexibility rather than stick with rigid plan	• Planning was controlled by specialist staff and not by line managers who have the responsibility • Power of some managers threatened by new procedures • Ability of entrenched interests to delay decisions	• Need to develop organisation that can cope with uncertainty • Short-termism • Over-emphasis on financial results • Lack of risk taking and entrepreneurial flair • Little toleration of the occasional failure

Note: Some comments might be regarded as applying to any form of strategy development rather than strategic planning as such. Note also the comment in the text on the research evidence used to support some of the comments.

Comment

Mintzberg is right in his emphasis on the need for innovative thinking, which may not be best served by a strongly bureaucratic strategic planning process. Overall, this book takes the view that Mintzberg is correct in his identification of the role for strategic planning: it summarises the decisions taken elsewhere and is useful for making strategy operational. Strategic planning is no substitute for careful and innovative thinking on the main strategic issues.

Three main styles of strategic planning that remain relevant today.

KEY STRATEGIC PRINCIPLES

- Strategic planning operationalises the strategy process in some organisations. It is no substitute for basic and innovative strategic thinking.
- The basic process may well cover background assumptions, long-term vision, medium-term plans and short-term plans. Importantly, new ideas are input into the process and revisions are a significant element of its development.
- Strategic planning has been heavily criticised by some researchers as being too bureaucratic and rigid in its approach, but attitudes are beginning to mellow as long as the process is narrowly defined.

CRITICAL REFLECTION

Strategic planning: to what extent is it needed?

Most senior managers and some strategists would agree that some form of strategic planning is essential in an organisation. The plan can be useful in setting out strategic and financial targets, as identified in the Balanced Scorecard, and in allocating resources between different parts of the business. Moreover, the analysis and logical process involved in devising and debating the strategies that underpin the plan is arguably of some benefit to the organisation, even if part at least is left to emerge from new innovations.

Nevertheless, the chapter has shown that there has been considerable scepticism about the benefits of strategic planning over the last ten years. Some strategists have rejected the whole notion of strategic planning. While this may go too far, it does raise the question of precisely what is meant to be achieved by a strategic plan, especially one that is developed to operate in the uncertain environment of many businesses at the present time.

To what extent is strategic planning useful? What constraints, if any, should be put on the process? And who should be responsible?

SUMMARY

- Implementation covers the activities required to put strategies into practice. The basic elements of this process are: general objectives; specific plans; the necessary finances; and a monitoring and control system to ensure compliance.
- There are three major approaches to implementation: comprehensive, incremental and selective. Implementation in small and medium-sized businesses may be less elaborate but should follow the same general principles.
- According to Pettigrew and Whipp, implementation is best seen as a *continuous* process, rather than as one following the formulation of the strategy. Hrebiniak and Joyce placed *boundaries* on implementation, depending on the ability of managers to consider every choice rationally and to evaluate the impact of implementation on the strategy itself. Emergent approaches to strategy imply that implementation needs to be considered not just as a single event but as a series of activities whose outcome may to some extent shape the strategy.
- When setting objectives and tasks, first establish who *developed* the strategy that is to be implemented. This will influence the implementation process. Individual objectives and tasks will follow from the agreed overall objectives. It may be necessary to experiment to find the optimal combination of events. In fast-changing environments, rigid objectives may be made redundant by outside events. Communication and co-ordination are vital to satisfactory implementation, and are especially important to ensure understanding of the plan and its underlying assumptions.
- The resource allocation process provides the necessary funds for proposed strategies. Where resources are limited, allocation of funds is usually from the centre of the organisation, using various decision criteria. Criteria for allocation include the delivery of the organisation's mission and objectives, the support of key strategies, the organisation's risk-taking profile and its relevance to the development of green strategies. In some circumstances, it may be necessary to re-allocate resources, for example if there are unusual changes in the environment. There is a risk that the resource allocation process will ignore the need to use resources more effectively and strategically.
- Monitoring and control systems are important in assessing strategy implementation and how the environment is changing. The necessity of obtaining information in sufficient time to take the required action is crucial. There are a number of ways in which strategic controls can be improved.

All rely on having simple, cost-effective and useful information about the organisation and its environment. It has been argued that strategy control and budgeting should be linked. This is not recommended because strategy monitoring is concerned with exploration, while budgeting is focused on achieving specific short-term targets.

- The Balanced Scorecard was developed as a method of translating abstract strategy into specific areas of company action to help strategy to work. The Balanced Scorecard combines quantitative and qualitative measures of the selected strategy. It acknowledges the different expectations of the various stakeholders and it attempts to link scorecard performance measures to the chosen strategy. The main benefits of the scorecard lie in its focus on turning strategy into implementation and the development of objectives that go beyond simple financial measures.
- There are four key principles behind the scorecard: *translating the vision* through clarifying and gaining consensus; *communicating and linking* by setting goals and establishing rewards for success; *business planning* to align objectives, allocate resources and establish milestones; and *feedback and learning* to review the subsequent performance against the plan.
- The four strategy perspectives that appear on every scorecard are: financial, customer, internal, future. These are translated using four steps – strategy objectives, setting targets, identifying measurement criteria and developing strategy initiatives – the targets are summarised as Key Performance Indicators (KPIs).
- Strategic planning makes the strategy process operational in some organisations, but it is no substitute for basic and innovative strategic thinking. The basic process of strategic planning may well cover background assumptions, long-term vision, medium-term plans and short-term plans. Importantly, the input of new ideas and revisions to the process are significant elements of its development. Strategic planning has been heavily criticised by some researchers as being too bureaucratic and rigid in its approach, but attitudes towards it are beginning to mellow as long as the process is narrowly defined.

QUESTIONS

1 Compare the Canon and Nestlé styles of strategic planning and discuss why they are different. Is one better than the other and, if so, which?

2 Does a small company need a formal strategic plan?

3 Apply the basic implementation process outlined in Figure 13.1 to the current procedures of an organisation with which you are familiar. Where does it differ and where is it the same? What conclusions can you draw about the process?

4 *'Nothing chastens the planner more than the knowledge that s/he will have to carry out the plan.'* (General Gavin, quoted by George Day) Discuss this comment in the context of the implementation process.

5 What are the implications of bounded rationality and minimum intervention in developing the strategic process?

6 How can objectives and tasks be communicated from senior management while at the same time motivating those who have to implement them?

7 *'If top management devotes more effort to assessing the strategic feasibility of projects in its allocational role than it does to the task of multiplying resource effectiveness, its value added will be modest indeed.'* (Gary Hamel and C K Prahalad) Discuss.

8 Devise a strategic plan for an organisation with which you are familiar and identify the main elements that you would control during the period of the plan. Consider whether you yourself can be wholly responsible for devising such a plan or whether you would, in practice, not only need to *consult* with others but to gain their *agreement* to the plan.

9 Explain briefly why strategic controls are necessary and indicate how they might be improved. Consider an organisation with which you are familiar and assess its strategic controls with reference to your explanation.

FURTHER READING

Hrebiniak, L and Joyce, W (1984) *Implementing Strategy*, Macmillan, New York is worth reading. An abridged paper based on this book appeared in the following: De Wit, B and Meyer, R (1994) *Strategy: Process, Content and Context*, West Publishing, MN, pp 192–202. For a more recent review, see Miller, S, Wilson, D and Hickson, D (2004) 'Beyond planning: strategies for successfully implementing strategic decisions', *Long Range Planning*, Vol 37, pp 201–218. An interesting practical paper: Michael K Allio (2005) 'A short practical guide to implementing strategy', *Journal of Business Strategy*, Vol 26, No 4, pp 12–21.

Kaplan, D and Norton, R (1996) *The Balanced Scorecard*, Harvard Business School Press, Boston, MA is important for this topic. See also Kaplan, D and Norton, R (2001) *The Strategy-focused Organization*, Harvard Business School Press, Boston, MA. Also worth reading are Ahn, H (2001) 'Applying the Balanced Scorecard concept: an experience report', *Long Range Planning*, Vol 34, Issue 4, pp 441–462 and Veen-Dirks, P and Wijn, M (2002) 'Strategic control: meshing the critical success factors with the Balanced Scorecard', *Long Range Planning*, Vol 35, pp 407–427. See also: Braam, G and Nijssen, E (2004) 'Performance effects of the balanced scorecard: a note on Dutch experience', *Long Range Planning*, Vol 37, No 4, pp 335–350 and Papalexandris, A, Ioannou, G and Prastacos, G (2004) 'Implementing the Balanced Scorecard in Greece: a software firm's experience', *Long Range Planning*, Vol 37, No 4, pp 351–366.

The classic study of different types of strategic planning is that by Goold, M and Campbell, A (1987) *Strategies and Styles*, Blackwell, Oxford and is well worth reading.

Arie de Geus wrote a useful article on strategic planning: (1988) 'Planning as learning', *Harvard Business Review*, March–April, pp 70–74.

Professor H Mintzberg has changed his views on strategic planning: (1994) 'The fall and rise of strategic planning', *Harvard Business Review*, January–February, pp 107–114. See also Mintzberg, H (1994) *The Rise and Fall of Strategic Planning*, Prentice Hall, New York. Note that Professor Colin Egan provides a logical and well-argued critique of Mintzberg's work in Egan, C (1995) *Creating Organizational Advantage*, Butterworth–Heinemann, Oxford, Ch 7.

NOTES AND REFERENCES

1 Sources for this case are the author's life-long support for Portsmouth Football Club and *Financial Times*: 6 August 1998, p 32; 11 March 1999, p 25; 21 July 2001, p 9; 22 July 2000, p 13; 29 July 2000, p 17; 18 August 2000, p 13; 27 October 2000, p 20; 29 March 2001, p 14; 11 August 2001, p 14; 24 August 2001, p 9; 2 September 2001, p 11; 6 October 2001, p 16; 7 December 2001, p 16; 23 February 2002, p 13; 1 March 2002, p 15; 9 March 2002, pp 12, 14; 3 May 2005, p 4 of 'Creative Business' special supplement; 16 December 2010, p 24; 17 December 2010, p 22; 12 April 2011, p 19. Manchester United Annual Report and Accounts 2004 – available on the web at www.ir.manutd.com/manutd/findata/kfd. Quote from *Daily Telegraph*, 22 January 2010 sourced from the web. UEFA official report 24 February 2010 on football finances, *UEFA benchmarking report 2009*: http://www.uefa.com/uefa/footballfirst/protectingthegame/clublicensing/news/newsid=1453119.html.

2 Day, G S (1984) *Strategic Market Planning*, West Publishing, MN, Ch 8.

3 Yavitz, B and Newman, W (1982) *Strategy in Action: The Execution, Politics and Payoff of Business Planning*, The Free Press, New York. It should be noted that Hrebiniak and Joyce (1984) also describe similar distinctions in *Implementing Strategy*, Macmillan, New York.

4 Day, G S (1984) Op. cit., Ch 8.

5 Author's experience based on strategy development in fast-moving consumer goods, telecommunications and consultancy.

6 Pettigrew, A and Whipp, R (1991) *Managing Change for Competitive Success*, Blackwell, Oxford, pp 26, 27.

7 Pettigrew, A and Whipp, R (1991) Op. cit., p 176.

8 Hrebiniak, L and Joyce, W (1984) Op. cit. An abridged paper based on this book appeared in: De Wit, B and Meyer, R (1994) *Strategy: Process, Content and Context*, West Publishing, MN, pp 192–202. For a more recent perspective: Sydow, J, Schreyogg, G and Koch, J (2009) 'Organizational path dependence: opening the black box', *Academy of Management Review*, Vol 34, No 4, pp 689–709.

9 Hunger, J and Wheelen, T (1993) *Strategic Management*, 4th edn, Addison-Wesley, Reading, MA, p 238.

10 Day, G S (1984) Op. cit., p 186.

11 Harvard Business School case (1983) *Canon Inc (B)*, reference number 9-384-151, and *Note on the World Copier Industry in 1983*, reference 9-386-106; Kono, T (1992) *Long Range Planning of Japanese Corporations*, de Gruyter, Berlin; *Financial Times*, 16 Feb 1996, p 31; *Canon Inc.*, Annual Report and Accounts 1994, 1998 and 2004 (English version); Hamel, G and Prahalad, C K (1994) *Competing for the Future*, Harvard Business School Press, Boston, MA. Canon annual report and accounts 2010, which is available on the web but appears to be difficult to download.

12 Galbraith, J and Kazanjian, R (1986) *Strategy Implementation*, 2nd edn, West Publishing, MN, p 98.

13 Goold, M and Campbell, A (1987) *Strategies and Styles*, Blackwell, Oxford, p 21.

14 Hamel, G and Prahalad, C K (1994) Op. cit., p 159.

15 References for Nestlé case: *Financial Times*: 6 May 1992, p 16; 15 May 1992, p 13; 20 April 1994, p 19. Goold, M and Quinn, J (1990) *Strategic Control*, Hutchinson Business Books, London, pp 118–119. Nestlé Annual Report and Accounts 2004 and 2010 available on the web at www.ir.nestle.com. The same website has various powerpoint presentations to investors, which detail the latest Nestlé thinking on its global organisation and have been used in the preparation of this case.

16 This section has benefited from Galbraith, J and Kazanjian, R (1986) Op. cit., pp 85–87.

17 Pettigrew, A and Whipp, R (1991) Op. cit., p 135.

18 This section has benefited from the paper by Bungay, S and Goold, M (1991) 'Creating a strategic control system', *Long Range Planning*, June, Pergamon Press, Oxford.

19 Bungay, S and Goold, M (1991) Op. cit.

20 Leadbeater, C (1997) 'Flying with a clear view', *Financial Times*, 1 April, p 17. Direct quote from David Norton.

21 Kaplan, D and Norton, R (1996) *The Balanced Scorecard*, Harvard Business School Press, Boston, MA, p 77.

22 Kaplan, D and Norton, R (1996) Ibid.

23 The evidence in this case comes from personal experience: the author was senior manager at Spillers plc corporate strategy headquarters and acted as liaison manager with the consultancy company.

24 Lester, T (1979) 'Slow grind at Spillers', *Management Today*, Jan, pp 59–114.

25 Day, G S (1984) Op. cit., p 189.

26 De Geus, A (1988) 'Planning as learning', *Harvard Business Review*, March–April.

27 Marx, T (1991) 'Removing the obstacles to effective planning', *Long Range Planning*, August, Pergamon Press, Oxford.

28 Loasby, B (1967) 'Long-range formal planning in perspective', *Journal of Management Studies*, October, pp 300–308; Lenz, R and Lyles, M (1985) 'Is your planning becoming too rational?', *Long Range Planning*, August, Pergamon Press, Oxford.

29 Hamel, G and Prahalad, C K (1994) Op. cit., p 283.

30 Exhibit 13.4 is developed from references 21, 22 and 26.

31 Mintzberg, H (1994) 'The fall and rise of strategic planning', *Harvard Business Review*, January–February, pp 107–114. See also his book (1994) *The Rise and Fall of Strategic Planning*, Prentice Hall, New York. Note that Egan provides a logical and well-argued critique of Mintzberg's work in Egan, C (1995) *Creating Organizational Advantage*, Butterworth–Heinemann, Oxford, Ch 7.

CHAPTER 14
Green strategy and sustainability

Video and sound summary of this chapter

LEARNING OUTCOMES

When you have worked through this chapter, you will be able to:

- outline the main elements of green strategy and sustainability and explain their importance;
- define and explain the additional elements involved in analysing the green strategy environment;
- explain the strategy implications of resource-based green strategy;
- identify how the purpose of an organisation changes as it adopts green strategy principles;
- explain the main implications of green strategy for knowledge, technology and innovation;
- outline the impact on strategy options, strategy choice and implementation from the perspective of green strategy and sustainability.

INTRODUCTION

Definition ▶ **Green strategy concerns those activities of the organisation that are focused on both sustaining the earth's environment and developing the business opportunities that will arise from such additional activities. Sustainability is the underpinning principle.** We begin with an important point of clarification. In many books and papers, green strategy is called the 'environment' or the 'natural environment'.[1] However, the words 'strategic environment' have been used in a different and broader context throughout this text – for example in Chapter 3. To avoid any confusion, this chapter uses the words 'green strategy' rather than 'environment' for the specific topic of strategies related to sustainability.

No one should be in any doubt about the need for fundamental change on the part of all organisations in both the public and private sector with regard to green strategy and sustainability. To quote from the International Institute for Sustainable Development: 'The tectonic changes that we face in the coming decades, including population increases, environmental degradation and socio-economic expectations, require bold thinking and new approaches . . . Lest readers imagine that this refers only to minerals, energy resources and similar commodities, there is no greater requirement than that posed by dependency on water as a precious and limited resource indispensable to human life and well-being.'[2]

This chapter summarises and brings together recent strategic thinking on green strategy with sustainability being the key underpinning logic in all its aspects. Significant academic work has now been undertaken in this area,[3] and this chapter draws on that material. It covers both strategic

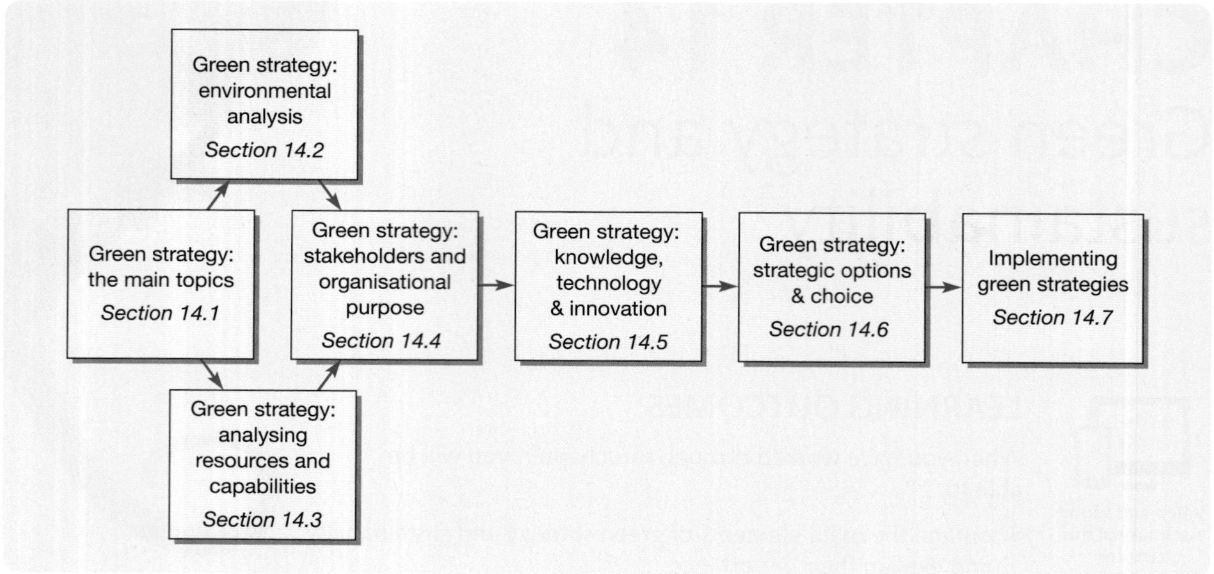

Figure 14.1 The main topics in green strategy

management and other fields of business such as corporate social responsibility, marketing, accounting and finance and production. However, the studies have focused primarily on ensuring that businesses meet or exceed sustainability *standards*. There has been rather more limited work on exploring the strategic business *opportunities* that might arise from such activities: for example, new industries developing solar power or wind energy. The main topics of green strategy broadly follow the chapters of this book – see Figure 14.1.

CASE STUDY 14.1

Prescriptive and emergent strategies: profits from the sun, wind and sea? Even from nuclear energy?

With the drive towards renewable energy, companies worldwide are beginning to commercialise the earth's natural resources. But profits are still to emerge in some cases. And major difficulties remain, as this case explains.

Renewable resources are already big business

As national economies develop and become wealthier, they need and consume more energy in areas such as electric power, transport and food processing. At the same time, the earth is warming up and becoming more polluted as a consequence of increased energy and greater consumption of manufactured goods. The outcome is that we need more power. But it needs to be renewable and it also needs to have low or zero emissions, especially with regard to carbon by-products.

Some national governments are now offering major financial support for low-carbon and renewable resource applications. Equally, some companies see major profit opportunities from renewable resources. In 2009, for example, the UK Carbon Trust produced a report which estimated that the total global investment in clean energy up to 2008 totalled £148 billion ($211 billion). Investment came from venture capital companies, small businesses, government departments and large companies through corporate research and development. Further growth was certain over the next 20 years, but the precise areas of growth remained unclear. Expansion depends on which technologies emerge as being the most cost-effective and also which technologies are most suited to particular countries: for example, some countries have more sun than others, thus favouring solar technology.

Sources of renewable energy

In terms of their contribution to total energy around the world, renewables accounted for around 20 per cent of total energy consumption in 2008 – see Figure 14.2. Fossil fuels

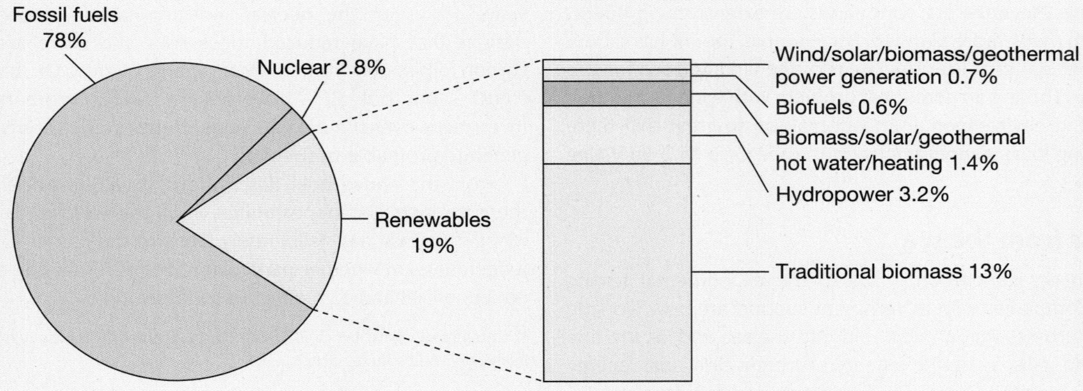

Figure 14.2 Renewable energy share of global final energy consumption 2008

Note: Fossil fuels include coal, gas and petroleum. Biomass is essentially plant material – from grass to wood – that is burnt to produce electricity. Geothermal is produced by boring into the central hot core of the earth. Hydropower typically comes from water contained behind large dams and then released through turbines to produce power – often called 'hydroelectric' power.

Source: REN21 Secretariat (2010) *Renewables 2010 Global Status Report*. Paris. Copyright © 2010 Deutsche Gesellschaft für Technische Zusammenarbeit (GTZ) GmbH.

Experimental power is being generated from the strong winds and tides of the coast of the Shetland Islands, Northern Scotland. But the costs may be too high to justify the major investment needed for large-scale use.

were still the largest source in 2008 accounting for 78 per cent of total use. However, virtually every government around the world was convinced that this source needed to be radically reduced by 2050. In essence, the problem with all alternative forms of energy at the present time is that the costs of production are higher than those for fossil fuel. There are two implications:

- Fossil fuels will continue to be the main source of energy until the costs of alternatives are reduced, for example by further advances in technology. The other possibility is that the cost of fossil fuel is raised, for example by extra government taxes on such fuel or by external factors such as war.
- There is a strong incentive to invest in new technologies to drive down the costs of renewable energy sources like the sun and the tide. But this pressure is, at least partly, driven by government policy rather than commercial considerations. Typically, public policy decisions are slower and lack the clearer sense of direction possessed by some business decisions.

For the purpose of this case, we focus on four methods of reduction: solar, wind, tidal and nuclear power.

Profits from solar power

This technology has existed for many years and is relatively mature. As a consequence, many companies are now investing in this form of renewable energy – both as manufacturers and as users. Importantly, the technology is so mature that large-scale production of solar panels is now being undertaken, especially in China and the USA. Economies of scale will bring down the production cost and take the costs of producing this form of renewable energy closer to the costs of fossil fuels. One of the technical problems for solar power is that the more northern countries receive lower amounts of sun, especially during the winter months. Hence, there is some incentive to develop other forms of renewable energy.

Profits from the wind

Many countries around the world now have both on-shore and off-shore 'wind farms' – essentially, groups of windmills that turn in the wind and generate power. The technology is partially developed, especially for land-based windmills. But the costs are still higher than fossil fuel and there is a technical problem with wind: its speed can be either too low to generate electricity or too high so that there is a danger of damaging the windmills. Nevertheless, wind farms are extensively in operation with many more planned. For example, the UK has set out extensive plans for licensing areas of the land and sea for this purpose. There is an additional problem with wind farms: their visual and environmental impact may be so great that there are strong local planning objections - see Case 18.2 on Viking Energy.

Profits from the sea

Tidal energy generation is still in the experimental testing stage. Companies with government support are now working to test turbines that are lowered into the sea and, as the tide rises and falls, generate energy. Turbines for tidal energy need to be sited where sea levels rise and fall dramatically: some geographical locations, such as northern Scotland, are particularly well suited to this. Technology and profits from this source of renewable energy have scope but are yet to emerge clearly.

Profits from nuclear power

Civil nuclear power generation has now been around for over 40 years. Some of the early reactors, such as Chernobyl, were so badly designed and managed that they have given the industry a poor reputation. Some nuclear reactors have also been poorly sited, like those at Fukushima, Japan, on the coast near a major geophysical fault line. Thus there are risks in nuclear power that the industry has not always recognised. Some people regard those risks as being so great that they oppose any further nuclear development. They also argue that there is a major problem over the storage of spent nuclear fuel which will hold its dangerous radioactivity for hundreds of years. However, the nuclear industry has developed new designs that have reduced these risks and there are zero carbon emissions from nuclear energy plants. On balance, some - but not all - governments favour more nuclear investment over the next 20 years. Hence nuclear power will generate profitable business.

From the above brief descriptions, it will be evident that there are risks and opportunities in all the areas of development. This case has deliberately left it to the reader to make judgements on whether particular forms of renewable energy are beneficial and cost-effective to the world.

Case questions

1 Which of the above four forms of renewable energies is predominantly prescriptive and which emergent? Why?

2 Which of the four areas have the greatest strategic risk? What underpinning strategy principles might be used to lower any such risks? [Consider, for example, the implications of the product life cycle, first mover advantages, joint ventures and alliances.]

3 Are commercial considerations, like profitability, the most important factor in deciding the investment and use of alternative forms of renewable energy? Or should governments intervene to support investment in some areas in any circumstances? And, if government action is appropriate, should this be undertaken regardless of the cost?

14.1 GREEN STRATEGY AND SUSTAINABILITY: THE MAIN TOPICS

In a major survey of 3,000 business executives in 2011,[5] researchers found that firms fully embracing sustainability as a key strategic issue were able to successfully implement profitable pre-emptive strategies in new socially and ecologically positioned market space. They also found that firms that were only casually adopting sustainability as a strategic initiative were unable to compete effectively in this new market space. In other words, green strategy delivers positive results for leading companies.

Within the overall topic, there are seven issues that companies need to consider:[6]

1 *Effective use of energy with moves towards electrification.* Safe and sustainable energy sources are essential. In practice, this will move organisations away from gas and oil towards other ways of generating energy. Many of these approaches are more environmentally friendly, e.g. the use of hydroelectric power and wind power.

2 *Sustainable use of natural resources.* There is a basic distinction between renewable resources – like water, soils and managed forests – and non-renewable resources – like oil, gas and some minerals. There is a need both to use renewable resources where possible and to use non-renewable resources in a careful and planned way. Any such strategy also needs to protect wildlife habitats, open spaces, lakes and wilderness.

3 *Protection of the biosphere and the development of carbon neutral organisations.* Many companies are targeting the lower use of carboniferous fuels like oil and gas over the next few years. The aim over time is either to use non-carbon fuels or to eliminate the emissions that arise from carbon-based fuels. Only airlines will have a fundamental difficulty in undertaking this task. However, they are already experimenting with bio-fuels to reduce emissions.

4 *Country self-sufficiency.* Countries need to become less reliant on importing energy where possible. Some countries have an abundance of alternative energy sources and others do not. But many are seeking alternative sources of energy, for example using solar or nuclear power to replace oil and gas.

5 *Greater energy and resource efficiency.* In both the production and the use of energy, many national governments and individual companies are researching and investing in more efficient sources of power generation. In addition, organisations are also seeking ways to use other resources – everything from mineral wealth to water – more efficiently. Thus research and development is continuing and companies are putting this whole approach as one of their key objectives in strategic planning.

6 *Reduction and disposal of waste.* Green strategy needs to include waste minimisation, recycling where possible and special strategies with regard to hazardous waste.

7 *Change of attitudes and lifestyles.* To achieve major change, a major shift in public attitudes is essential. Work and leisure, transport and infrastructure, town planning and architecture will all need to change. In many cases, this may mean a fundamental transformation in public attitudes at a national level.

All the above areas will provide both opportunities and problems for companies as they develop their green strategies. The underpinning principle relates to building a more sustainable planet. This explains why green strategy is now an important factor in strategy development for many organisations in both the private and public sectors.

Importantly and where relevant, virtually all the companies studied in this text have new comments on their green strategies. Many of these companies are now members of the *Global Reporting Initiative*, a worldwide reporting framework on sustainability which provides guidance on how organisations disclose their sustainability performance. It includes guidelines, sector supplements and technical protocols. The G3 Framework can be viewed at: http://www.globalreporting.org/reporting/reporting-framework-overview.

KEY STRATEGIC PRINCIPLES

- There are seven main trends that need to be considered in green strategy: electrification, sustainable natural resources, carbon neutral organisations, country self-sufficiency in energy, greater energy and resource efficiency within countries, waste disposal and changes in lifestyle with regard to energy generation and consumption.
- Green strategy will provide one of the next major business opportunities for some companies. Sustainability policies have the potential to lead to new technologies and new business growth. They represent a 'new wave' of innovation.

14.2 GREEN STRATEGY: ENVIRONMENTAL ANALYSIS

14.2.1 Basics

Up to the present time, green strategy has slowly emerged as a significant topic in the research and literature of strategic management.[7] There are some academic papers in eminent strategy journals on this topic,[8] but it 'does not figure prominently in top journals'.[9] There are at least three reasons for

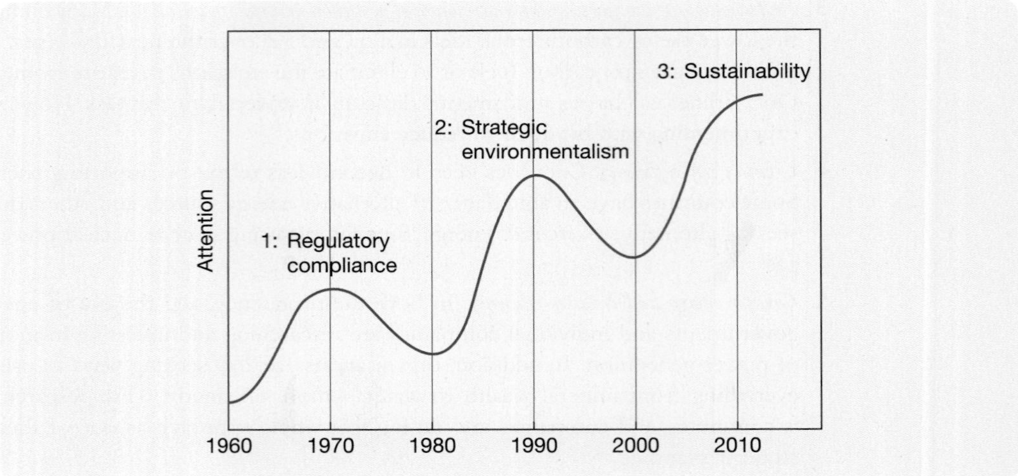

Figure 14.3 The three 'waves' of environmental management

Source: The Oxford Handbook for Business and the Natural Environment edited by Andrew J Hoffman and Pratima Bansal (2011) Ch 1 'Retrospective, Perspective, and Prospective: Introduction to The Oxford Handbook on Business and the Natural Environment' by Andrew J Hoffman and Pratima Bansal pp 3–25, © Oxford University Press, Figure 1.1 from p 5 by permission of Oxford University Press.

this. First, it is still an emerging topic that has stronger links in the past to scientific and engineering research than to social studies such as strategic management. Second, some commentators – particularly in the USA and the UK – dismiss green issues as being unnecessarily alarmist and largely unproven in their consequences. (This view is mistaken in the view of this author of *Strategic Management*, 7th edn.) Third, the topic has changed in nature from being one of regulatory compliance, then to saving the environment and ultimately to a new phase of positive business and public sector moves towards sustainability: see Figure 14.3.

The view taken by this book and by many organisations is that green strategy and sustainability are now important issues for both the public government sector and the private business sector. The topic begins by considering the strategic environment surrounding the organisation. Beyond the general analytical issues identified in Chapter 3, there are three main factors to be addressed in analysing the green strategy environment:

1 government legislation and directives;
2 business opportunities;
3 customer and consumer perceptions and pressure for change.

14.2.2 Government legislation and directives

Whether organisations agree or not, virtually every government around the world has now accepted the need to conserve the earth's resources and to reduce the pollution that arises from our activities on the planet.[10] Thus governments have enacted laws and made policy directives in line with these principles. Each country will have its own priorities, approaches and enabling framework.[11] It is the job of companies to assess these matters and then enact them as part of their strategies. The starting point is a full and careful analysis by the organisation of green issues in the country – or countries – where it operates. The outcomes of such a study, for example government targets on pollution and energy conservation, must then be built into the strategy of the organisation.

14.2.3 Business opportunities

According to a 2009 country study, green strategy initiatives were worth around $4.5 trillion in 2007. This figure was expected to grow to $6.4 trillion by 2015.[12] These activities include off-shore wind

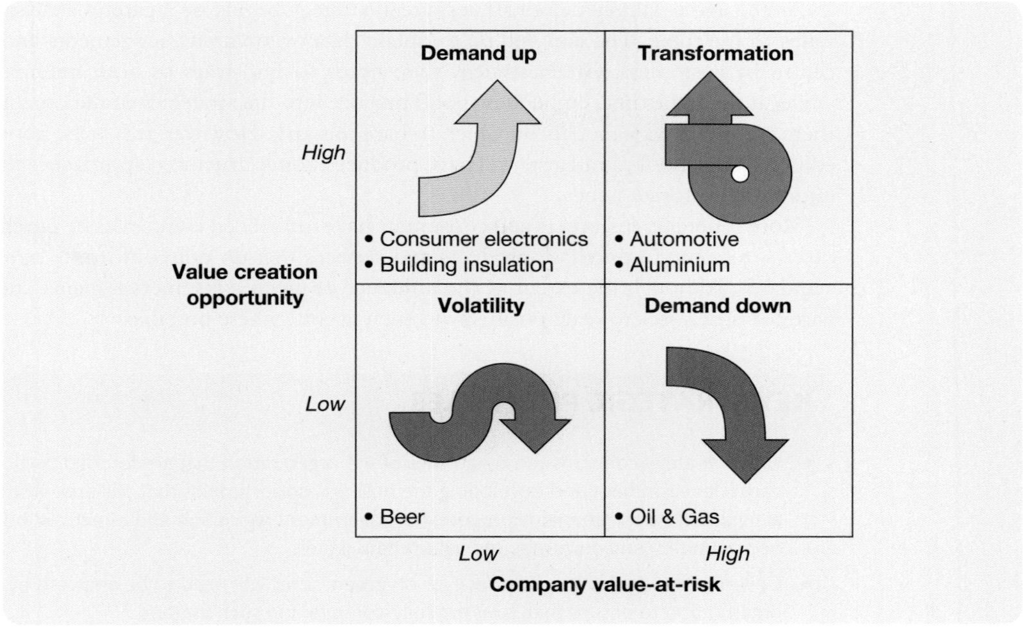

Figure 14.4 How climate change could create, transform or destroy company value

Source: Climate Change – A Business Revolution? Carbon Trust (2008) p 3

power, wave and tidal power, carbon capture and storage, and chemicals and biotechnology. They also include civil nuclear power, but this will need further analysis and consideration in light of the unfortunate problems with nuclear reactors in Japan in 2011. As a result of such work, there will be major demand for new green strategy businesses: everything from solar panels to wind farms, new lower emission car engines to more energy-efficient computers. It follows that there will be major business opportunities arising from green strategy, although they will be context-specific and difficult to analyse from a broader perspective.

In structuring green strategy business opportunities, it is important to recognise that there will be both gains and losses. For example, gains in green strategy will come from companies making building insulation and solar energy panels. On the other hand, lower consumption of oil and gas arising from the implementation of green strategy will lead to losses in the form of lower profits for companies in this area. However, increased demand for oil and gas products from emerging countries like India and China probably means that oil and gas company profits will still increase but at a lower rate than without green strategy. The UK-based Carbon Trust put together a matrix showing gains and losses with regard to the energy aspects of green strategy – see Figure 14.4. Essentially, the matrix argues that there will be a low-to-high range of value-creating opportunities arising from climate change. There will also be a low-to-high risk in terms of value generation for companies. This results in the four scenarios shown in Figure 14.4 with examples from different industries.

14.2.4 Customer and consumer perceptions and pressure for change

Some customers are strongly in favour of green strategy almost regardless of the cost. Some are indifferent and some are concerned about the extra costs involved in recycling, the higher costs of fuel and the inconvenience of new ways of working. Green strategy needs to recognise these issues and address them. For example, 66 per cent of UK customers in a survey in 2011 questioned the claims made by companies about their climate change activities.[13] However, the same survey also showed strong support for green strategy with 70 per cent of people wanting business to make compulsory disclosures of their carbon emissions.

As the above survey demonstrates, green strategy begins by a careful analysis of customer attitudes to the topic. The aim will be to obtain data on opinions, judgements and problems as perceived by customers. Green strategy then needs to find ways of both minimising any problems while, at the same time, embedding good practice into the strategies of the organisation. At present, there are no strategy models on which to bare this task. However, it is to be hoped that by the next edition of this book, strategists will have produced some structured approaches that will tackle these important customer issues.

More generally, customers and consumers have influenced companies by purchasing or – in some cases – refusing to purchase products and services that do not conform to agreed environmental standards. Although the extent of the influence of green consumers remains unclear,[14] it would be wise for businesses to react positively to such events, where possible.

KEY STRATEGIC PRINCIPLES

- Green strategy concerns those activities of the organisation that are focused on both sustaining the earth's environment and developing the business opportunities that will arise from such additional activities. It has three main components: government legislation and directives; business opportunities; and customer and value chain issues.
- Government legislation and directives on green issues will need to be analysed by every organisation to ensure that firms are fully compliant in such matters.
- Business opportunities arise because green strategy is still in the early stages of development. There are many new energy technologies, such as wind farms and waste disposal, which will provide new growth areas for organisations.
- Customers and consumers are broadly in favour of green strategies. In some cases, they have positively campaigned for change. Business needs to react positively where possible to such events.

14.3 GREEN STRATEGY: ANALYSING RESOURCES AND CAPABILITIES

Readers will recall from Chapter 4 that there are two related aspects to this topic: value chain analysis and resource-based analysis. This section therefore reflects this approach.

14.3.1 The green strategy value chain

From a resources and capabilities perspective, the green strategy value chain is not the same as the company value chain. Green strategy seeks to take a long-term – even idealistic – approach to value generated by the organisation. This may even be at the expense of the short-term cost increases that may arise from adopting lower carbon and other lower resource policies.

Definition ► **The green strategy value chain seeks out ways of reducing energy, lowering carbon content and adopting recycling policies, not only within the organisation but also with suppliers and customers. In addition, the green strategy value chain will involve every element and function, including those that perhaps do not always feature highly in many value chain analyses.** For example, an organisation might consider incentives amongst employees for ideas on developing and supporting green strategy. Equally, it might consider the use of water, which is a scarce resource and potentially subject to the United Nations CEO Water Mandate.[15] In essence, radical reconstruction and reconfiguring of the organisation's value chain may be required to deliver a long-term green strategy.

Within these general considerations, there are two major aspects:

1 green strategy value chain linkages;

2 green strategy value chain: benefits and costs.

14.3.2 Green strategy value chain linkages

In order to analyse the green strategy value chain, it is important to re-examine each element of the value chain. Chapter 4 outlined how most organisations are part of a bigger chain of business and public sector activities. Importantly from a green strategy perspective, every part of the value chain needs to consider green strategy issues and their impact on other parts of the value chain. For example, a company making solar panels might have asked its suppliers of engineering materials whether there were any ways to use lower levels of energy. In essence, green strategy applies across the value chain. In summary, there is a greater emphasis on seeking new solutions to green issues coupled with a need to be compliant with government policy and regulation. Figure 14.5 captures the main elements:

1 *Suppliers and inbound logistics*. Organisations need to discuss green strategy issues with their suppliers. For example, the pharmaceutical company GlaxoSmithKline (GSK) has estimated that 40 per cent of its carbon footprint stems from its supply chain. There may be benefits to both parties as a result of exploring green strategy issues. Such benefits and costs may also impact on the inbound logistics, such as transport and stock holding costs, of the supply chain.
2 *Infrastructure*. More radical reconstruction of the way that the organisation is built will often entail substantial capital costs, for example rebuilding using energy-saving materials. But infrastructure is not simply about building costs. It may also involve re-thinking the whole network of relationships that supply the organisation and deliver the outcome to customers. It might also involve the ingredients used in manufacturing products. For example, the pharmaceutical global company GSK has reduced the greenhouse emissions associated with its inhaler pharmaceutical products from 24 million tonnes of carbon dioxide in 1998 to 4.7 million tonnes in 2010. The sustainability guiding principle is that the long-term benefits must outweigh the costs. However, the benefits could be to *society as a whole* not just to the *individual* organisation.
3 *Production*. Over time, there will be a need to comply with new government regulations on green issues in every aspect of production. In addition, companies may wish to consider whether it is possible and desirable to move beyond these matters in the interests of enhancing their green strategies. They will also wish to engage with all their employees in tackling green strategy issues.
4 *Customers*. Many organisations will wish to underline their corporate governance and ethical stance by emphasising their green strategy. Moreover, some customers – perhaps even the majority over time – may come to demand a stronger green strategy stance from the organisation. Such actions are likely to include both communication with customers and investment in new technologies that improve energy efficiency and recycling.
5 *Services*. For some organisations, perhaps a minority, there will be opportunities to offer consultancy advice and technology information that will support green strategy.

Many companies and public sector organisations are now making significant efforts to become *carbon neutral* over time. This means that there will be no net greenhouse gas emissions from the sourcing of raw materials, or the manufacturing, distributing, using and disposing of the products from a company at that time.

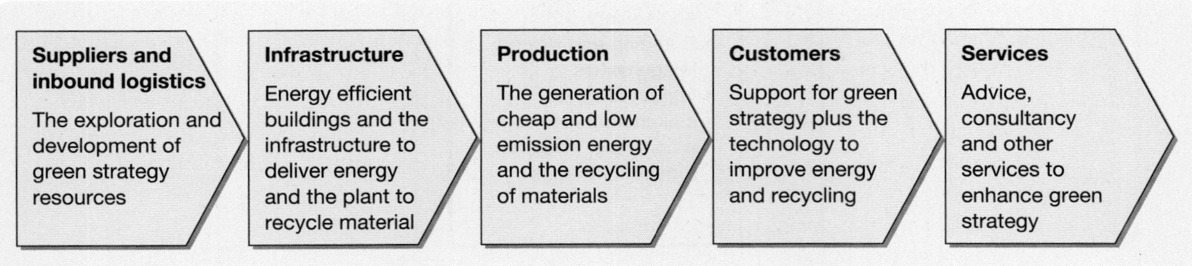

Figure 14.5 Green strategy value chain: linkages

14.3.3 Green strategy value chain: benefits and costs

From a green strategy perspective, green strategies will bring benefits both for the organisation and for its wider stakeholders – for example, employees, shareholders and the local community. Chapter 6 explores the concept of stakeholders in more depth. However, it is important to be realistic about the adoption of green strategy policies: there will be costs as well as benefits to the organisation. Figure 14.6 summarises the main areas that will need to be analysed. Most of these matters are covered elsewhere in this chapter so are not repeated here. However, the emergent and dynamic benefits and costs need careful monitoring. At the time of writing this text, many areas of green strategy are still developing for four reasons:

1. Green technologies are still the subject of both basic research and development and, for the more proven technologies, more advanced production technology research.
2. Costs of energy are rising because of both increasing demand and scarcity of supply.
3. The economies of scale associated with existing green technology will reduce costs over time as companies engage in larger-scale production.
4. Stakeholder attitudes to green strategy, including those of customers, are still developing.

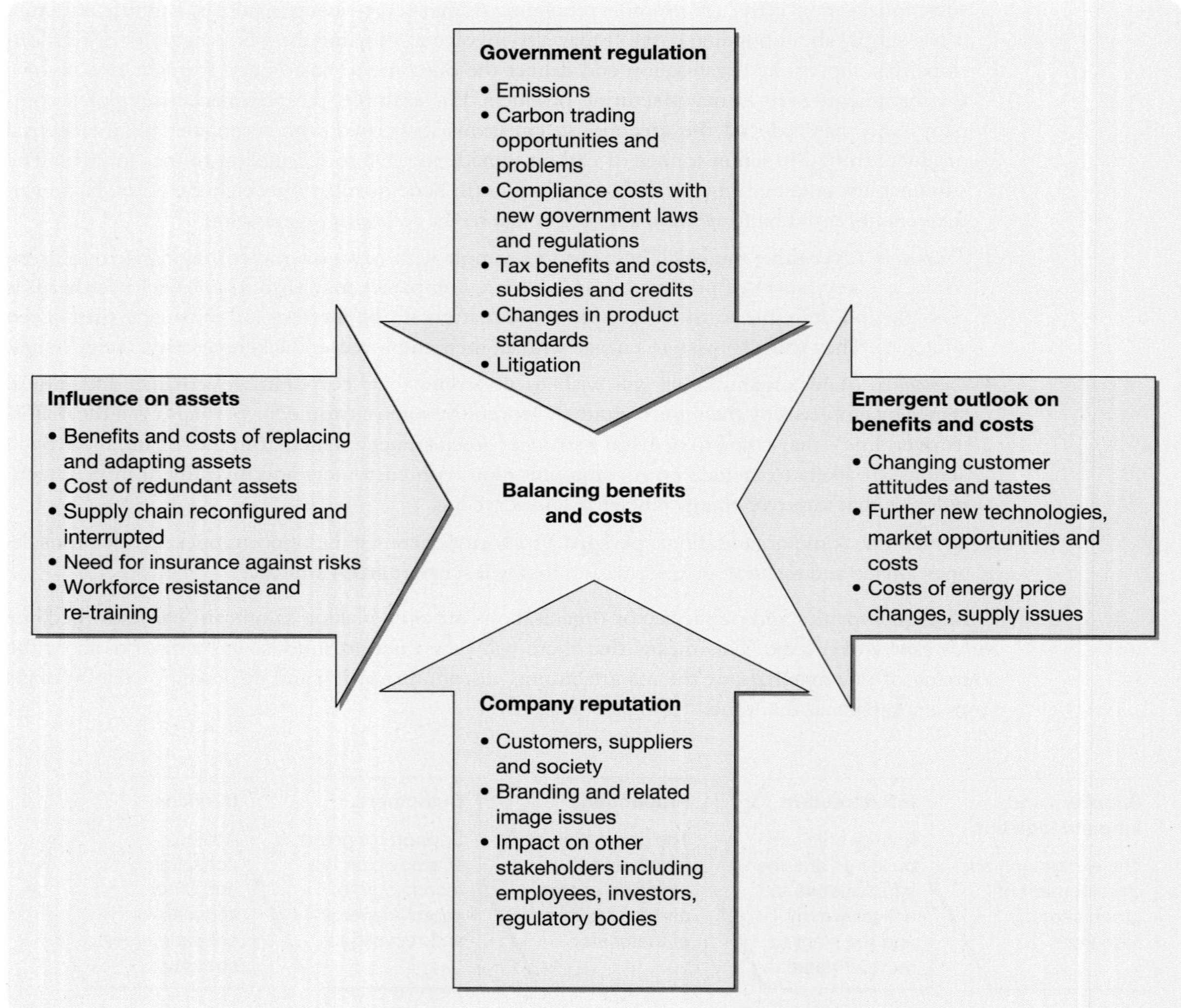

Figure 14.6 Green strategy value chain: benefits and costs

Hence the benefits and costs of green strategy are uncertain and must be considered from an emergent as well as a prescriptive process viewpoint.

14.3.4 Green strategy: analysis of resources and capabilities

Readers will recall from Chapter 4 that the resource-based view argues that the individual resources of an organisation provide a stronger base for strategy development than industry analysis. The reason is that they focus on competitive advantages of individual companies. Such resources can be divided broadly into tangible, intangible and organisational resources – see Section 4.6.1. However, some strategists have argued that this basic distinction misses a key aspect of resource analysis, namely that of the *natural environment*. 'It systematically ignores the constraints imposed by the biophysical (natural) environment.'[16]

In essence, the author of this paper, Stuart Hart, argued that the competitive advantage of an organisation needed to be judged from a 'natural-resource-based view'. This meant that the resources of an organisation had competitive advantage, especially if they were better than competitors at undertaking environmentally sustainable activities. For example, the Toyota car hybrid model, the *Prius*, was for some years reported to have lower emissions and be more fuel-efficient than its competitors. There are three aspects to such resources, each potentially involving strategic resources and capabilities: they are pollution prevention, product stewardship and sustainable development. Specific capabilities identified include:[17]

- *organisational capabilities* – the ability to organise for sustainability;
- *absorptive capacity* – the ability to assimilate new information on sustainability;
- *complementary assets* – the assets required to develop and market sustainability.

Comment

While identifying such resources and capabilities is highly commendable from a sustainability perspective, the approach may no longer deliver competitive advantage. The reason is that many organisations are now strongly engaged in green strategy and sustainability, thus reducing the opportunities for advantage in this area. For example, some car competitors have now caught up with Toyota's hybrid battery-plus-petrol car, the *Prius* – see Case 14.3 later in this chapter. However, this does not deny the importance of such activities and therefore the need to undertake the analysis.

KEY STRATEGIC PRINCIPLES

- Green strategy seeks out ways of reducing energy, lowering carbon content and adopting recycling policies, not only within the organisation but also with suppliers and customers. In addition, the green strategy value chain will involve every element and function, including those that perhaps do not always feature highly in many value chain analyses.
- The green strategy value chain has five main elements: suppliers and inbound logistics, infrastructure, production, customers and services.
- The green strategy value chain has both benefits and costs. These are captured under four headings: the influence on the assets of the organisation; government regulation; the company's reputation with its stakeholders; and the emergent outlook on benefits and costs as green strategy develops further.
- The resources and capabilities of an organisation can be analysed for their ability to deliver competitive advantages that are more sustainable than those of competitors. Three specific areas that might deliver such advantages include organisational capabilities, absorptive capacity and complementary assets. Because many firms are now engaged in this area, these three may not now be enough to deliver competitive advantage.

14.4 GREEN STRATEGY: STAKEHOLDERS AND ORGANISATIONAL PURPOSE

In identifying and developing the sustainable purpose of the organisation, stakeholders represent an important starting point as explored in Chapter 6. The range of stakeholders involved in green strategy is arguably wider. Moreover, some will have a great deal of power.[18] The reason is that sustainability and green strategy arouse strong opinions in some individuals and groups. These can be vocal and exert considerable pressure on other stakeholders: shareholders, managers, customers, etc. Such additional stakeholders include paid lobbyists, green activists, think tanks, rivals and business associations. They may all have interests and agendas that differ from those of the organisation itself. But they need to be considered in the development of the purpose of the organisation with regard to sustainability and green strategy.

Whatever the views of various stakeholder groups, the leadership of the organisation, i.e. the Chief Executive and senior board members, has prime responsibility for developing and adjusting the purpose of the organisation with regard to matters of green strategy and sustainability. For many companies, the issue for the leadership is how to respond to such green strategy pressure groups. This has been explored in a wide range of research.[19] It is best captured in *how* the leadership of the organisation will adjust its purpose and consequent policies to deal with issues relating to sustainability. Hoffman and Georg have summarised this process under four main headings:[20]

1 *Support of senior management.* The success of green strategy depends crucially on the backing of senior managers.[21] They need to institute management systems and policies that will enhance such strategies[22] and, possibly, appoint some managers as key implementers of such policies.[23]
2 *Framing and debate.* It is important that green strategy is clearly presented and discussed throughout the organisation. The issues need to be framed within boundaries of what is desirable and possible. They may also need to be debated and discussed in order to gain agreement and buy-in across the organisation.[24]
3 *Individual and managerial perceptions.* Green strategy needs to be implemented by individual managers. Thus the organisation's purpose with regard to such strategy is wholly dependent on individuals and their perceptions of the benefits and costs of such strategies. This will in turn be conditioned by the values and experience of individual managers.[25]
4 *The subsequent disclosure and reporting policies of the organisation.* It will often be necessary to publish the results of green strategy because of the pressure from stakeholders and also because of government requirements. The purpose of the organisation with regard to green strategy therefore needs to recognise such publicity in framing its objectives. Some of this activity may be undertaken in the annual report and accounts of companies.[26]

To summarise with regard to the purpose of green strategy, there have been important and influential pressure groups attempting to influence green strategy. They may operate at both government and company level: for example, organisations like Greenpeace and the World Wildlife Fund for Nature. But there are many more direct stakeholders in every organisation, ranging from the shareholders to the customers who will attempt to influence organisational purpose. A *stakeholder analysis* – see Chapter 6, Section 6.3 – with regard to green strategy is therefore essential in developing the sustainable purpose of the organisation. It will need to identify the parties that are directly or indirectly involved and affected by the organisation's operations. This analysis will then help to identify the relative power and the reactions of stakeholders to the green strategy options available to the company and influence the selection choice that will then need to be made.

KEY STRATEGIC PRINCIPLES

- In identifying and developing the sustainable purpose of the organisation, stakeholders represent an important starting point. The range of stakeholders is arguably wider with some having a great deal of power.
- The leadership of the organisation has prime responsibility for developing and adjusting the purpose of the organisation with regard to matters of sustainability. Within this general area, there will be a need to respond to the various green strategy pressure groups.
- There are four main aspects for an organisation developing its purpose with regard to sustainability: the support of senior management; the framing of and debate about the proposed green strategy policies; the perceptions of individual managers with regard to such policies; and the subsequent disclosure and reporting policies of the organisation.
- A stakeholder analysis with regard to green strategy is an essential element in developing the sustainable purpose of the organisation.

CASE STUDY 14.2

Green strategy: two problems with solar power

Although solar power has widespread government support and there is substantial demand for the product, there are at least two strategic problems that remain unsolved.

Government agencies – like the US Department of Energy – are now promoting competitions for the design of homes to use the power of the sun. Solar power has become big business.

Technology and solar power manufacturing

Back in 1861, Auguste Mouchout invented the first solar motor. In 1953, Bell Laboratories (now part of AT&T) created the first silicon solar cell able to generate electricity from the sun. Subsequently, many companies have developed ways of using the sun. Some, like Bell Labs, employ photovoltaic cells and others focus the sun's rays to heat water either by mirrors or by heat exchangers of various kinds. The key point here is that solar technology has not yet settled finally into one agreed route: scientists are still experimenting and developing new approaches.

There is nothing wrong with such experimentation in principle. However, from a business strategy perspective, this is a problem because it is more difficult for manufacturers to finalise the design of large plant to build solar generators if the technology remains uncertain. This means that it is difficult to obtain the economies of scale and thereby bring down the costs of manufacture. However, according to some experts, the technology is beginning to mature with regard to the manufacture of solar panels.

In spite of the problems over an agreed technology, at present the majority of solar power is generated by photovoltaic panels. There are some major manufacturers around the world, but many of the leading producers are centred in Germany with companies like Q-Cells and Solar World. In addition, solar panel manufacturing is also strong in China from companies like LDK Solar, Yingli and Suntech with over 80 per cent of their production being exported – often to Germany. In common with other industries, Chinese labour costs are lower than those in Germany and, in the case of solar panels, the Chinese government has been a keen supporter of this new technology for use in the domestic Chinese market.

The first problem – excess capacity

There has been one negative outcome of this new production investment activity. In 2009, there was world production capacity to produce 9,000 megawatts of solar panels while demand dropped from around 6,000 megawatts to 4,500 megawatts according to some estimates. This meant that some manufacturers were making losses even with the various subsidies that were available from different governments around the world. The costs of manufacturing were still too high when the fully installed solar electricity was compared with alternative sources of power. However, according to European estimates, demand soared again in 2010 to around 14,000 megawatts which at least meant that solar panel manufacturers were profitable again.

What is particularly interesting with regard to manufacture is that some of the world's most sophisticated electronics technology manufacturers, like Hon Hai and ACS of Taiwan, were beginning in 2011 to take an interest in solar panel manufacture. Hon Hai is the major assembler of Apple's iPhone, for example. Perhaps we are now beginning to move from experimental design into large-scale production technology. If correct, this should at last bring prices down and solve one solar problem.

The second problem – government subsidy

In order to reduce emissions, some governments around the world have been supporting solar power by various forms of subsidy. For example, the German government has insisted that the German electricity supply companies must buy all the power generated by solar energy at prices that are both fixed and high. This supports solar power electricity installation and puts the burden on customers because the German electricity supply companies simply pass on the extra costs in higher electricity prices. The outcome has been that Germany has the highest generation of solar power in Europe and in the world: 80 per cent of the world's installed solar panel capacity is in the European Union with much of that in Germany. However, this has been achieved at significant cost to German consumers and only with the effective support of the German government.

And that is the problem: solar power needs government support at the time of writing this case, either through direct subsidy or indirect government directives. In the jargon used by observers, solar power still does not have *grid parity* with the other methods of generating electricity.

According to one commentator, 'Part of going solar is changing the mindset, getting utilities who doubted the widespread use of such technology to see that it will be built and used.' But this is only part of the battle. There are also two more basic interconnected problems that are not yet fully resolved: the need for a more mature technology to bring down the costs of solar power generation and the need for governments to avoid having to subsidise solar power.

Case questions

1 The case argues that a mature solar energy technology is needed before production costs can come down. Which of the strategy theories in Chapter 5 is most closely aligned with this thinking? You might also like to look at Section 5.3.3 on the innovation flow process which explores maturing technologies.

2 Is pricing the major issue from a strategy perspective? Or are there other issues associated with the increased adoption of solar power?

3 If you were a major consumer of electricity, would you be willing to pay more for solar power because it was more renewable than electricity generated by coal or less risky than electricity generated by nuclear power? What are the essential issues that you would consider in coming to your decision?

14.5 GREEN STRATEGY: KNOWLEDGE, TECHNOLOGY AND INNOVATION

Given the changing pressures on organisations with regard to green strategy over the last 20 years, emergent strategy processes also need to be considered. Even solar power, which has been available for 20 years, is still subject to some uncertainty – see Case 14.2. We therefore need to supplement the three emergent areas discussed earlier in Chapter 7 with their implications for green strategy.

14.5.1 Knowledge creation and green strategy

In developing knowledge concepts for green strategy, the three 'A's concept captures the essence of the approach that is needed:[28]

- *Accentuate.* The first step is to audit current green strategy practices and develop them further, i.e. accentuate them. This will also include knowledge sharing within the existing organisation. Some of these practices will go beyond knowledge into physical areas like recycling and new energy saving systems. However, the principles behind all such initiatives remain a knowledge audit and knowledge sharing.

- *Acquire.* As we have seen above, many organisations acquire new knowledge from other firms, industry bodies and government institutions. In practice, acquisition can also mean joint ventures, sharing information and other forms of co-operation. Many organisations are highly likely to need to acquire new knowledge about green strategy.
- *Architecture.* One of the most important aspects of knowledge and green strategy is setting up the organisation structure – the architecture – to develop, enhance and implement green strategy. In a sense, this goes beyond the topic of knowledge into related areas. But the essential ingredient is again the knowledge foundation that underpins all such structures.

Given that the topic is still changing, green strategy knowledge needs to be considered in all its aspects.

14.5.2 Innovation and green strategy

Green strategy has arisen because of the need to sustain the earth's resources and use them more efficiently. It therefore needs a profound shift in attitudes and practice with regard to the existing resources of the planet. Such a change requires a thorough re-examination of the existing situation for each organisation and individual. In other words, green strategy will benefit greatly from a strong and focused approach to innovative ideas and processes relating to current practices and usage.

In addition to compliance with existing standards, the sustainability of the earth's resources has been identified by some writers as the next major business innovation opportunity. The need for change will produce new growth, just as earlier change produced possibilities in earlier times. Figure 14.7 captures some of these issues and provides an innovation perspective of green strategy in its historic context. In essence, sustainability policies have the potential to deliver new technologies and new business growth.

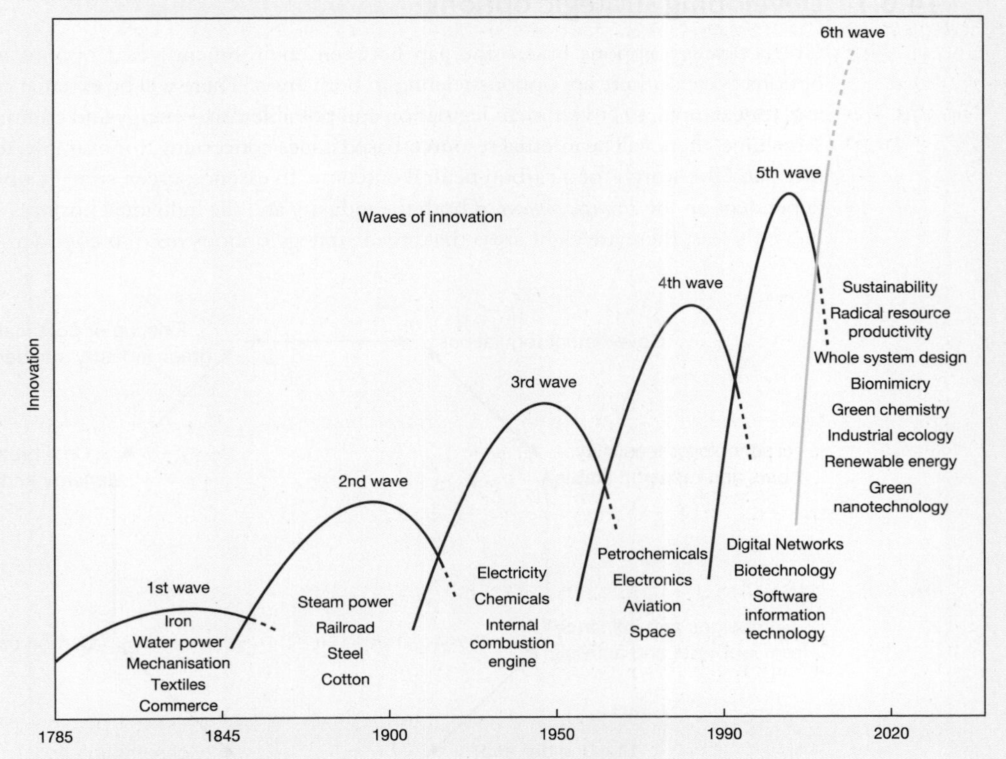

Figure 14.7 Sustainability as the sixth 'long wave' of business opportunity

Source: Hargroves, K and Smith, M H (2005) *The Natural Advantage of Nations: Business Opportunities, Innovation and Governance in the 21st Century*, London: Earthscan.

14.5.3 New technologies and green strategy

Over the past few years, green strategy has been linked with new technologies in two ways: First, some green strategy initiatives – for example, electric cars – have relied on fundamentally new *technology breakthroughs* for success. Second, other green strategies have made better use of *existing technologies*. However, they have needed *process technologies* – for example, the large-scale manufacture of solar panels – to reduce manufacturing costs and make the products price competitive with other traditionally manufactured products. From both perspectives, technology has made a vital contribution to the development of green strategy.

KEY STRATEGIC PRINCIPLES

- From a knowledge creation perspective, green strategy will benefit from the three 'A's concept: Accentuate current green strategy practices; Acquire new technologies; Architecture to set up the organisational structures required to implement new strategies.
- From an innovation viewpoint, green strategy has two aspects. The first relates to examining the use of existing resources to ensure that they are used most efficiently. The second suggests that sustainability may represent a 'new wave' of business opportunity that will provide new business growth.
- New technologies for green strategy can occur in two areas: technology breakthroughs and better use of existing technologies.

14.6 GREEN STRATEGY: STRATEGIC OPTIONS AND CHOICE

14.6.1 Developing strategic options

Green strategy options bridge the gap between environment-based options and resource-based options because there are options relating to both areas. There will be external considerations relating, for example, to government legislation and possible rising energy and commodity prices. At the same time, there will be internal resource-based issues concerning, for example, technology development and the search for a carbon neutral outcome. In essence, green strategy options will be wholly dependent on the *strategic context* of both the industry and the individual business within the industry. Nevertheless, there are eight areas that green strategy options need to consider – see Figure 14.8.

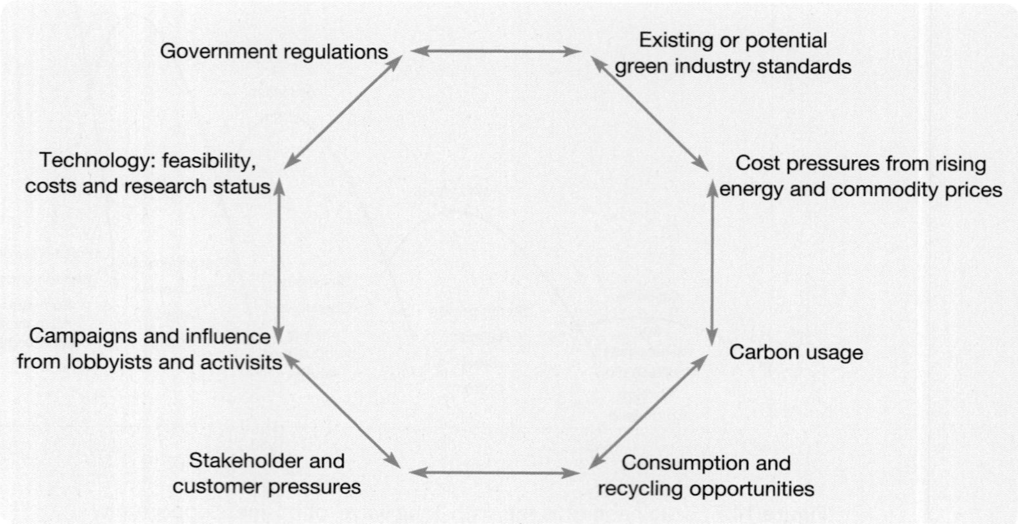

Figure 14.8 Developing green strategy options

While it is not possible to identify which green strategy options will apply to an individual organisation, the general areas that need to be considered are:

1. *Government regulations and future standards.* Companies will need to adhere to existing legislation with regard to green issues and also consider government targets and timing with regard to the introduction of new standards.
2. *Existing or potential industry standards on green issues.* In addition to government regulation, industries themselves may decide to set and regulate green standards. Some businesses may decide to take the lead in such matters and other businesses will decide to break away from such standards, if possible.[29]
3. *Cost pressures from rising energy and commodity prices.* Although some prices have declined, there has been a general tendency for these to rise over the past few years for two reasons: increased demand from newly developing nations and higher government taxes to incentivise greener usage.
4. *Carbon usage.* Some industries will be prime users of carbon such as coal-burning power stations while other industries will be low users such as the media industry. Companies will need to consider whether it is feasible and desirable to move towards being carbon neutral over time.
5. *Consumption and recycling opportunities.* Some industries will be major consumers of various manufactured materials such as electronics components and packaging. They will wish to consider options for reducing their consumption and for recycling.
6. *Stakeholder and customer pressures.* Green strategy will need to react to stakeholder pressure and customer opinion in developing business options.
7. *Campaigns and influence from lobbyists and activists.* Lobbyists on behalf of various public and commercial organisations will increasingly influence options. In some industries, such as the international whaling industry, activists have mounted concerted attempts – rightly or wrongly – to influence companies into particular courses of action.
8. *Technology.* The feasibility, costs and research status of new products and processes that deliver greener products and services will form an important aspect of business options. For example, the technology surrounding the development of electric cars forms a significant part of the effort of many world car manufacturers at the present time – see Case 4 in Part 6.

The relevance and relative importance of the various green strategy options will depend both on outside pressures influencing the organisation and on the competitive and other resources possessed by the organisation. Arguably the one option that is no longer available with regard to green strategy is for the organisation to do nothing.

14.6.2 Evaluating and selecting between options[30]

Beyond the basic evaluation concepts covered Chapter 10, such as cash flow and profitability, green strategy options selection involves a number of broader considerations. Perhaps the most important is the organisation's policy (or lack of it) with regard to green strategy: does it actually *possess* a green strategy? The company case examples throughout the text show that some companies have highly developed policies while a few are only now beginning to acknowledge the issue. The rest of this section makes the assumption that the organisation has chosen to develop green strategies as a matter of principle.

In developing and selecting green strategy, companies will make their decisions within the limits of their resources: for example, the finance available, the product range and the capabilities of the managers and employees. In addition, green strategy choice will depend on the nature of the company's business operations: high energy users like the steel industry will have different pressures compared with low energy users like internet providers. There will also be the pressures that will arise from the organisation's stakeholders that were identified in Section 14.4.

In addition to these considerations, there are three specific considerations with regard to evaluating and selecting green strategies:

1 strategic context;
2 existing and planned legislation and other government policies;
3 company-level incentives, costs, resources and timing.

Strategy context

As a broad general principle, green strategy selection will depend on the circumstances surrounding the organisation: the aims and aspirations of the country; the region within a country; and the policies of the industry within which the company operates. For example, Table 14.1 identifies the ten leading carbon-emitting countries and comments briefly on the strategic context for each country. Both countries and industries will set the context within which the company will then make its selection decisions.

Table 14.1 Green strategy context: the ten largest country carbon-emitters

Country	Carbon emissions 2008: million tonnes	Carbon emissions per head of population	Strategy context
The world's top ten emitters . . .			
China	6508	4.9	Central government policy favours lower emissions, but provincial governments are perhaps not so keen – new investment in greener energy in some sectors
USA	5596	18.4	Complex federal and state legislation but also much scepticism, especially from the right-wing media
Russian Federation	1594	11.2	Ambitious targets but renewed economic growth plus low-efficiency plant may make achievement difficult
India	1428	1.2	Poor infrastructure, oil-dependence and corruption will inhibit further reductions. But already one of the lowest per head in world
Japan	1151	9.0	Highly dependent on energy imports plus nuclear power – impacted by disaster at Fukushima Daiichi 2011
Germany	804	9.8	Strong government tariff policies have led to real reductions
Canada	551	16.5	Growing energy producer but national government targeting of greater efficiency not always supported at provincial government level
UK	551	8.3	Strong government incentives for industry to reduce emissions plus binding commitments on reduction
Islamic Republic of Iran	505	7.0	Trade sanctions have made it tough to invest in energy reduction with nuclear investment being highly controversial
South Korea	501	10.3	Highly dependent on imported energy with national government favouring new green initiatives
Some other countries for comparison . . .			
Italy	430	7.2	
Saudi Arabia	389	15.8	
France	368	5.7	
Brazil	337	1.9	
Egypt	174	2.1	

Source: author, based on data from IEA (2010) *CO_2 Emissions from Fuel Combustion: Highlights*, Paris.

Existing and planned legislation and other government policies

In spite of the failure of some international conferences like Copenhagen 2009 to reach substantive agreement on green policies, national and regional governments have often enacted or are planning legislation with regard to green strategy. They have done this because sustainable development cannot just be achieved by a single company. It needs to be seen as an activity that works through every part of the country within which the business operates. The choice of green strategies therefore needs to respond to such policies and initiatives.

Company-level incentives, costs, resources and timing

Both in theory and in practice, there are often incentives and costs for adopting green initiatives. Probably the most sophisticated of these is the European Union *Carbon Trading Scheme*. This is intended to encourage 11,000 industrial installations across the 27 member states of the European Union to reduce emissions. The EU sets emission limits and then forces polluting companies to buy allowances to cover their excess. There are incentives for the more efficient companies because they can exchange their unused allowances for cash or save them for future use. An extensive market has grown in trading these allowances – even leading to fraud and an estimated loss of €5 billion ($7.3 billion) in tax revenues as a result.[31]

Coupled with incentives and costs, there are also issues related to the resources and timing of green strategy. Companies often face trade-offs with regard to strategy changes. For example, does a company immediately close and replace a polluting plant with the consequent loss of sales? Or does it keep the plant open while building a replacement and face government fines for pollution?

In addition, some green strategy solutions may need resources that essentially remain unproven. Green technology is still developing in some areas with the costs and benefits still being difficult to determine. Companies may need to take a leap into the dark with regard to strategy choice in such circumstances: for example, Case 14.3 looks at the car companies developing new electric cars and argues that they do not really know the level of customer demand for such cars.

KEY STRATEGIC PRINCIPLES

- There are eight considerations in developing green strategy: government legislation; existing or potential green industry standards; cost pressures from rising energy and commodity prices; carbon usage; consumption and recycling opportunities; stakeholder and customer pressures; campaigns from lobbyists and activists; and technology issues.
- The precise development and choice with regard to green strategy options will depend on the situation and resources of the individual organisation.
- Green strategy selection assumes that companies wish to implement such strategies. Within this framework, selection will then be determined by the resources available to the organisation.
- There are three main areas that will influence green strategy selection and choice: the strategic context within which the decision is made; existing and planned legislation and other government policies; and company-level incentives, costs, resources and timing.

14.7 IMPLEMENTING GREEN STRATEGIES

As the International Institute for Sustainable Development points out, 'The current focus on environment, empowerment, education, enjoyment and ethics is not likely to be a passing fad. People are finally waking up to the need for organisations that protect the environment and our social well-being.'[32] In practice, this means that organisations need to think not only about how to develop green strategies but also how to implement them.

With regard to implementation, it is useful to begin by drawing a distinction between internal and external actions. Internal actions are those that take place within the organisation, beginning with a clear statement of what needs to be achieved coupled with plans to undertake, monitor and control green strategies. External actions focus on how such plans are communicated to the wider stakeholding community, including customers and investors. The guidelines set out in Exhibit 14.1 reflect this distinction.

EXHIBIT 14.1

Some guidelines on implementing green strategies

Internal actions

1 *Green strategy purpose*. Organisations need to begin by defining the overall principles of sustainability as they apply specifically to that organisation. This needs to be developed and endorsed by the organisation's Chief Executive Office in order to give real support.

2 *Developing operational targets to achieve sustainability*. Having defined the purpose of the green strategy, it is essential to identify specific goals and targets to deliver in these areas. These may be in the form of benchmarks, quantified changes in the use of energy and other resources and other relevant measures. These targets may then need to be subdivided into specific targets for different parts of the organisation.

3 *Define roles, responsibilities and timing*. Who will do what? And over what time period? In the early stages, it may be better to set up teams and ask them how they will achieve the targets that have been set, rather than simply imposing solutions from the centre.

4 *Topics for consideration and evaluation*. These will be specific to the organisation but may include any of the following: in-house waste, pollution prevention, recycling, better use of water, lower energy usage, alternative fuels, better design of equipment and so on. Importantly, these topics will have benefits and costs. Some may be low-cost such as simple recycling, but some may require major investment, which will need to be costed and evaluated. Generally, a start can be made on the simple, low-cost items with the more complex investments to come later after a benefit/cost evaluation has been completed.

5 *Publishing feedback and news on sustainability progress*. It is important to report on progress to achieving green strategy objectives. These also need to be set in the broader context of outside activity on sustainability by other companies and organisations. More general news on sustainability issues will inform and possibly initiate new ideas on further actions that can be undertaken.

External actions

1 *Annual report on sustainability in the organisation*. Many of the larger companies covered in this book now issue annual sustainability reports which are often linked with their main financial reports and accounts. This may not be appropriate for smaller organisations and companies. But even a simple summary of activities in the form of a press release will serve to summarise material for external stakeholders.

2 *Public relations activities*. Beyond an annual report, it is worth considering how to communicate with outside organisations on sustainability issues. This can be particularly important if a problem arises or a success occurs. It may be appropriate to appoint a particular person with responsibility in this area – especially a person who comes across as being clear, approachable and honest. These are important qualities for such public relations activities.

3 *Commitment to local and national community activities*. While this is not essential, some companies are now making clear and measured commitments to their local area that go beyond sustainability. Companies may wish to take a view on such activities.

4 *Developing external links and relationships*. Green strategy is still developing so it will be valuable in many cases to develop and link up with relevant outside organisations – perhaps professional groups, research bodies, non-governmental organisations and other interested parties.

CASE STUDY 14.3

Green strategy in the world car industry: who makes the rules?

Passenger car manufacturers around the world are under pressure from governments and customers to make cars more fuel-efficient and more sustainable. But who makes the laws and with what criteria?

R&D investment

From the perspective of the earth's resources and atmosphere, R&D to reduce the exhaust emissions and to lower the energy consumption of cars has become an important part of the business strategy of all car manufactures. Figure 14.9 shows that each major car manufacturer is at a different stage in its search for lower CO_2 emissions.

Although petrol engines and related car technologies are relatively mature, they still use expensive fuels and emit fumes into the air. In both the EU and the USA, government policy through legislation has been to encourage and support new more environmentally friendly automobiles. Car companies have therefore focused on developing 'greener cars', i.e. cars with either zero or very low emissions and cars with more fuel-efficient engines. As a result, the combined R&D expenditure of the ten leading car companies was around \$50 billion *per year* in the period 2005–2009: massive sums by any standards.

Hybrid cars: the 'petrol plus battery' model

One of the early leaders in green strategy was the Toyota car company. Toyota developed a totally new model of car - the new *Prius* (the word means 'ahead of time') - in the early 2000s. It was a hybrid power vehicle involving two forms of technology combined into one car engine. There was a high-efficiency petrol engine for low speeds in town coupled with a zero-emission electric motor for higher steady speeds on motorways - all combined into one engine. Honda also

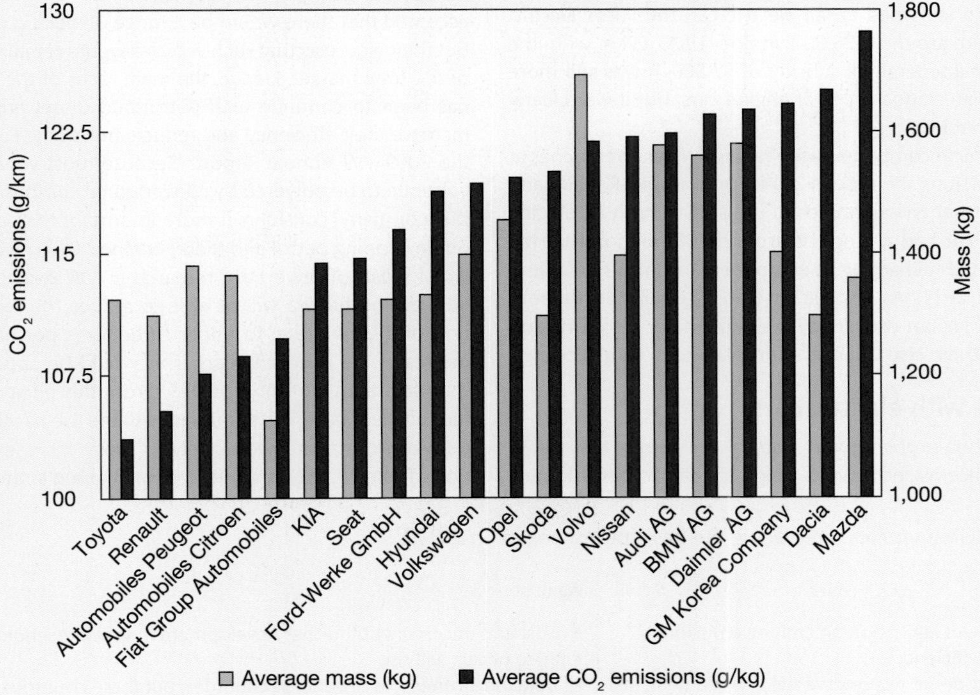

Figure 14.9 CO_2 emissions by car manufacturer, 2012

Note: The chart shows the average emissions from cars produced by Europe's large car manufacturers. The emissions are adjusted for the number of cars manufactured in a particular year and for the weight of the vehicles. For example, Fiat produces mainly smaller, lightweight cars with lower emissions. In other words, it is more sustainable to be on the left side of the chart.

Source: based on data from EEA (2013) *CO_2 emissions performance of car manufacturers in 2012*, European Environment Agency, Copenhagen.

developed similar technology. The Prius battery was relatively small compared to the petrol engine in these designs and was re-charged by energy from the brakes. These car models were priced from around $28,000 in 2013.

Amongst the American car manufacturers, GM also launched the *Chevrolet Volt* with a hybrid engine in 2011. However, it was different to the Prius with the electric battery being substantially larger and having a driving range of 40 miles on a single change. There was also a petrol engine to re-charge the battery and extend the driving range to over 300 miles. It was different from the Prius in that the Volt's petrol engine was simply used to re-charge the electric battery. It was not connected to the drive wheels like the Prius' engine. The Volt was priced around $41,000 before any government subsidies. The European version of the Volt was called the *Ampera* and was launched in 2012 with a higher price around $58,000. However, this price was expected to be reduced by government subsidies on 'green cars' of around $10,000.

All-electric cars

All-electric cars do not use petrol or diesel. They only have a battery and therefore have zero emissions. In 2010, Toyota announced a joint venture to develop an all-electric car with the well-known American all-electric car manufacturer, Tesla. Full details were not available at the time of writing this case. In 2013, Ford launched an all-electric car, the *Focus Electric*. It was priced around $35,000 in the USA. Even with the possibility of a federal tax subsidy of $7,500, it was still more expensive than standard petrol engine cars, but it was clearly more sustainable.

Other vehicle companies were taking similar approaches at the time of writing this case in 2014. For example, Renault and its major partner Nissan launched the *Leaf* with an all-electric engine. The car had a range of around 100 miles before the battery needed recharging. It was priced around $35,000 and launched in 2011. As Mr Carlos Ghosn, Chairman of both Renault and Nissan explained, 'We must have zero-emission vehicles. Nothing else will prevent the world from exploding.'

Problems with electric cars

There were two problems with battery-driven cars that posed particular concerns: the first was 'range anxiety'. Some customers feared that they would not be able to reach their destinations on one electric charge. Moreover, there were unlikely to be many re-charging points around the country in the early years for electric cars. The second problem was high price. Green cars were more expensive than similar petrol-driven models due to the high cost of battery production compared to petrol engine production. This was likely to remain a problem in spite of subsidies from national governments to encourage the take-up of green cars. Some commentators therefore predicted that green cars would primarily be bought by high-wealth customers. However, no one really knew.

These problems were summarised in a 2011 headline in the *Financial Times*, 'Electric charge is a leap of faith'. At the time of writing this case, the potential demand for green cars remained largely unknown. Some manufacturers were expecting them to account for 10 per cent of the total market demand, while others doubted this. For example, Dieter Zetsche, the CEO of one of the world's largest car and truck makers, Daimler, estimated that they would only capture between 1 and 5 per cent of the market.

Other approaches to sustainability

Daimler was not alone in suggesting that electric cars were not the main way forward for green car strategy. Volkswagen, Europe's largest car manufacturers, took a similar view. VW accepted that there would be a range of electric cars by 2020, but their view was that such vehicles would remain a small part of the total market. Hence, the main focus of the VW strategy has been to continue with petrol and diesel engines but to increase their efficiency and reduce emissions. To quote from the 2009 VW Annual Report: 'Because most vehicles will still continue to be powered by conventional combustion engines, the [company] considers it more important than ever to focus on developing petrol and diesel engines: Dr Tobias Lösche-ter Horst, head of drive train research at VW explained, "I have little doubt that we will be able to reduce the fuel consumption of a Golf Diesel to under three litres per hundred kilometres in the next ten years. This would be approximately a third less than current models."' From this perspective, more fuel-efficient petrol cars coupled with the use of other bio-fuels derived from plants were likely to prove more effective over time. Table 14.2 summarises the main green strategy issues.

Table 14.2 Greener cars – replacing the basic petrol engine in 2017?

For	Against
• Government legislation on limiting emissions and fuel efficiency • Customer desire to preserve the environment • Scientific evidence on global warming • Need for companies to keep up with competition • Increasing price of petrol • More public transport to provide an alternative to car travel	• Cost and uncertainty of further development in green technologies • Price of cars will rise • Demand strongest in developed countries, but these countries are not the fastest growing car markets • Low profitability of some green technology suppliers • Reaction against the increased use of bio-fuels because this has raised the price of all agricultural products • Insufficient powerpoints for re-charging electric vehicles

Issues for government and other public bodies

In principle, governments around the world have taken the decision to force manufacturers to design cars with greater fuel efficiency, lower emissions and higher sustainability. The problem facing both the governments and the car companies was that this was fine in principle, but how far should governments go? For example, should all governments adopt the same world standards? What would be the cost of such a move? What would be the proven benefits and would they outweigh the costs? The lack of agreement between nations at the Doha 2012 Climate Change Conference shows the difficulties involved. Coupled with differing views amongst car manufacturers, there was plenty of room for discussion.

Case questions

1 Some car manufacturers argue that sustainable green cars will still form a very small percentage of total car usage over the next few years. Government legislation will not be enough to increase demand for such cars. What are the problems faced by customers interested in buying such cars?

2 Should governments do more to support the spread of greener, more sustainable cars? At what cost? And with what underpinning principles?

3 Is this just a problem for countries with high wealth per head of the population, like the USA and Germany? Or should it concern countries with lower wealth like Russia, Brazil and South Africa? If it should also concern lower-wealth countries, what can they realistically do about it given their lower level of resources? Can car companies help here? If so, how and at what cost?

CRITICAL REFLECTION

Caution on green strategy development?

This chapter has focused on green strategy and sustainability. It has demonstrated that all such strategies have costs as well as benefits: there is no 'free lunch' for green strategy. What are the implications for companies? Should they develop green strategies almost regardless of the costs? Or should they take a more cautious approach? But what does 'caution' mean here? By what criteria should companies judge 'caution'?

SUMMARY

- Green strategy and the broader topic of sustainability concern those activities of the organisation that are focused on both sustaining the earth's environment and developing the business opportunities that will arise from such additional activities. It has three main components: government legislation and directives; business opportunities; and customer and value chain issues.
- There are seven main trends that need to be considered in green strategy: electrification; sustainable natural resources; carbon neutral organisations; country self-sufficiency in energy; greater energy and resource efficiency within countries; waste disposal; and changes in lifestyle with regard to energy generation and consumption.
- Green strategy will provide one of the next major business opportunities for some companies. Sustainability policies have the potential to lead to new technologies and new business growth. They represent a 'new wave' of innovation. Business opportunities arise because green strategy is still in the early stages of development. There are many new energy technologies, such as wind farms and waste disposal, which will provide new growth areas for organisations.
- Government legislation and directives on green issues will need to be analysed by every organisation to ensure that the firm fully complies in such matters.
- Customers and consumers are broadly in favour of green strategies. In some cases, they have positively campaigned for change. Business needs to react positively where possible to such events.

- Green strategy seeks out ways of reducing energy, lowering carbon content and adopting recycling policies, not only within the organisation but also with suppliers and customers. In addition, the green strategy value chain will involve every element and function, including those that perhaps do not always feature highly in many value chain analyses. The value chain has five main elements: suppliers and inbound logistics; infrastructure; production; and customers and services. It has both benefits and costs. These are captured under four headings: the influence on the assets of the organisation; government regulation; the company's reputation with its stakeholders; and the emergent outlook on benefits and costs as green strategy develops further.
- The resources and capabilities of an organisation can be analysed for their ability to deliver competitive advantages that are more sustainable than those of competitors. Three specific areas that might deliver such advantages include organisational capabilities, absorptive capacity and complementary assets. Because many firms are now engaged in this area, these three may not now be enough to deliver competitive advantage.
- In identifying and developing the sustainable purpose of the organisation, stakeholders represent an important starting point. The range of stakeholders is arguably wider with some having a great deal of power.
- The leadership of the organisation has prime responsibility for developing and adjusting the purpose of the organisation with regard to matters of sustainability. Within this general area, there will be a need to respond to the various green strategy pressure groups.
- There are four main aspects for an organisation developing its purpose with regard to sustainability: the support of senior management; the framing and debate about the proposed green strategy policies; the perceptions of individual managers with regard to such policies; and the subsequent disclosure and reporting policies of the organisation.
- A stakeholder analysis with regard to green strategy is an essential element in developing the sustainable purpose of the organisation.
- From a knowledge creation perspective, green strategy will benefit from the three 'A's concept: Accentuate current green strategy practices; Acquire new technologies; Architecture to set up the organisational structures required to implement new strategies.
- From an innovation viewpoint, green strategy has two aspects. The first relates to examining the use of existing resources to ensure that they are used most efficiently. The second suggests that sustainability may represent a 'new wave' of business opportunity that will provide new business growth.
- New technologies for green strategy can occur in two areas: technology breakthroughs and better use of existing technologies.
- There are eight considerations in developing green strategy: government regulations; existing or potential green industry standards; cost pressures from rising energy and commodity prices; carbon usage; consumption and recycling opportunities; stakeholder and customer pressures, campaigns from lobbyists and activists; and technology issues. The precise development and choice with regard to green strategy options will depend on the situation and resources of the individual organisation.
- Green strategy selection assumes that companies wish to implement such strategies. Within this framework, selection will then be determined by the resources available to the organisation. There are three main areas that will influence green strategy selection and choice: the strategic context within which the decision is made; existing and planned legislation and other government policies; and company-level incentives, costs, resources and timing.

QUESTIONS

1 Take the global market for solar power and explain the areas of customer analysis you would wish to consider in developing the strategy for a company setting up in this area.

2 To what extent is it worthwhile estimating customer demand when introducing a totally new green strategy product? What are the implications for strategy?

3 On the subject of global warming, the former US Vice President Al Gore commented: *'We have everything we need to begin solving this crisis with the possible exception of the will to act.'* Some detractors from his book, *An Inconvenient Truth*, have argued that his evidence and predictions are, at best, exaggerated and, at worst, plain wrong. Where do you stand on this? And what do your opinions mean for business strategy?

4 Take a market with which you are familiar and identify how it needs to change with regard to green strategy and sustainability. What implications does your distinction have for strategic management?

5 Compare and contrast the green strategies needed by the following three types of company: a branded breakfast cereal manufacturer, a large retail bank and a national charitable institution of your choice.

6 Should companies introduce green strategies regardless of their cost? What are the difficulties of this approach? In view of your answer, what problems do you foresee in practice with regard to green strategy?

7 In exploiting green strategy business opportunities, companies can copy existing market demand or find totally new product and services that meet unmet demand. How would you approach the task of making a choice between these two approaches? What evidence would you seek and what strategy process would you employ?

8 Are there any dangers in complying with government policy initiatives on green strategy and sustainability? Are there any circumstances where considerable caution is required?

9 *'A powerful force drives the world toward a converging commonality and that force is technology . . . the globalisation of markets is at hand.'* (Theodore Levitt) Discuss the implications for green strategy and sustainability.

FURTHER READING

There are many books that explore the subjects of this chapter in much greater detail. One good academic text is Hoffman, A J and Georg, S (293), *Business and the Natural Environment*, Routledge, London. The full text is expensive but could be borrowed from a library. An interesting government paper is Commission of the European Communities (2006) Green Paper: *A European Strategy for Sustainable, Competitive and Secure Energy*, COM (2006) 105 Final, Brussels. And then, of course, there is the popular text that has been heavily criticised by those challenging global warming: Al Gore (2006), *An Inconvenient Truth*, Bloomsbury, London.

On green strategy rather than the broader topic of sustainability, there are still relatively few papers. Two contrasting papers are: Siegel, D (2009) 'Green Management Matters Only if it Yields More Than Green: An Economic Strategic Perspective', *Academy of Management Perspectives*, Vol 23, No 3, pp 5–16, followed by Marcus, A A and Fremeth, A R (2009) 'Green Management Matters Regardless', *Academy of Management Perspectives*, Vol 23, No 3, pp 17–26. Many companies would now regard the second paper as being closer to their practice than the first. But both have merit.

NOTES AND REFERENCES

1 Hoffman, A J and Georg, S (2013) 'Introduction to business and the natural environment', in Hoffman, A J and Georg, S (eds), *Business and the Natural Environment*, Routledge, London, Ch 1. For example, Hoffman, A J and Georg, S (2013) describe the topic as the 'Natural Environment'. More broadly, this opening chapter from the four-volume series provides a valuable summary of the field. Professor Lynch fully acknowledges this source in developing this chapter.

2 International Institute for Sustainable Development (2011) *Annual Report*, 'From the Chair', Daniel Gagnier, p 2.

3 Hoffman, A J and Georg, S (2013) Op. cit.

4 References for the case 'Profits from sun, wind and sea? Even nuclear?': The Stationery Office (2009) *The UK Renewable Energy Strategy*, Cm 7686, Norwich; Renewable Energy Report 21 Secretariat (2010) *Renewables 2010 Global Status Report*, Paris; Carbon Trust (2009) *Investment Trends in European and North American Clean Energy 2003 to 2008*, London, p 4; Department for Business Innovation and Skills (2009) *The UK Low Carbon Industrial Strategy*, London; *Financial Times*: 'Climate of opinion', *Financial Times Supplement on The Future of Energy*, 4 November; 12 July 2008, p 15; 12 September 2008, p 21; 16 September 2008, Modern Energy Special Report; 17 April 2009, p 22; 14 August 2009, p 14; 18 August 2009, p 17; 19 August 2009, p 18; 2 December 2009, Understanding Energy Policy Special Supplement; 23 December 2009, Copenhagen Climate Change Summit Review supplement; 1 September 2010,

p 14; 26 October 2010, p 2; 29 November 2010, p 4; 6 January 2011, p 23; 15 February 2011, pp 11 and 24.

5 Haanaes, K, Balagopal, B, Arthur, D, Kong, M T, Velken, I, Kruschwitz, N and Hopkins, M (2011) 'First look: the Second Annual Sustainability & Innovation Survey', *MIT Sloan Management Review*, Winter, Vol 52, No 2, pp 77–83.

6 The author acknowledges the following sources in developing this section: Hoffman, A J and Georg, S (2013), Op. cit.; International Institute for Sustainable Development website: www.iisd.org; Hart, S (1997) 'Beyond greening: strategies for a sustainable world', *Harvard Business Review*, Reprint 97105, accessed free on the web courtesy of Vestas; Elkington, J (1994) 'Towards the sustainable corporation: Win-win-win business strategies', *California Management Review*, Winter, Vol 36, No 2, p 90; Crooks, E (2009) 'Climate of opinion', *Financial Times Supplement on The Future of Energy*, 4 November, p 5. The paper by Hart is one of the most useful in this field.

7 Hoffman, A J and Georg, S (2013) Op. cit. Their survey of citations on pp 6–8 presents strong evidence for the way that this has developed over the last 30 years.

8 See, for example, Hart, S (1997) Op. cit.; Elkington, J (1994) Op. cit.; Unruh, G and Ettenson, R (2010) 'Growing green', *Harvard Business Review*, June, pp 84–92; Unruh, G and Ettenson, R (2010) 'Winning in the green frenzy', *Harvard Business Review*, November, pp 100–115.

9 Hoffman, A J & Georg, S (2013) Op. cit., top of p 7.

10 See, for example, Commission of the European Communities (2006) *Green Paper: A European Strategy for Sustainable, Competitive and Secure Energy*, COM (2006) 105 Final, Brussels.

11 See, for example, the UK government papers: HM Government (2009) *The UK Carbon Industrial Strategy*, Department for Business, Innovation and Skills, London, www.hmg.gov.uk/lowcarbon.

12 Innovas (2009) *Low Carbon and Environmental Goods and Services: an industry analysis*, London, www.berr.gov.uk/files/file50253.dpf.

13 Carbon Trust (2011) Only 7% of the public believe company claims of action on climate change, 21 March, http://cts.force.com/EntryView?id=a0QD0000002XMYUMA4.

14 Peattie, K (2001) 'Towards sustainability: The third age of green marketing', *Marketing Review*, 2 (Winter), p 129. Pedersen, E R and Neergaard, P (2006) 'Caveat emptor – let the buyer beware: Environmental labeling and the limitations of green consumerism', *Business Strategy and the Environment*, Vol 15, No 1, pp 15–29.

15 Sourced from http://www.unglobalcompact.org/issues/Environment/CEO_Water_Mandate.

16 Hart, S (1995) 'A natural-resource-based view of the firm', *Academy of Management Review*, Vol 20, No 4, pp 986–1014.

17 Organisational capability: Sharma, S and Vredenburg, H (1998) 'Proactive corporate environmental strategy and the development of competitively valuable organizational capabilities', *Strategic Management Journal*, Vol 19, No 8, pp 729–753. Absorptive capacity: Delmas, M, Hoffmann, V and Kuss, M (2011) 'Under the tip of the iceberg: Absorptive capacity, environmental strategy, and competitive advantage', *Business & Society*, Vol 50, No 1, pp 116–154. Complementary assets: Christmann, P (2000) 'Effects of "best practices" on environmental management on cost advantage: the role of complementary assets', *Academy of Management Journal*, Vol 43, No 4, pp 663–680.

18 Unruh, G and Ettenson, R (2010) 'Winning in the green frenzy', *Harvard Business Review*, November.

19 Hoffman and Georg (2013) Op. cit., p 24.

20 Hoffman and Georg (2013) Op. cit., pp 25 *et seq.*

21 Dixon, S and Clifford, A (2007) 'Ecopreneurship: A new approach to managing the triple bottom line', *Journal of Organizational Change Management*, Vol 20, No 3, pp 326–345.

22 Douglas, T (2007) 'Reporting on the triple bottom line at Cascade Engineering,' *Global Business & Organizational Excellence*, Vol 26, No 3, pp 35–43.

23 Markussson, N (2010) 'The championing of environmental improvements in technology investment projects', *Journal of Cleaner Production*, Vol 18, No 8, pp 777–783.

24 Bansal, P and Clelland, I (2004) 'Talking trash: Legitimacy, impression management, and unsystematic risk in the context of the natural environment', *Academy of Management Journal*, Vol 47, No 1, pp 197–218.

25 Ramus, C and Steger, U (2000) 'The roles of supervisory support behaviors and environmental policy in "employee ecoinitiatives" at leading-edge European companies', *Academy of Management Journal*, Vol 43, No 4, pp 605–626. Sharma, S (2000) 'Managerial interpretations and organizational context as predictors of corporate choice of environmental strategy', *Academy of Management Journal*, Vol 43, pp 681–697.

26 Gray, R (1992) 'Accounting and environmentalism: An exploration of the challenge of gently accounting for accountability, transparency and sustainability', *Accounting, Organizations and Society*, Vol 17, No 5, pp 399–425.

27 References for solar power case: European Voltaic Industry Association, *2010 Market Outlook*, available on the web. *Financial Times*: 14 August 2009, p 14; 19 August 2009, p 18; 29 November 2010, p 4; 15 February 2011, p 24.

28 Unruh, G and Ettenson, R (2010) 'Going green', Op. cit.

29 Unruh, G and Ettenson, R (2010) 'Frenzy on green standards', Op. cit.

30 This section has benefited from World Business Council for Sustainable Development (1992) *Business Strategy for Sustainable Development: Leadership and Accountability for the 1990s*, International Institute for Sustainable Development with Deloitte & Touche, NY.

31 Chaffin, J (2011) 'Into the Air', *Financial Times*, 15 February, p 11.

32 This section and the exhibit use some ideas and concepts derived from the International Institute for Sustainable Development sourced from the web at www.iisd.org.

33 References for green cars case: Annual Reports and Accounts of Volkswagen, Toyota, Renault, Nissan, PSA, Ford, General Motors, Daimler, BMW, Honda and Fiat. *Financial Times*: 17 June 2011, p 16; 4 July 2013, p 16; 5 September 2013, p 9; 12 September 2013, p 21.

CHAPTER 15
Managing strategic change

Video and sound summary of this chapter.

LEARNING OUTCOMES

When you have worked through this chapter, you will be able to:

- understand the nature of strategic change and its implications for strategy developments;
- analyse the causes of change;
- outline the main approaches to managing strategic change;
- link a strategic change programme with the type of change required;
- draw up a programme of strategic change appropriate to the strategic task.

INTRODUCTION

Strategic management invariably involves change for people working in organisations. Sometimes they resist such proposals and make strategy difficult to implement; sometimes they are enthusiastic and make a significant contribution to the proposed developments. Understanding and exploring the impact of change on people is therefore important for strategy implementation.

As a starting point, it is useful to analyse the causes of strategic change. It is also important to understand the dynamics of the change process in the context of the strategies proposed. These can be used to suggest how such a change process can be managed in principle. Finally, a strategic change programme can be developed either on a one-off or permanent basis. The main areas to be explored are summarised in Figure 15.1.

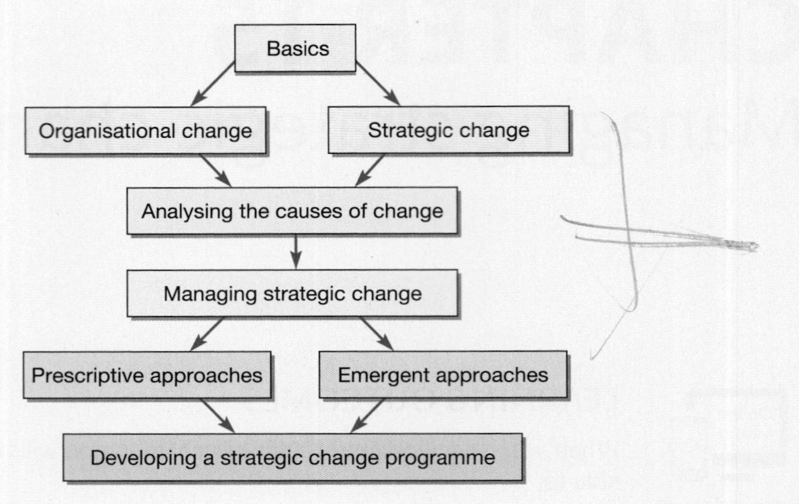

Figure 15.1 Managing strategic change

CASE STUDY 15.1
Strategic change at Nokia: the 'Doomsday Memo'

In February 2011, the chief executive of Nokia, Stephen Elop, sent out his famous 'doomsday memo' to senior staff. It did not make easy reading about the company's difficulties, so why did he send it? This case explores the reasons.

Background

As Case 9.2 explains in more depth, the world's leading mobile phone manufacturer, the Finnish company Nokia, was in some difficulty at the end of 2010. It was losing market share at both ends of the mobile phone market. At the top end, the share loss was to Apple's iPhone and to smartphones using Google's Android open software system. At the bottom end, low-cost mobile phones from southern China were much cheaper than similar Nokia phones. All this was in spite of the company increasing its R&D expenditure and its total number of employees – see Figure 15.2.

Stephen Elop joined Nokia from a senior position in Microsoft in autumn 2010. He then spent the first few months reviewing the company's position, talking to managers and employees. The company has operations in many parts of Europe and Asia so this took some time. He concluded that there was a lack of accountability in many parts of the organisation. There needed to be simplified decision making with less reference back to headquarters before decisions were taken. The culture needed to be more performance-based and less time serving. But, fundamentally, he also came to see that Nokia's strategy was in deep trouble. It was losing market share at the top end because its phones could not match the performance of their rivals on several key dimensions and, at the bottom end, its phones cost more to make than rivals.

Nokia's dramatic announcement that it was to change radically its existing range of software caused major uncertainty at the company's Finnish headquarters.

From a strategy perspective, Elop decided that radical strategic change was required. The difficulty was that any admission of problems would potentially harm Nokia's business and reduce morale within the company. But he still decided to go ahead: the situation was too serious.

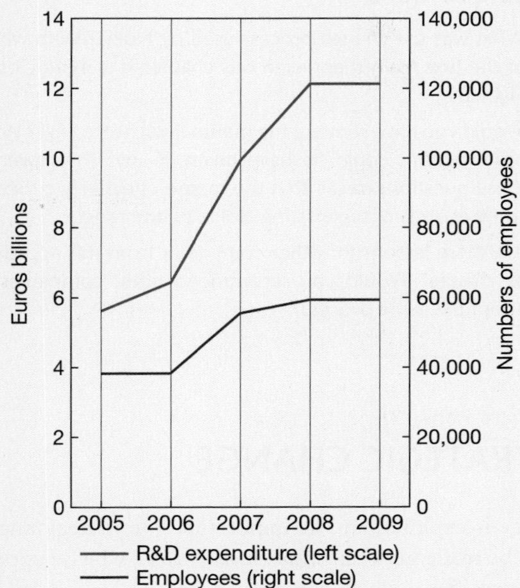

Figure 15.2 The rise in Nokia's R&D expenditure and employees 2005–2009

Source: author from Nokia annual report and accounts.

Strategic change at Nokia

Although it was vital to explain the change to the company, Elop and his senior colleagues also needed to develop future strategies. It was not enough to point out the problem. It was also important to show the way forward in any change plan in order to present the benefits as well as tackling the difficult cuts that would be required. In essence, Nokia first made two strategic decisions and then followed this up with the implications in terms of a strategic change programme.

The first strategic decision was to go ahead with Microsoft mobile software and get out of the Symbian software that had been the backbone of Nokia for many years. The second, related strategic decision was that around 4,000 Nokia employees would be made redundant and another 2,000 transferred to an outside company that would look after Symbian while it was still being used by customers. But how should Nokia explain this strategic change to Nokia employees who were totally unaware of what was about to happen? Elop decided that a serious shock was needed but that this needed to be followed by positive news. Hence, he sent out the 'doomsday memo' as a first step, to be followed by an announcement of the new link with Microsoft several days later.

On 7 February 2011, the well-constructed memo was sent as an email to senior managers. However, it was inevitable that it would quickly leak beyond this group to other employees and to the wider world. The message pointed out that Nokia was 'years behind' its rivals and the gap would increase unless a 'huge effort' was made to transform the company. 'The first iPhone shipped in 2007, and we still don't have a product that is close to their experience. Android came on the scene just over two years ago, and this week took our leadership position in smartphone volumes. Unbelievable.' Comparing the company to an oil worker on a blazing oil platform, 'We too are standing on a burning platform and we must decide how we are going to change our behaviours . . . We have more than one explosion . . . We have multiple points of scorching heat that are fuelling a blazing fire around us.' The latter point referred to the low-cost Chinese phone threat.

What happened next?

On 11 February 2011, Elop made a joint presentation with Steve Bullmer, chief executive of Microsoft on part of the Nokia way forward. It had chosen Microsoft's Windows 7 mobile platform. A few weeks later, a full deal was signed with Microsoft and, shortly afterwards, the announcement was made about the job losses. But at the time of writing this case, there was no substantive news on when the new smartphones would appear. It was also unclear what strategy would be developed by Nokia against the low-priced Asian phones. Elop then went on to explain the changes to groups of senior managers in various locations around the world. These were all-day meetings with full questions and answers from Elop and his senior team.

In spite of the lack of clarity in some areas, Nokia also announced a new senior management structure. It included a change taskforce run by the Nokia head of human resources that would be disbanded once the goals had been achieved. The taskforce covered nine areas:

1 Work with Microsoft to produce the new smartphones to regain market leadership.

2 Work on the low-end phone market by expanding web access and applications that would deliver new uses for such phones.

3 Invest in future disruptions to create next generation devices, platforms and user experiences. (This is a quote from Nokia and it is not entirely clear to the author of this case what this means.)

4 Build the new software systems that will deliver a complete smartphone experience to Nokia users.

5 Develop closer co-operation between the various parts of Nokia to ensure that sales, production and marketing are fully aligned.

6 Redevelop the Nokia management and governance structure to ensure that the company practices and processes are faster and more effective.

7 Develop a new and effective on-site R&D strategy.

8 Set up a programme office to lead change management overall.

9 Instigate a culture change programme to embed the right values, mindsets and behaviours.

The final outcome was that Nokia was acquired by Microsoft with major job losses, especially in Finland where Nokia was headquartered. In essence, all the above was not enough to save the company – see Case 9.2 for more information.

Note: If you want to read the full 'doomsday memo', you can find it at: http://blogs.wsj.com/tech-europe/2011/02/09/full-text-nokia-ceo-stephen-elops-burning-platform-memo/

 This case was written from published information only.[1]

Case questions

1 What was the change process used by Nokia? With which of the two main theories in this chapter is it more closely aligned?

2 Would you have sent out the memo if you were Elop? What other actions could he have taken, if any? In answering these questions, recall that the memo effectively criticised some aspects of the existing Nokia phone range.

3 Are there lessons for other companies from this approach to change? Would you recommend other companies to adopt the same process?

15.1 THE BASIC CONCEPT OF STRATEGIC CHANGE

In this section, the concept of strategic change is explored and its importance for strategy implementation is explained. A distinction needs to be made between *organisational change*, which happens in every organisation and is inevitable, and *strategic change*, which can be managed.

15.1.1 Organisational change

Change takes place continuously within organisations. The pace of change can be represented by two extremes:

1 *Slow organisational change*. This is introduced gradually, and is likely to meet with less resistance, progress more smoothly and have a higher commitment from the people involved.

2 *Fast organisational change*. This is introduced suddenly, usually as part of a major strategic initiative, and is likely to encounter significant resistance even if it is handled carefully. However, some prescriptive change may be unavoidable, for example, factory closure as part of a cost-cutting project.

Organisations usually prefer to choose slow change, where possible, because the costs are likely to be lower. In fact, much change follows this route, otherwise organisations would be in perpetual turmoil. Where there is a faster *pace* of change, it may be associated with strategic change, which is *proactive* in its approach.

15.1.2 What is strategic change?

Definition ► **Strategic change is the proactive management of change in organisations to achieve clearly identified strategic objectives.** It may be undertaken using either prescriptive or emergent strategic approaches. 'Proactive' means that the company takes the initiative to manage new strategies and their impact on people in an organisation.

Because strategy is fundamentally concerned with moving organisations forward, there will inevitably be change for some people inside the organisation: for example, the loss of jobs at Nokia in Case 15.1. However, strategic change is not just a casual drift through time but a *proactive search* for new ways of working which everyone will be required to adopt: for example, the sudden and dramatic changes at Nokia. Thus strategic change involves the implementation of new strategies that involve substantive changes *beyond the normal routines* of the organisation. Such activities involve:

> the induction of new patterns of action, belief and attitudes among substantial segments of the population.[2]

Thus the chief executive of Nokia began with a change management team and an announcement of the importance of changes in culture and values.

Many researchers and writers have explored the important topic of *organisational* change.[3] This text concentrates on those who have examined such concepts from a *strategic* perspective. Within this subject area, some researchers have seen the management of change as clear and largely predictable: the *prescriptive* approach (the actions of Nokia would probably fall into this category). Other researchers have formed the view that change takes on a momentum of its own and the consequences are less predictable: the *emergent* approach. (Emergent strategists might argue that in the Nokia case, although the initial consequences of Elop's actions were well known, the longer-term results were more difficult to predict and would take time to emerge.) In the emergent sense, change is not managed, but 'cultivated' (see Handy).[4]

It should be noted that emergent theorists may use the word *change* in a different way from prescriptive theorists:

- In prescriptive theories, change means the *implementation actions that result* from the decision to pursue a chosen strategy. In extreme cases, it is probable that the changes will be imposed on those who then have to implement them (such as the managers being forced to reapply for their jobs at BOC and later to redevelop the BOC strategy).
- In emergent theories, change can sometimes mean the *whole process of developing the strategy*, as well as the actions that result after it has been developed. This may involve experimentation, learning and consultation for those involved in the change.

We will return to this distinction in Sections 15.3 and 15.4.

15.1.3 Pressure points for strategic change

Strategic change is primarily concerned with *people* and the *tasks* that they perform in the organisation. They undertake their work through *formal organisation structures*, explored in Chapter 12. Groups of like-minded people also form *informal organisation structures* to pursue particular common interests: sometimes social groups, like the company sports club, sometimes commercial groupings, such as a group seeking a minor change in working practices. All such groups inevitably discuss, formally or informally, any new developments that affect their lives – for instance, the announcement or the rumours of strategic change. Importantly, such informal groups can abide by, interpret or change any element of the strategy implementation process: this can be advantageous, but it can also be a focus for problems if the group does not like the proposed strategies.

Whether the groups are formal or informal, they provide a channel of opportunities for senior management to influence strategic change and to be influenced by the comments of those affected by such changes. In the Nokia case, Stephen Elop was engaged in this task when he sent out his doomsday memo. He then followed this up with the joint presentation with Microsoft and the setting up of the change taskforce. He also made a series of presentations across the company.

Identification of such groups and individuals – for example, the Nokia senior managers – constitutes an analysis of the *pressure points for influence* in the organisation (see Figure 15.3). The pressure points provide important links between the basic strategic change process and the people involved.

In more general terms, strategic change borrows from a number of academic disciplines and does not have a clearly defined set of boundaries.[5] The main themes will be explored during the course of this chapter with some more specialist areas associated with company leadership and culture being addressed in Chapter 16.

15.1.4 Why is strategic change important?

In many cases, strategic change is accompanied by a degree of risk and uncertainty. Although risk assessment can be undertaken in an impersonal way at the corporate level,[6] uncertainty cannot be assessed in the same way at the *personal* level in an organisation.

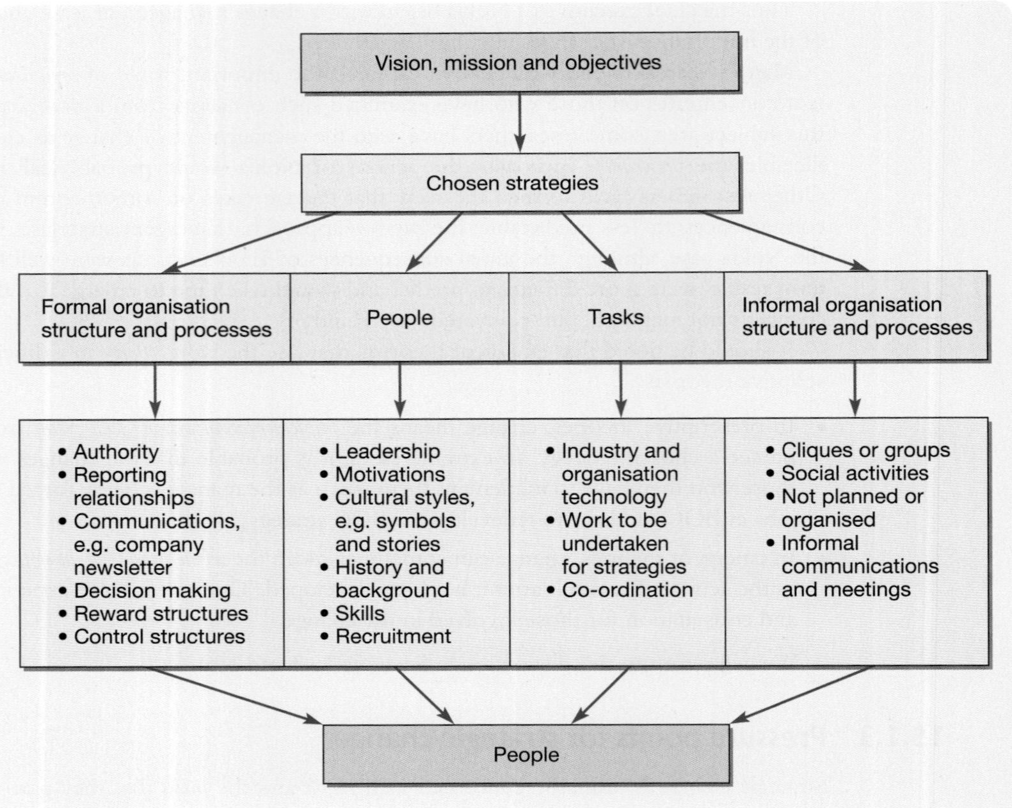

Figure 15.3 People and pressure points for influencing strategic change

Source: based on concepts outlined in Tichy, N (1983) *Managing Strategic Change*, Wiley, New York.

In some organisational cultures, individuals do not like the consequences of strategic change and seek to resist the proposals that are the cause of their problems. Strategic change may spark objections, thus making it difficult to implement. For example, initial reactions at Nokia to the call for action ranged from the understandable disappointment at the job losses to the recognition by some senior managers that change was badly needed.

In other organisational cultures, where learning and open debate have been part of the management process, change may be welcomed. However, even here, change will take time and will involve careful thought. Moreover, it will also be recalled from Chapter 12 that, even in a classic learning organisation such as the ABB of the late 1990s, there may still be some managers who do not like change.

To overcome problems associated with resistance to change, strategic change is therefore often taken at a slower pace – 'strategy is the art of the possible'. More consultation, more explanation and more monitoring of reactions are therefore involved in these circumstances. Figure 15.4 illustrates how the apparently simple process of strategic action is complicated by the reality of the many factors involved in successful strategic implementation.

All such discussion takes time and resources. For example, the cost at Nokia will not be clear for several years, but it will clearly be significant in terms of lost sales and profits while the company develops new smartphones and new low-cost strategies. Hence, strategic change is important because even successful change has an *implementation* cost for the organisation to set against the *direct benefits* identified from the new strategies. Although there are costs involved in strategic change, it may be possible to reduce them. A partial test of a successful strategic change programme is the extent to which such implementation costs can be minimised.

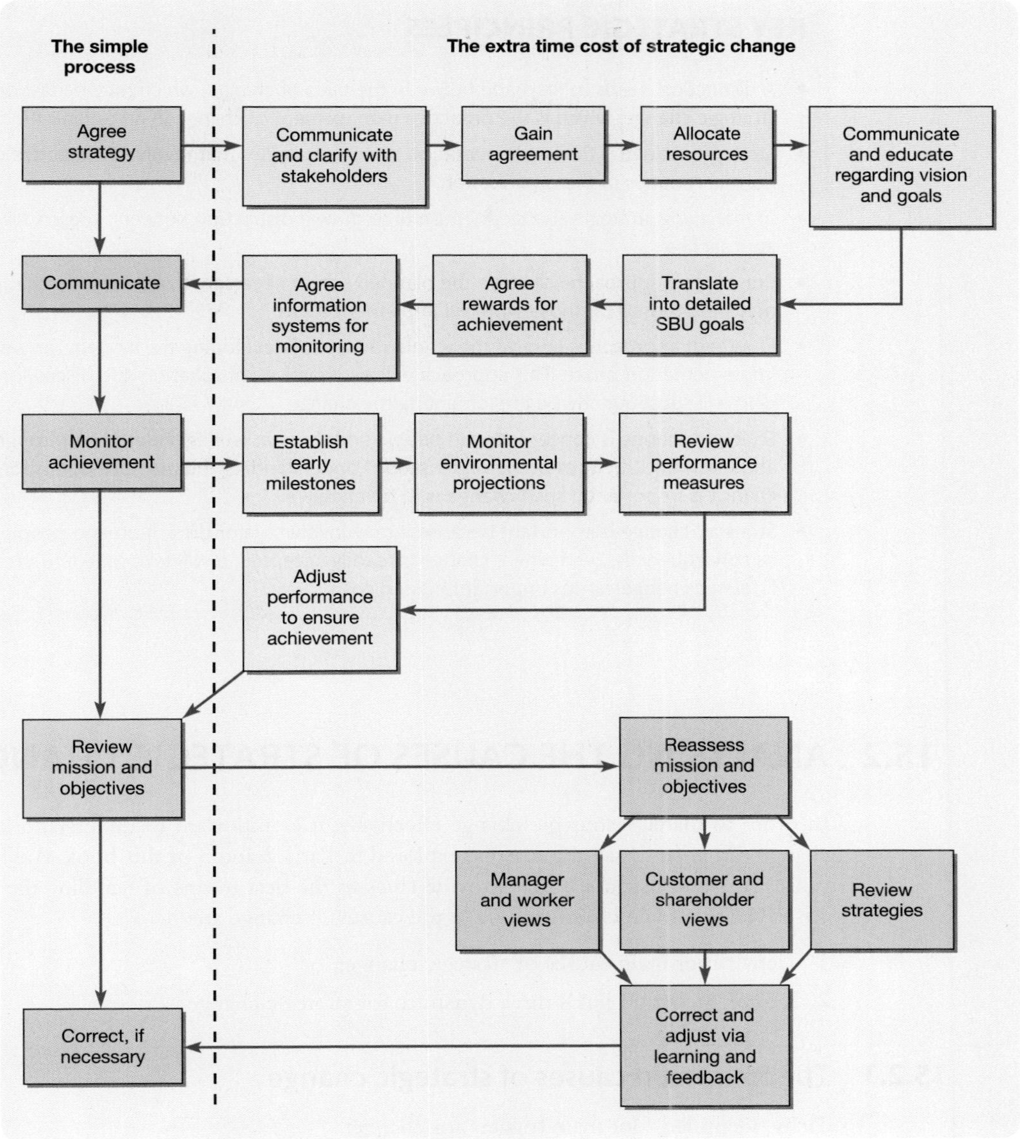

The simple process
The extra time cost of strategic change

Agree strategy
Communicate and clarify with stakeholders
Gain agreement
Allocate resources
Communicate and educate regarding vision and goals

Communicate
Agree information systems for monitoring
Agree rewards for achievement
Translate into detailed SBU goals

Monitor achievement
Establish early milestones
Monitor environmental projections
Review performance measures
Adjust performance to ensure achievement

Review mission and objectives
Reassess mission and objectives
Manager and worker views
Customer and shareholder views
Review strategies

Correct, if necessary
Correct and adjust via learning and feedback

Figure 15.4 Some time costs associated with the strategic change process

However, it is important not to exaggerate the negative effects of strategic change on people. Strategic change can also be positive: people may feel enthused by the new strategies. Their contribution may be more than a passive acceptance of the proposed strategies, resulting in even lower costs. Hence, another test of a successful strategic change programme might be the extent to which such costs are *reduced* beyond those identified in the strategy itself. All this will depend on the context of the change – the culture of the organisation, the way in which strategic change is introduced and the nature of the changes proposed. In brief, strategic change is context-sensitive.

Strategic change case study: *Shock tactics at BOC* – with three questions at the end of the case on strategic change plus indicative answers to the three questions on a separate page.

KEY STRATEGIC PRINCIPLES

- A distinction needs to be made between the pace of change, which may be fast or slow, and strategic change, which is the proactive management of change in an organisation.
- Strategic change is the implementation of new strategies that involve substantive changes to the normal routines of the organisation.
- In managing strategic change, it is useful to draw a distinction between prescriptive and emergent approaches.
- Prescriptive approaches involve the planned action necessary to achieve the changes. The changes may be imposed on those who will implement them.
- Emergent approaches involve the whole process of developing the strategy, as well as the implementation phase. This approach will also involve consultation and discussion with those who will subsequently be implementing the change.
- Strategic change is concerned with people and their tasks. It is undertaken through the formal and informal structures of the organisation. Understanding the pressure points for influencing change is important if such change is to be effective.
- Strategic change is important because it may involve major disruption and people may resist its consequences. Even where change is readily accepted, it will take time and careful thought. Strategic change carries important hidden costs.

15.2 ANALYSING THE CAUSES OF STRATEGIC CHANGE

In order to manage strategic change effectively, it is important to understand its causes. Strategic change can arise for all the reasons explored in Parts 2 and 3 of this book. Analysis of the specific causes is useful because it may provide clues to the best means of handling the change issues that arise. The two main classifications of the causes of change are:

1 Tichy's four main causes of strategic change;

2 Kanter, Stein and Jick's three dynamics for strategic change.

15.2.1 The four main causes of strategic change

Tichy[7] identified four main triggers for change:

1 *Environment*. Shifts in the economy, competitive pressures and legislative changes can all lead to demands for major strategic change.

2 *Business relationships*. New alliances, acquisitions, partnerships and other significant developments may require substantial changes in the organisation structure in order to take advantage of new synergies, value chain linkages or core competencies.

3 *Technology*. Shifts here can have a substantial impact on the content of the work and even the survival of companies.

4 *People*. New entrants to organisations may have different educational or cultural backgrounds or expectations that require change. This is especially important when the *leadership* of the organisation changes.

The implications of the above need to be considered in the context of the organisation's dynamic and complex structure. Tichy suggests that change is not only inevitable in such circumstances but can be managed to produce effective strategic results. This is explored later in the chapter.

15.2.2 Three dynamics for strategic change

Kanter, Stein and Jick[8] identified three causes of strategic change, one of which is the same as in the Tichy classification:

1. *Environment.* Changes in the environment compared with the situation in the organisation can lead to demands for strategic change.
2. *Life cycle differences.* Changes in one division or part of an organisation as it moves into a phase of its life cycle that is different from another division may necessitate change. For example, in a geographically diverse manufacturer such as Unilever, product ranges in developing countries would still be growing while similar products in developed countries might be in a more mature market phase. Typically, change issues relate to the size, shape and influence of such parts and involve co-ordination and resource allocation issues between them.
3. *Political power changes inside the organisation.* Individuals, groups and other stakeholders may struggle for power to make decisions or enjoy the benefits associated with the organisation. For example, a shift in strategy from being production-oriented to customer-oriented would be accompanied by a shift in the power balance between those two functions.

The description of such changes suggests that they relate not only to strategic change but also to other complex factors, such as the interplay between people and groups. The researchers suggested that the causes were constantly shifting, sometimes slowly and at other times faster. Essentially, such causal effects prompted the need at various points for substantive strategic change.

15.2.3 Analysis of causality

In practice, there is a need to define more *precisely* the causes that apply to a particular organisation. The above interpretations may supply some general pointers, but precision will prove more useful when it comes to managing strategic change. Equally, the causes described above raise important issues regarding how strategic change then takes place. This is examined in Sections 15.3 and 15.4 from the prescriptive and emergent change perspectives.

KEY STRATEGIC PRINCIPLES

- To manage strategic change, it is important to understand what is driving the process. There are numerous classifications of the causes, two of which are explored in this text.
- Tichy identifies four main causes of strategic change: environment, business relationships, technology and new entrants to the organisation, especially a new leader.
- Kanter, Stein and Jick identify three dynamics for strategic change: environment, life cycle differences across divisions of an organisation and political power changes.
- Precision regarding the causes of change is important in order to manage the change process effectively.

CASE STUDY 15.2

Counting on Carly

CEO Carly Fiorina directs strategic change at Hewlett-Packard

From the moment she joined the company as chief executive officer in 1999, Carly Fiorina began forging a new strategic direction for the US computer company Hewlett-Packard. She re-organised its organisational structure and re-oriented its organisational culture in her first two years. This case explores the way the company has changed since her arrival – both in organisational culture and business strategy.

The story is picked up again in Case 8 in Part 6 of this book. It ended in 2005 with Fiorina being sacked. But to understand the reasons, you need to know what happened in her first three years.

The HP Way: the 'old' organisational culture?

The Hewlett-Packard timeline.

Soon after Carly Fiorina arrived at Hewlett-Packard in 1999, she gave a presentation of her plans to the surviving joint founder of the company, Bill Hewlett. At this time, Bill was in a wheelchair and dying of cancer. But he remained fiercely (and rightly) proud of what he and his late partner, Dave Packard, had created: one of the world's largest computer and office equipment companies with a turnover of $42 billion and over 100,000 employees.

Named after its two founders, Hewlett-Packard had started in a converted garage in Palo Alto, California, in 1939 making audio oscillators for Walt Disney's *Fantasia* and scientific instruments for the US Navy. It grew steadily during the war years of the early 1940s on the back of US government contracts and then branched out into the areas of business and consumer electronics in the 1950s and 1960s.

Essentially, the company's two founders were particularly skilled at encouraging, supporting and then driving skilled employees to develop new products – moving into hand-held electronic calculators, personal and business computers, scientific instruments, electronic measurement devices and computer printers. The organisational culture of Hewlett-Packard was crucial to this rapid growth: it was called the 'HP Way'.

According to the founders' philosophy, the 'HP Way' encouraged and supported individual and small group engineering initiatives to develop business ideas. The whole atmosphere was ideas-driven and supportive, but it also had a hard-edged results side. Dave and Bill could often be seen walking individually around the Hewlett-Packard factories and offices – 'managing by walking around' as they used to call it. It was personal, friendly and socially aware. Its public face was summarised by HP – see Table 15.1 – but it is important to keep such an approach in perspective: many key growth initiatives were achieved by acquisition. Considerable efforts were made to bring such newly acquired companies into the 'HP Way', resulting in some delays to planned merger benefits.

Although the 'HP Way' was originally developed in the 1950s, it was still relevant 50 years later according to Hewlett-Packard's CEO, Carly Fiorina. In the HP Annual Report 2001, she wrote: 'We are now entering a period of computing that defies all limits and crosses all borders, in which everything works with everything else, everywhere, all the time.' She continued: 'Since I arrived at HP, we've taken aim at the heart of this transformation, and set a goal to re-invent this great company: to restructure and revitalize ourselves to recapture the spirit of invention that is our birthright, and apply it to meeting customer needs . . . As Bill and Dave understood, the real genius of the HP Way is that it's a legacy built on innovation, bold enough to embrace change and flexible enough to absorb it. The spirit of these original seven principles continues to guide us to this day.'

Although Carly Fiorina claimed that the company was still following the 'HP Way', it was not clear that the surviving founder, Bill Hewlett, believed her. New competitors and new technologies had entered the market place – IBM reborn, Sun Microsystems, Dell Computers, the Japanese company Canon – and Hewlett-Packard was beginning to lose its way. Certainly in 1999, the dying Bill Hewlett's only reaction to Carly Fiorina's presentation was a terse request to his nurse: 'Get me out of here.' And this was only just the beginning of Carly's battle with the old guard at HP.

Table 15.1 The seven elements of the HP Way

1 Recognise that profit is the best measure of a company's contribution to society and the ultimate source of corporate strength.

2 Continually improve the value of the products and services offered to customers.

3 Seek new opportunities for growth, but focus efforts on fields in which the company can make a contribution.

4 Provide employment opportunities that include the chance to share in the company's success.

5 Maintain an organisational environment that fosters individual motivation, initiative and creativity.

6 Demonstrate good citizenship by making contributions to the community.

7 Emphasise growth as a requirement for survival.

Source: Hewlett-Packard's report and accounts 2001 – the company comments that there were originally six elements, subsequently expanded to seven.

There can be few people who have been more charismatic than Carly Fiorina of Hewlett-Packard.

Early impact of Carly: the need to streamline the organisation

When Carly Fiorina arrived at Hewlett-Packard in early 1999, she quickly decided that there were fundamental problems with the company's organisation structure. The company was still organised as a series of separate divisions that allowed strong, decentralised, local initiative but meant duplication of valuable resources. The group had 83 product divisions, each of which was headed by a general manager with complete responsibility for all aspects of a business area from new product development to marketing. Importantly, the organisational culture of HP was also imbued with this long tradition of autonomy. The view was taken that duplication increased costs, so greater centralisation would reduce costs and increase profits.

'We have a lot of soloists in this company and what we need is an orchestra,' said Carly Fiorina. One of her best examples was the inefficiency created by the fact that HP had no fewer than 750 internal websites for employee training. 'Now why do we have that?' she asked.

The company had long recognised that there were major disadvantages with its decentralised structure. In his book *The HP Way*, Dave Packard himself told of an incident in the 1970s when working capital had suddenly started to rise for reasons that top management could not understand: it emerged that big customers were 'buying products from several HP entities to combine into a system. They were not paying for any of the products until they received the last one needed. We changed the procedure so that we were able to put the system together and check it before it was delivered.' Although decentralisation encouraged entrepreneurial activity and specialisation excellence, such an approach meant that the group co-operated badly. Moreover, it meant that even obvious benefits of co-operation, such as ensuring that the same company made the different parts of a personal computer (storage, drives, central processor, etc.) were not undertaken. Thus, simple economies of scale became increasingly difficult to achieve and this put HP at a major cost disadvantage against its competitors.

Carly Fiorina had previous experience of managing a fundamental re-organisation when she was chief executive of Lucent Technologies, the telecommunications equipment subsidiary of the major US telephone service company AT&T. She made her reputation at Lucent and was voted in 1998 'The Most Powerful Woman in American Business' on the cover of the American business magazine, *Fortune*. She joined HP in 1999 and came with a strong marketing and sales reputation that did not fit well with the organisational culture of the company. Essentially, the senior managers there were all engineers with a production-led approach to strategic issues. Fiorina was fearful on her arrival that she would be seen as 'marketing fluff' – someone who lacked strong operational skills. In fact, she was subsequently praised for her accomplished sales style and for bringing an important marketing approach to a high-technology company proud of its engineering history.

Two years after she arrived at Hewlett-Packard, she introduced a similar structure to that at Lucent. She combined the various operating companies into a very simple 'front end/back end' structure – see Figure 15.5. The front end would be customer-oriented and was essentially split into business and personal customers, with a separate section covering ongoing services. The back end would contain all the production and research functions, structured around product groups. In addition, there was a separate section devoted to services delivering ongoing and fee-earning relationships with major customers, who were not just buying products as such. The key to making such an organisation structure work is to develop the *links* across the company so that the front end and back end co-ordinate their efforts. HP attempted to solve this in three ways:

1 Keeping the structure simple – only three customer-oriented divisions.
2 Appointing a group of managers that reported to both front and back end executives.
3 Ensuring that back end units are not profit centres and therefore cannot sell their products direct to end-customers.

Perhaps not surprisingly, this re-organisation was not received well by some of the long-serving members of HP: 'The way it was done left a lot of product people feeling like the back end of the pantomime horse.' Some engineers complained that they were in danger of losing touch with customers. More

Front end:

- *Business Customer Organisation*: selling technology solutions to corporate customers – 20,000 employees
- *Consumer Business Organisation*: selling consumer items – 5,000 employees
- *HP Services*: delivering customer education, consulting and outsourcing – 30,000 employees

Back end:

- *Computing Systems*: makes servers, software and storage – 13,000 employees
- *Imaging and Printing Systems*: builds new printing and imaging products – 15,000 employees
- *Embedded and Personal Systems*: makes appliances, PCs and embedded solutions – 1,450 employees
- *HP Labs*: provides technological leadership for HP and invents new technologies – 850 employees

Group of managers reporting to both front and back end organisations

Figure 15.5 The new 2001 organisational structure at Hewlett-Packard

fundamentally, as one external business school professor commented: 'They are trying to reach synergies between divisions when all their traditions are about autonomy.'

Even after the subsequent re-organisation, the company's profitability did not improve - arguably for other reasons, such as a downturn in its markets - and the management response was that the situation might have been even worse if the re-organisation had not occurred. But this did not help Carly's case with those opposed to the changes. Carly was clearly fighting some fundamental attitudes at HP, but the battle was about to intensify further.

What strategy for the next five years? A new battle with the old guard at HP

Although there was clear business logic to the 2001 re-organisation, it was not enough in itself to solve the profit pressures that were now beginning to hit all computer and related companies around the world. The re-organisation had come at a time when three external factors were making business even more difficult for Hewlett-Packard:

1 There was a downturn in the world economy during the period 2001 onwards. Large companies and small customers were tempted to delay investment in new computers, printers and related services.

2 The after-effects of the dot.com bubble. During the late 1990s and early 2000, companies associated with the internet revolution had seen their share prices rise sharply and then fall as it was realised that the benefits of the World Wide Web would take longer to emerge and would not necessarily favour small, new web-based companies. The result was a sudden drop in demand for telecommunications products, including associated computer-related equipment.

3 Increased competition from companies such as IBM, Dell Computers and Sun Microsystems.

The results of these pressures were evident in the 2001 results of Hewlett-Packard: the worst set of profit figures for many years - see Table 15.2. The company needed a new strategy and it needed to do something fast. The result was a battle between two groups:

Table 15.2 Long-term perspective at HP - major changes needed in 2001

	1987	1988	1989	1990	1991	1992	1993	1994	1995	1996	1997	1998	1999	2000	2001
Sales ($ billion)	8.1	9.8	11.9	13.2	14.5	16.4	20.3	25.0	31.5	38.4	42.9	47.1	42.3*	48.8	45.2
Net income ($ million)	644	816	829	739	755	881	1,177	1,599	2,433	2,586	3,119	2,945	3,491*	3,697	408
Number of employees '000	82	87	95	92	89	93	96	98	102	112	122	125	84*	89	86

* After demerger of Agilent Technologies.

Source: company annual report and accounts.

- *the old guard at HP* – some of the earlier managers and the original Hewlett and Packard family trusts that still owned substantial blocks of shares in the company;
- *the new guard at HP* – represented by Carly Fiorina and her immediate colleagues who judged that there were no easy strategic solutions.

The old and new guard were to clash fundamentally on the new strategic directions for Hewlett-Packard in 2001. The story is followed through in Case 8 in Part 6 of this book. Eventually, Carly Fiorina was forced to leave the company in 2005. Even Chief Executive Officers can feel the impact of strategic change.

Hewlett-Packard supports the Global Reporting Initiative G3 Framework with a programme of sustainable developments on sustainability.

Sources: see references at the end of Case study 8 in Part 6 of this book.

Case questions

1 What were the main problems at Hewlett-Packard? Analyse the organisational culture and the power balance using concepts from Chapter 16. Identify also the business problems: strategic change needs to be seen in the strategic context of the business issues facing the company.

2 How would you categorise the strategic change analysis here?

3 What would you have done in 2001 if you were chief executive?

15.3 PRESCRIPTIVE APPROACHES TO MANAGING STRATEGIC CHANGE

In developing and implementing strategy, managers will need to consider how to *manage* the change process. For example, in the Hewlett-Packard case, the company clearly set out to manage its major organisational changes in 2001. Specifically, it undertook the following actions:

- It reassured its employees by careful announcements and explanations.
- It explained the reasoning behind making the new organisation structure more customer-focused.
- It promoted willing managers and ignored those who were against such change.

Two *prescriptive* routes for the management of change are examined in this section and then two *emergent* routes are examined in Section 15.4. The overall argument from the two sections is that the choice of prescriptive or emergent change is context-sensitive.

15.3.1 The three-stage prescriptive approach

During the late 1980s and early 1990s, research into change management by Kanter and her colleagues identified three major *forms* taken by the change process.[9] They linked these three forms with three *categories of people* involved in the change process, to produce a *three-stage process for managing change*. Their three forms were:

1 *The changing identity of the organisation.* As its environment changes, the organisation itself will respond. For example, it may need to react to a shift in the political stance of a national government. The dynamic is likely to be slow rather than fast, unless a political or other major revolution occurs.

2 *Co-ordination and transition issues as an organisation moves through its life cycle.* Relationships inside an organisation change as it grows in size and becomes older. Whether such a precise event occurs or not, the dynamic shifts associated with such change are predictable with regard to their pressures on groups and individuals. For example, the decision to create a separate division for a product range that is growing increasingly wide will give rise to change issues that are well known, but need management.

3 *Controlling the political aspects of organisations.* This results directly from the political pressures outlined in Section 15.2.2. Sometimes an orderly shift in power can be made but, occasionally, a more radical move is required – for example, the sudden departure of a chief executive 'after a clash over strategy and structure'.[10]

The three major categories of people involved in the change process were also identified:

1 *Change strategists.* Those responsible for leading strategic change in the organisation. They may not be responsible for the detailed implementation.
2 *Change implementers.* Those who have direct responsibility for change management (the programmes and processes that are explored later in this chapter).
3 *Change recipients.* Those who receive the change programme with varying degrees of anxiety, depending on the nature of the change and how it is presented. They often perceive themselves to be powerless in the face of decisions made higher up the organisation. In extreme cases they may object – for example some of the managers at Hewlett-Packard.

Essentially, the researchers observed that, in their sample, managing change was a top-down, prescriptive process. Emergent strategists would point to the obvious weakness in such an approach: the lack of knowledge and co-operation in advance is quite likely to cause anxiety and resistance. Prescriptive strategists would counter this by pointing to the difficulty of exploring a hostile acquisition with the change recipients before the acquisition takes place. Prescriptive strategists might cite a famous case from 1993, in which contact was made with future employees prior to acquisition, resulting in the workers eventually rejecting the offer. Volvo Car workers joined its Swedish management and a majority of shareholders in repudiating the proposed joint venture with the French car company, Renault.[11]

Comment

Kanter, Stein and Jick offer one way of structuring and managing aspects of the change process. However, their categories of people only give limited indicators of how to manage the process. Their model may also be more suited to major changes than the more common ongoing strategic process.

15.3.2 Unfreezing and freezing attitudes

In the 1950s, Lewin developed a three-step model to explain the change process:[12]

1 *Unfreezing current attitudes.* For change to take place, the old behaviour must be seen to be unsatisfactory and therefore stopped. Importantly, this need for change must be felt by the person or group themselves: it is a *felt need* and cannot be imposed. This process might be undertaken by leaking relevant information or openly confronting those involved.
2 *Moving to a new level.* A period of search for new solutions then takes place. This is characterised by the examination of alternatives, the exploration of new values, the changing of organisational structure and so on. Information continues to be made available to confirm the new position.
3 *Refreezing attitudes at the new level.* Finally, once a satisfactory situation has been found, refreezing takes place at the new level. This may well involve positive reinforcement and support for the decisions taken. For example, good news about the new position might be circulated, along with information about changes in status, changes in culture, reorganisation and reconfirmation of investment decisions.

Comment

This apparently simple model has been widely used to analyse and manage change. It tends to treat people as the objects of manipulation and does not involve them in the change process at all. However, it can be useful on occasions (see, for example, Figure 15.6 where the Hewlett-Packard case has been interpreted using the Lewin model).

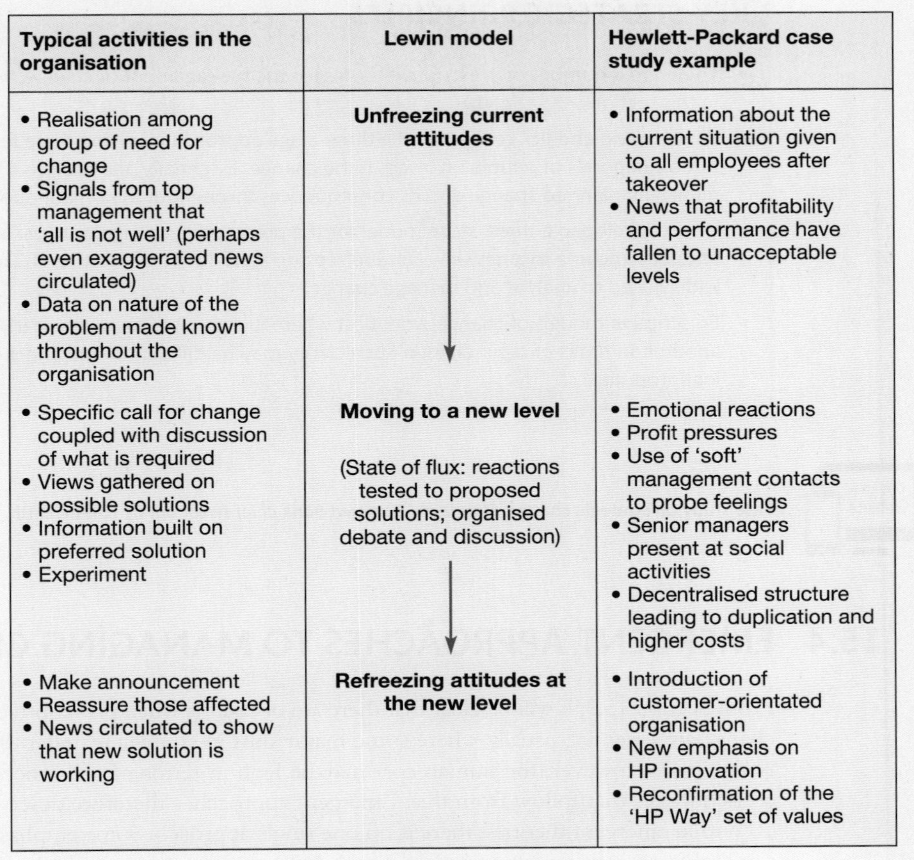

Typical activities in the organisation	Lewin model	Hewlett-Packard case study example
• Realisation among group of need for change • Signals from top management that 'all is not well' (perhaps even exaggerated news circulated) • Data on nature of the problem made known throughout the organisation	**Unfreezing current attitudes** ↓	• Information about the current situation given to all employees after takeover • News that profitability and performance have fallen to unacceptable levels
• Specific call for change coupled with discussion of what is required • Views gathered on possible solutions • Information built on preferred solution • Experiment	**Moving to a new level** (State of flux: reactions tested to proposed solutions; organised debate and discussion) ↓	• Emotional reactions • Profit pressures • Use of 'soft' management contacts to probe feelings • Senior managers present at social activities • Decentralised structure leading to duplication and higher costs
• Make announcement • Reassure those affected • News circulated to show that new solution is working	**Refreezing attitudes at the new level**	• Introduction of customer-orientated organisation • New emphasis on HP innovation • Reconfirmation of the 'HP Way' set of values

Figure 15.6 Hewlett-Packard re-organisation using the Lewin model

15.3.3 Comment on prescriptive models of change

There are other similar models that take a prescriptive approach to organisational change.[13] We have explored the criticisms of the prescriptive approach elsewhere in this book and can summarise the issues here with regard to change models.

- The assumption is made in prescriptive models that it is possible to move clearly from one state to another. This may not be possible if the environment itself is turbulent and the new destination state therefore unclear.
- Where major learning of new methods or substantial long-term investment is needed for the new situation, it may not even be clear when the new refrozen state has been reached – the situation may be soft-frozen (as it probably was at Hewlett-Packard, judging by the backroom comments afterwards).
- The assumption is also made that agreement on the new refrozen state is possible. This may be unrealistic if the politics within the organisation remain in flux. Given that prescriptive models involve only limited consultation, this assumption can be shown to have real weaknesses in some cultural styles characterised by competition and power building.
- Such models rely on the *imposition* of change on the employees concerned. This may be essential in some circumstances, e.g. factory closure, but, where the co-operation of those involved is needed or the culture works on a co-operative style, the prescriptive models may be totally inappropriate.

KEY STRATEGIC PRINCIPLES

- There are a number of prescriptive routes for the management of change: two were examined in this section.
- Kanter, Stein and Jick recommend a three-stage approach involving three forms of change and three categories of people involved in the change. Essentially, the route is a top-down guide to managing planned change and its consequences throughout the organisation.
- Lewin developed a three-stage model for the prescriptive change process: unfreezing current attitudes, moving to a new level and refreezing attitudes at the new level. This model has been widely used to analyse and manage change.
- Prescriptive models of change work best where it is possible to move clearly from one state to another. In times of rapid change, such clarity may be difficult to find and such models may be inappropriate.

Case study on strategic change: *Standard Chartered Bank chief swept out by culture clash.*

15.4 EMERGENT APPROACHES TO MANAGING CHANGE

From Section 15.3, it will be clear that there are occasions when prescriptive approaches to strategic change are essential, usually where some major shift in strategy is under discussion, such as in the Nokia case. However, the human cost may be high in terms of resistance to the changes and the consequences that follow from this. Emergent approaches therefore deserve to be investigated.

Within emergent theories, there is no one single approach. Some emphasise the need for responsiveness in an increasingly turbulent world. Others concentrate on the longer-term need to change an organisation's skills, style and operating culture fundamentally and over long time periods. It is these latter theories that are explored in this chapter, since they are more closely related to issues of strategic change. The two emergent areas chosen for examination have already been explored:

1 learning theory, as developed by Senge and others;[14]

2 the Five Factors theory of strategic change, as developed by Pettigrew and Whipp.

15.4.1 Learning theory

As we observed in Chapter 11 when considering learning in an innovative context,[15] the learning organisation does not *suddenly* adopt strategic change but is *perpetually* seeking it. The process of learning is continuous: as one area is 'learnt', so new avenues of experimentation and communication open up. In addition, the learning approach emphasises the following areas:

- team learning;
- the sharing of views and visions for the future;
- the exploration of ingrained company habits, generalisations and corporate interpretations that may no longer be relevant;
- people skills as the most important asset of the organisation; and, most importantly,
- systems thinking – the integrative area that supports the four above and provides a basis for viewing the environment.

It will be evident that the learning approach can work well where the company has the time and resources to invest in these areas. The objective is for the people in the organisation to shape its future over time. (The Hewlett-Packard case included elements of this in Carly Fiorina's comment, 'Since I arrived at HP, we've taken aim at the heart of this transformation.')

Arguably, learning would not be so applicable where there was a sudden change in strategic direction – for example, the HP 2001 reorganisation. The gradual assimilation of change and the ability of employees to guide their own destiny is limited, if rapid change is imposed by senior managers for outside commercial reasons. The learning approach appeared to offer little in the short term for Hewlett-Packard's 2001 predicament, for example.

Comment

The principle of the learning organisation appears to have a significant difficulty: precisely how and when companies should be developed into 'learning' organisations.[16] The outline concept is clear enough, but the practicalities of how this is achieved are vague and lacking in operational detail. Egan has commented on the definitional and conceptual ambiguity in the learning concept 'which has stifled the practical adoption of what could otherwise be an extremely powerful idea'.[17] Garvin has attempted to answer these difficulties by exploring the management and measurement of such new processes.[18] He suggests some first useful steps that might be adopted to begin the process, for example, *learning forums* or discussion groups in the organisation to tackle specific change issues.

15.4.2 The Five Factors theory of strategic change

Pettigrew and Whipp[19] (see Chapter 13) undertook an in-depth empirical study of strategic change at four companies: Jaguar cars, Longman publishing, Hill Samuel merchant bank and Prudential life assurance. They also undertook a more general examination of the industries in which the four companies were operating. Their conclusions were that there were five interrelated factors in the successful management of strategic change (see Figure 15.7):

1 *Environmental assessment.* This should not be regarded as a separate study but a separate function. All parts of the organisation should be constantly assessing the competition. Strategy creation emerges constantly from this process.
2 *Leading change.* The type of leadership can only be assessed by reference to the particular circumstances of the organisation. There are no universal 'good leaders'. The best leaders are always constrained by the actual situation of the firm. They are often most effective when they move the organisation forward at a comfortable, if challenging, pace: bold actions may be counterproductive.
3 *Linking strategic and operational change.* This may be partly prescriptive in the sense of a specific strategy for the organisation – 'This is my decision.' It may also be partly emergent in that the strategy may allow for evolution over time – 'But naturally our new strategy will evolve as we implement it.'
4 *Strategic human resource management – human resources as assets and liabilities.* These resources constitute the knowledge, skills and attitudes of the organisation in total. Crucially, some people are better than others at managing people. It is a skill acquired over time and needing a learning approach (see Section 15.3.1). Long-term learning is essential for the organisation to develop its full potential.
5 *Coherence in the management of change.* This is the most complex of the five factors. It attempts to combine the four above into a consistent whole and reinforce it by a set of four complementary support mechanisms:
   - *consistency* – the goals of the organisation must not conflict with each other;
   - *consonance* – the whole process must respond well to its environment;
   - *competitive advantage* – the coherence must deliver in this area;
   - *feasibility* – the strategy must not present insoluble problems.

Note that the five factors relate to the whole strategy development process, not just to the implementation process.

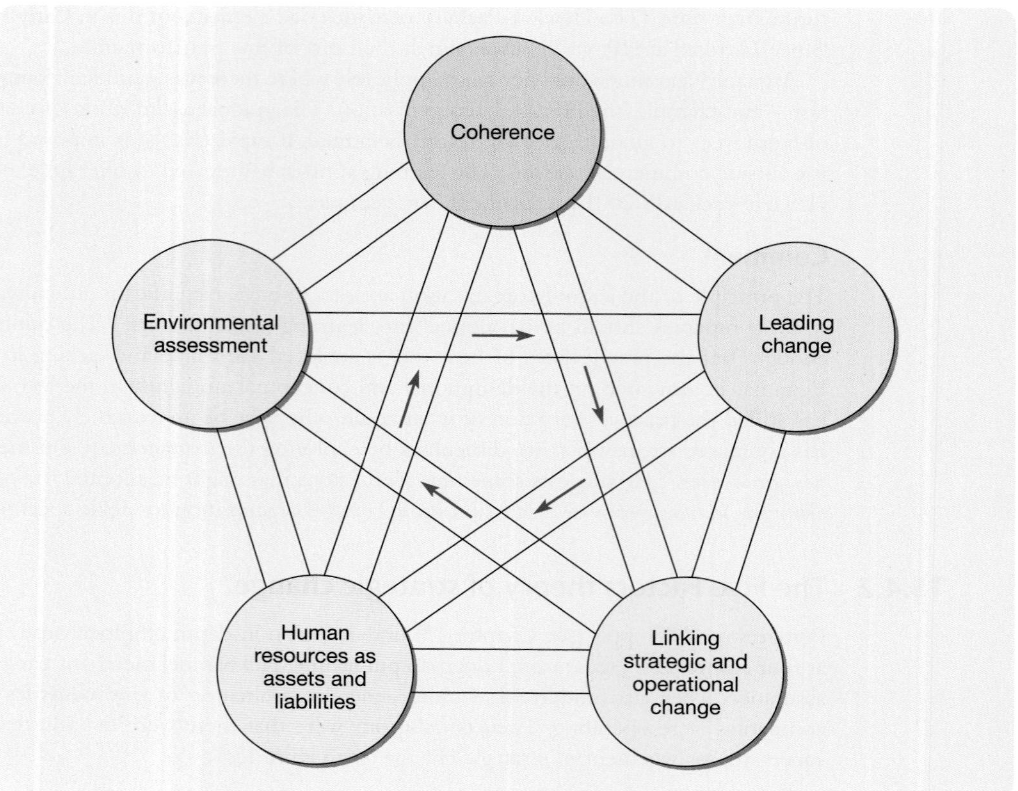

Figure 15.7 The five factors in the successful management of strategic change
Source: Pettigrew, A and Whipp R (1991) *Managing Change for Competitive Success*, Blackwell Publishing Ltd, p 104. Reproduced with permission.

To illustrate how the five factors might be used, the Hewlett-Packard re-organisation (see Case 15.2) has been analysed using this approach. The results are shown in Table 15.3. The model provides a useful way of taking the facts from a strategic change situation and structuring them to highlight the important items. Where data have not been gathered on one of the five elements of change, it highlights this area. The model may also suggest additional areas that need to be explored in the organisation in order to understand the dynamic of change, especially in the area of coherence.

Comment

Although the comprehensiveness of the model is its greatest strength,[20] it is also its most significant weakness. Some of the factors represent truths that most would agree with, but contain areas that are so generalised that they may provide only limited guidance on the difficult issues involved in strategic change. Thus, some of the five factors needed to be treated with caution.

- *Environmental assessment* is a well-known factor requiring constant monitoring. However, the more detailed comments against this heading in the model provide more limited guidance than those in Part 2 of this book.
- *Linking of strategic and operational change* is an important area of study, but many would regard this as being the same as the 'implementation' process discussed by other writers and explored in this book.
- *Leading change* and its complexity has been recognised as a change factor for many years.[21]
- However, the emphasis on *human resource assets and liabilities* is a welcome emphasis not present in some other analyses, such as Porter's generic strategies or portfolio matrices. Moreover, the identification, definition and logic of *coherence* as a major factor is also useful.

Table 15.3 Analysing the five factors for change at Hewlett-Packard

Factor	Hewlett-Packard analysis
Coherence	• Defined by the single act of re-organisation • The arrival of the new chief executive • Restatement of the 'HP Way'
Environment assessment	• Drivers of the business were identified – customers, etc. • Emphasis on customer-facing staff plus careful co-ordination with the back end staff
Strategic human resource	• Clear understanding of the old engineering culture of some employees • Communication emphasis, especially core messages management • Careful presentations to staff across the group
Linking strategic and operational change	• Links between back and front end staff • Attendance of senior managers at informal functions • Motivation and customer focus
Leading change	• Individual responsibility: the role of Ms Fiorina • Accessibility of senior managers • Focus on key factors for success: customer focus, more centralisation, new innovation

Note: The factors are in the order relevant to the Hewlett-Packard reorganisation.

15.4.3 Comment on emergent models of change

Both the Nokia and the Hewlett-Packard cases illustrate the difficulties of using emergent models of strategic change. For whatever reasons, both companies found themselves being forced to undertake completely different approaches to their strategy:

- Hewlett-Packard under pressure to raise profit margins by increased centralisation.
- Nokia's need for a highly charged message in order to change strategic direction.

It could certainly be argued that both companies had signalled the difficulties they were facing in computer markets and in international banking services, both to the Stock Exchange and to employees. However, the *emergent* models of strategic change, with their long-term approach to learning, provide only limited clues to interpreting the difficulties and suggesting how they might be tackled over this period. Nor, for example, is the 'Doomsday' memo at Nokia handled well by emergent models of change – such messages are sudden by definition. By contrast, the three-phase Lewin *prescriptive* model does provide a means of interpreting the events and their meaning for change. For instance, at Hewlett-Packard, the unfreezing came from Carly Fiorina's comments about the need for revitalising the company; the moving to a new level from the questioning of every aspect of the decentralised structure; the refreezing from the announcement of the new reorganised structure.

Emergent models of strategic change have a number of weaknesses that may make them difficult to employ:[22]

- The 'long-term learning' approach of Pettigrew and Whipp[23] necessary to achieve emergent strategies may have little practical value where an organisation faces a short-term unforeseen crisis. There is no guarantee that the 'learning' that has already taken place will be relevant to the crisis. Arguably, the crisis may partly have arisen because the learning was incorrect.
- In some emergent models, increased turbulence of the environment is assumed as a justification for the emergent strategies. Such generalisations about the environment need empirical evidence. There are a number of environments that are generally predictable.
- A reliance on a learning culture may be counterproductive for some managers and employees. Some managers may refuse to learn because they realise that such a process will reduce their power.[24] Empowerment of some employees may mean that others will have less power and may react accordingly.

Overall, the way forward proposed by some emergent strategists often amounts to the need to introduce change earlier so that the organisation is better able to adapt. This may not be sufficient at the time when a sudden change hits the organisation.

15.4.4 The choice between emergent and prescriptive strategic change

The choice between the prescriptive and emergent routes is context-sensitive. Potentially, organisations may wish to choose emergent strategic change management because it is less disruptive and therefore has a lower cost. However, there may be occasions when the strategic circumstances force prescriptive change. The choice depends on the situation facing the organisation at the time.

KEY STRATEGIC PRINCIPLES

- There are a number of emergent approaches to strategic change. The two explored in this section concentrate on the longer-term, learning culture routes to change.
- According to Senge, the learning organisation does not suddenly adopt strategic change but is perpetually seeking it. Hence, the organisation is using its learning, experimentation and communication to renew itself constantly. Strategic change is a constant process.
- Pettigrew and Whipp's empirical study of strategic change identified five factors in the successful management of the process: environmental assessment; leadership of change; the link between strategic and operational change; human resource aspects; and coherence in the management of the process.
- Emergent models of strategic change take a long-term approach and may have limited usefulness when the organisation faces short-term strategic crisis.
- The choice between prescriptive and emergent strategic change processes will depend on the situation at the time: ideally, emergent change should be chosen because it is less disruptive and cheaper. In reality, a prescriptive approach may be necessary.

CASE STUDY 15.3

Risky strategic change at EMI?

When Terra Firma acquired the UK record company EMI for $6.6 billion in 2007, the company 'unfroze' current attitudes by announcing the sacking of one third of the workforce. But what would happen if the proposed 'refreezing' business strategy was unsuccessful? This case explores the situation in early 2008.

The strategic task facing Terra Firma

After years of struggling to make profits, one of Britain's most famous record companies - EMI - was acquired by the private equity group Terra Firma in November 2007. The price paid was $6.6 billion, which some commentators regarded as high given that EMI had a history of strategic difficulties. For example, the two leading record companies, EMI and Warner, had been for years locked in battles to take over each other with the aim of cutting overheads in a combined operation. However, when Terra Firma came on the scene, it was proposing a different strategy and one that was quite radical for a record company.

Unfortunately for Terra Firma and Guy Hands - its chief executive - the acquisition of EMI was financed by a highly leveraged deal. This meant that it relied heavily on borrowed money from banks signed before the 2008 credit squeeze made finance more expensive. The pressure on Terra Firma and Guy Hands was quite significant. The critics' viewpoints were summarised in a *Financial Times* analysis: 'Mr Hands is the classic example of private equity overpaying in a boom and then resorting to crude cost cutting when times are tough.'

But Guy Hands hit back saying: 'The record business is stuck with a model designed for a world that has changed and gone forever.' He was seeking a radical new strategy for EMI in the record industry. He explained the background to his new strategy by pointing out that there were at least three major flaws in the profitability of the record industry:

EMI's new Owner, Guy Hands, has begun promoting the company across the music industry.
© Arnold Turner/Getty Images

1 The industry used major chart toppers to subsidise losses elsewhere. Hands commented: '300,000 sales can be massively successful and if we spend appropriately and creatively a record like that can be profitable.'

2 The large range of record labels in each company was supposed to produce economies of scale, but their complexity meant that this did not happen. Developing this further, Hands said: 'The major labels' response to the internet has been a massive failure of leadership, and their fall from grace should be taught as a cautionary tale at business schools.'

3 Individual promoters of a particular type of music (reggae, hip hop, etc.) claimed to be able to push their products to customers, regardless of customer demand, which had become increasingly varied. 'You don't need people with an "ear" for hits. People will tell you what they like. It's not magic. It's called market research,' explained Hands.

In essence, Hands said that EMI's culture must change from a bloated bureaucracy to a lean, customer-oriented business. And he was not a person to mince his words. According to one outsider: 'He rules Terra Firma with a rod of iron, so no one else speaks during negotiations.' Mr Hands himself described his style as, 'Blunt, direct and not very tactful.'

Certainly, Terra Firma had been involved in re-invigorating a number of major businesses over the past few years. Essentially, the Terra Firma strategy was to acquire a failing business, turn around the profitability and then sell the now-successful business for a substantial capital gain. It had successfully applied this approach to a chain of UK public houses, a motorway service operation and a waste treatment business. Nevertheless, in tackling a company in the record industry, Hands accepted that he was faced with a daunting task. Terra Firma knew that it would be difficult when it bought EMI. The company had done its analysis and identified many areas of the business that were capable of considerable improvement. Exhibit 15.1 summarises some of the difficulties at EMI and those reflected more generally in the record industry.

EXHIBIT 15.1

Problems of profitability at EMI

- Music is a 'people' business in terms of managing its principal assets - artists and music groups. However, only 6 per cent of EMI's staff were working in this area - called 'A&R' - responsible for finding new talent and developing existing artists.
- Only around 200 artists accounted for over half EMI annual sales - out of a total of 14,000 artists on its books. Equally, 80 per cent of EMI's digital revenues were delivered by 7 per cent of its digital contracts.
- 30 per cent of EMI artists had never produced a music album. The company was doubtful that some would ever do so. In a similar way, 85 per cent of new artists never make a profit for their record companies - even before taking account of overheads.
- EMI spent around \$140 million annually subsidising artists who would never make any money. In addition, EMI's annual marketing expenditure was operating around \$120 million over budget.
- EMI destroyed around 20 per cent of the CDs that it produced at an annual cost of around \$50 million.

The new strategy at EMI

Guy Hands had done his strategic analysis and quickly announced that he would sack one third of EMI's entire staff - 2,000 out of 6,000 employees - by June 2008. But he knew that this was not enough. He regarded the record industry in general, and EMI in particular, as being a *people industry*. The heart of the business revolved around recording artists, their agents and the entertainment industry. Relations with artists were critical to recorded music and already managers of several artists, such as the manager of Robbie Williams, had expressed unhappiness with Hands. The fear was that simply slashing people would strip out the best managers in a people business. Hands countered by saying that he was actually going to *increase* the numbers of A&R managers looking after artists. The staff cuts would come elsewhere in EMI.

Specifically, Hands had decided on a three-part strategy for EMI:

1. *Refocus the company on its A&R managers* – Increase the numbers and give them more scope to make deals and seek out new artists.
2. *Centralise many of the functions.* Sales, marketing, manufacturing, distribution and digital operations would be taken away from individual labels and into a new 'music services' division. The main job cuts would be in these areas. They would be placed under a new executive operation that would handle these tasks for all parts of the business. However, this meant that A&R executives would negotiate the deals with artists and then hand over responsibility to another part of the organisation to deliver the results. In the past, the A&R executive had responsibility for marketing and the other tasks listed above.
3. *Seek corporate sponsorship for the major EMI artists.* Hands wanted to attach individual brand names to his leading artists. This would bring in extra revenue in the same way that sponsorship deals at football companies delivered extra money to the game. However, some music industry experts were dubious about this approach: 'The recipe of bands, fans and brands is a potent mix that needs to be treated with great caution.' At best, this possible new revenue stream for EMI was proposed by Hands but remained untested.

Implementing strategic change at EMI

After only a brief period, Terra Firma and Hands announced the major job cuts to the financial press. They also diverted most of the Terra Firma staff to work at EMI. In particular, the company made two major appointments from the Terra Firma organisation into EMI:

1. Mike Clasper was appointed to the new position of head of music services. He was the former chief executive of British Airports Authority, being responsible for its sale to a Spanish company in 2006. His job was to put in place the new administrative structure in marketing, manufacture and other office services.
2. Pat O'Driscoll was appointed to head EMI's managers and, if needed, recruit new managers for the organisation. She was the former chief executive of the ready-meals manufacturer Northern Foods. She had plenty of experience of asking senior executives to leave during her time at that company.

Amongst the remaining senior and middle managers, around half of them would be re-interviewed for their jobs. They would have to convince O'Driscoll and her team that they had the 'skills, determination, ethical approach and the passion to do the job'.

To implement the new strategy, Hands called a meeting to announce the job cuts in early January 2008. Even before the meeting, he gave the financial press extensive interviews about the new strategy and announced the main elements of the cuts. His office also produced a 50-page booklet of explanation for employees.

In outlining the new strategy, Terra Firma said that the aim was to present a vision for the future of EMI alongside the reasoning for the changes. Hands explained: 'We are not trying to do something which is just tinkering . . . it will be much fairer and more objective . . . we are changing the organisation . . . In an ideal world there would be no pain in achieving gains. Unfortunately, we don't live in an ideal world.'

What happened next?

After the initial changes in 2008, some artists left the company complaining about the way that the company had changed. But others stayed. Importantly, a major legal dispute then took place. In essence, Terra Firma sued Citibank, which had sold the company to EMI. Terra Firma claimed that it had been misled by Citibank over the valuation of EMI and was seeking redress. After a lengthy court battle, EMI lost the case. EMI then became in default of various covenants made to Citibank and eventually EMI was broken up into two parts with the parts being sold to Vivendi/Universal and Sony – see Case 13 in Part 6 of this book.

 This case was written by Richard Lynch from published sources only.[25]

Case questions

1. In a 'people' business like the record industry, is it wise to take such an aggressive stance with regard to sacking some managers and asking many others to reapply for their jobs? Are there any alternative approaches?
2. By announcing the substantial job cuts, Terra Firma was arguably 'unfreezing' current attitudes. But does 'refreezing' at the next level need to be clear as to its outcome in terms of strategy? In considering this issue, you may want to consider that the new Terra Firma strategy, which separated A&R from marketing and delivery, largely remained untested and experimental at the time of the cuts.
3. Clearly, Terra Firma and its chief executive, Guy Hands, had plenty of experience in strategic change. Should other companies follow this example?

Checklist: Some barriers to implementing strategic change.

15.5 DEVELOPING A STRATEGIC CHANGE PROGRAMME

The starting point for any programme of strategic change is *clarity* regarding the changes required. These will relate back to the organisation's objectives explored in Chapter 6 but may include a more experimental element as well. In Case 15.3 on the UK record company EMI, there was clarity in the sense that substantial costs needed to be cut. However, some parts of the proposed strategy remained essentially unproven – for example, the new arrangement between the A&R managers and the new organisation that would deliver EMI's 'music services'. A strategic change programme may also include the introduction of a 'learning culture' as part of its way forward, but this was not proposed at EMI because faster change was required.

In practice, one of the main problems may be the resistance by managers to the changes that are proposed and another will be the need to persuade people to support the proposals. Both of these elements can be detected in the EMI case. It is therefore important to give these matters serious consideration at the commencement of the programme. The change programme needs to address four questions:

1 What areas of change are available?
2 What areas will we select and why?
3 Will people resist change? If so, how can this be overcome?
4 How will people use the politics of an organisation?

15.5.1 What areas of change are available?

In Section 15.1, four general areas of activity associated with people, referred to as pressure points for influence, were identified – formal organisation structure, people, tasks and informal organisation structure. These can be coupled with three main areas of strategic change activity[26] to produce the *change options matrix* shown in Figure 15.8. In practice, every organisation undertaking change will

	Areas of people activity → *Formal organisation structure*	*People*	*Tasks*	*Informal organisation structure*
Three main areas of strategic change: *Technical and work changes* from the strategy to be undertaken	• Organisation of work and reporting • Strategy and structure	• Selection, training • Matching of management style with skills • Routines	• Consider environment, technology, learning, competitor activity • Learn and carry out new tasks	• Understand and monitor • Feed with 'good news'
Cultural changes Style of company, history, age, etc.	• Managerial style • Mintzberg's subcultures *(Chapter 15)* • Handy's cultures *(Chapter 7)*	• Individual and corporate values matched • Management of groups and teams • Leadership choice	• Symbols, stories • Unfreezing • Make role models of key people • Clarify values • New recipes	• Awards, symbols • Develop networks • Encourage useful groups • Develop social activities
Political changes Interactions and power inside the organisation	• Formal distribution of power • Balance of power between departments	• Use available skills and networks • Match with new strategies • Incentives and rewards	• Lobbying • Develop structures • Influence formal and informal groups	• Attempt to manage • Make contacts • Network and circulate

Figure 15.8 Change options matrix

need to develop activities in most of these options. However, for most organisations, there will be a need to concentrate effort and monitor results. Hence, it will be useful to *focus and direct activities more tightly*: selection among the options will be a priority.

15.5.2 What areas will we select from the change options matrix and why?

The response to these questions will depend on the organisation, its culture and leadership. For example, organisations that have a history of top-down management might select items from the change options matrix that match this style of operating – that is, organisation of work and formal distribution of power – whereas organisations that have selected an open-learning, co-operative style of operating might select as their starting point team building and training and education. The clear implication is that it is essential to review the organisation's culture analysis: this is explored in Chapter 16 on leadership.

There are no universal answers. As we have seen, some researchers have recently tended to favour the more co-operative, learning organisation approach. However, it should be recognised that this may be a fashion of the turn of the century: only time will tell.

Whatever route is chosen, a more detailed answer to the question then needs to be followed through. As an illustration of the issues that can then arise, the *assumption* is made here that the co-operative, learning approach has been chosen. Within this route, Beer, Eisenhart and Spector[27] provide a detailed six-point plan on how to proceed, beginning by stressing that the areas to be selected for change should be chosen not by top management but by *those involved in the implementation process*. The six overlapping areas are:

1 *Mobilise commitment to change through joint diagnosis of business problems arising from the change objective.* One or more task forces might be employed here. They should represent all stakeholders in the organisation and be directed at specific aspects of the change objective.
2 *Develop a shared vision of how to organise and manage for competitiveness.* Senior management may lead the process, but the identification of the new roles and responsibilities is undertaken by those involved in implementation. Typically, this will be through the task forces.
3 *Foster consensus for the new vision, competence to enact it and cohesion to move it along.* This book has already explored vision, competencies and cohesion. The key new word is *consensus*, which the researchers suggest needs to come from strong leadership at the top. New competencies may be required, resistance may build and some individuals may turn out to be more reluctant than others. Difficulties may be overcome by teamwork coupled with training to provide support. However, it is likely that leadership will also be needed.
4 *Spread revitalisation to all departments, pushing it from the top.* Change is spread to the departments that supplied the members of the task force. However, such change cannot be forced onto departments. They must be allowed some freedom, but they can be guided and revitalised by top management.
5 *Institute revitalisation through formal policies, systems and structures.* Up to this stage, the process has contained a degree of freedom of choice, experimentation and action. Now the time has come to 'refreeze' the procedures, both to ensure commitment and understanding and to provide the basis for future monitoring and controls.
6 *Monitor and adjust strategies in response to problems in the revitalisation process.* Having 'learnt' an area, the organisation should be able to repeat the process as the environment continues to change and more is understood about the changes already introduced.

With the emphasis on joint task forces and learning through doing, it might well be asked what role senior management can perform. The researchers suggested they had three prime tasks:

1 *To create the prime conditions for change* – forcing recognition of the need, setting the standards and monitoring performance. Hewlett-Packard senior management is a good example here.
2 *To identify those teams and organisation units that had achieved successful change and then praise them as role models for the rest.* Exploring why there were so many websites at HP is one example here.
3 *To identify individuals and promote them on the basis of their success in leading change.*

EXHIBIT 15.2

Resistance to change

Why people resist change	Overcoming resistance
• Anxiety, e.g. weaknesses revealed or loss of power or position • Pessimism • Irritation • Lack of interest • Opposition to strategy proposals • Different personal ambitions	• Involving those who resist in the change process itself • Building support networks • Communications and discussion • Use of managerial authority and status • Offering assistance • Extra incentives • Encouraging and supporting those involved • Use of symbols to signal the new era

Finally, it should be emphasised again that this approach is suitable for one type of organisation but may not be appropriate for other types.

15.5.3 Will people resist change and how can this be overcome?

In practical terms, the issue of resistance to change is probably the chief obstacle to the successful implementation of strategic change. The reasons are many and the ways of overcoming them will depend on the circumstances. Exhibit 15.2 presents a list of some of the more common areas of resistance and suggests ways of overcoming them.

More positively, resistance will be less if the change is not imposed from outside but developed by those involved in the change procedures. Change will be more welcome if it is seen to reduce, rather than increase, the task of those involved and to be consistent with the values that they hold. Change is also more likely to be accepted if it offers an interesting challenge and a change from existing routine. Importantly, change is more likely to be appreciated if the outcome is genuinely valued by senior management, who have wholeheartedly supported the process as it has developed.

15.5.4 How will people use the politics of an organisation?

In the context of strategic change, politics starts by *persuading* people to adopt a new strategy. It may not be a question of meeting open resistance but rather one of different priorities, different power blocks or differences of opinion on the way forward. The first step is usually to establish the organisation's 'ground rules': that is, any criteria that it has for the acceptance of projects, such as minimum levels of profitability and so on.

The more difficult aspects of politics usually begin when these criteria have been met but there is still resistance. Politics then becomes *discussion, negotiation* and even *cunning* and *intrigue*. The Florentine diplomat and writer Nicolo Machiavelli (1469–1527) remains well known to this day for his insights into the ways that people use the politics of the organisations to which they belong.[28] His writing appears cynical, devious and self-serving, but he certainly understood management politics at its worst:

> It is unnecessary for a good prince to have all the qualities I have enumerated but it is very necessary to appear to have them.

On the subject of change:

> There is nothing more difficult to take in hand, more perilous to conduct, or more uncertain in its success, than to take the lead in the introduction of a new order of things.

Machiavelli saw little benefit in persuasion, except as a means of avoiding the alternative, which was to use direct force and possibly end up making enemies. His attitude was that reason mattered less than power, and human nature was best considered as acting for the worst possible motives. He would have chuckled cynically at such strategic change concepts as communication, discussion and empowerment.

In some organisations, Machiavelli still remains relevant today. Certainly, it is highly unlikely that major strategic change can be implemented if it meets strong political barriers. Strategists therefore have to be skilled not only at devising their proposals but also at building support for them through the organisation's political structure. Hence, it is important to understand how the *decision-making system* works in the organisation: this will include not only any final presentation but also the preceding discussions, consultations and lobbying. It may be useful to call for advice from those who have had previous experience of its processes.

Inevitably, the politics of an organisation will take time to understand. It will include the activities of other people and their interaction with strategy across a whole range of activities. People will have many motives: some good and some less attractive. They may employ many different types of activity that could loosely be described as political. Table 15.4 lists some that have been shown by empirical research to be important.

By definition, change involves moving from a previous strategy and therefore the starting point for the persuasion process might appear to be an attack on the existing strategy. However, politically this may be a mistake. It may force those who introduced the previous strategy to defend their decisions and therefore raise barriers to the new proposals. The people who are antagonised by the new strategies may be the very individuals whose support is vital for them.

Beyond these considerations, the person(s) responsible for seeking agreement to a new strategy will need to undertake several important tasks:

- identify potential and influential supporters and persuade them to support the new strategy;
- seek out potential opposition and attempt to change opinions or, at least, to neutralise them;
- build the maximum consensus for the new proposals, preferably *prior* to any formal decision meeting.

Finally, it is important to keep political matters in perspective. They are important, but this book has hopefully shown that strategy does not deal in certainties. It is an art as well as a science. This means that there is room for differing views and the use of judgement and debate in arriving at decisions. Strategy is the art of the possible.

Table 15.4 Politics in organisations[29]

Objective	Activities undertaken to achieve the objective	Reaction by superiors or rivals to the activities
Resist change or resist authority	• Sabotage • Rebellion	• Fight back • Institute new rules and regulations
Build power	• Flaunt or feign expertise • Attach oneself to superior • Build alliances with colleagues • Collect subordinates: empire build • Control resources	• Call bluff • Find heir • Re-organise department • Reclaim control of resources
Defeat rival	• Battles between units • Battles between staff and line managers • Expose mistakes (we all make them)	• Good leadership should provide balance
Achieve fundamental change in strategy, authority and leadership	• Form power group of key executives • Combine with other areas above • Inform on opponent • Leak damaging material to public media	• Intelligence essential • Recognise and cultivate those who are particularly influential • Seek out rival power groups • Respond with own leaks

KEY STRATEGIC PRINCIPLES

- The change options matrix sets out the main areas where change is possible: it is important within this to focus and select options.
- Selection from the matrix needs to be undertaken. This can best be undertaken by an understanding of the culture of the organisation: the cultural web can be useful here – see Section 16.3. A more detailed process to achieve change can then be planned out, with six overlapping areas providing a starting point.
- Resistance to change is probably one of the chief obstacles to successful strategy implementation. It is likely to be lower if strategies are not imposed from the outside.
- The politics of strategic change needs to begin by attempting to persuade those involved to adopt the new strategy recommendations. Beyond this, a Machiavellian approach may be necessary to ensure the desired changes are achieved. More generally, strategic change activities may include identifying supporters, attempting to change opposition views and building the maximum consensus for the new proposals. Preferably, this should be undertaken prior to any decision meeting.

CRITICAL REFLECTION

How important is ongoing strategic change in companies?

From the cases presented in this chapter, it is clear that one of the problems with the companies was that they only made changes after they were forced to change. Might it be better if all organisations were constantly engaged in some form of emergent change process?

Would this produce better strategy? And a better place to work?

SUMMARY

- In the management of strategic change, a distinction needs to be made between the *pace of change*, which can be fast or slow, and *strategic change*, which is the proactive management of change in an organisation. Strategic change is the implementation of new strategies that involve substantive changes beyond the normal routines of the organisation.
- In managing strategic change, it is useful to draw a distinction between prescriptive and emergent approaches. Prescriptive approaches involve the planned action necessary to achieve the changes. The changes may be imposed on those who will implement them. Emergent approaches involve the whole process of developing the strategy, as well as the implementation phase. This approach will also involve consultation and discussion with those who will subsequently be implementing the change.
- Strategic change is concerned with people and their tasks. It is undertaken through the formal and informal structures of the organisation. Understanding the *pressure points* for influencing change is important if such change is to be effective. Strategic change is important because it may involve major disruption and people may resist its consequences. Even where change is readily accepted, the changes will take time and careful thought. Strategic change carries important hidden costs.

- To manage strategic change, it is important to understand what is driving the process. There are numerous classifications of the causes, two of which are explored in this text, those of Tichy and Kanter, Stein and Jick.
  1. Tichy identifies four main causes of strategic change: environment, business relationships, technology and new entrants to the organisation, especially a new leader.
  2. Kanter, Stein and Jick identify three dynamics for strategic change: environment; life cycle differences across divisions of an organisation; and political power changes. Precision regarding the causes of change is important in order to manage the change process effectively.
- There are a number of *prescriptive routes* for the management of change, two of which are examined.
  1. Kanter, Stein and Jick recommend a three-stage approach involving three *forms* of change and three *categories of people* involved in the change. Essentially, the route is a top-down guide to managing planned change and its consequences throughout the organisation.
  2. Lewin developed a three-stage model for the prescriptive change process: unfreezing current attitudes, moving to a new level and refreezing attitudes at the new level. This model has been widely used to analyse and manage change.
- Prescriptive models of change work best where it is possible to move clearly from one state to another: in times of rapid change, such clarity may be difficult to find and such models may be inappropriate.
- There are a number of emergent approaches to strategic change. The two explored in this chapter concentrate on the longer-term, learning culture routes to change. According to Senge, the learning organisation does not suddenly adopt strategic change but is perpetually seeking it. Therefore, the organisation is using its learning, experimentation and communication to renew itself constantly. Strategic change is a constant process.
- Pettigrew and Whipp's empirical study of strategic change identified five factors in the successful management of the process. These were environmental assessment; leadership of change; the link between strategic and operational change; human resource aspects; and coherence in the management of the process. Emergent models of strategic change take a long-term approach and may have limited usefulness when the organisation faces a short-term strategic crisis.
- The choice between prescriptive and emergent strategic change processes will depend on the situation at the time: ideally, emergent change should be chosen because it is less disruptive and cheaper. In reality, circumstances may make a prescriptive approach necessary.
- In developing a change programme, the change options matrix sets out the main areas where change is possible: it is important to focus and select options from the matrix. This can best be undertaken by an understanding of the culture of the organisation.
- A more detailed process to achieve change can then be planned out, with six overlapping areas as a starting point. Resistance to change is probably one of the chief obstacles to successful strategy implementation. It is likely to be lower if strategies are not imposed from the outside.
- The politics of strategic change first require the persuasion of those involved to adopt the new strategy recommendations. Additionally, a Machiavellian approach may be necessary to ensure the desired changes are achieved. More generally, strategic change activities may include identifying supporters, attempting to change opposition views and building the maximum consensus for the new proposals. Preferably, this should be undertaken prior to any decision meeting.

QUESTIONS

1 How would you characterise the strategic changes at the three companies in this chapter - fast or slow? How would you describe their strategic management process - as prescriptive or emergent?

2 *'The twin tasks for senior executives are to challenge misconceptions among managers and to foster a working environment which facilitates rather than constrains change.'* (Colin Egan) Discuss.

3 Identify the pressure points for influencing strategic change in an organisation with which you are familiar.

4 If strategic change is important, why do some people find it difficult to accept and what are the consequences of this for the change process? How can these difficulties be overcome?

5 *'The sad fact is that, almost universally, organisations change as little as they must, rather than as much as they should.'* (Rosabeth Moss Kanter) Why is this and what can be done about it?

6 Given the problems associated with prescriptive change, why is it important and what can be done to ease the process?

7 Does the comment in this chapter that the way forward proposed by some emergent strategists often amounts to the need to start earlier mean that emergent approaches have little useful role?

8 Examining Hewlett-Packard in 2001 (see Case 15.2), use the change options matrix to determine what areas of change were available. What areas would you select to enact the proposed changes and why?

9 Analyse the politics of an organisation with which you are familiar. If you were seeking significant strategic change in the organisation, how would you approach this?

10 Leadership may be important for strategic change, but is it essential?

FURTHER READING

Bernard Burnes (1996) *Managing Change*, 2nd edn, Pitman Publishing, London, has a most useful broad survey of the areas covered in this chapter. See also Goodman, P S and Rousseau, D M (2004) 'Organizational change that produces results: the linkage approach', *Academy of Management Executive*, Vol 18, No 3, pp 7–21 and Mezias, J M, Grinyer, P and Guth, W D (2001) 'Changing collective cognition: a process model for strategic change', *Long Range Planning*, Vol 34, pp 71–95.

Professor Charles Handy (1993) *Understanding Organisations*, Penguin, Harmondsworth, is still one of the best available reviews of organisational change.

Kanter, R M, Stein, B and Jick, T (1992) *The Challenge of Organisational Change: How Companies Experience it and Leaders Guide it*, The Free Press, New York, has some thoughtful guidance on strategic change.

A useful article is that by Garvin, D (1993) 'Building a learning organisation', *Harvard Business Review*, July–August, pp 78–91.

Professors A Pettigrew and R Whipp (1991) *Managing Change for Competitive Success*, Blackwell, Oxford, has some important strategic evidence and insights.

NOTES AND REFERENCES

1 Sources for Nokia case: Nokia annual report for 2010. *Financial Times*: 26 January 2011, p 23; 28 January 2011, p 18; 10 February 2011, pp 1 and 15; 14 February 2011, p 10 (leader); 15 February 2011, p 17; 25 February 2011, p 13; 12 April 2011, p 14; 14 April 2011, p 16.

2 Schein, E H (1990) *Organisational Psychology*, 2nd edn, Prentice Hall, New York.

3 Burnes, B (1996) *Managing Change*, 2nd edn, Pitman Publish ing, London. Part 1 of this book presents a useful broad survey of this area.

4 Handy, C (1993) *Understanding Organisations*, Penguin, Harmondsworth, p 292 (see Ch 6 for further discussion of Handy and note that his view is emergent rather than prescriptive).

5 Burnes, B (1996) Op. cit., p 173.

6 Ansoff, I (1987) *Corporate Strategy*, 2nd edn, Penguin, Harmondsworth.

7 Tichy, N (1983) *Managing Strategic Change*, Wiley, New York, pp 18–19.

8 Kanter, R M, Stein, B and Jick, T (1992) *The Challenge of Organizational Change: How Companies Experience it and Leaders Guide it*, The Free Press, New York.

9 Kanter, R M, Stein, B and Jick, T (1992) Op. cit.

10 *Financial Times* (1996) 24 April, p 1.

11 *Financial Times* (1993) 1 November, p 19; 6 December, p 17.

12 Lewin, K (1952) *Field Theory in Social Science*, Tavistock, London.

13 Burnes, B (1996) Op. cit., pp 179–186 has a useful summary.

14 For other writers, such as Levinthal and March, and a wider review of the research, see the references on the learning-based strategic route forward in Senge, P (1990) *The Fifth Discipline: The Art and Practice of the Learning Organization*, Doubleday, New York, Ch 18.
15 Senge, P (1990) Op. cit.
16 Jones, A and Hendry, C (1994) 'The learning organisation', *British Journal of Management*, Vol 5, pp 153–162. Egan, C (1995) *Creating Organizational Advantage*, Butterworth–Heinemann, Oxford, pp 131–138, also has a useful critical discussion.
17 Egan, C (1995) Op. cit., p 135.
18 Garvin, D (1993) 'Building a learning organization', *Harvard Business Review*, July–August, pp 78–91.
19 Pettigrew, A and Whipp, R (1991) *Managing Change for Competitive Success*, Blackwell, Oxford.
20 Egan, C (1995) Op. cit., p 178.
21 See, for example, Handy, C (1993) Op. cit., Ch 4.
22 Burns, B (1996) Op. cit., pp 194–195.
23 Pettigrew, A and Whipp, R (1991) Op. cit., p 237.
24 Whittington, R (1993) *What is Strategy and Does it Matter?*, Routledge, London, p 30.
25 References for EMI case: EMI Annual Report and Accounts 2007 available on the web: www.emi.com/investors. *Financial Times:* 14 January 2008, pp 1 and 14; 15 January 2008, p 23; 16 January 2008, p 19; 19 January 2008, p 9; 18 September 2009, p 19; 10 February 2010, p 13; 11 March 2010, p 18; 25 September 2010, p 18.
26 Tichy, N (1983) Op. cit., pp 126, 135, 131.
27 Beer, M, Eisenhart, R and Spector, B (1990) 'Why change management programs don't produce change', *Harvard Business Review*, November–December, pp 158–66.
28 Machiavelli, N (1961) *The Prince*, Penguin, Harmondsworth.
29 There are four sources for this table: Machiavelli, N (1961) Op. cit.; Mintzberg, H (1991) 'Politics and the political organisation', Ch 8 in Mintzberg, H and Quinn, J B (1991) *The Strategy Process*, 2nd edn, Prentice Hall, New York; Handy, C (1993) Op. cit., Ch 10; and the author's own experience.

PART 5
Different strategy contexts and business models

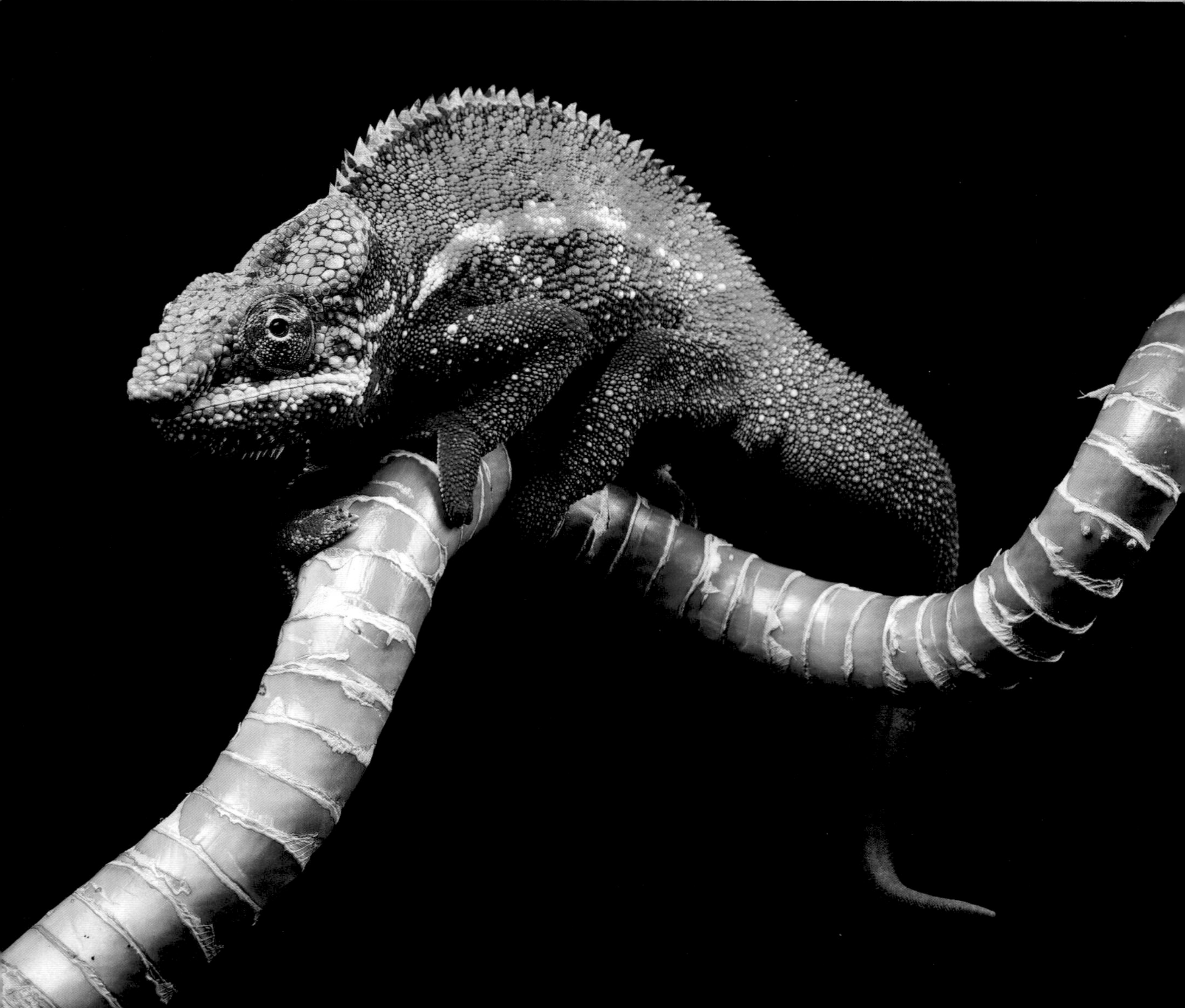

As we explored in Chapter 11, the context in which the strategy is developed can have a profound influence on the resulting strategies. This part of the book explores a number of situations in which strategy will be influenced by context. Specifically, we examine the way that leaders will influence strategy development. We then explore entrepreneurial strategy, public sector strategy and international and global strategy. Finally, this section explores business models and how they relate to strategy.

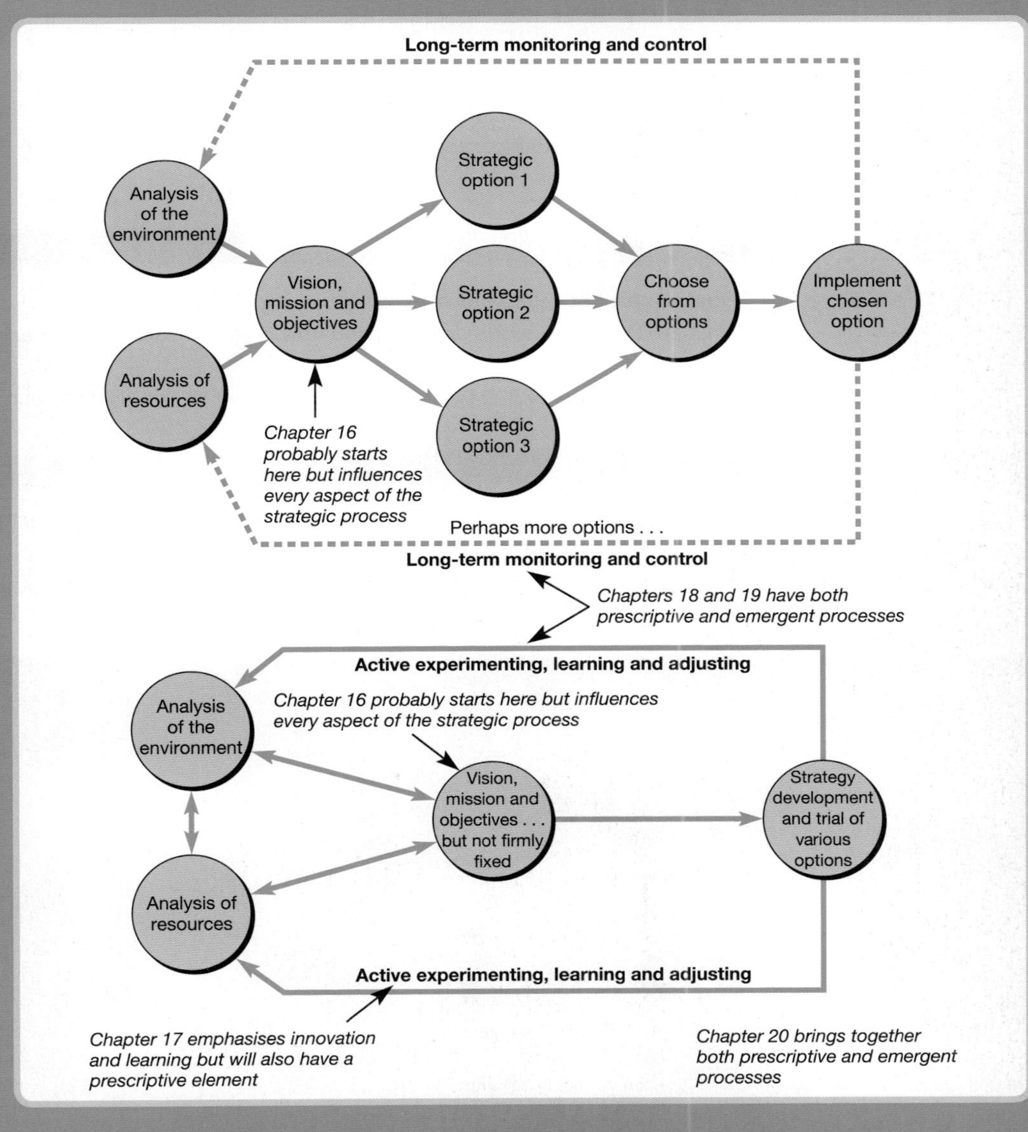

Key strategic management questions

CHAPTER 16 Strategic leadership	• What are the main elements of strategic leadership? • What makes a good leader? • How do leadership roles change over time? • How do leaders influence organisations and cope with power? • What are the main elements of successful strategic leadership?
CHAPTER 17 Entrepreneurial strategy	• What is entrepreneurial strategy? • How do entrepreneurs differ, especially with regard to risk taking? • What are the four main drivers of entrepreneurial strategy? • What are the main stages in implementing entrepreneurial strategy?
CHAPTER 18 Government, public sector and not-for-profit strategies	• What are the main strategy principles in this sector? • How do such strategies differ when profit is no longer the major part of the objective? • Is it possible to use the concepts developed for business strategy? Or do they need to be modified?
CHAPTER 19 International expansion and globalisation strategies	• What is meant by international expansion and globalisation? • What are the main theories involved and how do they relate to individual countries and companies? • What are the benefits and problems of company globalisation strategy?
CHAPTER 20 Strategy and business models	• What is the difference between a business strategy and a business model? • What are the main elements of a business model? • How do you identify the main strengths and weaknesses of business models? • How useful are business models?

CHAPTER 16
Strategic leadership

Video and sound summary of this chapter.

LEARNING OUTCOMES

When you have worked through this chapter, you will be able to:

- outline the main elements of strategic leadership;
- explain what makes a good leader;
- show how leadership roles change over time;
- outline how leaders influence and cope with power in organisations;
- explain the five main areas of successful strategic leadership.

INTRODUCTION

After relevant discussion and consultation, the top management team of the organisation takes the main strategic management decisions. Moreover, the same people lead and guide others in the organisation towards other, related strategic decisions. Strategic leadership is therefore a crucial component to gaining and sustaining the competitive advantage, where appropriate, of the organisation and to adding value to the organisation's activities.

This chapter explores this topic by considering first the nature of strategic leadership. It then looks at three major components – namely, the factors that make a good leader, how leadership roles can change over time and how leaders cope with power in the organisation. Finally, the chapter addresses the five specific components of successful strategic leadership: defining and communicating the organisation's purpose; managing human resource decisions; setting ethical standards; delivering the purpose to stakeholders; and sustaining the competitive advantages of the organisation over time. All these elements are shown in Figure 16.1.

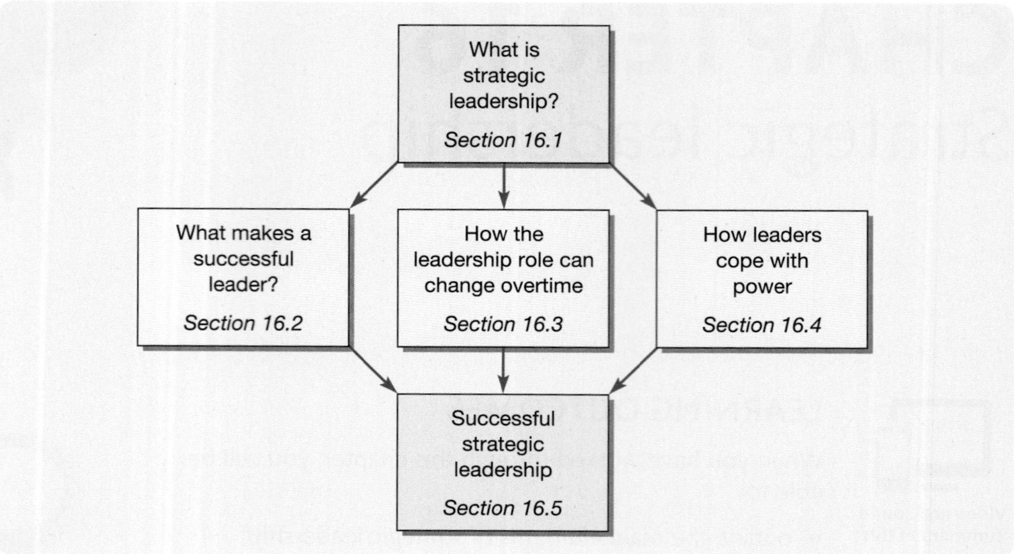

Figure 16.1 The main elements of strategic leadership

CASE STUDY 16.1

How Anne Mulcahy rescued Xerox

During the past 10 years, Xerox has reduced the size of its workforce, reorganised its operating companies and introduced a new organisation and culture to the company. This case examines the role played by its chief executive, Anne Mulcahy, in turning around the company.

Background

For 30 years, the US company Xerox has been engaged in a major global battle with its Japanese rivals, especially Canon and Ricoh. From dominance of the photocopying market in the 1960s, Xerox's market share has slowly been reduced. Its sales have risen, but not as fast as the market has grown. It has been the Japanese companies that have made all the running in terms of new products, higher quality, ease of use and maintenance-free equipment.

In 2004, Xerox Corporation had total sales of around $15.7 billion and net income of $859 million. This was a major recovery from its position in year 2000 when it made a loss of $273 million. This case examines the turnaround in strategy and organisation masterminded by its chief executive, Anne Mulcahy, over the four years to 2004.

Markets, competitors and customers

When Japanese companies decided to enter international photocopying markets in the 1960s, they had to find a way to overcome the dominance of Xerox. They chose to open up a new market segment: copiers for medium and small businesses that needed little maintenance and no regular service support. Xerox had a policy of always leasing its machines and then providing service engineers to maintain them: this was attractive to large companies with heavy printing demands, but smaller companies rapidly found the Japanese offerings more acceptable.

By 2000, Xerox had lost market share of the overall market. However, it still continued to maintain its market leadership in the high-end segment. Its competitive strengths still lay in its ability to provide a high level of service to customers. This was an area that the Japanese companies had never really attempted to match because of the high set-up costs and difficulty in obtaining minimum levels of business to make profits. Xerox had made several attempts to break into the lower end of the market. The last of these was around 2000. However, its strengths and cost structures were still largely geared to large company customers.

In 1993, its European subsidiary, Xerox Europe, undertook a survey of its customers' photocopying requirements: it found that they were spending 8 per cent of their turnover creating and managing documents, including creating and developing printed material, photocopying it, and filing and recording the results. This compared with 3 per cent of turnover spent on information technology. Moreover, up to 60 per cent of their customers' time was regularly spent on various activities associated with documentation. In 2001, the parent company Xerox America undertook a similar study and confirmed that its customers were still spending considerable time on

Xerox Chief Executive, Anne Mulcahy, transformed the company before handing it over in 2009.
© Jacob Silberberg/Getty Images News/Getty Images

documentation, but the nature of the work had changed - it was more concerned with electronic systems, the internet and accessing information electronically.

Problems in 2000

For a company with a strong range of products and some talented people, it may seem surprising that Xerox faced major problems in 2000. There were five main reasons:

1 Increased competition from Japanese and American companies - photocopying and printing was becoming highly competitive.

2 Failed re-organisation of its American salesforce had upset customers in its prime geographic area. The chief executive wanted Xerox to become more than a photocopier company. It needed to sell business solutions based on document work flows. This meant a major re-organisation of the company to provide industry specialists who would understand specific industries. It also involved drastically reducing the numbers of Xerox back office centres in order to lower the Xerox costs. The result of such a drastic change was little short of chaotic.

3 Problems in some of its new growth markets - particularly Brazil and Thailand.

4 Accounting problems in Mexico that eventually led to a Securities and Exchange Commission investigation with regard to equipment leasing in that country.

5 High levels of debt from excessive borrowing.

The result was that the chief executive officer, Rick Thoman, resigned. The Xerox board then chose as the new chief executive someone who had worked for the company for 25 years - Anne Mulcahy. Her job was to turn around the Xerox company, which by this time was in real difficulties. She spent her first 90 days talking to customers and employees: 'There was such confusion and complexity in the company that I could have wasted a lot of time addressing symptoms that were not at the heart of what was wrong.'

Turnaround 2000 in business and organisational culture

Anne Mulcahy's turnaround plan was simplicity itself:

- The company would have to cut overheads by $1 billion.
- It would have to close unprofitable activities.
- It would have to reduce its levels of debt finance by asset sales.

With colleagues, she then set about implementing these strategies. By 2002, the company had cut nearly 19,000 jobs. Costs were reduced by $1.2 billion. The complete small office/home division of Xerox was closed down because it was unprofitable. The company sold its half-share in Fuji Xerox back to its Japanese associate, the Fuji Company, in order to raise substantial finance. It also sold part of its customer financing business to GE Capital, again in order to raise finance and reduce its debts.

Importantly, Anne Mulcahy also started to change the company's culture. She had the dubious advantage that the company was clearly in trouble. This made it easier to explain to everyone that there was a real crisis and tough decisions would be needed. 'I used it as a vehicle to get things done that wouldn't have been possible in times of business as usual,' explains Ms Mulcahy. She used the crisis to obtain strategic change.

Her second step was to appoint a new management team. She was fortunate in that she knew her colleagues at Xerox well and wanted to promote from within where possible. 'I want to make sure someone feels ownership for every change initiative we have in place,' she said. 'Looking back, I think we had a lot of smart, articulate people - good presenters and good team players - who didn't necessarily like to take responsibility on their shoulders.' This meant that some of the people who were talented in other ways were not appropriate for the key management decisions that were now needed.

Beyond these changes, she did not alter the basic structure of committees and operations at Xerox. However, she did change the way that they were run. She herself describes an operations committee meeting: 'We were discussing customer satisfaction, an area where I think we should be doing better . . . The functional experts did a very nice job of presenting the process. We were all nodding and suddenly I had this feeling that this was the Xerox of the past. We were all going to go into conference rooms, we were all going to agree. . . . I just sat

Table 16.1 Xerox – financial results ($ millions)

	2000	2001	2002	2003	2004
Total revenue	18,751	17,008	15,849	15,701	15,722
Net income (loss)	(273)	(94)	91	360	859
Employees at year-end	91,500	78,900	67,800	61,100	58,100

there and said: "Time out". If I were putting my money on the table right now, right out of my wallet, would I bet that any of this is going to make a hoot of difference in terms of results? The answer is that I wouldn't put a dime on the table. It looks good. Nice presentations. Nice process. But at the end of the day we are not confronting the tough issues. I can't let us sit there and lull ourselves into that kind of discussion any more.'

Anne Mulcahy wanted a change in style and thought processes at Xerox and she wanted a shift in strategy beyond the short-term activities of the turnaround.

Shift of basic strategy

Given the time spent by its customers and its own strengths in servicing large customers, Anne Mulcahy decided to build on this but shift the emphasis of its basic business strategy. The company would make three main offerings:

1 *High-end copying.* It would continue to offer high-end copiers, printers and fax machines. This was its traditional area of strength and it had a highly skilled sales machine to undertake this task. This was the market where it competed against Hewlett-Packard, Canon and Ricoh.
2 *High-end production printing.* It would expand its interests in large-scale printing presses, such as those involved in magazine printing. This was the area of industrial printing where its main competitor was the German company Heidelberg.
3 *Document services and solutions.* It would offer consulting services and solutions for the archiving, documentation and printing problems of its client companies. It would help companies access archives containing 'millions of pages of R&D' or move millions of documents on to a company intranet in order to reduce costs. A new organisation, Xerox Global Services, was the result.

This implied higher degrees of service for all the document requirements of its customers, not just the photocopying part. The strategy shifted from simple photocopying towards offering a wider range of services and products to cater for the *document management* needs of its customers. Naturally, it continued to offer photocopying to those customers who preferred this.

In the early years, Anne Mulcahy recognised that it would take time for customers to see the benefits of its broader range. She noted that its rivals soon picked up the same themes: 'document management' and the 'document solution' were soon appearing elsewhere. However, Ms Mulcahy was convinced that its strategy was sound: it was built on its core skills and based on service. When done well, a service competitive advantage is immensely difficult for competitors to match because service is localised. However, the quality of that service is vital.

The situation in 2007

By 2007, Anne Mulcahy was able to comment: 'We've arrived at a place where the company is substantially different, focused on the future [with] all the heavy lifting behind us in terms of the shaping of the company for competitiveness.' This 'heavy lifting' involved cutting 30,000 jobs, outsourcing most of the Xerox heavy manufacturing and launching a joint venture with the leading Japanese company Fuji to deliver new co-operation on technology and sales. The three strategy areas listed above were also firmly on track.

So what about Anne Mulcahy herself who has had more than six years in the top job and 31 years with the company? 'Thirty one years is a long time. I'm well over the average of CEO tenures these days. The way I characterise it is that I'm not going to stay too long, but I'm not ready to go.'

By 2004, the company had recovered its market position. The new strategies were beginning to pay off – see the results in Table 16.1. By 2007, it was clear that Anne Mulcahy had led a significant turnaround at Xerox worldwide. In 2009, it was announced that Anne Mulcahy would step down as chief executive and be replaced by Ursula Burns, but Ms Mulcahy would remain as chairman.

Xerox has undertaken substantial measures with regard to sustainability. They can be viewed at: http://www.xerox.com/downloads/usa/en/e/EHS_Environmental_Sustainability.pdf.

Case questions

1 How would you summarise the strategies initiated by Anne Mulcahy in the face of strong Japanese competition?
2 Anne Mulcahy laid great emphasis on changing the Xerox organisational culture: how did she make the changes? What organisational, morale and human resource problems might arise as a result?
3 Given the success of Xerox in improving its profitability, what can other companies learn from the leadership of Anne Mulcahy and the Xerox experience? Would other companies need to adopt the Xerox culture and strategic approach if they wished to emulate the success that was achieved?

16.1 WHAT IS STRATEGIC LEADERSHIP?

Definition ▶ **Strategic leadership is the ability to shape the organisation's decisions and deliver high value over time, not only personally but also by inspiring and managing others in the organisation.** Such leadership begins with the top management team – the chief executive officer, other leading directors and, in large companies, the leading divisional directors.[2] For example at Xerox in Case 16.1, this has involved Anne Mulcahy and her fellow directors in a fundamental reappraisal of the company involving managers at many levels. They have had to take tough decisions on the Xerox product range, the ability of individual directors to deliver their areas of responsibility and profit, and the need to cut costs by reducing the number of employees at various Xerox factories around the world. All this has been done against the background of increasing global competition from companies like Canon and Ricoh – each seeking, along with other companies, to attack Xerox. The downturn in the US economy in 2008 added to the need for the strategic leaders at Xerox to consider carefully how they should respond to such outside pressures and continue to deliver to Xerox stakeholders.

Strategic leadership is therefore a complex balancing act between a number of factors. It involves coping with strategic pressures and changes in the environment outside the organisation, as we explored in Chapter 3. We also analysed the culture of the organisation in Chapter 4: this is an important background matter for leaders. Culture entails managing the human resources inside the organisation – possibly one of the most important strategic skills.[3] Leadership means more than merely responding to outside events. It includes inspiring and enthusing those inside the organisation with a clear direction for the future. This typically involves communicating with and listening to those inside the organisation with the aim of spreading knowledge, creating and innovating new areas and solutions to problems.[4] Importantly, leadership also means thinking and acting to develop the *future leaders* of the organisation.[5]

At its centre, strategic leadership entails developing and delivering the purpose of the organisation – see Chapters 6 and 7. The leaders do not undertake this task by themselves: they involve others in the organisation at many levels. The skill of the leaders comes in combining and managing such inputs, so that many in the organisation feel that they have made a contribution and, at the same time, are willing to follow and work towards the strategic direction defined by the leaders.[6] Three factors stand out in relation to this complex task:

1 How to lead so that others will follow: Section 16.2. For the most part, leaders will find that managers and employees work better if decisions are not imposed from the top.

2 How to shape the organisation's culture and style: Section 16.3. The atmosphere of the workplace and decision making are important in delivering results.

3 How to structure and influence decision making in the organisation: Section 16.4. Inevitably, there will be various groups seeking power within organisations and these need to be managed successfully.

KEY STRATEGIC PRINCIPLES

- Strategic leadership is the ability to shape the organisation's decisions and deliver high value over time, not only personally but also by inspiring and managing others in the organisation. Leadership not only involves the chief executive but the whole team at the head of an organisation.
- Leadership involves balancing a number of factors relating to strategy. These include the outside influences that impact on the organisation, from changes in the economy to increased competition. At the same time, leadership also means inspiring and leading people inside the organisation with a clear direction for its future. Ultimately, skilled leadership entails identifying and delivering the purpose of the organisation.

16.2 WHAT MAKES A SUCCESSFUL LEADER?

Definition ▶ **Leadership is the art or process of influencing people so that they will strive willingly and enthusiastically towards the achievement of the organisation's purpose.** As the case on Anne Mulcahy at Xerox demonstrates, leadership will have a significant influence on the performance of the organisation. However, the basic argument of this section is that the precise relationships between the two related topics of leadership and purpose are complex and depend on the specific circumstances. This means that it is difficult to provide prescriptive general principles on this relationship. Two ways are suggested in this section. One relies on the notion that leadership needs to avoid lasting conflict with subordinates. The other suggests that specific styles of leadership are likely to be associated with specific approaches to the development of purpose. Finally, this section argues that the most successful leaders need to go beyond defining the purpose of the organisation in a cold, abstract manner. Successful leaders will communicate and generate trust, enthusiasm and commitment amongst all those involved in the organisation.

16.2.1 Understanding the influence of leadership

Rupert Murdoch of News Corporation, François Michelin of Michelin Rubber, Bill Gates of Microsoft, Akio Morita of Sony, Anne Mulcahy of Xerox are all examples of leaders who have guided and shaped the direction of their companies. Leadership is therefore related to the purpose of the organisation. The essence of this aspect of leadership can be seen as the 'influence, that is the art or process of influencing people so that they will strive willingly and enthusiastically toward the achievement of the group's mission'.[7]

The organisation's purpose and strategy do not just drop out of a process of discussion, but may be actively directed by an individual with strategic vision.

> Visionary leadership inspires the impossible: fiction becomes truth.[8]

Leadership is a vital ingredient in developing the purpose and strategy of organisations. The potential that leaders have for influencing the overall direction of the company is arguably considerable. There is substantial anecdotal evidence to support this observation, though it is important to be aware of the hagiography (sainthood) that sometimes surrounds leaders – for example, the description of Rupert Murdoch in Case 8.4 portrays him in a generally favourable, if dominant, way. Nevertheless, in drawing up purpose and related strategy, it would be wise to consider carefully the personality, role and power of the leading person or group in the organisation.

Given the evident power that leaders may have in developing the company's mission and strategy, it is important to note some areas of caution based on research:

- Leaders should to some extent *reflect* their followers[9] and in some company cultures may need to be good team players if they are to effect change. Otherwise, they will not be followed.
- Vision can be eccentric, obsessed and not always logical.[10]
- It is certainly possible to exaggerate the importance of individuals when they are leading large and diverse groups that have strong company–political instincts.[11]

Certainly, these latter features are important in the modern, complex consideration of strategic management. Companies such as Philip Morris (USA), Royal Dutch/Shell (UK/Netherlands) and Toyota (Japan) may all be more comfortable with a corporate leader who is inclined to be evolutionary rather than revolutionary. To this extent, we may be suspicious of the hero worship of management saviours who have ridden with vision and purpose to the rescue of failing businesses. The same variations can be found in small business, not-for-profit and government organisations. In every case, leadership can have a profound effect on purpose.

16.2.2 Analysing leadership styles

In order to understand what makes a successful leader, it is useful to analyse the leadership role. However, in spite of extensive study reaching back to the 1950s, there is no general agreement on leadership analysis.[12] There are three main approaches:

Definition ▶ 1 ***Trait theories* argue that individuals with certain characteristics (traits) can be identified who will provide leadership in virtually any situation.** According to the research that has been done, such individuals will be intelligent, self-assured, able to see beyond the immediate issues and come from higher socio-economic groups. In recent times, such theories have been discredited because the evidence to support them is inconsistent and clearly incomplete in its explanation of leadership. On this view, successful leadership would be derived largely from the leader as an individual.

Definition ▶ 2 ***Style theories* suggest that individuals can be identified who possess a general style of leadership that is appropriate to the organisation.** For example, two contrasting styles would be the authoritarian and the democratic: the former imposes the leader's will from the centre and the latter allows free debate before developing a solution. According to the research, this has some validity, but leadership is much more complex than the simplicities of style. For example, it needs to take into account the varied relationships between leaders and subordinates, the politics of decision making in the organisation and the culture of the organisation. Such theories have therefore been downplayed in recent years. Successful leadership here would be defined by the leadership style.

Definition ▶ 3 ***Contingency theories* explore the concept that leaders should be promoted or recruited according to the needs of the organisation at a particular point in time. The choice is contingent on the strategic issues facing the organisation at that time and leaders need to be changed as the situation itself changes.** Thus the leader needs to be seen in relation to the group whom she/he will lead and the nature of the task to be undertaken. For example, recovery-from-disaster strategies will require a different type of leader from the steady development type of strategy. There is some evidence to support this approach, but it is still anecdotal and over-simplifies the leadership task. Successful leadership here would depend on the strategic context and related circumstances.

From a strategic perspective, the contingency theory approach holds the most promise for two reasons. It is the one that best captures both the leader and the relationship with others in the organisation, and it also identifies clearly the importance of the strategic situation as being relevant to the analysis of successful leadership.

Within contingency theory, there is one approach that is particularly used: it is called the *best-fit* analytical approach. This is essentially based on the notion that leaders, subordinates and strategies must reach some compromise if they are to be successfully carried forward. There may be some difference of views but, ultimately, the purpose of the organisation and the strategies to achieve that purpose will best be developed by some agreement between them. This is useful in strategic management because it allows each situation to be treated differently and it identifies three key analytical elements:

1 the chief executive officer or leader;
2 the senior/middle managers who carry out the tasks;
3 the nature of the purpose and strategies that will be undertaken.

Each of these is then plotted on a common scale, ranging from rigid (or heavily structured) to relaxed (or supportive and flexible). The best fit is then sought between these three elements. An example is shown in Figure 16.2. The result is inevitably vague but may prove useful in identifying the balance of style and its influence on people, strategies and purpose.

16.2.3 Successful leadership styles

Leadership style can vary from the *shared vision* approach of Senge to the *dominance* of individuals like the first Henry Ford or Margaret Thatcher in the UK in the late 1980s. Each style will influence the way that purpose is developed and the content that results.

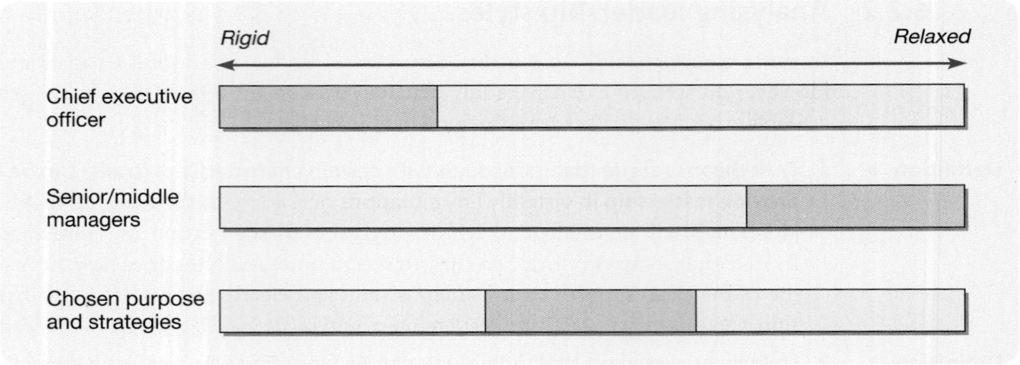

Figure 16.2 An example of the best-fit approach to leadership analysis

The leadership system that best describes the management style of the leader needs to be taken into account in the context of the organisation's purpose and strategy. Where the leader is dominant then she/he will be involved early. Where the leader is more consultative then early involvement will be on a more participative basis.

In essence, leaders and their organisations will wish to consider how they should be led. The choice of leadership style will ultimately depend on a number of factors that go beyond the personality and personal wishes of the individual. Some factors that will influence leadership style are shown in Exhibit 16.1.[13]

EXHIBIT 16.1

Factors influencing the leadership style of organisations

- Personality and skills of leader
- Size of company
- Degree of geographical dispersion
- Stability of organisation's environment
- Current management style of the organisation's culture
- Organisation's current profitability and its desire and need for change

16.2.4 The importance of trust, enthusiasm and commitment – the contribution of Bennis and Nanus

Successful leadership will influence many parts of the organisation. Thus, if leadership is to be successful, it cannot be regarded as just a cold and abstract analytical statement. The leader needs to generate trust, enthusiasm and commitment amongst key members of the organisation for the chosen purpose.

Amongst the most widely read writers on leadership in relation to the tasks of the organisation are Warren Bennis and Burt Nanus. These two US authors researched leadership amongst US organisations in the 1980s. They included failure as well as success and wrote a highly successful book full of short anecdotes and pithy conclusions on leadership and especially its people aspects.[14]

Their conclusions on successful leadership suggest that:

- Leaders need to generate and sustain *trust* in the strategy process and the general integrity of the organisation while developing its vision and mission.
- Leaders will deliver a more robust statement of purpose if they have generated and used the *intellectual capital* of the many people involved in the organisation. This means that leaders have tapped the knowledge, interest and experience of those below them in the organisation.

- Successful leaders need to demonstrate a *passion and determination* to seek out and then achieve the purpose that has been identified by the process.

16.2.5 Conclusions on successful leadership

Airport bookshops are full of leadership texts that claim to identify good leaders and the characteristics that are essential to fulfil such a role. These are usually prescriptive approaches to the leadership task and imply that all good leaders have particular attributes. But such books need to be treated with caution if contingent theories are correct, because such theories suggest that leadership depends on the strategic circumstances of the organisation. There is no one best way.

There is an additional reason for caution. The act of identifying leadership as a prime mover in the development of strategy reduces the role of other elements that are important. For example, team building and family ownership of the company can be equally important factors in certain types of organisation.

KEY STRATEGIC PRINCIPLES

- Leaders can have a profound influence on mission and objectives. They may be particularly important in moving the organisation forward to new challenges. However, in large and complex organisations their role is more likely to be evolutionary than revolutionary.
- There is no agreement on how to analyse leadership. Contingency theories are probably the most useful approach. They state that the choice and style of leadership is *contingent* on the strategic issues facing the organisation at that point in time.
- Within the context of contingency theory, the best-fit analytical approach can be used. It is useful in strategy because it allows each situation to be treated differently.
- Leadership style can vary from shared vision to dominance. The style needs to be modified to suit the strategic situation, with other styles being possible depending on the organisation and its environment.
- With regard to purpose, successful leaders need to generate trust in the strategic process. They need to draw upon the intellectual capital of the organisation and to demonstrate passion and determination.
- In some circumstances, leadership may be better served by allowing the purpose to emerge from the group working on a strategic task, rather than be imposed by the leader from the centre.

CASE STUDY 16.2

Ford Motors: strategy, leadership and strategic change

In 1994, Ford Motors was challenging its competitors with a new volume global strategy based on the Ford brand. By 1999, it had adopted a different strategy of acquiring major brands like Jaguar, Volvo and Land Rover. By 2001, it had sacked its chief executive and gone back to the basic business of delivering profits in its volume car business under Ford. By 2004, Ford had lost its second place in the world car market to Toyota. This case explores what happened, focusing particularly on the 'people' issues.

Ford's international operations

Ford was founded in the USA around the turn of the twentieth century. After rapid and innovatory development in its home country, the company's founder, Henry Ford, set up the first overseas factory in the UK in the late 1920s. Seventy years later, the company had major production facilities in the UK, Germany, Belgium and Spain. But these operations were part of a European Division that worked semi-independently of its US headquarters. In addition, Ford had manufacturing and marketing operations in South America, India and Australasia that were also operated partly independently of the US factory.

There was some central co-ordination, but production and models were still largely confined to a particular continent. The reasons were the need to meet local customer demand in terms of style, price-points and performance. The next sections track Ford's more recent history and strategies.

In terms of organisational culture, the company had several strong characteristics. First, it was still controlled from Detroit by the founding family. The company followed a robust approach to markets and people and, for many years, was more likely to promote Americans into the most senior positions. Henry Ford himself had antagonised the unions in the 1930s. This memory remained into the 1980s with the labour force being strong and well organised. The white-collar office workers were highly dedicated and in a clear hierarchical structure with regard to promotion and work dedication. The company was results-driven and supported those who were high achievers. It was in this context that various stories circulated about the senior managers that are described later in the case, after exploring the history of the company. An analysis of the organisational culture of Ford is shown later in this chapter as Exhibit 16.2: it is an integral part of this case.

Ford 1994 – global strategy project called 'Ford 2000' initiated by Alex Trotman

For many years, Ford had been attracted by the idea of a 'global' car. There were three good reasons for thinking that globalisation would deliver major benefits:

1 Major economies of scale and scope were expected in production.

2 Global manufacturers were able to negotiate global sourcing of car components, which would also deliver substantial additional cost savings.

3 Research and development on new models had become substantial, typically $8 billion. Spreading this cost across more production would bring down the cost per vehicle and also save duplication costs.

However, this would require massive reorganisation and co-ordination across a company as large as Ford, so it was not a project to embark upon lightly. In 1994, the company's chief executive, Alex Trotman, therefore launched a totally new project called 'Ford 2000'. Its objective was to develop a fully integrated global company by the year 2000. It was expected that there would be annual cost savings of $2–3 billion by the end of the decade and that this would present a serious challenge to Ford's competitors, like General Motors (USA) and Toyota (Japan). The Ford plan was put into operation in early 1995 and involved integrating all its operations into one company. Core engineering and production were simplified in order to achieve considerable savings. New models were designed around a reduced number of platforms that would also save funds. Jacques Nasser was put in charge of Ford's global automotive operations to implement the changes. He was so successful at killing off unprofitable vehicles, cutting costs and pressing suppliers and dealers for lower costs that he became known as 'Jack the Knife'. Substantial savings were made and Nasser was promoted to chief executive officer of the worldwide Ford Motor Company in 1999.

Ford 1999 – global niche strategy with Jacques Nasser

Nasser then went on to oversee another major change in strategy in the company – the global niche strategy. He argued that there was a shift in car demand across the world towards *niche* car markets – 4-wheel drive off-road vehicles, people carriers, small luxury town cars, sports cars, etc. Moreover, such vehicles had higher profit margins than the traditional Ford business of volume cars – like the Mondeo and Ka. 'What you're seeing are niche cultures,' explained Nasser. Customers want more than a metal box that stops and starts and looks just like the neighbour's car. For Ford, the new trend in customer niche strategy is 'a marvellous business opportunity'.

To meet such demand variations, the company under Mr Nasser embarked on at least five further ventures that would not even use the Ford brand name:

1 *Acquisition and development of Jaguar Cars.* Ford had bought the luxury company in the late 1980s and then spent billions of dollars developing new models, refitting factories and other activities. It kept the marque separate from its Ford 2000 project in order to emphasise the special niche. By the late 1990s, Jaguar had launched a series of models that were well received by the press and were attacking a market niche in which Ford had previously hardly any representation, namely the luxury segment of Mercedes-Benz, Rolls-Royce and Toyota's Lexus.

2 *Development of the Lincoln.* Ford had some representation in the luxury segment in the USA only under the Lincoln name. Another development under consideration was to introduce some of the leading Lincoln models to other parts of the world.

3 *Acquisition of Volvo Cars.* This Swedish company was acquired by Ford in 1999 for $6.5 billion in order to increase its representation in the upper market segments, where it had previously been only partially successful. Again, this would tackle new market niches where its rivals were stronger – for example, BMW and Mercedes-Benz. But, in this case, it would also deliver major cost savings in purchasing and logistics.

4 *Acquisition of Land Rover.* The British 4-wheel drive company was also bought by Ford in 1999 for $2.8 billion and used to develop its interests in this specialist car area. As with the other purchases above, Ford invested substantial new investment in people and machinery to modernise existing plant and develop new models over a number of years.

5 *Acquisition of KwikFit and consolidation of control of Hertz.* The European tyre, battery and exhaust-fitting company, KwikFit, was bought by Ford in the late 1990s for $1 billion in order to offer customers a complete range of services.

Henry Ford was the founder of mass car manufacturing and his legacy remains with the controlling interest of the present generation of the Ford family.

The company's link with the car rental company Hertz was also extended to take control of that company.

The new acquisitions were grouped together as a separate part of Ford, called the 'Premier Automotive Group'. The five-pronged global-niche strategy outlined above was expected to increase Ford's unit sales from 250,000 in 1998 to 750,000 in 2000. The new group was expected to deliver one-third of Ford's profits by 2005. Moreover, such sales would carry higher profit margins than those of its volume car range.

Ford 2001 and after – 'back to basics' strategy with Sir Nick Scheele and Bill Ford

In practice, the acquisitions did not work. The 'global niche' strategy took Ford's strategic focus away from its major activity of making profitable volume cars under the Ford brand name. The result was a profit disaster in 2001 – see Table 16.2. Although Nasser had not been solely responsible for the strategy, he paid the price and was asked to leave suddenly in late 2001. 'The board had reached a conclusion and, in reaching that conclusion, the sooner we told Jac [Nasser] the better,' said Sir Nick Scheele, the former chairman of Ford Europe and new chief operating officer. 'What we need is to get back to basics. We have had a terrible year for a variety of unrelated circumstances, but we have to move on.'

The Ford family – still important minority shareholders in the Ford company – had become increasingly disenchanted with the strategy, which was simply not delivering the company's objectives. Bill Ford, grandson of the founder Henry Ford, took over as chairman and chief executive of Ford. He then began an immediate drive to cut costs very substantially across every part of the Ford company. He focused on Ford's main business activities in North America and Europe:

- *Problems in North America.* A major cost-cutting exercise was begun in 2000 in North America to restore the profitability of this part of the company. Essentially, it was decided to axe five plants and 22,000 jobs in North America. Ford would also downsize activities at another 11 plants. In addition, it would also cut four low-profit models and sell $1 billion of non-core assets and cut the company dividend by one-third. The new chairman, Bill Ford, explained with the benefit of hindsight: 'We pursued strategies that were either poorly conceived or poorly timed. We strayed from what got us to the top of the mountain and it cost us dearly.'
- *Problems in Europe.* For all the claims about the new global strategy, the reality was that Ford's European market share was dropping alarmingly – down from 12 per cent in 1994 to 8.7 per cent in 2000. Coupled with plant inefficiencies, this caused the company to show a $1 billion loss in Europe in 2000. Radical action was therefore taken to cut capacity, with plant closures in the UK, Portugal, Poland and Belarus and plant cutbacks in most of Ford's other European plants. Global strategy did not appear to form a significant part of the European cutbacks.

In addition, Ford suffered a major drain on profits as it coped with the Firestone tyre debacle: some Ford cars fitted with Firestone tyres were involved in accidents that were blamed on the tyres and both Ford and Firestone were sued for damages. Moreover, Ford also became engaged in a price war on a number of its basic volume models and its cost base was too high to respond and still make a profit. Then came the tragic events of September 11 and the economic downturn in the USA. Over the next few years, Ford also faced increased pressure from its main US competitors, especially General Motors and Chrysler (part of DaimlerChrysler). In addition, Ford faced heavy competition from Toyota in Europe as the

Table 16.2 Ford sales and profits for the period 1999–2003 ($ millions)

Sales	2003	2002	2001	2000	1999
Sales	164,196	162,256	160,504	168,930	160,053
Net income/(loss)*	495	(980)	(5,453)	3,467	7,237
Total assets	315,920	295,222	276,543	283,390	270,249

* After tax and interest.

Source: annual report and accounts.

Japanese company began to build its market share in that continent. Toyota's Camry model was already the largest single selling model in the USA. By the end of 2004, Ford had lost its position as second largest car company in the world to Toyota: the web-based case 'Toyota: does it rely too heavily on production for world leadership' attached to Part 6 of the book picks up the story. Clearly this had a significant impact on the organisational culture and morale of the company around that time.

What happened next?

After a difficult period during the years up to 2009, Ford recovered well by focusing on its basic car range and sorting out its American and European operations. By 2011, it was probably the strongest of the American headquartered car companies.

Ford has been investing heavily in green strategy with regard to car design and new models. This is described in Case 14.3 earlier in this book.

Case questions

1 What were the main arguments put forward by the chief executives for the various Ford strategies over the past 10 years?
2 How did the various changes impact on leadership and human resources at Ford?
3 When a company makes a major shift in strategy, does it need to change its leader?

16.3 HOW LEADERSHIP ROLES CHANGE OVER TIME

As the Ford Motors case clearly shows, leaders change over time. But leadership roles can change even while the same leader remains at the head of the organisation. The previous section identified some important characteristics of various kinds of leaders. However, leaders are not static in their relationships both inside and outside the organisation. It is useful to consider this under two headings: changes of time and changes in relationship to two important groups of stakeholders.

16.3.1 How the leadership role changes over time

We know that leaders can shape organisations by influencing and directing the beliefs, style and values of those inside and outside the organisation. For example, Ford Motor Company encouraged and rewarded employees and managers who delivered results. Equally, Ford was quite ruthless in the way that it dealt with its chief executive officer, Jac Nasser, who failed to deliver on high-value acquisitions and to solve the substantial problems in the volume cars division. These decisions reflect the culture and values of the company, just as much as the immediate strategic issues that arise. Equally, they show how leadership roles can change from company expansion through acquisition to cost cutting to improve profitability.

Typically, the Chief Executive Officer of a major company will stay in the position for only five years – often much less. Research[16] has shown that the role of the leader will change during this time:

- *Early tenure.* The CEO learns rapidly and is willing to take risks. The leader declares any losses in the business in the first year. The responsibility for such losses is blamed on the previous CEO. The new CEO usually desires to bring a new perspective. Change is likely.
- *Mid-term tenure.* New initiatives continue, especially in the areas of expanding knowledge and skills. The performance of the organisation should improve with a range of set routines – called *heuristics* in Section 11.5.4. Change is less likely unless there are strong external pressures from competitors or technology.
- *Late tenure.* The leader is more likely to be committed to obsolete business models. The company may become risk averse and stale. There is only slow adaptation to external changes with a consequent loss of performance (and profits).

16.3.2 The changing leadership role with two key stakeholders

Changing CEO relationships can usefully also be considered in relation to two stakeholder groups: employees and customers. These relationships can change over time. They matter because employees deliver the strategy and customers buy the products or services.

In the early years of an appointment, the new CEO seeks information from a number of sources and engages in learning – perhaps by visiting customers and walking around various factory or office premises to meet employees. The aim is to understand and strengthen relationships with both stakeholder groups.

Later, strong CEOs have more comfortable and ongoing relationships both inside and outside the firm. This can lead to a united and committed workforce with trusted channels of communication. But it can also mean that the CEO is not picking up important changes amongst employees. Moreover, it may also lead to a disconnect with outside customers, markets and technologies.

What does this mean for strategy development and leadership? Leaders change over time. Their relationships with important stakeholders change so that they may no longer see how the external environment changes. There is a real danger of missing important developments. Some of these issues are captured in Exhibit 16.2 which analyses how Ford's leadership and culture changed as it was forced into a major change in strategy in 2001.

EXHIBIT 16.2

Leadership and culture at Ford Motor Company as it started to go 'Back to Basics' in 2001[17]

Environment:

- Highly competitive world market.
- Legacy issues in the USA as Ford coped with commitments to its former employees on health and pensions - profit pressures on the company.
- 'Green' issues surrounding car emissions.

Cultural factors specific to the organisation:

- History and ownership: highly significant - one of the founders of modern America - still strong family connections.
- Size: worldwide, complex, many interlinking parts.
- Technology: sophisticated but mature technology in petrol engines.
- Leadership and mission: strong vision for the future, but stumbled as leader sacked and new chief executive took over.
- Cultural web:
  - *Stories.* Too early for clear development but the new chief executive, Bill Ford, was inexperienced and therefore supported by a chief operating officer from Europe, who was well known - Sir Nick Scheele. The story of the actual sacking of the former chief officer, Jacques Nasser, was told in vivid detail around the company. Just a week before his sacking, stories were circulating that Nasser was laughing off his reported demise: 'It would be like someone saying you're about to be moved, and you know nothing about it.'
  - *Routines.* New routines were introduced to turn around the business - special meetings were called for all senior executives at the company's head offices. They were totally non-routine to emphasise the seriousness of the situation.
  - *Rituals.* The departure of Nasser was announced at a special employee meeting. Bill Ford's announcement 'received a standing ovation from cheering and whooping employees at Ford headquarters'.

- *Symbols*. The meeting rooms – called 'energy rooms' – to devise the new back-to-basics Ford strategy were not designed to be comfortable. Executives summoned to such meetings were told to make only brief presentations and given a simple agenda – 'Tell us how you are going to cut costs.'
- *Organisation*. A totally new team was set up to develop a revised cost-cutting strategy between November 2001 and the announcement of the new strategy in January 2002. This would be followed by thousands of job losses, the closure of four US car plants and the sale of non-core activities like KwikFit.
- *Control*. Some new controls were introduced, but the Ford system already had substantial systems for the monitoring of performance.
- *Rewards*. Given the nature of the crisis, the 'reward' was to keep your job. At the time of Nasser's departure, 20 top managers 'decided to retire', were reassigned to other jobs or were replaced.
- *Power*. A major power battle took place in the run-up to the sacking of Nasser. This was then followed by a period of stability that would see power concentrated such that the proposed changes could be made over the following three years to 2004–2005.

Identification of the basic cultural style of the organisation:

- Role culture: the large size of the Ford company makes this highly likely.
- But major new projects are sometimes conducted with task culture.

Strategic implications:

- Change likely to be slow, prescriptive and complex.
- Most decisions are taken under pressure as the company attempts to restore its profitability.
- Stakeholders such as managers, employees and union representatives will expect to be consulted.
- Shareholders and financial institutions will expect short-term action to halt profit problems.
- Note there is potential for conflict between the last two points above – employees and financial institutions.

KEY STRATEGIC PRINCIPLES

- Leadership roles change over time. In the early years, Chief Executive Officers (CEOs) learn rapidly and are willing to take risks. In the mid-term, they develop new initiatives and expand their knowledge and skills. Towards the end of their tenure, they may become risk averse and have difficulty in adapting to external change.
- Changing CEO relationships can be considered in relation to two key stakeholders: employees and customers. In the early years, the CEO will listen and learn from both employees and customers. Later, relationships become more formalised and comfortable with the possible danger that there will be a disconnect with outside important changes.

16.4 HOW LEADERS COPE WITH POWER

As strategic change occurs, leaders of organisations will have to cope with individuals and groups who are likely to have an active interest in the process. There may be pressure groups, rivalries, power barons and brokers, influencers, arguments, winners and losers. Some disputes may be disinterested and rational and some may be governed by strongly held views and interests. All these areas constitute the power issues of the organisation. **Power is therefore concerned with the exercise of authority, leadership and management in organisations.** Strategic change cannot be separated from such issues.

Definition ▶

If new strategies are resisted, then leadership power needs to take a pragmatic view of what is possible rather than what is ideal. For example, it may be highly desirable to alter radically a company's structure, but the cost in terms of management time may be too high in some circumstances, even with an imposed solution from the leadership. An analysis of the organisation's power situation is important as strategies are developed. Case 12.2 on Royal Dutch/Shell shows the difficulties that faced the new chairman of Royal Dutch/Shell in 2004 as he attempted to achieve radical change and impose his preferred solutions on the organisation.

16.4.1 What are the main elements of power in organisations?

As a starting point, leaders first need to recognise that it may be wishful thinking to attempt to 'manage change' in the sense of identifying where the organisation is heading and instructing everyone to take that route.[18] Leaders may find it more realistic and rewarding to 'cultivate change'. Research suggests that leadership power may be better directed towards encouraging a positive attitude to change, coupled with learning and persuasion.

There is nothing wrong with healthy competition between groups and individuals in an organisation. It can stretch performance and help groups to become more cohesive. It also helps to sort out the best. The difficulty arises when it gives rise to conflict and political manoeuvring. Leaders need to recognise that there are two principal reasons for organisational conflict:

1. *Differing goals and ideologies*. For example, different groups or individuals within an organisation may have different goals, make different value judgements, be given different and conflicting objectives, etc. There may also be a lack of clarity in the goals and objectives. It should be possible in the context of strategic change to ensure that conflict and confusion over goals are minimised.
2. *Threats to territory*. For example, some groups or individuals may feel threatened by others doing the same jobs, become jealous of other roles, be given instructions that cut across other responsibilities, etc. It is in this area that the greatest strategic difficulty is likely to arise. If savings are to be made or improved performance to be obtained, then it may be necessary to accept the conflict here.

Addressing the strategic change issue, Mintzberg[19] suggests that there are benefits from competition in organisations. It can be a force for achieving change. In this sense, power is an inevitable consequence of strategic change and needs to be accepted and channelled by the organisation's leadership for the best results.

16.4.2 How can leaders cope with power issues?

Right at the start of any strategic change process, leaders must clarify the organisation's objectives and the implications for individual parts of the organisation. If it is true that conflict arises as a result of confusion over objectives, then it follows that these need to be fully explored before other matters are raised.

In addition, five areas need to be addressed by the organisation's leadership:

1. *The extent to which the organisation has developed a culture of adaptation or experiment.* Such an approach will help when it comes to implementing agreed strategies later.
2. *The identification of major power groups or individuals* whose influence and support are essential for any major strategic change.
3. *The desirability or necessity of consultation rather than confrontation*, as the strategic analytical process continues.
4. *The role and traditions of leadership in the organisation* and the extent to which this may enhance the success and overcome problems associated with strategic change.
5. *The nature and scope of the external pressures on the organisation.*

These five areas are interconnected as a network of relationships – see Figure 16.3.

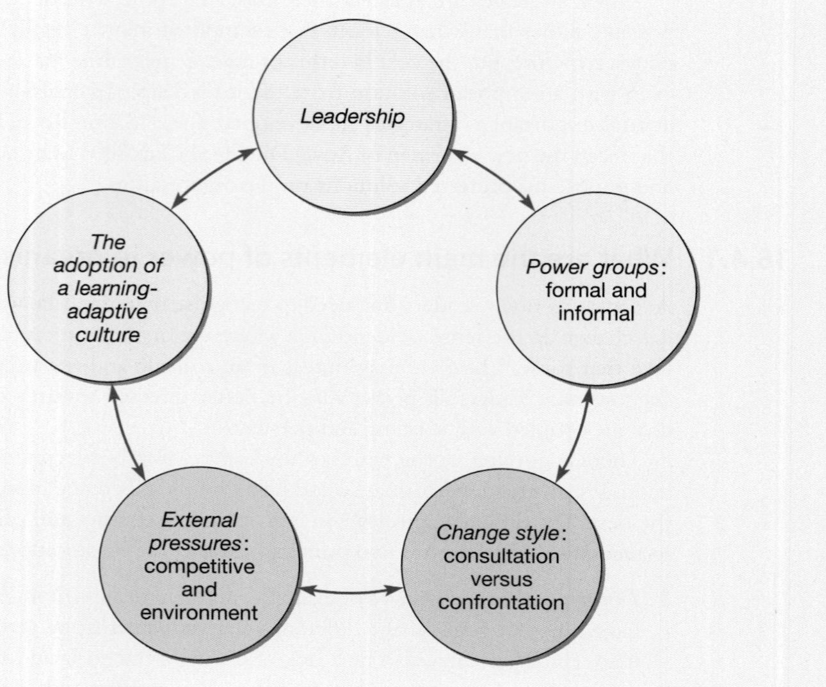

Figure 16.3 The political network of an organisation

KEY STRATEGIC PRINCIPLES

- Leaders need to consider what is possible in terms of change, just as much as what is desirable. They do not necessarily have unlimited power.
- Competition is healthy in organisations, except when it degenerates into unhealthy conflict and political manoeuvring.
- In working out how to cope with power issues, leaders need to survey power groups, leadership, the change style of the organisation, the adoption of a learning-adaptive culture and the nature of the external pressures.

CASE STUDY 16.3

Daimler: how three leaders influenced strategy

In 1985, the new chairman of Daimler – Edzard Reuter – developed a new strategy for the future of the company. Over the next 10 years, it turned out to be flawed. In 1995, the next new chairman of Daimler – Jurgen Schrempp – revised the strategy. In 2005, he resigned after the strategy again proved unsound. In 2005, another new chairman of the company – Dieter Zetsche – developed another new strategy for the company. At the time of writing, Zetsche was having some success. . . .

Daimler under Edzard Reuter: 1985–1995

When Edzard Reuter became Chairman of Daimler 1985, he became leader of a company that had been making quality cars for many years. With the support of its powerful shareholder, Deutsche Bank, Reuter soon announced a major shift in strategy. Daimler was to become an 'integrated technology group'. It would use its highly profitable cars and trucks to fund a strategic move into other businesses, whose main connection with the car business would be shared technology.

Over the next four years, the company spent $4.7 billion building an industrial conglomerate that made the group into the third largest company in Europe in terms of total sales. It acquired companies in the following areas:

- *Aerospace and defence* – Messerschmitt-Bolkow-Blohm, Dornier, Fokker as well as investing in Airbus.
- *Electrical engineering, electronics, rail engineering and domestic appliances* – AEG.
- *Financial services and software* – Debis.

The reasons for the shift in strategic thinking were essentially linked to a new vision of the company. Reuter decided that Daimler would emulate the highly successful Japanese and American conglomerates such as Mitsubishi and General Electric. Daimler was also keen to develop German industry as a global power in high-technology companies and to transform the European aerospace industry, where it could see real opportunities.

The process was seen to be a long-term move to develop Daimler into new areas that would be *mutually supportive* through technology. For example, as car pollution and traffic flow became greater problems in European cities, the vision was that cities would seek new ways to balance public and private transport. Daimler-Benz would draw up the new strategy for a city through its Dornier subsidiary, build the trains at AEG, the buses at Daimler-Benz and the new traffic control systems at TEMIC, which was a joint venture between AEG and Daimler Aerospace (Dasa). This process would require careful and complex co-ordination of the various large subsidiaries of the group by the centre. At the same time, each of these subsidiaries had its own product ranges to develop and sell: cars, aircraft, electronics, etc.

If all these aspects seem rather vague and unconvincing, they appeared that way to some employees at the time. They resented the interference from the centre in individual businesses. For example, the then chairman of Deutsche Aerospace, Jurgen Schrempp, was on public record[20] as describing the Daimler-Benz headquarters in Stuttgart as 'Bullshit castle'.

During the period 1985–1995, there were several unforeseen events in the environment that made it difficult for the company:

- German currency became even stronger, making Daimler's exports more expensive.
- Just as Daimler was investing in aerospace and defence, the political situation changed. There were substantial defence cutbacks as the cold war between the USSR and the West was reduced.
- The mid-range aircraft market took a major downturn with the acquisition of Dornier being particularly expensive and ill-judged.

In addition, the most expensive acquisition of the expansion period, AEG, proved to have some major difficulties. These related to the culture of the companies acquired, which were not easy to assimilate into the new group. In addition, it was judged that the product ranges were too broad and needed more focus: AEG was producing everything from nuclear power stations to refrigerators and typewriters. There was no attempt to focus on core areas of strength. The result was that

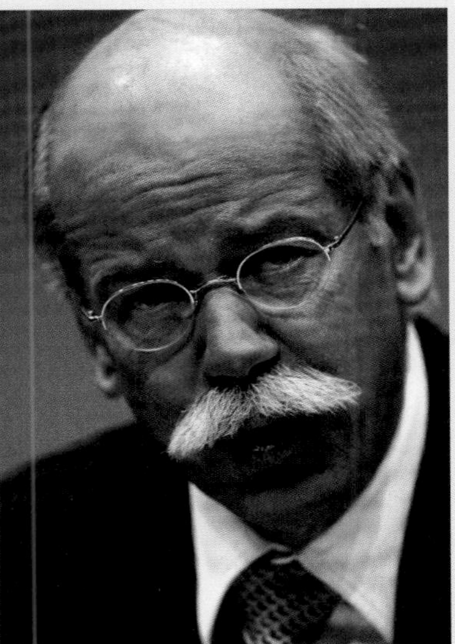

Daimler's strategy has changed radically under its three chief executives: from left to right, Edzard Reuter, Jurgen Schrempp and Dieter Zetsche.

between 1990 and 1995 AEG made a cumulative loss of around DM3.7 billion ($2 billion).

During the late 1980s and early 1990s, the profits from Daimler-Benz cars and trucks continued to subsidise much of the above. In 1995, the situation had become so bad that more drastic action was required. Edzard Deutz retired from the company. Daimler-Benz effectively transferred some assets of AEG to other subsidiaries and closed the rump of the company. It also withdrew its financial support from Fokker, the Dutch aircraft maker which was forced to close. However, Daimler continued its development of Airbus. The company had begun to define its new strategy as being essentially involved in *transport-based manufacture*. A new chairman was then appointed: Jürgen Schrempp from Dasa.

Daimler under its leader Jürgen Schrempp: 1995–2005

When Jürgen Schrempp took over as chairman of Daimler in 1995, the German group lacked focus strategically. It had the benefit of the well-regarded and highly profitable Daimler-Benz car and truck range, but also contained a loss-making aircraft manufacturing subsidiary, Fokker, and numerous other subsidiaries making everything from traffic lights to freezer cabinets; many of these units also had low profitability. Schrempp rescued the group by focusing on the car and truck business and selling the rest. But his vision went further than merely developing a profitable German transport manufacturing operation. He wanted to build a *global* car and truck company.

After considering various possibilities (including the acquisition of the Japanese car company Nissan), Schrempp did the deal in 1998 that would in his words 'change the face of the industry forever'. Daimler acquired the company that was third in the American market, Chrysler, for $38 billion. Although some commentators regarded the price as excessive, Daimler-Benz was very happy with the price of its North American purchase. Schrempp commented: 'We'll have the size, profitability and the reach to take on everyone.'

Around the same time, Daimler continued to pursue its global ambitions by buying 34 per cent of the Japanese car company Mitsubishi and taking a 10 per cent stake in the Korean car company Hyundai. In addition, Daimler also acquired further companies to support its truck interests in North America and elsewhere. The company also continued its programme of new models for its Mercedes flagship brand. Finally, it launched in Europe and America a new small car with the brand name Smart, using a totally new dealer network. The company was re-named DaimlerChrysler.

Unfortunately, although the German Daimler operation remained highly profitable, the Chrysler acquisition and joint ventures started to go wrong. In 2000, there were major problems over unsold cars and the slow introduction of new models. Moreover, the company culture of the German parent – technocratic, planned and precise – was at odds with the Chrysler culture – entrepreneurial, opportunistic and informal. The acquisition, which had originally been presented as a 'merger between equals', rapidly became a straight takeover. The American Chrysler Chairman and other senior colleagues left the company and Daimler put in its own top management team. The German company was determined to combine operations, cut costs and return to high profits. One of the parent company's top managers, Dieter Zetsche, was made managing director at Chrysler. But the new approach did not produce instant results – even in 2003, Chrysler was reporting a 12 per cent drop in sales and a $1.1 billion operating loss as new models were late coming to market and competition was increasing.

Around this time, Daimler's interest in Mitsubishi began to turn sour. In the late 1990s, DaimlerChrysler had identified Mitsubishi as an important partner in its global strategy and had paid $3 billion for a 37 per cent share of the Japanese company. Unfortunately for Daimler, its Japanese partner then ran into trouble with the Japanese government and with customers over quality and other issues. After considering the matter, Daimler decided to end its relationship with the Japanese company, despite the hole that this would leave in the German company's global strategy. It simply did not believe that it would get the returns it required, according to Manfred Gentz, finance director at Daimler.

Around one month later, DaimlerChrysler also ended its broad alliance with the South Korean car manufacturer Hyundai. The German company had acquired a 10 per cent share of the Korean company in 2000 for around $400 million. Daimler was able to sell for around $1 billion so it made a good profit. The problem was that Hyundai and DaimlerChrysler were unable to complete plans for a joint venture to manufacture commercial vehicles in South Korea. In addition, Hyundai had ambitions for its Chinese operations that were in conflict with those of the German company – essentially, they were competing in the Chinese market and this was unacceptable to Daimler. Again, this meant that another part of the DaimlerChrysler global strategy had ended.

In addition to all the other difficulties, the basic and highly profitable operations of its German subsidiary – Mercedes-Benz – were in trouble. In summary, these were:

- German manufacturing costs were too high.
- The new small Smart car was not meeting sales targets and was unprofitable.
- Mercedes models, especially the E-class, were subject to significant quality problems.

When interviewed in 2003, Schrempp had no doubts about the original merger with Chrysler: 'I still believe that our merger of equals was fantastic . . . we are making tremendous progress,' he said. The chief executive continued to receive the full backing of his executive board in spite of the difficulties that had arisen.

Daimler under its leader Dieter Zetsche: 2005 to the present

In mid-2005, it was announced by DaimlerChrysler that Schrempp was to step down as chief executive in late 2005. This was almost two years early. He was to be replaced by Dieter Zetsche, who had previously been responsible for the supposed turnaround at the company's US Chrysler Division.

Like the previous leaders of Daimler, Zetsche had a strategy for the company. He judged that it should focus primarily on its highly profitable German operations. He therefore proceeded to negotiate the sale of the US Chrysler operation to a group of merchant banks for $20 billion. Daimler retained a minority interest in the American company, but essentially Chrysler was allowed to operate as an independent company. The company was renamed Daimler again.

Reuter's strategy for the company was long forgotten. Schrempp's strategy for a global company was finally dead. Daimler had a new strategy developed by its new leader, Dieter Zetsche. Daimler was to be the leading car company in the quality and highly profitable premium car segment of the world car market.

Daimler has a strong policy on green strategy. Some elements of this are described in Case 14.3 earlier in this book.

Case questions

1 What were the three strategies of the leaders of Daimler? To what extent do each of the strategies fit with well-known strategy theories such as the competitive environment (Chapter 3), the resource-based view (Chapter 4), knowledge-based theories (Chapter 7) and theories about strategic management (Chapter 9)?

2 To what extent did the new strategies appear to derive primarily from the leader at the time? And to what extent were they justified by the strategic logic of the time?

3 Do powerful leaders make for powerful company strategy?

16.5 SUCCESSFUL STRATEGIC LEADERSHIP

There are five key subject areas that leaders need to address for successful and effective leadership (see Figure 16.4). We examine each of these in turn in this section.

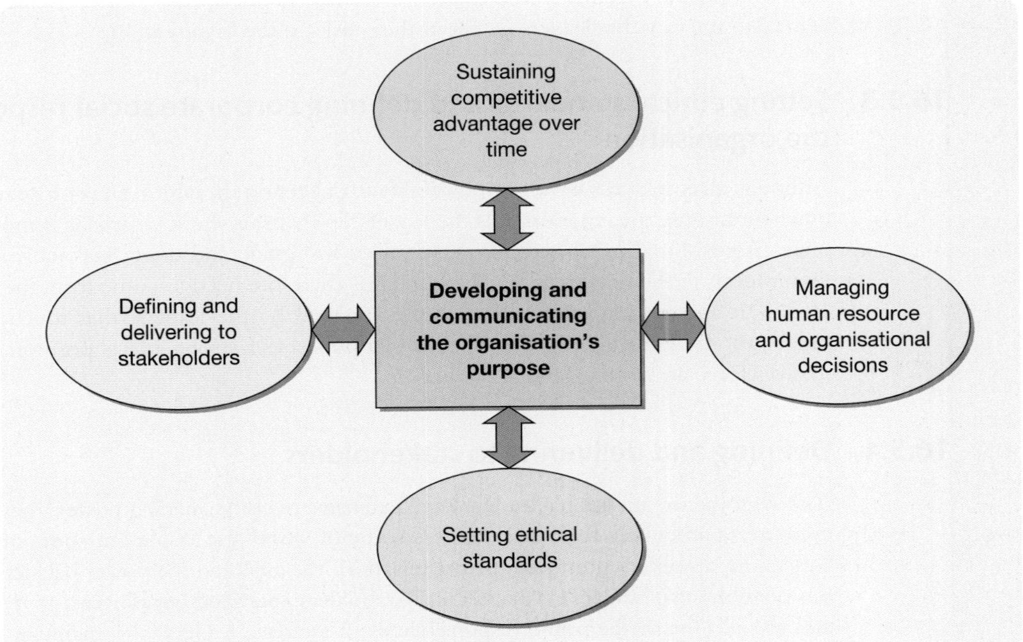

Figure 16.4 The five elements of successful and effective strategic leadership

16.5.1 Developing and communicating the organisation's purpose

In the first instance, strategic leaders are primarily tasked with determining the organisation's purpose and then communicating this to every part of the organisation. We explored the content of purpose in Chapters 6 and 7. In practice, this content is driven by the leaders of the organisation.[22] However, they do not normally do this alone: they will consult widely and gather contributions from many managers in the organisation. For example, DaimlerChrysler had extensive discussions both inside and outside the company with regard to its purpose of becoming a global leader in the car market and its acquisition of the Chrysler car company to achieve this. However, there may be occasions when it is inappropriate to engage in wide consultation – for example, during a takeover bid or company disposal when financial market rules may make such consultation difficult.

16.5.2 Managing human resource and organisation decisions

In addition to defining and developing purpose, strategic leaders need to motivate and reward managers and employees to deliver the agreed purpose. This forms an important part of the human resource decisions of the company.

Definition ▶ **Human resources are the skills, talents and knowledge of every member of the organisation.** Strategic leaders have a special responsibility to direct, develop and nurture employees in the organisation. For many strategists, human resources are one of the key competitive advantages of companies.[23] This means that one of the important leadership tasks must be to find, select and keep key employees.[24] For example, DaimlerChrysler has had an extensive management development programme for many years. It resulted in the identification of two of its recent chief executives, Jurgen Schrempp and Dieter Zetsche. In addition, the company also devotes substantial resources to hiring, selecting and training employees at all levels of the organisation – this is part of its ongoing purpose.

While people skills are vital, leaders also need to recognise that they have an equal responsibility to develop and maintain the culture of the organisation. We explored this issue earlier in this chapter, recognising the crucial role of leaders in setting the tone, atmosphere and standards that surround organisational culture.

Finally, strategic leadership will involve the reporting relationships and organisational structure that bind people together in the company.[25] These issues were explored in Chapter 12 and remain central to the way that leaders go about their tasks in the organisation.

16.5.3 Setting ethical standards and defining corporate social responsibility in the organisation[26]

Although all employees have a responsibility to deliver on the ethical and corporate social responsibility issues in the organisation, it is the leadership that sets the standards and monitors the achievement. As explored in Chapter 6, these values will guide and direct key activities – even at quite junior levels in the organisation. The standards therefore need to come from the top and be associated with an ongoing ethical programme, initiated by the leaders, that touches everyone in the organisation.[27] For example, DaimlerChrysler publishes a strong ethical position on key issues to all its workforce and to the general public.

16.5.4 Defining and delivering to stakeholders

Although the organisation's leaders have extensive decision-making power, they also have outside pressures, particularly from stakeholders some of whom are inside but some of whom have great bargaining power from outside the organisation. We explored the power balance amongst the various possible stakeholders in Chapter 6: shareholders, managers, employees, government institutions and so on. One of the prime responsibilities of strategic leaders is to maintain good relationships with such interested groups.[28] This will partly come from delivering year-end profits and dividends to shareholders in a commercial organisation and remuneration increases to employees and managers.

However, in practice, the relationship is more subtle and complex. For example, it is likely to involve dealing with financial institutions over raising new finance, share dividend policy, acquisitions and forms of co-operation. Equally, it can easily entail such issues as government negotiations on tax liabilities, government grants and employee prospects. For example, the demerger of Chrysler from the group was accompanied by extensive sessions at very senior levels with government, trade unions, commercial banks, merchant banks and key shareholders.

One of the major issues for strategic leadership is to prioritise the various demands on time and resource. This requires judgement and experience coupled with the use of outside advisers – often involving a public relations company. Professional help in dealing with these matters has become an important part of strategic leadership for virtually every organisation – large and small.

16.5.5 Sustaining competitive advantage over time

In Chapter 4, we explored the relationship between the value added by an organisation and its competitive advantage. In essence, organisations that wish to increase their value added can do this by increasing their competitive advantage. Hence, if strategic leadership is at least partially about growing the organisation's value over time, it is also about increasing the same organisation's competitive advantages. It is the responsibility of the organisation's leadership to preserve and enhance the competitive advantages of the organisation.[29]

In practice, this means activities like maintaining and improving products or service quality, enhancing the reputation of the organisation and investing in new company strategies across a range of activities.[30] It may also entail acquisitions and joint ventures, but leaders need to think carefully before moving into new areas that do not enhance competitive advantage. For example, it was not clear at the upmarket Daimler car company why the acquisition of the downmarket Chrysler brand would enhance the group's image. This underlines the important task that falls to the leadership to identify correctly the key competitive advantages and then to enhance them further.

KEY STRATEGIC PRINCIPLES

- In the first instance, strategic leaders are primarily tasked with determining the organisation's purpose and then communicating this to every part of the organisation.
- Strategic leaders have a special responsibility to select, nurture and develop employees in the organisation, especially those that are key to the organisation. They have a special responsibility to motivate and reward such employees. In addition, strategic leaders need to develop the culture of the organisation and to structure the reporting relationships that bind the company together.
- One of the key leadership tasks is to set and monitor the ethical and corporate social responsibility standards of the organisation. Such values need to come from the top.
- A prime role of strategic leaders is to maintain good relationships with stakeholders both inside and outside the organisation. Typically, there are multiple demands on the leaders' time and resource so leaders must judge how to handle this. Outside advisers have become increasingly common in helping senior leaders in such tasks.
- It is the responsibility of the organisation's leadership to preserve and enhance the competitive advantages of the organisation. Strategic leaders need to identify and support the key advantages of their organisations.

STRATEGIC PROJECT

The impact of new technology on such companies over the past ten years has made a substantial impact on human resource strategy. You might like to investigate other companies where there has been a similar change – for example, Kodak, which has been undermined by the collapse of the film business as cameras have become digital. You could consider the difficulties faced by national telephone companies as mobile telephones have gained in popularity and, in some countries like China and parts of Africa, come to dominate the market. You could first establish the basic situation by looking at the profit record of the companies themselves – often available on the web – and then follow this up by looking for public pronouncements, newspaper stories about changes in personnel and management.

CRITICAL REFLECTION

To what extent should leaders drive strategy from the centre?

In searching for the best leadership style, the early Chinese writer Lao Tsu argues:

> The wicked leader is he who people despise.
>
> The good leader is he who people revere.
>
> The great leader is he who the people say, 'We did it ourselves.'
>
> Lao Tsu

But is 'We did it ourselves' the best way for leaders to behave? Should they be more proactive and drive strategy from the centre of the organisation? The Xerox and Daimler cases both show that leaders can drive strategy from the centre, rather than rely on strategy initiatives from others lower down in their organisations. There is clearly some merit in this approach, which contrasts with the advice from Lao Tsu.

Perhaps a balance can be struck between the leader and the subordinates. But are there any guidelines? Do leaders always have to take final responsibility? What does 'leader' mean if the subordinates make all the major strategic decisions?

SUMMARY

- Strategic leadership is the ability to shape the organisation's decisions and deliver high value over time, not only personally but also by inspiring and managing others in the organisation. Leadership not only involves the chief executive but the whole team at the head of an organisation.
- Leadership involves balancing a number of factors relating to strategy. These include the outside influences that impact on the organisation, from changes in the economy to increased competition. At the same time, leadership also means inspiring and leading people inside the organisation with a clear direction for its future. Ultimately, skilled leadership entails identifying and delivering the purpose of the organisation.
- Leaders can have a profound influence on mission and objectives. They may be particularly important in moving the organisation forward to new challenges. However, in large and complex organisations their role is more likely to be evolutionary than revolutionary.
- There is no agreement on how to analyse leadership. Contingency theories are probably the most useful approach. They state that the choice and style of leadership is *contingent* on the strategic issues facing the organisation at that point in time.
- Within the context of contingency theory, the best-fit analytical approach can be used. It is useful in strategy because it allows each situation to be treated differently.

- Leadership style can vary from shared vision to dominance. The style needs to be modified to suit the strategic situation, with other styles being possible depending on the organisation and its environment.
- With regard to purpose, successful leaders need to generate trust in the strategic process. They need to draw upon the intellectual capital of the organisation and to demonstrate passion and determination. In some circumstances, leadership may be better served by allowing the purpose to emerge from the group working on a strategic task, rather than be imposed by the leader from the centre.
- Leadership role change over time. In the early years, Chief Executive Officers (CEOs) learn rapidly and are willing to take risks. In the mid-term, they develop new initiatives and expand their knowledge and skills. Towards the end of their tenure, they may become risk averse and have difficulty in adapting to external change.
- Changing CEO relationships can be considered in relation to two key stakeholders: employees and customers. In the early years, the CEO will listen and learn from both employees and customers. Later, relationships become more formalised and comfortable with the possible danger that there will be a disconnect with outside important changes.
- Leaders need to consider what is possible in terms of change, just as much as what is desirable. They do not necessarily have unlimited power. Competition is healthy in organisations, except when it degenerates into unhealthy conflict and political manoeuvring.
- In working out how to cope with power issues, leaders need to survey power groups, leadership, the change style of the organisation, the adoption of a learning-adaptive culture and the nature of the external pressures.
- In exploring the role and responsibilities of a good leader, the first task is determining the organisation's purpose and then communicating this to every part of the organisation. In addition, strategic leaders have a special responsibility to select, nurture and develop employees in the organisation, especially those that hold key responsibilities. They also have a special responsibility to motivate and reward employees. In addition, strategic leaders need to shape the culture of the organisation and to structure the reporting relationships that bind the company together.
- One of the key leadership tasks is to set and monitor the ethical and corporate social responsibility standards of the organisation. Such values need to come from the top. Another prime role of strategic leaders is to maintain good relationships with stakeholders both inside and outside the organisation. Typically, there are multiple demands on the leaders' time and resource so leaders must judge how to handle this. Outside advisers have become increasingly common in helping senior leaders in such tasks.
- It is the responsibility of the organisation's leadership to preserve and enhance the competitive advantages of the organisation. Strategic leaders need to identify and support the key advantages of their organisations.

QUESTIONS

1 Take an organisation with which you are familiar and show how the leader has influenced the organisation. To what extent is the leader reflecting the wishes of the members? And to what extent is the leader attempting to move the organisation into new areas that will stretch the people in the organisation? Does an organisation need to balance these two aspects of leadership? If so, how?

2 Analyse the leadership of the Daimler company from the perspective of contingency theory. Does such a theory provide an adequate explanation for the major changes in strategy described in the case?

3 How does organisational culture link with the leadership of an organisation? Give examples to support your view.

4 Using the evidence from the Xerox case, identify the leadership style of Anne Mulcahy. Use this analysis to explore how she went on to alter the culture of the company.

5 Using the Ford Motor Company as an example, explain how each of the three main leaders - Alex Trotman, Jacques Nasser and Bill Ford - influenced the strategic direction of the company. To what extent did they also influence the organisational culture of the company? Or did it stay much the same over the whole period?

6 Using Figure 16.3 on coping with power in organisations, explore how the power balance might be different in the following organisations: a multinational car company, a small computer software company, a privatised telecommunications service company like British Telecom or Deutsche Telekom, a local police station. Would a 'born leader' be able to lead each of these organisations?

7 '*Visionary leadership inspires the impossible: fiction becomes truth.*' (Westley and Mintzberg) Does such a bold comment apply to all organisations? Or only some? Why?

8 If leadership is complex and a balance between different factors, which of the five factors for successful leadership identified in Figure 16.4 comes first and which last? Give reasons for your views.

9 Was Lao Tsu correct in the opinion that, 'The great leader is he who the people say, "We did it ourselves" '? Some would argue that this is the sign, particularly in business, of a weak leader. What is your view and why?

FURTHER READING

On leadership: Bennis, W and Nanus, B (1997) *Leaders: Strategies for Taking Charge*, Harper-Collins, New York is a readable text with some useful insights. See also the special issue of *Academy of Management Executive* (2004) Vol 18, No 3, pp 118–142, on leadership including: Conger, J A, 'Developing leadership capability: what's inside the black box?'

The following leadership text is also worth consulting: Finkelstein, S and Hambrick, D C (1996) *Strategic Leadership: Top executives and their effects on organisations*, West Publishing, St Paul, MN. For the relationship between leaders and middle managers, the following is interesting: Raes, A M L, Heijltjes, M G, Glunk, U and Roe, R (2011) 'The Interface of the Top Management Team and Middle Managers', *The Academy of Management Review*, Vol 36, No 1, pp 102–126.

NOTES AND REFERENCES

1 References for the Xerox case: *Financial Times*: 24 September 1991; 25 August 1992, p 5; 13 January 1995, p 19; 13 February 1995, p 19; 28 April 1995, two-page advertisement; 7 January 2008, p 24; 22 May 2009, p 22. Lynch, R (1994) *European Business Strategies*, 2nd edn, Kogan Page, London, p 87; Xerox *USA Annual Report 1992* and *2004*. Xerox annual report 2010 appears to be available only in sections on the web and is therefore difficult to reference properly. There is a downloadable investor presentation for quarter 4, for the year 2010, but this makes no mention of green sustainable strategy. The sustainability statement is referenced at the end of the case itself.

2 Finkelstein, S and Hambrick, D C (1996) *Strategic Leadership: Top executives and their effects on organisations*, West Publishing, St Paul, MN.

3 Collins, J (2001) 'Level 5 Leadership: the triumph of humility and fierce resolve', *Harvard Business Review*, Vol 79, No 1, pp 66–76.

4 Teece, D J (2000) *Managing Intellectual Capital: Organisational, strategic and policy dimensions*, Oxford University Press, Oxford and New York.

5 Carey, D and Ogden, D (2000) *CEO Succession: A window on how boards can get it right when choosing a new chief executive*, Oxford University Press, New York.

6 Finkelstein, S and Hambrick, D C (1996) Op. cit.

7 Weihrich, H and Koontz, H (1993) *Management: Global Perspective*, 10th edn, McGraw-Hill, New York, p 490.

8 Westley, F and Mintzberg, H (1989) 'Visionary leadership and strategic management', *Strategic Management Journal*, Vol 10, pp 17–32.

9 Homans, G (1965) *The Human Group*, Routledge and Kegan Paul, London. Ch 7 on the 'Norton Street Gang' is illuminating and reflects research by Whyte in 1943.
10 Whittington, R (1993) *What is Strategy – and Does it Matter?*, Routledge, London, pp 47–49.
11 Miles, R E and Snow, C C (1978) *Organizational Strategy, Structure and Process*, McGraw-Hill, New York.
12 Handy, C (1993) *Understanding Organizations*, Penguin, Harmondsworth, Ch 4. This whole section has benefited from this excellent text.
13 Developed from the work of Bourgeois, L J and Brodwin, D (1983) 'Putting your strategy into action', *Strategic Management Planning*, March/May. The complete paper is reprinted in De Wit, B and Meyer, R (1998) *Strategy: Process Content and Context*, 2nd edn, International Thompson Business Press, London, pp 261–364.
14 Bennis, W and Nanus, B (1997) Op. cit.
15 Sources for the Ford strategy case include: *Financial Times*: 22 April 1994 (reprinted in the first edition of this text); 16 November 1998, p 12; 29 January 1999, p 1; 3 March 1999, p 14 (interesting article by Professor John Kay on globalisation in the car industry); 9 March 1999, p 25; an interesting series reviewing the Ford dynasty appeared in the *Financial Times* 29 October 2007, p 15 and succeeding dates.
16 This section has benefited from the literature summary in the following paper: Luo, X, Kanuri, V K and Andrews, M (2014) How does CEO tenure matter? The mediating role of firm-employee and firm-customer relationships, *Strategic Management Journal*, Vol 35, pp 492–511.
17 *Financial Times*: 29 November 2001, p 17; February 1992, p 14; 29 March 1994, p 30; 11 April 1994, p 20; 23 April 1994, p 11; 4 October 1994, p VII; 2 December 1994, p 17; 6 January 1995, p 17; 23 January 1995, p 10.
18 Handy, C (1993) Op. cit., p 292.
19 Mintzberg, H (1991) 'The effective organisation: forces and forms', *Sloan Management Review*, Winter, pp 54–67.
20 *Financial Times*, 11 July 1995, p 24.
21 References for Daimler-Benz: DaimlerChrysler Annual Report and Accounts 2004 available on the web. *The Economist*: 27 April 1991, p 87; 26 June 1993, p 77; *Financial Times*: 7 April 1993, p 26; 23 September 1993, p 24; 1 December 1993, p 49; 16 December 1993, p 21; 20 December 1993, p 13; 21 December 1993, p 3; 11 July 1995, p 24; 8 August 1995, p 13; 20 December 1995, p 25; 18 January 1996, p 27; 14 February 1996, p 23; 7 March 1996, p 28; 12 April 1996, p 23; 4 May 1999, p 26; 10 October 2000, p 24; 30 October 2000, p 26; 15 November 2000, p 46; 24 January 2001, p 37; 21 February 2001, p 30; 27 February 2001, p 20; 8 February 2002, p 28; 22 May 2002, p 16; 9 August 2002, p 27; 17 March 2003, p 28; 25 July 2003, p 25; 3 September 2003, p 31; 6 October 2003, p 28; 12 December 2003, p 30; 21 December 2003, p 32; 24 March 2004, p 26; 30 March 2004, p 23; 6 April 2004, p 21; 19 April 2004, p 28; 23 April 2004, p 19; 24 April 2004, p M1; 26 April 2004, pp 18 (Editorial) and 26; 30 April 2004, 22 (Lex); 4 May 2004, p 23; 11 May 2004, p 26; 18 August 2004, p 24; 29 October 2004, p 1; 11 January 2005, p 29; 3 March 2005, p 21; 21 March 2005, p 11; 1 April 2005, p 21; 2 April 2005, pp M1 and M6; 4 April 2005, p 26; 14 April 2005, p 15.
22 Finkelstein and Hambrick (1996) Op. cit.
23 McWilliams, A, Van Fleet, D and Wright, P M (2001) 'Strategic management of human resources for global competitive advantage', *Journal of Business Strategies*, Vol 18, No 1, pp 1–24.
24 Gratton, L (2001) *Living Strategy: Putting people at the heart of corporate purpose*, Financial Times/Prentice Hall, London.
25 Lundy, O and Cowling, A (1996) *Strategic Human Resource Management*, International Thomson Business Press, London.
26 Soule, E (2002) 'Managerial moral strategies – in search of a few good principles', *Academy of Management Review*, Vol 27, pp 114–124.
27 Trevino, L K and Brown, M E (2004) 'Managing to be ethical: debunking five business ethics myths', *Academy of Management Executive*, Vol 18, No 2, pp 69–81.
28 Hillman, A J and Keim, J D (2001) 'Shareholder value, stakeholder management and social issues: what's the bottom line?' *Strategic Management Journal*, Vol 22, pp 125–139.
29 Hamel, G and Prahalad, C K (1994) *Competing for the Future*, Harvard Business School Press, Boston, MA.
30 Kay, J (1993) *Foundations of Corporate Success*, Oxford University Press, Oxford.

CHAPTER 17
Entrepreneurial strategy

Video and sound summary of this chapter

LEARNING OUTCOMES

When you have worked through this chapter, you will be able to:

- explain the theory and practice involved in developing basic entrepreneurial strategy;
- identify the main characteristics of entrepreneurs, their risk taking and approaches to identifying opportunities;
- explore the four main drivers of entrepreneurial strategy – imagination, ideas, invention and innovation;
- explain the importance of competitive advantage and ownership in entrepreneurial strategy;
- outline the stages involved in implementing the entrepreneurial strategic opportunity.

INTRODUCTION

In this chapter, we explore the special aspects of strategy that apply to entrepreneurial activity. Entrepreneurs undertake new business ventures with the risk of either making significant profits or losses. They therefore make special demands on strategy that are not covered by the main strategy theories. This means that some of the concepts explored in this book need to be extended further for entrepreneurs and this is the purpose of this chapter.

It has been argued that entrepreneurship and strategy are parallel subjects.[1] That is not the approach of this chapter, which takes the view that entrepreneurial strategy is a special area of strategy rather than something completely different. The chapter covers the topic under the five headings that are shown in Figure 17.1.

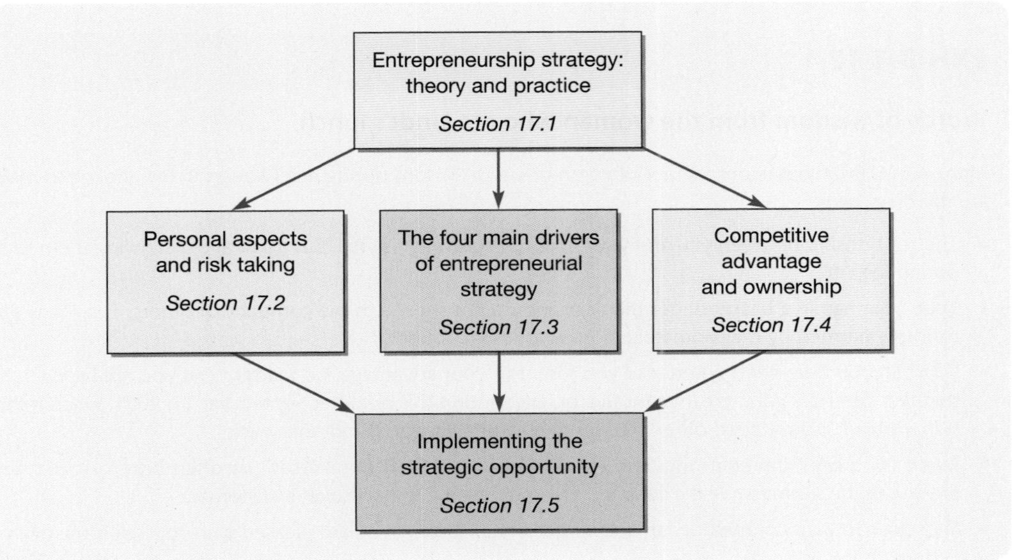

Figure 17.1 Exploring entrepreneurial strategy

CASE STUDY 17.1

FT

Chocolate maker savours its sweet desserts

Mary-Ann O'Brien has built her company by targeting the 'volume luxury' domain of the Belgians and Swiss.

Oh, to have been a fly on the wall at Lindt when the venerable chocolate maker found out it had lost an important long-term contract to supply British Airways. To lose to the Belgians would have been understandable – but not to a small Irish company – Lily O'Brien's Chocolates – run by a woman who just five years previously had bought her first set of chocolate moulds in a South African flea market for £12. 'Ah God, that was sweet. You can't imagine how I felt,' says Mary-Ann O'Brien. 'Here was Lindt, the granddaddy of them all, nearly 150 years old and steeped in so much tradition, and here's me, barely getting into my stride and pinching the contract from right under their noses.'

O'Brien had been eyeing the airline market after winning a contract with Aer Lingus. 'I just thought the Lindt brand looked tired, so I rang up British Airways and said it was all a bit dated and suggested we meet, saying I had a new, exciting range of chocolates and designs to offer. I asked the team to come up with a range of beautiful contemporary designs for packaging and our R&D department to come up with a range of 'dessert-like' sweets.' Soon, BA passengers were being served sticky toffee pudding, lemon meringue pie, raspberry mousse and lemon brulé as sweets. All these chocolates contained natural ingredients similar to those in desserts, be they lemon curd or real raspberries. 'The chocolates were an instant hit and we soon landed more airline contracts. As well as BA, we have Aer Lingus, Virgin, Continental, United and US Air.'

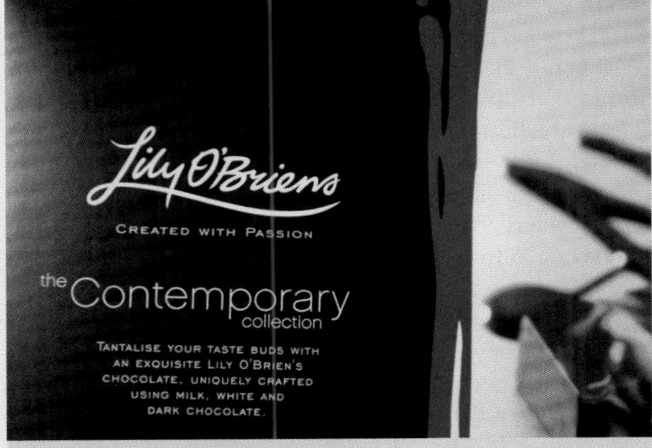

Lily O'Brien's Chocolates exploits the power of the internet for small entrepreneurial businesses.
Reproduced with permission from Lily O'Brien's.

There was a wobble when the airline industry went into a bit of a tailspin after September 11, 2001 and slashed spending, but Ms O'Brien hung in there, cutting costs with

EXHIBIT 17.1

Words of wisdom from the woman who ate Lindt's lunch

Mary-Ann O'Brien has learnt a series of common-sense lessons during her 12 years in the chocolate-making business. Here are the main ones:

- The relationship between you and your financial controller is vital. But try to avoid allowing them to be 'penny wise and pound foolish'.
- Keep your ego in a basket under the desk and do not show it in the company of others. Too many good companies are seriously harmed by megalomaniac bosses strutting around.
- Don't let your fear get the better of you. Use it to your advantage, no matter what you are facing. It is a cliché, but true, that fear can be a great creative motivator. Lily's found this out after September 11, 2001, when it thought it was facing ruin. Instead, it developed other markets and eventually got its old ones back.
- Don't shy away from confrontation. The longer you leave it the worse it so often becomes. But never show anger to anyone in the business, be it a supplier, an employee or, in particular, a customer.
- Stay close to your competitors and never get smug. The day you are pleased with yourself is the day your rival is stealing a march on you.
- Travel, and keep travelling, particularly in the USA. The number of ideas to be found there is staggering.
- If you don't know, do not be afraid to ask; and do not be afraid to hook up with a mentor.

new designs, and eventually regained most of the business. The airlines themselves lost substantial business and this impacted on their suppliers, such as Lily O'Brien's. The company responded by developing a new flow-wrapped airline chocolate product to replace the more expensive two-chocolate format. This innovation saved the airlines money and subsequently won the company the Mercury prize for cost-saving innovation on an airline. In 2004, Lily O'Brien's Chocolates (named after her daughter) shipped 8 million pieces on airlines alone. Lily O'Brien's employs more than 100 people in Newbridge, Co. Kildare, Ireland and had a turnover in 2004 of about €10 million ($11 million). The company exported to dozens of countries but mainly to those that serve the 'sweeter palate' – the UK, the USA, Canada and Australia. In the trade, her company was among the '55 percenters', chocolate makers with a minimum of 55 per cent cocoa in their products, which are described as 'luxury'. Some of the lessons learnt by the company over the past 12 years are summarised in Exhibit 17.1.

The company's long product list is headed by O'Brien's trade-mark Chocolate Crispy Hearts, her first commercial product, later augmented by dozens of handcrafted products from crèmes brûlées, mousses and pralines to truffles and nuts, all in milk, dark and white chocolate. 'We are a volume luxury chocolate maker, but all our products are hand-crafted,' she says. By volume, she means about 10–12 tonnes per week though that can rise to as much as 25–30 tonnes 'in a good week'. And good weeks there have been. So much so that a mezzanine extension was built at the factory over Easter 2004 to allow extra production.

This is all a far cry from Ms O'Brien's first chocolate-making experience. While on holiday in South Africa in 1992, she became friendly with the daughter of the owner of the hotel. At the time, she was recuperating from the debilitating illness myalgic encephalomyelitis or ME. One afternoon she was in the hotel kitchen, where a woman was stirring chocolate in a bowl. It turned out she was 'tempering' the chocolate – cooling it and removing air bubbles – before it was folded into moulds for setting. O'Brien was transfixed and the next day she bought a set of chocolate moulds. On her return to Ireland, she tried different recipes to see what worked. Often it was people such as her hairdresser who formed the tasting panel and, later, her first customers. 'Initially, I just worked in the kitchen of our flat and drove round delivering chocolates to customers.'

She took chocolate-making lessons in Belgium and became adept at the fiddly processes that make the difference between success and failure – often no more than 1°C either way in temperature. In 1993, she borrowed £30,000 for her first 'industrial scale' chocolate machinery and moved into a catering kitchen. Slowly, a business started to emerge – but it was still being run as a cottage industry. Later, a friend from the meat industry invested £40,000 in return for a significant share of the equity and encouraged her 'to stop thinking in kilos and start thinking in tonnes'. Funds from a Business Expansion Scheme allowed the company to spend nearly £1 million on modern machinery for the production line. 'I got my first big contract from Ireland's version of Waitrose which is called Superquinn. They said, "We won't let you make our truffles. The Belgians are doing that, but you can make our crocodiles and pigs." So I did. It started very small but, within a year, I had the whole of the Superquinn group and the Belgians were gone.' Lily's now supplies most of the British supermarket chains.

However, O'Brien realised her limitations. She does see herself as a seller, first and foremost. 'Give me a glass of vodka at lunchtime, and I'll talk all afternoon, it doesn't matter to whom: buyers, companies, you name it.' But chocolate-making is a scientific, complicated process with little room for the talk. So she has hired the best food technologists, designers and production, operational, financial and development staff she can find. 'They are all a class act, seriously, all of them,' she says. The learning curve has been all the more steep because chocolate-making is relatively new to Ireland (Lir and Butlers are fellow Irish chocolate businesses). The companies have benefited from the expertise of Bord Bia (the Irish Food Board) which has both helped expand their markets overseas and the producers tailor products to meet demand. Early research by Bord Bia uncovered an untapped sector of the market as 'self-indulgence'. This was where people wanted to buy luxury chocolates to treat themselves and wanted something better than Cadbury's but not quite as rarefied (or expensive) as the top Belgian brands.

In 2004, the company was hoping to see the opening of a Lily O'Brien's café, selling own-brand coffee as well as a new range of chocolates. 'I think the brand is strong enough now to expand in that area,' O'Brien says. She has come a long way since buying those first chocolate moulds. Not even Lindt could quibble with that.

This case was adapted by Richard Lynch from an article in the *Financial Times*, 20 April 2004, p 13, written by Eamonn Rafferty. The author is grateful to the Lily O'Brien's Company for correcting some data and adding some new information for this case. Richard Lynch is solely responsible for providing this adapted version of the original article and the Financial Times Limited does not accept any liability for the accuracy or quality of the adapted version.

Case questions

1 What do the dynamics of purpose, resources and the environment suggest about the strategic issues facing the company?

2 Did O'Brien develop a strategic plan or did she allow the company to develop in a more experimental way? Was her strategy prescriptive or emergent?

3 What lessons can entrepreneurs learn from a company like Lily O'Brien's Chocolates?

17.1 ENTREPRENEURIAL STRATEGY: THEORY AND PRACTICE

As Mary-Ann O'Brien demonstrates, entrepreneurship becomes the major focus of an individual's life. It involves seeking and developing opportunities – such as a demand for high-quality chocolates – and then finding outlets for them – such as the airline companies. Very often, entrepreneurs create opportunities – even new ones like the latest coffee shop concept at Lily O'Brien's Chocolates – and they usually take risks. In O'Brien's case, she clearly took a number of years of experimentation to develop products and there must have been times – like the period around September 11, 2001 – when she wondered if the business would survive. The key to taking risks in entrepreneurial activity is to shift them in your favour, balancing the risk and potential reward.[2]

Entrepreneurship is a major area of business activity that has developed its own literature and research. We begin our exploration of entrepreneurial strategy by putting some structure on the process by which the Lily O'Brien's Chocolates business was developed. This means looking at the practice as well as the theory.

17.1.1 The theory of entrepreneurial strategy

Definition ▶ **Entrepreneurship is a way of thinking, reasoning and acting that focuses on the identification and exploitation of business opportunities from a broad general perspective typically driven by the leadership of individuals or small groups.** The main elements of the entrepreneurial strategy have both prescriptive and emergent elements, but the opportunism of entrepreneurs is probably best captured by an emergent process. But just how do entrepreneurial opportunities emerge? There are a number of theories that underpin this process, but we will pick out three here:

1 creative destruction theory,
2 discovery theory,
3 creation theory.

Creative destruction theory

Definition ▶ **Creative destruction theory is based on the concept that innovative opportunities arise through competition and technology destroying previous market offerings.** Given that innovation is a key aspect of entrepreneurial activity, Joseph Schumpeter claimed that innovation is a 'perennial gale of creative destruction' which attacks existing industry competitors by undermining them with totally new competitive approaches.[3] Technological, political and social dramatic changes beyond the immediate market opportunity may also facilitate changes in the competitive landscape. For example at Lily O'Brien's, the top quality chocolate dominance of the Swiss company Lindt was changed by the new Irish competitor through the exploitation of new markets such as airlines to gain new sales opportunities.

For entrepreneurial strategy, the significance of the creative destruction approach is that it focuses on existing areas of customer need and drives the entrepreneur into new ways of satisfying them more efficiently or with higher levels of customer satisfaction than existing companies. The effect of this is to drive existing competitors out of business. The other implication of creative destruction theory is that the entrepreneur cannot afford to stand still because, by its very nature, every innovation by one entrepreneur will be replaced by another.

Discovery theory

Definition ▶ **Discovery theory is based on the premise that new opportunities already exist in the market place and are waiting to be discovered by entrepreneurs.**[4] Such opportunities sometimes arise from the dramatic changes in the competitive landscape identified above, the web being an obvious example that has transformed the way we do business. However, even if such rapid change is not available, those who have studied marketing will recognise the basic approach as one of identifying customers' unsatisfied needs at a point in time and then satisfying them through new entrepreneurial products.

Unlike creative destruction theory, there is no suggestion in discovery theory of destroying what is already present. The process relies essentially on searching for new areas of customer need. For example, at Lily O'Brien's, this might involve the development of a new high-quality product range for a specialist sales opportunity.

Creation theory

Definition ▶ **Creation theory is based on the hypothesis that new opportunities can be developed by entrepreneurs experimenting and creating a new market demand that did not previously exist.**[5] The creation process often involves an experimental learning process – trying new ways, gaining reactions to products and services and particularly relying on the *entrepreneur* as the essential source of such opportunities. Importantly, it is the action of the entrepreneur that is fundamental to the development of the new opportunity. Many of us will recognise such an approach which is often interwoven with the personality of the entrepreneur – Lily O'Brien, Richard Branson, Rupert Murdoch and many others. It is not difficult to imagine Lily O'Brien in her kitchen inventing new chocolate recipes and methods of presentation – see Case 17.1.

Theory and practice

So what are the implications for entrepreneurial strategy? First, there is no single theory that is generally accepted as defining the entrepreneurial strategy development process. Second, it is quite possible that each of the theories has something to offer depending on the strategic context. In our present state of knowledge, entrepreneurial strategy will continue to borrow from all three areas and others as well.

17.1.2 The practice of entrepreneurial strategy: a development model

Most small companies remain small[6] and the high-growth firm that creates real wealth is unusual.[7] In spite of this slightly discouraging beginning, many of us have knowledge of people who have made significant wealth from entrepreneurial activity. We have even identified some already in this book – for example, Sir Richard Branson at Virgin and Rupert Murdoch at News Corporation.

To develop beyond the small business, entrepreneurs need a *development model* that will allow them to expand the initial opportunity.

In developing the entrepreneurial process, the starting point is the business opportunity. This may be external to the company – for example, the demand for superior, hand-made chocolates at Lily O'Brien's must come from the customers of the company. Likewise, the technology behind the development of the Google web search engine. Equally, it may be internal to the company – for example, the invention of a new technology that can be exploited commercially. Thus the starting point for the organising framework must be the external and internal drivers that help to identify the business opportunity.

There are various ways to identify the opportunity:[8]

- The *prior experience* of individuals makes them more likely to identify new areas.
- *University contacts* to identify technology opportunities.
- *Previous knowledge*, perhaps developed from working in a company: this area is often called 'path-dependent prior experience'.
- *Experimenting with ideas*, perhaps even inventing something that did not previously exist.

Figure 17.2 shows these first elements.

According to McGrath,[9] the next step is to form a business to exploit that opportunity. There will often be a small nucleus of people who can form an internal team. It may be the most important and difficult entrepreneurial task to develop the team to exploit the opportunity successfully. More generally, most small companies will not have all the resources inside the organisation. It is for this reason that a separate 'external resource' area is identified in the development model shown in Figure 17.2.

Having assembled the resources, it is then usual to develop a separate limited company to serve the opportunity that has been identified. Once this has been completed, there is then a further stage where the products or services are launched onto the market place. Customers, distributors, suppliers and other stakeholders will then provide feedback from the market place that can be used to develop and shape the business opportunity further, if required. These elements then make up the latter part of the model shown in Figure 17.2.

In some modern entrepreneurial strategy theories,[10] the linear relationship of the model from left to right in Figure 17.2 is less pronounced. The flow is more experimental and creative with a strong emergent process with feedback at various points. In other models, the competitive resources

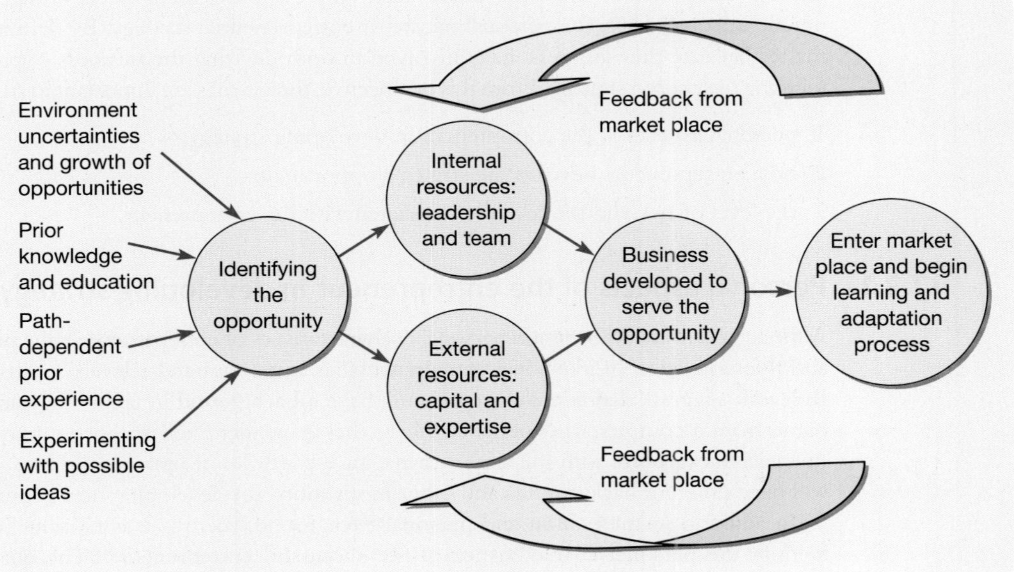

Figure 17.2 Model of the entrepreneurial process

of the participants – especially those who possess unique knowledge or technology – are emphasised as being crucial to the overall development and success of the business opportunity.[11] One area not shown in Figure 17.2 is the closure of unprofitable business activity. This last aspect is often overlooked in the enthusiasm of entrepreneurial activity, but it is important that business people learn how to walk away from failure and, if necessary, build up a totally new business venture.[12]

KEY STRATEGIC PRINCIPLES

- Entrepreneurship is a way of thinking, reasoning and acting that focuses on the identification and exploitation of business opportunities from a broad general perspective driven by the leadership of individuals or small groups.
- There are at least three theories concerning the emergence of entrepreneurial opportunities. The *creative destruction theory* argues that innovative opportunities arise through competition and technology destroying previous market offerings. The *discovery theory* is based on the premise that new opportunities already exist in the market place and are waiting to be discovered by entrepreneurs. The *creative theory* is based on the hypothesis that new opportunities can be developed by entrepreneurs experimenting and creating a new market demand that did not previously exist.
- In practice, it is possible to develop a model of the entrepreneurial process. The early elements of the model begin by identifying the external and internal sources that contribute to the business opportunity. The next stage is then to recruit the team plus the external resources that will exploit the opportunity. A business is then set up and the product or service is launched into the market place. The final stage of the model has a feedback mechanism from the market place that may modify or develop the opportunity further.

Checklist: Some possible issues on setting up a new entrepreneurial company.

17.2 ENTREPRENEURIAL STRATEGY: PERSONAL ASPECTS AND RISK TAKING

In the development of entrepreneurial strategy, there is one element that is stronger and possibly even unique in some cases: the personal nature of entrepreneurial strategy. By definition, entrepreneurs matter because they are personally involved in both devising the business opportunity and implementing the chosen strategy. From this perspective, three issues are important in strategy development:

1 personal aspects of the entrepreneur in developing strategy;
2 how entrepreneurs develop the strategic opportunity;
3 the level of risk and the rewards associated with the entrepreneur.

17.2.1 Personal aspects of the entrepreneur in developing strategy

Although there are no common personality characteristics of entrepreneurs,[13] the personal background and the motivation of individual entrepreneurs are important and relevant to strategy development. Research suggests that some entrepreneurs have a background in technology and invention, some come from a commercial experience where they have identified an opportunity and some from a financial background with the aim of managing a portfolio of opportunities.[14] Other entrepreneurs will have different backgrounds and other motivations for developing new ventures.

In addition to motivation and personal background, there is a significant body of research to identify the personal characteristics of the successful entrepreneur.[15] The qualities identified by research include areas like 'hard-working', 'confident' and 'receptive to new ideas'. We will return to this aspect of strategy development in the section on implementation later in this chapter.

Within the personal skills of the entrepreneur, one factor is particularly important: the ability of the entrepreneur to *transfer knowledge* within the business. This latter point is essential in both large and small businesses: the entrepreneurial capability of the firm is enhanced if knowledge is spread to all those involved in the enterprise, not just kept amongst one or two entrepreneurial individuals.

17.2.2 How can entrepreneurs learn and develop opportunities?

Beyond the external and internal sources outlined in the previous section, there are various theories about how entrepreneurs develop their opportunities: there is no single method. However, a useful starting point is *the experiential learning circle* developed by Kolb and Fry shown in Figure 17.3.[16] The underpinning assumption is that most entrepreneurs will be involved in some form of learning with regard to the business opportunity. **The experiential learning circle has four elements: concrete experience or knowledge; observation and reflection; formation of abstract concepts from the observation; testing of such concepts in new situations.** While the process is essentially circular and can begin at any of four positions, it is useful to start with some form of prior knowledge such as a technical entrepreneurial breakthrough – position 1 in Figure 17.3. Using this knowledge, some action is then undertaken such as the initial trial of the new opportunity and then seeing the effect of this: position 2 in Figure 17.3. The next step is then to consider whether a general principle can be formed from the previous steps – for example, whether the business opportunity has real potential and, if so, what are its main elements: position 3 in Figure 17.3. The fourth step is then to test this in a new situation – for example, a further development of the business opportunity: position 4 in Figure 17.3.

Definition ▶

In this particular model, individual entrepreneurial experience is fundamental to the development of the business opportunity. Importantly, the model makes demands of the entrepreneur at a personal level. Such an entrepreneur needs to have special skills:

- some specific experience or skill that is the basis of the business opportunity;
- being able to observe reactions to the opportunity without becoming over-enthusiastic in order to avoid distorting the main benefits and problems;
- conceptualising the main elements of the business opportunity;
- engaging in active experimentation to refine the business proposition;
- the ability to transfer the knowledge gained to other individuals – as discussed in the previous section.

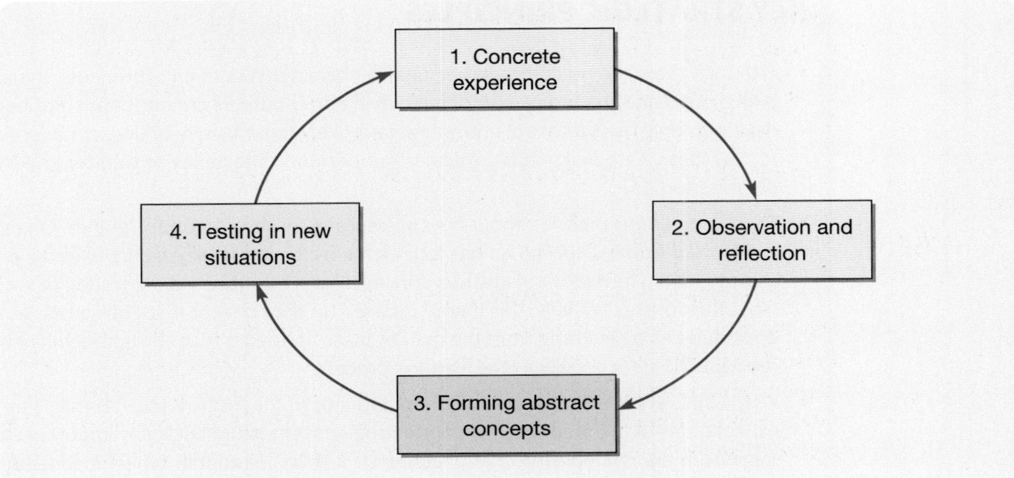

Figure 17.3 Experiential learning circle

Source: Kolb, D A and Fry, R (1975) 'Toward an applied theory of experiential learning'. In: Cooper, C (ed) *Theories of Group Process*, Copyright © 1975 John Wiley & Sons Ltd. Reproduced with permission.

17.2.3 Risks, rewards and uncertainty

In the words of the *Strategic Entrepreneurship Journal*'s distinguished co-editors, Dan Schendel and Michael Hitt:[17] 'Risk is inherent in entrepreneurship.' However, it is generally accepted that risks will only be taken if they are reasonable and the higher rewards that come with the risk are sufficiently attractive. 'Reasonable' here means in relation to the value judgement made by an individual with regard to his/her resources and expectations from life: it is difficult, perhaps impossible, to generalise about such matters especially for a single entrepreneurial business.

Beyond this point about value judgement with regard to risk, there is a need to make a distinction between two aspects of the entrepreneurial risk-taking process – namely risk and uncertainty.

Definition ▶ **Risk involves measurable inputs and outputs that are associated with known probability distributions of the outcomes of business actions. Nothing may be certain but the odds of a specific outcome are known.**[18] This means that risk is capable of statistical analysis using the various analytical tools.

Definition ▶ **Uncertainty may involve specific inputs but the outcomes are not fully defined in advance and perhaps not even clear after the event.** With uncertainty, it is not possible to make predictions with any confidence whatsoever. This means that it is not possible to develop probability distributions of possible outcomes based on statistical analysis.

Typically, considerations of risk and uncertainty apply when a business plan is developed for a specific entrepreneurial business opportunity and presented to an outside institution such as a bank in order to raise funds. The plan will contain estimates of sales, profits and costs that are likely to be delivered by taking business risks. Such numbers may appear to be the result of rational decisions and be capable of statistical risk analysis. In addition, the same numbers may also involve a high degree of uncertainty as well as risk and, essentially, may not be worth the paper on which they are presented.

In practice, steps can be taken to reduce the risk of entrepreneurial new ventures by undertaking further research, sending out products for market testing and other such activities. One of the main problems with regard to this form of risk-reduction arises with businesses that are already well established but wish to engage in entrepreneurial activities. To quote McGrath: 'The uncertainty reduction process for new ventures within an established organisation is usually conflict-ridden, because allocating resources to reduce uncertainty in a new idea implies denying resources both to other new ideas and to established organisational operations.'[19]

KEY STRATEGIC PRINCIPLES

- Although there are no common personality characteristics of entrepreneurs, the personal background and the motivation of individual entrepreneurs are important and relevant to strategy development. The successful entrepreneur is likely to be hard-working, confident and receptive to new ideas. One skill that is particularly important is the ability to transfer knowledge within the organisation.
- There are various theories about how entrepreneurs develop opportunities. One such theory is the *experiential learning circle*. This has four elements: concrete experience or knowledge; observation and reflection; formation of abstract concepts from the observation; testing of such concepts in new situations. Essentially, this theory is based on the concept that entrepreneurs develop new opportunities by learning from the market place. It implies that entrepreneurs need to develop the special skills associated with the learning process.
- Risk is inherent in entrepreneurship and depends in the first instance on the value judgements and expectations of the individual. In considering entrepreneurial risk, it is important to distinguish this topic from the related subject of uncertainty. Risk is measurable, while uncertainty is not so well defined. Risk can be reduced by undertaking further research. However, this may cause tensions in companies because the resources required for the risk research may need to be taken from other parts of the organisation, thus reducing opportunities elsewhere.

CASE STUDY 17.2

Strategy lessons from three entrepreneurs – Bill Gates, Luke Johnson and John Caudwell

Over the past 20 years, the three entrepreneurs described in this case have built positions of wealth and prestige. But they were not always successful, especially in the early days. This case explores some of their experiences and some possible lessons for entrepreneurial strategy

Bill Gates – chairman of Microsoft, the world market leader in personal computer software

When Bill Gates founded the world's leading computer software company Microsoft in the late 1970s, his small team of five members could hardly have envisaged how the company would develop over the next 30 years. Bill Gates himself complained that his competitors were readily copying all his early software ideas.[20] Essentially, the company had no competitive advantage over its rivals.

In the late 1970s, there was strong market growth in the American computer software market. However, the business opportunities were largely the same for all the main supplier companies. It was perhaps chance that gave Microsoft some luck. The dominant computer mainframe company, IBM, decided that it would not develop its own software for its new personal computer but would employ an outside company. In addition, IBM decided that it did not need to tie the software supplier, which was Microsoft, exclusively to IBM. Bill Gates was funded to develop the new software by IBM and was able to sell the software to anyone else for free – see Case 1.2 for more details. This gave Microsoft its opportunity:

> The software business is very American. The original technical advances were all made here. And the atmosphere that allowed it all to happen is here. That's how our original customers, including IBM, could be so open-minded about buying from a 25-year-old guy with a small company in Washington. They may have thought it was crazy at the time, but they said, 'Hey, if he knows so much about software, maybe he knows even more.'
>
> Bill Gates quoted in *Money* magazine, July 1986.[21]

However, the above comments do not explain how Microsoft's Windows came to dominate the personal computer software market. The process started with Microsoft's MS-DOS operating system being adopted by IBM on the establishment of IBM personal computers in 1981 as the industry standard. IBM failed to stop Microsoft encouraging widespread use of the MS-DOS system across other PCs. The development of an industry technical standard has been recognised in strategy as an important step to competitive advantage.

Following this initial success, an additional stage in Microsoft's progress was its successful defence of the Windows format against a patent infringement action by Apple Computers in the late 1980s. Microsoft argued that the Windows concept had originated at Xerox Palo Alto laboratories, not Apple. Microsoft then made its Windows software widely available to a number of computer manufacturers. This strategy was quite different to that of Apple who would not allow other companies to use its software. This allowed the user-friendly Windows format to build successfully on the earlier widespread adoption of MS-DOS. Subsequently, Microsoft has used its dominance of computer software to spread into a number of other areas, but Windows remains its prime source of competitive advantage.

In summary, Bill Gates and his colleagues moved from a company based on business opportunities to one with real competitive strengths through a combination of chance, leadership and astute strategic insight. Importantly, Microsoft was willing to borrow ideas from other companies where this was a legitimate business practice.

Luke Johnson – chairman of one of the UK's main terrestrial television channels, Channel 4

After studying medicine at Oxford University, Luke Johnson joined an advertising agency and then worked as a financial analyst in the City of London's financial district. In 1989, he bought a theatrical scenery business as an entrepreneurial opportunity: 'I wasted three years and made no money. It was a miserable experience but you learn from your setbacks.'

In 1993, Luke Johnson and a partner, Hugh Osmond, realised that there might be profits to be made in the changing tastes of England – specifically, a new taste for Italian food. They identified a medium-sized pizza restaurant chain called *Pizza Express* and staged a daring reverse takeover of the company. The risk paid off and they were able to build the new chain to such a degree that its sale in the late 1990s netted the two partners many millions of dollars. Looking back on the experience, Johnson commented: 'I think that a willingness to break the rules [without breaking the law] and punch above your weight is quite important [for entrepreneurs].' He went on to suggest that entrepreneurs needed to enjoy the thrill of taking risks and cultivate resilience to the inevitable failures. He pointed out that entrepreneurs were more likely to amass real wealth by building a company for subsequent sale rather than taking a high salary and expenses during the process of building the company.

John Caudwell – formerly chairman of the Caudwell Group – the largest distributor of mobile telephones in Europe

When John Caudwell sold his mobile telephone business in 2006, his company was worth $3.2 billion. However, Caudwell

All three entrepreneurs, from left to right, Bill Gates, Luke Johnson and John Caudwell, have developed highly successful businesses. What are their secrets of success?

did not begin his entrepreneurial career with mobile phones. He actually started by selling Belstaff motorcycle clothing. He made profits in the motorcycle clothing business by pitching his prices below his competitors, who then complained to the manufacturers Belstaff. The clothing company took the view that Caudwell was undermining the profitability of the whole market and stopped supplying him. After some difficult negotiations, Caudwell was allowed to sell his remaining clothing stock but had to find a new enterprise. He moved into selling cars.

Although John Caudwell then went on to build a reasonably successful car business, he was still looking for new opportunities. He began selling mobile telephones in the late 1980s as a new sideline with his cars. In the first eight months of 1987, he sold 26 phones but he persisted with the business. He was experimenting with how to sell mobile phones successfully to his customers because he could see the potential. For the first two years, he lost money on mobile phone sales, but he held firm in the belief that this was the future. In 1989, he pulled out of the car business entirely in order to focus on mobile phones and build a team to take the business forward.

Describing his business philosophy, Caudwell commented, 'I am aggressive. If anyone tries to stop me I'll try to smash their barrier down – whether it is a person or an object. But it has to be what I believe to be fair and ethical. If a big corporation is trying to stand in my way and damage my business – and this happens a lot – I will employ every strategy that I possibly can to get past the problem.'

More generally, John Caudwell believes that entrepreneurs need to be able to take the knocks and come back again when developing business. It is also important to be able to recognise growth opportunities and experiment. In addition, he also argues that to build a business it is important to be able to lead a team that includes people with different areas of expertise. Finally, 'Don't just focus on the business idea. Analyse yourself and see if you have personal qualities like . . . passion, drive and leadership.'

 This case was written from published sources only.[22]

Case questions

1 What are the common lessons from each of the three entrepreneurs? And what are the differences in approach?

2 To what extent was innovation important in entrepreneurial strategy at each of the three companies? How was any such innovation achieved? By technological advance? By copying other companies? By learning strategy?

3 What are the main lessons that other entrepreneurs can learn from the three companies?

17.3 THE FOUR DRIVERS OF ENTREPRENEURIAL STRATEGY: IMAGINATION, IDEAS, INVENTION AND INNOVATION

As our three entrepreneurs in Case 17.2 demonstrate, the essence of entrepreneurial strategy rests with the *four i's*: *imagination, ideas, invention* and *innovation*. All three business people have been single-minded at various times throughout their lives in pursuing these areas which lie at the heart of entrepreneurial strategy. These four drivers 'focus on the discovery or creation of new things, with advances from which society benefits through new value propositions that better serve the needs of some segment, or the whole of society'.[23] Each of our three entrepreneurs was able to create something new and fulfil a need in society: personal computer software, mobile telephone services, pizza restaurants. The question is, how to do this?

To develop the four i's, here are three principal methods: technology, innovation and new product or service development. We have already explored two of these – technology and innovation – in Chapter 7 of this book. We will therefore concentrate on the last element in this chapter – new product or service development. In addition in this section, we will explore the differences between undertaking this process in small versus large companies, because the process is more complex in the latter.

17.3.1 Ideas generation: new product and service development

As the entrepreneur John Caudwell shows in Case 17.2, it is essential to have a whole range of ideas to start the entrepreneurial process. He began with motorcycle clothing, went through car selling and ended up making his fortune with mobile phones. The key point here is that the process starts with a whole range of ideas, which are then reduced by a series of business criteria before a product or service is actually launched commercially as described below.

Ideas can come from anywhere but there are two techniques that will help the process:

Definition ▶
- **Brainstorming: the rapid generation of ideas by a group, often from a wide variety of backgrounds, without any evaluation of those ideas.**

Definition ▶
- **Focus group: a discussion of around five to eight people, selected for their relevance to the subject.** Typically, several groups are recruited to represent a specific target group. The resulting evidence explores qualitative rather than quantitative issues.

Brainstorming has the advantages of imagination, originality and enthusiasm. It is important that no criticism is allowed, not even a facial expression that implies disapproval. The reason is obvious – any critical comment and people will feel threatened, so the ideas will dry up. The session is helped if people are encouraged to link ideas together that may even appear to have only a distant relationship with one another.

Focus groups are used for a variety of market research purposes. They are led by a trained researcher and often stimulated with some simple research material such as a product concept on a board. They might begin with a general discussion around the broad subject area with ideas being generated and opposing views being sought. In the second part of the discussion, they might typically move on to examining a specific proposal or idea and giving their views and evaluation of this.

In addition to these two approaches to ideas generation and reaction, entrepreneurs often have their own ways of generating new business opportunities. They see an unmet customer need; they observe supply difficulties; they find a service not previously offered on the internet; they find ideas about a new service when visiting another country; and so on. The ideas stage of entrepreneurial strategy needs to be *open*, not restricted.

After the ideas generation stage, various other stages follow. These will vary with the individual organisation, but Figure 17.4 sets out a typical series of stages for a medium-sized company:

- *Screening* – the weeding out of the wilder ideas that always occur in any ideas generation session.
- *Business analysis* – a review of all the remaining ideas against the company objectives. Typically, there are some good ideas but not all will have the ability to generate sufficient profits against the company objectives.

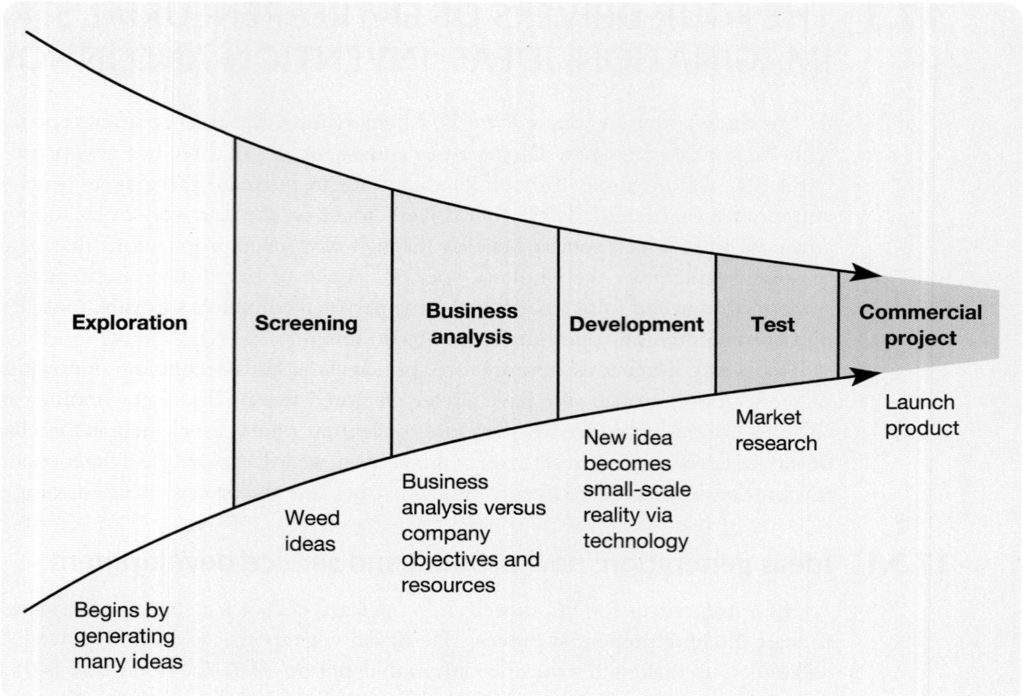

Figure 17.4 Developing and evaluating entrepreneurial ideas

- *Development* – the remaining ideas are then developed into experimental products or services. Again, some may fail here because the initial ideas simply prove impossible to realise in practice.
- *Testing.* Having developed some real products, they are then tested on a small scale against real customers – usually with real products in the home or office.
- *Commercial project.* Finally, those products that have proved attractive to customers in test are actually launched into the market place.

Inevitably, this ideas development process has many variations. The cases in Chapter 7 have other examples of routes to development: for example, the 3M process, which encourages individual employees to spend time generating their own ideas and then discussing them with others in the organisation. Importantly, the organisational culture of the company is supportive towards ideas development: employees are not criticised for failure. The four i's – *imagination, ideas, invention* and *innovation* – are the paramount starting point for entrepreneurs at this stage.

17.3.2 Entrepreneurial development inside existing companies: intrapreneurship

As mentioned at the beginning of this section, the creative development process can be more difficult inside companies. There are a variety of reasons – perhaps because of the past history of the company ('We tried that two years ago'), perhaps because of individual and unsupported opinions ('That'll never work'), perhaps because of the reporting structure of the company ('You'll never get that past the board').[24] There is strong research evidence to support the view that some, but not all, companies can block the ideas process: these areas were explored more fully in Chapter 12.[25] However, as we have also seen, some companies can be highly supportive of new ideas and innovation.

Definition ▶ **Intrapreneurship focuses on the identification and exploitation of creative and innovative opportunities within larger companies or organisations.** The process is somewhat similar to entrepreneurship but has the possible disadvantage of working inside an existing organisation with all its restraints. However, there are also significant *benefits* from operating within an existing organisation:

- Greater resources in terms of technology and research facilities: the $50 billion spent annually by car manufacturers on R&D for green strategy in Case 14.3 is an example.
- More network relationship contacts that allow for the cross-fertilisation of ideas: the 3M case in Case 7.4 is an example.
- Stronger support to bring ideas to market and then branding, marketing, distribution and sales structure in the market place: the Canon company in Case 13.2 is an example.

Intrapreneurship can be assisted by various company policies that support such developments.[26] They include: granting intrapreneurial employees some *ownership rights* to the innovation; treating intrapreneurial developments as a separate *profit centre* in an organisation, thus allowing the full benefits and credit to mature to the inventors; developing an *intrapreneurial team* with members being allowed a variety of role and alliances; and a system for *settling disputes* and rivalry between different teams so that intrapreneurship teams can compete but the problems do not become rancorous. Importantly, these approaches may work better in some national and company organisational cultures than others.

KEY STRATEGIC PRINCIPLES

- The four main drivers of entrepreneurial strategy are imagination, ideas, invention and innovation. There are three principal methods to create a new business opportunity: technology, innovation and new product and service development.
- With regard to new product and service development, two techniques will aid the process: brainstorming and focus groups. The former is particularly good at generating new ideas, even if some are totally impractical. The latter can assist the process of ideas generation in a more organised and specific process. After the ideas generation stage, a typical process for developing and evaluating entrepreneurial opportunities will involve five stages: screening, business analysis, development, testing and commercial project.
- Entrepreneurial activity is also possible in large companies and is called *intrapreneurship*. Intrapreneurship focuses on the identification and exploitation of creative and innovative opportunities within larger companies or organisations. It can be supported by various company policies that support such processes. These include ownership rights, profit centres, intrapreneurial team building and a system for settling disputes and rivalry between groups.

17.4 ENTREPRENEURIAL STRATEGY: COMPETITIVE ADVANTAGE AND OWNERSHIP

Unfortunately, it is not enough for entrepreneurs to develop and exploit new business opportunities: competitors may be able to imitate them, add something more and undermine the entrepreneur's business. This means that entrepreneurs need to be seeking ways to protect their competitive advantages. There are two principal means to undertake this task: developing sustainable competitive advantages and securing legal ownership.

17.4.1 Developing sustainable competitive advantages

In 1987, John Caudwell sold eight mobile telephones in eight months from his car sales showrooms. By the late 1990s, Caudwell owned the largest independent mobile telephone business in Western Europe – see Case 17.2. At the same time, other companies were entering the mobile telephone market across the continent; the market was growing and competition becoming fierce. How did an entrepreneur like Caudwell build and maintain such an important market position? The answer is that he identified and then made every effort to maintain his competitive advantages over time.

From Chapter 4 on competitive resources, we know that there is no unique formula for identifying and developing competitive advantage. We also know that this is a gradual process – one stage may lead to another as an idea develops and matures. The important point from an entrepreneurial perspective is to be constantly experimenting and watching customer reaction to products and services while, at the same time, monitoring and reacting to competitive activity.

Nevertheless, there are various aspects of competitive advantage that may lend themselves to entrepreneurial strategy:

- *Reputation and branding.* Even on a small scale in the market place, entrepreneurs can gain a reputation for offering value for money, exceptional service and more.[27]
- *Knowledge acquisition.* Technical innovation and knowledge may come from inside the organisation, in which case they may be patented – see the next section. However, they can also be acquired by licence or other means from outside companies, possibly even outside the country.[28]
- *Core competencies.* Entrepreneurs may have some specialist technical expertise that they can exploit but need to be constantly enhancing this.[29] 'Technological advances are the base for most innovations and in turn become a primary driver of change.'[30] The key here is to retain possession of such advantages, possibly by patenting.
- *Other unique resources.* There are some resources that are particularly difficult to replicate by competitors. Two of the most powerful are *teams* of innovators and *locational* advantages. Teams that work well together often have tacit knowledge – see Chapter 7 – that competitors find real difficulty in matching even over long time periods. Locational advantages may arise when a company has a particularly powerful geographical site – such as the Savoy Hotel in London or a Tesco or Wal-Mart superstore at a busy motorway interconnection – that competitors can only copy at great expense.

But, if Joseph Schumpeter is right, then all such advantages are governed by the *creative destruction* theory described earlier in this chapter: in essence, Schumpeter argued that competitive advantages are not sustainable. However, other strategy theories suggest that alternative methods for protecting and securing competitive advantage – such as patenting by legal ownership – need to be found.

17.4.2 Securing legal ownership

In addition to the ways described above, there are four methods of securing competitive advantage for entrepreneurial innovations and their related businesses over time.[31] The background principle

Definition ▸ here is called securing intellectual property. **Intellectual property is any product of human intellect that is intangible but has value in the market place.** It is called intellectual property because it results from the four 'i's' explored in Section 17.3.

There are four main means of securing intellectual property:

1. *Patent.* This is a registered legal document that grants ownership of the innovation. There is a lengthy and expensive legal process before such an advantage is given, usually by a special government office.
2. *Trademark.* This is essentially any word, symbol or other device to identify a product or service. Trademarks usually need to be registered with some form of governmental organisation. Most countries then have trademark laws that protect the entrepreneur from imitation products.
3. *Copyright.* This is a form of protection that gives the owner of a published work the legal right to determine how the work is used and gain royalties from its usage. The published work needs to be tangible – a book, a magazine article – and it is not possible to copyright an idea as such.
4. *Trade secret.* This is any formula, pattern, physical device or process that provides the owner of the information with competitive advantage. They may include marketing plans, financial forecasts

and technical information. Unlike the other areas above, there is no single legal framework or agency to provide protection. It would be necessary to pursue any infringement under secrecy laws, if they exist in a country.

In practice, the fundamental point to make about all these areas of protection is that they can easily involve heavy legal fees and expensive professional advice – either at the time of initially registering the protection or pursuing a competitor who has infringed the protection at a later stage. But they are valuable and often justify the costs, including the heavy management time, that is entailed in developing and registering them.

KEY STRATEGIC PRINCIPLES

- Because of the possibility that new opportunities might be imitated, entrepreneurs need to protect their new business ventures. There are two main means: developing sustainable competitive advantages and securing legal ownership.
- With regard to sustainable competitive advantage, there are no rules. However, various aspects lend themselves to entrepreneurial strategy: reputation and branding, knowledge acquisition, core competencies and other unique resources.
- From the perspective of securing legal ownership, there are four main methods: patents, trademarks, copyright and maintaining trade secrets. The first three can involve heavy legal fees and expensive professional advice. However, this can be justified by the protection provided for valuable new opportunities.

Case study: *eBay – the auction market that spans the world.* This case study has indicative answers to the case questions on the web as a separate page after the case.

CASE STUDY 17.3

Entrepreneurs pioneer a zero carbon house

Michael and Dot Rea have taken green strategy to its logical conclusion by building the first zero carbon house in northern Scotland. This case explains how they did it.

Early beginnings

Without any doubt, Shetland's natural beauty - 24-hour summer sun, clear air, abundant wildlife - is enough to attract some people to live there. It was in 1983 that Michael and Dot Rea bought there first house on the island of Unst, the most northerly island in the British Isles and part of the group known as the Shetland Isles. They were still living and working in southern England at the time. But they soon discovered the other side of Shetland: the wild seas, the winter gloom, the howling gales, even hurricanes. It was such wild storm that devastated their Unst house in 1991 and forced them to pull it down. But what to put in its place?

The idea for a zero carbon house

In 1992, the Reas started thinking about a completely new build on their land. They searched Canada, Scandinavia and the UK searching for a house design that would be relatively easy to heat and maintain. They had to consider that their house in northern Scotland would be on the same latitude as Anchorage, Alaska, with its wild extremes of weather. In the course of their search, they met Dr Jeff Kenna, the chief executive of Energy for Sustainable Development, which is one of the world's leading sustainable energy consultancy companies. It was Jeff who suggested that the Reas might consider building an eco house. It was the Reas themselves who then took this concept further by seeking to build one of the world's early zero carbon houses, i.e. a building that had no net carbon emissions and did not employ any carbon fossil products to produce heat, light and other energy activities. They identified three problems: first, design and build, second, financing and, third, promoting the new house.

Michael Rea explained, 'We want a warm, friendly house that will keep us in our old age. But we want to promote it because we think it needs promoting. If we're talking about carbon friendly, rather then telling people to change their light bulbs wouldn't it be better to design carbon friendly homes that serious builders could put up for sale?'

Designing and building the zero carbon house

After careful search, Michael and Dot Rea decided that they wanted a design that was as standardised as possible. They then followed up this approach by avoiding revolutionary designs. The new build would be timber-framed and would be an off-the-shelf design from one of Scotland's leading timber frame house companies, Scotframe of Inverurie. The new house would have strong insulation, a wind generator, solar panels and an air-to-heat pump. But none of this was totally new technology. What was different was a very early attempt to combine all these together into one house design.

In 2003, the long process of obtaining planning permission began. Ground clearing began in 2005 with the foundations following in 2006. The main timber frame and house was erected in almost hurricane force winds in late 2006. Internal insulation was then installed in 2007, followed by under-floor central heating, electricity cabling, plumbing and all the other aspects of modern house building. There were many problems, not least when a massive cylinder housing the heating slipped over during installation. The house was finally finished in 2008. Moreover, there were plans to build a greenhouse that would grow temperate plants like green peppers and frost-sensitive salad items with low-energy LED lighting and heat that was again zero carbon. In other words, there was self-sufficiency in energy for the production of some food. The whole process needed imagination, courage, persistence and some very hard physical labour.

The Reas' house on Unst is a zero carbon home. It has been designed and built with entrepreneurial flair and sponsorship from many green strategy companies.

Financing the build

For all entrepreneurs, financing is an important part of any project. However, for the Reas, this had some unusual aspects. They worked hard to obtain extensive sponsorship either in the form of building materials, labour or direct grants: the details of this important support are shown on the Rea's website listed at the end of this case. The key here was the dogged persistence and genuine enthusiasm of Michael and Dot Rea in the face of various difficulties.

Promoting zero carbon

Without doubt, the best way is to show that zero carbon works. The finished house in 2010 was so efficient that it barely used any electricity at all. What energy was being used was obtained from the air and sun: zero carbon. The Reas were promoting the new house through their website which was Google's fourth most visited website in the world. They were also engaged in consultancy, media visits and university and student support for various research projects.

Michael Rea explained, 'We are making a stand. We are making a statement, because global warming does worry us. And if it's something you feel passionate about, then the only way to demonstrate that it's achievable and workable is to do it. Next we would like to see houses like this spring up all over Shetland: and see the local community growing their own food all year round.' Dot added, 'I have been waiting 24 years for this house to be built. But it's just a standard house, an honest house, nothing fancy. It's a serious project in renewable design and energy efficiency, an experiment in joined-up technology.'

Note: The Reas' website is at www.zerocarbonhouse.com.

 This case was written after a visit to the house on Unst and extensive material from Michael Rea on the history of the build. The author records his thanks to Michael and Dot Rea for their help in preparing this case. He also acknowledges the other sources listed in the references.[32]

Case questions

1 What aspects of this zero carbon project are typical of other entrepreneurial activity? And what aspects are not typical?

2 What strategy lessons can other entrepreneurs draw from this case, if any?

3 Can green strategy and sustainability lead to other entrepreneurial business opportunities? What strategies would you employ to develop such opportunities?

17.5 IMPLEMENTING ENTREPRENEURIAL STRATEGY

Identifying the opportunity is only a part of the development of entrepreneurial strategy. The implementation stage may be just as challenging. According to Dan Schendel, 'It is one thing to see an opportunity, it is quite another to use and exploit opportunities.'[33] Much of the success of the zero carbon has come from the implementation of an initial idea – developing a combination of technology plus strong personal persistence to implement the zero carbon design. This section therefore explores implementation issues under three headings: personal aspects, implementation resources and drawing up a business plan.

17.5.1 Personal aspects of entrepreneurial strategy

Because of the personal nature of entrepreneurial strategy, we begin by reminding ourselves of the personal demands made on the entrepreneur and of the personal characteristics that are important in implementing entrepreneurial strategy. These are summarised in Exhibit 17.2.

EXHIBIT 17.2

What characteristics make a successful entrepreneur?

- Ability to focus on the task and the opportunity
- Hard worker in relation to the many hours needed
- Self-motivating to get started without support
- Resilient against the probable setbacks
- Confident and assertive in making proposals
- Information-seeking from many people and eager to learn from those able to contribute
- Attuned to seeking out business opportunities at all times
- Receptive to technology and other changes and also to shifts in customer and supplier demands
- Team builder and committed to others in the team
- Comfort with the power that early success will bring

Source: based on P Wickham (2006) *Strategic Entrepreneurship*, 4th edition, Pearson Education.[34]

17.5.2 Development of resources to exploit the business opportunity

In addition to the need for team building, there are various other resources that are essential to implementing entrepreneurial strategy. As outlined earlier, many entrepreneurial new ventures begin from a technology base. It is unlikely that many new companies will have all the knowledge and expertise to exploit such opportunities by themselves. Hence, many such companies will seek partners, either as joint ventures or alliances. The advantage of a joint venture is that it has the security of a legal framework, but the weakness is that the profits are shared with the partner. The alliance is a loser arrangement and runs the risk of the deal falling apart: this could be particularly painful if exclusive technology has been shared with a partner.

In addition to linkages with other companies, many new entrepreneurial ventures will need finance in the form of investment capital. Typically, this entails approaching a bank or a venture capital company. Such companies will want to take a hard look at the business opportunity. But their examination will also take in the people running the new venture, the scope and likelihood of competitive reaction and the growth potential. Accurate and well-developed projections of the costs of the new venture will usually be required. Bankers will be seeking a combination of realism from the entrepreneur that the projections are not too optimistic coupled with enthusiasm for the venture's future success.[35]

17.5.3 Development of realistic business objectives and a business plan

Once the initial resources are in place, there is then a need to develop a business plan. The key is to ensure that such a plan remains flexible and is able to learn from what happens in the market place. It is for this reason that the earlier model of entrepreneurial strategy in Figure 17.2 has a strong feedback mechanism to the 'environment' with specific, separate recognition of two points:

1 the chance outside events that can make or break an opportunity;

2 the need to adopt a learning-based approach with regard to ways of serving and developing the business opportunity. As O'Brien clearly indicated in Case 17.1, the customer is crucial to any such opportunity.

In structuring the business plan, the concepts developed earlier in this book can be used with some adaptation. The ten main elements are shown in Figure 17.5 and follow the prescriptive model structure developed earlier in this text. Arguably, an emergent approach could be used, but the prescriptive model has been chosen because of the specific need to satisfy outside investors, who will usually want some specific projections, as explained in the previous section.

From the topics outlined earlier in this chapter and the rest of this text, most of the elements of the entrepreneurial business plan, such as the analysis of the environment and resources, will be clear. However, the prescriptive model needs to be adapted for the lack of strategic options – there will be some, but the main task will be to define the business opportunity and then pursue this single-mindedly. There are then some six areas of implementation – target customers, distribution, pricing, quality and service, reputation and marketing, alliances and joint ventures – that then need to be developed. These topics have been covered either in this chapter or in earlier chapters so are not repeated here.

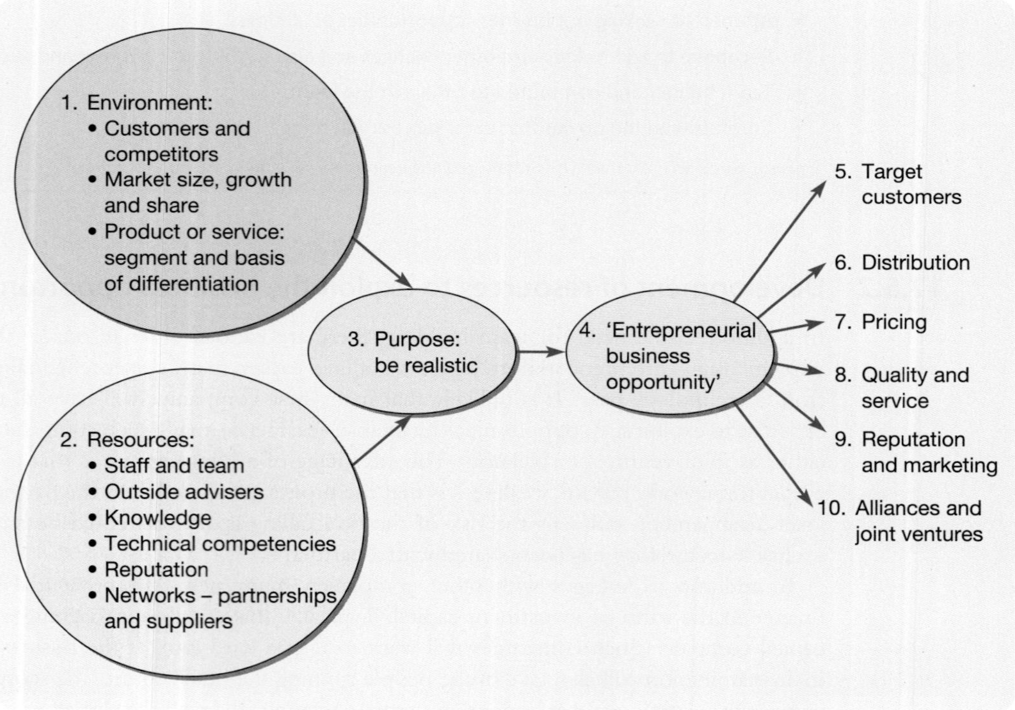

Figure 17.5 Entrepreneurial strategy: the ten elements of a business plan

KEY STRATEGIC PRINCIPLES

- To implement entrepreneurial strategy, there are three main issues: personal aspects, implementation resources and drawing up a business plan. With regard to personal aspects, one important skill required for many entrepreneurs is team building. In most cases, the entrepreneur will need other people to assist in implementing a new business opportunity.
- In the implementation stage, significant resources may be needed for the entrepreneurial venture. Technological resources are often a key component and may require either the recruitment of specialists or the use of joint ventures or alliances to supply such resources from other companies. In addition to technology, there is usually a need for financial support from banks and similar institutions. Banks will require a clear and well-argued plan before they commit funds to such new ventures: detailed and well-costed financial projections are often required. Bankers will be seeking a combination of realism from the entrepreneur that the projections are not too optimistic coupled with enthusiasm for the venture's future success.
- In developing a business plan for a new entrepreneurial venture, a prescriptive process can be employed, mainly because of the need to persuade outside bankers and investors to support the opportunity. However, the prescriptive model needs to be adapted for the lack of strategic options – there will be some, but the main task will be to define the business opportunity and then pursue this single-mindedly. There are ten elements associated with such a plan: environment, resources, purpose, entrepreneurial opportunity, target customers, distribution, pricing, quality and service, reputation and marketing, and alliances and joint venture activity.

CRITICAL REFLECTION

Does entrepreneurship have to be unstructured?

Some strategists argue that entrepreneurs need to seize market opportunities, wherever they arise. This means that they are essentially unstructured and opportunistic. However, when raising finance, many banks and other institutions insist that they need a prescriptive plan before they will risk their funds on such ventures. Who is right? Does entrepreneurship have to be unstructured?

SUMMARY

- Entrepreneurship is a way of thinking, reasoning and acting that focuses on the identification and exploitation of business opportunities from a broad general perspective driven by the leadership of individuals or small groups.
- There are at least three theories concerning the emergence of entrepreneurial opportunities. The *creative destruction* theory argues that innovative opportunities arise through competition and technology destroying previous market offerings. The *discovery theory* is based on the premise that new opportunities already exist in the market place and are waiting to be discovered by entrepreneurs. The *creative theory* is based on the hypothesis that new opportunities can be developed by entrepreneurs experimenting and creating a new market demand that did not previously exist.
- In practice, it is possible to develop a model of the entrepreneurial process. The early elements of the model begin by identifying the external and internal sources that contribute to the business opportunity. The next stage is then to recruit the team plus the external resources that will exploit the opportunity. A business is then set up and the product or service is launched into the market place. The final stage of the model has a feedback mechanism from the market place that may modify or develop the opportunity further.
- Although there are no common personality characteristics of entrepreneurs, the personal background and the motivation of individual entrepreneurs are important and relevant to strategy

development. The successful entrepreneur is likely to be hard-working, confident and receptive to new ideas. One skill that is particularly important is the ability to transfer knowledge within the organisation.

- There are various theories about how entrepreneurs develop opportunities. One such theory is the *experiential learning circle*. This has four elements: concrete experience or knowledge; observation and reflection; formation of abstract concepts from the observation; and testing of such concepts in new situations. Essentially, this theory is based on the concept that entrepreneurs develop new opportunities by learning from the market place. It implies that entrepreneurs need to develop the special skills associated with the learning process.
- Risk is inherent in entrepreneurship and depends in the first instance on the value judgements and expectations of the individual. In considering entrepreneurial risk, it is important to distinguish this topic from the related subject of uncertainty. Risk is measurable, while uncertainty is not so well defined. Risk can be reduced by undertaking further research. However, this may cause tensions in companies because the resources required for the risk research may need to be taken from other parts of the organisation, thus reducing opportunities elsewhere.
- The four main drivers of entrepreneurial strategy are imagination, ideas, invention and innovation. There are three principal methods to create a new business opportunity: technology, innovation and new product and service development.
- With regard to new product and service development, two techniques will aid the process: brainstorming and focus groups. The former is particularly good at generating new ideas, even if some are totally impractical. The latter can assist the process of ideas generation in a more organised and specific process. After the ideas generation stage, a typical process for developing and evaluating entrepreneurial opportunities will involve five stages: screening, business analysis, development, testing and commercial project.
- Entrepreneurial activity is also possible in large companies and is called *intrapreneurship*. Intrapreneurship focuses on the identification and exploitation of creative and innovative opportunities within larger companies or organisations. It can be supported by various company policies that support such processes. These include ownership rights, profit centres, intrapreneurial team building and a system for settling disputes and rivalry between groups.
- Because of the possibility that new opportunities might be imitated, entrepreneurs need to protect their new business ventures. There are two main means: developing sustainable competitive advantages and securing legal ownership.
- With regard to sustainable competitive advantage, there are no rules. However, various aspects lend themselves to entrepreneurial strategy: reputation and branding, knowledge acquisition, core competencies, other unique resources. From the perspective of securing legal ownership, there are four main methods: patents, trademarks, copyright and maintaining trade secrets. The first three can involve heavy legal fees and expensive professional advice. However, this can be justified by the protection provided for valuable new opportunities.
- To implement entrepreneurial strategy, there are three main issues: personal aspects, implementation resources and drawing up a business plan. With regard to personal aspects, one important skill required for many entrepreneurs is team building. In most cases, the entrepreneur will need other people to assist in implementing a new business opportunity.
- In the implementation stage, significant resources may be needed for the entrepreneurial venture. Technological resources are often a key component and may require either the recruitment of specialists or the use of joint ventures or alliances to supply such resources from other companies. In addition to technology, there is usually a need for financial support from banks and similar institutions. Banks will require a clear and well-argued plan before they commit funds to such new ventures: detailed and well-costed financial projections are often required. Bankers will be seeking a combination of realism from the entrepreneur that the projections are not too optimistic coupled with enthusiasm for the venture's future success.

- In developing a business plan for a new entrepreneurial venture, a prescriptive process can be employed, mainly because of the need to persuade outside bankers and investors to support the opportunity. However, the prescriptive model needs to be adapted for the lack of strategic options – there will be some but the main task will be to define the business opportunity and then pursue this single-mindedly. There are ten elements associated with such a plan: environment, resources, purpose, entrepreneurial opportunity, target customers, distribution, pricing, quality and service, reputation and marketing, and alliances and joint venture activity.

QUESTIONS

1 Looking at Lily O'Brien's Chocolates in Case 17.1, which of the three theories of entrepreneurial opportunity best explains the way that the business developed? Is it possible that more than one theory can be used to interpret the company?

2 Take a small organisation with which you are familiar - perhaps a student society or somewhere you have worked - do you see any opportunities for growth? If so, how might they be analysed from the perspective of its strategic environment and resources? And how might the organisation then use this to develop further?

3 Using the experiential learning circle, how might a small internet company employ such an approach to develop its business further? What are the stages in such a development? What are the problems in using such an approach?

4 Using Exhibit 17.2 as a guide, what personal characteristics do you think are particularly important for entrepreneurs? Will entrepreneurs fail if they lack some of these attributes or is this an idealised 'wish list' that does not need to be attained in practice?

5 If you were a banker reviewing a proposal for an entrepreneurial new venture, would you be more impressed by the numbers or by the enthusiasm of the presenters? How would you assess the risks and uncertainty contained in the proposal?

6 Commenting upon entrepreneurial activity, Luke Johnson said: 'I think that a willingness to break the rules [without breaking the law] and punch above your weight is quite important [for entrepreneurs].' Do you agree with both these opinions? What are the benefits and problems of 'breaking the rules'? Do you really need to 'punch above your weight', i.e. exaggerate your achievements and your current resources, in order to be successful?

7 Take a market that is still has scope for innovation - such as the provision of new services on the web - and investigate the entrepreneurial strategies that might be available for entering such a market. Identify those strategies, if any, that are more likely to deliver sustainable competitive advantage.

8 In entrepreneurial markets that are served by the internet, what strategies are available for the smaller business to gain market share and value added (see Cases 17.1 and 17.2 for some possible ideas)? You should consider whether such companies are exploiting all the available strategic opportunities.

9 Think of a small business opportunity - perhaps one of which you are aware or one that you would like to develop - and consider what steps you might employ to develop it. Use Figures 17.4 and 17.5 to help you in this process.

FURTHER READING

For a more detailed review of entrepreneurship, two books are recommended: Phil Wickham's textbook, *Strategic Entrepreneurship*, 4th edition, Prentice Hall, has a UK/European perspective. Bruce Barringer's book co-authored with Duane Ireland: *Entrepreneurship – Successfully Launching New Ventures*, Prentice Hall, Upper Saddle River, NJ, focuses mainly on American examples and is packed with useful insights.

Rita McGrath's chapter – McGrath, R G (2002) 'Entrepreneurship, small firms and wealth creation', in Pettigrew, A, Thomas H and Whittington, R, *Handbook of Strategy and Management*, Sage, London – provides a useful structure on entrepreneurship. A recent special issue also brings a different perspective: Cumming, D, Siegel, D S and Wright, M (2009) 'Special Issue: International Entrepreneurship, Managerial and Policy Implications', *Strategic Entrepreneurship Journal*, Vol 3, No 4, pp 283–296.

For a more academic approach, Volume 1 of the new research journal, *Strategic Entrepreneurship Journal*, published by John Wiley, has many useful papers and a fundamental review of the relationship between strategy and entrepreneurship. Well worth dipping into. Within Volume 1, there are two double issues – Numbers 1–2 and Numbers 3–4. From more recent issues, see Baron, R A and Henry, R A (2010) 'How Entrepreneurs Acquire the Capacity to Excel: A Constructive Perspective', *Strategic Entrepreneurship Journal*, Vol 4, No 1, pp 49–65.

NOTES AND REFERENCES

1 Schendel, D and Hitt, M A (2007) 'Strategy and entrepreneurship are independent constructs . . .', Introduction to Volume 1, *Strategic Entrepreneurship Journal*, Vol 1, p 3.

2 Timmons, J A (1999) *New Venture Creation – Entrepreneurship for the 21st Century*, 5th edn, McGraw Hill, Boston, MA, p 27.

3 Schumpeter, J A (1934) *The Theory of Economic Development*, Harvard University Press, Cambridge, MA.

4 Alvarez, S A and Barney, J B (2007) 'Discovery and creation: theories of entrepreneurial action', *Strategic Entrepreneurship Journal*, Vol 1, pp 1–26. This is a readable paper with a much more extensive review of the foundations of this theory and also that of the creative theory.

5 Alvarez, S A and Barney, J B (2007) Ibid., p 14.

6 Aldrich, H (1999) *Organizations Evolving*, Sage, Newbury Park, CA.

7 McGrath, R G (2002) 'Entrepreneurship, small firms and wealth creation', in Pettigrew, A, Thomas H and Whittington, R, *Handbook of Strategy and Management*, Sage, London.

8 Shah, S K and Tripisas, M (2007) 'The accidental entrepreneur: the emergent and collective process of user entrepreneurship', *Strategic Entrepreneurship Journal*, Vol 1, pp 123–140.

9 McGrath, R G (2002) Op. cit. Table 14.1, p 301.

10 See, for example, Alvarez and Barney (2007) Op. cit. and Shah and Tripsas (2007) Op. cit.

11 Helfat, C E, Finkelstein, S, Mitchell, W, Peteraft, M A, Singh, H, Teece, D J and Winter, S (2007) *Dynamic Capabilities: Understanding Strategic Change in Organizations*, Blackwell, Oxford.

12 Sarkar, M B, Echambadi, R, Agarwal, R and Sen, B (2006) 'The effect of the innovative environment on exit of entrepreneurial firms', *Strategic Management Journal*, Vol 27, pp 519–539.

13 Wickham, P A (2006) *Strategic Entrepreneurship*, Pearson Education, Harlow, Ch 3.

14 Jones-Evans, D (1995) 'A typology of technology based entrepreneurs', *International Journal of Entrepreneurial Research and Behaviour*, Vol 1, No 1, pp 26–47.

15 Wickham, P A (2006) Op. cit., Ch 5.

16 Kolb, D A and Fry, R (1975) 'Toward an applied theory of experiential learning', in Cooper, C (ed) *Theories of Group Process*, John Wiley, London. The author acknowledges the organisers, the Entrepreneurial Education Seminar, held over one day at the Academy of Management Annual Conference, Atlanta, 2006, where this theory was presented.

17 Schendel, D and Hitt, M (2007) Op. cit., p 3.

18 Schendel, D (2007) 'Moderator's comments on risk and uncertainty', *Strategic Entrepreneurship Journal*, Vol 1, p 53.

19 McGrath, R G (2002) Op. cit. p 310.

20 Ichbiah, D and Knepper, S L (1993) *Making of Microsoft: how Bill Gates and his team created the world's most successful software company*, Prima Publishing, Rocklin, CA, p 93.

21 Ichbiah, D and Knepper, S L (1993) Ibid., p 67.

22 Other sources for the three entrepreneurs case: www.microsoft.com – corporate relations; interviews with Luke Johnson and John Caudwell, *Later* magazine, September 2000, London; BBC website: bbc.co.uk/stoke/2006/08/07/john caudwell biog; www.lukejohnson.org accessed 2 February 2008.

23 Schendel, D and Hitt, M (2007) Op. cit., p 1.

24 All the quotes are taken from the personal experience of the author in his 20 years in various companies. He suspects that this anecdotal evidence is not untypical in certain large companies.

25 See, for example, Henry Mintzberg (1991) 'The innovative organization', Ch 13 in Mintzberg, H and Quinn, J B (1991) *Strategy: Process, Content and Context*, West Publishing, St Paul, MN, pp 731–746. Rosabeth Moss Kanter (1985) *The Changemasters*, Unwin, London. Both worth reading for concepts and ideas in this area.

26 These ideas have been taken from the Wikipedia section on 'Intrapreneurship' which summarises material from a number of sources – searched January 2008.

27 Kay, J (1993) *Foundations of Corporate Success*, Oxford University Press, Oxford.

28 Leonard, D (1998) *Wellsprings of Knowledge*, Harvard Business School Press, Boston, MA; Nonaka, I and Takeuchi, H (1995) *The Knowledge-Creating Company*, Oxford University Press, Oxford.

29 Hamel, G and Prahalad, H K (1994) *Competing for the Future*, Harvard Business School Press, Boston, MA, Chs 9 and 10.

30 Schendel, D and Hitt, M (2007) Op. cit., p 4.

31 This section has benefited from Chapter 12, Barringer, B R and Ireland, R D (2008) *Entrepreneurship: Successfully Launching New Ventures*, Pearson Prentice Hall, Upper Saddle River, NJ.

32 Other references for the zero carbon house case are: http://www.guardian.co.uk/environment/2008/may/19/greenbuilding.windpower; http://www.shetland-news.co.uk/features/Living/20carbon free on Unst.htm; http://computescotland.com/the-advent-of-eiggtricity-in-2008-624.php; http://www.zerocarbonhouse.com.

33 Schendel, D (2007) Op. cit., p 53.

34 Wickham, P (2006) Op. cit., Ch 5, pp 97–99.

35 Timmons, J A (1999) Op. cit., Ch 20.

CHAPTER 18
Government, public sector and not-for-profit strategies

Video and sound summary of this chapter.

LEARNING OUTCOMES

When you have worked through this chapter, you will be able to:

- explain why public sector strategy is different and why it is important;
- outline the two main public sector models and explain the concept of public value;
- analyse the public sector environment;
- analyse the resources of a public sector institution;
- explain how the purpose of a public sector institution can be developed and defined;
- outline the development of strategy in the public sector from the perspectives of context, content and process;
- develop either a plan to implement the selected strategy or an incremental approach for an emergent strategy.

INTRODUCTION

This chapter focuses on the special considerations that apply to strategy in the government, public and not-for-profit sectors. 'Government' means areas like defence and the law, which are the responsibility of the nation state. 'Public' means the provision of health, transport, energy and other services which may be the responsibility of the state or may have been privatised, depending on the political views of the government. 'Not-for-profit' means institutions that work for the common public good but are independent of the state – for example, charities, trusts and similar institutions. In order to avoid unnecessary repetition throughout this chapter, these organisations are simply called 'public' institutions and their strategies are called public strategies to distinguish them from the 'private' strategies of commercial businesses. The differences between the three different types of public sector institutions are discussed where required.

Why does public sector strategy deserve a separate chapter? There are two main reasons. The first is that the public sector in every nation around the world is important. Even for high-income countries such as the USA, where many services are devolved to the private sector, the wealth expended on the public sector is over 34 per cent of gross domestic product.[1] In other words, every country spends considerable sums on its public sector. Public sector strategy therefore matters and deserves to be explored in depth.

The second reason for a separate chapter is that the public sector is more complex and involves factors that do not apply in the private sector.[2] For example, companies like Kelloggs and Cereal Partners compete in the private sector breakfast cereal market. A measure of their success is their ability to deliver profits to shareholders and offer value for money products to customers. But in a public sector example like the local or national police force, there is no question of delivering a 'profit' on the police budget and a 'value for money' policing service needs considerable clarification if it is to have any meaning at all.[3]

If public sector strategy is so different, then it follows that the principles that have been explored for business strategy in the rest of this book may not apply in public sector strategy. For example, Chapter 5 explored competitive strategies like 'head-on' and 'flanking' attacks against a dominant competitor. These have little meaning where the state runs a monopoly such as its defence or police force.[4] We therefore need to reconsider the elements of business strategy in a public sector context.

An additional difficulty faces the business strategist in redefining its concepts for the public sector. Theories on *public sector administration* have been around for longer than those in business strategy.[5] This means that there is another stream of intellectual thought that needs to be considered in re-examining business strategy. It is not possible in one chapter to explore *all* the many public sector administration theories that have been developed. The approach of this chapter has been to focus only on those that have a direct connection with the rest of this book. However, the chapter contains sufficient references to allow the reader to follow up those areas that deserve greater depth. Interestingly, theories in public sector administration in the past 20 years have been moving closer to private sector concepts – as we shall see when we explore the *new public management* concepts later in the chapter.[6]

To explore strategic management in the public sector, we will follow the basic structure of the book as developed for business strategy. This approach is summarised in Figure 18.1.

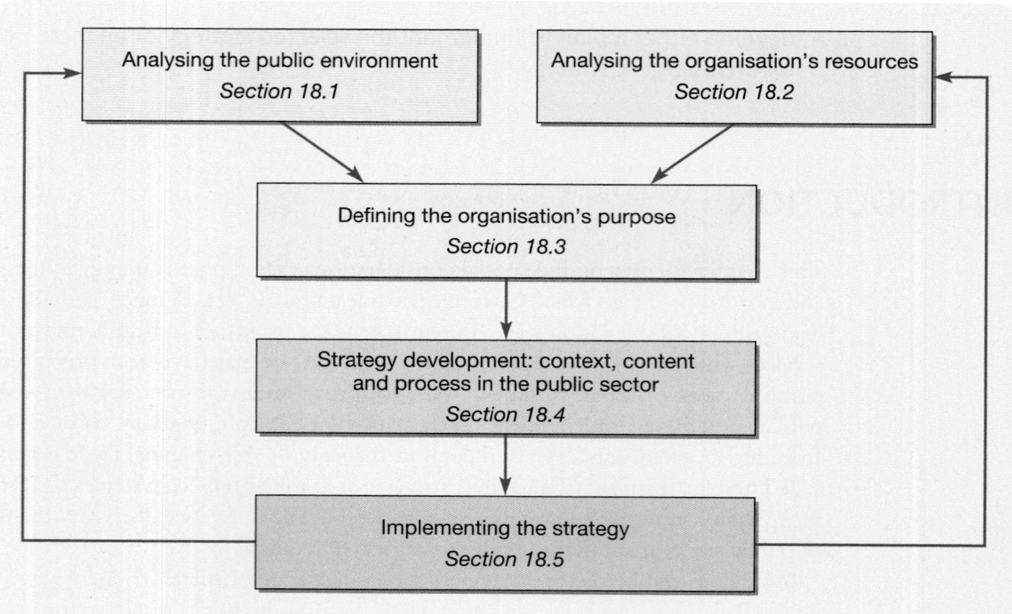

Figure 18.1 Developing strategy in public and not-for-profit sectors

CASE STUDY 18.1

Public sector strategy: how Galileo ended up in serious trouble

In 1999, politicians from European Union finally agreed the development and launch of a new global satellite system called Galileo. By 2012, political decision making and European company rivalries had delayed the project by seven years and tripled the initial cost. This case explores an extraordinary failure in public sector strategy.

Background

Some years ago, the US government launched a global network of satellites aimed to assist navigation everywhere in the world. Essentially, the signals from the satellites allowed virtually anyone on the planet with the right equipment to obtain an accurate fix on a geographical location: the Global Positioning System (GPS). In addition to its civilian use, the GPS is also used by the American military and its NATO allies for military purposes in time of conflict. There is also a Russian system, called GLONASS, that provides similar services.

In 2012, the GPS system was widely used in both military and civilian life: for example, there was a totally new market for car satellite navigation systems ('satnavs') that was entirely dependent on the GPS system. Mobile phone location systems also relied essentially on GPS signals. However, some countries within the European Union were not entirely happy with this arrangement for four reasons:

1 In theory at least, the US Government could switch off the GPS system at any time without consulting anyone.

2 For some European countries, the reliance on American military technology was seen as a serious military weakness. President Chirac of France was reported as saying that Europe risked becoming a 'vassal' of the USA.

3 European countries realised that their national defence companies risked losing key technological know-how and skills in satellite communications if they continued to rely on the US system and technology.

4 Some European nations also identified a world commercial business opportunity to sell satellite receivers and related services. According to some estimates, there would be world market demand for around 3 billion receivers worth around $250 billion by year 2020.

The problem for an individual European country and/or company was the heavy investment cost required to put up an alternative satellite system – around $3.5 billion in the late 1990s. This figure was beyond the resources of most individual European countries.

Europe's new Galileo satellite will compete directly against the American GPS system.

The Galileo joint venture

In 1999, the 15 countries (now 28) of the European Union agreed to the joint development of a pan-European satellite system to be called *Galileo*. The European Commission – the central administration of the EU – was granted a new frequency from the International Telecommunications Union to use with its proposed Galileo satellite system. Around the same time, each state within the EU agreed its share of the funding and design. Importantly, Galileo would use more sophisticated, new digital technology to deliver its positioning signals. This meant that in addition to a free signal, like the American GPS system, Galileo would also have another service called the Public Regulated Service (PRS): this latter service would *not* be free to the general public. The PRS would be encrypted so that it was available only on subscription from commercial organisations.

Galileo would also contain two other channel services: the first would only be available to Europe's military and defence establishments; the second would be used by its emergency services, such as the police and sea rescue. In summary, Galileo would be more accurate and have a wider range of services than the American GPS system as a result of using digital technology. In addition, the new European co-operative venture would make Europe independent of the American system. The EU Commission was so enthusiastic that it claimed that Galileo would create more than 150,000 jobs and generate an annual income of $10 billion. It would be a 'trump card that will greatly enhance Europe's influence in the world'.

After the final agreement amongst European nations, experimental contracts were then prepared and a complete timetable developed for the European launch. Prototype satellites were planned for launch in 2005 and, depending on the testing, the full Galileo system would become operational late in 2006. As matters then turned out, this timetable proved to be wildly optimistic. All these negotiations were dependent on basic progress with the Galileo system itself. Unfortunately, the Galileo satellite system was about to take a turn for the worse.

Crisis at Galileo

In May 2007, the German transport minister Wolfgang Tiefensee said that Galileo was in 'a deep and profound crisis. We have reached a dead end street.' The roots of the major problems had begun two years earlier. Originally, the EU expected that the private sector would provide most of the Galileo finance amounting to around $4 billion and therefore share most of the risk of failure. It was this principle that secured the approval of some EU governments - particularly the UK - who were dubious about the whole Galileo project: they considered that the private sector rather than the public sector would be taking much of the responsibility.

In addition to covering the risk, the big advantage of private sector funding was that the Galileo project would be open to competitive tendering from rival companies. Initially, two main consortia (a consortium is a group of companies) were bidding for the Galileo contract. The EU thought that their desire to gain the business would keep their bids low and the costs down. Each of the companies forming part of a consortium was a major company in an individual European country in either satellite manufacture or telecommunications. Unfortunately, political considerations within the EU destroyed this approach. The EU's awarding authority could not decide between the two bidders for fear of offending the national governments behind each of the companies. The result was that the two competitive bidders were combined into one single consortium. The combined company now had many of the EU's most powerful companies in the market: the major French and German aerospace company EADS, France's Thales and Alcatel-Lucent, the UK's Inmarsat, Italy's Finmeccanica, Spain's AENA and Hispasat and a German group called TeleOp that was led by Germany's largest telecommunications company Deutsche Telekom. Thus the bidding process to reduce costs had been lost.

Even this decision by the EU's awarding authority also had another major flaw. The authority never made any decision on how to split up the elements of the contract. This meant that, 'If the companies cannot get what they want, they go back to London, Paris or Rome' according to an anonymous person close to the negotiations.

After much further negotiation, the share-out of the contract was decided largely using political rather than industrial logic. For example, the headquarters would be in Toulouse, France, with operations run from London, England. Germany and Italy would operate control centres with a back-up in Spain.

What happened next?

The original plan was that Galileo would be fully operational by 2007. The first experimental Galileo satellite was launched in 2005 with another in 2006. Then Spain 'took the view that it should have as much as Italy and Germany. It was a matter of pride', according to an informed source. There was then another 18 months of negotiations.

Eventually, the EU gave the consortium a deadline of May 2007. The members of the single consortium then demanded new business terms from the EU. These included some guarantees about the profitability of the project for members of the consortium and also some special insurance in the event of a catastrophic failure of a Galileo satellite. The EU was in a weak position to argue since it was negotiating with a monopoly bidder for its business. The original estimated cost of Galileo was around $2 billion. The outcome of the new negotiations was that the EU governments were asked to find at least another $1.5 billion. This was finally agreed by the EU governments and four test satellites were planned for launch in 2011-2012.

In 2011, the consortium returned to the EU and said that the full system would need additional funds of around $2.5 billion. This would allow the launch of another 14 satellites in 2014 to complete the initial system. However, another 12 satellites would be needed to provide full global coverage and back-ups in the period from 2014 onwards.

To summarise, the original cost of Galileo had tripled from $2 billion to an estimated cost of $6 billion. The original completion date of the Galileo system was 2007. This was initially put back to the year 2011. The latest estimated completion date of the basic system at the time of writing this case (in 2011) was 2014 - seven years late.

In spite of this poor record, many European countries remained optimistic about the many potential uses such as mapping crop areas, tracking cargo and freight and assessing coastal erosion. The EU judged that the market for GPS systems had real potential: the market size was around $800 billion with a high annual growth of around 25 per cent. 'It is a fantastic project that has already lost a lot of time it cannot afford,' according to Karel van Miert, a former EU Transport Commissioner. But sceptics remained to be convinced that Galileo would even be finished by 2014.

Case questions

1 What were the main benefits from launching the Galileo satellite system? And what were the European Union's main mistakes? Do you think that the benefits outweighed the problems?

2 To what extent were the political difficulties predictable within the EU? How would you have handled these issues if you were a public sector official at the EU? Would you have changed the strategy? If so, in what way?

3 What, if any, are the lessons that can be learnt about public sector strategy from the Galileo experience?

Case study: *The World Bank: juggling the strategic environment.*

18.1 ANALYSING THE STRATEGIC ENVIRONMENT IN PUBLIC SECTOR STRATEGY

In public sector strategy, the analysis of the strategic environment is more complex than in the private sector. The main reason is that public sector strategy involves the wide-ranging and ill-defined subject of the *public interest*: **the public interest concerns both the objectives and the institutions that make and implement public decisions.** This basic concept in public sector strategy has two elements: the 'public' referring to citizens in general and 'interest' referring to the individual[8] wishes of the public.[9] The public interest is quite different from a company operating in a competitive market place. For example, the Galileo case shows that the public interest – as interpreted by national governments and various international agencies on behalf of their citizens – is important and quite different from a company selling its products in the market place. There are four main environmental factors that deserve to be analysed:

Definition ▸

1 the extent of the market mechanism in public service;
2 the concept of public value;
3 stakeholder power and complexity;
4 special issues in not-for-profit organisations.

After exploring these factors, this section then concludes by analysing the public sector environment.

18.1.1 The extent of the market mechanism in public service

We can explore this under three main headings:

1 the benefits of the market mechanism in the public sector;
2 the costs of the market mechanism in the public sector;
3 the balance between laissez-faire and dirigiste policies of national governments.

The benefits of the market mechanism in the public sector

In public sector administration theory, governments are assumed to take decisions on behalf of *all* their citizens, rather than a few. For example in the European Union's Galileo satellite investment, the funds were made available to *all* the relevant companies associated with their bids and the general public were not consulted. If the public goods and services must be available to all relevant parties, then public sector theorists have argued that this is most effectively and efficiently achieved through government agencies with centralised decision making:[10] for example, one agency to manage police services. In public administration theory, centralised decision making is regarded as being beneficial.

Taking decisions on behalf of all citizens is quite different from private markets where the 'buyer' can choose whether to buy a product from a 'seller'. The citizen has no such choice in public administration theory and, in market terms, the centralised public bureaucracy is effectively a monopoly. For many economists, a monopoly is unresponsive and inefficient as a service supplier. Centralised decision making is therefore not beneficial. Hence, there is a basic conflict in public service between *public administration* theory and *market economic* theory.[11] For many countries in the past 20 years, the view has shifted towards introducing market forces to reduce the price of public goods. For such countries, public administration theory has therefore moved closer to market economic theory.

The public sector approach accompanying this shift towards market forces has been to break up the state monopoly supplier of such goods into several companies, which then compete against each other on price and service levels in the market place. Competition is likely to reduce the costs of the former monopolistic state enterprise and therefore the prices paid by the customer: in essence, this is the *privatisation* of former state monopolies. Even in countries with a strong socialist tradition like China, there have been moves to privatise former state monopolies like civil air transport. The underpinning principle of privatisation is that market competition – often referred to as the *market mechanism* – is more efficient than monopoly in the management of state resources.

In some countries, this market-based approach has taken an additional form: co-operation between the public interest and private enterprise – called *public private partnerships* – with private finance and management being used to develop and subsequently administer public services. For example, private finance might be raised to develop a new state hospital in the public sector and then a private company appointed for a period of years to manage all the hospital services on behalf of the public. This co-operative approach remains controversial – particularly the allegedly high level of fees paid for the management contract – but is an example of another form of market mechanism in the public sector.

The costs of the market mechanism in the public sector

In addition to market-based benefits in public sector strategy, there are also costs associated with such an approach. There are two main areas: first, there are clear *limits* to how far the market approach can be implemented. Market theory suggests that failed products disappear from markets because they are not meeting demand. In principle, this would therefore suggest that any public sector body that is subject to market pressures and fails to deliver on its public sector objectives should be closed. While this may be possible for a failing school because there may be other schools, it is clearly not possible to allow a large regional hospital with specialist staff and equipment to fail. There is a cost to keeping such organisations open in terms of efficiency and lack of market pressures.

There is a second problem associated with introducing the market mechanism – the *transaction costs* of privatisation. There is a need to set standards, monitor progress, evaluate performance and other activities associated with giving former monopolies the freedom to undertake public services. If this were not done, such organisations might not deliver the full level of service previously provided by the monopoly: the market mechanism is powerful and can potentially distort performance. Setting such standards and monitoring the outcome has two main costs:

1 the public monitoring organisations needed to check on the activities of the newly privatised public sector organisations and ensure that they continue to deliver their public service obligations;
2 the administrative costs at the newly privatised organisations involved in providing data on their performance and related activities.

In theory, the benefit of the market mechanism should outweigh the two costs outlined above. In practice, there is some disagreement over such matters. Importantly in public sector strategy, it is essential to consider carefully the monitoring mechanisms, performance targets and their related costs in the development of strategy. It is also appropriate to build network contacts with those involved in the monitoring process – the public regulators – and discuss proposed strategy change with them.

The balance between laissez-faire and dirigiste policies of national governments

Definition ▶ In public sector policy, **the market mechanism is the means by which the state uses competition between suppliers, market pricing and quasi-market mechanisms to determine the supply and demand of goods that were previously state monopolies.** In both the EU and the USA, there are differing views on the extent to which the state should become involved in markets. In France, Italy and Greece, it has long been the tradition that state-owned companies and state intervention are important elements of the national economy. In the UK, New Zealand and the USA, the opposing view has been taken. The approach adopted is essentially a *political* choice made by those in power. The two approaches – often referred to as *laissez-faire* and *dirigiste* – are summarised in Table 18.1. Adam Smith, Karl Marx and many other political commentators have all contributed to the important political debate in this area. Table 18.1 is intended merely to summarise areas that are the most relevant to the development of strategic management.

Table 18.1 Two models of the public sector environment

Laissez faire: free-market model	Dirigiste: centrally directed model
• Low entry barriers • Competition encouraged • Little or no state support for industry • Self-interest leads to wealth creation • Belief in laws of supply and demand • Higher unemployment levels • Profit motive will provide basis for efficient production and high quality	• High entry barriers • National companies supported against international competition • State ownership of some key industries • Profit motive benefits the few at the expense of the many • Failure in market mechanism will particularly affect the poor and can only be corrected by state intervention • Need to correct monopolies controlled by private companies

In practice, the distinctions drawn in Table 18.1 are very crude. Some countries offer a *balance* between strong state-sponsored policies in some areas – for example, education, favoured industries (as in Singapore), investment in roads, power and water – and then couple this with a free-market approach in other areas – for example, privatisation of state monopolies or lower barriers to entry to encourage investment by multinational enterprises (MNEs). (MNEs are the large global companies such as Ford, McDonald's and Unilever.) Each country will have its own approach, so any public sector environmental analysis will have to be conducted on a country-by-country basis.

18.1.2 The concept of public value

Definition ▶ **Public value refers to the benefits to the whole of the nation from owning and controlling certain products and services.** For example, the national defence forces and the police service have a clear benefit to all the citizens of a country. The government, on behalf of the nation, takes the decision of which public goods and services should be under national control and which services should be controlled privately by business. In practice in many countries, there are some grey areas which are neither totally in government control nor totally private; the public value is therefore mixed. Figure 18.2 gives some examples.

Given the concept of public value, there are three important consequences for public sector strategy analysis:

1 Unlike a private sector market for a car or a hotel room, the public service for defence forces or clean air needs to be a binding collective decision for it to be effective. Public sector strategy needs to be enacted and supported by a *legal framework* and laws that bind, govern and distribute the public value. This legal framework needs to be analysed.

2 There is a need to ensure that the public value is genuinely available to all citizens, with everyone having a fair share or an equal opportunity – the concept of *equity*. This is fundamentally different from business strategy. The extent and nature of public equity needs to be analysed in developing public sector strategy.

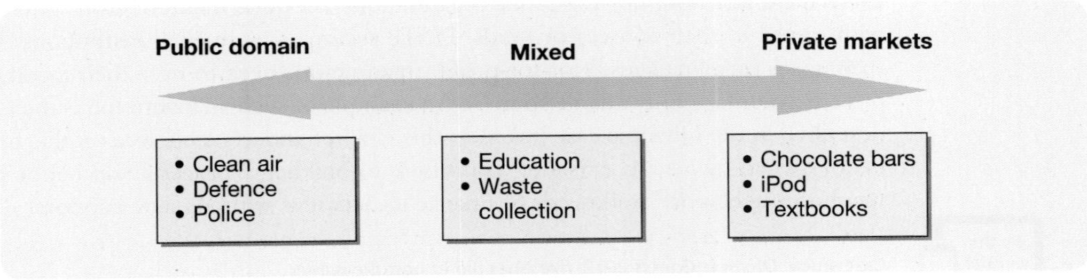

Figure 18.2 Public value is highest in the public domain

3 Occasionally, there is a need to remedy problems in distributing the public value: the market mechanism may fail after privatisation has occurred. Market failure can take many forms: for example, the newly privatised companies may attempt to control the market and keep their prices artificially high. The government may therefore appoint a special independent *public regulator* to oversee the results of privatisation and ensure full and fair distribution of the benefits of the public value arising from the privatisation. This is particularly important where public value is mixed with private wealth – for example, in a privatised telecommunications company. The mechanism for ensuring the fair distribution of public value therefore needs to be analysed.

As an example of the implications of the areas above, we can examine the European Union's handling of the Galileo satellite case. The *legal framework* environment analysis will cover the basic legal articles of association setting up the contracts for Galileo, the membership of its board and their responsibilities. The *equity analysis* will need to examine the way that funds are actually distributed by the Galileo overseeing authority so that its funds are distributed in accordance with the negotiated agreement and without undue influence. In the case of the Galileo contract, a *public regulator* is highly relevant given the strong element of competition involved in the distribution of the European Union's funds and given the way that the funds were then diverted according to various government pressures that bore little relation to the efficient use of resources.

18.1.3 Stakeholder power and complexity

In the public sector, stakeholder power is possessed by those citizens who are able to influence the decisions of the state. In practice, this may be through democratic elections, with a change of government leading to substantial changes in the services provided by the state. But it may be through other forms of state structure that do not rely on democracy. The difficulty here is that all such changes can be short-term and involve quite substantial and unpredictable changes in public sector strategy. Such uncertainty deserves to be analysed in developing public sector strategy.

In addition, there are other ways for citizens to exert their influence – pressure groups, campaigns, even riots and disturbances. For example, during the Galileo contract negotiations described in Case 18.1, press reports of the problems plus the various review meetings of the governing body exerted pressure for considerable change – not always for the better. This is important because it shows how public bodies can be lobbied and pressured in their decision making. A stakeholder power analysis can be undertaken – see Chapter 6 – but this may only show that the stakeholder group is more powerful than the politician who is theoretically directing the public service. We return to this matter in Section 18.3 on power and democracy.

18.1.4 Special issues in not-for-profit organisations

Although the definition of not-for-profit organisations is very broad, it will certainly cover charitable, voluntary and other public interest bodies that are not owned by the state. Such organisations are not concerned with the distribution of public value in the sense of delivering this equitably to all citizens. In addition, not-for-profit organisations are quite different from government institutions with regard to their sources of funds. Public sector governmental institutions derive their income from taxes on all citizens. Not-for-profit organisations need to raise their income from a variety of private, voluntary and variable sources. An example of such an institution is the Olympic movement described in the Olympic case linked to this chapter and available free on this book's website. This is not owned by a state, exists to 'contribute to building a peaceful and better world by educating youth through sport', and needs to finance its activities without state support.

Case study: *Olympic Games 2012: five cities bid to host the games.*

The main focus of an environmental analysis in such organisations will need to explore two main areas:

1. *The precise role and purpose of such organisations.* The role will define the environment in which the not-for-profit organisation exists and with whom it is engaged. For example, the role of the international Red Cross organisation (and Red Crescent in Muslim countries) is to bring humanitarian and disaster relief to those in distress around the world. Its environment is therefore that of other relief agencies, governments and countries needing such relief and the individuals in those countries benefiting from such work. In practice, this needs careful definition to ensure that the environment is adequately described.
2. *The fund-raising mechanism of the organisation.* Virtually every not-for-profit organisation needs financial support to undertake its work. Such organisations may even compete against each other for public support and public funds. For example, the public funds raised around the world in 2005 for the Asian tsunami disaster meant that some other public charities had difficulty in raising sufficient funds for their own activities. This suggests that an environmental analysis needs to examine carefully the current and future sources of funds of the organisation and the implications in terms of related, similar organisations. It also needs to explore the more general mood and public acceptance of the country or region in which the organisation operates, since this will impact on its ability to generate adequate funds.

18.1.5 Analysing the public sector strategy environment

We can summarise the implications of the discussion above by returning to the basic strategic environmental analysis undertaken in Chapter 3 and considering its implications for public sector analysis. This is shown in Table 18.2.

KEY STRATEGIC PRINCIPLES

- In public sector strategy, the analysis of the strategic environment is more complex than in the private sector. The main reason is that public sector strategy involves the wide-ranging and ill-defined subject of the public interest: the public interest concerns both the objectives and the institutions that make and implement public decisions. There are two main public sector models – centrally directed (*dirigiste*) and free-market (*laissez-faire*).
- The market mechanism is the means by which the state uses market pricing and quasi-market mechanisms to determine the supply and demand of goods that were previously state monopolies. In practice, over the past 20 years many states have moved to greater use of the market through privatising state-owned companies. Each individual country will have its own approach to the use of such mechanisms. A public sector environmental analysis will have to be conducted on a country-by-country basis. There are also two costs associated with the market mechanism: first, the cost of being unable to close inefficient services because they provide vital public services; second, the cost of administering the market mechanism to ensure that it serves the agreed public objectives.
- Public value refers to the benefits to the whole of the nation from owning and controlling certain products and services. But such value needs to be considered within the legal framework that binds and governs the value. In addition, public value requires the concept of equity to make sure that the value is distributed to all citizens. In some circumstances, public value needs a regulator to deal with any market imperfections.
- In the public sector, stakeholder power is possessed by those citizens who are able to influence the decisions of the state. Such power may be expressed through democratic elections but these can lead to short-termism in strategic decisions. Power can also be exercised through pressure groups and other forms of interest. Such power needs to be analysed.
- In the not-for-profit sector, an environmental analysis needs to consider the role and purpose of the organisation. It also needs to identify its actual and potential sources of funds. Such organisations cannot rely on public taxes to pay for their activities and need to seek voluntary contributions that will vary with a range of factors.
- The nine stages in environmental analysis used for business strategy can be adapted for use in public sector strategy analysis, though they need to be treated with caution.

Table 18.2 Analysing the public sector strategic environment[12]

Stage	Business strategy techniques	Can they be used in the public sector?
1 Environment basics – an opening evaluation to define and explore basic characteristics of the environment (see Section 3.2)	Estimates of some basic factors surrounding the environment: • Market definition and size • Market growth • Market share	Possibly but they need to be redefined: • Demand for a public service • Political will to supply the public service • The relevant funding and costs of supplying the service
2 Consideration of the degree of turbulence in the environment (see Section 3.3)	General considerations: • Change: fast or slow? • Repetitive or surprising future? • Forecastable or unpredictable? • Complex or simple influences on the organisation?	Yes, but perhaps not so easy to analyse. It will need judgement, especially on the influence of political and pressure groups • Is the environment too turbulent to undertake useful predictions? • What are the opportunities and threats for the organisation?
3 Green strategy	• Government policies • Market opportunities • Customer and industry attitudes	Yes – clear public interest issues plus opportunity for government to influence 'green' market
4 Background factors that influence the competitive environment (see Section 3.4)	PESTEL analysis and scenarios	Yes, definitely • Predict, if possible • Understand interconnections between events
5 Analysis of stages of market growth (see Section 3.5)	Industry life cycle	Possibly but not really clear what this could mean beyond the natural rhythm of country change
6 Factors specific to the industry: what delivers success? (see Section 3.6)	Key factors for success analysis	Yes in the sense that KFS will help identify issues with regard to the priorities needed for successful public sector strategy
7 Factors specific to the competitive balance of power in the industry (see Section 3.7)	Five Forces Analysis	• Possibly for 'customers' and even 'competitors' (many public sector institutions compete for funds) • 'Supplier' analysis is also relevant because governments should be powerful buyers • But difficult to see relevance of 'substitutes' and 'new entrants' in a monopoly
8 Factors specific to co-operation in the industry (see Section 3.8)	Four Links Analysis	• Definitely worth undertaking this analysis – the Galileo example shows its importance • Network analysis will also be useful
9 Factors specific to immediate competitors (see Section 3.9)	Competitor analysis and product portfolio analysis	• Difficult to envisage any significant benefit here
10 Customer analysis (see Section 3.10)	Market and segmentation studies	Customer analysis is useful but needs to be considered in relation to the broader concepts of public value and choice in the public sector

18.2 ANALYSING RESOURCES IN THE PUBLIC AND NOT-FOR-PROFIT SECTORS

As we saw in Chapter 4, the concept of sustainable competitive advantage underpins resource-based analysis in business strategy. However, the public sector has traditionally been regarded as not engaging in competitive activities – for example, the public fire and rescue service is non-competitive. If there is no competition in the public sector, then resource analysis will be quite different from its equivalent in business strategy. The first issue therefore is whether sustainable competitive advantage has any meaning in the public sector. If there is 'competition', then what form does this take?

The second issue with regard to public sector resources is the broader one of the *nature* of such resources beyond competitive issues and compared with business resources. By 'nature' is meant the range of resources available to the public sector strategist and the costs associated with public sector resources. The third issue is to identify the analytical tools for such work.

18.2.1 Does sustainable competitive advantage have any meaning in the public sector?

The Galileo satellite case perhaps implies that the company is unique and does not compete with other institutions. However, governments can divert or withhold funds if a company is under-performing and, in a sense, the Galileo satellite system therefore has had to compete for funds that might have been used for alternative projects within the European Union. The Shetland Islands case later in this chapter deals with the difficult choice between economic development and preserving wildlife – see Case 18.2. But it also explores the need for a public sector organisation to find finance to provide its services such as education, transport and local police. The Council may obtain some extra funds from its new wind farm development, if its plans are successful. Equally, it may also find funds from other sources such as local taxes and central government. But the Shetland Island Council arguably has no competitors. Do most public sector bodies conform to the monopolistic view of government and rarely engage in competition? The answer depends on the type of public administration model adopted by the nation – the *public sector administration* model or the *new public management* model. Resource analysis needs to begin by identifying which model is used by the state.

Definition ► For many years, **the *public sector administration model* was that of an organisation that did the bidding of its political masters.**[13] **In this model, a professional civil service enacted government legislation and administered the activities of the state on behalf of the government. The same public sector also contained public sector enterprises, such as electricity or telecommunications, that made the public pay for their monopolistic services.**[14] Competition played a relatively minor role in such a scheme: for example, one regional police force did not normally compete with another to make arrests. However, the annual budget of the police force – perhaps – 'competed' for funds from the government against the budget for other public services like defence and, in this sense, there was a small element of competition. Importantly, in this description of public services, there was little incentive for public employees to reduce their costs and increase their efficiencies because their services were essentially monopolistic.[15] More generally, such a model of public sector decision making did not lend itself to the rigorous economic logic of competitive advantage.

For many national governments around the world over the past 20 years, the situation has changed from the model outlined above, which has been replaced, at least in part, by the *new public management* Definition ► *(NPM) model.*[16] **New public management is a model of public sector decision making where the professional civil service operates with more market competition coupled with former state monopolies being divided and competing against each other for business from citizens. However, the nation retains some areas under state control, such as the defence of the nation.** The new model offered a set of ideas about how government can operate based to a much greater extent on the efficiencies derived from market competition.[17] There are six core issues in NPM[18] – productivity, marketisation, service orientation, decentralisation, policy and accountability – but from a strategy perspective the key issue is marketisation, so that is the issue explored here. This means that this section is not a full discussion of the many other aspects of NPM, which can be explored through the books listed at the end of this chapter.

NPM is based on two main assumptions.[19] The first is that demand for government services can be separated from the supply of those services. The second is that it is possible to introduce competition into the supply of such services. We can explore these assumptions by examining what has happened in those countries that have sold into the private sector previously nationalised industries. Examples of such state companies sold into the private sector include electricity generation and telecommunications services. After privatisation, demand for such services has not fundamentally changed, so the assumption that supply can be separated from demand has proved correct. Moreover, privatisation has taken place in such a way that the monopolies have been split into several competing companies, thus introducing competition into supply.

From a resource analysis perspective, it follows that competition does exist when a nation has adopted NPM policies. It is not possible to set out all the evidence in this brief review, but many researchers in both public sector administration[20] and strategy development in the public sector[21] support such a conclusion. This means that it is relevant to consider resource-based competitive analysis in the public sector. Such competitive advantages as tangible and intangible resources, core competencies, architecture, reputation, innovative capability and knowledge may all be explored in the public sector. The reader is referred back to Chapter 4 for a more comprehensive view of this area. It also follows that a SWOT analysis can be employed to summarise such issues – Chapter 8 sets out the main elements.[22]

Although the above argument has focused largely on government organisations, the same basic principles can be applied in not-for-profit organisations. This is explored more fully in Section 18.2.3.

18.2.2 The special nature of public sector resources

In addition to issues of competitive advantage, public sector resource analysis also needs to explore the special nature of public sector resources in four areas:

1 Sufficient and appropriate resources for purpose
2 Public power as a resource
3 The costs and benefits of public resources
4 Persuasion and education as a public resource.

Sufficient and appropriate resources for purpose – trade-offs and balances

As we have seen, some parts of the public sector are essentially monopolies – for example, defence forces and the fire and rescue service – and therefore do not compete amongst themselves. Nevertheless, such services do need to deliver the service identified by the nation and its politicians and they need to do this at 'reasonable' levels of cost (with 'reasonable' usually being defined by the governing politicians of the country). Nevertheless, many recent government initiatives in many countries have been directed at achieving greater efficiencies, higher levels of service and lower costs with the same service[23] – Pollitt and Bouckaert call these 'trade-offs and balances'.

Definition ▶ In order to undertake such tasks, **public sector resource analysis needs to assess whether sufficient and appropriate resources are available to deliver the purposes set by the state.** The first step in analysing resources is therefore to examine the objectives set by the state – for example, if a public sector ambulance is required to answer an emergency within 15 minutes, appropriate numbers of ambulances and trained medical staff need to be available. Public sector resource analysis then needs to set the service levels and other requirements of the state against the available resources.[24] Such an approach to resource analysis goes beyond the identification of competitive advantage and similar concepts from business strategy.

In analysing the required resources to deliver public sector objectives, one of the main difficulties rests with the words 'sufficient and appropriate'. The reason is that many state institutions will be able to make a case for more resources. To overcome this difficulty, careful exploration of the defined purpose and the tasks to be undertaken, coupled with comparisons from past experience and similar activities in other areas, will provide at least some of the answers. In practice, one of the main deciding factors is likely to be a government policy decision on 'trade-offs and balances' based on the political judgement of the public governing body. The case on the Kings Theatre at the end of this chapter captures many of the dilemmas and policy decisions required: public sector expertise, political pressure for re-election, pressure groups from within the local community. Resource analysis needs to consider these many complex aspects.

Public power as a resource

In strategic management, resource analysis often focuses on economic power, with cash and profitability as the dominant outcome. Even human resources like leadership and knowledge are often assessed by their ability to deliver profits or some form of added value to employees or management. In contrast, public resources have another dimension.

By definition, the nation state has an authority that is lacking to an individual business, however large. The state can be considered as having three distinctive, interactive systems that are not present in business: politics, a market economy and a system of public administration and the law.[25] Each of these is set within the larger context of a civil society of the nation – see Figure 18.3. The citizens of that nation both participate in and form judgements upon the legitimacy of that society and its institutions – not necessarily through a democracy.

From a public strategy perspective, this view of the state implies that citizens give their open or tacit approval to the events and decisions of the state. In this sense, citizens give power to public servants – for example, power to the defence forces to defend the state and support to the police and judiciary to uphold the law. This power can be mobilised at various times and forms a significant part of public sector strategy.[26] For example, the state can decide that it should lay increased emphasis on environmental 'green' issues in a way that is beyond that of individual businesses. **Definition ▸** **Public power is a resource possessed by nation states and consists of the collective decision making that derives from the nation state.** The analysis of such a resource is important in developing public sector strategy.

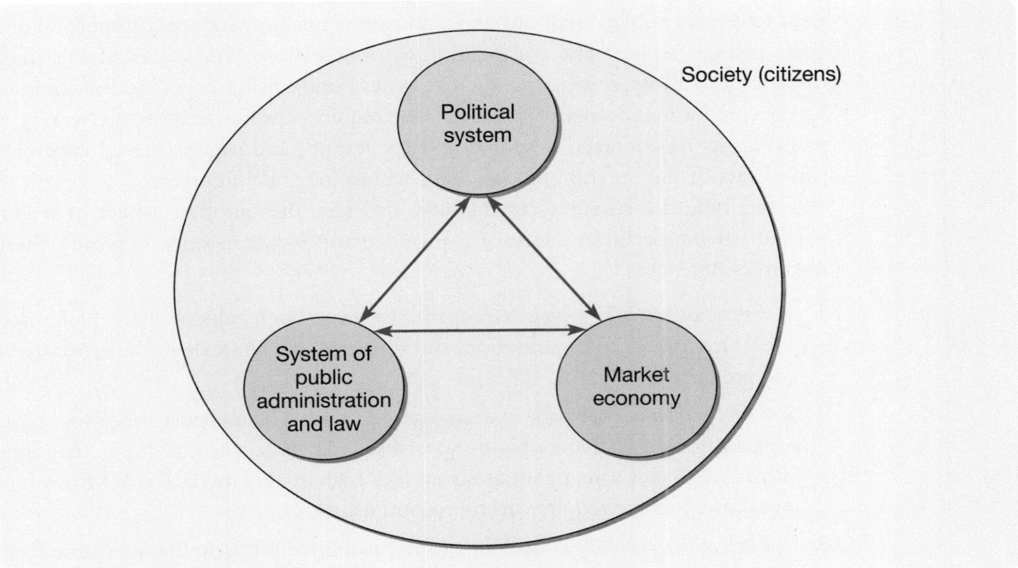

Figure 18.3 A simplified representation of the three main elements of the nation

Source: Pollitt, C and Bouckaert, G (2000) *Public Management Reform*, Oxford University Press. Used by permission of Oxford University Press.

The costs and benefits of public resources

Coupled with the state's exercise of power, there are also costs. Costs arise as the state goes about its business, investing in defence, in legal institutions and other areas of governmental activity.[27] They also include the costs associated with the misuse of power and the unintended side effects of political decisions[28] – for example, the higher costs associated with sorting waste when recycling becomes part of government policy in order to preserve the environment for future generations. Importantly, the state does not have unlimited funds for such activities because of the limitations on raising taxes. **Public resources need to be analysed for their ability to deliver the maximum benefit for the least cost. 'Benefit' here has a broader social definition than simply delivering shareholder profitability in the private sector** – for instance, social benefits associated with improvements in public health. This means that the task of the public sector manager has some similarities to that in the private sector but has a far wider brief and consequences. In practice in the public sector, this may require a strategic choice between making cost resource savings and improving performance through resource investment. It has been suggested that this can be resolved if there is some spare capacity in the governmental system or the possibility of employing new technology to improve efficiency.[29] Other resource-based solutions have included privatisation, as explored earlier, and setting public sector service quality and service standards in order to make comparisons across a part of the public sector – comparisons of health treatment in various parts of a country, perhaps.

Definition ▶

Persuasion and education as a public resource

Unlike individual businesses, the state has the opportunity to help individuals and groups improve their own lives by persuasion and education.[30] For example, the state can set up a public education programme to show citizens how to prevent fires. This may be just as useful and productive as the fire fighting service itself. This role for the state implies a public sector resource that is not readily available to individual businesses and needs to be considered in any resource-based analysis of public sector activity. **Public sector resource analysis therefore needs to consider whether persuasion and education are possible resources of the state and, if so, how and where they might be employed.**

Definition ▶

18.2.3 Some special characteristics of resources in the not-for-profit sector

Unlike the public sector, the resources of the not-for-profit sector will require funds that do not come from public taxes: there is a need to raise funds from private sources. The majority of such institutions need to rely on public donations and commercial business support of one kind or another. Inevitably, there is likely to be some competition to obtain those funds, even if this might seem somewhat distasteful to those engaged in such activity. Fund-raising expertise for some of these institutions has become a major area of resource that requires careful analysis – covering such resource areas as networks of contacts, branding and reputation, and organisational capability in energising the supporters of the organisation, many of whom may be volunteers.

Describing the resources in this way also identifies another aspect of resource analysis that is particularly important in the not-for-profit sector: *human resources*. Typically, there are three relevant resources here:[31]

1 *Voluntary help in raising funds and delivering the service*. Such helpers can be highly dedicated and provide a real strength to an organisation. But they can also be fickle in the sense that they are volunteers and are unpaid.

2 *Specialist technical knowledge in delivering the service*. The purpose of some types of not-for-profit organisations is to deliver highly specialised expertise – for example, the highly respected organisation Médecins sans Frontières provides high quality medical relief for refugees. Such specialist levels of expertise require careful resource analysis.

3 *Leadership and governance*. Each institution is unique but benefits over time from leaders who have the imagination and the ability to carry their workers, supporters and outside institutions with them as they develop and deliver their services. Arguably, this resource is even more important than in the public sector, because there is no acceptance and tradition of the public bureaucracy that is usually available to government institutions.

18.2.4 Analysing resources in the public sector

To summarise, the analysis of public sector resources will need to consider the main areas covered in Chapter 4 for business strategy: tangible, intangible and organisational resources; core competencies; architecture, reputation and innovative capability; and knowledge. In addition, the areas covered in more depth in this section need to be explored – public power, costs and benefits, persuasion and education – as possible resources available in the public sector. In not-for-profit organisations, this needs to be supplemented by an analysis of fund-raising and human resources.

The outcome of the resource analysis will identify the public organisation's strongest abilities and most effective actions and policies. From an administrative viewpoint, it will also set out the resources that it employs on a regular basis to perform well.[32] This latter point is important because the public sector is often involved in delivering an efficient administration with its routine tasks and legal frameworks that go beyond much of private sector activity.

One final aspect of public sector resource analysis also deserves to be emphasised – the necessary and appropriate resources to deliver the purpose of the organisation.[33] We explore purpose in the next section.

KEY STRATEGIC PRINCIPLES

- Public sector resource analysis needs to begin by examining which of the two public sector models - public sector administration or new public management - is adopted by the state. The *public sector administration* model consists of a professional civil service bureaucracy that enacts government legislation and administers the activities of the state on behalf of the government alongside state monopolies that supply services to the citizens. The *new public management* model is a model of public sector decision-making where the professional civil service operates with more market competition while former state monopolies are divided and compete against each other for business from citizens. However, the nation retains some areas under state control, such as the defence of the nation.
- The former does not support competitive advantage while the latter is underpinned by concepts of market competition in what was formerly the monopolistic state sector. Resource-based analysis in the public sector for the second approach will include similar concepts to those in business strategy - tangible, intangible and organisational resources, etc.
- There are four additional considerations that apply in analysing resources in the public sector: appropriate and sufficient resources for purpose; public power as a resource; the costs and benefits of public resources; and persuasion and education as a public resource.
- Public sector resource analysis needs to assess whether sufficient and appropriate resources are available to deliver the purpose and objectives set by the state. This means that resource analysis needs to identify public purpose and then assess resource requirements against this.
- Public power is a resource possessed by nation states and consists of the collective decision making that derives from the nation state. The analysis of such a resource is important in developing public sector strategy.
- With regard to costs and benefits of public resources, the task of the public sector manager is often that of obtaining the maximum benefit for the least cost. 'Benefit' here has a broader social definition than simply delivering shareholder profitability in the private sector. Such a balance needs to be considered in resource analysis in the public sector.
- Public sector resource analysis also needs to consider whether persuasion and education are possible resources of the state and, if so, how and where they might be employed.
- In not-for-profit organisations, there is a need to examine the fund-raising resource of the organisation. In addition, there is a specific need to examine human resources of such organisations in three areas: voluntary help, specialist technical knowledge and leadership and governance.
- The outcome of the resource analysis will identify the public organisation's strongest abilities and most effective actions and policies. From an administrative viewpoint, it will also set out the resources that it employs on a regular basis to perform well.

CASE STUDY 18.2

Windfarm or wildlife? A public interest dilemma for green strategy

Green strategy has forced a difficult choice in Shetland between a major windfarm to generate carbon free electricity and a threat to the wild, natural habitat of the Shetland Islands. This case explores the issues.

Early beginnings

Like the rest of the UK, the Shetland Islands Council is expected to support alternative sources of renewable energy. The islands are located nearly 200 miles (320 km) north of the Scottish mainland and have some of the highest and most reliable wind speeds in the world. This makes them attractive for land-based windfarms.

Back in 2003, both the local Shetland Islands Council (SIC) and Scotland's largest producer of electricity, Scottish and Southern Energy (SSE), independently decided that a new wind-farm complex should be explored for Shetland. Subsequently, the SIC handed over its interest in the project to another body, a charitable trust called the Shetland Charitable Trust (SCT). These two groups, the SSE and the SCT, then came together in a new company called Viking Energy.

As background, the Shetland Charitable Trust possesses around £180 million ($270 million) of funds donated by the oil industry for the inconvenience to Shetland from having a large oil terminal located at Shetland's Sullom Voe. The interest from this trust fund is used in Shetland for arts festivals, subsidised transport and other community schemes. The SCT is nominally independent of the SIC, but local Shetland councillors had the largest share of votes on both bodies at the time of writing this case.

Viking Energy

Set up in 2005, Viking Energy is 50 per cent owned by SSE, 45 per cent owned by SCT with the remaining 5 per cent owned by some local islanders who had previously invested in a small Shetland windfarm. The planning laws in the UK require that schemes of this nature prepare an Environmental Impact Assessment, which was initially done in 2006–0707. This was then followed by a period of consultation with the local communities in Shetland starting in 2007. A revised environmental impact assessment was then completed in 2009 and a formal planning application was then made. By that time, the objections from some (but not all) islanders to the scheme had been running for two years.

Viking Energy's proposal

After various surveys, SSE determined that a major new wind farm on central Shetland would provide a substantial renewable power source. However, the amount of power generated would be best served if it could be sent to the Scottish mainland. This meant that the construction of a 200-mile undersea cable was a crucial element of the proposal. In turn, this meant that a smaller scale windfarm for Shetland alone was not part of the proposal.

To generate and transmit renewable energy to the Scottish grid, Viking Energy proposed to construct 127 wind turbines, each 476 feet (145 metres) high. The site would be around 11 miles by 7 miles (18 km by 11 km) located on the northern part of the main island of the Shetland Isles. There would then be a cable running down the island and out to sea at the southern end. The development cost was estimated to be £685 million ($1.2 billion) for the windfarm plus another £500 million ($800 million) for the connecting cable to the mainland. The scheme would create only around 42 direct jobs but would generate an income of around £23 million ($38 million) per year for the SCT.

In addition, the proposal included habitat and heritage management schemes. However, it also involved the construction of over 60 miles of roads to service the windmills, cables to carry the power and a significant service infrastructure. The proposal was to build this across the largely untouched heather moorland, peat and bogland of central northern Shetland where birds, wild animals and people roamed freely up to that time. Viking Energy estimated that the carbon payback time would be around one year. But this figure was disputed by the objectors who produced figures claiming to show that it might be as much as 48 years.

At the time of writing this case, it was not clear how this £1.2 billion ($2 billion) project would be funded. It was assumed that SSE would be able to find their share of the total costs. However, the Trust has assets of only around £180 million. Nevertheless, it was estimated by Viking Energy that for various reasons the Trust would only need to find £30–60 million ($45–90 million). It was known that various banks, including the European Investment Bank, were willing to lend additional sums, but nothing had been agreed. Importantly, the high initial investment in this project was dictated by the large scale of the project and the related need to fund the cost of the cable to the mainland.

Objections to the proposals

Through contacts made using the local newspaper, the *Shetland Times*, and through local community groups, an organisation was set up called Sustainable Shetland. Its website is located at www.sustainableshetland.org/ and it has nearly 800 members. The organisation did not object to windfarm development in principle but did object to the size, impact and consequences of Viking Energy's proposals. Specifically, it complained to the UK Advertising Standards Authority (ASA) that one of Viking

In 2012, this was just one of the five windmills generating electricity on Shetland. But all this was about to change if the new proposals were approved by the Scottish Government.

Energy's leaflets was seriously misleading. The leaflet had been distributed to all households in Shetland. The ASA upheld three of the five objections and told Viking Energy that the leaflet could not be repeated in its current form. The ASA said, 'We told Viking Energy to amend their ad so that it did not claim that 50 per cent of profits would stay with the Shetland community; that it did not claim that a total of £25M to £30M would be injected into the Shetland economy every year; that it did not claim that upwards of £18M profits on average would go to Shetland Charitable Trust, and that it did not suggest the carbon payback time of the development was likely to be less than three years.' (The full adjudication is available at **http://www.asa.org.uk/ASA-action/Adjudications/2009/11/Viking-Energy-Partnership/TF_ADJ_47582.aspx**.)

More generally, the views of the majority of Shetland Islanders were unclear. A *Shetland Times*-commissioned poll in 2010 showed that one-third of islanders were in favour, one-third against and one-third undecided. Sustainable Shetland responded by pointing out that there were far more objections to the final plans submitted by Viking Energy than favourable comments: 2,735 versus 1,144 people. All these comments were considered by the Shetland Island Council when considering the public interest and approval procedure.

Formal public consultation and approvals

In accordance with normal UK planning procedures, Viking Energy presented its assessment first for local consultation across Shetland and then as a formal planning application for comments by the SIC. The main elements of the Viking Energy proposal can be viewed at **http://www.vikingenergy.co.uk/project-facts-figures.asp**. Various consultation and briefing meetings were held across Shetland in the years 2007–2009. As a result of these consultations, the windfarm was reduced in size from 150 to 127 turbines with the final application being sent to SIC in September 2010. The council must be consulted on the plans, but the final approval rests with the Scottish Government in Edinburgh. In December 2010, the Council approved the revised development.

Readers may find it odd that the company, Viking Energy, submitting plans to the Council is part-owned by a charitable trust whose members also sit on the Council. In other words, it would appear that the Council was being asked to support plans for a scheme of which it was a part-owner. Some members of the Council with an immediate interest withdrew from the planning meeting, but objectors to the scheme insisted that the relationship was still too close. Subsequently, this relationship has been the subject of a separate investigation by an independent lawyer for the Charities Commission which governs all trust activities in Scotland. The conclusion was that the relationship needed to be changed. But this does not seem to have persuaded the Council in the short term to reconsider its approval of the Viking Energy scheme.

In 2013, Viking Energy's scheme proposals were approved by the Scottish Government. The Government had to consider the following questions: Is the public interest best served by a major contribution to reducing the nation's carbon footprint with cheap renewable energy? Or is it better served by preserving the wildlife and natural habitat that would undoubtedly be disturbed by such a large-scale development? The Government chose to agree with Viking Energy.

But that was not the end of the matter. The development was then challenged legally in the Scottish High Court by the Sustainable Shetland organisation. At the time of updating this case, the legal decision was still pending.

Case questions

1 Where does the public interest rest in this case? Wildlife or windfarm? What criteria are needed to arrive at a decision?

2 Viking Energy's campaign was better funded than the objectors' response: is it inevitable that public sector strategy should be decided by this unequal debate?

3 In determining public green strategy, does it matter that the deciding local authority had an business interest in the application?

STRATEGIC PROJECT

At the time of writing the case, the decision of the Scottish Government to approve the project was being challenged in the Scottish courts by the objectors. You might like to check for the final decision which will be published on the *Shetland Times* website: **www.shetlandtimes.co.uk**.

18.3 EXPLORING THE PURPOSE OF PUBLIC AND NOT-FOR-PROFIT ORGANISATIONS

Public sector organisations face a difficulty that does not apply to business organisations. They are directed, at least in part, by politicians who need to be re-elected – unlike business leaders. This means that the purpose of a public sector body may change significantly after an election. It also means that long-term strategic direction can be difficult to sustain in the public sector. For example, it is possible that the leaders of the SIC – see Case 18.2 – will be defeated at the next election due to the unpopularity of their policies. What would then happen to any decision to press ahead with the Viking Energy windfarm development? The long-term direction of a significant part of Shetland Islands' strategy might be fundamentally altered.

In not-for-profit organisations, the reliance on voluntary, often unpaid assistance also means that such help is relatively unpredictable: it can even be withdrawn without warning for a variety of reasons. Moreover, unlike business organisations, many public sector bodies do not have shareholders expecting dividends and capital gains from their investments. Particularly in the not-for-profit sector, the objectives may well involve – perfectly justifiably – objectives that are more imprecise than shareholder value added. Such objectives may be difficult to measure and measurement may even be inappropriate: for example, the many voluntary groups that help the sick and dying deserve to be more than just a series of statistics. So how do public organisations develop their purpose? We examine this under three headings:

1 Stakeholders and the will of the people
2 Exploring and restating the purpose
3 Dilemmas and conflicts.

18.3.1 Stakeholders and the will of the people

In developing the purpose of public sector organisations, 'the key to success for public and non-profit organisations (and for communities) is the satisfaction of key stakeholders'.[35] The starting point in exploring the purpose has to be the opinions, views and judgements of the stakeholders. We explored stakeholder concepts in Chapter 6 and emphasised the need to analyse the influence of *stakeholder power*. The reader is therefore referred back to the earlier material on this important topic.

In addition to stakeholder theory, the public sector also relies on citizens expressing their opinions to politicians, arguably – though not necessarily – through their votes in public elections. This applies particularly to government organisations but can also apply to some not-for-profit bodies. Such a choice has its antecedents in the underlying principles to ascertain the will of the people developed by such scholars as Rousseau[36] and John Stuart Mill.[37] However, as pointed out by Nobel Laureate Amartya Sen,[38] similar thinking can be traced back to leaders in other non-Western countries including India and Japan, and some Muslim thinkers. He argues that 'democracy is best seen as the opportunity of participatory reasoning and public decision making – as government by discussion'. On this definition, democracy goes beyond voting in national elections every few years.

From a public sector strategy development perspective, there is a problem because some strategic decisions are complex and rely on expert knowledge. Sometimes it is difficult for the public to be fully informed about such matters, even if they participate in the 'participatory reasoning' of Sen above.[39] The relationship between informed public choice and its public sector consequences is therefore underpinned by an unavoidable tension. Namely, there is the need for the public debate and decision making to be mature and insightful while at the same time allowing citizens – even the ignorant – to express their opinion and even vote.[40] Britain's former prime minister Winston Churchill's observation that 'democracy is the worst form of government except for all the others' expresses the difficulty neatly.

In forming public sector strategy, there are times when ignoring the will of the people can invite problems. Hence, it is essential to attempt to understand the public perspective in developing purpose in public sector strategy. However, there are many ways to engage and represent the people around the world.[41] Churchill's comment on the weakness of democracy can be extended to the need for a range of methods to ascertain the will of the people in deciding the purpose of public sector strategy.

18.3.2 Exploring and restating the purpose

The starting point in defining the purpose of the strategy must lie with the basic mandate of the public sector organisation – What precisely is the organisation meant to do? Who is it meant to serve? There needs to be an identifiable social or political need that the organisation seeks to fill. This should be clarified, if necessary, by revisiting the formal charter or other legal, constitutional device that was agreed at the outset. This will lead to the mission of the organisation that, ideally, needs to be stated in a paragraph, using the principles explored in Chapter 6. An exploration of the strategic context in which the organisation is operating at a particular time will then suggest its purpose. For example, the mission of the European Union's Galileo satellite system to deliver a completely new and modern world navigation system, has led the company to re-examine its purpose, its timing and its delivery in the context of the changing interests of different national governments and companies.

For many public and not-for-profit organisations, the mission may also need to remind the stakeholders of the *inspiration* that originally led to the foundation of the organisation – in the case of volunteer organisations in particular, this may be what will drive them forward.[42] Such a purpose sometimes requires restating in strategy development.

18.3.3 Dilemmas and conflicts

One of the problems in public sector purpose is that many statements of purpose have to consider objectives that may conflict with each other.[43] For example, the European Union's Galileo satellite project has needed to find further funds to support the delays in developing the system while at the same time some, but not all, national governments have been highly critical of the way that the project has been managed. More generally, we can usefully identify two dilemmas that regularly impact on public sector strategy development:

1. *Steering versus rowing.*[44] Some commentators have argued that, in the setting of purpose in government strategy, government would work better if it concentrated on *steering* – setting policy, providing suitable funding to relevant public bodies and evaluating performance – rather than *rowing* – delivering the services. We do not need to resolve this matter here but simply recognise that this conflicting view of the role of government will impact directly on the ability to define strategic purpose.
2. *Improving public sector performance versus cost saving.* Commentators have varied in the emphasis they lay on these two different areas.[45] Performance improvements take as their starting point the need to adapt to the changing needs of society, new cultures and technologies. Cost saving begins by emphasising the need for the state to do less, cut back on public services and let market demand decide what is really needed. Again, we do not need to resolve this conflict here but recognise that such conflicts need to be identified and explored in the context of purpose.

In practice, these and other conflicts will vary with the strategic context of the time and the beliefs of the stakeholders. They need to be recognised and discussed. If they remain unresolved then it will be difficult for the purpose to be defined with sufficient clarity for strategy to be developed.

KEY STRATEGIC PRINCIPLES

- When developing the purpose of public sector organisations, the key to success for public and non-profit organisations is the satisfaction of main stakeholders. It is essential to conduct a stakeholder power analysis and seek the views of leading stakeholders.
- In addition to stakeholder theory, the development of public sector purpose also needs to reflect the general will of the people. Public opinion therefore needs to be identified and explored. It is sometimes difficult for citizens to develop an informed choice on complex issues, but such difficulties need to be recognised and resolved.
- The starting point in defining the purpose of strategy in the public sector must lie with the basic mandate of the public sector organisation, its role and its reason for its existence. This will lead to the mission of the organisation and a definition of its purpose in the context of the issues that it faces at that time.
- Many public sector organisations receive conflicting objectives. These need to be resolved if purpose is to be successfully defined and strategy developed.

18.4 CONTEXT, CONTENT AND PROCESS IN PUBLIC SECTOR STRATEGY

Having defined and clarified purpose, we are now in a position to develop strategies to deliver that purpose. It is possible to employ prescriptive models such as the options-and-choice approach of Chapters 8, 9 and 10.[46] The outcome, with some variations, is similar to that explored in the earlier chapters and is outlined briefly under the 'content' section below. However, given our focus on public sector strategy and the need to avoid repetition of areas covered previously, this section concentrates on the *differences* from business strategy. We examine this under three familiar strategy headings: context, content and process.

18.4.1 Strategic context

From the environmental and resource analyses, we established the chief differences in strategic context between public and business strategies:

- the change over the past 20 years from a public administration model of public sector strategy to a market-driven model in many countries;
- the dilemmas and contradictions that often exist between different policy directives in the public sector;
- the short-term and shifting nature of the political environment;
- the difficulty of raising funds and the reliance on specialist and voluntary human resources in parts of the not-for-profit sector.

Resource pressures to reduce numbers, privatisation of state monopolies and cost reduction policies all contribute to strategic context in the public sector. Shifting public attitudes on political, moral and social issues may determine the not-for-profit context. Such issues also need to be coupled with more radical changes in world environments when analysing strategic context in the public sector. For example, global warming, poverty and diseases, war and conflict, the increasing power of the internet and the ethical issues arising from biological advances all provide challenges in the public sector that may be important. Each public sector organisation will have its own list of factors against which to develop its strategy. The point here is that strategic context is arguably *broader* in the public sector than in business because of the wider role of government and not-for-profit institutions. The danger is that strategic context becomes over-complex. It can be focused by at least three methods:

1. *Developing some priorities with regard to strategic purpose* – identifying, possibly through group meetings, what will have a substantial impact on purpose and strategy.
2. *Using scenarios to develop some possible outcomes* for the leading strategic context issues. This will help to examine the consequences of particular situations.
3. *Keeping the strategic context analysis simple.* Complex and elaborate procedures are more likely to confuse than produce workable strategies.

18.4.2 Strategic content

Just as in business strategy, public sector content development can employ prescriptive strategy concepts of options-and-choice approaches.[47] In developing such options, Bryson recommends developing those that are both 'practical alternatives and dreams' for achieving the strategic purpose of the organisation.[48] He suggests that a useful procedure is to identify the barriers to achieving those outcomes and then ways of overcoming the barriers. Finally, he recommends that the chosen options are developed into specific proposals. Such an approach is not greatly different from business strategy, though the word 'dreams' might not appear in the latter.

In developing the strategic options, the question will arise as to whether the business strategy options outlined in Chapter 8 can be employed. The options fell into two distinct areas – those associated with the strategic *environment* – such as Porter's generic strategies – and those associated with strategic *resources* – such as cost reduction and the resource-based options. Can public sector strategy use these concepts?

Dealing first with environment-based options, Porter is probably the dominant strategist in this area. It is unlikely that business strategy environment options can be used in public sector strategy. To quote Professor Ewen Ferlie of London University: 'With its strong focus on markets, profitability and competitiveness, [Porter's] models are difficult to apply literally, as prices, markets and profits all remain underdeveloped in the public sector.'[49] Nevertheless, Ferlie concludes that Porter's approach does have some merit where market-based concepts have been introduced into the public sector: 'Porterian models may prove especially useful for public sector regulators and purchasers, guiding them in their market development tasks.'[50] Such approaches may therefore be more appropriate in *new public management* treatments of public sector strategy. In addition, strategy in the not-for-profit sector may benefit from options that identify the possibility of competition in the environment for funds and people.

Resource-based strategic options offer the opportunity to focus on those competitive resources that allow some public sector bodies to offer superior public service to others.[51] To quote Ferlie again: 'Resource-based models can be applied to public sector organisations, as their profile of intangible assets is surely closely correlated with their performance in such important managerial tasks as the management of strategic change.'[52] Hence, options based on public sector resource analysis are worth pursuing, including cost reductions where relevant.

We explore emergent approaches to options development in the next section.

18.4.3 Strategic process

Because of the uncertainties involved in the public sector – regime change at the political level and unforeseen cataclysmic events at the general level – some public sector strategists favour the *controlled chaos* or *logical incrementalism* of J B Quinn, explored in Chapters 7 and 12.[53] This consists of a series of small decisions within the overall purpose of the organisation, with the outcome of each step determining the next steps – in other words, an emergent process for strategy development. Beyond this concept, there seems to have been little exploration of the 'Learning-based strategic route forward' of Chapter 11. Nevertheless, the extended strategic options process called the *Oval Mapping Process*, developed by Professor Colin Eden of Strathclyde University along with Professor Bryson and others,[54] would seem to derive much of its basis from learning-based approaches.

An alternative to logical incrementalism that has found favour with some public sector strategists[55] is the approach recommended by Lindblom. He wrote a theoretical paper – it quoted no empirical evidence – some 50 years ago called 'The Science of Muddling Through' that is still quoted with approval today.[56] Essentially, Lindblom argued that it is impossible in public sector strategy to analyse fully all the options that are available: there are just too many factors involved, from political ideas through economic pressures to social trends. He set out an alternative strategic process that was more realistic and concentrated particularly on small-scale, incremental decisions. It differs from logical incrementalism in that Lindblom made no reference to using the outcome of one stage to decide the next. 'Muddling through' is more basic in that regard. Bryson argues that Lindblom's approach can have real merit in some circumstances: it reduces risk, breaks a project into small do-able steps, eases implementation, quickly makes real change, provides immediate reward and preserves gains.[57]

Pollitt and Bouckaert take a similar approach and favour small steps over major change in many situations in the public sector:

> To launch, sustain and implement a comprehensive strategy for reform requires certain conditions and these are seldom satisfied in the real world of public management reform . . . Thus talk of 'strategy' is usually an idealization, or post hoc rationalization of a set of processes which tend to be partial, reactive and of unstable priority.[58]

This all argues in favour of the realism of a small-scale, incremental process in public sector strategy development.

Comment

The strategic context of public sector strategy is relatively uncertain for a variety of reasons and it is also complex. There is little to be gained by speculating about whether it is *more* complex than business strategy. The essential point is that public sector strategy development has a number of dimensions that make it difficult to manage. This all suggests that radical change in public sector strategy needs to be treated with some caution – it can be done, but it requires a very clear vision, strong leadership and substantial resources which may need specialist training.[59] Incrementalism in public sector strategy may be the better option in many cases.

KEY STRATEGIC PRINCIPLES

- For a variety of reasons, the strategic context of public sector strategy is broader than its counterpart in business strategy. The danger is that it becomes more complex and difficult to handle. There are three main mechanisms to simplify the process: priorities, scenarios and simplicity.
- Strategic content in public sector strategy can follow the options-and-choice route commonly used in some business strategy. However, options associated with the strategic environment need to be treated with considerable caution because the market mechanism is still lacking in much of the public sector. Nevertheless, options derived from resource-based analysis can be employed.
- With regard to strategic process, the uncertainties of the public sector favour the use of 'logical incrementalism' as a process. An alternative is the 'muddling through' approach which reduces public sector strategy to a series of small decisions.
- Importantly, a number of strategists argue that major strategic decisions in public sector strategy usually require substantial commitment in terms of resources and leadership. Such an approach is not so easy in practice.

18.5 IMPLEMENTATION IN PUBLIC SECTOR STRATEGY[60]

As with business strategy, effective implementation of proposed strategies is essential in the public sector. Such activity needs to be carefully planned and is best undertaken quickly and smoothly. Beyond this, the form of implementation depends upon the scale of changes planned:

- *Major changes in strategic direction.* These need a strong group of supporters and implementers, a clear agreement on the change that is required, an understanding of the main elements of that change and adequate resources to carry out the task.
- *Incremental changes in strategic direction.* These represent the better option when some of those affected hold reservations about – even objections to – the proposed strategic change. It may be possible to undertake pilot projects, use learning-based approaches, circulate the results of first initiatives so others can analyse the consequences and so that adjustments can be made.

Beyond these basic matters, strategic implementation in the public sector needs to develop specific, testable plans in a number of specific areas:

- *Explanation and understanding of the value added.* If successful strategies add value, as has been argued throughout this text, then it follows that those implementing the strategy must clearly understand this added value, its purpose and the strategies by which it will be achieved. An education and explanation phase is therefore desirable. Agreement by those involved may also be necessary in order to overcome objections to such a strategy.
- *Fixing difficulties.* In most implementation procedures, problems will arise. It is important that such difficulties are recognised as they occur. This means building monitoring mechanisms and milestones into the process.
- *Summative evaluations.* It is desirable to find out if the purpose of the strategy has been achieved. This needs to be built into the implementation process. Bryson draws a useful distinction between two aspects of such a process: *outputs*, which are the actions produced by the strategies, and *outcomes*, which are the larger ramifications of such changes – especially the symbolic changes that occur.[61] He suggests that such an evaluation can be difficult and lengthy, but it is important to establish whether things are 'better' as a result of a new strategy. However, such an approach has also been used recently to justify an army of managers who do little beyond evaluating the results of strategic change – an obvious recipe for over-bureaucratic management.[62]
- *New organisations and culture.* It may be necessary to reorganise existing public sector areas and possibly to recruit or redefine management responsibilities. It may even be necessary to develop a new organisational culture to ensure long-lasting changes. These areas need to form part of the overall plan at the outset, but it should be recognised that they may take years to implement. Some recent public sector strategies in the UK have under-estimated the difficulties here.[63] In both the public and business sectors, people need to be given time to learn, adjust and adapt to new situations. The principles involved in this approach are explained in Chapter 15.
- *Recognise the need for flexibility.* There are very few public sector strategies that have a single, clear outcome. Many strategies will be challenged and others will need to adapt as events – including political changes – occur in the surrounding strategic context. Implementation therefore has to be alert to such issues and respond as they occur.

In the public sector, budget allocations for a period of time can often be a crucial factor in strategy implementation – 'no money, no strategy'. The difficulty is that such budgets are subject to political pressures and are often short-term, incremental and reactive. There are no simple ways to overcome this problem, but it is desirable if the strategic planning stage comes *before* budget setting. In addition, it may be important to recognise the importance of individual leaders in developing the strategy – agreement and ownership of a strategy are important factors in strategy development and are not confined simply to the 'implementation phase'. In this sense, this whole section on implementation needs to be re-evaluated as being part of a broader, ongoing strategy development process, rather than an add-on process after the strategy has been decided.

Comment

Finally, it is important to make the point that public servants involved in the development of strategy have an important responsibility with regard to strategy development. To quote Robert Reich:

> The core responsibility of those who deal in public policy – elected officials, administrators, policy analysts – is not simply to discover as objectively as possible what people want for themselves and then to determine and implement the best means to satisfying these wants. It is also to provide the public with alternative visions of what is desirable and possible, to stimulate deliberation about them, provoke a re-examination of premises and values, and thus to broaden the range of potential responses and deepen society's understanding of itself.[64]

KEY STRATEGIC PRINCIPLES

- Strategy implementation in the public sector needs to be carefully planned and is best undertaken quickly and smoothly.
- The form of implementation depends on the scale of what is proposed. Major changes need substantial support. Smaller changes are probably best treated incrementally.
- In implementing public sector strategy, it is important to identify the value added and then explain this to those involved in its implementation. It is also necessary to have a mechanism that can fix the inevitable difficulties that will arise as new strategies are implemented.
- It may be appropriate to have a summative evaluation of the strategy after it has been implemented to find out whether the planned improvements have been achieved. However, such an approach can be lengthy and time-consuming. It can also be over-bureaucratic.
- A new organisational structure and culture may be necessary for some new strategies. This will take time that needs to be built into the process from the beginning. Such processes should not be under-estimated and may require years to complete. There is also a need to build some degree of flexibility into the implementation process as circumstances change.
- The budget process can be crucial for new strategies and should ideally be undertaken after the strategy has been agreed. Importantly, this is only a part of a broader implementation process that needs to include the agreement of key decision makers. Arguably, implementation needs to be re-evaluated as being part of a broader, ongoing strategy development process, rather than an add-on process after the strategy has been decided.

CASE STUDY 18.3

'Should we close the Kings Theatre?'

A tough strategic decision for Portsmouth City Council

Portsmouth city councillors had a difficult strategic decision to make in July 2003: should they withdraw the city's financial support for the Kings Theatre, Portsmouth, UK?

The theatre had only been relaunched in 2001, but its subsidiary commercial operating company went bankrupt in early 2003 with over £200,000 debts. Closure would cause immense local anger and negate the 'Two Theatres' strategy of the city. But keeping the theatre open would be fraught with many financial problems and major risks. This case explores the strategic options available to the city.

Background

City councils are not required to make profits. They have a broader responsibility to their electorate – to provide a range of services from education and social services to the arts and sporting activities. They operate within limits defined by the national government on the services that *must* be provided locally – like education and social welfare – and services over which the council has some *choice* – like selecting the level of support for local libraries or local sport. This case explores this

Portsmouth's Kings Theatre became a major focus for political pressure with the threat of total closure

typical mix of strategic decisions in one particularly acute case – the possible closure of a well-loved local theatre and its sale to a national brewery chain as a public house.

With over 170,000 people and an annual budget of around £200 million, it might be thought that Portsmouth was well placed to provide live theatre for its citizens. The difficulty comes in balancing the various demands on the council's limited budget. The decisions are more difficult when activities have been under-funded in the past and when local pride and passion are involved. Local councillors are politicians and, understandably, want to be re-elected. The city is a major tourist venue as well as offering employment in a range of local companies. But Portsmouth's theatres were a victim of its past – it had four live theatres in 1950 that were packed every week. By the late 1990s, there were only two remaining major theatres – the Kings Theatre and the New Theatre Royal – plus a small Arts Theatre for experimental plays that was to be relocated to save money in mid-2003.The reasons for this decline were not hard to find – television, mass car ownership, the demand for nightclubs and more intimate entertainment.

It was against this background that the city council drafted its 'Two Theatres in Portsmouth' strategy in 1999 – see Exhibit 18.1. The concept was one theatre for major popular musicals, entertainment and drama – the Kings Theatre, with around 1,500 seats – and another theatre for smaller commercial productions such as small-scale experimental drama and concerts – the New Theatre Royal, with around 500 seats.

As Exhibit 18.1 also shows, the city's strategy across its two main venues was particularly difficult because both its major theatres were old and unmodernised. Portsmouth is unique in the UK as the only city with two beautiful old theatres designed by the great theatrical architect, Frank Matcham – there were only 23 Matcham theatres left in the whole of the UK in 2003. But the two unmodernised theatres were also an immense financial burden on the city, which the central government had done nothing to alleviate.

Competition from other theatres in the region

The nearby cities of Southampton and Chichester both had thriving theatres – see Exhibit 18.2. The Mayflower Theatre in Southampton and the Festival Theatre in Chichester had the benefit of substantial monies being spent on them in the 1980s. As a result, the rival theatres were already able to operate

EXHIBIT 18.1

Kings Theatre – the 'Two Theatres in Portsmouth' strategy

Kings Theatre

- 1,500 seats, to be used for major touring companies plus local amateur companies needing a large venue.
- Grade II* listed early twentieth-century beautiful building – never been modernised – poor car parking, away from city centre.
- Was relaunched by city council in 2001 as a non-profit theatre trust.
- Trust set up a limited company in 2001 with new manager/proprietor appointed – bankrupt with over £200,000 debts by early 2003 – company then liquidated.
- Needs minimum £7.5 million capital spend to modernise – possibly as much as £13 million to bring to the standard of competitors such as Mayflower Theatre, Southampton.

New Theatre Royal

- 500 seats, to be used for smaller touring companies, local drama education projects, Portsmouth University drama and music venue.
- Grade II* listed early twentieth-century beautiful building – never been modernised – partly burnt down so cannot take large scenery; city centre location, good parking.
- Needs minimum £5 million capital spend to modernise and create flexible performance space.

EXHIBIT 18.2

Kings Theatre, Portsmouth – the competitors

Mayflower Theatre, Southampton

- 1,800 seats, regular audience developed over years.
- Fully modernised theatre – compare to Kings Theatre, which is still using scenery handling built nearly 100 years ago.
- Takes top London musicals – King's Theatre will *never* compete here.
- City centre location, plenty of parking – compared with Kings Theatre, which is located away from Portsmouth town centre with poor parking for cars.

Festival Theatre, Chichester plus adjacent small experimental theatre

- 1,600 seats, strong local audience built over years.
- Modernised theatre, runs own productions – some transfer to London.
- Located on own site with good parking – just outside city centre.

Plus Portsmouth Guildhall Concert Hall and Portsmouth night clubs, comedy clubs plus other major venues in other local towns – e.g. Fareham, Havant.

more attractive, popular programmes. This meant that their seat prices were higher than the Kings Theatre – typically a yield of £12–14 per head compared to around £6–10 per head at the Kings. The competitors had developed loyal audiences over many years from a wide geographical area and would provide formidable competition to any refurbished Kings Theatre, Portsmouth.

Financing the Portsmouth two theatres strategy

> The [Kings] theatre could be solvent and operated successfully with continued subsidy at the present level.
>
> (Sam Shrouder, theatre consultant, after studying the Kings bankruptcy in April 2003)

Portsmouth city council took over the Kings Theatre in 2001. It gave an urgent capital injection of £300,000 and an annual subsidy of £135,000. It also decided to relaunch the theatre through a non-profit company and with a new director, David Rixon. He was given some freedom to test local customer demand during the period 2001–2003. The council always accepted that the first few years of the Kings Theatre would be experimental. However, no one bargained for the theatre actually going bankrupt in March 2003, with Mr Rixon resigning through ill-health.

How provincial theatres make profits

To understand the bankruptcy and judge its relevance to the long-term impact on the Kings Theatre, it is necessary to understand how provincial theatres make profits in the UK. Precise figures are not available, but it is likely that the Kings had an annual turnover of around £550,000. It was not open every week – probably around 30 weeks of the year. Some weeks there would be a full week of activity, perhaps with a local amateur theatrical company or with a touring opera or drama company. Other weeks, there might be just one or two nights with a well-known comedian or singer. It was the responsibility of the theatre's managing director – in this case, Rixon – to negotiate commercial terms with each touring company or individual artist. Typically in a modern theatre, the touring company would take 70 per cent or more of the revenue from that week – see Figure 18.4.

More than 200,000 seats were sold for 350 performances at the Kings Theatre during its 18 months of operation from late 2001 to early 2003. This was seen as satisfactory over this period. But the crucial matter to impact on the targets was the

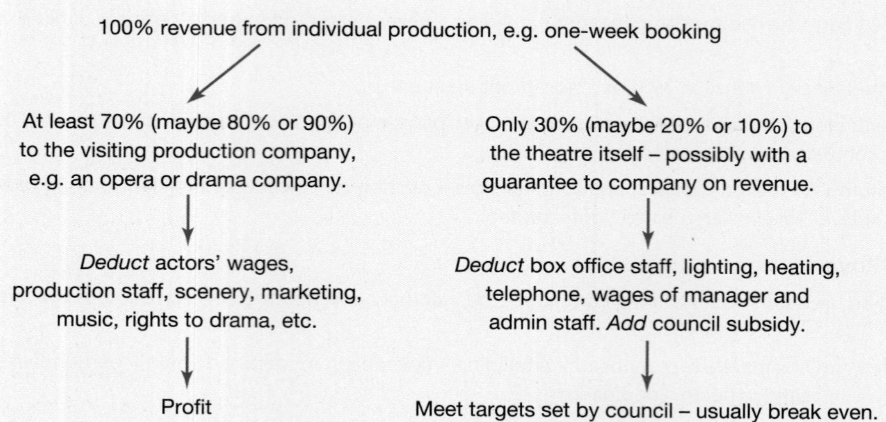

Figure 18.4 How local council-owned theatres achieve financial targets

bankruptcy of the theatre in March 2003. What precisely happened during the 18 months of operation that led to this situation was unclear. It is probable that some financial guarantees were given to touring companies that were too generous. In addition, there was probably some mis-management of costs, especially during the Christmas season in 2002–2003 which normally made a profit.

Strategic options for the future

There were three major options:

1 To provide new funds and new management to keep the theatre operating.

2 To sell the theatre to a national pub chain and convert it to public house entertainment venture.

3 To simply close down the venue and sell the land.

Option 1 Preserve the theatre

Many local people wanted to preserve the theatre. Unquestionably, there would be tremendous sadness among some members of the local and national theatre community if the Kings Theatre were to close as a theatre venue. 'Over my dead body' was how one well-known theatre expert expressed his views on the possible closure. Funds had been raised and excitement generated about the theatre's upcoming centenary in 2006. The city councillors were therefore under considerable voter pressure to choose this option.

'No political party is going to want to be seen as the one that closed the Kings' was how one observer summed up the local political pressure.

> A city with cultural ambitions like ours must be seen to do something with its theatres. That is the challenge.
>
> (Former council leader, Frank Worley, April 2003)

Hence, Portsmouth city councillors were faced with a strong local lobby that wanted to see the theatre preserved. This pressure was particularly acute because the local council was a hung council – each of the three main political parties had approximately equal representation – leaving decision making by one political party open to easy attack by the other two.

Option 2 Convert the theatre to a pub

Back in 1999 a UK national pub chain company – J D Wetherspoon – had expressed interest in purchasing the Kings Theatre as a public house entertainment venture. It said that it would preserve the fabric, spend funds to restore the interior and honour the grade II* listed status of the building. Importantly, the company had developed a proven tradition of preserving the fabric of historic buildings that it had acquired. But there would no longer be any live theatre for the general public.

The influential local newspaper, *The News*, had come out in favour of such a pub sale. The Arts Council of England was also in favour of this option. This was important because its views could influence the award of substantial capital grants and it could support local arts activity.

Option 3 Close down the venue and sell the land

This was a real option because it was not clear that options 1 and 2 were commercially viable. The funds generated from the sale could be used to help the other Portsmouth theatre, the New Theatre Royal, that was also under threat.

Expert recommendation of the leading council official

After careful consideration, the city council's leisure officer – David Knight – recommended to the council that the Kings Theatre should be closed and sold to the highest bidder. However, if possible, it should be preserved as a theatre and not just pulled down. He argued that the council's limited funds would be better deployed in developing the New Theatre Royal and such a policy was much more likely to find favour with the Arts Council.

Strategic choice by the elected city councillors

In spite of this expert recommendation, the council was not obliged to accept it. The council needed to make its decision about the future of the Kings Theatre at a full council meeting on 22 July 2003.

What happened next: the strategic choice made by Portsmouth city council.

 Richard Lynch wrote this case from the sources listed in the references at the end of the chapter.[65] The author would like to acknowledge the help of the former Portsmouth city council leisure officer, David Knight, in preparing this case. He is also grateful to Mike Allen, the theatre correspondent of the local newspaper, *The News*, Portsmouth, for his comments on an earlier draft of this case. All opinions, judgements and errors remain those of the author and do not reflect the views of the local council and its officers in any way whatsoever.

Case questions

1 What are the key strategy issues here? Political pressure and local choice? Customer demand? Theatre run with innovative flair on a tight budget? You may wish to use the strategy concepts of context, content and process to structure your answer.

2 What are the sustainable competitive advantages of the Kings Theatre? Are they strong or weak? You should use well-established resource-based strategy concepts – like reputation and core competencies – to develop your answer.

3 What would you recommend to the city council? Which strategic option would you choose? Why?

4 Having chosen an option, what is the strategic process that should then be adopted to implement that option? You may wish to identify the key players with whom the city council will need to bargain and what game plan will be required.

CRITICAL REFLECTION

Public sector strategy: increased service or lower costs?

One of the underpinning themes throughout public sector strategy in recent years is where to focus the effort. Some argue that it is important for the public sector to increase the quality of the service that it offers to citizens. Others argue that the public sector has become too large and it would be better to make cutbacks, even if this reduces the services offered to the public. Such a conflict needs to be resolved if strategy is to be developed, so an answer is needed. Where do you stand on this issue? What is your view?

SUMMARY

- In public sector strategy, the analysis of the strategic environment is more complex than in the private sector. The main reason is that public sector strategy involves the wide-ranging and ill-defined subject of the public interest: the public interest concerns both the objectives and the institutions that make and implement public decisions. There are two main public sector models – centrally directed (*dirigiste*) and free-market (*laissez-faire*). The market mechanism is the means by which the state uses market pricing and quasi-market mechanisms to determine the supply and demand of goods that were previously state monopolies. In practice over the past 20 years, many states have moved to greater use of the market through privatising state-owned companies. Each individual country will have its own approach to the use of such mechanisms. A public sector environmental analysis will have to be conducted on a country-by-country basis. There are also two costs associated with the market mechanism: first, the cost of being unable to close inefficient services because they provide vital public services; second, the cost of administering the market mechanism to ensure that it serves the agreed public objectives.
- Public value refers to the benefits to the whole of the nation from owning and controlling certain products and services. However, such value needs to be considered within the legal framework that binds and governs the value. In addition, public value requires the concept of equity to make sure that the value is distributed to all citizens. In some circumstances, public value needs a regulator to deal with any market imperfections.
- In the public sector, stakeholder power is possessed by those citizens who are able to influence the decisions of the state. Such power may be expressed through democratic elections but these can lead to short-termism in strategic decisions. Power can also be exercised through pressure groups and other forms of interest. Such power needs to be analysed.
- In the not-for-profit sector, an environmental analysis needs to consider the role and purpose of the organisation and also its actual and potential sources of funds. Such organisations cannot rely on public taxes to pay for their activities and need to seek voluntary contributions that will vary with a range of factors.
- The nine stages in environmental analysis used for business strategy can be adapted for use in public sector strategy analysis. But they need to be treated with caution.
- Public sector resource analysis needs to begin by examining which of the two public sector models – public sector administration or new public management – is adopted by the state. The public sector administration model consists of a professional civil service bureaucracy that enacts government legislation and administers the activities of the state on behalf of the government coupled with state monopolies that supply services to the citizens. The new public management model is a model of public sector decision making where the professional civil service operates with more market competition, while former state monopolies are divided and compete against each other for business from citizens. However, the state retains some areas under state control, such as the defence of the nation.

- The former does not support competitive advantage while the latter is underpinned by concepts of market competition in what was formerly the monopolistic state sector. Resource-based analysis in the public sector for the second approach will include similar concepts to those in business strategy – tangible, intangible and organisational resources, etc.
- There are four additional considerations that apply in analysing resources in the public sector. appropriate and sufficient resources for purpose; public power as a resource; the costs and benefits of public resources; and persuasion and education as a public resource. Public sector resource analysis needs to assess whether sufficient and appropriate resources are available to deliver the purpose and objectives set by the state. This means that resource analysis needs to identify public purpose and then assess resource requirements against this.
- Public power is a resource possessed by nation states and consists of the collective decision making that derives from the nation state. The analysis of such a resource is important in developing public sector strategy. With regard to costs and benefits of public resources, the task of the public sector manager is often that of obtaining the maximum benefit for the least cost. 'Benefit' here has a broader social definition than simply delivering shareholder profitability in the private sector. Such a balance needs to be considered in resource analysis in the public sector. Public sector resource analysis also needs to consider whether persuasion and education are possible resources of the state and, if so, how and where they might be employed.
- In not-for-profit organisations, there is a need to examine the fund-raising resource of the organisation. In addition, there is a specific need to examine the human resources of such organisations in three areas: voluntary help, specialist technical knowledge and the leadership and governance.
- The outcome of the resource analysis will identify the public organisation's strongest abilities and most effective actions and policies. From an administrative viewpoint, it will also set out the resources that it employs on a regular basis to perform well.
- When developing the purpose of public sector organisations, the key to success for public and non-profit organisations is the satisfaction of main stakeholders. It is essential to conduct a stakeholder power analysis and seek the views of leading stakeholders. In addition to stakeholder theory, the development of public sector purpose also needs to reflect the general will of the people. Public opinion therefore needs to be identified and explored. It is sometimes difficult for citizens to develop an informed choice on complex issues but such difficulties need to be recognised and resolved.
- The starting point in defining the purpose of strategy in the public sector must lie with the basic mandate of the public sector organisation, its role and its reason for its existence. This will lead to the mission of the organisation and a definition of its purpose in the context of the issues that it faces at that time. Many public sector organisations receive conflicting objectives. They need to be resolved if purpose is to be successfully defined and strategy developed.
- For a variety of reasons, the strategic context of public sector strategy is broader than its counterpart in business strategy. The danger is that it becomes more complex and difficult to handle. There are three main mechanisms to simplify the process: priorities, scenarios and simplicity.
- Strategic content in public sector strategy can follow the options-and-choice route commonly used in some business strategy. However, options associated with the strategic environment need to be treated with considerable caution because the market mechanism is still lacking in much of the public sector. Nevertheless, options derived from resource-based analysis can be employed.
- With regard to strategic process, the uncertainties of the public sector favour the use of 'logical incrementalism' as a process. An alternative is the 'muddling through' approach which reduces public sector strategy to a series of small decisions. Importantly, a number of strategists argue that major strategic decisions in public sector strategy usually require substantial commitment in terms of resources and leadership. Such an approach is not so easy in practice.

- Strategy implementation in the public sector needs to be carefully planned and is best undertaken quickly and smoothly. The form of implementation depends on the scale of what is proposed. Major changes need substantial support. Smaller changes are probably best treated incrementally.
- In implementing public sector strategy, it is important to identify the value added and then explain this to those involved in its implementation. It is also necessary to have a mechanism that can fix the inevitable difficulties that will arise as new strategies are implemented.
- It may be appropriate to have a summative evaluation of the strategy after it has been implemented to find out whether the planned improvements have been achieved. However, such an approach can be lengthy and time-consuming. It can also be over-bureaucratic.
- A new organisational structure and culture may be necessary for some new strategies. This will take time that needs to be built into the process from the beginning. Such processes should not be under-estimated and may require years to complete. There is also a need to build some degree of flexibility into the implementation process as circumstances change.
- The budget process can be crucial for new strategies and should ideally be undertaken after the strategy has been agreed. Importantly, this is only a part of a broader implementation process that needs to include the agreement of key decision-makers. Arguably, implementation needs to be re-evaluated as being part of a broader, ongoing strategy development process, rather than an add-on process after the strategy has been decided.

QUESTIONS

1 Take your own country and analyse the extent to which it employs *laissez-faire* or *dirigiste* policies in the public sector. How does this compare with other countries?

2 What public sector strategy would you expect the following organisations to have?

(a) A public library based in a small town.

(b) A voluntary group providing volunteers to visit the elderly and house-bound.

(c) A prosperous town with 100,000 inhabitants and a range of industrial activities from manufacturing to leisure.

(d) The police force associated with a region of a country.

3 'The need to improve service quality has been and remains a major pre-occupation for many public sector organisations and those who fund their activities.' (G Johnson and K Scholes (2001) *Exploring Public Sector Strategy*, p 250) Take an organisation with which you are familiar and consider this comment: is the comment correct for your chosen organisation? How has it been tackled? How should it be approached?

4 If you were asked to make the European Union's Galileo satellite project more responsive to public pressures, what would you do? In answering this question, you should take into account the existing structure of the institution.

5 Winston S Churchill commented: '*Democracy is the worst form of government except for all the others*' (see Section 18.3). Is this correct? What are the implications for public sector strategy?

6 Undertake a stakeholder power analysis for a public sector organisation of your choice: it could be a voluntary organisation like a student society or club. What are the implications of your analysis for the development of strategy in that organisation?

7 Why is it difficult to apply Porter's market-based concepts in public sector strategy? Do they have any relevance at all in a city-based fire and rescue service?

8 The chief executive of a not-for-profit charity serving those who are terminally ill has become worried by declining levels of income, believing the organisation has lost out to others that have a stronger public presence, and has turned to you for advice. What would you recommend?

9 '*To launch, sustain and implement a comprehensive strategy for reform requires certain conditions and these are seldom satisfied in the real world of public management reform.*' This is the view of Pollitt and Bouckaert – see Section 18.4. Are they being too gloomy about the prospects for radical reform of public sector strategy? Does this mean that major reform in the public sector is almost certainly doomed to failure?

ACKNOWLEDGEMENTS

This chapter breaks new ground in strategy textbooks. The author is therefore particularly grateful to three people who have commented on earlier drafts of this chapter: Dr Paul Baines of Cranfield University, Dr Paul Hughes of Loughborough University and Marc Coleman, former Economics Editor of the *Irish Times*. Any remaining errors and omissions remain solely the responsibility of the author.

FURTHER READING

Bryson, J M (1998) *Strategic Planning for Public and Nonprofit Organizations*, Jossey Bass, San Francisco, CA is one of the leading texts in this area and has strong, practical advice. There is also a more recent special issue that has some useful insights: Kochan, T, Guillen, M F, Hunter, L W and O'Mahoney, S (2009) 'Public Policy and Management Research: Finding the Common Ground', *Academy of Management Journal*, Vol 52, No 6, pp 1088 onwards.

Two books on public administration are Lane, J-E (2000) *The Public Sector: Concepts, Models and Approaches*, 3rd edn, Sage, London and Frederickson, H G and Smith, K B (2003) *The Public Administration Theory Primer*, Westview, Oxford. Both provide useful summaries of the basics of theories that follow a completely different academic tradition from strategic management.

A text with substantial cross-country empirical comparisons and interesting comment is Pollitt, C and Bouckaert, G (2000) *Public Management Reform: A Comparative Analysis*, Oxford University Press, Oxford, which is well written and thought-provoking.

Three recommended texts on strategic management in the public sector are: Joyce, P (1999) *Strategic Management for the Public Services*, Open University Press, Buckingham; Bovaird, T and Loffler, E (eds) (2003) *Public Management and Governance* Routledge, London; Johnson, G and Scholes, K (eds) (2001) *Exploring Public Sector Strategy*, Pearson Education, Harlow.

NOTES AND REFERENCES

1 Ferlie, E (2002) 'Quasi strategy: strategic management in the contemporary public sector', in Pettigrew, A, Thomas, H and Whittington, R (eds) *Handbook of Strategy and Management*, Sage, London.
2 Lane, J-E (2000) *The Public Sector: Concepts, Models and Approaches*, 3rd edn, Sage, London.
3 Frederickson, H G and Smith, K B (2003) *The Public Administration Theory Primer*, Westview, Oxford.
4 Lane, J-E (2000) Op. cit.
5 Lane, J-E (2000) Op. cit.; Frederickson, H G and Smith, K B (2003) Op. cit. and many other public strategy texts.
6 See many reviews. For example: Hood, C (1987) 'British administrative trends and the public choice revolution', in Lane, J-E (1987) (ed) *Bureaucracy and Public Choice*, Sage, London; Joyce, P (1999) *Strategic Management for the Public Services*, Open University Press, Buckingham; Pollitt, C (1990) *The New Managerialism and the Public Services: The Anglo-American Experience*, Basil Blackwell, Oxford; Pollitt, C (1993) *Managerialism in the Public Services*, 2nd edn, Blackwell, Oxford; Boyne, G A (2002) 'Public and private management: what's the difference?', *Journal of Management Studies*, Vol 39, No 1, pp 97–122.
7 The Galileo case was written by the author from numerous sources: The European Union has an extensive website devoted to the basic details of the project at http://europa.eu.int/comm/dgs/energy_transport/galileo/index_en.htm. *Financial Times*: 18 September 2003, p 24; 24 January 2005, p 20; 18 April 2005, p 28; 12 October 2006, p 9; 14 October 2006, p 6; 5 February 2007, p 6; 4 May 2007, p 7; 10 May 2007, p 13; 3 October 2007, p 26. *BBC News* from website: 6 March 2008 'Galileo demo sat to be despatched'; 5 January 2009 'Galileo, Europe's much delayed and costly satellite navigation project, takes a major step forward'; 26 October 2010 'Spaceopal named as Galileo European satnav operator'.
8 Some readers will detect a contradiction here but that is beyond the scope of this strategy text. You can explore it in: Lane, J-E (2000) Op. cit.
9 Lane, J-E (2000) Op. cit., p 6.
10 Frederickson, H G and Smith, K B (2003) Op. cit., p 193.
11 Back in the 1950s, Charles Tiebout attempted to resolve this problem by arguing that a theoretical competitive market could be created in a nation. It would need citizens to be mobile and different levels of public service to be offered in different parts of their country. If such citizens were able to shop around between local government areas for their preferred package of services and pay the taxes related to the choice that best suited their preferences, then such mobility would deliver 'the local public goods counterpart to the private market's shopping trip'. In essence, he was proposing a theoretical market in public services. Tiebold's hypothesis was that it was more efficient to have alternative government agencies competing rather than a centralised bureaucracy. For a fuller treatment, see Frederickson, H G and Smith, K B (2003) Op. cit., pp 193–194.
12 Bryson, J M (1998) *Strategic Planning for Public and Nonprofit Organizations*, Jossey Bass, San Francisco, CA.
13 Frederickson, H G and Smith, K B (2003) Op. cit., p 113; Lane, J-E (2000) Op. cit., p 2.

14 Lane, J-E (2000) Op. cit., p 305.
15 Lane, J-E (2000) Op. cit., p 304.
16 Pollitt, C and Bouckaert, G (2000) *Public Management Reform: A Comparative Analysis*, Oxford University Press, Oxford.
17 Frederickson, H G and Smith, K B (2003) Op. cit. has a comparison of the two systems on p 113.
18 Kettl, D (2000) *The Global Public Management Revolution: A Report on the Transformation of Governance*, Brookings Institute, Washington, D.C.
19 Lane, J-E (2000) Op. cit., p 307.
20 See extensive reviews in Lane, J-E (2000) Op. cit. and Pollitt and Bouckaert (2000) Op. cit.
21 See for example, Ferlie, E (2002) 'Quasi strategy: strategic management in the contemporary public sector', in Pettigrew, A, Thomas, H and Whittington, R (eds) *Handbook of Strategy and Management*, Sage, London; Bryson, J M (1998) Op. cit.; Bovaird, T (2003) 'Strategic management in public sector organizations', in Bovaird, T and Loffler, E (eds) *Public Management and Governance*, Routledge, London.
22 Bryson, J M (1998) Op. cit. uses SWOT extensively with many examples in both the public and non-profit sectors in his text.
23 Pollitt, C and Bouckaert, G (2000) Op. cit., Ch 7.
24 Bryson, J M (1998) Op. cit., Ch 5.
25 Pollitt, C and Bouckaert, G (2000) Op. cit., p 173.
26 See, for example, Hood, C (1983) *The Tools of Goverment*, Macmillan, London; Heymann, P (1987) *The Politics of Public Management*, Yale University Press, CT; Moore, M (1995) *Creating Public Value: Strategic Management in Government*, Harvard University Press, Cambridge, MA.
27 Lane, J-E (2000) Op. cit.
28 See for example, Bardach, E and Kagan, R (1982) *Going by the Book: The Problem of Regulatory Unreasonableness*, Temple University Press, PA; Wolf, C (1988) *Markets or Governments*, MIT Press, Cambridge, MA.
29 Pollit, C and Bouckaert, G (2000) Op. cit., p 170.
30 Osborne, D and Gaebler, T (1992) *Reinventing Government: How the Entrepreneurial Spirit is Transforming the Public Sector*, Plume, N Y; Alford, J (1998) 'Corporate Management', in Shafritz, J, *International Encyclopedia of Public Policy and Administration*, Vol 1, Westview Press, Boulder, CO.
31 Readers may care to note that this area remains somewhat under-researched. The author has therefore developed these comments from personal observation with the usual words of caution that derive from such an approach – partial, incomplete and a biased sample.
32 Bryson, J M (1998) Op. cit., p 30.
33 Bryson, J M (1998) Op. cit., Ch 5.
34 Sources for the Viking Energy case: in addition to the website sources quoted in the case, Professor Lynch made a 10-day visit to Shetland in August 2010. He interviewed seven local residents, some of whom were in favour of the proposal and some not. He also sourced further material particularly from the *Shetland Times* news stories which are available online.
35 Bryson, J M (1998) Op. cit., p 27.
36 Cranston, M (1968) (Trans and ed) *Jean-Jacques Rousseau – The Social Contract*, Penguin, Harmondsworth.
37 Mill, J S (1962) *Utilitarianism* – Edited with an Introduction by Mary Warnock, Collins/Fontana, London.
38 Sen, A (2005) 'The diverse ancestry of democracy', *Financial Times*, 13 June, p 19.
39 Lynch, R (2004) 'When majority opinion conflicts with expert judgment – the case of the Kings Theatre', *British Academy of Management Conference Paper*, St Andrews.
40 Lynch, R (2004) Ibid.
41 Wolf, M (2005) 'A more efficient Union will be less democratic', *Financial Times*, 15 June, p 19. This has an informed, if complex, discussion on such issues in the European Union. According to this argument, 'democracy' is more than just voting for European politicians every few years.
42 Bryson, J M (1998) Op. cit., p 27.
43 Pollit, C and Bouckaert, G (2000) Op. cit. Ch 7 has a long and interesting list of such conflicts and dilemmas which they discuss in detail.
44 Osborne, D and Gaebler, T (1992) *Re-inventing Government*, Addison Wesley, Reading, MA.
45 Bryson, J M (1998) Op. cit., p 159.
46 Bryson, J M (1998) Op. cit. Ch 7 provides a long and useful description in this area.
47 Bryson, J M (1998) Op. cit., p 33.
48 Bryson, J M (1998) Op. cit., p 33.
49 Ferlie, E (2002) Op. cit., p 289.
50 Ferlie, E (2002) Op. cit., p 289.
51 Bryson, J M (1998) Op. cit., Ch 5.
52 Ferlie, E (2002) Op. cit., p 289.
53 See, for example, Bryson, J M (1998) Op. cit., Ch 7.
54 Outlined in some depth with extensive references in Bryson, J M (1998) Op. cit.; Bryson, J M, Ackermann, F, Eden, C, Finn, C B (1995) 'Using the "*oval mapping process*" to identify strategic issues and formulate effective strategies', in *Strategic Planning for Public and Nonprofit Organizations*, Jossey Bass, San Francisco, CA, pp 257–275.
55 See, for example, Bryson, J M (1998) Op. cit., p 147 and Pollit, C and Bouckaert, G (2000) Op. cit., pp 183–187.
56 Lindblom, C (1959) 'The science of muddling through,' *Public Administration Review*, Vol 19, No 2, pp 79–88.
57 Bryson, J M (1998) Op. cit., p 147.
58 Pollitt, C and Bouckaert, G (2000) Op. cit., p 185.
59 Several research studies have shown that while the Margaret Thatcher privatisation reforms of the 1980s may have been presented as radical change, in practice, they were much more gradual and incremental, with the final outcomes being unknown at the start of the process. Quoted and referenced in Pollit, C and Bouckaert, G (2000) Op. cit.
60 This section of the chapter has benefited particularly from Ch 9 of Bryson, J M (1998) Op. cit.
61 Bryson, J M (1998) Op. cit., p 167.
62 One inevitable consequence of the introduction of the market mechanism into the public sector is the pressure for public servants to be accountable. This can 'distort priorities, consume time and effort in form-filling and produce changes locally that make no sense' – *Financial Times* Editorial, 31 January 2005, p 18. But, as the *FT* goes on to argue, there is good evidence that they have their uses and what is the alternative?

63 As one example, see Timmings, N (2005) 'Flagship hospital hit by barrage of changes', *Financial Times*, 31 January 2005, p 8.

64 Reich, R (1988) (ed) *The Power of Public Ideas*, Ballinger, Cambridge, MA. Quoted in: Alford, J (2001) 'The implications of "publicness" for strategic management theory', Ch 1 of Johnson, G and Scholes, K (eds) *Exploring Public Sector Strategy*, Pearson Education, Harlow. More generally, Ch 18 of *Strategic Management,* 7th edn, has benefited from Alford's introductory chapter to this edited book. It has also gained from the contributions of the other authors and the editors of this text.

65 Sources for the Kings Theatre case: The author has known the theatres of Portsmouth all his life. He declares an interest in the Kings Theatre, having made a small donation to its renovation fund in 2002. Other sources: *The News*, Portsmouth: 17 April 2003, p 5; 24 April 2003, pp 6, 8–9; 25 April 2003, p 22; 28 April 2003, p 5; 30 April 2003, p 6; 9 May 2003, p 11; 26 June 2003, p 6; 27 June 2003, p 10; 1 July 2003, p 6; 3 July 2003, p 5; 7 July 2003, p 5; 10 July 2003, pp 8 and 9; 10 July 2003, p 6; 11 September 2003, p 22; 21 February 2004, p 7. Interviews as outlined in the acknowledgements at the end of the case.

CHAPTER 19
International expansion and globalisation strategies

Video and sound summary of this chapter

LEARNING OUTCOMES

When you have worked through this chapter, you will be able to:

- explain what is meant by globalisation and distinguish it from international expansion;
- outline the main theories of international trade and explain their relevance to strategic management;
- identify the main institutions involved in international trade and investment and their influence on strategic management;
- explain the importance of trade blocks and their relationship with the development of strategic management;
- explore the main benefits and problems of globalisation strategies and comment critically on theories of globalisation;
- understand the main organisational structures needed to operate global strategy successfully;
- outline the main development routes and methods for global expansion.

Professor Richard Lynch has his own website specialising in international and global strategy. It has extra material including presentations, films, cases and other material. You can find it at: www.global-strategy.net.

INTRODUCTION

Video Parts 3 and 6

For some companies, international expansion and globalisation have become a vital aspect of strategy development and implementation. They present new opportunities to generate extra value added which deserve exploration. They may also entail increased competitive risk: international expansion may expose a company to new and sophisticated competitors. This chapter explores this topic.

The chapter begins by drawing a distinction between international strategy and global strategy: they are not the same. To understand international expansion, it needs to be viewed in the broader context of the topic of international trade and investment development. This involves the theories of international trade and the institutions that govern such activities.

Within this context, international and globalisation strategies then need to be explored: the particular benefits and problems need to be understood if such strategies are to be successful. Because of the increased scope of international operations, issues of organisational structure are also particularly important. In addition, the relationships between companies in international development, such as alliances and joint ventures, also need careful exploration because they may vary, depending on the markets and the countries. Figure 19.1 summarises the structure of this chapter.

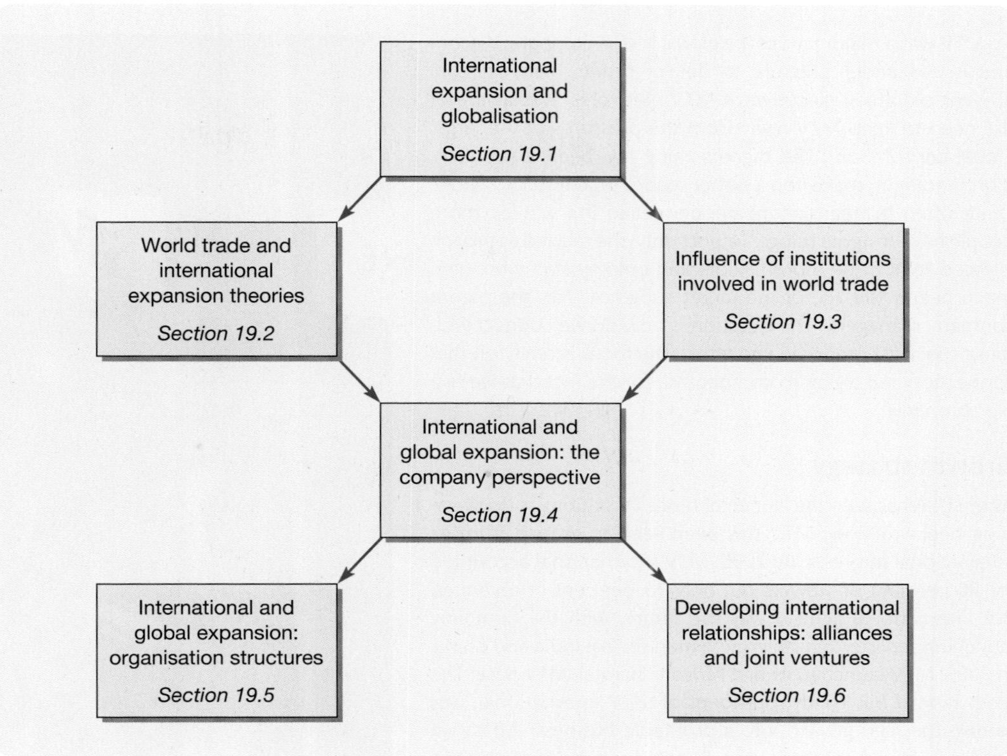

Figure 19.1 Exploring international and global strategy

International trade has its origins and theoretical foundation in the prescriptive topic of international economics. Thus some parts of international strategy seek prescriptive solutions. However, some of the more recent areas have taken more experimental routes which would fit more naturally within emergent strategic perspectives. Thus the early part of the chapter – on trade development – is more prescriptive, with emergent approaches being more appropriate later, in the section on company international expansion.

CASE STUDY 19.1

MTV: more local than global?

Around 1 billion people around the world see MTV every day, according to its American parent Viacom. Although there are global stars, like Madonna and Eminem, MTV mainly broadcasts through 40 national or regional music channels, each with a distinctive chart sound. This case explores the reasons why MTV's strategy is more local than global.

Programme content

When MTV began in 1981, it broadcast largely to its American home audience and its programme content was primarily music videos. By 2005, the US was still MTV's largest and most profitable market. But the programming had moved from simply music to include reality television programmes like the activities of *The Osbournes* and the baiting of celebrities on *Punk'd*. Nevertheless, music was still the central theme and the MTV Annual Music Awards were still able to cause controversy.

MTV pioneered the reality television format in 1992 with a programme called *The Real World*. It was about a group of young people living in an apartment in New York. It was originally planned to use actors but the company did not have sufficient funds, so it observed real people at zero cost instead. The company had the same low-budget, free-wheeling culture in 2005 – except for the vast sum it paid the Osbournes to have television cameras follow them for months. This was all part of the way of staying creative and in touch with its young target audience.

MTV was a major part of the global media company Viacom and it was under pressure to deliver profits. Tom Freston, 45-year-old chief executive of MTV Networks, was aware of the need to keep MTV away from the pressures of the large, global corporation: 'The bigness thing has been a problem. It's not going to make you a better record or a better TV show. Quite often it means more people get in the way or more people have to agree things.' Importantly, the relaxed approach allowed MTV to be more flexible and employ staff who were much nearer the age of the target audience than the parent company managers: 'The question is how do we connect with these specialist groups we go after? The focus is really on that connection and trying to compensate for the fact that we're a big company.'

Growth strategy

As the USA has seen the launch of more TV stations and advertising begin to slow, MTV has been seeking growth from its international interests. By 2005, MTV International accounted for 80 per cent of viewers but only 15 per cent of revenues. But international activity was the future, with the company launching services to high-growth markets like India and China. In 2005, MTV launched its first African channel, MTV Base. The main task of Bill Roedy, president of MTV International, was to turn the high growth into a profitable business. 'Africa we expect to be a big contributor. People look at Africa and see problems, but we also have to look at the positives. Its GDP growth is the second highest in the world behind growth in East Asia.'

China and India also represented major opportunities. 'The epicentre is shifting to the Far East and India,' commented Roedy. 'They are amazing markets but it's important not to get too euphoric about the numbers.'

Competition

Music downloading over the internet was becoming a major threat: Apple had led the way with its legal music site to millions of customers. In addition, the technology of broadband telecommunications would extend downloading to videos and mobile phones. MTV therefore needed to offer more than just music videos. In addition, it needed to take into account new ways of delivering its product. Japanese customers already accessed MTV more frequently by mobile telephone than by TV channel. Equally, in Korea, most homes had broadband and could download videos quickly and legally.

As a result, MTV was continuing to change its programme content with non-music offerings like *Jackass* and *Dirty Sanchez* and it was making all this available through the new media channels. But it faced the problem that much of this material was mainly American in humour and style. Its target audiences might be young and international, but they still mainly listened to national and ethnic recording artists – hence the need for local material alongside the global MTV brand name. The company has subsequently made some changes in its MTV strategy but the programming still remains partially local.

MTV's worldwide brand is adapted by each country or region to deliver its locally-based strategy within the global vision.

MTV's parent, Viacom, has been a firm supporter of green strategy and sustainability initiatives over the last few years.

 This case was written from published sources only.[1] Viacom's media brands include MTV, VH1, CMT, Logo, BET, Centric, Nickelodeon, Nick Jr, TeenNick, Nick at Nite, Comedy Central, TV Land, Spike TV and Tr3s as well as Paramount Pictures. For the most up-to-date information on MTV's company strategy, vision and positioning please see their annual report information available from www.viacom.com.

Case questions

1. What are the benefits of operating a global media strategy and what are the difficulties?
2. What are the market trends that will make it more difficult for MTV in the future?
3. Should MTV become more global with more programmes like Jackass, or more local with little global content?

19.1 INTERNATIONAL EXPANSION AND GLOBALISATION: THEIR MEANING AND IMPORTANCE

Video Part 3

For a series of structural reasons which we will explore later, international trading activities – *country exports and imports* – have increased substantially over the past 50 years. Moreover, in addition to trading, companies have also invested substantial capital sums in countries outside their home nation to set up factories and other facilities. The world is becoming more international and this has significant implications for strategic management. International expansion and globalisation issues are amongst the most important factors in the business environment influencing strategy development in the twenty-first century.

The early years of MTV show that such expansion is not just an issue for the major multinational enterprises (often abbreviated to MNEs) like the Ford Motor Company (USA) and Coca-Cola (USA). It may also be a significant issue for many rather smaller companies involved in international trade. It has also become increasingly important in not-for-profit activities such as international aid agency work and international rescue. However, this chapter concentrates on commercial activities for reasons of space.

As background to our understanding of globalisation, this section begins by looking at recent trends in world trade activity. It then uses this strategic context to explore the meaning of globalisation. Words like 'globalisation' and 'internationalisation' are used interchangeably to explore the strategic issues, but they are not the same. The distinction between them is important because it may lead to different strategic activities. Finally, the main strategic implications of globalisation are then examined in terms of the activities of both countries and companies.

19.1.1 The importance of world trade and investment: the strategic context

Definition ▸

In 1994, world merchandise trade amounted to $4,000 billion and grew by over 9 per cent over the previous year:[2] ***foreign trade* means the exporting and importing activities of countries and companies around the world.** At the same time, world output of goods increased by 3.5 per cent: *output* is the total production of goods by companies and public organisations aggregated together across the world. In fact, as shown in Table 19.1, world merchandise trade outstripped world output during the period 1970–90.[3] Countries are trading more with each other and faster than they are increasing their output. This should present continuing opportunities for the development of strategic management.

The reasons for the major increase in world trade are shown in Exhibit 19.1.

In many respects, world merchandise trade has come to be an important *driver* of country economic growth around the world. Strategic management has played a significant part in achieving this and, equally, has benefited from it. We are concerned here with the way international markets and industry structure interact with international company activity. Some industries cannot survive without overseas trade: for example, aerospace and defence companies such as Boeing (USA), Aerospatiale (France) and British Aerospace (UK) need sales beyond their home countries to make a profit. MTV, featured in Case 19.1, needs international sales since its national market in the USA is beginning to mature. Other industries simply benefit from being able to sell their products or services internationally.

Table 19.1 Comparison of world exports and world manufacturing value added

	1960–1970 (%)	1970–1980 (%)	1980–1990 (%)
Annual growth in world trade	9.2	20.3	6.0
Annual growth in manufacturing value added (1990 $)	n.a.	3.1	2.1

Source: UNIDO.[4]

EXHIBIT 19.1

The reasons for the major increase in world trade

- *New or enhanced trade blocks* have been agreed over the past 20 years, for example, the Single European Act 1986 certainly encouraged and supported trade across the EU. The ASEAN pact has been extended because benefits have been identified. New trade agreements are expected to keep this momentum for the next few years. There are several recent examples:
  1. The Uruguay Round of the General Agreement on Tariffs and Trade (GATT) was signed in December 1993 and was projected at the time to increase global welfare by between $213 and 274 billion in 1992 dollars by the year 2002.[5]
  2. The Mercosur Treaty has brought together Brazil, Argentina, Paraguay and Uruguay in South America to form a new regional trade pact.
  3. The North American Free Trade Agreement (NAFTA) was signed in late 1994 and brought increased trade between the USA, Mexico and Canada.
- *World and regional trade organisations* have themselves been strengthened and reformed: for example, the European Bank for Reconstruction and Development (EBRD) has been renewed following a difficult early period and has now begun to offer significant funds for development in Eastern Europe. The WTO, the World Bank and the IMF have also been strengthened. These institutions are explained in Section 19.3.
- *Multinationals* have become an important source of world sales and investment. According to UN estimates,[6] foreign sales by transnational corporations reached $5,500 billion in 1992. The same companies have accumulated $2,000 billion worth of FDI.
- *New technology* has made telecommunications, travel and media and all international communications much easier. This has brought countries together and influenced political and economic decision making.

19.1.2 The distinction between foreign trade and foreign direct investment

In addition to engaging in trading activities, companies may also engage in foreign direct investment (often abbreviated to FDI). It is important to distinguish between the two:

1. *Foreign trade* means the exporting and importing activities of countries and companies around the world – for example, MTV's export of *The Osbournes* TV programme from the USA.

Definition ▶

2. **Foreign direct investment (FDI) is the long-term investment by a company in the technology, management skills, brands and physical assets of a subsidiary in another country.** Such investment is then used to generate sales in that country, quite possibly replacing exports from the home country – for example, the FDI by MTV in its television network in South Africa.

The role of overseas trade and FDI has changed significantly for many companies and has come to be a direct part of strategic management. But an increase in *international* activity is not the same as an increase in *globalisation*.

19.1.3 Defining and exploring different types of international expansion

In analysing international company activity, Bartlett and Ghoshal distinguished between three different types of strategy:[7]

Definition ▶

1. *International* – **when a significant proportion of an organisation's activities are outside the home country and they are managed as a separate area.** For example, a small company engaged in exporting some of its product beyond its home country would be international according to this definition. The focus of such a business is its domestic operation, with international activity being an appendage to this.

Definition ▶ 2 ***Multinational* – when a company operates in many countries, though it may still have a home base.** One purpose of such operations is to respond to local demand. For example, the MTV music television company has many different operations to suit different music traditions, but they are all owned by its home-base operation in the USA. The business consists of a series of semi-independent operations, under a global brand name like MTV – see Case 19.1

Definition ▶ 3 ***Global* – when a company treats the whole world as one market and one source of supply.** There is only limited response to local demand – for example, Rolex watches or Disney's Mickey Mouse – see Case 8.1 for the latter. The focus of the business is one world market, with each of the operations delivering contributions to that activity.

These distinctions are important because they have different strategic implications:

- With the international activity, the primary strategic driver is the home market and the competitive advantage that it delivers, with international sales being subsidiary to this.
- With the multinational business, the competitive advantage is separately determined for each of the various national or regional markets in which the organisation is engaged.
- With the global business strategy, competitive advantage usually comes from common global brands and from concentrated production activity that has been sited to deliver significant economies of scale and resource sourcing. There may be some adjustment of the product or service for local needs but essentially it is the same around the world. The whole world is treated as one market.

In addition to the above on *company* activity, the term 'globalisation' is also used to cover three other topic areas:[8]

1. *Globalisation of economies, trade activities and regulatory regimes.* World economies are slowly coming together, with barriers to trade being lowered. We will explore this in Sections 19.2 and 19.3 below.
2. *Globalisation of industries.* Whole industries like the car industry, the aerospace industry and the paper and pulp industry are beginning to trade as one market rather than as a series of regional markets. We will explore this in Sections 19.4 and 19.5 below.
3. *Morality of globalisation.* It is argued by some commentators that the globalisation process has led some companies to pillage the environment, destroy lives and fail to enrich poor people as promised.[9] These are important issues that are beyond the scope of this text. However, the underlying principle of this book is that companies will act responsibly and in the interests of the wider community, as well as those of the owners of the organisation. These issues deserve our serious attention.

Comment

Those organisations that fail to distinguish between international, multinational and global strategy miss important elements of strategic development. Many companies that claim to be 'global' are not global in the sense set out above – they are merely selling in many parts of the world. This means that such companies are international or multinational, but it does not mean that they are global. In practice, as we will see later, the distinctions between these areas are not as clear as set out above, but they serve as a useful starting point in exploring global strategy.

19.1.4 International expansion and globalisation: the C–C–B Paradigm

In order to explore the relationships between companies and the many countries within which they operate, it is useful to identify the essential elements. These are set out in the C–C–B Paradigm shown in Figure 19.2. It is developed from an earlier paradigm by the international economist John Dunning, but has been substantially altered to concentrate on strategic management issues.[10] The main elements of the paradigm are:

- *C–C–B.* This refers to three essential components of the paradigm: the **C**ompany, the **C**ountry in which the company is operating and the **B**argaining that will take place between the company and the country.

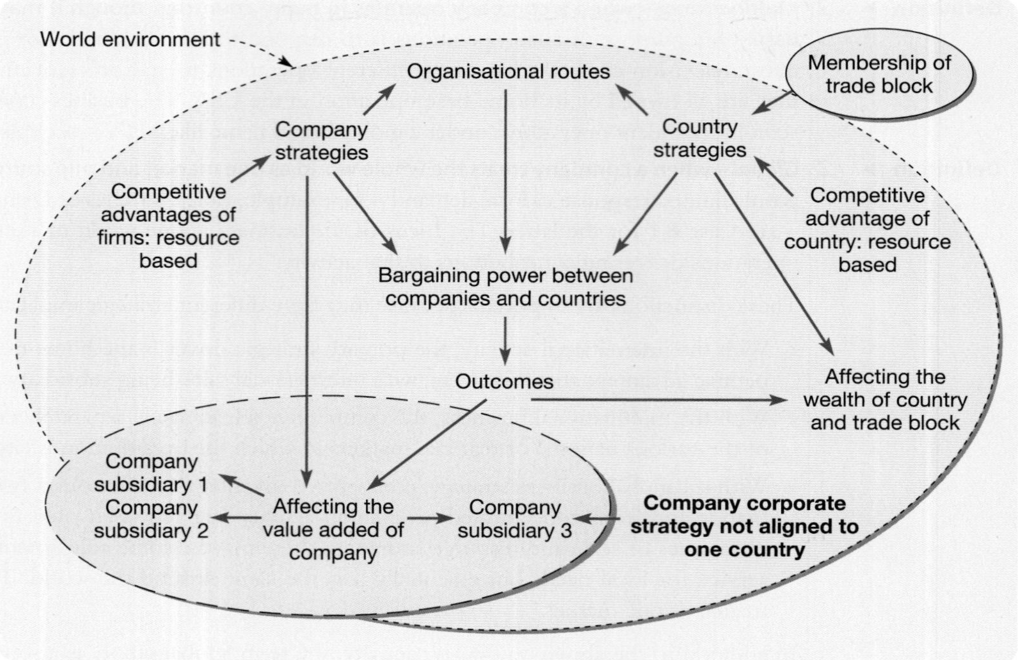

Figure 19.2 Companies in the global world: the C–C–B Paradigm

- *Underlying assumption of the paradigm.* Companies have different interests from countries. The conflict between these interests is resolved through bargaining between the two parties. The main areas of advantage can be identified by exploring the concept of competitive advantage – see Chapter 6 for companies and Section 19.2 below for countries.
- *Company.* Each company will have sustainable competitive advantages, based on its resources. For example, MTV has expertise in television programme development, local content development and its global brand name. These advantages will be used in developing its international strategy for individual countries.
- *Country.* Each country will have some competitive advantages, based on its resources. For example, these might include its physical location, such as Singapore's position on shipping routes between Europe and Asia. However, resources will also include the country's investment in education, such as Singapore's substantial investment in this area over the past 20 years, and its technical knowledge, such as Singapore's financial and electronics expertise developed over this period.
- *Bargaining power.* Companies and countries will negotiate with each other on the basis of customer market size, investment required, availability of investment incentives, country infrastructure and so on.
- *Outcomes.* The results of such bargaining will deliver *wealth* to the country receiving the trade and the FDI and *value added* to the company.
- *Value added of the company.* There may be more than one subsidiary of the company involved. Moreover, some subsidiaries may have other relationships with each other, not always inside the country. In addition, the stakeholders of the company are unlikely to be located in the country. The result is that the company's strategy will not necessarily be aligned to that of one country.

We will explore these elements further as we progress through the chapter.

19.1.5 Strategic management and international expansion – including globalisation

To deliver value added and sustainable competitive advantage, strategic management seeks two main opportunities from international expansion:

1 Market opportunities in many countries will deliver significant new sales, particularly as barriers to trade have been reduced over the past 50 years.

2 Production and resource opportunities will arise in some countries as a result of their special resources, such as the availability of low-cost labour, special skills and natural resources (like oil).

The result has been the creation of new international configurations of business that cover all the main elements of commerce: trade; services (such as advertising and technology); people (such as those needed to manage businesses locally); factor payments (such as profits, interest payments, licensing); and the FDI referred to above. In one sense, the principles of strategic management are just the same whether they are applied in one country or on a global scale. In another sense, there are some extra dimensions that arise from global competition and the interests of individual countries or groups of countries. We begin our exploration of these additional dimensions by exploring country issues in the next two sections of this chapter. We then turn to company issues in the following three sections of the chapter.

KEY STRATEGIC PRINCIPLES

- International expansion and globalisation are amongst the most important strategic influences in the business environment in the twenty-first century.
- International expansion has become an important driver of country economic growth. Companies have contributed to this and benefited from it.
- It is important to distinguish between foreign trade – exports and imports – and foreign direct investment (FDI) – the investment in capital, factories and people in foreign locations.
- It is important also to distinguish between three types of international and global expansion: *international*, where a significant proportion of an organisation's activities take place outside its home market, but it is still the domestic market that is the prime focus of strategy; *multinational*, where a company operates in many countries and varies its strategy country by country; and *global*, where a company treats the world as one market.
- Significantly, each of the three areas above implies a different international expansion strategy.
- The C–C–B Paradigm explores the resource relationships between the Company, the Country in which it operates and the Bargaining that takes place between the two. The twin purposes of such bargaining are to deliver increased value added to the company and increased wealth to the country.

CASE STUDY 19.2

TCL: global strategy at one of China's largest consumer electronics companies

Over the past few years, the Chinese television set manufacturer TCL has slowly been building a global strategy. It has acquired European and American companies as part of this process but has not yet been successful. What does this tell us about building a global strategy?

TCL's global objective

> We know it clearly that TCL is still far behind the mature world-class corporation. . . . To be a globally prestigious and most innovative enterprise is our prospect. It will definitely be fulfilled.
>
> TCL's Chairman, Li Dongsheng

This was the ambitious task set by the Chairman of TCL, one of China's largest consumer electronics companies, over the past few years. It would not be easy to achieve because TCL was competing industry giants, such as the Japanese companies Sony and Panasonic and the Korean companies Samsung and LG. The objective was made even more difficult because competition in China's home market was also fierce from other Chinese companies like Haier, Haisense and Konka. Another complication was that the industry's technology was changing from cathode ray tube (CRT) to flat panel plasma and liquid crystal display (LCD).

This case explores the difficulties faced by TCL and its strategies for building a global presence. TCL has faced setbacks along the way and, at the time of writing this case, was still not successful. But there are lessons to be learnt on global strategy from its experience so far.

The case has three sections:

- Company background and history
- Global market for television set manufacture
- Global strategy at TCL – progress to date.

Company background and history

TCL began as consumer electronics manufacturer, established in 1981 in Huizhou, Guangdong, China. The company was aligned to the local industry bureau and manufactured cassette tapes. In 1985, it identified a new trend in China's telecommunication industry and switched to producing telephones. Product innovation gave it market dominance in the industry, and from 1989 its products were exported to more than 30 countries. In 1996, it acquired the Hong Kong based TV manufacturer Lu's, whose products TCL were already selling in China through a long-term agreement. This move allowed TCL to enter into the TV set manufacture industry. Importantly, it also made history because it was the first Chinese state-owned company to acquire a foreign company.

TCL's international expansion started with emerging countries such as Vietnam. Choosing such a route was not by default but a deliberate plan. According to a TCL executive, the reason was that, 'There are 1.2 million overseas Chinese living in Vietnam and they are an important economic and social force in the country, which is undoubtedly beneficial to the Chinese companies investing in Vietnam.' Facing tough Vietnamese competition from other global brands, TCL chose a low-cost strategy as its source of competitive advantage. 'Instead of using the latest technology, TCL adopted second-hand facilitates which were suited to the local technological level and [these] enabled it to reduce the depreciation, therefore lowering the cost of the final products.'

TCL is one of China's leading consumer electronics companies. Its international expansion faced some problems, as the case explains.

Following this early success, TCL then began to develop its European and American business. In 2002, TCL began to integrate its international operations worldwide. It also took the decision to move into European and US markets, the world's two most mature and competitive markets. Brand and distribution building would be too slow and there were substantial quota restrictions on the import of Chinese televisions sets. TCL therefore acquired the bankrupt German company *Schneider* in 2002 and the American company *Govideo* in 2003.

In 2004, TCL took its international activities a stage further by signing two agreements with French companies: *Thomson* in television sets and *Alcatel* in mobile telephones. 'TCL's strategy is that we want to find strategic partners. We don't want to work alone and have to bear all the risk. That's because in these mature countries [Europe and the USA], the growth is relatively stable and entry barriers are high.' Thomson was important in Europe with its Thomson brand and distribution network and, in the USA, because Thomson also owned the *RCA* brand and related assets.

Essentially this was the third stage of TCL's international and global strategy – see Table 19.2. By 2006, the TCL Group

Table 19.2 The stages and strategies of the internationalisation process of TCL

Stages	Main objectives	Target location	International and global strategies
Stage One (1990–1997)	Leverage advantages of production capacity and low cost to produce for foreign companies	Domestic	Export, OEM, ODM
Stage Two (1998–2002)	Expand into developing countries with similar development and culture features	Developing countries	Export, FDI
Stage Three (2002–2006)	Penetrate into developed countries and gain complementary advantages (market access, technology and brand) from developed countries	Developed countries in EU and USA	Acquisition, joint venture and strategic alliances

Note:

OEM means Original Equipment Manufacturer: OEM companies make products that *other purchasing companies have designed* and then contracted for the OEM company to make. The products are sold under the name of the purchaser.

ODM means Original Design Manufacturer: ODM companies make products that the *ODM* companies have designed but sell them under the name of the purchaser.

had annual sales of 50 billion yuan ($6.4 billion) and was the market leader in the People's Republic of China (PRC) market by volume. As a result of these moves, the company became the largest supplier of cathode ray television sets in the world. The problem was that the global market was moving from CRT sets to flat screen sets.

Global market for television set manufacture

The world market demand for television sets was worth around $65 billion per annum in 2004 and was growing around 9 per cent per annum. Essentially, there were two market segments within this:

1 The more wealthy developed countries (North America, Europe, parts of Asia) where replacement demand for CRT sets was being replaced by new demand for higher technologies – plasma TV, LCD TV, high-definition television and a switch from analogue to digital television signals.

2 The less developed countries (Africa, South America, parts of Asia including Vietnam) where demand still existed for cheap, basic sets using standardised and well-established technology – largely based around the mature technology of the CRT.

National governments in Europe and the USA attempted to protect their own consumer electronics industries by erecting trade barriers. But all the leading companies had set up subsidiaries within these regions to reduce the impact of these measures.

Importantly, many of the components of television sets – semiconductors, switches, sockets, etc. – are common to the two main segments identified above, thus making it possible to serve both market segments without major additional investment. To reduce costs, the leading companies were sourcing many basic components and assembling their products in low-wage countries like China. This meant that TCL had no country-specific competitive advantage against the main global companies in television set manufacture. This presented a real challenge for any new entrant, including TCL.

With the standardisation of components, it was possible to gain economies of scale and scope, spread R&D and manufacturing investment over more worldwide sales – all major characteristics of a global strategy as defined in this book. In addition, many of the world's leading television set companies employed global branding: for example, Sony and LG appear in surveys of the world's leading brands. But true competitive advantage was difficult to achieve for the existing companies, let alone a new entrant like TCL.

Although this case focuses on the manufacture and sale of television sets, all the leading companies marketed other related consumer electronic products – digital video recorders, sound systems, video cameras, etc. The reasons were that such related products had similar components, the same distribution outlets and built on the same brand strengths. Any new company entering the television set market like TCL therefore needed to consider its strategy in the broader context of strengths in consumer electronics. A selected list of the world's leading consumer electronics companies, ranked by consumer electronics sales rather than television sales, is shown in Table 19.3. Based on this evidence, any new entrant into the consumer electronics market will face competitors that are large and with substantial resources – including those in related areas.

In summary, the main strategic problem facing all the companies, including TCL, was that the market was highly competitive, prices were falling and several of the major companies – Sony, LG and Sharp – were making little profit from their television set manufacturing (see Case 10 in Part 6 of this book on Sony for example).

Global strategy at TCL

By 2005, TCL's profits were under pressure: it made losses in 2005 and the first part of 2006. The company decided that it was over-stretched and needed to consolidate its resources if it was to achieve its global objectives. It therefore reduced its involvement in some peripheral areas of the business (personal computers, etc.) and focused solely on television manufacture. Specifically, it decided to drop its co-operation with Alcatel in mobile telephones. In November 2006, TCL announced that it was to restructure its European operation by closing down its production facilities in France, but keeping the R&D centre in Europe and restructuring its distribution.

Table 19.3 Selected list of the world's leading consumer electronics companies 2006 (All data in $ millions)

Company	Home country	Consumer electronics sales worldwide	Consumer electronics profits (loss) worldwide	Selected other products	Total sales including all other products
Sony	Japan	40,714	(264)	Games, films, semiconductors	63,893
Panasonic	Japan	34,100	1,631	Domestic appliances, property, semiconductors	76,100
Samsung	Korea	28,603	n/a	Telecommunications, domestic appliances, semiconductors	87,451
Philips	Netherlands	13,757	668	Medical systems, lighting, domestic appliances	40,121
LG	Korea	10,800	n/a	Domestic appliances, semiconductors	38,571
TCL	China	6,410	Loss in 2006	Mobile telephones, electronic components	6,410
Sharp	Japan	1,473	n/a	Information/calculators equipment, domestic appliances, electronic components	18,630

Note: Different companies have different definitions of 'consumer electronics' so the above data is a guide only.

Source: author from company annual report and accounts.

Although TCL has gained from its international strategy, there remained problems in four areas:

1 *High market entry barriers.* TCL faced strong protectionism in West Europe and North America in recent years.
2 *Cultural and managerial differences.* TCL found difficulties in penetrating some foreign markets due to its lack of familiarity with local culture. It also found difficulties in working with foreign partners after signing the cross-border deals.
3 *Lack of technical talent.* Technology leadership is one of the key success factors in this industry. Like any firm from a developing country, TCL has had a shortage of technical talent. This has directly contributed to its slow response to the technology changes in the industry, therefore missing an opportunity to catch up with its established rivals.
4 *Lack of managerial talent.* With rapid international expansion, TCL faced a severe shortage of managerial talent with international experience.

To overcome 'foreignness', TCL had entered the mature and competitive European and North American markets through acquisition of two local companies near bankruptcy: Schneider in Germany and Govideo in the USA. Although they were cheap to acquire, it turned out that their brands had a poor reputation and were a hindrance in achieving the objective of market penetration.

TCL then followed this by the joint venture with the French company Thomson, which owned the RCA brand in the USA. Vincent Yan, Chief Financial Officer of a subsidiary of TCL, explained later: 'We thought we could sell RCA as a premium brand, but in fact it had already deteriorated into pretty much a low-end brand.' Another of TCL's officials admitted, 'When we bought Thomson we knew its American business was going through a lot of troubles, but the European business was doing great, but we had underestimated the challenges involved in rescuing Thomson's business.'

This led a financial analyst to conclude: 'TCL's problem is that it does not have the experience or competence in managing acquisitions. It is too ambitious and is now paying the price.' By 2007, TCL had not yet overcome such problems in developing a global business.

Case questions

1 Using the benefits of global strategy outlined in this chapter, how does TCL rate against such benefits? And how does TCL rate against its competitors?
2 What were the problems faced by TCL in building a global strategy? Can they be overcome? How?
3 What would you recommend to TCL? Should the company continue to pursue a global strategy? If so, how? If not, what strategy should it adopt with its heavy commitments in Europe and North America?

19.2 WORLD TRADE AND THE INTERNATIONAL EXPANSION THEORIES

To understand the basis of company international expansion and globalisation, it is essential to explore why and how national markets have become increasingly global over the past 50 years. Between 1950 and 1996, world trade in merchandise goods increased by 1,500 per cent. Virtually all of this increased activity has been channelled through companies engaged in international activities. Globalisation is therefore capable of delivering major company strategic opportunities.

However, globalisation is also dependent on national government strategy. For example, the world consumer electronics industry would be totally unable to operate without the willing permission of governments to allow electronic exporting and importing when such countries have their own consumer electronics industries. We begin by exploring the theories of world trade, which have been mainly developed at the *country* rather than the *company* level. After setting the theories in historical context, we pick out some leading theories and then examine their strategic implications.

Until recently, world trade was mainly in commodities like agricultural products.[12] It turned down in the 1930s as countries attempted to protect their new industrial ventures. From the late 1940s, it has grown dramatically as countries have lowered barriers to trade and developed institutions to encourage international trade. The reasons for this growth are clearly relevant to strategic management but are complex and not easy to resolve.

Over the past 200 years, economists in particular have been developing theories to explain the growth and advantages of international trade. They have explored the benefits and problems in the context of empirical evidence that increased trade has generally been beneficial to those countries that have engaged in it.[13] The importance of such theories for strategic management is threefold:

1 They explain the way that nation states view their *bargaining position* with companies wanting to expand internationally.
2 They provide a *framework* in which to analyse the strategic management relating to international opportunities and threats.
3 They help to identify the *sustainable competitive advantages* of the nations that might be selected by companies to form part of an international strategic management.

Amongst the many theories of international economic growth, three can usefully be identified and contrasted for their impact on strategic management. They are explored in the sections that follow. There is no agreement amongst economists on the 'correct' theory: they all have some merit but all fail to capture the complexity of the full international strategic implications.

19.2.1 Theories of trade based on the resources of the country – the comparative advantage of nations

Definition ▶ **The comparative advantage of nations consists of the resources possessed by a country that give it a competitive advantage over other nations.** In the theories of the nineteenth century to the present day, some economists have argued that free trade between nations will deliver increased wealth. Early theories to support this argument relied on simple views of comparative labour costs between nations. More recent theories have concentrated on the economies of scale that arise as companies inside nations produce on a larger scale and thus reduce their costs. In both cases, these theories will depend on the resources of the country – such as the availability of raw materials and energy – along with the resources of the individual companies and industries within the country. They are often called *theories of the comparative advantage of nations*. None of these theories provides a complete explanation of the complex reasons for the growth in world trade.[14]

Whatever the reasons, evidence of the effects of removing some trade barriers during the period 1965–1995 came from the experience of Eastern Asia.[15] Singapore, Hong Kong and, later, South Korea and Taiwan lowered some trade barriers rather than protect their home industries. The four Asian newly industrialised nations raised their average real incomes per head from 20 per cent of those of the high-income countries (like the USA and the EU) in 1965 to 70 per cent by 1995. Contrasts were drawn between North and South Korea, mainland China and Hong Kong, West and East Germany. From the mid-1980s, mainland China itself began to take a different path, with successful results, especially in Shanghai and Guangdong Province. In the late 1990s, even countries like India that had feared the effects of trade liberalisation on their own national industries began to think again.

From a strategic management perspective, the significance of this theory is that it stresses the importance of identifying the resources of a country or region within a country as part of international strategy development.

19.2.2 'Diamond' theory of competitive advantage of nations – the contribution of Porter

Definition ▶ **Porter's diamond theory of international competitive advantage identifies a 'diamond' of four inter-related areas within a nation that assist that country to be more competitive in international markets – the four areas being factor conditions, competing firms within the country, support industries of the country and home demand.** In the late 1980s, Michael Porter embarked on a major empirical study of 10 nations and four major world industries.[16] His purpose was to identify those factors that contributed to national success in international markets. The countries surveyed were: Denmark, Italy, Japan, Singapore, South Korea, Sweden, Switzerland, the UK, the USA and West Germany. The industries were German printing presses, US patient-monitoring equipment, Italian ceramic tiles and Japanese robotics. The result was a diamond formed from four interrelated factors, as shown in Figure 19.3.

The four factors are as follows:

1 *Factor conditions*. Porter emphasised that competitiveness was not just a matter of comparative advantage. Resources can also be 'home-grown' and specialised. Thus, the provision of education, universities, excellent telecommunications goes well beyond natural resources but can assist in delivering national competitiveness. The success of countries like Singapore and Malaysia has depended, at least in part, on the national government's willingness to invest in these areas over long periods of time.

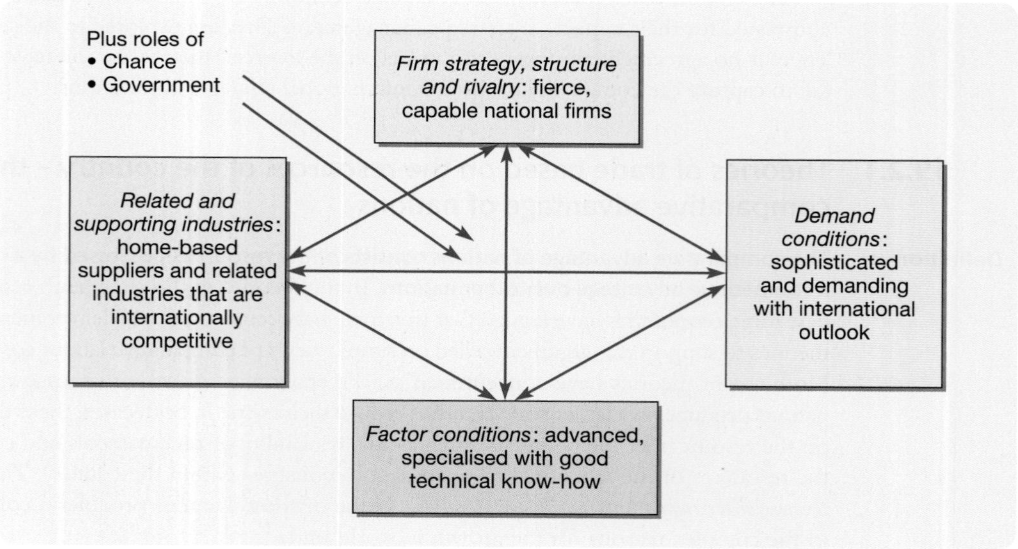

Figure 19.3 Diamond theory of competitive advantage

Source: reprinted with the permission of Free Press, a Division of Simon & Schuster, Inc., from *The Competitive Advantage of Nations*, by Michael E. Porter.

2 *Related and supporting industries.* Internationally competitive *suppliers* and other related industries represent a critical resource for international success. Clusters of such industries, each offering expertise and world-class service, can be vital. For example, Hollywood USA relies for its world success not just on film studios but on a range of other related companies in film recording, electronics, design and music.
3 *Firm strategy, structure and rivalry.* Fierce national *competition* will drive innovation, force down costs and develop new methods of competing that can then be used internationally by the same companies. For example, Porter argued that the global strength of the Japanese consumer electronics companies like Mitsubishi and Hitachi was directly related to the strength of the highly competitive home market for such goods.
4 *Demand conditions.* Highly sophisticated and demanding *customers* in a nation's home market will drive up innovation and quality. Porter pointed to the sophistication of Japanese cameras, like Canon, and the quality of German cars, like BMW, being the result of demanding national customers.

In addition, Porter identified two other factors that are important:

1 *the role of government*, which can influence any of the above by subsidies, regulation, investment in education and so on;
2 *the role of chance events*, which can shift competitive advantage in unpredictable ways: for example, war, inventions, oil price rises and so on.

From a strategic management perspective, this significant theory helps identify and select countries for production investment. It also provides evidence on the nature of customers and competitors in such countries. Importantly, it suggests that the size of a market matters less than its characteristics.

Comment

In spite of its clear relevance to the development of international and global strategy, Porter's theory has a number of difficulties:[17]

- *Sample.* Readers can work out which countries and industries were left out and what this might mean for the conclusions.
- *Government.* This is not included in the diamond but is crucial to many elements of it, such as national competition policy.
- *Chance.* This appears to be the only explanation for many events that may be crucial.
- *Company, not country, competition.* Porter took as his starting point the concept that countries compete in international markets. This is misleading because it is companies that compete – for example, Sweden and Finland do not compete on paper and pulp but pulpot and paper companies like SCA and Stora Enso do.
- *Multinational influence.* Porter totally ignores the major multinational companies, yet they are the main contributors to foreign trade and FDI. Dunning suggests that MNEs accounted for between 25 and 30 per cent of the GDP of the world's market economies in the mid-1980s. They were also responsible for around three-quarters of the world's commodity trade and four-fifths of the trade in technology and managerial skills.[18]
- *Home country advantage.* For some MNEs, the location of their home countries is largely irrelevant. The fact that ABB – see Case 12.3 – is located in Switzerland and Sweden has almost no bearing on its global strategies. This means that the basis of the Porter thesis – the 'home country' advantage (of Japanese consumer electronics, for example) – is irrelevant for such companies.

These and other criticisms suggest that the theory is only a partial explanation of complex issues. However, it does alert companies to important country issues that need to be addressed.

19.2.3 Theory of limited state intervention – attributed to the World Bank

In its work in supporting investment in developing countries over the past few years, the World Bank has had the opportunity to examine the areas of investment that deliver real increases in the

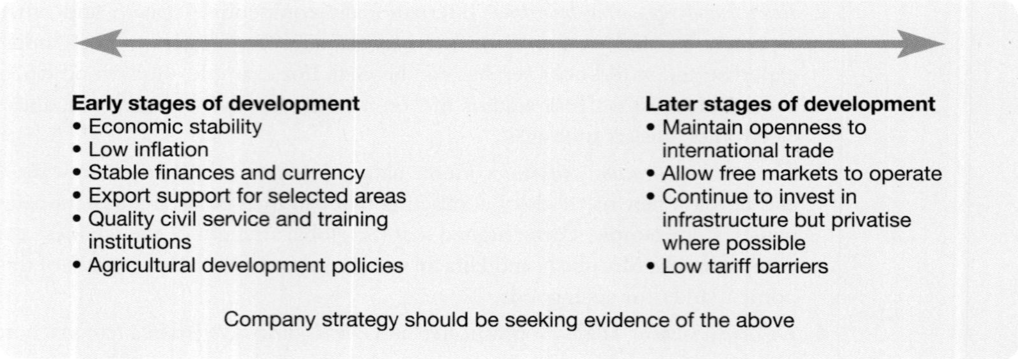

Early stages of development
- Economic stability
- Low inflation
- Stable finances and currency
- Export support for selected areas
- Quality civil service and training institutions
- Agricultural development policies

Later stages of development
- Maintain openness to international trade
- Allow free markets to operate
- Continue to invest in infrastructure but privatise where possible
- Low tariff barriers

Company strategy should be seeking evidence of the above

Figure 19.4 Theory of limited state intervention

wealth of countries. It has never published the results as a 'theory' as such, but its empirical findings can be found in its annual reports. It is these that have been summarised as the limited state intervention theory outlined in Figure 19.4.

Definition ► **Essentially, the theory of limited state intervention suggests that companies gained from national government investment in the early years in such areas as telecommunications and roads, but that as nations become more wealthy the state should withdraw its support and allow free market pressures to operate.** This means that state support for home-grown industries should be reduced if companies are to compete internationally.

From a strategic management perspective, the findings indicate the attitudes that companies should have towards government intervention. They indicate that companies should be wary of governments that deny open market access. Governments should also be seeking to stabilise the economy of a country and its currency as a matter of policy and should invest in its infrastructure and education. This provides clear guidance to companies on country selection for market potential and for production plant location.

19.2.4 Implications of international trade theories for strategic management

Overall, they point to the important role of government policy in several areas:

- *Developing basic infrastructures.* These concern such areas as water supplies, telecommunications and roads. It is difficult for company strategic management to make much headway in a country if the government is unwilling to invest in these areas.
- *Training and the quality of education.* These are also vital. The stock of human capital is an important element in the development of new investments because of the need to recruit and train nationals to work for the company. In selecting countries for international strategic development, this may be a major factor.
- *Economic stability and selected export stimuli.* Most organisations are able to work better if inflation is low and the economy is stable. In the early stages of development, there is also some evidence that governments can usefully support certain industries in terms of export assistance to stimulate early growth.
- *Competitive and open home market.* Although there is a risk that home industries may be swamped by large international companies entering the home market, this is not what has tended to happen in practice. When the home market is open, it has stimulated new entrants to open factories, creating jobs and thus wealth. For example, India has for years had home markets that were partially closed to international trade. Singapore and Malaysia have opened up their markets and benefited accordingly. And so have companies like Sony (Japan) and Philips (Netherlands) that have invested in such countries.

More specifically from a company perspective, it is important to examine the extent and nature of the main barriers that might exist to the opportunities associated with free trade: these are shown in Exhibit 19.2. In the short term, some barriers may be small and outside the more fundamental scope of strategic management. However, at a deeper level, such barriers may be fundamental to company survival and development. For example, the production plant investment by the Japanese car companies Nissan, Toyota and Honda inside the EU in the 1980s and 1990s was a direct strategic response, at least in part, to trade barriers and EU sensitivities in this area.

EXHIBIT 19.2

The main barriers to trade

- *Tariffs* – taxes on imported goods. They do not stop imports but do make them less competitive.
- *Quotas* – a maximum number placed on the goods that can be imported in any one period.
- *Non-tariff or technical barriers* – local laws or other technical means imposed by governments to make it difficult for imports to enter the country.
- Financial subsidies for home producers.
- *Exchange controls* – government control of the access its citizens have to foreign currency so that it becomes difficult to pay for imports.

KEY STRATEGIC PRINCIPLES

- Early theories of international trade concentrate on the *resources of the country.*
- They suggest that a reduction in trade barriers can be coupled with the economies of scale available to companies in explaining the growth of international trade over the past 50 years.
- Porter's *diamond theory of the competitive advantage of nations* identified four home country factors that explained why some countries were particularly successful internationally: factor conditions; related and supporting industries; firm strategy structure and rivalry; demand conditions. In addition, he identified two outside factors – government policy and chance – that were also significant.
- The *theory of limited state intervention* was attributed to the World Bank and identified the role of government in different stages of economic growth. As countries become more wealthy, governments should let free markets operate.
- Theories of international trade identify the role of government in encouraging international investment. They also help companies select which countries offer the best international prospects.

19.3 INFLUENCE OF INSTITUTIONS INVOLVED IN INTERNATIONAL TRADE

In any development of international and global strategy, it is useful to have some background knowledge of the main institutions involved and their roles in its development. Corporate strategists may meet them directly and will certainly encounter their policy decisions indirectly over time. It should be noted that the United Nations is not identified separately below. However, it has come to have an important policy role in a number of areas such as education, health and agriculture, which will have relevance to specific product strategy initiatives.

19.3.1 Three international trade institutions

In order to promote free trade after the mistakes of the 1930s, the major Western nations decided during the 1940s that they would need new bodies to oversee international trade. They attempted to establish three international institutions that would be directly relevant to companies involved in international trade:

1 *The International Monetary Fund* (IMF). The IMF is designed to lend funds to countries in international difficulty and to promote trade stability through co-operation and discussion. It has also provided a forum for the regulation of currencies up to 1973.
2 *The International Bank for Reconstruction and Development.* This is often called the World Bank. It was set up to provide long-term capital aid for the economic development of nations – roughly $10 billion per annum. It still provides lending for infrastructure, tourism and other projects, with the aim of long-term improvement in growth (see the web-based case study linked to Chapter 18).
3 *The International Trade Organization* (ITO). This was to be set up to regulate trade activity and sort out the trade disputes that had been so disastrous during the 1918–1939 period. It was never allowed to operate but the World Trade Organization, which was formed in 1995, was its direct successor.

The IMF and the World Bank were successfully inaugurated and continue to the present. Unfortunately, the USA failed to ratify the treaty setting up the ITO in 1948. As an interim measure, **Definition ▶** GATT was signed by 23 signatory countries in 1947. **GATT is the General Agreement on Tariffs and Trade. It is a treaty between nations that is designed to encourage and support world trade by providing an agreed set of trade rules and a means of adjudicating breaches of those rules.** It continued as the main mechanism to ensure free trade up to 1995. Exhibit 19.3 shows the main GATT principles. By the late 1990s, over 140 countries had signed the GATT because the results were seen to be beneficial.

EXHIBIT 19.3

The main principles of the GATT

There are three major principles:

1 *Non-discrimination*. Each country will give all other countries the same rates on import duties. Giving more to one country means giving more to all signatories (called *most favoured nation* status).
2 *Consultation*. When disputes arise, GATT brings the parties together and encourages compromise, rather than the squabbles of the 1930s.
3 *Sanctions for non-compliance*. Where no compromise is possible, then the WTO is empowered to adjudicate and impose a solution. It has semi-judicial status.

Over the period from 1947, GATT has sponsored eight major rounds of tariff and other trade barrier reductions to encourage world trade (barriers to trade are explored in the next section). Each negotiation round is named after the country or town where it was begun. The latest completed round was the Uruguay Round which started in 1986 and was signed in 1993.[19]

The World Trade Organization (WTO) was set up in 1995 to administer the GATT and to undertake the functions originally envisaged as being part of the ITO.[20] It has become a prime mover in the continued development of international trade and highly beneficial to those companies developing international strategic management. For example, the 'Banana War' between the USA and the EU in 1998–1999 was eventually decided under the GATT rules. The WTO judged that the USA was entitled to complete access for its banana exports and could apply sanctions against a range of EU companies if such entry was denied. The strategy of a large number of firms, including many that had no involvement with bananas, was affected by this move.

19.3.2 Developing countries and the GATT

Although GATT gave important protection to poorer and smaller countries when they reduced their barriers to large and powerful partners, such countries still felt that it assisted industrialised countries. They pointed to the fact that their share of world trade was declining. They therefore encouraged the United Nations to form the United Nations Conference on Trade and Development (UNCTAD). This body has been concerned with highlighting the trade concerns of the developing nations. It has a more limited role in the development of strategic management.

19.3.3 Institutions involved in currency regulation

In addition to trade, another major area of concern in 1945 was *exchange rates for currency* between countries: there is little point in fixing a price, regardless of tariffs, if the unit in which it is quoted then collapses. This will clearly have an immediate impact on company profitability. There had been real problems in this area in international trade in the 1930s. A system of largely fixed exchange rates was agreed internationally in 1944: the 'Bretton Woods' Agreement. This lasted until 1973 but was then replaced by floating exchange rates around the world. The IMF was set up to oversee the fixed system but did not disappear when the fixed system was discontinued. Today, it has more of a background role. It lends funds to countries in balance of payments difficulties and helps to support international trade stability through co-operation and discussion.

19.3.4 Importance of trade blocks

To pursue international strategy, companies usually need to negotiate with national governments. At its most basic level, this means that the company will need to assess the political attitudes of the government – see Chapter 3. This section concentrates on the international dimensions only.

Definition ▶ In addition to individual countries, various *trade blocks* have also developed around the world. **A trade block is a group of countries that have agreed to give each other preferential international trading terms.** The purpose of a trade block is to encourage trade between its members on the basis of the theories related to trade barriers and economies of scale. Because it is conducive to free trade, such a block may also help in stabilising a country's political and economic environment.

Some trade blocks have already been mentioned, one of the best known being the EU. Other well-known ones include ASEAN (Association of South East Asian Nations) and NAFTA (North American Free Trade Agreement). Each block is governed by its own rules: for example, the EU has a tight set of rules and relatively close degree of co-operation, while ASEAN is a looser grouping of countries, each having a stronger degree of independence.

For companies engaged in international expansion, the main tasks are to assess the opportunities in specific countries and the trade blocks to which such countries belong.

19.3.5 Conclusions for strategic management

At a senior level, there is increasing contact between the leading multinational companies and the main institutions outlined above. For smaller companies, there is always the possibility of *lobbying* to gain benefits and influence decisions that might be taken. For example, the world's leading banks are usually represented at the biannual conferences of the IMF and individual companies have made representations to the WTO. These are important areas of strategic influence for the senior officers of any company.

KEY STRATEGIC PRINCIPLES

- Three major international institutions have significant influence on international trade. The International Monetary Fund (IMF) oversees international payments. The World Bank provides long-term capital aid. The World Trade Organization (WTO) regulates trade activity and resolves trade disputes between nations.
- The General Agreement on Tariffs and Trade (GATT) is the general treaty covering trade between many nations of the world. Various rounds of tariff reductions have been sponsored under the GATT. They have opened up world markets over the past 50 years and significantly increased international trade.
- The United Nations Conference on Trade and Development (UNCTAD) represents the interests of developing countries in international negotiations.
- Trade blocks consist of countries that agree to give each other preferential trading terms. Strategic management will need to consider such blocks and their impact on trade.

CASE STUDY 19.3

Cadbury: will it ever gain global market leadership in chewing gum?

Over the past few years, one of the world's largest confectionery companies – Cadbury – developed a new global strategy for its chewing gum business. But it faced a long haul and needed heavy investment to gain global market leadership from the world market leader, the US company Wrigley.

Ultimately, the situation changed completely as both companies were transformed in the late 2000s – as explained at the end of the case.

Cadbury's move into global chewing gum

'We are really excited about gum,' explained Jim Cali, Cadbury's director of global gum operations in 2007, when launching the company's gum range into the UK for the first time. This case explores how Cadbury is beginning to develop a new global strategy in the chewing gum segment of the world confectionery market. It has four sections:

1 Worldwide confectionery markets and the key factors for success
2 Competition and opportunities in the world chewing gum segment
3 Global strategies in chewing gum at Cadbury
4 Acquisitions change perspectives in the late 2000s.

Trident was launched into the UK chewing gum market by Cadbury in 2007. The product needed to build strongly on Cadbury's strategic core resources and capabilities if it was to overcome the market dominance of rival products from Wrigley.

Worldwide confectionery markets and the key factors for success

For the year 2007, worldwide confectionery sales amounted to \$97 billion at *manufacturer's* selling prices (MSP). MSP are the prices at which manufacturers like Cadbury and Mars sell their products to retailers like Wal-Mart, Carrefour and Tesco, who then add their own profit margins and government taxes to determine their retail prices: this means that at *retail* selling prices the worldwide confectionery market was worth around \$140 billion in 2007. All market data used in this case study is by value, not volume.

In 2007, the worldwide market for confectionery was growing around 5 per cent per year – substantially above the average for many other packaged food products. This made the market attractive for manufacturers seeking new opportunities: the world consumer evidently has a sweet tooth.

Worldwide confectionery covers three main market segments:

1 *Chocolate and chocolate covered products* – for example, bars of pure chocolate like Mars' *Dove* and *Galaxy*, Cadbury's *Dairy Milk* and products like Nestlé's *Kit Kat* and Mars' *Bounty* that are covered in chocolate with other ingredients inside. This segment accounted for around 55 per cent of worldwide confectionery sales in 2007. The segment had higher profit margins than sugar confectionery for at least three reasons: more branding to add value, lower retail own-brand sales and higher sales in the more developed countries with higher income per head. Chocolate market growth was significantly below 3 per cent per year in developed markets, like Germany and the USA, but over 10 per cent in emerging markets, like Brazil and India. In practice, there are many different chocolate products, each positioned in different sub-segments of the chocolate market – see, for example, Figure 13.8.

2 *Sugar confectionery* – for example, boiled sugar sweets, toffees and jelly sweets. This segment accounted for 31 per cent of worldwide confectionery sales. The segment was virtually static in developed markets with growth just over 1 per cent per year, but was growing strongly in emerging markets at around 8 per cent per year. Growth in these latter markets was fuelled by population growth and greater affluence. Although there are many sugar confectionery products, the sub-segments of the market are more basic with less individual positioning than with chocolate products. Note that sugar confectionery is sometimes referred to as 'candy' in some strategy studies.

3 *Chewing gum* – for example, sticks of gum and gum tablets with soft centres. This segment accounted for 14 per cent of worldwide confectionery sales. Although it was the smallest segment, it was growing the fastest. Growth was over 5 per cent per year in developed markets and around 12 per cent per year (although from a smaller base) in emerging markets. The reasons for the higher growth rate in this segment are explained in the next section of this case. Profit margins were also higher. There are many sub-segments of the chewing gum market based on different flavours, ingredients such as 'sugar-free' and performance such as 'teeth whitening'. This variety has provided strategic opportunities for new entrants such as Cadbury.

The leading companies involved in worldwide confectionery are listed in Table 19.4. Importantly from a strategy perspective, the worldwide market was relatively fragmented with the five largest companies accounting for less than 40 per cent of

Table 19.4 World confectionery market: the market leaders 2007

Company	Home country	World market share by value in 2007	Selected brand names	Comment
Cadbury	UK	10.5%	Cadbury's Dairy Milk, Flake, Creme Eggs, Green and Black's Organic, Trebor, Maynards, Bassets, Trident, Stimorol and other gum brands	Only fifth in chocolate market segment – but leader in sugar segment and with representation in all three main segments
Mars	USA	9%	Mars, Snickers, Bounty, Twix, Milky Way, Dove, M&Ms	World market leader in chocolate segment
Nestlé	Switzerland	8.5%	Kit Kat, Crunchy, Rolo, After Eight	Second to Mars in chocolate segment
Wrigley	USA	5.9%	Juicy Fruits, Double Mint, Orbit and other gum brands	World leader in chewing gum segment
Hershey	USA	5.3%	Hershey, Reese's, Kisses, Skor, plus Cadbury, Rolo and Kit Kat brands in the USA only	Has nearly 90 per cent of its sales in USA, where it dominates the American market
Ferrero	Italy	4.8%	Ferrero Rocher, Kinder Surprise and related products, Nutella, Mon Cheri, Giotto	Range of specialist products plus a global strategy that is then adapted to local demand
Kraft	USA	4.5%	Suchard, Marabou, Daim	Particularly strong in chocolate in some European countries

Notes:

1. 'Confectionery' includes all the three segments of the world market: chocolate, sugar and chewing gum.
2. Mars, Nestlé and Kraft shares are for their confectionery business only. All have substantial sales in other markets beyond this category.
3. The major chocolate manufacturer Barry Callebaut is excluded from the above companies. The reason is that over 50 per cent of its $3.9bn 2007 sales are in the form of industrial chocolate sold to other food manufacturers to be used as an ingredient in other foods like chocolate-coated biscuits.

Source: author based mainly on company annual report and accounts – see references at end of chapter.

the total world market and the top ten for under 50 per cent. There are many companies that operate successfully in one country or one region of the world, partly for historical reasons and partly because of the nature of the key factors for success in confectionery markets.

Key factors for success in the confectionery business worldwide include:

- *Distribution*. Most confectionery items are low-priced individual items and many rely on impulse purchasing. It is therefore essential to have the products in-store and on display. The larger companies have invested heavily in sales teams and promotions to ensure this. Once shelf space has been gained in-store, this becomes a major competitive advantage of the company.
- *Branding*. Many products rely on brand names to attract customers – whether they are for children or adults. Marketing activity and expenditure to invest in the brand is therefore essential. Even national brands that are not available worldwide rely on the recognition and loyalty that are delivered by the competitive advantage of a brand.
- *Economies of scale and scope*. In this highly competitive market, retail price becomes a key factor. In turn, this means that many companies need to invest heavily in modern plant and packaging machinery. Hand-made confectionery at premium prices has a small niche in the market place but all the leading manufacturers rely on the low costs delivered by economies of scale and scope to remain competitive and profitable.

From a global strategy perspective, these key factors for success make it expensive for the leading world companies to develop their international business. Country-by-country detailed activity to gain distribution and invest in the brand becomes important. Economies of scale and scope are mainly achieved by focusing manufacturing on one or two locations: for example, Mars in Western Europe has only *two* main manufacturing locations in the Netherlands and the UK for its whole range of confectionery. In the same way, Cadbury manufactures its Creme Eggs at *one* factory in the UK for the whole of the European market.

Competition and opportunities in the world chewing gum market

The world market for chewing gum was worth $13.5 billion in 2007 and it was growing faster than other confectionery segments. In developed countries, the market was growing over 5 per cent per year and in emerging markets, it was growing around 12 per cent per year. Both the size and growth prospects make it an attractive market to enter.

Why were gum markets growing so fast when compared with other parts of the confectionery business? There were three main reasons:

1 *Innovation*. There has arguably been more product and packaging innovation in this product category than in many other areas of the confectionery business over the past few years. Thus, for example, we have had liquid-centred and hard-coated gums, healthy chewing gum, new flavours. To quote David Macnair, Cadbury's chief science officer, 'Gum is a very innovation sensitive category. It lends itself to a bewildering array of flavour and texture systems.'

2 *Health consciousness*. Demand has grown in the more developed countries for products with little or no sugar – feasible in chewing gum but not so easy in other sweet products that need sugar as part of the mouth feel. Other health benefits of gums include new products that freshen the breath or whiten teeth.

3 *Existing low per capita consumption in developing markets*. In 2005, Chinese consumption per head of the population was only 15 gum sticks per year, compared with 196 in the USA. Yet the Chinese people have long had a habit – along with Indian people – for chewing for recreational and other reasons.

For many years, it was the world chewing gum market leader, Wrigley, that was the most innovative. It was a well-run company with an admirable record in profitable growth. For example, its profit margins at around 22 per cent were amongst the highest in the confectionery industry. The company was started as a family company in Chicago, USA, in the late nineteenth century, as summarised on the company's website at www.wrigley.com. Even by the early twenty-first century, the company was still part-owned by members of the original family, though it had gained its first outside CEO.

With a world market share of 35 per cent, Wrigley was leader of the chewing gum market. It had strong brands, efficient production facilities and a distribution system that allowed it to deliver profitably even to small individual confectionery kiosks across the vast country of China. Market shares and brands of the leading companies prior to 2008 are shown in Table 19.5.

Although Cadbury had been involved in selling confectionery products for over 200 years, it only moved into the chewing gum segment in 1999 with the acquisition of the French market leader, the Hollywood brand, from Kraft. It followed this with the Danish market leader in 2002, Dandy, which owned the chewing gum brands Stimorol and Dentyne. In 2003, Cadbury acquired the American chewing gum company Adams for $4.6 billion. It was only now that the Cadbury's interests in chewing gum were transformed.

Adams' market share in the US chewing gum market was around 27 per cent at the time of its purchase by Cadbury. This then gave the company a solid base to raise the Adams' share to 35 per cent by 2007, mostly at the expense of Wrigley. The Wrigley US market share declined from nearly 70 per cent in the early 1990s to 59 per cent in 2007. The strategies adopted by Cadbury to increase its share are explained in the next section.

Importantly and unlike other sectors of the world confectionery market, Wrigley and Cadbury are the two main companies

Table 19.5 World's leading chewing gum companies 2007

Company	Home country	World market share	Selected leading company brands	Major areas of geographical strength
Wrigley	USA	35.0%	Spearmint, Juicy Fruit, Freedent, Double Mint	Market leader in the USA, Germany, UK, China, some Eastern European countries
Cadbury	UK	27.5%	Trident, Stimorol, Bubbaloo, Dentyne, Clorets, Hollywood	Market leader in France, Spain, Turkey, Japan, South Africa and a strong second in the USA
Lotte	Korea	7.0%	Lotte	Market leader in South Korea, Japan and some Asia Pacific countries
Perfetti Van Melle	Italy/Netherlands	6.5%	Mentos, Happy Dent, Fruitella, Chupa Chaps	Significant shares in some Western European countries but stronger in sugar confectionery
Arcor	Argentina	2.5%	Topline, Menthplus	Market leader in parts of South America
Haribo	Germany	1.5%	Gold Bears, Starmix	Mainly children's products including jellies

Source: author from company annual report and accounts – see references at end of chapter.

in chewing gum worldwide. According to Jim Cali, Cadbury's head of global gum, 'We have an active competitor in Wrigley, but a good competitor will push us and expand the whole category.' Companies like Lotte in Asia and Arcor in South America have regional importance, but the world strategic battle was between these two companies. And it is Cadbury's strategies that have begun to impact on Wrigley in recent years.

Cadbury's global strategies in chewing gum

Cadbury has six major global strategies. They were used in varying proportions in different countries around the world – a global/local approach to strategy development:

1 *Product innovation*. New flavours like raspberry and peach, new products like liquid centres alongside new packaging were employed to persuade new and existing customers. Kate Harding of Cadbury UK explained: 'The primary driver for the new growth we've seen is that we are bringing new people into the category. Some customers are buying their regular gum and then purchasing a new flavour on top of that, and 33 per cent of Trident buyers are completely new to chewing gum.' These clear advantages are offset by the investment in time and money in developing innovations in this market.

2 *Acquisitions*. Cadbury purchased a series of companies, including companies in France, Denmark, Turkey, Japan, Poland, South Africa (through Botswana), USA and Brazil. This strategy built presence internationally fast, but it had the disadvantage that Cadbury acquired a whole range of brands that were well known locally but did not constitute a single global brand name – unlike Wrigley.

3 *Brand investment*. In addition to its acquisition strategy, Cadbury has also invested heavily in new brand launches – Trident in the USA had a $50 million campaign in 2006 and in the UK $20 million in 2007. Such costs lower the short-term profitability of the brands in these countries.

4 *Focus on limited numbers of markets*. Because of the heavy brand investment involved – see above – Cadbury adopted a strategy of selecting a limited number of countries. In gum, it has chosen to focus on the USA, UK, Mexico, Russia, India, China, Brazil, France and Japan. These 'lead markets' were then used to launch into neighbouring countries. This both stretched the Cadbury resources and lengthened the timescale for global scale operations.

5 *Low manufacturing costs*. Cadbury adopted a strategy of factory closures and relocation to low labour cost countries. For example, some UK chewing gum products were made at the Cadbury factory in Turkey, where labour costs were lower than the UK. In addition, the company has been reorganised so that some decisions are taken centrally on purchasing raw materials and other related items: the company is attempting to gain the benefits of economies of scale and scope.

6 *Selected retail chain and trade focus*. Cadbury focused its efforts on seven leading retail shop chain customers and three trade channels. The company claimed that it was the only confectionery group with substantial presence in chocolate, sugar and chewing gum confectionery. Cadbury claimed, 'We have more total confectionery leading positions than our competitors in key markets.'

New acquisitions change perspectives in the late 2000s

In March 2008, the family-owned US company Mars made a $23 billion agreed bid for Wrigley. The combined company had a market share of 14.9 per cent. It took the world market confectionery leadership from Cadbury. From Cadbury's chewing gum perspective, Mars/Wrigley clearly presented a new and even more powerful competitor against its gum expansion.

In 2010, Cadbury itself was acquired by the American food company Kraft. Some of the UK assets were stripped out and moved to a European headquarters in Switzerland. Cadbury UK was a more limited entity with simply some factories and brand names. Its chewing gum business was reported to have lost momentum in all these changes. It was questionable whether Cadbury would ever gain global market leadership of the chewing gum market.

All the leading global confectionery companies have significant strategies in this area.

Case questions

1 Using the benefits of global strategy outlined in this chapter, how does Cadbury rate against such benefits? And how does Cadbury rate against its competitors?

2 What are the problems faced by Cadbury in building a global strategy? Can they be overcome? How?

3 Will Cadbury ever gain global market leadership in chewing gum? Why? How?

Five key resources for building a global strategy.

19.4 INTERNATIONAL AND GLOBAL EXPANSION: THE COMPANY PERSPECTIVE

Video Parts 3 and 6

We now move from issues concerning country competitive advantages to those relating to the company. This section explores basic issues surrounding international and global expansion strategies: the basic business case, the case for global strategy, the case for a global and local strategy, and some other international considerations. The following two sections explore organisational structures and specific entry routes and problems.

19.4.1 The basic business case for international expansion

In exploring international expansion, the starting point has to be the strategic business case and the impact on the company of any significant form of international expansion.

The contribution of Hymer

Although some basic products have been sold internationally for centuries,[22] the business logic for international expansion relied on two main arguments:[23]

1 a mature home market meant that higher growth might be achieved abroad;

2 higher rates of return could be earned outside the home country.

These two benefits needed to be set against the extra risks and costs of moving internationally – currency risks, political risks, economic risks and so on. Most economists thought for some years that a positive balance – rates of return from international expansion being greater than the risks and costs – was the reason that companies expanded internationally.[24] Hymer suggested that the reason for international expansion by companies investing in a country was more subtle. He pointed out that some companies chose to go further than simply take the low-risk option of exporting from their home countries. Why did they risk FDI in another country? The reason was to exploit the benefit of some hard-to-replicate competitive advantage of the company that could be used beyond the home country: brand, technology, patent, efficiency due to size, etc. He argued that this would enable the company to dominate a foreign market in the way that it dominated a home market. Professor Richard Caves then developed the arguments further, but the initial concept came from Hymer.[25] If a company has such a competitive advantage, then it may benefit from international expansion.[26]

19.4.2 The case for global strategy – the contribution of Ghoshal[27]

Global strategy means treating the world as one market and one interconnected source of supply. Some markets may be regional rather than global. For example, Cadbury has a series of chewing gum brands across Europe – Hollywood in France, Trident in the UK, Stimorol in Denmark – all of them operating nationally or regionally with no single brand around the world – see Case study 19.3. Companies need to explore the business case for extending this into operating a global market. Ghoshal set out a framework to explore the business case for a global strategy. He argued that there are three main areas of potential competitive advantage that will come from pursuing a global strategy:

1 *Exploitation of the comparative advantage of nations* – explored in Section 19.2.1 earlier in this chapter.
2 *Developing of economies of scale* – marginal cost improvements as a company increases in size.
3 *Achieving economies of scope* – cost savings achieved by transferring skills from one part of a business to another.

He suggests that there are three main outcomes to be obtained from a global strategy:

1 *Achievement of increased efficiency* from such areas as low cost leadership and differentiation – maximising the economic outputs of a company while minimising the inputs.
2 *Better management of risks* – offsetting the risks of one country by being involved in others can be beneficial in both economic and political terms. There may also be competitive and resource risks that can be lessened by a global strategy – for example, sourcing supplies from more than one country may have real benefits if a problem arises in a particular country.
3 *Stimulation of innovation and learning* may arise from sharing knowledge, ideas and insights across international barriers.

He then combined these into a matrix, which is shown in Exhibit 19.4. It structures the logical reasoning behind the development of a global strategy, but does not claim to provide simple answers. It should be seen as outlining areas for consideration rather than providing definitive guidance.

EXHIBIT 19.4

Global strategy – the logic behind the principle

		Competitive advantages of global strategy		
		National comparative advantage	Economies of scale	Economies of scope
Strategic outcomes from global strategy	*Achieved increased efficiency of current operations*	Benefiting from differences between nations on wages and cost of capital	Developing potential economies of scale in every area of business	Sharing of activities and costs across products and subsidiaries
	Better risk management	Managing different areas of risk arising from changes in the comparative advantages of different countries	Balancing the advantages of scale with strategic and operational flexibility	Diversifying product portfolios and spreading risks of options
	Stimulation of innovation and learning	Learning from different parts of world, different organisations and managerial systems	Benefiting from experience of cost reduction and new innovation	Shared learning and knowledge across different markets and businesses

Source: based on the late Sumanthra Ghoshal's 1987 paper on global strategy – 'Global Strategy: an organising framework', *Strategic Management Journal*, Vol 8, pp 425–440.

In 1983, Professor Theodore Levitt argued that global strategy can deliver extra value added and sustainable competitive advantage. There were two main factors that needed to be present to justify a global strategy:[28]

1 *Resources*. These may be more economically manufactured and sourced on a global basis.[29] It is a factor commonly used in the consumer electronics industry, where there are both economies of scale and considerable cost savings by manufacturing labour-intensive items in countries with efficient production equipment and low labour costs, such as some Asian countries. Companies such as Sony (Japan) and Philips (Netherlands) now operate in this way.
2 *Customer demand*. This is essentially the same around the world for some products. Companies such as Gucci (Italy, though actually owned by a French company), Rolls-Royce Cars (UK, though actually owned by a German company) and Nike (USA) make products that are essentially branded in the same way in all countries. In so far as there are any differences, then customers will be prepared to compromise as a result of the lower prices gained by the economies of scale from the global manufacturing operation outlined above.

George Yip has further developed the arguments in favour of globalisation.[30] He suggests that some organisations may fear being left behind. Moreover, the adoption of 'Western' values and customs has also contributed to globalisation because it promotes common customer demand. He lays particular emphasis on the ability of global products to spread the considerable costs of research and development across more countries – for example, the costs of drug development explored in Chapter 4.

Fundamentally, Yip argues that globalisation may increase the competitive leverage of a company, i.e. it may increase its competitive advantage as a result of its global scope. This presents the clear opportunity of globalisation. But it also raises the question of the number of markets that are truly global: even McDonald's has had to adjust parts of its menu to suit local tastes and dispense with the Big Mac completely in India. Rolex watches and Yves St Laurent clothing will arguably be global, but many other products may have to be significantly adapted to local needs.

Comment

Some strategists – particularly Ghemawat, Rugman and Verbeke – now suggest that there are real difficulties in developing a truly global strategy.[31] They argue that the major investment required, the need to downplay local customer tastes and the organisational and co-ordination difficulties associated with global strategy all suggest that such a strategy would be better replaced by strategies of 'semi-globalisation'. There is evidence to support such arguments, particularly in the more mature product areas such as food and drink.[32] We return to this topic in Section 19.4.5 below.

19.4.3 The case for a global/local strategy

Video Part 6b

In arguing the case for a global strategy, Levitt's arguments largely stopped with the two considerations outlined above. However, for many organisations the global considerations have to be balanced by the need to respond to variations in local demand: the case for the global/local strategy. This is sometimes summarised in the phrase: 'Think global, act local.'

About three years after Levitt produced his paper in favour of globalisation, Susan Douglas and Yoram Wind delivered a suitably robust response.[33] For most companies, there is likely to be a need for some local variation: even supposedly global companies like Nike – see Chapter 7 – need to have local variations simply because body sizes vary in different countries.

Local responsiveness clearly pulls in the opposite direction to the pressure for global activity. There are four main reasons behind this:

1 Customer tastes and conditions of usage may vary between countries.
2 National governments may be concerned that the interests of their countries are better served by some variation special to that country. This was explored earlier in this chapter.
3 Different technical standards, different legislation and other social issues may make it essential to produce products especially for a particular country. For example, it is still necessary for domestic

Table 19.6 The balance between global expansion and national responsiveness

Pressure for global strategy*	Pressure for international strategy but still responsive to national variations*
• Global or multinational competitors • High levels of investment or technology that need large sales for recovery, e.g. in production, branding or R&D • Economies of scale in production and purchasing • High levels of investment in marketing and brand building • Desire by customers for a global 'image' • Need to cut costs by seeking low labour sources • Global sourcing of raw materials or energy	• Differing competitors or distributors by nation or region • Need to adapt product extensively to meet national needs • Product life cycle at a different stage in local country • High skill levels in local country that will permit product adaptation to that country • Differing conditions of usage, e.g. climate • Pressure from governments for national activity, e.g. tariff or quota restrictions on global activity • National purchasing of key supplies essential

* These are not mutually exclusive.

electrical plugs and sockets to be produced for specific EU countries because of the different electrical connections (two- or three-pin) in each country.

4 Different national competitors may make it difficult to offer precisely the same competitive advantage in every market. For example, the UK chocolate company Cadbury had difficulty selling some of its chocolate block products in France and Spain because it faced stronger competition from the US multinational Kraft in these markets than in its home UK market – see Case 19.3. Subsequently, Kraft acquired Cadbury but that meant that there was no further opportunity for Cadbury to sell most of its products in France and Spain.

If local responsiveness is required, then this will dilute the value added that might be gained by the scale benefits of globalisation. However, many companies have found that such local issues can be accommodated within global expansion.

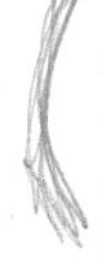

In practice, therefore, many supposedly global initiatives also need to accommodate significant national responsiveness. Even companies like Coca-Cola, Walt Disney and McDonald's provide some local variations in tastes, languages or national menu items respectively. The difficult strategic choice is often to find the *balance* between global expansion and local responsiveness. The global/national balance is summarised in Table 19.6.

19.4.4 Four prescriptive strategic options for international expansion

Video Parts 6b and 6c

Considering the issues explored above, companies have at least four options for international expansion.[34] They are essentially prescriptive in their approach and arise from a consideration of the benefits to be obtained by the two main factors: global strategy and national (or regional) demand. The four options are:

1 Some companies may decide to undertake purely global expansion (e.g. Gucci or Rolls-Royce cars).

2 Some companies opt for a global strategy *and* for national responsiveness (e.g. Toyota cars and Hewlett-Packard printers).

3 Some companies may need to be largely responsive to national demands and gain little from any form of global activity (e.g. Bata shoes).

4 Some companies may face *neither* of these pressures but still see opportunities to sell their products or services internationally (e.g. any domestic company that is willing to export some of its products).

The four options have been given names and are shown in Figure 19.5. However, it is important to note that the choice of one option does not preclude the choice of another at a later stage. For example, Yip argues that companies do not immediately choose the global option.[35] The global

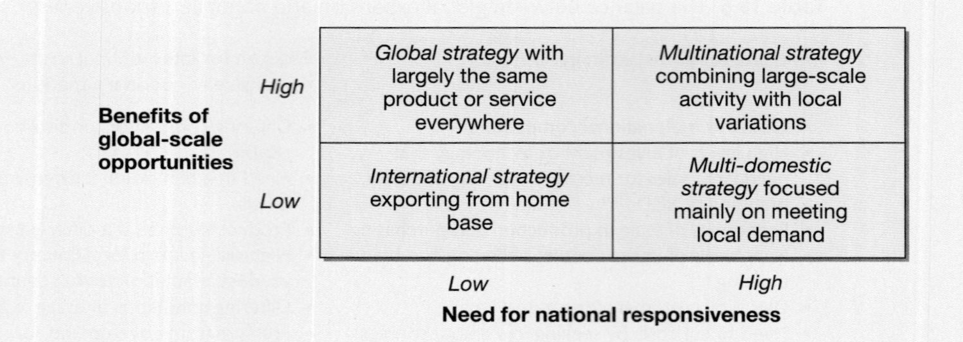

Figure 19.5 Four prescriptive options for international expansion

process will go through three stages that will take time and, arguably, some companies will not move beyond the first two stages. Yip's three-stage global process is:

- *Stage 1: Develop the core strategy* – the basis of competitive advantage. This is often developed for the home country first.
- *Stage 2: Internationalise the core strategy* – by launching it across a number of countries.
- *Stage 3: Globalise the strategy* – by seeking out the integration benefits that come from having one global market.

In practice, various other international strategy options have been identified. They are given various titles, with the following being representative:

- *Multicountry strategy*. This targets individual countries or groups of countries according to their customer potential and competitor presence. International co-ordination is secondary to a country-by-country expansion programme. For example, Danone (France) has marketed biscuits across Europe according to the local expansion opportunities rather than using a pan-European brand.
- *Global low-cost strategy*. This sources production where production costs are lowest and then sells globally. For example, Philips (Netherlands) manufactures radios in Hong Kong and sells them in Europe.
- *Global niche strategy*. The same product is sold in the same market niche in all countries of the world. For example, Dunhill (UK) and Yves St Laurent (France) products are presented in the same upmarket fashion in all countries.
- *International regional strategy*. Regions of the world will have their own production and there will be some regional or national variation in the products made and marketed, but the *global underpinning* of strategy is clear. For example, most car companies, such as Toyota (Japan) and General Motors (USA), follow such a strategy.

There are many other strategy variations that may also be chosen. The final decision will be *specific* to the product group and the organisation, but it may be assisted by the summary arguments presented in Table 19.6.

Case study: ***Tate and Lyle plc: globalisation to sweeten the profit line?*** **This case study describes the practical difficulties of developing a global strategy in the global sugar industry. Indicative answers are provided to the questions raised at the end of the case.**

19.4.5 Some other considerations in international expansion and global strategy

The global/local debate is not the only one that will guide international expansion. Two major issues are explored in the sections that follow: organisation structures and entry methods. However, there are issues in three other areas that need to be explored: competition, channels of distribution and government matters. These are summarised in Figure 19.6. All the issues may be important:

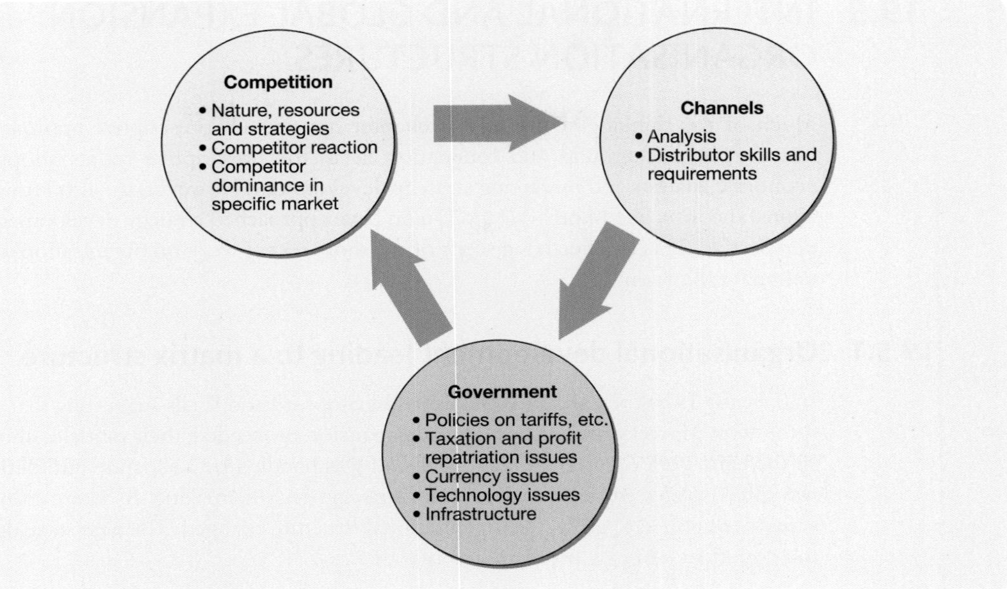

Figure 19.6 Three other considerations in global expansion

- *Competition.* Global expansion must take into account the activities of rival companies, their resources and position in target markets.
- *Channels of distribution.* These may be vital to product or service success. They need to be considered as a fundamental part of strategy development, where relevant.
- *Government.* Policy may impose excessive tariffs or other barriers. Even if the company can make profits, there may be substantive taxes and it may not be possible to repatriate any remaining profits to the home country. There may also be restrictions on the transfer of technology and poor country infrastructure – see earlier in this chapter.

KEY STRATEGIC PRINCIPLES

- International strategy expansion will follow the basic principles of strategy development. However, its greater complexity and uncertainty may mean that a staged development process is employed and selection is more complex. The starting point is clarity on the objectives and reasons for international expansion.
- Organisational history and culture, often based on home country senior management, also need to be considered.
- The case for a global strategy rests on two major elements: resources may be more economically procured and manufactured on a global basis. In addition, customer demand may be essentially the same around the world, thus allowing the world to be treated as one market.

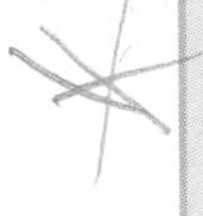

- The case for a strategy that is both global and local derives from the need to gain the benefits of a global market while responding to the needs of national market variations. Local variations may arise as a result of customer demand and conditions of usage, national governments, differing technical standards and different national competitors.
- In practice, there is often a need to balance both global and local issues in strategy development.
- At least four prescriptive options emerge from such considerations: global, international, multinational and nationally responsive. In practice, many other variations in international expansion strategies have been developed.
- Other considerations in international expansion include careful consideration of competitors, investigation of distribution channels and a full analysis of national government restrictions and requirements.

19.5 INTERNATIONAL AND GLOBAL EXPANSION: ORGANISATION STRUCTURES

Much of the thinking so far in this chapter has taken a prescriptive approach. This is probably because the background and foundation lie in the prescriptive routes adopted by international economic analysis and marketing strategy development. However, we also know that some organisational theorists like Mintzberg and Quinn have approached strategy development from an emergent perspective. This is reflected in some of the more recent work on organisational structures for international expansion.

19.5.1 Organisational development leading to a matrix structure

In the early 1970s, research was published by Stopford and Wells suggesting that organisational structures evolved over time as international expansion proceeded: their model is shown in Figure 19.7.[36] In the early period, international expansion was handled by a separate international division which was often isolated from the main areas of strategic decision making. As international sales and business activity continued to grow, the organisational structure changed. The next stage depended on whether the dominant strategic problem was that of:

- organising across different geographic parts of the world, leading to the *area division* structure;
- or organising across increasingly diverse product groups, leading to a *worldwide product group* structure.

Subsequently in the 1980s, the globalisation/localisation debate explored in the previous section led to a new organisational structure: the *matrix structure* where both area divisions and product divisions were employed.[37] This form of organisational structure was explored in Chapter 12 – the criticisms made then also apply here:

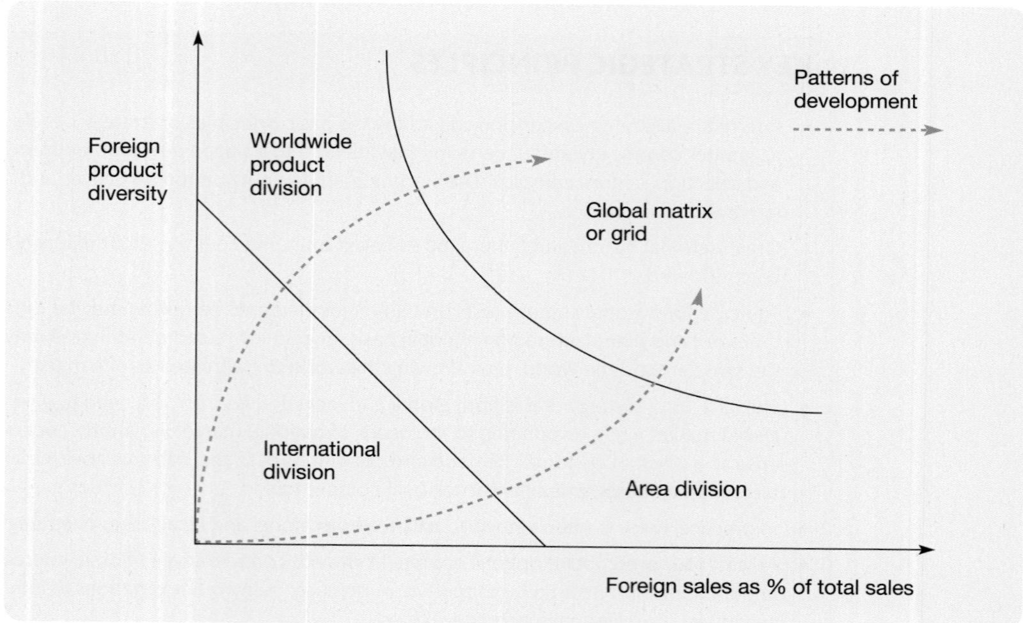

Figure 19.7 Structural stages model of international organisational expansion

Source: from *Managing the Multinational Enterprise* by John M Stopford and Louis T Wells. Copyright © 1972 by Basic Books, Inc. reproduced with permission of Basic Books, Inc, Pearson Education Ltd and the authors.

- Dual responsibilities, for example, area and product, are difficult to manage.
- The matrix amplified differences in perspectives and interests by forcing issues through a dual chain of command.
- Management became slower, more costly and possibly even acrimonious.

As a result, some larger companies, such as Unilever, tried and then abandoned the matrix organisation structure. At the end of the 1980s, along came a new organisational solution – the 'transnational structure'. It should be noted that this was *not* a new organisational form, but rather a way of conducting the business of a large international organisation.

19.5.2 Organisational structure: the transnational solution

In the late 1980s, Bartlett and Ghoshal published the results of a study of nine multinational companies that focused on the way that they organised their business and their ability to be both global and locally responsive. This placed considerable emphasis on the importance of innovation and technology development which was disseminated rapidly through the company.[38] The nine companies were grouped into three product areas:

1 *branded packaged goods* – Unilever (UK/Netherlands), Kao (Japan) and Procter & Gamble (USA);
2 *consumer electronics* – Philips (Netherlands), Matsushita (Japan) and General Electric (USA);
3 *telecommunications switching* – ITT (USA), NEC (Japan) and Ericsson (Sweden).

From an extensive study of the strategic requirements of these businesses and the way that each handled its main resources, the two authors identified both existing problems and the methods that these companies had developed to overcome them.

According to Bartlett and Ghoshal, the basic problem with a matrix structure was that it focused on only one variable – the formal structure – that could not capture the complexity of the international strategic task. They defined this task as being to reshape the core decision-making systems and management processes of large MNEs: their administrative systems, their communications channels and their interpersonal relationships. The authors argued that, in the complex and fast-moving environment of global business, it was difficult to use a simple 'structural fit' between strategy and structure in the way suggested by Chandler – see Chapter 12. What was needed was to build in *strategic and organisational flexibility*. They therefore developed the transnational form, which would have the following characteristics:

- *Assets and liabilities* – dispersed, interdependent, with different parts of the organisation specialising in different areas. Thus, one country/company might take the lead on one product, another on another product, but all would co-ordinate and co-operate fully.
- *Role of overseas operations* – within an integrated worldwide structure, each country or product group would make a differentiated contribution.
- *Development and diffusion of knowledge* – this would be developed jointly and shared around the world. Chapter 7 explored this concept.

The two authors commented that the transnational form was 'not an organisational form but a management mentality'.[39] They suggested from their empirical evidence that the locus of decision making was likely to vary:

- across functions like finance and marketing (some might need to be more centralised than others);
- across different product categories (some might be more global than others). Figure 19.8 is an attempt to capture the approach.

It was Kogut who later added an important word of caution: new organisational structures take longer to diffuse across MNEs than technological innovations.[40] This has the implication that the transnational form cannot simply be introduced overnight into a company. More recently, the internet has aided such developments and led to so-called 'netchising' in which firms create a network of

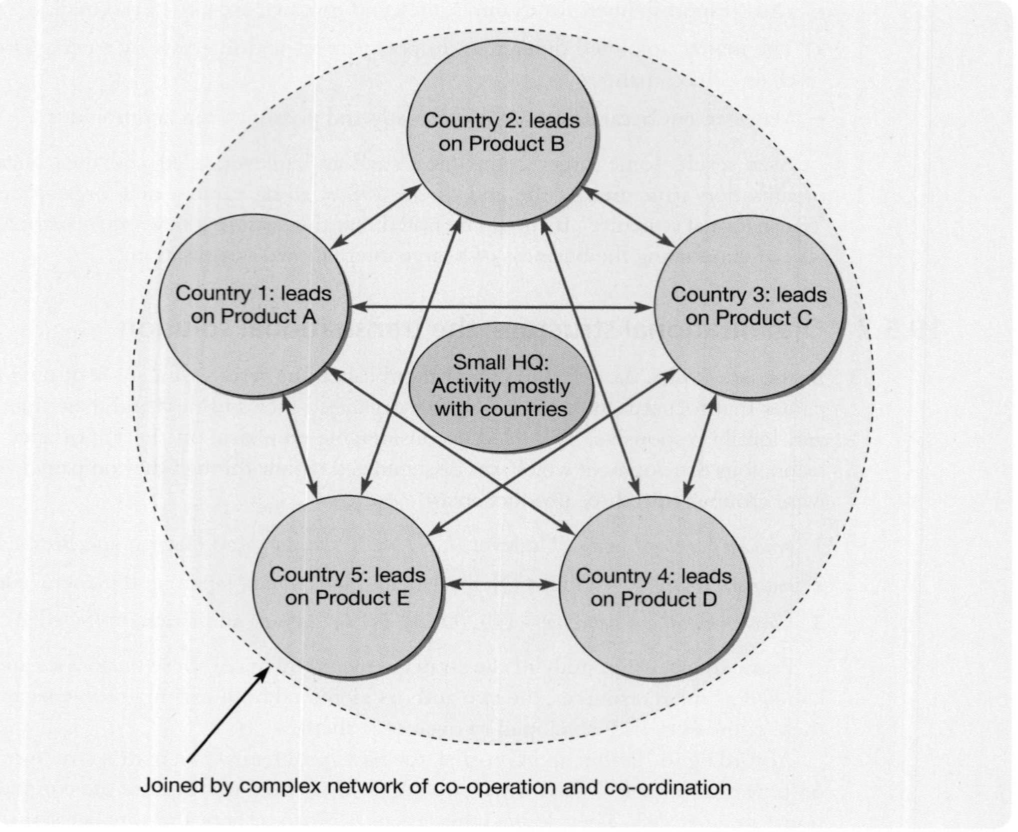

Figure 19.8 Transnational organisation: an example

related businesses that are highly integrated on an international scale.[41] Such network contacts have also been explored to allow international R&D centres to exchange knowledge in various configurations.[42]

Comment

This research has been highly influential in many large, international companies in terms of their style of operation. Essentially, it is emergent in its approach and emphasises the knowledge and learning aspects of organisational development in a way that is not captured in other models. Yet it was developed from observations on only nine companies. Moreover, its proposals remain essentially vague and without clear guidance on pressing issues like the relative roles of national companies and product groups. The re-organisation at Unilever in the late 1990s – see Case 9.3 – clearly borrows something from the approach but it was not enough to show the company how to balance the individual elements of its far-flung interests.

KEY STRATEGIC PRINCIPLES

- Organisational structures for international expansion often start by creating a separate division for international activities. As they grow in importance, such activities may then be re-organised either into a geographical area structure or one based on product divisions. This may then lead to a matrix structure with all its difficulties.
- The transnational solution to international organisation structure has been used by some companies. It involves dispersed and interdependent subsidiaries that are integrated into a worldwide operation.

Checklist for a company considering exporting outside its strong home market and facing foreign competitors in its home market.

19.6 DEVELOPING INTERNATIONAL RELATIONSHIPS SUCH AS ALLIANCES AND JOINT VENTURES

Many companies involved in international expansion have been re-thinking their relationships with other companies as customers, suppliers and associates. Many different outside relationships are possible – Chapter 8 outlined some of the major options. Two are explored in this section because they have particular relevance for international expansion: joint ventures and alliances. Exhibit 19.5 sets out some basic questions that need to be examined for both areas.

EXHIBIT 19.5

Some basic questions on the nature of international relationships

- *Nature* - who with?
- *Purpose* - what for?
- *Strategy* - how does it fit with the MNE's objectives and strategies?
- *Bargaining* - who gains what?
- *Verticality* - how are risks shared?
- *Behaviour* - what is expected of the venture by governments?

Source: Dunning, J H (1993) *Multinational Enterprises and the Global Economy*, Addison Wesley, Wokingham, p 240.

19.6.1 Basic forms of external relationships

In many circumstances, companies will decide that international expansion is best served by some form of external relationship with other companies. An external relationship means a contractual relationship between the *home* company and a *host* company in a foreign location. Essentially, the home company no longer has complete ownership of some aspect of its international strategy. There are three main reasons for developing external relationships:

1 *learning* – about the country and its culture, about the technologies contributed by the home and host companies and about the organisation and resources of its new host company;

2 *cost minimisation and risk reduction* – for example, lower-cost production sources, research, different regulatory systems and project economies;

3 *market factors* – international market access and distribution, competitive positioning, customer service.

The nature of the relationship is clearly important in determining the success of a new venture: *ownership* is an important starting point. Should the new venture be *wholly owned*, with the external relationships then applying to other elements of the value chain, such as suppliers and distributors? Or should it be a *joint venture*, in which both the home and host companies have shares? Or should it be simply an *alliance* with no shareholding involved and some rather weaker form of co-operation? The answers to these questions will vary with each company and its strategic situation. However, it is possible to provide some general guidelines on the factors that will determine the likely success of external relationships – see Exhibit 19.6.

EXHIBIT 19.6

Factors determining success of external relationships

- *Complementarity.* The partners should bring different resources to the relationship.
- *Agreement on objectives.* If this cannot be achieved, then the relationship will be difficult.
- *Compatible strategies and cultures.* They do not have to be the same but there should be some degree of empathy.
- *No surrender of key resources or core competencies.* The home partner must keep control of important strategic elements.
- *Stakeholder agreement.* There must be no conflict here.
- *Low risk of the host becoming a competitor.* It has occasionally been the case that a strong position has been established only for the host to set up in competition with the home partner.

19.6.2 Joint ventures[43]

Definition ► **A joint venture involves two or more companies creating a legally independent company to share some of the parent company's resources with the purpose of developing competitive advantage.** Joint ventures can take many forms, the most obvious one being a 50/50 shareholding in a joint company. An example of a recent successful operation has been that of the Cereal Partners joint venture. This is a joint company set up by the multinational food companies Nestlé (Switzerland) and General Mills (USA) – see Chapter 2 – with 50 per cent of the joint venture being owned by each of the two parents. It was formed to attack the breakfast cereal market around the world outside North America and has had some significant success. Such a share arrangement may not be appropriate in a different strategic context and with different strategic resources and competitors. It is essential to research well both the market and the chosen partner.

The main benefits that can arise from joint ventures between a large multinational and a local company are:

- risk reduction through sharing the project;
- rapid market access and speedy profits;
- the local firm's involvement and contacts, which may make the multinational more acceptable in the local community.

However, problems can arise from such joint venture activity:

- domination of the local market by the local partner so that the multinational remains insulated from direct customer contact;
- inability to work with the local partner for reasons of organisational culture, trust and national culture;
- the global objectives of the multinational may be in conflict with the national objectives of the local partner.

There is no simple way to determine the long-term success of joint ventures. Dunning is cautious, pointing to the difficulties of researching a topic with so many different variables.[44] Kogut is more pessimistic, commenting that they may succeed in mature markets, but success is less likely in fast-growing markets. The reason for the problem is that high growth is usually accompanied by the need for a rapid extra cash injection and at least one partner often has a problem with such demands.[45] Tomlinson is probably right to emphasise the *partnership nature* of a joint venture.[46] He argues that the joint venture must involve an opportunity for reciprocal benefits to both parties. Moreover, there needs to be mutual trust and forbearance to make the association work. This will ultimately mean compatible goals. It is also likely to imply a clear definition of asset ownership and specific areas of contribution so that the partners are clear on their respective resource contributions.

19.6.3 Strategic business alliances[47]

Definition ► **A strategic business alliance (SBA) is some form of contractual relationship designed to secure an international venture without involving a shareholding.** Recent years have seen a substantial growth in SBAs for several reasons: first, because the increasing cost of R&D has brought pressures to share such costs; second, because SBAs were found to deliver lower costs through shared economies of scale and scope; third, because SBAs brought other cost benefits as a result of the SBA partners specialising or rationalising their operations. Dunning has commented that: 'SBAs are deliberately designed to advance the sustainable competitive advantage of the participating firms.'[48] Here are some examples of SBAs:

- European and North American pharmaceutical companies have been operating SBAs to distribute new drugs without the expense of setting up totally new marketing networks.
- Telecommunications companies have been setting up world SBAs to deliver seamless telephone services to their major multinational customers around the world without being present in every country – see Case 11.2.
- National airline carriers have agreed SBAs to offer seamless ticketing across continents to their customers without opening offices in every airport.

In practice, the broad nature of such relationships suggests that there will be many reasons for SBAs. Exhibit 19.7 summarises the main reasons.

EXHIBIT 19.7

Reasons for international strategic business alliances

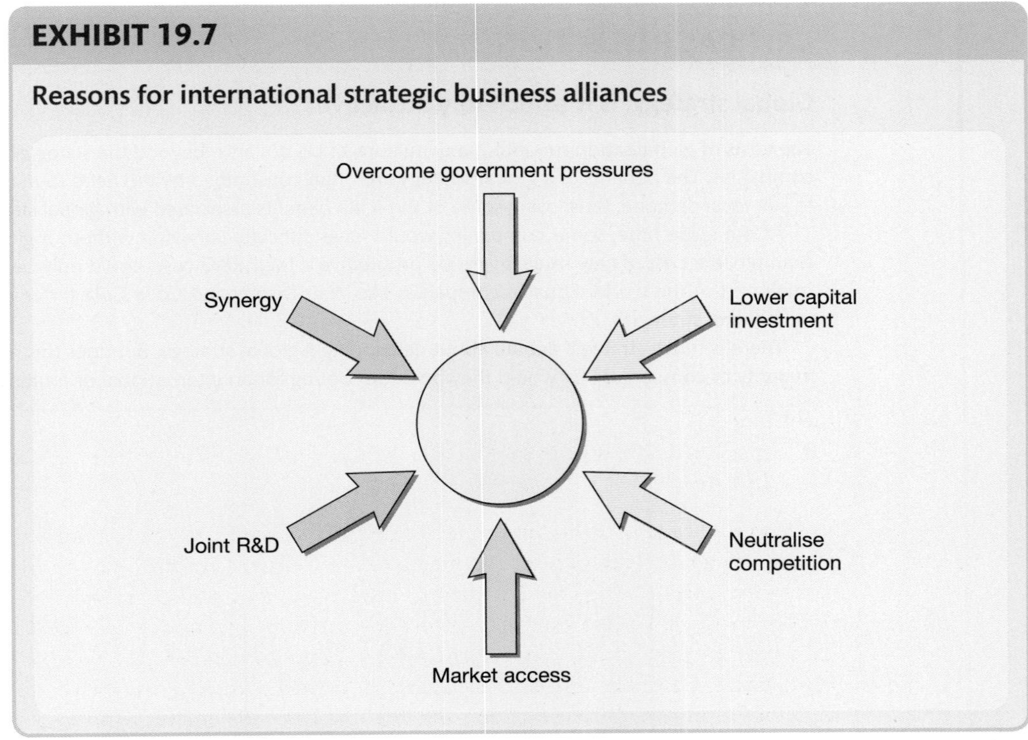

Professors Yves Doz of INSEAD and Gary Hamel of the London Business School investigated alliance relationships in the early 1990s.[49] They concluded that they were more likely to be successful when each partner was clear about the intent of the other and accepted that such relationships were likely to evolve over time. They also suggested that it was preferable for the governance relationships of the two parties in such alliances to be similar. The reason was that this would avoid conflicting objectives. It was important, too, that any national or organisational differences in culture were respected as part of the SBA. They also found that it was better if the participants were able to balance their needs inside the SBA with their other interests outside the partnership.

Although the above conclusions are useful, SBAs are difficult to research because they can take so many forms. It is therefore appropriate to be cautious about the long-term success of SBAs in international strategy development.

KEY STRATEGIC PRINCIPLES

- In developing international relationships with other companies, ownership issues need to be investigated. Joint ventures and alliances represent differing degrees of closeness in international co-operation.
- A joint venture between a multinational and a local company can provide rapid market access and local market involvement. However, the differing objectives of the two partners may lead to problems.
- Strategic business alliances cover relationships that do not involve a cross-shareholding. Benefits include cost savings and market access, but the nature of the linkage is essentially weak and it may not survive in the long term.

CRITICAL REFLECTION

Global strategy: is it sufficiently attractive?

The costs of globalisation run into many millions of US dollars - beyond the scope of all but the largest companies. The benefits of a global strategy are often constrained by the need to make local variations to suit local demand, thus losing some of the scale benefits associated with global strategy.

At the same time, some companies would have difficulty surviving without a global strategy - for example, the cost of new drugs might be prohibitive if their R&D costs could only be recovered from a small part of the world. Equally, companies like Walt Disney and Coca-Cola thrive on the benefits of their global strategies.

There is much strategic debate about developing a global strategy. But does this make sense for the majority of companies? Or would they be better opting for an international or multinational strategy?

SUMMARY

- International expansion and globalisation are amongst the most important strategic influences in the business environment in the twenty-first century. International expansion has become an important driver of country economic growth. Companies have contributed to this and benefited from it.
- It is important also to distinguish between three types of international and global expansion: *international*, where a significant proportion of an organisation's activities take place outside its home market but it is still the domestic market that is the prime focus of strategy; *multinational*, where a company operates in many countries and varies its strategy country by country; and *global*, where a company treats the world as one market. Significantly, each of the three areas above implies a different international expansion strategy.
- The *C–C–B Paradigm* explores the resource relationships between the **C**ompany, the **C**ountry in which it operates and the **B**argaining that takes place between the two. The twin purposes of such bargaining are to deliver increased value added to the company and increased wealth to the country.
- Theories of international trade identify the role of government in encouraging international investment. They also help companies select which countries offer the best international prospects. A number of theories can usefully be identified: some theories concentrate on trade barrier reduction and company economies of scale. Two theories are particularly useful: Porter's *diamond of national competitive advantage* and the *theory of limited state intervention* attributed to the World Bank.
- Three major international institutions have significant influence on international trade. The International Monetary Fund (IMF) oversees international payments. The World Bank provides long-term capital aid. The World Trade Organization (WTO) regulates trade activity and resolves trade disputes between nations.
- A trade block is a group of countries that have agreed to give each other preferential trading terms. Some blocks have stronger ties than others. All influence trade development.
- The case for a global strategy rests on two major elements: resources may be more economically procured and manufactured on a global basis. In addition, customer demand may be essentially the same around the world, thus allowing the world to be treated as one market. The case for a strategy that is both global and local derives from the need to gain the benefits of a global market while responding to the needs of national market variations. Local variations may arise as a result of customer demand and conditions of usage; national governments; differing technical standards; and different national competitors. In practice, there is often a need to balance both global and local issues in strategy development.
- Organisational structures for international expansion often start by establishing a separate division for international activities. As they grow in importance, such activities may then be re-organised either into a geographical area structure or one based on product divisions. This may then lead to a matrix structure with all its difficulties. The *transnational solution* to international organisation structure has been used by some companies. It involves dispersed and interdependent subsidiaries that are integrated into a worldwide operation.
- In developing international relationships with other companies, ownership issues need to be investigated. Joint ventures and alliances represent differing degrees of closeness in international co-operation.
- A joint venture between a multinational and a local company can provide rapid market access and local market involvement. However, the differing objectives of the two partners may lead to problems.
- Strategic business alliances cover relationships that do not involve a cross-shareholding. Benefits include cost savings and market access, but the nature of the linkage is essentially weak and it may not survive in the long term.

QUESTIONS

1. If international expansion is the most important strategic trend of the twenty-first century, should every organisation, even the smallest, develop international strategies? If so, what strategies might be adopted by (a) a medium-sized engineering company based primarily in one part of the world, such as Europe, and (b) a major grocery retailer whose sales are mainly in one country?
2. What different international expansion strategies are implied by international, multinational and global approaches to strategy development? Give examples to support your explanation.
3. Do theories of international trade help to explain why and how companies like MTV, General Motors and Tate & Lyle have developed internationally?
4. How do the major institutions of world trade influence strategy development?
5. Name two trade blocks and show how each of them influences the development of international strategy. In particular, identify any factors that are unique to each trade block.
6. How useful is Porter's diamond of national competitive advantage in the development of a company's business strategy?
7. *'Whether to globalize and how to globalize have become two of the most burning strategy issues for managers around the world.'* (George Yip) Comment critically on the usefulness of such generalisations in the development of international business strategy.
8. Does the 'transnational organisation' offer a solution to the difficulties facing major companies when they organise their international operations?
9. What are the problems with using alliances and joint ventures in international strategy development? How might they be overcome?
10. *'The adoption of a global perspective should not be viewed as the same as a strategy of global products and brands. Rather, for most companies, such a perspective implies consideration of a broad range of strategic options of which standardisation is merely one.'* (Susan Douglas and Yoram Wind) Do you agree with this comment? What, if any, are the implications for international business strategy?

FURTHER READING

Kogut, B (2002) 'International management and strategy', Ch 12 in Pettigrew, A, Thomas, H and Whittington, R (eds) *Handbook of Management and Strategy*, Sage, London is very readable and has a useful summary of global strategic thinking.

Professor Alan Rugman's text – Rugman, A M (2000) *The End of Globalization*, Random House, London – provides a more sceptical view of globalisation in his usual lively style. Read also the papers by Professor Ghemawat listed in the references below (note 27).

Dunning, J (1993) *Multinational Enterprises and the Global Economy*, Addison-Wesley, Wokingham has a very strong academic foundation and is a top-quality text if you are an economist.

Robock, S H and Simmonds, K (1989) *International Business and Multinational Enterprises*, Irwin, Homewood, IL is now out of print but is strong readable account of the main issues.

For a different approach to organisational issues on a global scale see: Saunders, C, Van Slyke, C and Vogel, D R (2004) 'My time or yours? Managing time visions in global virtual teams', *Academy of Management Executive*, Vol 18, No 1, pp 19–26.

Jones, G (1996) *Evolution of International Business*, Routledge/International Thompson, London is an excellent text for providing a historical context.

NOTES AND REFERENCES

1. References for the MTV case: Viacom and MTV websites. *Financial Times*: 10 October 2003, p 12. Times OnLine site www.timesonline.co.uk – 15 April 2005 – 'MTV grows into far more than music television'.
2. United Nations Industrial Development Organization (UNIDO) (1993) *Industry and Development Global Report 1993/94*, Vienna, p 81. Interesting and thoughtful material with additional references useful for essays and assignments.
3. Williams, F (1995) *Financial Times*, 4 April, p 3.
4. UNIDO (1993) Op. cit., pp 88, 89.
5. Woolf, M (1993) *Financial Times*, 16 December, p 19.
6. UNIDO (1993) Op. cit., p 81.
7. These are based on Bartlett, C A and Ghoshal, S (1989) *Managing Across Borders: The Transnational Solution*, Century Business, London, Ch 3.
8. I am grateful to one of the anonymous reviewers of the second edition of this text for prompting these important distinctions.
9. Harding, J (2001) 'Globalisation's children strike back', *Financial Times*, 11 September, p 14.

10 Dunning, J H (1993) *Multinational Enterprises and the Global Economy*, Addison-Wesley, Wokingham. See also: Dunning, J H (1995) 'Re-appraising the electic paradigm in an age of alliance capitalism', *Journal of International Business*, 3rd Quarter, pp 461–491.

11 Sources for the TCL case: web pages for company annual reports 2005 and 2006: www.tcl.com, www.sony.com, www.lg.com, www.samsung.com, www.panasonic.com, www.philips.com; Data Monitor 2005; Karabati, S and Tan, B (2005) 'Vestel Electronics: Transition into the Leading European TV Manufacturer', Koç University Graduate School of Business, Istanbul, Turkey, Case Number 605-015-1; Suppli 2006 television industry data – available from the web; *BusinessWeek* (2005) 'TCL multimedia's global agenda', 22 August; China Business Service (2006) 'TCL & the overseas (mis)adventure', 10 November, http://www.chinabusinessservices.com/blog/?p=391; *China Daily* (2006) 'TCL acts to tackle European losses', 12 September, http://www.china.org.cn/english/BAT/180816.htm; www.businessweek.com/magazine/content/03_46/b3858086.htm, 17 November 2006; Li, Dong Sheng (2006) 'Eagle's Reborn, a collection of written work published internally within TCL', 14 June; CFO Asia (2005) 'China's new globalizers', May.

12 One of the best books at tracking these developments is Kennedy, P (1992) *The Rise and Fall of the Great Powers*, Fontana Press, London.

13 Kennedy, P (1992) Op. cit., Ch 7.

14 Jepma, C J, Jager, H and Kamphnis, E (1996) *Introduction to International Economics*, Netherlands Open University/Longman, London, Ch 3.

15 World Bank (1993) *The East Asian Miracle*, Oxford University Press, New York.

16 Porter, M E (1990) *The Competitive Advantage of Nations*, Free Press, New York.

17 Useful critiques are contained in Rugman, A and Hodgetts, R (1995) *International Business*, McGraw-Hill, New York, Ch 10; Dunning, J H (1995) *The Globalization of Business*, Routledge, London, Ch 5.

18 Dunning, J H (1993) Op. cit., p 14.

19 See *Financial Times*, 16 December 1993, for a summary of the new Uruguay Round deal that had been negotiated over many months.

20 A useful short history of the WTO was published by the *Financial Times* as a supplement on the WTO's 50th birthday in 1998: 'The World Trade System at 50', *Financial Times*, 18 May 1998.

21 Sources for Cadbury case: web pages for company annual reports 2007 as follows: www.cadbury.com/investors; www.kraft.com; www.nestle.com; www.wrigley.com; www.hershey.com; www.barry-callebaut.com; www.perfettivanmelle.com; www.arcor.com; www.haribo.com; you can search for the Mars and Ferrero websites, but they only have limited data – private family companies giving away little; ICCO Annual Report 2006/7; www.convenience-store.co.uk/articles/51241; *The Independent*, 22 April 2002; *Guardian*, 31 October 2006; *International Business Times*, 7 March 2007; *Telegraph* UK, 26 March 2007; *Reuters*, 29 April 2008, 'Cadbury eyes Hershey as Mars chews up Wrigley'; 29 May 2008, 'Cadbury grabs US gum share from Wrigley'; *Timesonline*, 11 February 2007; *DNA Money Mumbai*, 24 November 2007, p 32; *Financial Times*: 19 September 2000, p 29; 3 September 2002, p 26; 2 September 2005, p 17; 11 September 2002, p 29; 19 October 2005, p 26; 22 February 2006, p 22; 2 March 2006, p 19; 4 March 2006, p 16; 24 April 2006, p 22; 9 May 2006, p 27; 14 March 2007, p 20; 16 March 2007, p 18; 1 June 2007, p 21; 20 June 2007, p 22; 11 October 2007, p 21; 12 December 2007, p 23; 20 February 2008, p 21; 29 April 2008, p 24; 1 May 2008, p 27; 1 April 2011, p 20. Brenner, J G (2000), *The Chocolate Wars – Inside the secret worlds of Mars and Hershey*, HarperCollinsBusiness, London. Note: The author spent five years as Marketing Director of a UK confectionery company so has detailed background knowledge of confectionery markets – albeit from the 1980s.

22 Kennedy, P (1992) Op. cit.

23 Chandler, A (1986) 'The evolution of modern global competition', in Porter, M E (ed) *Competition in Global Industries*, Harvard Business School Press, Boston, MA.

24 Kogut, B (2002) 'International management and strategy', Ch 12 in Pettigrew, A, Thomas, H and Whittington, R (eds) *Handbook of Management and Strategy*, Sage, London.

25 Caves, R E (1971) 'International corporations: the industrial economics of foreign investment', *Economica*, Vol 38, pp 1–27.

26 See the special issue of *Long Range Planning*, October 2000, Vol 33, No 5, pp 619–754.

27 Ghoshal, S (1987) 'Global strategy: an organising framework', *Strategic Management Journal*, Vol 8, pp 425–440. This paper is often difficult to access because it is more than ten years old and not always archived in libraries. However, it was reprinted in: Segal-Horn, S (1998) *The Strategy Reader*, Blackwell Business, Oxford.

28 Levitt, T (1983) 'The globalization of markets', *Harvard Business Review*, May–June, pp 92–102.

29 This argument is also supported by Hout, T, Porter, M E and Rudden, E (1982) 'How global companies win out', *Harvard Business Review*, September–October, p 98; Hamel, G and Prahalad, C K (1985) 'Do you really have a global strategy?', *Harvard Business Review*, July–August, p 139.

30 Yip, G S (1989) 'Global strategy – In a world of nations?', *Sloan Management Review*, Fall, pp 29–41. This article represents the clearest exposition of globalisation.

31 Ghemawat, P (2003) 'Semiglobalization and international business strategy', *Journal of International Business Studies*, Vol 34, pp 138–152. Ghemawat, P and Ghadar, F (2000) 'The dubious logic of global megamergers', *Harvard Business Review*, July/August, Vol 78, No 4, pp 23–32. Rugman, A M (2000) *The End of Globalization*, Random House, London. Rugman, A M and Verbeke, A (1992) 'A note on the transnational solution and the transaction cost theory of multinational strategic management', *Journal of International Business Studies*, Vol 23, No 4, pp 761–777. Rugman, A M and Verbeke, A (2003) 'Regional multinationals: the location-bound drivers of global strategy', in Burkinshaw, J, Ghoshal, S, Markides, C, Stopford, J and Yip, G, (eds) *The Future of the Multinational Company*, Wiley, Chichester.

32 Lynch, R (2003) 'Glitches in global strategy? Some evidence from the food and drink industry', Paper presented at the Academy of Management, Seattle, August.
33 Douglas, S and Wind, Y (1987) 'The myth of globalization', *Columbia Journal of World Business*, Winter, pp 19–29.
34 Prahalad, C K and Doz, Y (1986) *The Multinational Mission: Balancing Local Demands and Global Vision*, The Free Press, New York.
35 Yip, G S (1989) Op. cit., p 29.
36 Stopford, J M and Wells, L T (1972) *Managing the Multinational Enterprise: Organization of the Firm and Ownership of Subsidiaries*, Basic Books, New York.
37 For an extended discussion of this trend, *see* Turner, I and Henry, I (1994) Op. cit., pp 417–431.
38 Bartlett, C A and Ghoshal, S (1989) *Managing Across Borders: The Transnational Solution*, Century Business, London.
39 Bartlett, C A and Ghoshal, S (1989) Op. cit., p 17.
40 Kogut, B (1990) 'The permeability of borders and the speed of learning amongst countries', *Globalization of Firms and the Competitiveness of Nations (Crafoord Lectures)*, University of Lund, Lund. Quoted in Dunning, J H (1993) Op. cit., Ch 8.
41 Morrison, A, Bouquet, C and Beck, J (2004) 'Netchising: the next global wave?', *Long Range Planning*, Vol 37, No 1, pp 11–28.
42 Burkinshaw, J (2002) 'Managing internal R&D networks in global firms', *Long Range Planning*, Vol 35, pp 245–267.
43 Dunning, J H (1993) Op. cit., Ch 9, has a comprehensive survey of joint venture research. See also Kogut, B (1997) 'Globalization and alliances in high technology industries', *Financial Times Mastering Management*, Pitman Publishing, London, pp 491–494.
44 Dunning, J H (1993) Op. cit., p 245.
45 Kogut, B (1997) Op. cit., p 493.
46 Tomlinson, J W L (1970) *The Joint Venture Process in International Business*, MIT Press, Cambridge, MA.
47 Dunning, J H (1993) Op. cit., Ch 9, also has a useful survey of alliances. For a more recent review, see the three papers in *Long Range Planning*, Vol 36, No 6, pp 533–578.
48 Dunning, J H (1993) Op. cit., p 250.
49 Doz, Y and Hamel, G (1993) *The Competitive Logics of Strategic Alliances*, The Free Press, New York.

CHAPTER 20
Strategy and business models

Video and sound summary of this chapter

LEARNING OUTCOMES

When you have worked through this chapter, you will be able to:

- define a business model and distinguish it from a strategy;
- identify the different parts of a business model and show how they combine together;
- outline the main strengths and weaknesses of business models;
- evaluate their role and usefulness in implementing business strategy;
- focus on longer-term strategy issues including purpose, value added and sustainable competitive advantage.

INTRODUCTION

After developing the organisation's strategy, some – but not all – organisations choose to define and develop a business model for the organisation. The reason is two-fold. First, a business model helps to locate where and how value and profits are added in the organisation with the aim of preserving such areas.[1] Second, business models are useful in implementing and monitoring the chosen strategy. So, why do only some organisations identify a business model? Possibly because they regard their chosen strategy as being the same as their business model. In fact two concepts are not the same.[2] The chapter therefore begins by defining a business model and distinguishing it from a strategy.

Although the chapter explores business models, some of the concepts can be applied to the public sector. Public sector and not-for-profit organisations may wish to develop such a model – called a 'public sector model' – that will focus on delivering *value added* in the public sector rather than the profitability linked with the business sector. The essential reason for undertaking such a task is similar to that for a business – a need for a public sector organisation to define and differentiate itself from others within the sector and deliver its service to its public. For reasons of space and repetition, the public sector model is not explored further in this chapter.

After defining the business model, the question arises as to how it is developed: what are its main elements? This is not so easy to answer because there is only limited agreement on what constitutes a business model.[3] Importantly, there is no simple supporting logic to a business model. This chapter will review what we know and set out a method of identifying the model used by a company. Like most aspects of strategy and models, there are benefits and problems with business models. We therefore need to identify and explore these before outlining some conclusions on business models. The chapter then finishes with some brief and more general conclusions on strategic management.

The structure of the chapter is summarised in Figure 20.1.

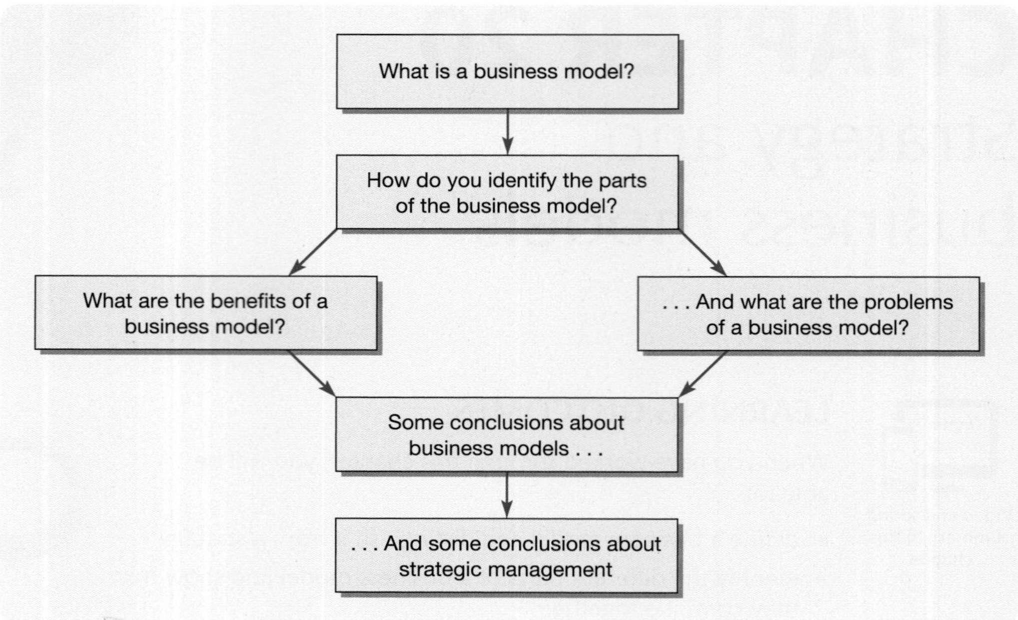

Figure 20.1 Developing a business model

CASE STUDY 20.1

The changing business model of Novartis

After the merger of two Swiss pharmaceutical companies the new company, called Novartis, needed to define its business model. But the model then changed as pressures from external markets and technology changed.

Background

Novartis was formed from two major Swiss companies, Ciba and Sandoz. With 1995 sales of $26 billion, Ciba was a medium-sized competitor in the global markets for pharmaceuticals and agricultural chemicals. In the same year, Sandoz had sales of $18 billion and was more heavily involved in pharmaceutical markets with a range of products that complemented those of Ciba. They were merged in 1995 to form the world's second-largest drugs company, with a market share of 4.4 per cent: at the time, only Glaxo Wellcome was larger, at 4.7 per cent. Subsequently, other global mergers have taken place and Novartis has dropped down the list, with around 4 per cent share.

After the merger, both Ciba and Sandoz also had non-drug businesses. The first step in defining the business model was the basic strategic question: 'What business are we in?' From a strategy perspective, it was decided that the new company – called Novartis – was essentially in two related business areas, namely pharmaceuticals and agribusiness. These two areas formed the business model of the company. The non-drug businesses were then sold. The decision to sell these businesses was a strategic choice: they were not part of the strategy and related business model.

In their merger, the two companies were following recent trends in the pharmaceutical industry, which had seen some global consolidations over the previous five years: for example, Smith Kline (USA) with Beecham (UK), Glaxo (UK) with Wellcome (UK) and then with SmithKleinBeecham and Pharmacia (Sweden) with Upjohn (USA). The strategy was to build a business model that focused on *larger size*. There were two major reasons for this model. First, the model enabled the company to spread its heavy R&D costs and marketing expenditures across a wider range of products. Second, it was also to counter the increasing negotiating power of distributors and government health bodies. However, some leading industrialists disagreed with this model and regarded dominance in specific drugs and critical mass as being more important.

Not all previous mergers had been successful: the GlaxoSmithKline merger went smoothly at the second attempt. But the Pharmacia Upjohn merger was generally regarded as a disaster because the organisational cultures of the two companies were so different and there was no dominant partner to put its stamp on the other, thus illustrating that the successful

Novartis' strategies – moving into new drugs and developing cheap generic copies – have consolidated the company's position as one of the world's leading pharmaceutical manufacturers.
© Fabrice Coffrini/AFP/Getty Images

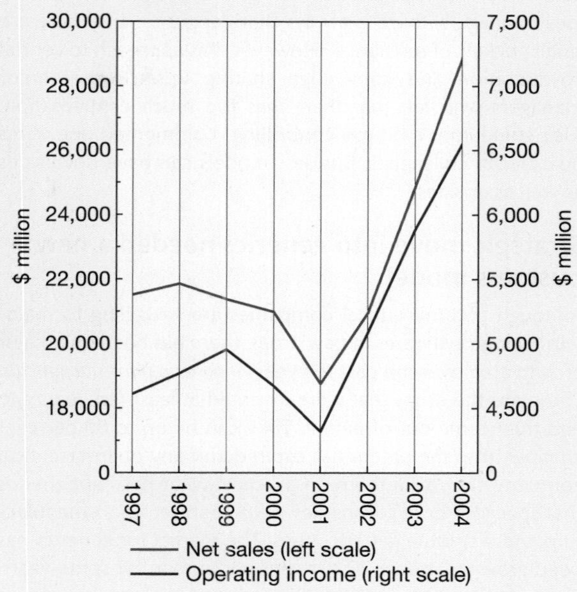

Figure 20.2 Novartis – performance of the company since the merger

Source: Novartis annual report and accounts 2004. Available at www.novartis.com – p 133 of the annual accounts.

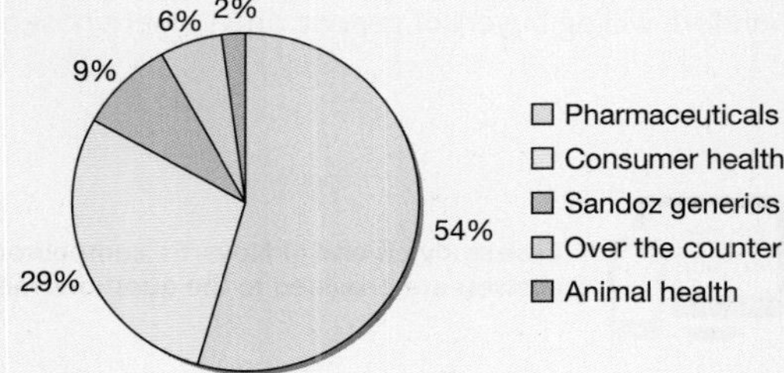

(b) Novartis net revenue by region 2004

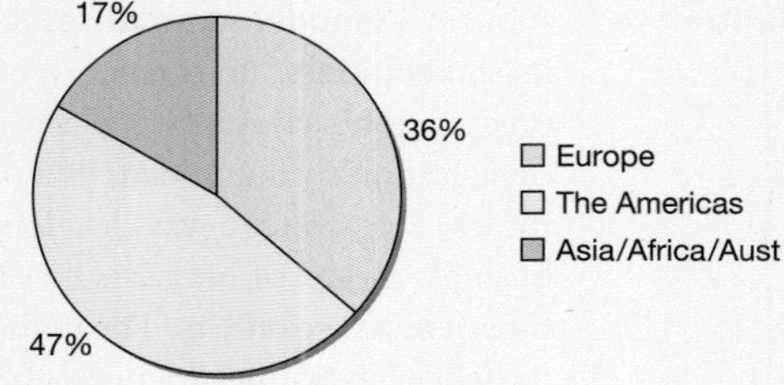

Figure 20.3 The main areas of Novartis business

business model is not just about size – it has many other dimensions, such as human resources and financial structure.

The new strategic task: growth

After the immediate period of the merger, sales held up strongly in the new Novartis. But in subsequent years, there were problems. The company's business model needed new drugs to re-invigorate its portfolio of products. It therefore invested around $2–3 billion each year in R&D, which was for some years amongst the largest budgets in the pharmaceutical industry. The company had a wide range of drug products but for some years had no single blockbuster that would alone deliver strong profits. For example, the company launched five new medicines in February 2001, but some did not live up to expectations. However, further drug approvals were gained in August 2001 so that the double-digit sales growth was still possible for at least another year. This has continued in later years with the success of new drugs such as Diovan for hypertension, Lotrel for cardiovascular treatments and Glivec for leukaemia. The company's record is summarised in Figure 20.2 and the source of its sales in Figure 20.3.

Other aspects of the business model

According to Dr Vasella, the company's business model was founded on growth, but this needed organisation and purpose. He believed that drug companies conducting research in a number of countries and subsidiaries often lacked the knowledge sharing necessary for the new breakthrough. For example, a small advance in one subsidiary might mean little to that company. Yet, if the same development was shared around the group, it might represent the final element in a major drug development for another part of the company. Thus, knowledge sharing was part of the business model of Novartis. 'That is why I hate fiefdoms,' says Dr Vasella. 'They are extremely bad for companies like ours. With decentralisation and strong local managers, there is always that danger . . . and there are small pockets of resistance.' However, this approach to central co-operation and knowledge sharing upset some senior managers who felt that there was too much centralisation: 'He's sometimes a bit too controlling,' commented one of his boardroom colleagues. Business models can have downsides as well as upsides.

Strategic move into generics needed a new business model

Although pharmaceutical companies are struggling to maintain their growth rates in new drugs, there has been one major growth area over the past ten years - *generic pharmaceuticals*. These are the drugs that were invented at least ten years ago and then came out of patent. They can be up to 80 per cent cheaper after the patent has expired and any pharmaceutical company can make them. In practice, what has happened is that specialist drug companies have been set up to manufacture and distribute generic drugs. The market for generics has been growing at over 20 per cent per annum for some years. For example, around $69 billion sales of patented drugs lost protection by 2009.

The difficulty for the major drug manufacturers was that generic drugs can be 80 per cent cheaper than the original product, i.e. the profit margins drop dramatically. In other words, generics are just commodity products that rely on low-cost, high-quality manufacturing techniques. They require core competencies that are different from the large R&D-oriented drug manufacturers typically spending $1 billion to get a new drug to market. The threat is that there are large customers - the major hospitals and health care providers - who are looking to cut prices and are therefore willing buyers of generic drugs where possible.

Why was this relevant to Novartis? Essentially because Novartis - unlike most of the other major pharmaceutical companies - took a strategic decision to move into generics: it changed its business model. It used its Sandoz brand as the basis of its activity and acquired two companies for a total purchase price of $8.3 billion in 2005. The deal made Novartis the largest generics pharmaceutical company in the world.

Subsequently, Novartis has developed its business model further. There are now five major trading divisions - pharmaceuticals, Sandoz generics, vaccines and diagnostics, Alcon eye care products and a consumer health division - plus a research division with over 6,000 scientists. Its business model was built upon its chosen strategy and was still showing significant growth.

Novartis has a strong record of green strategy and sustainability throughout the company.

 This case was written by Richard Lynch from published sources only.[4]

Case questions

1 Dr Vasella saw the way that the company was organised as being at the core of the company's business model. Are there any problems with this approach? And, if so, are there any solutions?

2 Will a strong R&D programme be enough to provide growth? Or does the company need to consider other aspects of strategy like knowledge, the resource-based view and learning-based strategy development? If so, how?

3 Can other companies learn from the experience of Novartis in developing its business model?

Case study on one of Novartis' competitors, Roche Pharmaceuticals: *Side-effects of age leave Roche reeling*. Indicative answers are provided to the questions raised at the end of the case.

20.1 WHAT IS A BUSINESS MODEL?

Definition ▶ **A business model summarises the logic of the firm, the way it operates and how it creates value for its stakeholders.**[5] In essence, a business model is a formula that captures the essential elements of an organisation's chosen strategy with the aim of delivering the company's profits (or a public sector organisation's value added) in a particular strategic context. The business model does not show how the chosen strategy was developed: that is the function of strategic management. For example, the business model of Novartis involves heavy investment in new pharmaceuticals with a research institute of 6,000 scientists. The company relies on the relatively high prices that it charges for new drugs to deliver its value added. At the same time, the company has also invested in the rapidly-growing generic pharmaceutical industry as another part of its business model: not all of the global pharmaceutical companies have this balanced product portfolio between new drugs and generics as part of their business model.

20.1.1 Defining a business model

Although the above definition captures the essence of a business model, it does not fully cover the many definitions that exist. For example, Baden-Fuller and Morgan list eight definitions that all emphasise different aspects of business models in one academic paper alone.[6] For example:

- Teece defines a business model as the relationship between creating value for the customer while capturing value for the firm with the firm's behaviour then reflecting this.[7]
- Itami and Nishino take the position that a business model is the combination of a profit model, an activity system and a learning project that can then be used to describe the firm and enable it to grow.[8]
- Zott and Amit consider a business model to be a system of interdependent activities that transcends the focal firm and spans its boundaries.[9]
- Gambardella and McGahan argue that a business model is a mechanism for turning ideas into revenue at a reasonable cost, emphasising the importance of innovation in the value chain.[10]

Why are there such differences in definition? The reason is that there is no single, established grounding for business models in either economics or in business studies.[11] Business models are used widely in discussing and resolving business issues, but there is no agreement on the underpinning logic. This makes the concept of a business model difficult to study.

20.1.2 Distinguishing between a business model and a business strategy

In spite of the wide use of the term 'business model' in the financial press, there has been only limited research on the concept in the leading strategy journals over the past few years. However, articles and papers regularly appear in the practitioner business press.[12] In addition, there has been some research in the context of entrepreneurial strategy.[13] However, it remains an under-researched area. In particular, the words 'business model' and 'strategy' have sometimes been used in the business press as if they were the same: they are not. Many strategists argue that it is important to distinguish between an organisation's *strategy* and its *business model.*

We begin with strategy. Strategy is the major actions by which an organisation's major objectives or goals are to be achieved over a defined period of time. This book has demonstrated how it always involves the strategic options and choices made by management – see, for example, Chapters 8, 9 and 10. Such choices involve the 'creation of a unique and valuable position' in the market place in the words of Professor Michael Porter.[14]

Business models are different: they do not involve choice because the choice has already been made at the higher strategy level. Moreover, they do not involve 'creation' in the sense used by Porter. Business models come *after* the creation of the strategy. Business models therefore are more associated with implementing the chosen strategy. They include an understanding of the logic of the strategic position but are more focused on the contingent plan that is the outcome of the strategy. The business model will therefore show how the company will compete and operate to deliver value for the firm's stakeholders.[15]

KEY STRATEGIC PRINCIPLES

- A business model is a formula that summarises the logic of the firm, the way it operates and how it creates value for its stakeholders.
- There is a clear distinction between the strategy of the firm and the business model. The strategy involves creating a unique position for the firm and involves making business choices. The business model summarises those choices and turns the strategy into an implementation plan for the organisation.

20.2 IDENTIFYING THE ELEMENTS OF THE BUSINESS MODEL

To identify the elements of a company's business model, the starting point is a summary of the core business strategy of the company. Every part of the business model must then be consistent with this core. For example, the Novartis pharmaceutical group has at least two business strategies. The first strategy is the classic research-based drug strategy with high development costs and strong marketing to health professionals. The second strategy at its Sandoz subsidiary involves taking existing drugs that have run out of patent protection and manufacturing them as cheaply as possible. In practice, it is possible to probe further to identify the company's core strategy: the next section outlines this.

After identifying the core strategy, the next stage in business model development is two-fold: first, to look outside the company at its customers and partners; second, to explore inside the company at the main functional areas of the firm. The identification of the elements of the business model is summarised in Figure 20.4.

20.2.1 Summarising the core strategy

The focus here is two-fold: where value is added in the organisation and what differentiates the organisation from its rivals. There are then two stages in this process:

1 Defining the product or service:
- *existing range and value elements* – the value chain can be used to go beyond simple description (see Chapter 4 for value chain);
- *customers* – who buys our product/service and why (see Chapter 3 for more detail).

2 Differentiation is then developed from:
- *analysis of competitive resources and capabilities* (see Chapter 4);
- *identification of other key resources* – not necessarily better than rivals but essential for business (the key factors for success (KFS) may provide a guide – see Chapter 3);

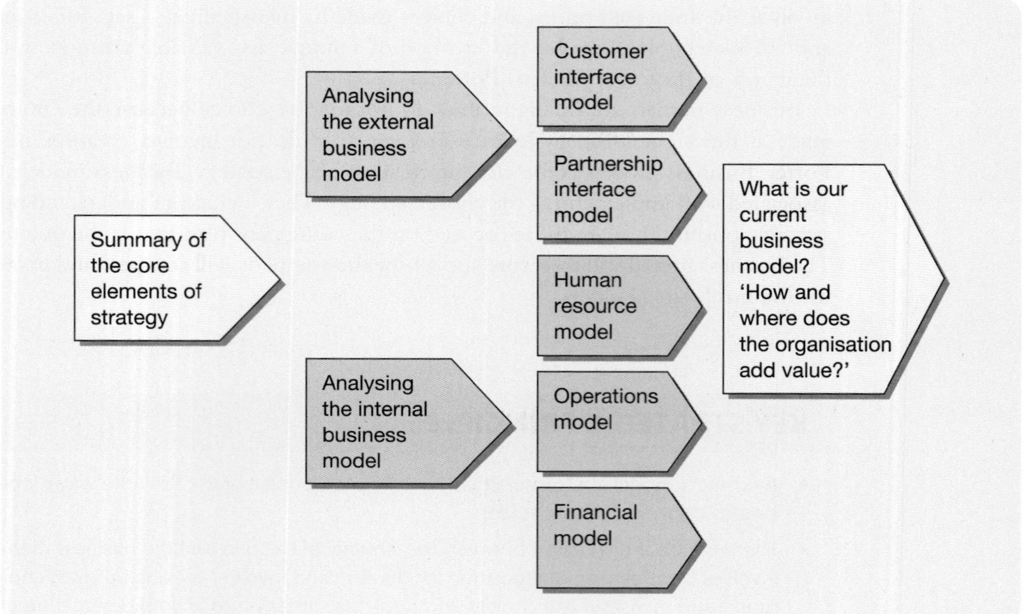

Figure 20.4 The main elements of the business model

- *conclusion* – why do customers buy our products/services rather than those of our rivals and with what benefit for value added?

20.2.2 Analysing the external business model of the company

After establishing the core strategy, the external business model of the company then looks outside the company at its customers and its partners. It does not look at its competitors because these do not deliver direct value to the company, though they may be important in assessing value added.

The customer interface model has at least five elements:

1. *Customer-driven strategy* – every part of the organisation needs to respond to customer issues and opportunities.
2. *Market positioning* – including specialist technology or unique location.
3. *Value for money* – price in relation to product or service – not necessarily the cheapest. In some models, the model could be the most expensive.
4. *Company reputation and branding* – knowledge, trust and service arising from years of trading and advertising.
5. *Customer relationships* – formal and informal links that bind customers to the company.

The partnership interface model has four main elements:

1. *Suppliers* – partnership with some suppliers, but perhaps distant and competitive relationship with others.
2. *Channel power* – links with distributors and channels of distribution – not necessarily partnerships.
3. *Alliances and joint ventures.*
4. *Other important links* – e.g. with government and with industry bodies that influence industry policy.

20.2.3 Analysing the internal business model of the company

The internal business model of the company then needs to analyse three main areas linked with the human resources of the company, the operations (production) and the financial resources and activities of the company.

The human resources model has three main elements:

1. organisational culture – 'the way we do things around here . . .' (see Chapter 4);
2. leadership style and substance (see Chapter 16);
3. organisation structure (see Chapter 12).

The operations model has five main elements:

1. make or buy decision, i.e. what do we manufacture and what do we buy from others?
2. total quality management;
3. cutting costs of manufacture, including supplier relationships, product design, factory layout and more effective use of labour;
4. improved and more efficient service, i.e. logistics and transport;
5. improved job performance and worker satisfaction.

The finance model has at least four main elements:

1. financing both existing and new developments;
2. tax and legal issues;
3. cash flow;
4. international transactions such as transfer pricing and currency.

In practice, each of these functional areas will have many more activities: for example, financial reporting in the case of the finance function. The above elements concentrate only on those aspects related to the analysis of the business model.

20.2.4 Simplifying the business model from the analysis

In practice, there are many possible elements in the above. There is a strong case for simplifying them. The reason is that they need to be debated, agreed and communicated throughout the firm, and this is difficult if they are long and complex. Casadesus-Masanell and Ricart suggest that there are two main ways of simplifying the business model analysis:[16]

1 *Aggregation*. This means zooming out from the detail, identifying key choices and their consequences in order to show how the main elements interact.
2 *Decomposition*. Some business models have elements that do not interact and can therefore be analysed in isolation from each other. It may then be possible to represent just a few key parts of the organisation in the model.

To show how aggregation can work, the complex business model for the low-cost airline Ryanair is shown in Figure 20.5 alongside the simplified model which more easily captures the main elements and is much easier to communicate and implement.

More generally, the business model can be summarised under four main headings, which are shown in Figure 20.6:

1 *Customer interface* – the target segments, the market positioning of the company, the pricing and related matters.
2 *Company strategic resources* – identifying and developing the strategic resources and capabilities that will deliver the value added through the human resources, finance and operations activities of the firm.
3 *Co-operators and partners* – working with the suppliers, distributors and other important linkages, like government, to deliver the long-term relationships that will enhance value added.
4 *Competitor differentiation* – monitoring, defining and sustaining the competitive advantages of the firm so that its value added is enhanced and not undermined by competitors.

Referring back to the Novartis case, it is possible to see how the company fits with the business model elements shown in Figure 20.6. For example, the customer interface will be with both the medical profession and with some large government institutions involved in health care – Chapter 3 summarises the main elements. Competitor differentiation will arise from the Novartis patents, its network of contacts and its reputation – Chapter 4 captures these elements. Co-operators and partners will particularly involve some large outside medical research organisations as well as some government bodies that go beyond customer relations – Chapters 4 and 5 summarise these areas. Company strategic resources will have two aspects: those relating to its main patented drugs and those delivering its generic drugs – Chapter 4 provides the underlying theory. Novartis' generics division will be highly focused on low-cost differentiation while the patented drugs will be more concerned with developing, testing and launching new drugs.

KEY STRATEGIC PRINCIPLES

- To identify the elements of a business model, the starting point is a summary of the core business strategy.
- There are two next steps: external to the company - customers and partners; internal to the company - the main functional areas of the business.
- The final step is to simplify the business model through either aggregation or decomposition.
- The summary will have four major headings: customer interface; company strategic resources; co-operators and partners; and competitor differentiation.

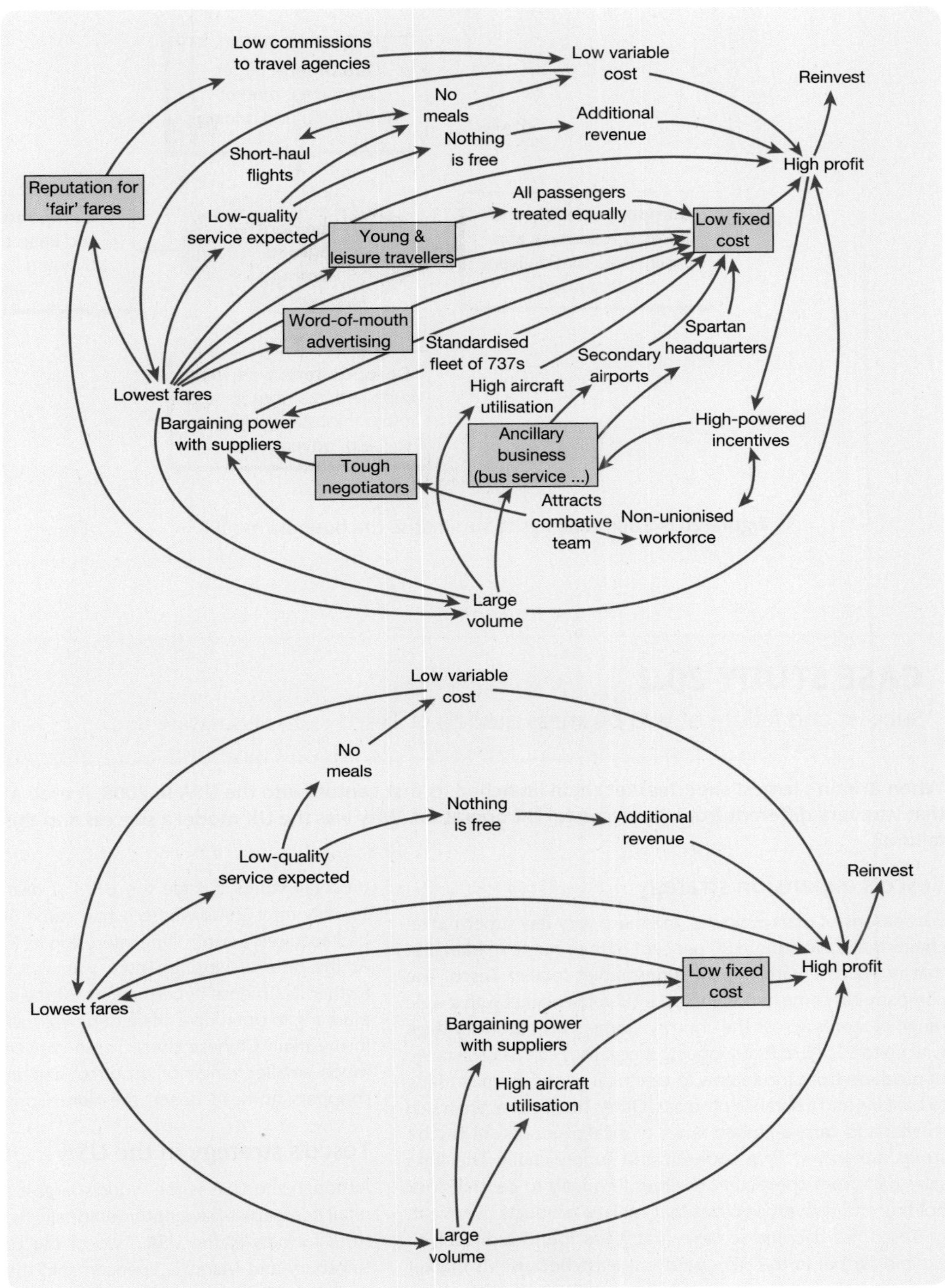

Figure 20.5 Ryanair simplified business model

Source: Casadesus-Masanell, R and Ricart J E (2010) 'From strategy to business models and onto tactics', *Long Range Planning*, 43, 195–215.

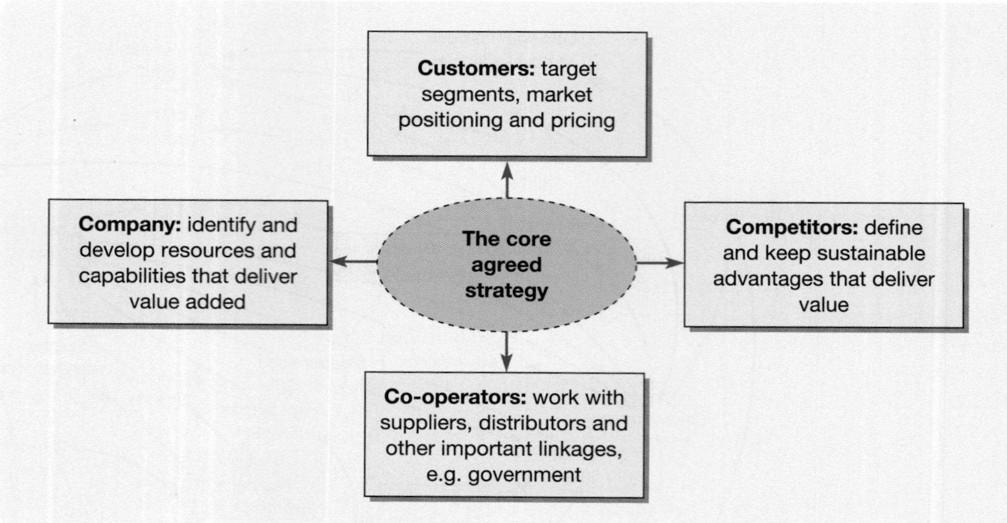

Figure 20.6 Four headings to summarise the business model

CASE STUDY 20.2

Success and failure of two business models at Tesco

When Britain's largest supermarket chain launched its first venture into the USA in 2008, it used a business model that was very different from its successful UK operation. Why was the UK model a success and the US model a failure?

Tesco's expansion strategy

For reasons of market power, there are very few supermarket chains that have around 30 per cent of their home market. But that is the case with the UK supermarket retailer Tesco. The company has come to dominate the UK retail market with a wide range of stores across the country. Some stores are very large with up to 50,000 sq ft of shopping space. They carry a wide range of products from food items to electrical goods, from clothing to banking and insurance products. Other Tesco stores are much smaller and carry a limited range of local products. All Tesco's stores are served by a sophisticated supply chain. This links sales data from computer checkout terminals to central stock holding and delivery vehicles that replace products overnight.

Tesco has become so large that it has found it difficult to expand further in the UK – partly, at least, because its market dominance has made the British competition authorities keen to ensure that the retail market remains competitive and prices stay low. Consequently, in recent years, Tesco has been forced to seek expansion outside the UK. Tesco's strategy has therefore been to develop major supermarket chains in such countries as Poland and the Czech Republic.

As a result of this international expansion strategy, some 80 per cent of Tesco's group capital expenditure in 2007 was on retail stores outside the UK. For example, it was moving steadily into China where it had some 50 hypermarkets and had acquired a controlling interest in its local partner, Tin Cao. At the time of writing, Tesco was also planning to develop further its Chinese hypermarkets. At the same time, Tesco was planning to open up a chain of new, small, convenience stores in the main Chinese cities. These convenience stores have a much smaller range of products and are located closer to shoppers' homes – hence, the name 'convenience'.

Tesco's strategy in the USA

Although the USA is the world's largest retail market, British retail companies have not traditionally had much success with store formats in the USA. Two of the UK's leading retailers, Sainsbury and Marks & Spencer, sold their US outlets during the 1990s. This was partly, at least, due to a lack of profitability because the USA is a highly competitive retail market. Possibly the most successful US retailer is Wal-Mart: the company operates very large, highly efficient, low-price stores mainly located near major shopping malls that require car access. Wal-Mart is the world's largest retailer by turnover and has expanded outside the USA into China and the UK, where it owns the ASDA supermarket chain.

In spite of this heavy competition, Tesco identified the USA as a market that it would like to enter. However, it needed to find a profitable strategy that would compete against companies like Wal-Mart. Tesco decided that its UK supermarket strategy could simply not compete against Wal-Mart - the American company was too efficient, too low-cost and too well-entrenched for Tesco to make headway. Tesco therefore needed another strategy.

After examining various possible approaches, Tesco decided that it would be best served by copying the strategy of two of its competitors in the UK: the German retailers Aldi and Lidl. When these two retailers decided to move into the UK in the early 1990s, they were faced with the large supermarket chains like Tesco, ASDA and others. In order to differentiate themselves, Aldi and Lidl brought their German retail strategies to the UK: small stores of around 5,000–10,000 sq ft, no frills or presentation, few if any major branded products and *very* low prices. They operated what is called the 'hard-discount' retail store concept. In effect, the two German chains offered a new concept in value for money to the British shopper. The result was that the two chains both had some real success, in spite of heavy competition from the major British retailers like Tesco.

Given the evidence of this success, Tesco decided that it would launch the hard discount retail concept in the USA. In early 2008, it began rolling out the first of 50 'Fresh & Easy' stores in California, USA. Tesco announced that it would be investing $500 million to develop a chain of 250 stores by the end of 2009. The chief executive of Tesco North America described this as a 'transformational' moment for the company. 'It is clearly scaleable but you can't push the pedal until you can convince shareholders it will work. We have got latitude to build a big business on the west coast before they hit the gas.' There were outline plans for 1,000 stores each of around 5,000 sq ft.

To keep costs low, the Fresh & Easy stores mainly sold a big non-branded range from identical store formats. There were self-service checkouts without cashiers and shelf-ready packaging. The aim was to reduce the number of staff needed in each store. There was also one totally new initiative that was not copied from Aldi and Lidl: Fresh & Easy would sell fresh ready meals and, unlike anywhere else in the Tesco business, the company set up its own manufacturing plant in California to make the meals. Again, the strategy was to reduce the costs. 'We could have asked one of our [UK] suppliers to come over and they would have jumped at it, but we felt we could do it ourselves,' explained John Burry, Fresh & Easy's chief commercial officer. 'We have lots of experience in this and the [profit] margin is better. Why pay someone else to do this?' The prepared food was going down so well with shoppers that there were availability problems in the first few weeks of operation.

Although there had been some early success, the Fresh & Easy concept was still facing problems in early 2011. It was making a loss with the store opening schedule also being delayed as a result: the trading loss in 2010 was £165 million ($270 million) with only 30 store openings in 2010 to make a total of 145 stores.

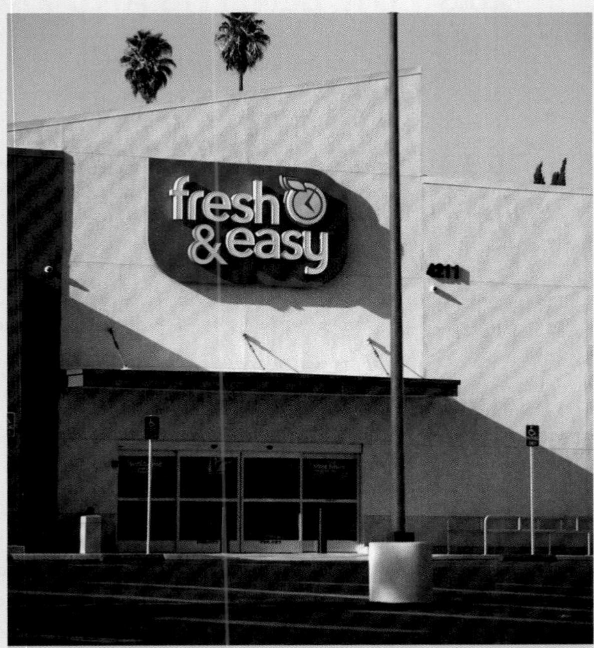

One of the world's leading retailers - the UK company Tesco - developed a totally new business positioning to enter the highly competitive US market.
Rex Features/Digital Beach Media

After five years of losses, Tesco finally decided in 2013 that the Fresh & Easy business model was not working. American customers wanted more choice in store, more opportunities to handle fresh products, less Tesco own-branded products and more well-known national brands. The company announced that it was pulling out of the USA at a cost of over $200 million.

In addition, Tesco was also facing problems with its large-store UK model in 2014. Its large-scale stores were threatened by two competing retail grocery models: the grocery discounters like Aldi and Lidl and the upmarket grocers like Waitrose. Tesco needed to rethink its business models.

Tesco has a good record of supporting sustainable strategies throughout both its UK and its international operations.

 This case was written from published information only.[17]

Case questions

1 What were the two main business models operated by Tesco described in this case? Why did the company develop a new model for the USA?

2 What are the benefits of defining a business model? And what are the problems?

20.3 THE BENEFITS AND PROBLEMS OF THE BUSINESS MODEL

Like most business concepts, there are benefits and problems in identifying and using a business model. It is important to know about these in order to judge the value and relevance of the concept.

20.3.1 The benefits of the business model

There are four main benefits of identifying a business model for a firm:

1 *Assists implementation* of the chosen strategy because it brings together some of the main strategic elements in a way that allows communication and debate across the organisation.
2 *Allows testing and debate* because the model clarifies the understanding and logic behind the strategy.
3 *Enables communication* of the strategy throughout the organisation because the business model provides a summary of the company's direction.
4 *Supports understanding and commitment* from all those people in the company not immediately involved in developing the core chosen strategy.

For example, the Tesco retail store case shows that the company operated at least two business models: one is for its large UK stores that are well-established and have a wide variety of goods on sale; the other was for its new venture in North America where it was competing against some very powerful existing supermarkets and where Tesco needed to find a point of differentiation that would prove attractive to customers and profitable to the company. The clarity and simplicity of the two business models at Tesco was relatively easy to communicate to all Tesco employees. In this sense, it assisted the implementation of the chosen strategy – even though it was ultimately unsuccessful.

20.3.2 The problems of the business model

There are two main problems with the business model concept:

1 *Largely prescriptive process.* It is primarily based on seeking differentiation from others in a reasonably predictable market place. Little emphasis is given to dynamic competition and none to fast-moving environments.
2 *Innovative structures, ideas and learning.* These aspects are largely ignored. This business model is usually presented as a static picture of a business in time. The emergent processes explored in this book are completely lacking.

20.3.3 Conclusions on the business model

The criticisms of the business model do not make the concept wrong, but they do show that the benefits – summarising and communicating a strategy – need to be set against the disadvantages, such as its lack of emphasis on innovation and learning.

Some strategists might argue that the business model is weak because it only looks at the past, not the future. However, others will say that this is not a fair criticism because examining the future is the function of strategic management, not the business model as defined in this text. Thus finally in this chapter, we return to the topic of strategic management.

KEY STRATEGIC PRINCIPLES

- There are four main benefits of a business model: it assists implementation; it allows testing and debate; it enables communication; and it supports understanding and commitment from people not immediately involved in development of the core strategy.
- There are two main problems with a business model: it is largely a prescriptive process; and innovative structures, ideas and learning are largely ignored.

20.4 STRATEGIC MANAGEMENT AND BUSINESS MODELS

20.4.1 Implementation and business models

As Chapter 1 pointed out, the separation in prescriptive strategy between analysis, options and choice, and implementation is useful. However, it does not really capture much of the ongoing strategy work that occupies organisations on a regular basis. Even where major upheaval occurs, such as the decision to close Tesco's Fresh & Easy stores, the venture will depend on how it is implemented over a relatively short space of time. Such issues will remain part of the longer-term strategic task of the organisation. But the business model will provide a template against which to judge a particular strategic venture – where, if anywhere, is valued added, for example.

Business models are only a first step in implementation. *Milestones* and *controls* need to be set up to oversee implementation issues:

- *Milestones* are used to measure precisely what progress of the strategy towards a final implementation goal has been made at some intermediate point. They are important because it is only by assessing activity while it is still in progress that useful corrective actions can be taken.
- *Controls* are employed to ensure that financial, human resource and other guidelines are not breached during the implementation process. For example, they might include cash flow, cost expenditures against budget, training programme achievement, plant installation procedures and many other tasks. They differ from milestones in that they are more detailed, ongoing and function-specific.

Some key guidelines on strategy implementation and control.

20.4.2 Re-examining the future environment and business models

In developing a coherent strategy, organisations may take the view that it is useful to identify the main trends that are likely to affect them over the next few years. This can be covered by business models by the use of scenario-based analysis – see Chapter 3 for an explanation of this. For example, both Novartis and other pharmaceutical companies have clearly found the need to re-examine the future pharmaceutical market as part of their development of strategy. Each pharma company can develop a business model for different scenarios: perhaps one where the patent stream remains as predicted, one where it becomes worse and one where several successful new drugs are patented and deliver significant value added.

There are two important areas of caution with regard to prediction. First, it will be recalled that part of the reasoning for scenario building was not *prediction* but rather *preparation* in the event of the unpredictable happening. Second, one of the most respected management writers, Peter Drucker, cautions against such predictions:

> It is not very difficult to predict the future. It is only pointless. Many futurologists have high batting averages - the way they measure themselves and are commonly measured. They do a good job foretelling some things. But what are always far more important are fundamental changes that happened though no one predicted them or could possibly have predicted them.[18]

Thus, although business models may help through scenarios, there are real problems with predicting the future. Nevertheless, it has even been argued that strategy should attempt to *shape* – not just predict – the future.[19]

20.4.3 The strategic purpose of the organisation and the business model

Beyond emphasising the importance of value added, business models do not really provide the detail that organisations will need when reconsidering their vision, purpose and mission. Moreover, organisations rarely stand still: some grow fast, like the producers of Facebook and Twitter. Some grow more slowly, such as major multinationals, unless they make a major strategic shift, like Novartis and Tesco. Some decline for a whole variety of reasons.

At a deeper level of purpose, business models fail to address the following four areas:

1 *Changes in the purpose of the organisation.* Does it actually matter if we decline? How important is it that we achieve our stated growth targets? The answers to these questions will relate to the values of the organisation and those of its management, employees and shareholders.
2 *Dynamics of sustainable competitive advantage.* How and where will we develop this further? What are the implications for the resources of the organisation?
3 *The culture and style of the organisation.* How do we undertake our work? What style do we wish to adopt? Again, these are fundamental questions that go beyond immediate business model issues to the underlying philosophy of the business.
4 *The values and ethical standards.* What values do we hold? Why? How do we wish to conduct ourselves? How do we measure up to these ideals? As organisations move into the new millennium, some have questioned previously held views on sustaining the environment, equal treatment for minorities, political affiliations and so on. These are legitimate matters of strategic management that go beyond business models.

This book has argued in favour of customer-driven quality, innovation and the learning organisation. It has also simplified purpose down to corporate social responsibility and value added. Strategy has been simplified down to the search for target customers and sustainable competitive advantage. Such considerations will not necessarily be appropriate for all organisations, but all will need to determine their long-term perspectives, whatever they are. Business models may be useful as a starting point here but they do not address the necessary detail.

Coupled with changes in the environment and in the organisation, new issues are constantly emerging in strategic management itself. Many of these go beyond business models. The research papers, journals, books and magazines quoted throughout this book will provide guidance on the subjects that are currently under study[20] – the subjects that make strategic management dynamic, stimulating, controversial and relevant to our future.

20.4.4 . . . and finally

Finally, it should not be forgotten that, in spite of all the attempts of strategic management to guide and cope with the future, there are always the *unpredictable* elements that are beyond strategic theory and the static nature of business models. In the words of the German chemical company, Henkel, 'To succeed in business, you need skill, patience, money . . . **and a bit of luck.**'[21]

KEY STRATEGIC PRINCIPLES

- Business models are only a first step in implementation. Milestones and controls are also needed.
- Many organisations attempt to re-examine the future environment. Business models can be coupled with scenario planning to predict future trends, but all such predictions must be treated with considerable caution.
- Business models fail to address four important areas of the strategic purpose of the organisation: changes in purpose; the dynamics of sustainable competitive advantage; the culture and style of the organisation; and the values and ethical standards of the organisation.
- There will always be an element of chance in strategic management. Luck will make a contribution to the development of workable proposals.

CASE STUDY 20.3

FT

Why a bigger business model does not necessarily mean better, but a green strategy helps

The story of the UK company Courtaulds highlights how large, diversified companies are not always best placed to withstand global competition. It also illustrates the increasing demand for green strategy initiatives.

In 1960, the UK textile company Courtaulds launched the fibre Courtelle in a range of Mary Quant designs. It was a strategic response to criticism of its earlier fibre, rayon. But Courtelle had no competitive advantage over rival, similar fibres that were already on sale. It was only when Courtaulds developed another new fibre called Tencel that it had a winning product. But it was all too late to save the Courtaulds Group, as this case explains.
Image courtesy of The Advertising Archives

Rise of China

The rise of China as a great exporting nation has been a huge boon for consumers in the West. But it has posed difficult problems for producers, especially those who are in direct line of fire from Chinese competition. Should they change their business model or should they battle on, hoping that innovation and superior technology will keep them ahead?

Nowhere has this dilemma been more acute than in man-made fibres, which have become dominated by Asian companies. Some 60 per cent of the world's synthetic fibre capacity is now located in China. The result has been a massive restructuring of the industry with most of the former leaders withdrawing from the market. Yet there is one European manufacturer, Lenzing of Austria, that has survived as a key player, not only in Europe but also in Asia. Peter Untersperger, chief executive, announced in 2010 an expansion of its plants in China and Indonesia and a third Asian site is planned in India. It has done this, moreover, in a sector of the industry – cellulosic fibres derived from woodpulp, which include rayon – that was once thought doomed to decline.

Courtaulds and Lenzing

The rise of Lenzing is the triumph of a specialisation business model. It is also a David-and-Goliath story that highlights why large diversified groups are not always best placed to deal with rising international competition. The Goliath in this case was Courtaulds, the British company that pioneered the development of rayon before the First World War but no longer exists.

When the original Lenzing plant was set up in 1938, Courtaulds was the industry giant. However, DuPont had just invented nylon, opening a new line of research that posed a threat to Courtaulds' main source of profit from its textile product called rayon. Nylon, polyester and acrylic fibres were 'synthesised' through polymer chemistry, and the leading producers were chemical companies such as DuPont, Hoechst and ICI. These fibres were more versatile than rayon and had easy-care properties that cotton and wool could not match.

How to reduce its dependence on rayon was a post-war pre-occupation of Courtaulds. By 1960, it had its own acrylic fibre (Courtelle) and was making nylon on a small scale. It had also diversified in other directions, including paints. Lenzing, by contrast, remained much more dependent on its core business model of cellulosic fibres. During the 1960s and 1970s, Courtaulds continued to diversify, principally in textile production of finished products and clothing. It had a diversified business model. The strategy was driven by Frank (later Lord) Kearton, who believed that through scale and new technology, textiles in Britain would 'cease to be a declining industry and have every prospect of become a growth industry once more'.

Problems with textile production

In 1975, when Lord Kearton retired, Courtaulds was a much bigger company with a substantial stake in fibres, including rayon. But the viscose process by which rayon was made caused environmental damage that was no longer acceptable in many countries. So the producers had to decide whether to spend large amounts of money to clean up the process or to withdraw. Courtaulds chose to stick with rayon but also to work on a novel cellulosic fibre made using a process known as solvent spinning. The research began in 1979 and at the end of that year, Christopher (later Sir Christopher) Hogg was appointed chief executive. His task was to bring order into the diversified business model that Kearton had created. The business model related to textiles production had proved to be a serious error, mainly because of rising imports from low-wage suppliers. This side of the group needed a great deal of sorting out. Hogg eventually demerged it as Courtaulds Textiles in 1990.

Results of the demerger

After the demerger, Courtaulds still had a diversified business model. The paints subsidiary, which had been expanded by further acquisitions, looked to offer the best prospects for growth. With the continuing contraction of the European textile industry, would it make sense to get out of fibres? An argument for not doing so was the progress that the researchers had made with solvent spinning. They had shown that the process was pollution-free, and that the fibre coming out of it - which was given the brand name *Tencel* ('tenacity' and 'cellulose') - was stronger than rayon and could be used to make finer yarns and lighter fabrics. The first *Tencel* plant in Mobile, Alabama, came on stream in 1992, and the initial response was enthusiastic. However, partly because of quality problems in converting yarn into fabric, the market developed more slowly than Courtaulds had expected. By the second half of the 1990s, the company found itself in a financial bind. It was spending heavily on the new fibre but not generating enough cash in the rest of the group. Its *Tencel* fibre manufacturing business model was in trouble. With the share price under pressure, Courtaulds was vulnerable to a break-up bid and, in 1998, Akzo Nobel of the Netherlands bought the diversified group.

Results of the takeover of Courtaulds

After the takeover, Akzo Nobel retained only Courtaulds' paints division. The fibres side was bought by CVC, a private equity firm, which sold the *Tencel* business to Lenzing in 2004. The Austrian company was by then producing its own solvent-based fibre, but Thomas Fahnemann, an ex-Hoechst manager, who had recently been appointed chief executive, believed that buying the Courtaulds plants would give Lenzing a dominant position in a promising sector of the market. He was right. While *Tencel* has not become a mainstream fibre, it has achieved part of what the proponents of the project in Courtaulds had hoped for. Although expensive compared with cotton or polyester, it was used in high-end garments where its exceptional softness and drape were valued. It also had the great advantage of 'greenness' - see Exhibit 20.1. The Lenzing business model that employed *Tencel* had found a market niche. The model was both profitable and sustainable.

As a cellulosic specialist, Lenzing was a logical home for the new fibre. Cellulosic fibres, of which rayon is still the most important, represent less than 5 per cent of the world fibre market - see Figure 20.7 - but they have some properties, notably absorbency, that the oil-based synthetics lack. As a textile fibre, rayon has recovered some lost ground in recent years, thanks in part to strong demand from China, and cellulosics are widely used in advanced industrial countries in non-woven applications. In spite of strong competition from Asian producers, Lenzing is well placed to serve both markets.

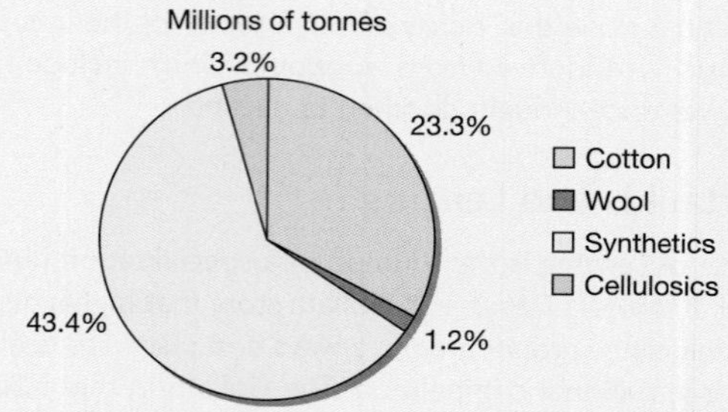

Figure 20.7 World fibre market 2008

EXHIBIT 20.1

The 'greenness' of *Tencel*

Many of the world's leading retailers are seeking to demonstrate their commitment to sustainability. This means, amongst other things, using products that are made from natural materials by processes that do not damage the environment. Marks & Spencer, for example, launched its Plan A programme in 2007. It was aimed at combating climate change, reducing waste and using more sustainable materials. The aim was to become the world's most sustainable large retailer. Greater use of organic cotton forms part of this plan, but *Tencel*, made from woodpulp by a process in which virtually all the chemicals are re-used, is also an option. 'Greenness' is also an important selling point for *Tencel* in non-woven applications. Absorbent and bio-degradable, it is well suited for disposable products, such as baby wipes and other hygienic, non-woven products. Costco, the big US discount retailer, which sells *Tencel*-based baby wipes, describes the fibre as 'the ideal New Age material', attractive to parents who want products for their children 'that are naturally made from raw materials but are also respective of the environment'.

Conclusion

Is there a moral to this story? One lesson is that large business models involving diversified companies are not necessarily better equipped to withstand international competition than small, specialised ones: there are dangers in business models that do too many things. Another is that violent changes in direction, such as Kearton's plunge into textiles production and clothing, can have disastrous consequences. Companies are generally well advised to concentrate on what they are best at and to build from there.

This case was adapted by Richard Lynch from an article in the *Financial Times* by Geoffrey Owen on 24 August 2010, p 10. The article was based on the author's book *The Rise and Fall of Great Companies: Courtaulds and the Reshaping of the Man-Made Fibres Industry*, published in September 2010 by Oxford University Press, Oxford. Richard Lynch is solely responsible for providing this adapted version of the original article and the Financial Times Limited does not accept any liability for the accuracy or quality of the adapted version.

Case questions

1 What were the main reasons why Courtaulds was broken up? What are the main strategy theories that help to interpret this strategy failure? Do you agree with the writer that this means that all large diversified companies are weaker than those that are more specialised?

2 What problems did Courtaulds find when it tried to innovate with Tencel? Should it have persisted? Are such problems typical of the difficulties facing innovative companies or are the problems unique to Tencel and Courtaulds?

3 Tencel has strong green credentials so why is it used in only a limited way in the industry? What strategies could be adopted to encourage its use more widely?

CRITICAL REFLECTION

Just how important is luck?

At the end of this summary chapter, the German company Henkel was quoted: 'To succeed in business, you need skill, patience, money . . . and a bit of luck.' If luck is a factor, then does this perhaps negate the value of the strategic content and process developed throughout the text? What is your experience? Does luck matter? What are the implications of your view for the development of strategic management?

SUMMARY

- A business model is a formula that summarises the logic of the firm, the way it operates and how it creates value for its stakeholders.
- There is a clear distinction between the strategy of the firm and the business model. The strategy involves creating a unique position for the firm and involves making business choices. The business model summarises those choices and turns the strategy into an implementation plan for the organisation.
- To identify the elements of a business model, the starting point is a summary of the core business strategy. There are two next steps: external to the company – customers and partners; internal to the company – the main functional areas of the business.
- The final step is to simplify the business model through either aggregation or decomposition. The summary will have four major headings: customer interface; company strategic resources; co-operators and partners; and competitor differentiation.
- There are four main benefits of a business model: it assists implementation; it allows testing and debate; it enables communication; and it supports understanding and commitment from people not immediately involved in development of the core strategy.
- There are two main problems with a business model: it is largely a prescriptive process; and innovative structures, ideas and learning are largely ignored.
- Business models are only a first step in implementation. Milestones and controls are also needed.

- Many organisations attempt to re-examine the future environment. Business models can be coupled with scenario planning to predict future trends, but all such predictions must be treated with considerable caution.
- Business models fail to address four important areas of the strategic purpose of the organisation: changes in purpose; the dynamics of sustainable competitive advantage; the culture and style of the organisation; and the values and ethical standards of the organisation.
- There will always be an element of chance in strategic management. Luck will make a contribution to the development of workable proposals.

QUESTIONS

1 Use the book's prescriptive model to analyse the business model at Novartis.

2 Is it possible to have rival companies with exceptionally effective business models against which to compare performance?

3 Using an example with which you are familiar, develop a business model to summarise its strategy. What are the strengths and weaknesses of the model that you have formulated?

4 Examine the Tesco strategic decision to close its Fresh & Easy stores using the various strategic processes explored in this text - prescriptive, learning-based, knowledge, etc. - to plot the way the decision was derived and comment on the usefulness of each process.

5 This book has highlighted 'customer-driven quality, innovation and the learning mechanism' as being particularly important in the development of strategic management. Are there other areas that you would wish to select and, if so, what are they and why would you select them?

FURTHER READING

There was a special issue of *Long Range Planning* in 2010 that has some excellent papers on the topic of business models: *Long Range Planning*, Volume 43, page 153 *et seq*. This chapter has benefited from this material.

To look into the strategic future, you might read Hamel, G and Prahalad, C K (1994) 'Strategy as a field of study: why search for new paradigms?', *Strategic Management Journal*, Special Issue, 15, pp 5–16. The 'Special Issue' of *Long Range Planning*, April 1996, also has an interesting review of this area. For a more recent perspective: Cummings, S and Angwin, D (2004) 'The future shape of strategy: Lemmings or chimeras?', *Academy of Management Executive*, Vol 18, No 2, pp 21–28, contains some interesting ideas and comparison between the 'old' and the 'new'.

NOTES AND REFERENCES

1 Casadesus-Masanell, R and Ricart, J E (2010) 'From strategy to business models and onto tactics', *Long Range Planning*, Vol 43, pp 195–215.

2 Baden-Fuller, C and Morgan, M S (2010) 'Business models as models', *Long Range Planning*, Vol 43, pp 156–171.

3 Teece, D J (2010) 'Business models, business strategy, and innovation', *Long Range Planning*, Vol 43, pp 172–194.

4 References for the Novartis case: Novartis Annual Report and Accounts 2013 – available on the web at www.novartis.com; *Financial Times*: 8 March 1996, pp 1, 17, 28; 19 March 1996, p 25; 11 April 1996, p 18 (Dr Håken Mogren's comments); 12 October 1998, p 15; 16 July 1999, p 27; 18 February 2000, p 26; 11 July 2000, p 34; 16 February 2001, p 25; 8 May 2001, p 19; 14 May 2001, p 27; 22 August 2001, p 20; 28 November 2001, p 23; 21 January 2004, p 12; 22 February 2005, pp 1, 28. See also Lynch, R (1994) *European Business Strategies*, 2nd edn, Kogan Page, London, pp 31–32, for an earlier exploration of global strategies in the drugs industry.

5 Casadesus-Masanell, R and Ricart, J E (2010) Op. cit.

6 Baden-Fuller, C and Morgan, M S (2010) Op. cit., p 158.

7 Teece, D (2010) Op. cit.

8 Itami, H and Nishino, K (2010) 'Killing two birds with one stone: profit for now and learning for the future', *Long Range Planning*, Vol 43, pp 364–369.

9 Zott C and Amit, R (2010) 'Business model design: an activity system perspective', *Long Range Planning*, Vol 43, pp 216–226.

10 Gambardella, A and McGahan, A M (2010) 'Business-model innovation: general purpose technologies and their implications for industry architecture', *Long Range Planning*, Vol 43, pp 262–271.

11 Teece, D (2010) Op. cit.
12 See as an example of *practitioner* articles, Gottfredson, M, Schaubert, S and Saenz, H (2008) 'The new leader's guide to diagnosing the business', *Harvard Business Review*, February, pp 63–73. Possibly the most useful collection of *academic* research papers on business models appeared in *Long Range Planning* in 2010 – referenced individually at various points throughout this chapter.
13 Barrninger, B and Ireland, D (2006) *Entrepreneurship – Successfully Launching New Ventures*, Prentice Hall, Englewood Cliffs, NJ.
14 Porter, M E (1996) 'What is Strategy?' *Harvard Business Review*, Vol 74, No 6, p 68.
15 This reasoning and distinction draws heavily on the paper by Casadesus-Masanell, R and Ricart, J E (2010) Op. cit.
16 Casadesus-Masanell, R and Ricart, J E (2010) Op. cit.
17 Sources for the Tesco case: www.tesco.com; *Financial Times*: 3 December 2007, pp 21 and 22; 28 January 2008, p 15; 22 September 2010, p 22 (with a useful long review on progress and future plans); 20 July 2011, p 19; 11 January 2012, p 18; 6 December 2012, p 25; 18 April 2013, p 19.
18 Drucker, P (1995) *Managing in a Time of Great Change*, Butterworth–Heinemann, Oxford, p vii.
19 Whitehill, M (1996) 'Introduction to foresight: exploring and creating the future', *Long Range Planning*, April p 146. This issue has a range of articles that tackle this subject from a number of perspectives, including those that believe it is a waste of time.
20 See, for example, Hamel, G and Prahalad, C K (1994) 'Strategy as a field of study: why search for new paradigms?', *Strategic Management Journal*, Special Issue, Vol 15, pp 5–16. See also *Long Range Planning*, April 1996.
21 Henkel, A G, Annual Report and Accounts: 1987.

PART 6

Integrative and longer case studies

1. Europe's leading airlines: budget strategy or bust?
2. Global beer and lager: exploring strategies in a mature market
3. SABMiller: South Africa goes quietly global
4. Prescriptive and emergent strategy: global car markets and the battle between the world's top car companies
5. PSA Peugeot Citroën: stuck in the strategy slow lane?
6. Risks and rewards in Russia: rescue strategy at AvtoVAZ cars
7. Competitive strategies: good news and bad news at Tata Motors
8. Strategic leadership and change: the rise and fall of CEO Carly Fiorina at Hewlett-Packard
9. Strategic leadership: what can companies learn from 'Chainsaw Al'?
10. Sony strategy: more restructuring or complete breakup?
11. Emergent strategy: what's the new smart strategy for PCs, media tablets and mobiles?
12. Prescriptive strategy: Dell's new strategy beyond commoditisation: too little and too late?
13. Emergent strategy: the competitive threat to Apple Music?
14. Emergent strategy: how Google's search strategy opened up the web (and earned a fortune for its inventors)

Four more cases:

- Heineken: What's the best strategy? Build brands or acquire companies?
- Toyota: does it rely too heavily on production for world leadership?
- Disaster and recovery: thinking outside the box at IBM
- Sorting out Sony: restoring the profits and the innovative fire

HOW TO ANALYSE AND PREPARE STRATEGY CASES

Tips on how to write up strategic projects

In addition to the cases shown throughout this book, there are some broader cases presented in the following pages. A case is a written description of a strategy situation. It often studies a real organisation at a point in time and describes the strategy issues that are present or that *appear* to be present – meaning that the organisation may not have fully understood its own strategic situation.

The objectives of analysing cases are:

- To *apply the theoretical concepts* that have been covered in this text. Importantly, you rarely need to describe in detail the theory in your case answer: you may assume that the reader (or listener to an oral presentation) will know this.
- To consider the *real-life complexity* of a number of factors affecting the business problem, rather than the single subject approach that may occur when a case is explored inside a specific chapter. Most strategy problems have several aspects that go beyond the subject matter of one chapter.
- To identify strategy issues and *make recommendations*.

Cases are not necessarily complete, although for most purposes you can usually work with the material in the case. In addition, some of the data in a case may not be relevant: this mirrors real life where managers need to *select the data* they use to resolve strategy issues.

Although questions are given at the ends of cases, such questions may not reflect the true issues underpinning the case. For example, a question might be asked about the competitive resources and capabilities of an organisation. However, you may wish to explore the competitive environment of the organisation before looking at competitive resources because this may influence the resources: for example, the competitive resource of a brand name may need to be seen in the context of the many brands already in that market place.

Nevertheless, for academic work, it is vital that *all* the questions at the end of a case are adequately answered. The mark sheet is often constructed with awards for specific points that cannot be earned unless these are addressed. For example, if you are asked to make recommendations, then you must make them.

Case preparation might usefully involve the following steps:

- Read the case fairly quickly.
- Read again, this time making some notes in relation to the questions or problems.
- Do a SWOT analysis on an organisation in the case – even if you are not asked for one – the process of doing this will help you understand the structure of the case and the data that are available.
- Then prepare a list of major issues based, for example, on either the prescriptive or emergent process models in this book. In practice, you may need to make a choice here between the two processes if the market is particularly uncertain. Perhaps you can use Section 3.3 on the *degree of turbulence* in the market place to help you decide:
  - if turbulence is high, then an emergent approach may be more appropriate;
  - if turbulence is low, then a prescriptive approach may be more useful.

  Importantly, even when turbulence is low, you might want to inject more innovation and experimentation into an organisation's strategy. In which case, you might opt for a more emergent approach – or perhaps both a prescriptive and an emergent approach.

- Here is a possible structure based on a prescriptive approach:
  - *Environment.* Work *selectively* through Exhibit 3.1. Only include the parts that are really useful unless you have been instructed otherwise. What are the major background factors influencing the organisation? Who are the customers? Who are the competitors? What is the size, share and growth of the market? And so on.
  - *Competitive resources.* Work *selectively* through Figure 4.9. Only include the parts that are really useful unless you have been instructed otherwise. What are the main tangible and intangible resources? What are the areas of organisational capability? What about core competencies? And so on.
  - *Purpose.* What is the purpose? If the purpose is not stated clearly, then you are entitled to assume a purpose – but you should make this clear in your presentation or report. You may also wish to be critical of the organisation's stated purpose – perhaps because it is unethical or insufficiently conscious of green 'environmental' issues or just simply too vague. Again, you should distinguish in your presentation between what the organisation says and what you have added.
  - *Strategy options.* You may like to demonstrate some of the other basic strategy concepts here – for example, using cost reduction processes or Porter's generic strategies. You are usually awarded higher marks for the use of strategy concepts. However, the good presentation uses such concepts with caution and indicates why they may be weak in practice.
  - *Strategy selection.* Here is the place where you can use your logic and clarity to argue your way through to some recommended strategies. Your choice of your recommended route needs to be clear and well argued – that means a comparison with other options with reasoning and data as to explain why you have chosen your option.
  - *Implementation.* Here is where you can perhaps set out a timetable, a discussion of the strategic change issues, or an estimate of the main resources needed. Remember all your recommendations have costs, including some costs that may be difficult to quantify – associated, for example, with strategic change.

You may judge that an emergent route is more useful. In this case, you will probably start with some of the same areas outlined above. However, your purpose will be more experimental and make recommendations associated with testing in the market place. You may also have a greater range of strategic options and perhaps not select between them but recommend experimenting with various possibilities. The emergent route probably provides fewer opportunities for demonstrating your logical and reasoning skills because it may not make a single recommendation. Bear this in mind when preparing your report – for example, by indicating some other areas of logic or by also undertaking some form of prescriptive analysis to sit alongside an emergent approach.

Some further areas of guidance:

- Remember there is no 'formula' for developing effective strategy.
- Do not write lengthy case introductions, nor pad out your analysis with a lengthy repetition of the material already in the case.
- Be practical: remember the organisation's resources, budgets, time constraints.
- State assumptions, which are acceptable as long as they are sensible.
- Be specific on your recommendations.
- Many universities and colleges require adequate and detailed references to the case material in your report – check with your tutor.
- Answer the question(s) asked.

Overall, the objective of a case is to provide you with an opportunity to apply in practice what has been learnt in theory. Marks therefore come from the application of the theory rather than a repetition of material in the case or a description of the theory. The evidence in the case and the application of logic and theoretical principles to that evidence are the foundation of a good case analysis and presentation.

CASE STUDY 1

Europe's leading airlines: budget strategy or bust?

After government deregulation in the 1990s and an 'open skies' agreement with the USA in 2007, Europe's leading airlines faced new competitive threats and opportunities from the budget airlines: some companies were expected to survive and some go bust. Do Europe's leading airlines need a budget airline strategy in order to survive?

Video and sound summary of this case

'We make money with falling air fares. And we make stinking piles of money with rising air fares. . . . It's scary' – Michael O'Leary, chief executive of the leading budget airline Ryanair in year 2000. Contrast this comment with the fate of three of Europe's leading national airlines – Swiss Air and the Belgian airline Sabena went bankrupt in 2001 and Alitalia was only surviving in 2007 with the help of the Italian government. Some low-cost, budget airlines have also disappeared – for example, Air Madrid, Buzz Air and Air Polonia – in the past few years. This case explores the strategic issues surrounding international airline markets, focusing particularly on Europe. The case begins by describing the three main factors driving strategic change: deregulation and 'open skies'; different models of airline profitability; and market pressures and opportunities. The case then provides some essential background on the European airline market and finally explores the way ahead for airlines.

Threats and opportunities from deregulation and 'open skies'

Between 1993 and 1997, European airline markets were steadily freed from government regulations on competition, pricing and services. This allowed the so-called low-cost airlines to open up new services across Europe. They exploited this opportunity by pricing air travel with fares that were substantially below those of the existing national airlines. The result was that totally new demand was stimulated – for example, weekend breaks in Dublin or Prague were suddenly within the reach of many more people.

Although the leading airlines were hit by this new competition, they still managed to make substantial profits. The reason was that such airlines traditionally earned their major profits from their *long-haul* routes – like Amsterdam to New York or London to Singapore. Their *short-haul* routes, i.e. those inside their home countries or within the European Union (EU), were rather less profitable and frequently incurred a loss. The long-haul market was particularly important for some airlines – see Table 1. Airlines with a high *proportion* of profitable long-haul routes and destinations – like Lufthansa, British Airways (BA) and Air France – were able to earn significant profits from such operations. Companies like Iberia, SAS and Alitalia had proportionately less long-haul turnover – for example, fewer people wanted to fly from Stockholm to New York than from Frankfurt to New York. Hence, the smaller airlines were unable to benefit to the same extent from profitable long-haul route networks.

On the long-haul routes, the major airlines were able to charge high prices because of special deals that existed between individual EU countries and other nations like the USA. In 2002, the European Commission, on behalf of the EU, challenged these agreements, arguing that they were against the open competition rules of the EU's Treaty of Rome. In 2007, a totally new deal was agreed between the EU and the USA. Essentially, it opened up all Europe's major airports to both other European airlines and to the leading US airlines by the year 2009. This led to greater competition and some reduction in airline ticket prices.

Although the open skies policy was fully operational by 2009, there were still major problems for airlines wanting to expand their flight operations. The difficulties arose from two sources. First, airlines could not simply operate from new airports. They had to obtain landing slots at each airport. In practice, there were still restrictions because the airports were only able to handle a specific volume of air traffic. Second, the USA was still operating restrictions on foreign, i.e. non-US, airlines operating inside the USA. This meant that there were still practical restrictions on European airlines attempting to find new routes in America. In practice, European and American airlines were finding ways around this through 'code sharing'. This is explained below.

Table 1 The importance of long-haul business for some leading airlines

Airline	Country of origin	Long-haul share of total turnover for airline (%)	Short-haul share of total turnover for airline (%)
British Airways	UK	63	37
Air France	France	57	43
Lufthansa	Germany	48	52
Alitalia	Italy	35	65
Iberia	Spain	32	68
SAS	Sweden, Denmark and Norway	15	85

Source: derived from annual report and accounts – note that figures are only approximate.

Two different models of airline profitability – *hub and spoke* versus *low cost*

In addition to controlled prices on long-haul routes, the main national carriers operated in other ways that generated profits. Specifically, such airlines worked to a substantially different model for profit generation from the low-cost, budget airlines. Table 2 compares the two main strategies that generated profits: there were some variations of individual airlines, but broadly the table summarises the main differences.

With the 'hub and spoke' strategy of the main international carriers, one of the main benefits comes from the economies of scale that derive from full loads over long distances. However, this will only benefit the main international hubs – like Paris, Frankfurt and London – and therefore only reduce costs for those airlines operating from those airports. In addition, it is complicated and expensive to operate the transfer system for baggage and passengers from the hub to the spoke. The high fixed costs mean that the 'hub and spoke' model is less attractive for the smaller international carriers. This was one of the reasons for the collapse of airlines like Swissair and Sabena: Zurich and Brussels respectively were not main hubs.

More generally, the main international carriers' strategies are essentially high-cost. The provision of on-board meals and other services is complicated to administer and expensive to clear. The frequent flyer programmes, the code sharing and the different classes of seating are all more costly to manage. The high costs mean that it is essential for the airlines to push up their passenger seat usage per flight – called the 'load factor' in airline jargon. In practice load factors are more complex. Table 3 lists the figures for the main European airlines. Notice how the low-cost, budget airlines have higher load factors in general than those of the leading hub and spoke airlines. The high-cost model is only likely to be profitable for the largest international airlines – the smaller international carriers need to merge to achieve the same results. Hence in 2004, Air France and KLM began a merger strategy. BA merged with Iberia in 2011.

Table 2 Two main strategies for airline profitability

The main international carriers such as Air France, Lufthansa and British Airways: hub and spoke model

- Fly 'hub and spoke': bring passengers from long-haul flights in large aircraft into a main airport *hub* – like Frankfurt or London. They then fly them on *spokes* to local destinations – like Munich or Vienna in the case of Frankfurt, or Edinburgh and Paris in the case of London.
- Form a 'code sharing' agreement with other international airlines – such that connecting flights can be booked seamlessly and loads shared: the 'Star Alliance' of Lufthansa, Continental, South African Airways and SAS Scandinavian is one example. The role of the three big airline networks cannot be over-estimated and membership is worth more to some airlines than to others. For example, Lufthansa is at the centre of Star Alliance and generates significant revenue (and profit) from its nodal position, especially from related businesses such as maintenance (Lufthansa Technik), catering (Skychefs) and market research/business advice (Lufthansa Consulting).
- Offer full-service: assigned seats, meals, etc. Arguably important on long-haul flights but less on short-haul ones where food and comfort matter less.
- Frequent flyer clubs to reward those who fly regularly with the same airline: useful but expensive to administer.
- Operate extensive business class facilities with their higher prices and profit margins.
- Operate different aircraft for the short- and long-haul destinations: more expensive to administer because the designs, servicing and maintenance are not standardised.
- Exploit government protection and limitations on routes: see above.

Budget carriers like Ryanair, easyJet and Air Berlin: the low-cost model

- Simple fare structure based on one-way tickets: easier and cheaper to operate internet booking and pricing and allows for higher pricing to maximise revenue from the last few available seats.
- Only fly point-to-point: there are no connecting flights. This means that budget airlines avoid delays that come from making connections, the extra baggage handling costs from linking flights, the more complicated route structures from such connections, etc.
- Rapid turnaround at airports – typically 25 minutes – on the principle that an aircraft only earns profits when it is flying and incurs cost when it is on the ground.
- Fly frequently with the emphasis on reliability: punctual timing, few cancellations, few lost bags – often a better track record than the long-haul operators.
- Fill the aircraft using dynamic pricing – low in the early days and rising as it fills. Note that most airlines, including the international carriers, now use this approach.
- Country focus – establish a profitable base with several routes in one country, then move on to another country.
- Use airports that have low landing fees – even if this means that the airport is further away from population centres. Note that not all low-cost carriers follow this strategy consistently.
- No food or other in-flight services – unless paid for on the flight. Clearing up food and waste paper delays the turnaround.
- Subcontract non-essential services like ground handling and often maintenance.
- Employ one model of aircraft for the whole fleet to reduce training costs, the stockholding cost of spare parts and so on.
- Few job restrictions plus extra pay for achieving efficiencies – even pilots in theory can help with the baggage.
- Operate high-density seating: e.g. Ryanair were reported to have taken out one mid-cabin lavatory to put in extra seats.

Note: The low-cost, budget carriers do *not* compromise on safety: companies like Ryanair and easyJet have an excellent safety record.

In June 2011, British Airways charged £149 for a morning flight from London Heathrow to Milan Malpensa Airport for a midweek date in July 2011 with a return one week later with 23kg luggage. The price from Ryanair – including a credit card charge and 15kg luggage – for a similar flight from London Stansted to Milan Bergamo was £124 for the same dates. BA's price was much closer to Ryanair's than similar flights in 2008.

With the low-cost, budget airline strategy, the profit position is much simpler and clearer. Low-price flights have been available for many years throughout Europe: the holiday charter air companies offered them by taking groups of tourists on holiday using special flights and dedicated aircraft. However, such flights were not available 'seat only' to the general public at scheduled times. This all changed with the *deregulation* of the European airline market in the 1990s. For example, in October 2001 a typical economy ticket on a scheduled flight from London Gatwick to Amsterdam cost $250 on BA and $170 on easyJet – but see the comment on the availability of tickets later in this section. The difficulty of BA and all the other leading European airlines is that they were unable to match the budget airline prices and still make a profit just by cutting out newspapers and coffee. But this pricing picture had changed by 2011: BA either cancelled some routes where it simply could not compete or reduced its fares on other routes, partly at least to fill the aircraft. For example, the easyJet price was $121 and the BA price was $145 on the same route. These prices in 2011 included the new higher tax rates on air travel introduced by national governments in an attempt to curb air travel and protect the environment.

For the budget airlines, low *price* itself is not a sustainable competitive advantage. However, lower *costs* than competitors are an advantage – as long as they can be maintained. The difficulty is that such a route to competitive advantage is well known. For example, Ryanair originally copied this approach from Southwest Airlines in the USA in the early 1990s: 'We went to look at Southwest. It was like the road to Damascus. This was the way to make Ryanair work' – Michael O'Leary, chief executive of Ryanair.

In spite of the attraction of low-cost strategies, it should be acknowledged that the level of service on the European budget airlines might be barely tolerable for some passengers. In addition, some European airports are far from tourist and business destinations. However, easyJet and Air Berlin have a deliberate policy of flying to main airports, even if the landing fees are higher. The aim is to attract business travellers, particularly those who need to save money such as small business managers and entrepreneurs. Moreover, the budget airlines often only offer the very low prices on the seats that they have difficulty in filling – just try to book a low-price seat during a main holiday weekend! Perhaps there is not so much competitive advantage on costs over the leading European carriers after all.

Business models: hub-and-spoke versus low cost

Looking at the data in Table 3, it is possible to draw the conclusion that the hub-and-spoke model has severe limitations: many of the international airlines in the table using this business model were loss-making in 2009. However, Turkish Airlines was profitable in spite of operating a hub-and-spoke model for some of its flights out of Istanbul. Equally, there is no simple relationship in the table between load factors and profitability: for example, Lufthansa was more profitable than Air France/KLM in spite of having a lower load factor. In practice, airline profitability is related to load factors, but there are also other considerations that impact on profitability.

Airlines have high fixed costs and often also expensive leasing payments on their aircraft. This makes them heavily dependent on high traffic volumes: the load factor measures this. But these same high costs also make the airlines highly vulnerable to changes in the economic cycle. Another problem for airline profitability relates to fuel costs. Back in 2008, fuel costs were around $61 per barrel. These rose to $75 in 2010 and are projected to rise further to $95 in 2011. This matters because fuel accounted for around 26 per cent of total airline costs in 2009. Some airlines hedge against fuel price rises, but this is not a long-term solution.

In order to overcome these profit pressures, the main strategy of the hub-and-spoke airlines was to take this further by co-operating or merging their services more deeply. This has taken two forms. The first has been a simple merger of airlines, such as that between Air France and KLM and that now agreed

Table 3 Comparing selected European-based airlines – budget airlines growing faster and more profitably

Airline	Country	Revenue $ million, year 2009	Operating profit (Loss) $ million 2009	Load factor (%)	Passengers (millions)	Strategic comment
Air France/KLM	France	38,262	(1729)	80.7	71	Air France/KLM merger improved efficiencies. But Paris/CDG base also used by budget airlines
Lufthansa	Germany	31,924	388	77.7	56	Picking up strategies from budget airlines – flexible pay, moved to internet ticket sales, etc. Acquired Swiss International 2006
British Airways	UK	12,057	(348)	78.5	32	Merger with Iberia not included in data – badly affected by industrial problems
Iberia	Spain	6,317	(665)	79.8	26	Many budget airlines offer cheap flights to Spanish destinations
SAS	Sweden, Denmark and Norway	6,256	(429)	71.6	21	Competition from Norwegian, Ryanair and easyJet to new destinations in Denmark and Sweden
Turkish Airlines	Turkey	4,659	479	70.9	25	Possibly fastest growing national airline
Alitalia	Italy	4,183	(392)	65.4	22	Has been under severe financial pressures for years
Virgin Atlantic	UK	3,679	37	82.1	6	Singapore Airlines own 49%
Austrian Airlines	Austria	2,951	(421)	74.0	10	Almost bankrupt in 2003. New strategy in 2004–2006 to focus on serving Eastern European destinations – Hungary, etc. Close relationship with Lufthansa
Aeroflot	Russia	2,849	359	69.5	9	Some protection from government
Finnair	Finland	2,708	(178)	75.9	7	Strong northern European competition
Some selected budget airlines						
Air Berlin	Germany	4,703	41	77.3	28	Not a 'true' budget airline – seats can be booked, free food, etc.
easyJet	UK	4,246	96	86.9	45	Stronger focus on main airports than its main rival Ryanair
Ryanair	Ireland	4,021	541	82.0	66	Remarkable growth in profit and passengers. But this includes passengers paying virtually nothing for a trip except for government taxes, etc.
Norwegian	Norway	1,259	98	78.0	11	Large network based around Scandinavia
Transavia	Netherlands	921	20	81.5	5	Budget airline subsidiary of Air France/KLM
Vueling	Spain	862	102	73.7	8	Spanish-based fast growing budget fleet
Germanwings	Germany	831	34	80.0	7	Budget airline linked with Lufthansa

Source: based on ATW World Airline Report 2010.

for 2011 between BA and Iberia. The benefits of sharing overheads, systems, aircraft financing and related costs are simple and clear.

The second form has been by developing and operating 'code sharing' agreements. Essentially, airlines around the world agree to co-operate with regard to the booking systems and seamless flight schedules. Thus flights are linked together to offer a more complete service. There are three main code sharing systems at present:

- *Sky Team* – including Delta and Air France/KLM. It shares around 460 million passengers annually.
- *Star Alliance* – including Lufthansa, United and US Airways and Singapore Airlines. It shares around 500 million passengers annually.
- *One World* – including American Airlines, BA, Iberia and Cathay Pacific. It carries around 350 million passengers annually.

There are some hints that the airlines would like to move from code sharing to a strategy of full merger. But these issues are subject to substantial regulatory investigation by the national competition authorities because they may substantially reduce competition. Most commentators expect any mergers to take many years.

One airline that has been determined to avoid a merger is the British-based airline Virgin Atlantic. It was profitable through a strategy of cutting back services as market demand fell, rather than seeking mergers. It operated code sharing agreements with some other airlines, but these were limited. Its Chairman, Sir Richard Branson, campaigned vigorously against the BA merger with Iberia and the possible extension of a further merger with American Airlines. But he was unsuccessful: BA finally merged with Iberia in January 2011. The problem for Branson was that, if such mergers went ahead over time, then this could leave his airline isolated. His additional problem was that Virgin Atlantic was 49 per cent owned by Singapore Airlines who had bought their share on a high valuation some years earlier. Singapore Airlines sold this stake to the American airline, Delta, in 2012 with the new alliance combining on some routes into London from 2013. Virgin Airlines made substantial losses on its business operations in 2010, 2012 and 2013.

European airline markets: customers and market segmentation

The European airline market can be broadly divided into two main market segments – business customers and leisure/domestic customers. Roughly 80 per cent of all customers fall into the latter category – they are travelling for holiday or domestic reasons such as study or visiting relations. They are important to fill the aircraft but do not represent the most profitable segment of the airline market. According to Michael O'Leary of Ryanair, 'In this business, it's low cost that wins. Ninety-nine per cent of people want the cheapest price. They don't want awards for the inflight magazine or the best coffee. The brand? Who cares? It has to be safe, on time and cheap. It's a bus service, it's transport.'

The other 20 per cent are business customers. They are paid for by their companies and are engaged on business-related activities. It is this latter group that is usually prepared to pay for full-fare tickets and travel in greater comfort. For the airlines, the business customers are therefore the most profitable. Given the higher profitability of business customers, one logical conclusion would be to segment the airline market further, targeting business customers in particular. This was done in 2006 by several companies launching business-class only airline services from various European destinations to the USA. However, all but one of these airlines had collapsed by 2009: Silverjet, Maxjet and Eos all disappeared mainly because of cost pressures from rising fuel prices. The only remaining dedicated business class airline is OpenSkies. It is owned by BA and operates daily services between Paris, New York and Washington.

Perhaps the most important strategic feature of the European airline market is the lack of strong market segments beyond the two above. This makes it difficult to operate dedicated niche strategies that target these segments with special prices, services and related activities. The lack of such segments has made it easier for the budget airlines to attack the leading European companies.

Strategic response to the competitive threat of budget airlines

In the face of the significant threat to their European routes, the response of the leading European airlines has been somewhat inconsistent. For example, BA decided in 1999 to launch its own low-cost airline, called *Go*. This was duly set up in 2000. Then in 2001, BA decided that its new strategy was to withdraw from the low-cost end of the market and concentrate on business passengers. The company sold *Go* to a management buyout in mid-2001. By the end of that year, BA announced a new strategy. It was restructuring its European airlines on low-cost strategic lines, but would not be setting up a separate airline. BA's strategy was to reduce its fleet costs by a series of measures that were not so different from the budget airline strategies.

In 2011, BA merged with the Spanish national airline, Iberia, to form the International Airlines Group (IAG). The merged group aimed to cut costs further by combining services, negotiating with trade unions to reduce the workforce and introducing new working practices. By 2013, the BA part of the group was back in profit but Iberia was still making losses.

Initially, Lufthansa's response to the budget airlines was different but equally defensive. Its immediate strategy was to offer low prices on its own domestic routes and to match Germania, one of its low-cost rivals. Ryanair then increased its presence in the German market and engaged in a very public battle with Lufthansa. This prompted a warning to Lufthansa from the German public competition office about selling seats below costs. In late 2001, Lufthansa withdrew its services from some UK/German routes where it faced heavy competition. In addition, the airline mounted a legal challenge to Ryanair's German advertising that called on Germans not to let 'Lufthansa strip you down to your underpants'. Ryanair obtained 1.5 million German passengers in 2002 and around 12.5 million by 2013. Finally, Lufthansa set up a new partially owned subsidiary – Germanwings – as its own low-cost airline, to benefit from German demand.

In addition to its budget airline strategies, Lufthansa acquired two smaller rival companies, Austrian Airlines and Swiss International Airlines. This had the benefit of delivering some additional economies of scale and scope to Lufthansa. But the company was still under considerable cost pressures in 2014.

The Dutch airline KLM responded to the budget airline challenge by setting up its own low-cost airline, Buzz. Subsequently, it sold the airline to Ryanair in 2004 who closed some of the routes and merged the rest into Ryanair. At the same time, KLM was also supporting two other low-cost airlines based in its home country – Martinair and Transavia. But the EU was not entirely happy with such arrangements because they had the potential to reduce market competition (an issue unresolved at the time of writing this case).

During this period, KLM merged its main company with Air France in order to save overhead costs. However, this merger was complicated and the full benefits only emerged after 2007. Air France itself had been concerned when its French competitor, Air Lib, collapsed in France. This released some air landing slots at Paris/Charles De Gaulle airport. easyJet attempted to take all these slots, but was only awarded a portion of them. SAS, Scandinavian Airlines, set up a series of deals with low-cost rivals Maersk in Denmark and Skyways in Sweden. However, these arrangements broke EU competition rules and needed to be re-negotiated. Around this time, Ryanair began operating budget flights to Scandinavian destinations. Many of Europe's leading airlines have thus far been unable to withstand the strategic challenge of the budget carriers in any substantive way.

In March 2002, a consortium of the leading European airlines launched its own website (www.opodo.co.uk) to sell airline tickets cheaply at the last minute and fill remaining aircraft capacity. It has proved a significant success in terms of offering a way for the major airlines to reduce booking costs and offer special deals to fill their aircraft. In addition, all airlines have now developed their individual extensive online internet booking facilities. The winners have been the ordinary customers; the losers have been the ticket agents who used to handle the bookings. The airlines themselves have gained no competitive advantage from such a move since they all offer the same facility.

Conclusion

In 2001, Ryanair and easyJet carried 7.4 million passengers and 7.1 million passengers. In 2013, the numbers were 82 million and 60 million, respectively – a remarkable increase by any standards. However, at least some of this increase had been achieved by opening up new market demand, rather than stealing passengers from the older airlines. Importantly, the increase had been undertaken profitably in contrast to the performance of most of the existing rivals. The low-cost airline business model was certainly viable.

The strategic growth issue for the budget airlines was whether demand would continue to increase – either through new short-haul destinations if available or, perhaps, through entering the long-haul market. Either strategy would need to be undertaken against a backdrop of rising fuel prices and also the increased willingness of governments to raise taxes on air tickets, thus pushing up prices and reducing demand.

The strategic issue for the older airlines was how to return to profitability on a long-term basis. In addition to the same cost and price pressures as the low-cost airlines, the older airlines faced another problem. Some of the Middle Eastern airlines were determined to increase their market shares on long-haul routes. For example, Emirates was reported to have around 60 Airbus A380 SuperJumbo Jets on order. This would significantly increase carrying capacity on such routes with all its implications for demand, pricing and increased competition. Moreover, the evidence from the USA was not encouraging. Many US airlines, with the exception of SouthWest which followed a budget strategy, had been in and out of bankruptcy for many years as a result of deregulation and excess airline capacity. Merger and acquisition were possible strategies for such airlines but they were not easy to achieve.

Perhaps the older airlines could learn more from Ryanair and easyJet?

 This case was written by Richard Lynch from published sources only.* The author would like to express his thanks to Professor Thomas Lawton, The Open University, for his comments on an earlier version of this case.

Case questions

1 Why is the development of strategic management important for the major European airlines?

2 Using the concept of the three major stages of strategic management, identify the possible main elements that might appear in a strategic plan for a low-cost airline.

3 What sustainable competitive advantages do the leading European airlines possess?

4 What strategies are needed for the main European airlines to survive? Can they learn from the budget airlines?

STRATEGIC PROJECT

Some of the world's airlines face severe financial pressures – for example, Air India and SAS at the time of writing this case. However, other airlines have managed to cope with such problems – for example, Singapore Airlines and Jet Airways of India. Why are some airlines more successful than others? What strategies have they followed? What external circumstances have helped them? You can obtain information to explore this by searching the websites of the major airlines. Then use the issues explored in this case to make a more general search of trends in airline passengers, attitudes of governments to competition, and fuel price pressures.

Note

* This case was written by author from numerous sources including: ATW World Airline Reports 2008, 2009 and 2010. *The Economist*, Special Survey, 12 June 1993; Annual Report and Accounts of Ryanair, easyJet, British Airways, Lufthansa, etc.; also from some selected *Financial Times* articles. For reasons of space, only the most recent articles are listed below. Earlier sources are listed in full in the sixth edition of *Strategic Management*. *Financial Times*: 8 June 2011, p 22; 21 October 2011, p 15; 8 January 2012, p 18; 16 January 2012, p 18; 31 January 2012, p 21; 7 February 2012, p 17; 9 February 2012, p 18; 21 February 2012, p 21; 1 March 2012, p 18; 5 June 2012, p 14; 7 December 2012, p 11; 6 December 2013, p 24; 19 December 2012, p 18; 28 February 2014, pp 16 & 21.

CASE STUDY 2

Global beer and lager: exploring strategies in a mature market

Although the annual global market for beer was massive in 2013, it was only growing slowly at just around 3 per cent per year. Moreover, it was dominated by four companies with a combined market share of over 50 per cent. These are all characteristics of a mature market. What are the best strategies for companies in such markets?

Video and sound summary of this case

Consolidation in world beer markets – size, growth and share

The world market for beers and lagers was valued at a massive $140–210 billion in 2012. Customers worldwide consumed 2,000 million hectolitres of beer and lager. The leading countries by production are shown in Figure 1: apart from German exports, beer is mostly consumed in the home country. It will be self-evident why the world's largest brewers have all been targeting the Chinese market over the past few years. The problem with the Chinese market is that profit margins are very low because beer is relatively cheap.

Over the 13 years to 2013, global beer markets followed a consolidation strategy. The number of independent brewing companies reduced and their share of the total market grew. The world's five largest brewers accounted for 19 per cent of sales in year 2000. Twelve years later, the world's four largest brewers accounted for 50 per cent of world sales and 75 per cent of global profits. The fifth brewer, the UK-based Scottish and Newcastle, was finally acquired and broken up by two of the other four in 2009. The consolidation strategy is typical of mature markets where a few firms come to dominate an industry and consolidate their market shares by acquisition and merger.

World beer markets are becoming increasingly competitive with companies developing differing strategies for different parts of the world.

In the nine years 2005 to 2013, compound annual growth in beer sales worldwide was around 3 per cent. But this masked a decline in developed world markets of minus 3.5 per cent and a growth in developing markets of plus 7 per cent. The

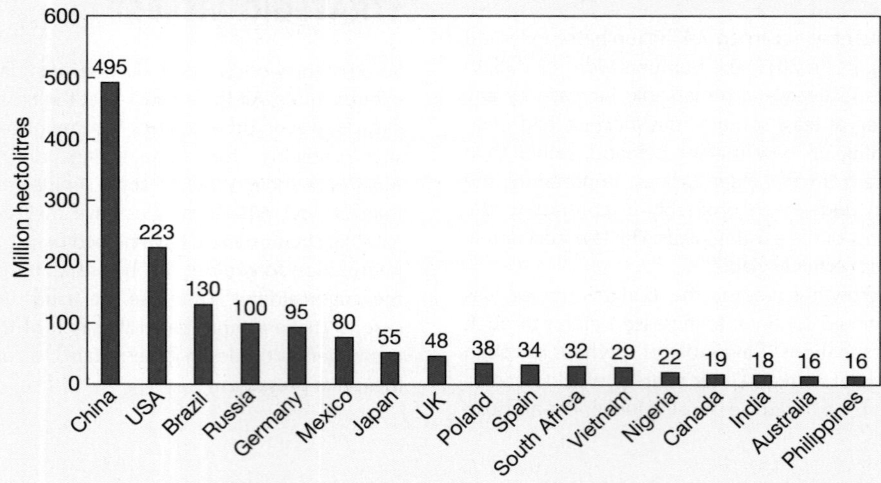

Figure 1 World beer production in 20 leading countries in 2012

Source: author from various industry estimates.

developing market growth level was higher than some other food and beverage categories and therefore attractive for companies seeking new opportunities.

The largest market growth areas were in China and Africa. Eastern Europe showed substantial growth in the early years but declined towards the end of the above period due to the reduced incomes of customers and the increased regulation and taxes from some governments. Some of the African growth came about with customers switching from the illegal brewing of alcohol to the purchase of legal drinks from the large brewers. Overall therefore, the relatively low level of growth worldwide obscured some significant differences in growth in individual countries and regions.

Such market differences were also reflected in the different relative strengths of the four main brewers in different regions of the world. For example, AB Inbev was particularly strong in North America – see Figure 2. In this case, the main reason was that the company owned Budweiser, the world's largest individual beer by sale volume. By contrast, Heineken was much more concentrated in Europe.

In terms of market share, consolidation was taking place in the world brewing industry through a combination of acquisitions and mergers: for example, 280 deals were completed between the years 2001 and 2006 with a total transaction value of $80 billion. Table 1 shows the most active players.

In 2011, the four leading world brewers were:

- *Anheuser Busch InBev* – this was formed from the European brewing company InterBrew, the South American company AmBev and America's largest brewer Anheuser Busch in 2008. InterBrew owns Stella Artois (Belgium), Labatts (Canada), Beck's (Germany) and Whitbread (UK) as a result of a series of takeovers in the 1990s. Brazil's *AmBev* – the market leader in South America – dominates the Brazilian market and is also strong in other South American markets: its main brand is Brahma. Brahma has now been launched worldwide as a result of the merger and positioned as a premium brand – higher quality and higher profitability. The claimed financial benefits of this merger are considered later in this section. In 2008, InBev merged with Anheuser Busch to form the world's largest brewer with the aim of further enhancing profitability in the combined group. Anheuser Busch was (and remains) the largest brewer in the USA with its flagship brand being the well-known Budweiser.
- *SABMiller* – whose activities are described in more detail in Case 3. Three major purchases have transformed the group in recent years – Miller Brewing in the USA in 2002, Grupo Empresarial Bavaria in 2005 in Latin America and Grolsch, the Dutch brewer, in 2008. However, US interests were proving difficult following heavy competition from Anheuser-Busch, as explored in Case 3.
- *Heineken* – a family company from the Netherlands that has moved onto the world stage. Its main brands are Heineken and Amstel. It is now beginning to build these into world, premium brands. Its activities are explored in Case 3 that follows.
- *Carlsberg* – controlled by a Danish charitable trust that has also been highly active in terms of acquisitions. The company has strong interests in some Western European countries, particularly Scandinavia. It has also developed its interests in some Eastern European countries. Much of this development has again been through acquisition.

Figure 2 provides some more detail on each company, especially with regard to strengths in regions of the world.

To some extent, company size matters in brewing. There are economies of scale in production and distribution. There are also scale benefits from building and promoting global brands, especially those that lend themselves to a premium price

Table 1 How the world beer market consolidated between 2000 and 2006

Company	Home country	World beer sales 2000 (million hectolitres)	Company	World beer sales 2006 (million hectolitres)
Anheuser Busch	US	120	InBev – see text	190
Interbrew	Belgium	76	SABMiller – see text	136
Heineken	Netherlands	74	Anheuser-Busch – combined with InBev in 2008	132
South African Breweries	South Africa	56	Heineken	122
AmBev	Brazil	56	Carlsberg	92
Miller Brewing	US	54	Scottish & Newcastle	50
Carlsberg	Denmark	47	Asahi	35
Scottish & Newcastle	UK	36	Kirin	33
Asahi	Japan	35		
Kirin	Japan	33		

Source: author, from trade estimates and company annual reports.

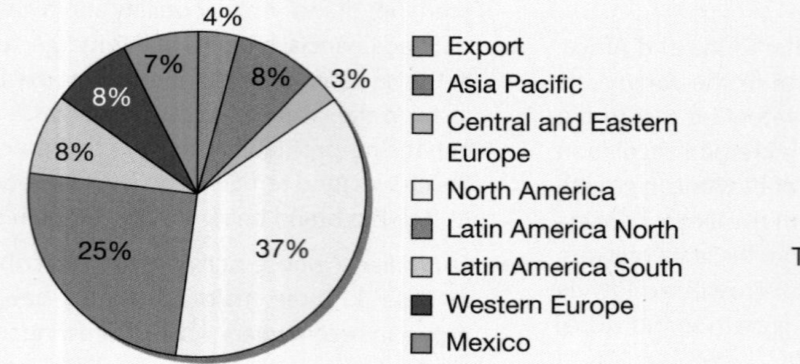

AB Inbev

Total turnover 2013:
US$ million 45,483

Total sales volume 2013:
million hectolitres 425

SABMiller 2013: Source of turnover

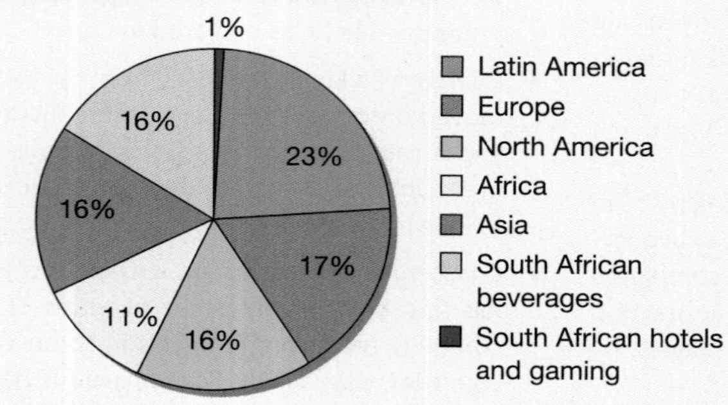

SABMiller

Total turnover 2013:
US$ million 34,487

Total sales volume 2013:
million hectolitres 242

Heineken 2013: Source of turnover

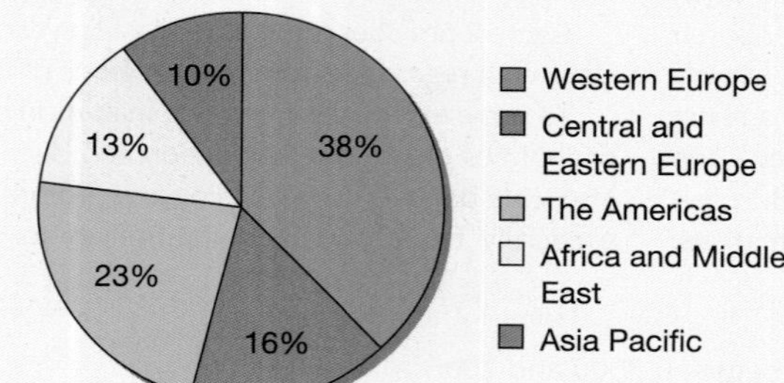

Heineken

Total turnover 2013:
US$ million 19,203

Total sales volume 2013:
million hectolitres 178

Carlsberg 2013: Source of turnover

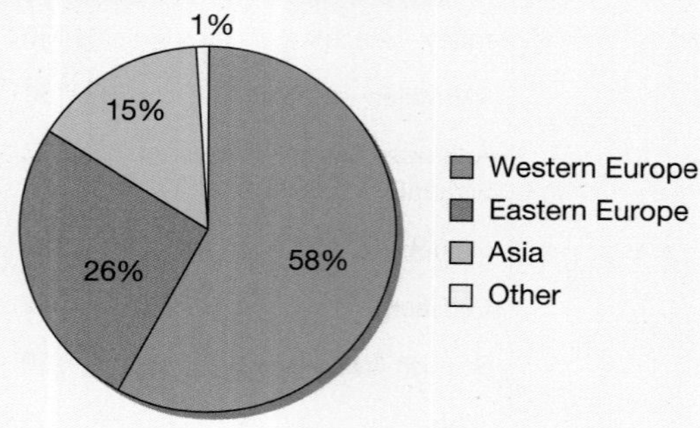

Carlsberg

Total turnover 2013:
US$ million 12,200
Total sales volume:
million hectolitres 139

Figure 2 Comparing the source of sales of the world's four leading brewers

Note: The Heineken and Carlsberg sources of turnover have been slightly simplified by the author.

Source: author from individual company report and accounts.

positioning – higher profit margins, customer loyalty. Companies like Heineken, Carlsberg and Anheuser-Busch (A-H) have worked hard to develop their world beer brands. The biggest world brand is Budweiser from AB InBev. It is the largest seller in its home country of America and it also has significant sales in other parts of the globe (but is not necessarily dominant).

Importantly for a mature market and unlike some other mature markets, there was no major excess production capacity in the world brewing industry. In some regional markets, the main brewers were actually building new plant, while in others they were closing down old plant and transferring production to more efficient locations.

To illustrate how size can matter in brewing strategy, InterBrew and AmBev estimated that there were substantial benefits from their merger in 2004 to form the company InBev. The company claimed that the combined group would be able to generate $350 million of annual cost savings per annum 'through a combination of technical, procurement and other general and administrative *cost savings*'. There would also be commercial savings of $175 million per annum. The company also obtained similar scale benefits from its later merger with Anheuser Busch.

AB Inbev was not the only brewer engaged in consolidation strategy in the industry. There have been a whole string of other mergers and acquisitions over the past few years. In 2007, Carlsberg and Heineken made a successful bid for one of the remaining major brewers: the UK-based Scottish and Newcastle (S&N). In 2011, SABMiller acquired the Fosters lager brand outside Europe for US$10 billion. In 2012, AB Inbev effectively took control of the large Mexican brewer, Grupo Modelo, for US$20 billion.

Finally, large size is not the only strategy in brewing. Some small companies can also be profitable: the *microbreweries* are described later in this case.

Global brand strategy: major strengths in local beer premium brands

From the visible levels of marketing support, it might be thought that the main strengths of the four major world brewers were in their premium global brands – Table 2 lists some of the major names. However, according to SABMiller, the international beer brands accounted for only just over 6 per cent of world consumption in 2009. Each of the major brewers has a whole series of brands that are largely confined to individual countries.

To take one example, Heineken owns the following brands in the UK: Newcastle Brown Ale, Strongbow (cider), John Smith, Kronenbourg 1664, Bulmers (cider), Amstel, Foster's and Heineken itself. In Ireland and around the world, its brands include Murphy's Stout. In Germany, it owns 31 brands – too many to list here. In China, it has minority stakes in breweries involving nine brands including Tiger. In India, it owns minority stakes in breweries selling beers with the Tiger and Kingfisher brand names. In Russia, its brands include the market leader, Baltika, In addition, there are also six other national brands and seven regional brands from its breweries spread across Russia.

Table 2 Leading brewing companies and their brands

	Home country	Selected international brand names
AB Inbev	USA and Belgium	Budweiser, Stella Artois, Becks
SABMiller	South Africa but HQ in London	Pilsner Urquell, Peroni, Miller, Grolsch
Heineken	Holland	Heineken, Amstel, Cruzcampo
Carlsberg	Denmark	Carlsberg, Tuborg, Kronenbourg 1664

Source: author from annual reports and accounts.

What is the reason for this proliferation of branding in the world beer market? Although it can be defined as a *world* market, it is in many respects *local*. Beer still remains local in many aspects of its strategy: for example, beer tastes vary around the world; different governments have different laws with regard to alcohol consumption; distribution in some countries is mainly through bars whereas in other countries the grocery supermarket has become the dominant seller. To quote the Chief Executive of the SABMiller group, Graham Mackay: 'Beer is a very local product. It's a local industry: brands are local, distribution systems are local; and customs are local, so we don't try to exert day-to-day operating management over every company from [our] London [head-quarters].' This aspect of strategy is explored further in the next section of this case.

In addition, urbanisation in many countries coupled with increasing wealth has meant that there is a significant demand for branded beers rather than home-brewed versions. Increased wealth has especially increased the consumption of branded *local premium* beers. Such beers have premium packaging, positioning and quality, but they are sold at prices closer to the local incomes of a particular country compared with the higher prices of the leading international brands like Heineken and Budweiser. This may mean that the international brands may be out of the price range of some local people (though the author of this case has personally observed the global brand Heineken on promotion in poor townships in Cape Town, South Africa). Whatever the pricing issues, the big global brewers were keen to promote their global brands in the long run. However, they recognised that this would take time and substantial investment.

Profitability, pricing and competition

Profitability

From a profit generation perspective, the world brewing industry has two extremes: the very large brewers and the very small brewers.

First, there are the large international breweries that have substantial economies of scale and scope, including the benefits of branding. One limiting factor here is the cost of transport.

It is expensive to transport heavy liquids (like beer) very long distances. In addition, some beers have a relatively short shelf life and lengthy transport times may shorten their time on final sale. Hence, many international breweries have regional production in countries with large geographical distances. In addition, countries often have different regional tastes in beer and are therefore better served by regional breweries.

Second, there are some very small breweries that often exist only in small communities: the *microbreweries*. These suffer because they do not have economies of scale. However, they do benefit from not having the high overhead costs of the international brewing companies. Microbreweries usually charge premium prices. Their products are positioned as exclusive, high quality, local brews and they often have high alcoholic strength.

In between these two extremes, the mid-size brewers may still be profitable. But they have tended to be acquired over time by the large international breweries.

Pricing and competition

Partly because of the strong brand advertising strategies of the leading world brewers, there was only limited price competition in the market place. However, there was some price competition – through local promotions, in-store pricing and similar strategies. Brewers also market local premium beers that met local demand but were still priced below the major international brands, as explained above.

Nevertheless, price competition was relatively subdued. Each of the main world brewers had similar cost structures to its rivals. There were some limited local advantages in some cases but low-cost coupled with low-price strategies were not generally pursued in the industry. The main world brewers did not co-operate on pricing strategy: that would be illegal. But they did watch each other closely and matched prices within each area of the market place. Importantly, they did not undermine each other on price in general terms.

More generally, there was another form of price competition. This took place *inside* the individual brewing companies like SABMiller, Carlsberg or Heineken. The large numbers of national, regional and local brands marketed by each of the main brewing companies meant that such brands competed against each other within the same company. The strategy here was for a company to offer brands in every conceivable niche and segment of the market. The outcome has been a *multi-brand strategy* for each of the major world brewing companies. Perhaps this goes some way to explaining why their world brands only accounted for 6 per cent of world consumption in 2009.

Case questions

1 What strategies are the major brewing companies adopting? Why?

2 What lessons, if any, can other firms in mature industries learn from the world brewing industry?

Note

* The references and evidence for this case are the same as for Case 3, which is the next case in this text.

CASE STUDY 3

SABMiller: South Africa goes quietly global

Over the past 15 years, South African Breweries (SAB) has transformed itself from a local South African holding company into the world's second-largest brewer of beer and lager. This case examines how it has quietly extended its global reach and faced up to some problems along the way.

Video and sound summary of this case

The birth of SABMiller: the South African Breweries

During the apartheid years, political sanctions made it impossible for South African Breweries (SAB) to move outside its home country, in spite of the profits from its dominant home market position. SAB therefore ploughed its profits back into a wide range of home businesses: clothing, retailing, textiles, plate glass and fruit juice were all investment targets. After sanctions were lifted, it began to move overseas. To fund the overseas expansion described below, SAB had sold the majority of its non-beer South African activities by 2001.

Even in the early 1990s, SAB made the important strategic decision that it needed to build from what it knew best - the brewing of beer and lager. The company already had the major share of its home market for beer with brands like Castle Lager. The company had the expertise to exploit the substantial economies of scale available in the brewing industry in brewing, bottling and distribution. In the early 1990s, there was little further scope in South Africa for SAB but it could see opportunities worldwide, where the brewing industry was still fragmented.

Beginning with Castle Lager in South Africa, SABMiller has built a worldwide group of brands over the last ten years.

SAB: the first international steps

Back in 1993, SAB made its first international acquisition. The brand was Dreher, Hungary's largest brewer. This was at the time when central Europe was moving away from domination by Russia and was beginning to privatise its former state enterprises. The opportunity was there for SAB to seize using its substantial South African profits. SAB subsequently admitted that it learnt some lessons from this acquisition. 'We made some mistakes when we first went in. You could argue that with our first acquisition in Europe, which was Hungary, we made serial mistakes. By the time we had got through a few of them, we knew what approach to take, what things to look out for, what things to do quickly and how to prioritise,' explained Graham Mackay, chief executive of SAB some years later.

Consistent with the vision, SAB's next step in 1994 was to move into the People's Republic of China in a joint venture with a Chinese government-owned brewery company. SAB took a 49 per cent stake and carefully and quietly began building its presence in that important country long before it became a target for Western companies. In the same year, SAB used its regional strengths and network contacts in Africa to begin moves into Tanzania, Mozambique and Zambia. All these moves were relatively modest and funded essentially from its existing profit stream.

In spite of its early problems in Hungary, SAB saw further opportunities in central Europe. In the period 1995–1999, it acquired leading breweries in Poland, Romania, Slovakia and Russia itself. Amongst these acquisitions was the Czech company Pilsner Urquel which had 44 per cent of its national market. SAB paid $629 million for the company. The problem was that the Czech brewer made only $17.2 million profit in 1998. Such low profitability would not support the purchase price without drastic action being taken. SAB's strategy was to take Pilsner Urquell back to its former brand glory in central Europe. It would modernise the plant, raise prices to position the product as a premium beer and use the central location of the Czech Republic as the springboard of all its central European operations. 'This is right on strategy,' said the chief executive, Graham Mackay. 'But not the end of the story. Czech brewing has a great reputation in eastern and central Europe and Pilsner Urquell the greatest of all. But there is still room for further consolidation [in the brewing industry] and we are here to participate.'

SAB becomes a world company

By 2000, SAB had played its strategy well. It had picked up dominant brands in central Europe, where it could exploit its core competencies. It had moved into markets with great growth potential - other parts of Africa and China. It had even bought a regional brewer in another country with great long-term protential - India. SAB acquired the Narang brewery,

Table 1 Results over 12 years of SABMiller's global expansion ($ million)

	2002	2003	2004	2005	2006	2007	2008	2009	2010	2011	2012	2013
Turnover	4,363	8,984	12,645	14,543	17,081	20,645	23,828	25,302	26,350	28,311	31,388	34,487
Profit for the year	293	296	645	1,141	1,440	1,649	2,023	1,881	1,910	2,408	4,221	3,274
Total assets	5,691	12,250	13,799	15,228	27,115	28,736	36,082	31,628	37,499	39,114	55,928	56,294
Earnings per share (US cents per share)	48.7	54	77.6	103.2	105	110.2	134.9	125.2	122.6	152.8	266.6	205.9

Source: author, compiled from SAB Miller company accounts.

even though it regarded the Indian market as highly regulated and immature. SABMiller also revised its joint venture relationship with the local Indian company, Shaw Wallace Breweries. The combined joint venture would become the second-largest brewing company in the Indian market, behind Heineken.

Although the company was building for the future, SAB was having difficulty in completing its global ambitions. Its rivals – Heineken, InterBrew and Carlsberg – dominated much of Western Europe. Anheuser-Busch with its Budweiser brand was steadily building its global status. Then, over the period 2001–2003, SAB made three major strategic moves:

1 *Central America*. In 2001 it acquired a 58 per cent interest in breweries in Honduras and El Salvador at a cost of $500 million.
2 *North America*. It spent $5.6 billion in 2002 to acquire the US brewer Miller from Altria (the former Philip Morris tobacco conglomerate). Miller was the second-largest brand in the USA. But its share was only 17 per cent against the market leader, Budweiser, which had 49 per cent. The market was described as being 'crowded and low-growth' and the Miller brand was described as 'ailing'. SAB was not buying success.
3 *Western Europe*. It spent $270 million to acquire the Italian lager company Peroni. This was the first time that SAB had moved into the more mature markets of Western Europe.

The largest of these acquisitions was the purchase of Miller. The company recognised this by changing its name to *SABMiller*. It had made the purchase partly to move into the largest beer market in the world – the USA. However, the company was forced to admit after six months that the problems were worse than it had anticipated on the purchase. The existing Miller chief executive who had been allowed to remain was sacked and a SAB executive moved in. 'We went into Miller with our eyes open. It will be a long turnaround, but we have no doubt we will fix the problems,' commented Graham Mackay one year later. However, even by 2008, SABMiller was still having trouble with this acquisition, as we will see later.

The outcome of SABMiller's strategic decision to become a major world company is shown in Table 1. As a result of its strategies, the company made a eight-fold increase in both its turnover and its profit before interest and tax. Earnings per share also more than doubled over the twelve years of expansion. But there were some major problems looming.

SABMiller's problems in North America

In 2004, SABMiller claimed to be turning around its new North American Miller brewing interests. But by 2008, it was still in trouble. Part of the reason was that the leading American company Anheuser-Busch (AH) regarded SABMiller as an important strategic threat and therefore started lowering beer prices across the USA, thus reducing profit margins for all companies. SABMiller's chief executive commented: '[Anheuser-Busch's] resort to a . . . price war when they weren't being attacked [by us] on pricing grounds in the first place is a reasonably extraordinary reaction.' The problem was that this interpretation did not solve SABMiller's US profit problems.

In addition, Americans were increasingly turning to wine rather than beer. This meant that the beer market was declining and, in turn, this had an impact on profitability. There are economies of scale in beer production and also in distribution, thus favouring the larger company Anheuser Busch (still independent at that time from InBev). All this meant that the profit margins at AH by 2007 were double those at its rivals – around 17.3 per cent versus 9.3 per cent and 8.9 per cent at Miller and Coors, respectively.

SABMiller needed a new strategy for its American operations. In 2007, it found this when it put its Miller operations in the USA into a joint venture with Coors. This gave the new company the size to compete better with AH. Marketing leadership of the new joint venture was being taken by Coors with the aim of saving $500 million annually. The strategy proved successful in that the new company improved its profitability, earning US$771 million in 2013. But the US beer market was still declining overall. The *MillerCoors* strategy therefore was to move the product range more towards premium-priced beers and ciders: revenue per hectolitre grew by a useful 3 per cent in 2013 as a result.

SABMiller quietly extends its global coverage

Elsewhere in SABMiller, its South African brewery and soft drink interests were still a major contributor to overall profits and an important source of funds for international expansion – see Figure 2 in Case 2 on the global brewing industry. Although there were problems in the USA, the company was extending its global reach and its strategy of premium branding to other parts of the world.

One striking aspect of SABMiller's global strategy was the way that it approached two family companies – Grupo Empresarial Bavaria in Colombia and Grolsch in Holland – with a view to both companies becoming part of SABMiller's worldwide coverage. Because of the close nature of family companies, this could only be undertaken quietly and with full respect for family interests. In addition, the competitors of SABMiller were also likely to have made approaches to these two well-known and resource-rich firms.

In 2005, SABMiller completed negotiations to acquire Colombia's largest brewer, Grupo Empresarial Bavaria, for $7.8 billion. Bavaria was an attractive purchase with leading market positions not only in Colombia but also in Ecuador, Peru and Panama. The Colombian company itself was paid with shares from SABMiller and regarded the whole process as being positive for itself. 'Bavaria is going ahead with a process of globalisation and consolidation,' said a Bavaria spokesman. 'We remain interested in strengthening that process, always looking towards the future and following the business cycles of the industry.'

In 2008, SABMiller completed yet another international acquisition with the purchase of the Dutch brewing company Grolsch for $1.2 billion. SABMiller explained that this acquisition would allow the company to add the Dutch beer to its portfolio of premium beers which they were beginning to promote to markets in South America and Africa.

In 2011, SABMiller then acquired the Australian-owned beer company Fosters for US$10 billion. Fosters is one of the biggest brands in Australia and also a major brand in the UK. The acquisition did not include the European Fosters brand, which is owned by Heineken.

Figure 1 shows how SABMiller has grown globally.

Strategies in 2014

After some years of hectic takeovers, the more recent period has been quieter. SABMiller had four main global strategies:

1 *Creating a balanced and attractive global spread of businesses.* There have been a whole series of acquisitions, as described elsewhere in this case. In addition, SABMiller has invested further in its Chinese operations through major support for its Chinese brand, Snow, to deliver 20 per cent of this rapidly growing market.

2 *Developing strong, relevant brand portfolios that win in the local market.* The company launched various locally based brands that capitalised on local trends or addressed local brand weaknesses: the local premium beers described earlier.

3 *Constantly raising the profitability of local businesses, sustainably.* This was undertaken through investment in local suppliers and further development of local brands.

4 *Leveraging SABMiller skills and global scale.* The company was exploring global purchasing to reduce costs. It also invested in new worldwide information technology systems that would save costs and enable faster sharing of quality information. Each of the various acquisitions of different companies over time would have had their own reporting systems prior to being acquired. Hence, this strategy was essential to deliver the full benefits that are available from a globally integrated operation over time.

In summary, SABMiller's main businesses were doing well, with substantial increases in sales, particularly in the local premium brands where the profit margins were higher. '[Looking at world beer markets,] there are only three or four top-tier global companies. My ambition is to stay there and offer a superior growth profile as a result of our acquisitions. We have never pursued size for the sake of size,' explained SABMiller's former chief executive Graham Mackay. He can take satisfaction from the way that SABMiller has been transformed quietly over 20 years from a local South African holding company into a major global brewer.

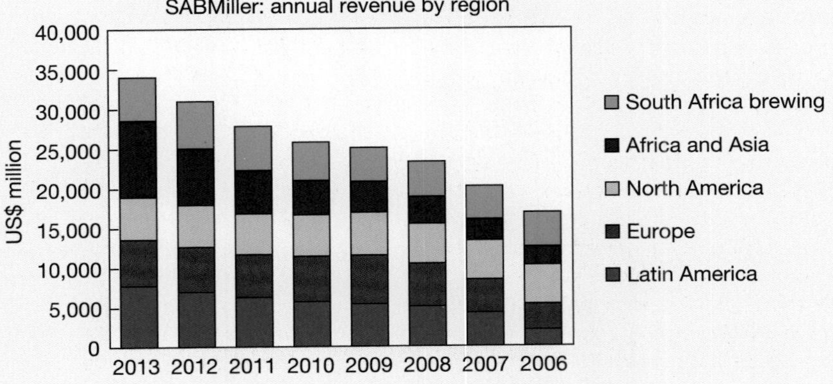

Figure 1 SABMiller goes quietly global . . . especially in Latin America, Africa and Asia

Source: author calculated from annual report and accounts for various years.

Case questions

1 What were the main strategic moves made by SABMiller over the past few years and what was the logic behind them? Would you conclude that they were more prescriptive or emergent?

2 Why was the move into the USA so problematic and what has the company done to put things right? How does the company's solution relate, if at all, to its global strategy of premium branding? How do you think that the main competitor, Anheuser Busch, will now react to the North American joint venture? Should SABMiller continue to pursue its business interests in the USA?

3 What lessons, if any, can other companies learn from the SAB strategy for growth in this mature world market?

Another global beer case study: *Heineken: What's the best strategy? Build brands? Or acquire companies?*

STRATEGIC PROJECT

This case focuses on SABMiller. The other leading brewery companies would all lend themselves to similar research from a strategy perspective. The starting point could easily be the websites of the various companies, which are readily accessible. One interesting approach would be to compare the international growth strategies of the leading companies - for example, the difficulties experienced by Carlsberg with some of its acquisitions (why?); the acquisition moves of Heineken, switching to brand building and then back to acquisition (why switch?); one of the former leading brewing companies was left behind and eventually taken over - Scottish & Newcastle (why?). There is plenty of scope for interesting projects here in international brewing.

Note

* This case was written by the author from numerous sources including: SABMiller Annual Report and Accounts for various years; InBev Annual Report and Accounts for various years; Anheuser-Busch Annual Report and Accounts 2004 and 2007; Heineken Annual Report and Accounts for various years; Carlsberg Annual Report and Accounts for various years; Scottish and Newcastle Annual Report and Accounts 2004 and 2007. All these companies have extensive websites which can be accessed quickly via any web search engine. Earlier sources for this are listed in *Strategic Management* 6th Edition. New sources from the *Financial Times*: 11 May 2011, p 21; 18 August 2011, p 15; 24 August 2011, p 18; 27 May 2013, p 21; 1 August 2013, p 14; 28 September 2012, p 11; 1 February 2013, p 15; 14 February 2013, p 14; 21 January 2014, pp 14 & 19; 20 February 2014, p 16; 27 February 2014, pp 16 & 18.

CASE STUDY 4

Prescriptive and emergent strategy: global car markets and the battle between the world's top car companies

Video and sound summary of this case

In 2008, the Japanese automotive company Toyota overtook its rival, the US giant General Motors, to become the largest car company in the world. However, in 2010, the German company Volkswagen said that its aim was to take global market leadership from Toyota by 2016. In addition, the other leading companies – GM, Ford and Renault/Nissan – remained ambitious to build their market shares. This case explores the battle between these five companies in the global automotive industry for volume car sales. It also adds some brief data on another leading French company, Peugeot Citroën.

The case begins by explaining the downturn in the world car industry in 2008–2009. It explores the strategic difficulties facing the car industry at that time. It then outlines the growing opportunities in developing markets and the prospects around the world for 2012 onwards. The case also summarises the production and customer issues facing the world car companies.

Downturn in world car markets 2008–2009

In 2007, world market demand amounted to 56 million passenger cars with the global market being worth around US$1,500 billion in monetary terms. However, the market then went into significant decline in 2008–2009 dropping up to 33 per cent in many Western markets – see Table 1. By 2009, the global market had declined to around US$1,200 billion. This was caused by the disastrous performance of the US economy and grossly irresponsible lending by the world's leading bankers. Such a decline had a dramatic effect on car company profits because economies of scale were (and are) important in the industry.

The profit problems were made worse because the potential supply of cars had been much greater than the demand for cars for many years in this world industry. For example, even in the 'profitable' year of 2007, the leading companies possessed global production capacity for around 73 million cars compared with worldwide customer demand of around 56 million cars. Inevitably, this excess production capacity problem became more acute when the world experienced the major economic downturn of 2008–2009.

The global automotive market is mature and fiercely competitive in developed markets but still growing rapidly in Asia. Companies like BMW – here promoting its small mini model in the USA – need strong export strategies to succeed.

Strategic difficulties for the leading car companies in 2008–2009

The first difficulty for all the leading companies was to survive the economic whirlwind that hit them in 2008–2009. Consumer demand was substantially down in many developed markets with an immediate impact on profitability and cash flow. Government support became essential during this period for most of the leading companies – price discounts on new cars, government funds to prop up balance sheets and government-supported negotiations to form new alliances and joint ventures.

The reason for government support related to the contribution of the car companies to the overall industrial economic health of many nations, especially in Japan, Europe and the USA. Automobile manufacture provided employment, tax revenues, international exports and leading-edge technologies. National governments supported their own national car companies and related car component companies at the expense of other foreign companies. They did this by various grants and import restrictions. Three examples are pertinent:

1. The largest German company, Volkswagen (VW), was part owned by one of the German states with consequently a strong interest in maintaining production and employment. The national government offered grants to customers for the purchase of new cars.
2. The three largest US car companies were given massive amounts of US government funds when they became unprofitable in 2008–2009.
3. The Indian government protected its own national car companies – like Tata Motors – by taxing foreign-made cars heavily and placing a large minimum investment barrier on any foreign car company wishing to set up a factory in India.

By 2010, it was clear that the worst was over and all the leading companies had survived. National government support was

Table 1 Estimates of global geographical sales of automotive vehicles including trucks and buses (Thousands of units)

	2009	2007	2002	2000	Comment
North American Free Trade Area	13,073	19,634	20,118	20,595	In year 2000, the three US traditional companies – GM, Ford and Chrysler – were dominant along with the Japanese company Toyota. By 2009, Chrysler was under the control of Fiat from Italy and the other two major companies were making losses.
Europe including Eastern Europe	18,827	23,123	19,172	20,158	Volkswagen, Fiat, PSA Peugeot Citroën and Renault were important companies in addition to Ford and GM. Fiat dominated the Italian market but was loss-making for several years 2000–2003 before returning to profitability in 2006.
South and Latin America, Africa and the Middle East	9,980	9,780	3,673	3,664	Several of the global manufacturers had regional production facilities – for example, Ford in Mexico and Volkswagen in Brazil.
Asia-Pacific, including Japan and Korea	23,303	17,767	14,373	12,880	Toyota was the largest company in its home Japanese market with Honda second. Hyundai was the leader in Korea. The four leading Indian companies – Suzuki Maruti, Tata, Mahindra and Hindustani – were very small by comparison.

Note: In analysing world automotive markets, the data can sometimes be confusing. Some companies – such as Renault – publish information on their sales and market shares based on the market for 'passenger cars'. Other companies – such as GM – define their markets to include trucks and commercial vehicles like buses and heavy lorries. This makes a comparison of data from the companies potentially confusing. Even though commercial vehicles have different industrial customers and different methods of distribution, many world companies are involved in both passenger and commercial markets because the technology and production methods are similar. This case therefore defines the market as that for *all* automotive vehicles, including buses and trucks.

Sources: based on data from General Motors 2009 Annual Report and Accounts plus data from OICA annual production data for 2009. There are good sources of *production* data but no single source of *sales* data.

therefore reduced, but import restrictions continued in the case of some countries. However, market conditions remained difficult in many countries.

In addition, there were three further fundamental strategic problems facing all the car companies, especially those operating internationally:

1 Profitability was under severe pressure from long-term high cost issues – like the pension and health provisions made to former employees of the US car companies (called 'legacy costs' in the industry). These were not so important for the newer car companies of India and Asia. But they were major issues for some of the European and American companies like Daimler, VW, Ford and GM.

2 Rising fuel costs made car ownership more expensive and therefore less attractive for many Western developed markets and other developing markets. Some larger car models – like those from BMW, Daimler and Jaguar Land Rover – were particularly hard hit with the need for massive new model and engine re-engineering. Even in America, where fuel costs were traditionally low, there was increasing public concern about the rise in fuel prices.

3 Increased awareness of the environmental consequences of motoring in terms of pollution and scarce resources had begun to impact on car design. Governments were bringing out new laws to enforce tougher car emission standards and better fuel economy. All motor manufacturers were therefore exploring new low-emission car engines. For example, the Indian company Tata had acquired shares in a Norwegian company that was developing an electric car engine. The French company Renault and its Japanese associated company Nissan developed a new all-electric car for launch in 2011. Indeed, all car companies are engaged in green strategies for three reasons: government legislation, the increasing price of fuel and the need to protect the environment. For this edition these vital strategies are explored in Chapter 14 which examines green strategy and sustainability.

Essentially, these issues led the world's leading car companies to seek radically new car designs.

In addition, basic restructuring of car companies was beginning to take place across parts of the industry to cut costs, reduce production capacity and return to profitability, especially in the USA. The US Government poured substantial public funds into major restructuring with the result that General Motors (GM), Ford and Chrysler closed dozens of car manufacturing plants. GM itself was threatened with being broken up in 2009 into a North American part and a separate European part with the latter being sold to new owners. In 2010, it was announced that GM would not be dismembered but would remain one company.

As a result of its restructuring, GM's American operations were delivering substantial profits by the end of 2011. However, its European operations, under the brand names Opel and Vauxhall, were making substantial losses. The reason was that European car manufacturing had not been restructured. As the *Financial Times* explained, 'Europe's car industry did not heal itself during the financial crisis [of 2008–10]. Detroit's producers closed dozens of car plants between 2006 and 2009 and now have operations supplying a resurgent market . . . But Europe is still saddled with capacity to make millions more cars than the market wants. Because of political and union pressure, too many high cost plants have been kept open at home when growth and profit have largely moved overseas.' In the period 2008–2011, only two car plants were closed in Europe: Opel in Antwerp and Fiat in Sicily.

In summary, reduced global demand, substantial model redesign and significant company restructuring put major financial pressures on the world's leading car companies in 2008–2009. American companies responded by restructuring, but European car companies were pressed into preserving jobs. In addition, the major growth in car markets was in the developing countries.

Growing markets in some developing countries from 2010 onwards

In spite of problems globally, some developing countries, like China, Brazil and India, were experiencing continued car market growth. Part of the reason was that such countries had much lower penetration of car ownership – see Figure 1 – while at the same time household incomes were increasing. However, these countries made up a smaller part of global demand than the developed nations – see Table 1 earlier in this case. The USA and the EU still accounted for around 60 per cent of the world market for cars in year 2008 though this percentage was declining. By 2010, China was the largest new car market in the world with India also growing fast. Brazil had much higher car penetration than these two countries but was still predicted to grow at 5–7 per cent per year up to 2016 – partly supported by the Soccer World Cup in 2014 and the Olympic Games in 2016, both of which would be held in Brazil. By 2018, two of the above developing countries were expected to be amongst the world's largest car markets. The top five in order were predicted to be China, the USA, Japan, Brazil and Germany. India was also beginning to catch up fast.

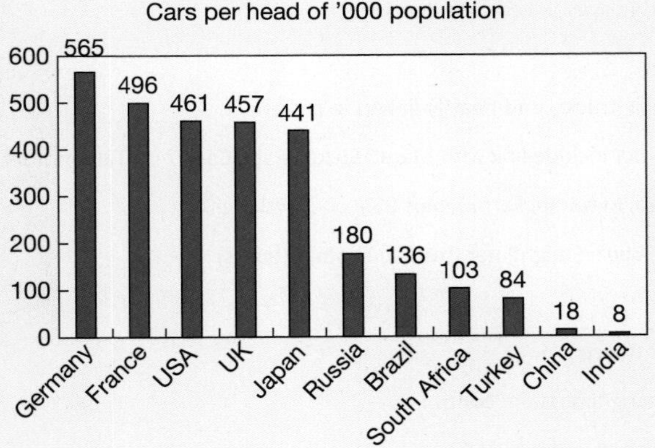

Figure 1 Latent customer demand higher in developing countries

Source: author using data from various internet databases, including the World Bank Annual Report 2008. However, the data has been adjusted by the author to account for increased demand in some developing countries such as China.

World car markets and companies – still fragile in 2012

By late 2009, the world car industry was recovering but had not returned to the levels seen earlier in the decade. Total sales of *passenger cars* amounted to around 50 million vehicles with truck and bus sales numbering around an additional 15 million *commercial vehicles* – see Table 1. The American and European economies were improving with many governments offering direct subsidies to car buyers to support sales and to underpin the contribution that car manufacturing made to their economies. However, these subsidies were short-term and had largely been withdrawn by 2012 except on the new, very low or zero fuel emission cars.

In addition to the withdrawal of subsidies, fuel prices were high and still increasing for three reasons. First, there was increased demand from Asia thus putting pressure on supplies. Second, governments in Europe put higher taxes on fuels, thus increasing prices with the aim of reducing consumption and migrating people to use public transport. Third, there was considerable political uncertainty in the area of the world's largest oil producing region: the Middle East. This had begun to impact on car usage and to shift demand to new, more fuel-efficient cars – perhaps benefiting the new electric and hybrid cars entering the market in 2011 and 2012.

Production over-capacity in the car industry was another factor adding to fragile car markets. One estimate for 2010 put the total global production capacity as high as 86 million vehicles including trucks and buses: a remarkable 18 per cent increase over 2007. Moreover, new production capacity was still being constructed in countries with strong growth such as China, Brazil and India. In addition, new capacity was also being added by many of the existing car companies in their traditional markets as they brought on stream new engine plant to handle new forms of engine, such as electric motors.

The problem of production over-capacity was particularly acute in Europe. As explained above, the US government supported radical restructuring at GM, Ford and Chrysler in the period 2009–2011. This led to the closure of 28 US car plants with these companies returning to profitability on their US operations in 2011. Similar government support in Europe resulted in the closure of only two European car plants with most of the European support being used to subsidise car prices and thereby increase European car sales for a short period. The outcome was that some, but not all, European car companies were making low profits or even losses on their European operations in 2011–2012.

With all these pressures, the world's leading car companies needed to focus on their competitive advantages in 2012. Many companies have areas of regional strength around the world: for example, VW, Fiat and Renault are important in their home countries – Germany, Italy and France, respectively. VW is the top-selling car company in the whole of the EU. Equally, two more of the world's largest car companies, Toyota and GM, have market leadership in Japan and the USA, respectively. Although these companies are 'global' in the sense of having significant sales in most of the world's major markets, most of them also have their highest market shares in one country or area of the world. This assists with economies of scale and scope, thus favouring the world's largest car companies – see Table 2.

However, such scale strategies are not sufficient in themselves. Large sales and market shares do not necessarily deliver high profitability. The largest unit sales in 2012 were achieved in the low-priced market segments – like the small cars segment with models such as the Renault Twingo, VW Golf and Ford Fiesta – where the profit margins were low. Smaller unit sales were achieved in the large, luxury segments – like those for luxury saloons from Toyota, BMW and Mercedes – where the profit margins were substantial.

In addition, the world's leading companies had strong brand names, some of which are shown in Table 2. Many also had good distribution networks and after-sales service. The problem was that, although such benefits were important contributors to key factors for success in the industry, they were weaker in providing competitive advantage. The reason was that strong branding and distribution strengths were common to many of the leading companies and the market was fragmented with many brands. However, they did provide barriers to entry against new car companies like those from China and India that were aiming to become global players. Distribution and after-sales service were amongst the reasons why Tata Motors from India and Geely from China acquired Jaguar Land Rover and Volvo, respectively.

Production strategy: economies of scale, supplier links and productivity

From a strategy perspective, the world automotive industry has the capacity to produce around 70–80 million units per year. In practice, most companies only produce what they are able to sell during a year, but there have been some exceptions as companies attempt to keep their plant operating during periods of low demand. The spare production capacity in the industry is particularly relevant because automotive companies rely on economies of scale and scope to deliver profits. Such economies reduce the costs of a company: conversely, spare capacity in the world car industry suggests that some companies are not able to achieve full cost reductions.

Labour productivity has become one of the classic measures of cost reduction strategy. Related cost reduction is also obtained using techniques like just-in-time, Kaizen and supplier relationships. The Japanese companies – Honda,

Table 2 Global car companies – larger but not necessarily more profitable (Ranked by approximate total vehicles sold in 2009)

Company	Home country	Total vehicle sales*	Selected brand names and models include:
Toyota	Japan	7.6	Daihatsu, Lexus, Aurus, Yaris, Corolla
General Motors	US	7.5	Buick, Cadillac, Chevrolet, Opel, Vauxhall, Saab (sold in 2010)
Volkswagen	Germany	6.3	Audi, Golf, Polo, Lamborghini, Bentley, Skoda, Seat
Ford	USA	4.8	Fusion, Lincoln, Mercury, Mondeo, Fiesta, Focus
PSA Group	France	3.6	Peugeot, Citroën Setra (trucks), Sterling (trucks), Western Star (trucks), Thomas Built (buses)
Nissan	Japan	3.5	Infiniti and heavily linked with Renault
Honda	Japan	3.4	Acura
Renault	France	2.3	Dacia, Mack (trucks) and heavily linked to Nissan
Suzuki	Japan	2.3	Data does *not* include link with Maruti Suzuki – see Case 7 on Tata motors
Fiat	Italy	2.2	Alfa Romeo, Maserati, Ferrari, plus 25% of Chrysler US
Daimler	Germany	1.6	Mercedes-Benz, Freightliner (trucks), Thomas (buses)
Hyundai	Korea	1.6	Kia
BMW	Germany	1.3	Mini, Rolls Royce
Chrysler	USA	1.3	Fiat beginning to acquire control
Mazda	Japan	1.2	Formerly linked with Ford US
Mitsubishi	Japan	1.0	
Tata	India	0.8	Jaguar, Land Rover

* Approximate numbers in millions based on company annual reports.

Source: author from company annual reports and accounts.

Nissan and Toyota – were pioneers in this area. However, many US and European companies have now caught up so that the previous competitive advantages of the Japanese companies in this area have now largely disappeared.

Productivity is not the only important production strategy: *build quality* has also become vital over the last 20 years. 'Build quality' refers to the lack of defects and inherent design flaws in new cars as they leave car factories. The competitive advantages of higher quality are sustainable in the sense that it takes several years to invest in the new plant that will produce cars of a higher quality. In addition, it will probably take at least as long to train and improve the workforce practices that deliver higher quality. Importantly, when companies build to a higher quality, they also reduce their manufacturing costs because there is less waste and fewer rejects that have to be recycled. Most of the world's leading companies have significantly improved their build quality, but differences remain: for example, see the quality comparisons published on the JD Power website: **www.jdpower.com**.

The labour productivity of car plants is also related to the capital investment in new machinery and other design features at individual plants – newer machinery is likely to make workers more productive. However, numerous studies have also shown that the *way* that the workers are employed and managed in the factory is also important – for example, the well-known *Toyota Production System* focuses on the workers and their working methods in the Toyota car plants rather than the machinery. Other companies have now adopted such approaches and invested heavily in new plant to improve productivity. But differences remain, based largely on company approaches to worker representation and co-operation in the factory: for example, VW was reported to have lower productivity at its German plants because of strong trade union agreements on working practices. This is explored in more depth in the sections relating to the five leading car companies below.

In manufacturing strategy, supplier relationships are also important. Every company only manufactures some parts of the car – for example, no major vehicle company makes tyres or batteries. If the outside suppliers are high-cost then this increases the costs of manufacture of the automotive companies. Toyota has traditionally been different from other manufacturers in that it has bought in more products from outside the company than a company like Ford, which has made car parts more internally.

However, the biggest reduction in costs comes not from supplier relationships but from research and development (R&D). The greatest cost reductions often arise from *redesigning* components rather than seeking cost reductions on the factory floor. Recent advances in R&D have also come from new electronic devices in the vehicle – electronic diagnostics, electronic sensors, etc. In addition, other more fundamental developments have emerged based on public and governmental pressure for more environmentally friendly vehicles.

Customer and quality strategies

Car markets have been heavily segmented for many years in many parts of the world in order to meet customer demand for different levels of performance, price points and standards of finish and quality. The main developments over the last few years have been two-fold:

1 The introduction of higher quality and add-on features as standard items – for example, satellite navigation, electric windows, extra safety bars and crash panels, in-car computers.
2 The launch of more fuel-efficient engines and lower emission exhausts.

In addition, car branding both for the basic manufacturer and for individual car models has also been a major strategic focus of many car companies. High levels of brand support and other promotional expenditure have built barriers to entry for new manufacturers. At the same time, they have provided sustainable competitive advantages for some individual companies.

Sustainable competitive advantage may also come from another important aspect of customer activity: after-sales service and dealer networks. All the world's leading car companies have extensive dealer networks with arguably little real differentiation. However, such services have delivered some competitive advantages for some individual companies in developed markets like the USA, Japan and Europe, where the top companies have good coverage with well-trained engineers. In developing markets like China, India and Brazil, the establishment of reliable networks has proved expensive and difficult, especially for countries spread over thousands of kilometres. In these countries, the global car companies have been seeking local partnerships through alliances or joint ventures to provide the same high levels of car service as in developed markets.

One area that has been both an opportunity and problem for car companies in the past few years relates to car quality and reliability and its impact on customer satisfaction. During the 2000s, Toyota built a strong reputation for reliability and this became a sustainable competitive advantage of the

In the global car market, one strategy relies on economies of scale to reduce costs. But the market is mature and supply outstrips demand for standard car models. Excess cars are then stored in massive car parks for future sale. Green strategies will make this situation even more complex.
© Corbis

company. The company lost this, to some extent at least, with the publicity surrounding sticky accelerator pedals and out-of-place floor mats in 2008–2009. The company then made extensive organisational changes to resolve these issues. Other companies, like Daimler Mercedes and Ford, have also had some quality issues that have needed to be rectified in the mid-2000s. These may have delivered short-term advantages to rival companies. However, all the above companies (and more not mentioned) have made strenuous efforts to resolve these matters at the time of writing this case with some considerable success.

Top five car companies: basic shifts in the global competitive battle

For decades, the two leading American car companies, GM and Ford, dominated the world car industry. They were the market leaders in the USA and also had significant market shares in Europe, although they were not necessarily the leaders. Then along came the Japanese car companies like Toyota, Honda and Nissan, with high quality and reliability, low-cost production and substantial marketing expenditure. The American companies were burdened around this time with 'legacy costs' associated with pensions and health commitments made with the US trade unions. Their world share declined – see Figure 2. In many ways, it was only support from the US Government that kept the leading US car companies in business during the 2000s.

In Europe, the leading European companies were able to hold their market positions, especially in their home countries. The German company, VW, was the market leader across Europe followed by the two French companies, Renault and PSA – the latter having two major brands Peugeot and Citroën. This case focuses on Renault because it is larger, but only when adding the market share of its Japanese associate, Nissan. PSA Peugeot Citroën is the subject of Case 5 that follows. Essentially, the strength of these major companies rests on their dominance of the home markets, Germany and France. Most companies also have other brands, e.g. VW owns Audi, Seat, Skoda and Rolls Royce cars. As Figure 2 shows, the European companies have been doing well in share terms over the last few years as the US companies and Toyota have declined. To understand why, it is necessary to examine the different strategies of each company. These are explored separately below.

From a strategy perspective, market share is not the only criterion by which to judge the competitive battle. Profitability and value added are at least as important. From this perspective, four of the five companies made substantial *losses* in either 2008 or 2009. The reason was the major downturn in world car markets during this time. Only VW out of the big five was able to report an operating profit for both these years. The detailed profit figures are not set out in this case because they were difficult to compare at the time of writing this case in early 2011. There were three problems: first, the different year-ends for the different companies; second, the differing ways and timing that each company reported its losses; third, there was a fundamental change in the way that at least one company, GM, restructured its trading and its balance sheet over this period – basically after bankruptcy and a bail-out by the US Government – making a comparison with earlier data difficult. Although the experience of the other four companies was not so drastic, they were all forced to undertake fundamental re-appraisals of their businesses and make substantial changes that were not easily captured in the financial data in the period up to 2009.

Nevertheless, data for 2007 and 2010 is now available and does provide an impression of the relative size of all five companies. This is therefore presented in Table 3. It is important to note that Renault and Nissan do not normally report their combined position as it is presented in the table. But, because they work so closely together and have cross-shareholdings, this is a legitimate approach to understand the combined market and investment power of these two companies. The table also compares the top five with the two next largest car companies,

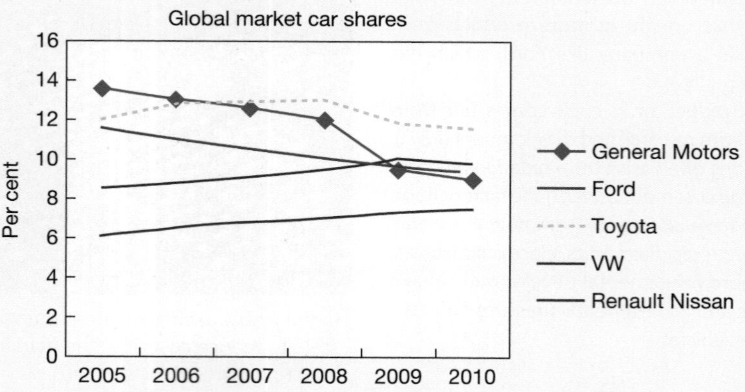

Figure 2 Global market shares of the world's leading volume car companies

Source: author from annual report and accounts.

Table 3 The top five ranked by 2007 turnover – much larger than rivals

Company	Country	Turnover 2007 US$ Mn	Production 2007 '000 cars only	Turnover 2010 US$ Mn	Production 2010 '000 cars only	Comment
Toyota cars	Japan	187,420	7,211	203,687	7,267	Fundamental re-appraisal of strategy in 2008–2009 after quality problems on some vehicles
General Motors	USA	181,122	6,259	135,600	6,267	Totally restructured by US Government and still a major global company
Volkswagen	Germany	160,079	5,964	166,743	7,120	Europe's market leader, not just in Germany with many other brands – see case
Ford	USA	154,400	3,565	128,954	2,959	The smallest of the five in terms of production and related economies of scale but still profitable
Nissan/Renault	Japan/France	148,000	4,927	146,000	5,548	Not normally combined together as one set of figures. The combination relates to the scale of their joint operations
Fiat	Italy	86,000	1,991	73,933	1,781	In 2007, this was the next largest car company. In 2011, Fiat was in the process of acquiring control of Chrysler Cars, the US company, in order to build towards the same size and scale as the top five above
PSA Peugeot Citroën	France	79,659	3,024	73,677	3,214	See Case 5 on PSA Peugeot Citroën

Source: author from annual report and accounts.

the Italian car company Fiat and the French company PSA Peugeot Citroën. It shows that the top five companies are way ahead of their rivals in terms of economies of scale and scope: key factors for success in the global volume car industry.

Two important notes:

1 Nissan and Renault have been combined together because of their close links: they normally report their financial performance separately

2 Daimler Mercedes had a higher turnover than Nissan/Renault. However, it is not included in the above because this turnover is misleading: it includes data from the turnover of the US company, Chrysler, which Daimler demerged part-way through 2007. The full, original Daimler ranking is shown in Case 7 on Tata Motors.

Toyota strategy summary – standalone strategy except in some developing markets

In around 2000, Toyota identified its purpose as being to take global market leadership by 2010. It called this its '2010 Global Vision Strategy'. During the 1980s and 1990s, the company targeted North America as its prime strategic focus. Along with Honda, Toyota launched cars of superior quality and with lower manufacturing costs than its US competitors. By 2003, Toyota was selling the most popular single car model – the Camry – in North America. Toyota produced many of its basic models in North America so it was unlikely to be affected again by changes in the Japanese yen. The company was a major employer in North America and was not merely outsourcing work to Japan.

In the 1990s, Toyota decided to attack the Western European market, which was the next largest market in the world at that time. They had been selling vehicles in Europe for many years but decided to build their first factory – at Burnaston in the UK – in 1995. This was then followed by other factories and a design facility in France in the late 1990s. Toyota was cautious about Europe for many years for two reasons: first, because the European vehicle industry was protected by trade barriers; and, second, by a voluntary agreement by the Japanese car companies to restrict their European sales. However, the EU removed such barriers in the mid-1990s and Toyota responded by a major drive into the region.

In earlier years, Toyota based its European strategy on selling cars that were reliable but were not perhaps the most attractively designed – arguably even dull. However, European car manufacturers like VW were rapidly able to replicate any competitive advantage based on quality. More recently, Toyota has begun to design cars specifically for EU markets: Shuhie Toyoda, head of Toyota's EU operations explains: 'In Europe styling and performance is generally high. European people enjoy driving their cars more than, for example, Americans. In 1999, we introduced the Yaris. That is a vehicle designed specifically for Europe. Until then, although we tried to develop a vehicle that would suit Europe, the main target was not Europe.'

But all was not completely satisfactory with Toyota Europe's strategy for two reasons. First, its factories were still not as efficient as Nissan - see later section. Its customers did not recognise Toyota quality as being the highest, reserving that accolade for VW. Moreover, profit margins on its European operations were small. Second, Toyota faced some real problems over quality and reliability with some well-publicised incidents that required the recall of some Toyota cars. The company has acknowledged that significant reform of its quality monitoring was required and claimed that matters had substantially improved by 2012. Partly as a result of such difficulties, Toyota made a loss in 2009 after enjoying substantial growth in both sales and profits over the period 1999–2008.

By the longer-term test of steady profitable growth, Toyota's strategy has been successful. It was partly built on the benefits of the Toyota Production System, which delivered lower factory costs. The strategy also included close relationships with its suppliers with the benefits of lower costs, lower inventory and flexible manufacturing. The company's design skills have also been important, for example in the early introduction of its hybrid car, the *Prius*. Its marketing skills have also contributed through strong branding and careful development of a powerful dealer network.

Apart from some production co-operation with competitors - Toyota shared a manufacturing plant with GM in North America, an R&D link-up with a Californian company making electric cars and a manufacturing plant with PSA Peugeot Citroën in the Czech Republic - Toyota never co-operated or acquired another company in Europe or America. This strategy was quite different from that of Ford - see below. However, the Toyota strategy in China and India was different because it entered into joint ventures with local partners. The reasons for this latter move relate to the barriers to trade in India and China coupled with the need to build local networks.

In addition, Toyota always had some doubts about a simple global strategy with the same basic model on sale everywhere. It has used model designs for its volume car ranges but then produced cars that were specifically designed for major regions of the world. For example, the *Yaris* small car was designed purely for the requirements of the European market and there were no plans to develop the model as a global car. In a similar way, Toyota developed its new car, the *Etios*, solely for the large and growing Indian market in conjunction with its local Indian partner, Kirloskar Motors.

In the three years up to 2010, Toyota suffered an immensely damaging series of problems associated with complaints about the quality and reliability of some of its models. In the USA, there were investigations as to whether Toyota knew about safety issues but ignored the consequences. The company itself accepted that there were some problems and recalled car models to rectify them. More importantly, Toyota recognised that it needed to reform thoroughly its quality control systems. For example, the first section of its annual report for 2010 was headed, 'A fresh start for Toyota - contributing to society through the production of safe and reliable vehicles.' At the time of writing this case, the company had begun to action a new organisation to change fundamentally the situation co-ordinated from its headquarters in Japan. But there was not a single foreigner on the Toyota main board in spite of major plant - and therefore quality issues - being located in the world's leading industrial countries.

GM strategy summary - hold market share, go bankrupt and then regroup

For many years, General Motors (GM) followed a strategy of volume building and market share in its traditional North American and European markets at the expense, if necessary, of profits. This has included a strategy of reducing its prices in order to hold its market share, especially in its home country.

GM's home country is the USA where it owns some of established brand names like Buick, Cadillac, Chevrolet and Pontiac. At one time, its North American operations included around 100 manufacturing, assembly and warehousing facilities. It was also involved for many years in Europe, where its brands include Opel (Germany), Vauxhall (UK) and Saab. It had ten production and assembly facilities in seven European countries.

After making substantial losses even before the downturn in world car markets in 2008–2009, GM went bankrupt with a rescue package funded by the US Government. The company then engaged in a major cost-cutting strategy reducing the number of brands, closing a number of factories and combining worldwide operations. For example, it sold the Saab brand to the Dutch company Spyder and completely withdrew the Hummer brand and models. GM emerged leaner in 2010–2011 as a result. Its joint venture in China was its leading profit earner at that time. The full outcome of its recovery from bankruptcy was yet to emerge at the time of writing this case. Importantly, GM's American operations were back into profit in 2011, but its European operations were loss-making. It was reported to be in discussion with Peugeot Citroën about the possibility of sharing some development and related costs in its European operations - see Case 5.

Ford strategy summary - first a global strategy, then acquisitions and then 'back-to-basics'

Global strategy

For many years, Ford was a leading company both in North America and in Europe. Its strategy during much of the 1990s was to gain the benefits of a global strategy. It made substantial attempts to integrate its operations on a global scale in the period 1995–1998. Core engineering and production operations were simplified and combined with common parts, common vehicle platforms and common sourcing from outside suppliers. The purpose was to achieve annual cost savings of around US$42 billion through economies of scale and through the spread of the development costs of a specific model across the sales in more countries. Substantial savings were achieved and Ford's profits then rose.

Acquisitions strategy

Following this success, the company then embarked on what it called a 'global niche' strategy. The company judged that world market demand was moving towards *niche* car markets - like off-road vehicles, people carriers - and this meant that the company should invest in these areas. The company therefore invested heavily by *acquiring companies* in its specialist brands in these areas - Jaguar cars, Lincoln luxury cars, Volvo cars, Land-Rover vehicles, Aston Martin sports cars. The strategy of acquiring rival companies in some cases - see Case 16.2 for more information - carries the major risk that it becomes difficult to gain sufficient economic benefits from the acquisition premium paid to buy such companies. An additional danger with the acquisition strategy was that the company was distracted by the need to integrate its acquisitions. Ford failed to invest sufficiently in its basic car ranges - like the Mondeo and the Fiesta in Europe - during the period 1999-2004. This allowed other companies to move ahead in these areas.

Back to basics strategy

With the benefit of hindsight, Ford's global niche acquisition strategy was then considered to be wrong and the Ford chief executive of that period, Jac Nasser, was sacked. A new strategy of 'Back to Basics' was introduced under the guidance of one of the members of the Ford founding family, Mr Bill Ford. Ford focused on the existing model range, improving quality while reducing costs. Ford also switched its efforts to redesigning its mid-sized cars to improve quality and equip them with many of the features found on more luxury models - higher driving positions, more storage space, etc. 'Redefining the North American saloon is a tall order, but that is what we set out to do,' says Phil Marten - Ford's group vice-president of product creation. Its success in pursuing this strategy was sufficient to ensure that Ford did not need to seek bail-out funds from the US Government in 2008-2009. Ford made losses, but these were sufficiently contained for the company to continue trading and maintain its global position over time. Importantly, Ford's increased emphasis on a quality strategy resulted in major growth in the company's quality and reliability ratings amongst customers. By 2012, it was one of the world leaders in these areas.

Renault/Nissan summary strategy - shared Chief Executive, shared suppliers and car parts, shared R&D but distinctive brands and different models

Nissan and Renault are two distinct companies, one French and the other Japanese. However, they share certain key assets and have cross-shareholdings. Hence, in the context of the world car industry, they have some of the benefits of a larger combined company, especially economies of scale in key areas. Nissan is the larger of the two companies in terms of volume and is therefore described first.

In the late 1990s, Nissan was the third largest of Japan's three major car companies after Toyota and Honda. Nissan was in serious financial trouble after being squeezed by its two Japanese rivals. Renault was a moderately successful French-based car company partially owned by the French state. Its CEO was Carlos Ghosn, a charismatic leader with the ability to turn around failing companies. Ghosn recognised that Renault needed to increase its scale beyond its French European base if it was ever to be successful. He persuaded Nissan to begin co-operation that led to Renault having 44 per cent of Nissan and Nissan having 25 per cent of Renault.

As part of the agreement, Ghosn became CEO of Nissan as well as Renault. He began to organise co-operation across a range of car models and designs. However, Renault was keen to preserve the semi-independence of Nissan. The Japanese company therefore continued to develop its own models and invest in its own factories in the USA, Europe and Japan. In 2010, Nissan had some of the world's most efficient car production facilities including its major European car plant at Sunderland, UK. It continued to produce distinctive models and had slightly higher total unit sales than its partner, Renault, in 2010.

Renault is French: the French government still has a 15 per cent minority stake in the company. Its main production and research facilities are located in France and it is one of the two French companies that competes strongly in the French domestic market, the other being Peugeot Citroën (PSA). Renault has a strong record in innovative and distinctive new car models such as the Espace, the Clio, the Twingo and the Mégane coupled with a strong record in vehicle safety features. But a major contributor to its recent success has been its co-operation strategy with Nissan.

In 2009, Renault claimed combined cost savings of over €1.5 billion from synergies with Nissan. It was seeking another €1 billion in 2010. These cost reductions have come from three major sources. First, the two companies share some common car parts, platforms and power trains. Second, Renault and Nissan combine together to purchase some car parts from outside suppliers that are the same and thus obtain lower prices from larger orders. Third, the two companies have shared R&D. For example, Nissan and Renault did not possess the resources to develop the new electric car model as separate companies. Nevertheless, the two companies retain their individual cultures and management, but with the same Group CEO to provide the combined vision and leadership where appropriate.

Volkswagen summary strategy - quality, multiple brands and locations but not the lowest costs

Founded in Germany back in the 1930s, VW retains its proud German roots. It has major manufacturing plants in many countries, but the hub of the company is the headquarters in the town of Wolfsburg, Germany. This is the organisational and emotional hub of the company.

Over the years, VW has acquired and invested in other companies: Seat in Spain, Skoda in the Czech Republic and

Bentley luxury cars in the UK. In addition, the company has developed its upmarket range with the separate Audi brand. All of these brands and models have been carefully positioned in different segments of the world car market. In addition, VW was one of the earliest companies into China with its joint ventures with the Chinese companies SAIC and FAW. VW brands now lead the Chinese market. More recently, the company took a 20 per cent share in the Japanese company, Suzuki. Part of the reason is that Maruti Suzuki is the market leader in the Indian car market - see the separate Tata case (Case 7). However, the two partners subsequently disagreed and, at the time of writing this case, Suzuki was seeking to disengage with VW.

In spite of all these world-scale links, the basic strategy of VW has strong German roots. The largest car production plant in the world is located at its headquarters in Wolfsburg, Germany. This means that the company produces vehicles that have a high reputation for quality and are strongly branded, for example the Polo, the Passat and the Golf. However, its German base also means that it has a high-cost labour strategy when compared with other car makers. The reason is that German companies have a strong culture and culture of co-operation and co-determination - *Mitbestimmung* - with the German car trade unions. This has the advantage of few strikes and high flexibility with regard to shifts in demand and production but has the disadvantage of higher labour costs. The VW view is that the *mitbestimmung* strategy has served the company well for many years and there is no need or desire for change.

Conclusion

According to the widely held view, world car companies needed to sell around 5–6 million units per year to be profitable. It was for this reason that the smaller Italian company Fiat took a 25 per cent share in the American company, Chrysler, in 2011 rising to 57 per cent in 2012. The company was pursuing cost and model synergies as a result. But the top five companies were still ahead with different strategies. Renault/Nissan was risking part of its future on its new electric car model. The two American-based companies, Ford and GM, were moving back into profitability from a lower cost base. But both Ford and GM still had to sort out their unprofitable European operations. VW's strengths in Asia and northern Europe were helping it through the depressed markets elsewhere in Europe.

Toyota was still the world market leader but had an unfinished strategy with regard to maintaining its reputation for low costs and reliability. VW had ambitions to surpass Toyota as world market leader, partly through its alliances with Chinese and Indian companies to benefit from the fast-growing Asian markets. But there was no guarantee that such a strategy would be successful and it was still relying on the petrol-driven car as the major means of growth. World car strategies still had a long way to go.

Finally, the strategies of the car companies PSA Peugeot Citroën, AvtoVAZ and Tata Motors are explored in the cases that follow.

Case questions

1 What were the main factors leading to uncertainty in the world car industry? What are the implications for the prescriptive strategies of the leading car companies? Is it possible to pursue prescriptive strategies in such circumstances?

2 What are the main competitive advantages of the leading car companies? Some strategists have argued that such advantages are now so common amongst all the leading companies that they no longer distinguish one company from another: do you agree?

3 How would you recommend, if at all, that Toyota responds to the ambition of VW to become the world's largest car company?

4 What lessons, if any, can other companies learn about the benefits and problems of the strategies of the world's leading car companies?

STRATEGIC PROJECT

You might like to follow up the strategic battle between the five market leaders to see how it has developed. VW has said that it wishes to take world market leadership. Both GM and Ford have been trying to catch up with Toyota for some years. Renault/Nissan were hoping to take the initiative with their new green cars alongside their existing range at the time of writing this case. Considerable data is available on the car market from the web, starting with the car companies themselves. The case references will point to further web data that would allow you to analyse the immediate past strategies of each of the three companies. It would then be possible to assess their present levels of success.

Note

* *Sources*: annual report and accounts of Toyota, GM, VW, Fiat, Ford, Renault and Nissan. Earlier information from the sources is fully listed in *Strategic Management*, 6th edn, so not repeated here. The new sources are from the *Financial Times*: 8 June 2011, p 22; 7 July 2011, p 22; 29 July 2011, p 19; 21 December 2011, p 25; 25 October 2012, p 19; 29 January 2013, p 19; 31 Janauray 2013, p 14; 15 March 2013, p 20; 12 April 2013, p 19; 14 May 2013, p 14; 20 November 2013, p 22; 26 November 2013, p 20; 6 December 2013, pp 23 & 26; 8 January 2014, p 21; 9 January 2014, p 9; 24 January 2014, p 18.

CASE STUDY 5

PSA Peugeot Citroën: stuck in the strategy slow lane?

Europe's second largest car company, PSA Peugeot Citroën, made losses on its car business in three of the five years 2008–2012. This has resulted in new strategies for survival and growth. But will they be enough? The case explores whether this famous French car company is still stuck in the slow lane of strategy development.

The case needs to be read in conjunction with the case 'Prescriptive and emergent strategy: global car markets and the battle between the world's top car companies'.

Video and sound summary of this case

The 2011 profit picture: in the slow lane or even temporarily off the road?

In the year 2011, the French company PSA Peugeot Citroën (shortened to Peugeot in this case) lost €499 million. Table 1 shows the profit record of the major divisions of the company over the last four years: it was the Automotive Division that was the problem. And the problem was becoming worse in 2012, as the case explains later. Peugeot cars were making heavy losses with a new strategy needed to turn around the company.

Table 1 shows that only Peugeot's two non-car operations were profitable in 2012. These were its car parts business, called Faurecia and its car financing business. The latter is called Banque PSA France and provides funds for customers to purchase cars. Faurecia benefited in 2011 from some small acquisitions by Peugeot that enabled the company to strengthen its profit position in this subsidiary. The *Financial Times* commented in early 2012: 'PSA [Peugeot] looks particularly fragile: the company burned through €1.6 billion of cash last year and is now selling assets to stay afloat.' Since that observation, the company has raised €3 billion in new funds as described later in the case.

Peugeot was well aware that its core business in car production and marketing was in serious difficulty. Philippe Varin, Chairman of the Peugeot Citroën Managing Board commented on the 2011 results: 'Deterioration in our business environment from the end of the first half [of 2011] led to very disappointing results from our Automotive Division. Other Divisions – Faurecia, Gefco and Banque PSA France – made a positive contribution to our results.' As explained above, Gefco was then sold to raise more finance.

Peugeot Citroen cars are familiar sights on the streets of Paris, supporting thousands of jobs in the French economy.

Table 1 PSA Peugeot Citroën operating profit (loss) contributions from main operating divisions (€ millions)

Peugeot Division	Main business	2012*	2011*	2010*	2009*	2008*
Automotive	Car production and sales	(5572)	(92)	563	(1820)	(711)
Faurecia	Car parts	428	651	420	(226)	(353)
Gefco	Transport and logistics	See below**	223	210	75	126
Banque PSA France	Bank for car loan purchases	390	1032	534	496	556
Other	HQ and group activities	252	(499)	9	59	(12)
Total		(4682)	1315	1736	(1416)	(394)

Notes:

* Important: PSA Peugeot Citroën changed the basis of its accounting practices over the years 2008–2011, thus making annual comparisons difficult. The above comparative figures are therefore approximate.

** The company sold 75 per cent of its transport and logistics business, Gefco, in September 2012 for €800 million. The aim was to raise cash for the rest of the business. It was therefore not included in the annual results for the year 2012.

Source: author from the company annual report and accounts for various years.

To overcome these problems, M Varin explained that the company would undertake the following strategies. 'We [will] implement a strong cash management programme. We [will] step up the cost measures announced last October [2011] from €800 million to €1 billion. In addition, we will launch [an] assets disposal programme . . . that will include property assets and the opening of Gefco's capital for a global amount around €1.5 billion. Our financial position remains robust and secured. . . . We will continue to expand globally especially with our second joint venture in China. [In addition], our two brands [Peugeot and Citroën] will pursue their marketing and upmarket drive.'

The Chairman was summarising the main strategies to recover the situation at the company in 2012 which included:

- investment to reduce costs further;
- sale of some assets;
- new business outside Europe – global sales;
- new car models that moved the company upmarket;
- further joint venture agreements in addition to China and Russia;
- new alliance with General Motors (GM).

These strategies are explored further in this case. However, it is important to note that the problems in the Automotive Division were not just in 2012. Peugeot's car division had also made losses in 2008 and 2009. This was in spite of the above business strategies, which were first announced in 2009 and included the search for new business outside Europe and the move to more upmarket car models.

Strategy: cost reduction

As the case on the world car industry explains ('Competitive strategy – global car markets and the battle between the top five companies'), car companies are highly reliant on economies of scale and scope. In addition, such companies also need strong brands, good distributors and quality servicing. In recent years, innovative new car designs – to reduce fuel consumption and emissions – have also become essential. All these fundamental parts of the business are costly to develop and maintain.

There are two additional complicating factors in the car industry in Europe. The first is that there is excess production capacity in the more mature markets of Western Europe. While the USA made great strides to close some car factories during the market recession of 2008–2009, there were few closures in Western Europe. The second is that the European car market declined substantially over the years 2009–2012. Any company that relied heavily on European sales was therefore particularly vulnerable.

Peugeot itself was given a French government loan of €3 billion and various European governments subsidised car prices to encourage car sales during the worst period of depression. But Peugeot repaid its loan in 2010 and 2011 and did not close any factories. The company's problem was that nearly half its unit production was in its relatively high-cost factories located in France. Moreover, in spite of using 'Lean Production' techniques, nearly half the company's employees were also located in France – see Figure 1. European employment law meant that it was expensive to make employees redundant and thereby reduce costs.

To complicate the cost reduction strategy further, Peugeot was firmly linked to the French Government and its leading politicians, who were seeking to maintain jobs in the French car industry. The company had a long and proud history of working with leading figures in French industry. Peugeot had been making cars since 1898. It was involved in the financial rescue of Citroën when that company went bankrupt in 1976. The PSA Peugeot Citroën company was still controlled by the Peugeot family in 2012 with 46% of the share voting rights. Thus the company and its family were well-connected to leading French political and business circles.

In 2011, the company announced a plan to cut 5,000 jobs in non-production parts of the company during 2011–2012 in order to reduce costs. However, this reduction was relatively small in the context of a company with nearly 200,000 employees of whom almost 100,000 were in France and another 65,000 in the rest of Europe. Arguably, such a cost-

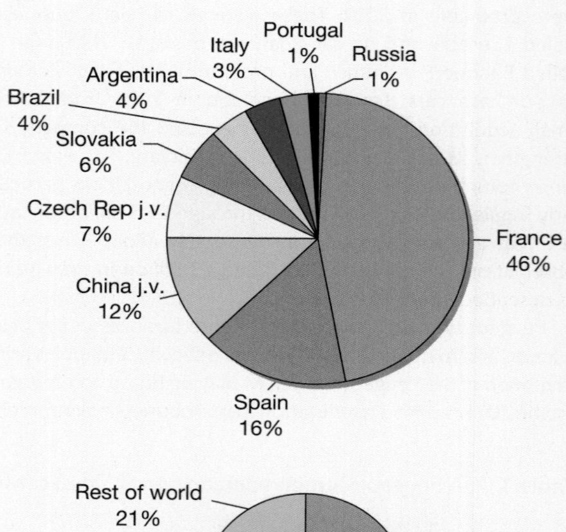

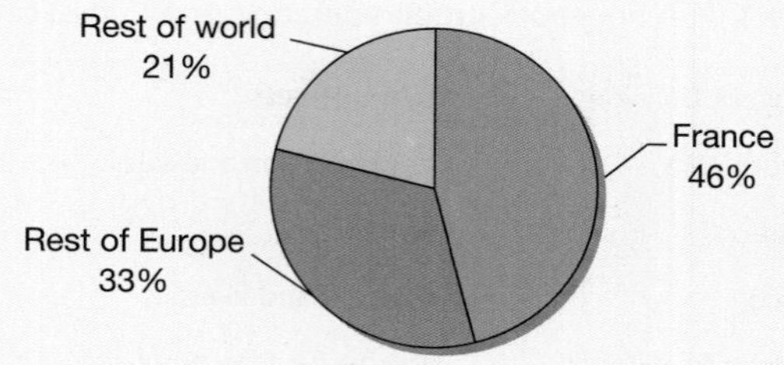

Figure 1 PSA Peugeot Citroën: location of units of production and employees 2010

Notes:
- For production, numbers show the percentage of total production units in each country – for example, France produced 46 per cent of all PSA company vehicles in 2010.
- For employees, numbers show the location of all Peugeot employees as a percentage of the total company employees.
- j.v. = joint venture with Dong Feng Motors in China.

Source: author from company reports and accounts.

cutting strategy was not deep enough. Peugeot was still in the slow lane with regard to its cost-cutting strategy.

In March 2012, Peugeot Citroën announced a new agreement to cut costs by linking with the US company, GM. This is outlined later in this case.

To achieve further cost reductions, the company decided to close one of the seven Peugeot factories in France: the company published plans in July 2012 to close its factory at Aulnay near Paris and to cut another 6,500 jobs. The company's Chief Executive, Philippe Varin, warned in 2011 that the company was in serious financial difficulties. He said that it was spending cash at a rate of €200 million per month in 2012 and did not expect to start generating free cash flow until 2014. His gloomy assessment was designed to indicate to France's powerful trade unions and the new socialist government that the cost-cutting measures were essential. 'The markets are experiencing a brutal, wide and ongoing decline,' he explained. The chief trade union at the company then commented that, 'War has been declared [by the company].' M Varin replied by pointing out that the company had lost €700 million on an operating basis in the first six months of 2012. This simply could not continue.

But, arguably, even the strategy of one factory closure was not enough to reduce costs. The closure strategy was further damaged by a new agreement in late 2013 with the French government and the French trade unions: there would be no further factory closures in France until 2016. This was part of an agreement to rescue the company in late 2013 that is described separately later in this case.

Strategy: new business outside Europe – global sales

As Figure 2 shows, Peugeot was highly reliant on Western European markets for its sales in 2012. Within this large geographic area, the company was even more dependent on two individual countries: France where it had around 30 per cent market share and Spain where it had around 20 per cent market share. By contrast, its share of the large German market was only 5 per cent.

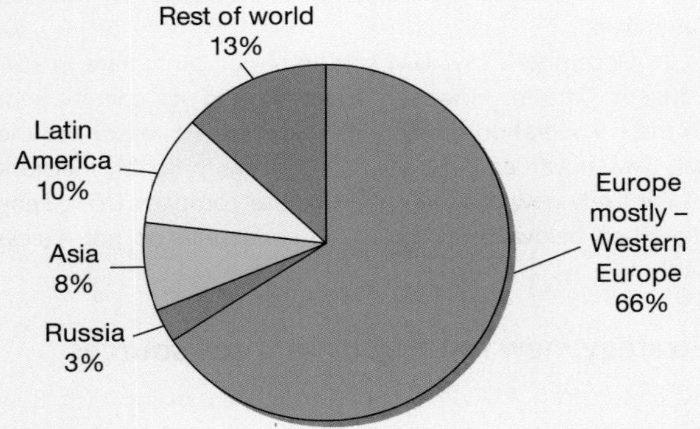

Figure 2 PSA Peugeot Citroen: source of sales 2012

Source: author from company reports and accounts.

Table 2 European car market: some leading market shares (Data: 12 months for 2010 and ten months to end October 2011)

	Country	Ten months to end October 2011	Year 2010
Volkswagen	Germany	21.6%	21.0%
Peugeot Citroën	France	13.2%	14.0%
Renault	France	10.1%	10.9%
Ford	USA	8.3%	8.3%
General Motors: Opel and Vauxhall	USA	8.1%	8.1%
Fiat	Italy	7.8%	8.4%
Daimler	Germany	5.6%	5.6%

Source: author from ACEA data available on the web.

Hence, although Peugeot Citroën was Europe's second largest car company by market share – see Table 2 – its sales were particularly reliant on two countries, namely France and Spain. The significant economic and market pressures of 2012 in those countries made it more difficult to sell cars. Peugeot's senior directors therefore wanted a new strategy that was less reliant on France and Spain and, more generally, Europe.

From 2009 onwards, Peugeot pursued its global strategy with the following specific developments in countries whose car markets were growing faster than Europe:

- Major expansion of its existing joint venture in China with the Dong Feng company located in Wuhan, central China. New plant was started in 2011 that would boost production capacity from around 450,000 per year units to 750,000 units by 2015.
- A totally new joint venture with the Chinese car company Chang'An Automobile in southern China was signed in 2011. This will focus on more upmarket car models and also produce light commercial vehicles (trucks). It will have a production capacity of 200,000 units per year by 2014.
- New production plant in Brazil and Argentina to lift capacity to around 350,000 cars per year from the previous level of around 250,000. Up to 2011, the company did not break even in Latin America.
- A new joint venture with the Japanese car company Mitsubishi in Russia, initially to produce around 125,000 units per year.

However, Peugeot's plans for a major entry into the fast-growing Indian car market were dropped in 2012. No clear reason was announced by the company, but it is probable that the company simply did not have the resources which were stretched following its profit problems. The company had no plans to launch its cars into the world's second largest car market, the USA. Nevertheless, the company was seeking to have 50 per cent of its sales volumes outside Europe by 2015.

Table 3 Peugeot location of car sales by market segment 2011

Segment	% Peugeot Citroën sales	Comment
Small cars	38%	Low profit margins, highly competitive
Mid-market	44%	Still competitive but profit margins higher
Premium	18%	More attractive with high profitability

Source: author from company annual report and accounts for 2011. Data was not published for 2012 but was unlikely to be substantially different.

Strategy: new car models that move the company upmarket

In addition to its heavy reliance on Europe, Peugeot also considered that it had problems with its range of car models. The company was over-exposed to the high volume but low profit small car segments of the market. These segments were also subject to strongly competitive price pressures. It had only limited sales in the premium car segment, where companies like Daimler, BMW and Jaguar Land Rover were able to deliver high profits with price being less important compared to performance, luxury quality and extra car features. Table 3 shows the location of Peugeot sales in 2011.

Peugeot was beginning to address the problem of its need for more premium car models with a series of new car launches. But this strategy would take time and was expensive in both design and marketing.

Strategy: new joint ventures

In addition to its joint venture in China, Peugeot was engaged in developing a number of other joint ventures. For example, it had co-operation agreements with Fiat on car engine development. The company had a joint car production unit with Toyota in the Czech Republic. It had also signed a joint venture agreement with BMW on the development of new generation of hybrid components for battery packs, generators and power electronics. Another joint venture agreement was the new Russian car plant with Mitsubishi mentioned above.

From a strategy perspective, many car companies were now engaged in joint ventures because of the high costs of R&D and the substantial capital sums involved in developing new factories. In addition, some countries still put barriers to trade against foreign companies and these were mainly being overcome by partnering with a local company.

Strategy: new alliance with General Motors

As the separate background case explains, the US car company GM was substantially restructured in the period 2009–2011. As a result, GM's American and worldwide operations were able to report healthy profits in 2011 and 2012. However, its European operations under the brand names Opel and Vauxhall made US$747 million loss in 2011 - even larger than the Peugeot loss in the same year. GM was determined to change its European fortunes.

Part of GM's European problem was that it had accepted a €1.5 billion loan from the German government in 2009 on the understanding that it would not close any German car plant until 2014 at the earliest. Peugeot received €3 billion from the French government with a similar agreement although the full details were never published. In spite of having repaid its loan, Peugeot still had obligations to the French government and the French unions.

In early 2012, GM and Peugeot companies announced that they were exploring a new alliance. GM planned to take a 7 per cent share of Peugeot. The companies would share vehicle platforms, components and modules. They would also create a global purchasing joint venture to buy components for the two companies in Europe with a combined annual purchasing power of US$125 billion. The two companies claimed that the synergies from their new alliance would amount to US$2 billion annually within five years. There would be a joint steering committee with an equal number of executives from both companies. The initial focus would be on small and medium-size passenger cars, multipurpose vehicles and small sports utility vehicles. The deal was still subject to regulatory approval at the time of writing this case.

Some analysts were doubtful if this was sufficient. 'Combining the two from a product perspective brings very little now,' explained Erich Hasser of Credit Suisse. He pointed out that the two companies both specialise in small and medium cars. To obtain the full synergies of the alliance, the companies would have to cut overlapping production capacity. But this may be against the government agreements outlined above. The *Financial Times* also pointed out that, 'Until now, [Peugeot] has guarded its independence.'

In any event, any such alliance would be politically and technically difficult. There would be issues of Peugeot family control in addition to any problems with the European governments. Moreover, European alliances did not have a strong success record in car strategy. Peugeot had attempted to form an alliance with Fiat in 2009 that was ultimately unsuccessful. However, as the background case explains, Renault has formed a successful alliance with Nissan so some observers remained optimistic.

In December 2012, GM sold its 7 per cent share in PSA Peugeot Citroën. However, it re-affirmed its commitment to the co-operation deal outlined above. The reason for the sale was never entirely clear, but it was probably because of the likely new deal with the Chinese company Dong Feng described below: US and Chinese companies do not necessarily mix.

Strategy: new funding from three sources

By early 2014, PSA Peugeot Citroën had major cash flow problems. This was solved by an injection of €800 million from the Chinese car company Dong Feng and €800 million the French government. The company was hoping to build a broader alliance with the Chinese car company, but this would take some years, possibly until 2020. In addition, another €1.4 billion was raised by a share issue, effectively diluting the shareholding of the Peugeot family so that it no longer controlled the company. This secured funding for the company's continued turnaround but it did nothing specific for the turnaround strategy.

Conclusion

PSA Peugeot Citroën was clearly experiencing a difficult trading period in 2012–2014. It had some competitive advantages that can be identified by reading the case. But it was still struggling to realise fully a new and successful strategy. It was heavily reliant on Europe's car markets where there was excess capacity in small cars. Moreover, its French production base was not low cost. For many commentators, its strategy was still stuck in the slow lane with no clear way forward.

 This case was written by Richard Lynch from published information. Sources: PSA Peugeot Annual report and accounts for various years. *Financial Times*: 2 February 2012, p 11; 16 February 2012, pp 16 & 19; 23 February 2012, p 19; 24 February 2012, p 12 (Editorial); 29 February 2012, p 25; 1 March 2012, pp 18 & 22; 7 March 2012, pp 10 & 21; 13 July 2012, pp 18, 19 & 22; 26 July 2012, p 20; 18 October 2012, p 17; 12 February 2013, p 21; 14 February 2013, p 14; 30 July 2013, p 16; 15 October 2013, p 18; 26 November 2013, pp 16 & 20; 21 January 2014, p 16; 20 February 2014, pp 16 & 19; 27 February 2014, p 20.

Case questions

1 Examine the changes in the strategic environment of the global car industry over the last few years and show how they have influenced the strategies of PSA Peugeot Citroën. Has the company's strategy managed such changes as well as its European rivals?

2 Analyse and then critically evaluate the main sustainable competitive advantages, if any, of PSA Peugeot Citroën. What does your analysis imply for the company's new strategy of building an alliance with GM?

3 In a relatively mature industry like the global car industry, to what extent is innovation a prime contributor to the strategies of a well-established companies like PSA Peugeot Citroën? If innovation is important, how can PSA Peugeot Citroën improve further? If it is not important, what other strategies are more important? Give reasons for your answer.

4 Comment critically upon the strategies of PSA Peugeot Citroën over the last four years, including cost cutting, developing upmarket models and moving outside its European base. What are the implications of your answer for the company's proposed new alliance with General Motors?

5 What strategies would you recommend for PSA Peugeot Citroën from 2014 onwards? Give the reasoning behind your answer.

CASE STUDY 6

Risks and rewards in Russia: rescue strategy at AvtoVAZ cars

For decades, AvtoVAZ has been Russia's leading car manufacturer. But it faces terminal decline unless its new owners, Renault and Nissan, can find a winning rescue strategy. What are the chances of success?

Video and sound summary of this case

Background

At its peak in the 1980s, AvtoVAZ employed over 250,000 people at its main factory in Togliati in the former socialist republic of the USSR. The company produced cars best known in the west under the brand name *Lada*. They were old-fashioned basic cars, often called 'clunkers', that were adequate when there was no market competition in the former one-party communist state. They were even exported to the West as cheap cars. But the exports were stopped in 1997 when the Europe introduced its first emission standards for car exhausts: *Lada* models would have failed the tests.

After the collapse of the USSR, Russian markets began to open up to Western products. Many of the world's leading car manufacturers began exporting to Russia during the early 2000. Some even set up assembly plants in the country. Although AvtoVAZ continued to hold the leading market share, it began to face new global models and new competitors.

To add to its problems, the year 2009 was a disaster for the Russian car market. The Russian economy went into serious decline as the country was affected by the world financial crisis. The domestic car market was hit particularly hard. AvtoVAZ had to be rescued by an injection of US$2 billion funds from the Russian government. It was no surprise that the company began looking for foreign partners – with the support of the government.

The foreign partners of AvtoVAZ

Even while AvtoVAZ was part of the communist state in the 1950s–1970s, the USSR government recognised that foreign help was required to improve the efficiency of its manufacturing and to design and build new vehicle models. The Italian car company Fiat was chosen in 1956 to help modernise the Russian company's outdated manufacturing plant with new equipment and some new models based on Fiat's Italian models. But this was not enough. For many of the following years, the company still had too many employees producing out-of-date vehicles.

After the break-up of the USSR in 1991, the new Russian state remained keen to support its domestic car industry. The old Fiat models did not survive the change. A new partnership was developed between AvtoVAZ and the American car giant General Motors (GM). But GM itself faced major profit pressures and the new co-operation never really produced any major change.

In 2010 and faced with the collapse of its leading domestic car manufacturer, the Russian government – totally understandably – sought another foreign partner: up stepped the French car maker Renault and its Japanese co-partner Nissan. They had initially invested over US$1 billion for a minority stake in the company in 2008. Sales were still declining with old Lada models and factory production was still inefficient after this investment. In spite of this (or perhaps seeing an opportunity), Renault/Nissan decided that they wanted control of the Russian company. After long negotiations, the two companies invested a further US$2 billion in 2014 to take a majority stake in the company with a minority 27 per cent still being held by a Russian government-owned company. Why did Renault/Nissan make such a risky investment?

This fuel station on the outskirts of St Petersburg serves the increasingly sophisticated Russian car market.

Risks and rewards in the Russian car market

Over the years 2008–2012, the Russian car market began to grow again – see Figure 1. However, the Russian car market declined by 5 per cent in 2013 due to weakness in the Russian economy. In addition, the AvtoVAZ market share continued to fall from 33 per cent to 30 per cent. The market share of foreign competitors continued to grow: for example, the Korean car company Hyundai/Kia increased its market share from 12.8 per cent to 13.3 per cent. Why? Although the AvtoVAZ models were newer, they were still poor compared to foreign rivals. There were therefore real risks for the takeover by Renault/Nissan.

So what was the potential reward for the new French/Japanese owners? Why did they invest over US$3 billion? In essence, it was the potential size of the Russian car market coupled with the market dominance of the AvtoVAZ company, which was supported by the Russian government.

The largest European car market in 2014 was Germany with 3.8 million cars sold. By comparison, the Russian market was

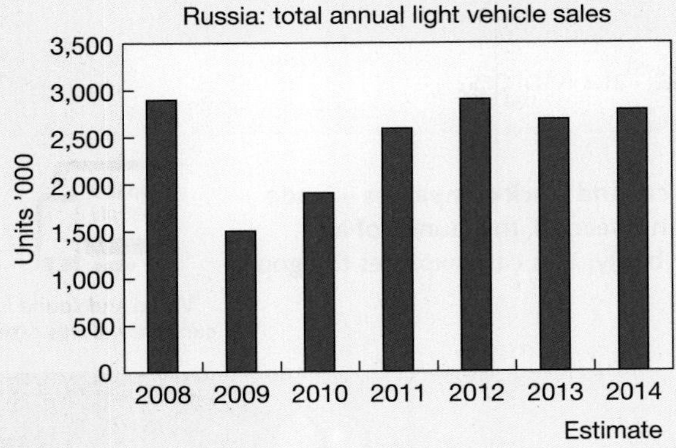

Figure 1 Russian car market – revived and then stalled

Source: author from various Russian car market estimates.

estimated to sell around 2.8 million cars in the same year. However, the population of Germany was around 85 million whereas the population of Russia was around 145 million: Russian car ownership per head of the population was much lower than German. Moreover, many of the cars on the roads in Russia were old stock and needed replacement. Analysts expected the Russian car market would grow substantially to around 5 million cars annually by the year 2020. This was an attractive proposition for foreign car companies – including Renault/Nissan.

Strategies for turnaround at AvtoVAZ

Arguably, the leading Russian car company AvtoVAZ was well placed to exploit this potential growth in the Russian car market. But it faced major problems: its model range was beginning to be replaced with cars from the Renault/Nissan range. But this would take time and would require some experimentation to judge the best models for the Russian market. Moreover, such a strategy had not worked at AvtoVAZ with the earlier new models from Fiat and GM. In addition, the company's manufacturing base was inefficient and unprofitable. For example, one of the first decisions of the new AvtoVAZ Chief Executive Officer, appointed in late 2013, was to reduce company employees by more than 12,500 people.

Despite these problems, AvtoVAZ had economies of scale from its large Russian car market share. It was therefore able to justify building a new car engine plant in Russia. Its smaller competitors with their lower scale of production were unable to justify the same investment. This was important because the Russian government introduced new import regulations that meant taxes were lower if 60 per cent of car components were manufactured inside Russia – potentially therefore giving AvtoVAZ a low cost advantage.

Importantly, the Russian government was broadly supportive of the new AvtoVAZ. It accepted that a major shakeup was required with a substantial injection of new technology and new models. These could only come from a foreign partner. This would preserve Russian jobs and develop the Russian car industry. It was therefore worth the leading Russian car company losing some independence. But the strategic risks were still there for Renault and Nissan.

Case questions

1 What are the strategic problems with relying on the growth forecast for the Russian car market? Are there any risks associated with buying a dominant market share of a company like AvtoVAZ? What strategies, if any, are available to overcome such problems and risks.

2 Identify the risks and rewards for Renault/Nissan and for the Russian government. Would you take these risks if you were the Chief Executive Officer of Renault/Nissan?

3 If you were a rival company like Volkswagen or Hyundai, what strategies would you adopt in Russia against AvtoVAZ?

Note

* This case was written by the author from numerous sources including: *Financial Times*: 13 December 2012, p 18; 16 January 2013, p 19. *Wall Street Journal*: 3 May 2012 'Renault-Nissan buy into Russia's aged auto giant'; 23 January 2014, 'Layoffs come after Russian vehicle sales fell 5.5% in 2013' and 'New AvtoVAZ broom sweeps clean'. *Reuters*: 12 December 2012, 'Renault Nissan seals Russian deal in quest for growth'; 14 February 2013, 'Renault-Nissan UniCredit create Russia finance venture'; 28 November 2013, 'Renault-Nissan to build second engine plant with AvtoVAZ'; 18 February 2014, 'Lada maker Avtovaz reports 2013 loss.' *Renault website*: 26 January 2013, 'Strategic partnership with AvtoVAZ'. *Automotive News Europe*: 20 January 2014, 'Suppliers enter, expand in Russia ahead of forecast sales surge'. *Economist*: 2 March 2012, 'Fiat's miserable failure in Russia underscores just how hard it is to do business there'.

CASE STUDY 7

Competitive strategies: good news and bad news at Tata Motors

In the two years to 2009, Tata Motors – one of India's leading car and truck companies – made two dramatic strategic moves: first, a world-class acquisition and, second, the launch of a revolutionary new car. One has turned out well and the other badly. This case explores the good news and bad news for the company.

Video and sound summary of this case

Two dramatic new strategies but with mixed success

In 2008, Tata Motors acquired two world car brands and their associated assets – Jaguar and Land Rover (JLR) – from the struggling US car company Ford Motors for $2.3 billion. Commenting on the occasion, the company said, 'This is a momentous time for all of us at Tata Motors. Jaguar and Land Rover are two iconic British brands with worldwide prospects. We are looking forward to extending our full support to the Jaguar and Land Rover team to realise their competitive potential.'

One year later, the same takeover was facing major problems. Sales at JLR were down 32 per cent compared to the previous year and the new purchase made a net loss of nearly $450 million in the 10 months since its purchase. Ratan Tata, Chairman of Tata Motors, commented in May 2009, 'If one had known there was going to be a meltdown, then yes [Tata went too far] but nobody knew. Both the acquisitions were made, I would say, at an inopportune time in the sense that they were near the top of the market.' Nevertheless, JLR returned to profitability in 2010. It has since proved to be a great success in world luxury car markets. That was the good news at Tata Motors.

Around the same time as Tata Motors acquired JLR, the company also impressed the world with the launch of India's cheapest new car model, called the *Nano*. Priced at around only $2,000 (1 lakh Indian rupees), the new car design was aimed at the large, low-priced car market in both India and other developing countries. The Nano embodied innovative manufacturing strategies and some neat, cost-saving features. Coupled with low Indian labour manufacturing costs, the Nano was designed to be the world's lowest-priced car while at the same time delivering profits to Tata. For various reasons, the launch was delayed from October 2008 to July 2009 with a consequent loss of sales and profits. The problems were compounded by further unexpected major difficulties with the Nano in 2010, as we will see later. By 2013, the Nano was only one of Tata's problems in the Indian domestic car market. That was the bad news at Tata Motors.

This case explores the strategic implications for the firm. Where does the company go from here? How does it tackle its problems in the Indian car market? How does it support JLR? Does it invest in other areas of the business where it has major strengths – like trucks and buses? What are its next strategic moves?

Tata Motors' traditional markets are mainly in India where the traffic – here near one of the new metro stations in New Delhi – is busy and growing fast. But Tata's acquisition of Jaguar Land Rover has given the company a global market perspective.

To explore these questions, the case has the following sections:

- Indian car and truck markets: stopped growing;
- Tata Motors and its competitors;
- Tata Motors: its resources and capabilities;
- Tata Motors: problems in the Indian domestic car market;
- Tata Motors: the successful acquisition of JLR after some early difficulties;
- Tata Commercial vehicle range builds on its strengths;
- conclusions: where now for Tata?

Indian car and truck markets: stopped growing

As the earlier case on the global car industry explained, all the car companies were heavily dependent on high volumes for their profits: economies of scale and scope remained key factors for success in this industry including India. In addition, all the major companies were engaged in new designs, particularly those associated with new engines. There were two pressures: to meet new emission standards and to produce engines that used either lower-cost fuels or alternative forms of power, such

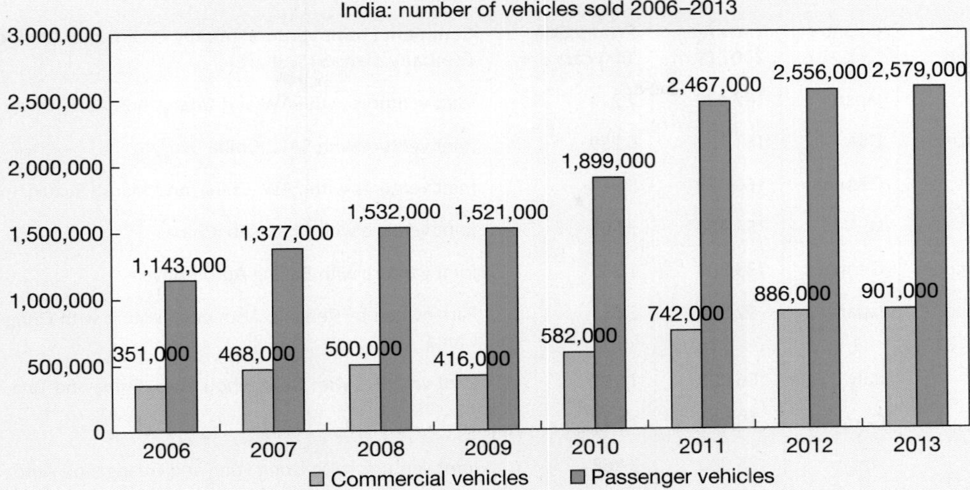

Figure 1 Indian vehicle markets have stopped growing

Source: author based on data from Tata Motors Annual Report 2013.

as electricity. For example, R&D expenditures by the ten leading car companies in 2007 were around \$50 billion alone. Hence companies such as Tata Motors and all its competitors in India were planning to invest heavily in new models and new more fuel-efficient engines over the period to 2016.

In 2013, the Indian home market for passenger cars was worth around \$9 billion at manufacturer's selling prices (MSP): this was small compared to the world market at around \$1,300 billion. World markets were beginning to recover from the downturn in 2007–2010 while the Indian market was in trouble. In 2009, it was growing at around 11 per cent per annum but it ceased to grow in 2013. The Indian market for commercial vehicles – trucks, three-wheelers and buses – was worth around \$7.5 billion, and had also halted.

Although the Indian car and truck markets are significant, they are small by world standards. But the 1 billion size of India's population, especially its growing middle class, suggests that the Indian market has great potential.

Table 1 shows the world's leading car companies and positions India's leading vehicle companies in that context. Anyone who has been stuck in one of the many rush-hour traffic jams in Delhi or Mumbai (like the writer of this case) might be surprised by the low position of the leading Indian companies. But many Indians have been too poor to afford to buy a car. They have relied instead on cheaper motorcycles: India is the world's largest market for two-wheelers. But this is now beginning to change with some growth during the years to 2009 in the market.

Foreign car companies, like the big five world companies, were primarily attracted to the Indian market for two reasons: first, existing car usage was lower than other countries, suggesting significant growth potential; second, there was good evidence of steadily increasing wealth in India to support greater car ownership. In addition, they expected long-term growth in the Indian economy coupled with the Indian Government's investment in a better transport infrastructure – roads and bridges – to make Indian markets more attractive.

Importantly when it comes to expansion strategies, the Chinese market may provide some lessons for India. The Chinese vehicle market has grown faster than that in India from two related strategies. First, the Chinese Government itself has supported foreign companies entering the Chinese market. It has placed restrictions on the share ownership of Chinese car companies, but otherwise it has encouraged foreign entry. Second, Chinese vehicle companies themselves have embraced wholeheartedly the strategy of joint ventures – see Table 1 – to develop rapidly the car production capacity of China. The result has been a more dynamic and open Chinese vehicle market than India. There have been almost no joint ventures between the world's leading car companies and Indian car companies.

After a dip associated with the world recession, both the Indian passenger car and commercial vehicle markets grew in 2010 – see Figure 1 – but then stalled. The reported reason was a lack of growth in the Indian economy. In spite of ths, the major global car companies were seeking ways into the Indian car market in 2014 – providing new competition for Tata Motors.

Tata Motors and its competitors

Because the Indian market for motor vehicles has enjoyed some protection in the past from the entry of world car companies, Tata Motors had only three major competitors in its volume home market in the years up to 2009. These were:

1 *Maruti Suzuki*. This company was controlled by the Japanese company Suzuki and was the market leader in the passenger car segment in India. The company is explored further in the section that follows.

Table 1 The leading world companies in the car industry ranked by turnover

Company	Country	Turnover 2007 ($m)	Production '000 cars only	Comment ('Joint venture' usually means that the local company owns 51% share)
Toyota	Japan	187,420	7,211	Joint ventures with FAW and Guangzhou Auto, China
General Motors	USA	181,122	6,259	Joint venture with SAIC, China
Volkswagen	Germany	160,079	5,964	Joint ventures with FAW, China, and Maruti Suzuki, India
Ford	USA	154,400	3,565	Joint venture with Chang'An, China
Daimler Mercedes	Germany	133,300	1,335	Joint venture with Beijing Automotive
Nissan	Japan	92,500	2,651	Part-owned by Renault. Also joint venture with Dong Feng, China
Fiat	Italy	86,000	1,991	Joint ventures with Guangzhou Auto, China and Tata, India
BMW	Germany	79,100	1,541	
Honda	Japan	76,000	3,868	Joint ventures with Dong Feng and Guangzhou Auto, China
PSA	France	73,600	3,024	Joint venture with Dong Feng, China
Renault	France	55,500	2,276	Pulled out of a new joint venture to set up own company in India; also has a larger car joint venture with Mahindra, India
Mazda	Japan	36,641		Joint venture with Chang'An, China
Hyundai	S Korea	32,334	2,292	Joint venture with Beijing Automotive, China
Mitsubishi	Japan	28,193		Joint venture with Beijing Automotive, China
FAW	PR China	24,613	1,436*	See above
Suzuki	Japan	21,200	2,284*	Joint venture with Chang'An Controlling interest (51%) in Suzuki Maruti, India
SAIC	PR China	20,731	1,137*	See above
Kia	S Korea	16,664		
Guangzhou Auto	PR China	14,724	510,000	See above
Chang'An Auto	PR China	7,860	850 E	See above
DongFeng Auto	PR China	7,782	638	See above
Beijing Auto	PR China	N/a	600 E	See above
Tata	India	5,778**	228	Includes joint venture with Fiat
Geely	PR China	5,640	185	
Suzuki Maruti	India	3,172	633	See above
Cherry	PR China	2,100	428	
Mahindra	India	1,775	100	Includes joint venture with Renault
Hindustan	India	1,230	N/a	Includes joint ventures with General Motors on trucks and with Mitsubishi on large cars

Notes:
E = Estimate by author based on published company data.
* Includes joint venture production, so numbers are double counted with the foreign car partners.
** Tata Motors includes turnover for trucks and buses, whose higher prices per vehicle explain why the turnover is higher while the production numbers are lower.
The large Russian car company – LADA – is excluded from the above data because turnover figures were not readily available at the time of writing this case. It would possibly be sited somewhere around SAIC/Kia in the table.
Chrysler did not file any meaningful data because it was part of Daimler up to 2007, then sold privately in 2008 and re-combined with Fiat in 2009. However, OICA data shows that the company produced 755,000 cars in 2007.

Sources: author's data sourced from the individual company accounts for turnover and from OICA 2007 data for production numbers, except for the Chinese companies sourced from their company accounts (because OICA significantly understates Chinese car production).

2 *Mahindra and Mahindra*. This company has a major presence in a special segment of the Indian vehicle market – the multi-utility vehicle (MUV) sector. These vehicles are larger than passenger cars and can be used to transport either passengers or commercial goods, depending on the precise configuration of the vehicle. Mahindra was market leader in MUVs with a share around 50 per cent. Mahindra also had a joint venture with the French car company, Renault. But Renault was beginning to develop separately – as explained below.

3 *Hindustan Motors*. This company tends to have a more specialist range of passenger cars, trucks and other commercial vehicles. It is the smallest of the four main Indian car companies and is owned by one of India's most famous family conglomerates, the Birla Group.

In addition, Tata Motors was facing new global competitors. Up to 2009, this was mainly in small sales of large and upmarket cars. The global companies did not target the main Indian car market: the sub-compact, smaller car during the early 2000s. However, by the late 2000s, they had all recognised that the large and growing Indian middle class was looking increasingly to quality, small car transport. The problem for the world's leading companies was that the entry barriers to the Indian market were high. What was the solution? Set up car plant inside India. As a result, Toyota, Ford and Renault had built or were building new Indian manufacturing plant:

- *Toyota*. The company had plant in Bangalore to produce the mid-range price Corolla. In addition, it launched a new Indian model, the *Etios*, in 2010 at a lower price point especially for the Indian market.
- *Ford*. Its factory in Chennai was making a new model, the Figo, especially targetted at the Maruti Suzuki range. The President and CEO of Ford worldwide, Alan Mullaly, explained that Ford had been involved in the Indian car market for many years but this was its first small car. 'We are entering the sweet spot of the Indian market. It's a game-changer for our Indian operation.'
- *Renault*. The company has built a major presence in the Indian car market over the four years from 2010. The *Fluence* and *Koleos* models were launched in 2011. An extensive distribution network through the country was completed in 2012, covering a minimum of 35 cities. In addition, a sales and marketing team has been built within Renault India.

All this meant greater competition for Tata Motors. The company's range of cars included more expensive models than the Nano and cheaper ones than the JLR range. Some of the Tata models would compete directly against the new Toyota, Renault and Ford cars.

Tata Motors: its resources and capabilities

Founded in 1954, Tata Motors forms a major part of one of India's most famous family conglomerates, the Tata Group. The company began as a manufacturer of commercial vehicles – trucks and buses – in association with the German company Daimler Benz. Daimler remains one of the world leaders in such vehicles, but the link with Tata was soon broken. Tata then developed an independent strategy and no longer had any connection with the German company. Given the protected nature of both the Indian passenger car market as well as the truck market, Tata then branched from commercial vehicles into passenger cars in 1991. It launched a series of car models over the next few years into different segments of the passenger car market. These are described later in this section.

In 2009, Tata Motor's commercial vehicle operations were one of the major resource strengths of the company. It was the market leader with over 60 per cent of the market in its home country India – see Figure 2. It had good relations both with the central Indian government and also with a number of the Indian state governments, all of whom were important customers for the large trucks and buses of this part of Tata's business. Tata commercial vehicles were also strong throughout neighbouring countries such as Nepal and Sri Lanka.

In addition, Tata has used its home strength in commercial vehicles to develop its worldwide operations. In 2004, it acquired the truck and bus operations of the Korean company Daewoo. In 2005, Tata bought a minority stake in a Spanish commercial vehicle company, Hispano Carrocera. In 2006, it formed a joint venture with a Brazilian company, Marcopolo which had strengths in bus and coach manufacture. Tata had also developed commercial truck and bus building production capacity in Argentina and South Africa. However, it had very limited operations in the world's two leading commercial vehicle markets, North America and Europe.

Turning to the Indian passenger car market, Tata Motors has not been able to gain the same market dominance as it possessed in commercial vehicles. Figure 2 shows its market share was weak and falling in the domestic Indian market: this was a major strategic problem for the company in 2013.

Over many years, Tata Motors had attempted to increase its share of the Indian market. In addition to its own designs, Tata developed a link with the Italian motor company Fiat and

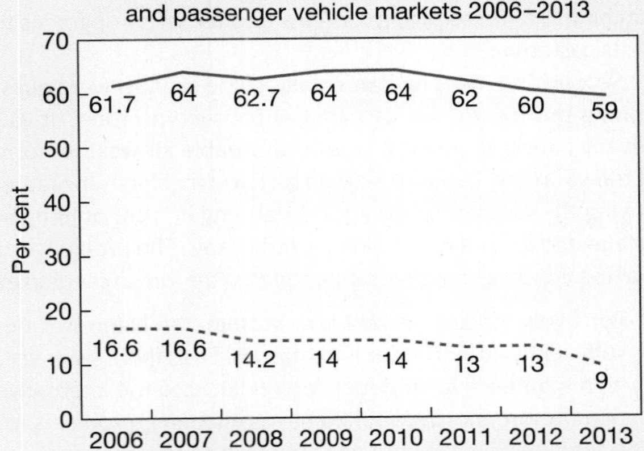

Figure 2 Tata dominates the Indian commercial vehicle market but not passenger vehicles

Source: author based on data from Tata Motors Annual Report 2013.

then used this to launch some Fiat designed cars. In addition, Tata also had access to Fiat's diesel engine technology – helpful with the increased pressures on greater fuel efficiency. In spite of all this activity, Tata's market share remained small and declining in the years to 2013. Neither the launch of the Nano, nor the arrival of the first JLR dealers in India in 2008–2009 had made a difference. This was not surprising in the case of JLR whose luxury cars would only ever take a small share of the Indian car market. But the lack of impact from the Nano was more significant.

As explained above, the Indian passenger car market has been dominated by Maruti Suzuki for some years with a share over 50 per cent. Maruti Suzuki's success has come because it has been better at developing models suited to the Indian market. This was not the only area where Maruti was better. For example, Maruti set up a company to sell used vehicles some years earlier than Tata, which only followed in 2008. Equally, Maruti was an early leader in developing a strong chain of support garages and service stations – vital in the massive Indian subcontinent – and also in providing driving schools to help its customers learn to cope with Indian's demanding road traffic. Arguably, these were company areas where Tata Motors was weaker than the market leader, Maruti Suzuki.

Tata Motors: problems in the Indian domestic car market

After four years of development work, the new Tata small car was launched with great publicity in 2008. It was priced at US$2,000 and was the world's cheapest car. It was hoped that the *Nano* would begin to eat into Maruti's dominant market share. However, Tata claimed that the main target of the Nano was not Maruti. The Nano was aimed at those Indian families who currently perch everyone on an over-laden motorcycle. Tata's objective was to expand the Indian passenger car market rather than attack a dominant competitor.

Although the Nano was initially well-received in the Indian domestic car market, there were two main problems with the car. First, there were reports of some Nanos spontaneously catching fire. These prompted Tata to offer safety upgrades to all its customers.

Second and more fundamentally, some analysts were questioning the Indian market demand for such a model. It was initially aimed at creating, 'a safe, affordable all-weather form of transport for . . . families riding on two-wheelers – the father driving the scooter, his young kid standing in front of him, his wife seated behind him, holding a little baby'. The problem was that this concept may have misinterpreted the Indian car market:

- For those Indians on *very low incomes*, the Nano was not sufficiently attractive for two reasons. First, there were very high maintenance and fuel costs relative to the alternative of a motorcycle. Second, there were parking problems for customers living in very poor housing conditions.
- For those Indians on *higher incomes*, the Nano was too basic. 'On your first car, you want something special with upmarket features . . . something that makes the car stand out'. If these explanations were correct, then the Nano did not appeal to either of the possible target groups.

Arguably, the launch of the Nano also took managerial and marketing focus away from the range of Tata cars serving the rest of the Indian car market. In particular, the company's range of mid-priced cars was under strong attack from competitors. The result was a significant decline in the whole range of models from Tata Motors in the years 2010–2013: Figure 3 shows the impact on sales and profits. Initially, sales rose dramatically after the JLR acquisition. But then the problems in the Indian domestic market hit home.

Tata Motors: the successful acquisition of JLR after some early difficulties

Around the same time as the announcement about the Nano, Tata Motors acquired the JLR company from the US company Ford Motors. JLR's passenger cars were positioned in the upmarket end of world cars with both high prices and high performance characteristics: Jaguar in luxury sports cars and Land Rover in off-road sports utility vehicles (SUVs). The JLR brands were pitched against heavy world competition from such other companies such as BMW, Mercedes Benz and Lexus (the luxury brand from Toyota).

At the time of the acquisition, JLR had a major programme of new models coming for launch over the period to 2016. Many of these models were designed to be both luxurious and able to meet the increasingly strict fuel efficiency and new higher exhaust emission standards being set in North America and Europe. The JLR headquarters were in the UK with three main UK plants, 14,500 employees and a major research facility.

From the outset, Tata Motors decided to manage its new acquisition separately from its Indian company – presumably for reasons of history, market positioning and resources. But this had the downside that Tata would not be able to share the JLR knowledge so easily across the Tata group. In the years to 2013, JLR announced that it was investing further in new models and recruiting several thousand more workers. It was also manufacturing one Land Rover model that would be shipped as parts to the Tata factory in Pune and re-assembled for sale in India.

The turnaround in JLR was reflected in the sales and profit figures for 2013 – see Figure 3. The upturn in turnover was entirely due to the new acquisition. The downturn – especially in profit before tax – was due to Tata's difficulties in the Indian car market. Without JLR, the company would probably have made a major loss.

Tata Commercial vehicle range builds on its strengths

Tata Motors announced several new models in its commercial vehicle range in the years 2010–2013. It was clearly putting significant resources behind this successful part of its business. But it faced competition from new entrants. For example, the world's leading commercial vehicle manufacturer, Daimler Benz, announced new models in 2010 aimed at developing countries like India. Specifically in India, Daimler Trucks acquired the 40 per cent shareholding that it did not already own in its Indian subsidiary and founded Daimler India Commercial Vehicles Pvt. Ltd. Daimler had reported profit problems in its Indian

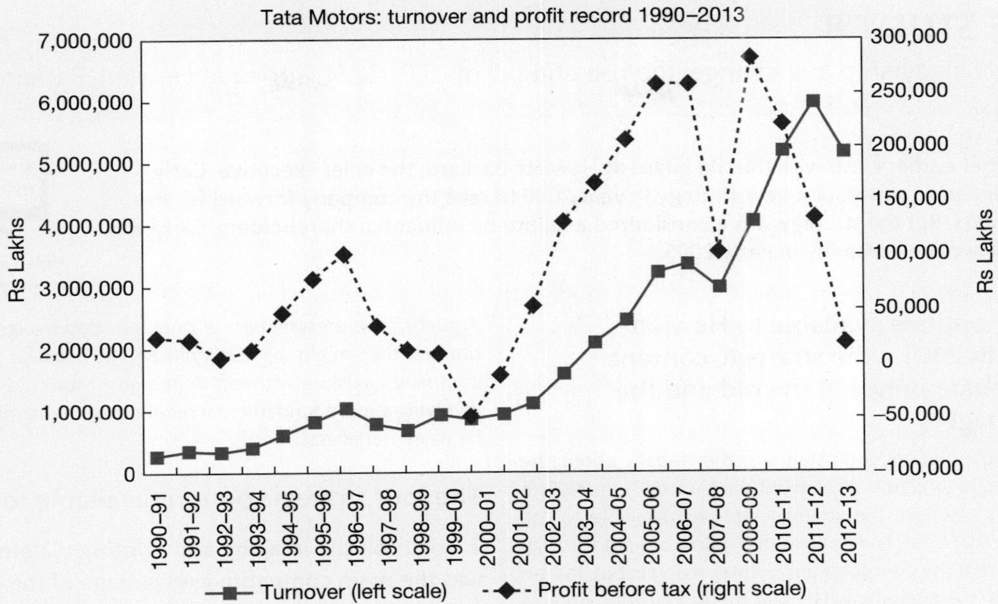

Figure 3 Tata Motors sales and profits tumble due to difficulties in the Indian domestic market, not Jaguar Land Rover

Source: author based on data from Tata Motors Annual Report 2013.

subsidiary in 2009 but was determined to make progress in coming years using its world-class truck and bus designs. Tata Commercial Vehicles would face a real competitive threat over time, not only in its dominant home market but in its various overseas operations where it was weaker.

Conclusions: where now for Tata?

From the perspective of global strategy, Tata Motors' strategic position was both weak and strong. Tata had a small and declining share of the Indian car market. It faced increased competition from its main domestic rival, Maruti Suzuki, and from the leading world car companies. The Nano had not solved the problem. However, it had launched a whole range of new models in 2013 and was optimistic about the future. But perhaps a joint venture with a foreign competitor would prove a better strategy for Tata?

And then there was the opportunity JLR. What should its strategy be for this part of the company? Should it continue to invest heavily? Could it leverage its Indian connections further to enhance sales? How best could it exploit a competitive resource that no previous Indian car company had ever previously possessed – two major global brands?

Although the Indian commercial vehicle market was growing more slowly, there was also substantial growth potential in its range of trucks and buses. Moreover, this was one area where Tata was the Asian market leader. Perhaps it should pursue this route more vigorously? Perhaps it should rebuild its former link with another of the world's leading commercial vehicle producers, Daimler-Benz, with a view to strengthening its world franchise? Perhaps Tata should continue to link up with other commercial vehicle manufacturers around the world but on a smaller scale? Would this fully exploit its knowledge and skills in commercial vehicles?

Case questions

1 From the perspective of Tata Motors, what are the main elements that you would highlight in a strategic environmental analysis? And what are Tata's main competitive resources and capabilities?

2 What are the implications of your analysis for Tata's future strategy? Does it continue to pursue all its current areas of growth? Perhaps it needs to be more selective in terms of its growth opportunities? Are there any that you would put first? Are there any that you would drop?

3 Are there any lessons that other companies can draw from Tata Motors' strategies over recent years? Consider strategies where Tata has done well and others where the company has done badly.

Note

* This case was written by the author from numerous sources including: Annual Report and Accounts for Tata Motors 2007–13, Maruti Suzuki 2008 and 2009, Mahindra and Mahindra 2008, Hindustan Motors 2008 all available on the web. References for the earlier case 'Tricky Time for Tata Motors' can be found in *Strategic Management*, 6th edn. New *Financial Times* references are as follows: 9 May 2011, p 19; 19 July 2011, p 22; 4 October 2012, p 26; 9 October 2012, p 23; 12 February 2013, p 19; 11 April 2013, pp 16 & 21; 21 July 2013; 10 September 2013, p 21; 6 December 2013, p 26; 7 February 2014, p 16; 11 February 2014, p 16; 7 March 2014, p 19.

CASE STUDY 8

Strategic leadership and change: the rise and fall of CEO Carly Fiorina at Hewlett-Packard

Following her earlier clash with the old guard at Hewlett-Packard, the chief executive, Carly Fiorina, needed to work out a new strategy in year 2000 to take the company forward for the next five years. But the strategy was a considered a failure by influential shareholders. Carly was forced to leave the company in early 2005.

Video and sound summary of this case

Strategic options available to Hewlett-Packard in 2001 – the strategic content of the debate between the old and the new managers

As a starting point to understanding the debate about the future strategic direction of Hewlett-Packard (HP) in 2001, it is relevant to explore the strategic options available to the company at that time. The options that follow are not the only way to segment the computer and printer markets but, rather, they present the options as HP saw them. The four options listed below follow the way that the company reports its business activities in its Annual Report and Accounts – see Table 1.

Table 1 HP: segment information – printing systems are crucial to profitability (all data in $ billions)

	2001	2000	1999
Net revenue			
Imaging and printing systems	19.4	20.5	18.6
Computing systems, e.g. 4 home and office computers	17.8	20.6	17
IT services, e.g. consultancy	7.6	7.1	6.3
Other	1.0	1.6	1.3
Adjustments	(0.6)	(1.0)	(1.1)
Total HP consolidated revenue	45.2	48.8	42.4
Net earnings before extraordinary items			
Imaging and printing systems	1.8	2.7	2.4
Computing systems, e.g. home and office computers	(0.4)	1.0	1.0
IT services, e.g. consultancy	0.3	0.5	0.5
Other	(0.3)	(0.1)	(0.1)
Corporate adjustments, including tax	(1.0)	(1.6)	(1.6)
Total HP consolidated earnings	0.6	3.6	3.1

Source: Hewlett-Packard report and accounts – note that numbers have been rounded so there may be some minor differences in totals.

Arguably, the presentation of only four options ignores other options that might be available to HP because it uses the company's existing segment definitions. More radical options involving a more fundamental redefinition of the market might be more beneficial.

The four strategic options available to HP

1 Focus on the imaging and printing systems: this was the main competitive advantage of the company

- The basic printer market is mature. It has several distinct segments:
- the low-end, low-price inkjet printers, where Epson and Canon are the market leaders – HP introduced a new range to counter this in the late 1990s;
- the middle-range market, where HP was clearly market leader;
- the high-end, high-performance volume printers where companies like HP, Brother and Canon have involvement.

2 Focus on the low-end personal computer market by acquisition of a rival

Although the market was large and still growing worldwide, it was now mature, with relatively few major technological advances and much of the value added taken by the branding and related strategies of the leading computer chip and software suppliers – Intel and Microsoft respectively – see Case 1.2 on IBM. Back in the mid-1970s, HP pioneered the personal computer and was one of the early manufacturers with a desktop PC. By the year 2000, the main PC manufacturer strategy for survival had become cost cutting. Dell began this process through its use of direct telephone selling, which cut out the *distributor's* margins and costs. Dell has subsequently followed this with a low-cost *manufacturing* strategy – using just-in-time procedures and flexible manufacturing to make PCs only for actual orders received rather than holding stock – see the later case on Dell Computers. PC customers have become increasingly value-conscious. HP's products were seen as reliable well-engineered, but not notably better than others.

The strategic option for HP was to reduce costs and build economies of scale through acquiring a competitor. It would then be necessary to rationalise the combined production and product ranges of HP and the acquired company in order to achieve the strategic benefits. For example, Compaq

Computers bought two smaller rivals during the 1990s - Tandem and DEC - then employed this strategy. However, Compaq found that it needed time to undertake such a rationalisation strategy and lost momentum in the market place during the cost-cutting process. Nevertheless, by 2000, the Compaq Presario was claimed to be the largest selling range in the personal computer market and Compaq also had a well-integrated product range in the computer server market. The new guard at HP were highly attracted to this strategic option, in spite of its difficulties.

3 Focus on the large computer server market

HP had some business in this area - see Table 1 - but was significantly smaller than the market leader, IBM. For the new guard, an attractive strategic option was to acquire a competitor that would give HP more scale in the server and IT market.

4 Focus on the computer IT consultancy market - also dominated by IBM but highly profitable

The market was worth approximately $100 billion in 2001 and annual growth was around 5 per cent. For many years, IBM has been the dominant player in this market. IBM has size, research facilities, skilled and knowledgeable staff and product range.

Intel Corporation's strategy of branding its computer chips worldwide (including China) has increased the competitive pressure on computer assembly companies like Hewlett-Packard.

Choice between the strategic options at HP and the consequences for strategic change - the acquisition of Compaq

HP decided that the company simply did not have the scale of its rivals and needed to undertake a major acquisition. The big business opportunity would come from major customers, who required single suppliers to provide comprehensive technology systems and services. Moreover, the industry was expected to slow down in terms of market growth and new technology - cost savings, rather than new technology, would therefore be the focus of strategy. The acquisition candidate would have to be large and possess heavy involvement in the IT sector to provide service for large customers. 'This is an industry that will consolidate and will required sustainable business models,' explained Carly Fiorina.

The search produced one candidate - Compaq Computers. This company was almost as large as HP and would bring a new dimension to the HP consultancy services. It was also strong in servers, personal computers and related businesses. Thus, Carly Fiorina launched a $21 billion takeover bid for Compaq in late in 2001.

After discussion, the Compaq managers and shareholders resolved to accept the bid in early 2002. Carly Fiorina's problem was that some of the shareholders of her own company - especially the members of the original Hewlett and Packard families - were against the deal. Led by Walter Hewlett, the son of Bill, they fought the acquisition of Compaq for months. The opponents issued three reports attacking the acquisition, including a specially commissioned survey that showed that large computing company mergers have consistently failed. Mr Hewitt commented: 'HP optimistically assumes it can succeed where others have failed before. Given that past computer mergers failed during the greatest IT spending boom in history, it is far riskier to attempt a complex global integration during the current severe recession in technology spending.' However, it would be wrong to simply see this just as a personal battle between the old guard and the new at HP: there were important strategic arguments that deserved to be understood.

After a protracted battle, Carly won the backing of 51 per cent of the shareholders of HP in May 2002. Compaq was to be absorbed into HP. But this was only the beginning of the strategic change that was then required to achieve the benefits of the Compaq acquisition: 'Fiorina wins the battle but now faces the war', was how the UK newspaper, the *Financial Times*, summed up the situation. HP had spent months working on the new merger organisation so was able to act quickly. It began by producing a combined new board of directors for the larger group, many of whom came from Compaq, including its chief executive Michael Capellas. The strategic change compared to five years earlier was remarkable. All the heads of the various divisions of Hewlett-Packard were new, with only the two senior staff directors remaining from the previous era - see Table 2.

With the senior managers in place, the next task was to gain the benefits of the acquisition. Walter Hewitt had repeatedly argued during the battle to secure the deal that technology

Table 2 Senior directors at HP – the changing of the guard between 1996 and 2001

1996		2001 **After acquisition of Compaq**	
Chairman, President and Chief Executive	Lewis E. Platt, age 55	Chairman and Chief Executive	Carleton S. Fiorina, age 47
President and Director	None	President and Director	Michael D. Capellas, age 47 (from Compaq – see text)
Executive Vice President Finance and Administration	Robert P. Wayman, age 51	Executive Vice President Finance and Administration	Robert P. Wayman, age 56
V.P. Human Resources	Susan D. Bowick, age 49	V.P. Human Resources	Susan D. Bowick, age 53
Executive V.P. Computer Organization	Richard E. Belluzzo, age 43	Executive V.P. Enterprise Systems Group	Peter Blackmore, age 54
Executive V.P. Test and Measurement Organization	Edward W. Barnholt, age 53	Executive V.P. Imaging and Printing Group	Vyomesh Joshi, age 47
Senior V.P. Research and Development	Joel S. Birnbaum, age 59	Executive V.P. Personal Systems Group	Duane E. Zitzner, age 54
Senior V.P. Corporate Affairs and General Counsel	S.T. Jack Brigham, age 57	Executive V.P. HP Services	Anne Livermore, age 43
Senior V.P. Measurement Systems Organization	Douglas K. Carnahan, age 55	Executive V.P. Worldwide Operations	Michael J. Winkler, age 56
Senior V.P. European Strategic Initiatives	Franco Mariotti	Senior V.P. Information Technology	Robert V. Napier, age 55
Director Internet Program	William Murphy	Senior V.P. Corporate Strategy and Technology	Shane V. Robison, age 48

Note: V.P. = Vice President.

mergers rarely work in practice – they were disruptive and involved too many painful cuts. Moreover, the merger would have to take place against the backdrop of a downturn in the computer industry.

HP's early merger strategy was to focus on customers: the company was keen to ensure that it lost no more than 5 per cent of its revenue base from such customers. Thus the company made early announcements regarding its combined product ranges, its branding policy, its combined website and drive to reassure major customers. HP needed to sort out such issues as overlapping product ranges without losing customers. Ultimately, the new HP needed to have the scale and service associated with an industry leader with a product range that would, in particular, serve the largest customers. By 2007, this complex process had been achieved. The strategy was so successful that earnings from operations more than doubled between 2005 and 2007 (see http://h30261.www3.hp.com/phoenix). In addition, HP regained worldwide market leadership in personal computers from its main rival, Dell Computers. Perhaps the company had been too hasty in sacking Carly?

In order to achieve the acquisition benefits, the combined company announced that it also needed to cut around 15,000 jobs – some 10 per cent of the combined workforce. It planned to undertake this task by the end of 2002 and expected to save $2.5 billion costs on an annualised basis. There were also some difficult organisational decisions to be taken – labour laws, software system incompatibility and tax issues made it difficult to achieve some quick savings. For example, some national labour laws required consultation before any redundancies. In some cases, this meant that the Compaq and HP sales teams were still in competition with each other until the merger was achieved. More generally, such cost cutting and major change was expected to impact on company morale. HP planned to move quickly in order to reduce such problems, but they were expected to take several years, given the additional problem of depressed conditions in the computer industry.

One person close to HP was quoted in the *Financial Times* as saying that the acquisition was never going to be easy but that Carly Fiorina had the full support of her new board. Turning around the company's entrenched culture would always be difficult and would attract criticism in some quarters. Continued board support for Carly now depended on her delivering the benefits of the merger. In truth, Carly had risked her job twice – first, in pursuing the merger against the old guard; second, in delivering the results of a new, larger and more streamlined Hewlett-Packard. Strategic change can sometimes carry real risks.

Carly is forced to leave HP

The cost savings were achieved, with $2.5 billion taken out of the costs of merged group. The difficulty was that Dell Computers continued to force the pace in the personal computer market. At the time of the takeover, HP's combined share of the worldwide PC market was 15.1 per cent and Dell's share was 14.5 per cent. In late 2002, Dell cut its prices but was able to cope with this because it had the best profit margins in the business. HP did not immediately follow because this would have swallowed up the profit margin gains from its merger. Eventually, HP was forced to reduce some prices. The result was that Dell's global market share climbed during 2003 to 17.2 per cent and Hewlett-Packard's share rose only slightly to 15.7 per cent.

Although HP regained some ground in 2003, Dell recovered market leadership with over 18 per cent of the market in 2004 and HP was struggling. Its strategy of taking on the low-cost market leader, Dell, was doomed to failure in a price-conscious commodity market. However, HP's printing business was doing well. It had also been helped by the Compaq computer server business that filled a gap in its range. But HP was still small in IT and consultancy services, which was the other booming area. By late 2004, it was in strategic trouble.

At HP headquarters, there were various changes in the main board of directors in early 2005. The people who had backed Carly Fiorina's appointment in 1999 resigned and were replaced by others who were more sceptical. It was only a matter of time before her position was reviewed. On 10 February 2005, HP made the announcement that had been expected: Carly Fiorina was sacked.

The London *Financial Times* thundered: 'Hewlett-Packard's decision to sack Carly Fiorina robs the corporate world of one of its most charismatic and articulate leaders and its most senior female executive. For all that, it was the right decision and one the board probably should have been made much earlier. Ms Fiorina's strategy had reached a dead end.' But that was not the view of the HP board – they still felt that the basic strategy was correct. But a new chief executive was needed to drive the company forward: Mark Hurd from the American company NCR was appointed from 1 April 2005. He then benefited from the many changes made during the era of Carly Fiorina. HP regained market leadership in personal computers from Dell Computers and HP's computer services operations began to deliver real profitability. Perhaps HP made a mistake in sacking Carly?

Carly Fiorina remains an important figure in American industry. In 2010, she stood as the Republican candidate for the US Senate seat of the State of California. She was unsuccessful but she still serves on the board of various organisations.

Case questions

1 What were the main changes made by Carly Fiorina? Analyse the changes using the models outlined in Chapter 15 and use Case 15.2 as well.

2 If you were appointed as chief executive at HP, what would you do now?

Note: Two further computer case studies are Case 12 relating to Dell and the web-based case study *Disaster and recovery: thinking outside the box at IBM*.

STRATEGIC PROJECT

Since 2005, HP has further developed its business model. It has copied the IBM strategy of moving into the computer services business. Why has it done this? With what benefits and problems? To explore this issue, you will find it helpful to read the case on the web, 'Disaster and recovery: thinking outside the box at IBM'.

Since this case study was written, Hewlett-Packard has announced that it was pulling out of PCs completely. Its new strategy would focus on computer software and related services – just like its great rival, IBM. HP made a bid for the British-based company Autonomy, valued at $11 billion, in August 2011. The British company's business was only in computer software and services. You might like to research this further as a strategic project. Why has HP made this major strategic move? What are the implications for its competitors?

Note

* This case was written by the author from numerous sources including: Company Annual Report and Accounts of Hewlett-Packard, Compaq, IBM, Dell, Sun, Microsoft and Intel. *Financial Times*: 28 March 1996, p 6; 14 November 1997, p 12; 21 January 1998, p 1; 9 November 1998, p 13; 13 April 1999, p 20; 20 July 1999, p 24; 16 November 1999, p 35; 7 December 1999, p 36; 1 December 2000, p 22; 19 April 2001, p 26; 9 May 2001, p 29; 22 August 2001, p 10; 9 January 2002, p 28; 31 January 2002, p 31; 1 February 2002, p 12; 21 March 2002, pp 20 and 28; 9 May 2002, p 27; 3 September 2002, p 28; 10 September 2002, p 27; 17 September 2002, p 28; 12 November 2002, p 27; 22 November 2002, p 32; 19 December 2002, p 12; 10 February 2003, p 9; 11 March 2003, p 28; 8 June 2004, p 29; 13 August 2004, p 12; 15 January 2005, p M5; 18 January 2005, p 31; 9 February 2005, p 24; 10 February 2005, pp 16 and 26; 11 February 2005, p 15; 30 March 2005, pp 27 and 29; 11 January 2008, p 26; 21 March 2011, p 27 (which describes something of what happened next). Further references are contained in the IBM case on the web and in Case 12 relating to Dell.

CASE STUDY 9

Strategic leadership: what can companies learn from 'Chainsaw Al'?

FT

Mr Al Dunlap made his reputation by aggressively pursuing only one strategic option – drastic cost cutting. His drastic approach earned him the nickname of 'Chainsaw Al'. Although his strategic options development might appear somewhat limited, he often achieved results. This case asks whether others have lessons to learn from this approach to strategy development.

Video and sound summary of this case

It was in June 1998 that Mr Al Dunlap was asked to leave his latest post. Seldom can a company announcement have caused so much pleasure to so many people. The news that 'Chainsaw Al', the chairman of Sunbeam Corporation (US) and champion of the slash-and-burn management style, had tripped on his own chainsaw sent a happy glow around the business world. It was like that moment in the television wrestling match when the hooded villain, who for the past half hour has been beating people senseless and chewing off their ears, suddenly gets his comeuppance. You know it is not for real, but it is cheering all the same. Mr Dunlap's pain is also cushioned, in his case, by millions of dollars of share options in Sunbeam. Still, it could not have happened to a nicer man.

His style is captured in his own book, *Mean Business*, which reads like the kind of manual he must have studied as a graduate of West Point Military Academy and later as a paratrooper and officer in charge of a nuclear missile installation. 'You're not in business to be liked. Neither am I. We're here to succeed. If you want a friend, get a dog. I'm not taking any chances: I've got two dogs.' Some people may conclude that in the caring, sharing 1990s, Chainsaw Al's approach to management – firing workers by the thousand, along with executives who failed to meet his targets – has gone the way of Tyrannosaurus Rex. They would be wrong. Instead, his downfall seems to be the result of three fatal mistakes.

First, he came to believe his own publicity. For most of his career, he has been a hired rottweiler, employed by Sir James Goldsmith and Kerry Packer to do their toughest jobs, and then popped back in his kennel with a hunk of meat and a few million dollars. The turnround of Scott Paper was his first solo effort, and it was staggeringly successful: the company sold out at a high price, and he walked away with about $100 million. He followed that with Sunbeam, which turned out to be a different story. Mr Dunlap's mantra is that if a business problem cannot be fixed in 12 months, it cannot be fixed at all, and he went into the US electrical home products company with chainsaw buzzing. In the new edition of his book, he claims: 'We took a company [Sunbeam] that was an absolute basket case and restructured it in seven months. Maybe somebody should buy copies of this book for all the CEOs and boards of directors out there with three-year restructuring plans.'

He had a chance in 1997 to walk off again as a hero, when the company was on a number of acquisition lists. But the share price had been talked up to a point where potential buyers turned away. It turned out that not all the company's problems can be fixed overnight. He may have sacked about half the workforce but in spite of his efforts – and what appears to have been a creative accounting approach to reporting the results for 1997 – Sunbeam was still in difficulties two years after Mr Dunlap arrived.

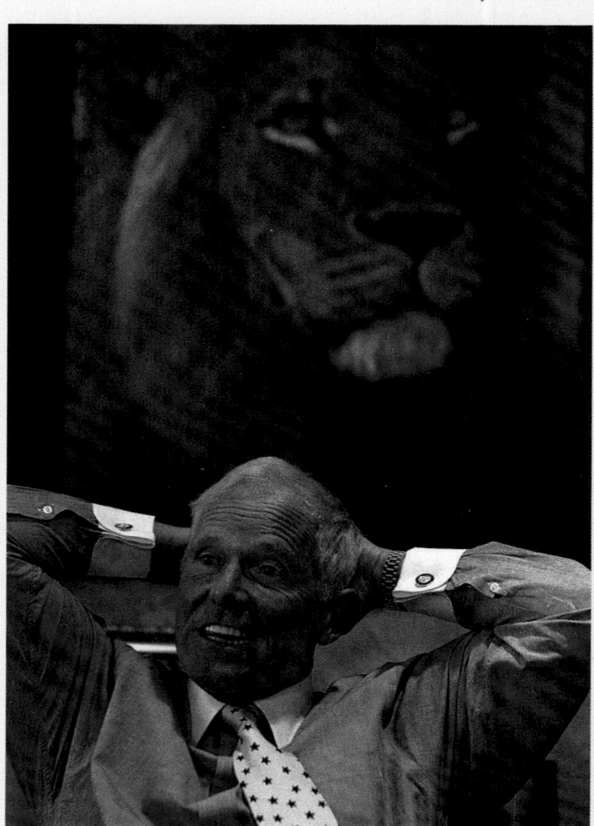

Al Dunlap gained his nickname 'Chainsaw Al' through aggressive cost-cutting strategies.

His second mistake was to disregard his rule: 'If you're going to be in business, you'd better understand that, above all, your goal is to make money for the owners.' He has not exactly fulfilled that promise. The share price fell from $53 in March 1998 to just over $15 in June of the same year. As the pressure mounted, he began to get a little crisp with Wall

Street analysts. He is reported to have told one critic: 'You son of a bitch. If you want to come after me, I'll come back at you twice as hard.'

But there were problems closer to home. The US financier Ronald Perelman sold his stake in a camping gear company to Sunbeam, partly for Sunbeam shares, in Spring 1998 when the shares were at a high point. He was said not to have been pleased when the value of his Sunbeam holding subsequently fell by several hundred million dollars. Mr Dunlap also required all his outside directors to have substantial shareholdings in the company, and to take their annual payment in the form of stock. So they, too, were displeased by the recent performance of the shares.

The third mistake was not to realise that times had changed. After one of the longest period of stock market share price increases in history, 1998 saw the beginnings of a sense in the USA that the rewards of success were not being shared widely enough. It was still acceptable to take tough decisions, but you should not glory in them. AT&T, the US's largest long-distance telecoms operator, was an example. In a speech in New York in 1998, its new chairman Michael Armstrong announced that 14,000 managers had applied for early retirement, many more than had been expected. His message was earnest and sincere: these managers were going with dignity, and were happy with the opportunity to start new lives. In this environment, Chainsaw Al – or, as Sir James used to call him, 'the Rambo in pinstripes' – looked increasingly out of place. Sylvester Stallone seemed to have given way to Leonardo DiCaprio.

America's economic success today certainly owes something to the work of Mr Dunlap and his kind over the past 15 years. Senior managers have been shaken out of complacency and self-indulgence: companies have cut costs and focused on their basic businesses. After surviving much pain and inner turmoil, US business has regained a competitive edge that is serving it well around the world. Other nations have lagged behind and need this treatment. In the interests of the world economy, the best thing to do with Mr Dunlap now might be to send him to Brussels to Europe's Parliament. 'Chainsaw Al' running the expenses of Europe's MEPs – now there's a thought.

Financial Times, 17 June 1998, p 15. Article written by Richard Lambert with a slight adaptation by Richard Lynch. All rights reserved.

Case questions

1 What are the main features of Mr Dunlap's approach to strategy development?

2 What are the consequences of Mr Dunlap's approach to the development of strategy? Does he really have a strategy beyond cost cutting?

3 Can other companies learn anything from Mr Dunlap's approach? Would you ever have employed him?

CASE STUDY 10

Sony strategy: more restructuring or complete breakup?

In the three years to 2013, Sony Corporation spent over US$1.8 billion 'restructuring' the business. Perhaps the time has come for a change of strategy? This case explores the case for a breakup of the Sony Corporation.

Video and sound summary of this case

American and Japanese leadership from 2005–2012

During the 1980s and early 1990s, Sony developed some major innovative consumer electronics products: for example, the Walkman, the games PlayStation and the Trinitron television. But it was then overtaken by other companies like Apple, Samsung and LG. The Sony innovative fire had slowly dimmed – see the web case 'Sorting out Sony: restoring the profits and the innovative fire'.

In 2005, the situation was so bad that Sony made the revolutionary first appointment of a non-Japanese, Sir Howard Springer, as its new Chairman with a Japanese colleague, Ryoji Chubachi, as its President. The company was hoping that Sir Howard would be another Carlos Ghosn, the Chief Executive Officer of the Japanese car company Nissan. Mr Ghosn, who was actually Brazilian, had turned around the loss-making vehicle company into a profitable global player – see Case 4 on the global car companies.

Although Sir Howard and Mr Chubachi set about their tasks with energy and care, they were thwarted by the Sony company culture. Sir Howard later commented, 'I would like to have gone after a lot of unprofitable businesses, particularly, and that would have involved a lot more headcount [that needed to leave the company.] But there is no enthusiasm for getting rid of any unprofitable businesses. Everyone is connected to something.' For example, the headcount at the company's electronics business declined 21 per cent over the ten years to 2013 while the business itself declined over 35 per cent.

During their time at Sony, the company was essentially a group of semi-independent companies that resisted co-operation and were reluctant to face up to the painful cuts in both manpower and product range that were required. Nevertheless, in his seven years as Chairman, Sir Howard did reduce costs, cutting employees, closing factories and moving production to cheaper locations – often overseas from Japan. However, as Figure 1 shows, the company's profit record was very poor over the seven years from 2007 to 2013. There were no significant profits at any time during Sir Howard's five-year tenure and losses in three of those years as the restructuring took its toll. There were still some fundamental weaknesses in the Sony product range at the end of his time at the company.

Up to recent times, Sony has been one of Japan's most respected and innovative companies.

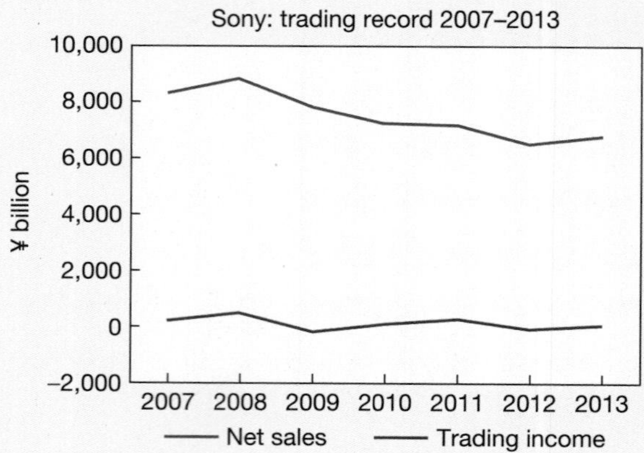

Figure 1 The impact seven years restructuring at Sony

Source: author from the Sony annual report and accounts for various years.

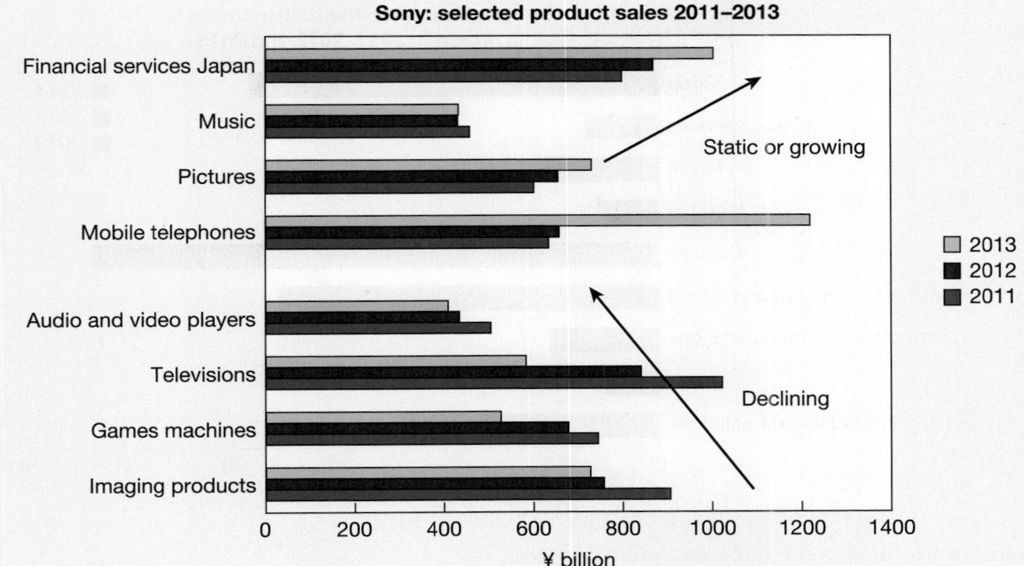

Figure 2 Sales of Sony products were still not growing across the company in the period 2011–2013

Note: The high growth in mobile telephones in 2013 was entirely due to full control being taken by Sony - see text.
Source: author from the Sony annual report and accounts for various years.

Restructuring the Sony product range from 2011–2013

Although some Sony product areas like films and music made steady profits, some parts of the business made heavy losses: see Figure 2. The Home Entertainments Division (HED) and the Devices Division were the main culprits. *HED* included the television manufacturing unit and *Devices* included semiconductors, personal computers and a chemicals company. Sony *Bravia* television manufacturing was heavily loss-making for some years and Sony *Vaio* personal computers also delivered no profits. Both product ranges were hit by strong competition, product innovation costs and low-cost manufacturing sourced from countries like China.

In 2012, Sir Howard retired as Chief Executive Officer at the age of 70. He was replaced by a new Japanese chief executive, Mr Kazuo Hirai. The new leader set about further changes, among them the demerger of the television business and the complete closure of the personal computer product range. In addition, he approved the purchase of the 50 per cent share owned by its joint venture partner, the Swedish company Ericsson. Sony wanted to have full control over a product range that was still growing and where its considerable technology expertise might be advantageous.

In addition, Mr Hirai was encouraged that some parts of Sony were still growing - see Figure 2. Moreover, although the Games division was declining during the period 2011-2013, it was expected to grow again with the launch of the new PlayStation 4 in late 2013. This increase would appear in the financial figures for 2014 and show that the Games division was growing again. The problem for Sony was that this increase did not solve the fundamental problems that remained at the group.

Restructuring or breakup?

In spite of spending US$1.8 billion in the years 2011-2013 on restructuring, Sony was still not expecting to make significant profits in 2014. It had actually set aside an additional US$500 million for more 'restructuring' during 2014. It financed the restructuring from Sony reserves and new debt and, more recently, from selling some assets such as its New York headquarters building. It was hoping to make a profit during the year 2014, but this depended, at least in part, on a decline in the value of the Japanese yen currency rather than any trading activity. One outcome of the restructuring strategy was that profitable and growing parts of the business - like the Music and Pictures divisions - were neglected in terms of investment because the majority of the funds were used to sort out the ailing parts of the company. Figure 3 shows that the majority of the funds invested in restructuring the group were in three product areas with the worst strategic problems: Devices division (where personal computers were located), Home entertainment and sound (where television manufacturing was located) and Imaging products and solutions (where there were profit problems with other Sony products.) The Music and Pictures divisions had required some restructuring funds, but they were fundamentally sound and profitable. This called into question whether Sony would be better broken up as a strategy.

What were the benefits of the current group structure? The original Sony vision had been developed back in the 1970s and 80s by Sir Howard's famous predecessor, Akio Morita. He argued that Sony should be both innovative and vertically integrated: from content such as music and films through to delivery devices like computers and televisions. As homes around the world moved towards new electronic

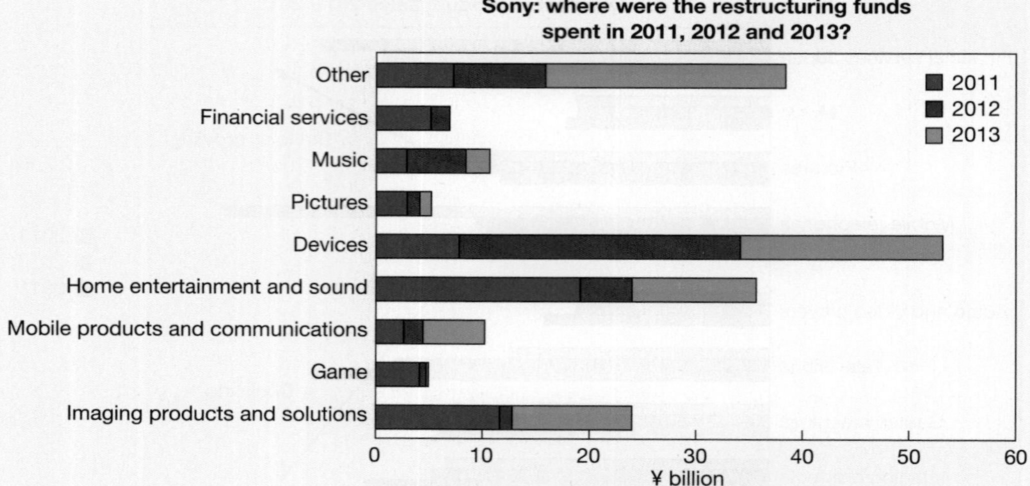

Figure 3 Most restructuring went to the least profitable areas

Source: author from the Sony annual report and accounts for various years.

devices and services, the Sony company would gain by offering the complete package: both products and services that were leading-edge and premium-priced to reflect their quality and performance. This vision of *convergence* and *synergy* between products in the consumer electronics market place is consistent with that of other companies such as Apple and Samsung: Apple music, Apple tv, Apple books, etc.

Unfortunately, television and personal computer manufacture had become commoditised – see the Dell Case 12. But the unique content owned by Sony music and films remained a competitive advantage for Sony. Moreover, its new games machine, the PS4, would provide a new global platform for delivering such content. There were arguably important synergistic benefits here and these areas were at least profitable – see Figure 4.

Set against this, the data in Figure 4 shows that some parts of the group had made substantial losses. They were arguably beyond turnaround. Moreover, one part of the Sony group, the Finance Services division selling insurance products only in Japan, contributed nothing to the synergy of the rest of the group.

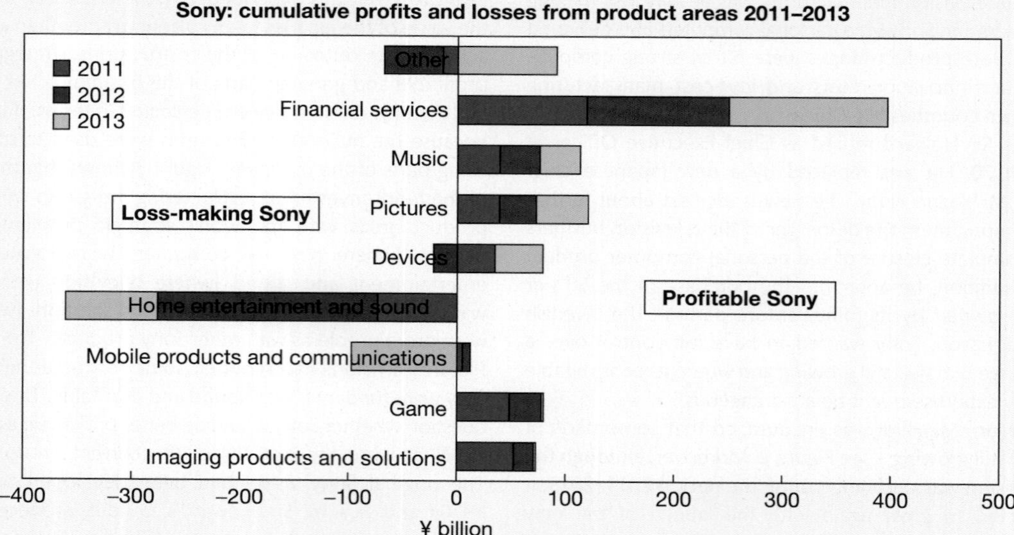

Figure 4 The product groups that delivered three years of profits and losses at Sony

Source: author from Sony annual report and accounts for various years.

However, it has to be admitted that Sony would have been in dire trouble over the last few years without the contribution of this division. But, given that some of the worst problems were over, that was arguably an argument for the breakup of the Sony. The Finance division could easily be sold. There was therefore a clear case for the breakup of the Sony group in 2014.

You might like to read the case *Sorting out Sony: restoring the profits and the innovative fire*. It traces the Sony history 2007–2011 in more depth and explains more about the Sony heritage from its foundation in 1946.

Case questions

1 Do customers really want convergence in consumer electronics? Both Apple and Sony suggest that they do. But what is the evidence? If customers do not want convergence, what are the implications for Sony?

2 What are Sony's main competitive advantages? How do they impact on the case for continued restructuring versus breakup?

3 What would you recommend to Sony? More restructuring or breakup?

Note

* Sources for Sony case: Sony Company annual report and accounts for years 2010, 2011, 2012, 2013. *Financial Times*: 27 May 2011, p 17; 17 August 2011, p 17; 29 July 2011, p 12; 25 January 2012, p 23; 21 February 2012, p 19; 28 February 2012, p 13; 28 February 2013, p 22; 21 November 2013, p 13; 29 November 2013, p 21; 8 January 2014, p 19; 9 January 2014, p 18; 7 February 2014, pp 14, 15 and 17.

CASE STUDY 11

Emergent strategy: what's the new smart strategy for PCs, media tablets and mobiles?

After years of growth, the global market for personal computers (PCs) was under attack in 2014 from new technologies, smart mobile phones and media tablets. What does this mean for the world's major personal computer companies like Hewlett-Packard and Dell? For software companies like Microsoft? And for smartphone companies like the dominant Apple and the smaller Chinese company ZTE? Perhaps even for computer games companies like Sony's PS4? What's the new smart strategy?

Video and sound summary of this case

Need for an emergent strategy?

After many years of development, the computer technology used in personal computers (PCs) was relatively mature: there was more storage capacity for video and film and new faster processors. However, most PCs still had a screen, a standard keyboard and a mouse. And the vast majority were still using software derived from the first IBM-compatible PCs of the 1980s. Technology had become standardised with limited competitive advantage between computer manufacturers, with heavy reliance on low-cost production and with competition based, at least in part, on price alone.

Around 2009, new technology finally began to take hold beyond PCs: new sharing networks on the internet, new and more powerful digital telephone networks, new forms of touch screen display and new information storage away from the PC itself in remote locations – *cloud computing*. Some strategists were even forecasting the end of the PC. However, the Chief Executive of Arm, one of the world's leading computer chip design companies, did not agree: 'There are all kinds of apocalyptic scenarios, but personally I'm not a believer in the end of the PC – it offers different functionality and there's no way we'll see PCs disappear over the next five years or so.' Nevertheless, significant changes were coming with major uncertainty in the market place.

Given such uncertainty, emergent strategies may be more appropriate. But what does this really mean? *What* emergent strategies? We explore the issues under four headings:

1 Trends in the PC market: slowing growth, commoditisation and cloud computing
2 Trends in smartphones and media tablets including the battle for the software standard
3 Trends in computer services: sharing sites, music, gaming, television broadcasting and information sites
4 Impact on individual PC companies.

Trends in the PC market: slowing growth, commoditisation and cloud computing

In 2010, the worldwide PC market was worth around US$175 billion and grew around 14 per cent compared to the previous year. By 2011, the market was declining due to the arrival of new portable devices like smartphones and tablets. There was still some growth in developing countries, like Brazil, Russia, India and China. But this was less than the decline that had begun in the developed countries of Europe and the USA: Figure 1 shows the overall picture.

This consumer electronics shop in Fukuoka, Japan, shows the vast range of branded products now competing in this fast-changing world market.

Over the years to 2015, the decline was expected to continue. The main reason was that mobile phones and media tablets were becoming more powerful and therefore able to replace some of the functions of PCs. In addition, the profit margins on the manufacture of PCs were becoming increasingly small. The average selling price of a PC was reported to have dropped from US$614 in early 2010 to US$544 in late 2013. Within this total, the average profit per PC was estimated to have dropped from US$15.71 to US$14.87 over the same timeframe. This delivered a profit margin on sales of 2.7 per cent in 2013 – hardly attractive for the long term.

Commentators noted that netbooks – the small and inexpensive PCs – had shown major growth in the years 2006–2009. But they were now declining rapidly with media tablets and ultra-light laptop PCs being the new developments. Products from these newer technologies are explored in the next section.

In addition to replacement demand, the PC strategy of the major companies like Hewlett-Packard (HP), Dell, Asus, Acer and Lenovo also faced two further problems: commoditisation and cloud computing. *Commoditisation* occurs when products

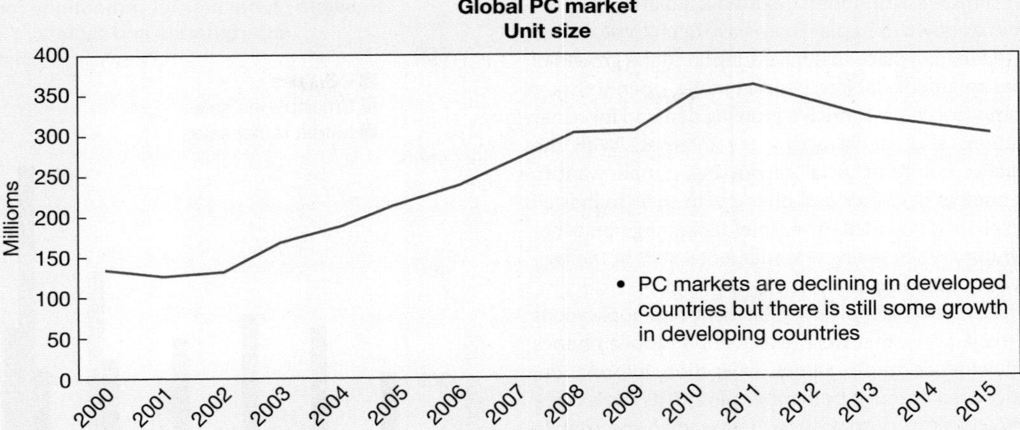

Figure 1 Global PC market projected to continue to decline

Source: author from various (and sometimes conflicting) industry estimates.

lose their ability to differentiate themselves from one another: they become commodities like sugar and oil, and sell mainly on price and volume. Commoditisation is a serious threat to profitability because the value added by the manufacturing process is low and competition is high. It is occurring in PCs because the technology has become standardised with a consequent move to sourcing components – like keyboards, hard discs and screens – from the cheapest producer. Companies like HP and Dell have therefore become assemblers of the various components rather than full manufacturers. They do assembly well and produce reliable products, but there is little differentiation beyond simple branding and design. The competitive advantage is therefore low and the value added is low. Dell's strategy problems with commoditisation are explored in more depth in Case 12.

Cloud computing also represents a serious long-term threat to PC manufacturers. The widespread and partially free internet has enabled software and hardware manufacturers to offer to store the computer data that is normally on the PC in a remote location – in the 'cloud'. This means that PCs can be simpler and cheaper because they do not need so much storage space – particularly attractive to some business users of PCs. But it also means that PCs will have even less equipment inside and therefore even lower value added. Cloud computing was developing rapidly as this case was being written in early 2014. Software companies like Microsoft and search companies like Google were promoting cloud computing heavily because their offer to store PC data would give them an even stronger grip on the information market. But customers still had to consider whether this was the best solution for them given that they would no longer hold data in their own storage areas.

Cloud computing was also relevant to smartphones and media tablets which had lower capacity for information storage. It was less certain how this would work, given that the scope, technical ability and design of these products was still developing.

Trends in smartphones and media tablets including the battle for the software standard

We need to be quite clear. Smartphones and media tablets are not entirely new. The *Newton* from Apple was launched in 1993 with the comment, 'We think there are going to be billions of these devices out there.' The Newton was withdrawn in 1998. The small, hand-held *Palm Pilot* was introduced in 1996 and delivered substantial wealth to that company for several years. It has now been replaced by the smartphone. The *Toshiba 1 Libretto* with a 15 cm screen and size similar to early netbooks was also launched in 1996. It lasted until 2001. Microsoft promoted the *Tablet PC* with a touch-sensitive screen and handwriting technology in 2002. However, its high price and consumer preference for a keyboard led to poor sales.

Nevertheless, the Tablet PC did not entirely disappear: it morphed first into the low-priced, mini-laptop range of netbook computers. Most PC companies produced models following the early success of the *Eee* netbook from the Taiwanese company Asus, in 2007.

Around the same time, Apple Computers launched the *iPhone*, which went on to sell over 40 million copies. The company then followed this up with the launch of the *iPad* media tablet in 2010 with sales of 10 million in 2011, 61 million in 2012 and 70 million in 2013. Both Apple products were high performance and premium-priced products. In 2006, the Canadian company RIM introduced the first versions of the *Blackberry* mobile smartphone. It was particularly strong in email communications as well as offering broader internet connectivity for the business customer. But it did not have the performance characteristics of the iPhone and was rapidly losing market share by 2012. Arguably, it is the success of the two Apple products that has prompted the introduction of many other similar smartphones and media tablets.

But it's not all down to Apple. There have been three further changes in the market place that have supported the growth of smartphones and media tablets: internet usage, open software and new computer chips. There is a growing demand for richer communications and media across the internet. 'With the almost addictive nature of social networking, people want to be on Facebook and Twitter and online with their friends all the time,' explained Phil McKenzie, chief technology officer at HP's PC division. 'We're seeing a fundamental shift in the way consumers use notebooks.'

Such a shift was also supported by the many new applications – 'Apps' in the jargon – that were available on mobile phones by simple downloads: music, games, navigation, information, etc. The major breakthrough both for Apple and its rivals came with the introduction of Apple Apps rather than the mobile phone itself. Apple Computers allowed software developers to write applications for the Apple system that were then subject to approval by Apple and from which Apple would take 30 per cent of any revenue generated by downloading of the application. Suddenly, phone users were able to access parts of the internet, new games and a wide range of other services that were previously unavailable through their existing mobile network operators. By 2013, Apple had around 750,000 Apps in its Apps Store.

Given the success of the iPhone, other mobile phone manufacturers have been seeking ways of satisfying this new demand. Google came up with one answer: a new software package called *Android* that the company made freely available to rival manufacturers of mobile phones. Google simply took a small percentage of the profit when mobile smartphone companies used its software in their phones. This software made it relatively easy for competing companies, like the Taiwanese company HTC and the Korean company Samsung, to launch highly successful smartphones. Again, the range of Android Apps grew dramatically to around 400,000 by the year 2013. By 2012, Android phones were outselling all others in the market place: the Korean company Samsung was particularly successful with its *Galaxy* range. Smartphone sales were growing rapidly around the world – see Figure 2.

In addition to growth from smartphones, there was also the growth of the media tablet. Apple launched its iPad media tablet in 2010. It was sold at a premium price but still proved highly successful in the market place. It could not be used as a phone, but its larger and well-illuminated screen allowed much bigger pictures to be viewed, including email, videos and photos. Arguably, it was the better display plus the new increasingly fast internet, 3G and later 4G, that made all the difference when compared to the previous historical products mentioned at the beginning of this section. Competitors like RIM, HTC and Samsung launched their own versions of the media tablet with some success, particularly Samsung. Moreover, like Apple, Google made the Android software available for tablet computers. The outcome was a major launch of such tablet devices: there were just over 50 million Android tablets sold in 2012, rising to 120 million in 2013. Android tablets from such companies as Samsung, Dell and Google itself were outselling the Apple tablets by 2013. The computer tablet market was projected to be larger than the PC market by 2014 – see Figure 2.

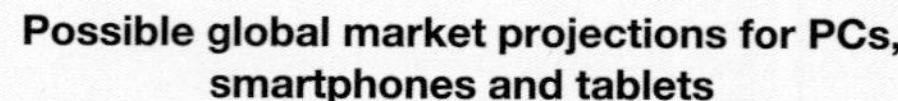

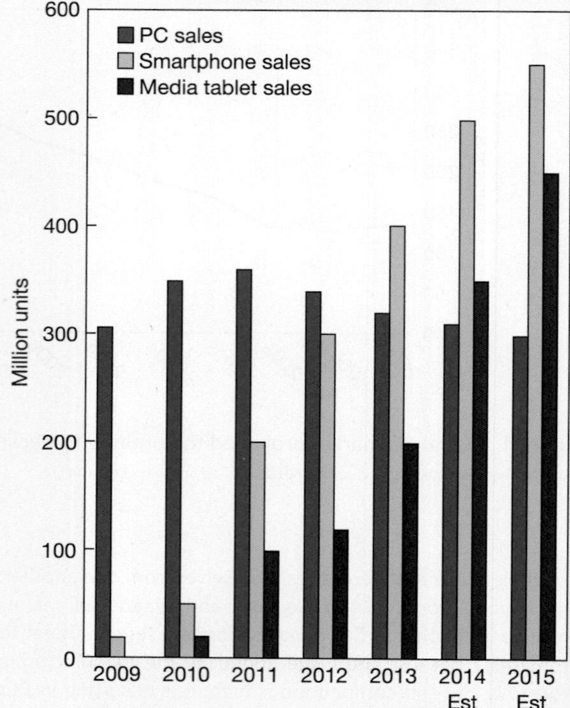

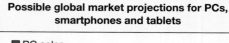

Figure 2 What will happen to PCs, smartphones and media tablets?

Note: PC sales include cheaper, cloud-linked models.

Source: author from various industry sources.

Trends in computer services: sharing sites, music, gaming, television broadcasting and information sites

Without any doubt, the popularity of Facebook and Twitter over the last few years has led to the increased use of mobile phones and tablets, although such site sharing began before the new smartphones were available. Yet the new devices are better because they have faster processors, increased ease of use and additional photo and video software. Some linking sites like Facebook and QQ in China have been particularly successful. Others like MySpace and Yahoo have found it more difficult to find a role in this changing market place. It would seem that one sharing network in a region of the world is destined to become dominant, but this takes time to develop. New sharing sites based on niche markets – like LinkedIn for professionals – are also emerging but there is no agreement, yet, on who will win.

In addition to sharing sites, music downloads have proved immensely popular both on the web and on individual smart-

Table 1 Apps around the world

Users of mobile apps worldwide by region 2012–2017 according to Portio Research

	2012	2013	2017
App users worldwide	1.2 billion	N/A	4.4 billion
Asia Pacific	30%	32%	47%
Europe	29%	28%	21%
North America	18%	17%	10%
Middle East & Africa	14%	13%	12%
Latin America	9%	10%	10%

Source: © Portio Research, in April 2014: http://mobithinking.com/mobile-marketing-tools/latest-mobile-stats/e.

phones – see Case 13 on Apple Music for more detail. Growth in music has been matched by increased growth in other areas for both business and personal use – see, for example, the separate cases on Travel websites in Chapter 11 of this text.

Amongst the most interesting strategy developments have been the ways that Apple came to dominate applications services in 2010–2012. According to one survey, Apple's App Store had revenues of US$1.7 billion by the end of 2010, but its share was reducing as the other applications grew in their respective services. However, Apps were becoming important around the world – see Table 1.

Some Apps had the ability to generate significant new revenue. Thus, in 2011, Apple announced that it was seeking not only 30 per cent of all revenue generated by its applications but also insisting that suppliers of applications gave Apple the same percentage on all revenue, even where this was generated by alternative methods like a rival network. Moreover, Apple would not provide customer information and addresses to its suppliers on subscribers who had taken out subscriptions. This meant that suppliers, like newspaper and music sites, would no longer have the possibility of further revenue from contacting their customers directly. Google responded by offering the same service on Android for a 10 per cent cut. Ultimately, this could lead to applications moving from the Apple Apps Store to rival platforms but only if they were as popular as Apple. 'Apple has invented a very clever system and perhaps it's the first real example of a very successful walled garden [to hold onto the revenue from its Apps Store] . . . probably Apple's walled garden will last a much longer time than the ones we have seen in the past but I think there is no recipe for eternal success,' commented Franco Bernabé, Chief Executive of Telecom Italia in 2011. However, the website VisionMobile has pointed out that for the majority of developers, App development is not financially rewarding: two thirds of developers earn less than US$500 per month from their applications.

More broadly, new strategies were bound to emerge over time from these powerful phone service companies. And, of course, there were similar dominant telephone service companies in the USA, China and India that might also explore similar strategies.

One final service area that was still in its early stages in 2014 was television broadcasting via the internet. New capacity and technology in broadband internet meant that it was becoming increasingly feasible to watch television programmes on computers, media tablets and smartphones. But the market itself was still in its early stages at the time of writing this case. Many of the world's leading broadcasters, including the BBC and ITV in the UK, and Disney and News Corporation around the world, were working actively in this new field. By 2014, new televisions from companies like Sony, Panasonic and LG had been launched with built-in connections to computers: *smart televisions*. In addition, companies like Netflix, Love Film and Now TV were offering totally new television services via the internet in many European countries – see Case 3.1 on Netflix and Blockbuster.

All these devices blurred the distinction between televisions, PCs, games machines, tablet PCs and smart mobile phones. Technologies and media devices were beginning to merge. There were totally new and unexploited business opportunities that required new, more experimental strategies.

Impact on individual PC companies

Inevitably with any emergent strategy process, the impact of these major changes in technology will be felt in different companies in different ways. The outcomes will depend both on the strategies that such companies have undertaken in the past and their responses to the trends in the market place. Elsewhere in this 7th edition of *Strategic Management*, you will find descriptions of the impact on Apple, Google, News Corporation and Nokia. In this section, we therefore focus on the leading PC companies. As a starting point, Figure 3 shows how the market shares of some of the leading companies have changed over the years to 2013. The changes in market share for some of the companies are discussed separately below.

Table 2 lists some brief business data for some of the leading companies in order to provide some measure of the scale

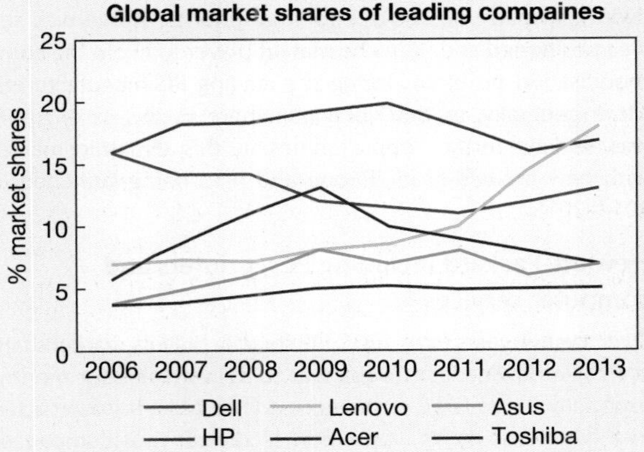

Figure 3 The varying fortunes for the leading PC companies: brief outline only

Source: author from various industry estimates.

Table 2 Results for selected leading PC and mobile companies in 2013

Company	Country	Sales US$ bn	Operating profit US$ bn	Sales margin %
Apple	USA	171	37	21.6
Hewlett-Packard	USA	113	7	6.2
Dell	USA	62	5.1	8.3
Lenovo	China	34	1	0.3
Acer	China Taiwan	12	(0.4)	(3.3)
Asus*	China Taiwan	8.3	0.2	2.4
ZTE**	China	12	(0.2)	(1.7)
Blackberry/RIM	Canada	11	(1.2)	(10.9)

Notes:
* Data for 2012 in the case of Asus.
** ZTE does not produce PCs, only mobiles – see company below.
Source: author from company annual report and accounts.

of their operations. It should be noted that the sales figures include products other than PCs: for example, HP sales include printers and ZTE sales include telecommunications exchange equipment.

Apple Computers

Given that Apple has positioned itself at the high end of most markets, it is perhaps not surprising that the company has some of the best profit margins in the industry. Apple stood alone in the benefits that it had gained up to that time from its innovative exploitation of the new technologies. The Apple market share of the PC market remained so small that it did not feature as one of the top five PC companies in 2010 – see Figure 3. The company had positioned itself differently from other PC companies for many years: heavily branded, premium priced, highly user-friendly, strong range of premium products, exclusive proprietary technology and software. Thus, even if it made no move into smartphones, Apple was still well positioned as a PC niche market player to avoid the commoditisation problems facing the leading PC manufacturers. More generally, as described elsewhere in this case, Apple was seeking further opportunities in this dynamic market with new models of its iPhone and iPad being launched in 2014–2015.

Hewlett-Packard including PCs, printers and computer services

Over the five years from 2006, HP steadily built its market share in PCs worldwide. Its strategy was to deliver value for money, especially for its large business customer base. It was assisted in this process by its acquisition of several rival companies, as described in more detail in the two other HP cases in this text – see Case 7 at the end of the text and Case 15.2. Importantly, the company had real strength in the related product category of computer printers which it continued to exploit over the years to give the company exposure to both the home and business customer.

In 2010, it engaged in a competitive battle with Dell Computers to acquire a company called 3Par that made corporate computer storage systems and data management products that helped reduce power and energy costs. Dell bid US$1.2 billion and HP trumped this with a successful bid of US$1.6 billion. The UK newspaper, the *Financial Times*, described the valuation as 'bonkers', because it was far in excess of the predicted profit stream and net assets of the company. But there were two advantages for HP: the new firm supported the HP strategy of building a one-stop shop for businesses wanting corporate technology services. It also made it more difficult for Dell to move into the same business area. Both companies had recognised the threat from commoditisation of PCs and were attempting to move into computer services – a similar strategy to IBM described in the separate IBM case on the book website.

Dell Computers – moving into computer services as well as PCs

Dell's story is set out in more detail in Case 12. But its strategic problem is well illustrated by its declining market share in Figure 3. The company had become an assembler of the final parts of the PC. It did this very successfully and efficiently. However, it was losing market share to its rivals as it attempted to deliver increased profits at the same time as shifting its strategy to higher value added products. Its main strategy was to move further into computer services.

Lenovo Computers

Lenovo is the leading Chinese PC company that came to prominence around year 2005 when it acquired all the IBM PC business, especially the IBM *ThinkPad*. Initially, this was successful because the IBM products performed well and had a good reputation with customers. However, the IBM products were positioned at the high, expensive end of the PC market. This caused severe problems for Lenovo when the world economy turned down in 2008 and 2009 and companies and individuals chose cheaper products. Lenovo then recovered its market position, especially in laptop computers. It was particularly strong in its home country China, where it was market leader. It claimed to avoid the problems of commoditisation through a strategy of PC innovation, but it was not a leader in smartphones or media tablets. Its strategy focused on the still-expanding markets in developing countries, especially China. The company's Chief Executive, Yan Yuanqing explained in mid-2012, 'China is an emerging market. In front-line cities (like Beijing), the market is saturated, (so) we are aggressively developing tier 2 and tier 3 cities. Computer penetration in these cities is still low, so that's why there's still room for growth.'

In addition to PCs, Lenovo was also moving further into mobile telephones with the acquisition of Motorola mobile phones from Google in 2014 for US$3 billion. This made Lenovo a third in the world market for mobile phone sales – albeit a distant third with 5% of the market compared with Samsung at 30% and Apple at 18% in early 2014.

In early 2014, Lenovo acquired IBM's low-server computer business for US$2.3 billion. This illustrates the ambition of this

Chinese company to become a world player in computer-related industries. However, at the time of writing this case, the purchase was in some doubt because some of the computers to be acquired were reported to be used by the US Government. Any involvement of a Chinese company might therefore be regarded as a security risk.

Acer Computers

This Taiwanese company increased its market share of the PC market significantly in the period up to the year 2010. But its share after this time has declined. It increased its share in part by acquiring two European and US companies: Gateway and Packard-Bell (which had no connection with HP). Acer also had a long record of innovation in PCs and laptops. The company used this strategy to differentiate it from mass-market PC companies with some success. In 2009, it introduced its first smartphone and followed this with a media tablet launch in 2010. This company had a premium performance strategy that was closer to Apple in some respects. However, it was using the common Android platform also used by its competitors. This would not help Acer to maintain its exclusivity because it delivered no competitive advantage over rival companies. By mid-2013, Acer was losing market share to its rivals and its profits had moved into loss: competition was too fierce, with rivals like Apple and Samsung delivering better products.

Asus Computers

Like Acer, Asus Computers is located in Taiwan. It has held its share of the PC market over the last few years while at the same time moving into tablets. It has a three-prong strategy to be a significant player in tablets and mobile phones as well as PCs. To achieve this, it has become a manufacturer of tablets on behalf of other companies: for example, it makes the Nexus 7 tablet for Google. Whether it will achieve its objectives in mobile phones is open to doubt: the market is highly competitive.

ZTE telecommunications equipment and mobiles but no PCs

ZTE is another leading Chinese company. It is mainly involved in the development and production of telecommunications equipment for mobile networks, exchanges and related activities. However, it does produce a range of mobile handsets and also launched its first media tablet in late 2010. Its products include the *ZTE Blade* and the *ZTE Skate* mobiles. These models tend to have a lower specification than some high-end models, like the iPhone, but they carry lower prices: an alternative value-for-money strategy that may work well in this market. Because it does not have the market presence of some of the leading companies, ZTE has also linked up with some of the major operators to produce phones that were renamed under their brands, e.g. the Orange network *San Francisco* model was essentially the same as the ZTE Blade. This may be a useful strategy for smaller companies.

In addition, ZTE has been investing heavily in research in the telecommunications market. It claimed to be one of the largest companies lodging new patents in the sector in 2013. The company was loss making at this time. However, this strategy may hold significant potential for delivering competitive advantage over time.

Research in Motion – Blackberry phone but no PCs

RIM is not the largest mobile telephone company, but it was certainly one of the most successful in terms of profitability and strategy up to 2011. Then it all went badly wrong. Prior to 2012, it developed a niche strategy aimed at emails and information for the business community. Its first smartphones were launched back in 1999 giving it first-mover advantage. The majority (58%) of its business was in the USA in 2010, but it claimed to have partners in 175 countries. One of the special features of its phones was that they ran on its own unique, secure network rather than on the main public mobile networks. RIM therefore delivered greater security than public networks – much to the dissatisfaction of some national governments, like those in India and some Arab countries, who have wanted access to its messages. But then three changes occurred. First, there was a major collapse of its networks in 2011. Second, Apple and Samsung launched rival phones that more user-friendly and with better technology. Third, its first media tablet in 2011 was a profit disaster as a result of poor technology compared with rivals. Blackberry fired its Chief Executive in early 2012 and was still in major profit trouble at the time of writing this case. Readers will find this company to be a good example of what can go badly wrong in emergent strategy.

Case questions

1 The case argues that the PC, mobile and media tablet markets are converging: do you agree? How would you define this market? What are the strategic implications of your definition?

2 What were the changes in the environment that led to the pressures and opportunities on the leading PC companies? Is the environment turbulent? If so, what are the implications for company strategy?

3 Given that innovation is important in this market, what recommendations would you make for a company engaged in this market place? Does it need to be an innovative leader or an innovative follower? Why and how?

Note

This case was written by the author from numerous sources including: Annual Reports and Accounts for the following companies: Hewlett-Packard, Apple, Nokia, Dell, Acer, Lenovo, Blackberry, Asus, ZTE. Previous references are given in *Strategic Management* 6th edn. New references from *Financial Times*: 2 June 2011, p 22; 4 August 2011, p 18; 24 February 2012, p 21; 8 March 2012, p 21; 4 May 2012, p 17; 30 July 2012, p 22; 24 August 2012, p 12; 22 May 2013, p 15; 5 June 2013, p 15; 5 September 2013, p 11; 29 November 2013, p 19.

CASE STUDY 12

Prescriptive strategy: Dell's new strategy beyond commoditisation: too little and too late?

The company's main competitive advantage was that it had lower manufacturing and distribution costs than most of its competitors in PCs (personal computers). But this advantage weakened substantially over the period 2005 onwards. The company was in strategic trouble and needed a new strategy. This case describes how PCs had become commoditised – low cost, little differentiation, low brand loyalty – and how Dell was developing a new strategy. But it was not clear if the company's new approach would bring renewed growth. Was it too little and too late?

Video and sound summary of this case

Dell: the need for new strategy

When Michael Dell first thought of selling computers by mail in his student room at Texas University in 1987, he could hardly have foreseen the consequences. By 2011, Dell was one of the market leaders in the worldwide personal computer (PC) market, with sales around US$61 billion. And Michael Dell, still aged only 40, was the eighteenth richest person in the USA. But the company was in trouble.

After many years of successful growth, Dell was beginning to slow down. The company's revenue stream was essentially flat between 2008 and 2011 with a dip in 2010 as a result of the worldwide economic downturn in that year. Table 1 shows that its operating income in 2011 was not significantly higher than in 2008. The company had begun to develop a new strategy away from commoditised PCs. But other companies, like the international market leader IBM, had already embarked on the same strategy some years earlier.

'We're committed to continuing our strategy to re-shape Dell's business as an end-to-end Information Technology (IT) provider,' explained Michael Dell, chairman and Chief Executive Office in mid-2012. 'We [are making] progress with the innovative IT solutions we're providing – notably our latest Dell servers, storage, networking and services that deliver customers enhanced productivity.'

Part of Dell's strategic problem was the rapid change in technology leading to the development of new media tablets and new computing power: see Case 11 on 'new smart strategy' for more details. In addition, Dell's business was concentrated in the USA which accounted for 52% of total sales in 2011. This meant that Dell was reliant on the economic growth of a relatively mature economy. But it also provided the opportunity to link with the high-technology service requirements of leading US companies and public institutions, as this case explains later, and also some high-growth areas of the USA in advanced internet technologies.

To understand fully Dell's new strategy, this case traces the origins of the company before explaining the main elements of its new approach.

Dell history

Michael Dell was 19 when he first had the idea of using mail order to cut the costs of selling PCs – no distributor profit margins; no inventory held to meet future customer demand; one centralised customer supply-base per country or region.

Michel Dell's company was founded in 1987. It now faces some difficult strategic issues.
Source: © Bob Daemmrich/Corbis

Within two years, he had launched into the USA and then Europe. 'We had 22 journalists turn up [for the launch] and 21 said it was a horrible idea,' says Dell. 'It wouldn't work. It was an American concept. I've been under-estimated, rejected; describe it any which way you want, but every time we opened new offices round the world, people said it wouldn't work.'

Perhaps journalists do have a point with regard to customer demand. Even today, some 30 per cent of European PCs are bought through shops and other distributors. Seventy per cent are bought through mail order and the worldwide web, although the percentage sold by mail order and the web is higher in the USA. Importantly, PCs bought by the web often have lower prices than shop-bought PCs. And, at least in the case of Dell, the lower price comes from Dell's lower manufacturing costs.

Table 1 Dell's trading record 2007–2011 (US$ millions)

	2007	2008	2009	2010	2011
Net revenue	57,420	61,133	61,101	52,902	61,494
Operating income	3,070	3,440	3,190	2,172	3,433
Total assets	25,635	27,561	26,500	33,652	38,599

Source: author from company annual report and accounts. The increase in assets was essentially the outcome of the acquisition strategy described later in the case.

Dell's early competitive advantage

Dell's advantage is much deeper than the costs it saves by selling via mail order and the web: some rivals, like Acer Computers, also sell using this method. What set the Dell Computer Company apart from its rivals was its manufacturing system. Most of its leading competitors, like Hewlett-Packard/Compaq and IBM, have their PCs made for them in low-cost labour in countries like Taiwan and China. From the beginning, Dell assembled virtually all its own PCs in-house, thus retaining at least part of the manufacturing profits. And Dell claimed to have the lowest manufacturing costs in the world. While this was true back in the early 2000s, it was much more open to challenge in 2012.

How did it achieve such low costs? The answer was by borrowing manufacturing concepts from the car industry and applying them rigorously, while strictly monitoring the results.

The Dell value chain in the 1990s

Unlike competitors who may have four *weeks'* stock of component supplies, Dell had only two *hours'* supply. It used just-in-time delivery to call off components from stocks held locally to its massive Round Rock factory in Texas: the cost of these stocks was borne by its suppliers, not by Dell. It used similar systems at its main European factory in Limerick, Ireland. This all meant that if a supplier, like Intel, launched a new computer chip, then Dell was not caught with high stocks of the old chip. Dell could introduce the new chip immediately and deliver an enhanced product to its customers.

In the Dell manufacturing system, parts came into the factory to fulfil actual customer orders - no PCs were made for stock, so there was no cost of holding stock. The detail of each customer order - RAM size, hard disc storage, CD-format, etc. - was turned into a white bar code label. Each label was then scanned and the relevant parts selected automatically by machine and placed in a box. Workers then assembled the parts, often using clips to fix them rather than screws because clips were faster. In many cases, the parts were colour-coded with the PC frame to make it easier to see where and how to fit them. This *attention to detail* was essential to the production of efficient, quality products.

PCs were then individually boxed, addressed and shipped immediately to customers, who could then be billed. There was direct telephone and computer tracking between the placing of the customer order and the factory floor - all the way through to final delivery.

Dell's monitoring and control strategy: the early 2000s

Importantly, such a system allowed very detailed and constant monitoring of order-taking, supplier delivery, factory production, customer delivery and so on. This highly analytical approach meant that *every* worker had detailed targets. These included sales and profit targets for senior managers, quality and production targets for factory floor workers, order-taking for sales personnel. Every quarter, every employee was assessed against profit, cost, quality and productivity targets.

This meant first that Dell knew where it stood in relation to its annual plan. But it also allowed Dell to lay off workers rapidly if demand fell - for example, the company said that it would eliminate 3,000 to 4,000 positions over two quarters after the IT spending market slowdown in 2001. It also meant that if suppliers, like Intel Corporation, lowered the price of computer chips then Dell could lower its PC prices quickly and announce them over the internet: Dell took around 80 per cent of its orders from the internet in the USA and found that customers compared prices before making decisions. The company said that employees found the system more interesting because they saw the product from start to finish. They were not merely a small part of an assembly line. Dell supported this by encouraging those assembling PCs to come up with ideas for better, lower cost ways of assembly.

In 2001, Dell reported its operating expenses at 10.2 per cent of sales. This compared at that time with 18.3 per cent at Compaq and 20.6 per cent at Hewlett-Packard. Essentially, Dell operated a *lean manufacturing system*. It concentrated on standardised technologies for high-volume production. It did not focus on product innovation. John Mendica, Dell's vice president of client products, formerly worked for Apple Computers. 'At Apple, demand is created through innovative products. At Dell, our innovation is around the business [production] model.'

New competitive threat for Dell: the late 2000s

In the early 2000s, this strategy was highly successful for Dell. But the standardised design of many PCs meant that other competitors were able to copy Dell's methods. In particular, some rival companies were assembling computers in countries that had much lower labour costs than Dell. By 2004, Dell was still focused on its businesses in the Americas, particularly the USA, and in Europe. These two areas accounted for over 80 per cent of its sales and profits. The company was having more limited success in the Asia/Pacific region.

For example, Dell was only fourth in the Japanese market and was having even more difficulties in another Asian country: China. The company had been forced to stop selling some of its low-end PCs in China. The reason was that Dell's costs and prices in the local Chinese market could not compete with the *very* low costs and prices of local Chinese PC manufacturers. Some commentators at that time were wondering what would happen if such Chinese companies began to market their low-priced products worldwide. One analyst said in 2005: 'It pierces the aura of invincibility [of the lowest possible costs] that Dell has - [the competitive claim] that it is so efficient that nobody can undercut Dell.'

Just one example to underline the problems facing Dell: the Chinese computer market leader, Lenovo, acquired the ThinkPad name and manufacturing rights from the major world computer company IBM in 2005. By 2010, Lenovo was the fourth largest PC manufacturer in the world and actively competing against Dell for its business. By 2013, Lenovo was the market leader: see Case 11. Lenovo was manufactured in China - a low-wage country and well able to compete against Dell's low cost manufacturing.

And, as many will know, Apple moved the manufacture of many of its products – including its highly successful Apple iPad and its laptops – to low-cost manufacturing operations in China.

What was Dell's response? It began to realise that its fundamental business model – low costs, made-to-order computers – was under severe attack from even lower cost manufacturers. The PC market had become *commoditised*: selling PCs was just like selling commodities like sugar, coffee or basic steel products. Market competition was based largely on the price of the commodity, little else. Sustainable competitive advantage from branding, core competencies, knowledge and many other areas had partially disappeared from the PC market.

Dell's new strategy beyond commoditisation: from the late 2000s

Given the difficulties in its existing strategy, Dell then began to move into a new, related business area to PCs: *computer services and software*. In essence, this was similar to the strategy of the world's leading computer company IBM which had made this strategic move some years earlier.

Dell began expanding its activities in the area of 'Enterprise solutions and services' by a series of acquisitions. In the period to 2011, it bought six companies in this area and was adding another two, namely SecureWorks and Compellent, in early 2012. In March 2012, Dell agreed to buy SonicWall, a provider of network and data security services for a wide range of companies, in a deal reported to be around US$1.25 billon. In July 2012, Dell agreed to acquire Quest Software for US$2.4 billion. This latter company was essentially involved in the related areas of computer storage, systems management, cloud computing and software. Quest customers were mainly large companies who needed back-up and recovery software and single sign-on solutions that allowed users to access multiple password-protected accounts with a single log-in.

Even prior to these new acquisitions in early 2012, Dell Services had a business worth US$7.7 billion in revenue and employing over 43,000 people. This area had become increasingly important to Dell: see Figure 1.

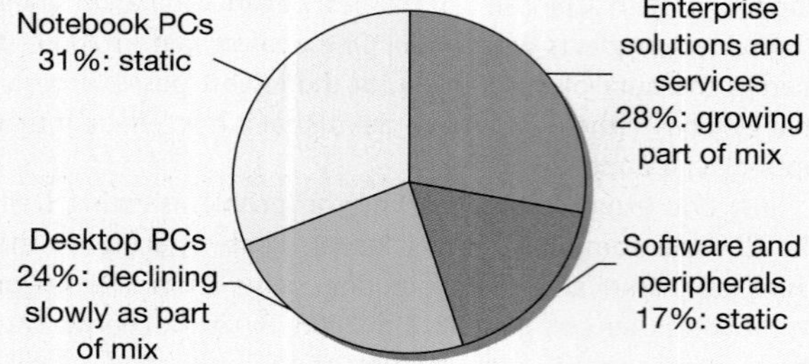

Figure 1 The contribution of Dell Enterprise Solutions and Services to Dell Group in 2011

Source: author from Dell annual reports and accounts.

Table 2 Dell's customer sales and profit margins in 2011

	Share of total Dell sales	Dell sales margin
Consumer	20%	1%
Small and medium business	24%	10%
Public sector business	27%	9%
Large companies	29%	8%

Note:

'Sales margin' is defined as the company's operating income (profits) as a percentage of its sales revenue. None of the Table 2 sales margins are particularly high. But the Consumer margin – largely related to PCs – is almost non-existent.

Source: author from company annual report and accounts.

The new strategy had the great advantage of higher profit margins than the cut-throat profits available in some parts of Dell's PC business. Although Dell does not publish its profit margins on its service business, its annual accounts do show the profit margins for the different sales mix of its businesses – see Table 2. This shows that consumer sales had very low margins. This business was the least likely to be to be buying its new Dell Enterprise Solutions and Services – illustrating the higher profitability of this service business.

Brian Gladden, Dell's chief financial officer, commented in 2012, 'We continue to shift the mix of our business during a challenging environment. Our enterprise solutions and services businesses now account for 50 per cent of our [sales] margin and we'll continue to make the necessary investments to maintain our progress.'

Although Dell had been involved in computer services for some years, it was from 2008 onwards that Dell began to expand more rapidly into the Enterprise Solutions and Services area – see Table 3. However, it was not easy for Dell to build a new venture in this area. Part of the reason was that it needed to operate a different type of company with different core skills associated with deeper levels of consultancy advice services than those linked to computer manufacture and marketing. Another reason was that it was expanding via an acquisition strategy, which is often difficult to undertake profitably. Good companies attract a premium price for their assets that may not be easy to recover from future profits.

At the same time as it was expanding into services, Dell could not afford to neglect its existing desktop and notebook business. In 2011, these still accounted for over half its total sales – see Table 3. Arguably, this was Dell's major strategic problem:

Table 3 Dell's revenue mix by product area

	2008	2009	2010	2011
Enterprise solutions and services	23%	24%	26%	28%
Software and peripherals	16%	17%	18%	17%
Desktops and notebooks	61%	59%	56%	55%

Source: author from annual report and accounts.

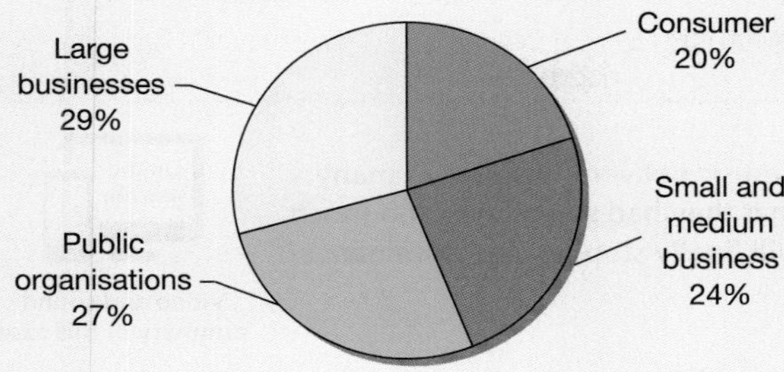

Figure 2 Dell's smaller customers were still important

it was still heavily reliant on a sales area that was proving increasingly competitive with rapidly changing technology, innovative rival products like media tablets and competitors like Apple that had sourced very low-cost manufacture.

Moreover, around 20 per cent of Dell's sales were still derived from small, personal PC sales – see Figure 2. It could not afford to abandon this market in the short term. In addition, even larger companies and public sector organisations were also seeking to use media tablets, smartphones and related products. It was not enough for Dell to rely on its new business in Enterprise Solutions and Services. Dell needed a product strategy.

Conclusion: too little and too late?

But all these new acquisitions came with costs. Had Dell paid too much for its new assets? How would the company integrate its new companies into the Dell Group? Would the company have the core skills and the flexibility to manage its new subsidiaries that were very different from its low-cost manufacturing competencies?

Some commentators were suggesting that the new Dell strategy was not a proven success. They also pointed out that its main rivals, IBM and Hewlett-Packard, had started down the move into computer services some years earlier. They suggested that there might not be enough market demand for a further company like Dell to move into this market, especially during a period of economic downturn. Fundamentally, they argued that Dell's strategy was merely a 'catch-up' strategy that copied competitors and lacked any distinctive competitive advantage.

But Dell was convinced that its new strategy would prove successful. For example, John A. Swainson, the president of Dell's new software group, said about its purchase of Quest Software, 'The addition of Quest will enable Dell to deliver more competitive server, storage, networking and end user computing solutions and services to customers.' But Dell was still behind its rivals.

In 2013, Michael Dell decided to take the company private again. He argued that it would be easier to make the required strategic changes if the company was no longer subject to the short-term, immediate results pressure of a public shareholding. 'As a private company, we are going back to our roots, to the entrepreneurial spirit that made Dell one of the fastest growing, most successful companies in history. We're unleashing the creativity and confidence that have always been the hallmarks of our culture. We will be able to serve our customers with a single-minded purpose and drive the innovations that will change our world for the better.'

After a protracted battle with some shareholders, Dell was effectively taken private in late 2013. But perhaps it was all too little and too late?

Source: this case was written by Professor Richard Lynch from published sources only. Sources include: Dell annual report and accounts for various years. *Financial Times*: 27 March 2013, p 19.

Case questions

1 Analyse how the strategic environment has changed over the last few years and assess the impact of such changes on Dell. To what extent, if at all, has the industry become less predictable? And what impact, if any, have such changes had on Dell?

2 Evaluate critically the sustainable competitive advantages of Dell and explain how these have changed over the last five years. What are the implications of your analysis for the company's new strategy of moving further into Enterprise Solutions and Services?

3 Dell does not appear to have been one of the industry's prime innovators in the years since 2005, unlike Apple and Samsung for example. Does Dell need to change? Or can Dell continue with its current strategy which places less emphasis on innovation and more on moving the company into the new area of service delivery?

4 Critically comment upon the Dell strategies undertaken by Michael Dell and his colleagues since 2005. Were there any other strategic options available to the company over this period?

5 Looking ahead from 2013, what strategies do you now propose for Dell? Give the reasoning behind your answer.

CASE STUDY 13

Emergent strategy: the competitive threat to Apple Music

After its launch in 2002, Apple's iTunes dominated the digital music delivery business in many countries around the world. Even the record companies felt that they had given away too much to Apple. But new companies are entering the market. Who will finally stop Apple's dominance? What is the role of emergent strategy?

Video and sound summary of this case

Major changes in home news and entertainment

Over the past hundred years, home music has undergone several major revolutions: first with the gramophone in the home; then with music from radio and television broadcasts; more recently, home personal computers and portable music devices like the iPod have access to music via the web. Now, the broadband revolution has begun in many countries providing greater communications capacity and speed.

As a result of these revolutionary changes, recorded music and music delivery companies around the world have begun to re-think their business strategies. To explore these issues, this case has four main sections:

1 World recorded music market
2 Compact discs versus digital music downloads
3 The main recorded music companies
4 Digital music: Apple iTunes dominates but for how long?

What strategies will stand the best chance of success? What can we learn from what has already happened? What scope do new technologies like mobile telephones and broadband bring for companies in the music business? This case identifies the main opportunities. But the market is moving so fast that emergent strategies may be the most effective way forward.

World recorded music market

Although the traditional record companies continue to lead the delivery of recorded music through the sale of compact discs (CDs), their grip on the market place continues to decline. World music sales were around $15 billion in 2013 with the market being largely stable over the previous year. CDs and singles accounted for 51 per cent of the total market (compared with 71 per cent in 2010) with digital music sales making up the other 39 per cent (up from 29 per cent in 2010). Performance rights accounted for another 7 per cent of the total with the final 3 per cent coming from royalty payments for the use of music in films, on television and computer games. The important shift from physical CDs to digital music delivery is likely to continue: Figure 1 shows the change over the five years to 2013.

The recorded music industry has accepted the change to new forms of delivery. Francis Moore, the chief executive of the international music body, the International Federation of the Phonographic Industry (IFPI) commented: 'The music industry has become a mixed economy of diverse consumer channels and revenue streams. This has been an amazing transformation, dramatically expanding the way artists reach their fans across the globe. It is now clear that music streaming and subscription is a mainstream model for our business. In 2011, there were 8 million paying subscribers to subscription services – today [2013] there are 28 million. Ad-supported and subscription streams are rising in most markets, helping grow overall digital revenues for record companies and artists.'

To support the market, the record industry has continued to invest in its artists. Record companies put around $5 billion back into the industry every year in recording, marketing and other promotional costs. This figure also included investment in artiste and repertoire work (A&R) of around $2.4 billion to explore and support new work. This works out at 16 per cent of revenue and is higher than many other industries. Some would say it is too high, given the low profits of some companies in the industry. However, the same A&R investment also earns revenue sources beyond the recorded music delivery market outlined above. Other profit streams include sheet music, live performances along with video and live television, radio and other publishing. There are also significant markets in audio equipment and performance venues. In total, it has been

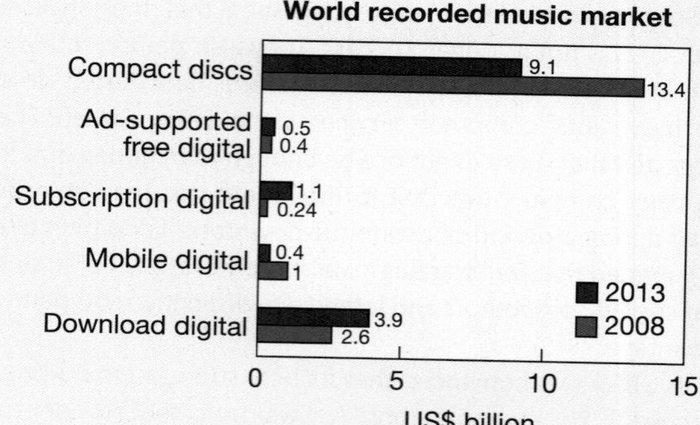

Figure 1 Digital delivery has grown significantly at the expense of CDs

Note: CDs are sold by the record companies. Download digital is dominated by Apple iTunes. Mobile digital is the music service of mobile telephone companies. Subscription digital and Ad-supported digital are from new companies that sell music listening delivered over the internet either by a monthly subscription or free with advertising.

Source: author based on industry data.

Music delivery is changing rapidly but companies do not yet know how. Experimental strategies will be important in this uncertain but exciting market.

estimated that the recorded music industry supports a broader music-related world market worth $160 billion annually.

Investing through A&R in individual artists and groups is still a risky business. It has been estimated that developing and marketing successful artists costs typically $1 million. This includes an artist's advance, the recording and video studio work, the tour support and promotion and marketing. The initial upfront investment in an individual performer is then recouped as the artist or group makes several albums of material over time. The whole process is highly risky for the record labels with only one in five, perhaps only one in ten, repaying the investment. The more recent proliferation of music outlets, including digital, has increased the distribution costs to the record companies.

For example, EMI had a roster of 14,000 artists in 2007 with just 200 of them producing most of the revenue. Around 85 per cent of the artists lost money for their EMI labels. The company explained that it spent annually $140 million subsidising the 15 per cent of artists who would never produce an album. Why does a record company spend so much for such poor value? Certainly, artists like Madonna and Elton John are brands in themselves and demand special treatment. The strategic difficulty is that, 'The recipe of bands, fans and brands is a potent mix and should be treated with great care,' according to a leading industry expert. In other words, the record artists argued that their creativity benefited from a degree of protection and investment.

Compact discs versus digital music downloads

Given the size of the market and the dominant shares of the leading record companies, it may seem surprising that such companies had profit problems. One of the main reasons in parts of the industry was that CDs had higher profit margins than web and other broadcast sales for the record companies and for the musicians.

Another reason for profit problems was illegal music sharing through the internet. However, this was not as great a problem in 2013 as it had been in the early 2000s according to the IFPI. There were two reasons for this. First, the record industry moved aggressively to close down illegal music file sharing sites. Second, the new Apple music model had monetised (commercialised) downloading by supporting payment for accessing music tracks digitally.

The balance between CDs and digital music varied in different parts of the world. Broadly, digital sales were now beginning to replace physical CD sales in many countries. Thomas Hesse, the president of global digital business at Sony Music, supported this view. He said that mobile music consumption had only 'scratched the surface' in the USA and that download services such as iTunes and Amazon had plenty more growth potential. Mr Hesse commented, 'There are grounds to believe growth will continue and accelerate again.'

This meant that the record companies needed to accept the inevitability of this shift in music delivery and adjust their strategies accordingly. One of the main problems was that one company's service, Apple iTunes, dominated digital delivery. But, as we shall see later, other forms of music delivery were beginning to threaten the Apple business.

The main recorded music companies

The recorded music companies, both large and small, matter in the music industry according to a report called 'Investing in Music' and published in 2010 by the IFPI and downloadable from the web.

The IFPI Chairman John Kennedy explained, 'One of the biggest myths about the music industry in the digital age is that artists no longer need record labels. It is simply wrong. The investment, partnership and support that help build artist careers have never been more important than they are today. This report aims to explain why. "Investing in Music" is about how the music business works. It explains the value that music companies add, helping artists to realise a talent that would typically go unrecognised and get to an audience they would otherwise not reach . . . Much of the value added by music companies is invisible to the outside world. Yet it is the investment and advice from labels that enable an artist to build a career in music and which, in turn, creates a beneficial ripple effect throughout the wider music sector.'

Turning to the companies themselves, there have been some changes in the market shares of the leading companies – see Table 1. In addition, ownership of most of the leading companies has changed over the period: the table provides some brief details. But such changes have made no fundamental difference to the industry structure. It is still dominated by the four main producers and, at the same time, characterised by a profusion of record labels, some of which are owned the major players.

The competitive advantages of the Big Four come from four related areas:

1 *Recording contracts*. Most of the world's top artists are signed up to one of the leading record producers. For example, Elton John, Cher, the late Michael Jackson's estate and Madonna all have exclusive contracts that provide sustainable competitive advantage for their record companies. George Michael's very public dispute with his record

company only highlighted the control that generally exists in the industry.

2 *High promotional barriers*. Entry barriers for new artists are high because of the marketing funds needed to promote international stars – as seen in the EMI data above. In addition, considerable expertise and networks are employed to promote and distribute records.

3 *Record sales through retail stores*. The majority of sales are through the leading recorded music retail stores. Gaining shelf space has been a barrier for the smaller companies and an opportunity for the large record producers because the latter have the bargaining power to handle such important retail distributors.

4 *Related contractual revenue from live concerts, television, radio and music publishing*. Many record companies have agreed contracts with their artists that bring additional revenue streams from such sources.

As mentioned above, most record companies have other sources of value added. For example, many record companies also have music publishing subsidiaries and rights to broadcast repeat fees that are highly profitable. Until recently, the record companies have never been involved with other related music industry activities like concert promotion. However, this has changed over the last few years. For leading artists like Kylie Minogue and Take That, the record companies are now negotiating broader promotional deals beyond simply CDs. For example, Robbie Williams was paid $120 million over five years for a deal that covered not only music but also fees from concerts, merchandise and other forms of branding. Essentially, this meant that the record producer was extending the music value chain from simply recording music into other aspects of the music industry – the performer, the tour promoter and the artist's agent.

Although existing record companies dominated traditional distribution, the internet has altered the balance towards new independent record labels over the past few years through online delivery. This can take place in a number of ways, including:

- Legitimate internet sites selling CDs and cassettes in competition with the high-street retail outlets. These sites will be supplied by the Big Four above, but independent labels can also sell their music. The three major companies have taken shares in one of the leading digital companies, Spotify, to protect their revenue interests. The danger is that they upset their traditional retail outlets.
- Digital juke boxes run by small, independent music companies like IUMA and MP3.com. In addition, some sites have been specially set up to distribute the music of new groups unable to get contracts from the Big Four. Each music group pays only $250 to put a recording on the site. Consumers can listen for free and download for only 99 cents. These include Spotify, Deezer and Pandora described below.
- Underground internet sites distributing music illegally from the Big Four without paying royalties, thus allowing others to download without buying the recordings. Napster was probably the most famous but was only one of many companies. Over the past four years, the record companies have slowly closed down most of these sites by aggressive legal activity. But there are still some active sites especially in Russia, if the earlier data from the IFPI is to be believed.

For 15 years, it was the illegal download route that alarmed the Big Four (now Three) recording companies. They developed what was claimed to be a 'pirate-proof' internet system to distribute their own music in response called Digital Rights Management (DRM). But after five years of development, the DRM proved, at least in part, a hindrance because it encouraged fans towards downloading illegal copies and the same software made it difficult to load personal stereo players. The breakthrough came with the Apple Computers' iTunes deal with all the leading record companies that revolutionised the record industry in 2002. For the first time, it was possible to download music legally for a payment and without the problems of DRM. By 2013, the legal download market was worth $3.9 billion annually with Apple the market leader with 70 per cent market share. Although some illegal downloading was still

Table 1 Leading global record producers

	Market share 2006 (%)	Market share 2008 (%)	Market 2013 share (%)	Comment
Universal	25	28	35	Following share transactions in 2006, the French group Vivendi owns 100%. The company bought part of EMI Music in 2011
Sony	22	20	26	In 2008, Sony acquired total control of company from the German group Bertelsmann. Sony acquired EMI music publishing in 2011
Warner	12	14	16	Warner Music separated from AOL Time Warner. It made several attempts to acquire EMI
EMI	12	11	0	UK-based group struggled with legal issues – see Case 15.3 – and broken up
Others	29	27	27	Share decline stabilised

Source: author from trade sources.

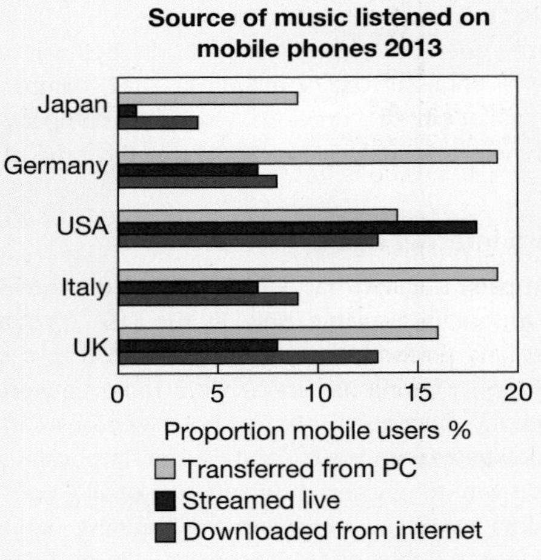

Figure 2 Mobile phone music mainly came from personal computers

Source: author from data in Ofcom International Market Communications Report 2013.

being undertaken, it was no longer a major competitive threat to the record companies.

Importantly, digital music needs to be put into perspective: it is not the only form of music listening. Full data is not readily available. However, some figures for *mobile phones only* make the point: the largest source of music for mobile phones was transferred from a PC for five leading developed countries. Live streaming and digital downloading from the internet were smaller sources – see Figure 2.

Digital music: Apple iTunes dominates but for how long?

By 2007, the record companies realised that Apple had gained dominance of the music online delivery industry and could therefore dictate prices and deals to the record companies. As a result, the record companies decided to encourage other delivery companies to enter the industry – they needed some competition for Apple. As a result, over 400 companies worldwide have been encouraged to take up the challenge of which there are 200 alone in Europe.

Five examples amongst many forms of new digital music services are:

1 *YouTube*, owned by Google, has free music of videos;
2 *Vodafone*, one of the European market leaders in mobile telephone services;
3 *Pandoro*, offering music tailored to individual tastes – see below;
4 *Spotify* and *Deezer*, the specialist music sites – see below;
5 *Amazon*, the market leader in online book and music shopping.

However, while Apple still dominated the market in 2014, some other companies were beginning to eat into this share. The main method of attacking Apple has been through music streaming, i.e. accessing recorded music through a computer online connection or through a mobile phone. Streaming grew rapidly over the five years to 2013 but was still smaller than music downloading – see Figure 3.

For reasons of space, this section of the case concentrates on only three companies, Spotify, Deezer and Pandora Radio. However, there are many other download services available. These include formidable competitors like YouTube and Vodafone as well as smaller companies – see the next section. Many other companies see real business opportunities in download services for digital recorded music.

Spotify

Spotify was launched in 2008 and was originally developed by two Swedish computer engineers. The company's business headquarters are in London, UK, but its research and development remains in Sweden. The main record companies above took minority shares in Spotify at its launch in 2008. But their shareholding has possibly been diluted with other venture capitalists investing further funds in later years.

Spotify offers digital music free if listeners are prepared to accept advertising. For a monthly fee of £4.99 or £9.99 depending on the service level required, Spotify will deliver advertising-free music that can be downloaded on any computer and shared with friends. The company claimed to have 40,000 fee-payers in 2009 soon after launch. This rose to 750,000 users willing to pay a fee at the end of 2010 and 7 million in 2014. The company made a major breakthrough in 2011 when it signed an agreement with the leading record companies to launch its service in the USA – the world's biggest music market. It also added a strong link with Facebook, the world's largest online social network that has proved a beneficial strategy.

Spotify allows access to a downloadable music library whereas iTunes allows access only to the track that has been

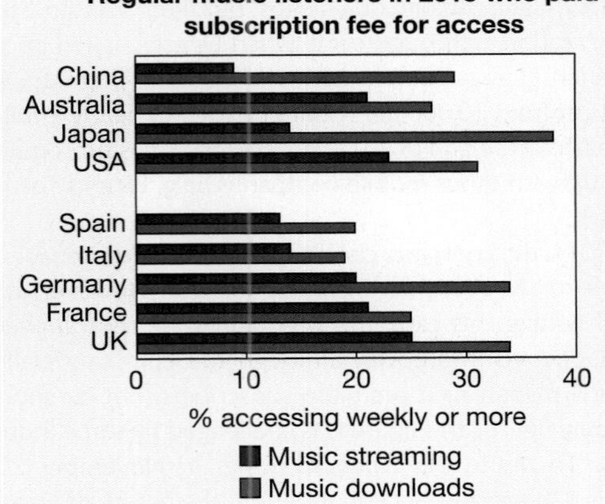

Figure 3 Downloads were still larger than streaming in 2013

Source: author from data in Ofcom International Market Communications Report 2013

purchased. Spotify music is still subject to DRM. Importantly, Spotify may be a new competitor to Apple Music, but that has not stopped Apple allowing the Spotify premium service (at £9.99) to be available as an App on the Apple App Store. Arguably, one of the reasons for this Apple generosity is that this allows Apple to insist to the national competition authorities that its market dominance is not anti-competitive.

Spotify was a private company at the time of writing this case in 2014 with limited disclosure of financial data. It was reported to have a turnover of US$570 million in 2012 with a net loss of US$77 million. The company therefore needed to raise finance to continue its operations. It was reported to have raised over US$450 million since its launch. Spotify claimed to have around 24 million active users in 2014 of whom 6 million paid for the premium service.

In March 2014, Spotify made a shock company purchase. It acquired The Echo Nest (EN) company for an undisclosed sum. EN works with the online services of radio companies using software that trawls the web to identify links between songs. It then supplies this data to radio companies to make music recommendations for radio playlists. This is not the same as the Pandora software described below, which is tailored to individual listeners. However, it does help Spotify customers in another way. Some customers feel overwhelmed by the vast Spotify music catalogue. This should help the company to suggest playlists. 'When you're on the way to the gym, we'll be able to select which of your friend's workout playlists would be most relevant for you.'

Deezer

Deezer began in France in 2007 and quickly ran into copyright problems with the leading record labels because it had not negotiated contracts. Like Spotify, it also had early financial demands that were not easily met. Both companies relied in the early days on selling advertising to pay for the service and this revenue stream was insufficient to cover the royalties to the record labels.

In 2009, Deezer launched a subscription service at €4.99 per month for higher quality downloads, but there was slow take-up. The real breakthrough came when Deezer signed up with the French Orange mobile network: Deezer's premium network went from 10,000 per month in 2010 to nearly 1 million per month by the end of 2011. The company has subsequently signed up with other mobile companies, e.g. EE and Telekom in the UK.

By 2014, the company claimed that the Deezer service was available in 182 countries, including the USA. However, at the time of writing this case, the USA launch did not appear to have happened. Moreover, although the company claimed to have 5 million paid premium subscribers (not far short of the Spotify figure), this figure was challenged by some industry experts. To quote the *Financial Times* in November 2013: 'There is a "huge misconception" about the nature of Deezer's subscribers that means that it is still a long way from catching up with Spotify . . . the paid subscribers figure includes an undisclosed number of subscribers to bundled telecoms deals who have not yet activated the service.' In other words, Deezer may be available on a mobile telephone but that does not mean that it is being actively used.

Deezer does not publish its accounts but was reported to have revenues of US$79 million in 2012, compared with US$60 million in the previous year. The company almost certainly was loss-making like Spotify at the time of writing this case.

Pandora Internet Radio

This company is somewhat different to the other two above. First, Pandora is available only in the USA, Australia and New Zealand. Second, the company began with a different technology – offering its service via a radio network. It has subsequently developed mobile phone versions and, in this sense, competes with Spotify and Deezer. Importantly, it also competes with the biggest music offering of all – YouTube.

Pandora works by observing the listening habits of an individual user. It then offers the songs or albums from various online retailers. Pandora monitors over 400 different musical attributes for each individual user and then combines these into 2,000 focus traits in order to make the suggested song selection for each user: 'We have pioneered a new form of radio.' In essence, it offers a unique internet radio service for each user – quite different from Spotify and Deezer, which do not have real-time monitoring of customers.

Pandora had revenues of US$427 million in 2013, having grown 56 per cent over the previous year. Its revenues were generated both by advertising (88%) and by a subscription premium service (12%). The company has been highly active with many new ideas such as linking up with all the major US car manufacturers to offer in-car radio services. The internet radio concept is really one to watch in the opinion of the author of this case (which is why it is included, in spite of the fact that Pandora cannot be heard in the UK). The Pandora Radio company can be accessed at www.pandora.com.

Conclusions on competitors to Apple Music

Although full *world* data is not available, market information from the *USA* market suggests that streaming was beginning to surge in 2013 at the expense of download music sales like Apple iTunes store. Specifically, US download single track sales dropped from 1.34 billion units in 2012 to 1.26 billion in 2013. Total download album sales at 118 million units were the same in 2013 as 2012. There was no full-year data for 2013 for digital streaming. But a mid-year report suggested that the market had grown by a massive 24 per cent to 50 million streams (but not units) in the first half of 2013.

Although this data might suggest that streaming was a threat to downloads, the data needs to be read with considerable caution. Just because someone paid a *subscription* to a streaming site, it does not necessarily mean that they *listened* to any music. Apple Music held the dominant share of the download market and would be therefore be particularly impacted by a major increase in streaming – unless, of course, Apple itself moved into music streaming. . . .

The market data makes the point that it is difficult to measure fully the sources and uses of music. For example, the

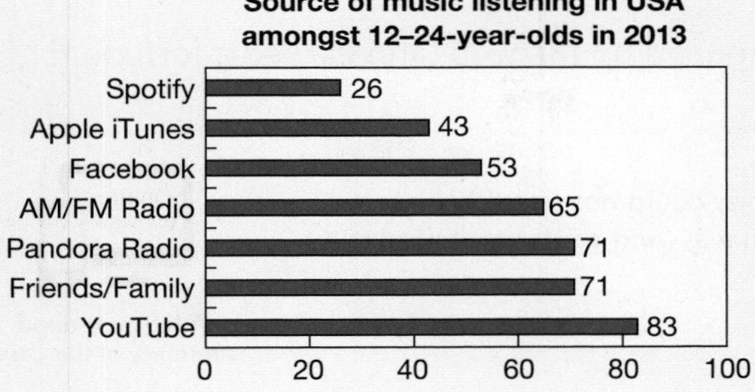

Figure 4 Music listening still ranges across many sources

Source: author derived from data from Edison Research linked with their publication 'The Infinite Dial 2013' © Copyright Arbitron Inc. and Edison Research 2013. All rights reserved.

use of an iPod, the purchase of a new CD, listening to radio, downloading some music all require different measures and may have anything from zero cost to monthly charges. To form some concept of what activity might take place, there is some data on music listening amongst a young group in the USA - see Figure 4. It is not conclusive, but suggests that there are still many alternatives to Apple Music, YouTube free music being just one. Certainly, Apple will face significant new competition in the digital music market over the next few years. The key will be how to compete and with what competitive advantages.

Case questions

1 Why has Apple been so successful in the digital download market? Is it only because of its first-mover advantage or are there other reasons?

2 Using emergent strategy concepts, what strategies would you now recommend for the digital music streaming companies like Spotify and Deezer? Have they anything to learn from Pandora? If so, what?

3 What lessons can be drawn from this case on the opportunities presented by new technology in the dynamics of strategy development?

STRATEGIC PROJECT

Substantial continuing growth in the internet will provide major strategic opportunities over the next few years for small and medium-sized enterprises (SMEs) in many industries. This case describes one example for the record industry. Identify further internet opportunities and use the concepts explored in this chapter and other parts of this book to develop strategies for SMEs.

Note

This case was written by the author from numerous sources most of which were listed in *Strategic Management*, 6th edn. The new sources are: Annual report and accounts of *IFPI 2013*; *Ofcom* Communications International Market Report December 2013; *Thomson Reuters* news services: 'Music service Spotify raises $250 million', 21 November 2013; *Financial Times* Syndication service: 7 November 2013, 'Media Doubts over Deezer's subscriber activity'; 4 January 2014, 'Digital music sales eclipsed as streaming services grow'; *Financial Times*: 2 June 2011, p 23; 6 June 2011, p 23; 15 July 2011, p 20; 8 November 2011, p 19; 14 February 2012, p 17; 12 April 2012, p 20; 12 July 2012, pp 19 & 20; 27 September 2012, p 20; 7 December 2012, p 20; 9 December 2012, p 21; 13 December 2012, p 4; 25 October 2013, p 18; 29 November 2013, p 23; 7 March 2014, p 22.

CASE STUDY 14

Emergent strategy: how Google's search strategy opened up the web (and earned a fortune for its inventors)

When Larry Page and Sergey Brin founded Google in 1999, they could not possibly have seen how it would develop. This case explores their strategy, which was (and continues to be) truly innovative, experimental and risk taking.

Video and sound summary of this case

'Don't be evil'

From the beginning, Larry and Sergey wanted to run an ethical company. They coined the credo 'Don't be evil' to describe the ethical principles behind the business. The atmosphere of the company reflected this approach. It was open, informal and innovatory. There were weekly company open meetings; all meals were provided by a well-known chef; there were bean bags to replace office furniture and a Lego model of a computer in the entrance hall. Employees work on the 70:20:10 principle – 70 per cent of their time on the immediate task, 20 per cent on related new ideas and the remaining flexible 10 per cent as they choose. The Google brand name itself was developed from the name commonly given to a very large mathematical number and the whole atmosphere was cerebral, geeky and fun.

The company consisted of the two partners and a few friends and colleagues. The 1999 turnover was $220,000 and it had the usual debts associated with a new start-up company. This was the booming era of new 'dot.com' companies when virtually any new internet company was able to raise funds and commentators were expecting the internet to revolutionise every aspect of business life – mistakenly as it turned out (see Cases 11 and 13 for more on this). Importantly, Google had something that was not shared by many other new internet companies of that time: it had an innovatory new technology.

Starting from nothing in 1989, Google has built a massive new business based on innovative and experimental strategies.

Google's innovatory technology

Back in 1999 when it all began, Larry and Sergey themselves were only in their early 20s. They had met whilst studying and researching computer technology at Stanford University in the mid-1990s. They found that they had a shared interest in searching and handling large pools of data. They subsequently commercialised this interest by developing a new and innovatory internet search engine. The two partners developed new search methods that went beyond what was previously available in two respects. First, they developed a new kind of server set-up that linked existing computers rather than using one large computer to undertake the search. This made the search faster because there was less queuing. Second, their search method did not count individual words, as in previous search methodology, but examined the entire link structure of the web to determine the most important sources of information. This made the search more comprehensive. The Google search was therefore better from the beginning than the existing searches supplied by companies like Yahoo!, Microsoft and Ask Jeeves.

However, although the technology was new, this did not necessarily deliver a profitable business. The new search engine was popular with computer users because it performed better than its rivals. The company found that it had no need to advertise because the growing communities of computer users rapidly spread its benefits. But Google had a problem because users were accessing its services largely free of charge: it needed to find a business model that would increase its turnover.

Google's new internet advertising services

From a small base in year 2000, Google has developed the internet advertising services that generate most of its revenue. Importantly from a strategy perspective, these were changed and developed over a number of years: there was no immediate breakthrough in its business model. Equally, the two founders recognised that they had only limited general business experience and made a considerable effort to recruit good people who would add to the team. In particular, they managed to attract Eric Schmidt from the computer company Novell in 2001 as their Chief Executive to manage the business and bring a wider range of skills to the company. By 2006, the company's turnover had grown to nearly $11 billion with profit after tax of over $3 billion. The full growth picture can be seen in Figure 1.

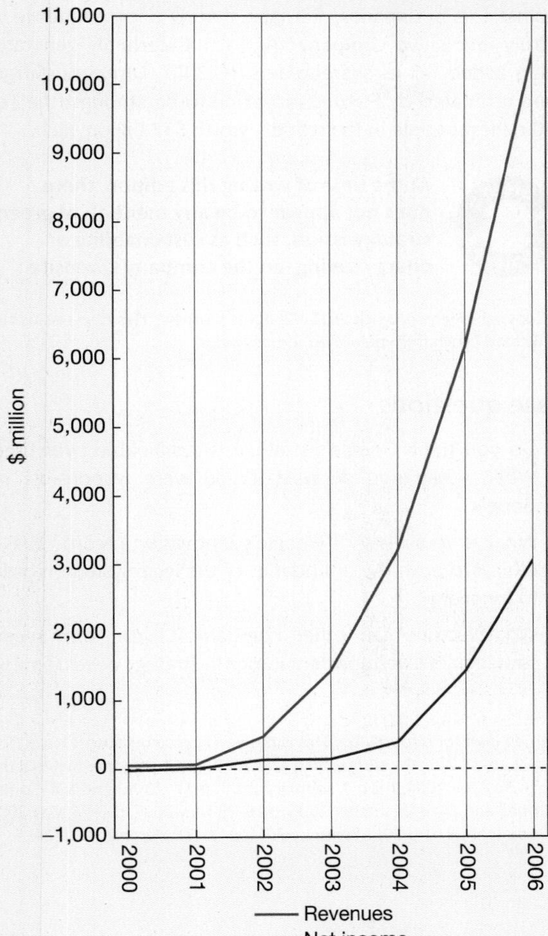

Figure 1 Dramatic growth in Google's business

Source: author from company accounts.

How and why has Google been so successful? There are seven principal reasons:

1 Google offers two services that meet real needs. The first – called AdWords – provides the opportunity to advertise services and products alongside each individual search undertaken by Google. The second is a service – called AdSense – to commercial web page providers, like newspapers, that delivers web advertising tailored to the web pages of that provider.

2 In spite of its laid-back and geeky image, Google has not hesitated to exploit its commercial benefits. For example, it introduced an auction process for available space on its AdWords search service. Equally, it negotiated large contracts with some publishers that involve guaranteed financial commitments that are highly profitable but carry some subsidiary risk.

3 Google has benefited from the rapid growth in the use of the internet worldwide over the past ten years.

4 Google has positioned itself as the world's leading provider of information. The company states that its mission statement is, 'To organise the world's information and make it universally available'. Thus Google has been accessing major world libraries and copying their extensive ranges of books and papers. Importantly, the company has been truly aggressive in this approach, upsetting some publishers by attempting to access copyright material without paying any fees.

5 Google has managed to stay ahead of its main rivals by introducing new services – like Google Maps – that offer new levels of search for its customers.

6 Google has good senior managers. Importantly, it has managed to retain and motivate its senior people over the past few years – particularly vital for a company that relies on innovation and 'out-of-the-box' thinking.

7 Google was lucky in its timing, its conjunction of senior people and its lack of strong competitors.

Google continues to innovate but is it always ethical?

By the law of large numbers, Google should have had difficulty in maintaining its high growth over time (see Figure 1). This was one of the reasons why it has been seeking new internet growth opportunities. Five developments stand out:

1 *YouTube*. In October 2006, Google bought the internet company YouTube for $1.65 billion in shares from its founders, Steve Chen and Chad Hurley. YouTube had only been running for just over a year and was still headquartered in offices above a pizza parlour in Silicon Valley California. But Google was attracted by the many enthusiasts who were posting videos onto its dominant webspace. As the UK newspaper *The Financial Times* pointed out, the two founders of YouTube set a record for the biggest financial payoff in the shortest time ever.

2 *Google Maps*. From 2007, Google started using special cars to photograph many streets in Europe and North America and link the results to its free digital maps. It introduced a totally new dimension in street views and helped to secure its earlier geographic Google mapping service in a new way. However, it also collected personal data from some households in the process and was investigated by many national government agencies for the ethics of collecting private data without the knowledge and permission of the home owners. Google has since said that this was done inadvertently and removed the data.

3 *Google Buzz*. This service was introduced as an alternative to the social network services provided by Facebook and Twitter. Google took an aggressive approach to using the existing personal details of those registered with its services to build an instant network. One outcome of this approach was to release personal data about Google subscribers without their permission. In 2011, the company made an agreement with the US Federal Trade Commission that its handling of personal data will be externally audited for the next 20 years – arguably an admission by Google that its ethical standards were not high enough in the past.

4 *Android mobile phone system*. The company has developed a totally new operating system that has been highly successful – see Case 11.

5 *Google copying of books in the public domain*. The company began scanning millions of books in the early 2000s with the aim of making them available online. The scans were done without the express permission of the copyright holders of the texts. However, Google made a legal settlement with the Authors Guild and the American Association of Publishers to pay a block royalty to copyright holders who had formally registered their title to their copyright. In March 2011, this agreement was blocked by the US courts as going too far: 'The [amended settlement agreement] would give Google significant advantage over competitors, rewarding it for engaging in wholesale copying of copyrighted works without permission, while releasing claims well beyond those presented in the case.' Google has arguably pushed the limits of its ethical boundaries with regard to copyright law. However, in fairness, Google has always followed the rulings of the legal system and also reached an agreement to pay royalties with representatives of some existing copyright holders.

What does all this mean for Larry and Sergey's original desire to run an innovative and ethical company? Google has never knowingly breached the law, but it has arguably pushed against the boundaries. Perhaps that is a consequence of a truly innovative company? And it has certainly generated value added for its shareholders. In 2007, Larry and Sergey were estimated by *Fortune* magazine to be amongst the Top 100 richest people in the world – worth $17 billion each.

At the time of writing this edition, there does not appear to be any mention of green strategy issues, such as sustainability or energy saving, on the company's website.

Case questions

1 Do you think Google's strategy is sustainable over time? What would you do next if you were responsible for Google?

2 What is your view of Google's innovation record? Was it ethical to push the boundaries of the legal system in order to innovate?

3 What lessons can other companies learn from recent strategies? How important is luck in strategy development?

Note

* Sources: Google Annual Reports 2000–2006 from Google website – see the section on investor information. This is the best source because it has a clear description of the various parts of the Google business and because it clearly sets out the risks facing the company to year 2007. The newspaper material that follows is vague and imprecise on these important strategic matters. *Financial Times*: 30 April 2004, p 31; 1 February 2005, p 17; 20 August 2005, p M6; 4 February 2006, p 10 – editorial; 6 March 2006, p 19; 11 October 2006, pp 14 (editorial) and 24; 8 December 2006, p 26; 23 May 2007, p 1; 26 May 2007, p 9; 21 September 2007, p 25; 27 September 2007, p 16; 21 August 2009, p 12; 21 December 2010, p 20; 7 February 2011, p 20; 31 March 2011, p 24.

GLOSSARY

Added value The difference between the market value of the output and the cost of the inputs to the organisation.

Agency theory Concerned with the added value that derives from one party – the *principal* – delegating the responsibility for one or more management decisions to another party – an *agent* acting on behalf of the principal – on the assumption that the agent is better placed better informed to make the optimal decision.

Architecture The network of relationships and contracts both within and around the organisation.

Attractiveness to stakeholders Strategy evaluation criterion associated with the strategy being sufficiently appealing to those people that the company needs to satisfy.

Backward integration The process whereby an organisation acquires the activities of its inputs (e.g. manufacturer into raw material supplier).

Balanced scorecard This uses strategic and financial measures to assess the outcome of a chosen strategy. It acknowledges the different expectations of the various stakeholders and attempts to use a 'scorecard' based on four prime areas of business activity to measure the results of the selected strategy.

Benchmarking The comparison of practice in other organisations in order to identify areas for improvement. Note that the comparison does *not* have to be with another organisation within the same industry, simply one whose practices are better at a particular *aspect* of the task or function.

Blue ocean strategy A strategy that focuses on untapped market space, demand creation and the opportunity for highly profitable growth.

Bounded rationality The principle that managers reduce tasks, including implementation, to a series of small steps, even though this may grossly over-simplify the situation and may not be the optimal way to proceed.

Brainstorming The rapid generation of ideas by a group, often from a wide variety of backgrounds, without any evaluation of those ideas.

Branding The additional reassurance provided to the customer by the brand name and reputation beyond the intrinsic value of the assets purchased by the customer. A specific name or symbol used to distinguish a seller's product or services.

Break-even The point at which the total costs of undertaking a new strategy are equal to the total revenue from the strategy.

Bretton Woods Agreement System of largely fixed currency exchange rates between the leading industrialised nations of the world. In operation from 1944 to 1973.

Business ethics See *Ethics*.

Business model A formula that summarises the essential elements of strategy that will deliver the company's profits in a particular strategic context.

Business process re-engineering The replacement of people in administrative tasks by technology, often accompanied by delayering and other organisational change. See also *Delayering*.

Capabilities The capabilities of an organisation are those management skills, routines and leadership that deploy, share and generate value from the resources of the organisation.

Capacity utilisation The level of plant operation at any time, usually expressed as a percentage of total production capacity of that plant.

Cash cows Products with high relative market shares in low-growth markets. See also *Portfolio matrix*.

Change options matrix This links the areas of human resource activity with the three main areas of strategic change: work, cultural and political change.

Changeability of the environment The degree to which the environment is likely to change.

Channel strategy See *Distribution strategy*.

Close-related diversification Different companies within a group may have different products or services but have some form of close affinity such as common customers, common suppliers or common overheads.

Collusive alliances Co-operative strategies in which firms seek to share information in order to reduce competition or raise prices. They are illegal in many countries.

Comparative advantage of nations This consists of the resources possessed by a country that give it a competitive advantage over other nations. See also *Diamond theory*.

Competitive advantage The *significant* advantages that an organisation has over its competitors. Such advantages allow the organisation to add more value than its competitors in the same market.

Competitor profiling Explores one or two leading competitors by analysing their resources, past performance, current products and strategies.

Complementors The companies whose products add more value to the products of the base organisation than they would derive from their own products by themselves – for example, Microsoft software adds significantly to the value of a Hewlett-Packard Personal Computer.

Complete competitive formula The business formula that offers both value for money to customers and competitive advantage against competitors.

Concentration ratio The degree to which value added or turnover is concentrated in the hands of a few firms in an industry. Measures the dominance of firms in an industry.

Consistency Strategy evaluation criterion associated with the strategy being in agreement with the objectives of the organisation.

Contend The constructive conflict that some strategists argue is needed by every organisation.

Content of strategic management The main actions of the proposed strategy.

Context of strategic management The circumstances surrounding and influencing the way that a strategy develops and operates.

Contingency theory of leadership Argues that leaders should be promoted or recruited according to the needs of the organisation at a particular point in time. See also *Style theory* and *Trait theory*.

Controls Employed to ensure that strategic objectives are achieved and financial, human resource and other guidelines are not breached during the implementation process or the ongoing phase of strategic activity. The process of monitoring the proposed plans as they are implemented and adjusting for any variances where necessary.

Co-operation The links that bring organisations together, thereby enhancing their ability to compete in the market place. See also *Complementors*.

Co-operative game Has positive payoff for all participants.

Co-operative strategy A strategy in which at least two companies work together with rivals or other related companies to achieve an agreed objective or to their mutual benefit.

Core areas of strategic management Strategic analysis, strategy development and strategy implementation from a prescriptive perspective only. For emergent strategists, the core areas will include knowledge, innovation, technology, strategy dynamics and related topics.

Core competencies The distinctive group of skills and technologies that enable an organisation to provide particular benefits to customers and deliver competitive advantage. Together, they form key resources of the organisation that assist it in being distinct from its competitors.

Core resources and capabilities The important strategic resources of the organisation, usually summarised as tangible and intangible resources of the organisation coupled with the organisational capabilities that deploy and share these resources.

Corporate governance The influence and power of the stakeholders to control the strategic direction of the organisation in general and, more specifically, the chief executive and other senior officers of the organisation.

Corporate-level strategy This has two meanings in the literature. First, corporate-level strategy means the strategic decisions that lead companies to *diversify* from one business into other business areas, either related or unrelated. Second, corporate-level strategy means the role of the *corporate headquarters* in directing and influencing strategy across a multi-product group of companies.

Corporate purpose The purpose and contribution of the central headquarters of a diversified group of companies.

Corporate social responsibility The standards and the conduct that an organisation sets itself in its dealings within an organisation and outside with its environment. See also *Ethics*.

Cost/benefit analysis Evaluates strategic projects, especially in the public sector, where an element of unquantified public service beyond commercial profit may be involved. It attempts to quantify the broader social benefits to be derived from particular strategic initiatives.

Cost of capital The cost of the capital employed in an organisation, often measured by the cost of investing in a risk-free bond outside the organisation coupled with some element for the extra risks, if any, of investing in the organisation itself.

Cost-plus pricing Sets the price of goods and services primarily by totalling the costs and adding a percentage profit margin. See also *Target pricing*.

Creative destruction theory Based on the concept that innovative opportunities arise through competition and technology destroying previous market offerings.

Creative theory Based on the hypothesis that new opportunities can be developed by entrepreneurs experimenting and creating a new market demand that did not previously exist.

Cultural web The factors that can be used to characterise some aspects of the culture of an organisation. Usually summarised as stories, symbols, power structures, organisational structure, control systems, routines and rituals.

Culture See *Organisational culture* and *International culture*. It is important to distinguish between these two quite distinct areas of the subject.

Customer-driven strategy The strategy of an organisation where every function is directed towards customer satisfaction. It goes beyond those functions, such as sales and marketing, that have traditionally had direct contact with the customer.

Customer profiling Describes the main characteristics of the customer and how customers make their purchase decisions.

Cyclicality The periodic rise and fall of a mature market.

Delayering The removal of layers of management and administration in an organisation's structure.

Demerger The split of an organisation into its constituent parts, with some parts possibly being sold to outside investors.

Derived demand Demand for goods and services that is derived from the economic performance of the customers. See also *Primary demand.*

Diamond theory of international competitive advantage Identifies a 'diamond' of four interrelated areas within a nation which assist that country to be more competitive in international markets – the four areas being factor conditions, competing firms within the country, support industries of the country and home demand. See also *Comparative advantage of nations.*

Differentiation The development of unique benefits or attributes in a product or service that positions it to appeal especially to a part (segment) of the total market. The products of the organisation meet the needs of some customers in the market place better than others and allow higher prices to be charged. See *Generic strategies.*

Dirigiste policy Describes the policies of a government relying on an approach of centrally directed government actions to manage the economy. See also *Laissez-faire policy.*

Discontinuity Radical, sudden and largely unpredicted change in the environment.

Discounted cash flow (DCF) The sum of the projected cash flows from a future strategy, after revaluing each individual element of the cash flow in terms of its present worth using the cost of capital of the organisation.

Discovery theory Based on the premise that new opportunities already exist in the market place and are waiting to be discovered by entrepreneurs.

Disruptive innovation This takes an existing market and identifies existing technologies that will offer simpler, less expensive products or services than have been offered previously. See also *Innovation.*

Distant-related diversification Although the different companies in the group will have quite different products or services, possibly using wholly different technologies, they will share the same underpinning core competencies or some other area of technology or service that would benefit from co-ordination by a central headquarters.

Distribution or channel strategy The strategies involved in delivering the product or service to the customer.

Diversification strategy This occurs when an organisation moves away from a single product or dominant business area into other business areas, which may or may not be related to the original business.

Diversified portfolio of products Companies that have a range of products serving many customers in different markets.

Division A separate part of a multi-product company with profit responsibility for its range of products. Each division usually has a complete range of the main business functions, such as finance, operations and marketing.

Dogs Products with low relative market shares in low-growth markets. See also *Portfolio matrix.*

Dominant logic The way in which managers conceptualise the business and make critical resource allocation decisions.

Double-loop learning Consists of a *first* loop of learning that checks performance against expected norms and adjusts where necessary, coupled with a *second* loop that reappraises whether the expected norms were appropriate in the first place. See also *Learning-based strategic route forward.*

Economic rent Any excess that a factor earns over the minimum amount needed to keep that factor in its present use.

Economies of scale The extra cost savings that occur when higher-volume production allows unit costs to be reduced. For example, a new, larger production plant produces products with the same quality but using fewer operatives, thus reducing unit costs. See also *Economies of scope.*

Economies of scope The cost savings developed by a group when it shares activities or transfers capabilities and competencies from one part of the group to another – for example, two products sharing the same sales team. See also *Economies of scale.*

Emergent change The whole process of developing a strategy whose outcome only emerges as the strategy proceeds. There is no defined list of implementation actions in advance of the strategy emerging. See also *Prescriptive change.*

Emergent strategic management A strategy whose final objective is unclear and whose elements are developed during the course of its life, as it proceeds. See also *Prescriptive strategic management.*

Empowerment The devolution of power and decision-making responsibility to those lower in the organisation.

Entrepreneurship A way of thinking, reasoning and acting that focuses on the identification and exploitation of business opportunities from a broad general perspective typically driven by the leadership of individuals or small groups.

Environment Everything and everyone outside the organisation: competitors, customers, government, etc. Note that 'green' environmental issues are only one part of this broader definition. See also *Changeability of the environment* and *Predictability of the environment.*

Ethics The principles that encompass the standards and conduct that an organisation sets itself in its dealings within the organisation and with its external environment. See also *Corporate social responsibility.*

Expansion method matrix Explores in a structured way the methods by which the market opportunities associated with strategy options might be achieved.

Experience curve The relationship between the unit costs of a product and the total units *ever produced* of that product, plotted in graphical form, with the units being cumulative from the first day of production.

Experiential learning circle This has four elements: 1. concrete experience or knowledge; 2. observation and reflection; 3. formation of abstract concepts from the observation; 4. testing of such concepts in new situations.

Explicit knowledge Knowledge that is codified and transmittable in formal, systematic language – often, but not necessarily, written down.

Feasibility Strategy evaluation criterion associated with the strategy being capable of being implemented.

Fit The consistencies, coherence and congruence of the organisation.

Floating and fixed exchange rates Currency exchange rates, such as the rate of exchange between the US dollar and the Yen, are said to *float* when market forces determine the rate, depending on market demand. They are *fixed* when national governments (or their associated national banks) fix the rates by international agreement and intervene in international markets to hold those rates.

Focus group A research discussion of around five to eight people, selected for their relevance to the subject.

Focus strategy Occurs when the organisation focuses on a specific niche (or segment) of the market place and develops competitive advantage by offering products especially developed for that niche (or segment). See also *Generic strategies*.

Foreign direct investment (FDI) The long-term investment by a company in technology, management skills, brands and physical assets of a subsidiary in another country.

Foreign trade The exporting and importing activities of countries and companies around the world.

Formal organisation structures Those structures formally defined by the organisation in terms of reporting relationships, responsibilities and tasks. See also *Informal organisation structures*.

Forward integration The process whereby an organisation acquires the activities of its outputs (e.g. manufacturer into distribution and transport).

Franchise A form of co-operative strategy in which a firm (the franchisor) develops a business concept and then offers this to others (the franchisees) in the form of a contractual relationship to use the business concept. Typically, the franchisee obtains a tried-and-tested business formula in return for paying a percentage of its sales and agreeing to tight controls from the franchisor over the product range, pricing, etc.

Functional organisation structure Structure based around the main activities that have to be undertaken by the organisation such as production, marketing, human resources, research and development, finance and accounting.

Game-based theories of strategy These focus on the decisions of the organisation and its competitors as strategy is developed – the *game* – and the interactions between the two as strategic decisions are taken.

Game theory Structured methods of bargaining with and between customers, suppliers and others, both inside and outside the organisation. Such structuring usually involves the quantification of possible outcomes at each stage of the strategy decision-making process.

Gearing ratio The ratio of debt finance to the total shareholders' funds.

General Agreement on Tariffs and Trade (GATT) International agreement between various countries around the world, designed to deal with trade disputes and support world trade.

Generic industry environment The study of those strategies that are particularly likely to cope with a particular market or competitive environment.

Generic strategies The three basic strategies of cost leadership, differentiation and focus (sometimes called niche) which are open to any business.

Global and national responsiveness matrix This links together the extent of the need for global activity with the need for an organisation to be responsive to national and regional variations. These two areas are not mutually exclusive.

Global product company This will often involve the global integration of manufacturing and one common global brand. There is only *limited* national variation. See also *Transnational product company*.

Global strategy When a company treats the whole world as one market and one source of supply. See also *International strategy* and *Multinational strategy*.

Green strategy Concerns those activities of the organisation that are focused on both sustaining the earth's environment and developing the business opportunities that will arise from such additional activities.

Green strategy value chain Seeks out ways of reducing energy, lowering carbon content and adopting recycling policies, not only within the organisation but also with suppliers and customers. In addition, the green strategy value chain will involve every element and function, including those that perhaps do not always feature highly in many value chain analyses.

Growth-share matrix See *Portfolio matrix*.

Heuristics Informal rules-of-thumb that provide simple decision rules to capture and summarise what has been learnt by one part of the organisation and then communicate this to other parts of the organisation.

Hierarchy of resources The four levels of resource that are the full resources of the organisation. The distinguishing feature of the higher levels is an increased likelihood of sustainable competitive advantage.

Historical strategy perspective According to this approach, the purpose of an organisation and its outcomes must, at least in part, be seen as being influenced by the organisation's present resources, its past history and its evolution over time. An organisation's previous history is a key determinant of its future development.

Holding company organisation structure (sometimes shortened to *H-Form* structure) Used for organisations with very diverse product ranges and share relationships where a central (holding) company owns various businesses and acts as an investment company with shareholdings in each of the individual enterprises. The headquarters acts only as a banker, with strategy largely decided by the individual companies.

Horizontal integration When an organisation moves to acquire its competitors or make some other form of close association.

Human resource audit An examination of the organisation's leadership, its people and their skills, backgrounds and relationships with each other.

Human resource-based theories of strategy These emphasise the importance of the people element in strategy development. See also *Emergent strategic management, Negotiation-based* and *Learning-based strategic route forward.*

Human resources The skills, talents and knowledge of every member of the organisation.

Industry- and environment-based theories of strategy Argue that profits are delivered by selecting the most attractive industry and then competing better than other companies in that industry.

Implementation The process by which the organisation's chosen strategies are put into operation.

Informal organisation structures Those structures, often unwritten, that have been developed by the history, culture and individuals in an organisation to facilitate the flow of information and allocate power within the structure. See also *Formal organisation structures.*

Innovation The generation and exploitation of new ideas. The process moves products and services, human and capital resources, markets and production processes beyond their current boundaries and capabilities. See also *Disruptive innovation.*

Innovation- and knowledge-based theories of strategy privilege the generation of new ideas and the sharing of those ideas as being the most important aspects of strategy development.

Innovation organisation structure Characterised by creativity, lack of formal reporting relationships and informality.

Innovative capability The special talent possessed by some organisations for developing and exploiting innovative ideas.

Intangible resources The organisation's resources that have no physical presence but represent real benefit to the organisation, like reputation and technical knowledge. See also *Tangible resources* and *Organisational capability.*

Intellectual capital of an organisation The future earnings capacity that derives from a deeper, broader and more human perspective than that described in the organisation's financial reports.

Intellectual property Any product of human intellect that is intangible but has value in the market place – often has a legal meaning for companies.

International culture Collective programming of the mind that distinguishes one human group from another. Distinguished from *Organisational culture.*

International Monetary Fund (IMF) International body designed to lend funds to countries in international difficulty and to promote trade stability through co-operation and discussion.

International strategy When a significant proportion of an organisation's activities are outside the home country and are managed as a separate area. See also *Multinational strategy* and *Global strategy.*

Intrapreneurship Focuses on the identification and exploitation of creative and innovative opportunities within larger companies or organisations.

Joint ventures Co-operative strategies where two or more organisations set up a separate jointly owned subsidiary to develop the co-operation.

Just-in-time System that ensures that stock is delivered from suppliers only when it is required, with none being held in reserve.

Kaizen The process of continuous improvement in production and every aspect of value added (Japanese).

Kanban Control system on the factory floor to keep production moving (Japanese).

Key factors for success (sometimes called *critical success factors*) Those resources, skills and attributes of the organisations in an industry that are essential to deliver success in the market place. Note that the emphasis is on *all* the companies in an industry. (Key factors for success are *not* about those factors that apply to an *individual* company.)

Knowledge A fluid mix of framed experience, values, contextual information and expert insight. It accumulates over time and shapes the organisation's ability to survive and compete in markets. Note that knowledge is *not* 'data' or 'information'.

Knowledge creation The development and circulation of new knowledge within the organisation.

Knowledge management The retention, exploitation and sharing of knowledge in an organisation that will deliver sustainable competitive advantage.

Laissez-faire policy Describes the policies of a government relying on an approach of non-interference and free-market forces to manage the economy of a country. See also *Dirigiste policy.*

Leadership The art or process of influencing people so that they will strive willingly and enthusiastically towards the achievement of the group's mission and purpose.

Learning The strategic process of developing strategy by crafting, experimentation and feedback. Note that learning in this context does *not* mean rote or memory learning.

Learning-based strategic route forward Emphasises learning and crafting as aspects of the development of successful corporate strategy. It places particular emphasis on trial and feedback mechanisms. See also *Human resource-based theories of strategy* and *Double-loop learning.*

Leasing A form of debt where the organisation hires an asset for a period, possibly with the option of buying it at the end of the period.

Leveraging The exploitation by an organisation of its existing resources to their fullest extent.

Life cycle Plots the evolution of industry annual sales over time. Often divided into distinct phases – introduction, growth, maturity and decline – with specific strategies for each phase.

Limited state intervention The theory of limited state intervention suggests that companies gained from national government investment in the early years in such areas as telecommunications and roads, but that as nations become more wealthy the state should withdraw its support and allow free market pressures to operate.

Logical incrementalism The process of developing a strategy by small, incremental and logical steps. The term was first used by Professor J B Quinn.

Logistics The science of stockholding, delivery and customer service.

Long-term debt A loan repaid over a period longer than a year. See also *Short-term debt.*

Loose–tight principle The concept of the need for tight central control by headquarters, while allowing individuals or operating subsidiaries loose autonomy and initiative within defined managerial limits.

Low-cost leader in an industry Has built and maintains plant, equipment, labour costs and working practices that deliver the lowest costs in that industry. See *Generic strategies.*

Macroeconomic conditions Economic activity at the general level of the national or international economy.

Market equilibrium The state that allows competitors a viable and stable market share accompanied by adequate profits.

Market mechanism The means by which the state uses market pricing and quasi-market mechanisms to determine the supply and demand of goods that were previously state monopolies in public sector strategy.

Market options matrix Identifies the product and the market options available to the organisation, including the possibility of withdrawal and movement into unrelated markets.

Market positioning The choice of differential advantage possessed by an organisation that allows it to compete and survive in a market place. Often associated with competition and survival in a segment of a market. See also *Market segmentation.*

Market segmentation The identification of specific groups (or segments) of customers who respond to competitive strategies differently from other groups. See also *Market positioning.*

Mass marketing One product is sold to all types of customer.

Matrix organisation structure Instead of the product-based multidivisional structure, some organisations have chosen to operate with two overlapping structures. One structure might typically be product-based, with another parallel structure being based on some other element, such as geographic region. The two elements form a *matrix* of responsibilities. Strategy needs to be agreed by both parts of the matrix. See also *Multidivisional organisation structure.*

Milestones Interim indicators of progress during the implementation phase of strategy.

Minimum intervention The principle that managers implementing strategy should only make changes where they are absolutely necessary.

Mission Outlines the broad general directions that the organisation should and will follow and briefly summarises the reasoning and values that lie behind it. See also *Objectives.*

Mission statement Defines the business that the organisation is in or should be in against the values and expectations of the stakeholders.

Monopoly rents Economic rent deriving from the markets in which the organisation operates. Such rents are associated with a company's unique position in the market place enabling it to influence market prices in its favour. See also *Economic rent.*

Multidivisional organisation structure As the product range of the organisation becomes larger and more diverse, similar parts of the product range are grouped together into divisions, each having its own functional management team. Each division has some degree of profit responsibility and reports to the headquarters, which usually retains a significant role in the development of business strategy. Sometimes this is shortened to *M-Form* structure. See also *Matrix organisation structure.*

Multinational enterprise (MNE) One of the global companies that operate in many countries around the world (e.g. Ford, McDonald's and Unilever).

Multinational strategy When a company operates in many countries, though it may still have a home base. See also *International strategy* and *Global strategy.*

Negative-sum game Actions of each party undermine both themselves and their opponents.

Negotiation-based strategic route forward Has both human resource and game theory elements. Human resource aspects emphasise the importance of negotiating with colleagues in order to establish the optimal strategy. Game theory aspects explore the consequences of the balance of power in the negotiation situation.

Net cash flow Approximately, the sum of pre-tax profits plus depreciation, less the periodic investment in working capital that is required to undertake the project.

Network-based strategy Explores the links and degree of co-operation present in related organisations and industries. It places a value upon that degree of co-operation.

Network co-operation Refers to the value-adding relationships that organisations develop *inside* their own organisation and *outside* it with other organisations.

Network externalities Refer to the development of an overall standard for a network that allows those belonging to the network to benefit increasingly as others join the network.

New public management model Consists of a model of public sector decision making where the professional civil service operates with more market competition and former state monopolies are divided and compete against each other for business from citizens. See also *Public sector administration model.*

Niche marketing Concentration on a small market segment with the objective of achieving dominance of that segment.

Objectives or goals Take the generalities of the mission and turn them into more *specific* commitments. They state more precisely than a mission statement what is to be achieved and when the results are to be accomplished. They may be quantified. See also *Mission.*

Oligopoly A market dominated by a small number of firms.

Organisational capability The skills, routines, management and leadership of its organisation. See also *Tangible resources* and *Intangible resources*.

Organisational culture The set of beliefs, values and learned ways of managing in an individual organisation. Note that it is important to distinguish this from *national* cultures.

Outsourcing The decision by an organisation to buy in products or services from outside, rather than make them inside the organisation.

Paradigm The recipe or model that links the elements of a theory together and shows, where possible, the nature of the relationships.

Parenting The special relationships and strategies pursued at the headquarters of a diversified group of companies.

Payback The time that it takes to recover the initial capital investment, usually measured in years.

Payoffs The results of particular game-plays. See also *Game theory, Zero-sum game, Co-operative game, Negative-sum game.*

PESTEL analysis Checklist of the political, economic, socio-cultural, technological, environmental and legal aspects of the environment.

Plans or programmes The specific actions that follow from the strategies. Often a step-by-step sequence and timetable.

Politics Concerned with the exercise of authority, leadership and management in organisations.

Portfolio matrix Analyses the range of products possessed by an organisation (its portfolio) against two criteria: relative market share and market growth. It is sometimes called the growth-share matrix.

Power This aspect of strategic leadership is concerned with the exercise of authority, leadership and management in organisations.

Predictability of the environment The degree to which changes in the environment can be predicted.

Prescriptive change The implementation actions that result from the selected strategy option. A defined list of actions is identified once the strategy has been chosen. See also *Emergent change*.

Prescriptive strategic management A prescriptive strategy is one whose objective is defined in advance and whose main elements have been developed before the strategy commences. See also *Emergent strategic management*, where such elements are crafted during the development of the strategy and not defined in advance.

Pressure points for influence The groups or individuals that significantly influence the direction of the organisation, especially in the context of strategic change. Note that they may have no *formal* power or responsibility.

Primary demand Demand from customers for themselves or their families. See also *Derived demand.*

Problem children Products with low relative market shares in high-growth markets. See also *Portfolio matrix.*

Process of strategic management How the actions of strategic management are linked together or interact with each other as strategy unfolds.

Profit-maximising theories of strategy Emphasise the importance of the market place and the generation of profit. See also *Prescriptive strategic management.*

Profitability The ratio of profits from a strategy divided by the capital employed in that strategy. It is important to define clearly the elements in the equation, for example, whether the profits are calculated before or after tax and before or after interest payments. This is often called the *return on capital employed*, shortened to ROCE.

Public interest Concerns about the objectives of the institutions that make and implement public decisions in public sector strategy.

Public power The resource possessed by nation states and consisting of the collective decision making that derives from the nation state.

Public resources Public resources need to be analysed for their ability to deliver the maximum benefit for the least cost. 'Benefit' here has a broader social definition than simply delivering shareholder profitability in the private sector.

Public sector administration model Consists of a professional civil service bureaucracy that enacts government legislation and administers the activities of the state on behalf of the government, coupled with state monopolies that supply services to citizens. See also *New public management model.*

Public sector resource analysis Needs to assess whether sufficient and appropriate resources are available to deliver the purpose and objectives set by the state.

Public value Refers to the benefits to the whole of the nation from owning and controlling certain products and services in public sector strategy.

Quota A maximum number placed by a nation state on the goods that can be imported into the country in any one period. The quota is defined for a particular product category.

Reputation The strategic standing of the organisation in the eyes of its customers and other stakeholders. It is the sum of customer knowledge developed about an organisation over time, including its brands among many other factors.

Resource allocation The process of allocating the resources of the organisation selectively between competing strategies according to their merit.

Resource-based strategy Stresses the importance of an organisation possessing some resources that deliver its competitive advantage over its rivals in the market place.

Resource-based view Stresses the importance of resources in delivering the competitive advantage of the organisation. It is often shortened to RBV. See also *Prescriptive strategic management.*

Resources The resources of an organisation are those assets that deliver value added in the organisation.

Retained profits The profits that are retained in an organisation rather than distributed as dividends to shareholders. These can be used to fund new strategies.

Return on capital employed Defined as the ratio of profits to be earned divided by the capital invested in the new strategy.

Reward The result of successful strategy, adding value to the organisation and the individual.

Reward systems The structured benefits paid to individuals and groups who have delivered strategies that add value to the organisation consistent with its agreed purpose.

Ricardian rents Economic rent deriving from the resources of the organisation. They are derived from resources that possess some real competitive advantage and allow the company to earn exceptional returns. See also *Economic rent.*

Risk Strategy evaluation criterion associated with a strategy that does not expose the organisation to unnecessary hazards or to an unreasonable degree of danger. Risk involves measurable inputs and outputs that are associated with known probability distributions of the outcomes of business actions. Nothing may be certain but the odds of a specific outcome are known. See also *Uncertainty.*

ROCE See *Profitability.*

Scenario Model of a possible future environment for the organisation, whose strategic implications can then be investigated.

Schumpeterian rents Economic rent deriving from new and innovatory products and services that allow the organisation to charge significantly above the costs of production. See also *Economic rent.*

Seven S Framework The seven elements are: superordinate goals, strategy, structure, systems, skills, style and staff. In some later versions, the first item was replaced by shared values.

Share issues New shares in an organisation can be issued to current or new shareholders to raise finance for new strategy initiatives. The word 'equity' is sometimes used in place of shares and the process is then called 'equity financing'.

Shareholder value added The difference between the return on capital and the cost of capital multiplied by the investment made by the shareholders in the business.

Short-term debt A loan repaid in less than one year. See also *Long-term debt.*

Small organisation structure Consists of the owner/proprietor and the immediate small team surrounding that person.

Socio-cultural theories of strategy Focus on the social and cultural dimensions of the organisation in developing corporate strategy. See also *Prescriptive strategic management.*

Split The variety of techniques that can be employed to develop and sustain the autonomy and diversity of large organisations.

Stakeholders The individuals and groups who have an interest in the organisation and, therefore, may wish to influence aspects of its mission, objectives and strategies.

Stars Products with high relative market shares operating in high-growth markets. See also *Portfolio matrix.*

Strategic alliances Co-operative strategies where organisations combine or share some of their resources without involving an exchange of shares or other forms of joint ownership.

Strategic business alliance A strategic business alliance (SBA) is some form of contractual relationship designed to secure an international venture without involving a shareholding.

Strategic business unit (SBU) The level of a multi-business unit at which the strategy needs to be developed. The unit has the responsibility for determining the strategy of that unit. An SBU is not necessarily the same as a division of the company: there may be more than one SBU within a division and SBUs may combine elements from more than one division.

Strategic change The proactive management of change in organisations in order to achieve clearly defined strategic objectives or to allow the company to experiment in areas where it is not possible to define strategic objectives precisely. See also *Prescriptive change* and *Emergent change.*

Strategic environment Everything and everyone outside the organisation: competitors, government, etc.

Strategic fit The matching process between strategy and organisational structure.

Strategic groups Groups of firms within an industry that follow the same strategies or ones that have similar dimensions and which compete closely.

Strategic intent A phrase that focuses on only the *essence* of the purpose of the organisation. It is sometimes phrased in a competitive context.

Strategic leadership This is the ability to shape the organisation's decisions and deliver high value over time, not only personally but also by inspiring and managing others in the organisation.

Strategic management This has at least three definitions. First, the identification of the *purpose* of the organisation and the plans and actions to achieve that purpose. Second, the identification of market opportunities, coupled with experimenting and developing competitive advantage over time. Third, the pattern of major objectives, purposes or goals and the essential policies or plans for achieving those goals.

Strategic planning A formal planning system for the development and implementation of the strategies related to the mission and objectives of the organisation. It is no substitute for strategic thinking.

Strategic space The identification of gaps in an industry representing strategic marketing opportunities.

Strategies The principles that show how an organisation's major objectives or goals are to be achieved over a defined time period. Usually confined only to the *general logic* for achieving the objectives.

Strategy as history The view that strategy must, at least in part, be seen as a result of the organisation's present resources, its past history and its evolution over time.

Strategy content The actual strategy that is finally selected to meet the objectives of the organisation.

Strategy context The circumstances surrounding the influencing the way that a strategy develops and operates.

Strategy process The process of communication and discussion amongst those contributing to and implementing the strategy.

Style theory of leadership Suggests that individuals can be identified who possess a general style of leadership that is appropriate to the organisation. See also *Contingency theory of leadership* and *Trait theory of leadership*.

Suitability Strategy evaluation criterion associated with the strategy being appropriate for the internal and external context of the organisation.

Survival-based theories of strategy These regard the survival of the fittest in the market place as being the prime determinant of corporate strategy. See also *Emergent strategic management*.

Sustainable competitive advantage An advantage over competitors that cannot be easily imitated. Such advantages will generate more value than competitors have.

SWOT analysis An analysis of the strengths and weaknesses present internally in the organisation, coupled with the opportunities and threats that the organisation faces externally.

Synergy The combination of parts of a business such that the sum is worth more than the individual parts – often remembered as '2 + 2 = 5'.

Tacit knowledge Knowledge that is personal, context specific and much harder to formalise and communicate – often, but not necessarily, hidden and not formally recorded.

Tangible resources The physical resources of the organisation such as plant and equipment. See also *Intangible resources* and *Organisational capability*.

Target pricing Sets the price of goods and services primarily on the basis of the competitive position of the organisation, the profit margin required and, therefore, the target costs that need to be achieved. See also *Cost-plus pricing*.

Targeted marketing See *Market segmentation*.

Tariffs Taxes on imported goods imposed by a nation state. They do not stop imports into the country but make them more expensive.

Taylorism Named after F W Taylor (1856–1915). The division of work into measurable parts, such that new standards of work performance could be defined, coupled with a willingness by management and workers to achieve these. It fell into disrepute when it was used to exploit workers in the early twentieth century. Taylor always denied that this had been his intention.

Three 'S' Framework for Dynamic Strategy has three main elements: 1. sensing the changes, 2. seizing the opportunities, 3. surveying the outcomes and responses.

Tiger economies Countries of South-East Asia exhibiting exceptionally strong economic growth over the past 30 years, including Singapore, Malaysia, Hong Kong, Thailand and Korea.

Total quality management (TQM) Emphasises the need for the whole company to manage quality at every level of the company.

Trade barriers The barriers set up by governments to protect industries in their own countries.

Trade block Agreement between a group (or block) of countries designed to encourage trade between those countries and keep out other countries.

Trait theory of leadership Argues that individuals with certain characteristics (traits) can be identified who will provide leadership in virtually any situation. See also *Contingency theory of leadership* and *Style theory of leadership*.

Transaction Cost Economics (TCE) Focuses on minimising the costs of production and the costs of transactions related to the operation and management of organisations.

Transactions continuum Based on the principle of the level of ownership by a diversified group, the transactions continuum represents the range of options that are available for ownership and control by the group: they begin at one end with an acquisition with 100 per cent ownership with divestment at the other end with zero per cent ownership.

Transcend Given the inevitable complexities of corporate strategy, some strategists argue that every organisation needs an approach to management that *transcends* these problems and copes with such difficulties.

Transfer price The price for which one part of an organisation will sell its goods to another part in a multidivisional organisation.

Transnational product company This usually involves some global integration of manufacturing coupled with *significant* national responsiveness to national or regional variations in customer demand. See also *Global product company*.

Uncertainty may involve specific inputs but the outcomes are not fully defined in advance and perhaps not even clear after the event. See also *Risk*.

Uncertainty-based theories of strategy These regard prediction of the environment as being of limited use because the outcomes of any strategy are essentially complex and unpredictable, implying that long-term planning has little value. See also *Emergent corporate strategy*.

United Nations Conference on Trade and Development (UNCTAD) A trade body set up to highlight the trading concerns of the developing nations of the world and promote their interests.

Unrelated diversification The different companies in a corporate group have little in common with regard to products, customers or technologies. However, they benefit from the resources of the headquarters with regard to the availability of lower-cost finance, quality of management direction and other related matters.

Validity Strategy evaluation criterion associated with the strategy and its related calculations and other assumptions being well-grounded and meaningful.

Value chain This identifies where the value is added in an organisation and links the process with the main functional parts of the organisation. It is used for developing competitive advantage because such chains tend to be unique to an organisation.

Value system The wider routes in an industry that add value to incoming supplies and outgoing distributors and customers. It links the industry value chain to that of other industries. It is used for developing competitive advantage.

Vertical integration This occurs when a company produces its own inputs (backward integration) or when a company owns the outlets through which it sells its products (forward integration).

Vision A challenging and imaginative picture of the future role and objectives of an organisation, significantly going beyond its current environment and competitive position. It is often associated with an outstanding leader of the organisation.

Weighted average cost of capital The combination of the costs of debt and equity capital in proportion to the capital structure of the organisation. See also *Cost of capital.*

Zero-sum game Has no payoff because the gains of one player are negated by the losses of another.

INDEX